Constitutional and Administrative Law

Macmillan Law Masters

Company Law   Janet Dine and Marios Koutsias
Constitutional and Administrative Law   Keith Syrett and John Alder
Contract Law   Ewan McKendrick
Criminal Law   Jonathan Herring
Employment Law   Deborah J Lockton and Tom Brown
Family Law   Samantha Davey
Land Law   Mark Davys
Medical Law   Jo Samanta and Ash Samanta
Sports Law   Mark James
Trusts Law   Charlie Webb and Tim Akkouh

Macmillan Law Masters

Constitutional and Administrative Law

Keith Syrett

Professor of Health Law and Policy, University of Bristol

John Alder

Emeritus Professor of Law, Newcastle University

Twelfth edition

macmillan
international
HIGHER EDUCATION

RED GLOBE
PRESS

This edition published 2021 by
RED GLOBE PRESS

Previous editions published under the imprint PALGRAVE

Red Globe Press in the UK is an imprint of Macmillan Education Limited, registered in England, company number 01755588, of 4 Crinan Street, London, N1 9XW.

Red Globe Press® is a registered trademark in the United States, the United Kingdom, Europe and other countries.

ISBN 978-1-352-01239-2 hardback
ISBN 978-1-352-01237-8 paperback

This book is printed on paper suitable for recycling and made from fully managed and sustained forest sources. Logging, pulping and manufacturing processes are expected to conform to the environmental regulations of the country of origin.

A catalogue record for this book is available from the British Library.

A catalog record for this book is available from the Library of Congress.

Publisher: Ursula Gavin
Assistant Editor: Christian Ritter
Senior Production Editor: Amy Brownbridge
Marketing Manager: Amy Suratia

Contents

Part IV Government institutions 205

As in previous editions, the aims of the book are, first, to explain the main principles of United Kingdom constitutional law in the context of the political and legal values that influence their development and, second, to draw attention to the main controversies. The book is intended both as a self-contained text for those new to the subject and as a starting point for more advanced students.

This is the first edition of the book with which John Alder has not been directly involved. John authored the first edition of this book over thirty years ago, and it is testament to his skill, erudition and clarity of expression that the essential framework of the text remains much the same, notwithstanding the hugely significant changes in the content of the subject matter over this three-decade period.

The structure of the text remains similar to previous editions. Part I concerns general principles. These include basic constitutional concepts and issues (Chapter 1), a broad account of the political ideals that have influenced the constitution (Chapter 2) and the sources of the constitution (Chapter 3). Chapter 4 provides a brief account of some constitutional landmarks. Chapter 5 provides an overview of the main institutions of government, the most important aspects of which are expanded in later chapters. In Part II, Chapters 6, 7 and 8 concern the underlying legal principles of the rule of law, the separation of powers and parliamentary sovereignty.

Part III concerns international aspects of the constitution. Chapter 9 explains the various ways in which international requirements are filtered into domestic law, the position of dependent territories, expulsion from the UK and the responses of the courts to international issues. Chapter 10 has been substantially revised to reflect the UK's withdrawal from the EU on 31 January 2020. In consequence, the discussion of EU institutions and principles of law (Sections 10.2 to 10.4) has been abbreviated, while that in Section 10.5, concerning withdrawal, has been expanded, albeit that the precise shape of the UK's future relationship with the Union will remain a matter of considerable uncertainty for some time yet.

Part IV is concerned with the main national and devolved legislative and executive institutions, and the relationship between them. (The judiciary does not have its own chapter but is discussed in various contexts, especially that of separation of powers.)

Parts V and VI deal with the rights of the individual against government. Part V concerns judicial review of government action, the core of administrative law and includes methods of challenging government action within the government structure.

Part VI deals with the fundamental rights of the individual. Chapter 21 concerns human rights under the ECHR. Chapter 22 relates these to the HRA. Chapters 23 to 25 focus on human rights issues of particular importance to the constitution. Chapter 23 deals with freedom of expression, focusing on press freedom where recent developments include official intrusion. Chapter 24 deals with government secrecy. Chapter 25, which has been substantially revised, discusses special powers, including emergency powers (including a discussion of the Coronavirus Act 2020), interception and surveillance and anti-terrorist measures.

As regards further reading, references to books and articles in the text are to writings that expand on the point in question. The 'Further reading' at the end of each chapter discusses fundamental and controversial general issues for those who require greater depth, or more ideas and points of view. These readings have been fully updated for this new edition. Short references within the text are to the 'Further reading'.

Unless otherwise stated, the main classical works cited throughout are as follows:

Bagehot, *The English Constitution*, ed. Crossman (8th edn, Fontana/Collins 1963)
Dicey, *An Introduction to the Study of the Law of the Constitution* (8th edn, Macmillan 1915, referenced as last edition for which Dicey was himself responsible); (10th edn, Macmillan 1958, ed. Wade)
Hobbes, *Leviathan*, ed. Minogue (Dent 1973)
Locke, *Two Treatises of Government*, ed. Laslett (Cambridge University Press 1960)
Mill, *Utilitarianism, On Liberty and Considerations of Representative Government*, ed. Acton (Dent 1972)

Montesquieu, 'L'Esprit des Lois', extracted in Stirk and Weigall (eds), *An Introduction to Political Ideas* (Pinter 1995)

Paine, *The Thomas Paine Reader*, ed. Foot and Kramnick (Penguin 1987)

Finally, I wish to thank the team at Macmillan for their assistance in preparing the new edition, and my family, without whose support it would never have seen the light of day.

This edition has been updated on the basis of material available on 1 January 2021.

Keith Syrett
January 2021

Table of cases

Table of legislation

Part I

The framework of the constitution

Chapter 1

Introduction: constitutional structures

The nature of the constitution: general issues

A constitution provides the governing framework of an organisation. Any organisation might have a constitution; for example, most sports clubs do so. In our case, the organisation is the state. A state is a geographical territory with a government that has effective control over that area.

A constitution has three purposes: first, to enable the organisation to run effectively; second, to define the powers of those in charge of the organisation; and third, to protect members of the community against the abuse of those powers. Thus, the late Lord Bingham, a leading judge, suggested that 'any constitution, whether of a state, a trade union, a college, a club or other institution seeks to lay down and define … the main offices in which authority is vested and the powers which may be exercised (or not exercised) by the holders of those offices' (*R v Secretary of State for Foreign and Commonwealth Affairs, ex p Quark Fishing Ltd* [2006] 1 AC 529, at [12]).

Friedrich (*Limited Government* (Prentice Hall 1974) 21) displays an idealistic approach to the idea of a constitution that stresses the (assumed) consent of the community: '[A] constitution is the ordering and dividing of the exercise of political power by that group in an existent community who are able to secure the consent of the community and who thereby make manifest the power of the community itself.' However, it is fanciful to assume that there is always a connection between the securing of power and community consent unless we consider 'consent' to include the absence of resistance to whoever is in power by a subservient community.

Constitutional law deals with the following matters:

- the choosing and removing of rulers;
- the relationships between the different branches of the government;
- the accountability of the government;
- the dividing up of powers geographically, for example the relationships between the central United Kingdom government and the devolved governments of Scotland, Wales and Northern Ireland, and those between the state and overseas bodies;
- the rights of the citizen in relation to government.

There is no hard and fast distinction between constitutional law and administrative law. Administrative law deals with the exercise of particular government functions such as planning, immigration and taxation, and the work of the numerous regulators, special tribunals and inquiries that decide disputes involving such government action. The administrative lawyer is especially concerned to ensure that officials keep within the powers given to them.

This book does not attempt to cover administrative law comprehensively, since the subject has its own separate texts (and is often studied separately and subsequently, as a discrete course). Chapters 17, 18 and 19 on judicial review of administrative action deal with the core of administrative law, which is the legal accountability of the government. Other matters relating to administrative law such as 'regulation', tribunals, public inquiries and ombudsmen are discussed in Chapter 20.

In almost all countries, the constitution comprises a special document or set of documents set above the ordinary law. This is called a written constitution, a codified constitution, or a Basic Law. In addition to setting out the main principles of the government structure and (sometimes) a list of individual rights, a written constitution may proclaim, usually in a preamble, some grand vision or moral message about the nature and purposes of the society (e.g. the US Constitution seeks to 'secure the blessings of liberty to ourselves and our posterity'). Importantly, a written constitution usually has a status superior to the rest of the law, in the sense that it can be altered only by an extraordinary procedure such as a public referendum or a special vote in the legislature, a device known as 'entrenchment'. The courts may have the power to set aside a law that conflicts with the constitution. Such a constitution is therefore protected against manipulation by the government of the day.

The United Kingdom has no written constitution of this kind and no grand vision about the nature of its society. Our constitution, such as it is, is composed of numerous ordinary laws and other rules and practices which have emerged over many centuries to deal with particular issues. In both its legal and its political aspects, the constitution relies on precedent in the sense of appealing to past decisions and practices. Its *legal* principles and rules, if written down at all, are to be found in the same documents as the sources of any law, namely:

▶ Acts of Parliament (statutes) passed by Parliament at the instigation of the regime in power at the time. Thus constitutional statutes are scattered throughout the centuries, each dealing with a particular concern of the day (for examples see Section 3.2). The constitution also evolves through the accumulation of many pieces of detailed legislation about particular topics, for example electoral law.
▶ Cases decided by the courts (common law). Again, these are scattered, dealing with specific matters and focusing narrowly on individual disputes which can arise in many and various contexts. The constitution therefore has to be pieced together by imaginative interpretation of a mass of particular rules and decisions.

Rules from these two sources are set out and can be changed in the same way as any other law. In other words, they are constitutional only because of the matters they deal with. How do we know what counts as constitutional? The question arises mainly because constitutional matters are sometimes given special treatment (see Section 8.4.3). Any guidance can only be vague and general. For example, Laws LJ said that a matter is constitutional if it 'conditions the legal relationships between citizen and state in some general overarching manner, or enlarges or diminishes the scope of what are now regarded as fundamental rights' (*Thoburn v Sunderland City Council* [2002] 4 All ER 156, [62]–[64]).

Craig ([2014] PL 373, 389) refers to horizontal, territorial and vertical dimensions of constitutions. Horizontally, a constitution sets up the main organs of government and distributes their powers; territorially, it divides powers geographically; and vertically, it governs the relationship between citizen and state. However, as Craig points out, a constitutional rule must also be especially important, thus introducing a vague subjective element (how do we define what is 'especially important'?) (see e.g. Section 1.4.1 Box).

The United Kingdom is probably unique in not having any written constitution. New Zealand is also sometimes said to have an unwritten constitution, but the New Zealand Constitution Act 1986, although it is an ordinary statute, sets out the basic structure of its government. Israel is said to have no written constitution, but it does have an organised collection of legislation recognised as constitutional by the Supreme Court. The constitution of Saudi Arabia is the Koran.

It is sometimes said that our constitution is 'part written'. While literally accurate – in that our constitutional laws are written down in the same way as any other laws – this description seems unhelpful since it ignores the fact that we have no special constitutional document with a higher status than other laws.

There are also many rules, practices and customs which are not 'law' at all. These get their force only because they are consistently obeyed as established practices. The most important of these are known as 'constitutional conventions'. Many basic constitutional arrangements rely on conventions; for example the selection of, and most of the powers of, the prime minister. Unlike laws, conventions are not directly enforced by the courts (Section 3.4.4). Some, although not all, are also unwritten.

There is no authority empowered to determine whether a convention exists and what it means. This depends entirely on general acceptance by the politicians and officials who run the government and those from whom they choose to take advice. There is no shortage of people who wish to give their opinions on constitutional matters and it is easy for the constitution to be influenced by networks of people having personal connections with those in power. Thus, Hennessy (*The Hidden Wiring* (Gollancz 1995) 15–30) describes the UK Constitution as generated by a circle of 'insiders' comprising senior officials, their friends and their academic and professional acolytes. He recounts the nineteenth-century claim that conventions embody 'the general agreement of public men' about 'the rules of the game' ((1995) 36, 37).

Our constitution is often described as 'organic', meaning that it develops naturally in the light of changing circumstances. We should not therefore expect the constitution to be straightforward and logical. It is a product of historical development and practical compromises generated by rival groups of power-hungry persons. In another metaphor, the common law UK Constitution has also been compared, with the implication that it is 'sound and lasting', to the work of bees making a honey-comb (see *Jackson v Attorney General* [2006] 1 AC 262, at [125] (Lord Hope)). Thus constitutional change may be disguised under the cloak of continuity, taking place in relatively small steps, in the interests of those in power at the time, without adequate scrutiny, and perhaps eventually changing the nature of the 'house'. Consider, for example, the progress of devolution of powers to Scotland, Wales and Northern Ireland, the series of anti-terrorism measures introduced in recent years, and the various constitutional implications of the UK's withdrawal from the European Union (Brexit).

It has often been suggested that we do not have a constitution in any meaningful sense. The democratic activist Thomas Paine (1737–1809) labelled the British government as 'power without right'. In *The Rights of Man*, Paine asserted that, without a written constitution authorised directly by the people, there was no valid constitution (first published 1791, ed. Foot and Kramnick (Penguin 1987) 220–21, 285–96). Similarly, Ridley (1988) claims that the United Kingdom has no constitution since he believes that constitutions must be superior to the government of the day and not changeable by it. The UK seems to fail this test. Insofar as any rules have a special status, this is based on no more than self-restraint founded upon respect for principles that are regarded by those in power as fundamental or 'constitutional'.

1.1.1 Constitutionalism

However, whether or not we have a constitution in a strict sense, the term 'constitutionalism' applies to the UK as a widely shared belief in favour of limited and accountable government. It includes the rule of law, which requires limits on government policed by independent courts, and 'responsible government', which requires government officials to be accountable for their actions to an institution representing the people.

Constitutionalism also favours the separation of powers between different governmental organs. For example, in *R (Evans) v Attorney General* [2015] UKSC 21, the Supreme Court was highly critical of the statutory power of the executive to veto a tribunal decision to require publication under the Freedom of Information Act 2000 (Section 24.2.1). This was described by Judge LJ in the High Court as a constitutional aberration ([2013] EWHC 1960 (Admin), at [1]).

It requires openness in government decision-making and open justice in the courts (*A v BBC* [2014] 2 All ER 1037, [27]). It also includes the protection of rights such as access to the courts and freedom of expression, described as inherent and fundamental to democratic civilised society (see Baroness Hale in *Seal v Chief Constable of South Wales Police* [2007] 4 All ER 177, at [38]–[40]).

1.2 The foundations of a constitution

A constitution can, of course, adopt any form of government. The most widely accepted explanation of the foundations of a constitution is a 'positivist' one. According to this theory, a constitution is 'legitimate' if enough of the people whom it concerns, both officials and the public, accept it so as to make it broadly effective, irrespective of the motivations for such acceptance. Thus, the foundations of the law depend upon a political state of affairs. UK law takes this pragmatic view in the context, for example, of recognising the legality of a rebellion (see *Madzimbamuto v Lardner-Burke* [1969] 1 AC 645: takeover of a British colony by a group of White settlers held not valid because they were not yet fully in control).

'Legitimacy' might also refer to an external standard that can be used to assess the constitution. The problem here, of course, is to identify what this external standard is. Lawyers, for example, might refer to 'the rule of law', meaning widely accepted but vague values, such as justice, as identified by themselves. Related to this are 'natural law' theories in which a constitution is valid only if it conforms to a set of objective moral principles. Apart from the question of who determines what these principles are, it may be preferable to treat moral principles as a standpoint for critiquing a constitution and proposing changes to it, rather than confusing this with questions of its *legal validity*.

1.3   Basic constitutional concepts

Three related ideas have dominated many modern constitutions, including our own. These are 'sovereignty', the rule of law and the separation of powers. Sovereignty means ultimate power without limit. Some, such as Hobbes (Section 2.3.1), argue that there must always be a 'sovereign' capable of having the last word in any conceivable dispute, particularly in an emergency. In any constitution, it might be difficult to locate sovereignty since government power is usually divided up. The sovereign need not be a single person: if it is not, rules are needed to ensure that its components can reach agreement. This raises problems as to whether the sovereign can change those rules and, if not, who can? However, in an extreme emergency, such as a threat of immediate attack, sovereign power might be exercised by a single person.

In the United Kingdom, the conventional view is that the sovereign is Parliament, as a combination of the monarch, the House of Lords and the House of Commons. However, the legal sovereign is not necessarily the political sovereign. For example, although Parliament has legal power to make any law, politically it is unlikely to be able to make a law to which the international money markets would seriously object.

The primary meaning of the rule of law is relatively uncontroversial – namely, that it is desirable to have rules known in advance which are binding on government and governed alike. This helps the organisation to run effectively by keeping order and producing certainty. However, this formal meaning of the expression 'rule of law' ignores the content of the rules themselves, whether they are morally good or bad, and the question of who makes them. For example, a concentration camp might be subject to the rule of law in this sense. A wider or 'substantive' version of the rule of law (Section 6.3) invokes certain moral and political ideas which are claimed to be especially associated with law. These include, above all, the notion of open justice policed by independent courts resisting the natural tendency of government towards secrecy (Section 23.3.4).

The separation of powers requires that government be divided up into different branches of broadly equal status and importance. From both a political and a legal perspective, this is to prevent any one branch of government having dominant power. Each branch can restrain the others since any major decision would require the cooperation of all branches. Governments usually comprise three primary branches. The legislature is the primary lawmaker, the judiciary settles disputes about the meaning and application of the law, and the executive carries out all the other government functions, implementing and enforcing the law. The difference between the three functions is hazy at the edges, but the basis of them is widely recognised. In contemporary society, the executive is likely to be the most powerful branch because it controls the resources, both physical and financial, of the state. Crucially, it is the executive that proposes most new laws to the legislature and appoints to the most important public jobs. Different countries have reached different conclusions as to the extent of the separation of powers since there is a trade-off between the interests of government efficiency (which points away from separation) and the desire to prevent abuse of power. For example, the United States has a relatively strict separation, but in the United Kingdom, separation is more limited. In the United States, a member of the executive headed by the president cannot be a member of the legislature, but in the UK, ministers who head the executive must (by convention) be Members of Parliament (MPs). We seem to prefer strong government to limited government.

Some constitutions make grandiose claims to shared ideals and purposes. For example, the Constitution of Ireland refers to 'seeking to promote the common good with due observance of Prudence, Justice and Charity so that the dignity and freedom of the individual may be assured, true social order attained, the unity of our country restored and concord established with other nations' (Preamble). The French Constitution famously refers to 'the Rights of Man' and the 'equality and solidity of the peoples who compose [the Republic]' (Art 1). The UK Constitution makes no such claims, at least explicitly.

Many constitutions contain a list of basic rights of the citizen; those of Germany and the USA are prominent examples. These rights vary, reflecting the political culture of the state in question. Constitutions also vary in the extent to which the courts may police these rights. In the family of liberal democratic states to which the United Kingdom belongs, these rights are primarily 'negative' rights; that is, rights not to be interfered with by the state. They include the right to life, the right to personal freedom, the right to a fair trial, the right to privacy and family life, the right to freedom of expression, the right to assembly and association, the right to freedom of religion and the right to protection for property. 'Positive rights', such as those to housing and medical care, might be regarded as equally important, but because these require hard political choices between priorities and large-scale public expenditure, they are generally regarded in the UK as matters for the ordinary political process rather than as firm legal rights. Enforcement by a court would be highly awkward and controversial. Nevertheless, positive rights appear in many constitutions, for example those of Poland, Portugal and South Africa. Some constitutions, for example that of Switzerland, also impose particular duties on citizens, such as military service and voting.

1.4   Written and unwritten constitutions: advantages and disadvantages

As we have seen, the constitutions of most countries are set out in a single document or related group of documents. These are generally superior to all other kinds of law in that laws which conflict with the constitution can be struck down by the courts. They also often contain entrenched provisions that protect the constitution from being changed by the government of the day, for example a referendum of the people or a two-thirds majority of the lawmaking assembly.

Even a written constitution will not include all the rules needed for governing the country. The precise contents vary considerably between different states. For example, the methods of voting are important by any democratic standards, but they do not feature in many constitutions other than as general requirements of fairness and equality. Some constitutions, such as that of the United States, are relatively short and expressed in general terms. Others, like that of Portugal, run to hundreds of detailed pages.

1.4.1   The merits of a written constitution

There is no consensus as to whether it is preferable to have a written constitution, although proposals to create one are regularly heard. The main purpose of a written constitution seems to be to usher in a new regime, or to signify a 'constitutional moment' or change of direction for a state as a result of revolution, grants of independence or domestic catastrophe. The device of a written constitution became widely used for these purposes from the late eighteenth century.

Since the late seventeenth century, the United Kingdom has not experienced such a constitutional moment. Most constitutional changes have been gradual and evolutionary, and the seventeenth-century 'constitutional moment' involved the assertion of an all-powerful Parliament, so making a written constitution pointless at the time (Section 4.5.1).

To mark the 800th anniversary of the Magna Carta, the Political and Constitutional Reform Committee of the House of Commons engaged in an extensive consultation as to whether the UK should have a written constitution, and what it should look like. While it acknowledged that the initiative for codifying constitutional rules should come from the executive branch, the Committee tentatively supported the creation of a written constitution on the basis that 'the public is entitled to know the processes by which it is governed and the fundamental rules on which the constitution is based' (HC 2014–15, 599, [58]): to which end it produced its own draft accessible summary constitution, with options for reform (ibid., Annex A). In its original consultation document (HC 2014–15, 463), the Committee set out the main advantages and disadvantages of adopting a written constitution as follows:

Advantages

- Publicity and accessibility: matters of such importance should be codified for all to see and understand.
- Democracy: the present unwritten rules are controlled by the elite and were appropriate to the deferential and class-ridden society of the past but not to today's more equal society. Constitutional changes can now be pushed through by governing parties to benefit themselves. Entrenched procedures that ensure parliamentary and popular support for constitutional changes are desirable.
- Sovereignty: the current fundamental principle that Parliament is supreme is unsuited to a modern democratic society in which the people should be sovereign. The people should therefore have a role in deciding what the constitution should include.
- Education: the absence of constitutional teaching in our schools makes it all the more important to have a single document. This would have great symbolic importance.
- Certainty: some of our unwritten constitution is highly uncertain, and some of its rules existing outside the law have dubious status. The uncertainty over the question of whether Parliament is sovereign (Section 8.5) is a conspicuous example, as is the question of the status of constitutional conventions (Section 3.4).
- Value: the special nature of constitutional principles makes it desirable to distinguish them from ordinary law. Thus in *Cullen v Chief Constable of the RUC* [2004] 2 All ER 237, at [46], Lord Hutton referred to a right which a democratic assembly representing the people has enshrined in a written constitution, the written constitution being 'clear testimony that an added value is attached to the protection of that right'. An example of the risks inherent in our unwritten constitution is the creeping erosion of individual freedom when restrictive legislation is continually added to (e.g. Section 23.7 and Chapter 25).
- Protecting weaker arms of government: parliamentary supremacy means that local government is not protected against central government, other than by political influences. The devolved governments of Scotland, Wales and Northern Ireland are also relatively unprotected. A written constitution would protect local government and also strengthen the separation of powers between the three branches of government whereas, at present, the executive dominates.
- National identity: a written constitution becomes a symbol of national identity and national pride (as in the USA, but not universally true).
- Coordination: constitutional reforms in the unwritten constitution are uncoordinated.
- Modernisation: 'The present "unwritten" constitution is an anachronism riddled with references to the past and unsuited to the social and political democracy of the 21st Century.'

Disadvantages

- It is 'unnecessary' because our constitution has proved stable and successful without the revolutionary 'constitutional moment' that calls for a written constitution (above). It might well be, however, that the divisions and uncertainties caused by the popular vote to leave the European Union in June 2016 and the various constitutional tensions which this has laid bare (see Section 10.5, and throughout this book), amount to such a 'moment'.
- It is flexible and evolutionary so as to respond to changing circumstances, enabling practical problems to be dealt with as they arise (see Lord Bingham in *Robinson v Secretary of State for Northern Ireland* [2002] UKHL 32, at [12]). This might be regarded as not wholly desirable depending on who deals with the problems.
- It reflects our 'British' character (although the committee does not say what this is: possibly deference to a ruling elite?).

▶ It enables decisions to be made by elected politicians rather than unelected judges. A written constitution would politicise the judiciary by requiring it to pass judgment on legislation, increase politically motivated litigation (of the type seen during the Brexit process) and expand judicial review of government action (this is sometimes also claimed as an *advantage* of a written constitution).

▶ There is already a wide range of pressures on ministers which serve as controls on their actions, decisions and policies. These include the opposition in Parliament, party backbenchers, departmental select committees, the House of Lords, the EU, the devolved governments, the media and the voter (objectors might claim that many of these are significantly weak).

▶ The unwritten constitution enables the executive to act quickly and flexibly 'to meet citizens' needs' (or to protect itself against criticism?).

▶ A written constitution would diminish the significance of the monarchy (arguably desirable).

▶ There are so many practical problems in deciding what to put into a written constitution that it is not worth bothering to do so since the matter is of low priority, carries little popular support and risks distracting and destabilising the country.

A written constitution will almost certainly be drafted in vague general language which must be interpreted in the light of the politics of the day and will thus change its meaning from time to time, allowing judges considerable freedom in applying it. For example, in *Plessy v Ferguson* 163 US 537 (1896), the US Supreme Court held that racial segregation was constitutional under the 14th Amendment of the Constitution ('equal protection of the law'), and in *Brown v Board of Education* 347 US 483 (1954) that it was not. Similarly, in *Lochner v New York* 198 US 45 (1905) the Supreme Court held that it was unconstitutional under the same provision for the law to regulate the relations between employer and employee, but in *West Coast Hotels v Parrish* 300 US 379 (1937), at a time of depression, the court upheld a law protecting women's wages.

However, because judges take differing approaches to interpreting the law, it is sometimes said that a written constitution could also encourage the use of abstract, linguistic, legalistic techniques at the expense of underlying political realities and human concerns. In the United States, there is continuing debate as to whether the constitution should be interpreted in the light of changing values, or restricted to the inferred intentions of its eighteenth-century founders. The 'right to keep and bear arms' in the Second Amendment is a particular, and hugely controversial, focus for this (see e.g. *McDonald v Chicago* 561 US 742 (2010)). Closer to home, the notion that the European Convention on Human Rights (ECHR) is a 'living instrument' that can be interpreted flexibly has caused resentment in some UK political circles and may result in a future repeal of the Human Rights Act 1998 (HRA), which gives the Convention effect in domestic law (Section 22.10).

A possible advantage of a written constitution is that it encourages a rationalistic process of constitutional design which ideally creates a constitution as a logical scheme in which inequality is relatively difficult to engineer. On the other hand, it can be argued that, in a matter as large and as open to disagreement as a constitution, human beings are not capable of sensible grand designs, and that the flexible trial-and-error approach favoured in the United Kingdom is preferable. Edmund Burke (1729–97), a prominent parliamentarian and conservative thinker, claimed that the constitution has special status by virtue of its being rooted in long-standing custom and tradition. Burke regarded attempts to engineer constitutions on the basis of abstract reason as ultimately leading to tyranny. This is because he believed that humans, with their limited understanding and knowledge, are inevitably at the mercy of unforeseen events, and that reasoning based on abstract general principles, by trying to squeeze us into rigid templates, is a potential instrument of oppression.

It is also argued, perhaps rather arrogantly, that the United Kingdom does not need a 'paper constitution' because our constitutional values, such as individual rights, are entrenched in the culture of the community itself and so support peace and stability. The fact that the United Kingdom invariably imposed written constitutions on its colonial territories was explained on the basis of their supposed immaturity. This attitude was influenced by the experience of the many revolutions in continental Europe during the late eighteenth and early nineteenth centuries, most importantly the

French Revolution and its series of regime changes from 1789 onwards. The then novel notion of a written constitution was associated with bloodshed, chaos and radical propaganda. For example, it was claimed in the House of Commons that 'we owe our superiority, in a great measure, to the freedom of our government and the blessings of our constitution' (HC Deb 8 November 1814, vol 29, col 39). Furthermore, Dicey, a leading jurist of the Victorian era whose analysis of the constitution has (as we shall later see) proved hugely influential, thought it an advantage that much of our constitution is embedded in the fabric of the common law made by the courts since this meant that practical issues are generated from below, rather than being imposed from above in a document that can be torn up at the whim of a transient political majority in Parliament.

However, there does not seem to be hard evidence that the relative stability of the United Kingdom has been due to our unwritten constitution as opposed to political and economic factors – not least the prosperity exacted from the British Empire of the nineteenth century and the ability of the ruling aristocracy to manage dissent by a mixture of repression and rewards (Sections 4.6 and 4.7). Conversely, the record of countries with written constitutions is mixed. The original US Constitution of 1788 has survived until the present day, although it has been amended sparingly from time to time. Argentina (1853), Belgium (1831), Luxembourg (1868) and Tonga (1875) have long-standing constitutions, but the first two have not had particularly stable governments. Switzerland is a highly stable country, but its constitution (most recent 1999) has been changed many times. Whether a regime is stable and whether a constitution is easily changed may well depend more on cultural and political factors rather than legal devices.

Moreover, it is questionable whether an unwritten constitution can address all of the problems of today. First, the population is much larger and more diverse (ethnically, religiously, culturally) than was the case for much of the nineteenth and early twentieth centuries, when, although democracy was increasing, most political influence lay with native-born male property owners with strong common interests. Secondly, it is not obvious that an unwritten constitution meets the needs of what is often called our 'multi-layered' constitution, where important powers are exercised by supranational bodies such as the European Union (EU – at least before Brexit) and by the devolved bodies in Scotland, Wales and Northern Ireland, as well as by the traditional Parliament and courts. Coordination between these bodies is important. These matters may call for clearer principles than are possible with an unwritten constitution.

Even in the absence of a written constitution, there are devices within UK law capable of limiting the ability of governments to make constitutional changes.

▶ It is arguable that a statute could 'entrench' a special rule by providing that the rule could be changed only by a special process such as a referendum (Section 8.5.3).

▶ The courts may give special weight and 'close scrutiny' to matters that they regard as constitutional (R (Evans) v Attorney General [2014] EWCA Civ 254: executive veto over court decision (Section 24.2.1)). It has been suggested that certain statutes are 'constitutional statutes' and that certain rights, such as freedom of speech, are constitutional rights that require the lawmaker to use very clear language to repeal or override (Sections 6.6 and 8.4.3). In R v Secretary of State for the Home Dept, ex p Simms [2000] 2 AC 115, at 131 (right of a prisoner of access to the press), Lord Hoffmann stated that we apply 'principles of constitutionality little different from those which exist in countries where the power of the legislature is expressly limited by a constitutional document'. Lord Steyn has remarked that to classify a right as constitutional strengthens its value in that the court is virtually always required to protect it (quoted by Cooke, 'The Road Ahead in the Common Law', in Andenas and Fairgrieve (eds), Tom Bingham and the Transformation of the Law (Oxford University Press 2009) 691).

▶ However, there may be disagreement as to what statutes or rights are 'constitutional'. Thus, in Watkins v Secretary of State for the Home Dept [2006] 2 All ER 353 (a prisoner's access to a lawyer), the House of Lords held that, in the absence of a written constitution, the notion of a constitutional right is too vague (see also A-G v National Assembly for Wales Commission [2013] 1 AC 792, at [80]: too uncertain). In R (Chester) v Secretary of State for Justice [2014] 1 All ER 683, at [35], [137], the Supreme Court held that the question of voting rights was not a fundamental feature of UK law.

- It has even been suggested that the courts could refuse to apply a statute that violates a fundamental constitutional principle (Section 8.5.6).
- The House of Lords Constitution Committee examines the constitutional aspects of bills and reviews constitutional developments (see HL 2001–02, 11; see Caird [2012] PL 4). The House of Commons Public Administration and Constitutional Affairs Committee considers general questions of constitutional reform.
- Proposed legislation that Parliament regards as 'of first-class constitutional importance' is examined by a committee of the whole House rather than by the normal 'standing committee' (Section 13.3.1).
- There is authority that compensation can be awarded against a public official who violates a 'constitutional right' even where no loss or damage has occurred (*Ashby v White* (1703) 2 Lord Raym 938: right to vote).

The argument about a written constitution therefore reflects deeper disagreements about whether public officials can be trusted, and whether democracy should be the ultimate principle of our society (Section 2.8). On balance, it may well be that contemporary changes in political society and institutional arrangements in recent years, coupled with a governmental system about which there is often considerable popular scepticism and disenchantment, make it desirable to make a break with the past and to establish a written constitution using a method that ensures the collaboration of the whole community. Time will tell.

1.5   The legal and the political constitution

Constitutional law depends heavily on its political context. Thus, the late Professor Griffith famously described the UK Constitution as a 'political constitution'. He remarked that 'the constitution of the United Kingdom lives on, changing from day to day for the constitution is no more and no less than what happens. Everything that happens is constitutional. And if nothing happened that would be constitutional also' ((1979) 19). Griffith seems to have meant that the constitution is the ever-changing interaction of the formal rules and the persons who interpret and operate them from time to time, all of whom have their own attitudes and prejudices.

Although our primary concern in this book is with law, it is therefore necessary to relate this to its political context. For the purposes of studying constitutional law, it is useful to attempt to distinguish between law and politics.

Unfortunately, there is no agreed meaning of 'politics', or of 'law'. For now, it is enough to say that 'law' means rules, principles and standards that are enforced ultimately by the physical force of the state and, in our case, policed by independent courts. Laws are recognised solely because they are made by designated institutions and procedures (in the UK, by the courts and Parliament). In a broad sense, 'politics' means the struggle for power between different interest groups, and in this sense, law is a distinctive aspect of politics in that it depends on and is influenced by political forces, and there is potential for conflict between the courts and the other branches of government.

Law can be distinguished from other aspects of politics in at least the following respects:

- It relies on impersonal and usually written sources of authority in the form of binding general rules.
- It emphasises the desirability of certainty, coherence and impartial and independent public procedures such as courts for settling disputes.
- Politics is concerned primarily with outcomes, for which law is only one among several instruments, and is more willing than law to use emotions, personal relationships, rewards and compromises in order to achieve those outcomes.

A useful way of framing the political context is the metaphor derived from Harlow and Rawlings (2009), of 'red light' and 'green light' theories. Red lighters emphasise the role of law as *controlling government*, in the interests of individual rights and the protection of autonomy. Green lighters favour the *collective goals of society*, which they believe are best carried out by the government through democratic mechanisms. They therefore see the role of law as being primarily to enable government to effectively achieve important public goals, such as education, health care and social welfare. Green light theory does not of course deny the importance of the individual, but emphasises collective and community means of protecting the individual and of preventing the abuse of government power. However, in reality, the approach taken by the law might be seen as a form of compromise between the two positions or, in Harlow and Rawlings's terms, 'amber light'.

The legal and the political constitution are interrelated in various ways. For example:

▶ Politics provides the purposes and values that underpin the constitution and give the law its content.

▶ Law operates as a delivery mechanism for particular political policies written into legislation.

▶ The accountability of government – constitutionalism – is both legal and political, and each acknowledges the other (e.g. Section 18.1). There is legal accountability to the courts through the courts' powers of judicial review of government decisions to ensure that they comply with the law. There is political accountability to Parliament in the form of the concept of 'responsible government', which requires the government to justify its actions to Parliament. However, for several reasons, including the domination of Parliament by the executive and limited resources, political accountability is weak. Other than the right to vote periodically for individual MPs, there is no direct accountability to the people.

▶ Conversely, values especially concerned with the legal process in the courts, which can be summarised as fairness and justice, feed into the political process. For example, how far should anti-terrorist policies be subject to the right to a fair trial (Section 24.6)?

▶ Within the law itself there is disagreement between different judges and groups of lawyers about political values. Because the limits of human competence mean that rules can never be entirely clear or complete, judges may be unconsciously influenced by their political beliefs in deciding between competing arguments. The best we can expect is an open and self-aware mind. Endless disagreement underlies both law and politics, and dissents are commonplace in judicial decisions. This is one reason why a diverse judiciary may be desirable.

▶ Politics determines the actual power relationship between the different branches of government: lawmaker, executive, judges, military and so on. For example, even if in law Parliament as the lawmaker is supreme, the executive is likely to be dominant if MPs are weak, self-seeking and subservient.

Griffith's view was that constitutional decisions should be (and, traditionally, were) made by political actors rather than unelected judges, and that political means of holding government to account (e.g. through a duty placed upon ministers to explain their actions and decisions in Parliament) were preferable to accountability through the courts. He took this view because he regarded these actors and mechanisms as inherently more democratic, and also because he felt that the judiciary was more liable to be susceptible to implicit political bias (of a right-wing character) as a consequence of its class and educational background. However, there has been a perceptible trend towards a legal constitution in recent years. The growth of judicial review, coupled with the enactment of the HRA (Chapters 17–19 and 22) and the impact of the law of the European Union (Chapter 10), has meant that legal mechanisms are now much more frequently invoked in order to render government accountable in the UK than was the case half a century or so ago.

1.6   The dignified and efficient constitution: deceiving the people?

It is often said that the glue that holds the unwritten UK Constitution together is the propensity of the British people to subservience and deference to officialdom. Writing in the mid-nineteenth century, Walter Bagehot regarded social class deference and superstition as the 'magic' ingredients that animated the constitution. Bagehot had a pessimistic view of the political sophistication of ordinary people and thought that government could only work effectively if its authority was buttressed by traditional institutions which commanded people's imagination and made them deferential to the rulers.

Bagehot distinguished between what he called the 'dignified' and the 'efficient' parts of the constitution. The dignified parts give the constitution its authority and encourage people to obey it. They involve the trappings of power, notably the monarchy that underpins the central government (Section 14.6) and the mystique of ceremony and ritual. Bagehot thought that it would be dangerous to shed the light of reality upon the monarchy since doing so would expose it as a sham. The efficient part of the constitution, which Bagehot located primarily in the Cabinet (although today this is less convincing, Section 15.4), carries out the working exercise of power behind the scenes. The distinction between the dignified and the efficient performs a useful function in a democracy by preventing working politicians from claiming to embody the state, a technique adopted by tyrants throughout history. For example, the monarch and Parliament have authority, the latter because it is elected, while the government has power without authority in its own right. It gets its authority only from Parliament.

On the other hand, the dignified element can reinforce tyranny by hiding reality. For example, in *McIlkenny v Chief Constable of the West Midlands Police* [1980] 2 All ER 227, at 239–40, Lord Denning MR took the view that it was better for the 'Birmingham Six' to remain wrongly convicted than to face the 'appalling vista' of the police being found to be guilty of perjury, violence and threats. The Scott Report into the sale of arms to Iraq (*Report of the Inquiry into the Export of Defence Equipment and Dual Use Goods to Iraq and Related Prosecution* (HC 1995–96, 115)) revealed that ministers and civil servants regarded it as being in the public interest to mislead Parliament, if not actually to lie, over government involvement in arms sales to overseas regimes. The Constitutional Reform and Governance Act 2010 prevents disclosure under the Freedom of Information Act 2000 of all correspondence between the Prince of Wales and ministers on the ground that it would weaken public confidence in the monarchy if people knew that the heir to the throne attempted to influence government (Section 24.2.1).

1.7 Types of constitution

There are several traditional ways of classifying constitutions. It must be emphasised that these are ideals or models, and there is no reason to assume that any particular constitution fits neatly within any single category. The types are:

Federal and unitary. In a federal state (such as the USA, Germany or Canada) the various powers of government are divided between different geographical units and a central government. Each unit is equal and independent and can exercise the powers given to it without the interference of the other level. In a unitary state, ultimate power is held by a single central government, although there may be subordinate units of local government with powers given and taken away by the centre. In law, the United Kingdom is strictly a unitary state with the central authority, Parliament, having absolute power.

How powers are allocated within a federation varies according to the history and political concerns of the state in question. There is usually a single citizenship of the central state, which is the internationally recognised entity. The federal government is usually responsible for foreign affairs, defence and major economic matters, while private law is usually the responsibility of the states. Criminal offences, social regulation and public services may be allocated to either level. Usually, particular matters are given to the federal level, with the residue left with the states: the 'reserved powers' model. Switzerland provides an extreme example, where the powers of the federal government are severely limited in favour of the autonomy of the cantons. The converse 'conferred powers' model is less common (e.g. Canada). The relative political power of each level depends on the circumstances of each country and cannot necessarily be ascertained from the law itself.

There may be demarcation problems to be resolved by the courts, so federal constitutions have a strong legalistic element. Each level might have its own courts, although in Germany, for example, there is a single court system. (In civil law countries such as Germany where the law, being codified, is more uniform, there may be less need for separate courts at each level than in a common-law country such as the USA.)

Federalism is practicable where the component units have enough in common economically and culturally to enable them to cooperate, while at the same time each unit is both sufficiently distinctive to constitute a community in its own right but insufficiently powerful to aspire to a role on the international stage. Thus, a delicate balance must be struck. The United States and Australia are relatively successful federations, whereas Canada, with its split between English-speaking and French-speaking regions, has sometimes been less stable. Yugoslavia, with its many ethnic tensions, was tragically unsuccessful once Soviet control was removed.

Dicey ((1915) 171) strongly opposed federalism, claiming that it tends towards conservatism, creates divided loyalties and elevates legalism to a primary value, making the courts the pivot on which the constitution turns, and perhaps threatening their independence.

In 1973, the Royal Commission on the Constitution (Cmnd 5460) argued against a federal constitution for the United Kingdom. It argued, first, that there would be a lack of balance since the units are widely different in economic terms, with England being dominant since it includes about 84 per cent of the population of the UK. There is a need for central and flexible economic management since the resources of the United Kingdom are unevenly distributed geographically, with much of the country comprising thinly populated hills. Secondly, echoing Dicey, the Commission argued that a federal regime would be contrary to our constitutional traditions in that it would elevate the courts over political machinery.

It may be best to think of federalism as a loose notion, a matter of degree comprising a range of relationships, rather than as a simple uniform model. From this perspective, the United Kingdom may be regarded as a state with certain federal features. The devolved governments for Scotland, Wales and Northern Ireland within the United Kingdom are not strictly federal, but in some respects have political and legal protection comparable to federalism (Section 16.1). From the strictly legal perspective, the principle that Parliament is sovereign preserves the unitary nature of the constitution. However, the Scottish referendum of 2014 revealed considerable tension within the devolved structure, not least because of the anomalous position of England, which lacks its own powers or legislative assembly (Section 16.6). That tension has persisted given that two of the constituent parts of the UK (Scotland and Northern Ireland) voted to remain in the European Union in the referendum of 2016, while the other two (England and Wales) voted to leave (Section 10.5.5).

Note that federalism can be distinguished from 'confederation'. A confederation exists where independent units agree to share some governmental institutions. Canada and the United States were once confederations. There are no modern instances, although the EU is sometimes regarded as a confederation. Thus, the two notions shade into each other, reinforcing the point that federalism is a loose notion.

Rigid and flexible. This concerns whether it is easy for those in power to change the constitution. In legal terms, a rigid constitution is where a special process, such as a referendum of the people, is required to change it. In a legal sense, the UK Constitution is highly flexible since it can be changed in the same way as any other law. However, whether a constitution is easy to change depends more on politics than on law. In a political sense, the status quo is not easy to change in the UK since those in power stand to benefit from it.

Parliamentary and presidential. The United Kingdom has a parliamentary system. In such a system, as applies to many Western European countries, the people choose representatives who form the legislature, Parliament. The head of government is the prime minister (the chancellor in Austria and Germany), chosen by the Parliament. The prime minister chooses and removes ministers, who are the leaders of the executive government. Sometimes, as in the United Kingdom, these must also be members of the legislature. Parliament scrutinises government activities, consents to laws and provides the government with finance. It can ultimately dismiss the executive by withdrawing its support. Parliamentary government therefore looks strong and accountable. However, in practice, the executive is likely to be dominant, not least because of the human tendency to defer to leaders.

In a parliamentary system, there is usually a separate head of state who might be a hereditary monarch, as in the United Kingdom, or elected by the people, as in Ireland. The head of state formally represents the state and is the source of its authority, but has little political power, except perhaps as a safety mechanism in the event of a serious political breakdown.

In a presidential system such as that of the United States, the leader of the executive, the president, is elected directly by the people independently of the legislature and holds office for a fixed period, subject (in some countries) to dismissal by the legislature. The president is usually also the head of state. Presidential government therefore gives the voter a greater choice. On the other hand, without a strong input from the legislature, accountability might be weak and, when the legislature and president represent different political parties, it might be difficult for the government to work effectively since its proposed laws may be blocked by the legislature.

The device of a separate head of state in the parliamentary system has the advantage of separating the authority of the state from its political powers. In a parliamentary system, the prime minister and other members of the executive are merely government employees who cannot (or, at least, should not) identify themselves with the state as such and so cannot claim reflected glory and immunity from criticism. The head of state has a symbolic role and also ensures continuity in the constitution. For example, if the government were to collapse, it would be the responsibility of the head of state to ensure that government continued. Apart from this exceptional situation, the Queen has little personal political power (Section 14.4), so that any respect due to her as representing the state does not carry the risk of tyranny.

Unicameral or bicameral. A unicameral constitution has a single lawmaking assembly. A bicameral constitution has two assemblies, each of which operates as a check on the other, the balance between them depending on the circumstances of the particular country. In the United States, for example, the Senate, the upper house, represents the states which compose the federal system, with the electors of each state, irrespective of its size, choosing two members; whereas the House of Representatives, the lower and larger house, is elected by the people generally, each state being represented according to the size of its population. Some European constitutions, such as those of Denmark, Sweden and Greece, are unicameral, and in most European constitutions, the upper house cannot override the lower house. It is questionable whether an upper house serves a useful purpose other than in a federal system in the US model, where each house can check the other from importantly different perspectives.

The UK Constitution is bicameral. The lower house, the House of Commons, with 650 members, is elected from the UK as a whole. The upper house, the House of Lords, with over 800 members, is mainly appointed by the prime minister, which contrasts with other European countries where the upper houses are mainly elected. The House of Lords cannot override the Commons. It serves as a revising chamber to scrutinise and amend legislation proposed by the lower house, thus providing an opportunity for second thoughts.

Monarchical or republican: monarchy, aristocracy and democracy. In a tradition dating back at least to Aristotle, there are three fundamental types of government: monarchy, or rule by one person; aristocracy, literally rule by a group of the 'best' people; and democracy, rule by the many, or the people as a whole. According to Aristotle, each form of constitution has its virtues, but also corresponding vices or deviations. The virtues exist when the ruler rules for the benefit of others; the vices when the ruler rules for the benefit of him or herself. According to Aristotle, the main merit of monarchy is its authority and independence since monarchs have a quasi-godlike status. The corresponding defect is despotism. The merit of aristocracy is wisdom; its defect is oligarchy, rule by a selfish group. The merit of democracy is consent of the community; its defect is instability, leading to mob tyranny. Aristotle postulated a vicious cycle in which a monarch becomes a despot, is deposed by an aristocracy, which turns into an oligarchy and is overthrown by a popular rebellion. The ensuing democracy degenerates into chaos, resolved by the emergence of a dictator, who takes on the characteristics of a monarch, and so on. Aristotle therefore favoured what he called 'polity', a 'mixed government' combining all three (but loaded in favour of what we now call the middle classes) and with checks and balances between different branches of government.

In those European countries where monarchy remains, the powers of the monarch are invariably limited, in some cases being purely ceremonial. The monarchy in these countries is hereditary within a family and thus relatively independent of political pressures. The UK has a 'constitutional monarchy', meaning that the monarch cannot make law or exercise executive or judicial powers. In this way, the risk of dictatorship is reduced and the monarchy serves as a harmless symbol representing the nation.

In 'republican' states, the head of state is elected either by the Parliament or by the people. As we shall see (Section 2.5), the notion of republicanism amounts to rather more than this. It embraces democracy in a wide sense, requiring equality in all aspects of government and, as such, has been of limited influence in the United Kingdom.

The United Kingdom retains an aristocratic element in the form of the House of Lords, one of the two parts of Parliament. The House of Commons, the members of which are elected as representatives of the people, is the more powerful part of Parliament.

Monist and dualist. This concerns the manner in which the constitution is receptive to international law in the form, for example, of treaties between nations or resolutions of the United Nations (UN). In a monist state, a treaty once ratified (confirmed) by the state is automatically part of that state's domestic law. For example, the Basic Law of the German Federal Republic, Article 25, states that the general principles of international law take precedence over domestic law and directly create rights and duties. The United Kingdom is a dualist state, in which international law is not binding in domestic law unless it has been adopted as part of our law, usually by an Act of Parliament.

The UK Constitution could be summarised as:

▶ uncodified;
▶ with an incomplete separation of powers: the judiciary being independent, but the executive and legislature partly combined;
▶ based on the rule of law and accountable government;
▶ unitary with some federal aspects;
▶ legally flexible;
▶ a constitutional monarchy;
▶ parliamentary;
▶ a representative democracy with an aristocratic element;
▶ bicameral;
▶ dualist.

1.8   Public and private law

Constitutional law is the most basic aspect of 'public law'. Broadly, public law governs the relationship between the government and individuals, and that between different governmental agencies. Private law concerns the relationship between individuals, and also deals with private organisations, such as companies. For reasons connected with a peculiarly English notion of the rule of law (Section 6.4) the distinction between public law and private law is less firmly embedded here than in the continental legal systems that inherited the distinction from Roman law. It was believed by Dicey that the liberties of the individual are best secured if the same law, broadly private law, governs officials and individuals alike so that officials have no special powers or status.

Attractive though this may be in certain respects (since it is premised upon formal equality), it is both unrealistic and arguably undesirable, given the huge powers that must be vested in the state to meet public demand for large-scale public services and government controls over daily life and the movement of the population.

Some writers have rejected the distinction between public and private law, at least on the level of fundamental principle, arguing that the same basic values and concepts pervade all law and that any given function could be carried out by the state or a private body (Section 19.5). It is difficult to deny that values such as fairness and openness are common to the private and public sectors, and that organisations such as charities that carry out functions for the benefit of the public on a non-profit basis have elements both of the public and of the private. This is particularly important today, when it is politically fashionable to entrust public services to profit-making private bodies. Moreover, there are numerous bodies not directly connected with the government that exercise vast powers over individuals, such as sporting and professional disciplinary bodies, trade unions and financial bodies. Beyond the core functions of keeping order and defence, there is no agreement in the United Kingdom as to what the proper sphere of the state is and which bodies are subject to public law.

Conversely, the Crown has the same legal powers as a private person, so government makes extensive use of private law in the contexts, for example, of contracts for the procurement of goods and equipment, employment and property. In this context, the government's economic power is so great (e.g. the purchase of NHS medicines), and its activities so wide-ranging, that it might be argued that these 'soft' powers should be treated as having a distinctive public law character.

There are important distinctions between public law and private law. These include:

- ▶ The government represents the whole community, and its officials (at least in principle) have no self-interest of their own. By contrast, a private company and an individual both have a legitimate self-interest, including the profit motive. It follows that government should be accountable to the community as a whole for its actions. By contrast, in the case of a private body, accountability might be regarded as an unacceptable intrusion on its freedom.
- ▶ Arguably, private law is fundamentally different from public law in that it concerns the voluntary interaction of individuals, calling for compromises, recognition of agreed solutions and concessions to vulnerability, whereas public law calls predominantly for general principles designed to structure and contain power. For example, in private law, a promise made is normally binding, whereas this is not usually the case in public law (Section 17.6.3).
- ▶ The government has the ultimate responsibility to protect the community against disruption and external threats. For this purpose, it must be entrusted with special powers to use force. As we shall see in Chapter 25, concerning emergencies, it may be difficult or impossible to reconcile this with our belief that all power should be curbed by law.
- ▶ The distinction between public and private law has particular implications in two main contexts. Firstly, there is the question of the scope of judicial review of decisions made by powerful bodies. This is limited to 'functions of a public nature' (Section 19.5). Secondly, the protection of the HRA applies mainly against public bodies and against bodies certain of whose functions are public functions (Section 22.5). A similar approach is taken in both contexts, the matter depending upon the extent to which the body in question is linked to the central government, for example, whether the body in question has special powers, whether it is controlled or financed by the government, and the public importance of its functions.

1.9 The direction of the constitution: reform

There is a widely shared belief that the constitution should not be subject to radical reforms but should evolve naturally, particular problems being dealt with as they arise. For example, there is strong resistance to altering the House of Lords on the basis that 'it works' (Section 12.3). This places constitutional reform at the mercy of the party politics of the day rather than subject to a special process designed to consider the long-term public interest. Ideally, there should be a special independent process to consider the issues and validate the new constitution.

The usual way of doing this is to hold a 'constitutional convention' composed of representatives of the main sectors of society. In a report issued in 2013 (HC 2012–13, 371), the Political and Constitutional

Reform Committee of the House of Commons saw value in establishing such an institution to reflect upon the consequences of recent rapid constitutional changes, and the possible future of the United Kingdom. The Conservative government elected in December 2019 promised to 'look at the broader aspects of our constitution' (including aspects such as the relationship between Parliament, government and courts, and the role of the House of Lords) following withdrawal from the European Union. To this end, it was proposed that a Constitution, Democracy and Rights Commission would be established in the first year of government. Unsurprisingly, since the government has been distracted by dealing with the COVID-19 pandemic, this has not yet happened and it seems likely that the proposal has been shelved, although Independent Reviews of Administrative Law focusing on judicial review, and and of the HRA were launched in 2020 (Sections 17.1, and 22.10).

Some commentators assert that there are general forces guiding the direction of the constitution. The 'Whig' view of history optimistically claims to find a progression from tyranny to democracy (Section 4.1). In this vein, Oliver (2009) suggests that four tendencies underlie constitutional reform. The first is towards 'principles'. These have been developed by the courts, for example the 'legitimate expectation' (Section 18.3.1) and 'proportionality' (Section 18.1.1), and also from within government, for example the 'Seven Principles of Public Life' (Section 5.9). The second tendency is towards 'governance', meaning reforming governmental processes. This would include, for example, the modernisation of parliamentary procedures. The third tendency, albeit perhaps hesitant and sporadic, is that of strengthening 'citizenship' in the sense of equality, for example the HRA and the Equality Act 2010. Oliver's fourth tendency is 'separation'. This would include devolution and the reforms to the court system made by the Constitutional Reform Act 2005, both of which enhance the separation of powers (Sections 7.5.3 and 7.6.2).

Bogdanor (2009) finds a tendency, albeit imperfect, towards dispersing power away from the centre and towards 'juridification' in the sense of using law rather than politics to make constitutional changes (see the discussion above on the 'political' and 'legal' constitution). There is also an increased reliance on written codes guiding the behaviour of politicians and officials. Some of these, such as the *Ministerial Code* (Section 15.1) and the *Cabinet Manual* (Section 3.4.1), are not legally enforceable. Others, such as the provisions governing MPs' salaries and expenses (Section 11.7.2), are statutory. It may be that these practices reflect public distrust in the capacity of those in power to govern without external constraints (Section 5.9).

Contemporary issues have placed the traditional model of the constitution under strain. In particular, the authority of state constitutions is challenged by globalisation, which in this context includes:

- the commitment to free markets by the powerful countries who control the main international organisations (the UN, the International Monetary Fund and the World Bank);
- a commitment, albeit less concrete, to international human rights and environmental standards, and the bringing to justice of political leaders who engage in international crimes such as genocide and torture;
- the ease with which money can be moved around the world;
- the international nature of problems such as terrorism, pandemics such as COVID-19, environmental protection and financial failure. State laws are sometimes ineffective, for example in dealing with terrorism, human trafficking and financial corruption;
- the fact that individual countries are increasingly dependent on others for resources and security.

The constitution provides filter mechanisms which to a certain extent recognise and control the influences of international actions and relationships on our own law and vice versa (Section 9.5), but otherwise, the law has not adapted well to globalisation. International affairs are still based on seventeenth-century ideas of self-contained sovereign states.

Summary

▶ Having read this chapter, you should have a general idea of some basic constitutional concepts and how they relate to the UK. Constitutions deal with the fundamental framework of government and its powers, reflecting the political interests of those who design and operate them and providing mechanisms for the control of government. The UK Constitution does not adequately address the international dimension of modern politics and economics.

▶ The UK Constitution is unwritten in the sense that there is no special constitutional document giving it a status superior to the ordinary law. The UK Constitution is made up of many ordinary laws and political conventions. Any special status depends on courts and officials giving it special weight when making decisions.

▶ The aim of a constitution is to manage disagreement in circumstances where collective action on behalf of the whole community is required. The UK Constitution provides a framework for this purpose. In particular, the courts protect basic individual rights.

▶ There is an underlying dispute as to how far constitutional disputes should be settled by courts or by elected bodies.

▶ There is a tendency in any form of government for powers to gravitate towards a single group. Thus, a primary concern of constitutional law is to provide checks and balances between different branches of government. We introduced the basic concepts of sovereignty, the rule of law, separation of powers and fundamental rights. However, the unwritten UK Constitution does not prevent power being concentrated in the hands of a wealthy minority.

▶ Political and legal aspects of a constitution should be distinguished, although the boundary between them is leaky and they have different perspectives. The legal aspects of the constitution are a distinctive part of the wider political context, each influencing the other. There are also important constitutional principles in the form of conventions and practices operating without a formal legal basis.

▶ The distinction between written and unwritten constitutions is of some but not fundamental importance. We compared the main advantages and disadvantages of written and unwritten constitutions without committing ourselves to one or the other since the matter is one for political choice. The UK Constitution is an untidy mixture of different kinds of law, practices and customs, and has a substantial informal element, which might lend itself to domination by certain networks or elites.

▶ We outlined the main categories of constitutions, emphasising that these are models and that actual constitutions need not closely correspond to any pure model. In particular, we discussed 'parliamentary' and 'presidential' models, the former concentrating power, the latter splitting it up. The UK Constitution is strongly parliamentary with perhaps a tendency towards federalism.

▶ The distinction between public law and private law is important, particularly in the context of the HRA and judicial review of powerful bodies. The courts have adopted a pragmatic approach to this question of classification.

Exercises

1.1 You are discussing constitutional law with an American legal expert who claims that the United Kingdom has no constitution. What does she mean, and how would you respond?

1.2 Sir John Laws ('The Constitution, Morals and Rights' [1996] PL 622) described a constitution as 'that set of legal rules which govern the relationship in a state between the ruler and the ruled'. To what extent is this an adequate description of the UK Constitution?

1.3 How well does the UK Constitution fit the various methods of classifying constitutions mentioned in this chapter?

1.4 'It is both a strength and a potential weakness of the British Constitution that, almost uniquely for an advanced democracy, it is not all set down in writing' (Royal Commission on the Reform of the House of Lords, Cm 4534, 2000) (the Wakeham Report). Discuss.

1.5 Should the courts have the power to overturn legislation?

1.6 Compare the merits of the parliamentary and presidential systems of government.

1.7 The government announces that, in the future, all proposals for new laws will be scrutinised in private by a 'forum' comprising the chief executives of the main banks and representatives of companies who contribute to the governing party. Are there any constitutional objections to this? Is further information needed to enable you to decide?

Further reading

Barber, *The Constitutional State* (Oxford University Press 2010)

Barker, 'Against a Written Constitution' [2008] PL 11

Blick, *Beyond Magna Carta: A Constitution for the United Kingdom* (Hart Publishing 2015)

Blick and Dickson, 'Why Does the UK Now Need a Written Constitution?' (2020) 71 NILQ 59

Bellamy, *Political Constitutionalism* (Cambridge University Press 2007) ch 1

Bogdanor, *The New British Constitution* (Hart Publishing 2009)

Bogdanor and Vogenauer, 'Enacting a British Constitution: Some Problems' [2008] PL 38

Ewing, 'The Politics of the British Constitution' [2000] PL 405

Feldman, 'None, One or Several? Perspectives on the UK's Constitution(s)' (2005) 64 CLJ 329

Feldman (ed), *Law in Politics, Politics in Law* (Hart Publishing 2013)

Finer, Bogdanor and Rudden, *Comparing Constitutions* (Oxford University Press 1995) ch 1

Gee, 'The Political Constitutionalism of JAG Griffith' (2008) 28 LS 20

Gee and Webber, 'What Is a Political Constitution?' (2010) 30 OJLS 273

Griffith, 'The Political Constitution' (1979) 42 MLR 1

Griffith, 'The Common Law and the Political Constitution' (2001) 117 LQR 42

Harlow and Rawlings, *Law and Administration* (3rd edn, Cambridge University Press 2009) ch 1

Hickman, 'In Defence of the Legal Constitution' (2005) 55 U Toronto LJ 981

King, 'The Democratic Case for a Written Constitution' in Jowell and O'Cinneide (eds), *The Changing Constitution* (9th edn, Oxford University Press 2019)

Leyland, *The Constitution of the United Kingdom: A Contextual Analysis* (Bloomsbury 2016)

Loughlin, *Sword and Scales* (Hart Publishing 2005)

Loughlin, *Foundations of Public Law* (Oxford University Press 2010) ch 10

Loughlin, *The British Constitution: A Very Short Introduction* (Oxford University Press 2013)

Munro, *Studies in Constitutional Law* (2nd edn, Butterworths 1999) ch 1

Oliver, 'The United Kingdom in Transition: From Where to Where?' in Andenas and Fairgrieve (eds), *Tom Bingham and the Transformation of the Law* (Oxford University Press 2009)

Poole, 'Tilting at Windmills? Truth and Illusion in the Political Constitution' (2007) 70 MLR 250

Qvortrup, 'Let Me Take You to a Foreign Land: The Political and the Legal Constitution' in Qvortrup (ed), *The British Constitution: Continuity and Change* (Hart Publishing 2013)

Ridley, 'There Is No British Constitution: A Dangerous Case of the Emperor's Clothes' (1988) 41 Parl Aff 340

Taylor, 'The Contested Constitution: an Analysis of the Competing Models of British Constitutionalism' [2018] PL 500

Tomkins, 'In Defence of the Political Constitution' (2002) 22 OJLS 157

Ward, *The English Constitution: Myths and Realities* (Hart Publishing 2004)

Chapter 2

Underlying political traditions

2.1 Introduction

Western European constitutions have been influenced by three broad and overlapping political traditions. These are loosely termed 'liberalism', 'republicanism' and 'communitarianism'. Each emphasises a different aspect of human nature and privileges different values. Liberalism, although relatively modern, is the dominant tradition. It is based on the notions of individual freedom and limited government. It assumes that the individual is the best judge of how he or she should live and that the state should not prefer one way of life over another. It therefore concentrates on limiting the power of the state.

Republicanism is an ancient notion inherited from classical Greece. It favours the concept of the 'virtuous citizen'. Drawing upon our social and cooperative nature as what Aristotle called 'political animals', republicanism concentrates on political involvement as equal citizens in governing ourselves and preventing any elite becoming dominant.

Communitarianism goes further in a collective direction. It emphasises our nature as herd animals that live by copying each other. It emphasises the virtues of sympathy and mutual support within the customs and traditions in which different communities are embedded. It is particularly concerned to protect the interests of groups such as ethnic minorities. The communitarian tradition is less prominent in the UK than in other European countries. For example, the French Constitution places liberty, equality and fraternity together. Within the UK, the provisions for devolved governments in Scotland, Wales and Northern Ireland embody certain communitarian elements, notably in the case of Northern Ireland concerning the interests of the different communities in the province (Section 16.4).

We would not expect a particular constitution to fit neatly into any single set of values; rather, we might expect to find values associated with all three traditions scattered throughout the constitution, with some more prominent than others depending on the circumstances at any given time. Moreover, each tradition has varying shades, so that in many contexts their practical conclusions overlap.

The three traditions might differ especially as to the extent to which they would protect fundamental rights such as freedom of expression. Liberalism would place an especially high value on individual freedom of expression, as, for example, does the US Constitution. Republicanism would regard freedom of expression primarily as an instrument to ensure citizen participation in government, and not as an end in itself. Republicanism and liberalism would concur in placing an especially high value on political freedom. To a communitarian, freedom of expression might be regarded as divisive, selfish and frustrating community values.

2.2 Liberalism

Liberalism is the dominant political belief in the UK and is sometimes invoked by the courts. For example, according to Lord Steyn in *R (Roberts) v Parole Board* [2006] 1 All ER 39, 'in our system the working assumption is that Parliament legislates for a European liberal democracy which respects fundamental rights'. However, given the different meanings of liberalism (below), such a generalisation is not particularly useful. Liberalism developed gradually from the seventeenth century, originating most prominently with John Locke (1632–1704).

It is difficult to identify concrete principles upon which all liberals agree. However, the following might be viewed as the main principles of liberalism:

▶ Liberalism emphasises the interests of the individual rather than the collective interests of the community. The state exists only to protect the interests of the individual.

▶ The interests of all individuals except those who harm others are worthy of equal concern and respect. This of course begs the question as to what counts as 'harm'. It might, for example, merely mean interference that the rulers themselves find unpleasant.

▶ Individuals should be free to follow their own chosen way of life ('autonomy'). Liberalism attempts to place constraints on government in the interests of individual freedom and to give the individual an area of private life that is out of bounds to the state. Liberal laws are therefore tolerant of minorities and dissenters. A problem here is the so-called liberal contradiction – namely, how far to tolerate a dissenter who threatens the security of the liberal state itself. For example, liberalism is secular in that it treats religion as a private and personal matter. This is a distinctive feature of European culture emerging from Protestant beliefs dating from the sixteenth century. This risks intolerance of groups who regard religion as pervading all areas of life, including government. In particular, it is a factor in contemporary conflicts between secular societies and fundamentalist religious groups (Section 21.4.4.3).

▶ Liberalism claims to be rational. It seeks a constitution that free and equal people would rationally support. It recognises that there is likely to be irreducible disagreement even among people of goodwill and so favours caution about state intervention.

▶ Liberalism is international and favours cooperation between nations. Thus, liberals broadly support organisations such as the EU that attempt to override national interests.

Liberalism is not universally admired, sometimes being condemned as selfish, uncaring and favouring the individual over the group. A modest defence of liberalism is that it at least tries to make room for other beliefs, recognising the desire to avoid conflicts. Liberal societies have been relatively stable and peaceful. Indeed, the desire for peace was the historical origin of liberalism, as a response to the religious conflicts that disrupted Europe during the sixteenth and seventeenth centuries. Once the bond supplied by a dominant religion had been dissolved, it became impossible to govern people of widely different beliefs without either conferring a large amount of individual freedom or resorting to oppression, which would ultimately destroy the community.

Liberalism is not wedded to any particular form of government. Liberals usually support democracy as the form of government most likely to secure individual freedom, but unlike republicans, do not value democracy as an end in itself, having no objection in principle to securing individual rights through the undemocratic means of a court. Moreover, in contrast to republicanism, liberalism is not especially interested in whether citizens directly participate in governmental decision-making, but accepts government by an elite accountable to citizens.

Liberalism would emphasise in particular the following:

▶ Decision-makers must be open and accountable. It must be borne in mind that mechanisms for making a decision-maker accountable are not the same for each kind of decision-maker. For example, it is arguably wrong to elect judges, since election risks compromising the independence of a court. Conversely, the arguments for elected lawmakers are strong since they can be removed if they make laws to which the people object. In both cases, it is normally important that the decision-making process be open and public, but sometimes confidentiality may be a competing concern, for example in cases involving the methods of the secret security services and in order to protect vulnerable people, such as children.

▶ Government power must be limited, and no single institution should have the last word so as to irrevocably to close off debate. For example, the lawmaker must not be able to bind future lawmakers (Section 8.4.3), and court decisions should allow dissenting judgments. The courts have an important role in protecting individuals against abuse of power and safeguarding fundamental rights, but there must be checks and balances between the courts and the lawmaker.

▶ Individual rights are respected, but are not necessarily absolute. There is considerable disagreement within liberalism as to when individual rights can be overridden.

▶ Departures from treating everyone equally must be justified. There must, in particular, be equal access to courts of law, and public office must be open to anyone with suitable qualifications.

2.3   Varieties of liberalism in constitutional thought

There are many varieties of liberalism, each applying the basic ingredients of freedom and equality in different ways. The following classical writers have influenced the development of constitutional thought in the UK and exemplify particular points on the map of liberalism.

2.3.1   Thomas Hobbes (1588–1679): the impersonal state and individualism

A fundamental change in political thinking emerged in the sixteenth century when the church and the state became separated. The idea of the state as an impersonal organisation intended to serve everyone was revived from classical antiquity by republican thinkers such as Machiavelli. Hobbes was one of the earliest English exponents of this approach and, although not himself a liberal, he generated ideas that are basic to liberalism.

Hobbes published his most influential work, *Leviathan*, in 1651, following a time of widespread political unrest when England was in the grip of religious turmoil and civil war between an authoritarian king and an equally authoritarian Parliament dominated by religious interests (of his other works, *The Elements of Law* is of particular interest).

He tried to explain the rationale of legal authority without drawing upon religion. Hobbes doubted whether it was possible to discover objective truth about anything. He had a strongly individualistic approach based on the equality of all citizens.

Hobbes believed that human affairs involve endless disagreement and therefore that a constitution has solid foundations only in the minimum government on which it is possible rationally to agree.

The basis of government, in Hobbes's view, was the need for certainty so as to make civilisation possible. Without certainty, in Hobbes's most famous aphorism, life would be 'nasty, brutish and short'. According to Hobbes, beyond the private sphere of family and personal relationships, society is driven by three impulses: competition, fear and the desire for power over others. We constantly strive to fulfil new desires in a never-ending and ultimately doomed search for what he called 'felicity'. Hobbes therefore argued that any government is better than none, and that 'the concord of many cannot be maintained without power to keep them all in awe' (*Elements of Law*, XIX, 4).

As with many liberal thinkers, Hobbes's idea of government was based on an imaginary 'social contract' according to which free and equal people would choose to give up their natural freedom in exchange for the benefits of government. This symbolises that government depends on the consent of the governed, hence Hobbes's relevance to contemporary democratic ideas.

The controversial question is what form of government free and equal people would agree to, and to this question, there is no generally accepted answer. According to Hobbes, the need for someone to settle disputes and keep order is the basic purpose of government. There must therefore be a single ultimate ruler, a sovereign, 'Leviathan', who has unlimited power and ultimately rules by force, to whom the people consent to surrender their natural freedom: '[A]ll the duties of the rulers are contained in this one sentence, the safety of the people is the supreme law' (by 'safety' Hobbes meant not just the preservation of life but also general justice and wellbeing; see *Elements of Law*, XXVIII, 1).

In order to minimise disagreement, the sovereign must be a single unitary body, an 'artificial man'. This could be either a monarch or an assembly. Hobbes's sovereign has no special qualifications for ruling, but is merely the representative of the community. The obligation of the sovereign derives from its gratitude to the people for the free gift of power. Hobbes believed that humans have certain 'natural' rights based on keeping promises, respect for individual freedom and equality: 'Do not that to another, which thou wouldest not have done to thyself' (*Leviathan*, XV). He also believed, anticipating modern liberalism, that the ruler should ideally leave the people as much liberty as possible without hurt to the public (*Elements of Law*, XXVIII). However, according to Hobbes, natural rights are no more than rational hopes or expectations and have no binding force unless the lawmaker chooses to protect them.

In Hobbes's view, because the sovereign itself needs security, the interests of the sovereign and the people naturally coincide since the sovereign needs to keep the people happy. However, it may be that the money provided by business interests coupled with modern technology – with its surveillance devices and weapons – makes a lawmaker less dependent on the happiness of the people than was the case in Hobbes's time.

Under that ultimate sovereign, there can be many different detailed government arrangements. Hobbes's government has only two crucial features. First, because of the uncertainty of human affairs, Leviathan must have unlimited power since otherwise there would be the very disagreement that the sovereign exists to resolve. However, Hobbes's Leviathan expresses itself through law, not random discretion.

Second, the sovereign exists for a single purpose, the welfare of his subjects, and has no authority to act for any other purpose. Thus, the sovereign should act so that 'the giver shall have no just occasion to repent him of his gift' (*De Cive*, III, 8). However, Hobbes was clear that it was for the ruler alone to decide whether it needed to exercise its powers, and he provided no legal remedy against a ruler that exceeded its power, regarding the matter as one for divine retribution.

Hobbes's ideas, although perhaps a one-sided view of human nature, underrating our sympathy and identification with others, are relevant to the modern constitution in that they identify recurring themes and claims. These include the following:

- Government depends on the consent of the people and is the representative of the people.
- The importance of certainty in the community. We associate this with the rule of law.
- The state has unlimited authority over all aspects of life, a contested notion that is central to constitutional debate. The contemporary question is whether there should be any individual rights that are sacrosanct.
- The most important function of government is the keeping of order and the protection of the people.
- A single sovereign to resolve disagreement. In our case, this is the doctrine of parliamentary supremacy.
- All citizens are equal. No one should have powers or rights or be subject to special obligations based on factors such as birth, custom, social status or religion.
- Freedom is the natural state of affairs, as opposed to a gift bestowed by authority. According to Hobbes, 'right is that liberty which the law leaves us' (*Elements of Law*, XXIX, 5). The sovereign can make any law, but unless it does so the individual is free to do what he or she likes: '[F]reedom lies in the silence of the laws.'
- The separation of politics from religion, church from state.
- The distinction between the public and the private spheres. In relation to areas of life not controlled by the state – namely, those where public order and safety are not at risk – what a person does is not the state's business.
- Laws concern external behaviour, not matters of personal belief or conscience. For example, under Art 9 of the European Convention on Human Rights (ECHR), freedom of religious belief is absolute, but the 'manifestation of religion' can be restricted on certain public interest grounds (Section 21.4.4.3).

Hobbes was not concerned with republican issues of participation in government. Nor did he tackle the problem of how to make government accountable. He did not deal with the problem that, in all but the simplest societies, power must in practice be divided up and rulers must rely on advisers, thereby creating potential disagreements. Hobbes disliked the common law because it is made by courts. In a long-running dispute with Coke, the Lord Chief Justice, Hobbes attacked the view of the judges that law is 'artificial reason' that resides in the learning of an elite group (i.e. themselves) as a childish fiction. He recognised a place for rules derived from natural reason which must be applied where there are gaps in the written law, but thought that these depended on the consent of the sovereign (*Elements of Law*, XXIX, 10). This dispute is echoed today in several contexts where one school of thought claims that the courts are the guardians of the values of the community (see Sections 8.5.6, 17.2 and 21.2).

2.3.2   John Locke (1632–1704): individual rights and majority government

Locke tackled the issue sidestepped by Hobbes – namely, the accountability of government. He is widely regarded as a founder of modern liberalism and constitutionalism. Locke's writings (*Second Treatise of Government*, 1690) supported the 1688 revolution (see Section 4.5), against the claims of absolute monarchy. They also influenced the US Constitution. Locke's approach was grounded in the Protestant religion, which stressed individual conscience and self-improvement by hard work, within a secular state which treats religion as a personal and private matter (Section 5.8).

Locke believed that individuals had certain natural rights which could be identified by reasoning about human nature. These are life, health, freedom and property. For him, the purpose of government is to protect these rights, particularly property, in the exceptional cases where conflicts arise. To this extent, Locke's government serves the same function as that of Hobbes. However, unlike Hobbes's, Locke's government has limited powers. Hobbes's and Locke's contrasting views still underlie much debate about the nature of the constitution.

Locke promoted a social contract theory, of a kind which is still favoured by some liberals. According to Locke, the people first hypothetically contract with each other unanimously to establish a government, and then choose an actual government by majority vote. The government undertakes to perform its functions of protecting natural rights and advancing wellbeing. Thus, unlike Hobbes's Leviathan, Locke's government is limited.

Locke's basic principles can be found in modern liberal constitutions. First, there is the idea that government depends upon the consent of the people. According to Locke, government should be appointed and dismissed periodically by a majority vote representing those with a stake in the community. Locke justified majority voting on the basis that the majority commands most force, but he recognised that there is no logical reason why a majority should be 'right' in relation to any particular issue. Second, Locke was concerned to limit the power of government in order to protect the rights and freedoms of the individual, which he considered primarily to be property and freedom of speech. However, liberals do not agree on how this should be done, for example whether by courts or by democratic mechanisms.

Locke himself did not favour detailed legal constraints on government, regarding the contribution of lawyers as 'the Phansies and intricate contrivances of men, following contrary and hidden interests put into words' (*Second Treatise of Government*, para 12). He relied on dividing up government power so that no one branch can be dominant: the separation of powers (see Chapter 7). He also insisted that governments should periodically be held to account by means of elections, and upheld, as a last resort, the right to rebel against a government that broke its trust.

Third, Locke promoted 'toleration' of different ways of life provided that these did not upset the basic political framework. For example, he did not favour toleration of Catholics, whom he regarded as subversive. Moreover, he drafted the Constitution of Carolina (in the United States) to accommodate slaves as property, since this advanced the economic system of the day. This apparent double standard is one of the alleged contradictions of liberalism. Thus, liberalism downgrades some interests to protect itself. This approach is seen today in the form of 'national security' to defend illiberal laws aimed at terrorism.

According to Locke, a criminal rejects the social contract and is therefore outside legal protection. This argument is sometimes used to justify the UK's blanket ban on convicted prisoners having the right to vote (Section 12.5.5). However, in *R (Chester) v Secretary of State for Justice* [2014] 1 All ER 683, Lord Sumption rejected this extreme position in favour of the more moderate version that a criminal can be temporarily barred from participation in society as a sign of society's disapproval.

Utilitarianism: David Hume (1711–76), Jeremy Bentham (1748–1832),
John Stuart Mill (1806–73)

Utilitarianism is arguably the dominant belief system influencing contemporary government and is closely related to democracy. Dicey, one of the most influential constitutional lawyers, was essentially a utilitarian.

Utilitarians believe that what is the right thing to do depends upon its consequences. This of course begs the question of what counts as a good consequence. Utilitarians favour the satisfaction of the wishes of as many people as possible; an approach which is attractive to the mindset of officials, but not necessarily to that of the lawyer since it may sidestep questions of fairness and justice. The case of *Copsey* (Section 2.4) affords an example.

David Hume, whose ideas influence the common law, was a founder of utilitarianism. He thought that government is a matter of practical compromise. He rejected the social contract as a fiction and regarded ideals of abstract justice as myths useful for persuading people to conform. Hume advocated a pragmatic society based on coordinating individual interests. He believed that our limited knowledge, strength and altruism provided the moral basis for a legal system. Contrasting with Hobbes, Hume thought that self-interest and our natural sympathy for others would generate basic principles of cooperation, including respect for private property, voluntary dealings and keeping promises. Hume favoured the common law as a vehicle for this, on the basis that the law is developed pragmatically in light of changing social practices and values.

Jeremy Bentham is the most celebrated utilitarian. He gave intellectual respectability to the idea of an all-powerful central government making general laws, which was accountable to a majority of the people. Using the slogan 'the greatest happiness of the greatest number', Bentham measured utility by counting people's actual demands, giving each equal weight ('each counts for one and none for more than one') and refusing to treat any preference as better than any other ('pushpin is as good as poetry'). Bentham's version of utilitarianism involves strong democratic controls to ensure that the law represents public opinion (see generally Craig, 'Bentham, Public Law and Democracy' [1989] PL 407). Bentham regarded law and courts as subordinate to utilitarian considerations. In particular, he regarded legal certainty and judicial independence, what we call the 'rule of law', as a sham. He thought that the idea of natural rights promoted by Locke was 'nonsense on stilts', claiming that rights were simply legal mechanisms, that law is merely a tool of government and public opinion is the ultimate authority.

Utilitarianism is replete with problems, particularly in relation to justice and fairness. For example, utilitarianism is consistent with slavery, in that the standard of living of a majority might be held to outweigh the loss of freedom of a minority. A utilitarian could reasonably posit that innocent people could be shot in order to disperse a public meeting or be kept in jail even if wrongly convicted in order to preserve public confidence in the police (see Lord Denning in *McIlkenny v Chief Constable of the West Midlands Police* [1980] 2 All ER 227, at 239–40). Utilitarianism also finds difficulty with the notion of rights and obligations. Why should I pay you what I have promised if I now discover a better use for the money? Can utilitarianism really give equal weight to all preferences without some non-utilitarian filter to exclude 'irrational' or 'immoral' preferences, such as those of paedophiles? These and other problems have been widely discussed, without clear agreement on a conclusion.

John Stuart Mill tried to reconcile utilitarianism with liberal individualism by claiming that maximising individual freedom is the best way to advance general welfare, since it encourages the virtues of creativity. He believed that happiness could best be achieved by experimenting with different ways of life. This led to Mill's emphasis on freedom of expression and his influential 'harm' principle – namely, that the only ground on which the state should interfere with individual freedom is to prevent harm to others. The state should not normally interfere paternalistically to protect a person for his or her own good. However, this begs the question of what counts as 'harm', since harm can be defined as anything we dislike. For example, does harm include 'offence' if someone pokes fun at my religious beliefs (see Chapter 23)?

Mill did not apply his harm principle to those who were unable fully to make rational judgments, such as children: uncomfortably, Mill seemed to extend this to colonised peoples. He was also a romantic, reminding us that ideas such as justice may not be purely rational, in the sense of being possible to pin down as legal rules, but have an emotional and spiritual dimension (see Ward, 'The Echo of a Sentimental Jurisprudence' (2002) 15 Law and Critique 107).

However, Mill, followed by Dicey, departed from strict utilitarianism in two ways. First, he believed that a person who makes independent choices and does not unthinkingly follow the majority is to be especially valued as having a better 'character'. Second, in contrast with Bentham's insistence that all pleasures are of equal value, he thought that the higher and more intellectual pleasures enjoyed by a well-educated minority were better than the lower pleasures enjoyed by the mob. Thus, some ways of life, notably those of the creative artist or the intellectual, are objectively better than others and can be favoured by the state. On the other hand, Mill would not have welcomed the contemporary practice of giving privileged access to government to business and financial interests.

The conflict between the different recipes of Mill and Bentham is reflected in contemporary legal and political issues, especially in relation to the question of the compromise between individual rights (Mill) and the wishes of the majority (Bentham). Not surprisingly, there is no overarching general principle. Sometimes, most notably in the increased respect given to minorities since the 1960s, Mill's values triumph. In other areas, most obviously that of state surveillance, a version of the general welfare has prevailed over individual freedom (Section 25.3).

2.3.4   Market liberalism (neo-liberalism): Friedrich Hayek (1899–1992)

Market liberalism claims to provide an objective method of resolving disputes. It is a form of utilitarianism. Market liberalism is concerned with harnessing what it regards as the primary human impulse of self-interest, in pursuit of the common good. It does so by encouraging competition between autonomous individuals relying on the allegedly objective measure of money. It gives the state a limited but strong role as a supposedly neutral umpire to ensure that free competition takes place. Its latest incarnation, neo-liberalism, has no compunction in using force to ensure conformity to its idea of freedom, thereby illustrating what opponents of liberalism regard as liberalism's inbuilt contradiction.

Market liberalism has been fashionable in UK government circles for several decades. A market liberal constitution requires a strong, highly centralised government as envisaged by Hobbes (Section 2.3.1). Indeed, the operation of any market system depends on a strong state to provide shared infrastructure such as roads, and security if things go wrong, as evidenced by the banking crisis of 2008, or the COVID-19 pandemic. The UK Constitution is therefore well suited to market liberalism (as, indeed, it is to any single-minded ideology) since a sovereign Parliament can easily be controlled by a cohesive group. For example, there are no legal restrictions preventing the state from transferring any of its functions to the private market.

There is no necessary connection between market liberalism and democracy or liberal beliefs in moral and social freedom. Indeed, because financial interests welcome stability, authoritarian and repressive governments can support market liberalism. A market liberal, such as former UK Prime Minister Margaret Thatcher, might claim to harness valuable human impulses in the economic sphere while suppressing what she or he regards as harmful human impulses elsewhere. As a form of utilitarianism, market liberalism does not value freedom for its own sake, but only as a means to an end, this end being wealth maximisation. Moreover, those lacking money who are excluded from the market are likely to be suppressed and many 'goods', for example health or the environment, are not easily reducible to a market.

Hayek was the outstanding champion of the relationship between market liberalism and the law. Hayek did believe that market liberalism was related to more general freedoms. According to Hayek, the state has neither the knowledge nor the competence to plan people's lives, and efficient solutions are best found through free interchange in the market, the price mechanism acting as a store of knowledge of supply and demand. The market encourages people to produce goods that others want. It also respects individual freedom, since people can decide for themselves what they want to buy or sell.

Hayek seems to assume that within a society which maximises individual freedom, shared understandings will emerge on which enough people agree for life to be harmonious: what he called the 'spontaneous order'. Hayek relied on the notion of the rule of law as a framework of certain general rules within which we can be 'free' to plan our lives. Following Hume (above), he favoured the common law since it produces rules generated from below by individual cases.

According to 'public choice' theory (an application of the theory of market liberalism to the state itself), politicians and officials are driven by self-interest. Thus, if left alone, they will try to maximise their incomes, expand their territories and spheres of influence, and minimise their workloads. Market liberalism may be attractive to politicians and officials partly because it provides an allegedly objective means of making policy since, according to market liberalism, the market can never be wrong. Thus, the role of the law is only to ensure that the market operates as freely as possible. Examples are the contemporary practices of privatisation and 'outsourcing' of public services such as the railways, utility companies, health services, elderly care homes, schools, and prisons, and the splitting up of many civil service operations into semi-autonomous 'executive agencies' run along the lines of private business (Section 15.9). Where goods and services cannot be competed for, regulatory mechanisms are created to simulate competitive price mechanisms, for example by setting targets and standards with accompanying rewards and penalties (Section 20.4).

2.3.5   Welfare liberalism: John Rawls (1921–2000): liberal justice and equality

Welfare liberalism recognises that individual freedom and market freedom may be of little value unless we have the basic resources, public and private, to live fulfilled and comfortable lives as social beings. Welfare liberalism therefore overlaps with communitarianism (in the USA the term 'liberal' is commonly used to mean this form of liberalism). Welfare liberalism, if it is to operate at a constitutional level, therefore requires positive protections for social goods such as health, security, education, dignity, friendship and leisure. Parliamentary supremacy means that UK law is capable of participating in these protections but, in practice, there is relatively little specific legal protection for welfare goals. The HRA concentrates on individual freedoms (but see Article 8 ECHR: respect for family life, Section 21.4.4.1). By contrast, European Union law, which (pre-Brexit) has had priority over domestic law, has a stronger welfare element, a factor which has traditionally troubled certain politicians from the right of the political spectrum, and led several of them to campaign (successfully) for the UK to leave the Union in the referendum of June 2016.

An influential version of welfare liberalism based on the social contract device is that of John Rawls:

> Our exercise of political power is proper and hence justifiable only when it is exercised in accordance with a constitution the essentials of which all citizens may be reasonably expected to endorse in the light of principles and ideas acceptable to them as reasonable and rational. This is the liberal principle of legitimacy. (*Political Liberalism* (Columbia University Press 1993) 217)

One problem with this is its reliance on the word 'reasonably', since we may disagree as to what is reasonable. Who decides what is 'reasonably expected' in a society made up of people with many different beliefs? To answer this question, Rawls constructed an imaginary 'original position' in which a representative group of people ignorant of their own circumstances, including sex, race or wealth, decide what would be a just constitution (*A Theory of Justice* (Oxford University Press 1972)). The purpose of this 'veil of ignorance' is to ensure equality and the removal of self-interested influences. However, one might argue that it also reduces people to clones, thinking as one and therefore not making an agreement at all in any real sense. Rawls was, of course, aware of this and later introduced the watered-down notion of an 'overlapping consensus'. This is a settlement that people from a wide variety of backgrounds might be prepared to acknowledge as reasonable. However, underlying all this is the liberal assumption that people want to agree and might be willing to compromise. It is by no means obvious that this is the case. Rawls acknowledges this, claiming that his arguments are political rather than philosophical and apply only in a community that is broadly sympathetic to liberal values ('Justice as Fairness: Political Not Metaphysical' in Freeman (ed), *Collected Papers* (Harvard University Press 1999); but see Skidelsky and Skidelsky, *How Much Is Enough? The Love of Money and the Case for the Good Life* (Allen Lane 2012), objecting to Rawls's idea of a neutral state as a misreading of liberalism).

Rawls identifies two fundamental 'principles of justice'. The first is that 'each person is to have an equal right to the most extensive basic liberty compatible with a similar liberty for others' (*A Theory of Justice*, 60). These liberties operate in the constitutional sphere. They include political freedoms, freedom of speech, personal liberty and the right to hold private property. This principle has priority over the second, the 'difference principle', which is concerned with allocating the resources of society: 'Social and economic inequalities are to be arranged so that they are both (a) reasonably expected to be to everyone's advantage, and (b) attached to positions and offices open to all' (*A Theory of Justice*, 60). Rawls is prepared to redistribute resources from rich to poor on the ground that much wealth is accumulated by chance, either through inheritance or through abilities that we happen to be born with. We therefore owe a duty to help the less fortunate. However, fundamental freedoms cannot be overridden in the interests of some other social goal. This distinguishes a liberal from a communitarian perspective.

2.3.6   Liberal pluralism: group liberalism

Liberal pluralism, sometimes called 'identity politics' or 'the politics of recognition', is similar to communitarianism and not always regarded as a kind of liberalism (see Anderson, *Constitutional Rights after Globalism* (Hart 2005); Galston (2005)). It requires the state to respect the identities and way of life of different groups such as national, religious, ethnic or sexual minorities, as well as political associations, trade unions, vocational groups and the like. It may therefore conflict with other liberal ideas of equality. The groups protected by pluralism might be disadvantaged because of the stereotype of the 'normal' person represented by the ruling group, in our case the White, able-bodied, heterosexual, culturally Christian male.

Baroness Hale stated in *In re G (Adoption) (Unmarried Couple)* [2009] 1 AC 173, at [122], that the protection of unpopular minorities is a particular duty of the courts. Liberal pluralism requires active steps to ensure that all such groups have the leverage to participate fully in the life of the community and to express their own identity against that of the dominant group, for example by being represented in public institutions, using their own language and giving effect to their own law and courts, as in the case of Islamic and Jewish laws. It is not enough merely to tolerate or attempt to integrate such groups into the mainstream, as is the dominant approach of UK law, since this implies only limited acceptance. The danger of identity politics is that it might encourage hostility between different groups, since its extreme 'identity' implies rejecting outsiders.

Liberal pluralism might therefore conflict with other kinds of liberalism, particularly where the values of the group conflict with more individualistic values; for example, a religious sect might claim that corporal punishment is part of its religion (*R (Williamson) v Secretary of State for Education and Employment* [2005] 2 All ER 1). A group might also claim that its way of life should be supported by the state (e.g. the provision and funding of religious schools), or should have special treatment to compensate for past injustices.

Liberal pluralism would place less stress on equality and rationality than would other forms of liberalism. Thus, there is the problem of a group whose values are authoritarian: the famous liberal dilemma of 'tolerating intolerance'. According to Lord Walker in *Williamson*, at [60], 'in matters of human rights the courts should not show liberal tolerance only to tolerant liberals'. For example, a common liberal claim is that liberalism contains universal truths derived from reason, and that a liberal law should not permit a religious group to prevent its members from leaving it. However, such freedom might be unacceptable to a religion that teaches, along the lines of positive freedom (Section 2.4), that compulsion is in a person's best interests. Some liberals suggest the proper approach is that the members of any group must accept that the state, in order to protect itself, can override their interests provided that the decision process used is fair to all interests. However, there may not be agreement as to what a fair process means (see Raz, 'Multiculturalism' (1998) 11 *Ratio Juris* 193).

In terms of constitutional arrangements, we would expect liberal pluralists to emphasise open and dispersed government and the equal representation of minority groups in public institutions such as the judiciary. The different devolved arrangements in Scotland, Northern Ireland and Wales (Chapter 16) could be presented as embodying this, at least to some degree. It is often suggested that one part of the legislature, the House of Lords, might comprise representatives of important interest groups. At present, the only such groups represented in Parliament are the aristocracy and Church of England bishops (Section 12.2). Liberal pluralism would also favour voluntary mechanisms to enable individuals to participate in society, for example tax breaks for charities and other voluntary bodies ('civil society').

Liberal pluralism might not be sympathetic to the idea of an overarching state law and might be required to respect different interpretations of the law according to the culture and traditions of different religious or ethnic groups, and to allow particular groups to use their own form of dispute resolution machinery, including courts. In the UK, voluntary methods of arbitration are permitted in respect of commercial disputes, and a variety of forms of marriage are recognised. However, these are subject to overriding requirements of the general law.

2.4   Freedom

The idea of freedom is central to liberalism. Some regard freedom as an end in itself: 'He who desires in liberty anything other than itself is born to be a servant' (De Tocqueville, *L'Ancien Regime* (1856) Patterson tr. (Blackwell 1947) 178). However, it is difficult to regard freedom as an end in itself, let alone the highest end. Do we, for example, regard Hitler's freedom to pursue his interests as something good in itself, although offset by the harm he did? Moreover, freedom may conflict with 'equality' since the strong are free to exploit the weak.

Freedom has different, vague and sometimes conflicting meanings. At the most basic level, liberalism contains a conflict between two ideas of freedom. This affects the extent to which different political groups regard state intervention as a good or a bad thing. There are two broad strands of thought:

1. *Traditional or negative freedom*, meaning the absence of interference, is what most of us understand by freedom. For example, negative social freedom as presented by Mill (Section 2.3.3) concentrates on the individual as 'author of his own life' – that is, freeing the individual from interference by the state. Economic liberalism relies on the idea of the free market and the belief that competing individuals pursuing their own self-interests are more likely to produce generally good outcomes than the state. The role of the state is a limited one of ensuring that the free market operates smoothly: a government with as few powers as possible beyond the basic functions of defence and keeping order.

   Social and economic freedom do not necessarily go together politically and do not lead to any particular conclusion as to how freedom should be protected, whether by a court or by democratic means. Arguably, economic liberalism depends on a certain degree of social conformity in order to ensure that enough people buy the goods on offer and to control those who lose out from the adverse consequences of competition.

   A fundamental problem with negative freedom is that some freedoms may conflict with others. Thus, the relative importance assigned to competing freedoms, such as freedom of the press against privacy (e.g. *Campbell v MGN Ltd* [2004] 2 All ER 995), may be controversial, and courts must sometimes choose between them: an exercise in which the idea of negative freedom is unhelpful. There seems to be no common measure to enable us to rank or compare different freedoms (e.g. *Copsey* below). Thus, when the law restricts freedom in order to protect the freedom of others as liberalism recommends (e.g. by restricting demonstrators in order to protect those going to work), it is not maximising freedom but only redistributing freedom among different people according to the lawmakers' preference as to which freedom is more attractive. This leads to a discussion of the second kind of freedom.

2. *Positive freedom*, an older idea, is freedom not to do what we want as such, but to control our lives by doing what is good for us. Freedom in this sense means exercising the power of reason to make choices that enhance the possibilities of our lives, thus 'liberating' our higher nature from our animal instincts and allowing us to control our own destinies (autonomy). For example, a drunk may have negative freedom but, having lost self-control, has no positive freedom. Plato (c428–c348bc), who recommended authoritarian rule, insisted: you are not free when you are a slave to your desires. Freedom is mastery by the rational self, mastery by knowledge of what is really good (Gorman, *Rights and Reason* (Acumen 2003) 33). Locke (Section 2.3.2) puts forward a version of positive freedom when he asserts that freedom means the exercise of specific rights protected by the law, whereas Hobbes treats freedom as the absence of law: 'By Liberty, is understood ... the absence of external impediments' (*Leviathan*, XIV).

The two kinds of freedom sometimes support each other, since negative freedom enables us to exercise choices. However, positive freedom is, in one sense, wider since it combats restrictions on our power to choose good things caused not just by interference by the state, but also by social and economic conditions such as poverty or a bad environment. It requires government action to limit negative freedom, such as distributing resources for services such as education, wealth and health care to enable people to make genuine choices and so take control of their lives.

In another sense, positive freedom is narrower in that it concentrates only on freedom to do good things. Positive freedom also allows us to claim paradoxically that obeying the law is 'freedom', in that law gives us a degree of rational choice by providing stability, which enables us to plan our lives. But there remains the difficult question of who decides what is good (below).

Attitudes of negative and positive freedom towards law therefore differ. Negative freedom concentrates on limiting state power, thus reflecting the red-light perspective (Section 1.5): the role for law is to protect autonomy from state interference, not as a tool for the state to intervene. Positive freedom (green light) is open to greater government control since it is consistent with the state designating what are valuable choices. The distinction between positive and negative freedom sometimes underlies disagreements in the courts. For example, in *Tomlinson v Congleton DC* [2003] 3 All ER 1122, the claimant had, despite warning notices, jumped into a pool owned by a local authority and broken his neck. The question was whether a local authority was obliged to do more to protect against this risk. Lord Hoffmann remarked – from the negative freedom perspective – that our liberal individualistic system meant that the 'nanny state' should not be encouraged and that, given there was a clear warning notice, the claimant should be responsible for his own safety. By contrast, Sedley LJ in the Court of Appeal took the view, characteristic of positive freedom, that the local authority should take precautions to guard people against their own irrationality.

According to Isaiah Berlin (2002), positive freedom has a sinister aspect. Who decides what is good and rational? Human affairs are notoriously prone to disagreement. How does one compare and choose between different freedoms which are 'incommensurable', meaning that there is no objective way of measuring their relative importance against each other? This is especially important in human rights law where two or more rights or values (such as freedom of expression and privacy) may conflict. For example, should one condone torture in the interests of good international relations (see *Jones v Ministry of Interior of Saudi Arabia* [2007] 1 All ER 113 (Section 9.5.2)), or perhaps in order to save the lives of others?

Positive freedom might justify the state claiming that a particular way of life, for example one based on a religious cult, an economic theory, or belonging to the European Union, is 'rationally' better than others and is therefore what the people would 'really' want if they could think properly, just as we say that someone who is drunk is not 'himself'. This justifies coercion in a person's 'own interests':

> Once I take this view I am in a position to ignore the actual wishes of men or societies, to bully, oppress, torture them in the name, and on behalf, of their real selves, in the secure knowledge that whatever is the true goal of man (happiness, performance of duty, wisdom, a just society, self-fulfilment) must be identical with his freedom – the free choice of his 'true,' albeit often submerged and inarticulate self. (Berlin (2002) 180)

For example, a person detained in a hospital for 'his own good' could be claimed to be not 'detained' at all, but freely submitting. Thus in *HM v Switzerland* (2002) 38 EHRR 314, the European Court of Human Rights held that placing an old lady in a care home was not a 'deprivation of liberty' since it was a responsible measure in the old lady's own interests (Section 21.4.2.3).

Berlin recognises that the state might sometimes have good reason for interfering with freedom. For example, in *HM v Switzerland,* Berlin's analysis would probably be that there was a deprivation of liberty, but one outweighed by a greater good. His point is that by lumping together freedom and other goods we are disguising hard choices between incommensurables. Thus, Berlin is concerned that decision-makers openly confront difficult choices. The best we can expect is a compromise that is widely acceptable.

Cases where religious sensibilities clash with employment illustrate the kind of compromises that have to be made. In *Copsey v WBB Devon Clays Ltd* [2005] EWCA Civ 932, Neuberger LJ referred to 'enlightened capitalism and liberal democracy' in deciding that an employer could require a Christian employee to work on a Sunday. It was held that Article 9 of the ECHR, freedom to manifest religion, requires a 'balance' to be struck between the reasonable needs of the employer and those of the employee, since Article 9 rights can be overridden on several grounds, including the 'rights and freedoms of others'. Perhaps a widely acceptable compromise was reached based on the utilitarian principle of the greatest good of the greatest number (although those subscribing to a religious faith might regard this as irrelevant). The employer had seriously tried to accommodate the employee's Christian beliefs about Sunday working, but in the circumstances, this would cause unfairness to other workers. There is some indication in the case, although the judges were not fully agreed on this point, that freedom of contract is to be ranked especially highly, so that an employee with religious objections would be free to get another job. Mummery LJ went further in a liberal direction, holding that an employer was entitled to adopt a secular regime. The secular approach means that religious interests must not be given special weight, or perhaps even feature in public life at all, so as to ensure equality. However, this conflicts with another cherished liberal belief, that of respecting an individual's choice of lifestyle.

2.5   Republicanism

There has been a recent revival of interest in republican ideas, stimulated by evidence of widespread apathy among voters and disenchantment with the integrity and competence of the political leadership (see e.g. Bellamy (2007); Tomkins (2005)). Republicanism means far more than its popular sense of the absence of a monarchy. Republicanism and liberalism overlap, but republicanism stresses equal citizenship and citizen participation in the processes of government. Originating in ancient Greece, revived in the Renaissance and developed in the seventeenth and eighteenth centuries (Machiavelli, 1469–1527; Harrington, 1611–77; Montesquieu, 1689–1755; Rousseau, 1712–78), republicanism builds on the idea of positive freedom (above). It stresses that the state exists for the benefit of all members of the community as free and equal citizens. Thus, rulers have no rights of their own (other than as citizens) but only duties to the community.

Republicanism has two main aspects that stress different meanings of the idea of 'freedom' (above). Firstly, it embraces the notion of virtuous citizenship and political self-determination by citizens collectively as equal participants in a democratic process. Republicanism stresses the right and the duty of citizens to participate in government. Positive freedom (above) links with this republican idea of democracy since we can rationally control our own lives if we participate in collective decision-making, what Constant (1767–1830) called 'the liberty of the ancients'. Thus, positive freedom might favour compulsory voting in elections. Rousseau (1712–78), for example, famously wrote that we should be 'forced' to be free, meaning that true freedom lies in collective participation by voting in public affairs. He assumed that each person would vote rationally in accordance with the public interest (the 'general will') rather than his or her selfish interests (the will of all) and that the minority who disagree with the outcome must therefore be 'wrong' (see Rousseau, *The Social Contract*, Cole tr. (1762), book 2).

Republicanism ideally favours direct democracy by means of an assembly of all qualifying citizens (qualification to be determined by those currently in power). Ignoring possible technological solutions, this is of course difficult to achieve except in relation to small local areas. Therefore, contemporary republicans such as Bellamy (2007) emphasise *representative* democracy by means of elected legislatures and also favour citizen participation through consultative mechanisms and the devolution of power to small units.

The principles of parliamentary supremacy, the devolution of powers to Scotland, Wales and Northern Ireland, and executive government responsible primarily to the elected House of Commons are broadly republican in character. Bellamy (2007) and Waldron (2001), drawing on the collectivist strain, suggest that improved democratic mechanisms are the appropriate republican safeguards rather than the courts' powers of judicial review.

The second form of republicanism invokes another meaning of freedom, what Pettit (*Republicanism: A Theory of Freedom and Government* (Oxford University Press 1997)) calls 'freedom as non-domination' as opposed to liberalism's 'freedom as non interference'. The republican concern is to ensure that no single person or group within the community can dominate others. This applies to private vested interests and democratic majorities as much as to government bodies. Apart from concern with a separation of powers between different branches of government and with protecting political freedoms, republicanism involves such questions as whether individuals should be able to buy access to political influence.

According to Pettit, this strain of republicanism influenced the Founding Fathers of the US Constitution. Freedom as non-domination recognises that, even if our rulers do not interfere with us and leave us to our own devices, we are nevertheless not truly free since our liberty depends entirely on the goodwill of the rulers. We are slaves who are at the mercy of (maybe a kind) slave master but are in the demeaning position of depending upon the arbitrary whim of another.

Freedom from domination therefore requires that the ruler be restricted by law from arbitrarily interfering with us, whether for good or for ill. It assumes that those in power cannot be trusted even if their motives are good and that they should therefore not have wide discretionary powers. Thus, this version of republicanism puts more faith in the courts than the democratic version. It is consistent with Dicey's version of the rule of law (Section 6.4.2). It can also be illustrated by the Constitutional Reform Act 2005, which places the independence of the judiciary, albeit imperfectly, on a legal footing. Previously, judicial independence was safeguarded largely by the self-restraint of the political and official community. It was widely accepted that the judges were, in fact, independent, but public confidence was thought to require full legal protection (Section 7.6).

Republicanism does not regard state interference as intrinsically bad but rejects only *arbitrary* interference. Interference is not arbitrary where it is carried out for the benefit of those who are subject to the interference – in other words for the public good. By public good is meant benefit which is common to all as members of the community as opposed to the benefit of the rulers themselves, or of sectional interests. Republican ideas therefore concentrate on constitutional mechanisms to ensure that government decisions are made for the public benefit.

These mechanisms include the following:

▶ the 'empire of law' (Harrington), or what we now refer to as the rule of law, meaning that all government power is limited by and must be exercised through legal rules announced in advance and binding both ruler and ruled;

▶ separation of powers, in order to ensure that no person or group is dominant: not only between executive, legislature and judiciary, but also in several other respects such as geographical jurisdictions;

▶ accountability mechanisms such as fair elections, independent scrutiny of public appointments, oversight bodies and openness in government decision-making. According to Pettit, a key principle is that of *contestability* by those who are subject to government, that is, all citizens. It must be borne in mind that mechanisms for making a decision contestable are not the same for each kind of decision-maker. For example, from a republican perspective it is arguably wrong to elect judges, however democratic this seems, since election risks compromising the independence of a court. Conversely, the arguments for elected lawmakers are strong since they can be removed if they make laws to which the people object. In both cases, it is normally important that the decision-making process be open and public and that there are mechanisms for individual complaints and grievances.

Particular constitutions may reflect these requirements in different ways and, in all likelihood, imperfectly. The UK Constitution with its commitment to representative and accountable government embodies general republican ideas, but in other respects, falls short of republican standards. For example, democratic government is imperfectly realised since we have an unelected head of state (the Queen), and one part of the legislature (the House of Lords) is also unelected. There is no attempt to ensure that government gives access on an impartial basis to those who wish to influence it. Public offices are theoretically open to all, but appointments often depend on the personal patronage of ministers.

Perhaps most importantly, large parts of the UK Constitution are beyond the law, based only on informal practices, conventions, or non-binding codes of conduct which rely heavily on trusting the rulers and their hand-picked networks of associates from business, the professions and the media to act without self-interest (Section 3.4). Parliament sometimes enacts laws of draconian severity with little discussion, relying on assurances from the government that in practice the laws will be applied only in special and limited circumstances (such as anti-terrorism legislation). Republicanism stresses that it is not enough that rulers in fact rule wisely and benevolently. In the interests of dignity, equality and freedom, all limits on the rulers must be secured by law so that the ruler cannot abuse his or her power. Anything less relies only on hoping that the 'slave master' will be kind. Occasionally, the law will intervene as a panic response following a conspicuous abuse of power such as the scandal concerning MPs' expense claims (Section 11.7).

Nor do we have a full separation of powers since certain senior members of the executive form part of Parliament, the lawmaker. According to the orthodox view, Parliament has unlimited lawmaking power, so that whichever group controls Parliament can exercise domination without legal constraint. The internal workings of Parliament and the electoral system used for UK elections are such that the will of the political party controlling the executive can, usually, be overcome only in exceptional circumstances (Section 13.1). On the other hand, it could be argued that Parliament has imposed these fetters on itself and that MPs who represent the people could, if they so wished, free themselves from executive control (the price being less efficient government).

Republicans differ as to the best form of constitution. Drawing on classical virtues combined with modern communications technology, some republicans favour the notion of deliberative democracy, where disputes are settled by ensuring that citizens have the opportunity to participate directly in rational decision-making. This seems to paint an idealised picture of groups of leisured and well-informed people with enough in common and sufficient goodwill to reach agreement.

Others regard this as unrealistic in a complex many-sided society in which many decisions require specialist expertise. Rather, a version of the representative system may be preferred, in which ultimate power is vested in an assembly chosen by the people in free and fair elections, to which the executive government is accountable (see Bellamy (2007)). Overlapping with communitarianism and group liberalism, the emphasis might be on elections based on the various trades, professions, regions, ethnic and other groups in the community. Proposals to reform the House of Lords have sometimes included these ideas (Section 12.3). The UK has provision for direct participation only exceptionally (see Section 2.8.3).

Those who support republicanism usually reject the notion that the courts should have the last word, and regard the constitution as being safer in political hands. For example, Tomkins (2005) places stress on the political doctrine that ministers are responsible to Parliament, regarding this as the golden principle of the constitution, while Bellamy (2007) stresses the importance of equal voting rights. Allan (2001), by contrast, regards the courts as guardians of republican ideals and would permit them to disapply legislation that violated fundamental democratic values. This runs counter to the view that it is offensive to submit to unelected authority on fundamental matters and that participation is 'the right of rights' (see Waldron (2001) 11, 12, 13).

Republicans are ambivalent about human rights. They recognise human rights, but in a more grudging way than liberals. A moderate republican would accept the idea of human rights, but as part of the general interest, and would therefore recognise more easily than a liberal that a right should give way to a social goal. It is sometimes suggested that the HRA embodies a moderate republican approach. Not only does it recognise that a social goal may often override a right, but it also leaves the final choice to Parliament rather than the court. However, republicanism and liberalism would both give special importance, but for different reasons, to freedom of political expression (Section 23.1). An extreme version of republicanism would regard possession of a right as conditional upon being a good citizen.

Republican and liberal approaches are illustrated by the reasoning of the majority and the minority in *R (Begum) v Head Teacher and Governors of Denbigh High School* [2007] 1 AC 100. The House of Lords held that a ban on the wearing of a strict form of Muslim dress at a school was not an unlawful interference with the right of freedom of religion. Two lines of reasoning were used. The majority held that the right to religious freedom was not infringed at all. The child concerned could have attended other, more flexible schools, and the style of dress chosen was not required by mainstream Islamic doctrine. This is consistent with a republicanism that imposes a standard model of the good citizen. Lord Nicholls and Baroness Hale held that a right had been infringed but was overridden by the important social purpose of fostering a sense of community by means of a dress code. This is nearer to the liberal approach because it recognises both the importance of the individual claim and that there is a dilemma. To the majority, the right disappeared within the wider public good, so that the problem of balancing the two competing claims was avoided.

2.6 Equality

Liberalism and republicanism presuppose that all people are equal. However, 'equality' has no clear meaning. Equality is merely a measure, the real question being 'equality of what?' For example, liberalism emphasises equality between individual freedoms, whereas republicanism is concerned with equality in the political process. We can distinguish broadly between 'formal' equality and 'substantive' equality. This is reflected in different versions of the 'rule of law' (Section 6.3). Formal equality is about procedures and appearances. It requires that everyone be treated the same in terms of the application of the law, for example the right to a fair trial. It does not mean that the contents of the rights are the same. That is a matter of substantive equality. For example, a landlord has more extensive rights over a house than a tenant and can often afford to go to court and get legal advice more easily, but the two sets of rights will be given equal consideration by a court. Unless we adopt the difficult position that everyone should be treated identically (which conflicts with freedom), substantive equality means only that we should not treat people differently without a good reason. Thus John Stuart Mill, widely regarded as a founder of British liberalism, said that 'all persons are deemed to have a right to equality of treatment except when some recognised social expediency requires otherwise' (*Utilitarianism*, ch. 5).

The substantial body of law concerning discrimination depends on finding good reasons to distinguish between different groups and which justify different treatment. We may disagree about what counts as a good reason. For example, in *R (Chester) v Justice Secretary* [2014] 1 All ER 683, the Supreme Court held that denying all convicted prisoners the right to vote in European elections was not discriminatory under EU law, on the ground that their conviction distinguished them from the normal voter. However, the precise link between voting and criminal conviction is unclear (Section 12.5.5).

While there is widespread agreement that we should not discriminate on grounds of personal characteristics that we cannot help, such as race or gender, it is controversial whether there should be equality in respect of the distribution of wealth or public services (equality of outcome). Should resource allocation be based on need (equality of opportunity) or on merit (equality of desert)? Why should people who happen to be born with talents that suit the interests of the community be better off for that reason? This raises political questions largely outside the scope of the law. Nevertheless, equality is of primary importance in combating action that arbitrarily targets unpopular groups.

For example, section 1(1) of the Equality Act 2010 imposes a duty on public bodies, when making 'strategic' decisions, to have regard to the desirability of reducing 'the inequalities of outcome which result from socio-economic disadvantage'. The Act also prohibits discrimination, meaning less favourable treatment by private persons and public authorities on the ground of certain 'protected characteristics'. These are age, disability, gender reassignment, marriage and civil partnership, pregnancy and maternity, race (including colour, nationality, ethnic or national origins), religion or belief, sex and sexual orientation. However, less favourable treatment can be justified if it is a 'proportionate means of achieving a legitimate aim' (Section 18.1.1).

2.7   Communitarianism

A thread of communitarianism linked to traditional conservatism is represented by the eighteenth-century political thinker and MP Edmund Burke, and more recently by Michael Oakeshott (1901–90). Burke believed that the constitution should be supported by custom and tradition generated within the community, and that rational attempts at constitution building are dangerous (Section 4.6). Burke believed in representative government, but supported an inherited aristocratic element, arguing that society was held together by respect for established rank and status. Burkian thinking finds modern expression in resistance to reform of the House of Lords (Section 12.3) and more generally in the heavy reliance on conventions, unwritten practices and understandings that characterise the UK Constitution (Section 3.4). The judge-made common law might also reflect this brand of communitarianism, in that it claims to derive from community values.

Oakeshott distinguishes between civil associations (Burke's 'little platoons') 'in which individuals and groups can pursue their freely chosen goals' by means of shared customs and understandings ('intimations') that cannot necessarily be formulated as rules, and 'enterprise associations' where the rulers impose their own goals on society through prescriptive laws. Mullender ((2012) 128 LQR 190) suggests that the decision of the Upper Tribunal in *Independent Schools Council v Charity Commission for England and Wales* [2012] 1 All ER 127 exemplifies the conflict between Oakeshott's two associations. The Charities Act 2006 requires that all charities must show that their activities carry public benefit. Charitable status has large tax benefits. This is particularly problematic in the case of private schools. The Charity Commission, which regulates charities and which consists of government appointees, has been said to attempt to impose its own ideas of what a charity should be like (enterprise association). Accordingly, it issued 'guidance' that there must be 'sufficient opportunity for people who cannot afford … fees to benefit in a material way that is related to the charity's aim' (*Public Benefit and Fee Charging* (2008) 9). The Tribunal held that the guidance was too interventionist and that, beyond the minimum threshold that its purposes did not exclude the poor, it was a matter for the trustees of each charity to decide how to run the school, and that it is not for the Charity Commissioners or the Tribunal or the Court to impose their own ideas of what is or is not reasonable (at [229]).

2.8   Democracy

The basic meaning of democracy is government by the people. This can mean different things. Thus, the European Court of Human Rights has pointed out that 'there is a wealth of historical, cultural and political differences within Europe, so that it is for each state to mould its own democratic vision' (*Animal Defenders International v UK* (2013) 57 EHRR 21, at [111]).

A prominent view, widespread among UK lawyers, is that courts and democracy go hand in hand since, according to the ideal of the rule of law, independent courts can ensure that government keeps within the powers given to it by the democratic lawmaker and that the rights of the individual are respected. However, this does not answer the question of who is to have the last word when there is no agreement (Section 8.5.6).

Fear and resentment of democracy remain part of the constitutional debate in the UK. Democracy in the limited sense of a periodic right to vote on occasions designated by Parliament was introduced slowly and reluctantly between the mid-nineteenth and mid-twentieth centuries, resisted by arguments that too much democracy is destabilising. Proposals to reform the House of Lords, which is currently wholly appointed, have foundered largely because of resistance to the idea of a wholly elected legislature (Section 12.3). The notion of the vote itself is disputed between those who regard it as a right to be overridden only for very strong reasons and those who prefer to treat it as a privilege conferred by the state on those it deems worthy (Section 12.5.5). The notion of a referendum of the people on important issues is also sometimes resented on the supposed basis that the people are not competent to decide such questions directly. The outcome of the referendum on membership of the EU in June 2016 is likely to underscore such a perception within a ruling elite which did not generally support withdrawal.

Karl Marx famously said that democracy is the 'solved riddle of all constitutions. Here … the constitution is brought back to its actual basis … and established as the people's own work' (see Marx, *The Riddle of All Constitutions* (Oxford University Press 2000) 149). Similarly (perhaps), democracy has been defined as 'the people of a country deciding for themselves the contents of the laws that organise and regulate their political association' (Michaelman, 'Brennan and Democracy' (1998) 86 California LR 399–400).

Based upon this definition, there is unlikely to be much democracy in the world, and yet most states label themselves democracies. Michaelman's aspiration is the republican one of direct citizen self-government by active participation, sometimes called 'deliberative democracy'. As noted above (Section 2.5), this might be practicable in a village where everyone knows everyone else, but it is unrealistic in contemporary nation states comprising millions of strangers with conflicting goals and interests, and where the complexity of society requires decisions to be made by specialists.

Democracy also means government with the 'consent' of the people, a more slippery notion. The people cannot consent to anything until there are rules determining who counts as 'the people' and how they express their wishes. For example, there are various disqualifications from voting, and different voting formulae fixed by those currently in power produce very different outcomes (Section 12.5.7). From the earliest times, democracy has meant decisions made by a majority. Liberalism favours majoritarian democracy, not for itself, but as the best way of protecting freedom. The liberal justification for majoritarianism is not that a majority is likely to be 'right', since this is clearly untrue, but that majority voting is fair since it treats everyone equally. However, majoritarianism has well-known problems. First, unless there is a simple choice between only two options, the mathematics of majority voting will not necessarily produce a majority preference. Second, objections to democracy, dating back to the time of Plato, include lack of expertise and susceptibility to persuasion by panic-mongers or plausible villains or ideologues. Thus John Adams, one of the founders of the US Constitution, feared 'elective despotism', and De Tocqueville (1805–59), commenting on the newly formed US Constitution, referring to the 'tyranny of the majority', said:

> I am trying to imagine under what novel features despotism may appear in the world. In the first place, I see an innumerable multitude of men, alike and equal, constantly circling around in pursuit of the petty and

banal pleasures with which they glut their souls… Over this kind of men stands an immense, protective power which is alone responsible for securing their enjoyment and watching over their fate. (*Democracy in America*, Lawrence tr. (Fontana 1968) vol 2, 898)

There is therefore a tension between individual freedom on the one hand, and democracy on the other. This underlies important issues in constitutional law, in particular whether the courts should be empowered to overturn Acts of Parliament on constitutional grounds (Section 8.5.6). Liberals are ambivalent about this.

2.8.1 Legal aspects of democracy

Democracy depends on certain legal protections. The main ones are as follows:

- Elections: fair and equal voting rights (Section 12.5).
- The regulation of political parties and the conduct of election campaigns (Section 12.6).
- The protection of MPs against interference (Section 11.6). In *R (HS2 Action Alliance) v Secretary of State for Transport* [2014] 1 WLR 324, the Supreme Court emphasised that a court cannot investigate the quality of any discussion that takes place in the legislature (Section 11.6.3; see also *R (Chester) v Justice Secretary* [2014], at [32]).
- Access to the courts to challenge government action (Sections 19.4 and 19.7).
- Freedom of expression, particularly of the media (Chapter 23).
- Freedom of association (Section 23.7). For instance, in *Redfearn v UK* [2012] ECHR 1878, the European Court of Human Rights upheld a person's right to belong to a racist political party. This was because of the importance of free political parties to the proper functioning of democracy.
- Access to government information (Section 24.1).
- Privacy, meaning rights to secrecy and anonymity as regards who we communicate with and who we vote for so that we can participate in the democratic process without fear of retaliation. Laws against state surveillance and monitoring of our communications (e.g. on the Internet) are therefore desirable (Section 25.3).
- The courts recognise the importance of democracy by refraining from interfering with the decisions of elected bodies with wide powers to make laws (see e.g. Sections 18.1, 19.7, 21.3.1 and 22.9.3).
- In the context of human rights, the European Court of Human Rights in Strasbourg has taken into account whether there has been a full democratic debate about the matter. For example, one reason why the UK's blanket ban on prisoners having the right to vote was contrary to the European Convention was that restrictions on human rights should be justified by considered debate rather than 'unquestioning and passive obedience to a historic tradition' (*Hirst v UK (No 2)* (2006) 42 EHRR 849; Section 12.5.5).
- There is also the fundamental question as to whether, in some circumstances, the courts should have the power to override Acts of Parliament (Section 8.5.6).

2.8.2 Representative democracy

The characteristic form of modern democracy is 'representative democracy'. This applies in the UK. The ideal is that of government that the people can choose, call to account and remove. The people choose representatives directly, who appoint others to assist them, subject to a clear chain of responsibility: thus combining the advantages of specialist decision-makers with control by the people. The representatives must explain their actions and must regularly submit themselves for re-election. A famous early statement is that of Fortescue (*On the Governance of the Kingdom of England* (1537)), who distinguished between *dominium regale*, the rule of the king alone, necessary in certain cases, for example to deal with an emergency, and *dominium politicum et regale*, the rule of the king with the assent of representatives of the community after discussion collectively in Parliament. More recently, in *R (Alconbury Developments) v Secretary of State for the Environment, Transport and the Regions*

[2001] 2 All ER 929, Lord Hoffmann informed us that in the UK 'decisions as to what the general interest requires are made by democratically elected bodies or by persons accountable to them' (at 980).

Representative democracy favours the more individualistic versions of liberalism since the citizen's only power is to vote as a private solitary act, without any requirement for discussion. Representative democracy relies upon a passive population led by an elite, provided that enough people vote to give those chosen some legitimacy. Thus, it is sufficient to comply with EU requirements of public participation in the making of government schemes affecting the environment that the scheme has been debated in Parliament (*R (HS2 Action Alliance Ltd) v Secretary of State for Transport* [2014]).

Republicans and communitarians who favour the active participation of citizens are less comfortable with representative democracy. Typically, the people choose a law-making assembly as the highest branch of government. In a presidential system, the people also vote for the head of state. Bentham and his utilitarian followers recommended that even judges be removable by the people since the people are the final court, but this is not the case in the UK.

Mill especially favoured representative democracy since it combines popular consent with a utilitarian reliance on experts. However, like many contemporary public officials, Mill distrusted 'the people'. He recommended skewing the voting system so that the highly educated had greater voting power and suggested that Parliament should include a quota of people with a 'national reputation'. He favoured a greater level of democracy at local level, not because it produced efficient government, but to enhance the abilities of local people to develop themselves by participating in public life. This does not fit the contemporary UK Constitution, where local government is largely constrained by central government so that local elected politicians have little significant power.

The term 'representative' is ambiguous. A representative assembly could be a 'portrait' or microcosm of those it represents, for example being representative in terms of the political balance of opinion or ethnic and racial groupings. Alternatively, it could be an agent of the people, not having any specified composition but made up of people chosen for their personal qualities or party membership. The practical significance of this concerns different types of voting system designed to produce different outcomes (Section 12.5).

Another basic issue is whether representatives are bound by the views of those who voted for them or should vote according to their own consciences. The UK Constitution has traditionally taken the attitude that representatives must not be bound by any outside commitments. For example, elected local authorities must not bind themselves in law to carry out any political mandate on which they are elected (e.g. *Bromley LBC v GLC* [1983] 1 AC 768). However, within Parliament, the Whip system encourages MPs to vote blindly for their party. Proceedings in Parliament cannot be challenged in the courts.

Representative democracy provides mechanisms for ensuring that the government is accountable to the electorate. Accountability is an ambiguous idea, but basically means that decisions must be explained and justified. The main accountability devices required by representative democracies are:

- ▶ the right to question the executive (Sections 13.5 and 15.7);
- ▶ policing financial limits on government spending (Section 13.4);
- ▶ independent review of government action;
- ▶ public access to information (Section 24.1).

Each of these depends on a separation of powers between different functions of government (and on safeguarding basic freedoms, including the freedom to form political parties and the freedom of the press to criticise government). The European Court of Human Rights and the UK courts have stressed the special importance of political freedom of speech in connection with the democratic process (e.g. *Culnane v Morris* [2006] 2 All ER 149; *Bowman v UK* (1998) 26 EHRR 1; *State of Mauritius v Khoyratty* [2006] 2 WLR 1330).

2.8.3   Participatory democracy

Sometimes called 'deliberative' or 'direct democracy', participatory democracy promotes direct participation by individuals and groups in decisions which affect them. It is favoured by republicans. The UK Constitution makes little provision for participation. Supporters of participation claim that it can harness 'reason' from a wide range of perspectives and enhance dignity and public education. However, participants are voiceless without rules and leaders who stage-manage their involvement.

Recognising that, in a complex society, full participation might be impracticable, many have argued (such as Hannah Arendt, 1906–75) that participation should apply to smaller units such as local government, charities and the workplace (civil society). Jürgen Habermas (1929–) suggests a form of deliberative democracy that he regards as appropriate to contemporary circumstances, in which the state is merely one among numerous community organisations, each comprising activists 'deliberating' on equal terms. The role of the law is to coordinate these units and to ensure that the discussions are open, fair and equal ('Three Normative Models of Democracy' in *The Inclusion of the Other* (MIT Press 1996)). Social networking technology opens up considerable scope not yet fully exploited, although it is also prone to 'fake news'.

Liberals, notably Mill, have objected that deliberative democracy is likely to attract busybodies, the self-promoting, the corrupt, the ignorant and cranks. It also favours the wealthy and leisured. However, representative democracy is also not immune from these distortions.

UK law provides for deliberative democracy only in a limited and piecemeal way:

▶ The jury system for serious criminal trials and in certain civil cases is the only example regarded as important enough to have constitutional status (Juries Act 1974). It has been suggested that citizens' juries should be enlisted to make decisions in constitutional cases as a response to the 'problem' of fundamental rights being determined by unelected judges.
▶ Statute provides machinery for referendums (Political Parties, Elections and Referendums Act 2000), which have become increasingly used in recent years (Section 5.10). It is often argued that the use of referendums would threaten the equality protected by representative democracy since a referendum is liable to be manipulated by vested interests.

The government usually consults interested parties (as designated by itself), and sometimes the public, when policies are proposed, although there is no general legal requirement to do so. In some cases, statute requires consultation, and the courts can ensure that the process is fair and is not merely window dressing. For instance, in *Berkeley v Secretary of State for the Environment* [2000] 3 All ER 897, the House of Lords held that a local authority was required to make environmental information relating to a proposal for a football stadium conveniently available to the public even though the council already had adequate evidence to enable it to make a decision. Lord Hoffmann suggested that public consultation was an end in itself and not merely an instrument of effective decision-making. However, vested interests with informal links with government officials or those who finance political parties may have an advantage in the consultation process.

▶ There are formal statutory public inquiries into many decisions relating to land development where those who can afford good lawyers have an advantage. The outcome is not normally binding on the government.
▶ The Localism Act 2011 introduces direct public involvement in certain land use planning decisions. There is also some participation in the provision for 'parish meetings' at local government level in small rural villages. However, these have little power other than in relation to local amenities such as playgrounds.
▶ There is provision for 'e-petitions' to the House of Commons (Section 13.6).

Participatory democracy shares with representative democracy a concern with freedom of expression, particularly freedom of the press and with public access to information. Thus, Lord Bingham pointed out in *McCartan Turkington-Breen v Times Newspapers* [2000] 2 AC 277 at 290–91 that a 'free, active, professional and enquiring press' was all the more important to support a participatory democracy, since the majority of people can participate only indirectly.

2.8.4   Political parties: market democracy

Political parties are essential in a democracy. They publicise and coordinate different opinions and, as Edmund Burke somewhat idealistically asserted, make it possible to achieve by discussion a notion of the common good (*On the Present Discontents* (1770) vol II). Without them, an elected assembly would be a rabble, and democratic governments would be unable to coordinate their policies. In Burke's time, MPs were usually of independent means as opposed to the paid functionaries of the present day, and party structures were relatively loose. A modern political party can usually exclude independently minded people as candidates for election and ensure that MPs vote in accordance with the party line.

Liberalism regards political parties as self-governing voluntary bodies even though they are central to government. In the interests of freedom, there is resistance to legal controls over political parties, for example in respect of how they raise funds. On the other hand, fair elections require certain controls – a tension characteristic of liberal democracy. For example, in the US case of *Buckley v Valeo* 424 US 1 (1976), restrictions on expenses for election advertising designed to ensure equal competition were held to violate the right to freedom of expression. A different view has been taken in the UK (Section 12.6).

'Market democracy' recognises the role of parties and argues that in contemporary circumstances elections provide only a limited choice. According to Max Weber (1864–1920) and Joseph Schumpeter (1883–1950), the voter's only power is to choose between products offered by competing party leaders who present themselves for election every few years. The vote provides the price mechanism.

Market democracy has significant implications for the constitution. No longer is the state the neutral umpire of Hobbes and Locke; it is a player in the game, making what the parties call 'an offer'. There is a danger that government will be captured by the vested interests of those who fund the parties. However, supporters of market democracy argue that competition will ensure that one party is unlikely to stay in control permanently, provided that the electoral system properly reflects the range of opinion – a proviso which is questionable in the UK. Society may have become too fragmented and diverse to fit into large-scale parties and may be represented more accurately by single issue or special interest pressure groups. Modern governments may therefore be chosen not on the basis of broad ideological or class differences, but on the basis of the personalities of the individuals standing for election. Moreover, market democracy encourages government policies to be expressed in terms of outcomes, targets and 'value for money' rather than in terms of fairness and justice. The emphasis on outputs also blurs the divide between the public and private sectors, since the means by which outputs are delivered ceases to matter.

Summary

▶ Having read this chapter, you should have some general theoretical perspectives which you can use to assess the UK Constitution.

▶ Constitutions are underpinned by an assortment of sometimes conflicting political values. Of these, liberalism has strong contemporary influence. Liberalism separates the individual from the state and emphasises limitations on state power in the interests of individual freedom. Liberalism overlaps with republicanism; however, the latter stresses equal participation as citizens and emphasises duties rather than individual rights. Both favour limited government.

Summary cont'd

▶ Liberalism also treats individuals as equal, the two ideas being capable of conflicting. Formal equality relating to fair procedures is a prime concern of the law. Substantive equality relating to the distribution of resources is primarily a matter of political choices.

▶ A review of significant writers who have influenced liberal ideas reveals different, and sometimes conflicting, forms of liberalism, depending on the importance and meaning given to individual freedom as opposed to the general public interest. These include liberal individualism, market liberalism, welfare liberalism and liberal pluralism.

▶ The distinction between positive and negative freedom illustrates the kinds of disagreement that arise within liberalism. Positive freedom emphasises our ability to choose reason to exercise choice and links with republican ideas of citizen participation in government. It may also lead to authoritarian attempts to impose rational solutions. Negative freedom is the freedom to be left alone. It may be seen as impractical and selfish.

▶ Republicanism can be contrasted with liberalism. Republicanism does not separate the individual from the state, but favours the notion of the virtuous, politically active citizen. It is associated with positive freedom and treats freedom as the right to participate in government. It stresses limited government and (usually) democratic rather than judicial controls over government. There are limited republican elements in the UK Constitution.

▶ A third tradition, communitarianism, is less influential in the UK. It is less sympathetic to human rights than liberalism and favours the interests of groups over those of individuals. The devolution provisions have some communitarian elements.

▶ There are differences between a parliamentary and a presidential democracy. The former concentrates legal power in the legislature and usually involves a separate head of state with limited power. However, in practice, the executive may come to dominate the legislature. The latter divides power between the executive and the legislature as equals, but the president is both head of the executive and head of state.

▶ Democracy has several variations, the main ones being representative democracy, deliberative democracy and market democracy. Representative democracy is the basis of the UK Constitution, but market democracy is, in practice, pursued by the political parties. Democracy is underpinned by ideas of constitutionalism and the rule of law, and the courts give particular importance to freedom of speech and the press in the context of democratic processes.

Exercises

2.1 How would (i) a liberal, (ii) a republican, (iii) a communitarian arrange for (a) the appointment of judges, (b) the method of lawmaking, (c) the settlement of a dispute as to whether a religious group should be permitted to have polygamous marriages?

2.2 What are the main principles of a republican form of constitution? Give examples of such principles in the UK Constitution.

2.3 Sedley (*London Review of Books* (15 November 2001)) describes a case where a French court upheld a ban on local funfairs where revellers had been permitted to shoot a dwarf from a cannon. The decision was made in the name of public morals and human dignity, even though the dwarfs made their living from the spectacle and were among the chief opponents of the ban. Discuss in relation to the views of Locke, Mill and Bentham.

2.4 Discuss the following legislative proposals from the perspective of different forms of liberalism:

(i) a ban on any religion that prevents its members from leaving it;

(ii) provision for a free market in unwanted babies;

(iii) a right for any person to have paid leave from work in order to practise his or her religion;

(iv) a ban on any person convicted of a crime from voting;

(v) a ban on 'faith schools'.

2.5 'A democratic constitution is in the end undemocratic if it gives all power to its elected government' (Sir John Laws). Explain and discuss.

2.6 To what extent does the common law reflect liberal or republican ideals?

Further reading

Allan, *Constitutional Justice: A Liberal Theory of the Rule of Law* (Oxford University Press 2001)
Bellamy, *Political Constitutionalism* (Cambridge University Press 2007) chs 1, 3–6
Berlin, 'Two Concepts of Liberty' in Hardy (ed), *Liberty* (Oxford University Press 2002)
Crick, *Democracy: A Very Short Introduction* (Oxford University Press 2002)
Dyzenhaus, 'How Hobbes Met the Hobbes Challenge' (2009) 72 MLR 488
Etherton, 'Liberty, the Archetype, and Diversity: A Philosophy of Judging' [2010] PL 727
Galston, *The Practice of Liberal Pluralism* (Cambridge University Press 2005)
Hammersley, *Republicanism: An Introduction* (Polity Press 2020)
Harden, *Liberalism, Constitutionalism and Democracy* (Oxford University Press 1999)
Hayek, 'Freedom and Coercion' in Miller (ed), *Liberty* (Oxford University Press 1991)
Kymlicka, 'Citizenship Theory' in *Contemporary Political Philosophy* (2nd edn, Oxford University Press 2002)
Laws, 'The Constitution: Morals and Rights' [1996] PL 622
Loughlin, 'Towards a Republican Revival' (2006) 26 OJLS 425
Loughlin, *Foundations of Public Law* (Oxford University Press 2010) chs 3–6
Mendes, *Constitutional Courts and Deliberative Democracy* (Oxford University Press 2013)
Pettit, *Republicanism: A Theory of Freedom and Government* (Oxford University Press 1997) chs 1–3, 5, 6
Sinnott, 'Constitutional Law and the Limits of Rawlsian Theory' (2020) 26 Legal Theory 124
Skinner, 'The Paradoxes of Political Liberty' in Miller (ed), *Liberty* (Oxford University Press 1991)
Tomkins, *Our Republican Constitution* (Hart Publishing 2005)
Tully, 'The Unfreedom of the Moderns in Comparison to their Ideals of Constitutional Democracy' (2002) 65 MLR 204
Waldron, *Law and Disagreement* (Oxford University Press 2001)

Chapter 3

The sources of the constitution

3.1 Introduction

As we saw in Chapter 1, the UK has no written constitution with a special legal status. The UK's unwritten constitution is constructed partly out of the general sources of law and relies partly on political 'conventions'. The legal sources include Acts of Parliament, the common law in the form of decisions of the higher courts and the 'laws and customs of Parliament' made by each House in order to control its affairs. The standard view is that statute law is the highest form of law in our constitution, although there is an argument that statute is subject to the 'rule of law', which is in the hands of the courts (see Section 8.5.6).

All constitutions rely to some extent on political understandings and practices even if they are not labelled as conventions, but because our constitution is unwritten we rely more heavily on such rules than most countries. There is no intrinsic difference between the content of a convention and that of a law. Any convention can be enacted as a law (e.g. the 'Ponsonby' convention concerning the ratification of treaties (Section 9.5.3)).

There are also 'practices' which may be of fundamental constitutional significance even though they are not in any sense binding as rules. The most obvious of these is the existence of political parties, through which contenders for power organise themselves. There is no legal or conventional requirement that there be political parties. Strictly speaking, a political party is a private voluntary organisation, albeit regulated to prevent it from abusing the electoral process (Political Parties, Elections and Referendums Act 2000). Because the leader of the majority party in the House of Commons normally becomes the prime minister, the internal rules of each party for choosing its leader are of fundamental constitutional importance. Indeed, it has been said that

> parties have substituted for a constitution in Britain. They have filled all the vast empty spaces in the political system where a constitution should be and made the system in their own image. (Wright, quoted in Nolan and Sedley (1997) 83)

3.2 Statute law

In *R (HS2 Action Alliance) v Secretary of State* [2014] 1 WLR 324, at [207], Lord Neuberger and Lord Mance, with whom a majority agreed, referred to important statutes dealing with constitutional matters as 'constitutional instruments' with a special status. They gave as examples:

- the Magna Carta 1215, of value symbolically rather than for its specific provisions, which recognised the principle that the monarch rules by consent and the rule of law;
- the Bill of Rights 1688, which, following the 1688 revolution, subjected the Crown to Parliament, and its equivalent in Scotland, the Claim of Right 1689;
- the Act of Settlement 1700, which regulated succession to the Crown and gave the senior judges security of tenure;
- the Acts of Union between England and Scotland 1707;
- the European Communities Act 1972, which made European law part of UK law (now repealed by the European Union (Withdrawal) Act 2018, which could itself be said to have 'constitutional' status);
- the HRA, which incorporated provisions taken from the ECHR into UK law;
- the Constitutional Reform Act 2005, which strengthened the independence of the judiciary.

Others might be added to the list. A problem here is that there is no objective way of deciding which statutes qualify for inclusion, short of a judicial decision on the point. The matter depends on how important the statute (or indeed a provision in an ordinary statute) is considered to be (see Sections 1.1 and 8.4.1). For example:

▶ the Parliament Acts 1911 and 1949, which made the House of Lords subordinate to the House of Commons;
▶ the Life Peerages Act 1958 and the House of Lords Act 1999, which reformed the composition of the House of Lords;
▶ the devolution legislation, although this has been applied somewhat inconsistently (Section 16.1);
▶ the Fixed Term Parliaments Act 2011, which removed the ancient royal prerogative power to dissolve Parliament;
▶ the European Union (Withdrawal Agreement) and European Union (Future Relationship) Acts 2020, which set out arrangements for Britain's withdrawal from, and its future relationship with, the EU.

Many other statutes have constitutional elements, such as those dealing with the structure of courts and tribunals, elections, complaints against government, controls over government finance, immigration, the media, police powers, the security services and freedom of information. It has been suggested that the Acts of Union with Scotland and Ireland have features of a proper written constitution (Section 8.5.2).

Three things might be noted about these statutes. First, they do not add up to a general constitutional code; they deal with specific issues and are usually responses to immediate problems. Thus, whether a statute is enacted depends mainly on the interests of the government of the day. For example, there are no statutes (other than some dealing with incidental matters such as pensions and salaries) limiting the powers of the prime minister or regulating the relationship between the executive and Parliament (contrast the devolved regimes in Scotland, Wales and Northern Ireland).

Second, although they have no special protection against repeal such as a written constitution might have, it has been argued that constitutional statutes may have a specially high status in the sense that they will be overridden by other statutes only if very clear language is used (*Thoburn v Sunderland City Council* [2002] 4 All ER 156 (Section 8.4.3); *Wilson v First County Trust* [2003] 4 All ER 97, at [179]–[185]; *H v Lord Advocate* [2012] 3 WLR 151, at [30]). This also applies to certain fundamental common law rights, such as freedom of speech, under what is called the 'principle of legality' (Section 6.6).

Third, it is sometimes suggested that a constitutional statute must be interpreted in a special way to reflect its political context and importance, for example the devolution statutes which created the governments of Scotland, Wales and Northern Ireland. Thus in *Robinson v Secretary of State for Northern Ireland* [2002] UKHL 32, Lord Hoffmann asserted (at [33]) that the Northern Ireland Act 1998 is to be construed

> against the background of the political situation in Northern Ireland and the principles laid down by the Belfast Agreement for a new start. These facts and background form part of the admissible background to the construction of the Act just as much as the Revolution, the Convention and the Federalist Papers are the background to construing the Constitution of the USA. (See also Lord Bingham at [11].)

However, the Supreme Court has subsequently held that, despite their constitutional status, the devolution statutes should be interpreted in the same way as ordinary statutes (Section 16.1). This may apply to constitutional statutes generally. *It does not mean that the constitutional background is irrelevant*, since every statute must be interpreted in its particular context. As Feldman (2014, 475) points out, over time the text of the statute becomes overlaid with meanings from different sources such as conventions, cases and political events. This can apply to any statute, although the complexity of constitutional affairs and the close interrelationship with politics makes the context especially important.

A few statutes have special symbolic influence beyond their practical application, as reminders of great events and important principles. This is true particularly of the Bill of Rights 1688 and the Act of Settlement 1700 (still in force), which established the legal framework for parliamentary democracy, and Magna Carta 1215 (enacted 1297). Although Magna Carta concerned specific disputes between the king and the leading landowners and has long been repealed, many of its general principles and sentiments are still invoked in constitutional debate. The most important and enduring principle is that even the king is subject to the law: the 'rule of law', a principle that differentiated England from the rest of Europe for many centuries.

Other ringing declarations inherited from Magna Carta include: 'to none will we sell: to no one will we delay or deny justice' and 'no freeman shall be taken or imprisoned or be outlawed or exiled or any other wise destroyed ... but by ... the law of the land' (see *R (Bancoult) v Secretary of State* [2001] QB 1067, Section 9.4). Magna Carta also includes the principles of proportionate punishment, no taxation without representation and the right to a fair trial.

Statutory instruments (Section 13.5.5) might occasionally have constitutional importance. These are laws made by the executive under powers delegated by an Act of Parliament, which are not subject to full democratic scrutiny. They usually concern very detailed and technical matters that do not raise general concerns. However, ministers are sometimes given wide powers to alter Acts of Parliament themselves, for example in relation to the powers of regulators (see Section 20.4). Moreover, statutory instruments have been used to create constitutions for some dependent territories of the UK.

3.3 The common law

The common law, developed by judges on a case-by-case basis, claims legitimacy as the embodiment of the values of the community given shape by precedent. Liberals and communitarians might both find the common law attractive, although republicans would have doubts about whether the common law meets the aspiration of citizen participation in government and might regret the emphasis of the law upon confrontation and rights rather than upon compromise. However, from a republican angle it might be claimed that all citizens are on an equal footing in the courts (subject to the obvious objection that the wealthy are at a practical advantage in being better able to afford lawyers).

Historically, the common law predates Parliament as lawmaker, since the common law emerged from customary laws that are sometimes claimed to go back to the ancient Britons. Indeed, the idea of an ancient common law constitution, threatened by the pretensions of monarchs, is part of the rhetoric of English constitutional debate, designed to instil reverence for precedent. Although judges are in theory Crown servants, from the seventeenth century it was established that the king cannot act as a judge himself but is bound by the law as made by the judges (see *Prohibitions del Roy* (1607) 12 Co Rep 64). This is an important marker establishing a separation of powers, of sorts.

There is a tension between the classical common law view of the constitution – advocated with varying degrees of emphasis by judges such as Coke (1552–1634), Hale (1609–76) and Mansfield (1709–93) and commentators such as Blackstone (1723–80) – and the modern political notion of the constitution as the application of unlimited democratic power vested in Parliament. Coke claimed that common law was the supreme arbiter of the constitution – an argument still pursued today. According to Coke, the common law is a matter of reason, but

> the artificial perfection of reason ... gotten by long study and experience ... No man (out of his private reason) ought to be wiser than the law, which is the perfection of reason. (*Institutes*, 1628, 1(21))

Artificial reason is, apparently, the collective wisdom of the judges. This classical view envisages the common law constitution as the product of the evolutionary development of community practices adapting the law in a practical way to meet changing circumstances. This is reflected in Hale's famous metaphor of the Argonauts' ship, where a ship whose design and purpose is identical to that which had set sail returns, but has been so often mended that no piece of the original remains (Hale, *A History of the Common Law* (1713) 40).

Hobbes (Section 2.3.1) roundly condemned Coke's claims. He denied that there is anything special about lawyers' reasoning and refused to accept that custom and tradition in themselves carry any legal authority. According to Hobbes, the rule of law derives from authority, subject to 'natural reason' which is available to everyone. He objected to the common law on the ground that disagreement between judges picking over conflicting precedents creates the very uncertainty that the law exists to prevent. Jeremy Bentham (Section 2.3.3) also objected to the common law on the ground that relying on precedent was irrational. We might also be cynical about the notion that the common law represents community values, and might regard it as the creation of professional lawyers, filtering experience through their own self-interest, even if subconsciously.

The distinctive characteristics of the common law have substantial influence on the constitution:

▶ The common law has largely developed through private law notions of personal liability and property rights, underlying Dicey's claim that the same rule of law applies to public bodies and private citizens alike (see Section 6.4). Arguably, this has frustrated the development of public law principles designed to hold government to account.

▶ The common law can claim to be embedded in community values. Notions such as the reasonable person, 'reasonable expectations' and right-thinking members of society surface in common law argument.

▶ The common law can be a focus for open and public debate about competing versions of justice (see e.g. *White v South Yorkshire Police Authority* [1999] 2 AC 455). The common law recognises disagreement about basic values appropriate to a democracy. Its driving force is dispute. Disagreement is kept open through the practices of separate opinions by individual judges and dissenting judgments. Judges can change their minds subject to the (relatively loose) rules of binding precedent.

▶ Some liberals argue that the courts are the guardians of fundamental freedoms and in extreme cases should have the power to override an Act of Parliament (Section 8.5.6). The conventional approach, characteristic of the UK's reliance on voluntary practices, is that there is an 'understanding' among the personal networks that make up the institutions of government as to their respective roles and limits.

▶ It is difficult to reconcile the judges' common law power to make law with either the separation of powers (see Section 7.6) or democracy. Supporters of the common law usually argue that the common law supports democracy by protecting its basic values such as freedom of speech against the danger that an elected government might pervert democracy by becoming tyrannical and overriding the interests of minorities. Against this, it can be argued that there is nothing to prevent judges from resisting change and that it is offensive to entrust an unelected, and unrepresentative, elite with the protection of fundamental values, the proper remedy against tyranny being to strengthen democratic mechanisms (see Waldron, *Law and Disagreement* (Oxford University Press 1999) 11–13). For example, in *Nairn v University of St Andrews* [1909] AC 147, during the height of the campaign for votes for women, the removal of the disqualification of women from voting was held to be a 'momentous and far reaching constitutional change' requiring the clearest statutory language.

▶ The courts are careful to respect the separation of powers to the extent that they are reluctant to develop common law principles in areas where Parliament has shown willingness to intervene (see *Re McKerr* [2004] 1 WLR 807: investigation of deaths; *Cambridge Water Co v English Counties Leather* [1994] 2 AC 264: environmental protection). They are also reluctant to develop the common law in controversial areas where they feel that Parliament has more legitimacy to act, for example assisted suicide (see *R (Nicklinson) v Ministry of Justice* [2014] UKSC 38).

3.4   Constitutional conventions

Conventions are rules that are politically, but not legally, binding. They are binding primarily by virtue of their acceptance by those in power (the term 'convention' literally means a 'coming together'). Conventions play a central part in the constitution. They deal with fundamental matters concerning the distribution of power and government accountability: for example, the principle that the monarch must act on the advice of ministers is a convention. Thus conventions may adjust the legal rules to the political reality.

Dicey ((1915) 432) claimed that 'conventions are designed to ensure the ultimate supremacy of the electorate as the true political sovereign of the state'. Along the same lines, Allan (*Law, Liberty and Justice* (Oxford University Press 1993) 253) concludes that conventions 'give effect to the principle of governmental accountability that constitutes the structure of responsible government'.

3.4.1   The nature of conventions

Constitutional conventions deal mainly with the relationship between the different branches of government: the Crown, the executive and Parliament, ministers and the civil service, the prime minister and the Cabinet, the central government and the devolved governments. There are, for example, no legal rules requiring there to be either a prime minister or a Cabinet, and most of the powers of the prime minister are conventional. Many of the central principles of the political constitution are conventions: for example, that the monarch must assent to all bills presented to her by Parliament, and that the Crown must act through ministers who are collectively and individually accountable to Parliament. Unlike a law which gets its validity because it is made in public by a recognised process, be that a statute or a court judgment, a convention is valid only in as much as it is generally respected. Conventions are evidenced by the opinions of those in influential positions. This might be discovered in government records, in academic writing or even in the biographies of eminent politicians.

Conventions are sometimes vague and uncertain in meaning. This in itself does not distinguish them from law. However, unlike a law proper, there is no authoritative way of settling a dispute about the meaning and application of a convention. Disputes must be settled by political means such as negotiation or parliamentary debate without the certainty of a conclusive outcome such as a court would provide. For example, no one is sure precisely what the recently established convention that Parliament must approve a government decision to go to war means (Section 14.6.3).

Another example comes from the General Election of 2010. When it appeared that a 'hung Parliament' without a clear majority to choose a prime minister was likely (as so it turned out), a self-selected group of civil servants, members of the Queen's entourage and invited academics drafted a set of principles to deal with the issue (see Blackburn, 'The 2010 General Election and the Formation of the Conservative–Liberal Democrat Coalition Government' [2011] PL 30). This then formed part of a lengthier document, the *Cabinet Manual*, which was published in October 2011 following a process of public consultation. This document explicitly acknowledges areas in which there are uncertainties (see e.g. [2.10]).

Conventions and law are sometimes intertwined in the sense that a convention has influenced the content of the law, such that the law cannot be understood without knowing the relevant convention. For example, many royal prerogative powers, legally in the hands of the Queen, are lawfully exercised directly by ministers without reference to the Queen, thus acknowledging the convention of ministerial responsibility (Section 15.7).

The absence of an authoritative decision-making process, or indeed any public and systematic discussion, reveals the absence of democratic legitimacy of conventions. Lord Simon of Glaisdale let the cat out of the bag in evidence to the Joint Committee on Conventions (HL/HC 2005–06, Paper 1212-1):

> [T]he great thing about the Salisbury Convention is that it works. Generally that is enough in this country… The last comment to make about it is that it is a constitutional convention and not constitutional law. In other words it is binding only politically and morally but not legally and only so long as it is convenient.

The obvious reaction to this is: convenient to whom? This question came to the fore in early 2019, when the Speaker of the House of Commons, John Bercow, permitted the tabling of an amendment by a backbench MP to a 'supplementary business motion', setting out the process for debate upon the Government's proposals for withdrawal from the EU, notwithstanding that there was an apparent convention that such motions could only be amended by government ministers. The Speaker stated that he was 'not in the business of invoking precedent, nor [was he] under any obligation to do so' (HC Deb, 9 January 2019). However, some two months later, he refused to allow the Government to table a further motion for a 'meaningful vote' on its Brexit deal, on the basis that there was a 'strong and long-standing' convention that a motion or amendment which is the same, in substance, as a question which has been decided during a session may not be brought forward again during that same session (HC Deb, 18 March 2019). These rulings called the Speaker's impartiality into question and led the Conservative Party to announce that it would field a candidate to oppose Bercow in an upcoming general election – this also being a break with the convention that a Speaker continuing in office is re-elected unopposed (in the event, Bercow announced his decision to stand down as an MP before the 2019 election took place).

The UK Constitution is not alone in generating conventions. Any constitution or set of formal rules is likely to be overlaid by unwritten customs and practices. This is partly because no set of written rules can deal with every possible situation, but also because all written documents fall to be interpreted in the light of the assumptions and beliefs, moral and political, of the interpreter. In the case of a constitution, there are numerous inputs of thousands of people over time, so that the nuances of the constitution are in constant flux.

3.4.2   The main conventions

Conventions help to ensure that the constitution reflects contemporary political values and to manage evolutionary constitutional change without generating political controversy by attempting to reform legislation. Most conventions concern the relationship between different components of government.

- Conventions relating to the monarch ensure that remaining prerogative powers are normally exercised only by or in accordance with advice received from ministers, who are accountable to Parliament. However, there are ill-defined circumstances in which ministerial advice need not be followed (Section 14.4).
- The chain of conventions embodied in the doctrine of ministerial responsibility to Parliament is of fundamental importance, being intended to ensure that the legal powers of the Crown are subject to democratic control. However, the supposed chain of accountability is not complete. Dicey anticipated neither the dominance of the executive in Parliament, nor the dispersal of executive power to miscellaneous bodies, including private companies, outside the central government structure (Section 15.10). Moreover, if ministerial accountability is to be effective, it assumes that Members of Parliament will act independently and not through party loyalty. In practice, accountability to Parliament is often accountability to the minister's own party.
- Other conventions concern the relationship between the two Houses of Parliament. For example, the 'Salisbury Convention' (Section 13.7) requires that the House of Lords should not oppose a measure sent to it by the Commons which was contained in the governing party's election manifesto, except perhaps where the matter is the subject of deep public controversy (see Turpin and Tomkins, *British Government and the Constitution* (6th edn, Cambridge University Press 2007) 643–45, 652–53).
- New conventions have been introduced to meet new challenges, for example to deal with the relationship between the central government and the devolved governments of Scotland, Wales and Northern Ireland. The 'Sewel Convention' requires that legislatures of the devolved territories should normally consent to any legislation made by Parliament that affects devolved matters (*Memorandum of Understanding*, Cm 5420, 1999). The Iraq War in 2003 created a convention that a government decision

to send armed forces overseas, at least on the ground, must be supported by a vote in the House of Commons. It has also been argued that there may be a right of the Prince of Wales as heir to the Crown to discuss policy with ministers, although this competes with the convention that the monarchy should not be involved with political controversy (see Brazier, 'The Constitutional Position of the Prince of Wales' [1995] PL 401). The extent of any such convention was considered by the Supreme Court in *R (Evans) v Attorney General* [2015] UKSC 21.

A fashionable recent device is that of 'concordats' agreed between participants, and intended to govern the relationship between different organs of government, or to set out practices. These may have the status of convention, at least if they are generally acted upon. There are many of these between government departments, agencies and the devolved institutions of Scotland, Northern Ireland and Wales and which clarify the relationship between these bodies. A Concordat made in 2004 between the government and the Lord Chief Justice concerning links between the judiciary and the executive underpins the reforms introduced by the Constitutional Reform Act 2005 (Section 7.4), a statute which might be seen as giving statutory form to existing conventions designed to secure the independence of the judiciary.

3.4.3   Identifying conventions

Many conventions are wholly unwritten, residing only in the opinions of those consulted about them. Some conventions and other practices and understandings are written down by officials in an uncoordinated profusion of 'protocols', 'memoranda', 'codes of practice' and the like. For example, the *Ministerial Code* (2019) issued by the Cabinet Office comprises a mixture of conventions, advice about ethics, practice and administrative matters designed to guide ministers in their relationship with Parliament and their ministerial departments. The consequence of the publication of the *Cabinet Manual* (2011), noted above, is that – in the words of the prime minister – 'for the first time the conventions determining how the government operates are transparently set out in one place'. However, note that the mere fact that a principle has been put in writing does not in itself make it a convention, but might be *evidence* of a convention (see Blick (2014)).

It is important to distinguish constitutional conventions from other forms of constitutional behaviour such as practices, traditions and, of course, law. It is necessary in particular to distinguish between conventions and practices, because conventions are binding but practices, however important, are not. The organisation of political parties, such as how they choose their leaders, is very important, but comprises practices rather than conventions.

It may be difficult to decide whether a particular pattern of behaviour amounts to a convention or merely a working practice. For example, doubt surrounds the role of the Cabinet, the practical importance of which seems to depend on the character of the prime minister at the time and the assertiveness of the Cabinet ministers (Section 15.4) (see now also the *Cabinet Manual*, Chapter 4).

There is a logical gulf between practice (what is) and rule (what 'ought' to be), although it must be conceded that well-established practices carry at least a presumption that they ought to be continued. This seems to be a basic psychological fact about human motivation. Furthermore, a practice ceases to exist if it is regularly broken. If a convention is broken, it ceases to exist only if no criticism follows. To this extent, conventions are at the mercy of raw politics.

However, Dicey does not distinguish conventions from practices. Dicey famously defined conventions negatively as anything that is not law ((1915) cxli). He stated that apart from laws:

> [t]he other set of rules consist[s] of conventions, understandings, habits, or practices which, though they may regulate the conduct of several members of the sovereign power, of the Ministry, or of other officials, are not in reality laws at all since they are not enforced by the courts.

Similarly, Munro ((1999) 81) argues that non-legal rules are best viewed as of one type, provided we accept that conventions vary in stringency. Thus, while conventions are binding, they do not all have the same degree of binding force. Some may have exceptions (such as the personal powers of the monarch; see Section 14.4); while others may not be regarded as important. However, this approach does not seem to cater for the fact that practices are not binding at all. Thus, Sir Kenneth Wheare defined a convention as 'a rule of behaviour accepted as obligatory by those concerned in the working of the constitution' (*Modern Constitutions* (Oxford University Press 1966) 102). The crucial matter is therefore the belief that there is an *obligation* to act in a particular manner. Jennings offered three tests to identify a convention (*The Law and the Constitution* (London University Press 1959) 136). First, are there any precedents? Second, do those operating the constitution believe that they are bound by a rule? Third, is there a constitutional reason for the convention? This has been accepted by the Canadian courts, although it is not clear why a court should have any say on the matter (*Reference re Amendment of the Constitution of Canada (Nos 1, 2 and 3)* (1981) 125 DLR (3d) 1).

In the absence of an authoritative decision-maker such as a court, there are plainly difficulties with precedents because there may be many occasions on which politicians disagree about the precedents they are supposed to follow (see the discussion above regarding the Speaker's rulings in 2019). This uncertainty clouds even established conventional rules, such as the choice of a prime minister (Section 15.2). Sometimes precedent is unnecessary because a convention might be created by agreement, for example by the Cabinet, or even laid down unilaterally by the prime minister or one of the Houses of Parliament (e.g. the Sewel Convention; Section 16.2). It is arguable, however, that a rule which is laid down in this way is better described as a 'soft law' to be put to the test and which becomes a convention only after it has gained general acceptance (see McHarg (2008)). A convention created by a formal agreement such as a concordat may perhaps be immediately binding.

Jennings' second test, that those subject to it regard themselves as bound by the rule, is subject to the difficulties discussed above. Moreover, the notion that conventions are essentially self-policing offends at least republican versions of constitutionalism, since it denies the notion of limited government. Jennings' third requirement of a reason for the convention is also problematic. Who decides whether such a reason exists, and if the rule is in fact obeyed, why should the reason matter?

3.4.4   The differences between law and convention: conventions and the courts

As we have seen, for Dicey, the distinction between legal and political rules depends on the absence of direct power to enforce conventions through the courts. However, many conventions function in a close relationship with laws since they direct how legal power will be exercised, or prevent the exercise of anachronistic legal powers: for example, the convention that the Queen must assent to bills presented to her by Parliament. Conventions provide principles and values that form the context of the law: as Jennings famously said, 'flesh which clothes the dry bones of the law'. Conventions are intertwined with law, operating as part of a single system, so that the difference between them might be regarded as superficial.

However, if law is defined as rules ultimately backed by state force and enforced through the courts, laws and conventions have clear differences. Munro (1999) points out that, unlike a convention, a breach of the law does not call into question its validity. He adds that individual laws do not rest upon consent – a widely disregarded law is nevertheless a valid law. A law does not lapse if it becomes obsolete, yet a convention can disappear if it is not followed for a significant period, or if it is broken without objection.

Another difference which is of vital importance is that laws emanate from definite sources – the courts and Parliament – with an authoritative mechanism (the courts) for deciding what each rule means and how it applies. In the case of conventions, there is no such authoritative source.

Nevertheless, Dicey's distinction between law and convention has been criticised as too rigid. Some laws are less binding than others. For example, procedural requirements stipulated by statute are sometimes dispensed with (Section 18.2). Nor can importance be a distinguishing factor. Conventions can be as important as laws; indeed some conventions may be more important than some laws. On the other hand, importance is irrelevant to the existence of a law, but perhaps not to the existence of a convention. It is also said that conventions are different from laws because they lack certainty. Munro (1999) demonstrates that certainty is not the issue. He argues that some social rules, such as the rules of cricket, can be clearly stated, but they are manifestly not laws. Moreover, many laws are uncertain and while the courts certainly rely on precedent they are free to depart from precedents in many cases.

From a functionalist perspective (i.e. one which is concerned with outcomes), Jennings argued that law and convention are at root the same thing, each resting ultimately on public acquiescence and serving the same function, social control. Certainly, the content of a convention is no different from that of a law, and a convention can be turned into law by enacting it as a statute (Section 3.4.6). But this does not help on a detailed level, for example to explain the different attitude of the courts to conventions and laws.

Perhaps the crucial distinction between convention and law concerns the attitude of the courts. The courts do not apply conventions directly. This means, first, that there is no remedy in the courts for breach of a convention as such, and secondly that the views of a court as to whether a particular convention exists and what it means are not binding. The existence and meaning of a convention are matters of fact that must be proved by evidence and not matters of law for the court.

On the other hand, the courts do not ignore conventions. In particular, a convention may form the political background against which the law has to be interpreted (see Box). Furthermore, statute may draw upon a particular convention, making it indirectly enforceable. For example, section 36(2) of the Freedom of Information Act 2000 exempts government information from disclosure if it prejudices or is likely to prejudice the convention of the collective responsibility of ministers of the Crown. Similarly, ss 2 of the Scotland Act 2016 and the Wales Act 2017 place the 'Sewel Convention' on a statutory footing.

The following cases illustrate the relationship between law and convention in the courts.

▶ In *Reference re Amendment of the Constitution of Canada* [1981], the Canadian Supreme Court, relying partly on British authority, recognised but refused to apply a convention. Under Canadian law, any amendment to the Canadian Constitution required an Act of the UK Parliament following a request from the federal government of Canada. The Canadian government wished to amend the Constitution so as to free itself from this legal link with Britain. The UK Parliament would automatically pass any legislation requested by Canada. However, there were important Canadian conventions on the matter. These required that the governments of the Canadian provinces be consulted about, and give their consent to, any proposed changes in the Constitution that affected federal–provincial relations. Some claimed that this had not been done. The Supreme Court was divided as to whether the convention in question existed. A majority held that it did, and went on to explain in some detail what the convention meant. Some of the judges doubted whether the court should even have gone this far, but, as long as we remember that the court's view about the meaning of a convention is not in itself binding, it seems acceptable. In any event, a larger majority held that, whatever the convention meant, it could not affect the legal rule that empowered the federal government to request an alteration to the Constitution. Thus, the convention could not be enforced by legal remedies. The judges also denied that a convention can ever crystallise into law, for example by becoming established over a period of years. This seems to be equally true of English law (see Munro (1999) 72ff).

▶ In *A-G v Jonathan Cape Ltd* [1976] QB 752, the government sought to prevent publication of the diaries of Richard Crossman, a former Labour Cabinet minister. This involved balancing the confidential nature of any material against any public interest in favour of its disclosure. The government relied upon the convention of collective Cabinet responsibility, arguing that this necessarily required that Cabinet business remain confidential to Cabinet ministers. The court refused to apply the convention as such. It held that the convention was relevant only to the problem of deciding where the public interest lay. It held that some of the diaries could be published because they dealt only with matters of historical interest and did not concern the activities of ministers still in office, which the convention was intended to protect. Thus the convention was a crucial strand in the argument, but not the law itself (see further Jaconelli (2005)).

▶ In *Carltona Ltd v Comr for Works* [1943] 2 All ER 560, the courts accepted the legitimacy of civil servants taking decisions that are in law the responsibility of the minister without reference to the minister personally. The reason for this was that, by convention, the minister is responsible to Parliament for the acts of civil servants in his department so that in law the civil servant can be deemed to be merely the instrument of the minister.

▶ In *R (Evans) v Attorney General* [2015], the Supreme Court ruled that the Attorney General was not entitled to issue a certificate under section 53 of the Freedom of Information Act 2000, which had had the effect of precluding disclosure of letters written by the Prince of Wales to ministers. This certificate had been issued to override the decision of the Upper Tribunal, which had determined that certain of the letters should not be exempted from disclosure under the Act. The Upper Tribunal had heard extensive evidence on applicable constitutional conventions in reaching its conclusions; the effect of the Attorney General's certificate was to redetermine the factual circumstances, including the meaning and scope of those conventions. Although it was open to the Attorney General to disagree with the decision of the Upper Tribunal, departure from findings of fact (including those as to the scope and applicability of conventions) would be lawful only if proper justification for doing so had been provided, which had not been the case in this instance.

▶ In *R (Miller) v Secretary of State for Exiting the European Union* [2017] UKSC 5, the Supreme Court considered whether the 'Sewel Convention' required the consent of the devolved legislatures to be given before the UK could trigger the process of withdrawal from the European Union. The Court held that the Convention had 'an important role in facilitating harmonious relationships between the UK Parliament and the devolved legislatures. But the policing of its scope and the manner of its operation does not lie within the constitutional remit of the judiciary, which is to protect the rule of law', [151].

3.4.5   Why conventions are obeyed

The main reason why conventions are obeyed is the adverse political consequences that might result from their breach. This produces the circularity that if a convention is not obeyed it may lose its binding force. For example, the supposed convention that a minister should resign if there has been a serious wrongdoing in his or her department is usually ignored unless and until a minister loses political support (Section 15.7). Dicey unconvincingly tries to link breach of convention to breach of law. He argues that even the 'boldest political adventurer' would be restrained from breaching conventions because (at least in the case of some conventions) it would eventually lead to the offender coming into conflict with the courts and the law of the land ((1915) 296–97). He gives as an example the consequences that might follow if Parliament did not meet at least once a year, or if a government did not resign after losing a vote of confidence. Dicey argues that the government would have no statutory authority for raising (some) taxes or spending money.

Not all conventions can be similarly treated. For example, the appointment of a non-Member of Parliament as a minister will not lead to any legal violation. The absence of adverse political repercussions may fortify ministers who give inaccurate parliamentary answers, but this failure is unlikely to lead to a breach of the law. If some conventions were breached, Parliament might be compelled to intervene to prevent a recurrence. Most famously this occurred after the Lords refused to pass the Finance Bill 1909, thereby disregarding the conventional principle that the Lords should ultimately defer to the wishes of the elected Commons. The Parliament Act 1911 removed the veto power of the Lords in respect of most public bills. If the sovereign (without ministerial advice) were to refuse to grant royal assent to a bill passed by both Houses, the prerogative power to refuse would surely soon be removed by legislation. Jaconelli (2005) suggests that many conventions are obeyed because they are reciprocal. The party in power, for the time being, accepts the constraints that conventions impose upon its behaviour in the expectation that the opposition parties will do likewise when they attain office. However, Jaconelli concedes that this would not apply to all conventions, for instance the obligation of the monarch to assent to a bill passed by Parliament. According to Jaconelli, prudence explains why such conventions are observed.

Conventions may apparently be breached or qualified (depending on one's viewpoint) as a safety valve where there is a conflict between what is normally constitutionally expected and current political consensus or expediency. In 1975 and 2016, the prime minister 'suspended' the principle of collective Cabinet unanimity to allow ministers to express their views openly in the referendum campaigns concerning membership of (what is now) the European Union. Collective responsibility was formally maintained during the (unusual) period of coalition government between 2010 and 2015, subject to limited 'agreements to differ' on particular policies where the Conservative and Liberal Democrat partners held highly divergent views, such as university funding and the renewal of the Trident nuclear deterrent.

3.4.6   Codification of conventions

Codification has different meanings and the fact that a set of rules is codified does not in itself determine the nature of the rules. First, it means an authoritative written version of the conventions in question. Strictly speaking, this means turning the convention into law in the form of an Act of Parliament, although promulgation as a Standing Order or Resolution of Parliament would give it legal effect within Parliament itself. Conventions might also be codified in a less authoritative sense and not legally binding, for example in the form of a report of a parliamentary committee, a ministerial announcement, a concordat or a Memorandum of Understanding. The *Cabinet Manual* may be regarded as the codification of conventions (as well as laws and other forms of rule) relating to the operation of central government (Blick (2014)).

The case for codification involves two distinct positions. The first asserts that conventions should be given legal force; the second that conventions might be codified within an authoritative text, but remain as non-legal political practices. However, even under the second version – which describes the status of the *Cabinet Manual* – it is plausible that the courts may rely on the codified conventions (see e.g. Sampford, '"Recognize and Declare": An Australian Experience in Codifying Constitutional Conventions' (1987) 7 OJLS 369).

The second approach to some extent addresses the lack of precision in some conventions and, if intended to be a comprehensive code, enables us to say with certainty which usages are, and which are not, conventional. Establishing the certainty of conventions also safeguards the neutrality of those who apply them. On the other hand, this approach might create uncertainty, for example as to the status of any interpretation of a convention that a court might give if the matter were to arise in litigation.

The more radical position, involving enactment as law, has the important advantage that it is likely to enhance public confidence in the integrity of government. Statutes must be widely published and the process of enactment is to some extent open and public. An example is the Constitutional Reform Act 2005. This reconfigured the relationship between the judges, Parliament and the executive in order to reinforce the principle of judicial independence (Sections 5.4 and 7.7), even though there was no serious argument that the judiciary was not in fact already independent. Another example is the Fixed Term Parliaments Act 2011 which replaced conventions concerning the removal or resignation of a government (Section 11.2). These statutes made changes to the arrangements rather than merely enacting the conventions. By contrast, the Constitutional Reform and Governance Act 2010 simply placed the 'Ponsonby Rule', a convention under which international treaties are to be laid before Parliament for 21 days before they are ratified by government on a statutory basis (Section 9.5.3).

On the other hand, the enactment of conventions might damage the flexibility of the constitution. It would be undesirable if conventions were to become fossilised and so impede further constitutional change. The enactment of a convention would bring the matter within the scope of the courts. It is arguable that democratic issues, for example whether a minister should resign, ought to be a matter of collective political decision, and thus fall outside the proper scope of the judicial function: certainly, this would be the view taken by a republican. But this depends on the particular convention. For example, the Sewel Convention, which restrains the UK Parliament from legislating on a matter within the powers of a devolved government, does not seem to be inherently non-justiciable (the convention has, in any event, been given statutory form: see Section 16.2). There might be practical difficulties in systematic codification. It would be impossible to identify all usages that are currently conventional, and after a code was established, further conventions might develop. A possible approach might be to enact only the most important and widely accepted conventions. This would place those selected outside the scope of the executive and locate more extensive power in Parliament. Constitutional development would then be a matter of statutory reform, which itself permits more open debate and discussion.

Summary

▶ The UK Constitution is embodied in individual statutes and in the common law, the latter being claimed to derive from the values embedded within the community. Statutes and common law principles that are regarded as 'constitutional' are given special treatment but within a context of considerable uncertainty. The common law introduces an element of openness, independence and flexibility into the constitution, although it challenges the idea of democracy.

▶ The UK Constitution is also embodied in customs and practices, the most important of which are conventions. Conventions are pragmatically intertwined with law but are not directly enforceable in the courts. There is therefore no authoritative mechanism for interpreting, identifying or enforcing conventions.

▶ Conventions are of fundamental importance in the UK Constitution. In their best light, they enable the constitution to evolve pragmatically in accordance with changing political values. In their worst light, they allow the government of the day and its favourites to manipulate the constitution in their own interests.

▶ There is disagreement about the definition of a convention. Accordingly, it is not always clear which forms of constitutional behaviour are conventions and which are mere practices. Conventions are binding rules of constitutional behaviour, while mere practices are not.

▶ Conventions are distinct from law, first in that there are no authoritative formal tests for the validity of conventions, and secondly because conventions are not directly enforced by the courts. However, there is no inherent difference in the content of laws and conventions, and the courts use conventions (as they do moral principles) to help interpret, develop and apply the law.

▶ Some commentators have argued that conventions could be incorporated into the law, but even if this is achieved, how many such laws would be suitable for scrutiny in a court (that is, 'justiciable')? Codification might offer certainty in respect of those conventions included in the code, but new conventions would be evolved after the code was introduced, and some flexibility in adapting existing conventions might be lost. Nonetheless, there have been moves to extend 'soft' forms of codification through documents such as the *Ministerial Code* and the *Cabinet Manual*.

Exercises

3.1 To what extent does the common law influence the character of the UK Constitution?

3.2 What is the meaning and significance of a 'constitutional statute'?

3.3 How are conventions recognised and enforced? Can they be distinguished from 'practices'?

3.4 Dicey claims that 'conventions are designed to ensure the ultimate supremacy of the electorate as the true political sovereign of the state'. Is this convincing today?

3.5 '[T]he great thing about the Salisbury Convention is that it works. Generally that is enough in this country...The last comment to make about it is that it is a constitutional convention and not constitutional law. In other words it is binding only politically and morally but not legally and only so long as it is convenient' (Lord Simon of Glaisdale, Joint Committee on Conventions (HL/HC 2005–06, Paper 1212-1)).

Discuss this statement from the point of view of democracy.

3.6 At the request of the government of an ally of the UK, the prime minister proposes to send military aircraft to Dystopia, a country in the hands of a terrorist army. The aircraft will support the land army of the ally in an attempt to defeat the terrorists. Advise the prime minister as to any constitutional requirements and explain the legal basis of your advice.

3.7 What is the role of courts in relation to conventions?

3.8 Should conventions be enacted into law or codified?

Further reading

Allan, *The Sovereignty of Law: Freedom, Constitution and Common Law* (Oxford University Press 2013)

Bagehot, *The English Constitution* (2nd edn, Kegan Paul 1902) ch 1

Barber, 'Law and Constitutional Conventions' (2009) 125 LQR 294

Blick, 'The Cabinet Manual and the Codification of Conventions' (2014) 67 Parl Aff 191

Bogdanor and Vogenauer, 'Enacting a British Constitution: Some Problems' [2008] PL 38

Feldman, 'The Nature and Significance of Constitutional Legislation' (2013) 129 LQR 343

Feldman, 'Constitutional Conventions' in Qvortrup (ed), *The British Constitution: Continuity and Change* (Hart Publishing 2013)

Feldman, 'Statutory Interpretation and Constitutional Legislation' (2014) 130 LQR 473

Hennessy, *The Hidden Wiring: Unearthing the British Constitution* (Gollancz 1995)

Jaconelli, 'The Nature of Constitutional Convention' (1999) 19 LS 24

Jaconelli, 'Do Constitutional Conventions Bind?' (2005) 64 CLJ 149

McHarg, 'Reforming the United Kingdom Constitution: Law, Convention, Soft Law' (2008) 71 MLR 853

Munro, *Studies in Constitutional Law* (2nd edn, Butterworths 1999) ch 3

Nolan and Sedley (eds), *The Making and Remaking of the British Constitution* (Blackstone 1997) ch 2

Perry and Tucker, 'Top-Down Constitutional Conventions' (2018) 81 MLR 765

Postema, *Bentham and the Common Law Tradition* (Clarendon Press 1986) chs 1 and 2

Sedley, 'The Sound of Silence: Constitutional Law Without a Constitution' (1994) 110 LQR 270

Wilson, 'The Robustness of Conventions in a Time of Modernisation and Change' [2004] PL 407

Chapter 4

Historical landmarks

4.1 Introduction

This chapter highlights themes and events that have influenced the structure of the UK Constitution. Our unwritten constitution has evolved under changing political pressures. This makes the historical context important as an aid to understanding. It is helpful to trace the gradual adjustment of institutions to different demands. History also helps to explain the survival of obsolete institutions which do not raise immediate problems or which benefit their members. However, it should be borne in mind that political and legal terms such as 'freedom' and 'sovereignty' may carry different meanings in different periods.

There are rival explanations of the history of the constitution, with the truth perhaps being a mixture of them. One extreme view is that history is driven forward by general forces, forces which individuals can influence but not fundamentally change. Another view is that the constitution is the outcome of an endless contest between rival self-serving factions competing for control over the institution of government and driven by personalities and chance events.

An example of the first view is 'the Whig View of History', promoted from the nineteenth century and linked to the idea that 'England' has a special identity. (The Whigs, part ancestors of the modern Liberal Democrats political party, were the more progressive of the two aristocratic parties that dominated politics from the middle of the seventeenth century to the late nineteenth century, the other party being the Tories.) This depicts the constitution as a happy unfolding story, from the tyranny of the Norman kings to modern democracy. Magna Carta (1215) and the seventeenth-century revolution which placed Parliament and the common law at the centre of the constitution are revered highlights of this narrative, which depicts democracy developing gradually until the present day, through a balance of strong central government and dispersed local administration (see e.g. Kellner (2009)). The king was subject to the common law based on the customs of the realm, and this ensured that absolutism never took root.

The other version of history identifies powerful groups who share self-interest or common beliefs and defend their powers and privileges against a succession of rivals, the outcome being determined primarily by force or chance. Individuals who enjoy exercising power over others can identify with any of these factions as appropriate to advance their own interests. Over time, these factions have included monarchs and their families, landowning aristocratic families, church leaders, the military, industrialists and, currently, business, professional and financial interests channelled through political parties.

Pervasive themes include periodic shortages of government funds triggering unacceptable demands for taxation, corruption within the ruling elite, ruthless suppression of dissent, fear of mainland Europe, and conflicts involving Scotland and Ireland. Religious quarrels and, until the Hanoverian settlement in 1814, instability in the succession to the monarchy, also played important parts.

Although there have been periodic uprisings and riots, there has never been a successful revolution on behalf of the common people. Those who campaigned for political equality were put down by force, notably the Peasants' Revolt of 1381, the 'Commotion' of 1549 and the Levellers in the mid-seventeenth century. The Chartists of the mid-nineteenth century lost popular support in times of prosperity. The 'revolution' of 1688, which is the basis of the present constitutional arrangement, was primarily a quarrel between groups within the governing elite. The extension of the right to vote from aristocratic control to a virtually universal franchise, culminating in 1948, was the result of continuing pressure against the ruling elite, but it took nearly 200 years to achieve and even now is set within a framework that favours the status quo (Section 12.5.6).

The following sections outline some important stages in the development of the constitution.

4.2 The Saxon period: origins of the Crown

The monarchy is the oldest institution and, in legal terms, still the keystone of the constitution. In theory, all legal power derives from the Crown. The withdrawal of the Romans in the fifth century put paid to a republican constitution. By the end of the tenth century, 'England', as a loose unity comprising rival warlords headed by a king, had emerged from rival kingdoms.

From pre-Norman times, the hierarchical and centralised character of English society was apparent. According to the myth of the 'ancient constitution', the king ruled subject to the consent of a council, the Witan, representing the leading citizens, and the idea of an 'English' nation was established. This is sometimes claimed to be the origin of Parliament, thus creating an appearance of continuity (which is taken to be a good thing).

By the end of the tenth century, a complex system of local government existed within the structure of counties that broadly remains today. This was controlled by royal representatives known as aldermen and sheriffs (these offices survive today, in characteristic English fashion, as ceremonial and social). There were local bodies within the counties organised into 'hundreds' and 'tithings' which acted as law enforcers, courts and tax collectors.

4.3 The medieval period: the beginning of parliamentary government and the common law; the formation of national identity

After the Norman Conquest (1066), the king claimed jurisdiction over the whole of England and, by the sixteenth century, over Wales. As Duke of Normandy, he also initially controlled much of France. The power of the monarchy derived from the hierarchical feudal system of landowning, with the king at its apex. The chief landowners and church dignitaries (the two often overlapping) formed the king's council of advisers which he could summon at will and through which he issued laws. Some of the original powers of the monarch survive today in the form of the royal prerogative (Section 14.6). The army comprised private forces raised by the king and other landowners, each of which had a feudal obligation to provide the king with resources. Until the Wars of the Roses ushered in the Tudor regime (from 1485), the Crown was held by a succession of warlords supported by rival landowning families. There were many disputes as to the succession.

Henry II (1154–89) introduced a centralised but flexible legal regime in the shape of the common law. The Assize of Clarendon (1166) established the king's power to administer law through judges and juries throughout the land. Justice was carried out in the king's name by travelling judges and by local Justices of the Peace. By the reign of Edward I (1272–1307), the common law was established as a general system of law developed by the judges through decided cases. It was accepted that even the king was subject to the common law.

Magna Carta (1215) (which was revised and reissued several times until 1300) was promoted, notably in the seventeenth century by Chief Justice Coke, as a foundation of the rule of law and as representing an allegedly ancient common law. In Magna Carta, King John promised to rectify a list of grievances presented by leading landowners and clerics. The king was forced to commit what were previously unwritten customs to formal writings. Some of the rights listed in Magna Carta are widely recognised as fundamental to the modern rule of law. These include the right to a fair trial, the jury, no punishment except by law, the rights of life, liberty and property, and no taxation without consultation with those affected, thus underpinning the development of Parliament and the common law.

Although it is no longer directly in force, the underlying principles of Magna Carta, especially that of the rule of law, influenced the seventeenth-century revolution, have been invoked in modern cases, and inspired other constitutions, notably that of the USA (see Thompson, *Magna Carta: Its Role in the Making of the English Constitution* (Octagon 1972)).

The king originally made law and governed through a council chosen by himself. The reign of Henry III (1216–72) saw constitutional conflict between the king, who wished to rule through the royal household, and the barons (the chief landowning families). Following the collapse of a period of baronial domination, Parliament began to develop as a distinct institution.

Parliament originated early in the thirteenth century as a meeting of leading landowners and officials summoned personally by the king at irregular intervals to transact important governmental business often including hearing appeals from the courts (the term means a 'parley or conference'). The House of Lords (which perhaps evolved from the Saxon Council of Elders, the Witan) was composed of the barons and church dignitaries. From time to time during the early thirteenth century, representatives from other groups were summoned separately, mainly to give information to the king.

Simon de Montfort, Earl of Leicester (1208–65), is credited with founding the House of Commons as a counterweight to the Lords by insisting in 1265 that representatives of local dignitaries, authorised to speak for their communities, be summoned together to Parliament, namely knights from country areas (the shires) and leading citizens from certain towns (burghers). This was the seed of the modern principle of representation. The first substantial representative Parliament was the 'Model Parliament' of 1295. Originally, the Commons sent representatives to the House of Lords, but from the middle of the fourteenth century, it met separately. The House of Lords was interested only in its own members, and the two houses made separate grants of money to the king (in 1640, Charles I tried to summon the Lords alone, but this was rejected as now constitutionally impossible).

The king could decide when to summon Parliament and did so irregularly, mainly when he needed to raise taxation. From the late thirteenth century, the king, in conjunction with Parliament, began to make laws; originally on the basis that Parliament was declaring the existing customs of the realm. A strong relationship developed between the House of Commons and the common lawyers, which was important for the future. Parliament, which had the status of a high court, was able to give final rulings on the law and to 'impeach' public officials for misconduct. (Impeachment depends on a resolution of the House and is unlikely to be used today, although it was suggested that Tony Blair, the then prime minister, should be impeached over the decision to invade Iraq in 2002, and Boris Johnson for unlawfully proroguing Parliament in 2019 (see Sections 14.6.4 and 19.7.1).) The notion of the 'High Court of Parliament' is still heard today.

By the reign of Henry IV (1366–1413), the Commons claimed primacy over the House of Lords in respect of taxation matters, an important precursor of contemporary principles. The Commons voted funds to the king in exchange for the redress of grievances, a principle that echoes in the modern Parliament. However, until the seventeenth century when royal pretensions became extravagant, Parliament was largely deferential to the Crown.

The fourteenth and fifteenth centuries saw constant struggles between the king and the barons. Representative parliaments gradually became an established feature of the constitution, although lawmaking was infrequent. The Speaker, a royal official, was introduced as a link between the king and the Commons, and the Commons claimed protection against outside interference. For example, there were claims during the reign of Richard II (1377–99) that, at least in judicial matters, Parliament was supreme. Parliament claimed independence, for example in 1404 when Henry IV tried to ban lawyers from the 'Unlearned Parliament', on the basis that they were interested only in themselves.

The reasons for the rise of a representative Parliament, which was unique in Europe, are obscure. It may be that Parliament was originally a useful tool of the king against obstructive barons, particularly when he needed to raise money. The Black Death epidemic of 1348–53, which wiped out half the population, left ordinary working people in a stronger political position as a result of labour shortages. The Peasants' Revolt or 'Great Uprising' (1381), when thousands of ordinary people marched on London in protest against corruption in the church, deprivation and excessive taxation, although ruthlessly suppressed, strengthened the political influence of ordinary people, if only as a warning to the Crown. John Ball (1338–81), an influential preacher who was executed after the Peasants' Revolt, promoted democratic ideals of equality that were taken up in later centuries, but which have never been fully realised.

During the fifteenth century, Parliament asserted itself. The forcible removal of the erratic Richard II (1399) in favour of his cousin Henry Bolingbroke (Henry IV), whose property Richard had confiscated, weakened the notion of the divine right of kings (which Charles I unsuccessfully tried to revive in the seventeenth century).

The Hundred Years War with France (1347–1453), which resulted in the final loss of French territories, impoverished the Crown, so that recurrent demands for taxation led to the increasing influence of the House of Commons. The war also destroyed England as a European power but stimulated the reinvention of a distinctively English culture, replacing the French domination that had existed since the Norman Conquest. In particular, English replaced French as the language of government. This made political influence more widely accessible.

The principle that lawmaking required the consent of representatives of the realm was recognised by the end of the fifteenth century. Thus, leading common lawyer Sir John Fortescue distinguished between *dominium regale*, as in France, where the king made his own laws and *dominium politicum et regale*, where the people assented to laws made by the king (*The Difference between an Absolute and Limited Monarchy* (1471)). Fortescue declared that 'nor does the king by himself or by his minister impose tallages, subsidies, or any other burdens whatsoever on his subjects, nor change their laws nor make new ones, without the concession or assent of his whole realm expressed in Parliament' (*de Laudibus Leges Angliae*, 'In Praise of the Laws of England' (c1470)). Of course, there is plenty of room for disagreement as to who counted as 'the whole realm' (see also *Duchy of Lancaster Case* (1561) 75 ER 325). By the beginning of the sixteenth century, the present structure of monarchy subject to Parliament and the common law was in place, but with the monarch still being the dominant player.

4.4 The sixteenth century, the Tudor period: the consolidation of the government

This period, the Renaissance, introduced both new and revived political ideas (assisted by the introduction of the moveable type printing press into England in 1476). The Tudor period, spanning the sixteenth century, saw the emergence in Europe of the modern concept of the nation state as a self-contained impersonal structure with absolute authority within its territory. The Renaissance state existed primarily for military purposes and depended for the authority of its ruling elite upon a permanent situation of competition or fear of war with other states.

In most of Europe, absolute monarchies lasted well into the nineteenth century. As a result of the medieval heritage, absolute monarchy had failed to take root in England. Nevertheless, until the American revolution at the end of the eighteenth century, the nation state in England was more secure than was the case in much of the rest of Europe, which remained riven by competing families, religions and traditional privileges.

This period saw the emergence of the modern type of executive, comprising ministers (the most important of whom, such as Thomas Cromwell (1485–1540), were styled secretaries of state), committees comprising the monarch's favourites and a bureaucratic structure of professional civil servants (the term itself was not used until Victorian times). Participation in government was no longer limited to the great aristocratic families and clergy, but extended to new professional classes, notably lawyers (such as Cromwell) and merchants. Laws made by the central state became commonplace.

The Protestant Reformation destroyed the dominance of the Catholic Church when Henry VIII created the Church of England as a state religion (Act of Supremacy 1534) and dissolved the monasteries, confiscating their property. The Laws in Wales Acts (1535, 1542) extended the jurisdiction of Parliament and English law and government into Wales. From the reign of Henry VIII, the English monarchs considered themselves also monarchs of Ireland, although English rule was resisted within Ireland until formal union in 1800.

There were successive problems concerning the legitimacy of the monarch. Underlying these was a hornets' nest of religious intolerance between the new Church of England, Catholicism and various sects of fundamentalist Protestants. This led to two centuries of religious conflict and, depending on who was in power at the time, threefold persecution between the Church of England, Catholics and dissenting fundamentalist Protestants.

Importantly, during the reign of Elizabeth I (1558–1603) the 'Puritans' grew in strength. So named by the government as a term of abuse, Puritans supported a 'pure' form of Protestantism based on individual responsibility. Many Puritans had returned from Europe, having fled there to escape persecution in Queen Mary's ruthless Catholic revival (1553–58). Puritans were dominant in the conflicts of the following century. Presbyterians were broadly their equivalents in Scotland.

The Reformation opened up a gulf, which still exists, between pragmatic English constitutional ideas and the more rationalistic mainstream European tradition. Protestant notions of individualism and freedom of thought, the foundations of democracy, began to circulate widely, as did classical republican ideas of equal citizenship (e.g. Sir John Harrington, 1561–1612), although the latter have not significantly influenced constitutional development in the UK (see Section 2.5).

In the early years of the century, England had been struggling economically as a result of many wars, competition with a burgeoning Europe and the decline of the staple wool trade. During Elizabeth's reign, the status of the monarchy and the finances of the government improved thanks to a policy of developing naval power, aggressive overseas trade and colonial adventures, all of which brought in money without the help of Parliament. Elizabeth therefore had relatively little need to call on Parliament. There was, however, friction between Elizabeth and Parliament concerning whether Parliament could discuss matters not raised before it by the Crown. This has echoes in the modern law of parliamentary privilege. In the last ten years of Elizabeth's reign, Parliament sat for only seven months.

Nevertheless, during the Tudor period, the independence of Parliament was promoted. Parliament was still spoken of as a court, reflecting the influence of lawyers in government and the fact that much government was carried out through court-like procedures. However, by the middle of the sixteenth century, it had become clear that Parliament was also a proper lawmaking assembly. The Reformation statutes showed that the monarch in conjunction with Parliament could make new laws of any kind, as opposed to merely declaring the existing law. It was widely assumed, but not settled, that this involved unlimited legal power. Parliament was promoted as uniting the important elements of the realm from the monarch downwards: 'The great corporation and body politic of the kingdom … with high, absolute and authentical powers' (Coke, *Institutes* (1644) 4(2); see Holdsworth, *History of English Law* (Sweet and Maxwell 1945) IV, 181–87).

Until the closing years of her reign, Elizabeth promoted a cult of monarchy based on personal prestige, buttressed by success against Spain and colonial spoils from the West Indies and North America. During her reign there was constant fear of subversion, supported by Catholic Europe. An elaborate state security system developed, underpinned by prerogative courts, most notably the notorious Star Chamber with its special laws (presaging contemporary immigration tribunals). As a result of security service activity, the Catholic Mary Stuart, who had been forced to abdicate as Queen of Scotland, and was a claimant to the English throne, was executed in 1587. This formed a precedent for the later execution of her grandson, Charles I.

4.5   The seventeenth-century revolution: the supremacy of Parliament over the Crown

The seventeenth century saw harmony between the three branches of government disintegrating. The century was a crucible of constitutional ideas, including sovereignty, representation and, to a limited extent, democracy. Religious conflicts between Catholics and Protestants were part of larger conflicts between rival European empires with whom English alliances shifted. The Treaty of Westphalia (1648), which ended many years of war across an exhausted Europe, introduced the notion that all states are equal and sovereign that underlies modern international law.

The Church of England, headed by the king, was confronted on the one hand by the Catholic Church and on the other by Protestant groups including the Puritans, who dominated Parliament. The Crown's need for war funds also played a leading role.

The Stuart monarchs who succeeded Elizabeth I in 1603 ruled the three separate kingdoms of England, Scotland and Ireland. There were uprisings in Scotland and Ireland, leading to financial and religious conflicts between the Crown and Parliament. This led to civil war in all three kingdoms, a period of republican rule and eventually to the 'revolution' of 1688, the foundation of the present constitution.

James I (1603–25) and Charles I (1625–48) attempted to revive the notion of royal supremacy and the supremacy of the Church of England. James began a process of colonisation in the north of Ireland by encouraging plantations in Catholic lands by settlers, mainly from Scotland. He also attempted to encourage political union with Scotland. Both James and Charles tried to use the royal prerogative to make law and to raise certain taxes, but respected the common law by accepting scrutiny by the courts.

See e.g. *Bates' Case* (1606) 2 St Tr 371: the king could tax import of currants since foreign affairs were exclusively a matter for him; *Darnall's Case: The Case of the Five Knights* (1627) 3 St Tr 1: the king could imprison without giving reasons; *R v Hampden* (1637) 3 St Tr 825: the king could tax for defence of the realm purposes; *Seven Bishops' Case* (1688) 12 St Tr 133: the king could not suspend the operation of statute (suspending power); but see *Thomas v Sorrell* (1674) Vaughan 330 and *Godden v Hales* (1686) 11 St Tr 1165: the king could release from legal obligation (dispensing powers).

The judges were servants of the Crown, but asserted their independence in deciding cases. Their position was ambivalent since they could be dismissed by the king and the judgments of the day were full of disagreement. James I and Charles I claimed that, under the constitution, the monarchy was the embodiment of the community and, as the 'fount of justice', guardian of the people's rights, an interpretation contested by Parliament and, somewhat more uneasily, by the common lawyers.

In *Prohibitions del Roy* (1607) 12 Co Rep 64, a landmark decision of the Kings Bench, Coke CJ asserted that the king, while nominally the head of the legal system, could not personally adjudicate in the courts, since the judges were the guardians of the 'artificial reason of the law', which was available only to a learned elite. As well as promoting the self-serving notion that the law was a matter of professional expertise in the hands of a 'priesthood' of lawyers, this relates to modern ideas of the separation of powers and the rule of law. Thus, Coke's principle has been used to prevent ministers from hiding behind any special privileges of the Crown (see *M v Home Office* [1993] 3 All ER 537). Coke claimed that the law was 'the golden metwand' that, if respected by the king, would protect both citizens and himself. The seventeenth-century philosopher Thomas Hobbes (see Section 2.3.1) strongly objected to what he regarded as Coke's inflated claims for the courts. Hobbes argued that the law should be based on ordinary reason accessible to all and not in the hands of an elite. See also *Case of Proclamations* (1611) 12 Co Rep 74: the king could not make law by proclamation.

Charles, impressed by the splendour of the absolute monarchy of Spain, promoted the medieval idea of the divine right of kings. However, he ran out of money and was under military pressure from rebellions in both Scotland and Ireland. In 1628, Charles accepted the *Petition of Right* presented by Parliament and derived from Magna Carta and the common lawyers, which listed grievances against the Crown including taxation and imprisonment without trial. Charles did not regard this as binding and, in 1629, dismissed Parliament. (It must be remembered that, until the eighteenth century, the meeting of Parliament was in law entirely up to the king, a fundamental constitutional lever.) However, in 1639, when Charles attempted to impose the Anglican prayer book on Scotland, the resulting uprising forced him to summon a Parliament, the 'Long Parliament', which sat from 1640 until 1660, albeit dormant or suspended for most of its life.

A short-lived compromise was reached in 1641 when the Star Chamber and other special prerogative courts introduced by the Tudors were abolished, together with various other prerogative measures. These events left English legal culture with a suspicion of special jurisdictions and a preference for the ordinary courts, reflected in Dicey's idea of the rule of law (Section 6.3).

In 1641, there was a Catholic uprising in Ireland which was widely blamed on the king, although it was probably engineered by his opponents. Reports of massacres inflamed opinion. Charles attempted to enter Parliament with soldiers and arrest a group of members for treason. However, they had fled, and the Speaker denied all responsibility other than as the servant of the House. (This event is recalled by the ceremonial opening of Parliament each year when entry is symbolically denied to the monarch.)

Civil war between the king and Parliament broke out in 1642, resulting, after 250,000 deaths and hardship and destruction throughout the country, in victory for Parliament in 1646. This was brought about mainly by the efficient 'New Model Army', recruited and trained under the leadership of Oliver Cromwell, a member of the middle-ranking gentry who became the leader of the parliamentary side. There was a wide-ranging constitutional debate at Putney between the Parliamentarians, including gentry and army officers, and the more radical army rank and file, represented by the Levellers, who proposed a written constitution. This 'Agreement of the People', echoing the earlier claims of the Peasants' Revolt (Section 4.3), was based on religious freedom, equality before the law and universal male suffrage (later qualified by excluding servants and beggars). However, Cromwell invoked custom and tradition in favour of more limited reforms. The Levellers, with their wider ideas of democracy, were defeated by force in 1649. The 'Rump Parliament', the remains of Charles's last 'Long Parliament', now claimed full power. In 'Pride's Purge' (1648), the army removed the moderate members leaving the 'Barebones Parliament'. Charles I was then tried by Parliament, which had set itself up as a court. He was executed in 1649. Charles's defence, correct in law, was that Parliament had no jurisdiction over him.

The House of Lords was abolished and a republic declared, promoted as the 'Commonwealth' of the three kingdoms. Rebellion in Ireland was ruthlessly suppressed, leaving a lasting legacy of anti-English sentiment. There was a further civil war generated from Scotland when Cromwell defeated Charles II, the heir of Charles I, at the battles of Dunbar (1650) and Worcester (1651). Charles went into exile in France, Germany and Holland.

In 1653, the remnants of Parliament were expelled and a military dictatorship, the Protectorate, was introduced. This included two attempts at a written constitution. The *Instrument of Government* (1653), made by the army, gave power to Cromwell as 'Lord Protector' together with a council and a single-chamber Parliament elected by property owners. This was superseded in 1657 by the *Humble Petition and Advice*, produced by Parliament, which gave Parliament greater authority but allowed Cromwell to choose his successor.

Cromwell, although refusing the title of king, increasingly took on the attributes of a monarch. After his death in 1658, his son Richard, whom Cromwell had nominated to succeed him, was unable to cope with the squabbling between the rival factions in the army and Parliament. With a massive inherited debt, the government fell apart.

General Monck, chief of Cromwell's occupying army in Scotland and who had previously fought for the king, invited Charles II to return from exile in Holland. In 1659, Monck's army marched into England and, after further quarrelling, Parliament dissolved itself. (In law, all of the Parliaments that had met since the time of Charles I were the continuation of his 'Long Parliament', which had never been dissolved.) This led to the triumphant arrival of Charles II, who had already been crowned king of Scotland and who took advantage of public weariness with the Puritans.

A self-appointed 'Convention' of political leaders invited Charles to resume the English and Irish monarchies unconditionally. He summoned a new Parliament, including those previously expelled, and the House of Lords was restored. The republican legislation was expunged from the statute book in an Act of Indemnity and Oblivion (1660), Charles's reign being backdated to the day after his father's execution. (However, those who had signed the death warrant of Charles I were excluded from the indemnity and executed, as were those involved in the uprising in Ireland of 1641.) Charles II (1660–85) was, at first, politically circumspect and careful of Parliament. He took little active part in domestic politics while contributing substantially to public culture and entertainment. Charles's reign saw the emergence of the two political parties that dominated government until the late nineteenth century and whose successors govern today. These were the Whigs, the ancestors of the modern Liberal Democrat Party, and the Tories (Section 4.6).

Charles was forced to ask for money from Parliament in order to pay for his failing war against Holland. In return, he assented to the Test Act of 1673 which debarred non-Church of England members, especially Catholics, from holding public offices. Such discrimination lasted until the mid-nineteenth century. The Treaty of Westminster (1674) ended his war with Holland, which now became an ally. As part of the settlement, Mary, daughter of Charles's brother James, the heir to the throne, married William of Orange, the ruler of Holland. Importantly, both were Protestant.

From 1674, anti-Catholic sentiment was revived and Charles was suspect, since he had a Catholic wife and his heir, James, was Catholic. Catholicism was associated in the public mind with absolute monarchy, an association that still impacts the constitution by preventing the monarch from being or marrying a Catholic. This led to the Exclusion Crisis (1679–81) in which Parliament attempted to bar James from the succession. In 1681, Charles used his prerogative power to block the Exclusion Bill and dismissed Parliament. He refused to summon Parliament again.

On Charles's death in 1685, James duly succeeded to the Crown. In that year, at the battle of Sedgemoor, James's forces brutally suppressed a small and amateurish rebellion supported by radical Whigs and rural workers led by the Duke of Monmouth, his illegitimate half-brother. Monmouth was executed.

4.5.1   The 'glorious' revolution of 1688: the foundation of the modern constitution

James II alienated majority political opinion by favouring Catholics and attempting to override Parliament under the royal prerogative ('suspending and dispensing' powers). This had some success in the courts, at least to meet emergencies (*Thomas v Sorrell* [1674]; *Godden v Hales* [1686]). James suspended the penal laws against Catholics in 1687 and 1688. In the *Seven Bishops' Case* [1688], the court rejected James's claim to override statute in pursuit of dissenters and recognised parliamentary privilege against the Crown. James also disqualified thousands of local parliamentary candidates who would not vote according to his wishes. The last straw was the birth in 1688 of James, a Catholic male heir to the throne. Seven leaders drawn from both the main political parties offered the Crown jointly to the Protestants William of Orange (James's nephew) and his wife Mary, James's daughter. This provided a veneer of tradition.

Supported by a large force of mercenaries, William landed in Devon proclaiming that his purpose was 'for preserving of the Protestant religion and restoring the laws and liberties of England, Scotland and Ireland'. His main interest, however, was to enlist England's support in his war with France. Force was not needed. James had dissolved Parliament and fled to France, and William was not resisted. The foundations of the modern constitution were then laid. A self-appointed 'Convention' conferred the monarchy on William and Mary subject to conditions placing Parliament in charge. The common law courts sided with Parliament, which may be one reason why the revolution was promoted as a revival of an established constitution rather than as a radical break with the past. The revolution was justified in two ways. On one premise, James II had abdicated, leaving a power vacuum which, according to the common law doctrine of necessity, must be filled in order to avoid chaos. On the other, a proto-liberal premise based on Locke who was a strong supporter of Parliament, James had broken his contract with the people by violating property rights, so entitling the people to rebel (Section 2.3.2). The revolution settlement attempted to deal with the problems that had led to the Civil War. The Convention promoted the Bill of Rights 1688, based on the Petition of Right 1628.

It prohibited the Crown from exercising key powers without the consent of Parliament, including the powers to make laws, to tax, to keep a standing army in peacetime and to override legislation. It also protected freedom of speech and elections in Parliament, ensured that Parliaments were summoned regularly, protected jury trial and banned excessive bail.

The Bill of Rights is still in force and has been copied in other constitutions. However, it was primarily concerned with the immediate grievances of the time. For instance, its provision that entitled Protestants 'to keep and bear arms' was a response to a recent ban by James II in favour of Catholics. (This provision, minus the Protestant element, was later copied into the United States Constitution with resulting problems to the present day.)

William and Mary then summoned a Parliament which ratified the Acts of the Convention (Crown and Parliament Recognition Act 1689). The Meeting of Parliament Act 1694 (the Triennial Act) required Parliament to meet at least every three years and limited the life of a Parliament to three years (now five years). Scotland accepted a settlement on similar terms. They were imposed upon Ireland.

The 1688 settlement also led to the creation of the Bank of England in 1694 as a semi-independent institution backed by Parliament which guaranteed the currency and through which the government could borrow money. This was an important reason for the success of the British government during the following century, since it gave the Crown a secure source of funds, strengthened business confidence and led to the growth of an overseas empire. The constitution would in future depend on finance and trade. Landholding and land taxes were also politically important.

Thus, the 1688 settlement put in place the main legal structures we have today. It was based neither on democracy nor on the fundamental rights of the individual, but on the supremacy of Parliament and the Protestant religion.

Thomas Paine, who fled the country in 1792 having been charged with sedition for denying that Britain had a constitution, said in *The Rights of Man* ((1791–92), IV):

> What is [the Bill of Rights 1688] but a bargain which the parts of the government made with each other to divide powers, profits, and privileges? You shall have so much and I will have the rest; and with respect to the nation, it said, for your share, you shall have the right of petitioning. This being the case the Bill of Rights is more properly a bill of wrongs and of insult.

The settlement led to further bloodshed since neither Ireland nor Scotland accepted it. Continuing his war with France (the Nine Years War), William together with German and Austrian allies (the Grand Alliance) defeated the deposed James II and his French and Irish supporters at the Battle of the Boyne in Ireland (1690) and put down an Irish rebellion (1691). The memory of the seventeenth-century massacres continues to resonate in Ireland. In 1692, William's forces massacred the Scottish MacDonald clan at Glencoe, an attempt at subjugating the Scots that would generate further bloodshed.

4.6   The eighteenth century: the parliamentary system and the rule of law

In the early eighteenth century, the revolution was consolidated. There remained concerns about the possibility of a Catholic succeeding to the Crown. The Act of Settlement 1700 therefore created a Protestant succession to the Crown of England by way of descent from Sophia, Electress of Hanover (a granddaughter of James I). Scotland reluctantly accepted the same succession and it was imposed upon Ireland.

The Act of Settlement required the monarch to be a member of the Church of England and not to marry a Catholic. It prohibited non-citizens from being Members of Parliament or the Privy Council (Sections 12.2 and 5.7). Importantly, it gave higher judges security of tenure and therefore independence from the Crown. Thus was founded the first 'constitutional monarchy' in Western Europe.

During this period, the Kingdoms of England and Scotland were legally united. A disastrous colonial venture in Central America (the Darien Scheme) in the 1690s had brought the Scottish government close to bankruptcy. Economic pressures from England, including bribery of leading politicians and restricting trade and immigration, led to Scotland accepting a treaty merging the two parliaments into the Westminster institution. Scotland retained its separate legal system and church (Union with Scotland Act 1706; Union with England Act 1707). There were 45 Scottish MPs out of 558 in the House of Commons and 16 members of the House of Lords out of 212. Periodic rebellions in Scotland on behalf of the Stuart dynasty were defeated finally at the Battle of Culloden (1746). This led to English exploitation of the Scottish Highlands and large-scale emigration to North America, which was soon to revolt against Britain.

The 1688 revolution had established that the king was subordinate to Parliament, but the political relationship between the Crown and the ministers who formed the executive remained unclear. In law, the monarch was the executive with prerogative powers to assent to legislation, to appoint and dismiss ministers, and to summon and dissolve Parliament, but unable to raise taxes or make law without the cooperation of Parliament. The Crown also had prerogative powers in relation to foreign affairs.

The political structure of the modern UK Constitution slowly emerged: a centralised system under which the powers of government are concentrated in ministers responsible to a Parliament which they can effectively control. A Standing Order of 1706 (Ord. 66) (which in substance remains today) established that Parliament can vote for public spending and taxation only on the initiative of the Crown, thus sowing the seeds of the modern executive dominance of Parliament. Ministers began to sit regularly in Parliament as 'The Treasury Bench'. This was the basis of the incomplete separation of powers we have today (Section 7.6.1).

A crucial event in the subsequent domination of ministers was that when Queen Anne, the last Stuart monarch, died in 1714, the only Protestant successor acceptable to Parliament was George, the Elector of Hanover and 58th in line to the throne. George I (1714–27) had little interest in British affairs and relied heavily on his Cabinet of senior ministers. The office of prime minister as leader of the government developed from about 1720, with the tenure of the notoriously corrupt Robert Walpole (known as 'Cock Robin'), whose control of the Treasury, the security service and party organisation were sources of patronage.

Walpole is credited with developing the Cabinet system and the House of Commons as the centre of parliamentary power. By liberally dispensing and withdrawing favours, he laid the foundations of modern party politics. The Whigs and the Tories were rival camps supported by mobs and alternating to form governments, sometimes for very long periods. The Whigs, who had sponsored the 1688 revolution, were on the whole more progressive, commercially minded, Protestant and egalitarian. The Tories were traditionalists, more supportive of the monarchy and the Anglican Church but sometimes suspected of Catholic and French sympathies. (These stereotypes ignore the many overlaps and cross-currents between members of the parties, as is the case today.)

Walpole was, in effect, the first prime minister, although the title was not formally adopted until the late nineteenth century, and for many years the office was sometimes regarded as unconstitutional, being inconsistent with collective government. This is an example of how constitutional conventions are gradually established by general acceptance (Section 3.4.3).

Until the reign of George III (1760–1820), the Crown accepted the implications of the 1688 settlement which put Parliament in control. However, George III attempted to revive the influence of the monarchy. The Crown ran what was in effect a political party known as the 'Court and Treasury Party', which was controlled by giving government jobs to its supporters and manipulating elections.

However, after the loss of the American colonies in 1783 (Treaty of Paris), the monarchy lost prestige and also substantial influence over ministerial appointments, which both became matters for the political parties. William IV in 1835 was the last monarch to dissolve Parliament on his own initiative, when he seriously misjudged public opinion. This power was then exercised by the prime minister until 2011 (Section 11.2). However, it was not until the reign of George V (1910–36) that the convention that the monarch must not intervene in political matters was universally acknowledged.

Until well into the nineteenth century, government was oligarchical, since elections to the House of Commons were not democratic. The House of Lords could veto legislation, although the Commons controlled the raising and spending of money by the Crown. Both main political parties were dominated by the aristocracy, which had considerable influence on parliamentary elections.

The electorate was limited, being confined to property-owners in rural areas and selected citizens in the towns (Section 4.7). The poor had no direct political influence. Thus, an Act of 1710 (9 Anne c 5) imposed a property requirement on membership of the House of Commons (except for the eldest sons of peers and knights and the representatives of Oxford and Cambridge universities).

The leadership was supported in rural areas by the gentry who had been at the heart of the seventeenth-century revolution. These were landowners of varying degrees of prosperity and little education, from whose ranks came the Justices of the Peace who kept order in the local communities. Reforms to Parliament later in the century endorsed the independence of the Speaker and gave protection to political minorities, allowing for a range of opinion and helping to keep Parliament in touch with public opinion. However, the government was, as it is now, substantially in control of the procedure of the House. There is an ancient right to petition Parliament, enshrined in the Bill of Rights 1688. This developed strongly until the mid-nineteenth century, although its procedure was and still is controlled by Parliament itself (Section 13.6).

At a time when most European states were absolute monarchies ruling by force, the British constitution was widely admired from outside as a stable regime. The notion of the 'mixed constitution' was promoted, in which monarch, Lords and Commons acted as checks on each other in a balanced clockwork-like machine.

Thus, George III proclaimed that:

> the obligation of each Briton to fulfil the political duties, receive a vast accession of strength when he calls to mind of what a noble and well balanced constitution of government he has the honour to belong; a constitution of free and equal laws, secured against arbitrary will and popular licence, a constitution in fine the nurse of heroes, the parent of liberty, the patron of learning and arts, and the dominion of laws.

The ruling elite in eighteenth-century Britain was prosperous, supplied as it was by a large empire based on the Americas and the slave trade. However, the century was also socially chaotic and volatile and, as today, there was a large gap between rich and poor. Towards the end of the century, the emerging industrial revolution generated the progressive population increases and growth of urban centres that continue today. There were continuing wars with France and Spain. There was friction over taxation between traditional landowning interests and the emerging trade and industrial interests. Between 1750 and 1830, statutory confiscations of common land (Enclosure Acts) and urban expansion created large-scale poverty and squalor leading to unrest and protest, which were brutally suppressed by the courts and the military. A large national debt was built up.

It became apparent that these factors threatened higher taxes and called for increased government powers to keep order and suppress the poor. The second half of the century saw serious rioting, particularly in London, related to food shortages as well as political freedoms. The taxation demands of the Crown were the immediate cause of the American War of Independence (1775–83). This led to the collapse of much of the empire and the weakening of the Crown at home.

Despite the eulogies for the constitution, the late eighteenth century saw considerable public unrest concerning corruption in government. Benjamin Franklin, one of the founders of the American revolution, wrote: 'Here numberless and needless places, enormous salaries, pensions, perquisites, bribes, groundless quarrels, foolish expeditions, false accounts or no accounts, contracts and jobs, devour all revenue, and produce continual necessity in the midst of natural plenty' (*Letter to Joseph Galloway*, London (25 February 1775)). Jefferson, a founder of the US Constitution, thought that the British system of government responsible to Parliament was inevitably corrupt (Stevens (2004) 24 LS 1, 2).

There was less violent dissent than in continental Europe. However, there were riots in support of the parliamentary reformer John Wilkes (1768–69) (see Box). The Gordon Riots in London triggered by poverty (1780) were savagely suppressed by the army. During this period, an active press continually pilloried government leaders and the royal family. This led to attempts, often unsuccessful, to use the laws of sedition and libel to restrain the press. However, the fundamentals of the constitution were not threatened.

Eighteenth-century politicians such as Edmund Burke, who entered Parliament in 1765, still influence contemporary debate. Burke favoured traditional ideas of monarchy, custom and the unwritten constitution as opposed to republican equality and abstract reason, which he feared would lead to chaos and tyranny. He grounded the constitution in the limited right to choose and remove a representative government (see *Reflections on the Revolution in France* (1790)).

Burke's rival Thomas Paine, who influenced both the American and the French revolutions, favoured republican ideas including broader ideas of democracy and the establishment of a code of fundamental rights.

John Wilkes (1725–97) influenced the constitution by raising in the press general issues that resonate today, especially in connection with government surveillance and attempts to restrict press freedom. He was a constant irritant to the ruling establishment of a kind absent today when the media is largely controlled by business interests. Wilkes campaigned for the political rights of ordinary citizens against the self-interest of MPs and ministers. His successful causes included parliamentary privilege from arrest (*R v Wilkes* (1763) 95 ER 737, Section 11.6) and freedom of the press, where he succeeded in outlawing general warrants. Between 1763 and 1774, there were public riots in his support. Wilkes was imprisoned and expelled from Parliament but later became Lord Mayor of London and resumed his seat in Parliament.

4.6.1   The courts and the rule of law

Judges had obtained security from dismissal by the executive and loss of pay in the Act of Settlement 1700. The same Act excluded judges from membership of the House of Commons, but not of the House of Lords, of which many judges were members. Until the early twentieth century, judges were politically appointed and were sometimes former ministers or military men. Judges were often guilty of corruption, although no more so than other officials. Until the reign of George III, judges had to be reappointed upon the death of a monarch.

During the eighteenth and early nineteenth centuries, the rhetoric of the rule of law was promoted as protecting individual rights, imagined as being grounded in ancient common law tradition:

> The poorest man may in his cottage bid defiance to all the forces of the Crown. It may be frail, its roof may shake, the wind may blow through it, the storm may enter, the rain may enter, but the king of England cannot enter. (Lord Brougham, *Historical Sketches of Statesmen in the Time of George III* (1845))

It was widely asserted that the relative moderation, stability and economic prosperity of this period were connected with a commitment to the rule of law. By contrast, 'France with its demagoguery, revolt, beheadings and … unruly mobs stood in English "common sense" as a dreadful warning of all that can go wrong, a sort of conceptual opposite to England's altogether more sensible ways' (Pugh, 'Lawyers and Political Liberalism in Eighteenth and Nineteenth Century England' in Halliday and Karpick (eds), *Lawyers and the Rise of Western Political Liberalism: From the Eighteenth to the Twentieth Centuries* (Clarendon Press 1997) 168).

Blackstone (1723–80), a leading lawyer, academic and MP (whose *Commentaries on the Laws of England* are still cited), praised the common law which he considered to be grounded in reason, the rule of law and the independence of the judges. However, Blackstone was already regarded as old-fashioned in the light of increasing demands for political freedom.

Because laws are often vague, reformers such as Bentham, who favoured utilitarian ideas of the public good, thought the law's claims to objectivity and balance were spurious and that the constitution was held together by aristocratic power and influence. 'Talk of balance, ne'er will it do: leave that to Mother Goose and Mother Blackstone' (Bentham, *Works*, quoted by Loughlin, 'John Griffith: An Appreciation' [2010] PL 649).

The record of the rule of law was mixed. It protected rights in the formal sense that everyone had access to the same courts and whatever rights a person had might be adjudicated impartially. This of course favoured the property rights of the affluent. However, Parliament passed harsh laws for the benefit of government supporters, which the courts were required to apply. These included the notorious anti-poaching 'Black Acts' (see Thompson, *Whigs and Hunters* (Allen Lane 1975)). Fears of revolution along the lines experienced in France generated blasphemy and sedition laws. The protection of *habeas corpus,* a court procedure preventing imprisonment without trial, was suspended several times. The Corresponding Societies Act 1799 outlawed radical political, trade union and cultural organisations.

On the other hand, freedom of the press and freedom from arrest and searches of property under general warrants issued by the executive or Justices of the Peace were successfully asserted in the courts (see *Wilkes v Wood* (1763) 19 St Tr 1153; *Leach v Money* (1765) 19 St Tr 1001; *Entick v Carrington* (1765) 19 St Tr 1029; *Wilkes v Lord Halifax* (1769) 19 St Tr 1046). In response to the Gordon Riots, the leading common law judge, Lord Mansfield, stated in Parliament that the executive has no special power to control riots, other than the power under the ordinary common law available to everyone of self-defence. This influenced Dicey's idea of the rule of law as comprising general principles binding government and private individual alike (Section 6.4).

Religious inequalities were gradually removed by statute, albeit motivated by a desire to recruit Catholics to the armed forces. The common law rejected slavery within England (*Somerset v Stewart* (1772) 98 ER 499) and the slave trade was abolished by statute. Some contemporary themes thus begin to emerge in this period. The constitution relies heavily on personal relationships within the governing elite. Patronage is exercised by the prime minister and political parties, who nominate candidates for election and recommend peerages and public appointments. The common law and Parliament are sometimes in tension.

4.7 The nineteenth century: reforms and democracy

After a series of violent rebellions against Protestant supremacy, the Acts of Union of 1800 joined Britain and Ireland, thus creating the present UK Parliament. The Irish Parliament was abolished in favour of Irish representation in the UK Parliament.

The political and economic circumstances of Britain continued to change. Rural communities dominated by aristocratic landowners were eclipsed by industrial cities and overseas trade. This led to the enactment of statutes acquiring land on a large scale for public works. In particular, the massive and rapid expansion of the railways from the 1820s involved a large increase in government intervention, reinforcing the influence of large companies over government and embedding parliamentary supremacy in the law (e.g. *Lee v Bude and Torrington Railway Co* (1871) LR 6 CP 576; *Edinburgh & Dalkeith Railway Co v Wauchope* (1842) 8 Cl and F 710). Corporate local authorities were created to provide the roads, utilities and public health services necessary to support business interests, but their powers were sometimes interpreted by the courts against the provision of welfare for the poor (e.g. *A-G v Fulham Corp* [1921] 1 Ch 440: power to provide 'washhouses' did not extend to a laundry service for working people; *Roberts v Hopwood* [1925] AC 578: power to fix wages must be exercised on a commercial basis).

Successive governments were weak and corrupt, still dominated by networks of wealthy families and industrialists. There were demands for democratic government by radical organisations, notably the Chartists (1837–54). Uprisings took place throughout Europe, especially in the 'year of revolution', 1848. However, uprising in Britain was on a lesser scale and followed economic fluctuations rather than any strong public desire for democracy. Public unrest was sometimes put down brutally (e.g. the 'Peterloo' massacre of reform campaigners in Manchester (1819)). This led to the notorious 'Six Acts', which severely limited political freedoms and made criminal prosecutions simpler.

Before the Reform Act 1832, the total electorate in England and Wales was 11,000: that is, about 4 per cent of the adult population, bearing little relationship to the distribution of the population. For example, the growing industrial cities of Leeds, Birmingham, Sheffield and Manchester had no MPs, while the predominantly rural south coast counties produced about 200. Elections were largely controlled by members of the House of Lords, by bribery or by selecting candidates. There was a property qualification to vote in the rural counties. In the boroughs (towns), the right to vote depended on local charters and customs. In many cases, this was attached to particular property and could be bought. There were numerous 'rotten boroughs' that had only a handful of electors, sometimes in the gift of particular families. For example, in 1830 Gatton (patron Sir John Wood) had two MPs and seven voters. The younger sons of members of the House of Lords were often guaranteed seats in the Commons.

However, fear of riots and protests against bribery and corruption led gradually to a more democratic electoral system. The first Reform Act of 1832 was intended to appease the middle classes, so as to split them from working-class reformers. Its introduction illustrates the capricious nature of constitutional reform in the UK. The 1832 Act was of great symbolic value, although its specific reforms were modest. It extended representation to northern cities, made a uniform reduction in the property qualification to vote and abolished the worst rotten boroughs. The electorate was increased to 18 per cent.

Thereafter, the removal of property qualifications was slowly and reluctantly conceded. Many more electoral constituencies were created, mainly in the urban areas corresponding to the distribution of the population. In 1872, secret ballots and a register of electors were introduced, reducing corruption and intimidation. Women were given the right to vote in 1928, after many years of opposition by the executive and the courts. The Representation of the People Act 1948 finally introduced equal voting rights for most adults.

Universal suffrage was resisted by arguments that the freedom of talented people to develop themselves would be curtailed by the inflated demands of the masses. It was argued that only those who paid taxes should be able to vote on how taxes should be spent. Democracy was also resisted by Dicey, the champion of the rule of law (Section 6.4), who thought that it was dangerously unpredictable. Dicey was also opposed to women having the vote on the ground that the franchise existed not for the benefit of the voter, but for the collective good. He suggested that voting required male attitudes since government ultimately depended on physical force. He also thought that extending voting rights would enable other 'unsuitable' people to vote. These attitudes still surface, especially in the context of reform of the House of Lords and votes for prisoners.

During Queen Victoria's reign (1837–1901), the monarchy reshaped itself as a symbolic representative of the nation, outside party politics. By the end of the nineteenth century, it was becoming established that the prime minister and most senior ministers must be members of the House of Commons, and it was increasingly claimed that the unelected House of Lords was subordinate to the House of Commons. Lord Salisbury (1885–92) was the last prime minister to sit in the House of Lords, presiding over a regime notorious for nepotism.

The civil service, which advises government and carries out its instructions, was caught between two stools. On the one hand, efficiency required it to be distant from day-to-day politics. On the other hand, ministers required loyal servants. The empire had once again expanded with increased control of territories in India and Africa. This stimulated the development of a professional civil service. Civil service recruitment and training were improved, with competitive examinations replacing the previous method of personal patronage. Various 'Place Acts' barred many categories of public official from membership of Parliament.

The extension of democracy led to debate about the place of common law. Traditional-minded lawyers, such as Dicey, defended the idea of the common law against what they perceived as threats from both democratic ideas and the authoritarian influences of continental Europe. Reformers despised the common law as an enemy of progress, democracy and efficient management. However, the broad justice-based system that predominated during the eighteenth century was challenged by more formalistic rule-based conceptions of law that suited the development of trade in the nineteenth century.

During this period of developing democracy, the courts endorsed the principle of parliamentary supremacy, but the contradiction between the common law and parliamentary supremacy was not resolved. Dicey is often credited with coining both the concepts of the rule of law and parliamentary supremacy, but never convincingly reconciled the two (Section 6.1). He argued that public opinion through the electorate would ultimately restrain Parliament: what he called 'self-correcting democracy'.

Utilitarian ideas produced radical reforms to the court system in the shape of the Judicature Acts 1873 and 1875, which introduced a unified court structure. However, the anomaly of the House of Lords as part of Parliament, being the final judicial appeal body, was restored by the Appellate Jurisdiction Act 1876. This was the result of a political deal concerning home rule in Ireland, thus illustrating the way in which constitutional reform can be driven by short-term party politics. This arrangement survived until 2005 (Section 5.4.1).

Until the early twentieth century, many High Court judges were political appointments. Reflecting the nature of the constitution, Lord Salisbury claimed that 'it is the unwritten law of our party system; that party claims should weigh very heavily in the disposal of the highest legal appointments. To ignore the party system would be a breach of the tacit convention in which politicians and lawyers have worked the constitution together' (quoted by Stevens (2004) 24 LS 1, 11).

From the 1870s, the question of Irish home rule dominated national politics, and there was debate concerning the desirability of a federal system. Traditionalists such as Dicey feared that parliamentary supremacy would be threatened.

4.8   The twentieth century: the rise of the executive

During the early years of the twentieth century, there was persistent hostility between the House of Lords, which had an inbuilt Conservative majority, and the Liberal government. This concerned in particular the continuing issue of Irish home rule and also the reluctance of the Lords to approve high taxation for welfare purposes. Edward VII attempted to intervene but died in the middle of the crisis in 1910. His successor, George V, reaffirmed the convention that the monarch must act on government advice. After a general election, the Lords backed down. The Parliament Act 1911 (Section 11.4) endorsed the supremacy of the Commons by removing most of the powers of the House of Lords to veto legislation.

Various attempts at compromise over Irish home rule failed, leading to violent rebellion. Most of Ireland left the UK in 1921, leaving the six counties of Northern Ireland as part of the UK, but continuing to be bitterly divided.

During the twentieth century, the balance of power between Parliament and the executive moved strongly in favour of the executive. MPs were becoming professional politicians, dependent for their livelihood on party support. At the end of the First World War in 1918, the property qualification for the franchise was finally removed, enabling all adult males and women over 30 to vote (extended to all adult women in 1928).

Elections became the mass campaigns with which we are familiar today. After the First World War, the Liberal Party collapsed, and the conservative Tories were confronted by the newly emergent Labour Party, then representing working-class interests and broadly in favour of a state with wide discretionary power. However, moderate coalition governments emerged and, perhaps partly due to the non-political monarchy, the UK avoided the extremes of fascism and communism that dominated Central Europe.

The British Empire began a process of dismemberment with the Statute of Westminster 1931. This freed the so-called white Dominions from parliamentary control (Section 8.5.1).

Impelled by the demands of a larger electorate, the executive began to increase in size and range of discretionary powers as successive governments provided a wider range of welfare services. These could be delivered only through large bureaucratic organisations making numerous detailed decisions, guided by a plethora of rules and technical specialists. During the twentieth century, it became more widely accepted that the state could regulate all aspects of our lives; whether it *should* do so was a matter not for the constitution but for the everyday political contest.

The traditional sources of law – Acts of Parliament and the courts – were supplemented by an array of tools that enabled the executive to act relatively quickly and informally without detailed parliamentary scrutiny. These included delegated legislation made by government departments under powers given to them by statute and wide discretionary powers conferred on ministers and local authorities (Section 13.5.5). Thousands of special tribunals staffed by government appointees were created to deal with the disputes generated by the expansion of state activity. These seemed to threaten the traditional idea of the rule of law, according to which the same general law should apply to all, administered in the ordinary courts.

Executive control over Parliament increased. Parliamentary processes were controlled by government supporters and were too amateurish to enable executive action to be thoroughly scrutinised. Statutory provisions were introduced which attempted to exclude scrutiny of governmental decisions by the courts. It was therefore feared that the executive had outgrown the constraints both of the rule of law and political accountability to Parliament.

The constitution responded in only limited fashion to these developments. In the interwar period, both ends of the political spectrum were concerned. Some believed that the executive had taken over; others that an individualistically minded judiciary would frustrate social reforms. In 1928, Lord Chief Justice Lord Hewart, a follower of Dicey, published *The New Despotism*, in which he asserted that the rule of law was under threat from the executive. This led to the establishment of the Committee on Ministers' Powers, whose terms of reference were 'to report what safeguards were desirable or necessary to secure the constitutional principles of the sovereignty of Parliament and the supremacy of the law'. Described as having 'the dead hand of Dicey lying frozen on its neck', the Committee's report (Cmd 4060, 1932) gave the constitution a clean bill of health. It recommended some strengthening of the powers of Parliament in relation to delegated legislation (Statutory Instruments Act 1946) and asserted the importance of control by the ordinary courts over the executive. There was, however, a powerful dissent from the socialist Harold Laski, who argued that judges were frustrating legitimate democratic policies. Thus the red light/green light divergence began to arise (Section 1.5).

The *Report of the Committee on Administrative Tribunals and Inquiries* (Cmnd 218, 1957, the Franks Committee) also recommended only marginal reforms. These improved publicity, strengthened the powers of the courts and introduced limited procedural reforms, including the duty to give reasons by most tribunals and by a minister following a public inquiry (Tribunals and Inquiries Acts 1958 and 1992). From the 1960s onwards, various 'ombudsmen' were set up to investigate complaints by citizens against government, but without legally enforceable powers (Section 20.2).

Later in the century, there were wider concerns about sovereignty. In 1973, the UK became a member of what is now the European Union (European Communities Act 1972), making European law binding in UK law. Concerns were also raised that the electoral system placed select groups in power and enabled the large political parties to control both the executive and Parliament. These complaints amounted to fears that the constitution had degenerated into an oligarchy that did little more than allow the people to choose periodically between groups of cronies. Indeed, in the eighteenth century, the French philosopher Rousseau had asserted that the British were slaves except at election time.

During the middle years of the century, reluctant to be seen to be challenging democracy, the courts adopted a low profile. They deferred to government decisions and predominantly took a narrow technical approach to their work. This reinforced the notions that law was objective and that judges were independent and above politics. However, from the 1960s, for reasons which remain unclear, the courts woke from what Sir Stephen Sedley has called their 'long sleep' (in Andenas and Fairgrieve (2009)) and began to interfere more actively with government decisions. Landmark cases during the 1960s form the basis of contemporary administrative law. These include *Ridge v Baldwin* [1964] AC 40: the right to a fair hearing; *Anisminic v Foreign Compensation Commission* [1969] 2 AC 147: no exclusion of judicial review; *Conway v Rimmer* [1968] AC 910: disclosure of government information in evidence; and *Padfield v Minister of Agriculture* [1968] AC 997: no unreviewable discretionary power.

Judicial independence, depending as it does on executive self-restraint, continued to be at risk. From the beginning of the century, High Court and Court of Appeal judges began to be appointed from the ranks of practising barristers. However, until the 1960s, about 25 per cent of High Court judges had been former MPs or parliamentary candidates, and political appointments to the Appellate Committee of the House of Lords were common until the 1930s.

From the 1960s, there was something of a sea change in Parliament as full-time professional politicians replaced lawyers in the House of Commons (the workloads of the latter no longer facilitated part-time work as MPs). Thus, the long-standing collaboration of lawyers in running the constitution propounded by Lord Salisbury (above) had all but vanished.

However, the Lord Chancellor still combined membership of the executive with leadership of the judiciary and responsibility for appointing most judges (the most senior judges were appointed by the prime minister). Indeed, in the 1980s, an expanded Lord Chancellor's Department assumed control of the court and legal aid system. This led to fears among the judiciary that independence was at risk. Judicial independence was also compromised by the practice of appointing judges to hold special inquiries into politically controversial issues (Tribunals of Inquiry (Evidence) Act 1921 (Section 20.3)).

From the 1960s, the courts were also increasingly exposed to politics. Governments introduced strongly ideological legislation such as that which promoted competition, or placed restrictions upon trade unions. These sometimes involved specialist courts, leading to pressure upon the notion of judicial impartiality. In the late 1970s, the judicial review process was reformed and was made more widely accessible (Section 19.4). This further raised the political profile of the judges. Moreover, well before the enactment of the HRA, increasingly liberal judges were drawing upon human rights concepts. The obligation to apply EU law, sometimes against the interests of the government, also put the judges under political scrutiny. There was sometimes vociferous criticism of the judges from government circles, again leading to worries about judicial independence (see Stevens (2004) 24 LS 1, 16, 20, 26).

4.9 The present century: distrust, reforms and an uncertain future

Despite the eulogies from the likes of Blackstone in the eighteenth century, the UK Constitution is unbalanced. This is because it entrusts unlimited legal power to Parliament and enables it to be politically dominated by the executive, which in turn is subjected to pressure from business and financial interests. Thus, the legal constitution depends on the political constitution. The notions of the separation of powers and judicial independence are frail.

A series of scandals from the 1980s onwards has exposed corruption and incompetence within central government and Parliament. They include the Westland affair, where ministers and civil servants appeared to conspire against each other (see Treasury and Civil Service Committee, HC 1985–86, 92), the 'arms to Iraq' affair, which involved allegations that ministers had tried to cover up breaches of United Nations sanctions against Iraq (see Scott Report, HC 1995–96, 115, and Section 15.7.2) and allegations that ministers had distorted intelligence reports in 2002 in order to justify supporting the USA in its invasion of Iraq (see Chilcot Report, HC 2016–17, 265). The exposure during 2009 of the extent to which MPs and peers had been abusing their expense allowances led to criminal convictions and the introduction of an independent statutory regulator for MPs (Section 11.7.2). There have been allegations that MPs, peers, civil servants and ministers give privileges to, and have received favours from, business interests (Section 5.9). The ability of a powerful executive to invade Iraq in 2002 on the basis of false information given to Parliament and the restriction of traditional civil liberties under the umbrella of combating terrorism weakened faith in the democratic process. The courts responded to this by asserting their independence and, to some extent, resisting the erosion of rights: most famously in *A v Secretary of State for the Home Department* [2005] 2 AC 68, where the House of Lords condemned the use of detention without trial against foreign terrorist suspects.

Bogdanor (2009) claims that the UK Constitution has recently been transformed by a dividing up and dispersal of power, both between institutions and geographically. The centrifugal forces noted by Bogdanor continue to be powerful within the constitution. Although the referendum on Scottish independence in 2014 resulted in a decision to remain in the United Kingdom, the continuing dominance of a nationalist party in Scotland and increased powers for the devolved legislature in Wales, as well as uncertainties over the post-Brexit nature of the border between Northern Ireland and the Republic of Ireland, place the future of the Union under continuing pressure.

That pressure has been exacerbated by the outcome of the referendum on the UK's membership of the European Union in June 2016, with the populations in two constituent parts of the United Kingdom (Scotland and Northern Ireland) voting to remain, while those in England and Wales voted to leave. Brexit has also exposed significant divisions between larger cities (many of which, including London, voted to remain in the EU) and other areas, and the leave vote has also been viewed by some analysts as reflective of a wider disconnection from traditional politics. As noted in several places later in this book, the lengthy process of withdrawal from the EU has also caused considerable tension within the constitution, notably between government on the one hand, and Parliament and the courts on the other. In the longer term, Brexit may act as a counterweight to the recent dispersal of power, as sovereignty – which has, to some extent, been pooled with other states during the period of UK membership of the Union – is 'reclaimed' by Westminster and Whitehall. However, whether the United Kingdom can survive this process geographically or even constitutionally intact is highly uncertain.

This sense of uncertainty has been exacerbated by the COVID-19 pandemic of 2020. The state acquired very strong, albeit temporary, powers, primarily by means of secondary legislation (but see also Coronavirus Act 2020) to restrict individual liberties in an attempt to limit the spread of the virus and expended considerable resources to seek to protect the economy. The long-term impact of these interventions is unclear at time of writing but seems likely to be significant, although it may also necessitate the postponement of other planned constitutional reforms (Blick 2020).

There has also been a process of 'juridification', meaning the introduction of a larger legal element and therefore an enhanced role for the courts in the constitution. However, the recent changes do not amount to systematic reform but have been responses to specific problems. Indeed, the absence of systematic reform may create its own problems because of unintended consequences. We shall discuss these changes in their contexts. The most important ones are as follows:

- devolution of substantial lawmaking and executive power to Scotland, Wales and Northern Ireland (Chapter 16);
- the HRA, which makes many rights drawn from the ECHR enforceable in UK courts (Chapter 22);
- the creation of the Supreme Court replacing the House of Lords, part of Parliament, as the highest appeal court (Section 5.4.1);
- removal of the Lord Chancellor, who is a member of the executive, from his traditional role as head of the judiciary and limiting the Lord Chancellor's powers over judicial appointments (Sections 7.6.3.1 and 7.7.3.1);
- a reorganisation of the tribunal system to make it more independent of the executive (Section 20.1);
- a large reduction in the number of hereditary peers eligible to sit in the House of Lords and reforms to penalise non-attenders (Section 12.2);
- replacing the royal prerogative power exercised by the prime minister to dissolve Parliament and so trigger a general election by a fixed term of five years with provision for Parliament to dissolve itself earlier (Section 11.2);
- changes in parliamentary procedure which have strengthened the role of the House of Commons in holding the executive to account (Section 13.5);
- putting the basic principles governing the civil service on a statutory footing, but without changing them (Section 15.8);
- through the Freedom of Information Act 2000, giving certain rights to acquire information from public bodies (Section 24.2);
- increased use of secrecy in the courts (Section 24.6);
- increased use of referendums (Section 2.8.3).

Summary

▶ The historical development of the constitution was driven by the gradual wresting of power from the monarch in favour of other interest groups, focused mainly on Parliament.

▶ The 1688 revolution created a settlement that still forms the legal basis of the constitution. It made the Crown dependent on Parliament and attempted to combine respect for continuity and a balance of forces with the principle of parliamentary supremacy. It left the judiciary in an ambivalent position which has yet to be fully resolved.

▶ During the eighteenth and nineteenth centuries, the modern principles of responsible parliamentary government were developed mainly through conventions. This increased the power of the executive at the expense of Parliament.

▶ Despite a tendency to corruption, democratic reforms were introduced during the nineteenth and early twentieth centuries, but without being a complete democratic basis for the constitution. The House of Lords remains an unelected part of the legislature. The common law and independent courts are regarded as important checks on government. In the late nineteenth century, the Lord Chancellor became responsible for the judiciary, thereby blurring the separation of powers but possibly acting as a check on the executive. In recent years, the courts have been much more active than previously in challenging government action.

▶ Latterly, there have been concerns about the increased power of the central executive, and a growing public lack of confidence in the integrity of public officials. These factors have generated limited constitutional reforms. Concern for the independence of the judiciary has reduced the role of the Lord Chancellor, and produced a new Supreme Court and an independent judicial Appointments Commission. The relationship between the courts and Parliament remains unresolved with some judges claiming the power to override Parliament.

▶ A process of diffusion of power away from central government and the Westminster Parliament to governmental institutions in Scotland, Wales and Northern Ireland remains ongoing. However, the end to the UK's half-century membership of what is now the European Union may 'claw back' some of the legal and political sovereignty which some regard as having been lost during that period. It remains unclear whether the UK will remain a unified state at the conclusion of this process.

Exercises

4.1 To what extent was the 1688 settlement a constitutional revolution?

4.2 Does the history of the UK Constitution reveal a march towards a greater democracy?

4.3 What do the events of the seventeenth and eighteenth centuries tell us about the process of constitutional change in England?

4.4 Do you agree with Jefferson that responsible government of the British type is inevitably corrupt?

4.5 Trace the history of the House of Commons, explaining its main successes and failures.

4.6 'Herein consists the excellence of the English Government, that all parts of it form a mutual check on each other' (Blackstone (1765)).

To what extent was this true in Blackstone's time, and is it true today?

4.7 To what extent have the judges influenced the development of the constitution?

Further reading

Blick, 'The Multiple and Profound Constitutional Implications of Covid-19', https://blogs.lse.ac.uk/politicsandpolicy/covid19-uk-constitution/ (2020)

Bogdanor, *The New British Constitution* (Hart Publishing 2009) ch 1

Chrimes, *English Constitutional History* (4th edn, Oxford University Press 1967)

Goldsworthy, *The Sovereignty of Parliament: History and Philosophy* (Oxford University Press 1999)

Kellner, *Democracy: 1000 Years in Pursuit of British Liberty* (Mainstream 2009)

Loughlin, *Foundations of Public Law* (Oxford University Press 2010) chs 1 and 2

Lyon, *Constitutional History of the United Kingdom* (2nd edn, Routledge 2016)

Sedley, 'The Long Sleep' in Andenas and Fairgrieve (eds), *Tom Bingham and the Transformation of the Law* (Oxford University Press 2009)

Vallance, *A Radical History of Britain* (Little Brown and Co 2009)

Van Caenegem, *An Historical Introduction to Western Constitutional Law* (Cambridge University Press 1995)

Wicks, *Evolution of a Constitution* (Hart Publishing 2006)

Chapter 5

An overview of the main institutions of the constitution

This chapter provides a summary of the most basic principles of the constitution. The more important topics relating to the central government and the judicial system are developed and discussed at length later in this book.

5.1 The basic structure of the constitution

The constitution takes the form of a *parliamentary democracy*, comprising the Queen as head of state and the three traditional branches of government: legislature (Parliament), executive (known as 'the Crown', but popularly referred to as 'government') and judiciary. Building on historical evolution, the legal part of the constitution is based on parliamentary supremacy. The Crown is the source of all legal power but cannot make law, create courts, raise an army or impose taxes without the consent of Parliament. The Crown must summon Parliament regularly and cannot dissolve Parliament without its consent. Griffith summarised the basic legal position as follows:

> Governments of the United Kingdom may take any action necessary for the proper government of the United Kingdom as they see it, subject to two limitations. The first limitation is that they may not infringe the legal rights of others unless expressly authorised to do so under statute or the prerogative. The second limitation is that if they wish to change the law, whether by adding to their existing power or otherwise, they must obtain the consent of Parliament. ('The Political Constitution' (1979) 42 MLR 1, 15)

From the perspective of the 'political constitution', the effect of an interlocking series of *conventions* is to ensure that the legal powers of the monarch are exercised in accordance with modern ideas of responsible parliamentary government. The powers of the Crown are exercisable by or on the advice of ministers. The office of head of state is a 'constitutional monarchy', the existence of which depends on Parliament. It has no significant political power, except in extreme circumstances of constitutional breakdown (Section 14.4). Ministers of the Crown are collectively and individually responsible to Parliament. Civil servants who implement and advise on government policy are responsible to Parliament, normally indirectly through ministers.

The UK Constitution has been portrayed from three perspectives, or 'models' (Le Sueur in Feldman (ed), *English Public Law* (2nd edn, Oxford University Press 2009), [1.86]). These are not necessarily rivals, but each provides a partial point of view. First, there is the 'Crown' model which emphasises formal legal matters (but appears not to reflect the reality of how power is exercised in practice); second, there is the 'Westminster model' which emphasises political matters and a centralised form of government through the responsibility of ministers to Parliament. This has been the traditional view of the Constitution.

The third model is the 'multi-layered fragmented governance model', according to which government powers are increasingly split between many different bodies both within the UK, for example the devolved governments of Scotland, Wales and Northern Ireland, and outside the UK (e.g. the EU). This is both a legal and a political model and has implications for the central legal doctrine that Parliament is omnipotent.

Under the third model, the constitution is not strictly federal, but unitary, since ultimately legal power remains concentrated in the central legislature of Parliament. However, this might be regarded as unrealistic. Substantial legislative and executive powers are devolved to Scotland, Wales and Northern Ireland, and there are legal and political mechanisms to protect the autonomy of these bodies. The powers of the EU have been, in practice, at least an external limit on Parliament so long as the UK remained a member of the Union. It is noteworthy that a desire to 'reclaim sovereignty' was influential in the Brexit process, suggesting that the second model outlined here retains considerable influence on public opinion.

5.1.1 The state

Unlike other European legal systems (see e.g. the Constitution of Ireland, Arts 4–6), the UK has no legal concept of the state. The nearest is the concept of the Crown (Section 14.1). Thus, in *R v Preston* [1993] 4 All ER 638 (at 663), Lord Mustill remarked: 'The Crown as the source of authority means that the UK has never found it necessary to create the notion of the "state" as a single legal entity'.

Where legislation refers to the 'state', its meaning depends on the context, for example the community as a whole (*Chandler v DPP* [1964] AC 763), the 'sovereign power' (*General Medical Council v BBC* [1998] 1 WLR 1573) or the executive branch of government (*D v NSPCC* [1978] AC 171). The civil service is unhelpfully defined as the 'civil service of the state' (Constitutional Reform and Governance Act 2010, s 3) (Section 15.8). Sometimes the 'state' refers to the whole system of government.

The non-statist nature of English law has at least the following important consequences:

▶ There is a distinction in statist constitutions between 'public law', which regulates the state itself and its relationship with citizens, and 'private law', which regulates the relationship between its citizens. The UK Constitution has not historically recognised such a distinction (see *Davy v Spelthorne BC* [1984] AC 262 (Section 19.6)). Officials are regarded as ordinary citizens embedded in the general private law. According to Dicey, this is an important requirement of the rule of law (Section 6.4) in that, unless a particular law provides otherwise, officials have no special powers or status and are individually responsible for any legal wrongs they commit. Thus the doctrine of *raison d'état* (broadly, 'national interest') as a general justification for government power is not recognised (*Entick v Carrington* (1765) 19 St Tr 1029). There are some advantages in the UK approach. Particular decision-making bodies must be openly identified and cannot hide under the general state umbrella.

  However, the contemporary fashion of contracting out government functions to private bodies has led to attempts to distinguish between public and private law and between public and private bodies and functions, particularly in connection with judicial review of government action, European law, human rights and access to information. This has led to some confusion. A watertight definition of a public body or public function has yet to be produced and these terms are not defined in the same way in each context. Sometimes a statute provides a list of bodies or functions regarded as public (e.g. Freedom of Information Act 2000 (Section 24.2)), but usually, the notion of public function is left undefined. For example, in *Poplar Housing Regeneration Community Association Ltd.* [2001] 4 All ER 604, Lord Woolf stated (at [65]), that '[w]hat can make an act, which would otherwise be private, public, is a feature or combination of features which impose a public character or stamp'.

▶ In a statist system, the state is both a creation of the law and the producer of law. Judges are the authoritative interpreters of the law, but not its creators, and do not traditionally have an independent lawmaking role. By contrast, the historical basis of the common law gives the courts an independent basis of legitimacy. The authority of the common law lies in community values. In the common law system, judges are regarded as individuals charged with doing justice on behalf of the Crown. However, in *R v Jones (Margaret)* [2006] 2 WLR 772, which concerned an attempt to accuse the government of a war crime in invading Iraq, Lord Hoffmann (at [65]) expressed concern about the theoretical difficulty of the court taking action against the 'state' of which it is a part (but see *M v Home Office* [1993] 3 All ER 537: Crown, courts and ministers must be separated (Section 7.5.3)).

What follows (unless stated otherwise, where the matter is for a devolved regime) concerns the constitution of the UK as a whole.

5.2 The legislative branch

▶ Parliament has unlimited lawmaking power (although this is sometimes challenged [Section 8.5]). The Queen in Parliament makes primary law in the form of Acts of Parliament (statutes). The Queen cannot make law without it being first proposed by Parliament (Bill of Rights 1688). By law, the royal assent is needed for all Acts of Parliament, so that in law the Queen could veto a bill. However, by convention, the Queen is obliged to give her assent to all bills submitted to her by Parliament.

- Parliament comprises the non-elected House of Lords and the elected House of Commons. It has three main functions. First, together formally with the Queen, it is the primary legislature (lawmaker). Secondly, Parliament provides the government with money: taxes cannot be raised without the authority of Parliament (Bill of Rights 1688). Thirdly, as a matter of convention, the executive is politically accountable to Parliament and ministers must appear before it to justify their decisions and actions.

- Parliament must meet at least every three years and so cannot be dispensed with (Meeting of Parliament Act 1694). By convention, Parliament meets annually.

- By convention, Parliament can require the executive to resign. The long-standing prerogative power that enabled the prime minister to dissolve Parliament was abolished by the Fixed Term Parliaments Act 2011, although this statute seems very likely to be repealed in the near future. Under the Act, Parliament is automatically dissolved at the end of five years and a general election held within a short time specified by statute. Within the five-year period, Parliament is dissolved following *either* a two-thirds vote of the whole of the House of Commons in favour of dissolution *or* failure to form a new government within 14 days of a majority vote in the Commons of no confidence in the government. However, it remains open to Parliament, since it is not bound by earlier legislation, to pass an Act specifying the date of an election *within* the five-year period, as occurred in October 2019 (Early Parliamentary General Election Act 2019).

- Although Parliament is the lawmaker and any MP can introduce a bill, in practice, almost all laws are prepared by ministers who formally propose them to Parliament. Parliamentary procedure is to a large extent controlled by ministers, although this is less obviously the case when a government has a small, or no majority – as happened frequently during debates on Brexit in 2019. The lawmaking role of Parliament is therefore usually to scrutinise, amend and give consent to government legislation.

- The elected House of Commons is superior to the House of Lords. Subject to an important exception, the House of Lords cannot veto public bills introduced in the House of Commons, but can delay a bill by no more than (about) one year; in the case of a 'money bill' by one month. The exception is a bill to prolong the life of a Parliament beyond five years. Thus, the House of Lords provides a constitutional safeguard to prevent a government from avoiding a general election.

Parliamentary elections are conducted for members to represent local constituencies by the 'first past the post' (FPP) method. This gives victory to the candidate with the largest number of votes and ignores all other votes. FPP therefore makes it difficult for minority parties to gain seats. (Different voting systems apply in the devolved regimes of Scotland, Wales and Northern Ireland and for the London Assembly and Mayor (Section 12.5.7).) A referendum on changing the voting system for Parliament produced a vote in favour of no change in May 2011.

5.2.1 Political parties

There is no law or convention requiring the existence of political parties and, as a matter of law, political parties are private associations. However, because parliamentary elections are organised on the basis of political parties and the executive is formed from the dominant party in Parliament, parties are a central feature of constitutional practice and an inevitable feature of a democracy. The pressures of party conformity are both strengths and weaknesses of government accountability, making independent scrutiny of legislation difficult, but providing a clear focus of responsibility when things go wrong.

The prime minister is normally the leader of the largest party and is chosen under internal party arrangements. Thus, the party rather than the electorate chooses the prime minister. For example, in 2019 Boris Johnson was chosen as leader by the Conservative Party following the resignation of Theresa May, who had herself been chosen by the party to succeed David Cameron.

The regulation of political parties poses constitutional problems. These primarily concern funding: whether this should be by private persons and organisations as is the case at present (Section 12.6.2). On the one hand, to restrict private funding could be seen as an interference with a basic freedom of political expression (the line taken in the USA). On the other hand, private funding could enable wealthy persons to buy influence in both Parliament and the executive.

5.3   The executive branch

- The core executive is the Crown. The term 'Crown' is used in this context, rather than 'Queen', but it is unclear what the term means (Section 14.1). The Crown includes the Queen as its formal head, ministers (holders of political offices, usually elected) and civil servants (other civilian Crown employees). The armed forces are also servants of the Crown. Other public bodies must be created by particular statutes.

- By convention, the Queen must appoint the person who is best placed to command the confidence of the House of Commons as prime minister to lead the executive. This is normally the leader of the largest party. The prime minister could, in law, be dismissed by the Queen. However, except in extreme circumstances (Section 14.4), the prime minister, along with all other ministers, is *required* to resign only following a vote of no confidence in the House of Commons (though he or she may choose to do so for other reasons, such as ill health or political pressure). The Queen must appoint and dismiss other ministers on the advice of the prime minister.

- All ministers must be MPs. Most must be members of the House of Commons, including at least the prime minister and ministers directly concerned with government finance. Hence, in this respect in particular, there is an incomplete separation of powers. The law prohibits many public officials from being members of the legislature (Section 12.4), but this does not apply to ministers.

- By convention, the Cabinet, a committee of about 25 senior ministers chaired by the prime minister, is responsible for government policy, coordinating the work of government departments and major decisions. Latterly, the Cabinet may have declined in importance, thus illustrating the tenuous nature of conventions. Its role has arguably been usurped by strong 'overlord' departments such as the Treasury and the Prime Minister's Office, and by informal committees appointed by the prime minister (see Burch and Holiday, 'The Blair Government and the Core Executive' (2004) 39 Government & Opposition 1). However, its importance depends largely on factors such as the personality of the prime minister and the strength of the governing party in Parliament.

- Government powers are mainly conferred by statute on individual ministers, but the Crown also has certain inherent common law powers under the *royal prerogative* which can be exercised independently of Parliament (Section 14.6). These include important powers relating to foreign affairs, such as making treaties and deploying the armed forces. The Crown also has 'ordinary' powers in common with other persons, such as owning property and making contracts, but these cannot authorise violating the rights of anyone. These powers give the government considerable leverage, for example in matters such as land ownership, financial dealing and the arms, transport and medicines trades. Other public bodies can be created only by statute and have no powers other than those specifically given to them by statute (see *R v Somerset CC, ex p Fewings* [1995] 1 All ER 513).

- By convention, all powers of the Crown must be exercised either by the Queen on the advice of ministers, or by ministers directly. A few, largely ceremonial powers require the involvement of the Queen as head of state, but otherwise, any Crown power can be exercised by a minister.

- A minister can normally exercise any power through a civil servant (*Carltona Ltd v Commissioners of Works* [1943] 2 All ER 560, Section 15.8.5). The civil service is a body of appointed Crown servants with the dual responsibility of providing impartial advice to the government and carrying out the day-to-day management and operations of the executive. It is governed by a mixture of statute, convention and royal prerogative. The civil service is therefore permanent, professional, impartial and independent of party politics: a reservoir of specialist expertise and experience that survives the periodic changes of government characteristic of a democracy. Critics of this arrangement point to tensions in that, although civil servants must be loyal to the government of the day, there is a danger that the civil service generates its own political culture in favour of avoiding change. There is, however, a special category of politically appointed 'special advisers' who are not required to be impartial. There is tension between these and the regular civil service (Section 15.8).

▶ The principle of responsible or accountable government is fundamental to the constitution. Ministers are responsible to Parliament. This means, first, *collective responsibility* for government policy in the sense that a minister who disagrees with such policy must resign. There is also *individual responsibility*, meaning that a minister must appear before Parliament and explain the conduct of his or her department. A civil servant has no direct responsibility to Parliament but is responsible to the minister in charge of his or her department. The minister, in turn, is responsible to Parliament. Thus, there is a chain of responsibility. By convention, ministers must always be MPs and, through parliamentary rules, they largely control the procedure of the House. Therefore Parliament is vulnerable to domination by the executive except at times when the governing political group is divided or weak (as was the case with the coalition government of 2010–2015, a period which produced a number of independent votes in the Commons; and again in 2019 when the Conservative Party had no overall majority).

▶ There are no constitutional principles requiring any particular structure of government departments. In recent years, the executive has become fragmented with around 400 separate bodies (e.g. the Environment Agency) created for a variety of purposes including specialist expertise, independence from political pressure and cost saving. Many of these bodies are concerned with regulating private activities and have enforcement powers (Section 20.4). They lack legal coherence. They are not normally part of the Crown, although they are appointed and funded by ministers. They are often called 'non-departmental public bodies' or more popularly 'quangos' (quasi-autonomous non-governmental organisations, a term which sums up their muddled character: being neither part of the central executive, nor private bodies (Section 15.10)). They could be regarded as a distinctive branch of government which is not fully subject to democratic control and with its leaders dependent on ministerial patronage. This makes accountability vulnerable, since responsibility may be shared between different bodies with no one taking overall responsibility, what Rhodes has called a 'hollowing out of the state' (*Everyday Life in British Government* (Oxford University Press 2011) 2).

5.4 The judicial branch

This section outlines the main constitutional features of the judiciary. Matters particularly affecting judicial independence and the separation of powers are discussed in Chapter 7, namely accountability, the appointment process and dismissal of judges. Structure, qualifications for appointment and the question of diversity are discussed here.

All courts must be created by statute and their powers are determined by statute. The courts act in the name of the Queen, but an important aspect of the separation of powers is that the executive cannot interfere in legal proceedings (*Prohibitions Del Roy* (1607) 12 Co Rep 64).

The right to a fair trial before an independent court is a fundamental feature of common law and also of the ECHR. The concentration of power in the other two branches of government without any overriding safeguards for judicial independence makes the position of judges in the UK especially vulnerable. However, it is sometimes suggested that in extreme cases the judges can override Parliament (Section 8.5.6).

The courts uphold the rule of law by means of judicial review of government action and by virtue of the fact that government officials are not generally protected against liability in the courts. Under the HRA, the courts can scrutinise government decisions and Acts of Parliament for conformity with rights derived from the ECHR. However, the 1998 Act does not empower the courts to overturn an Act of Parliament.

The judiciary was previously headed by the Lord Chancellor, who is also a government minister. The Constitutional Reform Act 2005 created a clear separation of powers by transferring many of the Lord Chancellor's functions to the Lord Chief Justice and the Chief Justice of Northern Ireland who now head their respective judiciaries. The Lord Chancellor is also Secretary of State for Justice, and as such is responsible for the administration of the courts in England and Wales (Section 7.6.3.1). There is no longer a requirement for the Lord Chancellor to possess a legal qualification.

5.4.1 The Supreme Court

The highest appeal court, the Supreme Court, was created by the Constitutional Reform Act 2005. It comprises up to the equivalent of 12 full-time Justices (Crime and Courts Act 2013, Sched. 13). Previously, the highest appellate body was part of Parliament, the Appellate Committee of the House of Lords, and its members sat in the House of Lords in its other roles. By making the highest appellate body a separate institution in accordance with the separation of powers, it was hoped to reinforce public confidence in the judges, both internally and at the international level.

The Supreme Court was introduced following a Cabinet reshuffle intended to remove the traditionally minded Lord Chancellor, thus illustrating the pragmatic aspects of constitutional reform. However, contemporary developments have put the independence of the judiciary under pressure. The courts have become more 'political' in the sense that they decide cases involving disputes between citizen and government under the HRA and, more recently still, in relation to aspects of the UK's withdrawal from the European Union. They are also required to adjudicate between governments by virtue of the devolution of powers to Scotland, Wales and Northern Ireland, and under EU law. There were also worries that the previous arrangements violated Article 6 of the ECHR, the right to a fair trial before an independent court. Behind these particular concerns was a general agenda of 'modernising' the constitution.

There was no serious doubt that, at least since the 1930s, the Law Lords were in fact independent of political pressures. Indeed, many thought that their presence in Parliament served the interests of constitutional balance by providing a channel of mutual influence and understanding. Thus, the characteristic British way of constitutionalism through personal relationships among the rulers clashed with republican ideas of government by law (Section 2.5).

The Supreme Court has the same jurisdiction as the former Appellate Committee of the House of Lords. Thus, it hears appeals in both public law and private law from all the UK jurisdictions other than Scottish criminal cases (Section 16.3.3). The Supreme Court also decides cases concerning the powers of the devolved governments of Scotland, Wales and Northern Ireland, replacing the Privy Council in this respect.

Eligibility for membership of the Supreme Court has been widened from exclusive reliance on senior judges (Constitutional Reform Act 2005, s 25; Tribunals, Courts and Enforcement Act 2007, ss 50–52). A Justice must (i) have held high judicial office in the UK for at least two years (meaning High Court or above, or the equivalent in Scotland or Northern Ireland); or (ii) satisfy the 'judicial-appointments eligibility condition'; or (iii) have been a 'qualifying practitioner', that is, a practising barrister or solicitor in Scotland or Northern Ireland for at least 15 years.

The 'judicial-appointments eligibility condition' is intended to encourage diversity in judicial appointments. It makes people other than judges and advocates eligible for judicial appointment (Section 5.4.3). Thus, an experienced legal practitioner or an academic lawyer who has never held senior judicial office could be preferred to a long-serving judge. Lord Burrows, a leading law academic, is an example in the current Supreme Court. The Supreme Court judges between them must have knowledge or experience in the practice of the law of each part of the UK, thus acknowledging the differences between English law and that of the devolved regimes (Constitutional Reform Act 2005, s 27(8)). As was its predecessor, the Supreme Court is unbalanced in relation with the devolved legal systems in that there are only two Scottish members and one each from Northern Ireland and Wales (see McCluskey, *The Supreme Court in Scotland: Final Report; Fraser v HM Advocate* [2011] UKSC 24).

Although the Supreme Court was originally promoted as no more than a presentational change, with its constitutional role and powers those of the previous House of Lords, the evolution of the constitution around it, most obviously the enactment of the HRA and the devolution statutes, has given it a more explicit constitutional role. The common law of judicial review of administrative action also has a constitutional dimension.

There are 12 Justices. Unlike many overseas constitutional courts, the Supreme Court usually sits in panels of five rather than *en banc* (which would avoid any suspicion of packing the panel, but risks stalemate). There may be panels of seven or nine in important cases; exceptionally, in highly important constitutional cases, such as *R (Miller) v Secretary of State for Exiting the European Union* [2017] UKSC 5 and *R (Miller) v the Prime Minister* [2019] UKSC 41, eleven judges may sit. There is a filter in that permission to appeal from the court below, or from the Supreme Court itself, is required. In criminal cases, the Court of Appeal must certify that there is a point of law of general public importance (Criminal Appeals Act 1968, s 33(2)). In other cases, it is the practice of the Supreme Court to apply a similar test. The filtering decisions are taken by a panel of three Justices and detailed reasons are not given.

R (Nicklinson) v Ministry of Justice [2014] UKSC 38 illustrates differing views among the Supreme Court Justices as to the constitutional role of the court. A nine-member panel was divided as to whether the court had the constitutional authority to address the wide and controversial issues about legalising assisted suicide. Lord Neuberger, Lord Mance and Lord Wilson held that the court had such authority, but took the pragmatic view that, in the circumstances, the court should not intervene since the matter was currently being considered by Parliament.

However, Lord Sumption, Lord Clarke, Lord Reed and Lord Hughes considered that, under the UK Constitution, these matters were not for a court to decide at all. Lady Hale and Lord Kerr agreed with Lord Sumption that Parliament was the only forum in which a solution could be found, but were prepared positively to intervene to make a declaration of incompatibility under the HRA (Section 22.5.2), thereby endorsing the notion of a 'constitutional partnership' between the branches of government.

It has been suggested that the Supreme Court has the potential to evolve into a constitutional court which might eventually claim to override statutes (see Hale, 'A Supreme Court for the United Kingdom?' (2002) 22 LS 36; Masterman and Murkens (2013)). Note, however, that its predecessor also made radical decisions in the field of judicial review, such as *Anisminic v Foreign Compensation Commission* [1969] 2 AC 147, and some of its members were prepared to question parliamentary supremacy on constitutional grounds (see *Jackson v A-G* [2006] 1 AC 262).

Cornes (2013) argues that institutional change unleashes new dynamics and that the stand-alone court has become a more clearly articulated constitutional court than its predecessor. The court has developed various publicity devices, including press releases, broadcasts of parts of its proceedings and easily accessible online reports intended to raise awareness and understanding of its activities outside the legal profession. Supreme Court judges also make public speeches relating to their work, indeed perhaps being less inhibited in this respect than when the highest court was part of Parliament and there was a particular need to display judicial impartiality.

According to Cornes, there is a danger that, as a result of media simplifications and dramatisations, the constitution becomes unbalanced in public perception in favour of judicial power against the democratic process. Such concerns seem to be echoed by the current Government, which appointed an independent panel to consider the process of judicial review (the Independent Review of Administrative Law), with a view to ensuring a balance between the rights of citizens to challenge executive decisions and efficient and effective government, in July 2020 (Sections 1.9 and 17.1). The Supreme Court itself takes a more nuanced, realist approach, regarding itself as a lawmaker, but with distinct limitations based on the desirability of conforming to principle and not competing with the democratic process. However, Cornes is concerned that the media might politicise and personalise discussion of the Court, for example in relation to the careers, views and personalities of individual Justices. This prediction appears to have come to fruition (see, e.g. 'Ex-barmaid with a spider brooch who spun legal web that snared PM', *Daily Mail*, 25 September 2019).

5.4.2   Other courts

This discussion is concerned primarily with England and Wales, as Scotland and Northern Ireland have distinct court systems. The internal structure of the court system will not be discussed here but can be studied in works on the English legal system.

The courts have traditionally been divided into *superior courts* and *inferior courts*. Superior courts comprise the High Court, which deals with major civil cases, the Court of Appeal and the Supreme Court. The High Court has power to decide its own jurisdiction and so can never act beyond its powers. Challenging its decisions depends on a right of appeal provided by statute in relation to the particular matter at hand. High Court, Court of Appeal and Supreme Court judges are 'senior judges'. They have strong protection against dismissal and reduction in salary (Section 7.7.3.2). Various specialised bodies are also designated as superior courts, although the effect of this is unclear. A body designated as a superior court is not equivalent to the High Court (see *R (Cart) v Upper Tribunal* [2012] 1 AC 663), and the term 'superior court' has no clear legal consequences. Its main significance is probably in connection with the personal liability of the judge (Section 7.4). All other courts are *inferior courts*. Depending on the particular statute, inferior court judges have a lesser degree of security of tenure and a lower level of protection against personal liability.

In addition to the court system, numerous special tribunals composed of both lawyers and lay persons decide specialised matters allocated to them by particular statutes. They are essentially simplified versions of courts of law, and provide simpler, cheaper and more expert ways of deciding relatively small or specialised disputes than the ordinary courts. These are most commonly disputes between individuals and government bodies. Tribunals were once called 'administrative tribunals' and were often regarded as closely bound up with the executive. Recent reforms have tied them more closely to the judicial system (Section 20.1).

5.4.3   Judicial diversity

Judicial appointments are made on the recommendation of the Judicial Appointments Commission or, in the case of the Supreme Court, a special Selection Commission (Section 7.7.3.1). Judicial appointments must be made 'on merit' (Constitutional Reform Act 2005, s 27(5)), or 'solely on merit' subject to the appointee being of 'good character' (other appointments (s 63)). (Good character does not therefore seem to be essential for the Supreme Court!)

Other than lay magistrates and tribunal members, judges are normally appointed from senior practising barristers. Before the Tribunals, Courts and Enforcement Act 2007, judicial appointments were restricted to barristers and solicitors having held rights of advocacy in the High Court for a prescribed period – at least seven, and often ten, years. This contrasts with the position in other European countries, where there is a separate judicial profession. The UK system has the advantage of drawing on talented people who are familiar with the workings of the court process. The disadvantage is that this might reinforce the perception of the legal system as a closed elite (the stereotype of white, elderly, privately educated males), which arguably hampers good judging and public confidence (see Etherton, 'Liberty, the Archetype and Diversity: A Philosophy of Judging' [2010] PL 727; Kirby in Lee (ed) (2011)). The Judicial Appointments Commission must have regard to the need to encourage diversity in all its functions (Constitutional Reform Act 2005, s 64), and the Crime and Courts Act 2013, Sched. 13, places a duty upon the Lord Chancellor and the Lord Chief Justice to take such steps as are considered appropriate for the purpose of encouraging judicial diversity, as well as permitting the preference of a minority candidate in the unlikely event of the merits of two candidates being equal. The Act also permits part-time appointments to the High Court, the Court of Appeal and the Supreme Court.

The Tribunals, Courts and Enforcement Act 2007 makes appointments available to professionals beyond those who practise in the senior courts. It introduces the general concept of the 'judicial-appointments eligibility condition' (ss 50–52): in the case of the Supreme Court, the senior courts and

Circuit Judges, this means solicitors and barristers (after pupillage) who have been qualified for five or seven years, depending on the post, and 15 years for the Supreme Court. The qualifying period must be one within which the candidate 'gains experience in law'. This is vague, stating that the candidate must be engaged in 'law related activities'. These are not confined to judicial activities but 'include' legal practice, consultancy, drafting legal documents, teaching or research, and can be full-time or part-time, paid or unpaid anywhere (s 52).

Certain junior judicial appointments are open to persons other than barristers and solicitors with specified 'other qualifications' and with the same requirement of gaining experience in law. The 'other qualifications' include only qualifications specified by the Lord Chancellor granted by the Institute of Legal Executives or by other bodies authorised to confer rights of audience or conduct litigation (patent and trademark agents and law costs draftsmen) (s 51(2)). Neither the broader base of eligibility nor the work of the Judicial Diversity Committee of the Judges' Council, established in 2013, has yet resulted in a significantly more diverse judiciary. As of 1 April 2019, 32 per cent of judges in courts, and 46 per cent in tribunals were women; 7 per cent and 11 per cent respectively were from a Black, Asian and minority ethnic (BAME) background (although some judges do not declare their ethnicity). Three out of 12 Supreme Court judges and nine of 39 Appeal Court judges were women, as were 26 of 97 High Court judges; the BAME figures for the latter two courts were just two and three, respectively, with no one from this background sitting on the Supreme Court.

5.5 Local government in England

Local authorities exercise a range of functions within geographical areas based on urban conurbations (unitary authorities), traditional counties, and areas within those counties, namely districts and parishes (communities in Wales). (Parishes have only limited functions relating primarily to local amenities, their main role being consultative in relation to local land use planning matters.) There are special provisions for London (Greater London Authority Act 1999), and a recent structure, the combined authority, which is discussed further below.

Local authorities take the form of an elected council, which is a corporate body with both legislative and executive powers. They have tax-raising powers and might therefore be considered to have some constitutional significance; and, indeed, they had considerable power during the Victorian era, when central government was much weaker than is the case today. However, local authorities have little financial independence, more than two-thirds of their resources being provided by central government in the form of grants or loans. Moreover, their tax-raising powers are regulated by central government. Local authorities are therefore accountable both to their electorate and to the central executive, thus distorting and confusing their accountability.

From both liberal and republican perspectives, local government could be regarded as providing a check and balance on central government in the sense of an alternative source of democratic power. Thus, Mill claimed that it is desirable in the interests of democracy and individual self-fulfilment for people to have closer contact with governmental bodies than is possible at central government level. In particular, local democracy generates different political perspectives and healthy disagreement and debate. On the other hand, particularly where personal welfare services, health and education are concerned, it may be perceived as unfair for different levels of service to be provided in different, sometimes neighbouring, areas (see *R v Gloucestershire CC, ex p Barry* [1997] 2 All ER 1 for judicial disagreement).

Local authorities are entirely creatures of statute (a series of constantly changing Local Government Acts based on the Local Government Act 1972) and, as such, are subject to comprehensive central government control. Local authority geographical boundaries are decided by the Secretary of State on the advice of a Boundary Committee (Local Government and Public Involvement in Health Act 2007). Although changes to local authority areas are often matters of considerable public concern, there is no provision for a public hearing, although representations by interested parties must be taken into account (s 9(3)).

Local authorities have executive powers in relation, most importantly, to land use planning, public health, local amenities, waste collection, the environment and trade. They have limited lawmaking powers to make by-laws for prescribed purposes, such as keeping order in public places and traffic control. Since the 1980s, local powers relating to education and housing have been drastically reduced in favour of central government and private bodies.

Their main functions are to deliver services designated by central government. This is usually subject to central government power to intervene, by means of devices such as consents, inspections, 'default powers' to take over a function, and appeals. Central control is often exercised in characteristic British manner not by using formal legal powers (although these exist in abundance), but through advisory circulars, letters and personal contacts. Thus, there may be the appearance of local independence, but without the substance.

Local government operates through structures designated by statute. The traditional model was that of a council divided into committees. However, the Local Government Act 2000 required councils to review their arrangements. Most authorities use a structure based on a council leader and 'executive' (Cabinet) responsible to the council. Sixteen councils (including London, which has special arrangements (Section 16.6)) have an elected mayor and executive structure more akin to a presidential system. This can be imposed following a referendum, which can be triggered by a public petition (Local Government Act 2000), by a two-thirds vote of the council (Local Government and Public Involvement in Health Act 2007) or by a referendum triggered by the central government (Localism Act 2011). Only Bristol has introduced a mayor by the last route. Powers can be exercised flexibly (most powers can be delegated to officers, members of an executive or other local authorities (Local Government Act 1972, s 101; Local Government Act 2000, s 13(2)).

The Localism Act 2011 introduces limited public involvement. There is a right to a referendum on any local issue, triggered by a petition of at least 5 per cent of the local electorate. Proposals to increase council tax by at least 2 per cent also require a referendum. The referendum is not binding. Subject to independent scrutiny, a local authority is required to make an order giving planning permission to land use development proposed by a parish council, or in certain cases a 'neighbourhood forum' comprising local residents and supported by a referendum of local electors. Land listed by the local authority as an 'asset of community value' nominated by a community organisation is protected against disposal. A local authority must also consider giving effect to a matter embodied in an 'expression of interest' put to it by a voluntary or community body or a charity or at least two local authority employees or other persons specified by the Secretary of State.

For many years, there have been complaints that local authorities have insufficient freedom to respond to local concerns. The Localism Act 2011 responds to this to a limited extent by conferring a general power on a local authority to do anything that an individual can do. Of course, this cannot involve violating the legal rights of another and is subject to judicial review on the normal grounds of fairness and rationality (*Shrewsbury and Atcham Borough Council v Secretary of State* [2008] 3 All ER 548, at [48]). The power is also subject to specific limitations (ss 2–4). Reflecting a constitutional fundamental, it cannot be used to make a charge for providing a service that it is required to provide, or without the agreement of the person concerned. Moreover, this general power cannot be used to avoid restrictions on other statutory powers. It cannot be used to alter constitutional or governance arrangements or 'contracting-out' arrangements. It cannot be used to make a profit but can be used for commercial purposes only if it applies also to non-commercial purposes.

The Cities and Local Government Devolution Act 2016 allows for devolution of powers from central government. These include powers over transport, housing, planning, policing and health and social care. The Act is intended to apply primarily to the largest city regions in England, but devolution is in principle open to other geographical areas should they wish. The Act contains generic provisions: individual 'deals' are struck between central government and local authorities, and will take effect through secondary legislation. The most high-profile of such arrangements is that struck with Manchester between November 2014 and July 2015, but a number of other areas have taken similar steps.

The Act provides for directly elected ('metro') mayors in combined authorities, the first elections being held in 2017. These authorities, which are established under the Local Democracy, Economic Development and Construction Act 2009, are created where they are considered likely to improve economic development, regeneration and transport. Leaving aside London, which has a different set of powers and budgets (see Greater London Authority Act 1999), there are currently ten such authorities in England, while Cornwall is a devolved unitary authority.

It is, as yet, too soon to determine how significant these developments will prove to be. They possess at least the potential to reverse some of the long-term drift of power in England away from the localities to the centre, which characterised much of the twentieth century. However, it is unclear how far they will progress in practice. The decision to withdraw from the EU, as well as the COVID-19 pandemic of 2020 means that, in the short to medium term, the priorities of central government have been elsewhere. On the other hand, the withdrawal of EU funding from certain of the activities carried out within local government, the focus on certain localities in the response to COVID-19 (e.g. 'local lockdowns'), coupled with pressures emanating in particular from governments in the devolved nations of the UK for some form of reconfiguration of the constitution, look likely to keep the issue of geographical diffusion of power high on the political agenda in the future.

5.6   The police and the prosecution system in England and Wales

The police are connected with the judicial system, so that, in accordance with the separation of powers, they should be independent of the executive. Moreover, from the origins of the police force (in London, 1829), there has been a concern that policing should be on a local basis with democratic accountability in order to avoid the risk of a repressive police state under government control. An accommodation must be struck between these concerns. This issue underlies the constitutional position of the police.

Although they are officers of the Crown, in the sense that their common law powers derive from the Crown's duty to keep the peace, the police are not Crown servants. Control over the police has been split three ways, a complex and tension-ridden arrangement that can be justified as a liberal mechanism for controlling power.

Firstly, there is the traditional status at common law of the 'constable' as an independent officer of the Crown with inherent powers of arrest, search and entry to premises, some common law and others statutory, and owing duties to the law itself to keep the peace (see Police Act 1996, s 10; *R v Metropolitan Police Comr, ex p Blackburn* [1968] 2 QB 118, at 136). All police officers and also prison officers are constables. Each police force is under the direction of its Chief Constable (in London, the Metropolitan Police Commissioner) with regard to operational matters (Police Reform and Social Responsibility Act 2011, ss 2, 4). Traditionally, Chief Constables have been independent in relation to operational matters.

Secondly, there is a tradition that the organisation of the police should be locally based and subject to democratic control so as to avoid the concentration of power associated with a 'police state'. Under the Police Act 1996, local police forces are organised on the basis of counties and amalgamations of county units. There are special arrangements in London comprising the Metropolitan Police and the City of London Police Force (Greater London Authority Act 1999). Funding is provided by local authorities by means of a share of local taxation and central grants.

Local police forces were traditionally supervised by local police authorities. These comprised a mixture of local councillors, magistrates and persons appointed by the Home Secretary, with elected members a bare majority. The presence of magistrates violated the separation of powers, reinforcing a common perception that magistrates have a privileged relationship with the police. Subject to the Secretary of State, the police authority appointed and removed the Chief Constable and certain other senior officers.

The threefold division of responsibility means that accountability over the police is confused and weak. The Police Reform and Social Responsibility Act 2011 attempts to focus police accountability.

The Act creates an elected Police and Crime Commissioner for each force to be elected every four years (s 50). The first elections were held in 2012. They attracted little public interest. The Commissioner's functions include funding, an obligation to issue a 'Police and Crime Plan' and requirements of public consultation and publishing information about policies. In London, the Mayor's Office for Policing and Crime has the equivalent functions.

The relationship between the Commissioner and the traditionally independent Chief Constable is murky. The Commissioner appoints and can suspend or remove the Chief Constable, and is responsible for securing the maintenance of the police force in the area, thus setting its budget and securing that it is efficient and effective (s 1(6)). The Commissioner must 'hold the Chief Constable to account' (s 1(8)), but has no direct powers to interfere with operational matters. The Chief Constable must have regard to the Police and Crime Plan for the area (s 8(2)). This is subject to guidance by the Secretary of State (s 8(5)).

There is a debate as to whether this level of democracy is desirable, since it might compromise the independence of the police. On the other hand, an elected Commissioner is a democratic counterforce against political interference by central government, which might be a greater threat to police independence. The Cities and Local Government Devolution Act 2016 allows for directly elected mayors for combined authorities to undertake the functions of the Commissioner for that area, if desired.

Thirdly, central government has wide powers over police forces conferred by statute, usually upon the Home Secretary (Police Act 1996, Part II; Police Reform Act 2002). The Home Secretary can provide funding, set objectives and make regulations concerning discipline and resources, including requiring the use of specified equipment. The Home Secretary can also require the merger of local forces and issue a national policing plan and 'policing protocol' concerning how police functions should be exercised (see Police Reform and Social Responsibility Act 2011, ss 77–78). As usual, the Home Office exercises informal influence through non-statutory 'advice', 'guidance' and personal networks.

Technical support for policing may be too expensive to provide locally, and modern crime, especially terrorism and cybercrime, is no respecter of local boundaries. To this end, the Crime and Courts Act 2013 created the National Crime Agency as an 'overlord' body which coordinates crime fighting by other agencies, carries out intelligence relating to all crime and investigates serious crime and organised crime. It is directly accountable to the Home Secretary. The Agency can request and, as a last resort, demand the help of other forces (s 5). Originally, the police themselves conducted most prosecutions. However, the Prosecution of Offences Act 1985 created a separate Crown Prosecution Service (CPS), which is under the control of the Director of Public Prosecutions (DPP). Crown prosecutors have powers to prosecute and conduct cases subject to discretion given by the DPP under the Act. The DPP is appointed by the Attorney General, who is answerable in Parliament for the CPS. In some cases, the consent of the Attorney General is required for a prosecution, particularly where political or large commercial interests are involved. The Attorney General has conflicting roles. S/he is the government's chief legal adviser and a member of the government itself, appointed and dismissed by the prime minister (Section 15.6.2). This blurring of roles is characteristic of the culture of UK government and sometimes attracts public suspicions of lack of independence. The CPS has power to take over most criminal prosecutions (s 3) or to order any proceedings to be discontinued (s 23). Except where an offence can only be prosecuted by a person named in the relevant statute (e.g. the Attorney General, or a specified public authority), any individual may bring a private prosecution, but the CPS can take over such a prosecution (s 6(2)). The Independent Office for Police Conduct has an independent role in investigating complaints against the police (Policing and Crime Act 2017).

5.7   The Privy Council

The Privy Council exercises both legislative and judicial powers. It is the descendant of the medieval 'inner council' (*curia regis*) of trusted advisers to the king. Over the centuries, most functions of the Privy Council were transferred either to Parliament or to ministers. Members are appointed by the Queen on the advice of the prime minister, and any British citizen is eligible. There are currently over

500 Privy Counsellors, including Cabinet ministers, senior judges, and miscellaneous worthies who have gained the approval of the prime minister. Cabinet ministers and leading opposition politicians are invariably appointed Privy Counsellors. One reason for such appointments is that Privy Counsellors swear an oath of secrecy, thus assisting government business to be kept out of the public domain.

Apart from its judicial functions (below), the role of the Privy Council is largely formal. Its approval is needed for certain important exercises of the royal prerogative, known as Prerogative Orders in Council, including, for example, laws for overseas territories, and also for Statutory Orders in Council, where Parliament gives power to the executive to make laws in this form. Approval is usually given by a small deputation of counsellors attending the Queen. The Privy Council also confers state recognition and legal personality by granting charters to bodies such as universities and professional, scientific and cultural organisations. It can exercise some degree of supervision over such bodies.

The Judicial Committee of the Privy Council is the final court of appeal for those few former British territories that choose to retain its services, in which capacity it is familiar with broad constitutional reasoning. Its role is to give advice on issues of law referred to it following a petition to the Queen. It originally comprised a mixture of politicians and judges, but the Judicial Committee Act 1833 limited membership to senior judges, thus acknowledging the separation of powers. Today, it comprises Supreme Court Justices together with judges of the country under whose laws the appeal is heard.

The Judicial Committee will usually consider an issue only when it has first been considered by the relevant local courts (see *Cayman Islands Chief Justice v Cayman Islands Governor* [2014] AC 198). It also has jurisdiction in respect of ecclesiastical courts, peerage claims, election petitions and appeals from the Channel Islands and the Isle of Man. Its former appeals jurisdiction in relation to the medical profession is now exercised by the Administrative Court and its jurisdiction in devolution appeals by the Supreme Court. Not being strictly a court, the Judicial Committee can give advisory opinions to the government (Judicial Committee Act 1833, s 4), although this is rare.

5.8   The Church of England

The relationship between church and state is ambivalent and can be explained only as a consequence of history. On the one hand, neither Christianity nor any other religion is part of the law as such (*Bowman v Secular Society* [1917] AC 406). On the other hand, we do not have a formal separation between church and state as exists in France or the US. As a result of events in the reign of Henry VIII (Section 4.4), the Church of England is the Established Church in England, and the Presbyterian Church of Scotland the Established Church in Scotland. The Anglican Church in Wales is not established (Welsh Church Act 1914, a measure passed without the consent of the House of Lords).

There are several particular connections between the Church of England and the state. These are sometimes justified even by supporters of other religions, on the basis that the church provides religious services open to all without discrimination and that it helps the state to curb the extremes of religious fanaticism.

- ▶ The monarch, as nominal head of the Church of England, must on succession be or become a member of the church (Act of Settlement 1700, s 3) and must swear an oath to support the Established Churches of England and Scotland (Act of Union with Scotland 1707).
- ▶ Church laws (measures) are legally binding and must be approved by Parliament (Church of England Assembly (Powers) Act 1919).
- ▶ There are special ecclesiastical courts, subject to control by the ordinary courts if they exceed their powers or act unfairly.
- ▶ The Queen, on the advice of the prime minister (which, as usual, is binding on her by convention), appoints bishops (see Ecclesiastical Jurisdiction Measure 1963).
- ▶ The 26 most senior bishops are members of the House of Lords until retirement.
- ▶ Finally, everyone has certain rights in connection with baptisms, weddings and funerals.

A church body is not a public authority as such, at least for human rights purposes (see *Aston Cantlow and Wilmcote with Billesley PCC v Wallbank* [2003] 3 All ER 1213; Section 22.7). However, particular functions available to the public, such as weddings and funerals, might be public functions and as such potentially subject to control by the courts.

5.9   Government standards of behaviour

The extra-legal nature of much of the UK Constitution makes arrangements heavily dependent on trusting those in power. This opens the way to oligarchy, where government is dominated by an elite, a self-selected privileged group which moves in interlocking family, social and professional circles. These groups are linked by a similar mindset and common values: what Lewis has called 'networks of conviviality which obscure the workings of the British state' (in McAuslan and McEldowney (eds), *Law, Legitimacy and the Constitution* (Sweet and Maxwell 1985) 125). Oligarchy arises in all forms of human organisation since most people are passive followers, but the UK Constitution is particularly vulnerable because, since the development of the parliamentary system in the eighteenth century, political power has become increasingly concentrated in the central executive.

Influential groups which can obtain access to the executive are therefore in a position to manipulate power. The nature of these elite groups changes over time (albeit that a common ingredient tends to be money). Indeed, it is often suggested that the willingness of the elite to open its doors to new members has contributed to the relative stability of the constitution. For example, during the postwar period until about the 1980s, the elite was dominated by traditional institutions, the learned professions, the older universities and the leading public schools (see Annan, *Our Age: A Portrait of a Generation* (Weidenfeld, 1990)). Latterly, although private education remains a prominent factor, the oligarchy has been dominated by business interests.

Oligarchy confronts the most fundamental ideals of republicanism: namely, equality of citizenship (Section 2.5). However, a liberal might find oligarchy less objectionable, provided that those in power do not curtail basic freedoms. There is a risk of corruption and nepotism, where public positions at a high level are dominated by people drawn from a restricted network of associates benefiting from the status quo and protective of each other.

Political thinkers over the centuries have worried about the corruptibility of those in power and it is widely acknowledged that people with power can easily abuse it, albeit sometimes accidentally or for good motives:

> Now it is a universally observed fact, that the two evil dispositions in question, the disposition to prefer a man's selfish interests to those he shares with other people, and his immediate and direct interests to those which are indirect and remote, are characterised most especially called forth and fostered by the possession of power … . [T]his is the meaning of the universal tradition, grounded on universal experience, of men's being corrupted by power. (Mill, *Considerations on Representative Government* (1861) ch VI)

John Adams, one of the founders of the US Constitution, asserted that:

> [D]espotism, or unlimited sovereignty or absolute power, is the same in a majority of a popular assembly, an aristocratic council, an oligarchical junta, and a single emperor. (Letter to Thomas Jefferson (13 November 1815))

Standard practices of oligarchy include patronage in jobs, positions and honours, payments for access to ministers and politicians, donations to political parties, hospitality and covering up wrongdoing and incompetence. The prevailing political fashion for 'contracting-out' public services to private organisations provides a fertile field for these practices. Senior government advisers and MPs frequently have active connections with lobbying groups, consultants and business interests, and, through the 'revolving door', senior officials and politicians exchange jobs and favours with private organisations with which they dealt while in office (but see Section 15.8.4).

Many public appointments and positions of privilege, most notably membership of the House of Lords and of 'quangos', and also positions as advisers or consultants, are made by the prime minister or other senior ministers. There is no legal mechanism to prevent appointments being made from insider networks or to prevent the same persons being 'recycled' through several positions.

Perhaps the most important contribution to elitism in government is the effective exclusion of those without plenty of money from the governmental process. The boards of public bodies and government are replete with representatives from finance, industry and the professions, but have comparatively few members of the general public or representatives of relevant interests such as patients, public interest groups, environmental campaigners or charities.

Oligarchical practices and mindsets may be inherent in all government. Moreover, in a democracy, it would be difficult to justify legal provisions restricting access to government and it is difficult (though not impossible) to impose restrictive requirements such as quotas for public appointments. A preferable method of reducing corruption and promoting accountability is to require openness and disclosure (transparency).

Many of the existing mechanisms for doing so are extra-legal. The prevalence of secretive personal networks and non-legal controls is usually defended by members of those networks along the lines that government can be more efficiently and smoothly carried out by this means and that officials are more likely to cooperate with voluntary measures. Even if this is true, it begs the question of whether it is worth the loss of public confidence involved.

There are some legal controls. Public officials are subject to the ordinary criminal law, including the Bribery Act 2010. There is a common law offence of misconduct in public office, comprising conduct which is likely to breach public trust that the duties of the office are being properly performed (see *R v Cosford* [2013] 3 All ER 649). In September 2019, the Greater London Authority referred to the Independent Office for Police Conduct the question of whether the prime minister, Boris Johnson, should be subject to an inquiry for such misconduct over allegations relating to his links with a businesswoman while he was London mayor; earlier in the year, an attempted private prosecution of Johnson for statements made during the EU referendum campaign was quashed by the High Court (*Johnson v Westminster Magistrates Court* [2019] EWHC 1709 (Admin)). There are also statutory offences of corruption (Public Bodies (Corrupt Practices) Act 1889; Prevention of Corruption Act 1916; Honours (Prevention of Corruption) Act 1925). The last was enacted in response to the sale of peerages on behalf of the then prime minister, Lloyd George.

Misconduct by MPs, including improper lobbying practices, is regulated by internal parliamentary rules enforced by Parliament itself, although MPs' pay and expenses are regulated by an independent body (Section 11.7). The House of Lords *Code of Conduct* does not prevent peers from lobbying ministers, but MPs have to declare lobbying connections as an interest in the register of MPs. There are disclosure requirements in relation to election campaigns and payments to political parties (Sections 12.6.1 and 12.6.2).

The Transparency of Lobbying, Non-Party Campaigning and Trade Union Administration Act 2014 responds to this by requiring some lobbyists to be registered with the Electoral Commission. This is a very limited provision. The Act applies only to substantial (VAT-registered) firms of commercial lobbyists who specialise in lobbying ministers and permanent secretaries. Thus, it excludes in-house lobbyists for business interests, individual lobbyists, voluntary bodies and lobbyists of MPs and peers (unless they are ministers). The Act says nothing about disclosure of lobbying by friends, family and personal associates of politicians. The Act falls to be interpreted by the courts in the context of Article 9 of the Bill of Rights, which excludes MPs from liability in relation to 'proceedings in Parliament'. A court would have to decide the extent of this protection and whether the Act's language overrides Article 9 (Section 11.6). The Act creates civil penalties imposed by the Electoral Commission on lobbyists for failing to register properly but does not otherwise restrict their activities.

Other disclosure requirements are non-statutory. The *Ministerial Code* (last updated August 2019) requires ministers, on appointment, to provide a full written list of all private interests which might be thought to give rise to a conflict with their public duties, and there are restrictions on lobbying government within two years of leaving public office. Official meetings with lobbyists and official hospitality with outside bodies are recorded. Some senior appointments involve the candidate appearing before a parliamentary committee, but this has no power to veto the appointment.

There is provision, again largely extra-legal, for general monitoring of official behaviour. The *Committee on Standards in Public Life* covers the whole field of government. It was appointed in 1994 by the prime minister as a permanent advisory committee. Its terms of reference include the UK Parliament, UK members of the European Parliament (prior to Brexit), central and local government and other publicly funded bodies. The Committee reports to the prime minister so that there is no independent mechanism, but its reports are published. It has become highly influential. Its recommendations are widely followed and sometimes incorporated into law. However, the Committee does not investigate individual complaints. In its first report (Cm 2850, 1995), under the chairmanship of Lord Nolan, the Committee promulgated seven 'Principles of Public Life' representing the core values of public service. They are 'selflessness, integrity, objectivity, accountability, openness, honesty and leadership'. They are supported by what Nolan called 'common threads', these being mechanisms used to embed the principles into governmental institutions. These are codes of conduct, independent scrutiny, and guidance and education.

The Nolan principles are enshrined in all governmental codes of conduct. For example, there is a *Ministerial Code*, a *Civil Service Code* and codes of conduct for MPs and the House of Lords. The codes are not usually enforceable by law and there is not always independent scrutiny. For example, the *Ministerial Code* is enforced by the prime minister and the House of Lords Code by the House itself. The Code of Conduct for MPs is policed by the Parliamentary Standards Commissioner who reports to the Standards Committee of the Commons (Section 11.7). The *Civil Service Code*, *Special Adviser's Code* and *Diplomatic Service Code* now have statutory backing but no specific enforcement mechanisms (Constitutional Reform and Governance Act 2010). The Localism Act 2011, s 27(2) requires local authorities to adopt codes of conduct.

The Nolan principles regarding public appointments are particularly important. It is regarded as improper for politicians to interfere with senior public appointments. The formula of 'appointed on merit by fair and open competition' has become standard usage. The Committee on Standards in Public Life has promulgated general principles of appointment according to open and published criteria that public bodies should follow, accompanied by independent representation on appointment bodies. Some bodies, but not those close to ministers, are policed by a non-statutory Commissioner for Public Appointments (Section 15.10).

5.10 Constitutional reform

During the last two decades, there have been significant constitutional changes. These have been introduced by successive governments in an uncoordinated way (Section 4.9). There has been no systematic attempt at constitutional reform. The constitution has, however, moved in the direction of increasing the use of formal rules. This might be regarded as evidence of a breakdown of confidence in the unwritten constitution. However, these rules are not confined to legal rules but include 'codes', 'concordats' and the like which lack clear methods of enforcement and have been made in a haphazard way.

There are no special provisions for constitutional reform, such as special procedures in the legislature, referendums or a constitutional convention comprising representatives from across the community, such as exists in Ireland. In *R (Southall) v Foreign Secretary* [2003] EWCA Civ 1002, it was said that there is no principle that fundamental constitutional change requires the approval of the electorate. This makes constitutional reform a matter of the politics of the government of the day and so vulnerable to party political bargaining. There are, however, a Public Administration and Constitutional Affairs Committee of the House of Commons and a House of Lords Constitution Committee, both of which publish valuable reports.

There are miscellaneous provisions for referendums on particular issues. These include:

- certain EU matters (Section 8.5.3). Additionally, the European Union Referendum Act 2015 made provision for the referendum of June 2016 which resulted in a vote to leave the EU;
- local government structures (Section 5.5);
- devolution (Section 16.1). A referendum in September 2014 on whether Scotland should become an independent state was defeated: the present First Minister is pushing for a second vote;
- a referendum was held on the voting system in 2011. The proposal to move to a form of proportional representation was defeated (Section 12.5.7).

Some constitutional changes have been brought about by political crises and have been preceded by a general election (e.g. the reduction of the powers of the House of Lords by the Parliament Act 1911).

Reforms, and proposals for reform, may also be driven by the desire of a new government which wishes to appear radical, but which subsequently loses momentum (e.g. the limited reforms to the royal prerogative made when Gordon Brown became prime minister in 2007 (Section 14.6.6)), or in order to minimise perceived limitations to its policy choices (as in the case of the Conservative Government elected in December 2019). The part-reform of the House of Lords in 1999 which comprised the removal of most hereditary peers has never been completed (Section 12.3). The major reforms to the judiciary in the Constitutional Reform Act 2005 may have been precipitated by infighting within government (Section 5.4).

There is a school of thought that rejects radical constitutional reform. This attitude has influenced, in particular, the many failed attempts to reform the House of Lords (Section 12.3). In *Hirst v UK (No 2)* (2006) 42 EHRR 849, the European Court of Human Rights rejected the UK's claim to deny the vote to prisoners partly on the ground, perhaps unfairly, that such decisions should be made by reasoned debate rather than unthinking tradition (Section 12.5.5).

One result of this erratic approach to reform is that obsolete principles or institutions which do not create short-term problems may remain unchanged (captured in the phrase, 'if it ain't broke, don't fix it'). For example, the connection between the Church of England, the monarchy and anti-Catholicism is still built into our constitution (Section 14.2), as is a limited hereditary aristocratic membership of the House of Lords, the survival of archaic institutions such as the Privy Council (Section 5.7) and archaic procedures in Parliament (e.g. Section 11.6.1).

Summary

- This chapter has identified the main features of the mix of law, conventions and political practice that form the constitution and points out important sources of conflict that will be followed up in more detail in later chapters.

- The Crown, which in law is the executive branch of government, must be distinguished from the Queen personally as head of state. By convention and law, the Crown as executive acts through ministers.

- The Queen in Parliament is legally the supreme lawmaker, but by convention, the Queen must assent to all bills presented by Parliament.

- Parliament comprises an unelected upper House with limited powers (House of Lords) and an elected lower House (House of Commons). The Queen must appoint the person best able to command the confidence of the House of Commons (usually the leader of the majority party) as prime minister and must accept the prime minister's advice in appointing all other ministers and also senior judges and other public functionaries.

- There are conventions to safeguard democracy against both legislature and executive. The executive must have the support of Parliament. By convention, Parliament must meet annually. By law, Parliament cannot last for more than five years, and before then Parliament can remove the executive by a vote of confidence. Parliament is automatically dissolved at the end of five years or, within that, by a resolution of two-thirds of the House of Commons or a statute providing for an early general election. The dissolution of Parliament triggers the summoning of a new Parliament, preceded by a general election.

Summary cont'd

▶ The executive formally comprises ministers of the Crown. Statutory powers are normally given to individual ministers and the central government is therefore fragmented.

▶ By convention, the executive is accountable to Parliament. In practice, however, the influence of political parties means that Parliament tends to be subservient to the executive. However, recent reforms in parliamentary procedure have strengthened the House of Commons.

▶ The Cabinet as the central policymaking body may be in decline with the rise of informal networks and powerful overlord departments, but much depends upon the strength of government in the Commons and the personality of the prime minister.

▶ Permanent civil servants are of two kinds. The senior civil service is responsible for advising ministers, developing policy and making rules and decisions. Other civil servants, usually organised as separately structured executive agencies, are responsible for delivering policies at an operational level. Civil servants are shielded from public responsibility for their actions by the doctrine of ministerial responsibility.

▶ Special advisers are a distinct group of civil servants. They are political appointees of ministers and their jobs terminate when their minister leaves office. They are not subject to the duty of a civil servant to be impartial. There are tensions between special advisers and regular civil servants who may regard themselves as being sidelined. However, special advisers cannot exercise any legal powers.

▶ According to the doctrine of ministerial responsibility, ministers are responsible to Parliament for the conduct of their departments and for agencies sponsored by their departments. The civil service is responsible to ministers but not directly to Parliament. Ministerial responsibility has become weaker in recent decades and its scope and effect are unclear.

▶ In recent years, executive powers have been distributed across a wide variety of public and private bodies outside the central executive, known as 'quangos', again obscuring ministerial responsibility.

▶ The judiciary is usually regarded as subordinate to Parliament. There can be a tension between the judiciary and the executive arising out of the courts' powers of judicial review. It has sometimes been suggested that the courts might override Parliament.

▶ The independence of the judiciary is vulnerable to the combined executive and legislature but has been enhanced following the Constitutional Reform Act 2005. Most notably, the creation of the Supreme Court, even though it formally has no new powers, has separated the judicial system from Parliament. There have been recent attempts to encourage diversity in judicial appointments but these have yet to yield significant change.

▶ The police are regulated by an unstable combination of an elected Commissioner, local and central government.

▶ The Church of England has particular constitutional links with the state.

▶ Weaknesses in the traditional methods of accountability have led to attempts to formulate standards of ethical conduct for persons holding public office. These do not generally have legal status and are usually enforced within government itself.

Exercises

5.1 Is it possible to identify the three most fundamental principles of the constitution? If so, what are they?

5.2 What mechanisms enable the executive to dominate Parliament? Are there any counter-mechanisms?

5.3 Is the Supreme Court a 'constitutional court'? Should it be?

5.4 How effective are measures to encourage judicial diversity? Is such diversity an important goal?

5.5 Jade, the Chief Constable of Barsetshire, instructs her force to give priority to protecting vulnerable persons against street crime and to ignore drug trafficking. Jacob, the local Police and Crime Commissioner, informs Jade that these policies are contrary both to the local Police and Crime Plan which gives priority to protecting 'persons of high net worth' and to an objective set by the Home Secretary of combating drug trafficking. Jade continues the same policies. Advise her. Would your advice be affected if Jade was informed that, when he was 17 years old, Jacob had been fined for a driving offence?

5.6 Assess the arguments for and against the Church of England having special constitutional status.

5.7 To what extent is the UK Constitution a liberal constitution or a republican constitution?

Further reading

Bell, 'Constitutional Transitions: The Peculiarities of the British Constitution and the Politics of Comparison' [2014] PL 446

Bogdanor, *The New British Constitution* (Hart Publishing 2009) chs 1, 2, 8, 10

Committee on Standards in Public Life, *Independent Reports,* http://www.public-standards.gov.uk

Cornes, 'Gains (and Dangers of Losses) in Transition – The Leadership Functions in the United Kingdom's Supreme Court: Parameters and Prospects' [2011] PL 509

Feldman, 'None, One or Several? Perspectives on the UK's Constitution(s)' (2005) 64 CLJ 329

Gay, 'The Regulation of Lobbyists' in Horne and Le Sueur (eds), *Parliament: Legislation and Accountability* (Hart Publishing 2016)

Gee, Hazell, Malleson and O'Brien, *The Politics of Judicial Independence in the UK's Changing Constitution* (Cambridge University Press 2015)

Hanretty, *A Court of Specialists: Judicial Behavior in the UK Supreme Court* (Oxford University Press 2020), ch 1

Hine and Peele, *The Regulation of Standards in British Public Life: Doing the Right Thing?* (Manchester University Press 2016)

Lee (ed), *From House of Lords to Supreme Court: Judges, Jurists and the Process of Judging* (Hart Publishing 2011)

Malleson, 'The Evolving Role of the UK Supreme Court' [2011] PL 754

Masterman and Murkens, 'Skirting Supremacy and Subordination: The Constitutional Authority of the United Kingdom Supreme Court' [2013] PL 800

Oliva, 'Church, State and Establishment in the UK in the 21st Century: Anachronism or Idiosyncrasy?' [2010] PL 482

Walker, 'Our Constitutional Unsettlement' [2014] PL 529

Windlesham, 'The Constitutional Reform Act 2005: The Politics of Constitutional Reform: Part 2' [2006] PL 35

Woodhouse, 'Delivering Public Confidence: Codes of Conduct: A Step in the Right Direction' [2003] PL 511

Part II

Fundamental principles

Chapter 6

The rule of law

The nature of the rule of law

The concept of the rule of law is central to Western civilisation, supporting the certainty that Hobbes (Section 2.3.1) emphasised as fundamental. In its most basic, 'core' sense, the rule of law means that it is desirable to be governed by rules, rather than by the discretion of rulers. This entails an independent body, a court, to settle disputes and peacefully restrain those in power from imposing their personal wishes on us. Thus, in *R (Unison) v Lord Chancellor* [2017] UKSC 51, the Supreme Court stated that 'At the heart of the concept of the rule of law is the idea that society is governed by law… Courts exist in order to ensure that the laws made by Parliament, and the common law created by the courts themselves, are applied and enforced. That role includes ensuring that the executive branch of government carries out its functions in accordance with the law' (at [68]).

The rule of law is an aspect of the broader notion of constitutionalism (Section 1.1.1). It derives from the origins of European civilisation. In the third century BC, Aristotle recommended 'a government of laws not men': 'it is better for the law to rule than one of the citizens so even the guardians of the law are obeying the law' (*Politics,* III, 16, 1087a). His reason for this included the belief that it is easier to find competent lawyers than wise rulers.

In England, the rule of law is claimed to go back to the Anglo-Saxon notion of a compact between ruler and ruled, under which obedience to the king was conditional upon the king respecting customary law. It was famously invoked by the thirteenth-century jurist Bracton as 'a bridle on power ': 'The King should be under no man but under God and the Law because the Law makes him King' (*On the Laws and Customs of England* (Thorne tr, Harvard University Press 1968) II, 33).

During the seventeenth-century disputes between king and Parliament, emphasis was placed on the common law and the independence of the judges from the king (e.g. *Prohibitions del Roy* (1607) 12 Co Rep. 64; Croke J, dissenting in *R v Hampden* (1637) 3 St Tr 825, 1130). According to Coke CJ (1552–1634), the rule of law protected both ruler and subject, the ruler against criticism, the subject against tyranny: 'The golden and straight metwand of the law and not the uncertain and eroded cord of discretion' (*Institutes* (1644) 4(37), (41)). The rule of law as proposed by Coke could, of course, be regarded as a bid for power by lawyers.

The rule of law in this general sense tells us nothing about the content of the law. It implies that the kind of tight, self-contained, logical reasoning that lawyers use is a protection for the individual and that it is dangerous to take into account less predictable factors, such as public opinion (along these lines see Sedley LJ in *Vellino v Chief Constable of the Greater Manchester Police* [2002] 1 WLR 218, at [60]).

The historian E. P. Thompson described the rule of law as 'an unqualified human good' (*Whigs and Hunters: The Origins of the Black Acts* (Allen Lane 1975) Afterword). In the context of condemning the oppressive property laws of the eighteenth century, Thompson argued that even a bad law is better than no law at all because, in order to give it credibility, a law has to be applied fairly and justly. This is preferable to the whim of a tyrant. Not everyone put on trial was convicted, even under the notorious anti-poaching 'Black Acts'. The rule of law is often claimed to be a necessary foundation of democracy. For example, by ensuring that officials keep within the powers given to them by the people and treat people equally, the rule of law is said to be both the servant and the policeman of democracy (Baroness Hale in *Ghaidan v Mendoza* [2004] 3 All ER 411, at [132]). In *A v Secretary of State for the Home Department* [2005] 2 AC 68, at [42], Lord Bingham, in rejecting an argument that courts are undemocratic, emphasised that independent courts under the rule of law are a cardinal feature of the modern democratic state. However, the rule of law is wider than democracy since the rule of law can operate in an undemocratic state, albeit perhaps with greater difficulty. In *R (Corner House*

Research) v Director of the Serious Fraud Office [2008] 4 All ER 927, at [65], Moses J said that the rule of law is nothing if it fails to constrain overweening power.

There is, however, a wider and more ambitious version of the rule of law. This is the idea, derived from Plato, that we should be ruled by 'philosopher kings': wise leaders. Some regard judges as fulfilling this role. Here, the courts announce and uphold the fundamental values of society. This wider version of the rule of law requires laws to be assessed and applied according to basic values of freedom and justice (or whatever the court considers to be sufficiently important). An outstanding example of this kind of judge was Lord Denning who dominated the judiciary (and had a large following of law students) throughout the middle of the last century (see Robson and Watchman (eds), *Justice, Lord Denning and the Constitution* (Glover 1981)).

These different perspectives may lead to disagreement in the courts. For example, in *HM Advocate v R* [2004] 1 AC 462, the Privy Council was faced with a provision that an accused person must be brought to trial within a reasonable time. The majority applied the legislation strictly, which meant that the trial was unlawful. However, Lord Steyn (a champion of a wide notion of the rule of law), dissenting, thought that this should be resisted on the ground of public reaction to letting the guilty walk free (see also the discussion of the *Anufrijeva* case (below)).

The wider version of the rule of law can easily merge into rhetorical shorthand for liberal values; for example, 'the sanctity of individual freedom and the security of private property rights, ensured by representative constitutional government' (Ferguson, *Civilisation* (Penguin 2012) 96). Thus, there are grandiose claims associating the rule of law with liberal beliefs such as dignity and freedom – for example in relation to the ECHR (see *Klass v Federal Republic of Germany* (1979–80) 2 EHRR 214; *Young, James and Webster v UK* (1982) 4 EHRR 38). The International Commission of Jurists argued that the rule of law 'should be employed not only to safeguard and advance the civil and political rights of the individual in a free society, but also to establish social, economic, educational and cultural conditions under which his legitimate aspirations and dignity may be realised' (Declaration of Delhi, 1959). The breadth of these definitions has led one eminent judge and commentator to state, pithily, that 'it is tempting to throw up one's hands and accept that the rule of law is too uncertain and subjective a notion to be meaningful' (Bingham (2010) 6).

In its basic sense, the rule of law has less welcome aspects. First, the desire for certainty and equality embodied by rules can cause injustice. For example, in *R (Animal Defenders International) v Culture Secretary* [2008] 1 AC 1312, the House of Lords upheld a general ban on political advertising. The rule was intended to prevent wealthy companies and individuals from dominating and distorting the democratic process. The claimants were a campaigning group, far from rich, whose activities enhanced the democratic process. Nevertheless, among other reasons (Section 23.3.2), their Lordships held that a general rule was necessary in the interests of certainty and to reduce the risk of abuse even if this produced hard cases (at [33]).

Secondly, the wealthy can take advantage of the law more effectively than the poor since they can afford better lawyers. Thus, the rule of law is said to encourage the rich and powerful to harass people who cannot fight back (Horowitz (1977)). Indeed, the law may become too burdensome. The UK produces about three times as much law as other democratic states. This results in complexity and cost, and adds to our dependency upon lawyers.

Thirdly, the rule of law could be regarded as mechanical and cruel, allowing officials to hide behind rules to avoid personal responsibility, ignoring sentiments such as compassion, mercy and common sense in favour of ruthless logic (see e.g. Hutchinson and Monahan (eds), *The Rule of Law: Ideal or Ideology* (University of Toronto Press 1987)).

However, the rule of law is not the supreme value and may be outweighed by other factors. For example, the police do not have to prosecute everyone; the Inland Revenue may release a taxpayer from a tax burden. Perhaps most importantly for our purposes, the right of Parliament to govern its own affairs and exclude the courts is an exception to the rule of law (Section 11.6.2).

Although the courts are reluctant to surrender their jurisdiction, they also refrain from interfering in matters of 'high policy' (Section 19.7). In *R (Corner House Research) v Director of the Serious Fraud*

Office [2008], the House of Lords held that a prosecuting authority could discontinue a prosecution for corruption involving members of the Saudi royal family on the ground that, had the investigation continued, the Saudi government would have withdrawn cooperation with the UK intelligence services, thereby increasing the risk of a terrorist attack.

There must also be wide emergency powers to deal with unforeseen and exceptional threats. However, even emergency powers can be hedged with legal safeguards, for example a requirement that they lapse after a set period (known as a sunset clause) (Section 25.1.1).

6.2   Practical application of the rule of law

The rule of law is most important as influencing the decisions of the courts, as illustrated by the cases in this chapter. However, the UK Constitution is not wholly derived from the rule of law since much of it is outside the law, depending on political practices, or at best conventions, between members of the ruling elite. These are policed by the same people who are subject to them, without the kind of independent decision-making that is fundamental to the rule of law.

The rule of law as understood in the UK is therefore not the same as the German concept of *Rechtsstaat*, which means that the state and the constitution as a whole should be embodied in legal rights. The rule of law directly applies only where the courts are involved, which is a relatively small part of constitutional activity (albeit an important one), focusing as it does on individual rights. However, the indirect influence of the courts in promoting public values may be more substantial.

The Constitutional Reform Act 2005 s 1 states that the Act does not adversely affect

(a) the existing constitutional principle of the rule of law, or
(b) the Lord Chancellor's existing constitutional role in relation to that principle.

The statute provides no further definition of the phrase. This has been viewed as a deliberate omission on the part of Parliament, which might well 'have preferred to leave the task of definition to the courts if and when occasion arose' (Bingham (2007) 68).

The rule of law may also have a political effect in restraining Parliament from enacting drastic legislation, for example interfering with the courts. A famous example was the Asylum and Immigration Bill 2003–04, which contained a clause excluding most asylum cases from judicial review. A robust challenge led by the Law Lords, including a suggestion of a campaign for a written constitution, led to the government dropping the clause from the Act (see Woolf, 'The Rule of Law and a Change in the Constitution' (2003) 63 CLJ 317, 328–29). Recent anti-terrorism powers have been limited to some extent by rule of law considerations (Section 25.1). However, challenges by asylum-seekers and other immigrants are still restricted and other aspects of the rule of law have been weakened by government intervention (e.g. Sections 9.7.1 and 24.6). The relationship between the rule of law in its wider sense and parliamentary supremacy has generated a debate as to which comes first. The predominant view is that Parliament has the last word, but there are respectable arguments to the contrary. These will be discussed when considering parliamentary sovereignty (Section 8.5.6).

The rule of law is widely recognised internationally, although its meaning is rarely specified. For example, the preamble to the UN Universal Declaration of Human Rights refers to the rule of law as 'essential'. The principle is embodied in the ECHR, signatories to which are stated to share a 'common heritage' which includes the principle (Preamble). The European Union claims to be based on the rule of law (Treaty of the European Union, Preamble). Article 28 of the German Basic Law refers to 'the principles of republican, democratic and social government based on the rule of law'.

6.3   Different versions of the rule of law

We have seen that the rule of law embraces a range of ideas. In this section, we shall outline three main versions of the rule of law, developing these in greater detail later. A broad distinction can be made between the rule of law as government *by* law (versions 1 and 2) and the rule of law as government *under* law (version 3). In principle, each of these versions builds upon the preceding, so that adherents to version 3 would endorse the other two versions, although there can be conflicts, as will be identified. The three versions are as follows:

1. *The 'core' rule of law*: This is the basic rule of law discussed earlier. It means government *by* law in the form of general rules, as opposed to the discretion of the ruler. All it requires is that the rules are validly made and applied. It does not specify their content. It assumes that general rules, even those made by a tyrant, are better than government by the unpredictable whim of a ruler, even a kind one. It implies 'equality' in the sense that everyone who falls within a given law must be treated the same under it, and that government must respect its own laws. This does not amount to much since there can be different laws for different groups of people (for example, landlords and tenants, or employers and employees). 'Equality' can be said to be satisfied if each individual in the group is treated equally under the laws relating specifically to the group. The core rule of law may therefore be consistent with hideously repressive regimes. As John Stuart Mill remarked, 'the justice of giving equal protection to the rights of all is maintained by those who support the most outrageous inequality in the rights themselves' (*Utilitarianism* (1863) ch 5).

2. *The 'amplified' rule of law*: The amplified rule of law claims that certain principles relating to fairness and justice are inherent in the notion of law itself as a guide to human conduct and that these moderate bad laws, for example a requirement that laws be announced clearly in advance and be applied by independent courts. It is not claimed that these principles cannot be overridden by other factors. The amplified rule of law is primarily procedural. It could conflict with the core rule of law, for example a rule which allows a witness in court special protection (e.g. *W (Algeria) v Secretary of State for the Home Dept* [2012] 2 All ER 699, Section 24.6).

3. *The 'extended' rule of law*: This is the most ambitious version. It claims that law encapsulates the overarching political values or general moral principles of the community – assumed to be liberal – such as freedom of expression and non-discrimination (Allan (2006)). It claims also to link law with republican ideas of equal citizenship. Insofar as this version relies upon vague and contestable concepts, it may conflict with the core rule of law. It is often claimed that the flexibility of this version of the rule of law allows the courts to respond to the changing values of society. This presupposes that courts are well placed to understand these.

In *R (Anufrijeva) v Secretary of State for the Home Dept* [2003] 3 All ER 827, different approaches to the rule of law led to judicial disagreement on the outcome of the case. A statute stated that the entitlement of an asylum-seeker to certain benefits terminated when the Home Office determined that asylum should be refused. A majority of the House of Lords held that this did not apply until the asylum-seeker had been informed of the decision, in this case several months later, so that the applicant could exercise her right to challenge the decision in the courts. Lord Bingham, however, dissenting, held that the court should follow the plain words of the legislation. Lord Bingham was thus staking out a core rule of law position, while the majority followed the extended rule of law approach. They took the view that, unless a statute explicitly says otherwise, it must be read so as to accommodate basic rights (the *'principle of legality'* (Section 6.5)) (see also *Seal v Chief Constable of South Wales Police* [2007] 4 All ER 177; Section 18.2).

Craig (1997) has distinguished between 'formal' and 'substantive' versions of the rule of law. The formal version centres on the shape and application of the law, whether it has been properly made, whether it is clear and fairly applied (thus reflecting the 'core' and 'amplified versions' above). There should be independent courts to interpret and apply the law, which should apply equally to those who fall within it. Without independent courts and equality, the notion of rules is meaningless (*R (Cart) v Upper Tribunal* [2010] 1 All ER 908, at [34]–[37]; *R (Privacy International) v Investigatory Powers Tribunal* [2019] UKSC 22). The substantive version opens out to the content of the law, whether it is fair, just, and reflects the values of society. Thus, it reflects the extended version. The danger of a broad approach is, of course, that it could reduce the rule of law to a discussion of whether the particular commentator approves of the law in question.

The different versions of the rule of law may confuse the debate about the relationship, if any, between the rule of law and democracy. The significant role of the judiciary in giving effect to the rule of law, especially in the wider version, where judges have the task of applying principles which reflect the values or principles of the community, superficially appears somewhat anti-democratic. Yet, such wider versions of the rule of law also assert that fundamental rights should be respected, and, as noted in Chapter 2, this is a key element of liberal democratic visions of the state. On the other hand, those favouring political solutions use a narrower version of the rule of law, which they associate with the importance of the democratic process as producing valid laws that should be obeyed precisely because they have been through that process. From this perspective, the judges have the more limited role of interpreting and applying laws validly made by Parliament, but not pronouncing on their wisdom or their conformity to a higher law. This may give precedence to representative democratic institutions, but it does not preclude those institutions from legislating in a manner which many might consider to be 'undemocratic', for example by overriding the rights of minority groups.

6.4 The core rule of law and Dicey's version of it

Hayek, the conservative political theorist (Section 2.3.4), is probably the most enthusiastic champion of the core rule of law. Hayek ((1960) ch 6) asserted of the rule of law:

> Stripped of all technicalities this means that government in all its actions is bound by rules fixed and announced beforehand – rules which make it possible to foresee with fair certainty how the authority will use its coercive powers in given circumstances, and to plan one's life accordingly.

The core rule of law is a requirement of the ECHR. Under many of its provisions, the state can override a right only if it acts 'in accordance with the law' or its action is 'prescribed by law'. For example, *R (Purdy) v DPP* [2009] 4 All ER 1147 concerned the DPP's discretion to prosecute the claimant's husband for murder for assisting her to travel to Switzerland to commit suicide to alleviate her suffering from a terminal illness. The House of Lords held that the right to respect for family life under the ECHR can only be overridden by a law that is accessible and clear enough to ensure that individuals could foresee, if necessary with legal advice, the consequences of their conduct. The DPP must therefore publish guidelines as to how he would exercise his discretion.

However, departing from the idea of the rule of law as rules set out in advance, Hayek favoured independent courts responding through the common law to concrete practical problems, rather than actions by governments which might have neither the skills nor the knowledge to plan for the future. However, Jeremy Bentham (Section 2.3.3) was unhappy with what he called 'Judge and Co'. He thought it strange that courts should be bound by precedent, since to him, this merely reproduced errors. He also thought that the common law, which he called 'dog law', was unjust in that we may be ignorant of the wrong until the case is decided (see Bentham's pamphlet *Truth versus Ashhurst* (written 1792, published 1823); also *R v Rimmington* [2005] UKHL 63, at [33]). However, he was not keen on the rule of law itself. He thought that laws should be no more than guidelines and, in the end, should give way to his master principle of the greatest happiness of the greatest number as determined by majority vote.

The core rule of law has an underlying, albeit somewhat disguised, political agenda. In common with many economic liberals, Hayek believed that the certainty created by the rule of law would encourage wealth creation through a free market and that the poor would be better off than under alternative regimes. Hayek suggested that a government that accepted the rule of law would not pick out individuals for special treatment, but be restricted to general rules applying equally to everyone. He recognised that his views were likely to lead to economic inequality and perhaps hardship, since liberal welfare principles may require officials to have discretionary powers to meet individual needs such as health and housing. He assumed that these were outweighed by the advantages of individual freedom.

Hayek's core rule of law can never fully be realised in practice. The meaning of a rule is rarely clear enough to be applied to every case, so discretion (meaning a choice between alternatives) is unavoidable. To self-styled 'critical' legal scholars, this inherent vagueness of law is a fundamental objection to the idea of the rule of law, which they regard as a mask for naked power. The standard liberal reply is that vagueness is a matter of degree and, in some circumstances, is to be welcomed as keeping alive valid differences of opinion (Kutz, 'Just Disagreement: Indeterminacy and Rationality in the Rule of Law' (1994) 103 Yale LJ 997). In practice, most laws have a widely accepted meaning. And even where laws are vague, there are widely accepted standards of 'practical reasoning', such as appeals to consequences, moral values, analogy with precedents, widely shared feelings and so on. In order to be legitimate, a judge's interpretation must not diverge far from public opinion. Even though there may be no objective 'right' answer, it is possible to justify a solution which would be widely accepted. This is how the common law might be reconciled with the rule of law. It claims to conform to widely accepted community standards: 'ordinary notions of what is fit and proper' (*MacFarlane v Tayside Health Board* [2000] 2 AC 59, at 108; *Invercargill City Council v Hamlin* [1996] AC 624, at 640–42).

6.4.1   The core rule of law and freedom

The core rule of law supports freedom in the sense that, outside the limits of a legal rule, we know that we are free from interference by officials. However, this is of little benefit if the lawmaker can make laws that drastically curtail freedom, such as laws restricting political activity (Sections 23.6.3 and 23.7).

However, Hayek thought that the core rule of law automatically supports freedom: '[W]hen we obey laws, we are not subject to another's will and are therefore free' ((1960) 153–54). This is a confusing claim. A common-sense view would assert that laws in their nature restrict freedom: as Hobbes put it, 'freedom lies in the silence of the laws'.

However, Locke, a founder of liberalism (Section 2.3.2), also thought that laws supported freedom, indeed that freedom means doing what the law allows: 'Law in its true notion is not so much the limitation as the direction of a free and intelligent agent to his proper interest and prescribes no further than is for the general good of those under that law' (*Second Treatise of Government* (1690) VI, 57).

The explanation of this difference is that Hobbes on the one hand, and Locke and Hayek on the other, are using different senses of freedom: Hobbes, the familiar 'negative' version meaning the absence of restrictions; Locke and Hayek the 'positive' version meaning the capacity to expand the possibilities of life and thus to enhance the autonomy of the individual (Section 2.4). Indeed, Hayek referred to freedom as the absence of *arbitrary* restraint, not all restraint. Hayek seems to have assumed that laws are made as a result of a rational process with which all would agree. In this sense, by obeying rational laws, we are apparently exercising freedom since as rational creatures we are 'obeying laws that we have made ourselves' (Kant). On the other hand, as Berlin pointed out (Section 2.4), positive freedom is trickery. Positive freedom assumes that all rational people would think the same, but there are different kinds of reason and, unless a law has a specifically freedom-loving content, there is no guarantee that it will offer good things to anyone except the friends of the lawmaker. The debate therefore seems to be playing on different meanings of freedom. Thus, the core rule of law needs to be supplemented by some idea of 'good law', or at least an inclusive lawmaking process, to have any serious chance of protecting freedom.

6.4.2   Dicey's version of the rule of law

In the late nineteenth century, Dicey promoted a version of the core rule of law tailored to English law and his own political beliefs, characteristic of a Victorian liberal, which centred upon private property, limited government and individual freedom (see Hibbitts (1994)). He claimed that constitutional law is based on general rules enforced through the ordinary courts. Dicey's rule of law has been of great influence among English lawyers, partly due to the clarity and apparent simplicity of his writing, but also, perhaps, because the legal profession sympathised with his political preferences. However, Dicey also promoted the equally influential idea that Parliament can do anything (Section 8.4.1). This does not seem to be reconcilable with his version of the rule of law.

In line with the orthodoxy of his time, Dicey had faith in science and believed that the scientific method could be applied to law so as to produce objective general principles with clear edges. We no longer have such faith and believe that at least some legal ideas, of which the rule of law is an example, are fuzzy, variable and laden with political value judgments (indeed, science itself is increasingly recognised as having these features).

Dicey formulated a three-fold version of the rule of law. His three aspects are inter-related but deserve separate treatment since some aspects stand the test of time better than others. They are as follows:

1. **The absolute supremacy or predominance of 'regular' law**

> No man is punishable or can be lawfully made to suffer in body or goods except for a distinct breach of law established in the ordinary legal manner before the ordinary courts (Dicey (1915) 110).

This aspect of the rule of law itself has three branches. First, that no official can interfere with individual rights without the backing of a specific law. This remains important today. In *R v Somerset CC, ex p Fewings* [1995] 1 All ER 513, which concerned an unsuccessful claim by a local authority to ban hunting on its land, Laws J, referring to one of the 'sinews' of the rule of law, said (at 524) that the principles that govern the application of the rule of law to public bodies and private persons are 'wholly different' in the sense that:

> the freedoms of the private citizen are not conditional upon some distinct and affirmative justification for which he must burrow in the law books...But for public bodies the rule is opposite and so of another character altogether. It is that any action to be taken must be justified by positive law.

Second, Dicey believed that government should not have wide discretionary powers. This must be significantly qualified today. Parliament regularly gives wide powers to officials to make discretionary decisions about the provision of public services. These frequently impact on the rights of individuals (e.g. land use planning decisions). However, Dicey did not rule out all discretionary power but only 'wide arbitrary or discretionary power of constraint'. He insisted on limits to and controls over the exercise of discretion. This aspiration is partly met by the courts' powers of judicial review of government action (Chapters 17–19). These include principles based on the purposes for which the power is given and standards of reasonableness and fairness.

Third, Dicey thought that all punishment should be meted out by the ordinary courts. This is no longer the case. For example, regulators and local authorities have wide powers to issue fines and other civil penalties, with only limited rights of appeal to ordinary courts. However, something of Dicey's belief is preserved in the capacity of the ordinary courts to supervise the activities of all of these bodies (*R (Cart) v Upper Tribunal* [2012] 1 AC 663; *R (Privacy International) v Investigatory Powers Tribunal* [2019]).

2. **No one is above the law/equality before the law**

Dicey meant that nobody, especially government officials, should be immune from the powers of the ordinary courts:

> Here every man, whatever be his rank or condition, is subject to the ordinary law of the realm and amenable to the jurisdiction of the ordinary [courts]. (Dicey (1915) 114)

Equality before the law in this sense is essential in the interests of public confidence (*Sharma v Browne-Antoine* [2007] 1 WLR 780, at [14]), and this aspect of Dicey's model has partly stood the test of time. Dicey did not mean that no official has special powers – this would have been obviously untrue. Dicey meant that 'every official, from the Prime Minister down...is under the same responsibility for every act done without legal justification as any other citizen' (ibid.). Officials as such enjoy no special protection from legal liability. For example, officials and private persons alike are liable if they use excessive force in defending others against criminal acts. And in *M v Home Office* [1993] 3 All ER 537, it was held that a minister cannot refuse to comply with a court order on the basis that he is a servant of the Crown (also *D v Home Office* [2006] 1 All ER 183). Thus, liability is personal to the individual official, who cannot shelter behind the state.

There are exceptions, but these require special justification. The rule of law requires that any immunities be limited to what is strictly necessary (*R v Chaytor* [2011] 1 AC 684). For example, judges are immune from personal liability in respect of their actions in court, Parliament is immune in relation to its internal proceedings, and MPs have certain immunities, but not from the ordinary criminal law (Section 11.6). The Crown has certain immunities (but Dicey's rule of law was influential in restricting these (Crown Proceedings Act 1947, Section 14.5)). In many cases, foreign governments and heads of state are immune from the jurisdiction of the UK courts (State Immunity Act 1978; Section 9.6.1). Public bodies are sometimes protected against legal liability in the interests of efficiency, particularly in cases involving discretionary decisions (e.g. *D v East Berkshire Community Health NHS Trust* [2005] 2 AC 373: false accusation of child abuse against parents).

However, Dicey's insistence that the same 'regular law' applies to all does not always work in favour of the citizen and, in view of the enormous expansion in government power since Dicey's day, must now be heavily qualified. It may be desirable to impose special restrictions on government because its capacity to do harm is often greater than that of the ordinary person. For example, in *Malone v Metropolitan Police Commissioner* [1979] Ch 344, it was held that the police could lawfully intercept telephone calls at common law because at the time there were no special laws in place to prevent this. Statute now endorses government power to intercept communications but imposes safeguards (Section 25.3).

On the other hand, there may sometimes be very good reason to place fewer restrictions on those performing public functions than upon private persons. Consider, for example, s 87(1) of the Road Traffic Regulation Act 1984, which provides that statutory provisions on speed limits shall not apply to vehicles being used by the police or emergency services, 'if the observance of that provision would be likely to hinder the use of the vehicle for the purpose for which it is being used on that occasion'. A 'privilege' of this type facilitates the undertaking of tasks which are in the interests of the community as a whole. It is therefore reflective of a 'green light' approach to the role of law (Section 1.5).

Dicey compared English law, where disputes between government and citizen were settled in the ordinary courts, favourably with French law, where there is a special system of law dealing with the powers of government (*droit administratif*, enforced by the *Conseil d'Etat*). Dicey thought (mistakenly) that special administrative courts would give the government special privileges and shield the individual wrongdoer behind the cloak of the state. This aspect of Dicey's teaching has been particularly influential. As recently as the 1970s, there was resistance to the idea of a distinction between public and private law.

Since then, however, the notion of public law has become accepted. There is now a special procedure for challenging government decisions, albeit within the ordinary court system (Chapter 19). However, in partial vindication of Dicey, attempts to distinguish between public law and private law have often foundered (Sections 19.5 and 22.7). There are also numerous special tribunals dealing with disputes between the individual and government (Section 20.1). However, they are usually subject to the supervision of the ordinary courts.

3. **The constitution is the 'result' of the ordinary law**

> [T]he general principles of the constitution are with us the result of judicial decisions determining the rights of private persons in particular cases brought before the courts. (Dicey (1915) 115)

This derives from the common law tradition. In line with the orthodoxy of his generation, Dicey believed that the UK Constitution, not being imposed from above as a written constitution, was embedded in the very fabric of society, dealing with concrete situations and backed by practical remedies in the hands of the courts. According to Dicey, this strengthens the constitution, since a written constitution may contain grand but vague abstractions and can also more easily be over-turned (this being especially the case in the UK because there are no special processes for amendment or repeal of laws which might be considered to have constitutional status). Moreover, because the common law developed primarily through the medium of private disputes, the constitution has individual rights as the basic perspective.

6.4.3   Dicey's rule of law today

It is easy to see that Dicey's version of the rule of law has only limited application to modern conditions, where Parliament frequently confers wide powers on the executive to carry out the broad range of functions expected of modern government. On occasion, Parliament also overturns fundamental principles of the rule of law, often in situations where there is a perceived threat to the security of the state, such as terrorism: for example in relation to open justice (Section 24.6) and no detention without trial (Section 25.1.1). On the other hand, Parliament is generally concerned to ensure that drastic powers have safeguards attached (see e.g. Section 25.5.4).

In this context, it is important to understand that, while Dicey sought to put forward a 'scientific' model of the UK Constitution, his model was nonetheless reflective of his particular political preferences. Dicey was a Victorian *laissez-faire* liberal, who favoured limited government and cherished individual autonomy, free from state interference. Understood in this manner, we can read the first two of Dicey's aspects of the rule of law as means of restricting broad governmental power so that the sphere of individual autonomous action remains as broad as possible. The third aspect can be viewed as exhibiting a preference for the individualistic approach of the common law, as distinct from a potentially collectively oriented (perhaps, socialist) expression of will by Parliament.

It follows that, if we do not share Dicey's political views as to the relationship between the state and the individual, we might wish to critique his model of the rule of law. This was the stance taken by a number of legal commentators in the early twentieth century, who adopted a more positive view of government's role, consistent with the development of the modern welfare state. For example, Sir Ivor Jennings wrote that if the rule of law 'means that the state exercises only the functions of carrying out external relations and maintaining order, it is not true. If it means that the state ought to exercise those functions only, it is a rule of policy for Whigs (if there are any left)' (*The Law and the Constitution* (University of London Press 1933) 311).

Nevertheless, Dicey remains relevant. He emphasises important principles which influence contemporary beliefs, most notably the principle that officials have only such powers as the law gives them, and that their decisions can be challenged in independent courts. Thus, at least outside the area of security and intelligence, attempts to exclude judicial review have been largely unsuccessful (Section 19.7). We might also note the requirement in contemporary human rights law that restrictions on rights must be based on clear laws or rules.

6.5   The 'amplified' rule of law

According to supporters of this wider version of the rule of law, the notion of law as rules necessarily implies certain basic principles. They concern the idea that, in order to guide conduct and be acted on, rules must be clear, look to the future (be prospective), and be applied impartially and publicly. There should be access to independent courts and a fair trial, particularly to challenge government action. See *R (Anderson) v Secretary of State* [2002] 4 All ER 1089, at [27], [39]; *Al Rawi v Security Services* [2012] 1 All ER 1.

The late Lord Bingham (2007, 2010), a distinguished senior judge, proposed a version of the amplified rule of law. His core notion was that 'all persons and authorities within the state, whether public or private, should be bound by and entitled to the benefit of laws publicly and prospectively promulgated and publicly administered in the courts'. Particular elements are that laws should:

- be intelligible and precise enough to guide conduct;
- minimise discretion, recognising that discretion cannot be removed completely;
- apply equally to all unless differences are clearly justified;
- give adequate protection to fundamental human rights (Lord Bingham acknowledged the lack of agreement as to whether this is an appropriate rule of law matter as opposed to a matter of politics);
- include machinery for resolving disputes without excessive cost or inordinate delay;
- provide for judicial review requiring decision-makers to act reasonably, in good faith, for the purposes for which powers are granted without exceeding the limits of those powers;
- embody fair adjudicative procedures;
- ensure that the state complies with international law.

Lord Bingham's approach probably represents a widely shared view as to what good law should be like in a liberal society.

Other versions embody similar ideas. The American legal theorist Lon Fuller (*The Morality of Law* (Yale University Press 1969)) includes the following principles as embodying the rule of law:

- generality: for example officials not being exempt from rules (*M v Home Office* [1993]);
- promulgation: so that laws can be known in advance (e.g. *R (Anufrijeva) v Secretary of State for the Home Dept* [2003]: decision to refuse an asylum-seeker status took effect from the date when the claimant was informed of it; *R (Kambadzi) v Secretary of State* [2011] 4 All ER 975, at [73]: published policies must be followed);
- non-retroactivity: no punishment without a law in force at the time the act was committed (ECHR, Art 7(1));
- clarity: a law should be sufficiently clear and certain to enable a person to know what conduct was forbidden before he did it (*R v Rimmington* [2005], at [32]–[33]). This is especially important in the context of human rights (*Gillan and Quinton v UK* [2010] ECHR 28, at [76]);
- consistent application: (e.g. *R v Horseferry Road Magistrates Court, ex p Bennett* [1994] 1 All ER 289: fair trial not given to a person brought before the court by kidnapping even if the court process itself is fair);
- the practical possibility of compliance: (e.g. *R v Secretary of State for Social Services, ex p Joint Council for the Welfare of Immigrants* [1996] 4 All ER 385: regulations which deprived asylum-seekers of benefits unless they claimed asylum status at the port of entry would frustrate their right of appeal);
- constancy through time: frequent changes in the law might offend this. A conspicuous example is the rapid changes in immigration law that have taken place in recent years (*R (Alvi) v Secretary of State for the Home Dept* [2012] 1 WLR 2208, at [11]; see *Odelola v Secretary of State for the Home Dept* [2009] UKHL 25: changes in immigration rules between applying to enter the UK and the decision).

Raz (1977) adds the following:

- access to legal assistance: (e.g. *R v Lord Chancellor, ex p Witham* [1997] 2 All ER 779: increases in legal fees denied access to courts for low-income people; *R v Grant* [2005] 3 WLR 437, at [52]: breach of lawyer–client confidentiality an affront to the rule of law; *R (Evans) v Lord Chancellor* [2012] 1 WLR 838, at [25]: unlawful as contrary to the rule of law to refuse legal aid funding to peace activists on grounds that government defence interests might be harmed). In *R (Unison) v Lord Chancellor* [2017] (introduction of fess regime for Employment Tribunals), the Supreme Court stated that 'the constitutional right of access to the courts is inherent in the rule of law' (at [66]);
- 'natural justice': in the sense of a right to a fair hearing before an independent tribunal (Section 18.3);
- 'openness': (e.g. *R (Middleton) v West Somerset Coroner* [2004] 2 All ER 465, at [5]: relatives of prisoners who died in police custody entitled to inquiry in public). The same principle supports the democratic public interest in judicial accountability and the free flow of information through press reporting (e.g. *R (Mohamed) v Secretary of State* [2010] 3 WLR 554, at [38]–[41] (Section 23.3.6)).

Related to the amplified rule of law is a political version of the rule of law derived from the republican tradition (see Section 2.5; Bellamy (2007)). From this perspective, law is a collective enterprise made by numerous people with many different interests – majorities and minorities alike. Indeed, any of us might sometimes be part of a majority and sometimes a minority. The focus is not therefore on courts alone, but on ensuring that the laws are made by a regular democratic process in which the representatives of all interests in the community have a voice. English law has not (yet) seriously engaged with this idea.

6.6 The extended (liberal) rule of law: 'the principle of legality'

As previously noted, this version of the rule of law includes, but goes beyond, the amplified rule of law. It seeks to restrain 'bad' laws by interpreting legislation in light of the shared values of the community. In some jurisdictions, courts might be empowered to strike down legislation which offends such common values.

In the UK Constitution, in which Parliament is sovereign, this approach has been applied by the courts as 'the principle of legality'. Fundamental rights, such as access to the courts, may be 'curtailed only by clear and express words and then only to the extent reasonably necessary to justify the curtailment' (per Lord Bingham in *R v Secretary of State for the Home Dept, ex parte Daly* [2001] 2 AC 532, at [5]; see also Lord Cooke at [30]). In this way, the rule of law claims to support liberal democracy. The principle of legality has been reinforced by the HRA (Chapter 22) and often overlaps with it. But the two routes to the protection of rights are distinct, one deriving from common law, the other from statute.

In *R v Secretary of State for the Home Dept, ex p Simms* [2000] 2 AC 115, at 131, Lord Hoffmann said:

> The principle of legality means that Parliament must squarely confront what it is doing and accept the political cost. Fundamental rights cannot be overridden by general or ambiguous words. This is because there is too great a risk that the full implications of their unqualified meaning may have passed unnoticed in the democratic process. In the absence of express language or necessary implication to the contrary, the courts therefore presume that even the most general words were intended to be subject to the basic rights of the individual.

The principle of legality applies both to procedural matters, thus encompassing the amplified rule of law above, and to matters of substance, such as freedom of speech and non-discrimination. Examples of the principle of legality include the following:

- personal freedom: *R v Secretary of State, ex p Pierson* [1998] AC 539; R (*Roberts*) *v Parole Board* [2006] 1 All ER 39, at [93]; *R (Ullah) v Special Adjudicator* [2004] 3 All ER 785, at [43];
- freedom of expression: *R v Secretary of State for the Home Dept, ex p Simms* [2000]: general powers to manage prison discipline were not enough to justify denying a prisoner access to a journalist; *Culnane v Morris* [2006] 2 All ER 149: election campaigns;
- privacy: *R (Daly) v Secretary of State* [2001]: search of a prisoner's belongings in his absence;
- access to the courts and fair trial: *R v Lord Chancellors Dept, ex p Witham* [1997]: regulations concerning legal costs made by the Lord Chancellor unduly restricting the citizen's right of access to the courts; *R (Cart) v Upper Tribunal* [2010] and *R (Privacy International) v Investigatory Powers Tribunal* [2019]: judicial review not to be excluded;
- *Al Rawi v Secretary of State for the Home Dept* [2012]: no secret court hearings;
- *HM Treasury v Ahmed* [2010] 2 AC 534: asset freezing of terrorist suspects with no provision for reasonable suspicion or a fair right to challenge.

The suggested link between liberalism, the rule of law and common law seems to be the idea that the law must be applied according to the values of those subject to it. The common law's independence from government means that it can plausibly claim to represent the values of the community. According to Allan:

> The principle that laws will be faithfully applied, according to the tenor in which they would reasonably be understood by those affected, is the most basic tenet of the rule of law: it constitutes that minimal sense of reciprocity between citizen and state that inheres in any form of decent government, where law is a genuine barrier to arbitrary power. (*Constitutional Justice* (OUP 2001) 62)

The former Court of Appeal judge, Sir John Laws, asserted that, because the courts derive their powers from common law and have no electoral mandate to pursue any particular policy, they must fall back on what he considered to be the only possible moral position, namely individual freedom: 'The true starting point in the quest for the good constitution consists in …the autonomy of every person in his sovereignty' ('The Constitution: Morals and Rights' [1996] PL 622, 623; also 'Law and Democracy' [1995] PL 72). However, such philosophical assumptions are controversial, and concepts such as freedom and equality are inherently vague and understood and applied differently by different groups.

6.7 The international rule of law

The idea of the rule of law comes under particular stress when there is a clash between different legal regimes, in particular between international and domestic law. International law as such is not automatically part of UK law, but international principles can filter into our law by various means (Section 9.5).

The idea of the rule of law is represented in international law by the notion of *ius cogens*, that is, certain absolutes that all nations are expected to recognise, such as prohibition against torture (*R v Bow Street Stipendiary Magistrate, ex p Pinochet Ugarte (No 3)* [1999] 2 All ER 97, at 198–99). Since the Second World War, there have been several attempts to draw up internationally binding codes of basic human rights and to promote liberal values under the banner of the rule of law. However, such concepts are contentious and sometimes vague, and are applied in different ways in different cultures. Indeed, in order to command support from as many nations as possible, treaties are often written in general language, so as to avoid clear commitments (see e.g. the Declaration of Delhi, Section 6.1).

International instruments include the United Nations Universal Declaration of Human Rights (1948), the Refugee Convention (1951) and the Torture Convention (1984). The International Criminal Court, dealing with war crimes, crimes against humanity and genocide, has been incorporated into UK law (International Criminal Court Act 2001; Section 9.6.4). Other international courts have been established on an individual basis, such as the court dealing with war crimes in the former Yugoslavia. Torture is an offence in the UK, wherever and by whomever committed (Criminal Justice Act 1988). Of most direct concern to UK law is the ECHR. Individuals have a right to petition the European Court of Human Rights in respect of violations by states, including the UK. The ECHR is given domestic effect through the HRA (Chapter 22).

Summary

- The rule of law is an umbrella term for assorted ideas about the virtues of law, mainly from a liberal perspective. They centre upon law as reason and law as administered by the courts as a means of controlling government. The rule of law in its core sense emphasises the importance of general rules as binding on government and citizen alike. The core sense of the rule of law is morally ambivalent since it can also be regarded as an efficient tool of tyranny.

- The meaning and importance of the rule of law are much contested. This is evidenced by the huge literature on the subject. The main areas of debate are as follows:

  - Is the idea of the rule of law more than empty rhetoric? It is sometimes regarded as signifying only that a law is good.

Summary cont'd

▶ Could an Act of Parliament be overridden on the ground that it conflicts with the rule of law, for example an Act that restricts access to the courts?

▶ Should the rule of law sometimes be overridden in favour of other values? For example, in an emergency should the government be free to act without constraint, or should law sometimes give way to compassion or mercy, or even to good relationships with dubious overseas governments?

▶ Is the regime of a tyrant who rules according to law, however repressive, in any sense a better regime than one ruled by a dictator who governs by personal whims? Is it ever justified to disobey the law?

▶ The rule of law as expounded by Dicey has significantly influenced the UK Constitution. Dicey advocated that government discretion should be limited by definite rules of law, that the same law administered by the ordinary courts should in general apply to government and citizen alike, and that the UK does not need a written constitution because the common law provides a firmer foundation for individual rights. This has influenced legal principles, processes and thinking, but is unsuited to the circumstances of modern government. It is also difficult to reconcile the rule of law in this sense with the principle that Parliament has unlimited power which can be harnessed by a strong executive.

▶ In an 'amplified' sense, the rule of law requires the law to reflect certain basic values derived from the nature of rules as guides to conduct. These centre upon the law being clear and accessible and upon the right to a fair trial. However, they are also consistent with repressive laws.

▶ In an 'extended' sense, the rule of law is claimed to be the guardian of the liberal values of the community, entrusted to the courts because of their role as sources of impartial reason. It is claimed to be translated into rights such as non-discrimination and freedom of expression. However, there is no reason to believe that these values or reason itself are the sole prerogative of courts, and they have to be accommodated against the social goals of elected governments. Why courts should have the power to do this is a theme to be pursued in later chapters.

▶ Other modern ideas of the rule of law include the increasing importance of international treaties which attempt to establish codes of fundamental rights and freedoms that governments should respect.

Exercises

6.1 Do you agree with Thompson that the rule of law is an 'unqualified human good'? Would an evil tyrant favour the rule of law?

6.2 To what extent does Dicey's version of the rule of law advance individual freedom and good government?

6.3 'The Rule of Law functions as a clear check on the flourishing of a vigorous democracy. Attempts to characterise the rule of law as the butler of democracy are false and misleading' (Hutchinson and Monahan). Critically discuss.

6.4 To what extent, if at all, is the rule of law conducive to equality?

6.5 Do the following violate the rule of law?

  (i) heads of state being exempt from legal liability;

  (ii) a statute banning press criticism of the prime minister;

  (iii) a statute that states that an allegation relating to the conduct of the security services cannot be made in the ordinary courts;

  (iv) a statute that gives discretion to the Education Secretary to decide what courses will be taught in universities;

  (v) a statute requiring that any law concerning the treatment of prisoners must be interpreted literally, without any presumption in favour of human rights.

6.6 'The rule of law clearly forms an essential element of liberal democracy and plays its part in providing a theoretical basis for an independent judiciary but it forms only one side of a balanced constitution' (Harlow). Explain and critically discuss.

Further reading

Allan, 'The Rule of Law as Liberal Justice' (2006) 56 U Toronto LR 283

Allan, 'Law, Justice and Integrity: The Paradox of Wicked Laws' (2009) 29 OJLS 705

Bellamy, *Political Constitutionalism* (Cambridge University Press 2007) ch 2

Bingham, 'The Rule of Law' (2007) 66 CLJ 67

Bingham, *The Rule of Law* (Penguin 2010)

Craig, 'Formal and Substantive Concepts of the Rule of Law: An Analytical Framework' [1997] PL 467

Dicey, *Law of the Constitution* (Macmillan 1915), chs IV, XII, XIII

Ekins, 'Judicial Supremacy and the Rule of Law' (2003) 119 LQR 127

Endicott, 'The Impossibility of the Rule of Law' (1999) 19 OJLS 1

Foran, 'The Rule of Good Law: Form, Substance and Fundamental Rights' (2019) 78 CLJ 570

Hayek, *The Constitution of Liberty* (Routledge 1960) 133–61, 205–19

Hibbitts, 'The Politics of Principle: Albert Venn Dicey and the Rule of Law' (1994) 23 Anglo Am LR 1

Horowitz, 'The Rule of Law: An Unqualified Human Good?' (1977) 86 Yale LJ 561

Jennings, 'In Praise of Dicey' (1935) 13 *Journal of Public Administration* 123

Jowell, 'The Rule of Law' in Jowell and O'Cinneide (eds), *The Changing Constitution* (9th edn, Oxford University Press 2019)

Loughlin, *Foundations of Public Law* (Oxford University Press 2010) ch 11

Poole, 'Questioning Common Law Constitutionalism' (2005) 25 LS 142

Raz, 'The Rule of Law and Its Virtue' (1977) 93 LQR 195

Syrett, *The Foundations of Public Law* (2nd edn, Palgrave Macmillan 2014) ch 2B

Taylor, 'The Contested Constitution: An Analysis of the Competing Models of British Constitutionalism' [2018] PL 500

Chapter 7

The separation of powers

7.1 Introduction: Montesquieu's doctrine of the separation of powers

The separation of powers is widely regarded as one of the pillars of a constitutional democracy. Its essence is that governmental powers should be divided so that no single person or body can exercise unlimited power and each branch of government requires the cooperation of the others. Article 16 of the (French) Declaration of the Rights of Man (1789) states that 'a society where rights are not secured or the separation of powers established has no constitution'.

The best-known version of the doctrine is that of Montesquieu, *The Spirit of the Laws* (1748), who adapted Locke's version (Section 2.3.2). Montesquieu divided government powers into legislative power: which he described as 'that of enacting laws'; executive power: 'executing the public resolutions'; and judicial power: 'trying the causes of individuals' (Book XI, ch VI, 174) (Locke's version had merged judiciary and executive and separated the conduct of foreign affairs (the federative power)). Montesquieu based his version on the English Constitution following the 1688 revolution.

The legislature (Parliament, in the case of the UK) makes the laws; the judiciary settles disputes and imposes sanctions for breaking the law. The scope of the executive power (the Crown and other bodies created by statute) is more difficult to define. The term 'execute' means to 'carry out'. The executive carries out the everyday tasks of government, which can be anything given to it by the lawmaker. Fundamentally, the executive implements the law and therefore commands the resources of the state, in particular the allocation of money and the use of force. In modern times, a key function of the executive is also to propose and prepare laws to be approved by the legislature. Thus, the law-making process is actually a combination of executive and legislature. The executive also includes the head of state, who represents the state in foreign affairs and has the ultimate responsibility for the welfare of the community.

The separation of powers is central to republicanism (Section 2.5) and is at least consistent with liberalism. It is not necessarily democratic. For example, the US Constitution with its strong separation of powers was devised primarily to prevent self-interested factions, including democratic majorities, from taking over the government. The UK Constitution is more ambivalent. All three branches originated with the Crown, but gradually evolved into separate institutions. However, the same people occupy key positions in the legislature and the executive, and parliamentary supremacy makes the separation of powers vulnerable. Thus, in *Jackson v A-G* [2006] 1 AC 262, at [125], Lord Hope fell back on the somewhat vague truism that the constitution depends upon 'mutual respect' between the branches of government.

Montesquieu's main aim was to protect liberty. He was no democrat and placed faith in aristocratic government subject to limits. He favoured what he called 'dissonant harmony'. He believed that disagreement was a healthy feature of politics and that the need for different interests to cooperate would prevent any power being used excessively: 'power must be checked by power'. Montesquieu thought that if any two of the three functions fall into the same hands, the outcome is likely to be tyranny. Each branch has different functions, but each can police the limits of the others. As Nolan J put it:

> The proper constitutional relationship between the executive and the court is that the courts will respect all acts of the executive within its lawful province, and that the executive will respect all decisions of the court as to what its lawful province is (*M v Home Office* [1992] QB 270, 314).

However, there must be an understanding as to which branch should have the last word in the event of a stalemate, since the separation of powers is capable of producing gridlock. The way this is done depends upon the particular political fears and worries of the day. Montesquieu most feared the legislature and disliked democracy. He favoured a monarchy as the executive, believing that this gave the constitution stability and continuity. According to Montesquieu, although the executive could not make laws or obtain finance without the support of the legislature, the executive could veto the proposals of the legislature. The executive could also dismiss Parliament, and Montesquieu thought that the executive should summon the legislature as and when needed. Montesquieu did not think that the legislature should have the power to remove the executive, since government must be continuous. Today, in common with the US Constitution, we usually regard the executive as the most dangerous branch. Thus Mill, influenced by de Tocqueville's writing on the emerging American democracy, feared 'the only despotism of which in the modern world there is real danger – the absolute rule of the head of the executive over a congregation of isolated individuals all equal and all slaves' (*Autobiography* (1873)).

For example, in the UK, Parliament can remove the executive, but the executive can no longer remove Parliament (Section 11.2, and see further *R (Miller) v the Prime Minister* [2019] UKSC 41).

Thus, the separation of powers does not necessarily mean that the three functions are always separate, but rather that with each function a separate body has the last word, and that the exercise of all power is subject to some kind of external check: the doctrine of 'checks and balances' – a term coined by John Adams, one of the founders of the American system of government. Hofstadter described the doctrine as '[a] harmonious system of mutual frustration' (*The American Political Tradition and the Men Who Made It* (Vintage Books 1948) 9).

7.2   The importance of the separation of powers in the UK

There is disagreement among academic writers as to the importance of the separation of powers in the UK. Dicey, perhaps the most influential exponent of the 'English' constitution, did not rank the separation of powers as one of its basic principles but mentioned it only in passing. Although Montesquieu took England as his model, it seems clear that he overstated both the possibility of a separation along his lines and its application in England. In particular, he did not accommodate the common law under which the judges, as well as Parliament, make law. Nor, according to Holdsworth ((1938) 721), did he appreciate how the various English institutions had developed, each on its own lines. Moreover, when Montesquieu was writing (after a visit to England in the early eighteenth century), the conventions which require the Crown to act on the advice of ministers chosen from the legislature had not clearly emerged.

The separation of powers in the UK is controversial. It is acknowledged that the UK Constitution does not have a full separation of powers in Montesquieu's sense. Separation of powers devices are scattered and unsystematic and applied pragmatically in particular contexts. They are strongest as regards the courts, weakest as regards the relationship between the legislature and the executive. It also seems clear that, in recent years, the UK has moved closer to recognising the importance of the doctrine, especially in relation to the courts. Here, the separation of powers supports the rule of law by requiring the courts to be independent of other branches of government (see *R (Unison) v Lord Chancellor* [2017] UKSC 51, [68] (Section 6.1)). In some contexts, however, it runs counter to the rule of law, especially in connection with the independence of Parliament from the jurisdiction of the ordinary courts (Section 11.6.2). The HRA, with its balance between the powers of the court, Parliament and the executive, could be regarded as a distinctive application of the separation of powers.

Marshall (*Constitutional Theory* (Oxford University Press 1971)) argues that the separation of powers is an umbrella for a miscellaneous collection of principles, each of which can be justified in its own right without using the concept of separation of powers, for example judicial independence. On the other hand, Barendt (1995), Munro (1999), and Syrett (2014), while not claiming that it is universal, regard the doctrine as a useful and important organising and critical principle.

7.3   Different kinds of separation of powers

The debate about the separation of powers may also be confused where different protagonists are using the concept of the separation of powers in different senses. In particular, separation of powers can mean:

1. Functional separation of powers, where one branch carries out tasks that strictly belong to another. This is seen in the law of judicial review, where the courts avoid intervening in government decisions merely because they disagree with them and would themselves have done differently (i.e. 'intervening on the merits' of the case).
2. Separation of personnel: where the same individual must not be a member of more than one branch. The huge exception in the UK Constitution is that ministers must also be members of the legislature.
3. 'Checks and balances': this requires each branch to have some control over one or more of the others to ensure that they do not abuse their powers. Again, judicial review is an outstanding example, as is Parliament's power to hold to account and remove the executive.

The strictest version of the doctrine, such as that adopted in the US, would aim at all three. However, even in such a case, it is likely to be impracticable to achieve complete separation since this would result in (at best) lack of coordination and (at worst) a state of gridlock in the system of government.

Moreover, if we wish to restrain power, it does not follow that this can be done only by dividing powers according to Montesquieu's three abstract forms of classification. For example, Claus (2005) argues that Montesquieu did not go far enough and that it is not the kind of power that matters, but the existence of checks and limits on all powers. The essential principle encapsulated by the separation of powers is that power should be divided, not that it should be divided in any particular way.

Power can be divided and checked in many ways, each having both benefits and problems. For example, there is a division between elected politicians and the professional civil servants who advise them and carry out their instructions (Section 15.8). Geographical divisions between central government and local governmental bodies, as in a federal system, are also restraining influences and relatively efficient in relating government functions to the wishes of different communities. Even 'quangos' (Section 15.10) may provide a valuable separation of power by focusing on specialist functions, albeit those who seek appointment on such bodies are not always conspicuous for their independence. The distinction between the dignified and the 'efficient' parts of the constitution also provides a form of separation of powers (Section 1.7).

On the other hand, the traditional division between legislative, executive and judicial functions is valuable by indicating different kinds of procedure for different jobs. For example, lawmaking requires the participation of a wide range of people meeting in public on equal terms; executive functions are likely to require decisions by small groups or by individuals with professional expertise, not necessarily in public. Judicial functions, above all, require impartiality and openness and are normally in public. There is no doubt that, out of all of the aspects of separation of powers, judicial independence is paramount (Section 7.4).

7.3.1   The mixed constitution

Montesquieu also favoured a different kind of separation of powers, namely the 'mixed constitution' based on Aristotle's three forms of government: monarchy, aristocracy and democracy (Section 1.7). Aristotle believed that any single form of government was unstable, leading to a permanent cycle of disasters. He therefore favoured a blend of democracy and aristocracy: democracy to provide consent, aristocracy to provide stability and wise leadership. The early Roman republic adopted similar ideas ('power in the people, authority in the Senate' – Cicero), but was later replaced by dictatorship ('what pleases the prince has the force of law'). For Montesquieu, all three elements of the mixed constitution should be represented in the legislature, since this was the supreme body. Thus the English legislature had two parts, one (the House of Lords) being aristocratic. Each element would check the others. The monarch could veto legislation (though convention now precludes this) but not initiate it: 'prevent wrong but not do wrong'. The aristocratic and elected elements would have to agree to make changes in the law.

Montesquieu, an aristocrat himself, believed that an aristocracy based on inheritance produced an independent, educated and leisured class which would protect freedom and curb the democratic element ('liberty is the stepchild of privilege'), while the other elements of the constitution could prevent the aristocracy from using their powers selfishly.

Blackstone (1723–80) also praised the English mixed constitution:

> Herein indeed consists the true excellence of the English government that all the parts of it form a mutual check upon each other. In the legislature the people are a check on the nobility and the nobility a check upon the people ... while the king is a check upon both which preserves the executive power from encroachments. And this very executive power is again checked and kept within due bounds by the two Houses ... For the two Houses naturally drawing in two directions of opposite interest, and the prerogative in another still different from them both, they mutually keep each other from exceeding their proper limits ... like three distinct powers in mechanics, they jointly compel the machine of government in a direction different from what either acting by itself would have done ... a direction which constitutes the true line of the liberty and happiness of the country. (*Commentaries on the Laws of England* (1787) 154–55)

The mixed constitution remains a significant element of the formal legal structure, in the form of the monarchy and the House of Lords as an aristocracy (Section 12.2). Fear of democracy still influences the constitution, many people favouring the continuance of the appointed House of Lords (Section 12.3) (note also Dicey's third element of the rule of law: Section 6.4.2). This raises the difficulty of whom we can trust to identify the 'best' so as to avoid Aristotle's corruption of aristocracy into an oligarchy of cronies.

7.4 Judicial independence and accountability

Judicial independence is an aspect of the rule of law in its own right. While it is a dimension of the separation of powers, it extends further. Article 6 of the ECHR requires 'a fair and public hearing ... by an independent and impartial tribunal established by law'. For example, in *Millar v Dickson* [2002] 3 All ER 1041, the Privy Council found a violation of Article 6 where the prosecuting authority, the Scottish Lord Advocate, was also responsible for renewing the appointment of a temporary judge: even though there was no complaint about the actual impartiality of the judge in question. As Lord Hope stated: 'Central to the rule of law is the principle that the judiciary must be, and must be seen to be, independent of the executive' (at [41]).

Article 6 does not require a formal separation of powers but requires that in the particular circumstances the court is not only independent but also appears to be so (*McGonnell v UK* (2000) 30 EHRR 289). Courts of a 'classic kind' must usually sit in public and be fully independent and impartial, and all decision-making bodies must be free from the appearance of bias (Section 18.4). Judicial independence therefore requires that judges in individual cases be protected from pressures that threaten their impartiality.

Judicial independence is frail in the UK Constitution since, in the absence of a written constitution, it depends largely on a shared understanding that the other two branches, which together are dominant, will respect it.

Judicial independence concerns both the judiciary as an institution (or 'branch') of government, and individual judges. There is a 'concordat' setting out a non-legally binding understanding of the relationship between the judiciary and the other branches (see House of Lords Select Committee on the Constitution, *Relations between the Executive, Judiciary and Parliament* (HL 2006–07, 151)). In particular, the Lord Chief Justice, who is head of the judiciary in England and Wales, must be consulted on many matters including budgetary matters (see *HM Courts & Tribunals Service Framework Document* (Cm 8882, 2014)).

Section 3 of the Constitutional Reform Act 2005 states:

1. The Lord Chancellor and other ministers of the Crown with responsibility for matters relating to the judiciary or otherwise to the administration of justice must uphold the continued independence of the judiciary.
2. The Lord Chancellor and other ministers of the Crown must not seek to influence particular judicial decisions through any special access to the judiciary.
3. The Lord Chancellor must have regard to:

   (i) the need to defend that independence;
   (ii) the need for the judiciary to have the support necessary to enable them to exercise their functions;
   (iii) the need for the public interest in regard to matters relating to the judiciary or otherwise to the administration of justice to be properly represented in decisions affecting those matters.

Judicial independence requires that judges should be protected against attacks on their conduct in court. Judges are immune from personal actions for damages in respect of acts within their powers or done in good faith (*McC v Mullan* [1984] 3 All ER 908; Courts Act 2003, ss 31–35). However, superior court judges may enjoy complete immunity (*Anderson v Gorrie* [1895] 1 QB 668). Under section 9(3) of the HRA, where an action for damages is brought in respect of a judicial act, there is no liability in respect of an act in good faith, except for an unlawful arrest or detention. Anything said in court by judges, advocates and witnesses is absolutely privileged against an action in libel and slander, but advocates are not protected against liability for negligence (see *Trapp v Mackie* [1979] 1 All ER 489; *Arthur JS Hall v Simons* [2000] 3 All ER 673). There are also restrictions under the law of contempt of court in respect of comments on court proceedings, which affect the freedom of the press (Section 23.3).

Murphy ('Rethinking Tortious Immunity for Judicial Acts' (2013) 33 LS 455) argues that the comprehensive legal immunity supposedly enjoyed by senior judges is excessive, and that arguments in its favour are either unsubstantiated or exaggerated. He claims that the interests of judicial independence and the rule of law would be adequately served by an immunity based on the tort of misfeasance in public office, which applies to all public officials.

A vital safeguard in the criminal process is that juries should not be vetted by the executive (*R v Crown Court at Sheffield, ex p Brownlow* [1980] 2 All ER 444) and cannot be required to give reasons for their verdicts or punished for giving or failing to give a verdict (*Bushell's Case* (1670) 6 St Tr 999).

7.4.1 Accountability

Judicial independence does not mean that judges should not be accountable. Accountability can be to a superior body, or to a peer group, or to the public. It can be legal, political or administrative (internal). It can be collective, applying to the institution of the judiciary as a whole, or individual.

In the light of the separation of powers, collective accountability suggests that the judiciary be legally and politically accountable only to the sovereign Parliament in relation (e.g.) to expenditure or the general pattern of activity. This form of accountability requires, among other things, the presentation of annual reports to Parliament (e.g. the Supreme Court's annual reports under the Constitutional Reform Act 2005, s 54).

Collective accountability to the public depends on the media and the public having access to information concerning the judiciary (Section 23.3.4). In this respect, the Supreme Court has been active in making its affairs accessible to the public by means, for example of making its premises accessible to visitors (it is one of the most popular destinations in London) and publicising its decisions (it operates live streaming and 'on demand' services for some of its judgments).

Individual accountability has two aspects. First, a decision-maker must explain and justify their actions. Second, a decision-maker might be corrected or penalised if their actions fall short of required standards. There is a need to ensure that accountability does not threaten the judge's impartiality.

Essential to legal accountability is a right of appeal against or review of the decision of a court (see *R (Cart) v Upper Tribunal* [2012] 1 AC 663; *R (Privacy International) v Investigatory Powers Tribunal* [2019] UKSC 22). There is usually a three-tier appeal system within domestic law, access to the European Court of Human Rights, and review by the senior courts of decisions of lower courts and tribunals. The Criminal Cases Review Commission refers possible miscarriages of justice to the Court of Appeal.

Judges are accountable politically to the public. This is an aspect of the wider principle of open justice, which has been said to be fundamental to democracy and the rule of law (*R (Mohamed) v Secretary of State for Foreign Affairs* [2010] 3 WLR 554, at [38]–[41]). Courts normally sit in public, disclose all material before them and give reasons for their decisions. Judicial decisions are therefore open to scrutiny by the media. It has been held that only in rare and extreme circumstances should the court's reasoning in a case not be published (Section 23.3.4). Traditionally, judges have not participated in public debate. However, in 1987, the Lord Chancellor relaxed the notorious 'Kilmuir' rules made in 1959 by the then Lord Chancellor which restricted such participation. The matter is now left to the discretion of the individual judge subject to the *Guide to Judicial Conduct* (see below). Judges often participate in public debate concerning general legal matters but avoid entering into matters involving competing party policies. In this connection, a judge might give a view as to what the law should be, relying on professional competence to remain impartial should the issue arise in a later case before that judge. For example, a number of senior judges have recently spoken on the relationship between UK courts and the European Court of Human Rights in Strasbourg.

The accountability of judges to Parliament is limited, in the interests of the separation of powers. According to the internal law of Parliament, cases in progress should not be discussed except in relation to matters of national importance or the conduct of ministers, and there should be no criticism of a judge's personal character, competence or motives except on a substantive motion for his dismissal. Backbenchers, but not ministers, may criticise individual judgments. By convention, ministers do not answer questions on cases in progress.

Administrative/internal methods of accountability used for other public servants, such as performance targets, are dubious for judges in that they may threaten the appearance of impartiality. However, there is a *Guide to Judicial Conduct* (2013, revised March 2019) enforced by internal disciplinary procedures backed up by the legal power to dismiss a judge. The Lord Chancellor (LC) (Secretary of State for Justice) and the Lord Chief Justice (LCJ) are jointly responsible for judicial discipline (Constitutional Reform Act 2005, s 108). The LC's disciplinary powers are limited to the removal from office of judges below the rank of High Court judge. The LCJ can reprimand and suspend a judge, but the agreement of the LC is required. Judges are to a large extent protected against dismissal, and judicial salaries are controlled by Parliament (Section 7.7.3.2).

7.5   Separation of function

Jennings (*The Law and the Constitution* (University of London Press 1933)) argued that there is no important difference between the three functions, the executive and the judicial being essentially a more detailed kind of lawmaking. While this may, in theory, be true, the practical distinctions between the functions of legislative, executive and judicial branches are reasonably clear. The legislature has no power of enforcement, its work being finished once it has enacted a law and delivered it to the world. The executive function is distinct in having the forces of the state under its control and in that it must be proactive in identifying tasks and taking action. The judiciary is distinct in that it is passive and can only decide particular cases brought to it by others and it requires the cooperation of the executive to use state force. Thus, the judiciary is often claimed to be the 'least dangerous branch', having no weapons at its disposal and no particular axe to grind.

7.5.1 Parliament and the executive

There is considerable overlap between the functions of Parliament and those of the executive. Although Parliament has no executive functions (except in relation to its own internal affairs), the executive is heavily involved in lawmaking. First, it is responsible in practice for most legislative proposals, so that Parliament's separate function lies in it having the last word to bring a law into effect.

Second, the bulk of legislation consists of delegated or secondary or subordinate legislation (the terms being synonymous) made directly by ministers and other executive bodies under powers conferred by statute. Such statutes typically lay down a general principle conferring power upon a minister to make detailed rules, the latter taking the form of secondary legislation. Delegated lawmaking powers may be very wide, even permitting the minister to alter Acts of Parliament past or future (the 'Henry VIII' clause; e.g. Legislative and Regulatory Reform Act 2006 (Section 20.4); European Union (Withdrawal) Act 2018 (Section 10.5.4)). It is also common for a statute to come into effect only when a minister triggers it.

Delegated legislation comes under many names, including regulations, orders, directions, rules and by-laws. Little hinges on the terminology used. However, a compendium term, 'statutory instrument', applies to most delegated legislation made by ministers and to Statutory Orders in Council issued by the Privy Council (which are in fact made by ministers) (Statutory Instruments Act 1946). Statutory instruments must be formally published, and, in accordance with the rule of law, it is a defence in criminal proceedings to show that an instrument has not been published and that it is not reasonable to expect the accused to be aware of it (s 4). However, it seems that failure to publish does not affect validity for other purposes (see *R v Sheer Metalcraft* [1954] 1 All ER 542).

Delegated legislation has often been criticised as an infringement of the separation of powers. It can be made without most of the public and democratic processes represented, albeit imperfectly, by Parliament. However, it is difficult to imagine a complex and highly regulated society that could function effectively if all laws had to be made by Parliament itself (see *Report of the Committee on Ministers' Powers* (Cmd 4060, 1932)). It also enables government to act swiftly, a plausible justification for the volume of secondary legislation which conferred far-reaching powers to respond to the COVID-19 pandemic. Most delegated legislation is subject to a limited amount of parliamentary scrutiny by means of being laid before the House, although this is usually nominal. There are also committees that scrutinise statutory instruments (Section 13.5.5).

Unlike a statute, the validity of delegated legislation, even if it has been approved by Parliament, can be challenged in the courts in the same manner as can most executive action.

Delegated legislation must be distinguished from what is often called 'quasi-legislation'. This comprises rules, standards, policies, guidance or advice issued, for example, in circulars by the government without statutory authority to make rules. Quasi-legislation is not strictly binding but must be taken into account and is in practice normally followed.

There is an important separation between Parliament and the executive in that the executive can make and ratify treaties binding in international law, but a treaty cannot alter rights and duties in domestic law unless confirmed by statute (Section 9.5). However, in certain areas, under the royal prerogative, the executive can make Orders in Council which have the force of law (Section 14.6).

7.5.2   Parliament and the judiciary

Our common law system means that the judges are also lawmakers and their function is not confined to interpreting laws made by others. Thus, whenever a court creates a precedent or gives a ruling on the meaning of legislation, it is making law, albeit in the latter case in conjunction with Parliament.

There are certain checks and balances, although these depend on the judges restraining themselves. One such check is the judges' duty to follow precedent so as to limit the possibility of making up new law according to a judge's personal preferences. Another is that the judges must make their law only in the context of the particular case before them and must avoid changing the law in matters of large social significance. For example, in *R (Nicklinson) v Ministry of Justice* [2014] UKSC 38 (see Section 5.4.1), the Supreme Court refused to intervene in the controversial area of assisted suicide. The constitutional reason for this was that a radical change in a socially and morally controversial area that raised many risks was not appropriate for a court to decide.

Another limit is the principle that a court must give way to Parliament. In *WH Smith Do It All Ltd v Peterborough City Council* [1991] 4 All ER 193, 196, Mustill LJ remarked that 'according to the doctrine of the separation of powers as understood in the UK, the legislative acts of the Queen in Parliament are impregnable'.

As a matter of cooperation and respect, Parliament and the courts generally avoid interfering with each other. A court cannot usually investigate parliamentary proceedings or challenge statements made in Parliament. In *Pickin v British Railways Board* [1974] AC 765, 799, Lord Simon of Glaisdale said:

> It is well known that in the past there have been dangerous strains between the law courts and Parliament – dangerous because each institution has its own particular part to play in our constitution, and because collision between the two institutions is likely to impair their power to vouchsafe those constitutional rights for which citizens depend on them. So for many years Parliament and the courts have each been astute to respect the sphere of action and the privileges of the other.

In relation to its own composition and internal affairs, the House of Commons has exclusive power to decide disputes and punish offenders (Section 11.6.2).

7.5.3   The executive and the judiciary

Although judges are, in theory, Crown servants, from the seventeenth century it was established that the king cannot act as a judge himself (see *Prohibitions del Roy* (1607) 12 Co Rep 64, Section 4.5). There is now a strong separation of powers between the courts and the other branches which has been often endorsed by the judges. As Lord Steyn put it in *R (Anderson) v Secretary of State* [2002] 4 All ER 1089, at [39]: '[o]ur constitution has never embraced a rigid doctrine of separation of powers. The relationship between the legislature and executive is close. On the other hand, the separation of powers between the judiciary and the legislative and executive branches of government is a strong principle of our system of government'.

In the same case, Lord Bingham emphasised that '[t]he European Court was right to describe the complete functional separation of the judiciary from the executive as "fundamental" since the rule of law depends on it' (at [27]) (see also *Duport Steels v Sirs* [1980] 1 All ER 529; *R v HM Treasury, ex p Smedley* [1985] QB 657; *R (HS2 Action Alliance) v Secretary of State* [2014] 1 WLR 324 at [110], [202]).

M v Home Office [1993] 3 All ER 537 concerned whether the court could treat the Home Secretary, a minister of the Crown, as being in contempt of court for disobeying a court order. The court rejected the argument that because the courts and ministers were both historically part of the Crown, the Crown would in effect be in contempt of itself. At first instance, Simon Brown J ([1992] 4 All ER 97 at 107), citing Montesquieu, pointed out that at least since the seventeenth century the courts had been recognised as an institution separate from the Crown itself and that the Queen had only a symbolic relationship with the three branches of government. Moreover, a minister exercising powers conferred on him by law was not to be treated as part of the Crown since to do so, as Lord Templeman remarked (at 541), would undo the consequences of the Civil War. Similarly in *R (Bancoult) v Secretary of State for the Foreign and Commonwealth Office* [2008] 4 All ER 1055, the House of Lords held that it had jurisdiction to review a Prerogative Order in Council since such an order was in reality made by ministers, not the Crown itself.

The question of what is a judicial function attracting the distinctive features of the judicial process has caused difficulty, notably in connection with the law of contempt of court and, until it was circumvented in the 1960s, in connection with the common law right to a fair hearing (Section 18.3). If, as Montesquieu thought, a judicial function is essentially the resolution of a dispute based on the finding of facts and the application of the existing law to those facts, there is no clear distinction between the judicial and the executive. Both may involve a policy choice as to what is the best thing to do, and many executive decisions include a judicial component as to the correct application of a law. For example, a local authority decision to grant permission for a nightclub to operate in a residential area may well involve a dispute between the owner and local residents as to whether the club is causing a nuisance. Ministers are often required to decide appeals against government decisions, even those in which their own department has an interest. Such decisions have a judicial element but may also raise political considerations that take them into the executive sphere. Decisions of this kind are sometimes called 'quasi-judicial' and raise concerns as to the extent to which the minister must be as impartial as if he or she were a judge (Section 18.4). Many judicial functions are exercised by special tribunals. These were once called 'administrative tribunals' and were regarded with suspicion as creatures of the executive. Today they are largely incorporated into the judicial system (Section 20.1).

Indeed, whether a matter is 'executive' or 'judicial' may depend not on any of its innate qualities, but upon the mechanism chosen to deal with it. For example, imposing a penalty by a court is a judicial function, but arguably an 'administrative penalty' such as a parking ticket imposed by a local official is not. Unlike a court, a minister or a traffic warden can seek out people to investigate and penalise.

What the separation of powers importantly requires is that each body should have the last word in relation to its particular function. Thus, by judicial review, the courts can review executive action and have the last word as to what a law means.

The separation of powers influences judicial review. For example, until recently the separation of powers was violated in that the Home Secretary played a prominent role in the sentencing process. The Home Secretary could decide the 'tariff' period that must be served in a life sentence before the prisoner became eligible for release on parole. The Home Secretary could also control the sentences of young persons imprisoned indefinitely 'at Her Majesty's pleasure'. In a series of cases, the European Court of Human Rights held that the involvement of the executive in the sentencing process is normally a violation of the right to a fair trial (ECHR, Art 6; see *R (Anderson) v Secretary of State for the Home Dept* [2002]; *V v UK* (2000) 30 EHRR 121). The Home Secretary's power has now largely been removed in favour of a judge or the independent Parole Board (e.g. Criminal Justice and Court Services Act 2000, s 60; Criminal Justice Act 2003, s 269).

However, in *R (Black) v Justice Secretary* [2009] UKHL 1, the House of Lords (Lord Phillips dissenting) upheld the power of the Home Secretary to override the Parole Board in the case of a 'determinate' sentence, meaning a sentence for a fixed period. The reason for distinguishing between determinate and indeterminate sentences is that in the case of a determinate sentence the sentence has already been decided by a judge. Any later intervention by the Home Secretary can therefore be considered not as part of the sentencing process but a matter of prisoner management. However, their Lordships suggested that the involvement of the Home Secretary, although lawful, was an undesirable anomaly.

A similar distinction can be drawn between fixing a sentence and the royal prerogative of mercy, which allows the executive to release a prisoner, for example on compassionate grounds or where new evidence comes to light throwing doubt on the conviction. It is arguable that the politically accountable executive is the most appropriate body to exercise this kind of power. Thus, the executive should periodically review an indefinite sentence, at least in the case of a young person, in order to refer it to the relevant body for possible reduction (*R (Smith) v Secretary of State for the Home Dept* [2006] 1 All ER 407). The prerogative of mercy (Section 14.6.1) remains with the Home Secretary, who can refer the matter to the independent Criminal Appeals Board, which can also directly refer doubtful convictions to the Court of Appeal (Criminal Appeals Act 1995).

The Attorney General has conflicting functions, which are so far unreformed. S/he is a member of the government and of Parliament, and the government's chief legal adviser. S/he plays a part in the judicial process, particularly in relation to decisions to prosecute, and is responsible for bringing legal actions against public bodies on behalf of the public interest (Section 15.6.2). The distinction between the executive advising as to the public interest in relation to a prosecution and bringing pressure to bear is a blurred one (see *R (Corner House Research) v Director General of the Serious Fraud Office* [2008] 4 All ER 927).

It is important for judicial independence that judges have no duty to advise the executive. However, judges are sometimes appointed to carry out investigations or inquiries into allegations against government or significant incidents. This carries the risk of compromising the independence of the judiciary by making it appear to be involved in politics (e.g. the Scott Report into arms sales to Iraq (HC 1995–96, 115) and the Hutton Report into the death of a government adviser in the context of the decision to invade Iraq (HC 2004, 247)). In some countries, such as the US and Australia, the practice of judicial inquiries of this kind is unconstitutional (see Drewry, 'Judicial Inquiries and Public Reassurance' [1996] PL 368). As part of the 'concordance' between judges and Parliament entered into in relation to the constitutional reforms of 2005, a senior judge must be consulted on any proposal to appoint a judge of the rank of circuit judge or above to hold an inquiry under section 10(1) of the Inquiries Act 2005 (Section 7.6.3).

Largely for historical reasons (they were once connected with the royal prerogative and the jurisdiction of the Lord Chancellor), some functions are exercised by courts which might be regarded as executive in that they do not necessarily involve disputes. However, they are usually non-political matters requiring impartiality. They include the supervision of charities (shared with the Charity Commission), aspects of the care of children, the winding up of companies and the administration of the estates of deceased persons.

Finally, magistrates' clerks are members of the civil service and as such part of the executive (Courts Act 2003). However, they have certain judicial functions and also advise magistrates on the law, participating in their private deliberations. The Courts Act 2003 makes some concession to their independence by providing that when exercising judicial functions, they are not subject to directions from the Lord Chancellor or any other person (s 29). The activities of magistrates' clerks do not violate judicial independence provided the clerk advises only on matters of law and procedure and not the actual decision, and any matters that the parties might wish to comment upon are raised in open court (*Clark (Procurator Fiscal Kirkcaldy) v Kelly* [2003] 1 All ER 1106). It is difficult to see how these protections are safeguarded given that the deliberations are in private. In *Kelly* the Privy Council relied on the 'well understood conventions' and the clerk's professional code as safeguards.

7.6 Separation of personnel

In view of the risk of bias or conflict of interest, the same individuals should not be members of more than one of the three branches, or exercise more than one function. This principle has traditionally been applied pragmatically against a background in which all branches of government are usually selected from overlapping networks of personal associates.

We have already seen that the UK Constitution does not comply with this, most importantly by its requirement that ministers must also sit in Parliament. In theory, this strengthens executive accountability to Parliament. In practice, due to the subservience of MPs, it enables the executive to dominate Parliament.

7.6.1 Parliament and the executive

The overlap between Parliament and the executive is at the heart of the 'political constitution'. All ministers must also be members of Parliament, and executive business has priority in parliamentary procedure. This strengthens the accountability of ministers while ensuring that government business can be achieved without the gridlock that a strict separation between Parliament and the executive could produce. In the nineteenth century, Bagehot (*The English Constitution* (Chapman & Hall 1867) 15) described the Cabinet as 'a hyphen which joins, a buckle which fastens the legislative part of the state to the executive part of the state. In its origin it belongs to the one, in its functions it belongs to the other'. However, the balance between the two elements is fragile, and it is widely believed that the pressures of the modern party system have tipped it in favour of the executive (Section 5.10). There is a clear conflict in that, as a parliamentarian, a minister should be concerned to maximise scrutiny of a government department, whereas, as a minister, he or she is concerned to defend the department.

There is some separation of personnel between Parliament and the executive. Not more than 95 ministers can sit and vote in the Commons (House of Commons (Disqualification) Act 1975, s 2(1)), thus preventing the government from packing the Commons with supporters. Other ministers can be members of the House of Lords without apparent limit. However, there are limits on the number of ministers who can be paid (Ministerial and Other Salaries Acts 1975, 1997). Nevertheless, there seems to be no shortage of MPs willing to be unpaid junior ministers, known as parliamentary private secretaries who, under the convention of collective responsibility (Section 15.7.1), must be loyal to the executive.

Certain officials for whom conflicts of role are especially likely (civil servants, police, regulators, members of the armed forces and so on) cannot be members of the Commons (Section 12.4). There are no such disqualifications from membership of the House of Lords.

7.6.2 Parliament and the judiciary

Separation of personnel between Parliament and the judiciary is especially important. This has mainly been upheld in the UK and recently strengthened. In particular, professional judges cannot be members of elected bodies (e.g. House of Commons (Disqualification) Act 1975). A professional judge who holds a peerage cannot sit or vote in the House of Lords (Constitutional Reform Act 2005, s 137).

As we have seen (Section 5.4.1), the Supreme Court was created by the Constitutional Reform Act 2005 in order to remove the anomaly that the highest appellate body was part of Parliament, namely the Appellate Committee of the House of Lords. By making the highest appellate body a separate institution and a proper court it was hoped to reinforce public confidence in the judges both domestically and at the international level.

7.6.3 The executive and the judiciary

Here, the separation of powers is at its strictest. Now that the Lord Chancellor is no longer head of the judiciary, there is no significant overlap of personnel between the executive and the judiciary (although symbolically the monarch is the figure in whose name justice is administered). Such problems as arise concern overlapping functions (above). The Judicial Committee of the Privy Council is formally part of the executive, but its members play no part in executive matters and its judicial functions in domestic law have largely been transferred to other courts (Section 5.7). The tribunal system has been significantly separated from the executive (Section 20.1).

7.6.3.1 The Lord Chancellor

Before the Constitutional Reform Act 2005, the office of Lord Chancellor violated both the separation of functions and of personnel in respect of all three branches. Often described as a walking contradiction of the separation of powers, the holder of this medieval office was the nominal head of the judiciary and was responsible for most judicial appointments. The Lord Chancellor was entitled to sit as judge and did so from time to time. The Lord Chancellor also presided over the House of Lords but, unlike the Speaker of the Commons, had no power to control proceedings since the House regulates itself collectively. More importantly, the Lord Chancellor was the minister who, holding the post of Justice Secretary, was responsible for the administration of the court system. There was therefore a conflict of interest in that, as a member of the government, the Lord Chancellor is bound by collective ministerial responsibility (Section 15.7.1). Like other ministers, the Lord Chancellor is appointed and dismissed by the prime minister and has no security of tenure to stand up to the prime minister.

The 2005 Act which addressed these matters (below) attracted considerable opposition from the legal establishment. It was argued that the overlapping roles of the Lord Chancellor supported rather than infringed the separation of powers by acting as a buffer or lubricant between the three branches. As a member of the House of Lords and therefore unelected, he had a certain independence from party politics. As a spending minister, he could seek to ensure that the courts are properly resourced, and, as a judge, he could defend the judiciary against executive interference. Moreover, it was suggested that the antiquity of the office is evidence of its value and that tradition and continuity should be respected. This kind of argument succeeded, insofar as the historic title and ceremonial trappings of the office have been retained.

The Constitutional Reform Act 2005 removed the Lord Chancellor as Speaker of the House of Lords, which now elects its own Speaker. The Lord Chancellor also ceased to be head of the judiciary, transferring this role to the Lord Chief Justice as President of the Courts of England and Wales (s 7).

The Lord Chancellor has, for most purposes, become an ordinary minister with some limited special functions attached. While the separation of powers is to some extent enhanced, there remain important conflicts. In particular, the Lord Chancellor also holds the nominally separate post of Secretary of State for Justice and as such controls the administrative and financial aspects of the courts and tribunals. The key executive powers to maintain the court system are exercised as Secretary of State for Justice, who is also responsible for prisons and the management of offenders, legal aid and human rights. However, the Courts and Tribunals Service is structured as a semi-independent executive agency with its own chief executive to represent its interests and account to Parliament.

The Lord Chancellor as such has a statutory responsibility to uphold the rule of law, although this carries no specific powers (Section 6.1.1). He or she also has powers in relation to the appointment of judges, albeit these are now more limited than was previously the case (Section 7.7.3.1). The Lord Chancellor is also responsible for judicial discipline, in conjunction with the Lord Chief Justice.

The other responsibilities of the Lord Chancellor are vaguely defined. S/he must ensure that the courts have such resources as s/he 'thinks are appropriate' for them to carry out their business (Constitutional Reform Act 2005, ss 50, 91).

The Lord Chancellor must 'have regard to': (i) the need to defend (judicial) independence; (ii) the need for the judiciary to have the support necessary to enable them to exercise their functions; and (iii) the need for the public interest in regard to matters relating to the judiciary or otherwise to the administration of justice to be properly represented in decisions affecting those matters (Constitutional Reform Act 2006, s 6(3)). Again, as Lord Chancellor, s/he has no specific powers in these respects.

As Secretary of State for Justice, the Lord Chancellor must compete for public money with other departments. This conflict could indirectly threaten both judicial independence and the rule of law: for example, he or she might seek to reduce staffing levels and to restrict legal aid (see e.g. Legal Aid Sentencing and Punishment of Offenders Act 2012).

There are limited safeguards. As noted above (Section 7.4), the Lord Chief Justice, who is head of the judiciary in England and Wales, must be consulted on budgetary matters. The Lord Chief Justice is responsible for the deployment of judges and tribunal judges (Crime and Courts Act 2013, s 20) and shares disciplinary powers with the Lord Chancellor (Section 7.4.1).

The direct access that judges had to Parliament through the Lord Chancellor is replaced by section 5(1) of the Constitutional Reform Act, which empowers the Chief Justice of any part of the UK to lay before Parliament or the relevant devolved assembly written representations on matters relating to the judiciary or the administration of justice that appear to him to be of importance. There are also many provisions which require the Lord Chancellor to consult or obtain the consent of the Lord Chief Justice.

The Lord Chancellor, like all ministers, must be a member of Parliament but need not be a member of the House of Lords. S/he must be 'qualified by experience' as a minister or member of either House of Parliament, or a practising or academic lawyer (Constitutional Reform Act 2005, s 2). Thus, the Lord Chancellor need not have a legal background and can be moved around in ministerial reshuffles or sacked liked any other minister, as happened when Michael Gove was replaced by Elizabeth Truss (the first ever female holder of the office) in July 2016. This is not conducive to judicial independence, as a prime minister can easily replace a Lord Chancellor with one whose perspective on the administration of justice is more favourable to government policy.

7.6.3.2 The Supreme Court

The separation of the Supreme Court from the protection provided to the Law Lords by the independence of Parliament arguably makes the court more vulnerable to executive interference. Gee suggests ([2013] PL 539) that the Office of Chief Executive of the Supreme Court, although held by a civil servant, provides a certain degree of constitutional protection. Under the Constitutional Reform Act 2005, s 48, as amended by the Crime and Courts Act 2013, s 29, the Supreme Court is largely independent from the Ministry of Justice. The Chief Executive is appointed by the President of the Court, is responsible for the non-judicial business of the court and is required to ensure that the resources allocated to the court 'are used to provide an efficient and effective system to support the court in carrying out its business' (s 48(4)). This dovetails with the Lord Chancellor's obligation (Section 7.6.3.1). The Chief Executive submits a bid to the Lord Chancellor for resources (s 50(1)). However, this bid is part of the Department of Justice's overall bid to the Treasury. The Lord Chancellor and the Treasury can therefore interfere with the court's bid for political purposes, should they so choose.

The Chief Executive also has a role in generating the strategy of the court and representing the court in dealing with political bodies including the devolved governments and international bodies.

The court's status as a non-ministerial department gives the Chief Executive an independent voice on behalf of the court. Unlike an ordinary government department, the Chief Executive is directly accountable to Parliament for the performance of his or her functions (Section 15.7). The Chief Executive does not therefore owe a constitutional duty to ministers and, Gee argues, has an independent constitutional role as representing the court. The President of the Court has no formal access to government. By contrast, the Lord Chief Justice, who heads the other courts, has direct access to both ministers and Parliament (Constitutional Reform Act 2005, s 5(1)).

7.7   Checks and balances

This is the most important aspect of the separation of powers. Checks and balances involve each branch having some control to police the limits of the others, but also require each branch to be protected against interference by the others. The checks and balances concept may therefore conflict with other aspects of the separation of powers. In the UK, in keeping with the 'insider' tradition, but violating republican aspirations to equality and citizenship, many checks and balances, such as the various commissions and committees dealing with standards of government, do not have legally enforceable powers to implement their recommendations.

Readers should identify checks and balances throughout the book. The HRA and judicial review are important examples. Some highlights will briefly be discussed here.

7.7.1   Parliament and the executive

The checks and balances between Parliament and the executive lie at the heart of the 'political constitution'. However, they are significantly weakened by the overlapping membership of the executive and House of Commons and the domination by the executive of the procedures of the House.

▶ The legislature is protected against the executive by statute and convention. The legislature can remove the executive, but, as a result of the Fixed Term Parliaments Act 2011, the executive can in principle no longer remove the legislature. The royal prerogative power to dissolve Parliament has been superseded by the Act, thus, what Montesquieu regarded as an essential balance in the constitution no longer exists. For example, a government that struggles against an obstructive Parliament would be unable to call for an election so as to put its case to the people. This indeed proved to be the case on several occasions in 2019; however, the 2011 Act was eventually circumvented by passage of the Early Parliamentary General Election Act 2019, and the subsequent election of a Conservative Government with a significant majority seems likely to result in the Act's repeal, in which case the prerogative power may resurface (Section 11.2).

▶ Parliament votes funds to the executive to enable the government to carry out its tasks.

▶ The executive must resign if it loses the support of the House of Commons. If an alternative government cannot command the support of the Commons, Parliament must be dissolved (Fixed Term Parliaments Act 2011, Section 11.2).

▶ Individual ministers must appear before Parliament and explain the conduct of their departments (Section 15.7).

▶ The House of Lords, the composition of which is not dominated by the executive, could be regarded as a partial check over the executive. However, under the Parliament Acts 1911 and 1949, the House of Lords cannot veto a bill introduced in the Commons, other than a bill to prolong the life of Parliament and certain other minor exceptions. In *Jackson v A-G* [2006] 1 AC 262, the House of Lords disagreed upon, but left open, whether there might be exceptional cases – for example where the executive was attempting to subvert fundamental democratic principles or abolish judicial review – where the Parliament Acts could not be used (Section 11.4).

7.7.2 Parliament and the judiciary

According to traditional doctrine, Parliament has unlimited lawmaking power, and an Act of Parliament cannot be overturned in the courts (but see Section 8.5.6). However, the courts also check Parliament, since they have power to interpret statutes independently. Thus, once a statute is enacted, Parliament loses direct control over it, and it moves into the domain of the courts.

There is therefore an accommodation between the two highest constitutional powers. On the one hand, the intentions of the democratic branch must be respected. On the other, the court is concerned to uphold the rule of law. In *Duport Steels Ltd v Sirs* [1980], Lord Scarman said:

> [T]he constitution's separation of powers, or more accurately functions, must be observed if judicial independence is not to be put at risk…[C]onfidence in the judicial system will be replaced by fear of it becoming uncertain and arbitrary in its application. Society will then be ready for Parliament to cut the power of the judges.

He meant that judges must observe the separation of powers by sticking to the language of legislation, even at the expense of their own views of what justice or policy should require. The orthodox view is that the courts must seek the 'intention of Parliament'. However, given that Parliament is a complex assembly of many hundreds of people, the notion of intention is to some extent a fiction. Parliament is assumed to give words their 'natural' or 'ordinary' meanings and to intend that a statute should be read against the background of basic values associated with rule of law. Furthermore, the intention of Parliament must be found primarily by reading the statute itself, not by giving effect to what the government or anyone else thought it meant (see *Wilson v First County Housing Trust* [2003] 4 All ER 97, at [139]; *R (Q) v Secretary of State for the Home Dept* [2003] 2 All ER 905, at [4], [5]).

The traditional approach is that the courts should not look at what was said in Parliament as an aid to statutory interpretation. The intention of Parliament is assumed to be identified by the objective language of the statute. This is not only to protect judicial and parliamentary independence (Section 11.6) but also because the rule of law implies that a statute should be read as understood by a member of the public (see Lord Hoffmann in *Robinson v Secretary of State for Northern Ireland* [2002] UKHL 32, at [40]). However, the courts take account of the purpose behind the statute in order to help them interpret it. To this end, they can consider background material such as official reports and White Papers. In the past, the courts have not, however, been able to consider *Hansard*, the official record of parliamentary debates. This supports the separation of the two branches. In this context, *Pepper v Hart* [1993] AC 593 presents problems. The House of Lords held that, where the language of an Act is ambiguous, the court can look in *Hansard* to discover what the promoters of the Act (usually ministers) intended. Thus, if applied liberally, *Pepper v Hart* could threaten the separation of powers and the rule of law by putting the executive in a privileged position. A statute is the collective enterprise of Parliament, over which the executive should not have special control.

The problem with *Pepper* is whether, as Lord Nicholls suggested in *Wilson v First County Trust* [2003], at [56]–[60], it does no more than remove an anomaly by permitting the court to use *Hansard* in the same way as it uses other sources, namely as an aid to the context. For example, in *Culnane v Morris* [2006] 2 All ER 149, the court was aided by the parliamentary debates in concluding that section 10 of the Defamation Act 1952 was not aimed at altering the general law (see also *Beckett v Midlands Electricity plc* [2001] 1 WLR 281, at [30], [34], [38]). If *Pepper* were to do more than this it would privilege the executive's view of what a statute means or, conversely, invite the argument that the minister should be bound by what he said in Parliament. Both would be constitutionally damaging. Thus, in *Jackson v A-G* [2006], at [97], Lord Steyn suggested that trying to discover the intentions of government from ministerial statements made in Parliament is constitutionally objectionable. And the cases since *Pepper* have taken a cautious approach, emphasising that it is for the courts to decide what a statute means and that the statements of ministers cannot control the meaning. It seems now that this limited approach is correct. In giving evidence to the Joint Committee on Parliamentary Privilege (HL 30/HC 100 2013–14, at [120]), the Lord Chief Justice said: 'We envisage that you look at *Pepper v Hart* to see the purpose of legislation that is opaque. Other than that, it does not apply, and you should not be referring to it. If you do it is a mistake' (see also *R (Public and Commercial Services Union) v Minister for the Civil Service* [2010] EWHC 1027 (Admin), at [42], [53]–[55]; *R v Secretary of State for Environment, Transport and the Regions, ex p Spath Holme* [2000] 1 All ER 884 at [211]; *Wilson v First County Trust* [2003] at [58], [59], [139], [140]; *Jackson v A-G* [2006] at [40], [98], [172]).

7.7.3   The executive and the judiciary

The Secretary of State for Justice is responsible for the administration of the court and tribunal system. The same person, as Lord Chancellor, also has important functions in relation to the appointment and discipline of judges. This requires checks and balances to meet the competing concerns of judicial independence and public accountability.

7.7.3.1 Judicial appointments

The judicial appointments system for England and Wales lacks the public accessibility for which a matter of such constitutional importance calls (see O'Brian [2014] PL 179). The executive, in the form of the Lord Chancellor, has an input into judicial appointments on the basis that a democratically accountable element is desirable. A stronger democratic input, such as the hearings by the US Congress, would create a risk that judicial appointments and behaviour would be politically partisan. On the other hand, since judges make decisions with political consequences and have considerable scope to be influenced by political preferences, it is arguable that their political views should be brought more clearly into the open.

The present regime was created by the Constitutional Reform Act 2005. The Act replaced a much-criticised informal regime which was in the hands of the Lord Chancellor and, in the case of appointments to the House of Lords, the prime minister. Its basic principle is that appointments are made on the recommendation of the Lord Chancellor who must recommend a person selected by the Judicial Appointments Commission or, in some cases, a special panel (see below). However, as another example of unsystematic constitutional change, the Crime and Courts Act 2013, s 20, Sched. 13 modifies this by transferring the Lord Chancellor's powers in the case of judges below High Court level, to the Lord Chief Justice, the head of the judiciary. The 2013 Act arguably tips the balance too far in favour of internal influence within the judiciary and away from accountability to Parliament (see generally O'Brian (above)). The Lord Chancellor retains overall responsibility for the appointment system with the power to make regulations (i.e. secondary legislation).

The centrepiece of the process is an independent Judicial Appointments Commission (JAC), which in substance makes most judicial appointments. A special Commission applies to appointments to the Supreme Court. These provisions are designed to limit the risk of political bias and to make it difficult for any interest group to dominate the appointment process.

All appointments must be 'on merit'. However, given the vagueness of the appointment criteria and the fact that the government system in the UK is pervaded by informal personal networks, it is doubtful whether it is possible to ensure that the appointment process is fully independent. The notion of 'merit' may invite those making appointments to appoint people similar to themselves.

Appointments to the Supreme Court (Constitutional Reform Act 2005, ss 25–31, Sched. 8) are made formally by the Queen (s 14) on the recommendation of the prime minister, who is required to recommend a person nominated by the Lord Chancellor, who in turn must nominate a person selected by the special Commission. The prime minister is therefore only a post box. The Selection Commission for the Supreme Court is appointed by the Lord Chancellor. It must comprise an odd number of not less than five. These must include at least one serving judge of the Supreme Court, at least one member of the Judicial Appointments bodies from each of England and Wales, Scotland and Northern Ireland, and at least one lay person. The Commission must consult the senior judges, the Lord Chancellor and the leaders of the devolved governments.

Appointments to the Court of Appeal (ss 76–84), to the High Court (ss 89–94) and of the Lord Chief Justice and other senior office holders (ss 67–75) are made by the Queen on the recommendation of the Lord Chancellor, who must recommend a person selected by the Judicial Appointments Commission. In the case of the Lord Chief Justice, the Heads of the Divisions of the courts and their deputies and Court of Appeal judges (Lords Justices of Appeal), there is a special Selection Panel of the JAC.

Judicial appointments below the High Court are made by the Queen, previously on the recommendation of the Lord Chancellor, but, under the 2013 Act, the latter is replaced by the Lord Chief Justice (head of the judiciary) thereby strengthening the separation of powers. Some deputy and temporary posts are to be appointed directly by the Lord Chief Justice with the agreement of the Lord Chancellor. Tribunal judges are appointed by the Senior President of Tribunals (Section 20.1.2). In all cases, a person selected by the JAC must be recommended. Fixed-term posts are renewable only by the Lord Chancellor.

There are arrangements to ensure the independence of the JAC. It is appointed by the Queen on the recommendation of the Lord Chancellor. It must comprise a lay chair plus members comprising judges, practising lawyers and lay members as specified by regulations made by the Lord Chancellor with the agreement of the Lord Chief Justice (currently 15). Lay members must outnumber judges and must include 'as far as practicable at least one person who appears to have special knowledge of Wales' (Constitutional Reform Act 2005, Sched. 12, para 6B). Civil servants are excluded from membership. Commissioners hold office for a fixed term that is renewable but cannot be longer than ten years in total. They can be removed on the recommendation of the Lord Chancellor on the grounds of criminal conviction, bankruptcy, failure to perform duties, unfitness or inability.

Lay magistrates are appointed by the Queen on the recommendation of the Lord Chief Justice who may seek advice from the Judicial Appointments Commission and must consult locally (Courts Act 2003, s 10; Crime and Courts Act 2013 Sched. 13, part 4). Consultation is usually through a local advisory committee. Although magistrates deal with relatively minor matters they account for the majority of criminal cases.

In all cases, the Lord Chancellor (or the Lord Chief Justice in the case of lower courts) has only limited power to override a selection made by the Commissions or panel (Constitutional Reform Act 2005, ss 29–31, 73–75, 82–84, 90–92). First, the Commission or panel must submit one name to the Lord Chancellor, who cannot put forward any other name. There are then three stages. At each stage, the Lord Chancellor's options are progressively reduced.

At Stage 1, the Lord Chancellor can accept, reject or require reconsideration. The Lord Chancellor can reject a selection only on the ground that the candidate is not 'suitable' and can require reconsideration only on the ground of inadequate evidence of suitability or evidence of unsuitability. He must give reasons. In the case of the Supreme Court, a reconsideration can also be required if the judges between them would not have knowledge or experience in practice of the law of each part of the UK.

At Stage 2: (i) following a *rejection* at Stage 1, the Lord Chancellor can either accept the selection or require reconsideration; *or* (ii) following a *reconsideration* requirement at Stage 1, the same or another name might then be selected. The Lord Chancellor can either accept this selection or reject it. Thus, the same person cannot be sent back twice for reconsideration and a new candidate does not get a chance of reconsideration.

At Stage 3, which is the outcome of a reconsideration requirement at Stage 2, the Lord Chancellor must either accept the selection or he can accept a person who at an earlier stage he required to be reconsidered but who was not resubmitted, thus allowing him second thoughts.

The Lord Chancellor's veto is exercised very infrequently.

There is a Judicial Appointments and Conduct Ombudsman, who can investigate complaints in individual cases against the Lord Chancellor, the Lord Chief Justice or the Commission by a person not selected and a person selected. The complaint must be of maladministration in the appointments process and cannot concern the merits of the appointment. The complaint must first be made to the Lord Chancellor, the Lord Chief Justice or the Commission (Constitutional Reform Act 2005, ss 99–105). The Ombudsman reports to the Lord Chancellor and the Lord Chief Justice. The report is not published and must not include names.

An aggrieved applicant can also seek judicial review of a decision purporting to be made under the appointment process.

The JAC is accountable for its general policies to Parliament through its annual report and appearances before parliamentary committees. The Lord Chancellor is accountable to Parliament under the normal principles of ministerial responsibility. However, the Lord Chief Justice and the President of Tribunals do not seem to be directly accountable.

7.7.3.2 Security of tenure: dismissal of judges

Senior judges – that is, judges of the High Court and above – have security of tenure designed to protect their independence. As a result of the 1688 revolution, they hold office during 'good behaviour' (Act of Settlement 1700, provisions now repealed). In itself, this is hardly conducive to independence since what matters is who decides whether they have misbehaved. Today, they can be dismissed by the Crown following a resolution of both Houses of Parliament (an important constitutional check in the hands of the House of Lords) and probably then only for misbehaviour (Senior Courts Act 1981, s 11(3)). An alternative interpretation of these provisions less sympathetic to the separation of powers is that the Crown (i.e. the prime minister) can dismiss a judge for misbehaviour without an address from Parliament, but on an address, a judge can be dismissed irrespective of misbehaviour. Section 33 of the Constitutional Reform Act 2005 preserves the ambiguity in respect of the Supreme Court. No judge has been subjected to these provisions since the nineteenth century, when a judge was dismissed for embezzling court funds.

In the case of judges of Northern Ireland and Scotland, there are additional safeguards (Constitutional Reform Act 2005, ss 133, 135; Scotland Act 1998, s 95).

In exceptional circumstances, a judge can be removed by the Lord Chancellor on medical grounds (Senior Courts Act 1981, s 11(8)). The Lord Chancellor can also suspend a judge pending an address or on grounds of criminality (s 108). Senior judges must retire at 70 (Judicial Pensions and Retirement Act 1993).

Other judges have limited security of tenure. Most powers of dismissal are exercised by the Lord Chancellor with the concurrence of the Lord Chief Justice on the grounds of inability or misbehaviour (e.g. Courts Act 1971, ss 17, 24; County Courts Act 1984, s 11; Courts Act 2003, s 22). Lay magistrates can also be removed for persistent failure to meet standards of competence prescribed by the Lord Chancellor and declining or neglecting their duties (Courts Act 2003, s 11).

Some junior judges, particularly tribunal judges (Section 20.1), are appointed either as temporary judges or for fixed terms which can be renewed and may be subject to special terms of appointment. This creates a risk to their independence of their being overanxious to please and might therefore engage the right to a fair trial under the ECHR (Section 7.4). In such cases, extension can be refused only on the ground of inability or misbehaviour or on a ground specified in the terms of appointment (e.g. Crime and Courts Act 2013, Sched. 13, para 35).

Most judicial salaries can be reduced only by Parliament (Judges' Remuneration Act 1965; Constitutional Reform Act 2005, s 14). However, the Lord Chancellor can increase salaries (Senior Courts Act 1981, s 12; Constitutional Reform Act 2005, s 34).

7.7.3.3 Judicial review

The courts provide a check over the executive by means of judicial review in the Administrative Court, where they try to draw a line between the *legality* of government action, which they are entitled to police, and the *merits* of government action, meaning whether a government decision is good or bad, which is a matter for Parliament and the electorate. However, the limits of judicial review are vaguely defined. In some cases, the courts will refuse to intervene or intervene only selectively; in others, they are much more intrusive. How this balance is struck is a politically controversial question (Section 19.7.1).

In *R v Secretary of State, ex p Fire Brigades Union* [1995] 2 All ER 244, 267, Lord Mustill said:

> It is a feature of the peculiarly British conception of the separation of powers that Parliament, the executive and the courts each have their distinct and largely exclusive domain. Parliament has a legally unchallengeable right to make whatever laws it thinks right. The executive carries on the administration of the country in accordance with the powers conferred on it by law. The courts interpret the laws and see that they are obeyed. This requires the courts to step into the territory which belongs to the executive, not only to verify that the powers asserted accord with the substantive law created by Parliament, but also that the manner in which they are exercised conforms with the standards of fairness which Parliament must have intended. Concurrently with this judicial function Parliament has its own special means of ensuring that the executive in the exercise of delegated functions, performs in a way that Parliament finds appropriate. Ideally it is these latter methods that should be used to check executive errors and excesses; for it is the task of Parliament and the executive in tandem, not of the courts, to govern the country. In recent years, however, the employment in practice of these specifically parliamentary remedies has on occasion been perceived as falling short and sometimes well short of what was needed to bring the performance of the executive in line with the law and with the minimum standards of fairness implicit in every parliamentary delegation of a decision-making function. To avoid a vacuum in which the citizen would be left without protection against a misuse of executive powers the courts have had no option but to occupy the dead ground in a manner and in areas of public life, which could not have been foreseen 30 years ago.

In this case, Lord Mustill was in a dissenting minority that refused to intervene in a decision of the Home Secretary not to make an order bringing into force a new Act dealing with criminal injuries compensation, but to introduce another, less generous scheme under royal prerogative powers. He considered that this was a matter for Parliament itself. The majority, however, considered that the matter was appropriate for the court as a check on executive discretion. They held that, although they could not require the Home Secretary to bring the Act into force, they could quash the prerogative scheme and ensure that he kept the matter under review. Thus different aspects of the separation of powers may conflict.

Summary

▶ The doctrine of the separation of powers means that government power should be divided into legislative, executive and judicial functions, each with its own distinctive personnel and processes, and that each branch of government should be checked so that no one can dominate the others.

▶ In Montesquieu's version, the separation of powers is complemented by the idea of the mixed constitution in which different class interests check and balance each other, particularly in the legislature. There is a vestige of the mixed constitution in the institutions of monarchy and the House of Lords. The idea of the mixed constitution shorn of its historical association with a hereditary aristocracy might still be valuable as providing a check over crude majoritarian democracy, linking with the idea of deliberative democracy.

▶ The question of judicial independence can be regarded as an aspect of the separation of powers but could be considered an issue in its own right, irrespective of other aspects of the doctrine. Judicial independence is safeguarded by the right to a fair trial and public trial under the ECHR. This applies more stringently to ordinary courts than to administrative bodies. There is a tension between judicial independence and ensuring that judges are accountable. Accountability methods include publicity, rights of appeal and review and internal disciplinary processes.

▶ The separation of powers comprises separation of function, institutions and personnel and includes the notion of checks and balances. The particular blend in any given case depends on the preoccupations of the particular country. There is disagreement among writers as to whether the separation of powers is a valuable idea or in what sense it applies in the UK. Separation of powers ideas have influenced our constitutional arrangements but in a pragmatic and unsystematic way.

▶ In the UK there is no strict separation of personnel, particularly between the legislature and the executive. Concern about executive dominance is the main driving force. However, there are many separation of powers mechanisms in the UK Constitution, particularly in relation to the judiciary and to membership of the House of Commons.

▶ The Constitutional Reform Act 2005 attempted to strengthen the separation of powers by creating a Supreme Court to replace the Appellate Committee of the House of Lords, injecting an independent element, the Judicial Appointments Commission, into judicial appointments and removing the Lord Chancellor's roles as head of the judiciary and Speaker of the House of Lords. It could be that aspects of these reforms, particularly in relation to the Lord Chancellor, strengthen institutional separation but weaken checks and balances.

▶ The power of the courts to review government action creates a tension between functional separation of powers and checks and balances.

▶ There are concerns about the relationship between the courts and Parliament, in particular in the context of the use of parliamentary proceedings in the interpretation of statutes.

Exercises

7.1 'The separation of powers is a misleading and irrelevant doctrine'. Discuss.

7.2 'In the government of this commonwealth, the legislative department shall never exercise the executive and judicial powers, or either of them: the executive shall never exercise the legislative and judicial powers, or either of them: the judicial shall never exercise the legislative and executive powers, or either of them: to the end it may be a government of laws and not of men' (Massachusetts Constitution 1780, Art XXX).

Does the UK Constitution live up to this?

7.3 'The intermingling of the executive and the legislature in the UK Constitution makes the doctrine of the separation of powers futile'. Discuss.

7.4 To what extent can the executive interfere with the courts?

7.5 'In some quarters the *Pepper v Hart* principle is currently under something of a judicial cloud…In part this seems… to be due to continued misunderstanding of the limited role ministerial statements have in this field' (Lord Nicholls in *Jackson v A-G* (2006), at [65]). Explain and critically discuss.

7.6 'The replacement of the Appellate Committee of the House of Lords put[s] the relationship between the executive, the legislature and the judiciary on a modern footing, which takes account of people's expectations about the independence and transparency of the judicial system' (Department of Constitutional Affairs (2003)).

Discuss in the light of the Constitutional Reform Act 2005.

7.7 'The office of Lord Chancellor is merely a token embellishment of the Ministry of Justice and serves no useful purpose'.

Discuss.

7.8 The government is experiencing a financial crisis. In order to save money, the prime minister proposes to the Lord Chancellor that no new appointments should be made to the staff of the Supreme Court for five years and that the court should refuse leave to appeal in at least 20 per cent of cases. Advise the Lord Chancellor.

7.9 Julian, a senior judge, is alleged to have been sexually harassing the junior staff of the High Court Registry. Parliament is not sitting, and the Lord Chancellor advises the Queen to make an example of Julian by dismissing him forthwith. Advise Julian. What would be the position if he was (i) a circuit judge or (ii) a lay justice?

7.10 (See also Sections 5.4.1 and 5.4.3.) There is a vacancy on the Supreme Court. A Selection Commission is convened. The Commission selects Sally, a barrister and university teacher who has worked for the last 15 years as a legal adviser to an organisation which campaigns on behalf of asylum-seekers. The Lord Chancellor sends Sally's selection for reconsideration on the ground that there is insufficient evidence that she is suitable. The Commission resubmits Sally's application to the Lord Chancellor, who sends it back again for reconsideration. The Commission now selects Clive, an eminent practising commercial solicitor who often advises the government and the Lord Chancellor's party on financial matters. Ten years ago, Clive entered into an agreement with the tax authorities to pay £100,000 income tax arrears in return for not being prosecuted. The Lord Chancellor accepts Clive's selection. Advise Sally, who heard that a colleague had informed the Lord Chancellor in private that she was 'a troublemaker' and who wishes to prevent the Lord Chancellor's recommendation going to the Queen.

Further reading

Barber, 'Prelude to the Separation of Powers' (2001) 60 CLJ 59

Barendt, 'Separation of Powers and Constitutional Government' [1995] PL 599

Bradley, 'Relations Between Executive, Judiciary and Parliament: An Evolving Saga' [2008] PL 470

Clarke, *The Limits of Judicial Independence* (Cambridge University Press 2011)

Claus, 'Montesquieu's Mistakes and the True Meaning of Separation' (2005) 25 OJLS 419

Ekins, 'The Intention of Parliament' [2010] PL 709

Gee, 'What Are Lord Chancellors for?' [2014] PL 11

Gee, Hazell, Malleson and O'Brien, *The Politics of Judicial Independence in Britain's Changing Constitution* (Cambridge University Press 2015)

Hazell, 'Judicial Independence and Accountability in the UK Have Both Emerged Stronger as a Result of the Constitutional Reform Act 2005' [2015] PL 198

Holdsworth, *A History of English Law*, vol X, ch VII (Methuen 1938)

Kavanagh, '*Pepper v Hart* and Matters of Constitutional Principle' (2005) 121 LQR 98

Keene, 'The Independence of the Judge' in Andenas and Fairgrieve (eds), *Tom Bingham and the Transformation of the Law* (Oxford University Press 2009)

Loughlin, *Foundations of Public Law* (Oxford University Press 2010) ch 15

McHarg, 'What Is Delegated Legislation?' [2006] PL 539

Masterman, *The Separation of Powers in the Contemporary Constitution: Judicial Competence and Independence in the United Kingdom* (Cambridge University Press 2011)

Further reading cont'd

Masterman and Wheatle, 'Unpacking Separation of Powers: Judicial Independence, Sovereignty and Conceptual Flexibility in the UK Constitution [2017] PL 469

Munro, *Studies in Constitutional Law* (2nd edn, Butterworths 1999) ch 9

Sedley, 'The Long Sleep' in Andenas and Fairgrieve (eds), *Tom Bingham and the Transformation of the Law* (Oxford University Press 2009)

Steyn, 'The Weakest and Least Dangerous Department of Government' [1997] PL 84

Steyn, '*Pepper v Hart:* A Re-examination' (2001) 21 OJLS 59

Syrett, *The Foundations of Public Law* (2nd edn, Palgrave Macmillan 2014) ch 2A

Vogenauer, 'A Retreat from *Pepper v Hart?* A Reply to Lord Steyn' (2005) 25 OJLS 629 (see also Sales, 'A Footnote to Professor Vogenauer's Reply to Lord Steyn' (2006) 26 OJLS 585)

Young, 'The Relationship Between Parliament, the Executive and the Judiciary' in Jowell and O'Cinneide (eds), *The Changing Constitution* (9th edn, Oxford University Press 2019)

Introduction

The doctrine of parliamentary sovereignty entails that Parliament has unlimited legal power to enact any law, and also that it cannot be overridden by another body. In *Jackson v A-G* [2006] 1 AC 262 at [9], Lord Bingham described the doctrine as the bedrock of the British Constitution. The classical doctrine of parliamentary sovereignty was most famously stated by Dicey ((1915) 3–4):

> Parliament means, in the mouth of a lawyer, ... the [Queen], the House of Lords and the House of Commons; these three bodies acting together may be aptly described as the '[Queen] in Parliament', and constitute Parliament. The principle of parliamentary sovereignty means neither more nor less than this, namely, that Parliament thus defined has, under the English constitution, the right to make or unmake any law whatever and further that no person or body is recognised by the law of England as having the right to override or set aside the legislation of Parliament.

It is easy to see that, from a political angle, this principle does not fit reality. Nobody could seriously believe that Parliament can make any law it wishes, and we know that the Queen has no political lawmaking power. What is the point, therefore, of the Queen being part of Parliament? We also know that most laws are, in practice, produced by the executive and that Parliament has insufficient time and expertise to do more than rubberstamp most of them.

Parliamentary sovereignty is therefore a legal, as opposed to a political, principle, meaning that a law made by Parliament in the above sense must conclusively be accepted as valid and obeyed by the courts (*Pickin v British Railways Board* [1974] AC 765). But valid laws might be condemned as unconstitutional in a broader political sense. Indeed, judges recognise that, at the highest level of the constitution, law and politics are inseparable. For example, in *R (Bancoult) v Secretary of State for the Foreign and Commonwealth Office* [2008] 4 All ER 1055 at [35], Lord Hoffmann identified parliamentary sovereignty with 'the unique authority Parliament derives from its representative character'. On the other hand, in *Jackson v A-G* [2006] at [120], Lord Hope said that '[p]arliamentary sovereignty is an empty principle if legislation is passed which is so absurd or so unacceptable that the population refuses to recognise it as law' (see also [126]–[128]). Thus, we might be concerned if the law is out of step with political reality.

Dicey himself distinguished legal sovereignty from political sovereignty. He described legal sovereignty as 'the power of lawmaking unrestricted by any legal limit' and contrasted this with political sovereignty, meaning the body 'the will of which is ultimately obeyed by the citizens of the state' ((1915) 27). By this Dicey meant the electorate, although a more cynical view today might wish to point to the financial and professional networks with privileged access to politicians (Section 5.9).

Dicey referred to both 'internal' and 'external' political limits on the lawmaker. Internal limits are those inherent in the rules and practices of Parliament. Within Parliament, a combination of the convention that requires the Queen to assent to all legislation and the law that subordinates the House of Lords to the House of Commons makes the House of Commons the supreme political body. The political and moral pressures imposed by constitutional conventions, patronage, and party discipline are also internal limits.

The external limits consist of what those subject to the law are prepared to accept. Parliament cannot, in practice, pass any law it wishes, and Dicey thought that pressure from the electorate would make democracy 'self-correcting' (see Craig, *Public Law and Democracy in the UK and the USA* (Oxford University Press 1991) ch 2). However, later in life, particularly after the powers of the House of Lords were curbed in 1911, Dicey came to realise that the executive was increasingly dominating Parliament ((1915) 'Introduction').

Dicey's version of the doctrine of parliamentary sovereignty is increasingly being questioned. Challenges to parliamentary sovereignty include external legal requirements, notably those of the EU (indeed, a major argument of the 'Leave' campaign during the Brexit referendum was that withdrawal from the EU would restore sovereignty), and claims that the courts under the common law are the ultimate guardians of the constitution (Section 8.5.6).

8.2 The basis of parliamentary sovereignty

Since we have no written constitution, the basis of parliamentary sovereignty is unclear. The matter is important in that it underlies contemporary questions about whether parliamentary supremacy can be changed. There is no logical reason, although it may be practically desirable, why there should be a single legal sovereign with unlimited powers. Indeed, Dicey himself denied that there was a logical need for an ultimate sovereign ((1915) 27), merely pointing out that evidence suggested that we have, in fact, adopted the doctrine of parliamentary sovereignty.

The most widely accepted explanation of parliamentary sovereignty is that it is no more than a belief (sometimes labelled as a 'hypothesis' or a 'rule of recognition') shared by the governing elite (or, at least, enough of them to make it effective) which has stood the test of time. It was generated by the 1688 revolution when Parliament implicitly claimed to be sovereign, a claim which has not been seriously contested. On this view, parliamentary supremacy 'is a political fact for which no purely legal authority can be constituted' (Lord Hope in *Jackson v A-G* [2006] at [120]). The doctrine would therefore change if the underlying political belief were to change. However, short of another revolution, it is not clear how we would know whether this had happened. The most plausible view is that Parliament, which originally claimed to be supreme, could itself withdraw that claim. Thus, in the *Factortame* case (Section 8.5.4), at 659, Lord Bridge took the view that parliamentary sovereignty can be altered by Parliament itself. If this is so then the doctrine is no more than a provisional working arrangement, albeit a very long-standing and fundamental one.

A rival explanation of parliamentary supremacy favoured by some lawyers and judges is 'common law constitutionalism'. This claims that the doctrine is based on the common law 'rule of law' under which the courts have voluntarily obeyed Acts of Parliament in the interests of democracy. Thus, in *Jackson v A-G* [2006], Lord Steyn, at [102] and Lord Hope, at [126] claimed that parliamentary sovereignty was, in the absence of higher authority, created by the 'common law' (see also Section 8.5.6).

It seems unlikely that anyone other than a lawyer would permit a court to exercise so fundamental a power. Indeed, the late Lord Bingham, after his retirement as the Senior Law Lord, wrote that the judges did not create parliamentary sovereignty and therefore could not change it (*The Rule of Law* (Penguin 2010) 167). Moreover, sovereignty of the courts seems historically implausible since the courts, who ultimately derive their power from the Crown, must surely have shared the Crown's surrender to Parliament in 1688.

The basis of this common law-centred belief is that, since the courts have to apply Acts of Parliament, they necessarily have a powerful role in deciding what parliamentary supremacy means, for example in deciding what counts as a valid Act of Parliament (Section 8.5.3), or where there is a conflict between an Act of Parliament and EU law (Section 8.5.4). The line between applying the doctrine and challenging it is fuzzy. In the famous case of *Marbury v Madison* (1803) 1 Cranch 14, the US Supreme Court took it upon itself to decide that it had the power to overturn legislation made by Congress. Crucially, however, it claimed to derive this power by implication from the written constitution.

Professor Wade (1955) famously combined both viewpoints. He upheld the conventional view that parliamentary supremacy is a unique 'political fact', based on the 1688 revolution. Indeed, he argued that any change would amount to another revolution. Yet he placed the matter in the 'keeping of the courts', which can authoritatively signify the 'revolution'. Indeed, Wade has argued that the cases concerning the UK's membership of the EU constitute such a revolution (Section 8.5.4). This places the courts at the heart of the constitution, a position that may not be convincing in a democracy. It is difficult to see why this unique foundational principle should be in the hands of the courts rather than of Parliament itself. The questions of what is the law, and who applies the law, are separate.

On the other hand, in partial support of Wade, judicial decisions, like political pressures, might influence changes in the doctrine of parliamentary sovereignty. There is no reason to assume that the doctrine will stand still. As Craig seems to suggest ([2014] PL 379, at 392), the role of the court is to place the doctrine in its broader legal context. However, whether the doctrine has actually changed is a larger political matter, which can become clear only when the new position is generally recognised.

According to Lakin (2008), the doctrine of parliamentary sovereignty is so uncertain that it is implausible to suppose that officials and the public have accepted it. Lakin argues that the doctrine is a myth and that only the courts can determine what is legally valid, since they apply the law. He sees no need for a concept of sovereignty as such, but prefers a network of principles in the hands of the courts as guardians of political morality. However, Lakin's argument seems vulnerable to the same objection as he makes to the traditional doctrine, namely that political morality is uncertain and also depends ultimately upon widespread acceptance.

8.3   The meaning of 'Act of Parliament'

Parliamentary sovereignty concerns only lawmaking power. Specifically, it is concerned only with an Act of Parliament (a statute). An Act of Parliament, as the preamble to every Act reminds us, is an Act of the monarch with the consent of the House of Lords and the House of Commons (subject to the Parliament Acts 1911 and 1949 (below)): the Queen in Parliament (see Lord Steyn in *Jackson* [2006], at [81]). Dicey's legal sovereign is therefore divided, comprising three bodies. Only in combination can they exercise the lawmaking power of Parliament. Even if we believe that the House of Commons is the political sovereign, a resolution of the House of Commons has no *legal* force, except in relation to the internal proceedings of the House (*Bowles v Bank of England* [1913] 1 Ch 57; *Stockdale v Hansard* (1839) 9 Ad & E 1).

Two questions arise from this. First, what rules create an Act of Parliament? Second, to what extent can the courts investigate whether these rules have been obeyed? There are complex procedural rules for producing a statute, but not all of them affect its validity.

Three levels of rule can be distinguished:

1. The basic definition of an Act of Parliament (statute) is a document that has received the assent of Queen, Lords and Commons. The preamble to a statute invariably recites that the required assents have been given. A court is not bound by a document that does not appear on its face to have received the necessary assents, but conversely must accept the validity of a document that does so appear (*Prince's Case* (1606) 8 Co Rep 1). This is called the 'enrolled Act rule'. It prevents the courts from investigating whether the proper internal procedures have in fact been complied with, and even whether the statute was procured by fraud. The official version of a statute was traditionally enrolled upon the Parliament Roll. Today there is no Parliament Roll as such, but two official copies of the Act are in the House of Lords Library and the Public Record Office.

   Indeed, some of the foundational cases on parliamentary supremacy concern this issue rather than wider questions (e.g. *Edinburgh & Dalkeith Rly v Wauchope* (1842) 8 Cl and F 710; *Lee v Bude and Torrington Railway Co* (1871) LR 6 CP 577). These cases were a product of the massive railway-building of the mid-nineteenth century when there was a competitive rush to promote Acts of Parliament authorising the taking over of land, with some promoters not holding back from bribing MPs. (*Pickin v British Railways Board* [1974] is a more recent endorsement of the rule, a case when fraud was alleged in the process of enacting a statute.)

2. In two cases, the basic requirements have been modified by statute. Most importantly, under the Parliament Acts 1911 and 1949, if the Commons so decides, and subject to important exceptions, a bill can become law without the consent of the House of Lords after a prescribed delaying period (Section

11.4). The Parliament Act 1911 partly excludes the courts by providing that a certificate given by the Speaker to the effect that the requirements of the Act have been complied with is 'conclusive for all purposes and shall not be questioned in any court of law' (s 3). However, this does not prevent the court from deciding the prior question of whether the bill falls within the 1911 Act at all (see *Jackson* [2006], at [51]). In principle, the court can investigate whether statutory requirements have been complied with.

Secondly, the Regency Act 1937 provides that the royal assent can be given by a specified Regent, usually the next in line to the throne, if the monarch is under 18, absent abroad or ill, and in certain other events. In this case, the court may also be able to investigate whether the Act has been properly applied.

3. There is a complex network of rules concerning the composition and internal procedure of each House. These include the various stages of passage of a bill, voting procedures and the law governing qualifications for membership of either House. They comprise a mixture of statute, convention and the 'law and custom of Parliament' enforced by the House itself. Apart from the enrolled Act rule (above), these are matters of parliamentary privilege and the courts cannot inquire into them (Section 11.6).

8.4 The three facets of parliamentary sovereignty

Dicey's doctrine has three separate aspects:

1. Parliament has unlimited lawmaking power in the sense that it can make any kind of law.
2. The legal validity of laws made by Parliament cannot be questioned by any other body.
3. 'Parliament cannot bind its successors' – that is, a Parliament cannot bind a future Parliament.

8.4.1 Freedom to make any kind of law

Dicey claimed that Parliament can make any laws it wishes irrespective of morality, fairness, justice and practicality. For example, the UK courts are bound to obey a statute which relates to matters anywhere in the world; whether or not the relevant overseas courts would recognise it is immaterial (e.g. *Manuel v A-G* [1982] 3 All ER 822: Canada). Parliament can also do the physically impossible. It has been said that Parliament cannot make a man a woman, or a woman a man, but this is misleading. The so-called laws of nature are not rules at all. They are simply recurrent facts. A statute which enacted that all men must be regarded as women and vice versa would be impractical, but it would be legally valid.

Dicey relied on examples of valid statutory provisions that are arguably grossly unjust. However, these do not prove that the courts would apply a statute that they considered even more unjust. Nevertheless, despite some recent dicta (Section 8.5.6), modern cases support Dicey. They include retrospective legislation (*Burmah Oil Co Ltd v Lord Advocate* [1965] AC 75; War Damage Act 1965) and statutes conflicting with international law (*Mortensen v Peters* (1906) 14 SLT 227; *Cheney v Conn* [1968] 1 All ER 779; (see also the discussion of the passage of the United Kingdom Internal Market Act 2020 (Section 10.5.6)) or with fundamental civil liberties (*R v Jordan* [1967] Crim LR 483). Thus, in *Madzimbamuto v Lardner-Burke* [1969] 1 AC 645, 723 Lord Reid put the orthodox position:

> It is often said that it would be unconstitutional for the UK Parliament to do certain things, meaning that the moral, political and other reasons against doing them are so strong that most people would regard it as highly improper if Parliament did these things. But that does not mean that it is beyond the powers of Parliament to do such things. If Parliament chose to do any of them the courts could not hold Parliament to account.

8.4.2 Parliament cannot be overridden

First, international bodies do not have the power in English law to declare an Act of Parliament invalid. International law can alter legal rights in the UK only if adopted by Parliament (Section 9.5).

Second, in the event of a conflict between a statute and some other kind of law, the statute must always prevail. However, this leaves open the possibility that a statute itself might authorise some other lawmaking authority to override statutes. This was probably achieved by the European Communities Act 1972 (Section 8.5.4), but still leaves it open to Parliament to repeal the Act in question, thereby destroying the authority of the other body. This has now been done by s 1 of the European Union (Withdrawal) Act 2018.

The most important dimension of this limb of Dicey's theory is that English courts do not possess the power to declare statutes to be invalid – that is, to 'strike them down'. There is no equivalent to the power which the US Supreme Court assumed for itself in *Marbury v Madison*. This provides an important reason why the UK Constitution has traditionally been considered to be 'political' rather than 'legal' in character. Challenges to laws made by Parliament can most fruitfully be expressed through political as distinct from legal channels, since the courts are limited in the action that they can take.

8.4.3   Parliament cannot bind its successors

In a sense this is a limit on Parliament, although it also means that each successive Parliament cannot be restricted by a previous statute, so preserving continuing parliamentary sovereignty. In other words, where there are two statutes of equal status we should prefer the later one since it represents the current intention of Parliament. This is a vital principle, closely associated with democracy, in that no generation should be able to tie the hands of the future. For example, Edmund Burke argued that the 1688 revolution had permanently enshrined a constitution which included the House of Lords. Thomas Paine answered this as follows: 'Every age and generation must be as free to act for itself, in all cases, as the ages and generations which preceded it. The vanity and presumption of governing beyond the grave is the most ridiculous and insolent of all tyrannies' (*Rights of Man* (1791)).

Thus, a statute cannot be protected against repeal. Indeed, where provisions contained in a later statute conflict with those in an earlier one, the later may 'impliedly repeal' the earlier. This is so even if the earlier statute states that it cannot be repealed (*Vauxhall Estates Ltd v Liverpool Corp* [1932] 1 KB 733; *Ellen Street Estates Ltd v Minister of Health* [1934] 1 KB 590). However, it must be stressed that the implied repeal doctrine is not an essential part of parliamentary sovereignty, since Parliament can in any case *expressly* repeal a previous Act. While it is consistent with parliamentary sovereignty, the implied repeal doctrine is merely a particular approach to statutory interpretation. Although Lord Maugham in *Ellen Street Estates*, at 597, said that it would be impossible to enact that there shall be no implied repeal, this has not turned out to be so. Indeed, the traditional implied repeal doctrine is no longer favoured and may apply only where the two Acts cannot be interpreted to fit together (*Henry Boot Ltd v Malmaison Hotel Ltd* [2001] QB 388, 402).

Indeed, some statutes are so important that they can be repealed only by express words, or possibly by necessary implication. In *Thoburn v Sunderland City Council* [2002] 4 All ER 156 at [62]–[64], Laws LJ stated that a 'constitutional statute', in the sense of a statute 'which conditions the legal relationships between citizen and state in some general overarching manner, or enlarges or diminishes the scope of what are now regarded as fundamental rights', would be so protected. In this way, parliamentary sovereignty might be reconciled with the rule of law. This was confirmed by the Supreme Court in *R (HS2 Action Alliance Ltd) v Secretary of State for Transport* [2014] 1 WLR 324 at [203]–[204], where it was suggested, but not decided, that an EU directive should not be interpreted to violate the basic principle in Article 9 of the Bill of Rights 1688 that the court should not scrutinise parliamentary proceedings (Section 11.6.3). In *H v Lord Advocate* [2012] 3 WLR 151 at [30], the Supreme Court took the view that nothing short of express language could overcome a constitutional statute. The 'principle of legality', which applies to common law rights (Section 6.6), operates in a similar manner.

Moreover, Parliament itself has secured statutes against implied repeal. For example, the European Communities Act 1972 (now repealed) did so (Section 8.5.4), as has section 3 of the HRA (Section 8.5.5).

8.5 Challenging parliamentary sovereignty

There are various arguments that Parliament can, after all, be legally limited. As we have seen, the foundations of the doctrine appear to rest only on general acceptance. In its origins, parliamentary sovereignty was a historical response to political circumstances, namely the rebellion against the Stuart monarchs. It does not follow that the same response is appropriate today. The Victorian period, during which Dicey promoted the doctrine, was one of relative stability and prosperity. The people (or at least the middle and upper classes) were benefiting from the spoils of empire, and the belief that Parliament could deliver progress and prosperity was still plausible. Latterly, different forces, both domestic and international, have arisen which have made parliamentary sovereignty appear parochial, politically unreal and intellectually threadbare. These forces include the global economy, devolution, membership of the EU and other international obligations, and the increasing powers of the executive over Parliament.

There is no longer a political consensus that Parliament should be legally unlimited and no compelling legal reason why it should be. The main challenges to parliamentary sovereignty are as follows.

8.5.1 Grants of independence

If Parliament were to pass an Act giving independence to a territory currently under UK jurisdiction, such as Scotland, could a later Act revoke that independence? For example, the Canada Act 1982 provides that 'no Act of the United Kingdom Parliament passed after the Constitution Act 1982 comes into force shall extend to Canada as part of its law' (s 2). The legal answer is: yes, as far as the UK courts are concerned (*British Coal Corp v R* [1935] AC 500; *Manuel v A-G* [1982]), although, as was pointed out in *British Coal*, this has nothing to do with political reality, since such a statute would be ignored in its target country. In *Blackburn v A-G* [1971] 2 All ER 1380, Lord Denning remarked that legal theory must give way to practical politics. All his Lordship seems to be saying is that politics is more important than law. On the other hand, a legal principle that is so out of line with common sense might well be worth reconsidering.

In the early days of the dismantling of the British Empire, the Statute of Westminster 1931 conferred an ambivalent form of independence upon the Dominions of Australia, Canada, New Zealand, South Africa and the Irish Free State. The Act retained a tie with Parliament by stating that an Act of Parliament shall not extend to the territory in question unless it has requested and consented to the enactment. This kind of procedural restriction raises special questions (Section 8.5.3).

8.5.2 Scotland and Northern Ireland: Acts of Union – was Parliament born unfree?

This is a more substantial challenge. The UK Parliament is the result of two treaties. First, the Treaty of Union with Scotland in 1707 created the Parliament of Great Britain out of the former Scottish and English Parliaments. The Treaty provided, among other things, that no laws which concern private rights in Scotland shall be altered 'except for the evident utility of the subjects within Scotland'. There were also powers securing the separate Scottish courts and Presbyterian Church 'for all time coming'. The new Parliament was created by separate Acts of the then Scottish and English Parliaments, giving effect to the treaties.

The traditional view is that the Act of Union is an ordinary Act, and that its provisions can be altered like any other Act, although it would seem that the Act of Union is a 'constitutional statute' and thus requires clear language to do so (Section 8.4.3). Some Scottish lawyers, however, argue that Parliament was 'born unfree', meaning that the modern Parliament cannot go beyond the terms of the Acts that created it, so that the protected provisions of the Act of Union cannot be altered by Act of Parliament. There are two versions of this. The first is that, in effect, the Union created a new Parliament combining the qualities of both the old Parliaments. In relation to the protected Scottish provisions, this does not necessarily have the quality of sovereignty inherent in the former English Parliament (Mitchell (1963) 79 LQR 196). Alternatively, and perhaps less plausibly, the Acts of Union were a form of written constitution binding both Parliaments (MacCormick (1978) 29 NILQ 1).

A contrary argument is that parliamentary sovereignty is an evolving doctrine that developed after the Acts of Union. The current devolution provisions try to endorse parliamentary sovereignty (Section 16.1), (although section 1 of the Scotland Act 2016 and section 1 of the Wales Act 2017 declare the 'permanence' of the Scottish Parliament and Government and Welsh Assembly (now Senedd Cymru/Welsh Parliament) and Government respectively, stating that they cannot be abolished except through a vote to that effect in a referendum). Section 37 of the Scotland Act 1998 expressly states that the provisions of the Act are to take priority over the Act of Union. On both views, however, it seems that the UK Parliament could repeal the Act of Union as a whole, for example were Scotland to become an independent state, as is not implausible in the relatively near future. The case of Northern Ireland is broadly similar. There was a Treaty of Union in 1798 which preserved certain basic rights in Ireland, including the continuance of the Protestant religion and the permanence of the Union itself. The Treaty was confirmed by the Act of Union with Ireland 1800, which created the present UK Parliament. The Act covered the whole of Ireland, but what is now the Republic of Ireland later left the Union. It might be argued that section 1 of the Northern Ireland Act 1998, which provides for the Union to be dissolved if a referendum so votes, would be invalid as contrary to the Act of Union. The 1998 Act makes no express reference to the relevant provisions of the Act of Union with Ireland, but provides that it overrides 'previous enactments'.

The issue has surfaced in a few cases, in all of which an Act of Parliament was obeyed. In *Ex p Canon Selwyn* (1872) 36 JP 54 (Ireland), the court denied that it possessed the power to override a statute. In two Scottish cases, *MacCormick v Lord Advocate* [1953] SC 369: arguing that Queen Elizabeth II of the UK is Elizabeth I in Scotland, and *Gibson v Lord Advocate* [1975] SLT 134: Scottish fishing rights, the courts avoided the issue by holding that no conflict with the Acts of Union arose. However, in both cases, the argument in favour of the Acts of Union was regarded as tenable, particularly by Lord Cooper in *MacCormick.* Nonetheless, his Lordship suggested that the issue is 'non-justiciable', that is, outside the jurisdiction of the courts and resolvable only by political means. On this view, a statute that flouts the Acts of Union may be unconstitutional, but not unlawful. In both cases, the courts left open the question whether they could interfere if an Act purported to make drastic inroads into the Act of Union, for example by abolishing the whole of Scottish private law. In *Jackson v A-G* [2006] at [106], Lord Hope acknowledged that the Acts of Union might not be repealable.

The devolution legislation of 1998 onwards gives wide lawmaking power to bodies in Scotland, Wales and Northern Ireland, but does not prevent Parliament from making laws in relation to those countries in respect of matters within the devolved powers (Section 16.1). However, in practice, Parliament is heavily restricted by convention from exercising its powers to intervene in the affairs of the devolved countries, although not completely so: see Section 10.5.5. It seems increasingly possible that political pressures may lead to legal sovereignty being surrendered in favour of a federal arrangement. It is also plausible that sections 1 of the Northern Ireland Act 1998, Scotland Act 2016 and Wales Act 2017, all of which specify that a referendum must be held if (respectively) it is proposed that Northern Ireland ceases to be a part of the UK, or if an attempt is made to abolish the Scottish Parliament and Government or Senedd Cymru/Welsh Parliament and Government, impose 'manner and form' restrictions on Parliament's capacity to legislate in these respects (see below).

8.5.3 Redefinition theory: entrenchment

Suggested most prominently by Jennings in *The Law and the Constitution* (University of London Press 1933), the redefinition theory attempts to circumvent the rule that Parliament cannot bind its successors. The argument has various labels, sometimes being called the 'new view', sometimes the 'entrenchment argument', sometimes the 'manner and form theory', and sometimes the distinction between 'continuing' and 'self-embracing' sovereignty.

In essence, the redefinition argument is that if Parliament can do anything, it can 'redesign itself either in general or for particular purpose', as Baroness Hale put it in *Jackson v A-G* [2006] at [160]. It can therefore redefine itself in such a way as to make it more difficult for a future Parliament to change the law that it wishes to protect. For example, suppose that a statute enacts a bill of rights and goes on to say that 'no law shall be passed that is inconsistent with the bill of rights, nor shall this statute be repealed expressly or impliedly without a referendum of the people'. Similarly, we might cite the real examples of section 1 of the Northern Ireland Act 1998, the Scotland Act 2016 and the Wales Act 2017, noted above. Various 'referendum locks' relating to changes in EU treaties and voting procedures were also contained in the European Union Act 2011, although this Act has now been repealed following the UK's decision to withdraw from the Union.

The core of the argument is that any lawmaker can only make law in accordance with the procedure laid down (call it P1), even if that procedure is created by itself, as Parliament is able to do. Therefore, if the lawmaking procedure is changed from P1 to P2, the new procedure (P2) must then be followed unless this new procedure is changed (either to P3 or back to P1, it does not matter). A document which purports to be an Act of Parliament but which has not been passed according to these basic rules has no legal force, so the courts must ignore it.

In our examples, Parliament has therefore added to the existing requirement of Queen, Lords and Commons a further requirement of a referendum, thus redefining itself for the particular purpose. An entrenched statute can still be repealed, but not without following the new procedure, that is, by holding a referendum as to whether the referendum requirement should be repealed. It is of course first necessary to interpret the measure that creates the entrenched procedure to discover what was intended (see *Jackson* case (Box below) and *Manuel* case (below)).

The redefinition argument can be attacked on three fronts:

1. (The argument students usually raise.) If Parliament were to ignore the special procedure by passing a statute in the ordinary way, the courts would simply obey the most recent Act of Parliament and thus treat the special procedure as impliedly repealed. However, this misses the point, since, according to the redefinition argument, a document that has not been produced under the special procedure *is not an Act of Parliament at all* and so must be ignored, just as an ordinary law would be ignored if it did not have the royal assent. Therefore, there are no competing statutes for the implied repeal doctrine to engage with.

2. It can be argued that any Act which confers lawmaking power subject to a special procedure is, in reality, delegating power to a subordinate body since, by definition, subordinate legislation is legislation made under the authority of another body and is inherently restricted by the terms of reference given to it. If this is so, then the superior body can always legislate to override the subordinate. However, this is a matter of interpreting what has happened. It is equally possible logically to regard this as a body redefining itself.

3. Professor Wade (1955) firmly rejects the redefinition argument. He argues that the meaning of 'Parliament' is 'fixed' by a rule derived from the 1688 revolution which is 'above and beyond the reach of Parliament': a fundamental constitutional principle which he takes to be in the hands of the courts and so a unique rule that is both 'political' and common law (Section 8.2). Wade argues that, because this rule gave Parliament its power, it cannot be altered by Parliament and any attempt to redefine Parliament would at best produce delegated legislation.

The notion of a higher rule does not seem necessary and is reminiscent of a magical incantation. Indeed, it raises the question of what makes the higher rule valid. The answer is general acceptance of it, and this could apply equally to a claim made by Parliament itself without the backdrop of anything 'higher' (Section 8.2).

However, even if we accept the idea of Wade's 'higher rule', why should the higher rule, supposedly made by those in charge of the 1688 revolution, not authorise its creature – Parliament – to alter the rule itself? Indeed, in *R v Secretary of State for Transport ex p Factortame (No 2)* [1991] 1 AC 603 at 659, Lord Bridge took the view that parliamentary sovereignty can indeed be altered by statute. It is also plausible that the fundamental rule is not fixed at a particular date but, in keeping with the nature of the unwritten constitution, evolves and changes. Indeed, the doctrine emerged in its modern form well after 1688, alongside the expansion of democracy in the nineteenth century.

In *Jackson v A-G* [2006], the House of Lords was confronted with the redefinition theory when, for the first time in a domestic context, it was asked to invalidate a statute, namely the Hunting Act 2004, which banned hunting with dogs. A majority seemed to support the redefinition theory. It was held that, although it was passed without the consent of the House of Lords under the Parliament Act 1949, the Hunting Act was indeed a fully-fledged statute which could not be challenged. Parliament had therefore redefined itself to mean only Queen and Commons in circumstances where the Parliament Acts were invoked (see Box).

There is judicial support for the redefinition theory from former UK territories (see *A-G for New South Wales v Trethowan* [1932] AC 526; *Harris v Minister of the Interior* [1952] (2) SA 428: South Africa; *Bribery Comr v Ranasinghe* [1965] AC 172: Sri Lanka). *Trethowan* went so far as to suggest that the court could grant an injunction to prevent a bill being submitted for royal assent if it did not comply with the entrenched procedure. These cases are of limited authority. They have been explained on the basis that the legislatures in these countries were not truly sovereign in the same way as the UK Parliament, since a UK Act had established the powers of the legislatures in question. However, in *Harris*, the Statute of Westminster 1931 had given the South African Parliament unlimited lawmaking power. Moreover, the court stressed that its reasoning did not assume that the legislature was subordinate. Indeed, in both *Trethowan* and *Ranasinghe,* there were dicta that the same arguments might apply to the UK Parliament. Thus it was said in *Ranasinghe* (at 198) that the legislature can alter the very instrument from which its powers derive.

In *Manuel v A-G* [1983], the Canada Act 1982 was claimed to be invalid in that it was enacted without relevant consents as required by section 4 of the Statute of Westminster 1931, which at the time applied to Canada as a former UK dominion. The purpose of the 1982 Act was to free Canada from its constitutional links with the UK. The Court of Appeal was prepared to recognise the possibility of redefinition. However, section 4 merely required that the Act had to *state on its face* that it had received the relevant consents. The 1982 Act did so state and the court could not investigate the internal proceedings of Parliament to see whether the statement was true. Obviously, the matter depends on the precise terms of the redefinition in question (a point to watch in any exam question!).

Jackson v A-G [2006] 1 AC 262

The Hunting Act 2004, which outlawed hunting with dogs, had been enacted under the Parliament Act 1949 without the consent of the House of Lords. The Hunting Act was challenged on two grounds:

▶ The first ground was that Parliament could not redefine itself by changing what counted as an Act of Parliament. Therefore, it was suggested that a law passed under the Parliament Act 1911 could only be delegated legislation, power being delegated by Parliament in 1911 to the Commons and Queen. Delegated legislation, unlike statute, can be challenged in the courts. The Hunting Act was passed under the Parliament Act 1949, which shortened the period for which the House of Lords could delay a bill. The 1949 Act was itself enacted without House of Lords' consent under the 1911 Act's procedure. It was assumed to be correct that, unless there is clear authority to do so from the parent Act, a delegate cannot enlarge its own powers. Therefore, on this argument the 1949 Act would be invalid, so the Hunting Act falls with it.

- The second ground (not directly relating to parliamentary sovereignty) was that, even if laws made under the 1911 Act are Acts of Parliament, nevertheless, as a matter of interpretation of the 1911 Act, there are implied limits intended by the 1911 Act which prevent the Parliament Act procedure from being used to further reduce the powers of the Lords and perhaps to make other constitutional changes. This would also make the 1949 Act invalid (since its effect was to reduce the period of delay).
- On the first ground, nine Law Lords held that Acts passed under the Parliament Acts were not delegated legislation but, as a matter of interpretation of the 1911 Act, they were intended to be full statutes and, crucially, that there was nothing to stop Parliament from doing this. The 1949 Act was therefore a proper Act of Parliament and the Hunting Act was also lawful. Thus, they endorsed the possibility of Parliament redefining itself. Lord Steyn at [81]–[86], [91]–[93] treated the definition of Parliament as a matter that Parliament itself could change (see also Lord Bingham at [35]–[36], Lord Carswell at [174], Lord Browne at [187], Baroness Hale at [160]).
- However, caution is required. It was stressed (at [25]) that the 1911 Act did not transfer power to a body other than Parliament or limit the power of the democratic House of Commons. It merely constrained the House of Lords. The courts might therefore draw back from accepting a more radical kind of redefinition, particularly one that limits democracy. Baroness Hale, in particular, left 'for another day' the question whether Parliament could redefine itself 'upwards', for example by requiring a referendum for a particular measure in addition to the normal procedure (at [163]).
- As to the second ground, which depended on the interpretation of the 1911 Act, a majority held that there were no limitations to be read into the 1911 Act preventing the Act itself from being altered so as to reduce the delaying period. The 1949 Act and the Hunting Act were therefore valid.
- However, there was disagreement whether, as a matter of interpretation, the Parliament Acts can apply to every bill to alter the Parliament Act 1911. This aspect of the case will be discussed later (Section 11.4).

A further issue was discussed. The Court of Appeal had suggested that a bill which made fundamental constitutional changes, such as abolishing the House of Lords altogether or violating basic democratic rights, could not be passed under the Parliament Acts, which could be read as implicitly limiting such fundamental changes. Their Lordships did not commit themselves on this point, but in the main rejected the argument. Lord Bingham [32], Lord Nicholls [61] and Baroness Hale, albeit ambivalently at [158], [159], [166], thought that there are no such limitations, although Lord Bingham [41] drew attention to the fact that the Parliament Acts weaken the checks and balances over a powerful executive. Lord Carswell [178] and Lord Browne [194] cautiously left open the possibility. Lord Steyn [102], perhaps endorsed by Lord Hope [107], [120], went furthest, taking the view that fundamental violations of the rule of law might be rejected by the courts – not merely those made under the Parliament Acts but also by the full Parliament (Section 8.5.6).

8.5.4 European Union law

The EU and its powers were created by a series of treaties between the Member States. Member States are obliged under the treaties to give effect to those laws that are intended under the rules of EU law to be binding within domestic law. However, as with all treaties, the law of the EU enters the legal systems of each Member State in accordance with the laws of that state. EU law will be discussed in more detail in Chapter 10, but we shall deal with the position as regards parliamentary sovereignty, while the UK was a Member State, here.

The European Communities Act 1972, which is repealed by section 1 of the European Union (Withdrawal) Act 2018, incorporated EU law into UK law. The Act stated that 'any enactment, passed or to be passed … shall be construed and have effect subject to the foregoing provisions of this section' (s 2(4)). The provisions referred to required, among other matters, that the English courts must give effect to certain laws made by the EU (s 2(1)). Section 3 of the Act also required UK courts to follow the decisions of the European Court of Justice (ECJ), the court of the EU (now called the Court of Justice of the European Union (CJEU)).

The effect of the above provisions seemed to be that a UK statute, even one passed after the relevant EU law, must give way to EU law. Not surprisingly, the CJEU, which is part of the EU system, favours the supremacy of the EU (see *Costa v ENEL* [1964] CMLR 425; *Internationale Handelsgesellschaft* case [1970] ECR 1125). But this is not enough in itself. As with all treaties, the matter depends entirely on whether a Member State, in accordance with its own law, has chosen to accept the supremacy of EU law. In the UK at least, a treaty cannot change the law unless incorporated into domestic law by statute (Section 9.5). Accordingly, in *R (HS2 Action Alliance Ltd) v Secretary of State for Transport* [2014] at [79], [203]–[205], the Supreme Court emphasised that EU law was part of UK law only by virtue of the provisions of UK law itself.

Section 5 of the 2018 Act, as amended by the European Union (Withdrawal Agreement) Act 2020, addresses the supremacy of EU law after Brexit (Section 10.5.4). According to subsection (1), the 'principle of supremacy' does not apply to any enactment or rule of law made after the end of the 'implementation period' ' (31 December 2020). However, subsection (2) provides that 'the principle of the supremacy of EU law continues to apply on or after [that date] so far as relevant to the interpretation, disapplication or quashing of any enactment or rule of law passed or made before [that date]'. This statutory articulation of the principle of the supremacy of EU law amounts to a recognition that the 1972 Act functioned to modify the principle of parliamentary sovereignty while the UK was a member of (what is now) the EU. This was done to give effect to the purpose and function of the Union, that is, to unite Member States in certain common goals, and the basis on which member states agreed to join, namely to subject themselves to EU law.

The judicial response to this principle of supremacy was best demonstrated by *R v Secretary of State for Transport, ex p Factortame* [1990] 2 AC 85, in which there was a clash between Spanish fishermen and the UK government. The Merchant Shipping Act 1988 limited registration of fishing vessels to those with a 'genuine and substantial connection' with the UK. The question of whether these requirements were compatible with EU law was referred by the High Court to the ECJ for determination. The question then arose as to whether the Spanish fishermen could lawfully be prevented from fishing *in the meantime* (i.e. before the ECJ had issued its ruling), given that the effect of doing so might be to deprive them of rights which they might have under EU law (the existence and effect of which would be established by the ECJ). Initially, the House of Lords refused to grant an injunction to prevent the Act being enforced, holding that it had no power to grant an injunction against the Crown to prevent the enforcement of an Act of Parliament. However, the House of Lords also referred to the ECJ the question of whether it was required by Community law to set aside any national rule which precluded it from granting an interim remedy (which, in this case, would have the effect of allowing the Spanish fishermen to continue to fish). The ECJ confirmed that this was indeed the case. In *R v Secretary of State, ex p Factortame (No. 2)* [1991], the House of Lords fell into line and 'disapplied' the UK statute. Lord Bridge said, 'By virtue of s 2(4) of the Act of 1972, Part II of the 1988 Act is to be construed and take effect subject to directly enforceable community rights…This has precisely the same effect as if a section were incorporated in…the 1988 Act…which enacted that the provisions were to be without prejudice to the directly enforceable community rights of nationals of any member state of the EC' (at 140).

Wade ((1991) 107 LQR 1) argued that *Factortame* signalled a constitutional revolution (Section 8.2) (see also *Equal Opportunities Commission v Secretary of State for Employment* [1994] 1 All ER 910, 919–20: provisions of a statute said to be 'invalid'). A somewhat different reading was that of Laws LJ in *Thoburn v Sunderland City Council* [2002], treating the 1972 Act as a constitutional statute (Section 8.4.3). According to this view, *Factortame* can be viewed as a case in which there was a strong *presumption of interpretation* against repeal: nothing short of an express statement along the lines of 'this Act is to override EU law' would suffice. No such statement existed in the Merchant Shipping Act 1988, nor could the latter be regarded itself as a constitutional statute, so EU law prevailed.

As the UK has now left the EU, the matters discussed here may appear to be largely of academic or historical significance. However, they do suggest that parliamentary sovereignty is not an immutable concept as Dicey seemed to suggest, but that it can be and has been modified in particular political and legal circumstances, albeit that it can also be 'reclaimed'.

8.5.5   The Human Rights Act 1998

By virtue of the HRA, a court must interpret a statute, 'so far as it is possible to do so', so as to comply with rights derived from the ECHR. If this is not possible, the court can issue a 'declaration of incompatibility' (Section 22.5.2). This does not override the statute, and the Act is clear that the court has no power to do so. The effect of a declaration of incompatibility is to invite the executive, in conjunction with Parliament, to change the law so as to comply with the ECHR. Thus, the Act does not directly restrict parliamentary sovereignty. However, along with the EU legislation and the devolution legislation (above), the HRA could be regarded, at least politically, as a brake on parliamentary sovereignty. This is especially the case as, in almost all instances, Parliament has legislated to change the law following the issuing of a declaration of incompatibility.

8.5.6   The common law/rule of law

This controversial issue arises out of uncertainty as to the basis of parliamentary supremacy (Section 8.2). It is sometimes suggested that parliamentary sovereignty may be conditional on compliance with fundamental values embodied in the rule of law so that in extreme cases the court might refuse to apply a statute. Early cases, such as *Dr Bonham's Case* (1610) 8 Co Rep 114a, possibly suggested that a completely unreasonable statute may be overridden, but, at least since the Stuart period, there has been no serious judicial challenge to parliamentary sovereignty.

However, in the absence of a written constitution, change cannot be ruled out. The test would be whether the claims of the courts become generally accepted. In 2003, Laws LJ claimed that the constitution is 'at an intermediate stage between parliamentary supremacy' and what he called 'constitutional supremacy' (*International Transport Roth GmbH v Secretary of State for the Home Dept* [2003] QB 728, at [71]). Other senior judges, notably Lord Hope and Lord Steyn (below), albeit countered by others including Lord Bingham and Lord Hoffmann, have expressed the view that the rule of law is sovereign. In *A v Secretary of State for the Home Department* [2005] 2 AC 68 at [42], Lord Bingham, in rejecting an argument that courts are undemocratic, emphasised that independent courts under the rule of law are a cardinal feature of the modern democratic state. However, he also said that ultimately the court should give way to Parliament.

Statements by judges in favour of their own sovereignty include the following:

▶ Lord Steyn in *Jackson* [2006] at [102] said that 'the Supreme Court might have to consider whether judicial review or the ordinary role of the courts was a constitutional fundamental which even a sovereign Parliament acting at the behest of a compliant House of Commons could not abolish'.

▶ In the same case, at [104], Lord Hope said that '[s]tep by step, gradually but surely the English principle of the absolute legislative sovereignty of Parliament is being qualified', and at [107]; and that 'the rule of law enforced by the courts is the ultimate controlling factor on which our constitution is based'.

▶ In the same case, at [159], Lady Hale said: 'The courts will treat with particular suspicion (and might even reject) any attempt to subvert the rule of law by removing governmental action affecting the rights of the individual from all judicial powers'.

▶ Writing extra-judicially about *Jackson* ([2006] EHRLR 243, 253), Lord Steyn said that 'the dicta in *Jackson* are likely to prevail if the government tried to tamper with the fundamental principles of our constitutional democracy, such as five-year parliaments, the role of the ordinary courts, the rule of law, and other such fundamentals. In such exceptional cases the rule of law may trump parliamentary supremacy'.

▶ In *AXA General Insurance Ltd v HM Advocate* [2011] 3 WLR 871, the Supreme Court held that the non-sovereign Scottish Parliament is subject to judicial review, but only in the most exceptional cases where the rule of law is threatened. Lord Hope, at [50], said that the position as regards the sovereign UK Parliament is 'still under discussion'. He suggested that, in light of the dangers of executive domination of Parliament, the court might intervene if Parliament were to abolish judicial review or diminish the powers of the courts in protecting the individual: '[T]he rule of law requires that judges must retain the power to insist that legislation of this extreme kind is not law which the courts will recognise' (at [51]). The other members of the court did not raise this issue.

▶ The late Lord Cooke, following Wade's approach (Section 8.5.4), suggested that an attempt by Parliament to override basic rights would be a 'revolution' on which the last word rests with the courts (in Andenas and Fairgrieve (eds), *Tom Bingham and the Transformation of the Law* Oxford University Press (2009) 689–91).

▶ In 2004 a government proposal to restrict judicial review of immigration decisions was defeated partly as a result of protests by judges based on the rule of law, among which were suggestions that the courts would not enforce such a provision (Section 6.1).

The courts have also suggested in their own favour that Parliament has become dominated by the executive (e.g. Lord Mustill in *R v Secretary of State, ex p Fire Brigades Union* [1995] 2 All ER 244 (Section 7.7.3.3); Lord Hope in *AXA General Insurance Ltd v HM Advocate* [2011], at [49], [50]; Lord Bingham in *Jackson* [2006], at [41]). Thus, the defence of Parliament, that it can make laws which are informed by a wider range of opinions than are available to a court and which carry the consent of those subject to them, can be presented as hollow. In *AXA* (above), Lord Hope emphasised (at [49]) that both sovereign and non-sovereign parliaments share the advantages of democracy which makes them best placed to know what is in the country's best interests but, in view of the dangers of Parliament being dominated by a party majority, 'the non-elected judges are best placed to protect the rights of the individual including those who are ignored or despised by the majority'.

A favourite liberal argument in favour of a court – implicit in Lord Hope's statement – is fear of what de Tocqueville called 'the tyranny of the majority'. The argument runs that 'democracy' is more than just the will of the majority and must be policed by certain basic rights of equality and freedom protected against the volatility, corruption or foolishness of the majority (see also Lord Hoffmann in *R (Alconbury Developments Ltd) v Secretary of State for the Environment, Transport and the Regions* [2001] 2 All ER 929, at [70]). The representative democracy that gives Parliament its legitimacy is an imperfect democracy that carries a risk of overriding minorities.

Thus, handing over power to a court is not anti-democratic (as might be thought), but, rather, a prudent 'pre-commitment' of a majority anxious to guard against its own weaknesses, for example discriminating against an unpopular minority or a panic overreaction to a supposed threat, such as that of terrorism. By removing at least fundamental rights from its control, the majority lessens the risk that it will misuse its power. Thus, in *R (Countryside Alliance) v A-G* [2008] 1 AC 719 at [114], Baroness Hale remarked that 'democracy is the will of the people, but the people may not will to invade those rights which are fundamental to democracy itself'.

Allan (2009) argues, along similar lines, that it is inconsistent with the political assumptions of a liberal society on which the rule of law is based that the legislature, or indeed any part of the government, should be all powerful. He claims that, in the common law tradition, the courts have the duty to protect the fundamental values of society. Relying on the fact that the court is concerned not with a statute generally, but with its application to the individual case, Allan suggests that the court can legitimately hold that a statute which appears to be grossly unjust does not apply to the particular case. This approach could be reconciled with parliamentary sovereignty on the basis that Parliament cannot foresee every implication of the laws it makes and can be assumed to respect the rule of law. Thus, in *Cooper v Wandsworth Board of Works* (1863) 14 CB (NS) 180 Byles J said that 'the justice of the common law will supply the omission of the legislature'.

Judicial supremacy is vulnerable to the republican attack in that it gives the last word to people we have not chosen, unelected judges. Thus, Waldron (*Law and Disagreement* (Oxford University Press 2001)), a leading opponent of judicial supremacy, draws on the republican argument that we sacrifice dignity, equality and control over our lives by letting unelected judges decide whether laws are valid. Arguably, this should be done by a democratic assembly in which the whole community can participate on equal terms.

The liberal values that the rule of law embraces are not peculiar to law. Ideas such as freedom and equality are the source of fundamental disagreement, which judges may be in no better position to resolve than anyone else. Indeed, Lord Bingham pointed out in *R (Countryside Alliance) v A-G* [2008] at [45] that the democratic process is liable to be subverted if, on a question of political or moral judgment, opponents of an Act achieve through the courts what they could not achieve through Parliament.

In the absence of a written constitution, we cannot rule out judicial rejection of parliamentary sovereignty. Indeed, the courts themselves inevitably have to decide the limits of their own powers when a case comes before them. Thus it has been said:

> Whoever hath an absolute authority to interpret any written or spoken laws, it is he who is truly the lawgiver and not the person who just spoke or wrote them. (Bishop Hoadley's sermon preached before King George I (1717))

There is a more moderate approach to such ideas, in the form of the 'principle of legality' (Section 6.6), under which clear statutory language is required to override a fundamental common law principle, so acting as a check and balance by ensuring that Parliament does not inadvertently or lightly override basic rights (see Lady Hale in *Jackson* [2006], at [159]). This might be seen to allocate dual roles to Parliament and courts. Thus, in *X Ltd v Morgan Grampian Publishers Ltd* [1991] 1 AC 1, Lord Bridge referred to the 'twin foundations' of the rule of law, namely 'the sovereignty of the Queen in Parliament in making the law and the sovereignty of the Queen's courts in interpreting and applying the law' (at 13). Similarly, in *Hamilton v Al Fayed* [1999] 3 All ER 317, 320, Lord Woolf MR referred to 'the wider constitutional principle of mutuality of respect between two constitutional sovereignties'.

Summary

- The doctrine of parliamentary sovereignty provides the fundamental legal premise of the UK Constitution. The doctrine means that an Act of Parliament must be obeyed by the courts, that later Acts prevail over earlier ones and that rules made by external bodies, for example under international law, cannot override Acts of Parliament. It does not follow that Parliament is supreme politically, although the line between legal and political sovereignty is sometimes blurred.

- Parliamentary sovereignty rests on frail foundations. Without a written constitution, it is impossible to be sure as to its legal basis other than as an evolving practice that is usually said to depend on the 1688 revolution. It is possible to maintain that the common law is really supreme. The question of the ultimate source of power cannot be answered within the legal system alone, but depends on public acceptance.

- Parliament itself is a creature of the law. The customary and statutory rules which have evolved since medieval times determine that, except in special cases, Parliament for this purpose means the Queen with the assent of the House of Lords and the House of Commons. However, this can be modified, as in the case of the Parliament Acts 1911 and 1949.

- The courts can determine whether any document is an Act of Parliament in this sense but cannot inquire into whether the correct procedure within each House has been followed.

- The doctrine has two separate aspects: first that the courts must obey Acts of Parliament in preference to any other kind of legal authority; and second that no body, including Parliament itself, can place legal limits upon the freedom of action of a future Parliament. The first of these principles is generally accepted, but the second is open to dispute.

- The implied repeal doctrine is sometimes promoted as an aspect of parliamentary sovereignty but is merely a presumption of interpretation. It would seem that some statutes can be repealed only by clear language.

- Grants of independence to dependent territories can probably be revoked lawfully in the eyes of UK courts.

Summary cont'd

▶ The possibility that parts of the Acts of Union with Scotland and Ireland are unchangeable is probably outside the courts' jurisdiction.

▶ The 'redefinition' argument proposes that, by altering the basic requirements for lawmaking, Parliament can redesign itself to impose restrictions on enacting legislation.

▶ Parliament limited the freedom of future Parliaments in relation to certain laws made by the European Union, but ultimately Parliament can override EU law and has now done so by repealing the European Communities Act 1972.

▶ The role of the common law as constituting 'dual sovereignty' through the courts' exclusive power to interpret Acts of Parliament leads to the argument that parliamentary sovereignty is conditional upon acceptance by the courts and that the courts might intervene if Parliament were to violate fundamental constitutional principles. This links with wider versions of the rule of law.

Exercises

8.1 Does the doctrine of parliamentary sovereignty have a secure legal basis?

8.2 To what extent can the courts investigate whether an Act of Parliament has complied with the proper procedure?

8.3 *Uncle George's Internet Student Guide to Constitutional Law* informs you that 'Westminster is Sovereign'. Is the Guide reliable, and if not, why not?

8.4 'Every age and generation must be as free to act for itself, in all cases, as the ages and generations which preceded it. The vanity and presumption of governing beyond the grave is the most ridiculous and insolent of all tyrannies' (Thomas Paine).

Discuss with reference (i) to the implied repeal doctrine and (ii) to the redefinition argument.

8.5 Consider the validity and effect of the following provisions contained in (fictitious) Acts of Parliament:

(i) 'There shall be a bill of rights in the UK and no Act to be enacted at any time in the future shall have effect, in as far as it is inconsistent with the bill of rights, unless it has been assented to by a two-thirds majority of both Houses of Parliament and no Act shall repeal this Act unless it has the same two-thirds majority.'

(ii) 'The Acts of Union with Scotland and Ireland are hereby repealed.'

8.6 'The sovereignty of Parliament and the sovereignty of the law of the land – the two principles which pervade the whole of the English constitution – may appear to stand in opposition to each other, or to be at best countervailing forces. But this appearance is delusive' (Dicey).

Discuss.

8.7 'The classic account given by Dicey of the doctrine of the sovereignty of Parliament, pure and absolute as it was, can now be seen as out of place in the modern United Kingdom' (Lord Steyn in *Jackson* [2006], at [103]).

'The rule of law enforced by the courts is the ultimate controlling factor on which our constitution is based' (Lord Hope, *ibid.*, at [107]).

Explain and critically discuss.

8.8 In view of concerns about demands for greater political rights for English cities, the government proposes to introduce a bill which cancels the next general election and gives the Secretary of State power to dissolve any city council. The bill provides that the decision of the Secretary of State shall not be challenged in the courts. Discuss any possible legal challenge to the bill.

Further reading

Allan, 'In Defence of the Common Law Constitution: Unwritten Rights as Fundamental Law' (2009) 22 Canadian Journal of Law & Jurisprudence 187

Bogdanor, 'Imprisoned by a Doctrine: The Modern Defence of Parliamentary Sovereignty' (2012) 32 OJLS 179

Craig, 'Constitutional Foundations, the Rule of Law and Sovereignty' [2003] PL 92

Davis, 'Parliamentary Supremacy and the Re-invigoration of Institutional Dialogue in the UK' (2014) 67 Parl Aff 137

Ekins, 'Acts of Parliament and the Parliament Acts' (2007) 123 LQR 91

Elliott, 'Parliamentary Sovereignty in a Changing Constitutional Landscape' in Jowell and O'Cinneide (eds), *The Changing Constitution* (9th edn, Oxford University Press 2019)

Goldsworthy, *Parliamentary Sovereignty: Contemporary Debates* (Cambridge University Press 2010)

Gordon, 'The Conceptual Foundations of Parliamentary Sovereignty: Reconsidering Jennings and Wade' [2009] PL 519

Gordon, *Parliamentary Sovereignty in the UK Constitution: Process, Politics and Democracy* (Hart Publishing 2015)

Jowell, 'Parliamentary Sovereignty Under the New Constitutional Hypothesis' [2006] PL 562

Knight, 'Striking Down Legislation Under Bi-polar Sovereignty' [2011] PL 90

Lakin, 'Debunking the Idea of Parliamentary Sovereignty: The Controlling Factor of Legality in the British Constitution' (2008) 28 OJLS 709

McConalogue, *The British Constitution Resettled: Parliamentary Sovereignty Before and After Brexit* (Palgrave Macmillan, 2020)

Munro, *Studies in Constitutional Law* (2nd edn, Butterworths 1999) chs 5 and 6

Oliver, 'Parliament and the Courts: A Pragmatic (or Principled) Defence of the Sovereignty of Parliament' in Horne and Drewry (eds), *Parliament and the Law* (2nd edn, Hart Publishing, 2018)

Wade, 'The Basis of Legal Sovereignty' (1955) 13 CLJ 172

Weill, 'Centennial to the Parliament Act 1911: The Manner and Form Fallacy' [2012] PL 105

Zhou, 'Revisiting the "Manner and Form" Theory of Parliamentary Sovereignty' (2013) 129 LQR 610

Part III

International aspects of the constitution

Chapter 9

The state and the outside world

9.1 Introduction: the idea of the state

The term 'state' derives from 'status' and originally meant a recognised function in the overall scheme of things. The contemporary idea of the state means a geographical area with its own government, which forms the basic legal unit of the constitution. From the point of view of international law, each state is a sovereign independent entity. The term 'nation state' is often used, but there is no necessary connection between the idea of a nation and that of a state, although the two terms are often used interchangeably. A nation is a cultural, political and historical idea, but is not a legal concept. It signifies a community marked out by shared cultural traditions: usually, but by no means always, coinciding with the legal entity of the state. Most legal systems derive their authority from the state, although there are important exceptions such as Sharia, Islamic law, which is based upon adherence to Islam. Some states, for example Saudi Arabia, have specifically incorporated Sharia law into their constitutions.

A nation may have a moral claim to be a state with its own laws and government (see Lord Hoffmann in *A v Secretary of State for the Home Dept* [2005] 2 AC 68) and the association of the ideas of nation and state can be used by those in power as a means of inspiring loyalty (e.g. the Constitution of Ireland, Article 9). As the history of Ireland, the Middle East, the Balkan states, Pakistan and many African states sadly reveals, the artificiality of state boundaries drawn by officials may generate violence and even genocide. The term 'country' has no legal significance and is used loosely to refer either to a nation or to a state.

The nation state has been the basic political and legal unit since the Treaty of Westphalia (1648) divided up the main territories after the Thirty Years War, in which religious and dynastic disputes affected most of Europe. The Westphalian settlement established the principle that states are equal internationally and independent in respect of their internal affairs and that, in international law, the state has primacy over religious and hereditary structures. Relationships between states are regulated primarily by agreement through the mechanism of treaties. There are many international treaties which try to impose overarching standards of behaviour in relation to common problems.

During the eighteenth century, stimulated by Enlightenment ideas of scientific reason, secularism and equality, the state developed as an impersonal command structure. This is broadly the position today. Under the influence of democracy, the state has become an all-purpose organisation with no inherent limitations to its functions or any consensus as to the relationship between citizen and state, other than the temporary accommodations produced by the balance of powers within the state.

Today, international obligations play an increasingly important part in constitutional disputes. International governmental bodies such as the United Nations, the World Trade Organization, the International Monetary Fund and the European Commission wield considerable influence over national governments. Influential businesses, such as banks and media organisations, can put pressure upon state governments. They have assets and operations scattered globally which can readily be moved around. Thus, while an international business is subject to state laws, enforcing these may be almost impossible. Contemporary problems require international cooperation and sometimes, shared laws. These problems include pandemics, such as COVID-19, environmental issues such as climate change, terrorism, financial wrongdoing, computer fraud and hacking, refugees, people trafficking, fugitive offenders, international trade and financial regulation.

Constitutional law must identify methods by which principles and rules made internationally can be filtered into domestic law and given effect without sacrificing fundamental constitutional principles, in other words trying to strike a balance between constitutionalism and international requirements. Specific issues include the following:

To what extent are international treaties and other forms of international law binding in UK law?
To what extent are foreign states and their officials subject to UK law?
What is the role of the law in relation to external matters, such as sending forces abroad or expelling people from the country?

The UK remains geared to the traditional model of the state, with international rights and obligations being filtered through the apparatus of domestic law. Thus, international law and domestic law are essentially separate systems. Unless a specific domestic link between them exists, most importantly by statute, the rules of international law cannot be directly applied in UK courts. However, the courts recognise the reality of the UK's international role to the extent that they will attempt to interpret the law to comply with an international obligation.

9.2 The UK as a state

The UK is a state in international law, but it is not a nation. Its legal and cultural basis is complex. The UK comprises England, Scotland, Wales and Northern Ireland, each of which, with the exception of England, has devolved self-government (Chapter 16). Before the union with Scotland in 1707, England was a nation state, but it is no longer a state. Great Britain, a name coined to express the union with Scotland, means England, Wales and Scotland collectively. Great Britain is not a state either, although the term is sometimes used in statute to mean the UK (e.g. 'British overseas territory'). The Channel Islands and the Isle of Man are not part of the UK. They belong to the Crown and have their own systems of law and government. There are various small dependent territories scattered around the world known as UK overseas territories.

The Queen is currently the head of the Commonwealth, which is a loose association of 53 former UK territories including Australia, Canada, India, New Zealand, Pakistan and several African, Asian and Caribbean states. The Commonwealth as such has no legal links with the UK, although a few of its Member States retain the Judicial Committee of the Privy Council as an appeal court (Section 5.7). Commonwealth citizens are treated for most purposes as aliens. Some Commonwealth citizens have certain political rights such as a right to vote or to stand for Parliament.

England and Wales have a single legal system governed by English law (although there are increasing calls for a distinct Welsh jurisdiction: see Chapter 16). Scotland and Northern Ireland have their own legal systems, which have much in common with English law, although Scotland has also been influenced by French civil law. In all jurisdictions, other than internal Scottish criminal cases, the highest appeal court is the UK Supreme Court.

9.3 Citizenship

Citizenship means full membership of a state. In UK law, citizenship is mainly concerned with the right to reside in the UK and with political rights. In its wider republican sense (which, it must be emphasised, is not its legal sense, Section 2.5), citizenship carries with it ideas of political equality, freedom, and participation in government with corresponding obligations to conform to the law, thus opening up the threatening possibility that citizenship depends on behaviour conforming to the policies of the government of the day. Some legal rights, notably under the Freedom of Information Act (Section 24.2), support this broad notion of citizenship, as does the denial of the right to vote to convicted prisoners (Section 12.5.5).

The unpleasant side of citizenship is that it entails 'exclusion', in the sense of an unwelcoming attitude to those regarded as non-citizens, who in UK law are labelled 'aliens'. Aliens can be denied entry and expelled in accordance with domestic law. However, this is limited by obligations under the ECHR (Sections 9.6.3 and 21.4). For example, in *A v Secretary of State for the Home*

Dept [2005], the House of Lords held that it was contrary to the HRA to discriminate between citizens and non-citizens in relation to anti-terrorism measures where there is a similar risk from both groups.

UK citizenship law is complex and has become increasingly restrictive due to many attempts to limit immigration following the collapse of the British Empire after the Second World War. It can only be sketched here. The British Nationality Act 1981 (BNA), as amended, is the main legislation. Although the label is 'British' citizenship, there is no citizenship of any other unit within the UK. There is also citizenship of the EU. However, this merely endorses certain rights which under European law apply to citizens of all EU states (Section 10.1). British citizens have lost EU citizenship after Brexit, although those with the necessary connections with other member states (especially, but not exclusively, Ireland) are able to retain it through those channels.

Citizenship can be based on birth in the UK, or on descent through a relative, or both. The following automatically have 'British' citizenship:

- Those born or adopted in the UK including the Channel Islands and Isle of Man (s 50). However, in the case of someone born on or after 1 January 1983, at least one parent must also be either a citizen or settled in the UK. In the case of a person born before 1 July 2006, if the parents are not married then this must be the mother.
- Those descended from a British citizen (s 2). At the time of birth, at least one parent must be a citizen other than by descent. Again, in the case of a person born before 1 July 2006, if the parents are not married, this must be the mother.
- Persons connected with former UK territories who were UK citizens, or who by virtue of specified family connections (patrials) had a right of abode in the UK, under the regime that existed before 1983 (s 11).
- Children of citizens who are government employees working overseas at the date of birth and certain persons connected with UK-dependent territories (below).

Citizenship can also be acquired by registration or naturalisation. **Registration** is a right mainly given to various categories of person who would have been entitled to citizenship under earlier regimes. The main examples are (i) persons who were born in the UK and either lived here until the age of ten or whose parent became a citizen or had an indefinite leave to remain; and (ii) persons at least one of whose parents was a citizen at the time of birth, the particular requirements depending on the date of birth (BNA, s 4; Immigration, Asylum and Nationality Act 2006, s 58; Borders, Citizenship and Immigration Act 2009, ss 44, 46, 47; Immigration Act 2014, s 65, sch 9).

In some cases under (ii), an applicant must also satisfy the Home Secretary that he or she is of good character. However, in *R (Johnson) v Secretary of State for the Home Department* [2016] UKSC 56, the Supreme Court held that a person who would, apart from his parents' marital status, automatically have been a citizen could not be refused registration on the ground of bad character. The claimant had been born in Jamaica to an unmarried couple, a British father and a Jamaican mother. He was not automatically a citizen because, in the case of those born out of wedlock before 1 July 2006, the mother has to be a citizen (above). In 1989 his father brought him to the UK at the age of four, where he had lived ever since. Having reached the age of 18 and having a serious criminal record he was not of 'good character' and the Home Office sought to deport him as a 'foreign criminal'. Had his parents been married, or his mother British, he would have automatically been a citizen. The Supreme Court held that he could not be deported. He was entitled to registration as a citizen because if his parents had been married he would have automatically been a citizen. Although the ECHR said nothing about nationality as such, a denial of citizenship affected personal identity within Art 8 of the ECHR and this triggered Art 14: discrimination (Section 21.4.4), since there is no rational justification for relating bad character to marital status.

A right of registration is also available to 'British subjects' which, despite the title, is a very limited group. Before 1949, it included citizens of all British territories, but it now applies mainly to persons born in former British territories who would otherwise be stateless (BNA, s 31). A limited group of citizens of Hong Kong, which the UK surrendered to China in 1997, have certain rights to registration as British citizens (British nationals (overseas)). Other Hong Kong citizens can acquire a British passport, although this in itself carries no legal rights, being essentially an identity document (British Nationality (Hong Kong) Act 1997; Borders, Citizenship and Immigration Act 2009, s 44). In July 2020, the government announced a new 'bespoke visa route', open from 2021, which would allow Hong Kong British nationals (overseas) citizens and their families, as well as those born after 1997 to a British national (overseas) parent, the right to apply for leave to live and work or study in the UK, and to apply for British citizenship after living in the UK for six years in total.

Naturalisation (BNA, s 6) is a matter for the discretion of the Secretary of State and is available to anyone, subject to requirements of residence, family association as prescribed by the Secretary of State, presence in the UK within a qualifying period of years, language, good character and 'knowledge of life in the UK' as prescribed by the Home Secretary (Nationality, Immigration and Asylum Act 2002, s 4; Borders, Citizenship and Immigration Act 2009, ss 39, 40). However, in *R(MM) v Secretary of State for the Home Department* [2016] 1 WLR 2858, Ousley J held that the Secretary of State's discretion was not a wide one. It was limited to the personal suitability of the candidate and did not enable the Home Secretary to refuse naturalisation in the public interest, in this case, to deter potential extremists by refusing to naturalise members of an extremist's family.

Citizenship is legally important mainly in the following respects:

It confers a right to enter and reside in the UK. There is an ancient common law principle that a citizen cannot be excluded from the territory. Under international law, except in special cases, a citizen cannot be denied entry to or removed from the country (*Al-Jedda v Secretary of State for the Home Department* [2014] AC 253). However, a citizen can be 'extradited' to another country to stand trial for a criminal offence or serve a sentence (Section 9.7.3).

The onus is on the person concerned to prove entitlement to enter the UK. In practice, a passport is usually sufficient evidence. A passport is a travel document issued by the Crown to a citizen in its discretion under the royal prerogative. Possession of a passport does not in itself confer any legal rights. However, someone with no passport is unlikely to be able to leave the UK, in as much as ships and airlines would be unwilling to take on such a person. The Crown could withdraw a passport, for example to prevent potential terrorists from training overseas, although this would be subject to judicial review.

British, Irish and Commonwealth citizens lawfully resident in the UK may vote in parliamentary and local elections (Representation of the People Act 2000) and elections for the devolved governments.

Non-citizens (other than Commonwealth and Irish citizens) cannot be members of either House of Parliament (British Nationality Act 1981, Sched. 7).

Honours cannot be conferred upon non-citizens, except Commonwealth citizens.

British citizens have a right to call upon the protection of the Crown when abroad, although this is not usually enforceable in the courts, which take the view that matters of diplomatic protection are not suitable for judicial decision except in extreme cases. The main consequence of the Crown's duty to protect British citizens abroad is that the Crown cannot require payment for such protection unless the person concerned voluntarily exposes himself or herself to some special risk (see *China Navigation Co Ltd v A-G* [1932] 2 KB 197; *Mutasa v A-G* [1980] QB 114).

British citizens abroad are subject to special taxation laws.

British citizens anywhere in the world owe 'allegiance' (loyalty) to the Crown (see *R v Casement* [1917] 1 KB 98).

As the UK is a monarchy, everyone within its jurisdiction, citizen and non-citizen alike, is a 'subject' of the Crown, owing allegiance to the Crown. Despite the word commonly being associated with subservience, the notion of a 'subject' is sometimes said to give valuable protection in that it presupposes a relationship of mutual respect between ruler and ruled. Allegiance has two main consequences. Firstly, in return for allegiance, the Crown probably cannot plead the defence of 'act of state' (Section 9.6.3). Secondly, the offence of treason is committed against the duty of allegiance. Thus, in return for 'allegiance' (loyalty) the Crown is obliged to protect the rights of the subject and keep the peace (see *Calvin's Case* (1606) 7 Co Rep 2a; *de Jager v A-G of Natal* [1907] AC 326; *R v Secretary of State for the Home Dept, ex parte Thakrar* [1974] QB 684, 709). Apart from renouncing citizenship, allegiance cannot be voluntarily surrendered. A person who holds a British passport is taken to owe allegiance even if s/he has never visited the UK and even if the passport has been fraudulently obtained (see *Joyce v DPP* [1946] AC 347).

Other legal rights and duties depend on presence in the territory or sometimes, particularly in relation to health and welfare services, a more specific connection such as lawful residence (see e.g. *R (A) v Secretary of State for Health* [2010] 1 All ER 87: access to health service denied to a failed asylum-seeker).

9.3.1 Removal of citizenship and statelessness

Citizenship can be renounced by registration with the Secretary of State (BNA, s 12). However, registration becomes ineffective unless the person in question acquires citizenship of another state within six months.

The UN Convention Relating to Stateless Persons (1954) defines a stateless person as 'a person who is not considered as a national by any state under the operation of its law', the term 'law' being broadly defined to include the practices of the executive in implementing the law, even if they fall outside the law itself, thereby conflicting with the rule of law (*Pham v Secretary of State for the Home Department* [2015] 1 WLR 1591).

The Home Secretary can by order remove citizenship:

(a) on the grounds of public good, unless deprivation of citizenship would make the person stateless whatever the cause: see *Al-Jedda v Secretary of State for the Home Department* [2014]); or
(b) where citizenship was acquired by fraud, false representation or concealment of a material fact (BNA 1981, s 40 as amended); or
(c) in the case of a naturalised citizen, if he has conducted himself in a way 'seriously prejudicial to the vital interests of the UK' even if he would otherwise be stateless, provided that the Secretary of State has reasonable grounds to believe that he is eligible for citizenship of another country or territory (Immigration Act 2014, s 66). The right of abode of a citizen of a Commonwealth country can also be removed on the ground of public good (Immigration, Nationality and Asylum Act 2006, s 57).

As a result of the exercise of this power, a person might be refused entry by another state. In *Pham v Secretary of State for the Home Department* (above), the Home Secretary made an order depriving the claimant, who was suspected of undertaking terrorism training in Yemen, of citizenship on the ground of public good. The government intended to deport him to Vietnam. Under Vietnamese law, the claimant was a Vietnamese citizen. However, on learning of the Home Secretary's action, the Vietnamese government refused to accept the claimant as its national. Nevertheless, the Supreme Court held that the claimant was not stateless. The reason was that no formal decision had been made by the Vietnamese government concerning the claimant's nationality and its refusal to accept him as a national had been after the UK order was made ([29], [67], [101]). The matter was referred back to a lower court to decide other issues, in particular whether EU law applied and whether the Secretary of State's decision was reasonable in domestic law.

Shamina Begum, an East London schoolgirl, travelled to Syria to join the Islamic State group in January 2015. She was deprived of her British citizenship by the Home Secretary on grounds of public good in February 2019. Begum sought to overturn the decision, and the Court of Appeal ruled that she must be permitted to return to the UK in order to exercise a fair and effective appeal against the determination, although this conclusion did not in itself reverse the decision on the deprivation of citizenship (*Begum v Special Immigration Appeals Commission and Secretary of State for the Home Department* [2020] EWCA Civ 918).

9.3.2 Non-citizens

Some categories of non-citizen have a right to live in the UK.

Those who were ordinarily resident in the UK without restrictions on 1 January 1983 do not need leave to enter and remain (Immigration Act 1971, as amended, s 1(2)).

The right of abode and treatment as citizens applies to citizens of Commonwealth countries who had the right to live in the UK under earlier legislation (Immigration Act 1971, s 2 as substituted by British Nationality Act 1981).

Under EU law, citizens of the EU, Switzerland and the broader European Economic Area (Norway, Iceland, Liechtenstein) and their families (subject to citizenship requirements) have a right to live and work within the UK. After five years' residence, the right can be certified as permanent. Those not working must be able to support themselves without recourse to public funds. Following Brexit, it will be necessary (from 30 June 2021) for these persons to apply under an 'EU settlement scheme'.

Citizens of the Republic of Ireland are not subject to immigration control, although there are passport checks (Immigration Act 1971, ss 1(3), (9)).

Certain other people, being members of countries belonging to the former British Empire and so victims of increasingly ungenerous immigration policies, attract privileges mainly in connection with immigration in circumstances too specialised to be discussed here.

The Home Secretary has discretionary powers to give other non-citizens leave to remain, either for specific periods or indefinitely. These powers are guided by the 'Immigration Rules' made by the Home Secretary 'as to the practice to be followed in the administration of the Immigration Acts' (Immigration Act 1971, s 1(4)). They comprise a mixture of policy requirements and discretionary guidance. The Immigration Rules are not strictly law but must be approved by Parliament and are published as parliamentary papers. Under general principles of judicial review, they must be followed unless there is a special reason not to do so (see *Hesham Ali (Iraq) v Secretary of State for the Home Department* [2016] UKSC 60, [15]–[17]).

Human rights standards apply to immigration decisions. This involves balancing the reasons for a refusal or deportation against the right in question under the principle of 'proportionality' (Section 22.9). The rights concerned come primarily from Art 8 of the ECHR: privacy and respect for family life, and Art 3: inhuman or degrading treatment (Section 9.7.4). Although the courts have sometimes been criticised for allegedly being over sympathetic to immigrants, they have accepted social cohesion as justifying strict immigration rules. Thus, in *R (Bibi) v Secretary of State for the Home Department* [2015] 1 WLR 5055, a husband was refused entry to join his wife because he could not speak English and could not afford lessons. The Supreme Court held that a language requirement in itself was proportionate under the right to respect for family life in Art 8 of the ECHR since it was rationally connected with the legitimate aim of social cohesion and went no further than was necessary. It was not unjustified discrimination since a general rule was desirable in the interests of clarity. However, in deciding individual cases, financial hardship should be taken into account.

Changing the immigration rules

A person seeking entry to the UK or one with permission to stay for a limited time is at risk that the governing policy will change, making him or her liable to removal. In *Odelola v Secretary of State* [2009] UKHL 25, the claimants were Nigerian doctors who had applied to work in the UK. While their applications were in progress the government changed the Immigration Rules so that only doctors with UK qualifications would now be admitted. The Supreme Court held that it was 'strictly a barren exercise' (at [25]) to ask whether the rules were law. They must be applied correctly but do not create legal rights in the full sense. The claimants could not therefore rely on the rules as they stood at the time of application but only those in force when the decision was made. There is no reason to assume that a government policy will not be changed. Thus, unless a person is given a specific promise that a policy will be applied to them, they have no 'legitimate expectation' (Section 18.3.1) that it will not be changed, only that the policy currently in force will be applied. Moreover, the constitutional presumption that laws should not be retrospective did not apply since the claimants had no legal rights.

However, in *Pankina v Secretary of State* [2011] 1 All ER 1043, the government attempted to impose an extra financial requirement on international students who wished to remain in the UK after graduating. It did this in the form of 'policy guidance' outside the Immigration Rules. The Court of Appeal held that the government cannot impose more obstacles to immigration than those set out in the rules themselves. It was suggested that because the Immigration Rules are heavily relied on, they have acquired a status similar to law. Moreover, the main requirements for leave to enter or remain must be set out in the rules and cannot be added on as extra policies (see also *R (Alvi) v Secretary of State for the Home Dept* [2012] 1 WLR 2208 and *R (Mayaya) v Secretary of State* [2012] 1 All ER 1491 endorsing this).

9.4 British dependent territories

9.4.1 The Channel Islands and the Isle of Man

The Channel Islands (the bailiwicks of Jersey and Guernsey, the latter including also the islands of Alderney, Sark and Herm) have a special status. They are not part of the UK, but their citizens are British citizens if they qualify under the normal rules (Section 9.3). They are subjects of the Crown, in the sense of the monarch, but are not subject to the UK executive.

The special position of the islands derives from feudal ownership by the Crown as successor to the Duke of Normandy. Sark in particular retains feudal features in its government and property-owning arrangements. The Crown makes laws for the islands, normally in the form of Prerogative Orders in Council giving royal assent to local laws. Each island has its own legislature, executive and courts. Parliamentary supremacy was extended to the islands by a Prerogative Order in Council of 1806. Thus, Parliament can make laws for the islands but, by convention, will do so only with the consent of the government in question. Such laws are rare. Moreover, there is a presumption of interpretation that an Act of Parliament will not apply to the Channel Islands in the absence of express words or necessary implication. The islands are therefore effectively self-governing. They pay no taxes to the UK and receive no money from the UK.

The common law does not apply, and the internal law of the islands is local customary law. Although the judicial review jurisdiction of the High Court applies, the local court system will normally be preferred (see *Ex p Brown* [1864] 3 LJ QB 193; *Ex p Anderson* [1861] 3 E&E 487). For example, the Supreme Court has held that, although they have jurisdiction to do so, the UK courts should not normally review human rights issues internal to the islands since the local courts are better equipped for this task (*R (Barclay) v Secretary of State for Justice* [2014] 3 WLR 1142: a case containing a good account of the general constitutional principles).

The position of the Isle of Man is broadly similar to that of the Channel Islands but supported by statute. The Crown's rights seem to derive from an ancient agreement with Norway, confirmed by statute (Isle of Man Purchase Act 1765 (repealed), Isle of Man Act 1958). Legislation is made by its partly elected legislature, the Tynwald, which is also its executive.

(See generally Royal Commission on the Constitution, 1973, Part XI and Minutes of Evidence VI, 7, 13, 227–34; *X v UK* (1982) 4 EHRR 188.)

9.4.2 British overseas territories

The UK retains some dependent overseas territories. Previously colonies or protectorates (a territory with its own government over which the Crown has powers under a treaty), they are now 'British overseas territories' (British Overseas Territories Act 2002). They are mainly scattered islands. They include Anguilla, Bermuda, the British Indian Ocean Territories (BIOT), the British Virgin Islands, Cayman Islands, Falkland Islands, Gibraltar, Montserrat, the Pitcairn Islands, St Helena, South Georgia and the South Sandwich Islands (SGSSI), and the Turks and Caicos Islands. Their citizens, British overseas citizens, can apply to register as UK citizens (British Overseas Territories Act 2002).

Except for residents of British sovereign bases in Cyprus, this is automatic for those who were citizens of the territory in question before 21 May 2002, but in other cases registration is discretionary. However, those born on or after that date in the overseas territory are entitled to British citizenship if a parent is either a British citizen, settled in the UK or settled in the territory in question. In the case of the Falkland Islands (which Argentina claims), all its citizens are entitled to British citizenship (British Nationality (Falkland Islands) Act 1983). Otherwise, their citizens are subject to ordinary immigration controls.

Former colonies occupy an ambiguous position. They are subject to parliamentary supremacy and the UK courts, but lack full legal protection. The rights of their inhabitants depend on the historical accident of how the territory in question came into British hands, often by unpleasant means. As in the case of the Channel Islands, Acts of the UK Parliament do not apply to them unless specifically so provided. By virtue of section 5 of the Colonial Laws Validity Act 1865, legislatures in overseas dependent territories have full power to make local laws, even if this is inconsistent with a UK statute of general effect or with the common law. This includes altering their own constitution but only in the 'manner and form' required by any UK law applying to the territory at the time (*R v Burah* (1878) 3 App Cas 889). This provides a safeguard against a regime manipulating legislative procedures in its own interests. It is not clear whether the protection of the HRA applies to dependent territories (Section 9.4.2.1).

The application of the common law and the powers of the UK executive depend on how the territory was acquired. There is a distinction between 'settled' territories and 'ceded or conquered' territories. A settled territory is one in which there were no developed political institutions when British settlers first arrived (such as SGSSI). A ceded territory previously had its own governmental institutions (e.g. BIOT) and was either ceded (given up) to Britain or conquered by force.

In the case of *settled* territories, the powers of the executive are restricted; the original settlers are deemed to have brought with them the English common law as it stood at the time of settlement (indeed, the common law reached what is now the USA by that route). This means that the limitations placed on the royal prerogative in England apply in that territory. Most significant are the restrictions laid down in the *Case of Proclamations* (1611) 12 Co Rep 74, after which the king could not introduce new laws without the consent of Parliament. In settled territories therefore, as in the UK, the Crown does not have the inherent power to make law. Laws can be made only under an Act of Parliament. Under the British Settlements Acts 1837 and 1945, statutory instruments made by ministers can create constitutions for each territory and delegate powers to local officials. Such powers are usually expressed as being for the 'peace, order and good government' of the territory, but it is unclear whether this ritual phrase has any specific legal effect (below).

In the case of *ceded* territories, the powers of the Crown are more extensive (*Campbell v Hall* (1774) 1 Cowp 204). The reason for the distinction is, of course, that extended powers were needed to suppress the existing governments in conquered territories. English common law does not automatically extend to the territory, which means that the *Case of Proclamations* does not apply. Thus, the Crown has full power to make law under the royal prerogative and to impose its own governmental arrangements and taxation including overriding fundamental rights (see *A-G for Canada v Cain* [1906] AC 542, 545; *R (Bancoult) v Secretary of State for the Foreign and Commonwealth Office (No 2)* [2008] 4 All ER 1055 at [96]–[101]). Governors can be appointed by the Crown ('commissioned') to make laws (in formal 'Royal Instructions' and in subsequent despatches).

Such powers are also usually expressed as being for the 'peace, order and good government of the territory'. However, it seems that this requirement does not limit the width of the prerogative lawmaking power and the courts will not inquire into the matter (see *Bancoult (No 2)* at [31], [47]–[50], [109], [127]–[130]). A similar requirement contained in a statutory instrument in respect of a *settled* territory might limit the executive's power since such power would be only subordinate.

The Crown can deprive itself of the prerogative lawmaking power. Lord Mansfield in *Campbell v Hall* (above) decided that, where there is a local legislature, the power is transferred from the Crown to the colony in question and cannot be recovered except by statute.

The prerogative in dependent territories

In *Campbell v Hall* (1774) the Crown had issued a proclamation empowering the governor of Grenada to establish a local legislative assembly. Despite the formally announced intention to decentralise government, the Crown had subsequently attempted to impose a new tax directly on the colony, and the court held that this was unlawful. Although the assembly had not actually been established, it was held that by promising to create one the Crown had lost its power to pass laws under the prerogative for that colony. The reason for this was that the Crown had sought investment and invited settlers to the colony, who would have relied on the promise to create a local assembly, an early example of the 'legitimate expectation' (Section 18.3.1). The quandary for Whitehall was that taxes had to be levied if the colonies were not to be a burden on British taxpayers, but, after *Campbell*, unless it continued with direct rule, the Crown had to rely on local assemblies to agree to the required taxation. It is unclear whether *Campbell* – the authority of which has never been doubted – is a decision that is now to be confined to its own facts, or whether it establishes a wider principle of constitutional law limiting the Crown's prerogative powers (Section 14.6), the boundaries of which remain unclear.

9.4.2.1 Control by the UK government

Dependent territories make their own laws through powers delegated to their legislatures by statute or, in ceded territories, the royal prerogative. However, the UK government may sometimes directly intervene, pursuing policies of its own. Where a British overseas territory of either kind has its own government, it may be that the Crown is 'divisible', meaning that the Crown in relation to the territory is a separate legal entity from the Crown of the UK (*R v Secretary of State for the Foreign and Commonwealth Office, ex p Indian Association of Alberta* [1982] QB 892; *R v Secretary of State for Foreign and Commonwealth Affairs, ex p Quark Fishing Ltd* [2006] 1 AC 529 [9], [20], [76]). If this is correct, the courts will assess the Crown's actions in relation to the interests of the territory in question and not those of the UK. Moreover, unless statute provides otherwise, the Crown should act on the advice only of the government of the territories concerned, not that of UK ministers (see Twomey, 'Responsible Government and the Divisibility of the Crown' [2008] PL 742).

However, the divided Crown doctrine may now be discredited and, perhaps in a common sense way, depends on the context. Where legislation concerns a matter internal to the territory, the doctrine may be useful. On the other hand, where the Crown legislates for purposes of UK policy which impacts on the territory, it seems artificial to treat the Crown as divided since the UK is internationally responsible for its dependencies.

Quark concerned a *settled* territory in the Antarctic with a rudimentary government and small population, South Georgia and the South Sandwich Islands (SGSSI). Local fishing restrictions were imposed by the Crown in the interests of the UK's relationship with neighbouring territories. The claimant argued that this violated its human right of private property. A majority of the House of Lords, Lord Bingham, Lord Hoffmann and Lord Hope, applied the divided Crown doctrine so as to hold that the UK HRA did not apply, since the Crown was not acting as a UK public authority but as the separate ruler of Quark, an Antarctic dependency. However, Baroness Hale and Lord Nicholls rejected the divided Crown doctrine as artificial. There was, however, another rationale supported by a majority, namely that the HRA does not apply to a dependent territory, unless the state in question has specifically extended the ECHR to that territory (Art 56). The UK had not done so in the case of the right in issue (Lord Hoffmann and Lord Nicholls thought that the HRA applied only within the UK itself irrespective of whether the Convention was extended, since international law and domestic law are separate).

However, later cases have modified this approach. Where the UK government directly intervenes in an overseas territory on its own behalf and is fully in control of the personnel concerned, for example by sending in troops, the HRA may apply whether or not the territory is a dependent territory (Section 22.3) (see *Keyu v Secretary of State for Foreign and Commonwealth Affairs* [2015] UKSC 69).

In *R (Bancoult) v Secretary of State for the Foreign and Commonwealth Office (No 2)* [2008], which concerned a ceded territory, namely the British Indian Ocean Territories (BIOT), the House of Lords rejected the divided Crown doctrine and held that the Crown could remove the rights of the inhabitants of a dependency for the purposes of UK policy (see Box). Lord Hoffmann, following the eminent eighteenth-century jurist William Blackstone (and changing his mind from what he said in *Quark*), stated that in relation to dependent territories there was a single undivided Crown (at [47]–[50]). In *R (Barclay) v Secretary of State for Justice* [2014] the Supreme Court suggested that the Crown could legislate for the Channel Islands in the wider interests of the UK, Lady Hale again denying the divided Crown doctrine.

Can dependent territories be sacrificed?

A wider issue behind the divided Crown doctrine is the extent to which the inhabitants of a dependent territory are protected where the UK government sacrifices their interests in pursuance of its own political interests. This is illustrated by the *Quark* case (above) and by the continuing saga of the displaced inhabitants of the Chagos Islands of BIOT. Although the judicial review powers of UK courts apply to overseas territories of both kinds, such territories appear to have little protection against a UK government determined to achieve some wider political purpose. In particular, according to *Quark* (above) the HRA and the ECHR do not normally apply to overseas territories (Section 22.3).

In *R (Bancoult) v Secretary of State for the Foreign and Commonwealth Office (No 1)* [2001] QB 1067, the court did protect the interests of the inhabitants of the territory, although this was short-lived. The Commissioner of the British Indian Ocean Territories (BIOT), which comprised a group of islands, had prerogative power to make law for the ceded territory. On the instructions of the UK government, he made an order (the Immigration Ordinance 1971) expelling the population of the Chagos Islands, resettling them elsewhere (the relevant events took place before the HRA came into force). The population consisted mainly of plantation workers, some of whose families had lived there for several generations. It was UK government policy to use the territory as a military base jointly with the US and for this purpose it wished to remove the inhabitants, falsely treating them as temporary workers so as to avoid problems with the United Nations. The Divisional Court held that the decision was unlawful since it bore no relationship to the interests of the inhabitants. Invoking Magna Carta, Laws LJ also thought that the prerogative power could not be exercised so as to exile a permanent inhabitant from the territory in which s/he has a right to live. However, Laws LJ suggested that, outside the most basic rights, the common law presumptions of the rule of law that require clear statutory authority for interference with individual freedom have only limited application to ceded territories, these having only a reduced rule of law (Section 6.6).

Following this decision, the Foreign Office announced that the islanders would be compensated and allowed to go home. However, subsequently, the Crown, under pressure from the USA, made a Prerogative Order in Council which purported to change the Constitution of BIOT by denying the exiled inhabitants a right of abode in the territory.

This was challenged in *R (Bancoult) v Secretary of State for the Foreign and Commonwealth Office (No 2)* [2008]. But the House of Lords effectively gave the UK government a free hand. It was held that the court had jurisdiction to review a Prerogative Order in Council. Such an Order was, in reality, made by ministers, not the Crown itself (an example of convention shaping the law: Section 3.4.2) and does not have the democratic credentials that made a statute unchallengeable. However, this Order was valid. Any right could be removed by a Prerogative Order in Council since this had full lawmaking powers. The royal prerogative was not limited by any requirement that the law must be for the benefit of the inhabitants of the territory and could prefer the interests of the UK as a whole. Moreover, the courts are very reluctant to interfere with powers exercised for reasons relating to international policy and will do so only in the clearest cases of wrongdoing. In this context, the policy concerns to maintain cooperation with the USA were a sufficiently rational basis for the decision, and any statement the government had made that the inhabitants could return was not sufficiently clear and unambiguous to create an enforceable 'legitimate expectation' (Section 18.3.1). The majority also held that any rights of the inhabitants been compensated with their agreement and that they were using the courts for a political campaign. The HRA could not apply because the UK had not extended the ECHR to the islands.

Lord Bingham (in his final case) and Lord Mance strongly dissented. They regarded the right to remain in the territory as a fundamental common law 'constitutional' right which applied to all UK territories. They applied the 'principle of legality' (Section 6.6), that only clear words in a statute could take away a constitutional right. In *Chagos Islanders v UK* 2013) 567 EHRR SE15, despite expressing misgivings about colonial relics, the European

Court of Human Rights held that the Islanders' claims were not admissible under the ECHR because the UK had not extended the protection of the ECHR to the Islands. Moreover, the court found the reasoning of the House of Lords majority adequate. The court made a similar decision in *Quark Fishing Ltd v UK* (2007) 44 EHRR SE4.

The Supreme Court was subsequently faced with a further claim by the Chagos Islanders, namely that *Bancoult (No 2)* should be set aside because the UK government had misled the court by failing to disclose some relevant documents relating to the feasibility of the inhabitants returning to the islands (*R (Bancoult v Secretary of State for Foreign and Commonwealth Affairs (No 4)* [2016] 3 WLR 157). The relevant expert report on geographical conditions had been amended so much that its reliability was questionable. A majority, careful to discourage the reopening of cases, held that the failure was the result of incompetence rather than intent, and that the case should not be reopened. A case can be reopened only if 'a significant injustice' has probably occurred or, in the case of fresh evidence, there is 'a powerful probability' of such injustice. This was not the case here since the outcome would not probably be different. A lower threshold might apply in the case of an egregious procedural breach and/or where there is difficulty assessing the consequences. Moreover, there must be no alternative remedy. Lady Hale and Lord Kerr dissented, holding that the threshold should be a much lower one, namely whether there is a 'real possibility' of a different outcome.

9.5 International law and domestic law

International law developed out of the concept of independent nation states emerging in the seventeenth century, primarily to deal with armed conflicts over claims to territory. More recently, international law has extended to concerns which also affect internal domestic law such as international crime, refugees, children, human rights, international trade and the environment.

The sources of international law are as follows: decisions of the International Court of Justice in the Hague; treaties between states, and between states and international bodies such as the EU and the UN; 'general principles of law recognized by civilized nations' including 'crimes against humanity' such as torture and genocide; cases decided by international courts and arbitration bodies; and, unlike domestic law, the writings of commentators: 'jurists'. This reflects the open-endedness of international law.

Other international instruments, for example declarations made by meetings of leaders, are sometimes called 'soft law', meaning that they are influential upon behaviour but not legally binding. The basic principle underlying all these sources is that international law derives its authority from the consent of equal states, whereas domestic law derives from an authority imposed from above. Custom and treaties are the most important sources of international law.

9.5.1 Customary law

Customary international law consists of the general practice of states coupled with a conviction that this is legally binding (*opinio juris*) or is required by social, economic or political necessity (*opinio necessitatis*) (Statute of the International Court of Justice Art 38; see *Mohammed v Secretary of State for Defence* [2016] 2 WLR 247, [220]). It is difficult to establish sufficient international consensus, particularly in areas of political controversy, and customary law is highly susceptible to cultural differences between the 195 states in the world. For example, in *Keyu v Secretary of State for Foreign and Commonwealth Affairs* [2015], the Supreme Court held that any rule of customary international law requiring an inquiry into the killing of civilians was only established during the last 25 years and so did not apply to a massacre taking place in 1948. In *Mohammed v Secretary of State for Defence* (above) there was a mass of conflicting opinion, leading the Court of Appeal to reject the government's claim that there was a rule of customary law permitting the taking of prisoners in a non-international armed conflict such as a civil war.

Customary international law is a source of the common law and so can be applied directly by the court (*Trendtex Trading Corp Ltd v. Central Bank of Nigeria* [1977] QB 529, 553). However, this principle is heavily qualified. Customary law gives way to fundamental domestic constitutional principles and values. It may be also excluded where the matter is covered by a domestic statutory regime (*R (Al-Saadoon) v Secretary of State for Defence* [2016] UKCA Civ 811; *Keyu v Secretary of State for Foreign and Commonwealth Affairs* [2015], [144–51]). In particular, customary law cannot create new crimes in the UK, since this should be done only by the democratic process of Parliament (*R v Jones (Margaret)* [2006] 2 WLR 772: campaigners who damaged military aircraft contrary to a domestic law had no defence of preventing the international crime of aggression since this was not a crime in English law).

The judges disagree on the part customary law should play in domestic law. In *Keyu* (above), Lord Mance said (at [150]): 'Customary international law, once established, can and should shape the common law whenever it can do so consistently with domestic constitutional principles, statutory law and common law rules which the courts themselves can sensibly adopt without it being for example necessary to invite parliamentary intervention or consideration'. Lord Mance was addressing the undecided issue of whether customary law enters domestic law by way of 'incorporation', that is, becoming part of the ordinary law, or 'transformation', retaining its distinct nature as a source of, but not part of, the law. If incorporation is the route, then the law might be inflexible, since it would be subject to domestic rules of precedent and it might be more difficult to respond to changing international principles. Lord Mance was therefore suggesting a middle way. On the other hand, in *Jones v Ministry of Interior of Saudi Arabia* [2007] 1 AC 270, followed by the Court of Appeal in *Al-Saadoon* (above), Lord Hoffmann stated that, contrary to ordinary common law techniques, 'it is not for a national court to "develop" international law by unilaterally adopting a version of that law which, however desirable, forward looking, and reflective of values it may be, is simply not accepted by other states'.

9.5.2 General principles of law

General principles of law, or *ius cogens,* include duties not to harm other states, for example by pollution, or unfair use of common resources such as waterways. They also include international crimes such as torture, genocide and war crimes, but not the crime of 'aggression', starting an unlawful war which is a violation of ordinary customary law. As yet, the increasing problems of slavery and human trafficking are not recognised as *ius cogens* (*Al-Maliki v Reyes* [2015] EWCA Civ 32). In the case of pollution and resource issues, enforcement largely depends on international arbitration, but international crimes are increasingly enforced through treaties to which effect is given in domestic law.

However, although domestic law will be interpreted in the light of such fundamental principles, even these cannot override domestic law (*Jones v Ministry of Interior of Saudi Arabia* [2007], [14], [27]; *Al-Maliki v Reyes* (above): immunities of foreign officials). Moreover, a state is not obliged to intervene with another state to insist that it does not use torture (*R (Youssef) v Secretary of State for Foreign and Commonwealth Affairs* [2016] 2 WLR 509).

9.5.3 Treaties

Today the main method for imposing international order is through treaties. A treaty (sometimes called a 'convention') is a binding agreement between states or international organisations and states. A treaty might be bilateral, that is, agreed between two states, or multilateral, where each state joins an existing treaty by 'accession'. In UK law, a treaty is negotiated and entered into under the royal prerogative by a minister or other authorised official.

After a treaty is agreed by representatives of each party, the terms of the treaty may provide that it must also be ratified according to the law of each state involved. Ratification, if required, brings the treaty into force at the international level, but not in domestic law, which depends on the law of each state. Under the terms of a treaty, for example the Climate Change Treaty, it may come into force only when a prescribed number of states have ratified (confirmed) it.

In the UK, treaties requiring ratification are ratified by ministers or by Order in Council under the royal prerogative, so that the consent of Parliament is not required (although the treaty which provided for the UK's withdrawal from the European Union was a special case: see Section 10.5.3). This lack of parliamentary control is unusual in democratic states. However, Part 2 of the Constitutional Reform and Governance Act 2010 brings in Parliament to a limited extent by enacting a convention, the 'Ponsonby Convention', under which a treaty was laid before parliament before ratification. Section 20 applies to all treaties requiring ratification, except certain EU treaties that require statutory approval, certain tax treaties and treaties made by UK dependencies and the Channel Islands and Isle of Man. The main provisions are as follows:

> The treaty must be laid before Parliament for 21 days and published in a way that the minister 'thinks appropriate'.
> If the House of Commons resolves that the treaty should not be ratified, the minister can lay a statement before Parliament that it should be ratified anyway and explaining why.
> After another 21 days, the treaty can be ratified unless the Commons passes a further resolution that it should not be ratified. This process can be repeated but, given the strength of the executive and the lack of background information available to Parliament, the executive is likely to prevail.
> If the House of Lords, but not the Commons, resolves not to ratify the treaty, it can be ratified anyway.

In cases which are exceptional (in a minister's opinion), a treaty can be ratified without complying with the above. Before, or as soon as possible after, ratification, the minister must lay a copy of the treaty before Parliament, publish it and lay a statement before Parliament explaining why the case is exceptional (s 22). Parliament can, of course, bring political pressure to bear on any proposed treaty under its normal processes, such as select committees, questions to ministers, and special debates.

Moreover, in *R (Miller) v Secretary of State for Exiting the EU* [2017] UKSC 5, the Supreme Court held that statute itself may be required to authorise the executive to make or alter a treaty that leads to a change in fundamental rights (Section 10.5.2).

In addition to ratification, any treaty that affects legal rights and duties, and one that involves spending public money, must be made enforceable in domestic law. In some states, such as Germany and Russia, international law, including treaties, is automatically part of domestic law: these are *monist* systems. In the UK, which has a *dualist* system, this is not so. Irrespective of ratification, a treaty cannot be enforced in domestic law unless it is first enacted by Parliament in a statute (see *MacLaine Watson and Co Ltd v Dept of Trade and Industry* [1990] 2 AC 418). This is separate from any parliamentary scrutiny needed before ratification (above). In other words, the wide prerogative power to enter into treaties is subject to the important safeguard that the executive alone cannot alter legal rights and obligations in domestic law. It seems also that withdrawing from such a treaty requires a statute if it involves a change in domestic law (*R (Miller) v Secretary of State for Exiting the EU* (above)).

A treaty might be incorporated by being fully enacted, in which case it is directly translated into statute law. Several important constitutional treaties have been enacted, including, for example, treaties giving foreign governments and their officials immunity from legal liability (Section 9.6.1). Alternatively, the requirements of a treaty can be introduced by enacting that a treaty shall be transmitted into domestic law automatically. The EU treaties are the most outstanding examples of this (European Communities Act 1972). The treaty which withdraws the UK from the EU, and that which governs the future relationship between the two, have also been enacted (European Union (Withdrawal Agreement) and European Union (Future Relationship) Acts 2020). The ECHR has not been incorporated as such, but most of its provisions have been given special domestic effect by the HRA.

It has been suggested that this dualist approach is too narrow, and that general principles of international law embodied in treaties concerning fundamental rights, such as freedom from torture and freedom of speech, should automatically be part of the common law irrespective of their enactment in statute (see Lord Steyn in *Re McKerr* [2004] 1 WLR 807). However, this has not had general support; see *R v Bow Street Metropolitan Stipendiary Magistrate, ex p Ugarte (No 3)* [1999] 2 All ER 97. Lord Kerr, dissenting in *R (SG) v Secretary of State for Work and Pensions* [2015] 1 WLR 1449, suggested that all human rights treaties should automatically be legally binding. The rationale behind this appears to be that the international rule of law embodied in human rights values should be all-pervading (see e.g. Malkani, 'Human Rights Treaties in the English Legal System' [2011] PL 554).

Reliance on statutory incorporation may cause problems since there might be gaps in the implementation of important treaties. An example is provided by the various UN Conventions against genocide, war crimes, crimes against humanity, torture, hostage-taking and other international crimes. These are intended to ensure that all countries apply these offences, wherever committed, in their domestic law. UK law has done so in some respects, but the record is patchy. For example, offences are not usually retrospective and apply to different dates where particular Acts came into force. Most apply only to UK citizens or offences committed in the UK (e.g. International Criminal Court Act 2001 (Section 9.6)), but some apply to anyone anywhere (e.g. Criminal Justice Act 1988, s 134: torture; Taking of Hostages Act 1982).

9.5.4   Applying treaties in the courts: incorporated treaties

A treaty is 'non-justiciable'. This means that a court cannot consider whether a treaty-making power has been unlawfully exercised, or review the content of a treaty, or prevent a minister from ratifying it (see *R v Secretary of State for Foreign and Commonwealth Affairs, ex p Rees-Mogg* [1994] 1 All ER 457). However, the court can use a treaty to help it interpret the law. The courts have taken a strict approach to applying treaties because of the danger of permitting executive lawmaking. However, they have recently become more liberal in their use of treaties and other international sources as aids to the interpretation of domestic law. This is due to a presumption that the UK's international obligations should be honoured.

There is a distinction between a treaty which has been incorporated into domestic law and an unincorporated treaty. Where a treaty has been incorporated, the courts should interpret it according to international law principles, including any documentation used in preparing the treaty (*traveux preparatois*) (*Al- Maliki v Reyes* [2016]; *Benkharbouche v Embassy of the Republic of Sudan* [2015] 3 WLR 301; *Assange v Swedish Prosecution Authority* [2012] 2 AC 471; *R (JS, Sri Lanka) v Secretary of State for the Home Dept* [2011] 1 AC 184). However, clear words in the statute ultimately prevail and domestic constitutional principles must be applied (*Pham v Secretary of State for the Home Department* [2015], [77]–[80]). For example, in *R (ST) (Eritrea) v Secretary of State for the Home Dept* [2012] 3 All ER 1037, the Supreme Court held that 'lawfully' in the Refugee Convention Article 32 which prevented a state expelling a refugee 'lawfully' on its territory, except on prescribed grounds, means lawful in domestic law. Even though the treaty must be interpreted generously according to its humanitarian purpose the court would not assume that it would override domestic law rights unless stated explicitly.

9.5.5   Applying treaties in the courts: unincorporated treaties

In the case of a treaty that has not been incorporated, the traditional position is that such a treaty may be used to help interpret a statute only if the statute is ambiguous since, otherwise, the executive would be making law in defiance of Parliament, thus violating the separation of powers (see *MacLaine Watson and Co Ltd v Dept of Trade and Industry* [1990]: the 'International Tin Council' case; *Brind v Secretary of State* [1991] 1 AC 696 at 748; Higgins (2009); Collins (2009)).

However, later cases have emphasised the 'strong presumption in favour of conforming to international obligations' (*Assange v Swedish Prosecution Authority* [2012], [122]). Indeed, the Supreme Court has held that other international materials such as UN reports should also be taken into account (*Pham v Secretary of State for the Home Department* [2015], [29]; Section 9.3.1; see also *Hounga v Allen* [2014] 1 WLR 2889, [51]–[52]). An unincorporated treaty can also be used, as can overseas judicial decisions, to help develop the common law (see *R (SG) v Secretary of State for Work and Pensions* [2015], [137], [239]–[244], [254]–[255]).

An unincorporated treaty might also be applied through administrative mechanisms such as discretionary immigration powers, as opposed to enacting a specific statute for the purpose. There may be disputes as to whether such a treaty has been properly implemented (see e.g. Liscombe and Beard, House of Commons Library SN/HA 4324 (2014); Modern Slavery Act 2015).

A court has no jurisdiction to make a binding interpretation of an unincorporated treaty or other questions of international law. The court cannot, therefore, decide whether the executive has correctly understood a treaty, but can ensure that it has taken the treaty into account, although the court is likely to be cautious in this regard (see *R (Corner House Research) v Director General of the Serious Frauds Office* [2008] 4 All ER 927 (HL, at [44], [62], [65], [67]); *R v Secretary of State for the Home Department ex parte Launder* [1997] 1 WLR 839).

An unincorporated treaty may also be taken into account if it is applied by the European Court of Human Rights in Strasbourg and so followed by the domestic courts under the HRA (Section 22.1). For example, *R (SG) v Secretary of State for Work and Pensions* [2015] UKSC 16 concerned whether the 'benefit cap' introduced by the government in 2006, which limited welfare payments, discriminated against women, specifically lone parents. An important issue was whether the UN Convention on the Rights of the Child 1989 (Cm 1976), which requires a child's best interests to be a 'primary consideration', should be taken into account. Clearly, a benefit cap was not in a child's best interests. The majority accepted that, in principle, an unincorporated treaty can be taken into account. However, it was held that, since the issue in the case concerned discrimination between men and women and did not *directly* concern any right of a child, in this case, the Convention need not be taken into account. Lady Hale and Lord Kerr took a broader view. Lady Hale took the view that the treaty should be taken into account as it was relevant to the ECHR test of proportionality. Lord Kerr held more radically that all human rights treaties should be considered legally binding (Section 9.5.3) (see also *R (T) v Chief Constable of Greater Manchester Police* [2015] AC 49: secrecy of children's criminal records: UN Convention on the Rights of the Child).

Treaties modifying human rights

In *R (Al-Jedda) v Secretary of State* [2008] 1 AC 332, an Iraqi citizen was interned by the army in a British army camp in Iraq. He alleged that his right to personal freedom, under Article 5 of the ECHR, had been violated. The House of Lords disagreed. This was because the European Court took the view that, in some circumstances, other international obligations, in this case, to comply with a UN peacekeeping resolution, could influence the application of the ECHR, in this case by modifying Art 5. The House of Lords, faced with a hard choice, held that the claimant's rights could be overridden to the extent that was necessary to comply with the UN resolution. (See also *Hassan v UK* [2014] ECHR 9936: international humanitarian treaty law gives powers of detention in international armed conflicts modifying the normal protection of the ECHR, e.g. no right to independent judicial review. Compare *Mohammed v Secretary of State for Defence* [2016], [251]: detention of Afghan prisoners by army in Afghanistan: international law does not give power to detain in a *non-international* armed conflict such as a civil war. See also *AH (Algeria) v Secretary of State for the Home Department (No 2)* [2016] 1 WLR 2071: UN Convention applied to limit rights of refugees.)

The overriding principle remains that international law cannot override clear principles of domestic law (*R (Bancoult) v Secretary of State for Foreign and Commonwealth Affairs* [2008] at [66]). In *R (A) v Secretary of State for Health* [2016] 1 WLR 331, a decision under a UN Convention called on the UK to overturn the ban on abortion in Northern Ireland. The Court of Appeal held that the Secretary of State did not have any obligation to mitigate the effects of Northern Ireland's harsh abortion laws by providing free abortions in England for women from Northern Ireland, although funding was later provided after an unsuccessful appeal to the Supreme Court.

9.6   Overseas relationships and the courts

9.6.1   State immunity

Where state immunity applies, a UK court has no jurisdiction over the case. State immunity belongs in the law of procedure, specifically 'impleader', that is, whether someone can be forced to appear before a court ('direct impleader') or whether his or her property can be seized ('indirect impleader'). The immunity is based upon the principle of 'comity' or respect for sovereignty (*The Parlement Belge* (1880) LR 5 PD 197). The immunity is personal to the state in question and is attracted where it would otherwise be open to legal liability. Thus in *Belhaj v Straw* [2017] UKSC 3, the Supreme Court held that UK ministers could not claim indirect state immunity in respect of the mistreatment of terrorist suspects by various states, since these states could not be made parties to the litigation. Once there was general common law immunity for acts of foreign governments, but as international transactions have increased, this has become more relaxed. Nevertheless, the importance of international relations requires a large amount of immunity (*Al Adsani v UK* (2001) 34 EHRR 273).

The position depends on the State Immunity Act 1978. This enabled the UK to ratify the European Convention on State Immunity 1978 (see also UN Convention on Jurisdictional Immunity of States and Their Property 2004). Before then, the common law had begun to restrict state immunity to sovereign activities (see *Benkharbouche v Embassy of the Republic of Sudan* [2015], [6]). The 1978 Act applies to civil and criminal actions against a state and its employees or agents. The state, meaning the 'executive organs of the central government', has complete immunity for the acts of its agents even where an agent is acting outside his or her instructions. The agent also has immunity.

The immunity is a blanket one and applies also to enforcing judgments of foreign courts. State immunity therefore challenges the rule of law. However, it has been held that the immunity does not violate Art 6 ECHR, the right to a fair trial, since the immunity is required under international law, to which the 1978 Act gives effect, and Art 6 must be taken to conform to international law (see *Jones v Ministry of Interior of Saudi Arabia* [2007], [14]; *Jones v UK* (2014) 59 EHRR 1; *Holland v Lampen-Wolfe* [2000] 1 WLR 1573; *Benkharbouche v Embassy of the Republic of Sudan* [2015], [16]). In *Belhaj v Straw* [2017], the Supreme Court left this point open.

The immunity covers all claims, even human rights violations including torture. In *Jones v Minister of the Interior of Saudi Arabia* [2007], the House of Lords held that torture carried out under the orders of the Saudi government was a governmental function, so that the officers of the state were immune from civil liability, even though torture is prohibited by the ECHR and by a fundamental principle of international law (Torture Convention (Cm 1775, 1990)) (see also *Al-Adsani v UK* (2001) 34 EHRR 273).

There are important exceptions. The main exception concerns commercial transactions such as sales, loans and contracts to be performed within the UK. Patents and trademarks, personal injury and property damage within the UK, the ownership, possession and use of property, commercial shipping matters and certain taxation matters are also outside the immunity.

Although contracts of employment made in the UK or to be performed there are outside state immunity, the Act preserves state immunity in employment cases concerning a national of the state concerned or a non-UK citizen not resident in the UK at the date of hiring or where there is agreement in writing (s 4(2)). It also preserves the immunity in the case of all employees working in an embassy (s 16(1)(a)). This has created problems in relation to contemporary concerns about forced labour. The immunity for embassy staff has been held to violate the ECHR and EU law. *Benkharbouche v Embassy of the Republic of Sudan* [2015] concerned a claim by a cook in an embassy for unfair dismissal and excessive working hours. The claimant invoked Art 6 of the ECHR, the right to a fair trial. The Court of Appeal decided that state immunity did not apply. It was held that there was no rule of international law requiring state immunity in respect of employment claims by service staff. Therefore sections 4(2) and 16(1), which create this specific immunity, fall outside the treaty and violate Art 6, which reflects international standards. (Cases such as *Jones* (above) differ since there the subject of the immunity fell within the treaty.) Under the HRA, the court cannot override a statute but can make only a non-enforceable declaration of incompatibility (Section 22.5). However, EU law also applied to the particular claim. Certain general principles of EU law contained in the EU Charter of Rights, in this case similar to the ECHR rights, took priority over domestic law (prior to Brexit). The court therefore 'disapplied' the statutory provisions which conferred the immunity against service staff (see also Section 9.6.2).

State immunity is a 'restrictive doctrine of immunity', meaning that its limits will be applied strictly since it weakens the rule of law. For example, in *NML Capital Ltd v Republic of Argentina* [2011] 4 All ER 1191, a majority of the Supreme Court held that the enforcement of a foreign judgment concerning a commercial transaction was not itself immune as a commercial transaction since the transaction itself was not in issue.

The property of the state cannot be enforced against, unless it is being used or intended for use for commercial purposes (ss 13(2)(b) and 13(4)). It is irrelevant how the property was acquired (see *AIG Capital Parties Inc v Republic of Kazakhstan* [2006] 1 All ER 284; *SerVaas Inc v Rafidain Bank* [2013] 1 AC 595).

Today, it is common for private companies to carry out functions on behalf of governments: 'separate entities' (State Immunity Act 1978, s 14). Here the immunity applies only to the 'governmental' functions of the body in question. In practice, this may be difficult to determine, but the immunity of the state cannot be circumvented by suing the separate entity (see *La Generale des Carriers et de Mines v FG Hemisphere Associates LLC* [2013] 1 All ER 409: separate status not conclusive, test is whether activities are integrated with those of government).

For example, *Kuwait Airways v Iraqi Airways (No 1)* [1995] 3 All ER 694 concerned the Iraqi invasion of Kuwait in 1990. Iraqi forces seized aircraft belonging to Kuwait and took them to Iraq. The Iraqi government later made a law transferring the aircraft to the state-owned Iraqi Airways, which used the aircraft for its business. The aircraft were later destroyed in a UN attack on Iraq, and the Kuwaiti airline sued Iraqi Airways for compensation. The House of Lords held that the Iraq government itself was immune under the 1978 Act, but that Iraqi Airways as a separate entity was not using the aircraft for governmental purposes. There was therefore no immunity. A governmental function therefore seems to mean the basic lawmaking, executive and judicial activities of government.

Out of respect for the dignity of the state, a serving head of state has complete immunity in both public and private matters (*Mighell v Sultan of Johore* [1894] 1 QB 149; State Immunity Act 1978, s 20). However, *former* heads of state are immune from liability only in relation to the 'proper functions of the state' (*Harb v Prince Abdul Aziz Bin Fahd* [2015] 1 All ER 77). In *R v Bow Street Metropolitan Stipendiary Magistrate, ex p Pinochet Ugarte (No 3)* [1999] UKHL 17, the House of Lords held that the former president of Chile, whom Spain had requested to be extradited to answer charges of torture, had no immunity because torture should not be regarded as a 'proper' function of the state. This is because all parties to the Torture Convention 1984 have agreed to make torture, wherever committed, a crime in their states. It is not clear whether the *Pinochet* principle applies to breaches of international law other than torture. Neither heads of state nor other officials have immunity from criminal liability under the jurisdiction of the International Criminal Court (Section 9.6.4).

9.6.2   Diplomatic immunity

Diplomatic immunity applies to representatives of foreign governments in the UK other than UK nationals. It is an expression of respect for another sovereign state. Diplomatic premises are also immune (e.g. rent and taxes). Under international law (Vienna Convention on Diplomatic Relations 1961; Vienna Convention on Consular Relations 1963; Diplomatic Privileges Act 1964), diplomats and consular officials and their households have complete immunity from criminal prosecution in their private capacity as well as on official business (e.g. traffic offences). (A consul is a state representative with more limited functions than a full diplomatic representative, usually serving outside a capital city.) The certification of diplomatic status by the state concerned is conclusive in the courts as to his or her official status (Section 9.6.3). In the controversial case of Harry Dunn, a teenager killed in a road accident by a car driven by the wife of a CIA operative working at a listening station in the UK in 2019, diplomatic immunity status was contested. Here, the woman had returned to the US following the accident, and it was argued that if any immunity did exist, it no longer applied after her return and that actions could thus be taken in US courts.

In *civil* liability, both official and private matters, for example marital disputes, are immune under the Convention, but *commercial* acts 'outside the official functions of a diplomat' are not. In *Al-Maliki v Reyes* [2016], domestic workers at the residence of a Saudi Arabian diplomat made claims of people trafficking, discrimination and failure to pay the minimum wage. This raises the human rights issue of forced labour and servitude under Art 4 of the ECHR. The Court of Appeal held that domestic employment was not 'a commercial act' since this was incidental to the diplomat's official functions and not for financial benefit. There was therefore full immunity. This is so even if the alleged wrongs were breaches of fundamental international law principles. It seems, therefore that, as with state immunity, a claim under the HRA is also excluded. The reasoning in the *Benkharbouche* case (Section 9.6.1) was not apparently available because domestic staff fall within the international convention to which the Diplomatic Privileges Act gives effect. In this respect diplomatic immunity is wider than state immunity. When a diplomat has left his or her post, the immunity continues in respect of official functions but, unlike the case of a serving diplomat, this does not normally include domestic service (see *Wokuri v Kassim* [2012] 2 All ER 1195, [23]–[25]: no immunity for ill treatment of domestic servant). Thus, a domestic servant's protection is highly context-dependent.

A representative of a state to a designated international organisation, such as a UN agency, is also entitled to immunity, as are the premises of the organisation. However, if permanently resident in the UK, such a representative is entitled to immunity only in respect of his or her official actions. An agency must be designated by a statutory Order made by the Foreign Secretary implementing a specific agreement made in international law under the Specialised Agencies Convention 1947. A certificate of the Foreign Secretary is conclusive in the courts as to his or her official status (International Organisations Act 1968, s 8). For example, *Estrada v Al Juffali* [2016] 3 WLR 243 concerned a divorce claim where the husband, a Saudi national, was certified as the representative of St Lucia to the International Maritime Organisation, a UN agency. The Court of Appeal held that, even though the husband had not in fact been performing any duties, the court could not go behind the certificate, even under Art 6 of the ECHR, the right to a fair trial. The arrangements made under international law must be taken as satisfying Art 6. For a court to investigate whether a position was genuine might harm international relations. However, the husband was held to be permanently resident in the UK since, given his marital history and lifestyle, his residence was not connected with his official duties. He therefore had no immunity.

The host state cannot enter diplomatic or consular premises (missions) without permission. Thus, an embassy might be resorted to by fugitives or asylum-seekers (such as Julian Assange in the Ecuadorian embassy in London), or used to commit offences. The Secretary of State can withdraw consent if the premises are not being properly used for diplomatic or consular purposes on certain grounds, for example on security grounds, subject to being satisfied that this complies with international law (Diplomatic and Consular Premises Act 1987, enacted following the shooting of a police officer during a siege of the Libyan Embassy in London).

The Secretary of State can withdraw diplomatic and consular privileges where the state in question does not offer the same privileges to the UK (Diplomatic Privileges Act 1964, s 3; Consular Relations Act 1968, s 2). Where a diplomat abuses his or her privileges, the Crown could require the offender to leave the country.

9.6.3 Act of state and justiciability

The common law doctrine of 'act of state' places limits on the court in cases involving foreign governments and the activities of the Crown overseas. The doctrine can arise in any litigation, not only where the foreign state is being sued, and so is distinct from the doctrine of state immunity (above). In *Belhaj v Straw* [2017], [95] Lord Mance emphasised that this is an evolving area of law and that the boundaries between domestic and international issues are increasingly blurred. The umbrella term 'non–justiciable' is often used in this context but is widely regarded as unsatisfactory, embracing as it does a variety of cases where, for different reasons, the courts are unwilling to intervene (see Section 22.9.3).

Act of State has three main meanings. These are:

(i)   a 'foreign' act of state
(ii) a 'domestic' act of state (an aspect of domestic judicial review law)
(iii) a defence to an action in tort committed abroad by the UK government ('Crown' act of state).

9.6.3.1 Foreign act of state

'Foreign' act of state means that UK courts will not normally question certain acts of foreign governments. The basis of the doctrine is respect for an independent sovereign state and its high-level officers (comity). Difficulties in obtaining evidence also play a part 'where there are no judicial or manageable standards… or the court would be in a judicial no-man's land' (*Buttes Gas and Oil Co v Hammer (No. 3)* [1982] AC 888 (at 938); *Shergill v Khaira* [2015] AC 359, [41], [42]).

In *Belhaj v Straw* [2017], the Supreme Court rejected the government's claim that there was a general principle protecting all sovereign acts of a foreign state. According to Lord Mance, the doctrine has three aspects. First, the validity of a state's own municipal law; secondly, actions within the state's territory at least in respect of its property; thirdly, acts of a state in relation to other states, outside its territory and so governed by international law. In relation to the second kind of case, Lord Sumption and Lord Hughes thought that personal injuries, as well as property rights, are included, but Lord Mance disagreed. The third head must be decided on a case-by-case basis. In all three cases, the underlying principles are 'comity', meaning respect for a sovereign nation and the separation of powers in respect of matters appropriate for the executive branch of government (at [225]). In *Belhaj*, the court emphasised that the doctrine cannot be based on avoiding diplomatic embarrassment for the government. Limits on the doctrine are as follows:

(i)   The doctrine does not apply to acts of courts and other judicial bodies.
(ii) The doctrine does not apply to commercial, as opposed to governmental acts.
(iii) The doctrine does not apply where the inquiry is only into whether events have occurred, as opposed to their legal consequences. In *Rahmatullah v Secretary of State for Defence* [2013] 1 AC 614, the Supreme Court was willing in principle to consider a case where US forces were detaining a prisoner of war in Afghanistan, but only as to who in fact controlled the prisoner, not the question of justification of the US government's actions.
(iv) Most important, and unlike state immunity, there is a public policy exception. In particular, foreign act of state does not apply to a serious breach of international law. *In Kuwait Airways v Iraqi Airways (Nos 4 and 5)* [2002] 2 AC 883, the House of Lords held that, by confiscating aircraft, the Iraq government had committed a flagrant breach of a fundamental principle of international law and this overrode any claim to foreign act of state. Lord Hope stressed that the reach of the law should evolve in keeping with contemporary circumstances.

In *Belhaj v Straw* [2017], the Supreme Court held that the then Secretary of State could not claim foreign act of state in relation to a claim that he had cooperated with the USA and other states in detaining and torturing asylum seekers. Lord Sumption and Lord Hughes based this on the international law doctrine of *ius cogens*, covering universally accepted fundamentals based on human rights.

9.6.3.2 Domestic act of state: margin of discretion

A 'domestic' act of state is a claim that certain decisions made by the Crown, usually under the royal prerogative in the field of foreign affairs or national security, cannot normally be challenged in the courts. In *Shergill v Khaira* [2015], [42] the Supreme Court held that the rationale for this is that such decisions do not normally engage legal rights. They also involve decisions of 'high policy', which the courts regard as the special province of the executive as a matter of the separation of powers or 'institutional competence'. This kind of decision is primarily political and lacks the objective standards which a court can assess. An act of state in this sense includes claims to territory, conferring sovereign immunity, or diplomatic immunity (e.g. *Mighell v Sultan of Johore* [1894]; *Engelke v Musmann* [1928] AC 433: the recognition of a foreign government; *Carl Zeiss Stiftung v Rayner & Keeler (No 2)* [1967] 1 AC 853: going to war and deploying the armed forces; *R v Bottrill, ex p Kuechenmeister* [1947] KB 41; *Smith v Secretary of State for Defence* [2011] 1 AC 1: the deployment of the armed forces was 'essentially non-justiciable' (Lady Hale)).

R (Gentle) v Prime Minister [2008] 1 AC 1356 was a claim by the mothers of servicemen killed in Iraq that the government had not complied with international law when it decided to invade Iraq. The House of Lords did not rule out intervention completely. Lord Bingham said that the court will intervene where there is a legal right but, in deciding whether a right exists, the restraint shown in 'matters of high policy', such as the making of treaties and the conduct of foreign relations, militates against such a right, [8]. In *R v Jones (Margaret)* [2006], Lord Hoffmann said that it is a 'constitutional principle' that the Crown's discretion to go to war was not justiciable. Lord Bingham, however, said that the courts would be slow to interfere with the conduct of foreign policy or the deployment of the armed forces, but did not wholly rule it out.

Other foreign policy decisions may be reviewable, particularly where human rights are involved since the courts must in principle decide all human rights cases (*R (Lord Carlile of Berriew) v Secretary of State for the Home Department* [2014] 3 WLR 1404, [30]; *Shergill v Khaira* [2015], [42]). In *R (States of Guernsey) v Secretary of State for Environment Food and Rural Affairs* [2016] EWHC 1847 (Admin), which concerned the suspension of fishing rights agreement between the UK and the Channel Islands, the High Court distinguished between three kinds of case. First, there is a 'forbidden area' where the court cannot interfere at all, which is very rare. Secondly, there are cases with a 'domestic foothold' where private rights are directly involved, or public law standards are in issue. Here the court can decide. Thirdly, there are cases such as diplomatic decisions affecting British citizens where there are no private rights directly in issue, but the court may decide the matter if it is necessary to do so to resolve some other issue. In that case, the court decided the matter, albeit in favour of the government, since the property rights of fishermen were directly in issue and decisions taken under the royal prerogative are reviewable by the courts (Section 14.6.4).

This kind of act of state may perhaps best be regarded as an extreme aspect of a wider principle which is not limited to foreign affairs, namely that of 'margin of appreciation' or 'margin of discretion' (Section 22.9.3). This is an elusive concept, difficult to define. The court will give special weight to the judgment of the executive on a particular matter where the executive has a special constitutional accountability or has specialised knowledge and experience not available to a court, foreign affairs being a typical example.

Where there is such a margin, the court will interfere with the assessment or judgment of the executive only in exceptional circumstances where the decision of the executive has no rational foundation. The extent of interference depends on the particular context and, especially, the subject matter of the power in question, its extent and the seriousness of the infringement of the right. Respect for international relationships is an important factor and raises sensitive issues sometimes leading to judicial disagreement. *R (Lord Carlile of Berriew) v Secretary of State for the Home Department* [2014] concerned a Home Office decision to ban a radical Iranian politician from entering the country to talk to a group of MPs because of fear of upsetting the Iranian government. A majority of the Supreme Court, Lady Hale and Lord Clarke reluctantly, would not interfere even though the Home Office evidence was uncertain. As Lord Sumption pointed out (at [33]), in a democracy, ministers should be politically responsible for this kind of decision since a court cannot be dismissed if things go wrong (see also Lady Hale, [105]). Lord Kerr dissented on the basis that the government gave too much weight to the Iranian attitude which was undemocratic and unreasonable.

Torture raises particular difficulty. Torture faced by an asylum-seeker can be fully scrutinised by the court since, under international law, removing a person to face a risk of torture is absolutely forbidden (*Chahal v UK* (1996) 23 EHRR 413). However, in *R (Youssef) v Secretary of State for Foreign and Commonwealth Affairs* [2016], the court refused to intervene in a torture case. The government joined with other states in order to place the claimant on a list of terrorist suspects in compliance with the UN Charter. The claimant may have been tortured in Egypt, which had requested the UN action. The Supreme Court held that it should review the decision with caution since the matter had been primarily entrusted to the Sanctions Committee of the UN. Provided that the Foreign Secretary did not use torture-tainted evidence himself, he did not have to investigate whether the evidence was obtained by torture (see also *R (Abassi) v Secretary of State for the Foreign and Commonwealth Office* [2002] EWCA Civ 1598 and *R (Al Rawi) v Secretary of State for the Foreign and Commonwealth Office* [2007] 2 WLR 1219: no diplomatic support for UK citizens imprisoned in Guantanamo Bay) (see Steyn, 'Guantanamo Bay: The Legal Black Hole' (2004) 53 ICLQ 1).

In *R (Bancoult) v Secretary of State for the Foreign and Commonwealth Office (No 2)* [2008], (Section 9.4.2), two majority judges held that matters concerning security policy and international relations were not reviewable ([109], [130]), Lord Hoffmann favoured a limited level of review ([58]) and two dissenting judges held that the decision was reviewable because a fundamental right was in issue ([72], [159]).

9.6.3.3 Immunity from liability in tort

Thirdly, the defence of 'Crown act of state' sometimes prevents the state being liable in tort for injuries it causes overseas. This version of act of state dates from the days of imperial aggression and international crises such as the Russian Revolution. The Crown is not liable for injuries caused in connection with *bona fide* acts of public policy overseas, provided that the action is authorised or subsequently ratified by the Crown (again, this is under the royal prerogative). It is for the court to decide whether an action is genuinely related to public policy (see *Mohammed v Secretary of State for Defence* [2016], [356–60]: detention of prisoners by army in Afghanistan (sent back to lower court to establish the facts); *Nissan v A-G* [1970] AC 179: British troops billeted in Cyprus hotel: not an act of policy; *Buron v Denman* (1848) 2 Ex 167: British naval officer set fire to barracks in West Africa in order to liberate slaves: Crown subsequently confirmed the action).

The defence of Crown act of state does not apply to acts done within the UK itself, except against 'enemy aliens', that is, citizens of countries with which we are formally at war (*Johnstone v Pedlar* [1921] 2 AC 262: US citizen imprisoned: Crown liable). This is because the Crown owes a duty to protect anyone who is even temporarily on British soil. Indeed, for the same reason, the defence may not be available against a British subject anywhere in the world. In *Nissan,* the House of Lords expressed divided views (see also *Walker v Baird* [1892] AC 491). It seems unfair to favour people with no substantial link with the UK merely because they happen to hold British passports.

The Crown can also be liable under the HRA for acts carried out abroad against persons under its control (Section 22.3). The defence of act of state cannot override a human right under the ECHR or a grave breach of international law (*Mohammed v Secretary of State for Defence* [2016], [373]; *Keyu v Secretary of State for Foreign and Commonwealth Affairs* [2015]).

9.6.4 International jurisdiction

International relations sometimes involve a tension between the legal and political standards familiar in the UK, and those in other countries. This relates in particular to immigration, security and crime. The topic is too large and varied to be dealt with in this book, so we will confine ourselves to sketching the main constitutional features. The UK has been jealous of its rights in relation to security and law enforcement and opted out of many EU functions concerned with policing and justice matters. Humanitarian concerns and need for cooperation with other states (comity) have led to important treaties which have been implemented in domestic law. Examples are as follows.

UK criminal law normally applies only within the territory, but some crimes such as torture are regarded as so heinous that they can be prosecuted wherever committed, irrespective of nationality (see Torture Convention 1984; Criminal Justice Act 1988, s 134). The International Criminal Court Act 2001 gave effect to the Statute of the International Criminal Court (The Rome Statute), a treaty that came into effect in 2002. The Home Secretary has a power to extradite suspects to the International Criminal Court based in The Hague and which can sit in the country concerned. The Act covers offences of genocide, war crimes and crimes against humanity. (The latter include enslavement, expulsion, torture, rape, forcible transfer of property, enforced prostitution, apartheid and other inhuman acts of a similar character which intentionally cause great suffering or serious injury to the body or mental or physical health.) The crime of aggression, which covers attacks upon other countries, has not been included to date because of difficulties of definition. The ICC can designate the UK as the state where a sentence of imprisonment is to be served.

The ICC has jurisdiction where the domestic jurisdiction is unable or unwilling to investigate. There is no state immunity, even for a head of state. A domestic court must deliver a suspect for extradition to the ICC on production of a properly issued warrant. The slowness of ICC procedure and its concentration on African states has been criticised.

Certain UN Conventions can be given effect by Order in Council under the United Nations Act 1947.

9.7 Removal from the UK

As an aspect of sovereignty, states have always had wide powers in international law to control entry and to expel aliens. At common law, aliens have no rights to remain in the UK, the matter being governed by the royal prerogative. Since the Immigration Act 1971, which was described by Lord Hope as a constitutional landmark (*R (Alvi) v Secretary of State for the Home Dept* [2012], [31]), most if not all prerogative powers have been replaced by statute. The legislation has been revised many times, impelled mainly by a desire to restrict immigration and, recently, to combat terrorism. The most recent general measure is the Immigration Act 2016.

A non-citizen can be removed from the UK in three cases: by expulsion under immigration law, by deportation on public interest grounds, or under extradition law, the last also applying to citizens.

9.7.1 Deportation and expulsion

Non-citizens, with certain exemptions based on residential status, can be deported on grounds 'conducive to the public good'. The deportation of a 'foreign criminal', meaning a non-citizen who is convicted of an offence and sentenced to imprisonment for at least 12 months, is deemed automatically to be for the public good and the Home Secretary *must* make a deportation order unless the deportation would be contrary to the ECHR (UK Borders Act 2007, ss 32 and 33). Commonwealth and Irish citizens are exempt from this automatic deportation but can be deported in other cases. In some circumstances, the Home Secretary can remove citizenship and might do so with a view to deportation (Section 9.3.1). There is also a general power to deport immigrants who require leave to enter or remain but do not have it. This replaces a variety of separate powers. There is a restriction on the removal of parents and children for 28 days after their appeal rights have been exhausted (Immigration and Asylum Act 1999, ss 2, 10; Immigration Act 2014, Part 1).

There are powers of arrest and search and a person subject to deportation can be detained indefinitely. Many detentions exceed a year, since there are practical problems in securing deportation including the refusal of other states to receive the deportee (Immigration Act 1971, sch 3 as amended).

There is a right of appeal to an Immigration Tribunal (Section 20.1), but this is limited to asylum, humanitarian and human rights claims (Immigration Act 2014, part 2). In other cases, there is provision for an 'administrative review' (Immigration Act 2014, s 15). As with all government action, these decisions are subject to judicial review. Indeed, immigration cases form the bulk of judicial review litigation. They are normally decided under the judicial review powers of the Upper Tribunal rather than by the High Court (Section 20.1). There are special arrangements for security cases including terrorist cases. The right of appeal is to the Special Immigration Appeals Commission (SIAC). The SIAC, created by the Special Immigration Appeals Commission Act 1997, has a membership appointed by the Lord Chancellor usually including a High Court judge as chair. It adopts a procedure under which information and publicity are restricted (Section 24.6).

In cases where there is no right of appeal, a decision made on national security grounds is subject to review by the SIAC on judicial review grounds (Immigration Act 2014, s 18). Under the Anti-Terrorism Crime and Security Act 2001, there is a right of appeal to the SIAC against a decision of the Home Secretary to certify that a person is an 'international terrorist'. The Home Secretary's decision cannot be challenged in any other way (s 30). SIAC itself is subject to judicial review in the High Court. Security matters may limit judicial review but do not exclude it completely (Section 25.1).

The power to deport a European Economic Area national (citizens of the EU, Iceland, Liechtenstein, Norway and for this purpose Switzerland) has been more limited during the UK's membership of the EU. A person with the right of permanent residence under EU Directive 2004/38/EC, the 'Citizenship Directive', which applies to all such nationals, could be removed only where the offender represents a serious threat to public policy or public security. This must normally be based on the risk of future offending.

This position has changed from 1 January 2021, although the UK has made clear that mere failure to apply under the EU settlement scheme (see 9.3.2) will not automatically result in deportation.

9.7.2 Asylum

The UN Refugee Conventions (Cmd 9171, 1951; Cmnd 3906, 1967) require the UK to give asylum to 'any person who…owing to a well founded fear of being persecuted for reasons of race, religion, nationality, membership of a particular social group or political opinion, is outside the country of his nationality and is unable, or, owing to such fear, is unwilling to avail himself of the protection of that country' (see e.g. *RT (Zimbabwe) v Secretary of State for the Home Department* [2013] 1 AC 152: a 'real and substantial risk' that a claim of loyalty to the regime by a politically neutral person would be disbelieved was enough to justify asylum (Section 23.1)).

The Refugee Conventions are intended to serve the objectives of the UN, namely international peace and security, and do not protect those in 'respect of whom there are serious reasons for considering that they have been guilty of acts contrary to the purposes and principles of the United Nations' (Art 1 F(c)), for example terrorism or crimes against humanity. The Refugee Conventions have been incorporated into domestic law by way of the HRA, EU law (Council Directives 2003/9/EC; 2004/83/EC, 2005/85/ EC) and the Nationality, Immigration and Asylum Act 2002. In dealing with asylum claims, the Supreme Court held that considerable weight must be given to the guidance of the United Nations High Commission for Refugees (UNHCR). For example, where an asylum-seeker is accused of terrorist acts, strong evidence and exceptional circumstances with an international dimension are required to justify refusing asylum (*Al Sirri v Secretary of State for the Home Department* [2013] 1 AC 745). Similarly, membership of an extremist group does not itself justify refusing asylum (*R (JS, Sri Lanka) v Secretary of State for the Home Department* [2011]). In the case of a child refugee, the best interests of the child must be a primary consideration (*R (TN (Afghanistan)) v Secretary of State for the Home Department* [2015] 1 WLR 3083: tracing family of an unaccompanied child).

There is a special 'fast track' procedure which applies where a state, designated by the Foreign Secretary, is treated as having 'in general' a low risk of persecution or contravention of the UK's human rights obligations (Nationality, Immigration and Asylum Act 2002, s 94(4); see *R (Brown) (Jamaica) v Secretary of State for the Home Department* [2015] 1 WLR 1060: homosexuality). Here the Home Secretary can treat an application as 'clearly unfounded' unless the asylum-seeker shows otherwise and an appeal on the facts can be brought only from outside the UK (s 92) (however, judicial review is available to challenge the legality of the decision).

9.7.3   Extradition

Extradition is a response to a request from another state to send a person to it either to be tried or sentenced for a criminal offence, or because that person has escaped from custody. Extradition therefore raises a conflict between mutual cooperation and the sovereignty of the UK. It also raises the question of whether the justice system in the other country is such that justice or human rights are at risk. There is no general obligation to extradite. The obligation to do so is based on treaties between the states in question. However, as Lord Phillips pointed out in *Norris v Government of the USA* [2010] UKSC 9 at [5], increasing international cooperation in the fight against crime has generated a number of treaties imposing such an obligation, not least with the US.

Extradition law is highly complex, and only the main considerations can be sketched here.

Under the Extradition Act 2003, requesting states are graded into two categories: First, there are the trusted *Category 1* states against which the individual's rights are limited. These are mainly EU members, but others can be added by Order in Council. A state which retains the death penalty cannot qualify (s 1). Extraditable offences are offences committed in the requesting state and not the UK, contained on a list of offences specified in the European Arrest Warrant Framework Decision of the EU Council (2002/584/JHA; Extradition Act 2003, Sched. 2) and punishable with at least three years' imprisonment. International crimes such as genocide are also extraditable (ss 64(6), (7)). Offences punishable by 12 months' or more imprisonment may also be extraditable even if partly committed in the UK, but must be offences both in the UK and in the requesting country.

In the case of a Category 1 state, where a designated authority in the requesting state issues a warrant to a designated authority in the UK certified as such by the Secretary of State (these are the usual prosecuting agencies), naming the suspect and specifying the offence, the offender must be arrested and brought before a senior district judge (lower-level criminal judge). The designated authority in the requesting state must be a judicial authority independent of the executive (see *Ministry of Justice, Lithuania v Bucnys* [2014] 2 All ER 235). A provisional arrest of a suspect in advance of a warrant is permissible. The court's function in relation to the warrant is limited to checking whether the accused is the right person, and the offence is an extraditable offence. The question of guilt or innocence is not investigated.

The court must order extradition unless certain 'extraneous considerations' apply, in which case the accused cannot be extradited. These include double jeopardy (s 12), lapse of time where extradition would be unjust or oppressive (s 14), discrimination (s 13), age (below the age of criminal responsibility in the UK, which is ten years), human rights (s 21) and 'speciality', meaning the absence of an agreement between the UK and the requesting state that the suspect will be dealt with only in relation to the matters specified in the warrant. There are provisions relating to the offence of hostage-taking under which a person cannot be extradited if his trial would be prejudiced because he cannot communicate with the authorities. There is an appeal to the High Court and with permission to the Supreme Court, but only if the High Court certifies that a point of law of general public importance is involved.

The UK's continuing participation in the European Arrest Warrant system, which underpins the preceding arrangements, was called into question by Brexit. The Framework Decision of 2002 continued to apply after 31 January 2020 until the end of the transitional period (31 December 2020). The agreement negotiated between the UK and EU in December 2020 (Section 10.5.6) provides for a fast-track system of extradition ('surrender') to replace the Warrant. Under this system, certain states may in future refuse to extradite their nationals to the UK, or may do so only under certain conditions.

In respect of *Category 2* states, which include all other states, the main differences are as follows:

 (i)   There must be an extradition treaty between the requesting state and the UK.
 (ii) The extradition request is made to the Home Secretary.
 (iii) The warrant is a UK warrant issued by a court.
 (iv) The offence must be an offence in UK law if it were committed in the UK.

(v) The court must be satisfied that there is sufficient evidence to justify the extradition, namely a *prima facie* case, in which there is evidence that, if proved, would mean guilt. However, in the case of requests from the US, the treaty dispenses with this safeguard (Extradition Treaty 2003, Cm 5821). There is no reciprocal provision on the US side and the arrangements are widely regarded as unfair.

(vi) After rights of appeal have been exhausted, the final decision is taken by the Home Secretary, who has a limited discretion (s 93). S/he can consider whether on the grounds of physical or mental condition extradition would be unjust or oppressive. S/he must also take into account whether the death penalty is involved and the speciality issue (above). However, under the Crime and Courts Act 2013, Sched. 20, human rights issues are decided by the court alone. The Home Secretary is not involved with Category 1 cases.

In both categories, the UK can refuse to extradite a person who was acting as an agent for the UK government on national security grounds if the conduct in question was not criminal in the UK due to authority given by the Secretary of State (s 203).

The Home Secretary has a power under the Crime (International Cooperation) Act 2003 to serve a foreign judgment on a person at the request of any foreign authority. In *R (Ismail) v Secretary of State for the Home Department* [2016] 1 WLR 2814, the chairman of a ferry company had been convicted in his absence of manslaughter in Egypt following a ferry disaster which killed 1000 people. The claimant had fled to the UK, claiming that any trial would be politically biased. The Supreme Court held that the Home Secretary need not consider Art 6 of the ECHR (right to a fair trial) since the service of the documents did not itself alter the claimant's rights and did not require the UK to take enforcement action. Therefore, as far as UK law was concerned, he was free not to leave the country.

9.7.4   Human rights restrictions on removal

Non-citizens have no right under the ECHR to enter or remain in the country but are protected against improper decisions to expel them. This applies whether they entered as an adult or a child or were born here (see *Maslov v Austria* [2009] INLR 47). Under the UN Refugee Conventions 1951 and 1967 a person, whether he or she is a refugee, cannot be removed to a country where he or she would be at risk of torture or inhumane or degrading treatment contrary to Article 3 of the ECHR. In *Chahal v UK* [1996], the European Court required an effective remedy in the form of 'independent scrutiny' to protect rights under Article 3.

In *R (Ullah) v Special Adjudicator* [2004] 3 All ER 785, the House of Lords extended this principle to the risk of serious violations of other rights under the ECHR, in that case, religious freedom (Art 9). The same applies to the right to a fair trial (Art 6; Section 21.4.2) and privacy and respect for family life (Art 8; Section 21.4.3). However, in cases other than Article 3 there must be a real risk of a flagrant breach of the Convention (*EM (Lebanon) v Secretary of State for the Home Dept* [2009] 1 AC 1198: Art 8; *Kapri v Lord Advocate* [2013] 4 All ER 599: Art 6: judicial corruption).

There is protection under Art 8 where removal would destroy family stability and, especially, the interests of children which the removal would disrupt. In Art 8 cases, the court must decide whether the decision is *proportionate*, that is, whether it impacts on the rights of the claimant excessively (Section 22.9). The court therefore has to weigh the government's reason for the removal against the effect on the claimant (*Huang v Secretary of State for the Home Department* [2007] 2 AC 167). This raises problems concerning respect for international relations, given the cultural and social differences involved. For example, in *HJ (Iran) v Secretary of State for the Home Dept* [2010] 3 WLR 386, the Supreme Court held that a person could not be expelled to a country where he or she would be unable openly to live as a homosexual. It was not enough that he would be 'reasonably tolerated'. However, it was emphasised that the UK is not entitled to impose its own values on other countries but only to protect the core entitlements recognised by the international community (see also *EM (Lebanon) v Secretary of State* (above): separation of mother and child was a flagrant violation, but the allegedly arbitrary and discriminatory nature of Lebanese family law was not sufficient in itself).

The Immigration Act 2014, s19, inserting part 5A of the Nationality, Immigration and Asylum Act 2002, attempts to influence the way in which the courts approach immigration cases under Article 8. It appears to endorse media propaganda that the courts are unduly sympathetic to Article 8 claims. Section 19 provides that the abilities to speak English and be financially independent are part of the public interest (but does not require these matters to be given special weight). However, 'little weight' should be given to private life or relationships with 'qualifying partners' (meaning British citizens who are settled in the UK), established while the claimant was in the UK unlawfully or where the claimant's immigration status is 'precarious'. This does not apply to the parental relationship with children who are citizens or have lived in the UK for more than seven years. In *Rhuppiah v Secretary of State for the Home Department* [2016] EWCA Civ 803 it was held that 'precarious' means having only a limited right to remain. It was also suggested that the statutory approach might be overridden where the private life in question has a 'special and compelling character'. An example might be where the claimant is a carer for the partner.

In deportation cases, the Immigration Rules provide that imprisonment for four years or other serious criminal factors should normally justify deportation unless there is a strong relationship with a child or partner who is settled or a refugee in the UK. This was upheld by the Supreme Court (Lord Kerr dissenting) in *Hesham Ali (Iraq) v Secretary of State for the Home Department* [2016].

Examples: removal and human rights

It is often claimed that the courts are unduly sympathetic to persons whom the government seeks to remove from the UK. What do the following cases suggest?

Problems arise where a deported person faces a trial in a country which has a different legal process from our own which is argued to be unfair. In *RB (Algeria) v Secretary of State for the Home Dept* [2010] 2 AC 110, the Supreme Court held that Abu Qatada (Othman), a terrorist suspect, could not resist deportation to Jordan on the ground that a trial in Jordan would not be independent of the government; even though in an English case the arrangements in the Jordanian court would violate the right to a fair trial. It was also held that it would not be a 'flagrant' denial of justice if torture evidence was used, although it would be if the accused himself was tortured. Moreover, the court was entitled to rely on assurances from the overseas government that a person would not be mistreated.

This was rejected by the European Court of Human Rights (*Othman (Abu Qatada) v UK* [2012] ECHR 56), holding that using torture evidence would indeed be a 'flagrant denial of justice'. Although assurances from the Jordan government could be taken into account, no assurances had been given about witnesses. The UK government was severely embarrassed, but, eventually, Abu Qatada agreed to return to Jordan, where he was acquitted on all charges due to lack of evidence.

In *Florea v Judicial Authority Carei Courthouse Romania* [2015] 1 WLR 1953, overcrowding in a jail was held to fall within Art 3 of the ECHR but the court would intervene only in severe cases where there was a risk to health.

In *GS (India) v Secretary of State for the Home Department* [2015] 1 WLR 3312, the Court of Appeal held that neither Art 3 nor Art 8 normally apply to removing a seriously ill person even though adequate treatment is not available in their home state and it is likely that they will die. There are exceptions, such as death bed cases where inadequate care to die with dignity is not available. In this case, one of the claimants was due for a live donor transplant. He could be protected because of the urgency of his case.

In *ZH (Tanzania) v Secretary of State for the Home Dept* [2011] 2 AC 166, the Supreme Court upheld an appeal against the removal of a mother under immigration control in the interests of the stability of the children's lives (see also *AA v UK* [2011] ECHR 1345: deportation of a child who had been convicted of rape was excessive given that there were strong family and community links and a previous record of good behaviour).

In *DM (Zimbabwe) v Secretary of State for the Home Department* [2016] 1 WLR 2108, the Court of Appeal held that the weight to be attached to relevant criteria, such as length of presence in the UK and family connections, is diminished where presence in the UK is unlawful. Very serious reasons are required to prevent deportation.

In *R (Agyarko) v Secretary of State for the Home Department* [2015] EWCA Civ 440, the Court of Appeal held that whether there are insurmountable obstacles to family life outside the UK is a factor to be taken into account but not an absolute requirement. Where an applicant knows that he or she has no right to be in the UK, a violation of Art 8 will be established only in an exceptional case. Separation from a spouse is not in itself such a case.

In 'foreign criminal' cases the balance is strongly in favour of deportation. In *R (Akpinar) v Upper Tribunal* [2015] 1 WLR 466 the claimant had arrived in the UK as a child and had been granted indefinite leave to remain as a child of refugees. The Home Secretary wished to deport him as a 'foreign criminal' (Section 9.7.1) since he had served prison sentences for various minor offences (mainly breaches of anti-social behaviour orders) in a young offenders institution. In *Maslov v Austria* [2009], the European Court had stated that, in the case of 'settled migrants' who had lawfully spent all or most of their childhood in the host country, very serious reasons are required to justify expulsion ([75]). The Court of Appeal held that *Maslov* did not require the Home Secretary to justify the deportation on the basis of especially serious offences. It held that the scales are heavily weighted in favour of deportation and the claimant must show exceptional circumstances to avoid deportation ([42]). On the other hand, the fact that an offence is very serious is not enough in itself to justify deportation and a balancing exercise must be carried out.

Similarly, in *Secretary of State for the Home Department v CT (Vietnam)* [2016] EWCA Civ 488, the claimant had served a prison sentence for attempted murder and been convicted of drug and firearms offences. The Court of Appeal held that, even where the interests of a child are involved as a primary consideration, the starting point is not neutral. In the case of a foreign criminal, it would almost always be proportionate to deport even taking into account the best interest of a child. In this case, the children would not have to live abroad and could remain with their mother. Long separation from their father would not be enough to prevent deportation.

In *extradition* cases, respect for international relations carries great weight and so may change the balance (*H v Lord Advocate* [2012] 3 WLR 151). In *Norris v USA* [2010], where no children were involved, the offence, obstructing justice, was of significant gravity and the importance of cooperating with the US outweighed the health effects on the claimant and his wife. By contrast, in *H v Deputy Prosecutor of the Italian Republic Genoa* [2012] 3 WLR 90, an appeal was allowed where an unwell husband would be left as sole carer for young children and the offence of importing drugs was regarded as 'of no great gravity'. But in *H v Lord Advocate* [2012], a husband and wife lost their appeal against extradition to the United States to face a much larger-scale commercial drug trafficking charge, even though the children were at risk of being put into care. The importance of combating crime and the desirability of a trial in the United States were held to be overwhelming.

Summary

- ▶ The UK Constitution has no unified concept of the state. This leads to a fragmented system of government but may protect individual freedom.

- ▶ Citizenship entitles a person to reside in the UK and has certain other miscellaneous consequences. There is no legal concept of the citizen corresponding to the republican notion of equal and responsible membership of the community.

- ▶ The UK Constitution does not distribute power geographically so as to limit the power of the state. The UK is therefore not a federal state, although it is arguably moving in this direction. The UK has devolved governments subordinate to the centre (see Chapter 16).

- ▶ British overseas territories are subject to the jurisdiction of the UK courts, but not to the HRA unless the ECHR has been extended to the territory. The lawmaking power of the UK government depends on whether the territory in question is a settled territory. The powers of the executive are wider in the case of a ceded territory.

- ▶ The traditional 'divided Crown' doctrine is questionable, and the cases conflict. It seems, however, that the UK executive can interfere with the rights of the inhabitants of a dependent territory for its own purposes.

- ▶ The Queen is head of the Commonwealth. This has no constitutional connection with the UK.

- ▶ International law does not automatically apply in domestic law but can be filtered into UK law by Parliament and the courts. Customary international law is recognised by the common law but subject to overriding domestic principles. A treaty is made by the executive and comes into force under the royal prerogative. There is no general requirement for parliamentary approval, but a treaty cannot alter domestic law without an Act of Parliament. There are provisions for parliamentary scrutiny of most treaties prior to their ratification by the Crown.

Summary cont'd

▶ The courts have taken a strict approach to applying treaties because of the danger of permitting executive lawmaking. However, they have recently become more liberal in their use of treaties and other international sources as aids to the interpretation of domestic law, there being a presumption that international obligations should be honoured. A treaty and other international documents can be used to interpret a statute which incorporates the treaty. Unincorporated treaties and other international sources can be used to help the interpretation of ambiguous statutes, and the common law where it is uncertain.

▶ Substantial immunity from the jurisdiction of the courts is given to foreign governments and their staff, international organisations and their staff, and heads of state by statute, reflecting international law. Similar protection applies to diplomats representing their governments, which in some cases extends to their private activities. There is some, but lesser, protection for former heads of state and former diplomats. The immunity itself has been upheld as complying with the ECHR, provided that its scope reflects international law. Where the immunity applies, even human rights claims are excluded.

▶ Foreign governments, and sometimes the UK government exercising functions in relation to foreign affairs, are protected by the overlapping common law doctrines of 'act of state'. This has at least three different meanings: an act of a foreign government that is non-justiciable; an act of foreign policy of the UK government that is not justiciable (or possibly justiciable in exceptional cases); and a defence to an action against the Crown for causing injury or damage abroad. However, important international standards such as human rights have made some inroads into these doctrines.

▶ There are arrangements for cooperation with other states in relation to criminal jurisdiction. There are different levels of extradition arrangements depending upon the relationship with the other state. There are special arrangements regarding the International Criminal Court.

Exercises

9.1 To what extent are UK-dependent territories able to make and apply their own laws?

9.2 'A treaty is not part of domestic law because, if it were, the executive would have lawmaking powers. On the other hand, the courts presume that Parliament intends to honour our international obligations.'

How are these statements reconciled?

9.3 Does the law governing removal from the UK strike an acceptable balance between the public interest and the rights of the individual?

9.4 Explain the difference between state immunity, diplomatic privilege and 'act of state'.

9.5 Jake, the ambassador to the state of New Britain, employs Jane as a housekeeper and Karl as a gardener at his home. He also requires them to help out at the home of his cousin, a businessman, in return for which his cousin supplies the ambassador with whisky. Jane and Karl claim that they are paid below the national living wage and are treated as slaves.

    (i) Advise them whether they can seek legal redress on the assumption that their claims are valid.

    (ii) What would be the position if Jake was the representative of New Britain to the International Trainspotters Organisation, a UN agency?

    (iii) Jake asks Jane to cook dinner for a party, which he holds at his residence, for the UK Foreign Secretary. Jane ruins the meal. In a rage, Jake attacks her, causing her serious injury. Advise Jane.

9.6 The UK government decides to recognise Cornwall as an independent state. In order to help the new Cornish government get established, the prime minister sends an army platoon to Cornwall as a peacekeeping force. Bill, a UK citizen, and Hilary, a US citizen, each own a hotel in Cornwall. Bill also runs a taxi business from his hotel. Hilary's hotel is damaged by British troops during a birthday party for their corporal. The Cornish head of state uses Bill's hotel as his office while a new residence is being built. He has not paid his bill for several weeks. Also, on the instructions of the Cornish government, Cornish soldiers commandeer Bill's fleet of taxis for use in military operations. Advise Bill and Hilary as to any remedies available to them in the English courts.

9.7 The (imaginary) island of Stark was settled by the UK in the seventeenth century. It has a population of 600. It is governed by a Commissioner employed by the Foreign Office, who is advised by an elected council. The UK government makes an Order requiring all the inhabitants to leave the island. The reason it gives is that it fears the island will soon be devastated by a volcano. George, whose family has lived on Stark for many years, is told by an American friend that the government's real motive is to hand the island over to the US for a naval base. Advise George as to whether he can successfully challenge the Order in the English courts. Would it make any difference if Stark had originally been seized by Britain from France?

9.8 The UK government wishes to deport Tess, a UK citizen who also holds a Utopian passport, for repeatedly claiming in the media that the Utopian government is corrupt. The UK is currently negotiating a very large arms sale to Utopia. How, if at all, can the government succeed? Would your answer differ if the government of Utopia withdrew Tess's Utopian passport?

9.9 Ed is a citizen of Dystopia who came to the UK five years ago as a postgraduate student. His permission to remain in the UK expires at the end of this year. Two years ago, he formed a relationship with Sarah, a UK citizen, and they are living together. Sarah has a three-year-old child, Paul. Sarah has now become seriously ill, and Ed intends to look after her indefinitely. Advise Ed as to his legal position as regards remaining in the UK after his visa expires. What is the position if Sarah is also a Dystopian citizen whose visa is due to expire and claims that she would be unable to obtain effective medical treatment in Dystopia and in consequence would be unlikely to live more than a few months?

9.10 While on a holiday visit to Dystopia, Mike, a journalist, was arrested, imprisoned and tortured by agents of the Dystopian government who believed he was a spy. He claims that, under an agreement with Dystopia, the British intelligence services provided information to the Dystopian authorities which led to his arrest. He wishes to sue the Dystopian government and the UK government. Advise him.

Further reading

Collins, 'Foreign Relations and the Judiciary' (2002) 51 ICLQ 489

Collins, 'Aspects of Justiciability in International Law' in Andenas and Fairgrieve (eds), *Tom Bingham and the Transformation of the Law* (Oxford University Press 2009)

Feldman, 'The Internationalization of Public Law and Its Impact on the UK' in Jowell and O'Cinneide (eds), *The Changing Constitution* (9th edn, Oxford University Press 2019)

Fox, 'In Defence of State Immunity' (2006) 55 ICLQ 399

Fripp, Moffatt and Wilford (eds), *Law and Practice of Expulsion and Exclusion from the UK: Deportation, Removal, Exclusion and Deprivation of Citizenship* (Hart Publishing 2015)

Higgins, 'National Courts and the International Court of Justice' in Andenas and Fairgrieve (eds), *Tom Bingham and the Transformation of the Law* (Oxford University Press 2009)

Lester, 'Citizenship and the Constitution' in *Halsbury's Laws of England Centenary Essays 2007* (LexisNexis Butterworths 2007)

Lowe, 'Rules of International Law in English Courts' in Andenas and Fairgrieve (eds), *Tom Bingham and the Transformation of the Law* (Oxford University Press 2009)

Malkani, 'Human Rights Treaties in the English Legal System' [2011] PL 554

Mance, 'Justiciability' (2018) 67 ICLQ 739

Murray, 'In the Shadow of Lord Haw Haw: Guantanamo Bay, Diplomatic Protection and Allegiance' [2011] PL 115

Sales and Clements, 'International Law in Domestic Courts: The Developing Framework' (2008) 124 LQR 388

Smith, Bjorge and Lang, 'Treaties, Parliament and the Constitution' [2020] PL 508

Southerden, 'Dysfunctional Dialogue: Lawyers, Politicians and Immigrants' Rights to Private and Family Life' [2014] EHRLR 252

Chapter 10

The European Union and Brexit

In a UK-wide referendum held on 23 June 2016, a majority voted to leave the European Union (EU), and the UK withdrew on 31 January 2020, although it remained subject to EU law until 31 December 2020. Brexit raises many constitutional issues and has been a politically complex and highly controversial process. It will be analysed in detail in Section 10.5, although readers will find references throughout this book. In the preceding sections of this chapter, we shall discuss the nature of the EU and its key institutions, as well as the main legal principles relating to the EU as they have affected the UK Constitution. Readers should also refer to Section 8.5.4, which discusses the impact of EU law on parliamentary supremacy.

10.1 Introduction: the nature of the European Union

The Treaty on European Union can be regarded as a constitution created by international law. Under successive treaties, the Member States transferred defined powers to EU bodies created by the treaties (*Parti ecoligiste 'Les Verts' v European Parliament* [1986] ECR 1339). *R (Miller) v Secretary of State for Exiting the European Union* [2017]. UKSC 5 provides a useful summary of the development of the EU in relation to UK law.

EU law has been part of UK law by virtue of the normal process for enacting a treaty into domestic law (Section 9.5.3). The EU treaties were made effective in UK law by the European Communities Act 1972. Redundantly, the European Union Act 2011, s 18 (now repealed by the European Union (Withdrawal) Act 2018), confirmed that directly applicable or directly effective EU law applies to domestic law only by virtue of statute.

The Supreme Court has emphasised that EU law and the jurisdiction of the European Court of Justice in domestic law depend on domestic constitutional law. In *Pham v Secretary of State for the Home Department* [2015] 1 WLR 1591, Lord Mance stated that European law is part of domestic law only to the extent that Parliament has legislated that it should be ([76]) (see also [90], and see *Miller* (above), [67]). Thus, in *Assange v Swedish Prosecution Authority* [2012] 2 AC 471, the Supreme Court held that aspects of EU law outside the 1972 Act operate only in international law. The courts of other Member States have also made it clear that EU law is valid in their legal systems only by virtue of their own constitutions (see *Brunner v EU Treaty* [1994] 1 CMLR 57, Germany; *Carlsen v Rasmussen* [1999] 3 CMLR 854, Denmark).

EU law therefore provides a sophisticated method of converting international law into domestic law (Section 9.5.3). This contrasts with the assertion of the European Union Court of Justice (CJEU) that the EU comprises a 'unique legal order' created by its members agreeing to surrender part of their sovereignty, and that EU law prevails over the laws of the Member States (*Costa v ENEL* [1964] CMLR 425). This assertion is valid from the perspective of EU law itself, but has applied to domestic law only insofar as our own constitution has accepted it. On the other hand, under our constitution, EU law is a source of law in its own right and not to be compared with delegated legislation: *Miller* (above, [68]), and the 1972 Act is unique in its legislative and constitutional implications (ibid, [90]).

The current treaties are the Treaty on European Union (TEU) and the Treaty on the Functioning of the European Union (TFEU). The TEU deals with general principles and the basic functions of the institutions. The TFEU deals with the specific composition, powers and processes of the institutions. It also deals with the EU Charter of Fundamental Rights (not to be confused with the ECHR, which exists independently of the EU and binds many more states).

What was originally called the Common Market was created after the Second World War as an aspiration to prevent further wars in Europe and to regenerate the European economies. The prototype was the European Coal and Steel Community created by the Treaty of Paris (1951). This was intended as an international control over the resources of war and is now abolished. Two other communities were created in 1957 by two Treaties of Rome. They were the European Community (formerly called the European Economic Community) and the European Atomic Energy Community.

The founder members were France, Germany, Italy, Luxembourg, Belgium and the Netherlands. Since then, membership steadily increased to 28 states. The UK became a member on 1 January 1973, after ministers ratified a Treaty of Accession on 18 October 1972. Effect in domestic law was conferred by the European Communities Act 1972 which took effect the day before ratification so as to ensure immediate compliance with EC requirements. Other current Member States are Denmark, Ireland (1973); Greece (1981); Portugal, Spain (1986); Austria, Finland, Sweden (1995); Cyprus, the Czech Republic, Estonia, Hungary, Latvia, Lithuania, Malta, Poland, Slovakia (2004); Slovenia, Bulgaria, Romania (2007); and Croatia (2013).

Most of the external territories of the Member States are not EU members but are dealt with in Part IV TFEU, which requires their welfare to be promoted. However, Gibraltar, as the only European UK dependency, is within the EU. There are special provisions for the Channel Islands and the Isle of Man for participation in EU economic arrangements, and special arrangements for the UK military bases in Cyprus (see Art 355 TFEU).

Members now include former communist countries, thereby altering the original balance and introducing a wide range of economic, political, cultural and religious perspectives that challenge the old-fashioned liberal paternalism of the founders. The idealistic founders deliberately created institutions that lacked direct democracy. They hoped that a unified 'European spirit' would eventually pervade the independent populations of the European nations, whereas the UK government originally envisaged the communities more pragmatically as a trading bloc. This tension remains and may well have influenced the Brexit vote.

The objectives of the communities were originally economic, primarily to encourage free movement of people, services, goods and capital between Member States. It was hoped that this would lessen the risk of further European wars. The organisation was also influenced by a desire to protect food supplies after the Second World War which, over time, became a policy to promote EU agriculture and fishing. This has left the EU with a substantial financial burden, in that about a third of its budget is still devoted to agricultural subsidies. However, the interests of the EU have steadily widened, partly by a process of interpreting the existing objectives liberally, and partly by the Member States formally agreeing to extend its areas of competence by means of new treaties over the decades.

The objects of the EU now include a wide range of political, economic and social matters such as the environment, employment protection, social welfare, transport, regional disadvantages, foreign policy, justice and security. Individual Member States have the right to opt out of some areas, but the four core 'freedoms of movement', namely of goods, of people, of services and establishment (setting up businesses), and of capital, that constitute the Single Market are sacrosanct. Moreover, 19 Member States share the 'internal currency', the euro. This involves large constraints over their financial policies policed by a European Central Bank, which has led to tensions between the wealthier northern countries, predominantly Germany, and the poorer southern states whose ability to respond to financial difficulties is restricted by membership of the euro. The UK, along with a minority of states, opted out of some functions, in particular membership of the euro and foreign policy, and had the right to 'opt in' to aspects of policing and justice. At the other end of the scale, groups of Member States can use EU institutions for 'enhanced cooperation' among themselves in respect of matters other than the Single Market (TEU Art 20).

Foreign policy, policing and immigration are subject to special provisions, and border controls are matters for individual states. In the light of contemporary concerns about international terrorism, these areas are subject to continuous review within the EU.

Thus, the aspiration towards universal principles cutting across cultural differences is far from achieved. There is no longer a unified EU, but one with a committed core of members together with more peripheral ones: what is sometimes called 'variable geometry' or, less kindly, a disintegrating EU. The effect on this of the departure of the UK from the EU is impossible to predict, although initial forecasts that Brexit would precipitate a swift break-up of the Union appear to have been wide of the mark.

The latest treaty, the Lisbon Treaty (on which the TEU and TFEU are based), is an attempt to rationalise and consolidate the European Union in the face of these tensions. It replaces an abortive Constitutional Treaty. Illustrating the political sensitivity of the idea of a written constitution, the Lisbon Treaty reproduces the main provisions of the earlier attempt, minus its constitutional rhetoric. The Lisbon Treaty is intended to strengthen the European Union as an international organisation, to strengthen links with domestic legislatures and to streamline its decision-making processes. It makes the EU, which was previously only a political label, a legal entity in its own right. EU citizenship is conferred automatically on citizens of Member States (TEU, Art 9; TFEU, Arts 20, 21). It probably does not create additional rights above those which EU law confers directly on nationals of the Member States (see *Pham v Secretary of State for the Home Department* [2015]). These include freedom of movement within the EU, 'the right to participate in the democratic life of the Union' and various rights of access to EU institutions.

In *R (Miller) v Secretary of State for Exiting the European Union*, [67], the Supreme Court acknowledged that the 1972 Act was a 'constitutional statute' which created a new source of law and a range of important rights in domestic law. The court identified three kinds of EU right which had been implemented in domestic law. Firstly there are rights such as employment rights which could be reproduced in domestic law alone; secondly, there are rights dependent on membership of the EU, such as those of UK citizens in relation to other EU states and of EU citizens in the UK (such as immigration rights); thirdly, there are rights which exist only in relation to the EU itself, such as the right to vote in EU elections and to refer cases to the Court of Justice of the European Union (CJEU). By contrast, some EU provisions do not take effect in domestic law, for example some matters of social policy. These are governed exclusively by the Crown's treaty-making powers in international law and cannot be adjudicated by domestic courts (*R v Secretary of State for Foreign and Commonwealth Affairs ex parte Rees-Mogg* [1994] 1 All ER 457).

EU competences pervade most aspects of national life. The EU has three kinds of power (TFEU, Arts 3–6):

1. *Exclusive competence* concerns customs, competition in relation to the Single Market, the euro, the common fisheries policy and common commercial policy. In these cases, Member States cannot legislate independently at all.
2. *Shared competence* includes the competences that do not fall into another category. Member States can legislate, at least until the EU has decided to intervene (see Case 804/479 *Commission v UK* [1981] ECR 1045).
3. *Supporting, coordinating or complementary functions* are primarily for the Member States, but the EU can exercise funding powers. This category includes health, industry, culture, tourism, education, vocational training, youth and sport, civil protection and administrative cooperation.

10.2 Institutions

The main EU institutions are as follows:

- Council of Ministers, known as the 'Council'
- 'Council of the European Union', European Council
- European Commission
- European Parliament
- Court of Justice of the European Union.

Other important community institutions governed by their own special provisions include the Court of Auditors in Luxembourg and the European Central Bank in Frankfurt.

The EU has lawmaking, executive and judicial powers which the treaties blend in a unique way, creating checks and balances, but requiring 'sincere cooperation' (TEU, Art 4). There is a separation of powers in relation to the Court. The other institutions are less clear-cut.

As well as being the main executive, the Commission has a significant legislative role in that only it can propose legislation, albeit the Council and the Parliament must usually give effect to legislation. The Commission also serves as the guardian of the treaties, ensuring that they are complied with by bringing actions in the courts against Member States. The Parliament, combined with the Council, has a substantial role in lawmaking and has certain powers over the Commission. However, the Commission is not accountable generally to the Parliament or any other body in the same way that a national executive would be. The Council has mainly legislative functions, while the overarching European Council is responsible for general policy direction and constitutional policy.

A primary concern of the treaties is to provide a balance between the interests of the Community and those of the Member States. Thus, TEU Article 4(2) requires that the Union shall 'respect the equality of Member States before the Treaties, as well as the national identities, inherent in their fundamental structures, political and constitutional, inclusive of regional and local self-government'.

Lawmaking is divided between the Commission, which represents the Union as such, and the Council, which comprises representatives from the Member States, together usually with the elected Parliament.

There is a system of checks and balances, for example where the consent of both the Council and the Parliament is needed for a measure proposed by the Commission. In accordance with both the separation of powers and the rule of law, each institution can bring an action in the Court to ensure the compliance of the other institutions with the limits on their powers and the notion of constitutional balance (Case 302/87 *Parliament v Council (Comitology)* [1988] ECR 56/15).

10.2.1 The Council of Ministers

The Council's main function is to approve or amend laws proposed by the European Commission, although in some cases it can ask the Commission to make a proposal. It also decides the budget, adopts international treaties and is responsible for ensuring that the objectives of the treaties are attained. The Council comprises a minister representing each Member State who must be authorised to commit its government. The membership fluctuates according to the business in hand.

Because of its membership of national politicians, the Council is biased towards national interests rather than towards an overall 'community view'. The way in which Council decisions are made is therefore all-important. When it considers draft legislation, it must meet in public (TFEU, Art 15). Certain decisions (albeit a shrinking category) must be unanimous, thus permitting any state to impose a veto. Unless the treaties state otherwise, Council decisions are made by a 'qualified majority'. Before the Lisbon Treaty, this was based on weighting according to the population of each state. The position now is that a 'double majority' is applied. This means a majority of 55 per cent of states, together making up at least 65 per cent of the population, thus reflecting the more varied membership of the EU. The 'blocking' minority of 35 per cent of the population must include at least four states (TEU, Art 16(4)).

Each state holds the presidency of the Council for six months. Holding the presidency therefore allows a state considerable influence in setting the legislative policies for the EU. The state holding the presidency must engage with the other Council members and also with the President of the European Council and the Foreign Affairs Representative.

10.2.2 The European Council

The European Council comprises the heads of state, together with the President of the Commission. It had existed informally for many years, but the Lisbon Treaty made it an EU institution with an enhanced leadership role. It provides the Union with 'the necessary impetus for its development and shall define the general political direction and priorities thereof' (TEU, Art 15(1)). It decides important policies including alterations to the treaties, the admission of new members and sanctions on Member States. It appoints the Commission (below) and other important officials and can make internal rules concerning the powers of the Council. It cannot, however, make laws.

The European Council is particularly important in relation to constitutional matters and foreign and security policies. Since its elevation to institution status, it may have tipped the balance of power away from the *supranational* elements of Commission and Parliament towards the *intergovernmental* element. It makes reports to the European Parliament after its meetings and also produces a yearly written report on the progress of the Union.

The Lisbon Treaty created the office of President of the European Council, whom the Council elects for two and a half years (TEU, Art 15(2)). The President is chair of the Council but has no executive powers. The President cannot hold any national elected office. There is also an office of High Representative for Foreign Affairs, who works with the Council to develop foreign policy and to represent the EU abroad (TEU, Art 18).

10.2.3 The European Commission

The Commission is the executive of the EU (TEU, Art 17). It includes the body of Commissioners each responsible for a policy area, and the permanent bureaucracy of the EU. The Commission represents the interests of the EU as such, although, since the EU is not a political entity but can work only through individual states, it is difficult to know what this means. Indeed, its members are nominated by the Member States. The Commission is required to be independent 'beyond doubt' of the member governments, thus counterbalancing the two Councils which represent the Member States. The Commission as a body is responsible to the European Parliament (TEU, Art 17.8; Section 10.2.4).

The five main functions of the Commission are (TEU, Art 17.1):

1. To propose laws or other initiatives for adoption by the Council. Although the Council or the Parliament can request the Commission to submit proposals the Commission normally has the exclusive right to propose initiatives for new laws which the other institutions then enact, modify or reject (TEU, Art 17.2). The areas of 'freedom, security and justice', including border controls and immigration, are special. Here a quarter of Member States can also propose initiatives (TFEU, Art 76);
2. In a few areas of EU competence, to make laws itself, either directly under powers conferred by the Treaty or under powers delegated to it by the Council;
3. As the guardian of the application of the treaties, to enforce EU law against Member States and the other EU institutions. The Commission enforces respect for the law by issuing a 'reasoned opinion', and, where it considers that a Member State or institution is in default, negotiating with the body concerned and, if necessary, initiating proceedings to remedy the default in the CJEU (Art 258);
4. To administer the EU budget;
5. To negotiate on behalf of Member States with international bodies and other countries in areas where given competence to do so, for example international trade negotiations.

The number of commissioners is determined by the European Council, which also fixes their salaries. The Commission currently comprises one member from each state irrespective of its size. There is, however, provision to reduce the number of commissioners to comprise two-thirds of the Member States on a revolving basis (TEU, Arts 17(4), 17(5); TFEU, Art 244).

The President of the Commission is elected by the European Parliament, on a proposal from a qualified majority of the European Council (TEU, Art 17(7)). The Council must 'take into account' the outcome of the previous election to the Parliament.

The European Council appoints the other commissioners with the 'common accord' of the President-elect, from candidates 'suggested' by the Member States (TEU, Art 17.7). Each commissioner is appointed for a renewable term of five years but must resign if required by the President (TEU, Art 17.6).

The appointment of the Commission as a body must be approved by the Parliament (TEU, Art 17). The appointment process takes place within six months of the elections to the Parliament, thereby strengthening democratic input. However, the Parliament cannot veto individual candidates without rejecting the whole Commission, so accountability is weak. Similarly, the whole Commission but not individual commissioners can be dismissed by the Parliament (TEU, Art 17.8). The President can be dismissed by the European Council for serious misconduct.

Individual commissioners have limited independence. The President assigns departmental responsibilities (directorates-general) to the other commissioners, who are required to conform to the political direction of the President.

10.2.4   The European Parliament

The European Parliament is the only directly elected institution. It does not initiate law and was originally created as an 'advisory and supervisory' body. However, it increasingly participates in the lawmaking process, especially so since the Lisbon Treaty. It currently has 705 seats. These are allocated in proportion to the population of each Member State, subject to a maximum of 96 (Germany) and a minimum of six seats so as to protect the smaller states (TEU, Art 14(2)). Elections are held every five years. Since 1977, Members of the European Parliament (MEPs) have been directly elected by residents of the Member States, the detailed electoral arrangements being left to each country.

A Parliament lasts for five years and is required to meet at least once a year. Its meetings alternate between Brussels and Strasbourg, with one week in Strasbourg as a plenary meeting each month and three weeks in Brussels for committee meetings. Its members vote in political groupings and not in national units. It meets in public.

The Parliament's three main functions are as follows (TEU, Art 14(1)):

1. Legislative functions jointly with the Council. As a result of a gradual extension of the Parliament's powers most lawmaking is now subject to the 'co-decision procedure', under which the consent of both Council and Parliament is required for a Commission proposal to become law.
2. Budgetary functions. The Parliament approves the EU budget jointly with the Council. It can veto only the whole budget: an extreme sanction.
3. 'Political control and consultation'. This group of powers is miscellaneous. The Parliament approves the appointment of the Commission as a whole and its President (Section 10.2.3). It also approves treaties, the admission of new Member States and certain other important matters. It must be consulted on the appointment of certain other senior officials. By a two-thirds majority of those voting, that is, also an absolute majority of all members, it can dismiss the entire Commission but not individual members of it. However, this sanction is extreme and unlikely to be exercised in practice.

It can question members of the Commission orally or in writing, hold committees of inquiry into misconduct or maladministration by other EU bodies and appoint an Ombudsman to investigate complaints by citizens, residents or companies based in Member States against EU institutions.

The consent of the Parliament is needed for certain matters, including some alterations to the EU treaties, the admission of new EU members or the withdrawal of exiting Member States (Section 10.5.6), and human rights sanctions against Member States (TEU, Art 7). Any citizen, resident or company based in a Member State can petition the Parliament on a matter that comes within the EU's field of competence and affects him, her or it directly.

10.2.5   The Court of Justice of the European Union (CJEU)

The CJEU comprises one judge from each Member State, appointed by 'common accord' by the governments of the Member States. Unlike senior national judges, a CJEU judge has limited security of tenure, being appointed for a term of six years, renewable at the option of the candidate's own government and dismissible by the unanimous opinion of the other judges and advocates-general, if 'he no longer fulfils the requisite conditions or meets the obligations arising from his office' (TFEU, Protocol 3, Art 6). On a rotating basis, half the judges resign every three years and are eligible for renewal or replacement at the option of their own governments. Their independence is, however, protected in as much as they have immunity from legal actions (TFEU, Protocol 3, Art 3).

As well as the judges, there are nine advocates-general (whom the Council of Ministers at the request of the President of the Court can increase to 11). An advocate-general provides the CJEU in open court with an independent opinion on the issues in individual cases. The opinion is not binding but is highly influential. The court itself gives a consensus decision and, unlike the common law style, its judgments are brief and without full reasoning.

The CJEU can sit in panels of three to five or as a Grand Chamber of 15. In certain cases prescribed by the treaties or where it considers that a case is of exceptional importance, it sits as a full court. Procedure mainly takes the form of written documents.

There is also the 'General Court' (formerly the Court of First Instance), also comprising one judge from each state. The General Court normally sits in panels of three or five. The General Court decides cases at first instance on matters within the jurisdiction of the CJEU other than those reserved to the CJEU itself by the Statute of the Court. There is a right of appeal on matters of law from the General Court to the CJEU.

The CJEU's task is to ensure that 'in the interpretation and application of the EU treaties the law is observed'. In this respect, it acts as a constitutional court. The 'law' consists of the treaties themselves, the legislation adopted in their implementation, general principles of EU jurisprudence developed by the Court, the *acquis communautaire*, which is the accumulated inheritance of community values, previous EU legislation and jurisprudence, and general principles of law common to the Member States, including the ECHR. International law such as human rights treaties, is also a source of general principles.

There is also 'soft law', comprising governmental agreements, declarations, resolutions and so on. These are not binding but must be taken into account. This enables changes to be introduced gradually, which can later harden into new treaty provisions.

The main jurisdiction of the CJEU is in the seven areas that follow:

1. *Enforcement action against Member States that are accused of violating or refusing to implement European law.* These proceedings are usually brought by the Commission but can be brought by other Member States, subject to their having raised the matter before the Commission. Exceptionally, the Court can award a lump sum or penalty payment against a Member State that does not comply with a judgment that the state concerned has failed to fulfil a treaty obligation. The EU has no enforcement agencies of its own.

2. *Judicial review of EU legislation and of the acts or the failure to act of community institutions* (TFEU, Arts 263, 265). In this respect, the CJEU acts as a constitutional court. Thus, the court can review alterations to the treaties themselves to ensure that they comply with the procedures in force at the time. As regards legislation, this review power of the CJEU applies only to *binding* acts of EU institutions and so does not apply to recommendations and opinions. The General Court cannot hear challenges to legislative acts or to most decisions of the Council (TFEU, Art 256(1); Statute of the Court, Art 51).

   The grounds of challenge are broadly similar to the domestic grounds of judicial review. Where, as is often the case, an EU power is exercised by domestic officials, the decision in question can be challenged in the domestic courts. The CJEU cannot pronounce on the validity of domestic legislation.

   An action can be brought by the other institutions or by Member States. An individual or private body can bring an action only where the community act in question is addressed to the individual in person and is of 'direct and individual concern to him or her'.

3. *Preliminary rulings on matters referred by national courts* (TFEU, Art 267). Any national court, or the parties to a case, where it is considered that a decision on the question is necessary to enable judgment to be given, may request the CJEU to give a ruling on a question of EU law. A court against whose

decision there is no judicial remedy in national law (i.e. the highest appeal court or any other court against which there is no right of appeal or review) *must* make such a request (TFEU, Art 267). Any court must make a reference if the *validity* of an EU law is challenged. The decision is one for the national court alone: there is no appeal to the CJEU on the matter. A court need not make a reference if it thinks the point is irrelevant or 'reasonably clear and free from doubt' (the *acte clair* doctrine), or if 'substantially' the same point has already been decided by the CJEU.

The role of the Court is confined to ruling upon the question of law referred to it. It then sends the matter back to the national court for a decision on the facts in the light of the Court's ruling.

The preliminary reference procedure has been described as the most effective engine of the European Union for legal integration and as an 'inter-judicial dialogue' embedding EU legal norms in national legal cultures 'in a much more immediate way than any other supra-national court could ever dream of' (Heyvaert, Thornton and Drabble (2014) 110 LQR 413).

4. Disputes regarding contracts entered into by the EU (TFEU, Art 340(1)).
5. 'In accordance with general principles of law common to Member States', damage caused by EU officials in the course of their duties (TFEU, Art 340(2)–(4)).
6. Issues between Member States, national central banks and the European banking system (mainly concerning the euro).
7. Disputes between EU bodies or agencies and their civil servants (TFEU, Art 270). This jurisdiction is exercised by a specialist Civil Service Tribunal with an appeal to the General Court (TEU, Protocol 3, Annex 1).

10.3 EU law and national law

The European Communities Act 1972, s 2(1) provides that all EU laws 'from time to time created or arising by or under the Treaties, … as in accordance with the Treaties are without further enactment to be given legal effect or used in the UK shall be recognised and available in law, and be enforced, allowed and followed accordingly'. In the case of other EU obligations applicable to the UK there had to be a transposition to UK law, usually in the form of a statutory instrument (s 2(2)). According to s 2 (4), any enactment passed or to be passed … shall be construed and have effect subject to the foregoing provisions'. We have seen that this affects the normal application of Parliamentary supremacy in as much as a domestic statute could not impliedly override an EU rule (Section 8.5.4). This was confirmed by the Supreme Court in *R (Miller) v Secretary of State for Exiting the European Union* (2017) ([66]). However the court emphasised that the fundamental 'rule of recognition' of the constitution is unchanged and that Parliament is ultimately supreme so as to override EU law by repealing the 1972 Act, as it has indeed done through s 1 of the European Union (Withdrawal) Act 2018.

Section 3 of the 1972 Act requires all courts to decide questions as to the meaning, validity or effect of EU law in accordance with the principles and decisions of the European Court.

10.3.1 EU law and its effects

Some EU measures take effect in domestic law 'without further enactment' (European Communities Act 1972, s 2(1)) and automatically became part of UK law while the UK was a Member State. This is determined by EU law itself.

The main kinds of EU legal instrument are as follows (TFEU, Art 288):

Treaties. Treaty provisions were directly enforceable in the UK courts (below). However, treaty provisions relating to the EU common foreign and security policy are not part of the treaties as far as UK law is concerned since the UK opted out of much of this area (European Communities Act 1972, s 1).

Regulations. These are general rules that apply to all Member States and persons. All regulations are 'directly applicable' and as such were automatically binding on UK courts, except where a particular regulation was of a character that is inherently unsuitable for judicial enforcement. Regulations rarely require transposing into domestic law and are legally complete on their face.

Directives. By contrast, a directive is not generally automatically binding but is sometimes so (below). A directive is used when there is a requirement to achieve a given objective, but it is left to the individual states to decide how to implement it. A directive may be addressed to all states or to particular states. A time limit is usually specified for implementing a directive.

Decisions. A decision is 'binding in its entirety', but if it specifies those to whom it is addressed, it is binding only on them.

Opinions and recommendations. These do not usually have binding force (TFEU, Art 288). There are exceptions concerned with financial deficits of Member States (TFEU, Art 126).

The treaties, the general principles of EU law (e.g. the Charter of Fundamental Rights) and regulations which by their nature are directly enforceable, are enforceable against anyone, state or private person, without the need for a domestic law to give them effect ('direct applicability'). By contrast, directives are mainly 'directly effective', a doctrine developed by the CJEU. To have direct effect, an instrument must be 'justiciable', meaning that it is of a kind that is capable of being interpreted and enforced by a court without trespassing outside its proper judicial role. In essence the legal obligation created by the instrument must be certain enough for a court to handle.

The criteria for direct effect are as follows:

1. The instrument must be 'clear, precise and unconditional'. It must not give the Member State substantial discretion as to how to give effect to it.
2. The claimant must have a genuine interest in the matter analogous to the *locus standi* requirement in domestic law (Section 19.4).
3. The time limit prescribed by a directive for its implementation must have expired. However, even a correctly implemented directive might be directly relied on if the way in which it is transposed does not give its full effect.

Where the direct effect doctrine applies, the national court must give a remedy which, as far as possible, puts the plaintiff in the same position as if the instrument had been properly implemented in domestic law. This might, for example, require national restrictions to be set aside or national taxes to be ignored.

Directives can be enforced only 'vertically', that is, against a public authority or 'emanation of the state', and not 'horizontally', against a private person (*Marshall v Southampton AHA (No 1)* Case 152/81 [1986] ECR 723). The reason for this limitation seems to be that the state, which has the primary duty to implement a directive, cannot rely on its failure to do so, an argument that it would be unfair to apply to a private body. Even where a European law lacks direct effect, the courts must still take account of it. In *Marleasing v La Comercial Internacional de Alimentacion* [1992] 1 CMLR 305, the CJEU held that all domestic law, whether passed before or after the relevant EU law, must be interpreted 'so far as possible' in order to comply with the EU law. In *Jessemey v Rowstock* [2014] EWCA Civ 185, the Court of Appeal took the view that a similar approach applies in EU Law to that under the HRA, namely that the court can distort or modify the language of an Act, but cannot make a change that 'goes against the grain of the Act' by contradicting its purpose and direction (Section 22.5.1).

Furthermore, where a directive does not have direct effect, an individual may still be able to sue the government in a domestic court for damages for failing to implement it. This was established by the CJEU in *Francovich v Italy* [1991] ECR I-5357, where the directive was too vague to have direct effect. Nevertheless, the Court held that damages could be awarded against the Italian government in an Italian court. The Court's reasoning was based upon the principle of giving full effect to EU rights. In order to obtain damages against the state for failing to implement an EU directive, the directive must confer rights for the benefit of individuals, the content of those rights must be determined from the provisions of the directive, and there must be a causal link between breach of the directive and the damage suffered.

This is a powerful and far-reaching notion. In domestic law, damages cannot normally be obtained against the government for misusing its statutory powers and duties (Section 19.2).

10.3.2 Fundamental rights

The ECHR is separate from the European Union. The ECHR comes under the auspices of the Council of Europe, which is a different organisation with its own court, the European Court of Human Rights (Section 21.3). The CJEU is not currently bound by the ECHR. However, the Court takes the jurisprudence of the Convention into account as a source of general principles of law. The European Court of Human Rights can consider whether an EU measure which is binding within a Member State complies with the Convention (*Matthews v UK* (1998) 28 EHRR 361). Under the Lisbon Treaty, the EU is required to accede to the ECHR (TEU, Art 6), and negotiations are currently in progress.

A gap in EU law was the absence of an enforceable Charter of Fundamental Rights. Since the Lisbon Treaty, however, the EU's Charter of Fundamental Rights has become directly enforceable against EU bodies and Member States. In this respect, the Charter has the same status as the treaties themselves (TEU, Art 6). The Charter must be interpreted in harmony with the ECHR (Art 52(3)) and, after accession of the EU to the ECHR, the Strasbourg court will provide a partial means of challenge to the CJEU. However, the Charter goes beyond the ECHR. In particular, it includes social rights such as workers' rights and rights of the elderly and children, data protection, and bioethics. It is structured on the basis of the republican concepts of dignity, freedom, equality, solidarity, citizenship and justice.

In the Lisbon Treaty, the UK partly opted out of making the Charter directly enforceable against the UK, or by our domestic courts, in respect of new freestanding rights. However, in the case of existing general principles of law, such as non-discrimination (TEU, Protocol 30), the Charter was binding in UK courts but only, of course, when applying EU law (see *RFU v Consolidated Information Services* [2012] 1 WLR 3333, [26]–[28]; *R (TN (Afghanistan)) v Secretary of State for the Home Department* [2015] 1 WLR 3083; *Benkharbouche v Embassy of the Republic of Sudan* [2015] 3 WLR 301). The UK opted out of the Charter in respect of asylum and immigration matters, and chose which rights to accept in the areas of justice and home affairs.

10.4 Proportionality and subsidiarity

The tension between the interests of Member States and those of the EU is expressed through the concepts of *proportionality* and *subsidiarity*. The principle of proportionality is that EU powers shall not exceed what is necessary to secure the objectives of the treaties (TEU, Art 5(4)). It is similar to the wider doctrine of proportionality which the courts apply in cases where decisions of government bodies are challenged under EU law and human rights law (Section 22.9).

Historically, subsidiarity was an authoritarian doctrine used by the Catholic Church to legitimise the level at which decisions should be taken within a hierarchical power structure; but it can also be a pluralist liberal principle that decisions should be made at a level as close as possible to those whom they affect. Subsidiarity entitles the EU to make decisions that cannot effectively be made by the Member States and, on the other hand, it enables the Member States to act for themselves where this is more appropriate. Subsidiarity was formally introduced into EU law by the Maastricht Treaty and is embodied in TEU Article 5(3):

> Under the principle of subsidiarity, in areas that do not fall within its exclusive competence, the Union shall take action only if and insofar as the objectives of the proposed action cannot be sufficiently achieved by the Member States either at central level or at regional or local level but can rather, by reason of the scale or effects of the proposed action, be better achieved at Union level.

The TEU gives an important role to national parliaments in connection with subsidiarity Article 12(b). Legislative proposals must contain a reasoned statement justifying the proposal in relation to both proportionality and subsidiarity. If one-third of the 'reasoned opinions' of member parliaments (each having two votes) raises an objection to an EU proposal on subsidiarity grounds (a quarter in the areas of freedom, security and justice), the Commission must reconsider it and give reasons for continuing with it. If a majority of national parliaments raise an objection, the Council by a 55 per cent majority or the Parliament by a majority must vote for it to proceed.

On the whole, the Lisbon Treaty maintained a balance between national and EU institutions and is not the charter for EU supremacy that was sometimes feared. The EU is arguably more like a confederation than a genuine supranational body but is perhaps best regarded as a unique legal order not reducible to other forms.

10.5 Leaving the EU: Brexit

Following a referendum on 23 June 2016, which, as a matter of law was merely advisory and not binding, the UK government decided that the UK should leave the EU under the provisions of the EU Treaties. Brexit raises several constitutional issues. A non-exhaustive list of these includes:

▶ the conflict between direct democracy and representative democracy in the context of a referendum;
▶ the relationship between domestic law and international law in respect of treaties;
▶ the role of the judiciary in a controversial political issue;
▶ the 'principle of legality' in relation to a constitutional statute;
▶ the scope of the royal prerogative;
▶ ministerial responsibility;
▶ the balance of power between legislature and executive, especially in respect of control of parliamentary proceedings, the privileges of Parliament and the calling of elections;
▶ problems relating to devolution in Scotland, Wales and Northern Ireland.

Certain of these issues are discussed in the remainder of this chapter, but readers will also find the implications of Brexit analysed throughout this book.

10.5.1 The referendum and the political context

Since joining the EU in 1973, the UK's membership has been controversial. An earlier referendum (1975) resulted in a 67 per cent majority in favour of remaining in what was then primarily a trading organisation and customs union. However, the objectives and powers of the EU have subsequently increased in favour of greater political union and wider objectives, while its governance has been less than impressive. In particular, a significant 'democratic deficit' is said to have emerged, with representative democracy in EU institutions being fragmented and incomplete. Anti-EU sentiment has consequently strengthened.

In the 2016 ballot, voters were asked simply whether they wished to leave or remain in the EU. On a turnout of 72.2 per cent, this resulted in a vote of 51.9 per cent to leave. The voting pattern was uneven. England voted to leave by 53.4 per cent, Wales by 52.5 per cent. In London, 59.9 per cent voted to remain, while majorities of 62 per cent in Scotland (turnout 67.2 per cent), and 55.8 per cent in Northern Ireland (turnout 62.7 per cent) favoured remaining. Under Art 355 TFEU, which deals with the various external territories of Member States, Gibraltar, which as the UK's only dependency within Europe is within the EU, voted to remain by 95.9 per cent (turnout 83.5 per cent). Thus, public opinion is highly divided, and the devolved constitution is under pressure.

Both the main political parties have a substantial 'Eurosceptic' element. In the case of the Conservative party, which is currently in power, the EU has been a central preoccupation at least from the 1980s, leading for example, to the resignation of Prime Minister Margaret Thatcher in 1990. Public opinion has been influenced by the limited democracy of EU institutions, by fears of immigration under the EU principle of freedom of movement, and by allegations of inefficiency, weak leadership, excessive legalism and extravagance within EU institutions. An appeal to old-fashioned ideas of national sovereignty and independence has also been characteristic of the debate.

The Conservative government promoted the referendum in order to placate its anti-EU members, and to outflank the emerging UK Independence Party. Then Prime Minister David Cameron attempted to renegotiate the terms of membership of the EU with the other Member States. However, the EU made only insignificant concessions, mainly consisting of minor changes to welfare benefits for immigrants. The UK was also to be exempted from the symbolic commitment in the preamble of the TEU to 'ever closer union of the peoples of Europe', a provision with little meaning and no direct legal effect.

For the purposes of the referendum, the Prime Minister dispensed with the normal convention of collective ministerial responsibility, so that Cabinet members could campaign and vote freely (24 favoured remain, 6 favoured leave). The government's own policy was to remain in the EU. This raises the question of the use of government resources and supposedly impartial civil servants for campaigning purposes.

The European Union Referendum Act 2015 addressed this by requiring that, for 28 days immediately before the referendum, government must not make any communication relating to the referendum question or that might encourage people to vote in the referendum. However, factual information could be provided: a difficult distinction to maintain. Those ministers who supported exit had only limited access to government resources even in their own departments. The campaigns themselves were funded by private donations, the leave side raising the larger amount (£8.2m to £7.5m).

The referendum result apparently took the government by surprise, since it had seemingly made no plans for the consequences of a vote to leave. Despite substantial support for leaving in the popular press, the government's campaign in favour of remaining was low-key. It presented remaining as the lesser of evils and concentrated on the economic risks of exit in the apparent belief that a majority could be persuaded into favouring the status quo.

The EU referendum and its aftermath illustrate the problems of a referendum in a parliamentary representative system in the context of a complex technical matter. The referendum tests the republican belief that a majority of people (Rousseau's 'general will' or 'the wisdom of crowds') ensures a rational outcome on the basis that, with large numbers voting, social and economic differences, eccentric attitudes or vested interests cancel each other out (Section 2.5).

The weaknesses of the referendum device were exposed. First, the terms of the referendum required a simple yes or no answer, but this ignores the many possible relationships the UK might have with the EU. These depended on negotiations with the EU as part of the leaving process and ranged from 'soft Brexit', participating in the free trade aspects of membership at the cost of accepting many EU rules and making payments to the EU, to 'no deal', where ties with the EU are abruptly cut off, leaving the UK to go it alone and seek trading relationships where it can (see Section 10.5.6).

Secondly, the detailed pros and cons of the EU itself were not examined in the referendum campaign, and the substantial exemptions from EU rules already enjoyed by the UK were not assessed. However, perhaps weaknesses within EU institutions, the faltering European economy, and the unattractiveness of the EU's leadership would have made a more positive case complex and difficult to present.

Thirdly, perhaps the most important single issue, immigration under the EU principle of freedom of movement, was avoided by the remain campaign but exploited by its opponents.

Finally, wider grievances may have influenced voters. In particular, the government may have underestimated the extent of public resentment (shared in European countries and the USA) against official behaviour, so that the referendum was an opportunity for retribution. There has been considerable media dissemination of the belief that an 'elite' network of venal and greedy politicians, professionals and business managers has exploited the political system. Average wages and living standards have fallen significantly since the banking collapse of 2008 and the subsequent bailout of banks by the government of up to £1626bn (National Audit Office (2016)). At the same time, the incomes of senior professionals, bankers and managers have substantially increased. This has fed into public distrust of 'experts', assumed to be members of this elite, who offered their opinions to the media, most of whom supported remaining in the EU.

The 2015 Act did not make the referendum result legally binding. However, there is a strong political obligation to honour a referendum result, even if it is not a constitutional convention. The Conservative election manifesto of 2015 also promised to honour the referendum result.

An immediate result of the referendum was that Prime Minister David Cameron resigned, to be replaced by Theresa May, who had supported the remain side. She immediately created a new Department for Exiting the EU under David Davis, a leading member of the leave campaign, and a Department for International Trade (under Liam Fox, another proponent of Brexit), which aimed to attract trade elsewhere to replace that lost by leaving the EU. These changes to our flexible constitution made under the royal prerogative without parliamentary approval were liable to create turf wars with other government departments, notably the Foreign Office (led by Boris Johnson, also a leader of the Brexit campaign).

May called a general election in April 2017 (obtaining a two-thirds majority for an early election under the provisions of the Fixed Term Parliaments Act 2011, see Section 11.2). However, the Conservatives failed to secure an overall majority at the ensuing election in June and were forced into a 'confidence and supply' agreement (see Section 15.2) with the Democratic Unionist Party of Northern Ireland in order to survive. This made the progress of passing the necessary legislation to withdraw from the EU extremely challenging, given that there was also no clear majority for leaving amongst MPs in the Commons (who, as representatives rather than delegates need not consider themselves bound by the views of their constituents). On several occasions over the following two years, MPs were able to gain control of the parliamentary process in efforts to soften the government position: an unusual scenario in a Parliament usually dominated by the executive (see Section 11.1).

May stepped down in July 2019 and was replaced as Conservative leader and Prime Minister by Johnson (note that both individuals were elected by their party rather than via popular vote: see Section 5.2). Johnson also faced difficulties with a House of Commons over which he held no majority, and controversially advised the Queen to prorogue (suspend) Parliament for a time in order to limit debate and opposition, an action which was ruled unlawful by the Supreme Court in *R (Miller) v the Prime Minister* [2019] UKSC 41 (Sections 14.6.4 and 19.7.1). Having attempted and failed on three occasions to gain the necessary two-thirds majority to trigger an early general election under the Fixed Term Parliaments Act 2011 (a motion of no confidence in the May government, which would have had the same effect, had also failed in January 2019). Johnson secured the passage – by simple majority – of the Early Parliamentary General Election Act 2019 (Section 11.2: the 2011 Act was not repealed, but under the doctrine of parliamentary sovereignty it could not bind the Parliament of 2019, which was free to legislate contrary to its provisions). Accordingly, a general election was held in December 2019, in which the Conservative Party won a substantial majority of 80 seats. The UK formally left the EU at 11pm on 31 January 2020 and entered into a transition period in its relations with the EU which ended on 31 December 2020 (Section 10.5.6).

For a useful summary of major events, see Walker, *Brexit Timeline: events leading to the UK's exit from the European Union* (House of Commons Library Briefing Paper 7960 (2020)).

10.5.2   Triggering the leaving process

Withdrawal from the EU required separate actions at EU and domestic levels. Withdrawal itself depends on the EU Treaties. Art 50 TEU provides machinery for a Member State to leave the EU. At the domestic level, the European Communities Act 1972 had to be repealed so as to remove EU obligations from domestic law and to put existing EU-based law onto a domestic footing while it is decided which particular laws to retain.

Art 50 TEU is designed to make it difficult to leave the EU. It requires the cooperation of the European Council (the heads of state), the Council (of Ministers), the Commission and the Parliament. Its essential provisions are as follows:

1. Any Member State may decide to withdraw from the Union in accordance with its own constitutional requirements.
2. A Member State which decides to withdraw shall notify the European Council of its intention. In the light of the guidelines provided by the European Council, the Union shall negotiate and conclude an agreement with that State, setting out the arrangements for its withdrawal, taking account of the framework for its future relationship with the Union… It shall be concluded on behalf of the Union by the Council acting by a qualified majority, after obtaining the consent of the European Parliament.
3. The treaties shall cease to apply to the State in question from the date of the entry into force of the withdrawal agreement or, failing that, two years after the notification referred to in paragraph 2, unless the European Council, in agreement with the Member State concerned, unanimously decides to extend this period.

Thus, under para 1, triggering Art 50 depends initially on the requirements of domestic law for giving effect to a treaty. The normal 'constitutional requirement' for giving effect to a treaty is a decision by the Crown through a minister under the royal prerogative, and this was initially what the government intended. However, as a result of the decision of the Supreme Court in R (Miller) v Secretary of State for Exiting the EU [2017], there is a short Act authorising the Prime Minister to trigger Art 50 (below). In Miller, an eight to three majority of the Supreme Court held that Article 50 could be triggered only by a clear statutory intention.

No such intention can be found in the European Communities Act 1972, nor in other statutes. The referendum has no legal significance. Miller provides an important account of general constitutional principles relating to treaties and has significance beyond the EU context, since it may mean that other important treaties which affect domestic law will not only have to be incorporated by statute but the executive's power to 'make, alter or revoke' them may also have to be authorised by statute, [132].

The case was argued on the assumption that triggering Art. 50 was irrevocable, thus inevitably leading to the UK leaving the EU. (However, it was subsequently ruled by the CJEU that unilateral revocation was possible (Wightman v Secretary of State for Exiting the European Union [2019] QB 199).) The majority based its decision on 'the ordinary application of basic concepts of constitutional law' (at [82]). First, the executive under the royal prerogative normally makes and revokes treaties. Secondly, a treaty in itself cannot change domestic law.

Thirdly, since the 1972 Act is important enough to rank as a 'constitutional statute', the clear intention of Parliament is required to change the basic rights it created: an aspect of the 'principle of legality' (Sections 6.6 and 8.5.6). Therefore, since membership of the EU was 'endorsed' by the 1972 Act, activating Art 50 without the consent of Parliament is unlawful in the absence of a clear intention in the 1972 Act that the prerogative could be so used. No such intention could be found in the language of the Act: and it is unlikely that given its importance, the 1972 Act contemplated ministers being able to leave the EU (see [61], [73], [76]-[78], [81], [83], [86], [87], [90]–[93]).

> We consider that, by the 1972 Act, Parliament endorsed and gave effect to the United Kingdom's membership of the (of the EU) in a way which is inconsistent with the future exercise by ministers of any prerogative power to withdraw from such treaties, [77].

By contrast, the dissenting judges (Lords Reed, Carnwath and Hughes) applied the same principles but with a different approach as to the ambit of the 1972 Act. They held, on the basis of the language of s.2, that the 1972 Act is 'inherently conditional' on the application of the EU Treaties to UK law (at [177]). In other words, the Act does no more than bring into domestic effect whatever the EU treaties require of the UK and therefore applies only if and while the UK is a member of the EU. This is a matter for the prerogative in the normal way. (The majority, led by its view of the importance of the matter, read the Act as being conditional only as regards treaty provisions *during* membership and not those *affecting membership itself.*) In contrast to the majority view that the prerogative can be exercised only if authorised by positive language in the statute, the dissent considered that the prerogative can be exercised unless specifically excluded by statutory language, which was not the case here. Lord Reed emphasised the 'compelling practical reasons' for the executive to manage foreign affairs (at [160]). He also held that the 1972 Act did not 'endorse' EU membership, but was neutral on the matter. He pointed out that the UK did not enter the EU by means of statute, but only by a treaty of accession ratified by the executive which process was entirely independent of the Act (at [194]–[197]). As regards the concerns of the majority about protecting fundamental rights, the dissent emphasised that the executive was responsible to Parliament for the exercise of its prerogative powers. The majority considered this to have constitutional dangers, encouraging the use of wide discretionary powers.

According to the dissent therefore, the *De Keyser* principle (Section 14.6.2) that an inconsistent statute excludes the prerogative does not arise, since the 1972 Act is not inconsistent with the continuation of the prerogative power.

Much was made in the *Miller* case, especially in the argument against the executive, of the doctrine of Parliamentary sovereignty. However, this was not in issue since both sides recognised that Parliament could intervene if it so wished. The dissenters pointed to the various statutes that had over the years limited the power of the executive to participate in altering EU treaties (e.g. European Union (Amendment) Act 2008, European Union Act 2011) pointing out that Parliament had not seen fit to include Art 50. The majority considered that under the 'principle of legality' nothing could be inferred from the silence of the Act (at [108]).

Following the government's defeat in the courts, the European Union (Notification of Withdrawal) Act 2017 was enacted. This short Act authorises the Prime Minister to 'notify under Article 50(2) of the Treaty on European Union, the United Kingdom's intention to withdraw from the European Union'.

10.5.3   The Withdrawal Agreement

Once the decision to leave the EU had been made, Art 50 was triggered by the UK notifying the European Council of its intention to withdraw, which it did on 29 March 2017.

The agreement was negotiated under TFEU, Art 218(3). This requires the Commission to make 'recommendations' following which the Council appointed the chief negotiator and authorised the start of negotiations. The negotiations, which formally opened on 19 June 2017, took place with a 'task force' headed by Michel Barnier, a former French foreign minister. The UK, as leaving state, could no longer participate in the discussions of the European Council or Council or in the decisions made by these bodies concerning it (TEU, Art 50(4)). Representatives from the UK could continue to participate in the European Parliament, and further elections for that Parliament were held in May 2019, with a newly formed Brexit Party winning the largest share of the vote.

There were three major matters at issue during the negotiations. First, the 'divorce bill', that is the amount due from the UK to the EU in settlement of its share of the financial obligations undertaken while it was a Member State. This amount was estimated as £32.9 billion as at the date of the UK's withdrawal, although the final settlement will be lower since, during the transition period following withdrawal (see below), the UK continued to contribute to the EU as if it were a member. It was argued that no settlement would be payable in the event of failure to reach a trade agreement with the EU.

Secondly, the rights of EU citizens living in the UK, of whom there were estimated to be around 3.7 million, and UK citizens living in the EU, of whom there were estimated to be 1.3 million, in 2019. In broad terms, continued residence is permitted, subject to fulfilment of specific national requirements (for EU citizens in the UK, see Section 9.3.2). However, the rights of those moving from the EU to the UK, and vice versa, after the end of the transition period were a matter for the negotiations of the future relationship: the Immigration and Social Security Co-ordination (EU Withdrawal) Act 2020 provides for the end of free movement of persons, making EU citizens subject to UK immigration controls.

The third, and most problematic, issue (especially domestically) was the impact of Brexit on the border between Northern Ireland and the Republic of Ireland. The latter is an EU Member State, meaning that this would be the only external EU land border between the EU and the UK. The border has been perceived as, in effect, invisible following the Good Friday Agreement of 1998 (Section 16.4), which is an international treaty. However, withdrawal from the EU would seem to require reinstatement of crossing controls and customs checkpoints, as free movement of persons and goods into the UK would no longer apply. This is highly sensitive given the recent political history of Northern Ireland and would seem to place the Good Friday Agreement at risk.

During the negotiations, the two sides agreed a Protocol (popularly known as the 'backstop'), which would have kept Northern Ireland within certain aspects of the Single Market, while the UK as a whole would have operated as a common customs territory in relation to the EU. This arrangement would potentially apply indefinitely, unless and until the EU and UK could devise a mutually acceptable alternative arrangement for the border.

On 14 November 2018, the UK and EU negotiating teams reached an agreement in principle on a Withdrawal Agreement, under which the UK would leave the EU on 29 March 2019. The Agreement was endorsed by the Cabinet, although this prompted several resignations by ministers who could not accept collective responsibility for it (Section 15.7.1), including that of the Brexit Secretary. However, because a statutory commitment had been made to give Parliament a 'meaningful vote' on the terms of any withdrawal (comprising both the Agreement and an accompanying, non-binding Political Declaration setting out the framework of the future relationship between the UK and EU) by way of s.13 of the European Union (Withdrawal) Act 2018, parliamentary approval was still required. In this respect, the Northern Ireland Protocol proved to be an irresolvable sticking point. The Democratic Unionist Party, on whose support the minority government relied, opposed the arrangement as a weakening of Northern Ireland's position in the UK. Many 'Eurosceptic' Conservative MPs were also concerned that a part of the UK might remain in the EU for an indefinite period. The House of Commons voted against the proposed Withdrawal Agreement on three separate occasions between 15 January and 29 March 2019.

It will be noted that the third of those defeats occurred on the date on which the UK had been scheduled to leave the EU. Parliament had already agreed to request an extension of Art 50 to 30 June 2019; the European Council had agreed to a shorter extension depending upon parliamentary approval of the Agreement. When the latter did not eventuate, a further extension to 31 October 2019 was agreed, with a final extension to 31 January 2020 (against the wishes of the new Prime Minister, Boris Johnson) being agreed in October 2019 as provided by the European Union (Withdrawal) (No. 2) Act 2019.

A new plan to deal with the Irish border issue was developed and agreed between the UK and EU in October 2019. This replaced the potentially indefinite 'backstop' with a time-limited arrangement under which Northern Ireland would remain aligned with the EU for a period of four years after the end of the transition period. There would be no customs or regulatory checks, or infrastructure on the border. Two months before the end of that period, the Northern Ireland Assembly would be asked to vote on whether to remain aligned with the EU. A vote against would result in continued alignment for a further two years while alternative arrangements to protect the EU single market were devised; a simple majority would result in continued alignment for a further four years; while 'cross-community support' would result in an eight-year extension. This term refers to a 'weighted majority of 60% of the members of the legislative assembly present and voting, including at least 40% of each of the nationalist and unionist designations'. It reflects the particular character of Northern Irish politics and constitutional arrangements (Section 16.4).

Having secured a majority in the general election of December 2019, Johnson was able to take the revised Withdrawal Agreement forward. The European Union (Withdrawal Agreement) Act 2020 received Royal Assent on 23 January: the specific requirement of a 'meaningful vote' on the terms of withdrawal being repealed by s 31 of the Act. As required by Art 50, the European Parliament signi-fied its approval, and final approval was given by the Council on 30 January (this being a formality, since the European Council had already approved the Agreement). The UK left the EU on 31 January and moved into a transition (or implementation) period, during which time its future trading rela-tionship with the EU was negotiated (Section 10.5.6). This period ended at 11pm on 31 December 2020 (s 39).

10.5.4 'EU law' in the UK after Brexit

Although the UK remained subject to EU law until the end of 2020, it was necessary to determine how the disentanglement of domestic law from EU law would take place thereafter. This matter is addressed by the European Union (Withdrawal) Act 2018, read in conjunction with the European Union (Withdrawal Agreement) Act 2020 (whose primary function is to implement the terms of the Agreement into domestic law, subject to the continuing sovereignty of Parliament to legislate con-trary to the Agreement if it so chooses (s. 38)).

EU laws have entered UK law by different routes, thus making disengagement a complex process. There are four main routes:

(i)   Laws made by EU bodies which apply in domestic law directly under the treaty itself by virtue of s 2(1) of the 1972 Act. Once the UK had left the EU, unless specifically preserved, these will automati-cally cease to apply. UK statutes have sometimes been overridden by EU rights. When the relevant EU rule ceases to exist, the domestic rule may therefore reactivate. This is because the EU rule has 'disapplied', not repealed, the inconsistent UK rule (Section 8.5.4).

(ii) Laws made under s 2(2) of the 1972 Act. This gives UK government bodies power to make various forms of subordinate legislation giving legal force to EU requirements. These have usually been made in order to implement EU Directives. They often reproduce the language of the Directive but are sometimes embellished for domestic purposes or in the interests of certainty.

(iii) Subordinate legislation made under other legislation for EU purposes or under the double authority of the 1972 Act and a domestic statute, for example many environmental laws.

(iv) Laws made directly by statutes including those required by Schedule 3 of the 1972 Act, such as imposing taxation or creating criminal offences. Many other statutes include particular provisions intended to cater for specific EU requirements.

Section 1 of the 2018 Act repeals the ECA 1972. However, ss 2–4 have the effect of preserving in force most existing EU law subsequent to the end of the implementation period. Three categories of 'retained' EU laws are specified: (a) EU-derived domestic legislation (s 2), which covers categories (ii) to (iv) above; (b) direct EU legislation (s 3), which applies primarily to regulations and decisions; and (c) a residual category of 'rights, powers, liabilities, obligations, restrictions, remedies and proce-dures' that are recognised and enforced by virtue of s 2(1) ECA: this mainly comprises directly effec-tive treaty provisions and, together with (b), covers category (i) above. The effect of these sections is that, as a general rule, the same laws apply on 1 January 2021 as applied when the UK was a Member State of the EU.

As regards the interpretation of EU law by the CJEU, this is addressed by s 6 of the 2018 Act. This specifies that UK courts and tribunals are not bound by CJEU decisions made from 1 January 2021 onward, but that they 'may have regard' to these in interpreting retained law (this appears to be broadly similar to the position which exists under s 2 HRA, see Section 22.2). However, s 6(3) pro-vides that any question as to the meaning of unmodified retained EU law will be determined in accordance with relevant pre-exit CJEU case law and general principles, with an exception for the UK Supreme Court and the High Court of Justiciary in Scotland, which may choose to depart from CJEU case law (s 6(4)). Controversially, s 26 of the 2020 Act gives ministers power to make secondary legis-lation which would allow specified lower courts and tribunals also to depart from CJEU case law in respect of retained laws, and the test which should be applied in determining whether to do so. This would seem to undermine the certainty and predictability which are core elements of the rule of law (Section 6.4).

Section 5 of the 2018 Act provides for two exceptions to the retention of law under ss 2–4. First, s 5(1) provides that the principle of the supremacy of EU law is not retained from 1 January 2021 onwards. This means that retained law does not prevail over post-exit enactments, as a straightforward application of the doctrine of parliamentary sovereignty would suggest (Section 8.4.3). However, under s 5(2), the principle continues to apply to EU-derived and retained law in relation to statutes and rules enacted or made *before that date*: thus, the former take precedence over other pre-exit domestic laws. This provision appears somewhat curious, since all of the law which is retained through ss 3–4 (that retained by s 2 already being domestic law) is no longer *EU law* but rather *domestic law* (albeit a particular variant thereof) as a consequence of the 2018 Act. Thus, the principle of supremacy – which, as stated in *Pham* [2015] and *Miller* [2017], only has effect in UK law through the ECA, which is repealed by s 1 of the 2018 Act – should not apply at all. As the House of Lords Constitution Committee notes (Constitution Select Committee, HL Paper 69 (2017–19), [91]), 'the "supremacy principle" is alien to the UK constitutional system: not only did it originate outside that system, it also sits uncomfortably with established constitutional principles, most notably the doctrine of parliamentary sovereignty'. It would seem, therefore, to have been more constitutionally appropriate to provide that retained direct EU law should be treated as having the status of an Act enacted on 1 January 2021, which would then prevail over pre-exit law through normal operation of parliamentary sovereignty.

The second exception is the Charter of Fundamental Rights, which is specified in s 5(4) not to be part of domestic law post-Brexit, although s 5(5) states that this does not affect any fundamental rights or principles which exist irrespective of the Charter. The meaning of the latter provision is not wholly clear, although it might be postulated that it covers the existing general principles of EU law (provided they are recognised by the CJEU as such before 1 January 2021: Sched. 1, para 2) as they apply to retained law (Section 10.3.2). However, it should be noted that Sched. 1, para 3 of the 2018 Act precludes the bringing of a legal action in UK courts based on a failure to comply with the general principles, thus limiting the function of these principles to acting as interpretative guides to the meaning of retained laws (compare *Benkharbouche* [2015]).

Two further exceptions are set out in Schedule 1: no retained law can be challenged on the basis that, prior to exit, the EU legal instrument was invalid; and there is no right to *Francovich* damages (Section 10.3.1).

The 2018 Act envisages that modifications of retained laws may, in future, be necessary. Under ss 8 and 11, ministers or devolved authorities, as appropriate, have power to make secondary legislation to address 'deficiencies arising from withdrawal'. The term 'deficiency' does not apply to a belief that the law in question is flawed, but rather because, after exit, it no longer functions effectively, is redundant, or refers to arrangements or rights that are no longer in place etc. (s 8(2); Sched. 2). This is a 'Henry VIII' power (Section 7.5.1) and, as such, controversial from the perspective of the separation of powers. However, the Act provides that the power expires after two years (i.e. 1 January 2023) (s 8(8); Sched. 2).

10.5.5   Brexit and devolution

There is no provision in Art 50 for part of a state to remain in the EU, although special access to the EU for Scotland, Wales and Northern Ireland could be negotiated. There were substantial referendum majorities in Scotland and Northern Ireland, but not in Wales, to remain in the EU. As has been seen, there is a particular problem concerning the land border between Northern Ireland and an EU state.

Under the Sewel Convention, which is statutory in respect of Scotland and Wales, the UK Parliament will not 'normally' legislate 'with regard to' devolved matters without the consent of the devolved legislatures (Section 16.2). However, in *Miller*, the Supreme Court reasserted the established principle that constitutional conventions are not law and cannot be enforced by the courts (Section 3.4.4). It held that the reference to the Sewel Convention in the Scotland Act (now also repeated in the Wales Act 2017 (Section 16.2)) merely acknowledges the convention as such and does not make it legally enforceable.

This issue became significant when consent was sought by the UK government for those provisions of the European Union (Withdrawal) Act 2018 which related to devolved matters. Both the Scottish and Welsh governments were concerned that, in an effort to avoid differentiated policies between the constituent parts of the UK once the obligation to comply with common EU rules had ceased (that is, the creation of a so-called 'internal market'), the UK government might indulge in a 'power grab' to reclaim certain powers which had been devolved. The 2018 Act provides, in section 12, for the issuing of delegated legislation to impose a temporary 'freeze' on devolved competences in relation to modification of retained EU law, so as to ensure that there is no divergence across the UK. And, even if fears of a redistribution of power proved to be unfounded, it was felt important that there should be proper negotiation and agreement between the four nations on the issue rather than this being a matter for decision by the UK government.

On this basis, both the Welsh and Scottish legislatures initially withheld consent for the legislation, although following a concession by the UK government, consent was given by Wales. By contrast, the UK Withdrawal from the European Union (Legal Continuity) (Scotland) Bill 2018 was passed by the Scottish Parliament to ensure continuity in respect of those areas devolved to Scotland after Brexit. Subsequently, under s 33(1) of the Scotland Act 1998 (Section 16.3.1), the Attorney General and the Advocate General for Scotland referred to the Supreme Court the question of whether the Bill was within the legislative competence of the Scottish Parliament.

In *The UK Withdrawal from the European Union (Legal Continuity) (Scotland) Bill – A Reference by the Attorney General and the Advocate General for Scotland (Scotland)* [2018] UKSC 64, the Supreme Court ruled in favour of the UK government. The argument that the entirety of the Continuity Bill was beyond the legislative competence of the Scottish Parliament was rejected on the basis that the Bill did not concern international relations (including relations with the EU), which are reserved to Westminster by Schedule 5 of the Scotland Act 1998, but rather with the implications of withdrawal from the EU for the domestic legal system (at [33]).

However, the Supreme Court held that clause 17 of the Bill, the effect of which would have been to make the exercise of the power in the Withdrawal Act to make secondary legislation to modify deficiencies arising from withdrawal (see above) subject to prior consent by Scottish ministers, was beyond competence (at [52]). This was because Schedule 4 of the Scotland Act 1998 precludes the Scottish Parliament from modifying the 1998 Act. Since s 28(7) of that Act preserves the unqualified legislative supremacy of the Westminster Parliament (Section 16.3.1), the limitation imposed by clause 17 on the freedom to legislate amounted to an impermissible modification of the Scotland Act.

Various other provisions of the Bill, including clauses which would have maintained the EU Charter of Fundamental Rights and the *Francovich* principle in Scots law after exit, were also held to be beyond competence. This was because Westminster had enacted supervening legislation – the Withdrawal Act – before the Continuity Bill had received Royal Assent; and *that* Act had been specified as protected against modification by the Scottish Parliament under Schedule 4 of the Scotland Act 1998 (European Union (Withdrawal) Act 2018, Sched. 3, para 21(2)). It did not matter that the conflicting clauses in the Continuity Bill did not expressly amend the Withdrawal Act: implicit amendment or disapplication was enough ([99]).

The decision of the Supreme Court has not ended the controversy over devolved powers. Consent was also withheld to the Withdrawal Agreement Act 2020 by the Welsh and Scottish legislatures, joined this time by the reinstated legislature in Northern Ireland. There remain continued concerns that the legislation accords powers to ministers in Whitehall to make decisions on devolved matters, and on the balance of devolved powers, without agreement of the other nations. The Scottish Parliament has also voted to withhold consent to what became the United Kingdom Internal Market

Act 2020, which sets out the framework for the operation of trade between the constituent nations of the UK after exit. One sticking point was the requirement that all nations have to accept standards at the level set by any one of them, which may result in a 'race to the bottom'.

From the perspective of constitutional principle, it is arguable that legislating in the absence of the consent of the devolved legislatures is not a breach of the Sewel Convention which, as noted above, is subject to the qualifying word 'normally'. Legislation to give effect to the UK's withdrawal from the EU, and the future internal consequences of this, could be viewed as unique rather than normal. From a political perspective, however, these events reveal the continuing, and considerable, tensions in the UK's quasi-federalist, asymmetric model of devolution (Chapter 16). When these are combined with a strong nationalist movement in Scotland and the difficulties previously outlined in respect of the Northern Irish border, it becomes apparent that Brexit not only represents a significant change in the UK's external relations, but also presents a threat to its internal arrangements.

10.5.6   Future relations with the EU

As noted above, following withdrawal on 31 January 2020, the UK entered into a transitional, or implementation, period during which negotiations about its future relationship with the EU, particularly in respect of trade, were to take place. Although it was no longer a Member State, during this period the UK continued to be subject to EU law and was within the customs union and single market. The intended direction of this future relationship was set out in the Political Declaration which accompanied the Withdrawal Agreement, although this was not binding.

Although negotiations commenced in March 2020, the timetable for talks soon became problematic because of the COVID-19 pandemic. Provision did exist in the Withdrawal Agreement for an extension of up to two years, but the British side signalled that it did not wish any such extension to take place. This significantly increased the chances that it would be impossible for an agreement to be concluded before the end of the implementation period on 31 December 2020 – the 'no deal' scenario, in which the UK's future trading relationship would be governed by the rules of the World Trade Organization, with the possibility of agreements subsequently being reached in specific sectors, although these might take some time to negotiate. In such an eventuality, tariffs would be imposed on UK goods entering the EU, with the UK imposing tariffs on EU goods. This would have been likely to prove very damaging to the UK economy, certainly in the short-term.

As negotiations progressed, it became apparent that there were three main obstacles to reaching an agreement. These were, first, fisheries: that is, the amount of fish which EU vessels would be permitted to catch from 2021 onwards, with the UK side arguing for priority to be given to British boats in British waters as an independent coastal state outside the EU's Common Fisheries Policy. Secondly, there were differences over the so-called 'level playing field', that is the set of common rules and standards which would prevent UK businesses gaining a competitive advantage over those operating within the EU – this turned mainly on labour and environmental standards, and on the availability of state subsidies for business. Thirdly, the process by which any disputes relating to the agreement would be resolved was a matter of concern. In particular, the UK was opposed to any involvement of the CJEU as a mechanism for policing the agreement, even where questions were raised relating to the interpretation of EU law. It was also necessary to reach agreement on how to implement in practice the arrangements for the Northern Ireland border which had been set out in the Withdrawal Agreement.

The negotiations proved lengthy and, on several occasions, appeared to have reached an impasse. From a constitutional perspective, one of the most controversial episodes was the insertion of clauses into the Bill which became the United Kingdom Internal Market Act 2020, which would have permitted ministers to issue secondary legislation which would disapply, or modify the effects of parts of the Protocol to the Withdrawal Agreement, notwithstanding any inconsistent international law (see Section 9.5.4). This was justified as an exercise of the sovereignty of Parliament, and was intended to be used only if the EU was to act in 'bad faith'. The clauses were rejected by the House of Lords but were reinstated when the Bill returned to the Commons; however, they were removed prior to Royal Assent when the EU and the UK reached an agreement on the arrangements for Northern Ireland on 8 December 2020.

Following several personal interventions by prime minister Boris Johnson and the President of the European Commission, Ursula von der Leyen, an agreement (the EU-UK Trade and Cooperation Agreement) was finally concluded on Christmas Eve 2020, just one week before the end of the transition period. The Agreement consists of three main 'pillars': trade (covering not only trade in goods and services but also matters such as investment, competition, air and road transport, energy and sustainability, data protection and social security coordination); security, with cooperation on law enforcement and criminal justice, particularly in relation to cross-border crime and terrorism; and governance of the Agreement, with a joint Partnership Council supervising its operation, supported by a network of other committees. The Agreement is subject to review on a five-yearly basis and may be terminated by either party with twelve months' notice, while certain areas of cooperation may be terminated separately without affecting the rest of the agreement (notably, the provisions on law enforcement and judicial cooperation in criminal matters will be terminated if the UK withdraws from the European Convention on Human Rights, and the Agreement also notes that cooperation on such matters is based on 'the importance of giving effect to the rights and freedoms in that Convention domestically', which may impact upon any proposals for reform of the HRA (see Section 22.10)).

Under Article 218 TFEU, the consent of the European Parliament must be obtained prior to adoption by the Council of a decision concluding the Agreement. Given the late date on which negotiations ended, this did not prove possible prior to the end of the transition period. Accordingly, the Council unanimously adopted a decision authorising the signature of the Agreement and its provisional application on 28 December 2020, with the consent of the Parliament expected to be secured at a later date: the agreement will thus not formally be ratified until 1 February 2021 at the earliest. For its part, the UK Parliament passed all stages of the European Union (Future Relationship) Act 2020 in one day, 30 December 2020, providing for the application of relevant provisions of the Agreement in domestic law. It was argued that this 'this process represent[ed] an abdication of Parliament's constitutional responsibilities to deliver proper scrutiny of the executive and of the law' (Hansard Society blog, 'Parliament's role in scrutinising the UK-EU Trade and Cooperation Agreement is a farce', 29 December 2020, https://www.hansardsociety.org.uk/blog/parliaments-role-in-scrutinising-the-uk-eu-trade-and-cooperation-agreement). The legislatures in Scotland and Northern Ireland refused to signify their consent to the legislation, while the Welsh Senedd 'noted' the agreement between the EU and the UK but refused to vote on a consent motion due to lack of time for sufficient scrutiny.

Summary

▶ The EU exists to integrate key policies of Member States, with the aims of providing a Single Market and creating a powerful European political unit. The constitution of the EU is an evolving one. Some functions are exclusive to the EU, while others are shared with Member States. The UK opted out of several areas of EU activity, and the EU Charter of Fundamental Rights (not to be confused with the ECHR) was only partly enforceable in UK courts.

▶ EU law was incorporated into UK law by the European Communities Act 1972, which:

(i) made certain EU laws, for example the treaties, regulations and some directives, automatically binding in the UK;

(ii) required other laws (e.g. directives) to be enacted in UK law either by statute or by regulations made under the 1972 Act;

(iii) obliged UK courts to decide cases consistently with principles laid down by the European Court of Justice. In some cases questions of law must be referred to the CJEU.

Summary cont'd

▶ The main policy and lawmaking bodies are the Council, which is the main lawmaking body; the European Council of heads of state, responsible for policy direction and making key appointments; the appointed European Commission, which is the executive of the EU; and the elected European Parliament, which participates in the lawmaking process and has powers to control the Commission and the EU budget. Taken together, these bodies are meant to balance the interests of national governments and those of the EU as such, but not to follow strict separation of power ideas.

▶ The Court of Justice has some characteristics of a constitutional court by reviewing decisions of EU institutions and giving preliminary rulings in domestic cases. Together with the Commission, it enforces EU law against Member States.

▶ Not all EU law is directly binding on Member States. The treaties, regulations and general principles of law are binding. Other laws are binding if they satisfy the criteria of 'direct effect' created by the CJEU. Directives can have direct effect against public bodies (vertical direct effect) but not against private bodies (horizontal direct effect). The requirement that domestic law be interpreted so as to conform to EU law may alleviate this in certain circumstances.

▶ The process for the UK to leave the EU has been highly complex and politically controversial. It has required actions and negotiations at the international and domestic levels. The precise nature of the UK's ongoing relationship with the EU is unlikely to be clear for some time.

▶ The Brexit process raises numerous constitutional issues which are explored throughout this book. Perhaps the most visible of these have been those which involve the relationship between prerogative and statute (*Miller* [2017]) and the prime ministerial exercise of prerogative powers (*Miller* [2019]), the balance between the executive and Parliament (especially when a minority government is in power), powers of ministers to modify laws under the European Union (Withdrawal) Act 2018, and relations between the devolved nations and the UK government. Politically, the most difficult question has been that of the Northern Irish border, and it remains unclear whether this has been satisfactorily resolved.

Exercises

10.1 Explain the constitutional structure of the European Union. To what extent is it federal? Does it conform to the separation of powers?

10.2 It is a requirement of membership of the EU that a Member State have a democratic form of government, but it has often been remarked that the EU would not satisfy the conditions for membership of itself. Do you agree?

10.3 Explain the distinction between the differing forms of EU law and their effects in the legal system while the UK was a Member State.

10.4 Does the European Union (Withdrawal) Act 2018 provide a coherent basis for the disentanglement of EU law from the domestic legal system?

10.5 Many of those in favour of leaving the EU argued during the referendum campaign that sovereignty had been lost during the UK's membership. Do you agree with this claim? (Consider also the material contained in Chapter 8.)

10.6 'The process of withdrawal from the EU has brought to the fore the various weaknesses of the unwritten British constitution'. Discuss.

Further reading

Anthony, 'Brexit and the Common Law Constitution' (2018) 24 European Public Law 673

Barnard and Peers (eds), *European Union Law* (3rd edn, Oxford University Press 2020) chs 1, 3, 4, 5, 6, 9, 10

Birkinshaw, 'Brexit's Challenge to the UK's Unwritten Constitution' (2020) 26 European Public Law 29

Blick, *Stretching the Constitution: The Brexit Shock in Historic Perspective* (Hart Publishing, 2020)

Brexit Special Extra Issue [2017] PL

Craig, 'Casting Aside Clanking Medieval Chains: Prerogative, Statute and Article 50 After the EU Referendum' (2016) 79 MLR 1041

Craig, 'Brexit and the UK Constitution' in Jowell and O'Cinneide (eds), *The Changing Constitution* (9th edn, Oxford University Press 2019)

Dougan, *The UK After Brexit: Legal and Policy Challenges* (Intersentia 2017)

Elliott, 'The Supreme Court's Judgment in *Miller*: in Search of Constitutional Principle' (2017) 76 CLJ 257

Elliott, *The UK Constitution After Miller: Brexit and Beyond* (Bloomsbury 2020)

Phillipson, 'A Dive into Deep Constitutional Waters: Article 50, the Prerogative and Parliament' (2016) 79 MLR 1064

Part IV

Government institutions

Chapter 11

Parliament: constitutional position

Introduction

In this chapter, we will discuss Parliament generally. In the following two chapters, the composition and procedures of Parliament will be discussed more closely. Parliament comprises two Houses, the appointed House of Lords and the elected House of Commons. As a result of the seventeenth-century conflict between the monarchy and Parliament, it was established that the monarch could not make law or raise taxes without the consent of Parliament and that Parliament should be free from royal interference (Section 4.5). These powers formed the platform for the subsequent development of Parliament's roles of maintaining the executive and holding it to account. Together with the court-centred rule of law, this forms the basis of modern constitutionalism.

Parliament's functions are to:

- Enact legislation. Apart from the limited powers of the Crown under the royal prerogative (Section 14.6), no other body can make law without the power being specifically conferred by Parliament. Tomkins (2003) suggests that because most legislation is, in fact, prepared by the executive, it is more appropriate to regard Parliament's role as that of scrutinising and approving legislation. However, even though ministers are also MPs, there are important differences between laws made by the executive as such (namely subordinate legislation under powers conferred by statute and laws made under the royal prerogative) and those enacted by Parliament itself. In particular, under the general law of judicial review, the courts can examine whether the procedure for making subordinate legislation is fair and reasonable, but cannot do so in the case of Acts of Parliament (see *Bank Mellat v HM Treasury (No 2)* [2013] UKSC 39);
- 'Sustain' the government by providing it with money by voting for taxation. Now that the Crown has little independent power, Parliament is ultimately responsible for ensuring that government carries on;
- Hold the government to account and redress the grievances of the people by scrutinising government action and, ultimately, removing a government;
- Debate upon public matters of public concern as a focus for the nation;
- Serve as a recruiting ground for ministers. Parliament acts as a flawed means of translating the popular vote into the appointment of an executive, since by convention whichever party or coalition of parties commands a majority in the House of Commons is entitled to form a government. Owing to the distortions of the electoral system, a popular majority does not necessarily translate into a parliamentary majority (Section 12.5).

A dominant feature of the UK Constitution is the existence of a *parliamentary executive*. This is derived from conventions under which the leader of the government (the prime minister) must command the confidence of the House of Commons, the executive depends on the support of the Commons, and all ministers, although chosen by the prime minister, must be MPs. The prime minister and all Treasury (finance) ministers must be members of the House of Commons. Other ministers could be appointed as members of the House of Lords, thus enabling the prime minister, on whose advice the Queen must appoint both ministers and members of the Lords, to appoint friends and supporters who have not been elected to the Commons.

Most laws are proposed by the executive, and many laws are directly made by the executive as delegated legislation. Thus, in practice, Parliament does not make law itself, but scrutinises proposals from the executive, amends them and gives its consent. Individual MPs can propose legislation, but the time available for this is so limited that such attempts rarely succeed. Control of parliamentary business and the timetable in the House of Commons is largely in the hands of the government party, although this has recently been slightly modified (Section 13.1), and the government frequently lost control during the debates on Brexit during 2019.

A strong two-party adversarial system developed in the UK Parliament from the early twentieth century, during which highly disciplined parties funded by private interests emerged. One reason for this is that most MPs are paid professional politicians dependent on party conformity. Each party has a highly organised 'whip' system dedicated to enforcing party discipline and persuading members to vote in the required way.

It is widely acknowledged that the executive is normally dominant over Parliament. Two factors in particular strengthen its power.

First, under the procedural rules of the Commons, government business has priority and a government minister organises the business of the House. Recent reforms have, to some extent, increased the influence of backbench MPs (Section 13.1), but this is insignificant in relation to the government's power to control the extent to which proposed laws are discussed. The House of Lords is not dominated by the government, but its proposals can be rejected by the Commons and laws passed without its consent using the Parliament Acts (Section 11.4).

Secondly, there is the 'first past the post' (FPP) voting system for Parliament, which generally results in an executive being formed from the majority party. Coalition government is unusual. This contrasts with systems of proportional representation (PR) used in many countries under which seats are distributed among the parties according to their share of the total vote (Section 12.5.7). PR is likely to weaken the power of the larger parties, allowing MPs greater independence. The present system has been justified on the basis that it usually produces a strong government.

However, executive domination of Parliament should not be overstated. Reflecting the separation of powers, Parliament is a separate institution with significant powers and distinctive functions, and it can resist the executive if it is so minded, as it did frequently during the Brexit process. The following factors are significant in establishing Parliament's position:

▶ Apart from approximately 100 ministers, members of the executive cannot be members of the House of Commons, thus reinforcing the separation of powers (Section 12.4). Government proposals must be publicly explained in Parliament, and ministers must justify their decisions in public if required to do so by Parliament. The dual role of ministers as MPs means that a minister must have regard to the voters as well as to the authority of the government, thus providing a check on executive power.

▶ The independent Speaker, who chairs the Commons, is responsible for ensuring fair and focused debate, with ministers answering questions properly, and for protecting the interests of minorities.

▶ The Opposition, the second-largest party in the Commons, is a formal institution protected by the law of parliamentary procedure – a government and prime minister in waiting. It has a duty to oppose government policy, short of frustrating the governmental process, and forms a 'shadow Cabinet' ready to take office. There is funding designated by the House of Commons ('Short Money', named after Edward Short, the MP who proposed it) for the parliamentary work of Opposition parties. This is determined by a formula based on the number of seats and votes the party received in the previous election. There is also funding for the Opposition leader's office.

▶ The House of Lords is less subject to party discipline than the Commons and may not have a government majority.

▶ While there is no law to this effect, it is often claimed that an MP has a duty to exercise independent judgment on behalf of all his or her constituents and not merely those who voted for him or her. However, in practice, many MPs mechanically support the party that sponsors them, although there are a few independent voices. Occasionally, an MP changes parties. Previously, unless he or she becomes disqualified to sit in Parliament (Section 12.4), an MP could not be removed until the next election. However, the Recall of MPs Act 2015 has expanded the situations in which an MP may be 'recalled' by their constituents, triggering a special election which may remove the sitting member.

▶ There have been recent reforms to the procedures in the House of Commons which strengthen the position of backbenchers (Section 13.1).

The relative power of Parliament and the executive fluctuates according to the political circumstances of the day and is therefore itself a constitutional check between the two democratic bodies. Public opinion and the cohesion of the ruling groups are important factors. For example, during the period of coalition government from 2010 to 2015, and again when the Conservative Party had no overall majority from 2017 to 2019, there were a significant number of rebellions and independent votes in the Commons, and the Speaker encouraged backbench participation, sometimes controversially so (Section 3.4.1).

11.2 The meeting of Parliament

Reflecting its early history as an assembly of advisers to the monarch, Parliament cannot convene itself and must be summoned by the monarch, originally under the royal prerogative. The abuse of this power was a major contribution to the seventeenth-century revolution. This resulted in statutory intervention. Under the Septennial Act 1715, as amended by section 7 of the Parliament Act 1911 (now replaced (below)), a Parliament could not last for more than five years, after which a general election must be held. Moreover, 'Parliament ought to be held frequently' (Bill of Rights 1688, Art 13) and must meet at least once every three years (Meeting of Parliament Act 1694). By convention, Parliament meets annually, backed by administrative necessity, for example to authorise taxation and public spending. In practice, Parliament is usually in session for about eight months in the year, with a long recess over the summer.

The termination (dissolution) of a Parliament was radically reformed by the Fixed Term Parliaments Act 2011. Described as 'constitution making at its worst' (Brazier (2012) 128 LQR 315), this was enacted with little public discussion (see Political and Constitutional Reform Committee HC 2010–11, 436). The Act removed (or at least suspended) the long-standing royal prerogative power to dissolve Parliament at any time (exercised on the advice of the prime minister, which must usually be accepted). The power to dissolve Parliament was a weapon in the hands of a prime minister and could be used to time an election to the advantage of the ruling party. The Act is intended to remove this possibility and to reinforce stability. This is particularly so where there is a coalition government. However, it also seriously restricts the ability of a prime minister who takes office between elections (as Theresa May and Boris Johnson did in 2016 and 2019, respectively) to seek a popular mandate from the public by dissolving Parliament and calling an election. This might be thought to be bad for democracy.

The Act imposes a statutory timetable for dissolution and subsequent general elections as follows. Parliament can be dissolved only by this process:

▶ A general election must be (and was) held on 7 May 2015 and thereafter on the first Thursday in May every five years after the previous general election (s 1). An 'early general election' must be held in either of the following cases (s 2):

  1. if a motion for an early general election is passed by two-thirds of the whole number of seats of the House of Commons, including any vacancies, or
  2. if the House of Commons passes a vote of no confidence in the government by a majority of those voting and there is no motion of confidence passed within an alternative government within 14 days.

▶ The date for the 'early general election' is set by royal proclamation on the recommendation of the prime minister (s 2(7)). This allows time for any outstanding parliamentary business to be completed. However, no time limit is set.

▶ Where the previous election was an 'early general election' the next regular election is held in the fourth year after that election if it was held before the first Thursday in May (s 1(4)). Thus, a government cannot last beyond five years between elections. However, subject to the approval of both Houses, the prime minister can extend the polling date of any general election by not more than two months.

- Parliament is automatically dissolved at the beginning of the 25th working day before the date set for the election whether normal or early. 'Parliament cannot otherwise be dissolved' (s 3(2) and Electoral Registration and Administration Act 2013, s 14).
- The Act does not make clear the position in the unlikely event of the prime minister refusing to make a recommendation as to the date of an early general election. This would prevent dissolution. The monarch seems to have no discretion independently of a recommendation from the prime minister. It is arguable that, in an extreme case, the courts might require the prime minister to make a recommendation (below). Nor is it clear what would happen if a government were simply to resign without a vote of no confidence taking place. It is now clear, however, that the government can circumvent the provisions of the Act by securing the passage through Parliament of a further Act specifying a different date for an election from that which would be provided by the 2011 Act (Early Parliamentary General Election Act 2019).
- 'Once Parliament dissolves' the monarch may issue a proclamation summoning the new Parliament and appointing the date for its first meeting (s 3(4)). This will presumably be on the advice of the existing prime minister who will remain in office unless and until the Queen appoints a successor (Section 15.2). At the same time, the Lord Chancellor issues the writs that call upon the election officers to start the election process (Section 12.5.3). There are no statutory provisions relating to the date for the new Parliament to meet other than the three-year requirement (above). Usually, a new Parliament meets within a few days of the election.
- The different matter of 'proroguing' Parliament is not affected by the 2011 Act and is governed by the royal prerogative (s 6(1); and see *R (Miller) v the Prime Minister* [2019] UKSC 41, Sections 14.6.4 and 19.7.1). The 2011 Act arguably does not abolish the royal prerogative power to *dissolve* Parliament, but it certainly suspends it while the Act remains in force (Section 14.6).
- It has been suggested that, because the Act places the dissolution of Parliament on a statutory basis, the courts might become involved. However, those aspects of the process concerned with the resolutions of the Commons are subject to parliamentary privilege and so are not reviewable (Section 11.6.2). The powers of the prime minister under the Act are not subject to privilege since they are not within the internal affairs of the House. For example, should a prime minister refuse to set an election date the courts might interfere (see *R v Secretary of State for the Home Department parte Fire Brigades Union* [1995] 2 All ER 244). Such matters have usually been seen as non-justiciable in the sense that they raise political issues more suitable for the democratic branch of government (Section 19.7.1), but the outcome of *R (Miller) v the Prime Minister* [2019] demonstrates that this is not a certainty.

On one analysis, the Act removes a significant 'check and balance' of the traditional separation of powers, in that it makes it more difficult for the executive to dismiss the legislature. Montesquieu thought that the executive should be able to dismiss an obstructive legislature since the continuity of the government was paramount. Writing in the eighteenth century, he praised the British system as a balance of equal constitutional forces (Sections 7.1 and 7.2). However, Montesquieu did not anticipate the extent to which executive power and party control would increase over the following centuries. His fear was the power of the elected mob over the aristocracy. By contrast, prime ministers have used the power of dissolution as a threat to keep the House of Commons subservient, or for political advantage to call an election at a time favourable to themselves.

The 2011 Act can, of course, be altered or repealed. Its future seems highly uncertain. Although the first Parliament following its enactment lasted the full five years, each of the subsequent two Parliaments were brought to an end early. An election was held in June 2017, after a motion for an early general election was passed by the requisite two-thirds majority. The minority Conservative government failed to secure that majority on three separate occasions in 2019, but Parliament subsequently enacted (by simple majority) the Early Parliamentary General Election Act 2019, under which an election was held in December of that year. Both major political parties promised in their manifestos for that election to repeal the Act if elected.

Section 7 of the Act requires that it be reviewed by a committee, the majority of whose members must be MPs, between June and November 2020. A Joint Committee (consisting of members of both the Commons and the Lords) was established in November 2020, but prior to completion of its deliberations, the government published a draft bill which, if enacted, would repeal the Act. One difficult issue is whether the prerogative power to dissolve Parliament, which has been in abeyance while the Act has been in force (see above), will be 'automatically' restored on repeal. The draft legislation seeks to address this by providing that the powers relating to the dissolution of Parliament and calling of a new Parliament which were previously exercisable by virtue of the prerogative will be exercisable again as if the 2011 Act had never been enacted: but it is unclear whether this would in fact operate to revive the prerogative power or whether the power will now be based upon the newly-enacted statute (see Young, 'The Draft Fixed-term Parliaments Act 2011 (Repeal) Bill: Turning Back the Clock?', UK Constitutional Law Association Blog, 4 December 2020, https://ukconstitutionallaw. org/2020/12/04/alison-l-young-the-draft-fixed-term-parliaments-act-2011-repeal-bill-turning-back-the-clock/). The bill also contains an 'ouster clause' (Section 19.7.2) which purports to exclude the exercise of the power from review by the courts.

The life of Parliament cannot be extended without the consent of the House of Lords since a provision that does so is excepted from the procedures of the Parliament Acts 1911 and 1949, which enable statutes to be passed without the consent of the Lords. Thus, to some extent, there is protection against an attempt by the executive to keep itself in power. It is arguable, however, that this safeguard can be removed in two stages, first by using the Parliament Act procedure to repeal section 2(1) itself and then by bypassing the House of Lords under the Parliament Acts (Section 11.4).

During the election period, the meeting of Parliament is postponed by the monarch by 'prorogation' under the royal prerogative (see Prorogation Act 1867). The effect of prorogation is to suspend Parliament until recalled by the monarch. The power of prorogation is not affected by the 2011 Act (s 6(1)). This might be appropriate, for example, if the election does not produce a clear winner to form or continue the government.

A Parliament is divided into 'sessions'. These are working periods usually of a year (but there is no fixed timetable), and usually running from November (about 170 sitting days). Sessions are ended by being prorogued by the monarch under the royal prerogative, thus being under the control of the prime minister on whose advice the monarch, by convention, must act. It was the exercise of this power which was at issue in *R (Miller) v The Prime Minister* [2019], when Boris Johnson advised the Queen to prorogue Parliament ostensibly to bring a lengthy session to an end, but with the additional goal of limiting parliamentary debate on the terms of the UK's withdrawal from the EU. The case is discussed more fully in Sections 14.6.4 and 19.7.1.

A new session is summoned by the monarch by proclamation. Again, there is no fixed time, but, in practice, pressure of business means that the new session starts a few days after the old one has ended. Although there is no constitutional requirement for this, each session is opened by the monarch, with an address from the throne which is written by the government and outlines its legislative proposals. A general debate on government policy takes place over the following week. Within a session, each House can be adjourned at any time by resolution of the House. Adjournments apply to daily sittings, and the breaks for holidays and over the summer. The remainder of the session (generally following the summer break) is used to finish outstanding business. The Speaker can suspend individual daily sittings of the Commons for disciplinary reasons.

There is machinery for recalling each House by proclamation while it stands prorogued (Parliament (Elections and Meetings) Act 1943, s 34) and also under emergency legislation (Civil Contingencies Act 2004). As usual, this is on the advice of the prime minister. An adjourned Parliament can be summoned by proclamation (Meeting of Parliament Act 1694) and also by the Speakers of both Houses at the request of the prime minister, or perhaps at the request of the leader of the Opposition. However, it does not seem to be possible for ordinary MPs to recall Parliament in order to debate any crisis that may arise while Parliament is not sitting: for example, calls to recall Parliament to debate Brexit during the summer recess of 2019 were resisted by the government. This again illustrates the subservience of Parliament to the executive.

During the COVID-19 pandemic, no more than fifty MPs were permitted to sit in the Commons chamber at any one time. Arrangements were made for remote participation for those who had self-certified that they were unable to attend for medical or public health reasons connected to the pandemic.

11.3   The House of Lords

The purpose of the House of Lords, or Upper House, is to act as a check on the House of Commons by scrutinising bills and providing an opportunity for second thoughts. In the UK, the appointed House of Lords is subordinate to the elected House of Commons. This is secured by the Parliament Acts 1911 and 1949 and by conventions, notably the 'Salisbury Convention', which requires the Lords to accept proposals contained in the government's election manifesto. The House of Lords should also defer to the Commons on matters of government finance since this is a matter between the Crown, which asks for money, and the Commons, which supplies it.

The House of Lords is unusual among second chambers in the following respects:

▶ Its members are not elected. Most of them are appointed by the Crown (by convention, the prime minister). There are also 26 senior Church of England bishops. Until the House of Lords Act 1999, the bulk of members were hereditary peers whose descendants enjoyed permanent seats. As the first stage of a reform programme, the 1999 Act removed all but 92 hereditary peers. Substantial further reform seems unlikely (below).
▶ The House is one of the world's largest legislative chambers, having more than 800 members compared with 650 in the Commons. However, attendance is on average only around 60 per cent. Members (other than the bishops) sit for life, subject to voluntary or mandatory withdrawal under the House of Lords Reform Act 2014 (Section 11.7.3). Members other than those who serve as government ministers receive no salaries in respect of their parliamentary duties. However, they are entitled to an allowance of £305 per day's actual attendance and may claim some travel expenses.
▶ Members have no constituencies and in this respect are democratically accountable to no one. About 25 per cent of the members are 'cross-benchers', who are independent of political parties.
▶ By long-standing practice, the proceedings of the House are regulated by the House itself without formal rules or disciplinary sanctions, members being treated as bound by 'personal honour'. This has not prevented some peers from abusing their position, and there is now a *Code of Conduct* (4th edition, HL 2015, 3). This is policed by a Commissioner for Standards, with the assistance of the House's Committee for Privileges and Conduct.

11.3.1   Reform of the House of Lords

Being undemocratic, the position of the House of Lords is controversial. It could be variously depicted as a constitutional abomination, a valuable ingredient of a mixed constitution, or a historical survival that, from a pragmatic perspective, might nevertheless have some useful functions. The Parliament Act 1911 removed the power of the House of Lords to veto most legislation. Its preamble stated that this was a precursor to replacing it by a second chamber 'constituted on a popular basis' and 'limiting and defining' its powers. However, there has been no agreement as to how that should be done. In 2000, the Wakeham Report (Royal Commission on the House of Lords, *A House for the Future* (Cm 4534, 2000)) endorsed the conservative view that the House of Lords should remain subordinate to the Commons (thus ensuring the clear democratic accountability of the government), that it should provide constitutional checks and balances, and that it should provide a parliamentary voice for the 'nations and regions of the United Kingdom'. Despite numerous consultations, government papers and parliamentary debates and reports (see White Paper, *House of Lords Reform* (Cm 7027, 2007) for a useful history) no agreed proposals for further reform of the House of Lords have emerged – a pattern that has been repeated since 1911. The most recent attempt at reform, the House of Lords Reform Bill 2012, ended in failure after a significant number of Conservative MPs dramatically rebelled against the proposal supported by their party's leadership (Section 12.3).

In January 2020, it was suggested that the House might move to York, at least while the Palace of Westminster is undergoing refurbishment from 2025, and possibly permanently, to 'reconnect' with the public. However, this proposal seems to have been abandoned when it failed to receive support from the body charged with organising the restoration of the Palace.

11.3.2 Role of the House of Lords

The usual justification for the existence of a second chamber in the UK is that it acts as a revising chamber to scrutinise the detail of legislation proposed by the Commons and to allow time for second thoughts, thus acting as a constitutional safeguard against the possible excesses of majoritarianism and party politics. According to the Wakeham Report (above), the functions of the second chamber include, and should continue to include, the following:

▶ to provide advice on public policy, bringing a range of perspectives to bear that should be broadly representative of UK society, and in particular to provide a voice for the nations and regions of the UK and ethnic minorities and interest groups. The present composition of the Lords obviously does not reflect this aspiration, but the proposed move to York (although now unlikely to take place) may signal ambitions for a greater regional role in future;
▶ to act as a revising chamber, scrutinising the details of proposed legislation within the overall policies laid down by the Commons. By convention, supported by the Parliament Acts 1911 and 1949 (Chapter 13), the House of Lords does not discuss matters of government finance, this being a matter solely for the Commons;
▶ to provide a forum for general debate on matters of public concern without party political pressures;
▶ to introduce legislation as a method of relieving the workload of the Commons. Any bill other than a financial measure can be introduced in the Lords;
▶ to provide ministers: thus unelected persons can be appointed as ministers. However, by convention the prime minister and the Chancellor of the Exchequer must be members of the Commons;
▶ to provide committees on general topics, such as the European Union Committee (which scrutinised many of the preparations made for Brexit), and the Science and Technology Committee. These are highly respected;
▶ to enable persons who have made a contribution to public life, other than party politicians, to participate in government. It is often claimed that the House of Lords is a valuable source of expertise, in that outstanding persons from all walks of life can be appointed. However, the expertise of the House may be patchy and skewed in favour of persons who have been subservient to government. Membership is dominated by former officials, politicians and leading members of the elite professions and business interests. There have been allegations that seats in the Lords can be bought (Section 12.2). Moreover, appointment to the Lords is likely to be towards the end of a career, thus risking expertise which is out of date. Conversely, those with active expertise may be infrequent attenders. Moreover, it has been suggested that the House of Commons may command greater expertise on certain issues (see Bochel and Defty, 'A Question of Expertise: The House of Lords and Welfare Policy' (2010) 63 *Parliamentary Affairs* 66);
▶ to act as a constitutional check by preventing a government from prolonging its own life, in respect of which the Lords has a veto (Parliament Act 1911 (below)). The consent of the Lords is also needed for the dismissal of senior judges (Section 7.7.3.2);
▶ to act as a constitutional watchdog. The House has no specific powers for this purpose but has a Constitution Committee which examines the constitutional implications of bills brought before the House.

These functions can be pursued in the House of Lords partly because its procedure and culture differ significantly from those of the Commons. In particular, party discipline is less rigorous, and the House of Lords is less partisan than the Commons. Members of the House of Lords, other than bishops, are removable only by statute (including under the House of Lords Reform Act 2014) and are therefore less susceptible to political pressures than MPs. The House as a whole controls its own procedure, making it relatively free from party constraints and is subject to less time pressure than the Commons. Its members have a considerable accumulation of experience and knowledge. The House of Lords cannot therefore easily be manipulated by the government, is attractive to external lobbyists and can ventilate moral and social issues in a non-partisan way.

11.4 The Parliament Acts

Under the Parliament Acts 1911 and 1949, subject to a delaying period intended to give time for the Commons to reconsider, most public bills (Section 13.3.1) can be enacted without the consent of the House of Lords, thus ensuring that the democratic will prevails. The 1949 Act reduced the period during which the Lords can a delay a bill from about two years to one year.

The Lords can reject a bill in two parliamentary sessions provided it is sent to them at least one month before the end of each session and no more than one year elapses between the second reading in the first session and the date the bill passes the Commons in the second session (Parliament Act 1911, s 2, as modified by 1949 Act). After the second session, the bill can receive the royal assent without the consent of the Lords. (However, if the Commons amends a bill after it has come back from the Lords in the first session, then it may not count as the same bill unless the amendments were suggested by the Lords.)

In the case of a 'money bill', the Lords can delay only for one month, provided the bill is sent to them at least one month before the end of a session (Parliament Act 1911, s 1). A money bill is a public bill that, in the opinion of the Speaker, deals exclusively either with central government taxation spending, borrowing or accounts. This definition is narrow since few bills deal exclusively with these matters.

The Speaker must certify that the Parliament Act procedure has been followed, and his certificate cannot be questioned in a court (Parliament Act 1911, ss 2(2), 3). However, this applies only to the question of compliance with the internal procedure. A court can decide whether a bill falls within the limits of the Parliament Act in the first place, as seen in *Jackson v A-G* [2006] 1 AC 262 at [116].

There are three main exceptions where the Parliament Acts do not apply (Parliament Act 1911, s 2(1)). They are:

(i) a bill to prolong the life of a Parliament beyond five years, thus ensuring that a government cannot use its majority to keep itself in office;
(ii) a bill introduced in the Lords itself;
(iii) a private bill (Section 13.3.2) and a Provisional Order Confirmation bill (an obsolete process for approving large building projects).

The Parliament Acts do not apply to delegated legislation, which sometimes requires the approval of Parliament. In November 2015, the House of Lords voted to delay a government proposal (contained in delegated legislation which had been approved by the Commons) to limit eligibility for tax credits. Arguing that the Lords had breached the principle of the supremacy of the Commons on financial matters, the government responded by ordering a review of the Lords' powers in respect of delegated legislation, which recommended that a new procedure be created to enable the Lords to invite the Commons to 'think again' when a disagreement takes place, allowing the Commons to assert its superiority if it chose to do so ('Secondary Legislation and the Primacy of the House of Commons', Cm 9177, 2015). This proposal has not yet been acted upon.

Before 1991, the 1911 Act was used only three times (Government of Ireland Act 1914; Welsh Church Act 1914; Parliament Act 1949). Since then, it has been used four times for relatively minor purposes

(War Crimes Act 1991; European Parliamentary Elections Act 1999; Sexual Offences (Amendment) Act 2000; Hunting Act 2004).

- The conventional view is that, subject to the limits specifically mentioned in the 1911 Act, any statute can be enacted under the Parliament Acts including, for example, one abolishing the House of Lords. In *Jackson v A-G* [2006] the House of Lords held that the changes made to the 1911 Act by the Parliament Act 1949, which reduced the powers of the House of Lords still further and was enacted without its consent, were effective since Acts passed under the Parliament Act procedure were fully fledged statutes (see Section 8.5.3).
- However, it is not clear whether this would apply to an alteration to the Parliament Acts to remove the limitations on the use of the Acts set out in the 1911 Act, such as an Act extending the life of a Parliament. Clearly, this could not be achieved directly under the 1949 Act. However, arguably it could be achieved in two stages. First, by using the Parliament Acts, the Commons might alter the 1911 Act itself so as to remove them. It would then, using the altered Parliament Acts, pass a statute, for example extending Parliament's life to ten years. Lord Bingham, at [32], and Baroness Hale, at [164], [166], took this logical view, holding that there were no limitations in the Parliament Acts 1911 other than those expressly set out. Therefore, the courts could not prevent this, however politically undesirable it might be. However, a majority (Lords Nicholls, at [59], Steyn, at [79], Hope, at [118], [122] and Carswell, at [175]) suggested that this manoeuvre would be unlawful as subverting the clear intention of the 1911 Act. Lord Rogers, at [139], was sympathetic to this view. Lords Walker and Browne did not express a view.

It seems clear, however, that the House of Lords could be abolished under the Parliament Acts (see Pannick [2012] PL 230).

11.5 The functions of the House of Commons

The main functions of the Commons are as follows:

- Choosing the government indirectly, by virtue of the convention that the person who commands a majority of the Commons is entitled to form a government, as the person best placed to command the confidence of the Commons. The Commons has no veto over individual appointments nor can it dismiss individual members of the government (another prime ministerial power);
- Sustaining the government by supplying it with funds and authorising taxation. The size and complexity of modern government means that parliamentary control over finance cannot be exercised directly. Parliamentary approval of the executive's budget and accounts is largely a formality. Detailed scrutiny and control over government spending takes place mainly within the government itself through the medium of the Treasury (Chapter 15). However, a substantial parliamentary safeguard is provided by the National Audit Office, headed by the Comptroller and Auditor-General (Section 13.5.4);
- Legislating. Any member can propose a bill, but in practice, the parliamentary timetable is dominated by government business, and legislation is usually presented to Parliament ready-drafted by the executive. This is why Bagehot thought that the absence of a strict separation of powers made the UK Constitution an effective machine for ensuring government by experts. There are certain opportunities for private members' bills, but these rarely become law (Section 13.3.1);
- Supervising the executive by scrutinising its activities. By convention, ministers are accountable to Parliament and must appear in Parliament to participate in debates, make statements, answer questions and appear before committees (Section 15.7). Policy announcements should be made to Parliament before releasing them to the media, although there is no clear convention to this effect and the principle is now very frequently ignored. The House of Commons can require a government to resign by a vote of no confidence, or it can trigger a dissolution of Parliament under the Fixed Term Parliaments Act 2011 (Section 11.2). These sanctions are rarely used since the resignation of the government is likely to result in a general election, putting the jobs of MPs at risk;

- Redressing grievances raised by individual MPs on behalf of their constituents. There are certain opportunities to raise grievances in debates, but they are usually pursued by correspondence with ministers or by the Parliamentary Ombudsman (Section 20.2). Every constituent has a right of access to his or her MP, which can be exercised by visiting Parliament if necessary. Individuals may also petition Parliament;

- Debating matters of public concern. Again there are limited procedural opportunities for such debates, although the creation of an additional debating chamber in 1999 has significantly expanded this role (these are known as 'Westminster Hall debates').

11.6 Parliamentary privilege

In *R v Chaytor* [2010] EWCA Crim 1910, at [5]–[7], the Court of Appeal said that 'properly understood, the privileges of Parliament are the privileges of the nation and the bedrock of our constitutional democracy'. It is important, as part of the separation of powers, that a legislature can control its own affairs and that its members be protected against outside interference so that they can speak freely. (The report of the Joint Committee on Parliamentary Privilege, HL 30/HC 100, 2013–14 provides a useful overview of this subject.)

Interference by the Crown with parliamentary business was an ingredient of the seventeenth-century revolution (see *R v Eliot, Holles and Valentine* (1629) 3 St TR 293: king forcibly dismissed Parliament, Sir John Eliot holding the Speaker down in an attempt to prevent this). As a result, at the beginning of every Parliament, the Speaker symbolically asserts the 'ancient and undoubted privileges' of the House of Commons against the Crown. The House of Lords also has privileges. The devolved legislatures of Scotland, Wales and Northern Ireland do not have parliamentary privilege but are protected against liability for defamation (e.g. Scotland Act 1998, s 41).

Some parliamentary privileges are mainly of historical or symbolic interest. These include the collective right of access of the Commons to the monarch. Members of the Commons also enjoy immunity from civil, as opposed to criminal, arrest during a period from 40 days before to 40 days after every session. In the case of peers, the immunity is permanent and seems to be based on their status as peers rather than membership of the House (*Stourton v Stourton* [1963] 1 All ER 606). Now that debtors are no longer imprisoned, civil arrest is virtually obsolete, being concerned mainly with disobedience to court orders. The Joint Committee on Parliamentary Privilege (above) recommended the abolition of this privilege. Members and officers of both Houses can be excused from jury service (Juries Act 1974), and the House can exempt members from giving evidence in court.

The two most important privileges overlap. They are:

(i) the collective privilege of each House to control its own composition and proceedings;
(ii) freedom of speech in Parliament (Art 9 Bill of Rights 1688).

We shall discuss these below. The courts accept that Parliament has the exclusive power to regulate its own internal affairs, but claim the right to determine the limits of parliamentary privilege (see *R v Chaytor* [2011] 1 AC 684).

11.6.1 Contempt of Parliament

Breach of a specific parliamentary privilege is one kind of 'contempt' of Parliament. A parliamentary privilege is a special right or immunity available either to the House collectively (e.g. to control its own composition and procedure) or to individual members (e.g. freedom of speech). Contempt is a general term embracing any conduct, whether by MPs or outsiders,

> which obstructs or impedes either House of Parliament in the performance of its functions or which obstructs or impedes any member or officer of the House in the execution of his duty or which has a tendency directly or indirectly to produce such results (Erskine May, *Parliamentary Practice* (Butterworths 1997) 108).

This is very wide. It includes, for example, abuses by MPs of parliamentary procedure, breaching confidences, refusing to obey a committee (the most common form of contempt), causing disruption in the House and improper or dishonest behaviour by MPs. It also includes conduct by outsiders, such as the press, for example publishing MPs' home telephone numbers (*Daily Graphic Case* (HC 1956–57, 27)), accusing MPs of drunkenness (*Duffy's Case* (HC 1964–65, 129)) or making press allegations of conflict of interest by MPs. Contempt not only protects the 'efficiency' of the House but also its 'authority and dignity'. On 4 December 2018, the House of Commons voted in favour of a motion finding ministers in contempt for a failure to publish full legal advice concerning the EU Withdrawal Agreement (Section 10.5.3). This was the first time ministers had been found to be in contempt in modern parliamentary history. In response to the motion, the government made legal advice available to inform a Commons vote on the Withdrawal Agreement which took place the following week.

Perhaps the most striking feature of contempt of Parliament is that Parliament accuses, tries and punishes offenders itself. This is an aspect of the wider principle that Parliament claims to look after its own affairs without outside interference. The ordinary courts have no jurisdiction over the internal affairs of Parliament (below), and there are no independent safeguards for the individual. This is a violation both of the separation of powers (in its functional sense) and the rule of law concerning the right to be judged by an independent court. It also confronts the right to a fair trial under Article 6 of the ECHR (Section 21.4.1.3; see *Demicoli v Malta* (1992) 14 EHRR 47). However, the immunity of Parliament from interference by the courts is reinforced by the HRA, which provides that Parliament is not a public authority for the purpose of the Act (s 6(3); Section 22.5). This prevents a challenge under the Act being brought against Parliament.

The procedure for dealing with a contempt of the House of Commons, or a breach of privilege, is as follows (see Committee of Privileges, Third Report, HC 1976–77, 417):

1. Any member can give written notice of a complaint to the Speaker.
2. The Speaker decides whether to give priority over other business.
3. If the Speaker decides not to do so, the member may then use the ordinary procedure of the House to get the matter discussed. This would be difficult in practice.
4. If the Speaker decides to take up the matter, the complaining member can propose that the matter be referred to the Committee of Privileges or that some other action be taken, for example an immediate debate. A select committee can in certain cases refer a contempt against itself direct to the Committee (HC Deb 18 March 1986, vol 94, cols 763–64).
5. The Committee investigates the complaint. The Committee reports back to the House, which decides what action to take. This could be a reprimand, suspension or expulsion from the House, or imprisonment for the rest of the session, renewable indefinitely. A power to impose a fine was last used in 1666. The procedure is entirely up to the Committee and has been widely criticised as archaic and unfair. Witnesses are examined, but there is no right to legal representation. The accused has no legal right to a hearing or to summon or cross-examine witnesses. Parliament is not subject to the HRA (Section 22.5) so the right to a fair trial cannot be invoked.
6. The Speaker also has summary powers to deal with disruptive behaviour in the House or breaches of the rules of debate. He or she can exclude MPs and others from the Chamber until the end of the session (HC Standing Orders 24–26) and make rulings on matters of procedure. The Speaker of the House of Lords has no procedural or disciplinary powers.
7. The Joint Committee on Parliamentary Privilege considered whether contempt of Parliament should be endorsed or regulated by statute. It rejected this on the ground that it would be undesirable for the courts to interfere with the internal affairs of Parliament. However, the Committee recommended that procedural safeguards for those appearing before the Committee of Privileges should be formalised by the House. These include asking for matters to be considered in private and an opportunity to respond to allegations.

The House of Lords can also punish for contempt. Its powers include a fine. It can suspend but not expel a member (but see also Section 11.7.3).

11.6.2   'Exclusive cognisance'

Each House of Parliament claims exclusive control over its internal affairs against both the other House and outside bodies. This is an important aspect of the separation of powers. It was originally based on the premise that Parliament has its own peculiar law which was not known to the courts, but its contemporary rationale was described by the Joint Committee on Parliamentary Privilege (above) as a 'doctrine of necessity' meaning that protection should be confined to what is essential for the effective functioning of Parliament (see *Canada (House of Commons) v Vaid* [2005] 1 SCR 667 at [4]). The courts, while they cannot interfere with the application of the doctrine, can decide its limits (*R v Chaytor* [2011]). This exemplifies the comity between the two branches that informs the separation of powers (Section 7.5.2).

For example, although the qualifications for being an MP are fixed by statute, each House has the exclusive right to regulate all internal proceedings and to expel members (*Bradlaugh v Gossett* (1884) 12 QBD 271: atheist refusing to take the oath). The courts cannot decide whether the procedures for enacting legislation have been properly followed; whether they are honest, fair, adequate; or probably, whether they comply with any EU requirements (see *Pickin v British Railways Board* [1974] AC 765: allegation of fraud; *R (HS2 Action Alliance Ltd) v Secretary of State for Transport* [2014] 1 WLR 324: EU (Section 11.6.3)). No one can be prevented from placing a matter before Parliament even where they have contracted not to do so (*Bilston Corp v Wolverhampton Corp* [1942] Ch 391). The courts cannot order a minister to present a matter to Parliament even where a change in the law is required by European law (*R v Secretary of State for Employment, ex p Equal Opportunities Commission* [1992] 1 All ER 545). Nor can they give their opinion whether a matter has been given adequate scrutiny in Parliament.

However, the validity of delegated legislation can be challenged in the courts even if it has been approved by Parliament, although the parliamentary process itself cannot (see *Hoffmann-La Roche v Trade and Industry Secretary* [1974] 2 All ER 1128; *Bank Mellat v HM Treasury (No 2)* [2013], at [38]–[49]; (Section 13.3.1.1). In *R (HS2 Action Alliance Ltd) v Secretary of State for Transport* [2014] at [205], it was tentatively suggested that, even in the case of a bill, the court might be able to examine material which the government collected at an earlier stage. However, in considering whether government action is unreasonable the court will be especially deferential to decisions that have been approved by Parliament (Section 19.7.1).

The exclusive cognisance privilege only applies to the internal affairs of the House. Resolutions of the House of Commons cannot alter the general law. This requires a statute (*Stockdale v Hansard* (1839) 9 Ad & E 1; *Bowles v Bank of England* [1913] 1 Ch 57). The Ombudsman, who investigates citizens' complaints against the executive and reports to Parliament, is not protected by privilege because s/he deals with external matters (Section 20.2). By contrast, the Parliamentary Commissioner for Standards, who polices the conduct of MPs and so is concerned with matters internal to the House, is subject to privilege and so is not subject to review by the courts (Section 11.7.1). The position, as regards the Independent Parliamentary Standards Authority (IPSA), which polices salaries and expenses arrangements (Section 11.7.2), is unclear since IPSA has both external and internal aspects.

The scope of the privilege may change over time, as the activities of Parliament change in response to new circumstances. For this reason, the Joint Committee on Parliamentary Privilege (Section 11.6, at [47]) rejected a suggestion that the scope of the privilege be codified.

Exclusive cognisance has two aspects. First, it includes the management and administration of Parliament, such as control over the premises (precincts), arrangements for salaries and expenses, libraries, catering etc., all of which support Parliament as an independent institution. Secondly, it ensures that MPs are not impeded from performing their duties, namely lawmaking, scrutinising the government and representing constituents in the House. This second aspect overlaps with the separate privilege of freedom of speech (below).

On a wide view, the first aspect has sometimes been thought to include anything that happens within the precincts of the Houses of Parliament (the Palace of Westminster). Parliament has control over the precincts in the sense that permission is required to enter, even by the police. In 2008, the police searched the parliamentary office of Damian Green, a shadow immigration minister, in connection with an investigation into a leak of information from the Home Office. This may have been politically unwise and an overreaction, but since the Speaker had apparently given permission it was not a contempt of the House (see Bradley, 'The Damian Green Affair – All's Well that Ends Well?' [2012] PL 396).

In *R v Grahame-Campbell, ex p Herbert* [1935] 1 KB 594, the Divisional Court held that the House of Commons bar was exempt from the liquor licensing statutes and so could sell drinks without restriction. The rationale was that a statute does not apply to Parliament unless it expressly states so. This has been criticised and may be incorrect. The report of the Joint Committee on Parliamentary Privilege (Section 11.6, at [126]) recommended that a statute should normally state that it applies to Parliament.

Not all matters relating to the House fall within the privilege. Older cases established that the privilege does not apply to breaches of the peace, treason or sedition (*Seven Bishops' Case* (1688) 12 St Tr 133). In *R v Chaytor* [2011], the Supreme Court held that the privilege applies only (i) to decisions made by parliamentary bodies and (ii) to MPs in the performance of their 'core' or essential functions of legislating, holding government to account and representing constituents, but not to ordinary management matters, activities that might take place in any institution, for example theft or fraud or the treatment of staff. In some cases, such as use of research facilities in the House, the distinction may be difficult to make.

In *R v Chaytor* [2011] (which contains a useful review of the authorities), three MPs claimed to be protected by the exclusive cognisance privilege against prosecution in the ordinary courts for making fraudulent claims for parliamentary expenses. The Supreme Court held that parliamentary privilege is subject to the rule of law and so it is for the Court to determine its limit. The Court was not bound by decisions made by parliamentary bodies, although it would treat them with respect. For example, it may sometimes be more suitable or fairer for an MP to be dealt with by Parliament itself.

The Court held that the exclusive cognisance privilege was not available in respect of the expenses claims. Lord Phillips said that Parliament can waive (give up) its exclusive cognisance privilege, and has done so for many years in respect of the administrative management of the two Houses including statutory interventions (at [74], [89]–[92]). There is a distinction between the making of administrative rules of the House, including decisions by parliamentary committees on such matters as expenses and salaries. These rules remain subject to privilege and cannot be reviewed by the courts. However, in respect of matters relating to the *application* of the rules to individuals, Parliament has permitted the ordinary authorities to act and, where there is an overlapping jurisdiction, will cooperate with outside authorities (at [89]–[92]). Ordinary civil actions and criminal matters against individuals are not therefore protected. Thus, the prosecution of the MPs in question was lawful. Moreover, according to Lord Clarke, although the point remains open, the individual cannot invoke a privilege that Parliament has waived and, except by statute, Parliament cannot withdraw this long-standing waiver (at [131]–[132], cf. Lord Rodgers at [124]). It was also left open whether a statute only applies to activities within the Palace of Westminster if it expressly states as much (at [78]).

Lord Rodgers held that, even without waiver, the privilege applied only to matters directly related to the core functions of an MP, and there was nothing in the allegations which related in any way to these. The other members of the court agreed with both Lord Phillips and Lord Rodgers. Therefore Lord Rodgers would exclude most administrative matters and questions of ordinary legal liability from the privilege. See also *Corporate Officer of the House of Commons v Information Commissioner* [2009] 3 All ER 403: expense claims are subject to Freedom of Information Act.

11.6.3 Freedom of speech

Freedom of speech is the central privilege of an individual MP, who must be at liberty to speak and write freely and frankly without pressure from outside bodies, whether participating in a debate, asking questions of ministers, acting in a committee or raising the problems of his or her constituents. Moreover, people who communicate with MPs about concerns with public officials also deserve protection against retaliation from the executive or police. Parliamentary privilege in relation to the freedom of speech of an MP has been upheld by the European Court of Human Rights as a proportionate way of securing the independence of the legislature (*A v UK* (2003) 36 EHRR 917; *Hoon v UK* [2014] ECHR 1442).

Article 9 of the Bill of Rights 1688 (part of the revolution settlement for the purpose of protecting Parliament against the Crown) states:

> The Freedom of Speech or Debates or Proceedings in Parliament ought not to be impeached or questioned in any court or place out of Parliament.

Article 9 overlaps with the exclusive cognisance privilege discussed above. In *Chaytor* (above) the Supreme Court explained the difference, namely that exclusive cognisance is a privilege belonging to the House as a whole and can be waived by it. Neither the House nor the individual MP can waive Article 9: at [63]. Only a statute can do so. For example, the Defamation Act 1996, s 13, permits an MP to use things said in Parliament in evidence provided that the MP waives his or her own immunity. However, the Joint Committee on Parliamentary Privilege (Section 11.6) recommended that this be repealed.

In *R (HS2 Action Alliance Ltd) v Secretary of State* [2014], there was an attempt to use EU law in defiance of Article 9. It was argued that parliamentary procedure was not sufficiently independent and rigorous to satisfy EU Directive 2011/92 concerning strategic environmental impact assessment of a 'plan or project'. The Directive requires information to be supplied and public participation. The claimants argued that the parliamentary process was inadequate and tainted due to the ignorance of MPs, the constraints of the party system and the lack of time for debate. The Supreme Court held that these matters were not its concern: at [109], invoking Article 9 and the separation of powers: at [110], [202]. The court held that the parliamentary process fell within an exemption in the Directive (Art 1(4)) for legislative procedures. The procedure satisfied the exemption in that MPs are supplied with adequate information and have the power to make changes. It was therefore a genuine means of discussion and debate. The court held that the relevant Directive did not require parliamentary processes to be investigated in depth, only that they were not a formality or sham. A clash with Article 9 was avoided by holding (perhaps dubiously) that this level of scrutiny did not violate Article 9. Had the court decided otherwise, parliamentary supremacy would have been in issue (Section 8.5.4).

Article 9 embodies a clash between two constitutional principles which are both important to democracy. On the one hand, it protects a vital constitutional interest: namely, that MPs should not be subject to pressures from outside which might prevent them from performing their duties properly. This calls for a broad reading of Article 9 (see *Pepper v Hart* [1993] AC 593, 638). On the other hand, in *Chaytor* (above) the Supreme Court held that, since Article 9 violates the rule of law (in its wide sense) and restricts ordinary legal rights, in particular freedom of speech, it should not be construed broadly (see also *A-G for Ceylon v De Livera* [1963] AC 103, 162; *Prebble v Television New Zealand* [1995] 1 AC 321, 340). The main limit on the scope of Article 9 is what is meant by 'proceedings in Parliament'. In 1688, it was probably thought that the phrase was self-explanatory. It certainly includes speeches and written or oral questions by an MP in the House, or in committee proceedings. The work of a modern MP goes beyond this. Much of an MP's time is spent in dealing with constituents and attending meetings in the UK and abroad with ministers, officials, pressure groups, local authorities, business organisations and so on. In *R v Chaytor* (above), the Supreme Court took a narrow approach. It held that Article 9 applies only to the 'core' or essential business of Parliament: at [62]. The false expense claims made by the MPs did not relate to this and scrutiny of expense claims by the courts would not inhibit an MP from performing his essential duties: at [48]. Lord Rodgers, with whom the others agreed, said that Article 9 could not cover matters outside the scope of the exclusive cognisance privilege (above).

Anything said in the Chamber as part of the business of the House and in committees or reports related to the business of the House is certainly protected. Parliamentary committees often visit locations around the country, and interference with their proceedings wherever they take place is a contempt of Parliament (e.g. a disturbance at Essex University in 1969, HC 1968–69, 308). On the other hand, even within the House itself, speech unrelated to parliamentary business enjoys no privilege (see *Re Parliamentary Privileges Act 1770* [1958] AC 331). In *Rivlin v Bilankin* [1953] 1 QB 485, for example, libellous letters about a private matter posted within the precincts were not protected. Similarly, statements made by MPs in election campaigns or at public meetings are not protected (*Culnane v Morris* [2006] 2 All ER 149).

Statements in the media where an MP may repeat or comment on something said in Parliament raise problems. Such statements are within the more limited protection of 'qualified privilege' which anyone can claim (Section 11.6.4), but are not normally covered by parliamentary privilege. Thus, an MP could be liable if he or she repeats in the media, or anywhere else, anything said in Parliament. In *Buchanan v Jennings* [2005] 2 All ER 273, an MP in a television interview endorsed a defamatory statement he had made in the New Zealand Parliament by saying that he 'did not resile' from the statement. The Privy Council held that he could not claim parliamentary privilege for the interview since this was not part of his parliamentary functions.

However, repetition of a statement before an official body may be protected by Article 9. In *Makudi v Baron Triesman of Tottenham* [2014] 3 All ER 36, the Court of Appeal attempted to strike a balance by introducing a new principle, taking the law into uncertain territory outside the language of the statute (see Joseph (2015) 131 LQR 12). The defendant, a member of the House of Lords, had given evidence to a parliamentary committee raising concerns about some members of FIFA, the governing body of international football. He undertook to take his concerns to FIFA. He repeated the allegations in a subsequent review of the matter held by the Football Association. It was held that this was also protected by Article 9. First, there must be a public interest in the repetition of what was said in Parliament. Second, there must be a sufficiently close relationship between both occasions that the prospect of his obligation to speak is reasonably foreseeable at the time of the first occasion, and his purpose in speaking is the same or very closely related. However, the limits of an MP's duties are vague. For example, MPs appear to have a duty to inform their constituents of their activities. Therefore, placing a link on a website to an MP's speech in Parliament would be protected by parliamentary privilege but reproducing the speech may not be. The onus is on the MP to show that he falls within the immunity since this is an exception from the basic assumption of equality before the law (see *Chaytor* (above) at [41], [42]).

Another area of uncertainty in respect of Article 9 concerns things said or written to or by MPs as part of their wider duties on behalf of their constituents, for example a letter complaining to the Secretary of State about an NHS hospital. In the case of *Strauss* (HC 1956–57, 305), the House of Commons by a tiny majority (218 to 213) rejected a recommendation by the Committee of Privileges that such letters should be protected by parliamentary privilege. *Strauss* concerned a complaint about the activities of the London Electricity Board (LEB). It is not clear what the reasons for the Commons resolutions were, and the vote may have been on party lines. On the basis of *Chaytor* (above), a letter from an MP is privileged only if it is to do with a matter currently being debated in the House or is the subject of an official parliamentary question. One way of distinguishing *Strauss* is that the LEB was not a government department, so the minister to whom Strauss wrote was not directly responsible to Parliament for its activities.

Other examples under Article 9

In *R v Greenaway* [1992], unreported (see [1998] PL 356), the court held that parliamentary privilege did not apply where an MP took a bribe, because the offence occurred when the bribe was received and therefore the court did not need to investigate what went on in Parliament (*Greenaway* was doubted in *Chaytor* (above) at [42]; see *US v Brewster* 408 US 501 (1972) 524–5). In *Hamilton v Al Fayed* [1999] 3 All ER 317, an MP was accused of taking bribes, but since parliamentary processes themselves were not the subject of the action Article 9 did not apply. However, protection could apply where an MP acts on a bribe, for example in a debate. In *Rost v Edwards* [1990] 2 All ER 641, the Register of Members' Interests was held not to be protected on the basis that it was a public document;

compare *R v Parliamentary Commissioner for Standards, ex p Al Fayed* [1998] 1 WLR 669: report of Commissioner to Parliament protected. The Joint Committee on Parliamentary Privilege (Section 11.6.7) suggested that *Rost* should be reversed as an anomaly. Article 9 should also protect the 'briefing papers' written by civil servants for ministers, but presumably only where they directly relate to a parliamentary question or bill or statement for which the minister is responsible. Ordinary departmental papers would not be protected, since these relate directly only to the executive, not Parliament.

The most important aspect of Article 9 concerns the use of parliamentary material in the courts. Article 9 concerns challenges to, or criticism of, what is said. It does not exclude the use of parliamentary material in court to establish the facts of what was said in Parliament, provided that the parliamentary processes or things said in them are not criticised. For example, parliamentary proceedings can be used as evidence that a matter has in fact been considered by Parliament. Going beyond that raises problems of inhibiting discussion in Parliament, particularly in committees, and creating uncertainty in the courts (see Joint Committee on Parliamentary Privilege (Section 11.6, at [32]–[35])).

Parliamentary proceedings can also be used in judicial review cases, for example to discover what government policy is, or whether consultation has taken place. Although evidence of something a minister said in Parliament cannot be used to determine whether he or she is acting honestly (*R v Secretary of State for Trade, ex p Anderson Strathclyde* [1983] 2 All ER 233, 238–39), it can be used as evidence of the reasons for executive action (*Toussaint v A-G of St Vincent and the Grenadines* [2008] 1 All ER 1).

However, the court cannot assess the *quality* of any debate (*Wilson v First County Trust* [2003] 4 All ER 97 at [62]–[67]; *R (Williamson) v Secretary of State for Education and Employment* [2005] 2 All ER 1 at [17]; *R (HS2 Action Alliance) v Secretary of State for Transport* [2014]). Nor can the court use something said in Parliament or a committee to support a particular conclusion of law, since this opens up questioning by the other party (*Office of Government Commerce v Information Commissioner* [2008] EWHC 774 (Admin), cf. *R (Reilly) v Secretary of State for Work and Pensions* [2013] EWCA Civ 66 and *R (Pelling) v Secretary of State for the Home Department* [2011] EWHC 3291 (Admin), where courts endorsed committee reports).

Under the controversial *Pepper v Hart* rule, statements in Parliament can sometimes be used as an aid to statutory interpretation (Section 7.7.2). In *Pepper v Hart* [1993], the House of Lords took the view that the purpose of Article 9 was only to prevent MPs from being penalised for what they said in the House. However, in *R v Forsyth* [2011] 2 AC 69, the Supreme Court refused to look at parliamentary debates in order to decide whether a statute which gave power to the government to penalise individuals who funded the Iraq government had an implied time limit. The Court took the view that, unless fundamental rights were at issue, there would be a 'real risk' of breaching parliamentary privilege.

As with any liberty, the price to be paid is that an MP might abuse privilege to make untrue allegations against persons who cannot answer back, or to violate privacy. An example occurred in September 2019, when the Conservative MP and Leader of the House of Commons, Jacob Rees-Mogg, compared a senior doctor who had warned of possible shortages of drugs after Brexit to the disgraced anti-vaccination doctor Andrew Wakefield: Rees-Mogg subsequently apologised after the named doctor, David Nicholl, had threatened to sue him if he repeated the statement outside Parliament (see also Watt [2019] PL 469).

Thus, the limits of freedom of speech have to be defined. There are therefore limitations placed upon members' freedom of speech by Parliament itself. The Speaker, who presides over the House of Commons, has a duty to control procedure impartially. Internal rules exist to prevent MPs misusing their privilege of freedom of speech, for example by attacking people who cannot answer back or by commenting upon pending legal proceedings. For example, 'the invidious use of a person's name in a question should be resorted to only if to do so is strictly necessary to render the question intelligible and the protection of parliamentary privilege should be used only as a last resort' and 'in a way that does not damage the good name of the House' (see HC Deb 17 March 1986, vol 94, col 26). 'Impeached or questioned' also includes attacks on MPs in the media. However, Article 9 has not been invoked in respect of media criticism of what was said in Parliament, short of cases of extreme contempt of Parliament (Section 11.6.1).

11.6.4 Qualified privilege

Independently of parliamentary privilege, an MP performing his or her official duties may be protected by 'qualified privilege' (Section 23.4.1). Qualified privilege is not confined to MPs. It is available to anyone who has a legal or moral duty to make the statement in question in the particular context. Qualified privilege is narrower than parliamentary privilege. It does not give complete immunity but covers only statements made in good faith and taking proper care. It applies only to defamation (the law relating to statements that damage reputation), whereas full or 'absolute' parliamentary privilege covers every kind of legal action. It is a defence to an action, so the MP must subject herself or himself to the burden of legal proceedings. Even if she or he eventually wins, the expense and uncertainty of litigation may discourage an MP from speaking freely.

Qualified privilege applies to cases where an MP repeats outside Parliament something he or she has said in Parliament (Section 11.6.3). In *R v Rule* [1937] 2 All ER 772, it was held that a constituent's letter to an MP has qualified privilege. It could also apply to a media interview or press statement (*Church of Scientology v Johnson-Smith* [1972] 1 QB 522), or a statement made in an election campaign (*Culnane v Morris* [2006]: anti-BNP leaflets). Political freedom of expression is regarded as of the highest importance, and the scope of qualified privilege is correspondingly generous (*Culnane*). In a democracy, the public has a general interest in receiving information and opinions from MPs.

However, it is doubtful whether an MP who merely repeated what s/he had said in the House could claim qualified privilege because the statement would already be accessible to the public. An MP who makes a defamatory statement that is not related to his or her parliamentary duties would not have qualified privilege (this would seem likely to have applied in the case of Rees-Mogg, noted above). Nor, perhaps, would messages on social media such as Twitter, since these are arguably not sufficiently public in character.

11.6.5 Publication of parliamentary proceedings

A controversial aspect of contempt of Parliament concerns public access to parliamentary information, which arguably should be unrestricted except where the disclosure would harm the public interest. However, parliamentary committees often sit in private and 'leaks' of reports of select committees have been prohibited since 1837, although action is only likely to be taken if the leak causes substantial interference with the function of a committee. The House of Commons has waived any more general right to restrain publication of its proceedings and has authorised the broadcasting of its proceedings, subject to a power to give directions. It has also undertaken generally to use its contempt powers sparingly (HC 1967–68, 34, [15]).

There is also statutory protection for documents published by order of Parliament and correct copies, such as *Hansard*, have full parliamentary privilege (Parliamentary Papers Act 1840, ss 1, 2). The publication by the press of fair and accurate extracts or abstracts from authorised reports of parliamentary proceedings have 'qualified privilege', meaning that they are protected if the publisher shows that they are published in good faith without malice (s 3), as are broadcasts of parliamentary proceedings (Defamation Act 1952, s 9; Broadcasting Act 1990, s 203(1)). The Joint Committee on Parliamentary Privilege (Section 11.6) recommended that the definition of 'broadcast' should be extended to include electronic media, and that this privilege should include fair and accurate reports as well as extracts and abstracts. In any event, other press reports, including parliamentary sketches and (probably) broadcasts and internet reports, are protected by the general law of qualified privilege already, provided that they are honest and fair (*Wason v Walter* [1868] 4 QB 73; *Cook v Alexander* [1974] QB 279). Section 15 of the Defamation Act 1996 protects fair and accurate reports of legislative proceedings and other public meetings anywhere. Here, it is for the claimant to show that the publication was not in good faith.

11.6.6 The courts and Parliament

As we have seen, the courts do not intervene in the internal affairs of the House. On the other hand, where parliamentary activity involves the rights of persons outside the House, the courts have intervened at least to the extent of deciding whether the privilege asserted by Parliament exists. Both the rule of law and the separation of powers are engaged in this context. In a famous eighteenth-century controversy that asserted basic rule of law values, the courts held that parliamentary officers have no power to deprive citizens of voting rights: 'where there is a right there is a remedy' (*Ashby v White* (1703) 2 Ld Raym 938; see also *Paty's Case* (1704) 2 Ld Raym 1105). In *Stockdale v Hansard* [1839], it was held that parliamentary privilege did not protect reports published by order of the House from being the subject of libel actions. The subject matter of these disputes is only of historical interest. Parliament no longer controls elections, and *Stockdale v Hansard* was soon reversed by statute (Parliamentary Papers Act 1840). Nevertheless, the general principle about the power of the courts remains relevant.

Parliament has never accepted that *Stockdale v Hansard* was correctly decided. Thus, in the *Sheriff of Middlesex* case (1840) 11 Ad & E 273, Parliament imprisoned the two holders of the office of sheriff for enforcing the court's judgment in *Stockdale v Hansard*. Not surprisingly, the sheriffs applied to the court for release, but the court (which had itself decided *Stockdale v Hansard*) held that it was powerless to intervene. Parliament had the undoubted right to commit to prison for contempt, and it did not have to give reasons. Unless some improper reason was disclosed on the face of the committal warrant, the court must assume that Parliament was acting lawfully even though the judges knew otherwise. Whether this principle applies in modern times rests with Parliament's – or the courts' – political sense. The courts are unwilling to take action that might be considered trespassing on Parliament's preserve. Parliament too has shown restraint in asserting claims to privilege. This standoff could be regarded as an example of the comity which it is claimed that the separation of powers requires. Thus, it has been claimed that there is a voluntary, mutual respect between the two institutions (*Hamilton v Al Fayed* [1999] 333–34). In *Chaytor* [2011] (Section 11.6.2), the Supreme Court held that it was settled that the court can decide the limits of parliamentary privilege, and the Joint Committee on Parliamentary Privilege has endorsed this (Section 11.6.1).

11.6.7 Reform of parliamentary privilege

The Nicholls Report (Report of the Joint Committee on Parliamentary Privilege, HL 43–1/HC 214–1, 1998–99) recommended reforms. It suggested the enactment of a code of parliamentary privilege to include modest reforms largely intended to clarify the relationship between Parliament and the courts. They include the following:

- 'Place out of Parliament' for the purposes of Article 9 should be defined to include courts and tribunals empowered to take evidence on oath but not tribunals of inquiry if both Houses so resolve.
- The offence of abuse of public office should include MPs.
- MPs should be subject to the criminal law relating to corruption.
- Members of the Lords should be compellable before Commons' committees.
- Parliament's 'exclusive cognisance' should be confined to 'activities directly and closely related to the business of the House'. A similar principle was applied in *Chaytor* (Section 11.6.2).
- Contempt by non-members should be dealt with by the ordinary courts and limited to a fine.
- Freedom from arrest should be abolished.

The 2013 report of the Joint Committee on Parliamentary Privilege endorsed most of the Nicholls proposals and accepted that the courts could determine the limits of parliamentary privilege. However, it disagreed with the idea of a code and with statutory reforms, other than a few specific ones which have been mentioned above (Sections 11.6, 11.6.3 and 11.6.5). In the light of experience in Australia (Parliamentary Privileges Act 1987), the Committee took the view that a code would be inflexible and over-complex. Enactment as a statute might raise problems by confusing the relationship between the courts and Parliament. The government accepted the Committee's conclusions (see Cm 8771, 2013).

11.7 Standards in the Commons

Following the recommendations of the First Report of the Committee on Standards in Public Life (Cm 2850, 1995), there is a *Code of Conduct* for MPs (HC 2014–15, 1076). In keeping with parliamentary privilege, this is policed by the House itself.

The primary duty of an MP is to be an independent representative of his or her constituents. There are obstacles to the independence of MPs. First and foremost, there are party loyalties. Second, many MPs are sponsored by outside bodies, including trade unions and business interests, which may contribute towards their expenses. Some MPs accept employment as paid or unpaid 'consultants' to businesses and interest groups, such as the Police Federation, or hold company directorships. MPs are also frequently offered 'hospitality', or gifts, or invited on expenses-paid 'fact-finding' trips. There are also 'all-party' subject groups of MPs which involve relationships with outside bodies (see HC 1984–85, 408). Except in the case of a private bill, a member is free to vote on a matter in which she or he has a personal interest. There is therefore a risk that MPs are susceptible to lobbying by private interests.

It is often said that sponsorships and consultancies enable MPs to keep in touch with informed opinion outside Westminster and to develop specialised knowledge. They also enable MPs without private means to supplement their parliamentary salaries. The process of enacting legislation is also helped by consultation with interested parties. There is much 'lobbying' of civil servants, and it is desirable that this should be counterbalanced by MPs having their own access to outside interests. On the other hand, apart from the risk of corruption, some MPs might also spend time in company boardrooms that may generate little understanding of social problems and would be better spent helping their constituents. Compromises are therefore made.

In the *Brown* case (HC 1946–47, 118), an MP sponsored by a trade union was dismissed by the union for not advocating its interests in Parliament. The Committee of Privileges voted that a contract could not require an MP to support or represent his or her sponsor's interests in Parliament, nor could the sponsor punish the MP for not doing so. However, it was not contempt to dismiss a consultant if, for whatever reason, the employer or sponsor was unhappy with his or her services. This somewhat evasive compromise does not seem to take the matter much further. It would be a contempt to threaten to dismiss an MP unless she or he took a certain line in Parliament but not, apparently, to dismiss her or him after the event. Arguably, pressures from local constituency parties would also be contemptuous.

Since the seventeenth century, resolutions of the House have declared that certain kinds of external influence are in contempt of Parliament. The latest distinction seems to be between promoting a specific matter for gain, which is forbidden, and acting as a consultant generally, which is acceptable. There have been many resolutions attempting to capture this elusive matter.

For example, a resolution of 1995 which amends a resolution of 1947 (HC 1994–95, 816) (see HC Deb 6 November 1995, vol 265, cols 604, 661) states:

> It is inconsistent with the dignity of the House, with the duty of a Member to his constituents, and with the maintenance of the privilege of freedom of speech, for any Member of this House to enter into any contractual agreement with an outside body, controlling or limiting the Member's complete independence and freedom of action in Parliament or stipulating that he shall act in any way as the representative of such outside body in regard to any matter to be transacted in Parliament; the duty of a Member being to his

constituents and to the country as a whole, rather than to any particular section thereof: and that in particular no Members of the House shall, in consideration of any remuneration, fee, payment or reward or benefit in kind, direct or indirect, which the Member or any member of his or her family has received, is receiving or expects to receive –

(a) advocate or initiate any cause or matter on behalf of any outside body or individual, or
(b) urge any other Member of either House of Parliament, including Ministers, to do so by means of any speech, Question, motion, introduction of a bill, or amendment to a Motion or a Bill.

A further resolution restricts the extent to which a member may participate in a delegation to ministers or public officials; see *Code of Conduct* for MPs (HC 2014–15, 1076, at 38).

The *Code of Conduct* forbids paid advocacy, prohibits payment for promoting or opposing any matter in Parliament, requires openness and frankness, and forbids the use for gain of information received in confidence for the purpose of parliamentary duties.

There are also criminal offences involving members of public bodies. Misconduct in public office is a common law offence, and there are also offences under the Public Bodies (Corrupt Practices) Act 1889, the Prevention of Corruption Act 1916, and the Bribery Act 2010. However, it is arguable that an MP is not a 'public servant' and does not hold a public office as such, so is outside these offences (see *A-G's Reference (No 3 of 2003)* [2004] EWCA Crim 868).

MPs must enter information about their financial interests in a Register of Members' Interests (see the *Code of Conduct* for MPs, chs 1 and 2). The categories of interest required by the register have been strengthened to include full details of an employment contract, the provision of services such as consultancy, company directorships, employment or offices, professions and trades, names of clients, financial sponsorships, overseas visits as an MP, payments received from abroad, land or property, shareholdings and 'any interest or benefit received which might reasonably be thought by others to influence the member's actions in Parliament'. However, the precise value of such payments need not be entered. It has been estimated that MPs earned £3.35m in total from external sources in 2018.

As a result of allegations concerning tax avoidance, members of both Houses of Parliament are deemed to be resident, ordinarily resident or domiciled in the UK for tax purposes and so are fully liable for UK tax (Constitutional Reform and Governance Act 2010, s 41).

11.7.1   The Parliamentary Commissioner for Standards

Following the First Report of the Committee on Standards in Public Life (Cm 2850, 1995) the House of Commons appointed a Parliamentary Commissioner for Standards empowered to investigate complaints of misuse of the Commons Register and to report to the Standards and Privileges Committee of the House of Commons (HC Standing Orders (Public Business) (1995) No. 150). The Commissioner can also investigate complaints by MPs and the public concerning the Code of Conduct, and give advice to MPs. The decisions of the Commissioner are subject to parliamentary privilege and so are not subject to judicial review (*R v Parliamentary Comr for Standards ex p Al Fayed* [1998]). The Commissioner is an independent officer of the House of Commons, appointed for a non-renewable fixed term of five years.

The Commissioner cannot investigate the interests of ministers acting as such, thus reflecting the separation of powers. There is no independent mechanism to regulate ministers. Compliance with the *Ministerial Code* is a matter for the prime minister (Section 13.5.1). Independent inquiries in the form of a Royal Commission, or under the Inquiries Act 2005, can be held into ministerial misconduct. However, these are set up by ministers. The Tribunals of Inquiry (Evidence) Act 1921, under which Parliament could order an inquiry, was repealed by the 2005 Act.

11.7.2   The Independent Parliamentary Standards Authority

The Independent Parliamentary Standards Authority (IPSA) is responsible for the salaries and expenses of MPs and has a role in the administration of MPs' pensions. Revelations in the press during 2008–09 that many MPs had been abusing their expenses claims caused considerable public concern. This led to legislation which, for the first time, introduced an element of outside policing into the affairs of Parliament. MPs' expenses had previously been dealt with relatively informally within the House.

IPSA is a statutory body (Parliamentary Standards Act 2009, modified by the Constitutional Reform and Governance Act 2010). It has no jurisdiction over the House of Lords. The Acts go to considerable lengths to make IPSA independent. The members of IPSA must comprise a Chairman, a former senior judge, a qualified auditor and a former MP. Apart from this, no MP or former MP may serve. Members hold office for five years, renewable for one further term of three years, and can be removed only on an Address from both Houses of Parliament. Thus, they have similar status to a senior judge.

The members of IPSA are appointed by the Queen on an Address from the Commons on the nomination of the Speaker on the recommendation of the Speaker's Committee (below), subject to the usual mantra of appointment on merit by fair and open competition ('OMFOC'). The Act does not prescribe how the appointment process should be conducted. In fact, MPs play no part in the selection of the nominee, and the appointment process is subject to the Code for Public Appointments made by the Public Appointments Commissioner. An independent panel is used.

IPSA determines the salaries and expenses of MPs, and polices the expenses system. There is a compliance officer appointed by IPSA for five years, non-renewable. The compliance officer reviews the rejection of an expenses claim by IPSA and investigates misuses of the expenses scheme. An investigation can be carried out on the compliance officer's initiative or at the request of the MP concerned, or at the request of any individual, including therefore, a member of the public. There is a right of appeal from the compliance officer to the ordinary tribunal system. IPSA can recover improper payments through the ordinary courts. There is a penalty of up to £1000 for failing to provide information to IPSA. MPs' expense claims must be published, containing such information as IPSA considers appropriate, and IPSA must make an annual report to the House of Commons.

The Speaker's Committee for IPSA approves appointments to IPSA and that of the compliance officer. This Committee comprises the Speaker, the Leader of the House (a government minister), the Chair of the Committee on Standards and Privileges, five backbench MPs who are nominated by and can be replaced by the House and three laypersons who have never been MPs. The latter are appointed by resolution of the House.

In *Chaytor* [2011] (Section 11.6.2), it was conceded that the expenses scheme, as it existed before the introduction of IPSA, was protected by parliamentary privilege. However, IPSA may not be protected by parliamentary privilege. The 2009 Act states that nothing in it affects Article 9 of the Bill of Rights 1688 (s 1), but this in itself does not determine the matter, since the question is what Article 9 covers (Section 11.6.3). It is arguable that IPSA is not covered by privilege, given its statutory basis and the fact that the expenses system is linked into the general legal system and publicised. Indeed, IPSA may be vulnerable to accusations of interfering with proceedings in Parliament under Article 9. For example, an MP might plausibly complain to the Standards Committee that the expenses scheme is so mean that it prevents him from performing his functions. IPSA has attracted criticism from MPs as being overly bureaucratic and its staff have been subjected to abuse from some MPs. Its hasty creation and immediate modification perhaps illustrate how constitutional reform in the UK is often driven by panic reaction to short-term problems.

11.7.3 Standards in the House of Lords

There is a 'custom' that the House of Lords should not be subject to formal regulation. It is said by its members that it should rely on their 'personal honour' (Seventh Report of the Committee on Standards in Public Life, Cm 4903, 2000). However, no reason has been offered as to why members of the Lords are more honourable than members of the Commons. Previously, with the possible exception of treason, a member could not be deprived of a peerage or expelled for misconduct without statutory authority, nor could a member resign, although he or she could take a leave of absence. It is customary for membership not to be regarded as a full-time commitment and many members have outside interests, including full-time jobs.

This position has changed as a consequence of the enactment of the House of Lords Reform Act 2014. The Act enables a member of the Lords to retire or resign (s 1), to be excluded on the basis of non-attendance at any stage in the preceding session (s 2), or to be excluded upon the commission of a serious offence (s 3) (see also House of Lords (Expulsion and Suspension) Act 2015).

There is a House of Lords *Code of Conduct* (HL 2015–16, 3) embodying the Nolan principles of public life. This includes a Register of Members' Interests. The register was originally voluntary in respect of non-financial interests. However, as a result of the Seventh Report of the Committee on Standards in Public Life (Cm 4903, 2000), it was made compulsory (see HL 1994–95, 90 at 98). It is, however, less stringent than the Commons Register.

The *Code* also provides for an independent House of Lords Commissioner for Standards who investigations allegations against members involving misuse of their position or undisclosed financial interests. A complaint can be made by anyone, including a member of the public. The Commissioner's work is overseen by reports to the House of Lords Committee for Privileges and Conduct. The first Commissioner, appointed in May 2010, was a former chief constable; the second, who took office in June 2016, is the former President of the Law Society of England and Wales. IPSA does not apply to the House of Lords, which polices its own expenses claims.

Summary

- Parliament has developed primarily through the party system. It has the competing functions of sustaining the government and holding the government to account. It scrutinises legislation, provides the executive with finance, debates matters of public concern and redresses grievances. The executive is usually too powerful and complex for Parliament to be fully effective, although recent reforms have to some extent improved this (Section 13.5). However, Parliament is nevertheless a public forum in which the executive can be forced to appear and explain its actions.

- There is a network of laws and conventions to ensure that Parliament lasts no more than five years, that it meets annually and that it can remove the government. The former prerogative power to dissolve Parliament exercisable by the prime minister has been curtailed by the Fixed Term Parliaments Act 2011, but this seems very likely soon to be repealed.

- After the 1688 settlement, the House of Lords was regarded as holding the constitutional balance of power, but by the twentieth century, it had become subordinate to the elected House of Commons. The Lords was given a new lease of life by the introduction of life peers in the 1960s, but the constitutional role of the House remains controversial. By convention and law, the Lords must ultimately defer to the Commons. It is primarily a delaying and revising chamber. Since the bulk of the hereditary peers were removed in 1999, the House of Lords has become more aggressive in resisting the executive. The House of Lords is less subject to party pressures than the House of Commons. The rules of procedure and party discipline in the House of Lords are more relaxed than those in the Commons. Because of the control over the Commons exercised by the executive, a second chamber is desirable, but there is no agreement as to how the hereditary element in the Lords should be replaced. At present, the House of Lords is accountable to no one.

- Parliament can protect itself against interference from without and within through the law of parliamentary privilege and its powers to punish for contempt. Parliament can enforce its own privileges, free from interference by the ordinary courts. The main parliamentary privileges are Parliament's exclusive control over its own affairs and freedom of speech. There are difficulties in regard to what counts as parliamentary proceedings for these purposes. These are confined to matters related to the core business of the House and purely internal matters within the precincts of the House. MPs and the media also have qualified privilege in the law of defamation, but this is limited.

- There are safeguards against conflicts of interest for MPs, including the Register of Interests and the Parliamentary Commissioner for Standards. There are similar but somewhat less stringent safeguards in the House of Lords. There is no independent mechanism to enforce standards against ministers. IPSA was created to determine and police MPs' salaries and expenses but does not apply to the House of Lords.

- There has been conflict between the courts and Parliament as to who decides whether a claimed privilege or contempt exists. It is probably recognised that the courts have the power to do so.

Exercises

11.1 'It has been a source of concern to some constitutionalists that the effect of the 1911 [Parliament] Act and more particularly the 1949 Act has been to erode the checks and balances inherent in the British Constitution' (Lord Bingham in *Jackson v A-G* [2006] at [41]).

Explain and discuss.

11.2 The government wishes to complete an ambitious programme of reforms to the tax laws which was in its previous election manifesto and involves large increases in taxation for wealthy property owners. A general election is due before it can introduce the measure it wishes. The prime minister, who has a large Commons majority, thinks it would be a good idea to postpone the election for a year claiming that 'the people are behind me'. However, the Leader of the House of Lords objects to this. Advise the prime minister what, if anything, he can do to postpone the election. What would be the position if the government threatened to resign immediately?

11.3 'It is well known that in the past there have been dangerous strains between the law courts and Parliament – dangerous because each institution has its own particular part to play in our constitution, and because collision between the two institutions is likely to impair their power to vouchsafe those constitutional rights for which citizens depend on them. So for many years Parliament and the courts have each been astute to respect the sphere of action and the privileges of the other' (*Pickin v British Railways Board* [1974] (Lord Simon of Glaisdale)).

Explain and illustrate.

11.4 'Whatever matter arises concerning either house of parliament ought to be examined, discussed and adjudged in that house to which it relates and not elsewhere' (Blackstone's *Commentaries* (1765–69)).

Is this an accurate statement of the modern law?

11.5 'It is not unduly idealistic to regard the integrity of Members' judgment, however constrained it may be by the party system, and the devotion of their time to the job to which they have been elected, as fundamental values worth not only protecting but insisted on' (Sedley).

Discuss in relation to the outside interests of MPs and peers.

11.6 'Parliament does not make law, but merely approves it.' Discuss.

11.7 Bulldog, an MP, makes a speech in the House of Commons in which he strongly criticises Placeman, the head of a National Health Service body, for allegedly taking bribes from drug companies. He relies for this on a briefing paper prepared by Fawn, a civil servant. Bulldog is later asked in a television interview whether he stands by the allegation. He replies, 'You must refer to my speech.' Bulldog also publishes a copy of his speech on his website. Placeman issues a writ for libel against Bulldog and Fawn. Contending that this is a matter of parliamentary privilege over which the court has no jurisdiction, both refuse to enter an appearance or to defend the action. Meanwhile, the House of Commons resolves that any judge, counsel or party who takes part in such proceedings will be guilty of contempt. Discuss the position of Bulldog and Fawn and any possible action that may be taken against Placeman if he proceeds with the action.

11.8 i. Ivan, an MP, is prosecuted for buying alcohol in the House of Commons bar to give to a person who is underage (his son). Advise him whether he can claim parliamentary privilege.

ii. Jill complains that the expenses she has been allowed by IPSA are not enough to enable her to attend Parliament regularly. Advise her.

iii. The Department of Transport has prepared supporting documents for a bill to authorise a new railway line passing through the constituency of Ken, the leader of the Opposition. Ken believes that the documents include fraudulent material. Advise him whether he can prevent the documents being placed before Parliament.

Further reading

Archer, 'The House of Lords, Past, Present and Future' (1999) 70 Pol Q 396

Blackburn, 'The Summoning and Meeting of New Parliaments in the United Kingdom' (1989) 9 LS 165

Evans, 'Privilege, Exclusive Cognisance and the Law' in Horne and Drewry (eds), *Parliament and the Law* (2nd edn, Hart Publishing 2018)

Forsyth, 'The Definition of Parliament after *Jackson*: Can the Life of Parliament Be Extended Under the Parliament Acts 1911 and 1949?' (2011) 9 Int J Constit L 132

Holdsworth, *History of English Law*, vol X, 539–550 (Methuen 1938)

Joseph, 'Parliament's Attenuated Privilege of Freedom of Speech' (2010) 126 LQR 568

Kelly, Hamlyn and Gay, 'The Law and Conduct of Members of Parliament' in Horne and Drewry (eds), *Parliament and the Law* (2nd edn, Hart Publishing 2018)

Lord Lisvane, 'The Courts and Parliament' [2016] PL 272

Munro, *Studies in Constitutional Law* (2nd edn, Butterworths 2000) ch 7

Riddall, 'The Second Chamber: In Search of a Complementary Role' (1999) 70 Pol Q 404

Russell, *The Contemporary House of Lords: Western Bi-Cameralism Revived* (Oxford University Press 2013)

Ryan, 'The Fixed Term Parliaments Act 2011' [2012] PL 213

Ryan, 'Bills of Steel: The House of Lords Reform Act 2014' [2015] PL 558

Tomkins, 'What Is Parliament For?' in Bamforth and Leyland (eds), *Public Law in a Multi-layered Constitution* (Hart Publishing 2003)

Chapter 12

The composition of Parliament and parliamentary elections

12.1 Introduction

The composition of Parliament raises key questions about the legitimacy of the constitution. Which of the different kinds of democracy (Section 2.8), if any, best captures the UK's arrangements? Can a non-elected element in the legislature be justified? Do the voting rules give fair representation and cater for the different functions of Parliament? What restrictions should there be on the right to vote, stand for election or participate in an election campaign? Liberal freedoms such as freedom of expression may conflict with the aspiration of equality.

12.2 The House of Lords

The dominant feature of the House of Lords is that it is not elected, its members having been chosen by the executive in one form or another. Apart from senior Church of England bishops who sit *ex officio*, and 92 hereditary members, its members, titled 'peers', are appointed by the Queen on the advice of the prime minister. There is, however, a limited form of internal election in that, under the House of Lords Act 1999, on the death of a hereditary member, the remaining hereditary members can elect a replacement hereditary peer (below).

Once appointed, a member is entitled to remain for life, subject to the provisions of the House of Lords Reform Act 2014 (Section 11.7.3). The House of Lords therefore reflects the idea of the 'mixed constitution' favoured by Montesquieu (Section 7.3.1). The hereditary principle, based on landholding peerages originally conferred by the Crown in return for services, was the historical basis of the House of Lords. Today, the House of Lords is mainly an appointed 'aristocracy' since an automatic link between inheritance and political influence is no longer acceptable, at least openly. Moreover, even if it is considered that landholding should qualify for influence in government, inheritance of a peerage is no longer linked to landholding (Administration of Estates Act 1925).

There are six disqualifications for membership of the House of Lords. These are as follows:

1. non-citizens other than Commonwealth and Irish citizens. A non-resident Commonwealth citizen can sit in the Lords but not in the Commons (see Act of Settlement 1700, s 3, as amended by the Constitutional Reform and Governance Act 2010, s 47);
2. persons under the age of 21 (SO2 – Standing Order);
3. undischarged bankrupts (Insolvency Act 1986, s 426(A));
4. persons convicted of treason until their sentence is served or pardoned (Forfeiture Act 1870, s 2);
5. a peer (thus, not including a bishop (below)) who is certified by the Lord Speaker on the basis of the register of attendance as failing to attend for the whole of a session (at least six months) without leave of absence or other disqualification. The peer automatically ceases to be a member (House of Lords Reform Act 2014, s 2). This is a generous provision; one day's attendance avoids disqualification and actual participation is irrelevant. Thus, the problem of a peer who signs in, collects his allowance and does nothing else is not addressed;
6. a peer certified by the Lord Speaker of conviction for a criminal offence and sentenced to prison or ordered to be detained for more than one year. Again, the peer automatically ceases to be a member (House of Lords Reform Act 2014, s 3).

Professional judges cannot sit or vote in the House or its committees (Constitutional Reform Act 2005, s 137).

A member of the House of Lords can otherwise be removed only by statute, although the House of Lords Reform Act 2014, s 1, permits the member to choose to retire or resign: there is no provision for automatic retirement at a specified age. The House can also suspend a member for the rest of the session if he or she abuses his or her position, for example by selling favours.

Protocol 1, Article 3 of the ECHR requires states to hold free elections to the legislature. In *Matthieu-Mohun v Belgium* (1988) 10 EHRR 1, the ECHR held that this requires at least one chamber to be elected. However, one of the judges stated that the elected element must comprise a majority of the legislature and the non-elected element must not have greater powers than the elected element. The present House of Lords violates the majority condition, there being currently 650 seats in the House of Commons and more than 800 members of the Lords.

The membership of the House of Lords comprises the following three categories:

1. *The Lords Spiritual.* These are the Archbishops of Canterbury and York, the Bishops of London, Durham and Winchester, and 21 other diocesan bishops of the Church of England, these being the senior bishops in order of appointment. Bishops are appointed by the Queen on the advice of the prime minister, the practice being that the prime minister chooses one from a list of nominations provided by the Church authorities. The bishops vacate their seats in the Lords on ceasing to hold office. They are not peers and can vote in parliamentary elections. (Dignitaries from other faiths may of course be appointed to the House of Lords as ordinary peers.) Other than on historical grounds, it is difficult to see why the Church of England should be so privileged.

2. *Hereditary peers.* Dukes, marquises, earls, viscounts and barons. Until the House of Lords Act 1999, the hereditary peers (around 800 in all, although many did not attend regularly) formed a majority, thereby biasing the House of Lords in favour of conservative interests. Attendance was erratic and unpredictable except where the personal interests of the peerage were at issue.

   At common law, a peer cannot surrender his or her peerage. However, under the Peerage Act 1963, a hereditary peerage can be disclaimed for life. This would enable the former peer to vote and to stand for election to the Commons. The peerage must be disclaimed within 12 months of succeeding to it (one month if the new peer is an MP) or within 12 months of coming of age. The succession to the peerage is not affected. A peer who disclaims his or her title cannot again become a hereditary peer but could be appointed a life peer (below).

   The House of Lords Act 1999 (intended as part of a larger reform which has stalled (below)), provides that no one shall be a member of the House of Lords by virtue of a hereditary peerage. This is subject to an exception, negotiated to prevent the peers from completely rejecting the Act. Under this exception, the House can retain 90 peers, together with the Earl Marshall and the Lord Chamberlain, who are royal officials. Under the relevant Standing Orders, any vacancy can be filled by an election by the remaining hereditary members. The elected peers comprise 75 peers elected on the basis of party balance, together with 15 elected as deputy speakers and committee chairs. Peers who are not members of the House of Lords can stand for and vote in elections to the House of Commons (s 3). As a result of the 1999 Act, no single party is likely to command an overall majority in the House.

3. *Life peers.* Life peers (about 700) are appointed by the Queen on the advice of the prime minister, with the rank of baron. Originally, life peers could not sit in the House of Lords, but under the Life Peerages Act 1958, which was enacted in order to regenerate the House of Lords, they can now do so. A life peerage cannot be disclaimed. Life peerages are intended to enable hand-picked people to play a part in public life. No reason need be given for the conferring of a peerage, and it is unlikely that the conferring of honours or titles is subject to judicial review (Section 19.7.1). By convention, appointments are usually made on particular occasions including the New Year, the Queen's official birthday, and the dissolution of Parliament. Appointments usually include the following categories: retiring ministers and MPs, a limited number of outstanding contributors to public life, and an unspecified number of 'working' party political peers. The proportion of party-political peers is negotiated between the parties. Individuals are also appointed to the Lords so that they can be ministers without having to stand for election. This raises a problem of legitimacy (see Yong and Hazell, *Putting Goats Among the Wolves:*

Appointing Ministers from Outside Parliament (The Constitution Unit 2011)). Leading business people and associates of the prime minister have commonly joined government by this route. The prime minister's conventional power to appoint life peers is subject to a non-statutory House of Lords Appointments Commission. The Commission is appointed by, and reports to, the prime minister and is only advisory. It is composed of a cross-bench peer as chair, three peers nominated by the main parties and three non-party political persons. The Commission vets proposals for political appointments on the ground of propriety, mainly by examining application forms for evidence of misconduct. It also administers a process for a small number of non-party political appointments. Any British or Commonwealth citizen over 21 can apply for appointment. The criteria for appointment are a record of 'significant achievement', 'independence of political parties' and 'an ability to contribute to the work of the House'. The last of these criteria invites preference to be given in the manner of a private club to those with whom the existing members feel personally comfortable; the number of these so-called people's peers has diminished over time.

There is no direct correlation between the composition of the Lords and the distribution of votes at a general election, although the coalition government of 2010–15 expressed a commitment (which was not fulfilled) to make membership of the House reflective of the share of the vote secured by political parties at the preceding general election (for criticism, see Russell, *House Full: Time to Get a Grip on Lords Appointments* (The Constitution Unit 2011)). Because a member generally stays until death, the pattern of appointments made by previous governments is a controlling factor. For example, in January 2020, there were 245 Conservative peers, 180 Labour, 92 Liberal Democrats, 49 non-affiliated (a category which includes some peers who have resigned from other parties, such as Lord Sugar, entrepreneur and star of *The Apprentice* TV programme) and 15 'others' who are affiliated to other parties (it is noteworthy that the Scottish National Party, which currently has 47 MPs, has no members of the House of Lords as a result of party policy). There are 186 cross-benchers forming a recognised group without specific party commitment. The members of the House of Lords are overwhelmingly White (approximately 7 per cent are from ethnic minorities) and male (576 men and 218 women).

12.3 Reform of the House of Lords

There is substantial agreement among politicians and academic commentators that the House of Lords should be reformed. This is primarily because an appointed House is regarded as out of place in a democracy, but also because of the increasing size of the House and the belief that some of its members are inactive or disreputable. However, there is no consensus on the shape of any reform, and most attempts at reform have failed. The House of Lords itself is likely to resist reform, but there is no doubt that any reforms can be enacted by the Commons alone under the Parliament Acts (see *Jackson v A-G* [2006] 1 AC 262).

The issue of Lords reform is worthy of discussion because it exemplifies some fundamental features of the UK Constitution. These include, first, its conservative evolutionary nature which is resistant to fundamental change; second, the absence of any special machinery for constitutional reform, so that reform proposals are usually mixed up with ordinary party politics and therefore dominated by the immediate concerns of the government in power; third, a distrust of democracy; and fourth, a concern with the pre-eminence of the executive. It is also worth remembering that it is difficult to address particular reforms in isolation since the various aspects of the constitution are often interdependent.

On the one hand, there is a body of opinion, probably a majority, that the House should be elected, but with no agreement as to the details of this. On the other hand, there is substantial opinion in favour of a House made up of 'experts' chosen by other experts. However, there is a consensus that the second chamber should remain subservient to the House of Commons with the latter sustaining the government and having the last word on legislation. This preserves a clear line of accountability and the power of the executive, which would be threatened by a stronger Upper House.

Subsequent to the Parliament Act 1911 (Section 11.4), which was a response to a crisis, only five limited reforms have been made. These were the Parliament Act 1949, which modified the 1911 Act by reducing the delaying period to meet the needs of the post-war reforming government; the Life Peerages Act 1958 (Section 12.2), which was relatively uncontroversial; the Peerage Act 1963, which enabled peeresses in their own right to sit and enabled a hereditary peer to disclaim his or her peerage (Section 12.2). The House of Lords Act 1999 was the largest but incomplete measure. This removed most of the hereditary element, leaving uncertainty as to what to do next. The House of Lords Reform Act 2014 makes relatively minor reforms concerning resignation, attendance and criminal convictions (Section 12.2).

There are several reasons why House of Lords reform has proved intractable. First, Lords reform is not urgent given also that the Lords performs certain functions reasonably effectively; nor does it command significant interest among voters to be a priority; nor is it in the personal interest of most existing politicians and their acolytes in the media, business and academia. This means that reforms have been stalled by arguments over detail or delaying tactics or mixed up with other issues. For example, the major reform proposal of 2012 was withdrawn because of an unlikely combination of Conservatives who objected to various aspects of the proposed electoral arrangements for the House of Lords, and Labour members who objected to the limited time available for discussion, possibly hoping to displace other government measures.

Second (and as this example demonstrates), reform crosses party boundaries, making party discipline weak. This disagreement reflects profound differences between those who favour the evolutionary pragmatic nature of the UK Constitution and so prefer marginal, if any, change and those of a more rationalist bent who favour radical change. Thus, those arguing in favour of the status quo claim that the House of Lords has 'worked', subject to interventions from time to time to deal with particular problems. It is argued along the lines of the mixed constitution (Section 7.3.1) that the present appointed House mainly comprises the best people (aristocracy in its original sense) who modify the excesses of democracy. As a result, when moderate proposals are introduced, both groups may object to them. This was the fate of the reform bill in 1968, which was defeated by a combination of conservatives to whom the status quo was untouchable, and socialists for whom the bill was too limited. The Conservative politician Enoch Powell is reputed to have said at the time that the House of Lords should no more be questioned than should an oak tree.

Third, and most importantly, there is a fear that an elected House might either duplicate or rival the House of Commons, thereby weakening the accountability (or power) of the executive. It is argued that attempts to codify the relationship between the two Houses by statute so as to protect the dominance of the Commons risk bringing the courts into the political arena. However, the relationship could be regulated by the internal rules of each House and so remain outside the jurisdiction of the courts (Section 11.6).

On the other hand, an entirely appointed chamber may lack public credibility and reinforce the patronage that currently undermines various aspects of the constitution. A mix of the two elements risks the unelected element being marginalised as undemocratic. Moreover, there is no agreement as to the pool from which any appointed element should be chosen. One possibility would be from representatives of major community interests such as regional legislatures, business, charities, churches, ethnic groups, the professions and local communities. However, it could prove impossibly complex and controversial to achieve an acceptable balance of interests. Another model, which seems to have some current support, would be a chamber based upon regional representation, but it is not clear how this fits with devolution of power to Wales, Scotland and Northern Ireland.

Lord Bingham, a former senior judge, suggested that a second chamber be purely advisory, with no lawmaking powers, but designed as a senate of experts to give independent advice to the House of Commons (see Bingham (2010)). He proposed that the composition of the House be similar to its present composition, and that it should select its own membership. It is questionable whether such a body would be able to establish public confidence in its political impartiality and, as with the current House, its membership would be likely to be dominated by persons who conform to the interests of those in power. The notion of unbiased expertise is, in any event, highly questionable.

Mill (*Representative Government* (1861) ch 13) argued that a second chamber should primarily act as a partial check on the majority and should ideally embody 'the greatest number of elements exempt from the class interests and prejudices of the majority, but having in themselves nothing offensive to democratic feeling'. He considered that, in every constitution, there should be a centre of resistance to the predominant power, 'and in a democratic constitution, therefore, a nucleus of resistance to the democracy'. He recommended including experts in a second chamber, recruited primarily from persons distinguished in the public professions, such as the judiciary, armed forces and civil service. However, although he thought that the question of a second chamber was relatively unimportant, it could be justified (in both liberal and republican terms) on the basis of the corrupting effect of absolute power and as a mechanism for producing compromise. Mill's preferred solution was proportional representation in the House of Commons (below), which would make it more difficult for any majority faction to be dominant.

A democratic possibility would be random selection from the whole adult community, as is currently the case with jury service. However, this raises many practical and economic problems and is probably unrealistic (see Phillipson (2004)).

There is no significant support among politicians for the outright abolition of the House of Lords. This might be a rational and cheap solution – and it should be noted that a significant number of states do possess only one legislative chamber – but the essential functions of the Lords, namely scrutinising proposed legislation and acting as a check on constitutional abuse, would still have to be undertaken. The former function could be dealt with by advisory committees, but the latter would seem to point towards a written constitution with an enhanced role for the courts.

The following is a brief chronicle of the various attempts at reform.

The Parliament Act 1911 removed the power of the House of Lords to veto most public bills introduced in the Commons (Section 11.4). The Bryce Conference of 1917–18 (*Conference on the Reform of the Second Chamber* (Cd 9038, 1918)) attempted to tackle the problem of the composition of the House of Lords but was unable to agree. The Parliament Act 1949 further reduced the delaying power of the Lords (Section 11.4). In 1958, the introduction of life peers reinvigorated the House to a certain extent. In 1968, an all-party conference proposed removing voting rights from most of the hereditary element and introducing the concept of 'working peers', mainly life peers, who would form a permanent nucleus of the House. The bill to introduce these reforms was abandoned because of opposition from both sides of the House of Commons (above).

The Labour government of 1997–2010 intended to reform the House of Lords in two stages. Stage one comprised the House of Lords Act 1999 (above), the main result of which was to remove most of the hereditary element. Stage two did not take place.

A Royal Commission on the House of Lords (*A House for the Future*, Cm 4534, 2000) (the Wakeham Report) examined the composition of the House of Lords in isolation from wider questions of constitutional reform and therefore did not question the role and powers of the House of Commons or those of the executive. Wakeham endorsed the existing roles of the House of Lords as subordinate to the Commons, providing limited checks on the executive, a revising mechanism for legislation and a 'constitutional long-stop' to force the government to have second thoughts. The Report rejected the extremes of an all-elected second chamber and one made up of 'experts'. It proposed a balance of representatives from the main interests in the community with about one-third elected. Elections would be on a 15-year cycle, with one-third being elected every five years to ensure that the outcome did not duplicate elections to the Commons. An independent statutory commission would appoint all other members, taking account of regional, ethnic, gender and religious concerns.

A White Paper (*The House of Lords: Completing the Reforms*, Cm 5291, 2001) broadly adopted these proposals but weakened them in favour of a larger element of government control over the House of Lords. This was not well received and was followed by proposals from the Public Administration Committee (Fifth Report, HC 2001–02, 494–1), the House of Commons and the political parties for different permutations of elected and appointed members. In 2002, a joint committee of both Houses set out seven options ranging from complete election to complete appointment. None of these were approved by the Commons, while the Lords voted for an all-appointed House (HL 17/HC 171, 2002–03).

Revised proposals were set out in a White Paper which remains of value for its historical summary and references (*House of Lords Reform*, Cm 7027, 2007). These proposals were not well received. This was superseded by the White Paper, An Elected Second Chamber, Cm 7438, 2008, which favoured an elected House with the same functions and powers as now. However, it left open the most contentious matters, namely whether there should be an appointed element and the voting system to be used. For example, a form of proportional representation would ensure a different distribution of seats from the House of Commons. In order to avoid the political balance of the upper house reflecting that of the Commons, its members would sit for terms of 12 to 15 years, with staggered elections.

Following proposals by a Joint Committee of both Houses, the Conservative–Liberal Democrat coalition government introduced a bill to the Common in 2012. This provided for a House of Lords of 450 members paid £300 per day. It comprised an elected element of 80 per cent elected in eight regions by the 'open' party list system (Section 12.5.7), every 15 years on a five-year cycle coupled to general elections. (This device of relatively long periods of membership seems to be widely accepted and might reinforce the different roles of Lords and Commons and avoid the problem of the political composition of one chamber mirroring the other.) The remainder would mainly be appointed on a non-party basis as 'experts' by an independent commission, but there would be only 12 bishops. There would be provision for expelling non-attenders and criminals. The bill was withdrawn in August 2012 as a result of resistance by Conservative MPs and lack of support from the Opposition.

The House of Lords Reform Act 2014 was a private members bill which made reforms relating to resignation, non-attendance and expulsion following conviction for a serious offence (Section 11.7.3).

12.4   Membership of the House of Commons

Anyone can be a member of the House of Commons, other than the following:

1. non-citizens other than Commonwealth citizens with indefinite leave to reside in the UK or citizens of the Irish Republic (Act of Settlement 1700, s 3 as modified by Electoral Administration Act 2006, s 18);
2. people under the age of 18 (Electoral Administration Act 2006, s 17);
3. persons detained as mental patients (Mental Health Act 1983; there are special provisions for removing sitting MPs under this Act, involving two medical reports at six-month intervals);
4. peers who are members of the House of Lords (peers can sit in the devolved legislatures);
5. bishops who sit in the House of Lords (House of Commons (Removal of Clergy Disqualification) Act 2001);
6. bankrupts, until five years after discharge unless the discharge certifies that the bankruptcy was not caused by the debtor's misconduct (Insolvency Act 1986, s 426(A));
7. persons convicted of election offences (below);
8. persons convicted of treason, until expiry of the sentence or pardon (Forfeiture Act 1870);
9. persons convicted of an offence and sentenced to prison for more than one year while actually in prison or unlawfully at large (Representation of the People Act 1981, designed to prevent convicted terrorists in Northern Ireland from standing);
10. persons holding certain public offices (House of Commons (Disqualification) Act 1975).

The last of these disqualifications is an example of the separation of powers. One aftermath of the seventeenth-century conflict between Crown and Parliament was that the Commons became fearful that the Crown might bribe members by giving them jobs. The Act of Settlement 1700 therefore provided that nobody who held Crown office or a place of profit under the Crown could sit in the Commons. This would, of course, have prevented ministers from sitting, meaning that the constitution would have had a much stricter separation of powers. However, this part of the Act was repealed by the Succession to the Crown Act 1707, and the current position is as follows:

1. Under the House of Commons (Disqualification) Act 1975, not more than 95 ministers may sit and vote. There are usually about 20 ministers in the House of Lords.

2. The Ministerial and Other Salaries Act 1975 (as amended) fixes the salaries of the various grades of minister and limits the number of paid ministers of the government to 83, plus about 30 other specialised political office holders such as whips; also four law officers. However, a government can (and will) increase its loyalists in the House by appointing unpaid parliamentary secretaries.

3. The House of Commons (Disqualification) Act 1975 debars certain other holders of public office from sitting in the Commons. The main examples are:

- full-time judges of various kinds;
- regulators of privatised undertakings;
- civil servants;
- members of the regular armed services and police (other than specialised forces such as railway police);
- members of foreign legislatures. However, by virtue of the Disqualifications Act 2000 a member of the Irish legislature (the Oireachtas) can be a member of the Commons;
- members of certain public boards and undertakings;
- holders of the offices of Steward or Bailiff of the Chiltern Hundreds or the Manor of Northstead. These are meaningless titles in the gift of the Chancellor of the Exchequer. A successful application for one of these offices has the same effect as resigning or retiring, for which there are no specific rules.

In the event of a dispute about a disqualification, the Judicial Committee of the Privy Council may make a declaration on the application of any person (1975 Act, s 7). The House may also refer a matter to the Privy Council for an opinion (Judicial Committee Act 1833, s 4).

12.5 The electoral system

Election law is found primarily in the Representation of the People Acts 1983 and 1985 and the Parliamentary Constituencies Act 1986. Important changes were made by the Representation of the People Act 2000, the Political Parties, Elections and Referendums Act 2000, the Electoral Administration Act 2006, and the Electoral Registration and Administration Act 2013.

12.5.1 The purpose of elections

We can critically assess the electoral system only in relation to its aims. Is it intended (i) to secure fair democratic representation; (ii) to produce effective government; (iii) to produce 'accountable' governments; or (iv) to provide a local representative? No electoral system has yet been devised that successfully combines all of these goals. Underlying these conflicting aims is the difference between 'representative democracy' and 'market democracy' (Sections 2.8.2 and 2.8.4). Protocol 1, Article 3 of the ECHR provides a general and vague standard, limited to representative democracy: 'Free elections at reasonable intervals by secret ballot, under conditions which will ensure the free expression of the opinion of the people in the choice of the legislature'. There is no requirement that the people choose the executive government, or that each vote should have equal weight.

There is a conflict between the law of the electoral process and practical politics. The legal basis of democracy in the UK is that the electorate in each constituency chooses an individual to represent the constituency in the House of Commons. However, this is distorted by the convention that the executive government must be supported by the House of Commons and is usually drawn from the majority political party. Thus, election candidates are overwhelmingly members of, and chosen by, political parties. Elections are fought and funded between the parties on a national battlefield, and one vote has to serve three not necessarily compatible purposes: namely choosing a local representative; choosing the governing party; and choosing a prime minister.

As noted above, the ECHR requires free and fair elections but does not require any particular kind of electoral system. The essence of Protocol 1, Article 3 is primarily as a collective right, namely to free expression of the opinion of the people as a whole (*R (Chester) v Justice Secretary* [2014] 1 All ER 683 at [130]). An electoral system must not discriminate against particular groups of citizens, although a political party cannot apparently challenge the electoral system on the basis that it is placed at a disadvantage (see *Lindsay v UK* [1979] 3 CMLR 166; *Matthieu-Mohun v Belgium* [1988]; *Liberal Party v UK* (1982) 4 EHRR 106).

The courts are likely to adopt a low level of review in relation to electoral machinery because of their sensitivity to interfering with the province of Parliament (*R v Boundary Commission for England, ex p Foot* [1983] 1 All ER 1099).

12.5.2 The Electoral Commission

The Electoral Commission is a 'quango' (Section 15.10) established as an independent public body to regulate the electoral system and the conduct of elections. Created by the Political Parties, Elections and Referendums Act 2000 with wide-ranging functions, it was a response to the concerns of the Fifth Report of the Committee on Standards in Public Life (*The Funding of Political Parties in the United Kingdom*, Cm 4057, 1998). This came against a background of reduced public confidence as a result of worries about the funding of political parties by wealthy business interests.

The Commission has had mixed success and was the subject of the Eleventh Report of the Committee on Standards in Public Life (*Review of the Electoral Commission*, Cm 7006, 2007). The Committee found that the Electoral Commission was unclear about its role as regulator and was passive and timid in investigating abuses. The report pointed out that the Commission's staff lacked relevant expertise and experience, this being due to the requirement that the Commission be independent, thus raising a familiar tension between efficiency and the appearance of fairness. The report recommended that the Commission's structure and processes should focus more strongly on regulation. In particular, its statutory remit as a regulator, as opposed to a monitor, should be clarified.

These recommendations were implemented by the Political Parties and Elections Act 2009, which has extensively amended the 2000 Act. The main functions of the Electoral Commission are as follows:

1. It reviews and reports to the Secretary of State such matters relating to elections and referendums as it may determine from time to time.
2. It registers political parties and keeps records of their accounts and donations to them, thereby bringing what had previously been regarded as private concerns into the open.
3. It has powers to investigate infringements of election requirements and to impose penalties (Political Parties and Elections Act 2009).
4. It provides for public access to information relating to the financial affairs of political parties.
5. It is responsible for periodic reviews of constituency boundaries.
6. It must be consulted on changes in electoral law.
7. It prescribes performance standards for the local authorities which administer elections (Electoral Administration Act 2006).
8. It advises broadcasters in relation to party political broadcasts.
9. It promotes understanding of electoral systems in the UK (Political Parties and Elections Act 2009, s 8).
10. It is involved, together with local authorities, in pilot schemes for alternative methods of voting such as electronic and postal ballots, making voting facilities available in shops or extending voting times.
11. Subject to modifications by the Secretary of State, it can make 'policy development grants' to registered political parties with at least two sitting MPs for the purpose of preparing their election manifestos.

The Electoral Commission has ten members. It is appointed by the Queen on an Address from the House of Commons on a nomination by the Speaker in consultation with the party leaders. The

Speaker's Committee on the Electoral Commission, which comprises relevant ministers and back-bench MPs (Political Parties, Elections and Referendums Act 2000, Sched. 2), must determine the appointment process. A member can be dismissed on an Address from the House of Commons on various grounds of incapacity, misbehaviour or failing to perform duties (Sched. 1). Members can be reappointed on the recommendation of the Speaker's Committee.

The Commission's members must not be members, officers or employees of political parties or holders of elective office. Nor must they have had such connections or been registered party donors (below) within the last five years. A member ceases to hold office if he or she becomes an election candidate. However, four commissioners are nominated by the political parties from persons with political experience, one of whom must be from a party other than the three largest parties (Political Parties and Elections Act 2009, s 4).

The Electoral Commission reports to the Secretary of State and is accountable to Parliament via the Speaker's Committee. An advisory Parliamentary Parties Panel comprising representatives of all parties which have at least two sitting MPs submits representations or information relating to political parties to the Commission.

12.5.3 General elections and by-elections

A general election occurs when a Parliament is dissolved. The election process is triggered by writs issued by the Lord Chancellor and the Secretaries of State for Scotland and Northern Ireland when the previous Parliament dissolves (Fixed Term Parliaments Act 2011, s 3(3)).

A by-election takes place when there is an individual vacancy in the House. The House itself decides the election date and, by convention, the motion is proposed by the party to which the former member belonged. There is no time limit for this. When the House is not sitting, the Speaker can issue the writ for a by-election (Recess Elections Act 1975).

Procedural matters for an election are set out in 'Parliamentary Election Rules' (Representation of the People Act 1983 (RPA) Sched. 1). The writs are sent to returning officers in each constituency. The returning officer is either the Sheriff in a county constituency (a largely ceremonial Crown officer) or, in other cases, a mayor or council chairman (RPA 1983, s 24). The returning officers are responsible for the conduct of the election including decisions as to qualifications of voters and candidates. Registration officers, who are normally local authority chief executives, make the detailed arrangements.

Section 48 of the Constitutional Reform and Governance Act 2010 requires the returning officer to take reasonable steps to begin the count of votes as soon as practicable within four hours of the poll closing at 10 p.m. The constitutional tradition of the UK is that power should be handed over with brutal speed. If a clear majority in favour of another leader emerges, the incumbent prime minister is expected to resign on the following day.

The law is concerned with fairness between candidates and with preventing fraud, disruption or confusion. To this end, it requires clear lines of accountability for the conduct and spending of the parties and candidates. Elections also raise questions of freedom of expression. This might conflict with fairness, for example if well-financed candidates dominate the media. This is especially important now that elections are largely fought through print and social media rather than personally within local communities. English law, on the whole, seems to favour the interests of fair elections over those of individual freedom of expression.

12.5.4 Candidates

A candidate must provide a deposit of £500 (forfeited if 5 per cent of the vote is not won) and be supported by ten signatures (RPA 1983, Sched. 1). The nomination paper must state either that the candidate stands in the name of a qualifying registered party or that they do not purport to represent any party (s 22). The latter applies to candidates standing as independents, to the Speaker seeking re-election or if the nomination paper provides no description. A party is any organisation or person that puts up at least one candidate, so a one-person party is possible (s 40). Each political party must be registered with the Electoral Commission under the Political Parties, Elections and Referendums Act 2000. In order to qualify for registration, the party must provide its name, its headquarters address and the names of its leader, treasurer and nominating officer. These can be the same person. It can also provide the name of its campaign officer, and if it does so the campaign officer will have some of the responsibilities of the treasurer (s 25). It must also have a scheme approved by the Commission for regulating its financial affairs. It can also provide up to 12 descriptions of itself. The Commission can refuse to register a name or description on the following grounds: having more than six words; being obscene or offensive or where publication would be an offence; being misleading, contradictory or confusing; being in a script other than roman or containing words prohibited by the Secretary of State (Electoral Administration Act 2006, ss 28, 48, 49). This seems to create a significant possibility of executive censorship. Similar rules apply to party emblems (s 29).

A registered political party is subject to accounting and audit requirements (Political Parties, Elections and Referendums Act 2000, Part III; Electoral Administration Act 2006). Accounts must be lodged with the Electoral Commission and must be available for public inspection (s 46). The law has therefore now acknowledged that political parties are more than private clubs and that they should be subject to external financial controls. However, this creates a risk of state interference with political freedom.

12.5.5 Eligibility to vote

The right to vote is fundamental to democracy. This raises the question of whether there is a consti-tutional right to vote which can be restricted only in extreme circumstances, or whether the franchise is a privilege conferred by the state and the subject of ordinary political decision-making. Although it does not directly create a right to vote, Protocol 1, Article 3 of the ECHR (above) requires a state to justify restrictions upon voting rights (*Hirst v UK (No 2)* (2006) 42 EHRR 849). However, in *R (Chester) v Justice Secretary* [2014] at [35], [137], the Supreme Court held that the question of voting rights for prisoners was not a fundamental feature of UK law.

Under section 1 of the Representation of the People Act 2000, to be eligible to vote a person must be:

1. 18 years of age on the date of the poll;
2. a British citizen, a citizen of Ireland or a 'qualifying' Commonwealth citizen (i.e. one who is entitled to reside in the UK) (EU citizens have previously been able to vote in English local elections and elections in the devolved regimes; following Brexit, the position in England is likely to depend on reciprocal arrangements made with particular countries, while the intention is to allow EU citizens to continue to vote in the devolved regimes for the time being);
3. registered on the electoral register for the constituency. To qualify for registration, a person must be 18 years of age or due to be so within 12 months beginning on 1 December following the date of the application for registration and resident in a dwelling in the constituency on the date of the application for registration: 'rolling registration' (see RPA 2000, ss 3–7 replacing RPA 1983, ss 5, 7).

'Resident' means the person is normally living at the address in question as his or her home. It is a question of fact and seems to focus on whether the dwelling is the applicant's home for a substantial period, as opposed to being a guest or a lodger for some particular purpose. The fact that a person may have more than one home is important but not conclusive:

> Regard shall be had in particular to the purpose and other circumstances, as well as to the fact of his presence at or absence from the address on that date … for example, where at any particular time a person is staying at any place other than on a permanent basis he may in all the circumstances be taken to be at that time (a) resi-dent there if he has no home elsewhere, or (b) not resident there if he does have a home elsewhere (RPA 2000,

s 3; see e.g. *Fox v Stirk* [1970] 2 QB 463: student resident in college entitled to registration; *Hipperson v Newbury Electoral Registration Officer* [1985] QB 1060, 1073: protesters camping outside airforce base entitled to registration; *Scott v Phillips* [1974] SLT 32: holiday home does not qualify).

A person may therefore be validly registered in more than one constituency but can vote only once. Temporary absence at work or attendance on a college course does not interrupt residence if either the applicant intends to return to the actual residence within six months and will not be prevented from doing so by performance of that duty, or the dwelling would otherwise be his or her permanent residence and he or she would be in actual residence (RPA 2000, s 3).

There are special provisions for the benefit of certain people who may be absent for long periods. Detained persons are not resident where they are detained. However, remand prisoners and mental patients who are not offenders are deemed to be resident where they are detained if they are likely to be there long enough to satisfy the residence requirement. Alternatively, they can make a 'declaration of local connection'. Members of the armed forces who make a 'service declaration' and merchant seamen can be registered in the place where they would otherwise live (RPA 1983, s 15; Electoral Administration Act 2006, s 13). People living overseas who would otherwise qualify to vote can make an 'overseas electors declaration' (RPA 1985, s 1). They must either have been registered in the constituency during the last 15 years, or, if they were too young, a parent or guardian must have been so registered.

A problem with the registration arrangements was that registration depended on the householder providing the names of eligible voters living in the house. The Eleventh Report of the Committee on Standards in Public Life (Cm 7006, 2007) proposed that registration by households be replaced by individual registration. This is designed to combat fraudulent postal voting whereby one member of a household can return votes on behalf of others. This was implemented by the Electoral Registration and Administration Act 2013 and came into effect in July 2014. However, there is some evidence that this resulted in lower levels of registration, especially among students in university towns (see *Guardian* 31 January 2016). Even if they are on the register, the following have no right to vote:

▶ members of the House of Lords, other than bishops sitting *ex officio*;
▶ convicted prisoners and persons detained in mental hospitals as offenders (except for contempt of court or refusing to pay a fine), including persons unlawfully at large (RPA 1983, s 3; RPA 2000, s 2). A common law mental capacity test was abolished by the Electoral Administration Act 2006;
▶ persons convicted of election offences (Section 12.6.4);
▶ illegal immigrants and asylum-seekers waiting for a decision (Political Parties, Elections and Referendums Act 2000, s 2).

In *Hirst v UK (No 2)* [2006] (which has become a focus for those who regard the court as too interventionist), the European Court of Human Rights in Strasbourg held that the blanket exclusion for prisoners violates the right to free elections. The Court held that the right to vote is not merely a privilege, but a vitally important Convention right. However, it did not go so far as to treat it as an absolute right. It was held that the UK's automatic absolute bar was not proportionate, there being no legitimate policy reason for excluding *all* convicted prisoners irrespective of such matters as the nature of the offence, or the length of the sentence: at [82]. Moreover, there had been no adequate parliamentary consideration of the matter, and it was wrong to rely only on tradition: at [79]. (This criticism may be unfair since the matter was reviewed in 2000 when remand prisoners were enabled to vote; see Lord Sumption in *R (Chester) v Justice Secretary* [2014], at [136]–[137].)

The UK was required to introduce a more limited ban and, in *Greens v UK* (2010) 53 EHRR 710, the Strasbourg court conceded that states have a wide discretion as to what provision to make. It gave the UK six months to introduce new laws. In *Scoppola v Italy (No 3)* (2012) 56 EHRR 663, the Strasbourg court held that a disqualification for those serving sentences for three or more years together with provision for rehabilitation was valid and that the decision to disqualify did not have to be made by a court.

Parliament has not changed the law and in 2011 voted overwhelmingly against change, thus defying Strasbourg. (It will be recalled that, as an international body set up by treaty, the decisions of the Strasbourg court are not binding in UK law unless made so by statute (Section 9.5).) A draft bill (Voting Eligibility (Prisoners) Bill 2012) sought to give the vote to prisoners serving 12 months or less and those in the last six months of their sentence but was not introduced to Parliament. An underlying problem is that there is no consensus on what the purpose of the ban is. Is it a further punishment, or intended to encourage civic responsibility, or expulsion from participating in public affairs as a mark of disapproval? (See *R (Chester) v Justice Secretary* [2014] at [91–93], [125–31].)

Chester turned on the extent to which Strasbourg decisions should be respected by UK courts under the HRA (Section 22.2). The Supreme Court followed *Hirst* on the basis that it should follow Strasbourg decisions unless the issue concerned a fundamental principle of UK law and no such principle was in issue here. However, the court did not intervene on the ground that, given the uncertain scope of any law, the specific rights of the claimants were not necessarily affected. Lady Hale pointed out that, since they were convicted murderers, it is unlikely that whatever law was introduced would give them the right to vote (at [99]). In relation to elections to the European Parliament, the Supreme Court held that the ban was not discriminatory under EU law, since the singling out of convicted prisoners for this purpose was not arbitrary (see also the decision of the Court of Justice of the European Union on the (separate) right to vote in European Parliament elections under the Charter of Fundamental Rights of the EU (Section 10.3.2), *Delvigne* [2016] 1 WLR 1223).

In *McHugh v UK* [2015] ECHR 155, the Strasbourg court endorsed the approach taken in *Chester*. It reiterated that the UK was in breach of the Convention but held that the claimants were not entitled to compensation. Thus, against a background of resentment in government (and some judicial) circles about the role of the Strasbourg court, a temporary compromise was reached.

In November 2017, the government announced that, without amending legislation, it was proposing to take two steps: first, to explicitly notify prisoners that on conviction they would lose the right to vote; and second, to permit those released on temporary licence in the community (a process under which offenders can commute to employment in the community, thus preparing themselves for return to society) to vote. The Council of Europe accepted that these measures would suffice to comply with the *Hirst* judgment, and closed the group of cases in September 2018. However, the UK has been criticised for its 'minimalist compliance' with the original ruling (see Andreas von Staden, 'Minimalist Compliance in the UK Prisoner Voting Rights Cases', ECHR Blog, 16 November 2018, http://echrblog.blogspot.com/2018/11/guest-blog-minimalist-compliance-in-uk.html).

12.5.6 The voting system

There are problems with the workings of all voting systems. A system that always produces a majority may be impossible. For example, in an election where there are three candidates, different majorities might prefer A to B, B to C and C to A.

The electoral system for Parliament is that of 'first past the post' (FPP), or 'relative majority'. This gives the seat to the candidate with the largest number of votes. This is rarely an overall majority. FPP is particularly defective in terms of democratic representation, in that it ignores the votes for all but the winning candidate. Moreover, the actual number of votes is irrelevant. The outcome may depend on a small number of 'swing' voters in a few marginal seats. Nevertheless, when translated into seats, FPP very often produces a strong majority government.

For example, in 2005, Labour won an overall majority, gaining 355 seats with 35.2 per cent of the vote, the Conservatives had 198 seats with 31.7 per cent, and the Liberal Democrats 62 seats with 22 per cent. In England, the Conservatives, with 600,000 more votes than Labour, won 90 fewer seats. In the 2019 election, the Conservatives won 365 seats with 43.6 per cent of the vote, with Labour winning 202 seats (32.2 per cent of the vote); the next largest party was the Scottish National Party with 48 seats on 3.9 per cent of the vote. The latter performance demonstrates how a party whose support is geographically concentrated is favoured by FPP over one whose support ranges more broadly: the Liberal Democrats secured 11.6 per cent of the national vote, but only won 11 seats.

In Parliament itself, the members always vote by simple majority in a straight yes/no way between two propositions. The combination of these two forms of voting means that any particular law might command the support of less than 20 per cent of the public.

However, the FPP system is simple and transparent, offering voters a clear choice. It encourages accountable governments that are supported by substantial numbers of voters. A party stands or falls as such at an election and it must answer on its own record. Generally, it cannot blame any minority parties and, unlike in systems with proportional representation (below), governments cannot usually change without the consent of the electorate (below). It also produces a direct link between the constituency and the individual MP, reinforcing accountability.

12.5.7 Other voting systems

The choice between voting systems is between the claims of strong government, fairness, reflecting the majority will and protecting minorities. No voting system has yet been devised that reconciles all of the competing demands upon it. Complex systems of proportional representation (PR) are widely used in an attempt to achieve fairness and protect minorities. They rely on mathematical formulae to make the outcome correspond more closely to the distribution of the vote (see Farrell, *Electoral Systems: A Comparative Introduction* (Macmillan 2011)).

PR systems usually necessitate negotiations between political parties and can produce unstable governments held together by shifting alliances between small and large parties, thus weakening accountability. However, Germany and the Scandinavian countries, which use PR systems, appear at least as stable as the UK. Arguably, a degree of instability is desirable in a liberal society where there is no agreement as to the right answer to social and political problems. The main forms are as follows:

▶ *The party list*. Under the 'closed list system', the voter chooses only the party, individual seats being allocated by the party in accordance with the party's share of the vote. Various formulae can be used to calculate the precise share required. The party list system has been said to destroy the principle of local representation and to put excessive power into the hands of party leaders. This method is used for elections to the European Parliament. Under an 'open party list' system, the voter can choose between the names on the list, sometimes subject to a pre-set ranking. In Germany, a party must achieve at least 5 per cent of the votes or three seats.

▶ *The additional member system*. This system combines FPP and the party list system. It has the advantage of retaining a connection between the MP and the constituency while ensuring representation for minorities. It is used for elections to the Scottish Parliament, the Welsh Parliament/Senedd (Sections 16.3.1 and 16.5.1;) and the London Assembly (Greater London Authority Act 1999, s 4). A proportion of candidates are elected on the FPP principle in local constituencies. This is topped up by a second vote in a larger regional constituency, either for an individual candidate or from an open party list. Each region is allocated the same number of seats (e.g. five in the Welsh regions, seven in the Scottish), and an 'electoral region figure' is produced. The electoral region figure is the number of votes won by that party divided by the number of seats won by the party's candidates in the local constituency elections plus one. The candidate or party with the highest electoral region figure wins the first seat. The second and subsequent seats are awarded on the same basis, in each case after a recalculation to take account of seats already won. Thus, the fewer the seats won by a party in the local constituency elections, the better the chances of winning a seat in the regional election. A person cannot, of course, take a seat in more than one constituency.

▶ *The single transferable vote*. This is probably the method that best reflects voting preferences. It is used for elections in Northern Ireland, where the desire to neutralise conflicting political forces dominates the constitutional arrangements (Section 16.4; see Northern Ireland Act 1998, ss 8, 28, 34). Each constituency can elect a given number of members. Votes are cast for candidates in order of preference. There is an 'electoral quota' for each constituency, calculated according to a formula based on the number of voters divided by the number of seats plus one. The quota is the winning post. A candidate who obtains the quota based on first preferences is elected. Any surplus votes over the quota are transferred to other candidates according to the second preference on the winning candidate's voting slips. This may produce more winners who reach the quota. The process is repeated until all the seats are filled. If no candidate reaches the quota, the candidate with the lowest number of votes is eliminated, and his or her votes distributed among the other candidates. This system enables voters to choose between different candidates within the same party since all seats within a constituency could be fought by each party. It also prevents wasted votes and protects minorities. On the other hand, it weakens the direct link between constituency and member.

▶ The *alternative vote (AV) system* is a compromise non-PR system that attempts to produce a single candidate with majority support. The candidates are voted for in order of preference, and there are several rounds. After each round, the candidate with the lowest vote is eliminated and his or her votes distributed among the others until a winner with a clear overall majority emerges. If there is still a deadlock, a winner might then be chosen by lot. This system seems unfair in that it takes account of the second preferences only of those who supported losing candidates. On the other hand, it keeps a strong link between the member and the constituency. It is the system used for elections for the Mayor of London (Greater London Authority Act 1999, s 4) and some local authorities.

▶ AV was recommended for the UK in 1910 by the Royal Commission on Electoral Systems. In 1998, the Independent Commission on the Voting System (Cm 4090) recommended the introduction of the *AV Plus* voting system. This combines the alternative vote in single-member constituencies with a system of topping-up from a party list. Under the Parliamentary Voting Systems and Constituencies Act 2011 a referendum was held in 2011 on whether AV should be used for parliamentary elections. The proposal, which, unsurprisingly, had little support from the larger parties, was rejected with 67.9 per cent against on a turnout of 42.2 per cent.

▶ Finally, the *double-ballot system* is used in France. A candidate who gets an overall majority in round one is elected. Failing that, there is a second ballot which only those who achieved a certain proportion of the vote can enter (in France, 12.5 per cent). The candidate with the most votes in the second round wins.

12.5.8 The constituencies

In an ideal election system, there would be the same number of voters in each constituency. This is not the case in the UK. The population is not evenly distributed across the country, so each vote does not carry equal weight. Constituency boundaries and voting patterns are significantly influenced by geography. For example, the largest constituency, the Isle of Wight, has about 113,000 potential voters; the smallest, Na h-Eileanan (Western Isles), 21,000. It is tempting for a government to 'gerrymander': that is, to alter the constituency boundaries in favour of its own party. The natural trend over time is for traditional boundaries to favour conservative parties, since the old industrial conurbations which formed the basis of many constituencies are losing population in favour of suburbs and rural areas.

There is semi-independent machinery for fixing electoral boundaries (Parliamentary Constituencies Act 1986). This is currently the responsibility of the Secretary of State for Justice, subject to four independent Boundary Commissions for England, Wales, Scotland and Northern Ireland (Parliamentary Constituencies Act 1986). A range of criteria, including the number of voters and local community boundaries, are applied and there is substantial discretion. The dilemma is the conflict between fairness in the sense of equality of votes and the desire that an MP should represent a genuine geographical community.

There must be a review of the number and boundaries of constituencies. Previously, this was at intervals of between eight and 12 years, including provision for public hearings. A review may take several years to complete, and once made could well be out of date. However, the Parliamentary Elections and Constituencies Act 2011 introduced a requirement for a five-yearly review. The Commission consults in the local area and must consider any representations, but there is no requirement for a formal public hearing.

A report of the review is submitted to the Secretary of State, who is required 'as soon as may be' to lay the report before both Houses of Parliament, together with a draft Order in Council giving effect to it (s 3(5)). Each House must approve the Order, which is then submitted to the Queen in Council. It then becomes law.

The most recent review was completed in 2018 but has not yet been approved by Parliament; consequently, the 2019 election was fought on boundaries which had not been altered since 2010. The Parliamentary Constituencies Act 2020 removes the obligation to comply with the 2018 review, restores an eight-year cycle for reviews (following the next review, due in 2023) and removes the parliamentary process for approval by requiring the report to be submitted to the Speaker (who chairs the Commissions) rather than to the Secretary of State, with no requirement for Parliament to approve the draft Order in Council.

The main criteria are as follows (Sched. 2, as amended by the Parliamentary Voting Systems and Constituencies Act 2011):

1. Currently, there are 650 constituencies. The Parliamentary Voting Systems and Constituencies Act 2011 reduced the number of constituencies to 600, but the 2020 Act retains the higher number.
2. There must be a separate City of London constituency.
3. Each country of the UK has an 'electoral quota'. This is a rough average of voters per constituency. It is calculated by dividing the total electorate by the number of constituencies on the date when the Commission begins its review. It cannot be updated during the course of a review. For England, the quota is roughly 70,000. At present, few constituencies correspond to the quota. However, the Parliamentary Voting Systems and Constituencies Act 2011 requires that the number of voters in each constituency should vary only between 95 per cent and 105 per cent of the electoral quota, thus favouring equality over community. There are, however, special provisions for the Isle of Wight, the Western Isles of Scotland and the exceptionally low-population areas. No constituency should be larger than 13,000 square kilometres.
4. Other factors to be taken into account, as amended by the 2011 Act, include:

   ▶ existing constituency boundaries and European Parliament constituency boundaries;
   ▶ local ties;
   ▶ the inconvenience involved in altering boundaries;
   ▶ special geographical considerations. These include the size, shape and accessibility of a constituency.

The report and the Order in Council can be challenged in the courts, but the chances of success are small. The time factor is important. As we have seen, no court can interfere with parliamentary procedure, so that the Secretary of State could not be prevented from laying an order before the House or be required to lay an Order (*Harper v Home Secretary* [1955] Ch 238). Moreover, by virtue of section 4(7), the validity of any Order in Council which purports to be made under the Act and which recites that approval was given by each House 'shall not be questioned in any legal proceedings' (but see Section 19.7.2).

A report must therefore be challenged before it is submitted to the Secretary of State. Even here the chances of success are slim. There is no statutory mechanism for challenging a review, but judicial review would apply. The court will respect the subjective judgment of the Commission and would interfere only if the review was arbitrary or made in bad faith, seriously disproportionate, or if a statute was violated. Moreover, out of respect for Parliament, a court would not normally make an order that prevents the report from going to Parliament. At most, it would make a declaration (a non-binding opinion, *see R v Boundary Commission for England, ex p Foot* [1983]).

12.5.9 Voting procedures

Voting is traditionally in person at a designated polling station. However, any person otherwise qualified to vote can have a postal vote. 'Absent voters' are permitted to vote by a proxy, who must also be a registered voter (Representation of the People Act 2000, Sched. 4). Absent voters must provide a signature and date of birth as a protection against fraud (Electoral Administration Act 2006, s 14). They include people on the register for that year but no longer resident in the constituency; service and overseas voters; disabled people; people with work or education commitments; and people who have to make a long journey.

The ballot is secret in the sense that the vote itself is cast in privacy. However, there is no protection for postal votes and, by comparing the registration number on the voting slip with the register of electors, it is possible for officials to discover how a voter cast his or her vote. Indeed, this is necessary to prevent multiple voting. There are provisions intended to prevent ballot papers being examined except for the purpose of detecting election offences (Representation of the People Act 2000, Sched. 1). Offences of stealing votes were created by the Electoral Administration Act 2006 (s 40).

12.6 Election campaigns

The election campaign at constituency level has long been regulated by laws designed to ensure fairness between the candidates campaigning in their local areas. The law was open to the charge that it did not properly address national party politics, with its massive financial backing from private donors, or modern methods of campaigning, including the intensive use of the media. The Political Parties, Elections and Referendums Act 2000 attempts to bring the law up to date by addressing these realities (see *The Funding of Political Parties in the United Kingdom*, Cm 4443, 1999).

12.6.1 Campaign expenses

UK law concentrates on regulating campaign spending but does not put a limit on donations to political parties (see Webber (2012)). The controls are intended to ensure that expenditure is open to public scrutiny and that no candidate has an unfair advantage or can buy votes (see *R v Jones* [1999] 2 Crim App Rep 253). In the US, restrictions upon election expenses have been held to violate freedom of speech (see *Citizens United v Federal Election Commission* 558 US 50 (2010)). A counterargument is that equality of resources is a better safeguard of democracy in the long run.

The main controls over election expenses are as follows (Representation of the People Act 1983 applies unless otherwise stated):

1. Every candidate must have an election agent who is accountable for the conduct of the candidate's campaign. A candidate can appoint himself as agent. There are controls over receipts and expenses out of the candidate's own pocket (ss 73, 74).
2. There is a maximum limit upon the amount that can be spent on behalf of any individual candidate in respect of 'the conduct or management of an election' (s 75; Political Parties, Elections and Referendums Act 2000, s 132). The amount is fixed by the Secretary of State on a recommendation from the Electoral Commission (RPA 1983, s 76A(1)(b)). Limits apply to the 'short' campaign period, namely the normal period of 25 working days between the dissolution of Parliament and the day of the election (see Section 11.2). If a Parliament lasts for more than 55 months, there are further limits for a 'long' campaign period of four months before the date of dissolution. The amount depends primarily on the size of the constituency and the number of voters. For the 2015 election, the government, against the advice of the Electoral Commission, raised the amount per candidate by 23 per cent to about £20,000 for the 'short' period and £45,000 for the 'long' period. This favoured the then incumbent Conservative Party which has substantial private funding, although the Opposition made no attempt to require a parliamentary vote.

There is no fixed definition of an election expense. Some expenditure, for example to canvassers, on posters (except to advertising agents), on hiring vehicles to take people to vote and on broadcasting from abroad, is banned completely (ss 101–12). Reasonable personal expenses can also be incurred (s 18).

3. Candidates are entitled to free use of schools and public buildings for meetings (ss 95, 96). Each candidate can send one election address to each voter post-free (s 91).

4. The Political Parties, Elections and Referendums Act 2000, Part V extended controls over campaign expenditure by registered political parties at national level. The campaign period for this purpose is 365 days, ending with polling day (Sched. 9, para 3(7)). Campaign expenditure includes party political broadcasts, advertising, market research, rallies, press conferences and transport (Sched. 8). It also includes the provision of property, services and facilities to a party either free or at more than 10 per cent below the commercial rate (s 73). There are overall limits on expenditure based on the number of constituencies contested, amounting to about £30,000 for each constituency (s 79). All campaign expenditure must be authorised by the party treasurer who must deliver a return of expenditure to the Electoral Commission (ss 75, 80, 82). This must be made available for public inspection (s 84).

5. 'Third-party campaigners', such as pressure groups, are restricted in promoting candidates during the campaign period. No expenditure over £700 can be incurred with a view to promoting a candidate without the authority of the candidate or agent, thus counting as part of the candidate's expenses (Representation of the People Act 1983, s 75; Transparency of Lobbying, Non-Party Campaigning and Trade Union Administration Act 2014; c.f. *Bowman v UK* (1998) 26 EHHR 1: earlier limit of £5 held to be restriction on freedom of expression: does the higher limit make a difference?).

6. Indirect support is also restricted by the Political Parties Elections and Referendums Act 2000 (PPERA), as amended by the Transparency of Lobbying, Non-Party Campaigning and Trade Union Administration Act 2014. The general campaign expenditure of a third-party campaigner, as opposed to expenditure exclusively targeted to a particular constituency, is regulated by the Electoral Commission. Only a registered body can spend more than £20,000 in England or £10,000 in any of Scotland, Wales or Northern Ireland within 365 days of the date of the election.

To be registered, an individual or organisation must be based in the UK. 'Regulated campaign activity' means activity intended to promote a party or a policy or issue related to the election. There are certain exceptions including newspaper editorial matter, broadcasts, personal expenses and the value of services provided free by individuals (PPERA 2000, s 87).

For example, a leaflet put out by an animal rights pressure group is regulated if the concerns of the group feature in the election. These provisions may restrict the freedom of expression of campaigning groups: for example where a pressure group publicises a cause such as reducing poverty by issuing factual material which might be related to the election, but where there is no specific intention to influence the election.

12.6.2   Donations to political parties

There are no restrictions on the size of donations to a political party. Attempts to impose such restrictions could fall foul of the right to freedom of expression, as well as affecting the self-interest of politicians. Party donations have been a subject of serious concern, given that wealthy individuals, some resident overseas and non-taxpayers, may be in a position to influence political parties by means of gifts and loans which may be anonymous. Such controls as exist are not intended to outlaw payments, but to bring them into the open and ensure accountability.

The Power Commission (2006) suggested that political parties should be funded by the state, so as to avoid being unduly influenced by wealthy individuals. On the other hand, state funding attracts state control, which may also be undesirable. Moreover, it is not easy to produce a formula for payments that would be democratically fair and would not favour the status quo.

There is currently no general state funding for political parties. However, policy development grants of up to £2 million are available from the Electoral Commission to parties with at least two

MPs and money is provided by each House of Parliament to opposition parties for their parliamentary duties ('Short Money' (Section 11.1)).

Introduced by the PPERA, controls were tightened by the Electoral Administration Act 2006 and the Political Parties and Elections Act 2009. They apply to donations, loans and credit facilities of more than £200 to political parties. They are not confined to the election campaign. 'Donation' is widely defined to include gifts, sponsorship, subscriptions, fees, expenses and the provision of non-commercial services (PPERA, s 50). A registered party cannot accept a payment if it is not made by a 'permissible donor' or if it is anonymous (PPERA, s 54(2); Electoral Administration Act 2006, s 61). A permissible donor must be registered to vote in the UK or be a business, trade union or registered political party based in the UK. In the case of a company, the shareholders must have approved the donation and the amount must be disclosed in the directors' report (PPERA, s 140, Sched. 19).

There are particular disclosure requirements. These were imposed as a result of failure by political parties to adequately check the sources of donations. In the case of a donation of more than £7500, there must be a written declaration of its source, including whether the donor is an agent for someone else (Political Parties and Elections Act 2009, s 9). Exceptions to the duty of disclosure include voluntary services provided by an individual, various payments made under statute, payments to MPs by the European Parliament, and the hire of stands at party conferences for a payment deemed reasonable by the Commission.

It is arguable that non-taxpayers should not participate in elections. The Political Parties and Elections Act 2009, s 10, provides that no donations or loans amounting to more than £7500 in a single calendar year can be made to a political party unless the donor makes a declaration that he or she is resident or domiciled in the UK for tax purposes. However, this provision comes into force by a ministerial order and has not yet done so. A substantial number of 'tax exiles' give money to political parties.

A party must report relevant donations or loans of more than £5000 regularly to the Electoral Commission (ss 63, 65, 68, 96; Electoral Administration Act 2006, ss 56, 57). This has caused problems since the person responsible for reporting is not clearly identified. The Commission keeps a public register, but this must not include the address of a donor who is an individual (s 69). Impermissible payments must be returned or, if the donor or lender cannot be identified, given to the Commission (s 56). The court can order a payment to be forfeited (s 58) (see *R (Electoral Commission) v City of Westminster Magistrates Court* [2010] 1 All ER 1167).

12.6.3   Broadcasting and the press: freedom of expression

Rules that attempt to ensure that the parties are treated fairly must be balanced against freedom of expression under Article 10 of EHCR. Campaign publicity has qualified privilege in the law of defamation, so there is no liability if it is published in good faith (*Culnane v Morris* [2006] 2 All ER 149). The same applies to the press and broadcasting (see Section 23.4). There are further controls over the broadcast media, reflecting its power to influence a campaign:

1. Political advertising is unlawful *at any time* except for party political broadcasts made by agreement between the BBC, Ofcom (the Office of Communications) and the main parties (Communications Act 2003, s 321(2)). This is intended to enhance the fairness of democratic debate by preventing domination by the wealthy. However, it also restricts campaigning groups by denying them publicity. The ban was upheld by the Strasbourg court in *Animal Defenders International v UK* (2013) 57 EHRR 21 (see Section 22.9.3.2). Only registered political parties can make party political broadcasts (Political Parties, Elections and Referendums Act 2000, s 37). These do not count as election expenses (Representation of the People Act 1983, s 75(1)).

2. There is a general duty on Ofcom to preserve good taste and balance and impartiality in all political broadcasting (Communications Act 2003, s 6). The BBC is not governed by statute but operates under a royal charter and an agreement with the Home Office. However, since 2017, Ofcom performs certain

regulatory functions in respect of the BBC in accordance with the charter and agreement (Communications Act 2003, s 198). Ofcom forbids the expression of editorial opinion about matters of public policy, excluding broadcasting matters. The independent broadcasters are protected by the HRA in respect of the right of freedom of expression (Section 20.4). However, as a public body, the BBC may not be entitled to such protection (Section 22.7).

In principle, the broadcasters' duties are enforceable by the courts. However, the idea of political impartiality is both vague and complex and the courts are reluctant to interfere in party political matters. For example, must there be balance within the context of every specific subject? How much coverage should minority parties enjoy? The court will not intervene with the broadcasting authority's decision except in a case of bad faith or complete irrationality (see *R v Broadcasting Complaints Commission, ex p Owen* [1985] QB 1153; *R (ProLife Alliance) v BBC* [2003] 2 All ER 977). Each broadcasting authority, in consultation with the parties, must adopt a code of practice concerning the participation of the parties in items about the constituency (Representation of the People Act 1983, s 93 as amended).

3. It is an illegal practice (Section 12.6.4) for a person to 'use or aid, abet, counsel or procure' the use of broadcasting stations outside the UK for electoral purposes, except where the matter is to be retransmitted by one of the domestic broadcasting companies (Representation of the People Act 1983, s 93 as amended). However, this may not prevent overseas stations from directly broadcasting to voters and does not control the internet. Indeed, considerable political propaganda is now disseminated via social media and there seem to be no relevant controls, other than the general limits on election expenditure.

Apart from the particular controls over broadcasting, under RPA 1983, s 106 it is an illegal practice (below) for any person to make a false statement of fact in relation to a candidate's personal character or conduct for the purpose of affecting the election result, unless the person making the statement had reasonable grounds to believe, and did believe, that it was true. Section 106 therefore curbs freedom of speech in the interests of the standard of political debate but risks involving the judiciary in politics.

In *Watkins v Woolas* [2010] EWHC 2702 (QB) (upheld in *R (Woolas) v Speaker of the House of Commons* [2012] QB 1), an MP was convicted under section 106 for making a false statement that an opponent encouraged support from Muslim extremists. Even though this had significant political implications, it was held to be a matter of personal character or conduct because its basic meaning was that the candidate condoned violence. Trying to strike a balance between freedom of expression and democratic standards, the court distinguished between the personal and the political, holding that a 'political' statement falls outside section 106. The court took a narrow view of the meaning of political statement, limiting it to statements relating to the candidate's official position, which thus limited free expression (see Hoar (2011) 74 MLR 607). However, it was emphasised that even false political statements made carelessly should be protected in the interests of democratic debate (*R (Woolas) v Speaker of the House of Commons* [2012] at [124]).

12.6.4 Election disputes

There is an Election Court, comprising two judges. Either a voter or a candidate may, within three months of the election, lodge a petition to the court. The court can disqualify a candidate, order a recount or scrutiny of the votes, declare the result, invalidate it and order a fresh election (Representation of the People Act 1983, s 159). The decision takes the form of a report to the Speaker, which the House of Commons is bound to accept (s 144(7)). Even though it comprises High Court judges, the Election Court is subject to judicial review by the High Court (see *R (Woolas) v Speaker of the House of Commons* [2012]).

Election offences result in the offender being disqualified as a candidate or prevented from sitting in Parliament. The extent of the disqualification depends upon whether it is a 'corrupt practice' (everywhere, ten years) or an 'illegal practice' (in a particular constituency, five years). 'Innocent' illegal practices can be overlooked (s 167). A corrupt practice involves dishonesty, improper pressure on voters or improper expenditure. Illegal practices concern breaches of various statutory requirements and raise questions of freedom of expression (above).

There are also offences concerning misuse of the voting process which are prosecuted in the ordinary courts (Electoral Administration Act 2006).

Summary

▶ The House of Lords is unelected and, with over 800 members, is one of the largest legislatures in the world. Attempts to reform its composition, with the exception of the removal of most of the hereditary peers in 1999, have had little success.

▶ The voting system for Westminster parliamentary elections is currently the simple plurality, 'first past the post' system. Voting systems must cater for the incommensurables of effective government, accountable government and democratic representation. It is questionable whether the electoral system is adapted to its modern task of choosing governments, whether it is truly representative of public opinion, and whether it is fair to all candidates. We briefly compared different kinds of voting system, including the alternative vote and proportional representation. Variations of PR are used in elections to the regional legislatures.

▶ The machinery for regulating constituency boundaries gives a certain amount of protection against political interference, which has been strengthened by the enactment of the Parliamentary Constituencies Act 2020. It is difficult to challenge decisions made by this process in the courts.

▶ The law governing the conduct of elections, which had previously ignored national politics in favour of the individual election at local level, has been reformed to regulate campaign expenditure at national level, including spending by third parties on election campaigns and sponsorship of political parties. The independent Electoral Commission has wide responsibilities in relation to the finances of political parties and the conduct of elections. This is intended to bring greater openness and accountability to political parties.

▶ Controls over election broadcasting are designed to ensure fairness between the parties in accordance with their popular support and are more stringent on their restrictions over the press. However, there is little regulation of the internet and social media.

Exercises

12.1 'In a democracy there is no point in an Upper House of the legislature. If both Houses are elected, there is a problem of duplication. If the Upper House is not elected then it is not legitimate.' Discuss.

12.2 The prime minister makes the following recommendations to the Queen for elevation to the peerage:

(a) George, a banker who has made large donations to the prime minister's party, and who was told by an adviser to the prime minister that his donations should be worth a peerage.

(b) Clara, an artist whose application was rejected by the House of Lords Appointment Commission on the ground that she would not 'fit in' with the culture of the House of Lords because she had been convicted of drug-related offences.

(c) Benjy, the prime minister's brother-in-law, who has recently been defeated in an election to the House of Commons.

Advise the Queen as to the legality of these proposals and as to the constitutional implications, if any. What are her powers in the matter?

12.3 To what extent can common ground be found in the attempts to reform the House of Lords since 1911? What reforms would you suggest?

12.4 Do the present arrangements for designating parliamentary constituencies contain adequate safeguards against gerrymandering?

12.5 Should prisoners be allowed to vote?

12.6 To what extent has the law successfully regulated the funding of political parties? Should there be legal restrictions on the amount of all private donations to political parties?

12.7 A general election is to take place within the next year.

   (a) The Campaign for Free University Education proposes to distribute leaflets and hold meetings during the election campaign in various university towns.

   (b) Donald, a wealthy businessman resident in the US, wishes to make an anonymous loan of £5 million to any political party that will campaign to withdraw the UK from the EU. He also proposes to advertise in the national press and on TV in favour of repealing the anti-hunting law in the UK.

   (c) Clive, who is resident in the Channel Islands, wishes to donate £8000 to the Get Back Into Europe! party.

   Discuss the legality of these proposals.

12.8 During an election campaign, Damien, a supporter of one of the candidates, wrote to a newspaper stating falsely that Joanna, a candidate for a rival party, did not live in the constituency, was a member of an animal rights group that advocated violence, and in a previous job as an accountant had often made false expenses claims. Discuss any legal liability.

12.9 'Reforms of the electoral system through the introduction of a single transferable vote ... would revitalise the operation of political processes and make a major contribution to the development of a more accountable, effective system and a more influential citizenry' (Oliver). Discuss.

Further reading

Ballinger, *The House of Lords 1911–2011: A Century of Non-Reform* (Hart Publishing 2012)

Bingham, 'The House of Lords: Its Future' [2010] PL 261

Bogdanor, *The New British Constitution* (Hart Publishing 2009), ch 6

Bryan, 'Lions Under the Throne: The Constitutional Implications of the Debate on Prisoner Enfranchisement' (2013) 2 Camb J Int Comp L 274

Committee on Standards in Public Life, *Thirteenth Report, Political Party Finance: Ending the Big Donor Culture* (Cm 8208, 2011)

Ewing, *The Cost of Democracy: Party Funding in Modern British Politics* (Hart Publishing 2007)

Grist, 'Challenging Elections in the Courts' [2015] PL 375

Marriott, 'Alarmist or Relaxed: Election Expenditure Limits and Freedom of Speech' [2005] PL 764

Phillips, *Strengthening Democracy: Fair and Sustainable Funding of Political Parties* (HMSO 2007)

Phillipson, 'The "Greatest Quango of Them All"' [2004] PL 352

Power, *Party Funding and Corruption* (Palgrave Macmillan, 2020), ch 6

Power Commission, *Power to the People: An Independent Inquiry into Britain's Democracy* (Rowntree Trust 2006)

Royal Commission on the Reform of the House of Lords, *A House for the Future* (Cm 4534, 2000) [Wakeham Report] (and see (2000) 64 MLR 82)

Russell, *The Contemporary House of Lords: Western Bi-Cameralism Revived* (Oxford University Press 2013)

Webber, 'The Polycentricity of Political Financing' [2012] PL 310

Chapter 13

Parliamentary procedure

Introduction

It is only through procedures for debating, questioning and voting that the voice of Parliament as a collective institution can make itself known. It will be recalled that there is no strict separation of powers between the executive and the legislature in that all ministers must also be MPs, and the most important ministers must be members of the elected House of Commons. This has democratic strengths, ensuring that ministers must appear in public and are directly answerable to Parliament, but where the government has a strong majority it weakens the independence of Parliament.

The procedural rules attempt to ensure that Parliament, as representative of the people, can perform its four sometimes conflicting tasks. These are:

1. enacting legislation;
2. sustaining the government by providing it with funds and ensuring that government business can be adequately dealt with;
3. holding the executive to account;
4. redressing individual grievances.

Parliamentary procedure is adversarial, presupposing a government and Opposition constantly in conflict. The rectangular layout of the chamber reflects this. Government and Opposition confront each other on either side, and the seats are symbolically arranged two sword-lengths from each other. Other European legislative chambers are characteristically semi-circular in layout, representing a more conciliatory ethos, with the parties, usually elected by proportional representation, merging into each other.

The adversarial nature of parliamentary procedure is mitigated by what are known as 'usual channels'. These involve informal cooperation between the parties so as to ensure that the procedures operate smoothly and fairly. For example, absences from votes may be arranged in 'pairs' so as to maintain party balance. Party whips have the responsibility of liaising between the government and backbench MPs and imposing party discipline. On occasion, however, these processes break down. For example, in July 2018, the Conservative Party chairman was criticised for breaking a 'pairing' agreement with Liberal Democrat leader Jo Swinson, who had recently given birth.

It is widely acknowledged that the voice of Parliament is often stifled by executive dominance. Furthermore, most legislation is proposed and prepared by the executive so that the main role of Parliament is to scrutinise and approve bills, rather than to initiate them.

Generally, the government controls the day-to-day procedures of the House of Commons and, unlike the case in many other democracies, can timetable its own business. It can invoke procedures which enable a bill to be passed with little discussion (Section 13.3.3). Under Standing Order (SO) 14, government business has priority, and under SO 48, financial measures can be initiated only by the Crown. Twenty days per year are set aside for Opposition business. Only once since 1978 has the government lost an Opposition Day debate (on the Gurkhas in 2009), but more recently there has been a trend for MPs from the governing party to abstain on such debates, leading to claims that the government is failing to accord Parliament sufficient respect.

Through its whips (party managers), the government attempts to ensure that party members vote loyally, and the Chief Whip advises the prime minister upon the careers of ministers and MPs. A disloyal member might have the 'whip removed', which amounts to expulsion from the party. These pressures are especially strong when dealing with matters claimed by government to involve security (see Howe and Walker, 'Lessons Learned from Political Constitutionalism? Comparing the

Enactment of Control Orders and Terrorism Prevention and Investigation Measures by the UK Parliament' [2014] PL 267).

It is clearly vital that government business should not be obstructed, but also important that reasonable time be available for the concerns of backbenchers representing their constituents. To this end, a Backbench Business Committee was established in 2010 to control the agenda during times set aside for non-government business (about one day a week). This preserves a limited space free of direct government control (see Procedure Committee, *Review of the Backbench Business Committee*, HC 2012–13, 168). The method of appointing parliamentary committees has also been revised to give backbenchers greater influence.

As became apparent during debates on the withdrawal from the European Union in 2019, it is for the House collectively to control its own procedures, so it could, if it so wished, radically transform itself. In some countries, influenced by the doctrine of separation of powers, there are provisions which prevent the procedure from being controlled by the executive.

Parliamentary procedure is based upon Standing Orders made by each House, customs and conventions, and rulings by the Speaker of the Commons. The authoritative manual of parliamentary procedure is Erskine May, *Parliamentary Practice* (2019: https://erskinemay.parliament.uk/). The finance, administration and staffing of the House of Commons are supervised by the House of Commons Commission, which comprises a group of MPs chaired by the Speaker (House of Commons (Administration) Act 1978), now supplemented by two external members and two officials (the Clerk and Director General of the House of Commons): House of Commons Commission Act 2015. It does not have a government majority and is therefore independent of the executive.

There has been a series of measures to 'modernise' the procedure of Parliament. Characteristic of constitutional reform in the UK, these are unsystematic. Initially, the proposals involved more rigorous timetabling of business to enhance efficiency, although this fostered greater government control (see *Modernisation of the House of Commons: A Reform Programme* (HC 2001–02, 1168)). The *Power Report* (Rowntree Trust 2006) recommended that select committees should get enhanced powers, that there should be limits on the powers of the whips and that Parliament should have greater freedom to initiate legislation, petitions and inquiries independently of the executive.

Some of these measures were introduced following the report of the Select Committee on Reform of the House of Commons (the Wright Committee) in March 2010 (House of Commons Reform Committee, *Rebuilding the House* (HC 2008–09, 1117); see Political and Constitutional Reform Committee, *Revisiting 'Rebuilding the House': the Impact of the Wright Reforms*, HC 2012–13, 82; *Revisiting 'Rebuilding the House': the Impact of the Wright Reforms: Government Response*, HC 2013–14, 910). The Wright Committee's recommendations were designed to strengthen the collective power of the Commons, give individual members greater influence, and make the proceedings of the House more transparent, so as to increase public ability to influence and understand parliamentary business. Most of the Committee's recommendations were implemented by Standing Order. These were that:

1. a Backbench Business Committee should allocate business in the House of Commons. This initially applies only to non-government business (above) but would eventually extend to most government business. However, the latter (a 'House Business Committee') has not yet materialised;
2. backbench members should have greater control over the membership of select committees of the House (Section 13.5.3);
3. more time should be made available to debate select committee reports and the government's response to them;
4. backbenchers should have greater opportunity to initiate debates.

The Wright Committee also recommended that the Opposition should have greater control over the timetabling of the 20 Opposition Days available for debating subjects of its choosing, that the government should not decide for how long its business should be debated without reference to the House, that aspects of the 'estimates' (Section 13.4) should be more thoroughly debated, and that backbenchers' motions should be voted on. These recommendations have not been formally implemented.

13.2 The Speaker of the Commons

The office of Speaker, 'the first commoner', symbolises the historical development of the House of Commons. The Speaker presides over meetings of the Commons and is the intermediary between the House and the Crown. Originally, the Speaker was a Crown servant, but since the seventeenth century has asserted independence from the Crown. When Charles I entered the chamber to arrest the Five Members (1642), Speaker Lenthall replied: 'I have neither eyes to see nor tongue to speak in this place but as the House is pleased to direct me, whose servant I am here'. Thus, the Speaker represents the rights of the House against the Crown.

Since the nineteenth century, it has become established that the Speaker is independent of party, cannot hold ministerial office and takes no part in debate. The Speaker is required to be impartial between the political parties. The Speaker controls the procedure, keeps order and is responsible for protecting the rights of all groups within the House, particularly those of minorities. S/he has considerable discretion. The Speaker makes procedural rulings, decides who shall speak and has summary powers to suspend members or terminate a sitting. In terms of the conduct of particular proceedings, the Speaker need not normally give reasons for decisions. The Serjeant at Arms is the enforcement agency responsible to the Speaker. There is also a Deputy Speaker and deputies to him or her. One of these presides when the whole House is sitting as a committee, as it does in relation to financial matters (Section 13.4).

The Speaker is elected from among its members by the House at the beginning of each Parliament. The election may be unchallenged, but if there is more than one candidate, a secret ballot is held. An absolute majority of over 50 per cent must be obtained; the 'Father of the House', the longest-serving member, runs the election. Traditionally, a newly elected Speaker has to be dragged to the chair, a reminder that this was once a dangerous post. The Speaker can be removed by the House. There has been no removal of a Speaker since 1695 (Sir John Trevor for corruption), but in 2009, Speaker Martin resigned amid allegations that his conduct was overprotective to MPs accused of excessive expense claims, and in 2015 an unsuccessful attempt was made to oust John Bercow (see also Section 3.4.1).

13.3 Legislative procedure

Most bills are prepared and presented to Parliament by ministers. The procedure may be divided into three stages (see Constitution Committee, *Parliament and the Legislative Process*, HL 2003–04, 173, [9]). These are 'pre-legislative scrutiny', 'legislative scrutiny' and 'post-legislative scrutiny'. At present, despite a proposal by the Law Commission (Law Com No 302 (2006)), there are only limited arrangements for post-legislative scrutiny by the House itself, although some individual statutes provide for this (e.g. Fixed Term Parliaments Act 2011, Coronavirus Act 2020, and much anti-terrorist legislation). Apart from this, departmental select committees can carry out scrutiny within three to five years of royal assent (*Post-Legislative Scrutiny: The Government's Response*, Cm 7320, 2008).

The main distinctions are between public bills and private bills. There are also special arrangements for financial measures.

13.3.1 Public bills

A public bill is a bill intended to alter the general law. The formal procedures in the House are only the tip of the iceberg. Any member can propose a bill (a private member's bill), but almost all public bills are promoted by the government and introduced by ministers. Private members' bills have priority on 13 Fridays (the House does not otherwise sit on Fridays, so few MPs are likely to be present). Private members' bills are usually defeated at the 'second reading' (see below) unless they are bills that the government supports. However, there is controversy over the perception that the government may 'hijack' this process, which came to the public attention when a private members' bill with government support which made 'upskirting' a criminal offence was blocked by a backbench Conservative MP in June 2018, supposedly for this reason. A government bill was later passed (Voyeurism (Offences) Act 2019).

13.3.1.1 Pre-legislative scrutiny

Before their formal introduction, public bills go through various processes within the administration, involving the formulation of policy and principles, and consultation with outside bodies (*Code of Practice on Consultation* (2008)). There is no legal requirement of consultation, or probably even a convention. In *Bank Mellat v HM Treasury (No.2)* [2013] UKSC 39, which concerned a Treasury Order freezing the assets of a foreign bank, Lord Sumption (at [39]) emphasised that, in the case of primary legislation made by Parliament itself, there was no duty to consult or even to be fair. However, this does not apply to subordinate legislation made by ministers which Parliament does not make itself but may scrutinise (Section 13.5.5): here, the court can examine the validity of the legislation, although it cannot scrutinise the parliamentary process itself. Nonetheless, it is reluctant to hold that the procedure was unfair if it has been subject to parliamentary scrutiny.

The bill is then sent to the Parliamentary Counsel for drafting. Some bills, particularly those dealing with commercial matters, are drafted with the aid of outside lawyers. The relationship between the draftsmen and the government is similar to that of lawyer and client. The draftsmen work under considerable pressure of time, and there is continuous consultation with government departments. Some bills relating to reform of the general law are prepared by the Law Commission. Important bills may be foreshadowed by Green Papers, for consultation; or White Papers, which state the government's concluded opinions, albeit sometimes open to further discussion. Both are published. There has been substantial criticism of the drafting of contemporary legislation (see Greenberg (2015)).

As part of a programme of modernisation of Parliament, important bills have been published as draft bills for 'pre-legislative' discussion with public consultation before the formal process is started. Draft bills are considered by a select committee or a public bill committee.

13.3.1.2 Legislative scrutiny

The final version of a bill is approved by the Cabinet and then introduced into Parliament. Except for financial measures, which must be introduced by a minister in the Commons, a bill can be introduced into either House. The same stages apply in each House. Relatively uncontroversial bills are likely to be introduced in the House of Lords, which eases pressure of time in the Commons.

Parliament debates each bill in a process that distinguishes between general principles and detail. Parliamentary debates consist of a motion and a question proposed by the chair in the same form as the motion. Following debate, the question is put and voted upon, the result being expressed as a resolution or order. At any stage, there may be amendments proposed, but in all cases, issues are presented to the House one at a time for a yes or no vote by a simple majority.

The stages of a public bill are as follows:

- *First reading*. A formality which ensures that the bill is printed and published.
- *Second reading*. At which the main principles of the bill are discussed. In theory, once a bill has passed this stage, its principles cannot later be challenged. Occasionally, the second reading is dealt with by a special committee. After second reading there is a 'programme motion' timetabling the bill, and there may be a vote authorising any expenditure concerning the bill.
- *Committee stage*. The bill is usually examined by a public bill committee, with a view to suggesting detailed amendments. Unlike a select committee, which exists for the whole of a Parliament, a public bill committee is set up only for the purpose of a particular bill. Its membership of up to 50 is based upon the strength of each party in the House, so it is difficult for amendments to be made against the wishes of the government. Opponents of a bill sometimes deliberately cause delays by discussing matters at length in committee. However, the chairman has the power to decide which amendments should be discussed and a business subcommittee allocates time for discussion. The parliamentary draftsman may be present, and civil servants or experts might be called to give evidence.

▶ Sometimes a bill is referred to a committee of the whole House. This might happen for example when the bill is uncontroversial or, at the opposite extreme, where it is urgent, highly controversial or a 'major bill of first-class constitutional significance', although the meaning of this is unclear (for example the Bank of England Bill 1997, which transferred power to fix interest rates to the Bank, went to an ordinary public bill committee). A government can effectively neutralise the committee stage by obtaining a resolution that a committee of the whole House shall deal with a bill. This means that the bill is unlikely to be examined in detail. This device was used in 2010 for the Academies Bill, which allowed qualifying schools to remove themselves from local authority into central control. Occasionally, a specialised bill is referred to one of the permanent select committees.

▶ *Report stage.* The bill is returned to the House, which can then vote upon the committee amendments and consider further amendments. The Speaker can select the amendments to be debated. In principle, this allows the House an opportunity for detailed scrutiny. However, most of the limited time available (a few hours) is used up with government amendments, leaving little scope for intervention by backbenchers. The report stage can be dispensed with where the bill has been discussed by a committee of the whole House.

▶ *Third reading.* This is the final vote on the bill. Only verbal amendments are usually possible at this stage (SO 77), but the bill as a whole can be opposed.

▶ If started in the Commons, the bill is then sent to the House of Lords. The role of the House of Lords is to improve the bill by scrutinising it in detail and suggesting changes. The House of Lords is not expected to reject a bill on principle although, under the Salisbury Convention (Section 13.7), this may strictly apply only to a bill that forms part of the government's election manifesto. By convention, the House cannot discuss financial measures. If the Lords veto the bill or make amendments, it is returned to the Commons. If there is continuing disagreement between the two Houses, the Parliament Act procedure can be triggered (Section 11.4).

▶ Otherwise, the bill is sent for royal assent. This is usually notified by commissioners at the prorogation ceremony that ends each session (Royal Assent Act 1967). By convention, the monarch must always assent, except possibly in the unlikely event of the prime minister advising to the contrary. In this case, however, the government would be at odds with the Commons, and so required to resign.

▶ Once a bill has received the royal assent, it becomes law. However, it is often provided that an Act or parts of it shall take effect only when a minister so orders. A minister's decision whether or not to bring an Act into effect can be subject to judicial review (see *R v Secretary of State for the Home Dept, ex p Fire Brigades Union* [1995] 2 All ER 244). It is also common for an Act to confer power on ministers to make regulations without which the Act itself cannot operate. These might include a 'Henry VIII clause' under which a minister is empowered to alter the Act or other statutes.

▶ If a public bill has not become law by the end of a session, it lapses. However, some bills can be carried over into the next session (SO 80A (HC 1997–98, 543)). This must be authorised by a resolution of the House, which is of course usually under the control of the governing party.

Some bills can be passed without debate, but with scrutiny by a joint committee of both Houses. These are bills of a largely formal nature to consolidate other legislation without making significant changes or to repeal redundant statutes. The Law Commission prepares these bills.

13.3.2 Private bills

A private bill is one directed to particular persons or places, for example a bill to build a new section of railway line. It is not subject to the Parliament Acts. Private bill procedure allows both local and national perspectives to be examined and is therefore suitable for very important private schemes: for this reason, such bills were especially common in the Victorian era. The procedure includes a special committee stage involving petitions by interests concerned, which are considered by a select committee. There can be legal representation. Although private bill procedure involves outside elements, it is still wholly within parliamentary privilege. Therefore, the courts cannot intervene on the ground that the procedure has not been properly followed, or even that there has been fraud (*Pickin v British Railways Board* [1974] AC 765).

A public bill with a private element is called a 'hybrid bill' (e.g. the High Speed Rail (London–West Midlands) Bill 2013–14 to authorise a new railway, involving acquiring land from thousands of specific individuals and bodies). A hybrid bill is subject to the public bill procedure, except for the committee stage when it is examined by a select committee in the same manner as a private bill. Private bill procedure has been much criticised, not only because it is slow and antiquated, but also because it fails to provide opportunities for the public to be directly involved in debating schemes that may have serious environmental impact, for example new railway lines. In the HS2 case (*R (HS2 Action Alliance) v Secretary of State for Transport* [2014] 1 WLR 324), it was argued that the procedure was not sufficiently independent and rigorous to satisfy EU Directive 2011/92 concerning strategic environmental impact assessment of a 'plan or project'. The Directive requires information to be supplied, and public participation. The court held that the procedure satisfied the Directive in that MPs are supplied with adequate information and have the power to make changes. It was therefore a genuine means of discussion and debate, despite the influence of political parties on the parliamentary process.

However, Article 9 of the Bill of Rights 1688 would have prevented the court from investigating whether the particular process was adequately carried out (Section 11.6.3). It was held that the Directive as applied by the CJEU required only that the legislative process was not a formality or a sham. This could be established without violating Article 9. Otherwise, a conflict with parliamentary sovereignty might have arisen (Section 8.5.4).

There is a range of alternative procedures for large-scale schemes. The main examples involving Parliament are as follows:

▶ *The Transport and Works Act 1992* applies primarily to large rail and waterway projects. A Secretary of State authorises projects after consulting local authorities and affected parties and after an environmental assessment. A public inquiry must be held into objections. The Secretary of State can refer proposals of national importance to Parliament for debate.
▶ *Provisional orders* made by ministers, again following a public local inquiry, are confirmed by a provisional order confirmation bill, the committee stage of which involves a select committee at which interested parties can be heard. It is not subject to the Parliament Acts. This procedure is rarely used.
▶ *Special parliamentary procedure* involves a ministerial order which is subject to a public inquiry and also to a hearing before a special parliamentary committee. It can be debated on the floor of the House. This procedure is less cumbersome than the procedure for private bills or provisional order confirmation bills. It gives the authority of Parliament to sensitive proposals but is rarely used.

13.3.3   Government control over procedure: cutting short debate

By virtue of its majority and the submissiveness of the government's supporters, the government is usually in a position to control the timing of debate. Moreover, the parliamentary timetable is usually crowded, with the result that many, if not most, clauses of a bill are not discussed at all. The passage of a bill can be timetabled in advance under a 'programme motion' by the government (SO 83A–83I; for background see Modernisation Select Committee Report (HC 1997–98, 190); Procedure Committee Report, *Timetabling Legislation* (HC 2003–04, 325): government's response (HC 2003–04, 1169)). This applies to most government bills and increases the government's control over Parliament. The government might 'fast track' a bill by drastically curtailing debate so that the whole process might be complete within a few days or less (see Constitution Committee, HL 2008–09, 116). There are other procedural devices to cut short the time spent on debate. The main devices are:

▶ *Closure*. A motion in the House or in a committee that the question now be put. This must be supported by at least 100 members and means that the matter must immediately be voted upon (SOs 36, 37). The Speaker can also cut short debate when s/he thinks there has been adequate discussion. Except in the case of private members' bills, closure motions are rare, but are important as a last resort.
▶ *Guillotine*. A minister may propose a timetable for a bill, a motion that cannot be debated for more than three hours (SO 83).

▶ There is a limited safeguard for the independence of the House in that a *business* or *programme committee* comprising backbench members appointed by the Speaker divides up the time allocated to bills that have been subject to a programme motion (SO 83B) or guillotine (SO 82) in relation to a committee of the whole House or at report or third reading stage.

▶ *Kangaroo*. The Speaker at report stage, or the chairman of a committee, selects clauses or amendments for discussion.

13.4 Financial procedure

Financial controls have developed pragmatically over the centuries. They are a confusing mixture of statute, convention, common law, parliamentary customs and practice. They reveal the untidiness of the UK Constitution.

The dependence of the executive on money voted by the people is an essential feature of a democratic constitution. It is a fundamental principle, embodied in both law and convention, that the House of Commons controls public finance and that proposals for public spending can be initiated only by the Crown: 'The Crown requests money, the Commons grant it and the Lords assent to the grant' (Erskine May, *Parliamentary Practice* (Butterworths 2019) para. 33.2). On the other hand, modern government finance is so large and complex that parliamentary control may be unrealistic. It is widely accepted that, particularly in relation to advance scrutiny of government demands for money, parliamentary control is ineffective. The Commons can only scrutinise taxation and expenditure proposals very superficially, relying heavily on what the government tells it and having limited resources to carry out independent scrutiny. In practice, the most substantial control over government finance is exercised internally by the Treasury (Chapter 15). The independent National Audit Office is effective in relation to scrutiny of past expenditure.

Financial procedure is based on an ancient distinction between 'ways and means' – raising money – and 'supply' – allocating money to the purposes of the executive. This is somewhat artificial since the two are closely related. By virtue of the Bill of Rights 1688, the Crown cannot raise taxation without the consent of Parliament. The basis of the principle that the Crown cannot spend money without the consent of Parliament is partly long-standing custom endorsed by the common law (*Auckland Harbour Board v R* [1924] AC 318) and partly statute, in that payments out of the Consolidated Fund, the government's bank account, require statutory authority (Exchequer and Audit Departments Act 1866, s 11).

The Crown comes to the Commons to ask for money in the form of the 'estimates' for each government department. Financial measures can be proposed only by a minister. The Commons can reduce the estimates, but not increase them. The survival of a government depends upon the Commons voting it funds, and the refusal of the Commons to do so is equivalent to a vote of no confidence so that the government must resign. By convention, the House of Lords cannot amend measures relating to central government finance and, under the Parliament Act 1911, can delay bills that are exclusively concerned with raising or allocating central government money only for one month.

Taxation and expenditure must first be authorised by resolutions of the House of Commons. Amendments cannot be made outside the terms of the resolution, thus strengthening the government's hand. The enactment of the legislation is a formality, any serious discussion itself limited, having taken place months earlier when the government presented its public spending proposals according to a timetable of its choosing.

There are three main financial measures (see Brazier and Ram (2004) chs 1 and 2 for a clear account). First, the Finance Act raises taxation. The royal assent to a taxation measure is expressed in the words *la Reyne remercie ses bons sujets, accepte leur benevolence et ainsi le veult* ('the Queen thanks her good subjects, accepts their kindness and thus assents'), as opposed to the normal *la Reyne le veult*. Second, an Appropriation Act, usually in May, allocates amounts out of the Consolidated Fund to the Crown according to the estimates ('votes') presented for each government department for the current financial year, that is until the following April. It also confirms spending that has been authorised provisionally by other legislation for the current and previous years. Third, Consolidated Fund Acts authorise interim spending until the following Appropriation Act and may also authorise additional spending from time to time. These bills have no committee or report stage but go straight from second to third reading.

Central government money does not come exclusively from taxation. Governments borrow large sums of money in the form of bonds and on the international money markets. Money is also raised from landholding, from investments both in the UK and overseas and from trading activities. These sources of finance are not subject to detailed parliamentary scrutiny, although statutory authority is required in general terms for borrowing (National Loans Fund Act 1968).

13.4.1 Taxation procedure

The key taxation event is the annual 'budget' resolution proposed by the Chancellor, usually in March (although this is nowadays substantially anticipated by an 'Autumn Statement' which usually takes place in the preceding November). The budget speech sets the general economic framework of government policy and proposals for tax changes. The budget resolution is followed by the annual Finance Bill. This includes taxes (notably income tax) that must be authorised afresh each year, albeit that they are enforced and administered under permanent legislation (Income and Corporation Taxes Act 1988). Some taxes, mainly indirect taxes such as customs duties, are authorised by permanent legislation, although their rates can be changed at any time. Constitutional principle has been preserved in the case of EU law by the requirement in the European Communities Act 1972 that laws affecting taxation, for example VAT, must be implemented by a statute.

The effect of the budget resolution is that the tax proposals become law with immediate effect but lapse unless embodied in a Finance Act that becomes law by a specified time. This is 5 August if the speech is in March or April, otherwise within four months (Provisional Collection of Taxes Act 1968). The main parts of the Finance Bill are considered by a committee of the whole House. This procedure illustrates the constitutional principle that resolutions of the Commons cannot by themselves change the law but need statutory backing (*Bowles v Bank of England* [1913] 1 Ch 57). However, unless an aspect of the Finance Bill is especially controversial, it is subject to little scrutiny. For example, ministers inserted provisions into the Finance Act 1984 which exempted MPs' expense claims from normal taxation (see Little and Stopworth (2013) 76 MLR 83).

13.4.2 Supply procedure

Most public expenditure must be authorised annually by the Appropriation Act, which approves the government's estimates. These estimates are made under the supervision of the Treasury. They include 'votes' setting out the government's proposed allocation of funds between departments. Thus, the Commons approves both the global sum and the executive's broad priorities. However, the Appropriation Act is very short and general, merely listing the broad functions of each department to be financed, allocating a global amount, designating a grant from the Consolidated Fund (the government's main bank account) and setting a limit to 'appropriations in aid', that is money that can be raised from fees and charges and so on. Moreover, the Act deals only in cash, so contemporary methods of 'resource accounting', which includes other government assets, may not fall properly within parliamentary controls (see Daintith and Page (1999) 166).

Parliamentary control over the estimates is largely a formality. The Appropriation Act and Consolidated Fund Acts are usually passed without debate. Debates on the estimates have been replaced by the 20 Opposition Days, which allow the Opposition parties to raise anything they wish, and by special 'adjournment debates' following the passage of the Acts. The latter allow issues to be discussed without a vote.

The Act appears to authorise payment to the Crown rather than to the individual department, thus reinforcing the Treasury's power to control other departments by presiding over the internal allocation of funds. However, in *R v Lords Commissioners of the Treasury* (1872) LR 7 QB 387, it was said that the Treasury is obliged to pay the sums in question.

There is an arcane debate as to whether the Appropriation Act alone is sufficient to make lawful particular items of expenditure that fall within its general provisions. This is worth briefly considering as it raises wider concerns as to the role of internal understandings and influences as against legal constraints in the constitution (see Daintith and Page (1999) 35, 174, 203–06). One view is that, in addition to the Appropriation Act, specific powers must be conferred either by statute or under the royal prerogative. In other words, the Appropriation Act authorises the Crown to use the government's bank account for purposes that are lawful but does not in itself make any *particular* purpose lawful. On the other hand, if an act of the Crown does not involve interfering with the legal rights of others, why should the Crown require specific powers, since as a person it can do anything that the law does not forbid, including, presumably, spending its money? On this argument, the Appropriation Act that puts the money into the Crown's hands should be a sufficient legal basis for spending.

Where a statute confers specific spending powers, this supersedes any general power derived from the Appropriation Act (e.g. *R v Secretary of State for Foreign and Commonwealth Affairs, ex p World Development Movement* [1995] 1 All ER 611; *R v Secretary of State for the Home Dept, ex p Fire Brigades Union* [1995] 2 All ER 244). However, a later Appropriation Act could possibly validate past unlawful expenditure. A Concordat in 1932 between the Treasury and the Public Accounts Committee assumed that an Appropriation Act could override limits in other statutes but stated that it was 'proper' that permanent spending powers and duties should be defined by particular statutes. Other government statements are inconsistent (see Daintith and Page (1999) 205). It may be that the courts would be reluctant to read general provisions in an Appropriation Act as overriding specific provisions in other Acts (see *Fisher v R* [1903] AC 158).

Some items of expenditure are permanently authorised by particular statutes. These are called 'Consolidated Fund Services'. They include judicial salaries, royal expenses and interest on the national debt. The Government Trading Act 1990 gives permanent authority to the financing of certain commercial services such as the Post Office by means of a Trading Fund. In practice, most government spending is the subject of long-term commitments (e.g. pensions), thus leaving little flexibility.

13.5 Supervision of the executive

Supervision of the executive depends upon the doctrine of ministerial responsibility and relies in the last resort upon the convention that the House of Commons can require the government to resign. In modern times, the role of Parliament has been weakened by the party system and the difficulty of obtaining information from the government. It should also be remembered that not all government activity requires formal parliamentary authority. This includes royal prerogative powers, such as going to war and other matters concerning foreign affairs (and also property and commercial transactions, such as buying and selling weapons, carried out under ordinary private law powers). Parliamentary scrutiny is also limited by the practice of transferring government functions to bodies outside the central government. The main procedures for scrutiny of the executive are discussed in this chapter. Particular issues of ministerial responsibility are discussed in Chapter 15.

13.5.1 Questions to ministers

Questions can be written or oral and must be about a matter for which the minister is responsible. About one hour each day is allowed for oral questions to ministers, the departments being on a fortnightly rota. Questions are selected at random by the Speaker. The prime minister has one oral session of 30 minutes each week for which any MP can put down a question. In other cases, there is a rota of three ministers per day, but members must ballot for the privilege of asking an oral question. Except in the case of Prime Minister's Questions, two weeks' advance notice must be given, but a member may ask one unscheduled supplementary question. Civil servants who brief ministers, while required by the *Civil Service Code* to be as open as possible with Parliament, are skilled in anticipating possible supplementaries, which need only bear a tenuous relationship to the main question. Sycophantic questions are frequently asked by government supporters.

There is provision for an urgent question to be asked without prior warning as a 'private notice' question (SO 8(3)). This must relate either to matters of public importance or to the arrangement of parliamentary business. The Speaker's permission is required, and the minister must attend on the same day. There have often been fewer than a dozen permitted urgent questions per session, although the Speaker has recently encouraged their use as a means of increasing the influence of the Commons.

Oral questions are of limited value as a means of obtaining information. Written questions, of which there are many thousand per session, can be asked without limit and the answers are recorded in *Hansard*, the official parliamentary journal. Oral questions are of value mainly as a means of ensuring that ministers present themselves in public to acknowledge their personal responsibility for their departments and of assessing the personality and parliamentary skills of the minister.

The *Ministerial Code* (2019) requires that ministers must be as open as possible with Parliament and give accurate and truthful information to Parliament, correcting any inadvertent error at the earliest opportunity (see also Cabinet Office, *Guidance to Officials on Answering Parliamentary Questions*, HC 1996–97, 671, annex C). However, answers might be perfunctory or incomplete. The *Ministerial Code* is enforceable only by the prime minister.

Ministers can refuse to answer on various grounds, including cost, government efficiency, commercial sensitivity, confidentiality and the 'public interest', and cannot readily be pressed upon a refusal to answer. Some specific matters are excluded. These include matters relating to the monarchy and personal criticism of a judge. Matters subject to litigation in UK courts cannot be discussed, subject to exceptions ruled on by the Speaker in connection with civil litigation relating to ministerial decisions or matters of national importance. Exemptions covered by the Freedom of Information Act 2000 also apply. Reasons must be given for refusing to answer. MPs have often expressed frustration that ministers are not always prepared to provide full and timely answers to parliamentary questions. The Public Administration and Constitutional Affairs Committee monitors the government's responses to questions. There is no coercive machinery to compel a minister to offer a prompt, relevant and full answer in Parliament, and it is unlikely that Parliament would use its contempt powers to compel ministers to answer questions.

13.5.2 Debates

There are various opportunities for debates; all involve limited time. However, ministers must respond if required and thus, like questions, debates require government to present itself in public. The different kinds of debate include:

> ▶ *Adjournment debates*. These can be on any matter for which a minister is responsible. The most common is a half-hour daily adjournment debate which can be initiated by a backbencher. The topic is chosen by the Speaker. There is a weekly ballot (SO 9). There can also be adjournment debates following passage of a Consolidated Fund or Appropriation Act (Section 13.4), emergency adjournment debates (which are rarely permitted) and 'recess' debates, in which miscellaneous topics can be debated for up to three hours. Amendments cannot be moved to adjournment motions, so adjournment motions can be used by the government to restrict the Opposition. Adjournment debates do not result in a formal vote and a minister's response cannot be questioned. They usually do little more than enable a member to draw attention to him or herself but might give publicity to an issue.

▶ *Opposition Days*. Twenty Opposition Days are dispersed through the session which allow the Opposition parties to raise anything they wish.

▶ *Emergency debates*. The Speaker must hold that the matter is urgent, specific and important and should have urgent consideration. Only three minutes are allowed for the application. If permission is granted there can be a three-hour debate. Such debates are rare: there have only been 51 since 1979, although eight such debates took place in relation to withdrawal from the European Union.

▶ *The debate following the Queen's Speech at the opening of a session.*

▶ *Censure motions*. By convention, a government is expected to resign if defeated on a censure motion (also called a no confidence motion). The government must provide time to debate the motion. Until the 1970s, the convention also seemed to include other government defeats on important matters, but the latter seem no longer to require resignation. The possibility that a government can be defeated on a major part of its programme but also remain in office strengthens a weak government by providing a safety valve for dissidents within its party. Since 1964, a government has resigned only once following a censure motion (1979). On that occasion, the government was a minority government; however, another weak government, that of Theresa May, survived such a vote in January 2019. A no confidence motion has no particular form: either government or Opposition can declare any vote to be one of confidence. Such a vote does require the government to publicly defend itself.

▶ *The budget debate* (Section 13.4.1).

▶ *Early day motions*. This procedure allows an MP to put down a matter for debate without a fixed date. Early day motions are hardly ever debated. Their function is to draw public attention to a particular issue. They may be supported by a large number of members across parties, amounting in effect to a petition.

▶ *Procedural debates, such as points of order*. These must nominally relate to the practices of the House but might be used ingeniously to raise a broader issue.

▶ *Ministerial statements which can be followed by questions and discussion*. The Speaker can require a minister to attend and make a statement.

▶ *Westminster Hall*. This sits in a large committee room on three weekdays. It is a supplement to the main chamber as a forum for debates initiated by backbenchers on less contentious business for which time might not otherwise easily be found. Decisions must be unanimous and otherwise are referred to the main House. Ministers must be available to respond every other week, whereas in the main chamber they must respond if required to any debate.

13.5.3 Select committees

A select committee is appointed from backbenchers for the whole of a Parliament. A select committee must be distinguished from a public bill committee, the function of the latter being to scrutinise particular bills. A select committee's function is to investigate matters of its choice within the areas to which it is allocated. A select committee is supposed to be independent of government, but there is the possibility that committee members will try to curry favour with ministers, for example by discussing proposed committee reports with them.

There are four main kinds of select committee:

1. Committees charged with investigating the expenditure, administration and policy of the main departments and reporting to the House (SO 130). There is no prime minister's committee as such, but the prime minister voluntarily appears twice per year before the Liaison Committee, which is composed of the chairs of the other committees. The Intelligence and Security Committee is statutory and subject to special restrictions (Section 25.3).

2. Committees dealing with important general concerns. These include communications, environmental audit, European scrutiny, public accounts, public administration and constitutional affairs, and regulatory reform, among many others.

3. The Backbench Business Committee (Section 13.1) is chosen by backbenchers and can designate matters for debate, other than government business. It has a limited time allocation given by government of 35 days in each session (SO 9), but apart from that is free of government control.

4. Committees dealing with matters internal to the House such as standards, privileges and procedure.
5. The Speaker's Committee on the Electoral Commission deals with electoral matters (Section 12.5.2); there is also a Speaker's Committee on IPSA (Section 11.7.2).

Some select committees are joint committees of the Lords and Commons. These include human rights, national security strategy and statutory instruments.

The work of the departmental select committees is coordinated by the Liaison Committee, elected by the House. Previously, committees were appointed mainly by party managers. However, as a result of the recommendations of the Wright Committee (Section 13.1), chairs of departmental and other important select committees are now elected by the House (although the *distribution* of chairs between the parties is still decided by party managers). Members of select committees are chosen by secret ballot within party groups according to the strength of their representation in the House. Select committees may also recruit outside advisers, such as academics.

Committee proceedings are open to the public unless the committee resolves to meet in closed session. Decisions are made in private. Strictly speaking, evidence taken by a select committee cannot be published without the consent of the committee, unless and until it becomes part of the formal record of Parliament. However, evidence given in public can be published (SOs 135, 136).

A select committee will frequently issue a report, which is published. The government may make a published response. The government is not required to take action on a committee's report, but the committee can monitor the response of the government and publish a further report. A committee has limited powers of enforcement of its report which depends on a vote of the whole House.

A select committee has power under Standing Orders to send for 'persons, papers and records' at any time, even when Parliament is not sitting, and failure to attend, refusal to answer questions, or misleading the committee could be a contempt of the House. However, enforcement of committee powers would require a resolution of the House, although the Committees on Standards and Privileges possess the power to compel attendance (SO 149(6)). Assurances have been given that ministers will attend and give information to committees; there have been occasional difficulties in summoning outsiders as witnesses, although the embarrassment of receiving a summons is usually sufficient 'soft power' to secure compliance (see House of Commons Library Briefing Paper 6208, 2016, at [2.1]). Civil servants attend only with the permission of ministers and cannot be compelled to speak. Their evidence is also significantly limited (Section 15.8.5). Parliamentary committees can take evidence on oath (Parliamentary Witnesses Act 1871), although they do so only exceptionally. Ministers have sometimes relied on these ambiguities and weaknesses as a means of shielding the inner workings of government from publicity. This is tempered by a general undertaking by ministers to cooperate with committees, for example by explaining why evidence cannot be given.

Select committees are not limited as to the matters they can examine, but in practice may have limited ability to probe deeply. Time, party discipline, the doctrine of ministerial responsibility and the rules of parliamentary procedure can combine to frustrate their activities (see Liaison Committee, *Shifting the Balance: Select Committees and the Executive*, HC 2000–01, 321). Committee members do not always have the skills of focused questioning to confront evasive officials and may be tempted to promote themselves with soundbites in the hope of being quoted in the media.

On the other hand, persistent questioning is possible, expertise can be developed, and the committees are relatively non-partisan, sometimes chaired by an Opposition member. A committee is not confined to examining the activities of government departments but can carry out wider-ranging investigations in matters relevant to their departments. For example, in February 2009, after the near collapse of the banking industry, senior bankers were grilled by the Treasury Committee. Select committees have drawn public attention to important issues and have exposed weaknesses in governmental policies and procedures. Their capacity to do this may have an important deterrent effect on government departments.

13.5.4 Supervising expenditure

As we have seen, money raised by central government goes into the Consolidated Fund. The control of spending from the Consolidated Fund is the responsibility of the Commons, but given the size and complexity of modern government, this is clearly an impossible task for an elected assembly. In practice, direct parliamentary control over expenditure is very limited. More substantial, if less independent, controls are imposed within the government machine itself (Section 15.6.1). These are based on a mixture of statute, royal prerogative, convention, insider networking and the inherent power of any employer to administer its workforce.

In medieval times the Court of Exchequer supervised government spending, but the modern courts have relinquished this responsibility in favour of Parliament.

The courts are therefore reluctant to interfere with central government spending decisions which are subject to parliamentary scrutiny (see *Nottinghamshire CC v Secretary of State for the Environment* [1986] AC 240). However, in *R v Secretary of State for Foreign and Commonwealth Affairs, ex p World Development Movement* [1995], a Foreign Office decision to give a large grant to the Malaysian government for the Pergau Dam project was set aside by the Court of Appeal on the basis that the project had no economic justification. The governing legislation required that the decision be based on economic grounds, which, crucially, the Court equated with 'sound' economic grounds. This has the potential to give the courts a wide and possibly undesirable power of review. On the other hand, the matter only came to light because of the intensive, adversarial process of the Court. The internal process of control had not revealed the misapplication of public funds.

Spending by central departments and other public bodies related to the centre is scrutinised on behalf of Parliament by the Comptroller and Auditor-General, who reports to the Public Accounts Committee of the House of Commons. With characteristically British equivocation, the Comptroller is semi-independent of the executive, being an officer of the House of Commons but appointed by the Crown on a motion from the House of Commons proposed by the prime minister with the agreement of the chair of the Public Accounts Committee (Budget Responsibility and National Audit Act 2011, s 11). The Comptroller holds office for ten years and cannot be reappointed. He or she can be removed only on an Address from both Houses of Parliament (s 14). The Comptroller is not directly concerned with the merits of government policy, but rather with the efficient and economical use of money (National Audit Act 1983, ss 6, 7). However, it is difficult to separate these two concerns.

The Comptroller is supported by the National Audit Office (NAO), structured on a broadly similar independent basis (Sched. 2). The NAO scrutinises the accounts of central government departments and those of some outside bodies dependent on government money, such as universities. The NAO carries out two kinds of audit; 'Certification audit' is based on financial accounting practice, and 'value for money audit' is based on the wider concerns of the 'economy, efficiency and effectiveness' of government expenditure (National Audit Act 1983, s 6). This is not meant to include the substantive merits of government policy, although the line between them may be difficult to draw. The NAO is also concerned with matters of 'regularity, legality, propriety and probity'.

The Budget Responsibility and National Audit Act 2011 places the Office for Budget Responsibility (OBR) on a statutory basis. The OBR is intended to provide an objective assessment as to how far the government is achieving its fiscal goals (tax and public spending) and its policies for managing the national debt. It is required to report at least twice yearly on the sustainability of the public finances. This includes making fiscal and economic forecasts and assessing whether the 'fiscal mandate' has been achieved (this is the means by which the Treasury will attain its fiscal objects as set out in a 'Charter for Budget Responsibility' prepared by it (s 1)). The report must be published and laid before Parliament. Its members are semi-independent, being appointed and dismissed by the Chancellor of the Exchequer. The appointment and dismissal of the Chair and two other members (the Budget Responsibility Committee) require the consent of the Treasury Committee of the Commons.

The Constitutional Reform and Governance Act 2010, Part V introduced a technical but useful reform intended to make government accounts more transparent. The Act gives the Treasury power to direct that information be included in government accounts coordinating and aligning the different accounting methods used by government departments and designated 'quangos' (see House of Commons Liaison Committee, *Financial Scrutiny: Parliamentary Control over Government Budgets*, HC 2008–09, 804; Chief Secretary to the Treasury, *Alignment (Clear Line of Sight) Project*, Cm 7567, 2009).

13.5.5   Scrutiny of delegated/subordinate legislation

Significant and broad powers are often conferred on ministers to make delegated legislation, much of which is detailed and technical. An important recent example is the extensive use of delegated legislation to confer powers to take various actions in response to the COVID-19 pandemic: 249 such statutory instruments having being laid by the end of September 2020. Concern over lack of scrutiny of these led the government to promise MPs that votes would be permitted on further delegated legislation 'where possible'.

It is, however, impracticable to subject all delegated legislation to detailed democratic scrutiny. Thus, delegated legislation is subject to a limited degree of parliamentary control by being laid before one or both Houses for approval. Neither House can usually amend delegated legislation, but either could introduce a motion requesting the government to do so.

Originally the laying process was haphazard, but as a result of public concern about 'bureaucratic tyranny' (see *Report of Committee on Ministers' Powers*, Cmd 4060, 1932), limited reforms were made by the Statutory Instruments Act 1946. A statutory instrument made after the 1946 Act came into force is defined as such either if it is made by Order in Council, or if the parent Act expressly provides. Thus, there is no legal obligation on governments to comply with the controls in the 1946 Act. However, in practice, most delegated legislation takes the form of a statutory instrument.

A statutory instrument has to be laid before the House only if its parent Act so requires. The laying procedures typically require only that the statutory instrument be 'laid on the table' of the House in draft or final form for 40 days, subject to annulment by a vote of the House – the 'made negative' procedure. The fate of the instrument therefore depends upon the chance of a member seeing the document and securing a debate.

Some important statutory instruments are subject to a 'made affirmative' procedure, under which there must be a positive vote to bring them into effect. Such instruments are usually referred to a public bill committee. There are also 'special' or 'super-affirmative' forms, used occasionally. These require advance scrutiny by a committee and involve twofold scrutiny. The House can propose amendments. For example, orders changing the counter-terrorism functions of the National Crime Agency are subject to the super-affirmative procedure (Crime and Courts Act 2013, Sched. 23).

The 1946 Act requires that statutory instruments be published 'as soon as may be', unless there is a special reason for not doing so (s 3). Failure to publish may not make the instrument invalid, but provides a defence to prosecution, provided that the accused was unaware of the instrument and that no reasonable steps had been taken to publicise it (s 3(2); see *R v Sheer Metalcraft Ltd* [1954] 1 All ER 542). Failure to lay a statutory instrument before Parliament does, it seems, invalidate the instrument. (See *R (Alvi) v Secretary of State for the Home Dept* [2012] 1 WLR 2208: code of practice under Immigration Rules (not statutory instruments, but required to be laid in a similar way). Compare *R (Munir) v Secretary of State for the Home Dept* [2012] 1 WLR 2192: non-binding aspects of immigration rules not within laying requirement.)

The Joint Committee on Statutory Instruments is responsible for scrutinising statutory instruments laid before Parliament. The committee is not concerned with the political merits of the instrument but is required to draw the attention of Parliament to specified constitutional matters. These are as follows:

- Does the instrument impose taxation or other forms of charge?
- Does it exclude control by the courts?
- Is it retrospective without the express authority of the parent Act?
- Has there been unjustifiable delay in laying or publishing it?
- Is there doubt as to its legal validity or does it appear to make some unusual or unexpected use of the powers under which it was made?

- For any special reason does its form or purport call for elucidation?
- Does its drafting appear to be defective?
- Any other ground other than those relating to policy or merits.

There is also a House of Lords Secondary Legislation Scrutiny Committee. This can examine the policy merits of statutory instruments laid before the House. The Delegated Powers and Regulatory Reform Committee of the House of Lords considers proposals to give ministers powers to make statutory instruments. It also examines the powers of ministers to alter statutes under the Public Bodies and Regulatory Reform Act 2006.

13.6 Redress of grievances

Members of the House of Commons have a duty, and the House collectively has a right, to seek the redress of the grievances of subjects of the Crown. This dates back to the medieval origins of the House of Commons arising from the Crown's need to ask Parliament for money, which request is granted in return for the redress of grievances.

No parliamentary time is reserved for the redress of grievances as such. An MP is able to give publicity to a grievance by placing it on the parliamentary record. Apart from that, the process is haphazard. The main procedures available are questions, adjournment debates, early day motions and, perhaps most effective, informal communications with ministers, although the latter are not always protected by parliamentary privilege (Section 11.6.3). All of these suffer from the inability of an individual MP to force disclosure of information. There are other opportunities by way of the debates and motions that were discussed above, but these suffer from limited time and the absence of voting. An MP can also refer a matter to the Parliamentary Ombudsman (Section 20.2). Finally, there are public petitions that members can present on behalf of their constituents (SO 153). The right of the subject to petition originally the king, and later Parliament, dates from the thirteenth century, reflecting the history of the Commons as a means of raising grievances with the monarch. On receipt (each petitioner's name and address must be supplied) petitions can be formally presented to the House or, most commonly, are placed in a green bag behind the Speaker's chair and read out before close of business each day. A petition can be about any subject and is published in *Hansard*. A petition can also be presented to the House of Lords, but this is rare.

There is also provision for e-petitions. A petition which receives 10,000 signatures will receive a response from government, while one with 100,000 supporters is eligible for a Commons debate, although this may be in 'Westminster Hall' (Section 13.5.2). The petition system therefore offers a form of public engagement. It is controlled by the Petitions Committee, a select committee of the Commons which was set up in 2015. An e-petition may trigger an inquiry by the Committee itself. In some respects, this has been a considerable success: the Westminster system is the parliamentary e-petition system with the highest usage in the world, but it is not clear that it has had any marked effect on policy (Leston-Bandeira 2019). Notably, a petition to revoke Article 50 and remain in the EU, which received over 6 million signatures, had no lasting effect on Brexit.

Members habitually deal with grievances outside the formal parliamentary framework, acting in effect as generalist welfare officers. A letter from an MP is likely to be dealt with at a higher level in the civil service hierarchy than would otherwise be the case. Perhaps much of this work could more appropriately be done by other agencies, such as local authorities.

13.7 House of Lords procedure

The House of Lords regulates its own procedure, which is less adversarial and party-dominated than the Commons. There is no party whip and less reliance on formal procedural rules. The Lord Speaker is elected by the House but does not have the disciplinary powers available to the Speaker of the Commons, the only power being to put a question to the vote (SO 18). Under the House of Lords

(Expulsion and Suspension) Act 2015, the House may pass a resolution to expel a member or to suspend for a limited time.

Any bill other than one involving government taxation or expenditure can be introduced in the House of Lords. Such a bill is not subject to the Parliament Acts (Section 11.4). A bill introduced in the House of Commons and passing all its stages then goes to the House of Lords. The procedure in the House of Lords is broadly similar to that of the Commons, except that the committee stage usually takes place before a committee of the whole House. The House can call upon considerable specialist expertise from among its membership, even if some of it may be somewhat out of date. This is often regarded as a justification for an appointed Upper House.

According to the 'Salisbury Convention', the House of Lords must respect the 'mandate' which the electorate is assumed to have given to the government in its election manifesto. The Salisbury Convention was articulated by Lord Salisbury in 1964 when the House of Lords had an inbuilt Conservative majority. However, now that most of the hereditary element has been ejected (Section 12.2), this is no longer the case. The scope of the convention is therefore unclear, particularly as the Parliament Acts protect the power of the Lords to delay legislation.

The Parliament Acts do not apply to delegated legislation, so the House of Lords can veto a statutory instrument. However, it has done so only on one occasion in the last 30 years, when it vetoed two measures relating to the election for the Mayor of Greater London, one of which would have denied free mailing to candidates (HL Deb 20 February 2000, cols 184–85). Nevertheless, the House has asserted the existence of the power and even votes to delay delegated legislation can be controversial (see Section 11.4).

The House of Lords is a valuable forum for general and topical debates since its members are less subject to electoral pressures than MPs and are recruited from people with a wide range of expertise. Except for committees of the whole House and some minor committees, all committees in the House of Lords are select committees existing for the whole Parliament, which can therefore accumulate expertise. Select committees in the House of Lords deal with topics rather than departments, reflecting the role of the upper house as a forum for the detailed discussion of important issues free of immediate party pressures. Reports of select committees of the House of Lords, notably those of the European Union Committee and the Science and Technology Committee, command considerable respect. On the other hand, as a consequence of the senior judges no longer being members of the House of Lords (Section 7.6.3.2), substantial legal expertise over a wide variety of subjects has been lost.

Ministerial accountability in the House of Lords is limited since only a minority of ministers, none of them at the most senior levels, sits in the upper house. Questions are normally addressed to 'Her Majesty's Government' rather than to individual ministers.

Summary

▶ Parliament does not embody a strict separation of powers, the executive being in practice the dominant force. Parliamentary procedure is designed to ensure that government business goes through, but subject to Parliament's duty to control the executive. Recent reforms have attempted to strengthen the independence of Parliament as against the executive, and the process of withdrawal from the European Union demonstrated that the House of Commons retains some capacity to determine its own processes, contrary to an (admittedly weak) government's wishes.

▶ We outlined the lawmaking procedure as it applies to public bills and private bills. We then looked at the procedural framework within which the Commons attempts to make legislation, hold the government to account, control public finance and redress citizens' grievances. The timetable is largely under the control of the government, as are procedural devices for cutting short debate. However, there are provisions giving time for backbenchers and the Opposition. There are mechanisms for approving government spending and taxation proposals and scrutinising government expenditure, notably the office of Comptroller and Auditor-General and the Public Accounts Committee. In general, however, the House of Commons is not equipped for detailed control of government expenditure. In recent years, the emphasis has switched to internal controls over expenditure, through the Treasury (Chapter 15).

Summary cont'd

▶ Other devices for parliamentary control of the executive include specialist select committees and the Parliamentary Commissioner for Administration. These devices have implications for ministerial responsibility (Section 15.7). This is because they involve investigating the activities of civil servants and they raise questions about the relationship between ministers, civil servants and the House of Commons. Select committees provide a valuable means of publicising issues and are probably the most effective means of parliamentary scrutiny of the executive.

▶ Delegated legislation is often required to be laid before the House, but unless the affirmative procedure is used, it may not get serious scrutiny. The Joint Committee on Statutory Instruments monitors delegated legislation on constitutional grounds.

▶ Procedure in the Commons is dominated by the government through its power to propose business and its control of a majority of votes. Government proposals take up most of the available time. Members of Parliament have no privileged access to government information, so their debate is not especially well informed.

▶ The House of Lords regulates its own procedure. The Lord Speaker does not have the disciplinary powers available to the Speaker of the House of Commons. Its committees are valued for their expertise.

▶ The conventional assessment of Parliament is that it has become subservient to the executive – certainly when the latter is powerful – primarily because its members have capitulated to party loyalty, reinforced by the electoral system and the dual role of ministers as members of both executive and Parliament. Parliament, according to this view, is at its worst as a method of controlling government finance, poor at supervising the executive and lawmaking, but better at redressing individual grievances, although this owes much to the work of members outside the formal parliamentary procedures. On the other hand, Parliament provides a forum where the executive must defend itself in public and expose the strengths and weaknesses of its leaders. The possibility of defeat in an election may encourage members to distance themselves from an unpopular government and act as a limited constitutional check.

Exercises

13.1 'The role of Parliament is not to run the country but to hold to account those who do' (Gladstone). Is this correct? To what extent does the procedure of Parliament perform this role successfully?

13.2 'The virtue, spirit and essence of a House of Commons consist in its being the express image of the feelings of the nation. It was not instituted to be a control on the people. It was designed as a control for the people' (Edmund Burke). 'Parliament really has no control over the executive. It is a pure fiction' (David Lloyd George). To what extent do these statements represent the contemporary constitution?

13.3 'The key to democracy is the power to control public finances'. Are the powers of Parliament in this respect adequate?

13.4 A group of Opposition MPs believes that a senior government minister has been holding secret discussions with a defence equipment company concerning the possibility of engineering an uprising by anti-Western elements in an African state, so as to sell weapons to the government of that state. In an answer to a question in the House, the minister denies that the government has any involvement with the state in question. Advise the group as to their chances of obtaining a thorough investigation into the matter.

13.5 Compare the strengths and weaknesses of parliamentary questions and select committees as a means of controlling the executive. To what extent have recent reforms improved the position?

13.6 'Parliament can in principle do what it likes but lacks a mechanism independent of the party system controlled by government, in particular to initiate independent inquiries.'

Explain and critically discuss.

13.7 Compare the procedures of the House of Commons and the House of Lords. To what extent do these reflect the different constitutional functions of the two Houses?

13.8 How far can backbench MPs play an effective role in Parliament?

Further reading

Benton and Russell, 'Assessing the Impact of Parliamentary Oversight Committees: The Select Committee in the British House of Commons' (2013) 66 Parl Aff 772

Brazier and Ram, *Inside the Counting House* (Hansard Society 2004)

Daintith and Page, *The Executive in the Constitution* (Oxford University Press 1999)

Greenberg, 'Dangerous Trends in Modern Legislation' [2015] PL 96

Howarth, 'The House of Commons Backbench Business Committee' [2011] PL 490

Johnson, 'Select Committees: Powers and Functions' in Horne and Drewry (eds), *Parliament and the Law* (2nd edn, Hart Publishing 2019)

Judge, 'Whatever Happened to Parliamentary Democracy in the United Kingdom?' (2004) 57 Parl Aff 682

Kelly and Maer, 'Parliamentary Reform and the Accountability of Government to the House of Commons' in Horne and Le Sueur (eds), *Parliament: Legislation and Accountability* (Hart Publishing 2016)

Laws, 'What Is the Parliamentary Scrutiny of Legislation For?' in Horne and Le Sueur (eds), *Parliament: Legislation and Accountability* (Hart Publishing 2016)

Lee and Larkin, 'Financial Control and Scrutiny' in Horne and Drewry (eds), *Parliament and the Law* (2nd edn, Hart Publishing 2019)

Leston-Bandeira, 'Parliamentary Petitions and Public Engagement: an Empirical Analysis of the Role of E-petitions' (2019) 47 Policy & Politics 415.

Norton, 'Parliament: The Best of Times, the Worst of Times?' in Jowell and O'Cinneide (eds), *The Changing Constitution* (9th edn, Oxford University Press 2019)

Tucker, 'Parliamentary Scrutiny of Delegated Legislation' in Horne and Drewry (eds), *Parliament and the Law* (2nd edn, Hart Publishing 2019)

14.1 Introduction: the nature of the Crown

We saw in Chapter 5 that constitutional law in the UK has no concept of the state as such and some-times uses the notion of 'the Crown' as a substitute. The Crown is an ill-defined concept. The difficulty derives from the gradual evolution of the constitution from a position where the king or queen personally ran the government, to one where the monarch exercises power only through others. Nevertheless, the fiction persists that this power is still monarchical. This provides a good illustration of how, in pursuing the illusion of continuity, our rulers may mystify and distort a relatively simple concept, that of a monarch, to fit contemporary concerns.

The term 'Queen' is normally used to refer to the Queen acting personally, whereas the term 'Crown' is used as shorthand for the central executive branch of government, for example in 'Crown property' or 'Crown immunity'.

As head of state, the Queen has the undefined responsibility of being the ultimate guardian of the constitution. No minister appears to have this responsibility even though the Ministry of Justice, headed by the Lord Chancellor, is administratively responsible for constitutional matters. By convention, the Queen must act on the advice of ministers, thereby separating the 'dignified' from the 'efficient' constitution and preventing the prime minister from pretensions to the role of head of state. However, most Crown powers are exercised directly by ministers with no involvement of the Queen at all. Thus, Sir Robert Armstrong, the then Cabinet Secretary, said that 'for all practical purposes, the Crown is represented by the government of the day' (Hennessy, *The Hidden Wiring* (Gollancz 1995) 346). In appointing a prime minister, and thus a government, the Queen must choose the person best placed to command the confidence of the House of Commons (generally, the leader of the party with a majority of seats), an essential link between monarchy and democracy. However, ministers cannot shelter behind the dignities and privileges of the Crown. Thus, a minister exercising powers conferred directly by statute is not to be treated as part of the Crown, since to do so, as Lord Templeman remarked in *M v Home Office* [1983] 3 All ER 537, 541, would undo the consequences of the Civil War. Similarly, in *R (Bancoult) v Secretary of State for the Foreign and Commonwealth Office* [2008] 4 All ER 1055, the House of Lords held that it had jurisdiction to review a Prerogative Order in Council since such an order was in reality made by ministers and not by the Crown itself.

The Queen is:

▶ head of state, and as such formally appoints ministers, bishops and most judges, and makes other senior public appointments;

▶ part of the legislature, albeit by convention with no substantive powers. Her formal consent is required for an Act of Parliament and she summons and dissolves Parliament. It has been settled since the Bill of Rights that, apart from a residue of special royal prerogative powers (Section 14.6), the monarch has no independent lawmaking powers;

▶ as the Crown, formal head of the executive for the UK, the devolved governments and dependent territories. In relation to each government, the Crown has traditionally been regarded as a separate entity (cf. Section 9.4);

▶ source of the authority of the judiciary, although since *Prohibitions del Roy* (1607) 12 Co Rep 64, it has been clear that the Queen cannot participate in or interfere with judicial proceedings;

▶ as the Crown, prosecutor of criminal offences. By statute, the independent Crown Prosecution Service carries out this role under the Director of Public Prosecutions, who is accountable to the Attorney General (Prosecution of Offences Act 1985);

- head of the Church of England;
- head of the armed forces;
- head of the Commonwealth, which is a loose association of former UK territories. The role has symbolic political importance but carries no legal powers.

Thus, although historically the source of all power was the Crown, a separation of powers has evolved according to which the Crown is mainly the executive arm of government.

The historical process of removing power from the monarch (Chapter 4) has left ambiguities and confusions concerning the legal nature of the Crown. There is no generally accepted view on this matter (see McLean (2004) 24 OJLS 129). It is not clear whether the Crown means:

- the Queen as an individual; or
- a corporate body with one member, namely the Queen – a corporation sole akin, for example, to a bishop. In *Calvin's Case* (1608) 7 Co Rep 1a, it was said that the Crown has two inseparable capacities, one being a 'natural' person, the other a mystical 'body politic' which is immortal (see also *Duchy of Lancaster Case* (1561) 75 ER 325, 327). Hence the maxim 'the monarch never dies';
- Neither the individual nor the corporation sole theory explains the modern principle that the Crown as the executive acts through ministers. However, the corporation sole theory seems to fit the Queen in her role as head of state, separating her from her private capacity;
- a kind of company together with ministers (corporation aggregate); see Maitland, 'The Crown as Corporation' (1901) 17 LQR 131, 140;
- or merely a 'brand name' with no legal identity as such. For example, for purposes of civil liability, the defendant is a designated government department (Section 14.5). Maitland ((1931) 418) regarded the Crown (as opposed to the monarch) as a fiction, a cover for ignorance; Munro (*Essays in Constitutional Law* (2nd edn, Butterworths 1999) 255) as a convenient abstraction.

In *Town Investments Ltd v Dept of the Environment* [1977] 1 All ER 813, the House of Lords disagreed as to the legal nature of the Crown. The question was whether an office lease taken by a minister, using the standard formula 'for and on behalf of Her Majesty', was vested in the minister or the Crown since, in the latter case, it would be immune from taxation. The House of Lords held that the lease was vested in the Crown. Lord Diplock thought that the Crown was a fiction, a legal shell overlaid by conventions. He seemed to favour the corporation sole model. Lord Simon of Glaisdale said that the expression 'the Crown' symbolises the powers of government that were formerly wielded by the wearer of the crown and reflects the historical development of the executive as that of offices hived off from the royal household. He stated that the legal concept best fitted to the contemporary situation was to consider the Crown as a corporation aggregate headed by the Queen and made up of 'the departments of state including ministers at their heads'. His Lordship attached two clarifications (the second of which may be questionable) (at 833): 'First the legal concept still does not correspond to the political reality. The Queen does not command those legally her servants. On the contrary she acts on the formally tendered collective advice of the Cabinet.' Second, 'when the Queen is referred to by the symbolic title of "Her Majesty" it is the whole corporation aggregate which is generally indicated. This distinction between "the Queen" and "Her Majesty" reflects the ancient distinction between "the King's two bodies", the "natural" and the "politic"'.

The 'corporate aggregate' explanation may be plausible, according to which the Crown is akin to a company acting through many members designated by the law, in this case, ministers (this explains not only why the Queen must act on the advice of ministers but also why the powers of the Crown are exercised automatically by ministers) (for a useful critical account see Weait and Lester, 'The Use of Ministerial Powers without Parliamentary Authority' [2003] PL 415).

Thus, it has been said that the powers of the Crown are 'channelled' through ministers, who for this purpose *are* the Crown (see *R v Secretary of State for Foreign Affairs, ex p Quark Fishing Ltd* [2006] 1

AC 529 at [12], [19], [78]–[79]). However, in *R (Bancoult) v Secretary of State for the Foreign and Commonwealth Office* [2008] QB 365 at [114], the Court of Appeal turned this on its head, suggesting that ministers govern through the instrumentality of the Crown, thereby making the Crown into a kind of tool (a power drill?), but reflecting the reality rather better. Thus, the Crown may be a redundant concept, mysticism obscuring political reality. On the other hand, in the absence of a legal notion of the state (Section 5.1), this is all we have.

Statutory powers are usually conferred directly on ministers, who cannot then claim to be acting on behalf of the Crown. In *M v Home Office* [1993], the Home Secretary attempted to rely on Crown immunity to deport an immigrant in defiance of a court order. The House of Lords held that he was liable in his official capacity for contempt of court. He was separate from the Crown and was not protected by any Crown immunity. In that case, Parliament had conferred the power in question directly upon the Secretary of State. Sometimes, however, statutory powers are conferred on the Crown as such (e.g. Bank of England Act 1998, s 1(2): appointment of Governor of Bank). Property is often vested in the Crown since not all government departments have their own legal personality.

If the monarchy were to be abolished, a different explanation would have to be found as to the basis of legal power. This could lead to a written constitution. Thus, even though the role of the monarch herself is relatively insignificant, the monarchy remains the keystone of the constitution.

14.2 Succession to the monarchy

Under the 1688 settlement, Parliament obtained the power to designate who shall be the monarch. The Act of Settlement is primarily concerned to ensure that Catholics are excluded from the monarchy. It provides that the Crown is to be held by the direct descendants of Princess Sophia (the granddaughter of the deposed James II). The monarch does not apparently have to be a British citizen. However, there are provisions designed to prevent a monarch dragging the country into foreign disputes. If the monarch is not 'a native of this kingdom of England', any war for the defence of a foreign country needs the consent of Parliament (s 3). The holder of the Crown must be, or become, a communicating member of the Church of England and must not be or marry a Catholic (s 3). Several members of the royal family have been excluded from the line of succession for this reason. Under the Royal Marriages Act 1772, a member of the British royal family directly descended from George II cannot marry without the consent of the monarch, subject, if over the age of 25, to an appeal to Parliament.

The rules of descent are based upon the medieval law governing succession to land, under which preference is given to males over females and to the older over the younger. The land law rules required sisters to hold land equally (co-parcenaries). However, in the case of the Crown, the firstborn prevails (although the matter has not been litigated).

The Act of Settlement 1700 might violate the HRA, being discriminatory in relation to sex, religion and the exercise of property rights (the succession being arguably a property right). However, the Succession to the Crown Act 2013 removes significant disqualifications. First, in the case of a person born after 28 October 2012, no preference must be given on gender grounds. Second, there is no longer disqualification for marriage to a Catholic. Third, the requirement of consent to marriage applies only to the first six in the line of succession. The succession was last altered when Edward VIII abdicated in 1936 and his brother, the next in line, succeeded (His Majesty's Declaration of Abdication Act 1936). It is not clear whether the monarch has the power to abdicate without an Act of Parliament. Since monarchy is a status conferred by law and without a voluntary act, the answer is probably not. The Crown's titles are also determined by statute (Royal Titles Act 1953).

When the monarch dies, the successor immediately and automatically becomes monarch. A special Accession Council, composed mainly of members of the House of Lords, proclaims the successor. This is confirmed by the Privy Council. Whether these bodies have a power of veto is unclear. One view is that the Accession Council reflects the mythical 'ancient constitution', according to which the monarch was appointed with the consent of the 'people'. The monarch is also required to swear a coronation oath of loyalty (Act of Settlement 1700), although the Coronation ceremony has no legal significance. It is not clear who resolves the question of a dispute to the succession. Possibly, it should be Parliament in its capacity as a court, or the Privy Council advising the putative monarch.

For succession to take place smoothly the demise (death) of the Crown does not affect the arrangements for the meeting of Parliament or an election unless the demise occurs between seven days before the date of the dissolution of Parliament and the date fixed for the election (Section 11.2). In these circumstances, the election is postponed for 14 days (Fixed Term Parliaments Act 2011, Sched.). If the monarch is a minor, ill or absent abroad, the royal functions are exercised by a regent, or councillors of state. These are the persons next in line to the throne (see Regency Acts 1937–53). In such cases certain bills cannot be assented to – most importantly a bill for altering the succession to the Crown.

14.3 Financing the monarchy

The official expenses of the monarchy and of those members of the royal family who perform public duties were traditionally funded from the Civil List in return for the monarch surrendering to Parliament the hereditary income from Crown property (the Crown Estate). The Civil List was an amount granted by Parliament at the beginning of each reign. Under the Sovereign Grant Act 2011, the Civil List is replaced by a more streamlined and transparent arrangement. This comprises a grant from the Treasury (£85.9 million for 2020–21) to cover the Queen's official duties: the Sovereign Grant. The amount of the grant is to be decided by the Royal Trustees according to a formula based on 25 per cent of the net surplus from the Crown Estate or the previous year's grant, whichever is the greater. There are provisions for the grant to be renewed six months after the end of each reign. There is also a reserve fund which, if used, is deducted from the next year's grant. Income from the Duchy of Cornwall, which is owned by the Prince of Wales, is also deducted. The revenues of the Crown Estate (a net profit of £343.5 million in 2018–19) are still surrendered to Parliament under the Civil List Act 1952. The accounts of the royal household are audited by the government and laid before Parliament.

Many of the royal expenses are funded directly by government departments, such as the upkeep of some Crown buildings, security, travel and entertaining political dignitaries. However, sections 11 and 13(8) of the 2011 Act clarify that the government is not responsible for the upkeep of the royal palaces. The Queen has considerable personal wealth, there being no clear line between this and assets derived from the monarchy as an institution. Even in her private capacity, the Queen is exempt from taxes unless statute specifically provides otherwise. However, the Queen has entered into a voluntary agreement to pay tax on current income and personal capital.

14.4 The functions of the monarch

The modern functions of the monarchy can be outlined as follows:

1. *to represent the nation*. For this purpose, the monarch participates in ceremonies and public entertainments. It is often said that the popularity and public acceptance of the monarchy is directly related to the fact that the monarch has little political power and is primarily an entertainer. It is not clear why a modern democracy requires a personalised 'leader'. There is a strong element of superstition inherent in the notion of monarchy, hence the importance of the link between the monarch and the Established Church;
2. *to 'advise, encourage and to warn'*. The monarch has access to all government documents and regularly meets the prime minister. The monarch is entitled to express views in private to the government, but there is no convention as to the weight to be given to them;
3. *certain formal acts*. These include:

    ▶ assent to statutes;
    ▶ Orders in Council made in the Privy Council (Section 5.7), which give effect to important decisions, laws under the royal prerogative and some statutory instruments regarded as especially important;

- appointments of ministers, ambassadors, bishops and judges;
- proclamations, for example dissolving and summoning Parliament or declaring a state of emergency (where the presence of the Privy Council is required);
- awarding peerages, honours and medals.

14.4.1 Personal powers of the monarch

Apart from the award of certain honours, by convention, the monarch must exercise all her powers on the advice of or through ministers. Until after the reign of George V (1910–34), monarchs occasionally intervened in connection with ministerial appointments and policy issues. The abdication of Edward VIII (1936) probably spelled the end of any political role for the monarch. However, it has been suggested that in certain special cases the monarch can, and indeed must, exercise personal power. There is little precedent and no principles as to whose advice she should take. Although the monarch must, as far as possible, avoid intervening in politics, as head of state, the monarchy is the ultimate guardian of the constitution and must intervene where the normal machinery of government has broken down. The most basic principle is that the government must retain the confidence of the House of Commons.

However, most of these special cases have depended on the monarch's ultimate power to dismiss the executive and dissolve Parliament, regarded by Montesquieu as an essential check and balance in the constitution (Section 7.1). This power has presently been suspended, by section 3(2) of the Fixed Term Parliaments Act 2011 (Section 11.2). The monarch might, however, retain some power in respect of the appointment of a prime minister (Section 15.2). She might also refuse to appoint peers to the House of Lords if the prime minister asked her to do so in order to flood the Lords with his supporters. However, the exercise of these powers ultimately depends on endorsement in a general election which, under the 2011 Act, only the House of Commons can bring about.

It has also been suggested that the royal assent to a bill might be refused. The monarch has not refused assent since 1707. However, the Queen might conceivably refuse assent where the refusal is on the advice of the prime minister, for example, in the unlikely event of a private member's bill being approved by Parliament against the wishes of the government. Here, two conventions clash. It is submitted that the better view is that she must still give assent because the will of Parliament has a higher constitutional status than that of the executive.

It has also been suggested that the Queen has a residual discretion to refuse assent to a statute that violates fundamental constitutional principles (see Twomey, 'The Refusal or Deferral of Royal Assent' [2006] PL 580; Blackburn, 'The Royal Assent to Legislation and the Monarch's Fundamental Human Rights' [2003] PL 205). This turns the monarchy into the equivalent of a Supreme Court, which seems implausible. However, the matter has not been tested.

There is an internal manual that sets out a controversial practice under which the consent of the Crown and the Duchy of Cornwall (which provides income to Prince Charles) is obtained in respect of any bill that affects their interests. A long list of bills has been published on which either the Queen or Prince Charles was consulted (*Guardian* 11 January 2013); see also *Guardian* 7 February 2021.

14.5 Crown immunities

The Crown has special privileges in litigation. The monarch cannot be made personally liable in any court. More importantly, at common law, no legal action would lie against the Crown in any of its capacities in respect of its property rights and contracts, or in respect of damage or injuries caused by the Crown (torts). This gap in the rule of law was avoided by the Crown's practice of voluntarily submitting to the jurisdiction of the courts. In the case of actions involving property and contract, this was through a procedure called a 'petition of right'. In the case of a tort, the individual Crown servant who committed the tort could be made liable and the Crown would pay the damages.

There is also the maxim 'the King can do no wrong'. This means that wrongdoing or bad faith cannot be attributed to the Crown. For example, at common law, the Crown could not be liable for wrongs committed by its employees because unlawful acts of its employees were necessarily committed without its authority. However, the maxim has never prevented the courts from deciding whether a particular action falls within the lawful powers of the Crown. Invalid acts as such are not wrongful acts (see *Dunlop v Woollahra Municipal Council* [1982] AC 158). Moreover, individual Crown officers can be accused of any kind of wrongdoing.

The Crown Proceedings Act 1947 subjected the Crown to legal liability, as if it were a private person, for breaches of contract, for the wrongs of its servants and for injuries caused by defective Crown property. Section 1 permits action for breach of contact against the Crown; section 2 permits action in tort but only where a private person would be liable in the same circumstances. However, the Act still leaves the Crown with several special privileges. The most important are as follows:

▶ No court order can be enforced against the Crown, so the claimant's right to damages depends upon the Crown voluntarily paying up. Similarly, no injunction lies against the Crown or against a Crown servant acting on behalf of the Crown (Crown Proceedings Act 1947, s 21). However, this applies only in civil law cases involving private rights. In judicial review cases where the legality of government action is in issue, and in cases involving the enforcement of EU law, ministers cannot claim Crown immunity (*M v Home Office* [1993]; *R v Secretary of State for Transport, ex p Factortame (No 2)* [1991] 1 AC 603).

▶ In an action for breach of contract, the Crown can plead 'executive necessity'. This means that it can refuse to comply with a contract where it has an overriding power to take some action in the public interest (*Amphitrite v The King* [1921] 3 KB 500; *Commissioners of Crown Lands v Page* [1960] 2 QB 274). Either there must be some definite prerogative power that overrides the contract, or the contract must conflict with a statutory duty. Governments cannot cancel contracts without compensation merely because of policy changes.

▶ The Crown is not liable in tort for the acts of its 'officers' unless the individual officer was appointed directly or indirectly by the Crown and paid wholly from central government funds (s 2(6)) (the term 'officer' includes all Crown servants and ministers).

▶ The Crown is not liable for wrongs committed by 'judicial' officers (s 2(5)), that is, judges or members of tribunals. A person exercising judicial functions also enjoys considerable personal immunity (Section 7.4).

▶ Until 1987, a member of the armed forces injured on duty by another member of the armed forces or while on military property could not sue the Crown if the injury was pensionable under military regulations (s 10). This caused injustice because it was irrelevant whether or not the victim actually qualified for a pension. The Crown Proceedings (Armed Forces) Act 1987 abolished this rule, but the Secretary of State can restore it in times of war or national emergency.

▶ The Crown is not bound by an Act of Parliament unless it expressly or by necessary implication binds the Crown. Necessary implication is a strict notion. It is not sufficient to show that the Crown is likely to cause unfairness and inconvenience or even that the exemption is against the public interest (*Lord Advocate v Dumbarton DC* [1990] 2 AC 580). It has to be established that the statute would be unworkable unless the Crown were bound (*Cooper v Hawkins* [1904] 2 KB 164: 2 mph speed limit for tractors did not bind the Crown). It is debatable whether the Crown can take the benefit of statutes where it is not bound by them. For example, the Crown can evict a tenant free of statutory restrictions, but could the Crown as a tenant resist eviction by a private landlord by relying on the same statutory rights that it can ignore as a landlord?

14.6 The royal prerogative

The royal prerogative comprises special powers, rights and immunities vested in the Crown at common law. Identifying each of these powers and their scope is problematic since there is no authoritative source. This uncertainty is a concern because as a matter of constitutional principle – in particular, the rule of law – those exercising power should be able to identify authority justifying its exercise. The prerogative can be explained historically as the residue of the special rights and powers conferred on the monarch by medieval common law. Some aspects might also be justified in Hobbesian terms (Section 2.3.1) on the basis that a residue of discretionary power is always needed to protect the community against unexpected dangers.

Lord Denning in *Laker Airways Ltd v Dept of Trade* [1977] QB 643 considered that the Crown had a general discretionary power to act for the public good in certain spheres of governmental activity for which the law had otherwise made no provision. This interpretation is, however, inconsistent with the rule of law as famously invoked in *Entick v Carrington* (1765) 19 St Tr 1029. Here, the court emphatically rejected a claim of 'executive necessity' that officers of the state had a general power to enter and search private property. The better view is that, although the Crown has certain discretionary powers in relation to emergencies, such as the requisitioning of property, the prerogative comprises a finite number of miscellaneous powers, rather than one general power to act for the public good.

Some prerogative powers were based upon the position of the monarch as chief landowner within the medieval feudal system. Others are inherent in the notion of sovereignty, derived from the responsibility of the monarch to keep the peace and defend the realm. This duality may have corresponded to the distinction drawn in seventeenth-century cases between the 'ordinary' and the 'absolute' prerogatives, the latter being discretionary powers vested in the king and arguably beyond the reach of the courts.

From the sixteenth century, theories of absolute monarchy became dominant in Europe but were less influential in England. Thus, in 1611 it was made clear that the king could legislate only within areas of prerogative allowed to him by the existing law (*Case of Proclamations* (1611) 12 Co Rep 74). The debate therefore shifted to exploring the limits of the prerogative. The Stuarts attempted to extend the prerogative and to impose taxes, imprison without trial and override the ordinary law. However, even they submitted themselves to the courts and, in a series of famous cases punctuating the political conflicts of the time, the scope of the prerogative was inconclusively argued (Section 4.5). An issue pervading these cases was whether the king or the court decides whether the state of affairs exists that triggers the prerogative power, for example an emergency. This issue has echoes even today (e.g. *Nissan v A-G* [1970] AC 179; Section 9.6.3.3). The outcome was revolution culminating in the 1688 settlement (which provides the framework of the modern law). This can be summarised as follows:

▶ In principle, the royal prerogative remains but must give way to statute where this covers the same subject matter (*A-G v De Keyser's Royal Hotel Ltd* [1920] AC 508) (Section 14.6.5).
▶ No new prerogatives can be created (*BBC v Johns (Inspector of Taxes)* [1965] Ch 32). However, old prerogatives can be extended to apply to new circumstances provided that their basic function remains the same (e.g. *Malone v MPC* [1979] Ch 344: interception of mail extended to telephone tapping (Section 25.3)). The prerogative can be controlled by the courts through judicial review, although the extent of such control depends upon the type of prerogative power in question and the context (Section 14.6.4).
▶ The Bill of Rights 1688 outlawed certain aspects of the prerogative, including the power to suspend laws without parliamentary consent. The Bill of Rights also banned taxation under the royal prerogative. Modern judges have taken this further by refusing to imply a power to raise money in any way unless clear statutory language is used (see *A-G v Wilts United Dairies* (1921) 37 TLR 884: tax on milk; *Congreve v Home Office* [1976] QB 629: increase in TV licence fee; *McCarthy & Stone (Developments) Ltd v Richmond upon Thames LBC* [1991] 4 All ER 897: charge for giving advice).

14.6.1 The scope of modern prerogative powers

There is no authoritative list of prerogative powers. Only the courts or Parliament can determine the scope of the prerogative. Prerogatives embrace a variety of subjects, most of the important ones concerning foreign affairs.

The main prerogative powers are as follows. (Those marked * are traditionally performed by the Queen personally, usually on the advice of ministers and sometimes in the Privy Council. Others are exercised directly by ministers.) Many domestic prerogative powers have been wholly or partly superseded by statute (Section 14.6.5).

In relation to domestic affairs:

▶ the appointment and dismissal of ministers;*
▶ the summoning, prorogation and dissolution of Parliament* (the latter superseded by statute (Section 11.2));
▶ royal assent to bills;*
▶ grant of peerages, honours and titles* (some being in the Queen's personal gift);
▶ the appointment and regulation of the civil service. A general framework for the civil service was enacted by the Constitutional Reform and Governance Act 2010 (Section 15.8);
▶ the commissioning of officers in the armed forces;
▶ security:
  (i) the Crown has a residual power to keep the peace within the realm, for example by deploying the military or issuing the police with weapons (*R v Secretary of State for the Home Dept, ex p Northumbria Police Authority* [1989] QB 26; *Chandler v DPP* [1964] AC 763). In relation to emergencies, the prerogative has largely been superseded by statute (see Section 25.4);
  (ii) to control entry to the UK (*A-G for Canada v Cain* [1906] AC 542). Recognised as one of the oldest powers of a sovereign state, this has mainly been superseded by statute but may still apply in wartime (see *R (Alvi) v Secretary of State for the Home Dept* [2012] 1 WLR 2208 at [27]–[31]; Section 14.6.5).
▶ the appointment of Queen's Counsel (senior barristers);
▶ the prerogative of mercy: releasing convicted persons from punishment (Section 7.5.3);
▶ the granting by the Privy Council of a royal charter to bodies such as universities, learned societies, charities or professional associations that gives the body the status of a legal person and signifies state approval of its activities (see e.g. Section 23.3.2). A royal charter cannot confer powers other than those possessed by private persons;
▶ the regulation of charities; mainly superseded by statute;
▶ the care of the vulnerable: children and the mentally ill; superseded by statute;
▶ the Attorney General's power to institute legal proceedings in the public interest and to stop criminal proceedings.

In relation to foreign affairs:

▶ the making of treaties;
▶ the declaration of war (formal declarations of war are not currently made);
▶ the deployment of the armed forces on operations overseas;
▶ the recognition of foreign states;
▶ the accreditation and reception of diplomats;
▶ the governance of some overseas territories;
▶ the granting and revoking of passports.

Finally, there are prerogatives based on feudal landholding. The most important of these are the Crown's ownership of the seashore and tidal waters, rights to *bona vacantia*, that is, property without any other owner, and rights over certain living creatures, notably swans.

14.6.2 Two kinds of prerogative power?

There is ambiguity as to what a prerogative power is. Blackstone (1723–80) regarded the prerogative as confined to the special powers which the king enjoys alone in contradistinction to others and not to those which he enjoys in common with any of his subjects (*Commentaries on the Laws of England* (1st edn, 1765–69) 111). However, Dicey ((1915) 282–3) described the prerogative as including all the non-statutory powers of the Crown, including the 'private law' powers of ownership, employment, contracting and so on apparently possessed by the Crown as a legal person in common with everyone else. These are sometimes called 'ordinary' powers, sometimes 'third source' powers or 'residual' powers (e.g. *Shrewsbury and Atcham BC v Secretary of State* [2008] 3 All ER 548).

Blackstone's distinction seems unreal in as much as all Crown powers are important politically and in the way they are exercised they are indistinguishable from powers that Blackstone would regard as genuine examples of the prerogative. For example, the Crown has enormous economic power (sometimes called *dominium* power); a defence contract or health service contract made with the Crown could affect the livelihoods of millions. The Crown may be a property owner in common with others, but its economic and political power surely puts it in a special position and calls for additional controls. There is much to be said for Dicey's view and for treating all common law powers alike. It is true that the residual powers cannot directly violate individual rights, but they can nevertheless have serious consequences, for example in terms of livelihood or reputation (e.g. *R v Secretary of State for Health, ex p C* [2000] 1 FCR 471: creating a sex offenders register).

The cases conflict. In *Council of Civil Service Unions (CCSU) v Minister for the Civil Service* [1985] AC 374 (*CCSU*; also known as the 'GCHQ case') the House of Lords treated control of the civil service as part of the royal prerogative, holding that it could review the validity of an Order in Council varying the terms of employment of certain civil servants. Lord Diplock thought that the distinction between special and ordinary powers of the Crown is artificial and that all common law powers of the Crown are prerogative powers. In *R v Criminal Injuries Compensation Board, ex p Lain* [1967] 2 QB 864, a government scheme to pay compensation to the victims of crime was treated as prerogative, thus enabling the court to review errors of law made by the board running the scheme. The scheme was financed out of money provided by Parliament but was not statutory. Since anyone can give away money, this scheme would not count as royal prerogative under the Blackstone definition. However, in *A-G v De Keyser's Royal Hotel Ltd* [1920], Lord Parmoor favoured Blackstone, so the matter remains unsettled. Since both types of power can be reviewed, the question may be an academic one with no practical consequences and attention should focus on the particular power in issue (e.g. *R (Sandiford) v Secretary of State for Foreign and Commonwealth Affairs* [2014] 4 All ER 843).

14.6.3   Political control over the prerogative

Most prerogative powers are exercised by ministers. These powers include some that are among the most significant powers possessed by any government, for example a decision to deploy troops, and the power to make a treaty. The constitutional problem concerns a lack of democratic control over officials claiming to act under the prerogative. As common law powers, prerogative powers do not need to be approved by Parliament, so there is a gap in democratic accountability. Decisions taken under the prerogative are essentially decrees with no formal accountability other than the limited possibility of judicial review.

The absence of any statutory requirement for parliamentary approval thus raises profound questions in a modern democracy (see Public Administration Committee, *Taming the Prerogative* (HC 2003–04) 422). The UK Constitution is perhaps unique in allowing government such extensive and imprecise powers that are not granted by the legislature. In some cases, however, the exercise of a prerogative power must be confirmed by statute. These cases include treaties that alter the existing law and certain EU treaties (Section 9.5.3). Under the Constitutional Reform and Governance Act 2010 a treaty has to be laid before Parliament before ratification, although Parliament cannot prevent ratification under this procedure (Section 9.5.3).

There is also an emerging convention that a decision to deploy the armed forces must be approved by Parliament. However, the scope of this is unclear. For example, does it apply to the deployment of troops in a peacekeeping role as opposed to armed conflict? What about emergencies? This convention emerged only after the government decision for a full-scale invasion of Iraq was supported by the House of Commons in March 2003 (on the basis of false information provided by the then prime minister). Since then, the Commons has voted to support a decision to assist rebel forces in Libya (2011), and the government accepted a vote not to do so in Syria (2013), interpreting that as applying to all armed intervention in that country. The new convention is acknowledged in the *Cabinet Manual* (2011), at [5.38].

Some parliamentary control is possible over the prerogative, first because all government functions depend on money which must be authorised by Parliament, and second through the doctrine of ministerial responsibility, although this may be after the event. These methods of control are weak since Parliament has insufficient resources adequately to investigate government spending, and there is, in any case, normally an automatic majority for the executive. Moreover, government spending is usually authorised by a blanket departmental allocation or met out of a general contingency fund or a retrospective vote. Although conventionally ministers are responsible to Parliament, at least one prime minister has expressed the view that 'it is for individual Ministers to decide on a particular occasion whether and how to report to Parliament on the exercise of prerogative powers' (HC Deb 1 March 1993, vol 220, col 19W).

By convention, the prime minister cannot be questioned about advice given to the sovereign concerning certain prerogative powers, such as the granting of honours and appointments, and the dissolution of Parliament (the latter now being governed by the Fixed Term Parliaments Act 2011). The reason is that these powers are exercised personally by the monarch, even though the monarch must usually act on the advice of the prime minister. In addition, ministers sometimes refuse to be questioned about prerogative powers relating to foreign relationships, national security matters and the prerogative of mercy. However, Parliament, if it wished, could insist on investigating these. Whether their exclusion is justifiable upon any basis other than the mystique that has traditionally attached to the prerogative is debatable. They involve wide discretionary powers, but that in itself could be an argument for, rather than against, political accountability.

14.6.4   Judicial control

The courts have developed sophisticated rules for judicial review of the exercise of statutory powers (Chapters 17–19). These do not (at least in theory) entitle the courts to make the government's decisions for it but are designed to ensure that government keeps within the limits of its powers and complies with basic standards of fairness, reasonableness and relevance. Is there any reason why the same should not apply to the prerogative?

Historically, the courts exercised only limited control over the prerogative. If a prerogative power was disputed, a court could determine whether it existed and, if it did, what it empowered the executive to do, but the monarch was the only judge of how to exercise the power. For example, in the *Saltpetre Case* (1607) 12 Co Rep 12, the king had the power in an emergency to enter private land and was held to be the sole judge of both whether an emergency existed, and what measures to take. Accordingly, before the speeches in the House of Lords in *Council of Civil Service Unions (CCSU) v Minister for the Civil Service* [1985], it was assumed that the courts could determine the existence and limits of a prerogative power, but could not interfere with how it was exercised.

However, in *CCSU*, the House of Lords held that decisions made under prerogative powers are in principle reviewable on the same basis as decisions made under a statutory power. But this does not mean that this jurisdiction will always be exercised. The power must be of a 'justiciable' nature, which means that it must be suitable for the courts' scrutiny. This is no longer resolved by looking at the source of the power (statute or prerogative), but at its subject matter and its suitability in the context of the facts of the case, the particular grounds of review, and the political role, expertise and knowledge appropriate to the court. In many cases, these factors apply to prerogative powers. In *CCSU*, Lord Roskill listed prerogative powers he regarded as wholly non-justiciable because their nature or subject matter was not amenable to the judicial process. These included the making of treaties, defence, the prerogative of mercy, the grant of honours, the dissolution of Parliament and the appointment of ministers.

Lord Roskill's list has not fully stood the test of time. The prerogative of mercy has been held to be reviewable (*R v Secretary of State for the Home Dept, ex p Bentley* [1993] 4 All ER 442; *A-G of Trinidad and Tobago v Lennox Phillip* [1995] 1 All ER 93). The power to make Orders in Council governing a dependent territory is reviewable, as is the prerogative power to assent to a law enacted by the Sark Parliament

(R (Bancoult) v Secretary of State (No 2) [2008]; *R (Barclay) v Secretary of State for Justice* [2014] 3 WLR 1142 (Section 9.6)). The power to issue a passport is reviewable because it is an administrative decision affecting the right of individuals as opposed to a matter of 'high policy' (*R v Secretary of State for Foreign and Commonwealth Affairs, ex p Everett* [1989] 1 All ER 655).

In *R (Miller) v the Prime Minister* [2019[UKSC 41, the Supreme Court determined that the prerogative power to prorogue Parliament (which is to be distinguished from dissolution, see Section 11.2) could be reviewed. The Court interpreted the question which it had to determine not as one concerning the *manner* in which a prerogative power was exercised, but rather the *extent* of the power, specifically where 'the boundary between the prerogative on the one hand and the operation of the constitutional principles of the sovereignty of Parliament and responsible government on the other hand' lay (at [52]). The Prime Minister's decision to prorogue was therefore justiciable.

Justiciability will be considered in greater detail in the context of judicial review generally (Section 19.7.1). In summary, in cases involving high policy decisions, especially those relating to foreign affairs, or where there is a wide political discretion, judicial review is likely to be excluded. The threshold of successful challenge is likely to be high. At the other extreme, a more intensive standard of review is likely in respect of routine administrative decisions (*R v Secretary of State for Foreign Affairs, ex p Everett* [1989]: passports).

> Other prerogative powers have been held to be reviewable. These include the powers to make ex gratia payments to the victims of crime (*R v Criminal Injuries Compensation Board, ex p P* [1995] 1 All ER 870), to compensate farmers affected by the foot and mouth epidemic (*National Farmers Union v Secretary of State for the Environment, Food and Rural Affairs* [2003] EWHC 444 (Admin)), to issue warrants for telephone tapping (*R v Secretary of State for the Home Dept, ex p Ruddock* [1987] 2 All ER 518) and to adopt a policy of discharging gay men from the armed services (*R v Ministry of Defence, ex p Smith* [1996] QB 517). In *R (Sandiford) v Secretary of State for Foreign and Commonwealth Affairs* [2014], the Supreme Court held that the rule against 'fettering discretion' does not apply to prerogative powers (Section 17.6.3).

14.6.5 Prerogative and statute

Since Parliament is sovereign, statute can abolish a prerogative power. How easily can this be achieved in the light of the courts' approach to interpretation? Express words or necessary implication certainly do so. Problems arise where Parliament has enacted statutory provisions dealing with the same subject matter as the prerogative without clearly abolishing the prerogative powers. Where an area of governmental activity is subject to both a statutory and a prerogative power, the statutory power may supersede the prerogative power. Whether or not it does so is a matter of interpretation of the statute. It depends first on whether the statute is intended to bind the Crown (Section 14.5) and second on whether the statute is intended to replace the prerogative.

There is uncertainty as to when the statute is regarded as prevailing. In *A-G v De Keyser's Royal Hotel Ltd* [1920], the House of Lords took a wide view. It was held that, where a statute comprehensively covers the same ground as a prerogative power, the prerogative power cannot be exercised. The Crown took possession of the hotel ostensibly under a statute that conferred a right to compensation. It was nevertheless argued that the Crown had a prerogative power to take possession of land during an emergency and that no compensation was payable under this prerogative power. The House of Lords upheld the property owner's claim, holding that the occupation of the hotel had taken place under statutory powers. The prerogative had been superseded by a comprehensive statute regulating this field of governmental activity and it would be meaningless for the legislature to have imposed limitations on the exercise of governmental power if these could merely be bypassed under the prerogative.

However, in *R v Secretary of State for the Home Dept, ex parte Northumbria Police Authority* [1989] QB 26, the prerogative was not overridden. The Court of Appeal held that the Home Secretary could use the prerogative power to keep the peace to supply the police with weapons even though statute gave local authorities the power to provide the police with resources. The Court said that the prerogative power was overridden only when its exercise was actually inconsistent with a statutory power (see at 44, 45).

On this basis, *De Keyser's* could be regarded as an example of inconsistency (the statute provided a right to compensation, the prerogative did not). On the other hand, in support of the wide view, *Northumbria* can be explained as one where the statute did not intend to provide a comprehensive regime. It is also plausible that the decision in *Northumbria* was simply incorrect (Vincenzi (1998) 121).

The decisions of the Supreme Court in *R (Munir) v Secretary of State for the Home Dept* [2012] 1 WLR 2192, [23]–[26] and *R (Alvi) v Secretary of State for the Home Dept* [2012] 1 WLR 2208 seem to support the wide view. It was held that, despite a provision which appeared to preserve the prerogative, the Immigration Act 1971 has created a comprehensive regime governing immigration so that prerogative powers no longer apply except possibly in wartime. (The government had failed to lay statutory rules before Parliament as the Act required.)

However, dicta of Lord Hope (with whom the others agreed) in *Alvi*, at [28], are ambivalent. Consistent with the wide view, Lord Hope said: 'Where a complete and exhaustive power is to be found in the statute, any powers under the prerogative which would otherwise have applied are excluded entirely.' However, he went on to say: '[A]ny exercise of a prerogative power in a manner or for a purpose inconsistent with the statute will be an abuse of power'.

In any case, prerogative power must not be exercised in a manner that, in substance, conflicts with the intention of Parliament. In *R v Secretary of State for the Home Dept, ex p Fire Brigades Union* [1995], the Secretary of State had power to make a commencement order bringing into force legislation intended to establish a particular regime for compensation for victims of crime. It was held that he could not refuse to bring the statute into effect with a view to establishing an alternative scheme under the prerogative. However, as their Lordships remarked, the case is not strictly an example of a conflict between statute and prerogative. The statute was not yet in force, and the gist of their Lordships' reasoning was that, by committing himself to the prerogative scheme, the minister had disabled himself from bringing the statute into force (see also *Laker Airways Ltd v Dept of Trade* [1977]: inconsistency).

A curious example of the relationship between statute and prerogative, Section 33(5) of the Immigration Act 1971, provides: 'This Act shall not be taken to supersede or impair any power exercisable by Her Majesty in relation to aliens by virtue of her prerogative'. If so, there is no right of appeal and the courts' more limited powers of judicial review provide the only remedy. There is a basic right to a hearing (see *IR (Sri Lanka) v Secretary of State for the Home Dept* [2011] 4 All ER 908).

In *R (G) v Secretary of State for the Home Dept* [2012] 1 All ER 1129, the prerogative power was used to exclude an anti-Israeli agitator (following revocation of the claimant's citizenship under statute). However, the decision seems doubtful. In *R (Alvi) v Secretary of State for the Home Dept* [2012], Lord Hope suggested that, in the light of contemporary human rights standards that require clear legal procedures, the prerogative power no longer has any practical effect. In *R (Munir) v Secretary of State for the Home Dept* [2012], at [25]–[26], the Supreme Court suggested (obiter) that the prerogative power was confined to times of war.

It has been argued that the common law powers which the Crown shares with ordinary people (Section 14.6.2) can be extinguished only by clear statutory language (*R (Hooper) v Secretary of State for Work and Pensions* [2006] 1 All ER 487 at [46]–[47], but leaving the point open; cf. *Shrewsbury and Atcham BC v Secretary of State* [2008], suggesting the wider approach).

It is not clear whether repeal of the statute revives the prerogative power. In other words, is the prerogative power abolished or merely suspended while the Act is in force? (See *A-G v De Keyser's Royal Hotel Ltd* (above) at 539; *Burmah Oil Co v Lord Advocate* [1965] AC 75, at 143; *R (Munir) v Secretary of State for the Home Dept* [2012], at [33].) The point has not so far arisen. It seems to depend on the intention of the particular statute (see Section 11.2 for a contemporary example).

14.6.6   Reform of the prerogative

It has often been suggested that prerogative powers should be put on a fully statutory basis. On the whole, however, the government apparently prefers to leave reform of the prerogative to the traditional evolutionary constitutional process. It stated in 2009 (Ministry of Justice, *Review of the Executive Royal Prerogative Powers: Final Report*, at [111]–[12]):

> Some of the remaining prerogative powers could be candidates for abolition or reform, but their continued existence has – at the minimum – no significant negative effects. In many cases it is positively useful… The government has concluded that it is unnecessary, and would be inappropriate, to propose further major reform at present. Our constitution has developed organically over many centuries and change should not be proposed for change's sake. Without ruling out further changes aimed at increasing parliamentary oversight of the prerogative powers exercised by ministers, the government believes that any further reforms in this area should be considered on a case-by-case basis, in the light of changing circumstances.

This position is not difficult to understand given the flexibility which these powers confer upon ministers, and their relative lack of accountability.

The main reforms that have been proposed included increasing parliamentary oversight of treaties, the management of the civil service, war powers and reform of the office of Attorney General. Only the first two have been implemented (Sections 9.5.3 and 15.8); the Fixed Term Parliaments Act 2011 also places dissolution of Parliament on a statutory footing (see Section 11.2). The Public Administration Committee (Section 14.6.3) took the view that some prerogative powers, for example a power to press men into the navy, may have lapsed through disuse. Similarly, the ancient writ of *ne exeat regno*, which prevents persons from leaving the country, is sometimes regarded as obsolete. However, there is no doctrine of obsolescence in English law.

Summary

- In this chapter, we first discussed the meaning of the term 'Crown'. The Queen as head of state, the monarchy, must be distinguished from the Crown as the executive. The legal nature of the Crown is unclear, but the dominant view is that the Crown is analogous to a company (corporation aggregate), its members being ministers. Ministers exercise the powers of the Crown directly.

- Succession to the monarchy depends on statute, thus reinforcing the subordinate nature of the monarchy.

- The monarch has certain personal political powers which should be exercised in times of constitutional crisis. These include the appointment of a prime minister, the dissolution of Parliament and the appointment of peers.

- At common law, the Crown was immune from legal action. Some of this immunity has been reduced by the Crown Proceedings Act 1947, but the Crown is still immune from enforcement and has certain special defences. There is, however, no general doctrine of state necessity as justifying interference with private rights. Certain acts of the Crown give rise to immunity from legal liability.

Summary cont'd

▶ The Crown's executive powers derive from three sources:

(i) statutes;

(ii) the royal prerogative, that is, the residue of special common law powers peculiar to the monarch;

(iii) powers possessed by virtue of the fact that the Crown is a legal person with basically the same rights and duties as any adult human being. The Crown can therefore make contracts, own property, distribute money and so on. There is a dispute as to whether this kind of power is part of the royal prerogative.

▶ No new prerogative powers can be created.

▶ Prerogative powers can be reviewed by the courts unless they concern a 'non-justiciable' subject matter or issues such as foreign relationships.

▶ While prerogative powers are subject to some parliamentary scrutiny, in practice, political control over prerogative power is limited.

▶ The prerogative must give way to statute, although the precise scope and extent of this is unclear. The matter depends on the interpretation of the particular statute.

Exercises

14.1 Compare the royal prerogative with parliamentary privilege (Chapter 11) with reference to (i) its purposes, (ii) its history and sources and (iii) the extent to which it can be controlled by the courts.

14.2 Which analysis of the nature of the Crown best fits the law?

14.3 'The UK has a constitutional monarchy.' Explain and critically discuss.

14.4 For all practical purposes, the Crown is represented by the government of the day (Sir Robert Armstrong, former Cabinet Secretary). Is this a correct statement of the law?

14.5 To what extent are royal prerogative powers subject to control by Parliament?

14.6 The Railways (Suspicious Persons) Act 2021 (imaginary) gives the operators of railway stations in the UK power to remove any person from any railway premises in the UK. The Home Secretary requests Network Rail, which operates many railway stations, to ban all photographers from railway premises in the interests of 'national security'. Network Rail refuses to do so. The Home Secretary seeks your advice as to whether she can use powers under the royal prerogative to impose such a ban. Advise her.

14.7 Advise the Queen in the following cases:

(i) There has just been a general election in the UK. The existing government has obtained the largest number of seats in the Commons but without an overall majority. The Opposition is negotiating with a minority party to form a government. The prime minister refuses to resign.

(ii) What would be the position if the Opposition had obtained the largest number of seats in the Commons and the government was negotiating with the minority party?

(iii) The government is defeated in a vote on the annual Finance Act. The prime minister refuses to resign.

(iv) The prime minister has just been sacked as party leader. However, due to an agreement with the Opposition and a minority party, she could still command a small majority in the Commons.

14.8 The Queen's birthday honours list has just been published. It includes ten knighthoods for retiring senior civil servants whose careers have included no recorded achievements and three of whom are related to the chair of the Honours Committee (a civil servant). There were no honours for the winners of gold medals in the recent Olympic Games. A spokesperson for the Honours Committee explains to the press that 'the athletes were just doing their jobs'. Discuss whether there are any methods of challenging these awards.

Further reading

Blackburn, 'Queen Elizabeth II and the Evolution of the Monarchy' in Qvortrup (ed), *The British Constitution: Continuity and Change* (Hart Publishing 2013)

Bogdanor, *The Monarchy and the Constitution* (Clarendon Press 1995)

Craig, 'The Supreme Court, Prorogation and Constitutional Principle' [2020] PL 248

Hameed, 'The Monarchy and Politics' [2016] PL 401

Harris, 'The Third Source of Authority for Government Action Revisited' (2007) 123 LQR 225

Loughlin, *Foundations of Public Law* (Oxford University Press 2010) ch 13

Maitland, *The Constitutional History of England* (Cambridge University Press 1931)

Ministry of Justice, *The Governance of Britain: Review of the Executive Royal Prerogative Powers* (Ministry of Justice 2009)

Public Administration Committee, *Taming the Prerogative: Strengthening Ministerial Accountability to Parliament* (HC 2003–04, 422)

Sunkin and Payne (eds), *The Nature of the Crown: A Legal and Political Analysis* (Clarendon Press 1999)

Tomkins, *Public Law* (Clarendon Press 2003) ch 3

Twomey, 'Challenging the Rules of Succession to the Throne' [2011] PL 378

Vincenzi, *Crown Powers, Subjects, Citizens* (Pinter 1998)

Chapter 15

Ministers and departments

15.1 Introduction

This chapter concerns one of the central issues of the constitution, namely the accountability of the executive branch of government. We shall be concerned with conventions, more than with law in the strict sense. The structure and powers of the central executive depend on powers being channelled from Parliament and the Crown, usually to ministers, and upon the general principle, which combines law and convention, that ministers can exercise power through civil servants. The *Ministerial Code* (most recent edition, 2019), issued by the Cabinet Office, provides a general framework for the conduct of ministers. The *Code* is not legally binding and so cannot be enforced by the courts (*R (Hemming) v Prime Minister* 2006] EWHC 2831 (Admin)). Nor is it a convention, although it contains statements of conventions. It is ultimately enforced only by the prime minister through the power to appoint and dismiss ministers.

There are few legal controls over the organisation of government departments or the relationship between ministers, civil servants and Parliament. A major problem is the absence of clear rules regulating the relationship between individual government departments. The size and structure of the executive have not normally been regarded as a matter of constitutional significance, although it is, of course, central to the role of government. The most important matters are governed by convention. The Constitutional Reform and Governance Act 2010 has finally given statutory effect to the basic principles of the civil service but without changes of substance. Some general principles are published in the *Ministerial Code* and the *Civil Service Code* (2015). Unlike the *Ministerial Code*, the *Civil Service Code* is arguably statutory and may therefore be enforceable in the courts.

The relationship between ministers, civil servants and Parliament is governed by the conventions of collective and individual ministerial responsibility, but there is no consensus as to what precisely these conventions mean, and no method of enforcing them other than by Parliament itself. It is widely accepted that Parliament is dominated by the executive. This is the result of our incomplete separation of powers where all ministers are members of Parliament and, under parliamentary rules, in a position to dominate parliamentary business (Section 13.1). Apart from the tribalism inherent in political culture, MPs depend on the approval of their party leaders for advancement. Moreover, under the convention of collective ministerial responsibility, MPs who are government ministers must support the government or resign. Approximately 100 MPs out of a total of 650 in the Commons are ministers.

The abuse of executive dominance was remarked upon by Lord Bingham, at [41], and Lord Steyn, at [71], in *Jackson v A-G* [2006] 1 AC 262. Lord Bingham thought that this was outside the concerns of the courts. Lord Steyn was more equivocal (Section 8.5.6). In the same case Lord Hope, at [125], relied on the characteristic British evasion that the constitution depends on 'mutual respect' between the institutions of government.

However, executive domination must not be overstated, since there are provisions enabling Parliament, if it so wishes, to control the executive and much depends on shifting political factors such as the size of electoral majorities, and the public support enjoyed by the ruling group (Section 11.1; see also *R (HS2 Action Alliance Ltd) v Secretary of State* [2014] 1 WLR 324 (Section 11.6.3), where the Supreme Court accepted that objective examination was possible in Parliament).

15.2 Appointment of the prime minister

The role of the prime minister, an office which dates from the eighteenth century, was originally that of acting as an intermediary between the monarch and the government, and chairing the Cabinet. The main principles relating to the office are matters of convention. Today, the powers and influence of the prime minister have enormously increased, so that the office-holder is effectively head of the government and perhaps eclipses the Cabinet (below) as a policymaker.

The prime minister is appointed by the Queen subject to the following conventions. These are somewhat vague (although they are now set out in a written, non-legally binding form in the *Cabinet Manual* (2011)):

▶ The prime minister must be a member and have the confidence of the House of Commons. The size of the popular vote is constitutionally irrelevant. As far as possible, the Queen must take no initiative and must not influence the choice of prime minister. The monarch normally acts on the advice of the outgoing prime minister who, of course, must follow the above convention.

▶ The prime minister is therefore usually the leader of the political party with the largest number of seats in the Commons. In the case of a 'hung Parliament', where no single party has a majority, a leader might gain the support of the Commons by forming a coalition between two or more parties, as was the case between 2010 and 2015 with the Conservative and Liberal Democrat parties. Alternatively, a minority government might be possible with the looser support of other parties as a 'confidence and supply' arrangement, under which the minority party agrees to sustain the government but can differ on other matters. There were minority governments in 1974, 1977–79, 1996–97, and 2017–19.

▶ The usual process is as follows: if the existing government wins the election, the incumbent prime minister continues in office, or if not, the existing prime minister approaches the Queen, offers his or her resignation and advises her as to the succession. In cases where there is no general election but where the office becomes vacant owing to resignation (such as that of David Cameron in 2016 and Theresa May in 2019), an internal party leadership election process will determine the successor.

▶ The Queen then requests the successor to form a government. If there is no clear-cut successor, it appears that the existing prime minister has the first right to try to form a government (*Cabinet Manual* [2.12]). Failing this, informal discussions between political leaders, advised by civil servants if necessary (in which case the approval of the Cabinet Secretary, authorised by the incumbent prime minister, must be obtained: *Cabinet Manual* [2.14]), seem to be the only mechanism for gauging Parliament's support. It is a fundamental principle that the Queen should be kept out of politics and that there must be continuity of government. So, if a new prime minister cannot be found, the former prime minister will continue in office. However, if the new or existing prime minister is defeated on a vote of confidence in the Commons then, unless by the end of 14 days there is a vote of confidence in a new government, Parliament must be dissolved and a new election called (Fixed Term Parliaments Act 2011; Section 11.2). This could be indefinitely repeated.

After an election, a new Parliament meets on the date already fixed by proclamation, although the meeting could be prorogued (postponed) under the royal prerogative. There is no formal timetable for forming a government, although the practice is to act quickly. Where there is a clear election winner, any change of government is dramatically quick, taking place immediately after the election results are known. In 2010, when there was no overall majority, the process took five days.

15.3 The powers of the prime minister

The powers of the prime minister are mainly derived from convention. Whether the prime minister can exercise dominant power therefore depends on the political forces of the day, and not least the personalities involved. Powers are also scattered in statute, custom and practice, royal prerogatives and 'nods and winks' derived from the British culture of sycophancy. The prime minister exercises the most important prerogative powers. Apart from political powers (below), these include overall responsibility for security, control of the civil service and the mobilisation of the armed forces. The prime minister also has statutory powers in sensitive political areas (e.g. Police Act 1997, s 9; Intelligence Services Act 1994, s 2; National Minimum Wages Act 1998; National Audit Act 1983, s 1). In recent years, prime ministers have also assumed control over foreign policy, which has the attraction of providing opportunities for self-promotion without the chore of detailed administration. The main conventions are as follows:

▶ The prime minister appoints and dismisses all government ministers and determines their status and pecking order. S/he also has powers of appointment in relation to many other important public posts (a mixture of statute and convention).
▶ The prime minister controls the Cabinet agenda, formulates its decisions and allocates government business. In this way, Cabinet discussion can be bypassed and matters entrusted to selected prime ministerial supporters, smaller groups of ministers or advisers; or indeed anyone, since there are no controls over a prime minister taking advice. Ministers' energies are centred upon their own departmental interests. Few have the time or knowledge to concentrate upon issues outside their departmental concerns.
▶ Except for the unlikely event of intervention by the monarch, impeachment by Parliament or removal by his or her party under its rules, there is no formal machinery to get rid of a prime minister. A vote of no confidence in the House of Commons can only bring down the government as a whole.
▶ The prime minister is head of the internal security services.
▶ The prime minister is the channel of communication between Queen and government.
▶ The prime minister is the main spokesperson for the nation and in many contexts, such as international meetings, acts on behalf of the head of state. As such s/he has unique access to the media. The prime minister's press office holds a key position. There is a danger that, in terms of public perception, the prime minister is perceived as a head of state, thereby eclipsing the monarchy.

There are limited checks and balances that prevent the prime minister using powers arbitrarily. In the main, they rely on the unlikely event of the prime minister's supporters turning against him or her. Their inadequacy can be illustrated by the then prime minister's decision to invade Iraq in 2003, where, despite limited information being given to both Cabinet and Parliament (see the Chilcot Report, Section 4.9), a vote in the Commons endorsed the decision. The checks and balances include:

▶ defeat of the government in a vote of confidence in the Commons;
▶ the Queen's legal power to dismiss the prime minister, as occurred in Australia in 1975. If she were to dismiss the prime minister, she would then appoint a replacement who would be subject to a vote of confidence in the Commons (Section 15.2);
▶ the risk of dismissing Cabinet ministers who may enjoy political support in their own right. In practice, a prime minister's freedom to appoint ministers may be limited by party considerations;
▶ the absence of a separate prime ministerial department (apart from a Private Office). However, prime ministers may have a substantial staff of political special advisers. There has been a recent effort to bring the prime minister's office, the Cabinet Office and the Treasury closer together;
▶ the possibility of a prime minister being deposed as party leader and therefore losing the support of the Commons. The influence of senior backbench MPs may be significant. The resignation of Margaret Thatcher in 1990 provides an example.

15.4 The Cabinet

The Cabinet is the policymaking body that formally coordinates the work of government departments. It comprises all Secretaries of State and includes other ministers chosen by the prime minister, some of whom attend without membership as such. Its proceedings are confidential.

The Cabinet originated in the seventeenth century as a group of trusted Privy Counsellors called together to give confidential advice to Charles II. The term was originally one of abuse and referred to the king's 'closet' or anteroom. An attempt was made in the Act of Settlement 1700 to prevent 'inner caucuses' from usurping the functions of the Privy Council, but the provisions were never implemented and were later repealed. George I (1714–27) leaned particularly heavily on party leaders, and from his reign onwards the monarch ceased to attend Cabinet meetings, substituting the prime minister. During the reign of George III (1760–1820), the convention emerged that the monarch should generally consult the Cabinet. The eighteenth-century Cabinets served the vital purposes of ensuring that the executive could command the support of the Commons and presenting the monarch with a united front. From a mid-nineteenth-century perspective, Bagehot regarded the Cabinet as the 'buckle' that held the government together (Section 7.6.1).

The Cabinet has no legal powers as such. However, statute law recognises the status of the Cabinet by protecting Cabinet secrecy (Health Service Commissioners Act 1983, s 12; Parliamentary Commissioner Act 1967, s 8(4)), and sometimes powers can be exercised only by a minister of Cabinet rank (e.g. Data Protection Act 2018, s 27(12)). According to the *Ministerial Code* ([2.2]), the business of the Cabinet and ministerial committees consists in the main of (i) questions which significantly engage the collective responsibility of the government because they raise major issues of policy or are of critical importance to the public; and (ii) questions on which there is an unresolved argument between departments. Cabinets usually comprise between 20 and 30 ministers, including the heads of the main government departments and certain other senior officeholders. Other ministers and civil servants often attend Cabinet meetings for particular purposes, notably the Chief Whip, who forms a link between the government and its backbench supporters.

Cabinet business is frequently delegated to committees and subcommittees, or informal groups of ministers and other persons such as civil servants and political advisers. This is an inevitable consequence of the complexity of modern government and is an important method by which the prime minister can control the decision-making process. There are two kinds of formal Cabinet committee: (i) ad hoc committees set up on a temporary basis to deal with particular problems; and (ii) named permanent committees, for example home affairs, economic affairs and parliamentary business and legislation. The names and membership of these committees are published (www.gov.uk/government/publications/the-cabinet-committees-system-and-list-of-cabinet-committees). The Butler Report (Section 15.7.1) criticised the contemporary practice of policymaking by informal groups and individuals selected by the prime minister without written records and without the Cabinet being fully informed. Indeed, the tendency to bypass the Cabinet raises the question whether the Cabinet is a convention of the Constitution, or only a working practice (Section 3.4.3).

Collective Cabinet responsibility (Section 15.7.1) ensures that every member of the government is bound by decisions approved by the Cabinet, whether or not the full Cabinet has discussed them. Thus, it is sometimes said that the Cabinet has become merely a rubberstamp or 'dignified' part of the constitution. The secrecy surrounding the workings of the Cabinet is also an aspect of collective responsibility and makes objective analysis (and accountability) difficult. Other practical limits upon Cabinet power are that its meetings are relatively short (about two hours per week), its members have departmental loyalties, and its agenda and procedure are controlled by the prime minister.

The Cabinet Office services and coordinates the work of the Cabinet and records its decisions for implementation by departments. It comprises about 100 civil servants headed by the Cabinet Secretary, who also coordinates other Whitehall committees, designates most of their chairmen and, as head of the civil service, reports to the prime minister. Arguably, these three roles create fundamental conflicts of duty.

15.5   Ministers

A minister is defined by section 8 of the Ministers of the Crown Act 1975 as an officeholder under Her Majesty. It is for the Queen, on the advice of the prime minister, to designate the number and titles of ministers and to appoint and dismiss ministers. Some ministers have separate legal personality as corporations sole. By convention, a minister must be an MP and most ministers, particularly those in major spending departments and the Treasury, must be members of the House of Commons. In principle, any number of ministers can be appointed. However, there are statutory limits on the number of ministers who can sit in the Commons, and also the number of paid ministers in either House (Section 12.4). There are about 100 ministers, ranked as follows:

- *Cabinet ministers*. Most Cabinet ministers head departments, but some offices are traditionally without departments and can be assigned to special or coordinating work by the prime minister. These include the Chancellor of the Duchy of Lancaster and the Lord President of the (Privy) Council. The Leader of the House of Commons is responsible for managing government business in the House. The most important departments are traditionally headed by Secretaries of State. These are the successors of the powerful officials created by Henry VIII to control the central government.
- *Ministers of state and parliamentary under-secretaries of state* (where the head of the department is a Secretary of State). The two law officers, the Attorney General and the Solicitor General, who deals primarily with internal matters, are also of this rank.
- *Parliamentary secretaries*. These are mainly recruited from the House of Commons and assist more senior ministers with political and administrative work.
- *Parliamentary private secretaries*. These are MPs who act as unpaid assistants to individual ministers.
- *Whips*. The whips control party discipline and provide a channel of communication between government and backbenches. They are formally officers of the royal household. The Chief Whip is not a member of the Cabinet but attends Cabinet meetings and consults with the prime minister on matters such as the appointment of ministers.

By convention, a minister must head each government department to ensure ministerial responsibility to Parliament. Ministers are often appointed for their political or parliamentary skills, or for reasons of political balance and reward for loyalty. They do not necessarily have the skills, interest or experience to run complex departments. Unlike the position with most other parliamentary systems, there is a practice in the UK of 'reshuffling' ministers at roughly two-yearly intervals so that only exceptionally does the same person hold office for the duration of a Parliament. During a reshuffle, ministers may be sacked or reallocated, and junior ministers or backbench MPs promoted. This is a prime ministerial tool to enforce party loyalty and perhaps to deflect public attention from policy failures. It can also engender incompetent government by inexperienced politicians who are likely to leave office without taking responsibility for the consequences of their failings.

15.6 Government departments

There are no constitutional requirements relating to the organisation of government departments. Most can be freely created, abolished or amalgamated by the prime minister. For example, the Ministry of Justice was created in 2007, taking over the functions of the Department of Constitutional Affairs (created in 2003) and parts of the Home Office. This has implications for the separation of powers (Section 7.5; see *Relations between the Executive, Judiciary and Parliament*, HL 2006–07, 151 [19]).

The only statutory limitations concern restrictions upon the number of ministers who can sit in the House of Commons (Section 12.4) and provisions relating to particular offices, notably the Lord Chancellor (Constitutional Reform Act 2005). The Treasury also has a special position.

The organisation of departments is sometimes regarded as a matter of royal prerogative, but could also be the right of the Crown, as of any private organisation, to organise itself as it wishes, thus illustrating a possible weakness in our non-statist constitution. In the nineteenth century, committees of the Privy Council or special bodies were set up to deal with new governmental responsibilities, but, as the work of government increased, separate permanent departments headed by ministers were created. These have been expanded, abolished, split up or combined as circumstances dictated, without apparent constitutional constraints.

Some government departments and ministers, notably the Treasury and the Lord Chancellor, trace their origins back to medieval times. The other 'great offices of state', the Home Office and the Foreign Office, are nineteenth-century creations of the royal prerogative. Other departments are either statutory or, more commonly, set up by using the prerogative to create a Secretary of State, at least in relation to his statutory powers over them. Some departments, such as HM Revenue and Customs, have substantial administrative and financial independence, with powers conferred directly upon them. They are known as non-ministerial departments. However, a minister remains constitutionally responsible for them, at least in relation to any statutory powers he possesses in respect of them.

Because English law has no umbrella concept of the state (Section 9.1), government property is sometimes held by the Crown, often through the Crown Estates Commission, sometimes by ministers, and sometimes by departments created with legal personality. This has caused problems in deciding in what capacity a given asset is held (e.g. *Town Investments v Dept of the Environment* [1977] 1 All ER 813; Section 14.1). Provision must also be made for transferring rights and liabilities between ministers and from ministers to other agencies. Under the *Carltona* principle (Section 15.8.5), functions entrusted to a minister can be exercised by a civil servant in his/her own department but not transferred to other ministers or to anyone else. These matters are dealt with by standardised legislation (e.g. Ministers of the Crown Act 1975; Deregulation and Contracting Out Act 1994). Under the Civil Service (Management Functions) Act 2002, a minister can transfer the management of civil servants to any other Crown servant. This is intended to allow ministers to create semi-independent 'executive agencies' (Section 15.9). There is a curiosity that, since the office of Secretary of State is in law a single office, the various Secretaries of State can interchange functions and assets without the need for legislation.

For the purposes of litigation, a list of appropriate departments is maintained by the Treasury. In cases of doubt, the Attorney General represents the Crown (Crown Proceedings Act 1947, s 17). Criminal cases are prosecuted in the name of the Queen.

15.6.1   The Treasury

The prime minister is the First Lord of the Board of the Treasury, a body that never meets. By convention, the Chancellor of the Exchequer is the responsible minister. The Treasury is an overlord and coordinating department in that it is responsible for the economy as a whole, allocates finance to government departments, supervises their spending and is responsible for the tax-gathering agencies and the Bank of England.

The Treasury has special constitutional significance, and its activities provide a good illustration of the mix of legal and informal controls that typify the UK Constitution and make the exercise of power obscure. There is a general 'understanding', the basis of which lies in internal practices based on 'ancient authority', that the Treasury both authorises and polices departmental expenditure (see Daintith and Page (1999) 109–26). The support of the Public Accounts and Public Administration Committees of the House of Commons also authorises Treasury power. Thus, the Treasury can strongly influence, if not control, the spending priorities of other departments.

The Treasury also plays the role of gatekeeper to Parliament, through which it authorises and presents government spending and taxation proposals. Parliament depends on an initiative from the Treasury since (by convention) the Crown's recommendation is required for all taxation and public expenditure. Moreover, it is arguable that Parliament votes money to the Crown rather than to any particular department (Chapter 13). This gives the Treasury a powerful lever since it can approve allocations to individual departments. The Treasury fixes the overall levels of expenditure for each department and can set objectives against which the effectiveness of spending is measured. It approves spending proposals by departments, either in general or in relation to especially sensitive items. Thus, a strong Chancellor can concern himself with the business of every government department as a rival power centre to the prime minister. This was apparently the case during the Labour government led by Tony Blair, leading to confusion and hostility within the government organisation.

Treasury pre-eminence is backed by specific legal powers. First, the Treasury has statutory power to approve payments from the Consolidated Fund and the National Loans Fund (the government's main bank accounts) and to place limits on other sources of income such as fees and charges (Government Resources and Accounts Act 2000, ss 2, 3). Second, the Treasury approves the form and method of the accounts of government departments (ss 5, 7). Under these powers, the Treasury is in a position to decide what count as public assets and expenditure, and thereby to determine the extent to which public bodies can raise private money. Third, the Treasury can authorise additional payments to departments (s 6), and many items of expenditure require Treasury consent under particular statutes. It is unlikely that in the absence of a plain violation of statute, matters of economic policy would be subject to judicial review (see *R v HM Treasury, ex p Smedley* [1985] QB 657: payments contrary to statute).

The Treasury appoints an Accounting Officer for each department who is responsible for the management of the department (Exchequer and Audit Department Act 1866, s 22). This is usually the head (Permanent Secretary) of the department and, in the case of an executive agency, its chief executive. The Comptroller and Auditor-General examines departmental accounts and reports unauthorised expenditure to the Treasury, which can either authorise it or report the matter to Parliament (Exchequer and Audit Departments Act 1921, s 1).

The Budget Responsibility and National Audit Act 2011 requires the Treasury to prepare and lay before Parliament a 'Charter for Budget Responsibility' which sets out its objectives and the means by which they will be attained. The Act also establishes an Office for Budget Responsibility, the role of which is to examine and report on the sustainability of public finances (see Section 13.5.4).

The Bank of England has some independence. A statutory body, it administers the government's bank account and, in conjunction with the Treasury and the Financial Conduct Authority, regulates other banks (Bank of England Act 1998). Subject to the statutory objectives of maintaining price stability, supporting the economic policies of the government and complying with inflation targets set by the Treasury, it is responsible for monetary policy (primarily, fixing interest rates) and for issuing currency. Its directors are appointed by the Crown and can be dismissed on prescribed grounds with the consent of the Chancellor of the Exchequer, and 'in extreme economic circumstances', it is subject to directions from the Treasury. The Bank is also subject to scrutiny by the Treasury Select Committee and is required to publish the minutes of its Monetary Policy Committee, an annual report and an annual inflation report.

15.6.2 The law officers

As members of the executive, MPs, and also connected with the legal process, the law officers infringe the separation of powers in respect of all three branches of government. Governed mainly by convention, they occupy a vague area of dubious independence, lack of accountability and conflict of interest characteristic of the UK Constitution. The Attorney General is the chief law officer. S/he is assisted by the Solicitor General, to whom s/he can delegate functions (Law Officers Act 1997). The Attorney General and the Solicitor General are ministers and therefore MPs. Like all ministers, they are appointed and dismissed on the advice of the prime minister. By convention, although s/he is not a member of the Cabinet, the Attorney General attends Cabinet meetings. The Attorney General has the following main functions:

- representing the government in legal proceedings, including intervening in any legal proceedings to put the government's view;
- giving confidential legal advice to the government. The government has no obligation to obtain independent legal advice;
- acting as legal adviser to the House of Lords and House of Commons: another potential conflict of interest;

- having political responsibility for the Crown Prosecution Service, the Serious Fraud Office, with powers under various statutes to consent to the prosecution of certain offences and under the prerogative power to interfere to prevent a prosecution (*nolle prosequi*);
- bringing legal proceedings on behalf of the general 'public interest', either on own initiative or on the application of any member of the public (a relator action). This might include an action against a public authority, including the government of which s/he is a member. No Attorney General has challenged his/her own government, although there have been many proceedings against local authorities whose decisions have been contrary to central policy;
- referring questions of law to the Court of Appeal where an accused person has been acquitted of a criminal offence, or requesting a more severe sentence for a convicted person;
- by tradition, holding the position of Leader of the Bar, even though it is important that the legal profession should be seen to be independent of government.

The law officers are entitled to consult other ministers but, by convention, they act independently. Their claim to independence does not fit easily with their collective responsibility for government policy. The law officers may make statements to, but are not required to answer questions in, Parliament. The Attorney General's advice to ministers is confidential, a convention that has been defended by the inappropriate analogy of a lawyer's advice to a private client. Moreover, the Scott Report (*Report of the Inquiry into the Export of Defence Equipment and Dual Use Goods to Iraq and Related Prosecution*, HC 1995–96, 115) revealed an official culture in which the advice of the Attorney General was treated as if it had legal force, a practice condemned by the court in *R v Brown* [1993] 2 All ER 75. The Attorney General's decision whether or not to intervene in legal proceedings cannot be challenged in the courts (*Gouriet v Union of Post Office Workers* [1978] AC 435). However, the Privy Council has hinted that this might be reconsidered (*Jeewan Mohit v DPP of Mauritius* [2006] UKPC 20, [21]). Thus, the law officers are uniquely unaccountable.

The Attorney General's two roles as government lawyer and representative of the public interest are sometimes in conflict. For example, in 2007 the Attorney General was required to obtain an injunction preventing the BBC from reporting allegations relating to the Prime Minister's Office selling peerages. We have only the predictable assertions of successive Attorney Generals that they can be trusted – a notion offensive at least to republicans (Section 2.5), but a recurring theme in the UK Constitution.

In 1924, the government fell because the Attorney General acted on instructions from it in relation to a prosecution of an anti-government journalist. In 2002, the government claimed that it was lawfully entitled to invade Iraq on the basis of advice from the Attorney General, over which he had changed his mind. The Chilcot Report, published in 2016 (Section 4.9), did not rule on the legality of the invasion, but did note that the Attorney General should have been asked to provide written advice to Cabinet as to his reasons for concluding that the invasion was now lawful. Reform proposals to make the law officers compliant with the separation of powers have not been implemented (see Select Committee on the Constitution, *Reform of the Office of Attorney General*, HC 2007–08, 93).

15.7 Ministerial responsibility

Ministerial responsibility defines both the relationship between ministers and Parliament and the relationship between ministers and civil servants. Ministerial responsibility has two aspects:

1. All members of the government are *collectively responsible* to Parliament for the conduct of the government.
2. Each minister is *individually responsible* to Parliament for the conduct of his or her department.

Ministerial responsibility developed during the eighteenth and nineteenth centuries, corresponding to the rise of the House of Commons and the decline in the power of the Crown. Its original purpose was as a weapon against the monarch by achieving coherence among politicians with divergent views (there being no party machinery in the modern sense). Ministerial responsibility is a matter of convention, although it is recognised by the law (e.g. Freedom of Information Act 2000, s 36(2)(a)(i); Section 24.2), and the *Ministerial Code* provides a written statement of certain of its elements.

While the rule of law might be the cornerstone of the legal constitution, ministerial responsibility is the cornerstone of the political constitution. Ministerial responsibility in a broad sense gives the constitution a republican element (Section 2.5). However, it is arguable that the doctrine is so nebulous and so damaged by executive domination of Parliament that it currently has little value as a constitutional principle.

Tomkins (*Public Law* (Clarendon Press 2003) 134) identifies three 'fault lines' in the doctrine. These are, first, a lack of openness in government; second, 'ownership', in the sense that the government itself can influence the meaning and enforcement of the doctrine; and third, and most importantly, the pressures of party domination. These work together to weaken Parliament.

'Responsibility' is sometimes used interchangeably with 'accountability'. Both terms have a range of meanings (see Public Service Committee, HC 1995–96, 313, [14]–[21], [32]). They include obligations to provide explanation, information, acknowledgement, review and redress. Sometimes resignation may also be expected. The particular combination appropriate in any given case depends upon the circumstances. In addition to ministerial responsibility as such, there are instruments such as the Freedom of Information Act 2000, the *Codes of Conduct* for MPs and civil servants and the Cabinet Office *Guidance to Officials on Drafting Answers to Parliamentary Questions*, which inform the notion of openness and accountability. More generally, the openness and accountability of government are required by the fourth and fifth Principles of Public Life, namely accountability and openness, set out by the Committee on Standards in Public Life (Section 5.9).

Ministerial responsibility does not mean that Parliament (except through statute) can give orders to ministers or lay down policies. Parliament does not itself govern, and to this extent, there is a separation of powers. Ministerial responsibility means only that ministers must discharge their duties in a manner that has the continued support of the Commons, and that they must give an account of their actions and decisions. If the Commons so votes on a motion of confidence, the government collectively must resign.

Ministerial responsibility also provides information to arm opponents in the adversarial conduct of British political debate. Indeed, it is a characteristic of the parliamentary system of government that there is a continuing struggle on the part of MPs to gain more information than ministers are willing to provide.

On its face, the convention can be acclaimed as a device to ensure accountable government. Another view is that the convention favours 'strong' government because by focusing only on Parliament it allows ministers to govern with little effective supervision since Parliament has neither the will nor the resources to hold ministers effectively to account (see Flinders (2000)). Ministerial responsibility may also be out of line with the practices of modern government, in particular the techniques of privatisation and devolved public management. In this context, the convention actually shields government from public accountability because the impugned decision may have been taken in an agency that has been hived off from central government. Although in principle, the minister remains fully responsible, the vague meaning of responsibility enables ministers more easily to evade blame the further away they are from the location of decision-making. The party system and the tradition of secrecy within the civil service have also played a part in breaking the chain of accountability through Parliament to the electorate.

15.7.1 Collective responsibility

Collective responsibility applies to all government ministers. It was developed originally so that government and Parliament could put up a solid front against the king. It suggests collegial government that is at odds with the legal basis of government, with powers given to individual ministers. It serves the constitutional function of creating a clear line of responsibility.

Collective responsibility has four aspects:

1. It requires all ministers to be loyal to the policies of the government whether or not they are personally concerned with them (solidarity). Collective responsibility therefore applies even though many important decisions are made elsewhere and are not fully discussed by the Cabinet as a whole. Resignation is required before a minister can speak out on a particular issue. Nevertheless, as a convention, collective responsibility may be adapted to new circumstances and the prime minister can apparently modify it over a particular issue.
2. It requires the government as a whole to resign if it is defeated on a vote of confidence in the House of Commons.
3. It requires that the process by which a Cabinet decision has been taken should be confidential (see *Ministerial Code*, [2.1], [2.3]).
4. It protects ministers against personal responsibility since collective responsibility can be used to justify an individual avoiding blame. For example, the Butler Report into intelligence failures relating to Iraq (*Review of Intelligence on Weapons of Mass Destruction: Report of a Committee of Privy Counsellors*, HC 2003–04, 898) absolved all ministers and civil servants from blame for misleading the public on the basis that the various falsehoods were 'collective'. (Butler himself was a former head of the civil service.) Collective responsibility and individual responsibility (Section 15.7.2) can therefore come into conflict.

The drastic sanction of a vote of confidence is the only method by which Parliament can enforce collective responsibility, but governments have rarely been defeated in this way in modern times. In 1924, Ramsay MacDonald's Labour government resigned, and in 1979, so did James Callaghan's Labour government. Both were minority governments.

The coalition government of the Conservative and Liberal Democrat party which was in office between 2010 and 2015 gave rise to some disagreements between the parties, for example in respect of welfare cuts, elections, environmental matters and taxation. Although there is no formal constitutional difference between a coalition government and any other, the desire of each party to keep its identity involved a suspension of collective responsibility on certain matters, at least to the extent of disagreements being made public. Ministers were also permitted to campaign against the government's position on membership of the EU in the run-up to the referendum in 2016 (Section 10.5.1).

The relationship between prime minister and Cabinet has an important impact on how well collective responsibility works in practice. The collegial model of government, which emphasises the participation of all Cabinet ministers in decision-making, disguises the dominance of the prime minister in the formulation of policy. There are no formal checks and balances. The extent to which the prime minister can exercise an authoritarian style depends upon the composition and mood of the Cabinet, the attitude and cohesion of the party and the Commons, the temper of the electorate and not least the personal style of the prime minister. If undue reliance is placed on a select group of senior ministers (the 'inner Cabinet') or unelected 'cronies', if too many 'private deals' are struck with individual ministers, or if too many controversial policies are effectively formulated in Cabinet subcommittees, ministers may feel less inclined to loyalty. Serious embarrassment can result where senior ministers resign, having concluded that the workings of the Cabinet have strayed unacceptably far from the collegial model. Geoffrey Howe's resignation over European policy in 1990 resulted from his concern about the prime minister's apparent distaste for collective decision-making. This resignation played a pivotal role in ending Mrs Thatcher's tenure in 1990.

It could be argued that collective responsibility is no different from the solidarity expected within any organisation. Ministers can discuss policy differences in private, confident that all will support the decision that is eventually reached. The presentation of a single view also adds authority to the government's position because it disguises the compromise nature of many governments. This argument begs the question whether government can be compared with, say, a large private sector company. Given that an important value of democratic government is to manage disagreement without suppressing it, it may be desirable for government not to speak with a single voice but to recognise the provisional nature of any decision reached. It can also be argued that the doctrine of collective responsibility could contribute to a general public disenchantment with politics if ministers were seen to vote in support of policies they were believed not to support.

15.7.2 Individual responsibility

Sir Edward Bridges, the Permanent Secretary to the Treasury, expressed the classical interpretation of the doctrine of individual responsibility in 1954, after the 'Crichel Down affair' (Section 15.7.3; see Public Service Committee, HC 1995–96, 313, at [8]). He stated that a minister is responsible to Parliament for the exercise of all executive powers and every action taken in pursuance of those powers. This emphasises that a minister must always answer questions and give a full account of the actions of his or her department. This is so whether or not the minister is personally at fault for what has gone wrong, and is subject to only limited exceptions, related among other things to commercial confidence, national security and some macroeconomic issues.

Individual ministerial responsibility is concerned with a chain of accountability from Parliament through ministers to civil servants. Ministerial responsibility protects civil servants from direct public responsibility since they owe their loyalty to the government and especially to the minister in charge of their department. Thus, civil servants appear before Parliament only with the permission of ministers and on terms set by ministers.

Beyond that, its meaning and scope are unclear: first, in respect of what 'responsibility' entails, and second, in respect of what actions the minister is responsible for. Ministerial responsibility is primarily enforced by Parliament. Most specifically, it requires that ministers provide information to Parliament by means of answers to parliamentary questions, evidence to select committees, formal ministerial statements and letters to MPs. Within the executive, the prime minister is responsible for enforcing ministerial responsibility and therefore, indirectly, for defining it.

Ministers are certainly responsible for their departments, but much less clearly so in relation to executive agencies sponsored by their departments. There does not seem to be direct responsibility for non-ministerial government departments, or for 'quangos', although in both cases ministers are responsible for the exercise of their specific functions in relation to these bodies (Sections 15.9 and 15.10).

Ministers have attempted to limit their responsibility by making various distinctions and by seeking to ensure that their civil servants are not subject to direct scrutiny by Parliament. Generally, Parliament has deferred to ministers in these respects rather than asserting its undoubted right to have the last word.

First, it has been claimed that responsibility applies only to 'policy' matters, as opposed to 'operational' matters, which are deemed to be failures properly to implement policy. This has been particularly evident following the radical restructuring of government in the 1990s, with the majority of civil servants working in semi-detached executive agencies under the day-to-day direction of chief executives with only limited departmental control (Section 15.9). This restructuring has tended to confuse lines of accountability. In *Williams v Home Office (No 1)* [1981] 1 All ER 1151, the court drew a distinction between acts done by civil servants in the exercise of statutory functions conferred on ministers, and routine management matters, saying that the latter are not to be regarded as the act of ministers. This is questionable in terms of the traditional doctrine of ministerial responsibility but perhaps represents a more realistic view of the nature of modern government.

The policy/operational dichotomy is a vague one. Indeed, the two are often inextricably interconnected. The effect has been to make it more difficult for Parliament to find out who is to blame when problems arise. For example, is prison overcrowding a matter of policy (a consequence, for example, of tougher sentencing rules), or operation? Thus, ministers can exploit confusion by intervening where they perceive electoral gains, as in the events leading up to the dismissal of Derek Lewis, the head of the Prison Service, following allegations of interference by the Home Secretary in the detailed administration of the service (see *Review of Prison Service Security in England and Wales and the Escape from Parkhurst Prison on Tuesday 3rd January 1995* (Cm 3020, 1995) (the Learmont Report); Lords Public Service Committee, HL 1997–98, 55, [341]).

Ministers may also interfere in 'operational' matters while declining to answer questions about them, claiming that such matters fall within the responsibility of the chief executive. Moreover, since it is the minister who decides what is policy and what is operation, ministers can effectively determine the extent of their constitutional responsibilities. The House of Lords Public Service Select Committee concluded that it was not possible effectively to separate policy from operations, and that such a division was not desirable (HL 1997–98, 55, [348]).

Secondly, ministers have distinguished between 'accountability' and 'responsibility'. This seems to divorce the circumstances in which a minister must give to the House an explanation of the actions of his department (accountability) from cases in which a minister must accept the blame for departmental mistakes and resign (responsibility). In *The Civil Service: Taking Forward Continuity and Change* (Cm 2718, 1995, [27]–[28]), the government stated that Parliament can always call a minister to account for all that goes on in his department, but it added that a minister cannot be responsible in the sense of having personal knowledge and control of every action taken, and cannot be personally blameworthy when delegated tasks are carried out incompetently or errors of judgment are made at an operational level. Coupled with this is a reluctance by ministers to subject civil servants to independent scrutiny, thereby creating an 'accountability gap' (Section 15.8.5).

The accountability/responsibility distinction was rejected in 1996 by the Public Service Committee of the Commons (above), but accepted by the Scott Report on the Arms to Iraq affair (HC 1995–96, 115). It entails that ministers be prepared to offer a complete explanation of any error to Parliament, but that they are not obliged to take the blame. There is a duty to offer reasons by way of justification in the face of criticism. Experience reveals, however, that ministers have not always been willing to give a full account of their actions. Notoriously, the conclusion of the Scott Inquiry was that there were numerous examples of ministers failing to give full information about the policies, decisions and actions of government regarding arms sales to Iraq (HC 1995–96, 115, K8.1, [27]) and that this had undermined the democratic process (D4.56–D4.58). Answers to parliamentary questions in the affair had been 'designedly uninformative' because of a fear of adverse political consequences if the truth were revealed (D3.107). Following revelations of this kind, it became clear that there should be a renewed commitment to the doctrine of individual responsibility combined with a need to clarify the obligations entailed by it. This led to the adoption by the government of the *Ministerial Code* (latest revision 2019), which, in effect, amounts to a 'Ministerial Code of Ethics'. The *Code* (at [1.3]), sets out the following principles of ministerial conduct:

1. The principle of collective responsibility applies to all Government Ministers.
2. Ministers have a duty to Parliament to account, and be held to account, for the policies, decisions and actions of their departments and agencies (Section 15.9).
3. It is of paramount importance that ministers give accurate and truthful information to Parliament, correcting any inadvertent error at the earliest opportunity. Ministers who knowingly mislead Parliament will be expected to offer their resignation to the prime minister.
4. Ministers should be as open as possible with Parliament and the public, refusing to provide information only when disclosure would not be in the public interest, which should be decided in accordance with the relevant statutes and the Freedom of Information Act 2000.
5. Ministers should similarly require civil servants who give evidence before parliamentary committees on their behalf and under their direction to be as helpful as possible in providing accurate, truthful and full information in accordance with the duties and responsibilities of civil servants as set out in the *Civil Service Code*.
6. Ministers must ensure that no conflict arises, or appears to arise, between their public duties and their private interests.

7. Ministers should not accept any gift or hospitality which might, or might reasonably appear to, compromise their judgment or place them under an improper obligation.
8. Ministers in the House of Commons must keep separate their roles as Minister and constituency Member.
9. Ministers must not use government resources for party political purposes.
10. Ministers must uphold the political impartiality of the Civil Service and not ask civil servants to act in any way which would conflict with the *Civil Service Code* as set out in the Constitutional Reform and Governance Act 2010 (see Section 15.8.1).

However, there is no genuinely independent method of enforcing the *Code*, which has no legal force. The *Code* states that the prime minister 'is the ultimate judge of the standards of behaviour expected of a Minister and the appropriate consequences of a breach of those standards' (at [1.6]). Thus, the prime minister is both a setter of standards and responsible for their enforcement. It provides that he may refer a possible breach of the code, having consulted with the Cabinet Secretary, to the Independent Adviser on Ministers' Interests, a post created in 2006. The Adviser is appointed by the prime minister, rather than via open competition, and has to date been a retired senior civil servant. The Commons Select Committee on Public Administration (HC 2010–12, 1761) recommended that the Adviser should have power to initiate investigations in the absence of the matter being referred by the prime minister, and to conduct short preliminary investigations to establish the facts of the case, but this has been rejected by government. There has been criticism of the apparent unwillingness of the prime minister to refer alleged breaches to the Adviser (see House of Commons Library Briefing Paper SN 03750 (2015)). The apparent weakness of this mechanism was demonstrated in November 2020, when the prime minister refused to sack the Home Secretary, Pritti Patel, following an investigation which concluded that she had breached the *Ministerial Code* ([1.2]) by bullying civil servants in her department. This refusal led the Adviser, Sr Alex Allan, to resign.

15.7.3 Ministerial resignation

Ministerial resignation engages both collective and individual responsibility. This is because, when resignation takes place, it saves fellow ministers from having to offer support for the beleaguered minister under the principle of collective responsibility. One interpretation of the convention is that resignation is required for every serious departmental error, regardless of the personal blame of the minister. Characteristically of conventions, such a convention, if it ever existed, seems to have been destroyed by disuse. The 'Crichel Down affair' (Cmd 9220, 1954), which involved serious civil service misconduct in relation to government confiscation of land, was once thought to have required resignation. However, Sir Thomas Dugdale's resignation in that case probably owed more to political misjudgement and a lack of parliamentary support. Lord Carrington resigned as Foreign Secretary in 1982 when his department failed to spot the invasion of the Falkland Islands by Argentina.

It seems that resignation is only constitutionally required in three categories of case:

1. where a minister has knowingly misled Parliament (except in the very limited cases where this is justified: Public Service Committee, HC 1995–96, 313, [32]). However, an honest, even if unreasonable, belief in the accuracy of information given to Parliament can be a lifeline to beleaguered ministers. The Scott Inquiry found that William Waldegrave unreasonably clung to the view that government policy governing the sale of arms to Iraq had not changed (HC 1995–96, 115, D4.1–D4.7), but Waldegrave did not resign. Similar questions arose after Lord Falconer's refusal in 2001 to resign in respect of the funding and sale of the Millennium Dome;
2. where the minister is personally to blame for a serious departmental error;
3. in cases of personal dishonesty or wrongdoing, at least when the minister is politically vulnerable. Examples include David Laws in 2010 for breaching rules on MPs' expenses at a time when the matter

was the subject of considerable public agitation, and Andrew Mitchell in 2012, after an alleged altercation with a police officer in Downing Street. Private misconduct unrelated to a minister's duties might also lead to resignation, but perhaps only where the minister becomes politically vulnerable. However, Woodhouse argues that personal indiscretions are relevant because they affect the public credibility of the minister concerned ('Ministerial Responsibility in the 1990s: When Do Ministers Resign?' (1993) 46 Parl Aff 277).

Nevertheless, raw politics, including the support of the prime minister and media attention, rather than constitutional obligation, is surely the best explanation of ministerial resignations. For example, David Laws' resignation in 2010 involved only a technical breach of expenses rules, but came in circumstances of significant public anger at MPs' conduct generally.

15.8   The civil service

The civil service is a professional, permanent and independent part of the executive. Its purpose is to assist the government in formulating its policies, to carry out decisions of the government and to administer services for which the government is responsible. More broadly, the civil service, being an institution independent of changing governments, gives the constitution continuity and stability and is a source of expert advice and 'institutional memory'. In the last resort, where ministers fail, the civil service must keep the government functioning.

The civil service might also be regarded as another component of the separation of powers, providing a check and balance against politicians. However, civil servants have no constitutional status or independent powers of their own but can only exercise powers channelled from ministers. In some countries, notably the USA, the senior civil service is overtly political, its leaders being appointed in accordance with the preferences of the president. In the UK, attempts are made to protect the independence of the civil service. However, in accordance with UK constitutional culture, these have not until recently been backed by law.

There is no meaningful legal definition of a civil servant. The Constitutional Reform and Governance Act 2010, following the Tomlin Commission on the Civil Service (Cmnd 3909, 1931), unhelpfully refers to 'the civil service of the State'. This may include every person who serves the Crown other than the military, ministers holding political offices and holders of judicial offices. The armed forces are, of course, also Crown servants but are subject to a distinctive legal regime. The police are not civil servants, because they are not employed by the Crown. Thus, the definition of a civil servant is partly negative, meaning a Crown servant other than those falling into special categories (see Sandberg, 'A Whitehall Farce? Defining and Conceptualising the British Civil Service' [2006] PL 653). Only around 1.5 per cent of civil servants, the senior civil service, are responsible for policymaking. The remainder are responsible for service delivery, either in executive agencies or non-ministerial departments (Section 15.9).

Management of the civil service is currently vested in the Minister for the Civil Service – who is the prime minister. The Treasury also has powers over the civil service. Each government department is managed by its Accounting Officer, usually of the highest rank of Permanent Secretary. The Accounting Officer's activities can be examined by Parliament, by means of the Public Accounts Committee and the Comptroller and Auditor-General. According to the *Ministerial Code* (at [5.3]), the Accounting Officer is personally responsible for the 'propriety and regularity of the public finances for which he or she is responsible; for keeping proper accounts; for the avoidance of waste and extravagance; and for the efficient and effective use of resources' in the department, thus raising the question of ministerial responsibility (below).

There is tension from two directions. On the one hand, the civil service must offer impartial advice and expertise to governments of all political colours. On the other hand, it is required loyally to carry out government instructions. The argument that UK civil servants should have wider duties to the Crown as distinct from duties to the government of the day has not succeeded (see Public Service

Committee, HC 1995–96, 313, [169]). The contrary proposal, namely that senior civil servants should be appointed by each incoming administration from its supporters, as in the USA, also lacks significant support.

Ministers (especially those who are weak) may therefore complain that they are dominated or subverted by their civil servants. Civil servants may complain about political interference with the impartiality and influence of the civil service. These tensions are particularly acute in connection with a kind of civil servant known as a special adviser. Special advisers are party political advisers appointed directly by ministers and working closely with them. They were formally recognised by a government announcement in 1974 but have probably always existed. They are temporary civil servants appointed for the purpose of providing 'assistance' to ministers, a purpose which goes beyond advice (Constitutional Reform and Governance Act 2010, s 15). Unlike other civil servants, they are not required to be impartial or objective and they need not be appointed on merit by fair and open competition. There is no legal limit on the number of special advisers. In December 2019, there were 109 posts attached to UK government ministers, 44 of them in the prime minister's office. Special advisers lose their posts when their minister does so, or after a party's defeat in a general election.

Special advisers are therefore a link between the political and the permanent parts of the government. There has been concern that their activities, particularly in relation to communication with the media, may threaten the reputation of the civil service for impartiality. There is also a concern that permanent civil servants may be denied access to ministers and that their role will be reduced to carrying out orders from special advisers (see Select Committee on Public Administration HC 2000–01, 293; Committee on Standards in Public Life (Cm 1817, 2000; Cm 5964, 2003)).

The position of special adviser has been placed on a statutory basis by section 15 of the Constitutional Reform and Governance Act 2010, which applies to the UK government and to the devolved governments of Scotland and Wales. The powers of special advisers have, in principle, been constrained (below). However, accountability has not been increased other than by requiring an annual report to Parliament concerning the number and cost of special advisers (s 16).

15.8.1 The statutory framework

Following recommendations by the Committee on Standards in Public Life (see Cm 5775, 2003), the Constitutional Reform and Governance Act 2010 enacted a framework of principles regulating the civil service. This replaces the previous mixture of royal prerogative rules and conventions. The 2010 Act does not apply to the security services, the Northern Ireland civil service or civil servants serving wholly outside the UK.

Most importantly, the Act has nothing to say about the detailed relationship between civil servants, ministers and Parliament, so that the disagreements surrounding these conventions remain.

The main provisions of the Act are as follows:

▶ The Civil Service Commission, previously existing under the royal prerogative, is established as a corporate body with its own legal identity. The Commission hears complaints relating to violations of the *Civil Service Code*, disciplinary and recruitment matters, but has no enforcement powers. It also monitors recruitment practices (ss 2, 9, 11, 12, 14). It is directly involved with senior civil service appointments.
▶ Managers must have regard to the need to ensure that civil servants who advise ministers are aware of the constitutional significance of Parliament and the conventions governing the relationship between Parliament and Government (s 3). The Act does not state what these are.
▶ The *Civil Service Code* must be published and laid before Parliament (s 5). The Code must require civil servants to carry out their duties with integrity, honesty, objectivity and impartiality. However, special advisers need not be objective or impartial (s 7). In addition, the *Ministerial Code* requires ministers to uphold the impartiality of the civil service and to give due consideration to its advice.

▶ The Minister for the Civil Service must publish a *Special Adviser's Code* which must be laid before Parliament (s 8). Special advisers cannot authorise expenditure from public funds nor manage other civil servants, except other special advisers, nor exercise statutory or prerogative power (s 8(5)). A special adviser must be appointed by the minister personally, subject to the approval of the prime minister (s 15). The terms of the appointment require the consent of the Minister for the Civil Service.

15.8.2 Recruitment

Civil servants, other than special advisers, short-term appointments and statutory Crown appointments, such as the Governor of the Bank of England, must be appointed by a fair and open competition (Constitutional Reform and Governance Act 2010, s 10). Specific qualifications for appointment are prescribed by and published in the *Civil Service Management Code* (most recent edition, 2016). Normally only a Commonwealth citizen, a British protected person or a citizen of the Republic of Ireland can be appointed.

The recruitment process is supervised by the Civil Service Commission, which must publish 'recruitment principles' (s 11). These can create further exemptions from the open competition requirement, for example when someone with particular expertise or experience is needed. In such cases, the Commission must approve the appointment and can participate in the appointment process. In the case of senior appointments, ministers can be consulted but, by convention, do not make the decision. Senior appointments must be approved by the Civil Service Commission. However, some senior appointments are approved by the prime minister, and the head of a department (Permanent Secretary) is appointed by the prime minister in all cases on the advice of the Head of the Home Civil Service.

Ministers can appoint anyone they wish to advise them outside the civil service, there being no safeguards in place. For example, in 2010, Lord Browne, a former chairman of British Petroleum, was asked to advise the prime minister in relation to reducing the costs of running the executive. There was no formal appointment process, nor apparently any element of competition. It is arguable that business persons are unlikely to be successful government appointees, often being unfamiliar with the practices of consultation, openness and detailed accountability that are desirable in a democracy.

15.8.3 Legal status

According to one view, a civil servant, traditionally being subject to the royal prerogative, has no contract of employment and cannot enforce the terms of his or her employment other than those laid down by statute. At common law, the Crown can dismiss a civil servant 'at pleasure', that is, without notice and without giving reasons (*Dunn v R* [1896] 1 QB 116). This is consistent with the view that there is no contract. On the other hand, it has been held that there can be a contract between the Crown and a civil servant, but that as a matter of public policy the contract can be overridden by the Crown's power to dismiss the civil servant at pleasure (*Riordan v War Office* [1959] 3 All ER 552). On this second analysis, other terms of employment such as pay and conditions are enforceable against the Crown.

Modern cases have stressed that there is no inherent reason why the relationship cannot be contractual (see *Kodeeswaren v A-G for Ceylon* [1970] AC 1111; *R v Civil Service Appeals Board ex parte Bruce* [1988] 3 All ER 686; *R v Lord Chancellor's Dept, ex parte Nangle* [1992] 1 All ER 897). The Employment Act 1988 deems there to be a contract between the Crown and a civil servant for the purpose of making a civil servant liable for industrial action (s 30). Indeed, senior civil servants are required on appointment to enter into a written contract with specified periods of notice (*Civil Service Management Code*, [11.1.8]). However, the Crown can probably still dismiss at pleasure and a contractual term that says otherwise is not enforceable (see *Civil Service Management Code*, [11.1.1]). This can be regarded as a matter of public policy.

15.8.4   Discipline

Civil servants, like other citizens, may be protected by judicial review. However, in *Nangle* (above) it was held that judicial review did not apply to internal disciplinary decisions unless a formal adjudicative process is involved (but see *Bruce* (above) and *R v Civil Service Appeals Board ex parte Cunningham* [1991] 4 All ER 310). Moreover, internal remedies must be used before resorting to the courts. Most civil servants are also protected by statutory unfair dismissal rules administered by industrial tribunals (Employment Rights Act 1996, s 191).

Special machinery applies to security issues. A minister can, by issuing a certificate, remove any category of Crown employee from the employment protection legislation on grounds of national security (Employment Rights Act 1996, s 193). A civil servant who is suspected of being a security risk is given a special hearing, but without the normal rights of cross examination and legal representation, before a panel of 'three advisers'. These usually comprise two retired senior officials and a High Court judge.

Problems arise when a civil servant considers that his or her integrity is compromised, for example by being required to act for politically partisan purposes, or possibly to break the law. Obeying the orders of a superior is not a defence in English law. The orthodox doctrine is that civil servants owe an absolute duty of loyalty to ministers (above), and the *Civil Service Code* imposes a lifelong duty not to disclose official information without authority.

There are internal mechanisms to enable civil servants to express issues of conscience. These include a right of appeal to the independent Civil Service Commission (above) and special provisions relating to the Official Secrets Act 1989. Judicial review may also be available.

Civil servants cannot be MPs (House of Commons (Disqualification) Act 1975, s 1(1) (b)). The political activity of civil servants is also restricted according to the level in the policymaking hierarchy. The majority are unrestricted except while on duty, or in uniform, or on official premises. An 'intermediate' group can take part in political activities with the consent of their head of department. This includes clerks, typists and officials performing specialist non-political jobs. A 'restricted' group of senior officials directly involved in policymaking cannot take part in national politics at all but can indulge in local politics with the consent of their head of department. However, whole departments can be exempted. Civil servants are also prohibited from taking gifts or doing other things that could create a conflict between their private interests and their official duties. There are restrictions (including waiting periods) placed upon former civil servants who wish to take up new appointments or employment outside the service. These are designed to ensure that the civil servant is not influenced in carrying out official duties by the hope or expectation of future employment; to prevent exploitation of privileged access to contacts after having left the service; and to prevent a firm or organisation from gaining advantage by employing a former civil servant who has knowledge of government policy and commercially valuable or sensitive information about competitors (*Civil Service Management Code*, [4.3]).

15.8.5   Civil servants and ministerial responsibility

Under the *Carltona* doctrine (*Carltona v Commissioner for Works* [1943] 2 All ER 560), a minister can lawfully exercise any of his statutory powers through a civil servant in his department, and need not personally exercise any power unless statute specifically so requires (e.g. Immigration Act 1971, s 13(5). The decision remains that of the minister – the civil servant and the minister being indivisible in law (see also *Bushell v Secretary of State for the Environment* [1981] AC 75; *R (Alconbury Developments Ltd) v Secretary of State for the Environment, Transport and the Regions* [2001] 2 All ER 929). The *Carltona* principle does not apply to delegation to other departments, or outside the civil service. Thus, statute is required to give a minister wider powers of delegation (e.g. Extradition Act 2003, s 101: decisions to senior officials in civil and diplomatic services).

The classical doctrine has been that, as civil servants have no powers of their own and so cannot take decisions or do anything except and insofar as they are subject to the direction and control of ministers, a civil servant has no direct responsibility to Parliament and cannot be called to account by Parliament. Civil servants are therefore accountable to ministers, and ministers accountable to Parliament. In particular, advice given to ministers by civil servants cannot be disclosed without the permission of ministers (see Freedom of Information Act 2000, s 35). According to the government, civil servants appear before parliamentary committees only with the consent of their ministers. Ministers therefore shield civil servants from outside scrutiny. In return, civil servants are loyal to ministers and owe no other allegiance, thus emphasising the minister's own accountability to Parliament.

Their evidence before select committees (Section 13.5.3) has been limited to describing their actions taken on behalf of ministers, as opposed to their conduct generally. Thus, civil servants cannot give evidence about the merits of government policy, or the consultation process within government, or the advice they gave to government. Indeed, ministers have sometimes forbidden civil servants from appearing, in particular on the grounds of national security, 'good government' and 'excessive cost'. There are also conventions that civil servants should not give evidence about the conduct of other officials or matters before the courts and evidence from papers of a previous government or a different political party (see Cabinet Office, *Giving Evidence to Select Committees: Guidance for Civil Servants* (2014)).

The relationship between ministers and civil servants can cause an 'accountability gap'. This is because accountability can break down where a minister blames a civil servant for some failure and subsequently directs that individual not to appear before a select committee. Notoriously, the Secretary of State for Trade and Industry refused to allow the civil servants involved in aspects of the 'Westland affair' to appear before the Commons Defence Select Committee (see HC 1985–86, 519; Cmnd 9916, 1986). This problem has, in part, been addressed in the *Ministerial Code*. Although civil servants still give evidence to select committees under the direction of ministers, the minister must insist that civil servants be as helpful as possible in providing accurate, truthful and full information (at [1.3(e)]). However, Parliament still lacks effective power to compel ministers to answer questions and the decision on who best represents a minister in front of a select committee rests with the minister concerned (see Cabinet Office, *Giving Evidence to Select Committees: Guidance for Civil Servants*, [11]–[13]).

The Scott Inquiry (above) revealed how civil servants have sometimes acted independently of ministers, or in the expectation of subsequent ministerial ratification of their actions (HC 1995–96, 115, D3.40). This exposed the constitutional fiction that civil servants only give advice to ministers. Civil servants concealed important questions from ministers and may even have defied ministerial instructions. Moreover, as discussed above, ministers have attempted to pass responsibility to civil servants, first by distinguishing between policy and operational matters and second by distinguishing between 'accountability' as a duty to explain, and 'responsibility' as liability to take the blame (Treasury and Civil Service Select Committee, HC 1993–94, 27, [120]). It has long been accepted that, as Accounting Officer, the permanent head of a department must appear before the relevant parliamentary committee. *Giving Evidence to Select Committees: Guidance for Civil Servants* (at [12]) states that there is a presumption that ministers will agree to the request of a select committee for a named official to appear but, as noted above, the matter is ultimately one for the minister, who may offer to appear in person. Moreover, civil servants cannot disclose or discuss the advice they gave to ministers, only the action they took on behalf of ministers (ibid., at [33]). However, the *Ministerial Code* provides some protection to the civil service. If the Accounting Officer considers that a minister's action breaches requirements of propriety, regularity or value for money, he or she may set out objections in writing and, if the minister decides to override the objections, the Accounting Officer may 'seek' written instruction, and the Comptroller and Auditor-General must be notified (at [5.4]–[5.5]).

15.9 Executive agencies and non-ministerial government departments

Since the 1980s, many government functions have been removed from the traditional civil service structure of a pyramid topped by ministers and transferred to semi-separate 'executive agencies' (originally called 'Next Steps' agencies), sometimes competing for work with private bodies, for example to run prisons.

Executive agencies are part of the civil service and remain subject to control by ministers. Each agency has a sponsoring government department, and most departments have several agencies. Examples include HM Courts and Tribunals Service, UK Visas and Immigration, the Driver and Vehicle Licensing Agency, the Prison Service and the Met Office.

The division between an agency and its sponsoring department is that responsibility for 'service delivery' should reside with the agency, while policy matters should be reserved for the department acting under direct ministerial control. 'Framework agreements' made between the agency and the sponsoring department (sometimes with the Treasury as a party) establish the relationship between the two. The framework agreement contains the strategy and financial arrangements under which the agency will work. It sets out the objectives of the agency and the division of responsibility between the agency and the department.

Agencies are permitted to run themselves semi-independently from their sponsoring government department, recruiting their own staff and managing themselves by copying the practices of private businesses. A chief executive for each agency is appointed by the minister, usually for a fixed period, to be responsible for its day-to-day management.

The chief executive is responsible to the minister but, as Accounting Officer, also appears before select committees of Parliament to answer MPs' questions about the functioning of the agency, but not policy matters. Controversially, this suggests that a convention may have been emerging under which agency chief executives are directly responsible to Parliament in their own right. MPs have also been encouraged to approach chief executives directly on behalf of their constituents, and chief executives answer written parliamentary questions. The answers are published in *Hansard* in order to avoid the bypassing of Parliament which might occur if chief executives responded directly to individual MPs.

Executive agencies are distinct from non-ministerial government departments. These have long existed. They are departments which carry out basic governmental functions but, in the interests of stability and impartiality, are not subject to direct political control. They are normally created by statute and have a separate legal identity. They are, however, servants of the Crown and their staff are civil servants. They include, among others, HM Revenue and Customs, the Crown Prosecution Service, the Serious Fraud Office, the Charity Commission and the regulators of energy companies.

Non-ministerial departments are headed by a civil servant who, unlike in the case of a ministerial department, is directly accountable to Parliament. A minister has powers over it which depend on the particular statute. Normally a minister appoints the chair or board. Dismissal powers vary according to the extent of independence and security desired. Sometimes a minister has power to give non-binding 'guidance' or binding 'directions'.

15.9.1 Ministerial responsibility

The fragmentation of government departments, coupled with the privatisation of some governmental activities (the 'hollowing out' of the state), has placed the classic model of accountability under strain. In principle, ministerial responsibility applies in full to executive agencies (*Ministerial Code*, [1.3(b)]), but the policy/operational distinction discussed above complicates the matter. The Commons Public Service Committee stated that ministers remain accountable for what goes on in agencies just as in their departments (see HC 1995–96, 313, [84]–[91], [109]–[23]; Cabinet Office, *Modernising Government* (Cm 4310, 2002)).

The *Carltona* principle (Section 15.8.5) applies to executive agencies when they are exercising functions delegated by a minister by means of the normal framework agreement (see *R v Secretary of State, ex p Sherwin* (1996) 32 BMLR 1; cf. Freedland, 'The Rule against Delegation and the *Carltona* Doctrine in an Agency Context' [1996] PL 19, arguing that this should only be the case where there is a clear line of decision-making from the minister). In *Sherwin*, Brightman J thought that there might be activities of an executive agency which no one would reasonably connect with the minister but gave no example.

It seems that ministerial responsibility is limited in the case of a non-ministerial government department to circumstances where a minister possesses specific statutory powers in relation to the department. This is appropriate since bodies of this kind frequently exercise quasi-judicial powers akin to those of courts or tribunals so that it is important that politicians maintain a separation.

15.10 Non-departmental public bodies: 'quangos'

The UK Constitution has no general concept of government, or the state, and there are no constitutional limitations on the kind of bodies that can be created to act on behalf of government. Thus, there is a bewildering profusion of specialised bodies created at different times for particular political purposes. Functions are conferred on many miscellaneous specialised bodies outside the central government: these are usually created by statute but sometimes informally (see *Public Bodies* (2019): for example, the Environment Agency controlling waterways and regulating pollution; Natural England regulating nature conservation; the Arts Council which funds the arts; and the British Council, which promotes knowledge and understanding between the people of the UK and other countries). These bodies (currently about 235, but their numbers are constantly changing) are often called 'quangos' (quasi-autonomous non-governmental agencies), but there is no legal significance in these labels.

Quangos are not part of the Crown, so their members and staff are not civil servants, and they are not directly headed by a minister. Thus, they fall outside the traditional chain of accountability between Parliament, ministers and civil servants. However, depending on the particular statute, ministers have certain important functions in relation to them which usually enable a minister to dominate.

Quangos enable selected functions to be exercised outside the constraints of central government, giving at least an appearance of greater independence than in the case of a government department. This might be because a function is specialised, or is regarded as uncontroversial, or requires impartiality akin to the judicial function, or is a problem that a particular minister prefers to pass on to someone else. Quangos therefore embody a fundamental constitutional dilemma arising out of clashing incommensurable values (Section 1.9) in that the aspiration towards independence from political pressure conflicts with the need for accountability.

Some functions which might be expected to call for impartial expertise retain at least some involvement by ministers, presumably because they are politically sensitive: for example the approval of company takeovers or mergers. To add to the complexity, some specialist bodies whose functions are similar to those of quangos are within the central government as non-ministerial departments (above). Being part of the Crown, non-ministerial departments are responsible to Parliament for all their activities. The existence of quangos is therefore a pragmatic matter without a coherent constitutional basis.

Quangos may be classified into five main functions. Many bodies have more than one function, raising questions about conflicts of interest. The main functions are:

(i) service providers, such as Homes England or the National Gallery;
(ii) risk assessors, who provide government with specialist information and who may also have enforcement powers, for example the Environment Agency;
(iii) boundary watchers, who ensure that providers pay regard to the public interest and do not abuse their powers, for example the Care Quality Commission, which monitors, inspects and regulates care services to make sure they meet fundamental standards of quality and safety;
(iv) auditors concerned with ensuring that the public money is properly spent, such as the Office for Budget Responsibility ;
(v) adjudicators who resolve disputes, such as the Independent Agricultural Appeals Panel. These bodies provide accountability but also raise questions about their own accountability.

Tribunals (Section 20.1) are also regarded as non-departmental public bodies but are best regarded as part of the judicial system.

Quangos are usually managed by boards appointed by ministers. They provide a useful source of patronage, whereby a minister can give posts on the boards of quangos to persons s/he wishes to favour or keep quiet. The same people are often recycled between several quangos. Some include representatives of particular interests or local councillors.

The main quangos can be divided into advisory bodies and executive bodies, although many have both functions. Advisory bodies, such as various health, education, trade, scientific and agricultural authorities and committees, have no decision-making power but give independent advice to ministers, thus legitimising government policy. Advisory bodies can be created by ministers, or indeed anyone else, without statutory authorisation.

Executive bodies such as the Environment Agency require statutory powers. Their powers include granting licences and permits, requiring registration, enforcing compliance with standards and procedures by means, for example, of inspections, and auditing accounts and other documents. They might also carry out operations such as flood relief work. There are also a few statutory 'public corporations' that run operational services. During the 1980s, many public corporations were converted into private companies, supervised by a new breed of regulators (Section 20.4). The surviving public corporations are constituted either by statute or under company law on the model of private companies. These may be wholly or partly owned by the government in the form of shareholdings or under statute, for example the Independent Broadcasting Authority, the Post Office and, as a result of the financial crisis in 2008, some banks. This kind of body may be subject to the commercial pressures of a private company, so that public accountability is even more blurred.

The Bank of England is a special type of quango of central importance to government. It was created after the seventeenth-century revolution in order to support loans to the Crown and, as such, was crucial to the development of a powerful state. Nationalised after the Second World War, its activities are interrelated with those of the Treasury. Its independence is safeguarded by statute (Bank of England Acts 1946, 1964, 1998). It administers the government's bank account. It has responsibilities relating to the stability of the economy, including the money supply and determining the basic interest rate. It lends to other banks and is the lender of last resort on behalf of Parliament. It also regulates the financial services industry in relation to governance and financial security (Financial Services Act 2012). Its Governor appears before Parliament in his own right.

Quangos are formally independent of government. Setting up a quango therefore enables a minister to avoid direct responsibility. However, ministers are likely to have substantial powers of control, sometimes including power to give general directions for which they are accountable to Parliament. Board members are usually appointed by a minister and funding is mainly provided by ministers from funds voted by Parliament to the minister's department. In addition, ministers may produce non-statutory 'advice', 'guidance' or 'concordats' regulating the relationship between the quango and government departments, or informally exercise influence over compliant members of quango boards.

In theory, quangos might provide a vehicle for diverse democracy where independent opinions can be publicly expressed. This may, however, be more apparent than real. Independently minded persons are unlikely to be appointed to the boards of quangos. Members of quangos are usually appointed for fixed periods, and quangos can be created or dissolved either by statute or by ministers at any time.

The constitutional accountability of quangos is unclear and indirect since these are not government departments yet are normally funded mainly by Parliament.

Other constitutional issues are, first, whether a body is part of the Crown so as to enjoy legal immunities (in the case of statutory bodies the statute will usually make this clear; most quangos are not part of the Crown); second, whether it has any genuine democratic element, this being unlikely; third, the extent to which it is accountable to Parliament; and fourth, whether it is a public authority for particular purposes such as the HRA (as it usually will be: Section 22.7). Bodies with powers conferred by statute may also be immune from liability for damages provided that they do not exceed their statutory powers (see e.g. *Marcic v Thames Water Utilities* [2004] 1 All ER 135; *X (Minors) v Bedfordshire CC* [1995] 2 AC 633).

The appointment of members of quangos has been subject to concerns that they are chosen from a pool of persons linked by personal, professional, business or political relationships. This problem of patronage is not confined to quangos and is inherent in the political side of the constitution (Section 5.9). As a result of the work of the Committee on Standards in Public Life, the process for ministerial appointments of members of the main quangos, and some non-ministerial government departments and public corporations, is subject to general regulation, monitoring and audit by an independent Commissioner for Public Appointments, who is appointed by the prime minister under the royal prerogative (Public Appointments Orders in Council 2019). However, the Commissioner has advisory powers only and does not take part in individual appointments.

The Cabinet Office has issued a *Governance Code on Public Appointments* (2016) which includes a requirement for open advertisement of vacancies and to ensure that the selection is on merit and that the process is open, transparent and fair, and encourages diversity. The appointment principles include a role for independent assessors and 'proportionality', which enables simplified procedures to be used in the case of less important roles. Reappointments are permitted, but only following a satisfactory performance appraisal. However, it is doubtful that the *Code* can fully address the problem that the pool of applicants is likely to be dominated by insiders.

Quangos have limited protection against interference by ministers. Under the Public Bodies Act 2011, a minister can abolish, modify or alter the funding arrangement of many quangos. However, the minister cannot exercise these powers so as to prevent the quango from acting independently of ministers in cases where the quango exercises judicial powers, or where it has enforcement activities in relation to obligations imposed on a minister or which exercises oversight or scrutiny of the actions of a minister (s 7). An Order made by a minister under the Act is subject to parliamentary scrutiny by the 'special affirmative procedure' (Section 13.5.5). Significant numbers of quangos have been abolished under this Act: the total stood at 904 in 2010.

Since quangos are normally funded by Parliament and their accounts are laid before Parliament, in principle, they are accountable to it. A select committee might summon the chief executive or chair of a quango to appear before it and disclose documents. Enforcement of this obligation might, in some cases, require a resolution of the Commons (Section 13.5.5). However, the parliamentary process is geared towards the hierarchy of ministers and their departments so that in practice, accountability may be sporadic. Ministers may be accountable to Parliament for their own involvement, in relation to appointments, funding and general oversight and policy. Some quangos closely related to government departments are subject to the Parliamentary Ombudsman (Section 20.2).

There are also numerous voluntary bodies and private companies, for example charities such as the National Trust, housing associations and the Royal Society for the Prevention of Cruelty to Animals, which carry out functions for the public good, sometimes under contract on behalf of the government with state funding, and occasionally subject to special statutory provisions (e.g. National Trust Act 1907). It must be established in each context whether the body itself or a particular function of the body is regarded as public or private (Section 19.5). These bodies are not subject to direct political accountability but are accountable only to their own members.

Comparison between quangos, executive agencies and non-ministerial government departments (NMDs):

▶ Executive agencies are not separate legal entities but are part of the Crown. Their staffs are therefore civil servants. Quangos are separate legal entities or committees of individuals. Their staffs are not civil servants. NMDs are separate legal entities but part of the Crown.

▶ Ministers are responsible for the acts of executive agencies. Ministers are only responsible for the acts of quangos and NMDs in relation to the actual involvement of the minister.

▶ Executive agencies may exercise powers on behalf of ministers under statute or the royal prerogative. Quangos may freely give advice to anyone who will listen but have no legal powers unless conferred specifically by statute. NMDs have direct statutory powers.

- An executive agency is required to carry out instructions from ministers as to any of its activities. A quango is nominally independent of ministers, except where the minister has statutory power to intervene. However, this difference may be unreal given the desire of those chosen to be members of quangos to please their patrons. Ministers may have specific statutory powers in relation to NMDs.
- As Accounting Officer, the chief executive of an executive agency must appear before parliamentary select committees, but on behalf of the minister. The leaders of quangos and NMDs appear in their own right (Section 15.7).
- Executive agency appointments, in common with most civil service appointments, are subject to regulation by the statutory Civil Service Commission with a view to preventing political involvement (Constitutional Reform and Governance Act 2010, ss 11–14). Quangos and NMDs are subject to regulation by the non-statutory Commissioner for Public Appointments.

Summary

- The prime minister has significant powers under the royal prerogative, pre-eminently to dissolve Parliament (subject currently to the Fixed Term Parliaments Act 2011), to appoint and dismiss ministers and to control the government agenda. However, these are largely convention, and determined political opposition could limit a prime minister.

- As a body, the power of the Cabinet has decreased in recent years, with decisions effectively being made by smaller groups within and outside the Cabinet and by departments of the executive.

- There are few constitutional laws or conventions concerning the detailed distribution of functions between departments. Political and administrative considerations, rather than constitutional principle, determine the number, size, shape and interrelationship of government departments. The creation of bodies outside the framework of the Crown is of greater constitutional and legal significance.

- The convention of ministerial responsibility is central to the UK Constitution. Collective responsibility means that all members of the government must loyally support government policy and decisions, and must not disclose internal disagreements. Individual responsibility means that each minister is answerable to Parliament for all the activities of the department under his/her control. It also means that civil servants are not personally accountable. From these principles follow (i) the traditional notion of the civil service as anonymous and politically neutral, having a duty to serve with unquestioning loyalty governments of any political complexion; (ii) the secrecy that pervades the British system of government.

- The traditional doctrine of ministerial responsibility may be out of line with the practices of modern government and functions effectively to shield the government from accountability. In particular: (i) Cabinet decisions are rarely made collectively; (ii) many government bodies are not directly controlled by ministers, the creation of executive agencies reinforcing this; (iii) civil servants are increasingly expected to make political decisions and to be responsible for the financial management of their allotted activities; (iv) public functions are increasingly being given to special bodies or private bodies. Thus, the traditional chain of accountability between Parliament, ministers and civil servants is weakened.

- In law, civil servants are servants of the Crown. They can be dismissed 'at pleasure', that is, without notice and without reason being given. However, the modern cases suggest that there can be a contractual relationship between the Crown and a civil servant and that a civil servant can be protected by the law of judicial review.

- In light of the convention relating to ministerial responsibility, civil servants are regarded as servants of the government of the day with an absolute duty of loyalty to ministers. Their advice to ministers is secret, and they appear before Parliament only with the consent of ministers. They are supposed to be non-political and neutral, responsible for giving ministers objective advice and for carrying out ministerial orders. However, 'special advisers' need not be neutral or appointed on merit. Their existence creates tensions within the civil service.

- The internal arrangements for the carrying out of government business involve entrusting individual civil servants with considerable decision-making responsibility and, in recent years, with financial accountability within the government machine. Many civil servants work in executive agencies, hived off from the central departmental structure and outside the direct control of ministers. This has led to tensions between traditional ideas of ministerial responsibility and the actual channels of accountability, and has raised problems in connection with the supposed distinction between policy and operational matters.

Exercises

15.1 Consider whether the relevant laws and conventions support Bagehot's view that the Cabinet is the central institution of the UK Constitution.

15.2 A general election has just been held. The prime minister's party has won the largest number of votes but has only 45 per cent of the seats in the Commons. The Solidarity Party, with 10 per cent of the seats, is willing to support the prime minister's party but only if he resigns in favour of a candidate supported by the Solidarity Party. Advise the Queen as to the constitutional position.

15.3 Although it has a substantial majority in the House of Commons, the government has difficulties in getting Parliament to approve its policies, mainly because many of its backbenchers are discontented, claiming that the voters are unhappy. Green, the prime minister, is unpopular and behaving increasingly eccentrically, but refuses to resign. Advise the Queen as to the constitutional position. Advise Tina, the Leader of the Opposition, whether a legal action to remove Green might succeed.

15.4 'Ministerial responsibility is, in practice, an obstacle to the availability of information and to the holding of government to account' (Oliver). Discuss.

15.5 To what extent can Parliament and the public scrutinise the activities of a civil servant?

15.6 When should a minister resign?

15.7 Critically evaluate the constitutional significance of special advisers.

15.8 The government creates an executive agency to regulate motorway service areas. The Secretary of State for Consumption delegates to the agency his statutory powers to ensure the 'adequate provision of motorway services'. Under a contract made with the Secretary of State, the agency promises to achieve certain targets, including a clean environment. The agency employs Grasper plc to run the Crusty Group of service areas. Due to cuts in its budget from government, the agency does not check Grasper's performance, but increases its chief executive's annual bonus by 100 per cent. A newspaper subsequently discovers that many of the catering staff employed by the Crusty Group are illegal immigrants, and that several of them have contracted food poisoning. In response to a parliamentary question, the Secretary of State asserts that the matter is no concern of his and he knows nothing about it. He also refuses to permit the agency chief executive to appear before the Select Committee for Consumption. Discuss.

Further reading

Appleby, 'Reform of the Attorney General: Comparing Britain and Australia' [2016] PL 573

Bamforth, 'Accountability of and to the Legislature' in Bamforth and Leyland (eds), *Accountability in the Contemporary Constitution* (Oxford University Press 2013)

Burnham and Piper, *Britain's Modernised Civil Service* (Palgrave Macmillan 2008)

Daintith and Page, *The Executive in the Constitution* (Oxford University Press 1999) chs 1–6

Feaver and Sheehy, 'The Political Division of Regulatory Labour: A Legal Theory of Agency Selection' (2015) 35 OJLS 153

Flinders, 'The Enduring Centrality of Individual Ministerial Responsibility within the British Constitution' (2000) 6 *Journal of Legislative Studies* 73

Poole, 'The Executive in Public Law' in Jowell and O'Cinneide (eds), *The Changing Constitution* (9th edn, Oxford University Press 2019)

Sampson, *Who Runs This Place?* (John Murray 2004) chs 1–4, 7, 8

Samuels, 'Abolish the Office of the Attorney General' [2014] PL 609

Vennard, 'Prime Ministerial Succession' [2008] PL 302

Yong and Hazell, *Special Advisers* (Hart Publishing 2014)

16.1 The background to devolution in the UK

In relation to Scotland, the Supreme Court has called the devolution legislation a fundamental constitutional settlement (*H v Lord Advocate* [2012] 3 WLR 151, [30]). However, typical of constitutional change in the UK, the devolution provisions for Scotland, Wales and Northern Ireland were made without regard to any general system of constitutional reform and left fundamental issues unresolved. These include the position of England and its regions, financial issues that underlie democratic accountability and the pathway of future changes.

This showed itself in the chaotic arguments surrounding the referendum in Scotland of September 2014, in which a proposal for Scottish independence was defeated by a majority of 55 to 45 per cent. At a late stage in the campaign, the UK government was panicked into undertaking to give Scotland increased taxation powers, apparently without considering the impact of such an undertaking on the wider issues, and potentially unravelling the structure of government throughout the UK (Section 16.6). The devolution arrangements in Northern Ireland are unstable due to the absence of a clear settlement between the two power-sharing political groupings. The restricted – although expanding – form of devolution given to Wales has also created some instability.

The UK is a union of what were the separate states of England and Wales, part of Ireland and Scotland. It is far from being a unified territory, having been cobbled together over the centuries by conquest and treaties. The history of the three territories is very different and reflected in different devolution arrangements.

Scotland has the most extensive powers. Scotland was a separate kingdom often at war with England until the mid-sixteenth century. During the civil wars of the seventeenth century, its northern Catholic population and southern Protestants (Covenanters) mirrored the religious conflict in England, and violent resistance to the Protestant settlement lasted until the mid-eighteenth century. The Act of Union 1707 brought together the two states, nominally as equals (Section 4.6). Scotland kept its separate legal system, but its Parliament was assimilated into the English Parliament, which became the Parliament of Great Britain.

Wales was a group of principalities conquered by England during medieval times. Since Tudor times its laws and government have been assimilated with those of England (Act of Union 1536). Wales had no governmental organisations of its own until 1965, when the Welsh Office was created as a department of the UK executive. The devolved powers of Wales have traditionally been more limited than those of Scotland and Northern Ireland, but have grown significantly as the devolution settlement has matured.

The turbulent history of Ireland has left a legacy of grievance which dominates the devolution arrangements. Laws made by the Irish Parliament had been subject to English control since 'Poyning's Law' (1494). However, until Tudor times, England effectively controlled only an area around Dublin called the Pale. Successive governments attempted to extend control to the whole of Ireland and, during the seventeenth century, there was a policy of extensive settlement of Protestants, mainly from Scotland. There was violent repression of dissent.

The union with Great Britain, which formed the United Kingdom (Act of Union 1800), was created because of a failure to control Ireland as a colony. It abolished the ancient Irish Parliament, and Irish MPs now sat in the UK Parliament. In 1922, after a civil war, Ireland became an independent state within the British Commonwealth: the Irish Free State (Anglo-Irish Treaty 1921). However, Northern Ireland immediately resumed membership of the UK under the treaty. The present Republic of Ireland came into existence following a referendum in 1937.

Between 1922 and 1972, Northern Ireland had its own Parliament and internal self-government. However, the permanent majority commanded by the Unionist, mainly Protestant, community was regarded by the Nationalist, Catholic minority as repressive and discriminatory, and between 1968 and the late 1980s there was continuous violent conflict, extending to the British mainland. These conflicts led to direct rule by the UK government from 1972.

Northern Ireland could be regarded as a prototype for devolution in that various devices were introduced, unfamiliar to the UK Constitution, in a series of attempts to achieve peace, sometimes short-lived but resurfacing in the current law. They included a devolved lawmaking assembly, the referendum, proportionate representation and a bill of rights. Special anti-terrorist measures also played a part (Section 25.5).

Before the introduction of devolved government, the internal affairs of Scotland and Wales were governed by the UK central executive. This took the form of 'administrative devolution' to ministers for each territory. There was no specific democratic power base or accountability mechanism linking the ministers to their regions since the relevant minister might have an English constituency. In 1973, the Royal Commission on the Constitution (Cmnd 5460) asserted that government in the UK was overcentralised, and recommended devolved government. Referendums were subsequently held in Scotland and Wales which foundered because they failed to obtain the required two-thirds majorities in favour of change. The Labour government that took office in 1997 was supportive of devolved government as part of an agenda of constitutional reform in favour of dispersing power. Further referendums (this time requiring only a bare majority) produced majorities in favour of devolution. In Scotland, the majority was 74.29 per cent on a 60.23 per cent turnout, in Wales 50.3 per cent on a 50.1 per cent turnout. The referendum in Northern Ireland included other matters concerning the relationship with the Republic of Ireland (majority 71.1 per cent, turnout 81.5 per cent). There was a corresponding referendum in the Republic of Ireland which concerned a constitutional change under which the Republic modified its long-standing claim to govern the whole of Ireland.

Legislation was enacted to give devolved powers to a Scottish Parliament (Scotland Act 1998, with further powers granted by the Scotland Acts 2012 and 2016), a Northern Ireland Assembly (Northern Ireland Act 1998) and, to a lesser extent, a Welsh Assembly (Government of Wales Act 1998). The Government of Wales Act 2006 increased the powers of the Welsh regime and restructured its government. This involved a further referendum with a 63.5 per cent majority in favour of wider powers on a turnout of 35.4 per cent. The powers of the Welsh Assembly remain more limited than those of the others but have gradually increased by way of the Wales Acts 2014 and 2017.

16.2 The structure of devolution

The devolution statutes could be regarded as embodying a form of constitution for each territory. The basic devolution arrangements are entrenched in the devolution statutes which specifically provide that they cannot be altered by the devolved regimes (below). On the other hand, the devolution arrangements are not wholly stable in that they can be altered by Parliament at any time. The Welsh provisions in particular have been substantially altered, with Scotland also gaining more powers in recent years. The devolution arrangements for the three territories have many features in common, but there are important differences. This is sometimes called 'asymmetric devolution'. There are three fundamental differences.

First, Wales does not have its own legal system, there being a single legal system for England and Wales, although there are increasing calls to establish a separate Welsh jurisdiction (see National Assembly for Wales, Constitutional and Legislative Affairs Committee, *Inquiry into a Separate Welsh Jurisdiction* (2012); Commission on Justice in Wales (2019)). Scotland has its own legal system, with substantive law different from English law in many respects. Northern Ireland also has its own legal system, although its laws are more closely related to English law.

Second, in the cases of Scotland and Northern Ireland, the Acts do not specify the powers of the devolved governments but specify what they cannot do: a 'reserved powers' model. They can legislate on any other matter. Initially, Wales could legislate only on matters specifically assigned to it in the legislation: a 'conferred powers' model; however, the Wales Act 2017 places Wales on the same footing as the other two systems.

Third, there are particular restrictions upon the composition and powers of the Northern Ireland Assembly and Executive designed to ensure power sharing between the main political groups, reflecting the troubled history of the province.

All three devolved structures are based on the separation of powers with legislature, executive and judiciary as separate institutions. They are modelled broadly on the UK parliamentary system. Thus, ministers who lead the executive must be members of the legislature, and the executive must be supported by the legislature. However, they have different voting systems from Westminster, which make strong executive governments less likely. The devolution framework created by statute has given legal substance to matters that in the UK parliamentary system are only convention.

The devolved governments are funded mainly by grants from the UK Parliament. There is therefore only partial accountability to their own voters. Scotland and Wales have some tax-raising powers, including a rate of income tax. Northern Ireland currently has no tax-raising powers. In relation to the continuing role of the UK government, there is a Secretary of State responsible to the UK Parliament and a committee of Parliament for each devolved country.

There are provisions for dealing with issues that cross boundaries and for settling disputes between the different layers of government. First, there are political mechanisms which give protection to the devolved governments so that the arrangements are sometimes called 'quasi-federal'. Under the 'Sewel Convention', which copies the arrangements made during an earlier period in Northern Ireland, the UK Parliament does not normally legislate for a devolved territory without the consent of its legislature (see Cabinet Office, *Memorandum of Understanding and Supplementary Agreements* (2013), at [14]–[17]). This provides a constitutional safeguard and ensures that UK officials consider the possible impact on the devolved areas when preparing legislation. The Convention has been placed on a statutory footing by s 2 Scotland Act 2016 and s 2 Wales Act 2017. It is given effect in the devolved legislatures in respect of UK bills by means of 'legislative consent motions' (also known as 'Sewel motions'). However, because it remains sovereign, the Westminster Parliament can legislate irrespective of consent, as it did in respect of the European Union (Withdrawal) Act 2018, the European Union (Withdrawal Agreement) Act 2020 and the European Union (Future Relationship) Act 2020 (Sections 10.5.5 and 10.5.6).

Second, there are also non-legally binding 'concordats' between each UK government department and the devolved administrations. These put in place principles for coordinating the activities of the governments, for example through a joint ministerial committee, but may buttress the kind of secretive informality characteristic of the UK Constitution (see *Memorandum of Understanding and Supplementary Agreements* (2013); Poivier, 'The Function of Intergovernmental Agreements' [2001] PL 134; Rawlings, 'Concordats of the Constitution' (2000) 116 LQR 257).

Third, there are statutory provisions for cooperation. These provide for shared functions, and enable functions to be transferred in both directions between the UK government and the devolved regimes (see e.g. Scotland Act 1998, ss 56, 57, 63, 108, 109). Thus, although devolution does not in law affect parliamentary supremacy, it is vital to recognise that political pressures may well do so in practice.

As already noted, devolution is an evolving process. The Scotland Act 2012 gave increased powers to the Scottish government, most importantly in respect of taxation. The Scotland Act 2016, which gave effect to the recommendations made in light of the 'no' vote in the independence referendum of 2014, devolved a variety of further powers, allowed the Scottish Government to set rates and bands of income tax, assigned a portion of VAT to the Government, and declared that the Scottish Parliament and Government are to be considered permanent parts of the UK's constitutional arrangements, not to be abolished without a decision of the people of Scotland voting in a referendum. The powers of the Welsh Assembly were expanded by the Government of Wales Act 2006, while the Wales Act 2014 devolved certain taxation powers to the Assembly and made provision for a referendum on a power to set rates of income tax. The referendum requirement was removed by the Wales Act 2017, with a

Welsh rate of income tax being set from April 2019. The 2017 Act also moved Wales to a 'reserved powers' model (see above), recognised the permanence of the Welsh Assembly (which was renamed the Senedd Cymru, or Welsh Parliament, in 2020) and Government, and provided that they are not to be abolished without a decision of the Welsh people in a referendum, as well as according further legislative powers to the Parliament. The Welsh and Scottish models of devolution are therefore increasingly converging, notwithstanding that support for nationalist political parties is considerably stronger in Scotland than in Wales.

The future trajectory of devolution is very difficult to predict in light of the UK's decision to leave the EU. England and Wales voted to leave, but Scotland and Northern Ireland to remain. This has created considerable ongoing tensions, as outlined in Section 10.5.5. It is plausible that the long-term outcome of this difference of views, when set alongside the imperative to establish a common framework to ensure the efficient working of the 'internal market' post-Brexit, will point to the need for the relationships between the distinct parts of the UK to be placed on a more solid constitutional footing than is presently the case. On the other hand, a further independence referendum in Scotland seems highly likely to eventuate in due course. The considerable difficulties concerning the post-Brexit border in Northern Ireland (Section 10.5.3) also present an existential threat to the continuation of the UK as presently constituted.

16.2.1 Legal limits on the devolved lawmakers

There is a similar general framework but different legal limits on the devolved lawmakers in the three regimes. In all cases, the devolved lawmakers and governments cannot exceed the limits on their powers imposed by the respective UK Acts (Scotland Act 1998, ss 29, 30; Government of Wales Act 2006, ss 94, 95; Northern Ireland Act 1998, ss 6, 7). The courts are responsible for ensuring that these limits are respected, thus giving them a strong constitutional role (see *The UK Withdrawal from the European Union (Legal Continuity) (Scotland) Bill – A Reference by the Attorney General and the Advocate General for Scotland (Scotland)* [2018] UKSC 64, 'the Scottish Continuity Bill case').

In order to decide whether a law enacted by a devolved lawmaker is within its limits, there is a two-stage test. The court must look at the purpose and effect of the law in question: first, to see whether it affects a matter outside the devolved power; and second, if it does so, whether this is merely incidental or consequential, in which case it is valid (e.g. Government of Wales Act 2006, s 108(5)).

There are extra provisions concerning alterations to Scottish private and criminal law so that, even if the alteration is incidental or consequential, it is invalid if it is 'special' to a matter reserved to the UK Parliament (Scotland Act 1998, Sched. 4). The meaning of 'special' is obscure. It may mean 'important' (see *HM Advocate* v *Martin and Miller* [2010] UKSC 10).

This approach is similar to the federal approach under which, when examining the scope of a law, a court should concentrate on its basic purpose, ignoring any merely incidental straying outside its territory: the 'pith and substance doctrine' used, for example, in Canada (see *Gallagher v Lynn* [1937] AC 863, 870; *A-G v National Assembly for Wales Commission* [2013] 1 AC 792: *A-G's Reference Re Agricultural Sector (Wales) Bill* [2014] UKSC 43; Aroney (2014)).

For example, in *HM Advocate v Martin and Miller* [2010], the Supreme Court held that a Scottish Act that increased the power of the sheriff to impose a sentence on summary conviction of a criminal offence for up to 12 months was valid, even though it impinged upon the topic of road traffic, which was reserved to the UK since this was incidental only. However, there was a strongly expressed dissent from Lords Rodger and Kerr, who thought that the matter was 'special' to a reserved matter.

This leads to the question of whether the devolution arrangements can be regarded as 'constitutional statutes'. This requires Parliament to use very clear language if it wishes to override them (Section 8.4.2). In *H v Lord Advocate* [2012] at [30] the Supreme Court held that the Scotland Act was a constitutional statute that could be repealed only by express language.

More controversially, a constitutional statute may also fall to be interpreted more broadly than other statutes in the light of the fundamental concerns of the particular community. In *Robinson v Secretary of State for Northern Ireland* [2002] UKHL 32, a majority of the House of Lords held that this was the case in relation to the Northern Ireland Act (Section 3.2).

However, neither the majority solution nor the more ordinary approach of the minority successfully dealt with the constitutional issue in question (Section 16.4). Subsequently, the Supreme Court has held that, despite their constitutional importance, the devolution statutes should be interpreted in the same way as ordinary statutes (*A-G v National Assembly for Wales Commission* [2013] at [80]; *AG's Reference Re Agricultural Sector (Wales) Bill 2013* [2014]). In reaching this conclusion, the judges emphasised the need for clarity and certainty in the devolution arrangements (see also *Imperial Tobacco Ltd v Lord Advocate* [2012] UKSC 61 at [14], [15]). However, even in the case of ordinary methods of interpretation, the context and purpose of the Act are relevant (Section 3.2). Moreover, this conclusion may now be questionable in light of the permanence of the constitutional arrangements in Scotland and Wales as stated in the ss 1 of the Scotland Act 2016, and of the Wales Act 2017.

Related to the question of constitutional interpretation is that of federalism (Section 1.7). Strictly speaking, there is no federal element since the devolution arrangements do not affect the unlimited legal power of the UK Parliament to make laws for the devolved regions and also to override laws made by the devolved regimes (e.g. Scotland Act 1998, s 28(7)). However, Lady Justice Arden ((2014) PL 189, 194) has suggested that devolution is in reality federalism because '[t]he actual label is not important. It means a stable relationship under which in fact two sets of political institutions exercise mutually exclusive powers in the same territory'. Thus, the federal principle requires that there should be mutual respect for the freedom of each unit of government.

In this context, the political concepts of autonomy and independence can be distinguished. An autonomous body may have a superior, but the superior allows the body a large degree of self-government which it respects. An independent body has no superior, as in a true federal system. A republican (Section 2.5) would probably reject the notion of autonomy in this context on the basis that a kind slave master remains a master.

The legislation gives some guidance with a view to reducing conflicts. The courts are required to 'read down', that is to say interpret, laws made by the devolved lawmakers narrowly, 'if such a reading is possible', to make the law valid as within the powers of the legislature in question (Government of Wales Act 2006, s 154(2); Scotland Act 1998, s 101; Northern Ireland Act 1998, s 83; see *A-G v National Assembly for Wales Commission* [2013]). However, these provisions are triggered only where the legislation in issue is ambiguous.

The devolution structure could reasonably be regarded as essentially federal if both the political conventions and the legal provisions are taken into account (especially now that the 'Sewel Convention' has been given statutory recognition). Indeed, the history, politics and cultures of the three communities seem to have sufficient similarities, overlaps and differences to make federal arrangements appropriate. However, federalism has traditionally been viewed as an inappropriate political structure for the UK, since one constituent element (England) is so dominant as regards its population and resources. Further devolution to regions of England might provide a way forward in this regard, but support for such a move has largely been lacking (Section 16.6).

The following sections discuss the main features of each regime. Unless stated otherwise, the relevant provisions in Wales and Northern Ireland are similar to those in Scotland. The detailed matters that are devolved to each regime are significantly different but will not be discussed here. They are set out in schedules to the statutes.

16.3   Scotland

Under the Act of Union 1707, Scotland has its own judicial system, while its Church, although not 'established' in the sense that the Crown and Parliament are not part of its governance, enjoys independence by statute (Church of Scotland Act 1921). There is an argument that the UK Parliament cannot override these aspects of the Act of Union, although section 37 of the Scotland Act 1998, which makes the Act of Union subject to the 1998 Act, assumes that the UK Parliament can do so (Section 8.5.2). The Scotland Act 1998 created the greatest freedom of the three regimes. There is a Scottish Parliament and a Scottish government responsible to it.

Scottish devolution claims to uphold four basic aspirations (see Report of the Consultative Steering Group on the Scottish Parliament, *Shaping Scotland's Parliament* (1998), at [2]; Procedures Committee of the Scottish Parliament, *The Founding Principles of the Scottish Parliament*, SP Paper 818 (2003)). These are political guidances rather than legally enforceable provisions. They are:

- sharing of power between the people, Parliament and the executive;
- accountability of the executive to the Parliament and the Parliament to the people;
- accessibility, openness, responsiveness and participation;
- promotion of equal opportunities.

However, the structure of the devolution legislation, like that of the UK parliamentary system, relies on a central executive responsible to Parliament and with no direct involvement of the people other than voting in party-oriented elections. On the other hand, the introduction of proportional representation and the relatively stronger powers of the Parliament in relation to government appointments may marginally alter the balance in favour of Parliament relative to Westminster.

16.3.1   The Scottish Parliament

The Scottish Parliament can enact Acts on any matter other than those specified in the 1998 Act (below). Acts of the Scottish Parliament require royal assent (Scotland Act 1998, s 28). The validity of the procedure leading to an enactment does not affect the Act's validity (s 28(5)) but otherwise, Acts of the Scottish Parliament that are outside its competence 'are not law' (s 28).

The UK Parliament retains its full power to legislate for Scotland, thus overriding the devolution provisions (s 28(7)): see the Scottish Continuity Bill case [2018], [52]. UK statutes apply in Scotland only expressly or by necessary implication. Although sometimes called 'primary' legislation, Acts of the Scottish Parliament are strictly subordinate legislation, owing their validity only to the Scotland Act 1998. They can be set aside by the courts not only if they are outside the devolution provisions, but also under the domestic law of judicial review. However, the courts are unwilling to review a decision made by a high-level democratic body and will review the Scottish Parliament on judicial review grounds only in exceptional cases.

AXA General Insurance Ltd v HM Advocate [2011] 3 WLR 871 concerned a challenge to a Scottish Act which reversed recent case law which had removed employer's liability for certain asbestos-related illnesses. As a creation of statute, the Scottish Parliament was a subordinate body and therefore was subject to judicial review under domestic law. However, as an elected body, the Scottish Parliament was entitled to a wide margin of discretion in relation to questions of social justice such as this, and the Act was not manifestly unreasonable. The court went further. Given the democratic credentials of the Scottish (and the Welsh and Northern Ireland legislatures), judicial review would be limited. The court would ensure that the Parliament complied with the statutory limits on its power contained in the devolution legislation. Other than that, judicial review would apply only in exceptional circumstances, not present here, namely where the Parliament violates the rule of law. The ordinary judicial review standards of irrationality, unreasonableness or arbitrariness (Section 18.1) would not apply. Lord Hope, at [51], suggested that, in light of the dangers of executive domination of the Parliament, the court might intervene if the Parliament were to abolish judicial review or diminish the powers of the courts in protecting the individual: the rule of law requires that judges must retain the power to insist that legislation of this extreme kind is not law which the courts will recognise. More radically, Lord Hope also suggested that the same argument might apply to the UK Parliament (Section 8.5.6).

The following are the main limits on the power of the Scottish Parliament (s 29):

▶ Although it can alter UK statutes, it cannot, except in minor respects, amend the Scotland Act 1998 itself or various UK statutes (Sched. 4), including the parts of the Act of Union dealing with free trade. In the Scottish Continuity Bill case [2018], various provisions of the Bill which were inconsistent with the European Union (Withdrawal) Act 2018 were held by the Supreme Court to be beyond the competence of the Parliament, as the 2018 Act had been included in Sched. 4 (Section 10.5.5).

▶ It cannot alter any law that 'would form part of the law of a country or territory other than Scotland, or confer or remove functions exercisable otherwise than in or as regards Scotland'. The UK government can specify these functions (s 30(3)). This is of particular significance in relation to fishing.

▶ It was unable to override European law (s 29(2)(d)) (see now European Union (Withdrawal) Act 2018, s.12 and Section 10.5.4). It cannot override Convention rights (s 29(2)(d)), meaning rights in the ECHR specified in the HRA (Section 22.1). Thus, the court can overturn devolved legislation that violates a Convention right, something not possible under the HRA itself.

▶ It cannot remove the powers of the Lord Advocate as head of the criminal prosecution system and investigator of deaths (s 29(2)(e)).

There are 'reserved matters' on which only the UK Parliament can legislate (s 30, Sched. 5). Reserved matters can be altered by Order in Council (s 30(2)) but without affecting things already done (Scotland Act 2012, s 9). They include the most basic functions of government and important constitutional matters including the devolution arrangements themselves. Thus, the 2014 referendum in Scotland on a proposal for independence required an Order in Council, even though it was only advisory. The main reserved matters include: the civil service; the registration and funding of political parties; the Union with England; the UK Parliament; the higher Scottish courts; international relations (see the Scottish Continuity Bill case [2018], [33]); defence and national security; treason; fiscal, economic and monetary policy; currency; financial services and markets; money laundering; border controls; transport safety and regulation; media policy; employment regulation; certain health matters; the regulation of key professions; and social security. The regulation of elections (see also Scotland Act 2016, ss 3–10); drug control, drink-driving limits and certain speed limits were added by the Scotland Act 2012 Sections 1, 19, 20 and 21.

The Scottish Parliament has limited borrowing and tax-raising powers. Under the Scotland Act 2012, Scotland has power to vary income tax by up to 10 per cent, control over stamp duty on land transactions and landfill tax, and power to borrow in order to maintain its level of revenue. The Scottish rate of income tax came into effect in April 2016, initially at 10p in the pound, cancelling out a reduction in UK income tax of the same amount.

As noted above, the Scotland Act 2016 makes further changes in the wake of the 2014 independence referendum. These give substantial added powers to the Scottish Parliament, which has been described (by the UK government) as 'one of the most powerful devolved parliaments in the world' (*The Herald*, 23 February 2016), while leaving the main economic levers with the UK government. There are provisions for guarding against *ultra vires* legislation. A person in charge of a bill must, on or before its introduction in Parliament, state that in his or her view the provisions of the bill would be within the legislative competence of Parliament (s 31(1), as modified by Scotland Act 2012, s 6). The Presiding Officer, who submits bills for royal assent (s 32), must, on or before its introduction, 'decide whether or not in his view' the bill is within the powers of the Parliament (s 31(2)). These statements do not block the bill but generate political accountability. The Advocate General, the Lord Advocate or the UK Attorney General can require a bill to be referred to the Supreme Court (s 33), as happened in the Scottish Continuity Bill case [2018].

Somewhat controversially due to the 'colonial' flavour of such a power, the Secretary of State can prohibit a bill from being sent for royal assent where she or he 'has reasonable ground to believe' that the bill would be incompatible with international obligations, or the interests of national security or defence, or would have an adverse effect on the law relating to reserved matters (s 35) (see also section 58 in relation to the Scottish government).

The UK government can make subordinate legislation remedying *ultra vires* Acts of the Scottish Parliament and the Scottish government (s 107). A court or tribunal can protect people who may have relied on invalid laws by removing the retrospective effect of the invalidity or suspending the invalidity to allow the defect to be corrected (s 102).

The Parliament comprises 129 members elected by the additional member form of proportional representation (Scotland Act 1998, ss 6–8; see Section 12.5.7). Seventy-three candidates are elected on the 'first past the post' basis in local constituencies. This is topped up by a second vote on the 'open party list' basis for 56 candidates in eight regions. There is, therefore, more likely to be a coalition government involving more than one party in Scotland than is the case in the UK.

Entitlement to vote (s 11) includes adult resident citizens of the UK and EU citizens (EU citizens cannot vote in UK parliamentary elections). The voting age has been reduced to 16 for elections to the Scottish Parliament and for local elections (Scottish Elections (Reduction of Voting Age) Act 2015).

Before 1998, Scotland was entitled to at least 71 seats in the UK Parliament, thus making it over-represented in terms of its population. Section 86(1) of the Scotland Act 1998 abolishes this entitlement and places Scotland under the same regime as England in terms of the criteria for defining constituencies (Chapter 12). This has reduced the number of Scottish MPs to 59. Originally the constituencies for the Scottish Parliament were the same as those for the UK Parliament. However, by virtue of the Scottish Parliament (Constituencies) Act 2004, the link between the two has been severed.

Membership of the Scottish Parliament is subject to similar disqualifications to those applying to the UK Parliament, mainly the holding of certain public offices (s 15; Section 12.4). However, unlike in the UK Parliament, a citizen of an EU country can be a Member of the Scottish Parliament (MSP) (s 16). The same person cannot be a candidate in more than one constituency but, unlike the case in Wales, can stand in both a regional election and a local constituency election in the same region (s 5). The constituency election has priority. If the candidate wins the constituency he or she must be excluded from the regional count. The same person can be an MSP and a UK MP.

The Presiding Officer, elected by the House for the duration of the Parliament (s 19), has a larger role than is the case with the UK Parliament. This includes submitting bills for royal assent (below), recommending the appointment of the first minister, advising a dissolution (below) and proposing the date of the general election.

The Scottish Parliament sits for four years, after which it is automatically dissolved. A general election must be held on the first Thursday in May in the fourth year after the previous ordinary general election, after which the Parliament must meet within seven days (s 2) (the Presiding Officer may vary this by up to one month (s 2)). The date for the election must not be the same as for a UK general election (Fixed Term Parliaments Act 2011, s 4).

The Parliament can be dissolved earlier by the Queen in two cases (s 3). In both cases, the power to dissolve is triggered by the Presiding Officer fixing a date for an 'extraordinary general election'. The first case is following a two-thirds majority resolution of the Parliament, and the second is where the Parliament fails to designate a first minister within 28 days of the post becoming vacant. This could arise where the government is defeated on a vote of confidence requiring the first minister to resign (as with the UK Parliament there is no time limit specified for this election). However, the new Parliament must meet within seven days after the election. In the UK there is no fixed date (Section 11.2).

The Parliament and its members do not enjoy parliamentary privilege, although its members do have absolute privilege in defamation (s 41; Section 11.6). Parliament has the right to require any person, including ministers, to attend, give information and disclose documents in relation to matters for which the Scottish government has responsibility (ss 23–25). This contrasts with the murkiness of the practices surrounding ministerial responsibility in the UK (Chapter 15). In practice, however, the Scottish Parliament seems largely to have followed the Westminster model, according to which the executive dominates parliamentary processes and decides what, and how much, information to disclose.

There have been innovations in practice that have made the Scottish Parliament more proactive than the UK Parliament. Scottish committees not only scrutinise the executive and revise legislation, but may initiate legislation and conduct inquiries that involve direct engagement with the people. A public petitions system has been introduced, and there are Internet-based information and discussion mechanisms.

The Scottish Parliament has enacted a substantial amount of legislation, particularly concerning social matters and public services, which has markedly distinguished the regime from its Westminster counterpart. These include free personal care for the elderly, greater support for students, rescue packages for fisheries and the victims of foot and mouth disease, land reform, mental health and freedom of information.

16.3.2 The Scottish Government

The Scottish Government (Scotland Act 2012, s 12) comprises a first minister, ministers, junior ministers and law officers (Lord Advocate and Solicitor General (Scotland Act 1998, ss 44–50)). The Crown is the formal head of the Scottish Government. The Crown in relation to Scotland is separated from the Crown in relation to the UK, so that they can enter into property transactions with each other, for example (s 99).

Within the devolved areas, the Scottish Parliament can confer functions on Scottish ministers either individually or collectively (s 52). Powers under UK statutes and royal prerogative powers previously exercised by UK ministers are automatically transferred to Scottish ministers (s 53). In order to provide flexibility, additional functions outside devolved matters can be given to Scottish ministers either alone or jointly with UK ministers by Order in Council (s 63). The principles for forming and dismissing the Scottish Government are broadly similar to the conventions applying to the UK government (Section 14.1). However, the Scottish rules give significant roles to the Presiding Officer and the Parliament:

- The monarch appoints the first minister on the nomination of the Parliament (s 46). The Presiding Officer recommends the nomination to the Queen (s 46(4)). Presumably, she must accept.
- The Parliament must nominate the first minister within 28 days of a 'triggering' event (s 46). This means:
    (i) a general election or extraordinary general election (above);
    (ii) the resignation of the first minister. The first minister can resign at any time and must do so if the government is defeated on a vote of confidence. The first minister remains in office until a successor is appointed (s 45(3));
    (iii) the first minister ceases to be a member of the Scottish Parliament, except on dissolution, when the trigger event is (i) (above).
- If there has been no nomination after 28 days, the Parliament is dissolved, leading to an extraordinary general election and thus starting the process again. If the first minister cannot act, or the office is vacant, the Presiding Officer appoints an acting first minister from among MSPs (or former MSPs in the event of a dissolution; s 45(4), (5)) (there is no UK equivalent; the Cabinet makes the arrangements).
- The monarch appoints other ministers and law officers (the Lord Advocate and Solicitor General) on the nomination of the first minister with the agreement of the Parliament (ss 47–49). All ministers, but not the law officers, must be MSPs (ss 47, 48). (The UK convention is that the monarch appoints all ministers and law officers on the advice of the prime minister. All must be MPs or members of the House of Lords.)
- The first minister can dismiss ministers (ss 47(3), 49(4)). The first minister can dismiss law officers only with the approval of the Parliament (s 48(1)). (Under the UK convention the monarch can dismiss ministers and law officers on the advice of the prime minister.)
- Ministers and law officers can resign at any time and must resign if they are defeated in a vote of confidence (ss 47(3), 48(2), 49(4)). They lose office immediately, except that the Advocate General continues in office for essential functions until a replacement is appointed (ss 47(3)(d), 49(4)(d), 48(3)). (The UK has a similar convention but after a vote of confidence ministers and law officers do not lose office until they are replaced.)

> ▶ Ministers lose office if they cease to be MSPs, except on dissolution, when they stay in office until the election (ss 47(2)(e), 49(4)(e)). (The UK convention is that ministers must resign if they cease to be MPs, except on dissolution.)
>
> ▶ The law officers are the Lord Advocate and the Solicitor General for Scotland. They can, but need not, be MSPs. They can participate, but cannot vote in, the Parliament (s 27). Unlike ministers, they cannot be dismissed without the agreement of the Parliament (s 48(1)). The Parliament cannot interfere with the independence of the Lord Advocate as head of the criminal prosecution and investigation of death systems (ss 29(2)(e), 48(5)). (The UK law officers are ministers and MPs and dismissible by the prime minister (Section 15.5).) There is also an Advocate General for Scotland, who is responsible for giving advice on Scottish matters to the UK government (s 87).
>
> ▶ Ministers in the UK government cannot hold office in the Scottish Government (s 44(3)). However, MSPs can sit in the UK Parliament and be UK ministers.

The civil service is part of the UK civil service and is subject to the UK law regulating the civil service. Management of the civil service is not a devolved matter. Civil servants are, however, appointed by, and presumably responsible to, Scottish ministers (s 51). Thus, there may be a conflict of loyalty. However, since the Crown in relation to the Scottish Government is a different entity from the Crown in relation to the UK government (s 91), their primary loyalty is to Scottish ministers. They are, however, responsible to Scottish ministers only in relation to functions exercised by those ministers. Conflicts of loyalty might therefore still arise in relation to functions exercised jointly by Scottish and UK ministers.

16.3.3   The courts

Scotland has its own legal system with separate courts and separate substantive law, which has been influenced by continental civil law as well as by English common law. Final civil appeals are decided by the Supreme Court, which has jurisdiction over the whole of the UK, while criminal appeals are decided wholly within the Scottish courts. However, under the Scotland Act 2012, ss 35–36, devolution issues of compatibility with Convention rights under the ECHR are to be decided by the Supreme Court even in criminal cases. There are currently two Scottish Justices of the Supreme Court, one from Northern Ireland and one from Wales (which is not (yet) a separate jurisdiction) (Section 5.4.1).

English and Scottish civil law have much in common, although property law has many differences. Scottish criminal law and procedure is markedly different from that in England, which has the potential to create problems of cooperation. In *Stuart v Marquis of Bute* (1861) 9 HL Cas 440, 454, Lord Campbell LC said: 'As to judicial jurisdiction, Scotland and England, although politically under the same Crown and the supreme sway of one united legislature, are to be considered as independent foreign countries, unconnected with each other' (see also *R v Manchester Stipendiary Magistrate, ex p Granada Television Ltd* [2000] 1 All ER 135).

The most senior Scottish judges (the Lord President of the Court of Session and the Lord Justice Clerk) are appointed by the monarch on a recommendation from the prime minister on the nomination of the first minister (s 95). Other judges are appointed on the recommendation of the first minister.

In some respects, Scottish judges appear to have stronger protection against political interference than their UK counterparts (Section 7.7.3.2). Senior judges can be dismissed for inability, neglect of duty or misbehaviour only on a recommendation by the first minister following a resolution of the Parliament (s 95). The resolution can be made only on the basis of a written report from a tribunal, chaired by a member of the Privy Council who has held a high judicial office, concluding that the judge is unfit for office on one of these grounds. In the case of the Lord President and the Lord Justice Clerk, the prime minister must be consulted.

16.3.4   Devolution issues (s 98, Sched. 6)

The courts have a special role in relation to 'devolution issues'. These are:

- whether the Parliament has exceeded its powers;
- whether a member of the government has acted outside his or her devolved competence or violated Convention rights or European Union law;
- any other question about whether a function is within devolved competence;
- any other question arising by virtue of the Act about reserved matters.

A devolution issue can arise in any legal proceedings or can be brought before a court by means of a reference by the Lord Advocate, who can also defend any proceedings, or by the more political Advocate General. In English and Welsh courts, the UK Attorney General can bring devolution proceedings, and in Northern Ireland courts, the Attorney General for Northern Ireland.

A devolution issue is ultimately decided by the Supreme Court, either on appeal, by way of a reference from a lower court or directly on a reference by any of the above law officers (as in the Scottish Continuity Bill case [2018]). There need be no proceedings in existence. This has been said to be an essential part of the constitutional settlement ensuring that the rule of law is respected throughout the entire range of the activities of the Scottish Government (*H v Lord Advocate* [2012], at [31]). In the case of a reference in respect of a Scottish minister, the action in question must be stalled, a safeguard denied against the UK executive.

In *H v Lord Advocate* [2012], the Supreme Court stressed that Scottish ministers have no powers other than those conferred by or under the Scotland Act. Thus, ministers cannot act incompatibly with Convention rights even if they are acting under a UK Act (because it is only the Scotland Act, s 53, that enables them to do this). As a devolution issue, this is independent of the HRA itself (*Somerville v Scottish Ministers* [2007] 1 WLR 2734). Therefore, the provisions of the HRA, which allow public authorities to override a Convention right when enforcing a UK statute (Section 22.6), do not apply to Scottish ministers. Thus, without the constraints of the HRA, a distinct Scottish version of human rights could develop (subject to the future of the Act within the UK; see further Chapter 22).

There is an exception where only the HRA itself applies. This concerns the prosecuting and criminal investigation role of the Lord Advocate under UK statutes so as to ensure that these powers are the same throughout the UK (s 57(3)).

However, it is only the actions of the Scottish Government *itself* that are devolution issues (Sched. 6, para 1(d)). In *Kinloch v HM Advocate* [2013] 2 AC 93, the Supreme Court held that the police are not part of the Scottish Government so that the issue of police violation of privacy was not a devolution issue. Therefore, only the ordinary operation of the HRA applied. Under the HRA, Scottish Acts cannot be overridden, but UK Acts applying in Scotland can (Section 22.6).

16.4   Northern Ireland

Following a long period of stalemate between the Unionist and Nationalist communities (Section 16.1), a series of agreements created a basis for inter-community negotiations (Anglo-Irish Agreement 1985; 'Downing Street Declaration' (Cm 2422, 1994)). These led to the Belfast, or Good Friday, Agreement (Cm 3883, 1998) between the UK and Irish governments and the main political parties in Northern Ireland. This is the basis of the current arrangements. The Good Friday Agreement provides for the restoration of devolved government, the amendment of the Irish constitution to accept that Northern Ireland is currently controlled by the UK, and the creation of various consultative bodies representing the interests of the UK, Northern Ireland and the Republic of Ireland (North/South Ministerial Council, British–Irish Council, British–Irish Intergovernmental Conference). The Good Friday Agreement was endorsed by 71 per cent of voters in Northern Ireland and 94 per cent in the Republic of Ireland in separate referendums.

The Northern Ireland Act 1998 attempts to ensure a balance between the competing communities. It is sometimes characterised as an example of deliberative democracy and liberal pluralism (Sections 2.3.6 and 2.8.3). It restricts the political freedom of the legislature and executive to a greater extent than is the case in the rest of the UK. Ministers are directly elected by the Assembly in accordance with the balance of the parties within it. Thus, the system is very different from the UK's traditional system, which concentrates power in the leader of the largest party. The Northern Ireland devolution settlement also provides for the possibility of a vote in a referendum to leave the UK and for the Republic of Ireland to participate in the affairs of Northern Ireland. The Assembly's powers are more limited than is the case with Scotland. Moreover, the UK Secretary of State has stronger powers.

The following are the main provisions of the Northern Ireland Act 1998:

- Northern Ireland remains part of the UK, and the status of Northern Ireland will be altered only with the consent of a majority of its electorate (s 1). If a referendum favours a united Ireland, the Secretary of State is required to 'make proposals' to implement this by agreement with the Irish government (s 1).
- The overriding power of Parliament to make law for Northern Ireland is not affected by the Act (s 5(6)). UK statutes apply in Northern Ireland only expressly or by necessary implication.
- The Northern Ireland Assembly is elected by a single transferable vote (Section 12.5.7).
- The Assembly sits for a fixed four-year term. An election must be held every four years on the first Thursday in May. The Assembly is then dissolved within a minimum period fixed by the Secretary of State. The Assembly is also dissolved on a resolution supported by two-thirds of the total number of seats or if a Chief Minister and Deputy Chief Minister cannot be elected within six weeks of the first meeting of the Assembly or of a vacancy (below), as happened in January 2017: the Assembly being suspended for three years, until January 2020. The Secretary of State fixes the date of resulting election (ss 31, 32).
- If 30 members petition the Assembly in relation to any matter to be voted on, the vote shall require cross-community support (s 42).
- The Assembly can legislate generally in relation to matters exclusively within Northern Ireland except in relation to matters that are excluded (s 6). As in Scotland, the Assembly's powers have been subject to EU law and the rights protected by the HRA. It can raise certain taxes but not the main taxes that apply generally throughout the UK. Unlike in Scotland, excluded matters are of two kinds: 'excepted' matters and 'reserved' matters, listed in Schedules 2 and 3. The Assembly cannot legislate on excepted matters unless ancillary to other matters. It can legislate on reserved and ancillary matters with the consent of the Secretary of State (ss 6, 8, 10). Policing and justice finally became devolved matters in 2010. Discrimination on the grounds of religious belief or political opinion is outside the competence of the Assembly, and certain statutes (European Communities Act 1972; HRA; parts of the Justice (Northern Ireland) Act 2002) cannot be altered (s 7).
- The Presiding Officer introduces bills to the Assembly. If the Presiding Officer decides that a bill is outside the powers of the Assembly he must refuse to introduce it (s 10) (cf. Scotland, where the bill is not blocked).
- Acts of the Assembly require royal assent (s 5). Unlike the case in Scotland, where this is a matter for the Presiding Officer, the Secretary of State submits bills for royal assent (s 14). S/he can refuse to submit a bill if s/he thinks it is outside the competence of the Assembly or contains provisions incompatible with international obligations, the interests of defence or national security, the protection of public safety or public order, or would have an adverse effect on the operation of the single market within the UK.

- The first minister lacks the discretionary power of a UK prime minister to appoint or dismiss other ministers and the previous power (currently limited by the Fixed-Term Parliaments Act 2011), to dissolve the legislature. Instead, there is a bipartisan arrangement for power sharing, ensuring that both Unionists and Nationalists play a part. The first minister and deputy first minister are elected jointly by the Assembly from its members. This requires a majority of the Assembly and also separate majorities of Unionists and Nationalists (s 16). The first and deputy first ministers must both lose office if either resigns or ceases to be a member of the Assembly.

- Following problems arising out of a failure by the Assembly to elect a first and deputy first minister within the stipulated period, which was then six weeks (see *Robinson v Secretary of State for Northern Ireland* [2002]), the Northern Ireland (St Andrews Day Agreement) Acts 2006 and 2007 introduced an amended procedure. This requires the largest and second-largest parties, through their 'nominating officers', to nominate a first and deputy first minister respectively within 14 days of a vacancy. This process must be repeated until both posts are filled (s 16A).

- Subject to a maximum of ten, which can be increased by the Secretary of State (s 17(4)), and to the approval of the Assembly, the first and deputy first ministers jointly decide on the number of Northern Ireland ministers heading departments and forming a Cabinet. Ministers are then nominated by the political parties from members of the Assembly in accordance with a formula designed to reflect the balance of parties in the Assembly (s 18). Assembly committees must also reflect party strengths.

- A minister can be dismissed by his or her party through its nominating officer and loses office on ceasing to be a member of the Assembly other than after a dissolution (s 18). Ministers collectively lose office when a new Assembly is elected, where a party is excluded on a vote of confidence, where a new determination as to the number of ministers is made or as prescribed by Standing Order (s 18).

- Ministers and political parties can be excluded for up to 12 months (renewable) by the Assembly on the grounds that they are not committed to peace or have otherwise broken their oath of office (s 30). The motion must have the support of at least 30 members (from a total of between 96 and 108) and must be moved by the first and deputy first ministers jointly or by the Presiding Officer of the Assembly if required to do so by the Secretary of State. The Secretary of State must take into account the propensity to violence and cooperation with the authorities of the excluded person. The resolution must have cross-party support.

- Ministers must take a pledge of office which includes a *Ministerial Code of Conduct* (s 16(10), Sched. 4). The *Code* requires the 'strictest standards of propriety, accountability, openness, good community relations and equality and avoiding or declaring conflicts of interest'. Any direct or indirect pecuniary interests that members of the public might reasonably think could influence ministers' judgment must be registered. The *Code* is similar to the *Ministerial Code* for UK ministers and requires compliance with the Nolan Principles of Public Life (Section 5.9). In Northern Ireland, unlike the rest of the UK, it might therefore be enforceable in the courts.

- The Attorney General for Northern Ireland is the government's principal legal adviser and representative. Although the Attorney General cannot be a member of the Assembly, s/he can participate in its debates but cannot vote. The Attorney is appointed (for a single term of five years) and dismissed by the first minister and the deputy first minister jointly. The office has greater security than its Scottish equivalent, in that dismissal is only on the ground of misbehaviour or inability and requires a proposal from a special tribunal (s 24). There is also an Advocate General for Northern Ireland, who shares certain functions with the Attorney General. The post of Advocate General must be held by the UK Attorney General (Justice (Northern Ireland) Act 2002, s 27, Sched. 7). Thus, governmental legal arrangements are less independent than is the case in Scotland since the Advocate General is appointed and dismissed by the UK prime minister without safeguards.

- Northern Ireland has its own legal system, but the substantive law is closely related to English common law.

- As in Scotland, devolution issues can arise in any legal proceedings and can also be referred directly to the Supreme Court (s 79, Sched. 10). In Northern Irish courts, the power to do so and to defend legal proceedings lies with the UK Attorney General and the Attorney General for Northern Ireland.

However, as well as the law officers, the first minister and the deputy first minister acting jointly may refer a matter directly to the Supreme Court, a provision not paralleled in the other jurisdictions. There is a separate civil service for Northern Ireland, but the functions of the Civil Service Commissioners (dealing with appointments and standards) are reserved matters (Sched. 3).

▶ There are human rights and equal opportunities commissioners with powers to advise government and support legal proceedings.

16.5 Wales

Wales was never a separate state but consisted of a fluctuating group of kingdoms that were gradually assimilated by the English. Until the sixteenth century, they had separate legal systems which may have been coordinated from the tenth century (see Jenkins (ed), *Hywel Dda The Law* (Gomer Press 1986)). However, England took over the whole of Wales and imposed the English language, law and administration (Acts of Union of Wales 1536, 1542). There were Welsh representatives in the English Parliament, and a separate Welsh Assembly was abolished in 1689. A single court system for England and Wales was introduced in 1830.

Although there have always been voices in favour of Welsh independence, the political pressures have tended to be less clear than in the case of Scotland, and in economic terms, Wales and England are more closely assimilated. According to Rawlings (*Delineating Wales* (University of Wales Press 2003) 63), the original devolution arrangements were a 'Wales of bits-and-pieces', muddled between the 'three faces' of what he called 'Welsh Office Plus'. First, an extended administrative arrangement under which only subordinate laws could be made; second, 'the new politics', an assembly that combined lawmaking and executive powers; third, a separation between legislature and executive implemented through a committee structure. The 2006 Act developed the third version as a reduced version of the Scottish model, but the Wales Act 2017 has brought Wales much closer to the Scottish pattern of devolution, as Wales has moved from a conferred powers to a reserved powers model.

Wales presently has no separate legal system, but s 1 of the 2017 Act declares the existence of a body of 'Welsh law' made by the Assembly and ministers, which, while not affecting the scope of devolution, nonetheless forms part of the law of England and Wales. It is the existence of this body of law which has led to calls for the recognition of a separate Welsh jurisdiction (see above).

16.5.1 The Welsh Parliament/Senedd Cymru

Under the Government of Wales Act 1998, both lawmaking and executive powers were vested in a National Assembly for Wales, with provision for delegation to committees and secretaries. This was a hybrid of a local government model based on committees formed out of an elected assembly, and an administrative model based on the former Welsh Office of the UK government. The Assembly was confined to making subordinate legislation under powers that were previously exercised by UK ministers. Otherwise, it had to make application to the UK Parliament if it wanted powers. In 2004, the Richards Commission recognised that, in practice, the Welsh Government had initiated considerable legislation, albeit without coherent principles, and recommended that it be given wider powers. Accordingly, the Government of Wales Act 2006 substantially increased the powers of the Assembly, although they were still less than in Scotland. It also created a separation of powers between the Assembly and ministers on a similar basis to that in Scotland, transferring executive powers from the Assembly to the Welsh ministers. It replaced most of the 1998 Act. The new powers of the Assembly were triggered following a referendum held in 2011 (majority of 63.5 per cent).

Under the 2006 Act, the Welsh Assembly, by enacting an 'Assembly Act', could do anything that could be done by an Act of Parliament, but only on the particular subjects (fields) designated by the Act. Thus, unlike the position in Scotland and Northern Ireland, the need for a positive power to make a law still applied. As in Scotland, the powers of the Assembly have been subject to EU law and Convention rights under the HRA, and also to restrictions limiting the creation of criminal offences and the alteration of certain statutes. In *A-G v National Assembly for Wales Commission* [2013], the Supreme Court upheld an Assembly Bill intended to increase the powers of the Welsh Government by removing a statutory requirement for the consent of the Secretary of State to changes in certain local government by-laws. Lord Hope held that within the prescribed fields the powers of the Assembly were to be treated as similar to those of the Scottish Parliament. Assembly Acts are therefore subject only to limited judicial review (Section 16.3.1).

The Wales Act 2014 empowered the Assembly to pass laws in relation to certain taxes, and a Welsh income tax came into effect in April 2019.

The Assembly, now renamed Senedd Cymru/Welsh Parliament under s 2 of the Senedd and Elections (Wales) Act 2020, of 60 members is elected by a method similar to that in Scotland, with 20 members elected in five regions, and 40 in local constituencies. However, unlike in Scotland, a person cannot stand in both regional and local constituency elections (ss 7, 17). The Assembly sits for a fixed term of four years but can be dissolved earlier by a two-thirds majority or if a first minister is not nominated within 28 days, as in Scotland (ss 5, 47).

16.5.2 The Welsh Government

A first minister is chosen by the Senedd and appoints and dismisses other ministers and deputy ministers from Senedd members (ss 46–51 Government of Wales Act 2006). However, the approval of the Assembly is not required for ministerial appointments. Instead, the total number of ministers and deputy ministers is limited to 12.

A Counsel General, responsible for giving legal advice to the Government, must also be appointed and can be removed on the recommendation of the first minister with the agreement of the Senedd. The Counsel General loses office when a new first minister is appointed (s 49). Safeguards for the independence of the law officer are therefore less than in Scotland and Northern Ireland. S/he can, but need not, be a Senedd member.

Welsh ministers are financially responsible to the Senedd, for which purpose there is an Auditor-General (s145). However, unlike the position in Scotland, their accounts are regulated by the UK Treasury (s 141).

A Senedd Commissioner for Standards seeks to promote, encourage and safeguard high standards of conduct in the public office of Senedd members. There is a *Code of Conduct* (2016), complaints of the breach of which may be investigated by the Standards of Conduct Committee. There is also a Public Services Ombudsman (Public Services Ombudsman (Wales) Act 2005). This is a stronger version of the Ombudsman mechanism than the Parliamentary and Health Service Ombudsman (see Section 20.2). Unlike the latter, the Public Services Ombudsman can receive complaints directly from the public and has jurisdiction over the Senedd and Government, local authorities, health authorities and social landlords. The Ombudsman's report may be published, and the authority concerned must also do so unless the Ombudsman excludes publication in certain circumstances on public interest grounds (s 21). In the event of non-compliance, the Ombudsman can refer the matter to the High Court.

The Government of Wales Act 2006 has a communitarian edge. Welsh ministers are empowered to promote or improve the economic, social and environmental wellbeing of Wales (s 60) and under the rubric of 'inclusiveness' must consult widely, advance various social and cultural concerns, and prepare strategies dealing with sustainable development, the voluntary sector, equal opportunities and the Welsh language. There must also be a 'Partnership Council' comprising ministers and local authority representatives (s 72).

16.5.3 The courts

There are provisions similar to those in Scotland for the courts to deal with cases raising devolution issues. These can arise in any legal proceedings or on a reference from the Counsel General, the UK Attorney General, or the law officers of the other devolved regimes in cases arising in their jurisdictions (Government of Wales Act 2006, Sched. 9). (Because of the separate legal system in Scotland, the Attorney General has no equivalent power to intervene in proceedings arising in Scotland.) The Counsel General and UK Attorney General can also refer a question of whether a legislative provision is within competence directly to the Supreme Court (s 112). There is no requirement for the Supreme Court to include a Welsh member, although it presently does.

In the current absence of a separate Welsh legal system, a Welsh devolved powers case could, in theory, be brought in any English court. However, there is a branch of the Administrative Court in Cardiff dealing with judicial review cases against Welsh government bodies. In due course, this may develop distinctive constitutional principles. In *R (Deepdock) v Welsh Ministers* [2007] EWHC 3347 (Admin) at [20], it was suggested that there should be a presumption that public law cases involving Welsh public authorities should normally be heard in Wales.

16.6   England

The asymmetric nature of devolution has given rise to an anomaly as regards England. England, comprising 84 per cent of the population of the UK, has no elected institutions of its own. England is governed by the central UK government. Therefore Scottish, Welsh and Northern Irish members of the UK Parliament have been entitled to vote in debates affecting exclusively English matters for which they are not accountable to the voters, whereas English MPs cannot vote on matters which fall within the scope of devolution. Indeed, a UK government might be kept in power on the strength of Scottish or Northern Ireland votes. For example, in 2004, by a majority of five, the Labour government won the vote in favour of increasing university tuition fees in England by virtue of its Scottish supporters, whereas from 2017 to 2019 the minority Conservative government was kept in office by support from the Democratic Unionist party of Northern Ireland.

This problem of England (often called the 'West Lothian question' after the constituency formerly represented by the late Tam Dalyell, a relentless pursuer of the matter) has been ignored for many years as a constitutional 'abeyance' (Section 1.9). It became more serious following the Scottish referendum of September 2014. The solution adopted was to change the Standing Orders of the House of Commons to give effect to the principle of 'English votes for English laws'. The Speaker is now obliged to certify bills which relate only to England (or to England and Wales, in cases where the matter in question was not devolved to Wales), and that comparable policy decisions are devolved elsewhere in the UK. In such instances, a legislative Grand Committee of English (or English and Welsh) MPs vote on a 'consent motion' prior to the bill's third reading. In effect, therefore, such bills require double approval (or are subject to a double veto): first, from MPs in Westminster as a whole, and second, from the Grand Committee (see House of Commons Library Briefing Paper 7339 (2015)).

A more radical suggestion is that greater powers, including taxation, be devolved to the English regions or larger cities. There has been recent progress in this direction: the Cities and Local Government Devolution Act 2016 provides for the implementation of 'devolution deals' with local authorities in England, which transfer resources and powers (notably over housing, transport, planning and policing). The first of these was agreed with bodies in Greater Manchester in July 2015. However, it is unclear how far the economic and other uncertainties generated both by Brexit and by the COVID-19 pandemic will impact upon this process. It is perhaps significant that a dispute between the mayor of Manchester and the UK government over the package of financial support payable as the city went into the highest level of COVID-19 restrictions in October 2020 resulted in the latter getting its way.

There is a more long-established form of regional devolution for the London region in the form of an elected mayor and Assembly (Greater London Authority Act 1999). The Assembly is elected on the basis of 'first past the post' (Chapter 12), together with an 'additional member' from a party list in accordance with the party's share of the vote, thereby reflecting public opinion to a greater extent than is the case with Parliament. The mayor and Assembly have certain executive powers in relation mainly to transport, policing, land use planning, housing and local amenities.

Summary

▶ Legislative and executive power has been devolved to elected bodies in Scotland, Northern Ireland and, more gradually, Wales. The UK Parliament has reserved the power to legislate in respect of many matters and has a general power to override the devolved assemblies. Their legislation is subordinate legislation, which is invalid if it exceeds the limits prescribed by the devolution statutes. The devolved legislatures are in principle subject to judicial review, although the courts will be circumspect in reviewing the acts of an elected body. Unlike a UK statute, legislation violating Convention rights protected by the HRA is invalid. This does not depend on the HRA itself (which also applies in the devolved territories).

▶ If political constraints are taken into account, the devolution arrangements come close to a federal system in which each body respects the autonomy of the others. However, the courts are ambivalent as to how far the devolution statutes should be regarded as 'constitutional', and the Sewel Convention has not always been observed, notably during the steps leading to Brexit.

▶ Elections to the devolved bodies are partly by proportional representation. The Scottish and Welsh executives are structured according to the UK parliamentary system. However, the balance of power is more in favour of the Parliament than is the case in the UK system. The Northern Ireland system is primarily concerned to achieve a balance between different political factions and is more restrictive than is the case with Scotland.

▶ There is no devolved government in England, other than on a limited basis to London and some urban areas and regions. Representatives from the devolved countries could therefore vote in the UK Parliament on purely English matters. This matter has been addressed through a change to the Standing Orders of the House of Commons.

Exercises

16.1 To what extent can devolution in the UK be regarded as a federal system?

16.2 'The devolved regimes are autonomous but not independent.' Discuss.

16.3 Compare the rules governing the appointment and removal of the Scottish and Northern Ireland governments. Which is the more democratic?

16.4 Compare the methods in the UK and Scotland (i) for dealing with a hung Parliament and (ii) for choosing the leader of the government.

16.5 Assess the arguments for and against a separate Welsh legal system.

16.6 Has the 'West Lothian question' been satisfactorily resolved?

16.7 What safeguards are there in the devolved regimes (i) for ensuring that the devolved lawmakers do not exceed their powers and (ii) for ensuring that the UK government respects the independence of the devolved governments?

16.8 On 4 May, elections take place in Scotland. The Socialist Party gets the largest number of seats in the Scottish Parliament (40 per cent). The Freedom Party, which came third with 15 per cent, agrees to support the Socialists to nominate Cherie, the leader of the Socialists, as the next first minister. The Socialists and the Freedom Party together hold 55 per cent of the seats of the Parliament. In response to its support, Cherie promises to appoint two members of the Freedom Party as ministers.

On 4 June, the Parliament nominates Cherie for appointment as first minister. The Conservatives, who came second in the election, oppose the nomination. The General Secretary of the Socialist Party, on behalf of the Scottish Parliament, submits the nomination to the UK prime minister, who advises the Queen to accept it.

Once Cherie is appointed as the first minister, she decides to appoint as ministers exclusively members of her political party, irrespective of whether they have been elected as MSPs. Nick, the leader of the Freedom Party, claims that the first minister has breached her promise and warns her that she will face severe consequences and that he will use the most drastic measures at his disposal.

After this controversial commencement, the Socialist government declares that it is going to develop an extremely ambitious programme for Scotland. In its electoral programme, the Socialist Party had promised a stronger voice for Scotland in both the UK and Europe, and therefore the government announces a bill concerning legally binding international agreements between Scotland and other European states. This bill will be introduced in the Scottish Parliament by Dave, a Scottish minister. The Secretary of State for Scotland informs Edinburgh that he will block this bill if they decide to put it forward.

Discuss the constitutional position in respect of each of these events.

Further reading

Aroney, 'Reserved Matters, Legislative Purpose and the Referendum on Scottish Independence' [2014] PL 422

Birrell, *Comparing Devolved Governance* (Palgrave Macmillan 2012)

Bogdanor, *The New British Constitution* (Hart Publishing 2009) ch 4

Colley, *Acts of Union and Disunion* (Profile Books 2014)

Commission on Justice in Wales, *Justice in Wales for the People of Wales* (2019)

Dickson, 'Devolution in Northern Ireland' in Jowell and O'Cinneide (eds), *The Changing Constitution* (9th edn, Oxford University Press 2019)

Hannant, 'Justifying a (Welsh) Legal Jurisdiction' [2019] PL 665

Hazell, *The English Question* (Manchester University Press 2006)

Himsworth and O'Neill, *Scotland's Constitution: Law and Practice* (3rd edn, Bloomsbury 2015)

Leyland, 'Multi-layered Constitutional Accountability and the Refinancing of Territorial Governance in the UK' in Bamforth and Leyland (eds), *Accountability in the Contemporary Constitution* (Oxford University Press 2013)

McHarg, 'Devolution in Scotland' in Jowell and O'Cinneide (eds), *The Changing Constitution* (9th edn, Oxford University Press 2019)

Rawlings, 'Riders on the Storm: Wales, the Union and Territorial Constitutional Crisis' (2015) 42 JLS 471

Rawlings, 'The Strange Reconstitution of Wales' [2018] PL 62

Rawlings, 'The Welsh Way/Y Fford Gymreig' in Jowell and O'Cinneide (eds), *The Changing Constitution* (9th edn, Oxford University Press 2019)

Silk, 'Devolution and the UK Parliament' in Horne and Drewry (eds), *Parliament and the Law* (2nd edn, Hart Publishing 2019)

Smyth, 'English Votes for English Laws' in Horne and Drewry (eds), *Parliament and the Law* (2nd edn, Hart Publishing 2019)

Tierney, 'The Three Hundred and Seven Year Itch: Scotland and the 2014 Independence Referendum' in Qvotrup (ed), *The British Constitution: Continuity and Change* (Hart Publishing 2013)

Part V

Administrative law

Chapter 17

The grounds of judicial review, I: illegality and *ultra vires*

17.1 Introduction: the constitutional basis of judicial review

Judicial review has ancient origins (see *Keighley's Case* (1609) 10 Co Rep 139). Sometimes called the 'supervisory jurisdiction', judicial review is the High Court's power to police the legality of decisions made by public bodies. Judicial review cases are decided by the Administrative Court, part of the Queen's Bench Division of the High Court (the Upper Tribunal also has certain judicial review powers (Section 20.1)). Judicial review applies to all public bodies, including courts and tribunals other than Parliament, which is protected by privilege (Section 11.6), and the High Court itself. Judicial review applies to government decisions and actions that affect individual rights and interests, and also to general statements of government policy, at least where they relate to individual rights (e.g. *Gillick v West Norfolk AHA* [1986] AC 112: guidance on contraception).

Although partly regulated by statute, judicial review is essentially a creation of the common law, so that the courts themselves control its scope and limits: although the Independent Review of Administrative Law established by the government in 2020 (Section 1.9) has been tasked, among other matters, with considering whether it should be codified in statute. It is an essential aspect of the rule of law (see *R (Alconbury Developments Ltd) v Secretary of State for the Environment, Transport and the Regions* [2001] 2 All ER 929 at 981; *R (Cart) v Upper Tribunal* [2012] 1 AC 663 at [71]–[73]).

Judicial review strikes an accommodation between competing aspects of the separation of powers. On the one hand, the principle of checks and balances requires that government action be subject to review by independent and impartial tribunals. On the other hand, judicial review operates within the context of the parliamentary accountability of the executive; from this latter perspective, the functional separation of powers pulls in the other direction by requiring the court to avoid trespassing into the political territory of Parliament and the executive.

The courts strike this accommodation mainly by claiming not to be concerned with the 'merits' of government action, that is, whether it is good or bad, but only with whether governmental decisions fall within authorising legislation and meet legal standards of fairness and 'reasonableness'. This can be presented as reflecting the rule of law in both its basic and its wider senses.

However, these principles are vague, and there is considerable room for debate as to the proper limits of the courts' powers. Moreover, the judicial review principles are flexible in that the depth of review, the range of grounds available and the selection of remedies vary with the context. At one extreme, the courts may refuse to interfere altogether where they consider that a matter is unsuitable for the legal process, for example an international treaty (Section 9.5.3). In other cases, while not excluding review entirely, the courts may intervene only exceptionally. This is often called 'deference' but is really an application of the separation of powers (Section 19.7.1). In particular, courts respect the sphere of democratic bodies, especially Parliament, albeit they have long been alive to the dangers of a dominant executive (see *R v Secretary of State, ex p Fire Brigades Union* [1995] 2 All ER 244 (Section 7.7.3.3); *AXA General Insurance Ltd v HM Advocate* [2011] 3 WLR 871, Section 8.5.6). The HRA has added a further dimension to judicial review by creating additional grounds for challenge (although some of these overlap).

Judicial review is a last-resort method of challenge, and there are procedural barriers intended to prevent it being too easily taken up (Section 19.3). Other and cheaper methods of challenging government decisions exist, for example through tribunals, statutory regulators, ombudsmen (see Chapter 20) and MPs. However, these may be questionable either because of the absence of enforcement or investigatory powers or because of a lack of independence (see *R v Secretary of State for the Home Dept, ex p Fire Brigades Union* (above), at 267 (Lord Mustill)).

17.2 The legal basis of judicial review

The legal basis of judicial review is disputed, reflecting the wider debate as to the nature of our constitution. There is a large (and rather repetitive) literature on this issue. One perspective bases judicial review on freestanding common law principles, according to which powerful bodies must act in accordance with wide rule of law values of fairness and rationality (*Dr Bonham's Case* (1610) 8 Co Rep 114a; *Bagg's Case* (1615) 11 Co Rep 936; *Cooper v Wandsworth Board of Works* (1863) 14 CB (NS) 180). This draws inspiration primarily from liberal ideas and from the history of the common law as claiming to be the embodiment of community-based values of fairness and justice.

The other perspective gives greater emphasis to parliamentary supremacy, democracy and the rule of law in its narrower sense. It assumes that, because most government powers are created by Acts of Parliament, the courts' job is to ensure that powers do not exceed the limits set out by Parliament: the *ultra vires* doctrine. The underlying principle is that of parliamentary supremacy. The courts must obey a statute. Conversely, decisions or actions outside the scope of a statute have no legal effect. To its supporters, this provides a more substantial and democratic basis for judicial review than does the common law. However, both approaches can be made to fit the facts, and the historical evidence is inconclusive.

Both approaches conform to possible meanings of the separation of powers and the rule of law. The *ultra vires* approach is biased towards the functional aspect of the separation of powers (Section 7.5); the common law approach towards checks and balances. One difference between the two approaches is that the *ultra vires* approach would not permit the courts to override an Act of Parliament. The common law approach is, in itself, neutral on this issue. However, some of its adherents claim that the courts might be able to override a statute in an extreme case (Section 8.5.6).

Another difference between the two approaches is that the common law approach has less difficulty in understanding how judicial review can apply to bodies whose powers do not derive from statute. For example, royal prerogative powers and other non-statutory powers exercised by public bodies are subject to judicial review (*CCSU v Minister for the Civil Service* [1985] AC 374; *R v Panel on Takeovers and Mergers, ex p Datafin plc* [1987] QB 815). The common law might also be the basis for extending judicial review principles, similar to those applied to government, to powerful private bodies (e.g. sports regulatory bodies and powerful commercial companies) that exercise control over important aspects of public life. Proponents of the *ultra vires* doctrine accommodate this possibility by suggesting that there need not be a single basis for judicial review. Thus, the extent of judicial review depends on political choice rather than an abstract conceptual theory.

Even the *ultra vires* approach accepts that the judges are developing their own principles in accordance with the 'amplified' or 'extended' versions of the rule of law, in particular, the 'principle of legality' according to which basic rights cannot be infringed unless Parliament uses very clear language (Section 6.6). This approach claims that judge-made rules are part of Parliament's 'constructive intention', by which is meant that Parliament is assumed to intend that these principles be implied into the exercise of every statutory power, because Parliament is taken to respect the rule of law. There are many presumptions of statutory interpretation which require courts to assume that Parliament intended to act fairly while allowing the court considerable room to decide what this means. Judicial review may be regarded as an application of this. The difference between the two approaches is that, according to the common law view, Parliament *tolerates* judicial review, whereas on the *ultra vires* view Parliament somehow *authorises* judicial review.

Forsyth (1996) suggests that the *ultra vires* doctrine is a useful 'fig leaf' which gives constitutional respectability to what is happening and at least reminds us that Parliament has the last word. However, Forsyth's fig leaf could also be taken to hide something we would prefer not to see, namely that the *ultra vires* doctrine is an empty vessel for whatever happens to be the prevailing judicial fashion.

There is substantial judicial support for the *ultra vires* doctrine as the basis of judicial review (e.g. *Boddington v British Transport Police* [1998] 2 WLR 639; *Credit Suisse v Allerdale BC* [1996] 4 All ER 129 at 167; *Page v Hull University Visitor* [1993] 1 All ER 97 at 107). On the other hand, in *CCSU v Minister for the Civil Service* [1985] Lord Diplock famously abandoned the *ultra vires* doctrine by classifying the grounds of judicial review under the three, judge-made broad heads of 'illegality, irrationality and procedural impropriety', claiming that the law should not pursue 'fairy tales'. *In R v Secretary of State for Education, ex parte Begbie* [2000] 1 WLR 1115, at 1129, Laws LJ suggested that the root concept behind judicial review is 'abuse of power'. However, this seems too vague to be helpful.

17.2.1 Appeal and review

Judicial review must not be confused with an appeal (for discussion, see *Michalak v General Medical Council* [2017] UKSC 71, at [20]–[22]). An appeal is a procedure which exists only under a particular statute or, in the case of a voluntary body, by agreement. An appeal allows the appellate body to decide the whole matter again unless the particular statute or agreement limits the grounds of appeal, for example to questions of law only. An appeal therefore may involve a thorough reconsideration of the whole decision – including its merits – whereas judicial review is concerned only with ensuring that legal standards are complied with. Depending on the particular statute, an appellate body might be a court, a tribunal, a minister or indeed anyone. A claim for judicial review is possible only in the High Court or the Upper Tribunal.

An appellate body can usually substitute its decision for the first instance decision, although in some cases its powers are limited to sending the matter back to be decided again by the lower body. In judicial review proceedings, unless there is no doubt as to the right decision, the court cannot make the decision itself but must send the matter back to the decision-maker with instructions as to its legal duties.

Unlike an appeal, which can be decided only by the body specified, the invalidity of government action can be raised not only in the Administrative Court but also by way of 'collateral challenge' in any proceedings where the rights of a citizen are affected by the validity of government action (e.g. *Boddington v British Transport Police* [1998]: defence to prosecution for smoking contrary to railway by-laws alleged to be *ultra vires*). This is because an unlawful government decision is, in theory at least, of no effect in law (void/a nullity) and can be ignored, thus vindicating the rule of law (*Entick v Carrington* (1765) 19 St Tr 1029). In the case of an appeal, the offending decision is fully valid until the appeal body changes it.

17.3 Classification of the grounds of review

Unfortunately, there is no general agreement on how to classify the grounds of judicial review, and textbooks take different approaches. For example, a broad distinction is sometimes made between what is called 'excess of power', where the decision-maker acts outside the limits on his power imposed by statute, and 'abuse of power', where the decision-maker misuses power, for example by acting unfairly. The most usual way to organise the grounds of judicial review is, however, on the basis of Lord Diplock's classification in *CCSU v Minister for the Civil Service* [1985] at 410–11, that is, under the three heads of 'illegality, irrationality and procedural impropriety'. Illegality means that the decision-maker must correctly apply the law that confers power. Irrationality means that the decision must not be unreasonable (the term being used in a special sense (Section 18.1)). Procedural impropriety includes a failure to comply with procedural requirements imposed by statute and also the common law principles of fair procedure or 'natural justice', namely a right to a fair hearing before an unbiased decision-maker. However, the House of Lords has emphasised that these heads of challenge are not watertight compartments, but sometimes run together (*Boddington v British Transport Police* [1998], e.g. *Wheeler v Leicester City Council* [1985] 2 All ER 1106 (Section 18.1)). In this chapter, we shall discuss illegality. The other grounds are discussed in Chapter 18.

It might be helpful at this point to provide a checklist outlining all three concepts:

1. *Illegality*
   ▶ 'narrow' *ultra vires*, or lack of jurisdiction, in the sense of straying beyond the limits defined by the statute;
   ▶ errors of law and (in certain cases) errors of fact;
   ▶ 'wide' *ultra vires*, or acting for an ulterior purpose, taking irrelevant factors into account or failing to take relevant factors into account; fettering discretion.
2. *Irrationality*
   ▶ *Wednesbury* unreasonableness. This could stand alone or be the outcome of taking an irrelevant factor into account;
   ▶ lack of proportionality, at least under the HRA.
3. *Procedural impropriety*
   ▶ violating important statutory procedures;
   ▶ lack of a fair hearing;
   ▶ bias;
   ▶ failure to give reasons for a decision;
   ▶ frustration of a 'legitimate expectation' (although the expectation may not always be procedural in character: see Section 18.3.1).

17.4 Illegality: 'narrow' *ultra vires*

Illegality concerns *ultra vires* in its basic sense, namely a requirement that the decision should fall within the statute that confers the power. The doctrine is based on the principle of the rule of law that a public authority can interfere with the freedom of others only if specifically authorised by law to do so. Thus, in *R v Somerset CC, ex parte Fewings* [1995] 1 All ER 513, a local authority attempted to ban stag hunting on land that it owned. The Court of Appeal held that the Council was not entitled to rely on its ownership of the land as a private landowner might but must justify the ban by reference to a statutory power (Section 17.6.2).

The focus is therefore upon statutory interpretation. Most government bodies are statutory; for example, local authorities and tribunals and most central government powers are conferred by statute on individual ministers. In the case of courts and judicial tribunals, the terminology of 'lack' or 'excess' of *jurisdiction* is often used. (Jurisdiction means 'area of power' and 'lack' or 'excess' of jurisdiction means here the same as *ultra vires*.)

Here are some famous examples of *ultra vires*. In *A-G v Fulham Corp* [1921] 1 Ch 440, a local authority had power to provide a 'wash house' for local people. It interpreted this as authorising the provision of a laundry service for working people, who could leave washing to be done by staff and delivered to their homes. This was held to be unlawful in that 'wash house', according to the court, meant a place where a person can do their own washing.

This raises the possibility of political bias in interpreting statutes. For example, the court might have been influenced by a prejudice against local bodies spending taxpayers' money on welfare services. If the court had read the statute against an assumption of democratic freedom, the outcome might have been different. More recently, in *Bromley LBC v GLC* [1983] 1 AC 768, the House of Lords held that an obligation to provide an 'efficient and economic' public transport service meant that the Council could not subsidise the London Underground for social purposes. Among other lines of reasoning, it was held that 'economic' meant that there was an obligation to break even financially (see also *Prescott v Birmingham Corp* [1955] Ch 210: free transport for pensioners held *ultra vires* under a power to charge such fares as the council thought fit since no 'fare' was charged; *Roberts v Hopwood* [1925] AC 578: 'wages' should not include a social welfare element). These cases suggest that the courts take a narrow approach and are reluctant to read a statute as authorising a local authority to be guided by radical political ideologies.

Where the scope of a statute is unclear, the courts rely on presumptions of interpretation in the light of ideas of the rule of law. They will thus read a statute as overriding certain principles only if it uses clear words: the 'principle of legality' (Section 6.6). Examples include *R v Secretary of State for the Home Dept, ex p Simms* [2000] 2 AC 115 at 131 (freedom of expression); *Congreve v Home Office* [1976] QB 629 and *McCarthy & Stone v Richmond upon Thames LBC* [1991] 4 All ER 897 (no taxation without statutory authority); *R v Secretary of State for the Home Dept, ex p Pierson* [1998] AC 539 (retrospective use of powers); *Raymond v Honey* [1983] 1 AC 1 (prisoner's rights); *Anisminic Ltd v Foreign Compensation Commission* [1969] 2 AC 147, and *R v Lord Chancellor's Dept, ex p Witham* [1997] 2 All ER 779 (access to the courts).

There is some leeway in the *ultra vires* doctrine in favour of the government. The courts will permit an activity that, although not expressly authorised by the statute, is 'reasonably incidental' to something that is expressly authorised. For example, in *Akumah v Hackney LBC* [2005] 2 All ER 148, the House of Lords held that it was lawful to clamp cars in a car park attached to a block of local authority flats under a scheme that required tenants to obtain parking permits at a cost of £2. The Council had statutory power of 'management, regulation and control' over the 'dwelling houses' and this should be interpreted broadly to include the regulation of car parking since this affects the quality of life of the residents. This was the case even though the council could have made parking regulations under other, more specific legislation. However, the House of Lords was not asked to rule on the legality of the particular scheme, thus leaving it open whether making a charge or clamping was lawful.

A narrow approach was taken in *McCarthy & Stone* (above), where a charge for giving advice in connection with planning applications was held not to be incidental to the authority's planning powers. Giving advice was not expressly authorised and was itself an incidental function. The House of Lords took the view that something cannot be incidental to the incidental. Moreover, there is a presumption, dating from the Bill of Rights 1688, that taxation cannot be imposed without clear statutory authority (but is a charge for a service taxation?) (see also *A-G v Crayford UDC* [1962] Ch 575: voluntary household insurance scheme reasonably incidental to the power to manage council housing because it helped tenants to pay the rent; *Hazell v Hammersmith and Fulham LBC* [1992] 2 AC 1: interest swap arrangements, made by several local councils to spread the risk of future changes in interest rates, were not incidental to the council's borrowing powers because they concerned debt management rather than borrowing as such).

17.5 Errors of law and fact

'Error' or 'wrong' in this context means a mistake: wrongly believing something to be true. (This is worthy of note because sometimes the term 'error' is used as a loose label for all grounds of judicial review.) A typical error of law would be to misunderstand the meaning of a legal term (e.g. what is meant by 'residence' in a dwelling). Errors of law must be contrasted with errors of fact. A typical error of fact is a mistake about something happening in the real world (e.g. whether a person was actually in the dwelling).

The question of whether the court can review decisions on the ground of legal or factual errors has caused problems. There is a clash of principle. On the one hand, if the court could intervene merely because it considered that a mistake had been made, it would be trespassing into the merits of the case, showing disrespect for the deciding body and violating the separation of powers. A reviewing court is not necessarily in a better position than the original decision-maker to decide every question.

Thus, according to the traditional doctrine, it has been said that if a body has jurisdiction to go right, it has jurisdiction to go wrong (Lord Reid in *R v Governor of Brixton Prison, ex p Armah* [1968] AC 192 at 234). It has also been said that permitting the court to intervene merely because a mistake has been made threatens the rule of law by creating uncertainty, so it is better that a decision should stand even at the expense of the occasional injustice (*R v Bolton* (1841) 1 QB 66) (see also *R v Nat Bell Liquors* [1922] 2 AC 128: false evidence not reviewable).

On the other hand, the rule of law surely calls for a remedy if a decision-maker makes a clear mistake. Moreover, contemporary expansion of judicial review has encouraged the courts to take a more aggressive approach than the traditional doctrine would suggest. The courts have therefore adopted a compromise. Almost all errors of law and some errors of fact can be challenged. However, they have reached this position only after much technical wrangling.

Even under the traditional doctrine, some errors were reviewable. A rationale that was popular in the nineteenth century and still exists is the doctrine of the 'jurisdictional', 'collateral' or 'preliminary' question. According to this doctrine, if a mistake relates to a matter that defines the scope of the decision-maker's power, then the mistake makes the resulting decision *ultra vires* or outside jurisdiction. This applies equally to mistakes of law and mistakes of fact. For example, in *White and Collins v Minister of Health* [1939] 2 KB 838, the Secretary of State had power to acquire land 'other than a garden or parkland'. It was held that the court could interfere if it thought that the minister had wrongly decided whether the claimant's land was parkland. The doctrine can be justified on rule of law and separation of powers grounds that a minister should not be allowed to expand his own powers (see Farwell J in *R v Shoreditch Assessment Committee, ex p Morgan* [1910] 2 KB 859 at 880). The matter was said to depend on Parliament's intention. Thus, if the statute uses 'subjective language': for example 'if the minister considers that the land is parkland', the matter would be for the minister to decide. The court would interfere only if his decision was flawed in some other respect, for instance if it was completely irrational (Section 18.1).

It was suggested that a jurisdictional error is an error committed at the *beginning* of the decision-making process which made the body go entirely outside its allotted sphere ('excess of jurisdiction') and that errors committed subsequently were 'errors within jurisdiction'. For example, suppose a body has power to fix the rent for a 'furnished dwelling'; in order to decide whether it has jurisdiction, it must first decide whether the dwelling in front of it is 'furnished'. A mistake about this would go to its jurisdiction. Mistakes which it committed later, for example in calculating the rent, would not.

Although this approach is plausible it seems arbitrary to rely only on the order in which matters are decided. Suppose, for example, a magistrate has power to decide whether 'a minor was drunk in charge of a vehicle at night'. Which of these several matters, if any, are 'jurisdictional'? A second device, which flourished during the 1960s but has largely been superseded, is the doctrine of 'error of law on the face of the record', or patent error (*R v Northumberland Compensation Appeal Tribunal, ex p Shaw* [1952] 1 KB 338). This allows the court to quash a decision if a mistake of law can be discovered from the written record of the decision without using other evidence. This provided a practical compromise by allowing obvious mistakes to be rectified without reopening the whole matter. Many bodies are required to give written reasons for their decisions as part of the record and the courts were liberal in what material they regarded as part of the record. However, the doctrine is very formalistic, and mistakes of fact could not be challenged at all.

17.5.1 Error of law

Perhaps without intending to do so, the speeches of the House of Lords in *Anisminic Ltd v Foreign Compensation Commission* [1969] triggered a revolution in treatment of errors of law, making the older doctrines largely redundant and defying the traditional reluctance to interfere. *Anisminic* appears to have made all errors of law reviewable, at least in principle. The Foreign Compensation Commission (FCC) was established by statute to adjudicate on claims to compensation for war damage in connection with an Arab-Israeli war. Under complex regulations, it had to decide many questions, one of which was that the owner of the damaged property and the owner's successor in title must be British subjects. The FCC had interpreted the term 'successor in title' as including a purchaser. This led it to refuse compensation to Anisminic, a British company which had sold its property to an Egyptian company. A majority of the House of Lords held that, as a matter of law, a purchaser was not a successor in title because the term 'successor in title' in this context was intended to mean only someone who succeeds to property on the death or winding up of its original owner. According to the majority, this made the decision not just wrong, but outside the FCC's jurisdiction.

Anisminic has been widely viewed as deciding that any mistake of law affecting a decision makes the decision *ultra vires*. The reason for this seems to be the loose way in which the majority characterised a jurisdictional error as taking an irrelevant matter into account, failing to take a relevant matter into account or 'asking the wrong question'. In the case itself, an irrelevant matter had been taken into account that Parliament did not intend, namely the nationality of the Egyptian company.

All mistakes could logically be presented under those heads. *Anisminic* arguably takes the court beyond its proper constitutional limits by enabling it to second-guess the decision-maker on any issue of law. Indeed there are dicta in *Anisminic* itself denying that all errors of law are jurisdictional, and Lord Morris strongly dissented (at 174, 189, 195, 209; see also *Pearlman v Governors and Keepers of Harrow School* [1979] QB 56; *South East Asia Fire Brick Sdn Bhd v Non-Metallic Mineral Products Manufacturing Employees Union* [1981] AC 363).

However, the view that all errors of law can, in principle, be reviewed is widely accepted, and the issue is probably closed. In *CCSU v Minister for the Civil Service* [1985] at 410, Lord Diplock said that understanding correctly the law that regulates the decision-making power is *par excellence* a question for the courts (see also *R (Cart) v Upper Tribunal* [2012], at [17]–[18], [39]–[40], [110]; *Re Racal Communications* [1981] AC 374; *O'Reilly v Mackman* [1982] 3 All ER 1124; *Page v Hull University Visitor* [1993]; *Boddington v BTP* [1998] at 158).

The courts have, to some extent, drawn back from *Anisminic*. They have recognised that some matters raise specialised issues which the expert tribunal or government decision-maker is better equipped to decide than the court. For example, in *Re Racal Communications* [1981], Lord Diplock suggested that *Anisminic* did not apply to decisions of lower courts where questions of law and questions of fact were inextricably mixed up. In *Page v Hull University Visitor* [1993], it was held that the specialised rules of universities should be conclusively interpreted by the university visitor. In both these cases, it was recognised that unfair or unreasonable decisions could be reviewed. In *R (Cart) v Upper Tribunal* [2012], it was held that, in view of the high status of the tribunal, the court would interfere only in exceptional circumstances.

17.5.2 Error of fact

Anisminic has not been applied to mistakes of *fact*. Errors of fact are not normally reviewable, since the courts regard the initial decision-making body as in the best position to find the facts. However, possible injustices invite exceptions, although these might be explained on the basis that the particular error falls within another head of review. The exceptions are as follows:

▶ The old doctrine of the jurisdictional/preliminary question (Section 17.5) applies both to errors of law and to errors of fact, where it is sometimes called the 'precedent fact' doctrine. This allows the court to decide the question of fact itself. For example, in *Khawaja v Secretary of State for the Home Dept* [1983] 1 All ER 765, the Home Secretary could deport an 'illegal immigrant'. The House of Lords held that the court could decide whether the appellant was, in fact, an illegal immigrant and was not limited to deciding whether the minister's decision was unreasonable. The problem is to decide what kind of case falls within the doctrine. This depends upon the statutory context. In *Khawaja*, the court was influenced by the fact that the decision involved personal freedom, so that a high level of judicial control was required. By contrast, in *Bugdaycay v Secretary of State* [1987] AC 514, the question was whether the applicant was a 'refugee'. This question was only one of several given to an immigration officer to decide under immigration rules and involved a large element of subjective value judgment, so could not be regarded as a precedent fact (at 522–3). A finding of fact which is completely unreasonable in the sense that it has no evidential basis is reviewable (*Ashbridge Investments v Minister of Housing and Local Government* [1965] 1 WLR 1320 at 1326). Unreasonableness in this sense is a ground of review in its own right (Section 18.1).

▶ A clear and undisputed error. In *R v Criminal Injuries Compensation Board, ex p A* [1999] 2 AC 330 at 344, Lord Slynn said that 'misunderstanding or ignorance of an established and relevant fact' is reviewable but emphasised that this is no more than an application of ordinary review principles (see also *Secretary of State for Education and Science v Tameside Metropolitan BC* [1977] AC 1014 at 1017). By contrast, judicial review does not include a reinvestigation of disputed facts, unless the decision is perverse (*Adan v Newham LBC* [2002] 1 All ER 931). In other words, the courts will not attempt to investigate factual disagreements or to weigh evidence but will intervene in clear cases. In *R (A) v Croydon LBC* [2009] 1 WLR 2557, a refugee was eligible for housing only if there was a child in need. It was held that the court could interfere where there was an objectively right or wrong answer (i.e. whether there was a child) but not on the question of need, which was a subjective value judgment. It was also held that the court would look at the quality of the initial decision-making process: the better it was, the less willing the court would be to interfere. The distinction made in this case is sometimes described as being between 'hard' and 'soft' edged questions (see also *R (Al-Sweady) v Defence Secretary* [2009] EWHC 2387).

This is the nearest the law gets to error of fact as an independent ground of review. However, this level of review may be insufficient to satisfy ECHR Article 6: right to a fair trial (Section 21.4.1.3, and see also *R (Kiarie) v Home Secretary* [2017] UKSC 42: Article 8). In general, it might be preferable in cases both of law and of fact to allow judicial review only where the decision is an *unreasonable* one, for example where proper consideration was not given to the matter. This provides a safeguard without infringing the competence of the decision-maker. A right of appeal can be provided by statute where a more detailed scrutiny is required. This is an important feature of judicial review which emphasises the way a decision is reached rather than the outcome in isolation.

17.6 'Wide' *ultra vires*: improper purposes and relevance

These aspects of illegality arise in the context of discretionary powers where the governing statute does not define the extent of the powers precisely. They are sometimes labelled 'abuse of discretion'. Even though the decision-maker keeps within the express language of the statute:

▶ it may act for an improper purpose; or
▶ it may be influenced by irrelevant factors; or
▶ it may fail to take relevant factors into account.

These grounds apply even where the statute appears to give the decision-maker an unrestricted, subjective discretion, using such expressions as 'if the minister thinks fit', since even the widest discretionary power is, in principle, reviewable (although it may sometimes be difficult to square such review with the *ultra vires* approach described in Section 17.2: can this form of review really be said to be about giving effect to Parliament's intention, where Parliament seems to have conferred unfettered discretion?). It is for the court to decide what factors are relevant and what are the purposes of the Act (see *Padfield v Minister of Agriculture, Fisheries and Food* [1968] AC 997: a minister who had wide subjective discretionary power to refer an issue to a committee of investigation must not be influenced by considerations that do not advance the policy and objects of the particular Act).

17.6.1 Improper purpose

This is where a decision-maker acts for a purpose of his own outside the statute. In *R v Secretary of State for Foreign and Commonwealth Affairs, ex p World Development Movement* [1995] 1 All ER 611, the government had statutory power to give financial aid to other countries for 'economic' purposes. It decided to give a grant to Malaysia for the Pergau Dam project. The Court of Appeal held that Parliament must have intended the word 'economic' to include only 'sound' economic decisions, so the court was entitled to infer that the decision had been made primarily for an ulterior purpose (e.g. of facilitating an arms sale arrangement). This seems to come near to the courts trespassing on forbidden territory by interfering with the merits of the decision since the court could deepen its investigation into any statutory function by saying that Parliament must have intended that function to be carried out 'soundly' (see Irvine [1996] PL 59). On the other hand, parliamentary scrutiny had been ineffective, so the court's role may be justifiable (from a separation of powers perspective) as the only available constitutional check.

In *Porter v Magill* [2002] 1 All ER 465, the leader of a local authority had embarked upon a policy of selling off the authority's housing. This in itself was a lawful policy. However, sales were concentrated in marginal electoral wards with a view to attracting votes for the Conservative Party. The House of Lords held that the policy could not be justified on the basis of legitimate housing purposes. A democratic body can hope for an electoral advantage as the incidental outcome of its policies (and choose between alternative legitimate policies for electoral reasons), but it cannot distort policies to seek electoral advantage. In other words, a matter may lawfully be taken into account along with other relevant matters but cannot be the predominant purpose of the decision.

17.6.2 Irrelevant considerations

The decision-maker may be broadly acting for the proper purpose but may take an improper route to achieving it by taking into account an irrelevant matter or failing to take into account a relevant matter. As usual, the starting point is the language of the statute, but where wide discretionary powers are concerned this may not be helpful, and the courts have leeway to impose their own view as to what is relevant. Thus, the concept of relevance sets out conditions of proper decision-making, and the courts are policing the boundaries of the democratic process. For example, in *R v Secretary of State for the Home Dept, ex p Venables* [1997] 3 All ER 97, public opinion, in the shape of an opinion poll in the *Sun* newspaper, was not relevant where the Secretary of State reviewed the sentence in a notorious child murderer case, since his judicial function must be exercised using his independent judgment. Moreover, factors which are relevant must be clearly explained. For example, if a policy refers to 'exceptional circumstances' the authority must be able to indicate as far as possible what these might be (*R (Rogers) v Swindon Primary Health Care Trust* [2006] EWCA Civ 392: refusal to provide cancer drug).

In deciding what factors are relevant, the court can look at background evidence, for example official reports that influenced the legislation in question, and also things said in Parliament as to government policy. However, statements made in Parliament cannot be used as evidence that a minister has acted in bad faith, since this would violate parliamentary privilege (Section 11.6). An unequivocal statement as to the scope of a provision might, however, prevent a minister subsequently from attempting a different explanation (*R v Secretary of State for the Environment, Transport and the Regions, ex p Spath Holme* [2000] 1 All ER 884: were rent control powers limited to anti-inflation measures or of wider scope?).

A decision-maker must take into account all relevant government policies and guidance, including international obligations, even though these do not necessarily have the force of law. In *R (Bulger) v Secretary of State for the Home Dept* [2001] 3 All ER 449, the court, drawing on international obligations, held that in fixing the length of time a convicted child offender must serve, the Secretary of State must take into account the welfare of the child and keep the child's progress and rehabilitation under review. The courts have also held that local authorities should concern themselves with local issues as opposed to general issues of national or international politics (*R v Lewisham LBC, ex p Shell UK Ltd* [1988] 1 All ER 938).

The courts may seek to protect individual interests against bureaucratic zeal. In *R v City of Westminster Housing Benefit Review Board, ex p Mehanne* [2001] 2 All ER 690, legislation required the board to reduce a claim when it considered that the rent was unreasonably high, 'having regard in particular to the cost of suitable accommodation elsewhere'. The board interpreted this as preventing it from taking into account the claimant's personal circumstances, including his wife's pregnancy and his reduced income as a refugee. The House of Lords held that personal circumstances were relevant, pointing out that the phrase 'in particular' invited other factors to be considered. Lord Bingham said that 'in the absence of very clear language I would be very reluctant to conclude that the board were precluded from considering matters which could affect the mind of a reasonable and fair minded person' (at 697).

In *R v Somerset CC, ex p Fewings* [1995], the council had banned hunting on its land for ethical reasons. The Court of Appeal held that, under the governing statute which gave them power to 'manage' land, the moral question of cruelty was a relevant consideration. However, it was not open to a council merely to impose the personal moral views of its members; it was necessary to consider what was for the 'benefit' of the area, as the statute provided.

In some cases, the courts have appeared to restrict the powers of local authorities to innovate in order to compel them to conserve taxpayers' money by adopting 'business principles' in fixing wages, fares and prices at the expense of local democratic freedom (see *Roberts v Hopwood* [1925]; *Prescott v Birmingham Corp* [1955]; *Bromley LBC v GLC* [1983]). However, it has been stressed that the scope of what is relevant should be responsive to changing community values (see *Pickwell v Camden LBC* [1983] QB 962).

In relation to general factors such as hardship or expense, or political or moral considerations (as in *Fewings*, above), unless the statute plainly requires otherwise, the decision-maker may have discretion to decide what is relevant in the particular circumstances. The court will interfere only where the authority exercises its discretion unfairly or unreasonably (see *Ashby v Minister of Immigration* [1981] NZLR 222 at 224: 'obligatory' and 'permissible' considerations; *R (FDA) v Secretary of State for Work and Pensions* [2012] 3 All ER 301: effect of changes to public sector pensions on national economy).

An important instance of this issue arises where it has had to be decided whether a decision-maker is entitled to take financial cost into account. This is especially important when financial cuts mean that public services are under pressure. For example, in *R (Condliff) v North Staffordshire Primary Health Care Trust* [2011] EWCA Civ 910, it was held that a hospital could decline to provide medical treatment on the basis of clinical factors alone, without taking into account the personal circumstances of the patient since this was a non-discriminatory and fair way of allocating scarce resources (Section 21.4). In *HSE v Wolverhampton City Council* [2012] UKSC 34, the Supreme Court held that, in deciding whether to revoke a planning permission, a local authority could take into account the cost to the public of the compensation involved.

There is a dilemma where a local authority refuses to provide a welfare benefit to which a person may be entitled on the grounds that it does not have sufficient resources. If the court were to order the authority to provide the benefit, it could be accused of interfering with democratic choice. If it were not to do so, there may be unfairness (a so-called 'postcode lottery') if different standards are applied in different local areas. In *Southwark LBC v Tanner* [2001] 1 AC 1 at 9–10, Lord Hoffmann warned against judicial intervention in a field which is so very much a matter of the allocation of resources in accordance with democratically determined priorities.

In this kind of case, the court interprets the particular statute to determine whether the duty to provide the benefit is intended to be absolute (mandatory), or permissive, which would allow the authority to take its resources into account. Words such as 'shall' or 'may' are indicative but not conclusive, and the whole statutory context must be examined. The importance of the matter, the desirability of uniformity and resource implications are taken into account.

In *R v Gloucestershire CC, ex p Barry* [1997] 2 All ER 1, a majority of the House of Lords held that a statutory duty to give such assistance as was 'necessary' to meet the 'needs' of a disabled person allowed the authority to take into account its resources as part of the meaning of 'necessary'. However, an authority should provide an explanation of how it prioritises competing needs (see *R (KM) v Cambridgeshire CC* [2012] 3 All ER 1218).

In *R (G) v Barnet LBC* [2004] 1 All ER 97, the House of Lords held that the duty imposed on local authorities by the Children Act 1989 to 'safeguard and promote' the welfare of children provided only broad aims which the authority should bear in mind. The Act therefore gave the authority a discretion to choose between competing demands and to take cost into account, and the court would interfere only if the discretion were to be exercised unreasonably. This is sometimes labelled a 'target duty', reflecting the fact that not all needs can realistically be met in full.

In *R (Conville) v Richmond on Thames LBC* [2006] EWCA Civ 718, the Court of Appeal held that a statute which required the Council to give a tenant a 'reasonable opportunity' to secure other accommodation did not allow it to take its own circumstances into account in deciding what was reasonable (see also *R (M) v Gateshead Council* [2007] 1 All ER 1262; *R v East Sussex CC, ex p Tandy* [1998] 2 All ER 769; *R v Sefton Metropolitan BC, ex p Help the Aged* [1997] 4 All ER 532; *R v Newham LBC, ex p Begum* [2000] 2 All ER 72).

The relevance principle does not require the decision-maker to give any particular weight to a given matter. In general, the appropriate weight to be given to a factor is a political matter that is not for the court. The decision-maker can choose which of the competing factors to prefer, provided that a relevant consideration is not completely ignored. For example, in *Tesco Stores v Secretary of State* [1995] 2 All ER 636, the House of Lords held that, in accordance with a government circular, a planning authority must take into account an offer from Tesco to contribute to the building of a new road in the area in return for planning permission. However, it could give the offer 'nil' weight in influencing its decision.

The court is not entirely excluded from matters of weighting:

▶ A statute might expressly or implicitly indicate that special weight be given to some factors.
▶ According to the 'principle of legality' special weight must be given to the fundamental rights of the individual (Section 6.6).
▶ Similarly, matters falling within the HRA attract the 'proportionality' principle, which is essentially one of weighting, requiring as it does a strong reason to override a human right (Section 22.9).
▶ A 'legitimate expectation' might be given special weight (Section 18.3.1).
▶ The court can interfere if the decision-maker has acted irrationally in relation to matters of weighting (Section 18.1).

An improper purpose or an irrelevant consideration is not automatically fatal. The court will not set aside a decision if the factor in question would not objectively have made any difference to the outcome. In this sense, the line between legality and merits is blurred. In the context of improper purposes, this is sometimes expressed as the 'dominant purpose' test. The following are illustrations:

▶ In *Westminster Corp v London and North Western Railway* [1905] AC 426, the local authority had power to construct public lavatories. It incorporated a subway into the design of its lavatories, and it was objected that this was its real purpose. This was held to be lawful on the basis that the subway was merely incidental. Although it could be used by people to cross the street, it was also an appropriate method of reaching the lavatories. By contrast, in *Webb v Minister of Housing and Local Government* [1965] 1 WLR 755, the local authority had power to construct coast protection works. It incorporated a promenade into a scheme, compulsorily acquiring a number of houses for the purpose. This was held to be unlawful on the ground that more land was acquired than was needed for a coastal protection barrier. The whole scheme was invalid, and the good part could not be separated from the bad.

▶ In *R v Lewisham LBC, ex p Shell UK Ltd* [1988] 1 All ER 938, the council decided to boycott Shell's products on the ground that Shell had interests in South Africa, which, at the time, was subject to apartheid. It was held that the policy could have been lawfully justified on the ground of promoting good race relations in the borough. However, as the council had tried to persuade other local authorities to adopt a similar policy, it had gone too far, its purpose being to put pressure on Shell.

▶ In *R v Secretary of State for Social Services, ex p Wellcome Foundation* [1987] 2 All ER 1025, irrelevant commercial factors were taken into account, but the decision could be justified on proper health grounds.

17.6.3   Failure to take relevant factors into account: fettering discretion

It is unlawful to fetter a discretionary power imposed by statute. Officials fetter their discretion by binding themselves in advance to decide in a particular way, without being prepared to consider all the circumstances of an individual case on its merits. Thus, this is an extreme example of a failure to take relevant factors into account.

Discretion can be fettered in many ways since administrators may find this is an attractive method of disposing of cases without too much effort or responsibility. Examples of unlawful fetters include the following:

▶ rigid application of rules, 'guidance', or policies made within the government. Unless the rule is made legally binding by a statute or subordinate legislation, it is unlawful to treat it as absolutely binding (*R v Port of London Authority, ex p Kynoch* [1919] 1 KB 176). An official can, of course, take into account guidelines drawn up within the government and give them very high priority. Indeed, government would be impracticable without them. Moreover, fairness and certainty require policies to be published and followed (see e.g. *R (Purdy) v DPP* [2009] 4 All ER 1147: prosecution policy in cases of assisted suicide). No more is required by the rule against fettering than that the decision-maker must keep an open mind by considering whether in any given case an exception to the policy should be made. This is a vital protection for the individual against official intransigence.

▶ In *British Oxygen Co v Minister of Technology* [1971] AC 610, there was a valid policy that grants would be payable only in respect of products above a certain cost. Nevertheless, the possibility of making an exception should have been considered. As Lord Reid put it (at 625):

[A] Ministry or large authority may have had already to deal with a multitude of similar applications and then they will almost certainly have evolved a policy so precise that it could well be called a rule. There can be no objection to that, provided that the authority is always willing to listen to anyone with something new to say.

For example, in *R v Secretary of State for the Home Dept, ex p Hindley* [2001] 1 AC 410, a 'whole life tariff' set by the Home Secretary for a convicted murderer was lawful, provided that it was open to periodic review, even if an exception was extremely unlikely. In *R (Lumba) v Secretary of State for the Home Dept* [2012] 1 AC 245, the Supreme Court held that a blanket policy to detain all foreign national prisoners on completion of sentence pending deportation was unlawful, unless individual cases were considered as possible exceptions. Administrative convenience is no excuse;

▶ rigid application of party-political policies, without making an independent judgment (*R v Waltham Forest LBC, ex p Baxter* [1988] QB 419);

▶ acting solely in accordance with electoral mandates (*Bromley LBC v GLC* [1983]). These can, of course, be given great weight (*Secretary of State for Education and Science v Tameside Metropolitan BC* [1977]);

▶ agreements and contracts that contradict a statutory obligation (*Ayr Harbour Trustees v Oswald* (1883) 8 App Cas 623; *Stringer v Minister of Housing and Local Government* [1971] 1 All ER 65). Contracts are always binding and so inevitably fetter the future exercise of a discretion. However, the principle seems to be that a contract is invalid only if it is inconsistent with a clear statutory obligation (see *R v Hammersmith and Fulham LBC, ex p Beddowes* [1987] 1 All ER 369);

▶ acting under the dictation of another body (*Lavender & Son Ltd v Minister of Housing and Local Government* [1970] 3 All ER 871). But consulting another body and even relying on the decision of another body unless an objection are raised is lawful (see *R v GLC, ex p Blackburn* [1976] 3 All ER 184).

In respect of statements made by officials, the doctrine of estoppel familiar in private law areas such as contract, under which in certain circumstances a person is bound by a promise or statement on which another relies, does not apply in public law (*Western Fish Products v Penwith DC* [1981] 2 All ER 204: developer wrongly told that he would not need planning permission; *R (Reprotech (Pebsham) Ltd) v East Sussex CC* [2003] 1 WLR 348: council subcommittee resolution recommending grant of planning permission for waste treatment plant not binding). The justification for this harsh principle is the public interest that government decisions should be made according to law and that public bodies should be free to revise their position if circumstances change. On the other hand, a citizen who is misled by an official is the victim of unfairness. However, in this kind of case, the citizen may have a 'legitimate expectation' that the statement should be honoured. This alleviates the harshness of the rule to some extent (Section 18.3.1).

There is, of course, no unlawful fetter where the decision-making power has been validly delegated to the official in question (Section 18.2) and has been lawfully exercised. Here the decision will be binding. However, it may be difficult for the citizen to discover whether this is in fact the case. It is not enough (as it would be in private law) that the official reasonably appears to be authorised ('ostensible authority'). However, in *South Buckinghamshire DC v Flanagan* [2002] 1 WLR 2601, where the council's solicitor made a decision, it was held that ostensible authority can validate a decision provided that the official *could* under statute have made it although he had not in fact been authorised to do so. In other words, the decision must not be *ultra vires* the statute.

The rule against fettering discretion seems to apply only to statutory powers and not to prerogative or other common law powers. In *R (Sandiford) v Secretary of State for Foreign and Commonwealth Affairs* [2014] 4 All ER 843, the Supreme Court upheld a blanket policy not to fund legal representation for British citizens facing criminal proceedings abroad even in death row cases. The policy itself, intended to avoid practical problems, was not unlawful and it could be applied without exceptions. However, the policy was being kept under review. The reason for this distinction seems to be that, unlike a statutory power, there was no 'external originator' of the power which must have contemplated that it might be appropriate to exercise the power in a different manner in different circumstances: rather, 'they are intrinsic to the Crown and it is for the Crown to determine whether and how to exercise them in its discretion', at [61].

In fettering discretion problems, particularly those involving policy fetters, four distinct questions arise:

1. Is the policy itself lawful? Apart from questions of *ultra vires* (above), the policy must not be inconsistent with any relevant published policy (see *Lumba* (above) [34]–[39]; *R (Mayaya) v Secretary of State for the Home Dept* [2012] 1 All ER 1491).
2. Has the policy been applied too inflexibly so as to fetter discretion?
3. The reverse situation: has an exception been made to the policy which itself is unlawful? For example, in *R v Port Talbot BC, ex p Jones* [1988] 2 All ER 207, the council's policy was to allocate housing on a first-come-first-served basis. However, it allowed a person standing for election to the council to jump the queue so that she could qualify as a local resident. This was held to be unlawful so that the policy should have applied. Had the house been allocated because, say, of special hardship, the decision might have been lawful.
4. Does fettering the discretion also engage the issue of legitimate expectations? This will be discussed in the next chapter (Section 18.3.1).

17.7   Nullity: void and voidable decisions

According to the rule of law and the *ultra vires* doctrine, an invalid government act should be a nullity (void) and have no legal consequences. Indeed, this has been emphasised by the courts (e.g. Lord Reid in *Ridge v Baldwin* [1964] AC 40; *Anisminic Ltd v Foreign Compensation Commission* [1969] at 171, 195, 207; *Secretary of State for the Home Dept v JJ* [2008] 1 All ER 613 at [27]).

Thus, if a decision is held in judicial review proceedings to be a nullity then, in principle, it should be treated as never having had legal effect, and its consequences unwound. For example, in *Ridge v Baldwin* [1964], a Chief Constable dismissed without a hearing was held still to be in office and so entitled to his pension rights. In *Secretary of State v JJ* [2008], it was held that a void Control Order made by the Home Secretary under anti-terrorist legislation could not be amended to make it lawful. Similarly, in *R (Lumba) v Secretary of State for the Home Dept* [2012], the Supreme Court rejected the government's contention that it was not liable for false imprisonment on the basis of an unlawful decision because the same decision could have lawfully been made (however, this prevented the claimant getting substantial compensation).

On the other hand, it may be impractical and even unjust to ignore a decision since its invalidity can be exposed only once a court has ruled as much. In that sense, a decision is only voidable: valid until set aside by a court. This is reinforced by the fact that all judicial review remedies are discretionary, so in judicial review proceedings, the court does not have to set aside even an *ultra vires* decision. By contrast, where a decision is challenged collaterally, for example as a defence to a prosecution, the court has no discretion. Thus, a different outcome is possible depending solely on which route is taken for the challenge (see *Credit Suisse v Allerdale BC* [1996] at 167).

The concept of nullity does not always result in justice. In particular, a third party might have to rely on a decision that seems to be valid at the time. This applies especially to procedural flaws that may not be obvious (indeed the issues overlap (Section 18.2)). In *DPP v Head* [1959] AC 83, a woman was improperly confined in a mental hospital as a result of an invalid medical procedure. A man charged with having sexual relations with a patient 'detained' under the Mental Health Acts successfully argued that, due to the invalidity, the patient was not 'detained' under the relevant Acts. On the same analysis, the officials who administered the hospital would have made numerous decisions affecting the detainee on the assumption that the initial order was valid. A public body might rely on its own invalid actions to escape its liabilities. For example, in *Credit Suisse v Allerdale BC* [1996], a local authority successfully argued that a guarantee which it had given was *ultra vires* and so not enforceable against it (see Local Government (Contracts) Act 1997 reversing this).

If due to the initial infection of an invalid decision, all consequential acts had to be unpicked, the result would be chaos. For instance, would everyone granted a driving licence under a regulation which later turned out to be invalid find themselves guilty of an offence?

There are various ways of attacking this problem, none of them entirely satisfactory:

1. Argue that only the most serious defects make a decision void, while others make it only voidable in the sense that it might be set aside for the future only (see *Bugg v DPP* [1993] QB 473 at 493). This had been rejected as lacking coherence by the House of Lords in *Anisminic v Foreign Compensation Commission* [1969], which took the view that all defects make the decision a nullity (cf. Lords Browne Wilkinson and Slynn in *Boddington* [1998]).
2. Claim that there is a 'presumption of validity', meaning that, until it is set aside, a decision must be treated as valid, but if successfully challenged it can be set aside retrospectively, that is, treated as if it never existed (see *Hoffmann-La Roche v Secretary of State* [1974] 2 All ER 1128; *Calvin v Carr* [1980] AC 574). In that sense, all decisions would be voidable only. This does not address the problem of third parties who rely on a decision. However, a distinction is sometimes made between defects which are obvious (patent) and those which can be discovered only by further investigation (latent); only the former can be ignored (cf. *Smith v East Elloe RDC* [1956] AC 736: 'bears the brand of invalidity on its forehead'). This kind of argument is probably unfashionable today.
3. Use judicial discretion according to all the circumstances of the particular context so as to enable an *ultra vires* decision to have legal consequences if it is just to do so. Thus, in *London and Clydesdale Estates v Aberdeen District Council* [1979] 3 All ER 876, the House of Lords held that a certificate of compensation for a compulsory purchase order which failed to give required information about a right of appeal was *ultra vires*. However, the certificate was not a complete nullity and could have legal consequences until the court set it aside. For example, there could be an appeal against it to the Secretary of State, thus enabling the amount of compensation

to be altered. Lord Keith remarked that the distinction between void and voidable should be avoided as inappropriate and apt to confuse (at 894). Lord Hailsham referred to a 'spectrum of possibilities' and did not encourage the use of rigid legal classifications: 'The jurisdiction is inherently discretionary' (at 883).

The Court of Appeal exercised discretion in *R (Corbett) v Restormel Borough Council* [2001] EWCA Civ 330, where a local council tried to rely on its own unlawful act. A landowner had relied on an *ultra vires* planning permission for building work which the authority then tried to deny. It was held that, in order to do justice, the permission should be treated as valid so as to enable it to be cancelled, which would entitle the landowner to compensation under the statute. Schiemann LJ recognised (at [16]–[17]) that this was a clash between two notions of the rule of law, that of legal certainty and that of the 'principle of legality', which required protection of basic rights (Section 6.6).

4. Professor Wade deals with the conundrum by using the concept of 'relative nullity', meaning that an invalid decision is indeed a nullity but only if challenged in the right court by the right person in the right way ('Unlawful Administrative Action: Void or Voidable?' (1968) 84 LQR 95). For example, a claimant may be out of time to bring an action, in which case the decision must stand, and a third party can rely on it.

5. Forsyth (1998) suggests a distinction between an act valid in law and an act that exists in fact. This refers to the situation where an invalid decision has a chain of consequences where it is relied upon by other officials or citizens who assume that it is valid – the 'domino effect' or 'the theory of the second actor'. The crucial question of interpretation is whether the validity *in law* of the first act is a precondition to the validity of the second decision, or whether a decision *in fact* is sufficient. For example, in *R v Wicks* [1998] AC 92 the House of Lords held that a developer could be prosecuted for disobeying a planning enforcement notice even though the notice was invalid since the statutory requirement was only for a notice that existed *in fact*, that is, one that appeared to be valid.

6. Distinguish between the decision itself and the preliminary steps leading to it. These are not necessarily void and so the whole process need not be unpicked (see *Shrewsbury and Atcham BC v Secretary of State* [2008] at [57]–[58]).

Summary

- Judicial review is constitutionally ambivalent. On one hand, it supports the rule of law, parliamentary supremacy and democracy by enabling the courts to police the limits of government power. On the other hand, the courts are open to the complaint, based on the separation of powers, that they are interfering with the decisions of democratically elected bodies. The basis of this complaint is that the courts interpret the legislation in question in light of their own values and presumptions, which are not necessarily democratic.

- Judicial review therefore claims not to be concerned with the merits of a government decision, but with whether the decision-maker has kept within legal limits and followed broad principles of fairness and rationality. The grounds of judicial review are loosely classified under the heads of illegality, irrationality and procedural impropriety.

- The constitutional basis of judicial review is contested. According to one view, it depends on the *ultra vires* doctrine. The alternative view is that judicial review is a freestanding part of the common law, but subject to parliamentary supremacy. Proponents of the *ultra vires* doctrine cater for the fact that much of the law is actually judge-made by claiming that Parliament intends and so implicitly authorises legislation to be interpreted according to principles of judicial review.

- A statutory decision-maker must act within the limits of the statute, including what is 'reasonably incidental' to the statute. The courts apply presumptions of statutory interpretation, notably 'the principle of legality', in policing the limits of statutory powers.

- Procedural flaws raise particular problems in that, despite the rule of law, the courts are reluctant to invalidate decisions on purely technical grounds. Various devices have been used to enable the court to respond to the justice of the particular case.

- With some specialised exceptions, the court will review a decision on the ground of error of law although this sits uneasily with the notion of *ultra vires*.

- Review for mistakes of fact is limited since this might involve a reviewing court going outside its proper sphere. Clear errors of fact may be reviewable, and an error of fact might also fall within one of the other grounds, for example irrationality (Chapter 18). The interpretation of broad subjective terms in a statute may be classified as mixed questions of law and fact to limit review.

Summary cont'd

▶ A decision-maker also acts *ultra vires* by acting for an improper purpose, taking an irrelevant factor into account, or failing to take a relevant factor into account where this affects the outcome of the decision. Matters directly related to the statute must always be taken into account. Broader factors can be taken into account subject to the court deciding their relevance in the particular case.

▶ Fettering discretion concerns the application of a self-created rigid rule, policy or undertaking in a case where, under a statute, the decision-maker must exercise a discretion. A decision-maker can adopt guidelines but cannot treat them as absolutely binding.

▶ An *ultra vires* decision is strictly speaking of no effect (nullity/void). However, this may cause injustice in some cases. As with procedural flaws, the courts have tried to take a flexible approach, but without clear principles emerging.

Exercises

17.1 'The simple proposition that a public authority may not act outside its powers (*ultra vires*) might fitly be called the central principle of administrative law' (Wade and Forsyth). Discuss.

17.2 Dumbo City Council owns and manages the Dumbo Leisure Centre which, by statute, must be accessible to the public at all reasonable times. It has statutory power to make regulations for the purpose of 'good order' within the Centre.

(i) One regulation provides that no person may sell or buy goods from any stall or vehicle within the precincts of the Centre unless the seller displays a permit in a prominent place on the stall or vehicle. A fee is payable for the issue of a permit. George operates a burger bar from a van in the Centre's car park without a permit. Advise George.

(ii) The council places notices around the Centre promoting the opinions of councillors on the issue of using live animals for medical experiments. Mary objects to the council's advertisements. Advise Mary.

(iii) Another regulation made by the council requires all users of the centre to purchase accident insurance from the council. Advise Dave, who refuses to do so and is banned from entering the Centre.

17.3 When can mistakes of law and fact be challenged in the courts?

17.4 By statute, a tribunal composed of expert economists has the power to decide the 'appropriate level of fares' that can be imposed by 'public transport' undertakings operating 'outside the London area'. George operates a car hire service based in London that includes journeys to and from various regional airports for which he makes a surcharge based on fuel costs. He also gives free transport to pensioners on a Monday evening. The tribunal orders George to lower his charges in order to withdraw the concession to pensioners. George claims that he is not operating outside the London area, that he is not a public transport undertaking, and that the tribunal has miscalculated the cost of fuel. He also claims that the tribunal is not entitled to prevent him giving concessions. Advise him.

17.5 Under the Sports Act 2021 (fictitious), the Minister of Sport has power 'where he considers it necessary in the interest of public safety and good order, to require the admission of paid spectators to any sporting event to be subject to showing membership cards at the entrance'. The minister, interpreting 'sport' as including any activity that is competitive, has made an order requiring entrance to chess competitions to be subject to the showing of membership cards. The minister has been advised that chess events are an important source of the Opposition party's finances. In another case, the minister has revoked the membership cards of all the members of a football club because the club has failed to provide adequate refreshment facilities for visitors. Discuss.

17.6 Assume that local authorities have statutory power to control the disposal of household waste within their local areas. Bristowe City Council makes the following regulation: 'Each household must produce, if required to do so by an authorised officer, a standard sized bin containing a reasonable amount of recyclable waste. Failure to do so will incur a penalty at the discretion of the authorised officer'.

(a) Alf fails to produce a bin. He claims that his bin was recently stolen. The authorised officer tells him that he has no choice but to impose a penalty.

(b) Bill produces a bin containing only a small amount of waste. He explains that he has recently been absent abroad. The officer, who considers that Bill is lying and who has fallen behind with his performance target, imposes a penalty on Bill.

(c) Clara's bin is filled to overflowing. The officer imposes a penalty on her on the ground that the amount of waste produced will impose an excessive financial burden on the government.

Advise Alf, Bill and Clara as to any grounds on which they can challenge the regulations and the decisions in their individual cases.

Further reading

Adams, '*Ultra Vires* Revisited' [2018] PL 31

Allan, 'Constitutional Dialogue and the Justification for Judicial Review' (2003) 23 OJLS 563

Boughey and Crawford, 'Reconsidering *R (on the application of Cart) v Upper Tribunal* and the Rationale for Jurisdictional Error' [2017] PL 592

Craig, 'The Common Law, Shared Power and Judicial Review' (2004) 24 OJLS 237

Elliott, *The Constitutional Foundations of Judicial Review* (Hart Publishing 2001)

Endicott, *Administrative Law* (4th edn, Oxford University Press 2018) chs 2, 9

Forsyth, 'Of Fig Leaves and Fairy Tales: The *Ultra Vires* Doctrine, the Sovereignty of Parliament and Judicial Review' (1996) 55 CLJ 122

Forsyth and Elliott, 'The Legitimacy of Judicial Review' [2003] PL 286

Forsyth et al. (eds), *Effective Judicial Review: A Cornerstone of Good Governance* (Oxford University Press 2010)

Halpin, 'The Theoretical Controversy concerning Judicial Review' (2001) 64 MLR 500

Hare, 'Separation of Powers and Error of Law' in Forsyth and Hare (eds), *The Golden Metwand and the Crooked Cord* (Clarendon Press 1998)

Harlow and Pearson, *Administrative Law in a Changing State* (Hart Publishing 2008)

Lui, '"Fairness" for Mistake of Fact: A Mistake in Fact' [2020] PL 428

Murkens, 'Judicious Review: The Constitutional Practice of the UK Supreme Court' (2018) 77 CLJ 349

Murray, 'Escaping the Wilderness: *R v Bolton* and Judicial Review for Error of Law' (2016) 75 CLJ 333

Nason, *Reconstructing Judicial Review* (Bloomsbury 2019)

Perry, 'The Flexibility Rule in Administrative Law' (2017) 76 CLJ 375

Poole, 'Legitimacy, Rights and Judicial Review' (2005) 25 OJLS 697

Tomkins, 'The Role of the Courts in the Political Constitution' (2010) 60 U Toronto LJ 1

Williams, 'When Is an Error Not an Error? Reform of Jurisdictional Review of Errors of Law and Fact' [2007] PL 793

Chapter 18

The grounds of judicial review, II: beyond *ultra vires*

This chapter continues the discussion in Chapter 17. It includes grounds of review that are less clearly linked to the notion of *ultra vires* and which therefore especially raise issues of the proper limits of the courts' role. It is important to bear in mind that the level (sometimes called the 'intensity') of review – in other words, the depth of the court's investigation – varies with the context. The court will scrutinise a decision more rigorously according to the seriousness of its impact on the individual. On the other hand, the court will show respect for a democratic decision-maker, an expert body, or a decision which appears highly 'political' in character (such as those entailing the allocation of limited resources), and will usually be less intrusive in such cases (Section 19.7.1). As so often, an accommodation must be struck between competing concerns.

18.1 Irrationality/unreasonableness

Irrationality or 'unreasonableness' can be used to challenge the exercise of discretion or findings of law and fact (Section 17.5). Although the question of what is reasonable must, as always, be decided in the context of the particular statutory power, this ground of review operates as an external control, in that it draws on values not directly derived from the statute. Indeed, the notion of 'unreasonableness' is so vague that it seems to invite the court to impose its own opinion of the merits in place of that of the decision-maker.

Against this, the separation of powers, coupled with practical considerations, suggests that the courts should be cautious in interfering with the decisions of the executive on vague grounds such as unreasonableness. The former Lord Chancellor, Lord Irvine (1996), suggested that three broad reasons lay behind this: first, respect for Parliament, which conferred decision-making power on the body in question; secondly, limited judicial expertise in matters of policy concerning the general public interest; thirdly, what he called the 'democratic imperative', namely that government is judged by the electorate every few years. Lord Irvine's third rationale seems misplaced, since the electorate cannot vote in respect of individual decisions.

The courts have struggled to give the notion of unreasonableness a limited meaning. The starting point and baseline is usually called '*Wednesbury* unreasonableness' after Lord Greene's speech in *Associated Provincial Picture Houses Ltd v Wednesbury Corp* [1948] 1 KB 223. Lord Greene said, obscurely, that the court will interfere only where a decision is 'so unreasonable that no reasonable authority could ever have come to'. In that case, the court upheld a condition that no child should attend a cinema in the town on a Sunday. (Of course, perceptions of what is unreasonable may change over time!)

Other attempts have been made to capture this elusive idea. For example, the decision must be 'beyond the range of responses open to a reasonable decision-maker' (*R v Ministry of Defence, ex p Smith* [1996] QB 517; *R v Chief Constable of Sussex, ex p International Trader's Ferry Ltd* [1999] 1 All ER 129 at 157). In *CCSU v Minister for the Civil Service* [1985] AC 374, Lord Diplock said that the courts will interfere only where a decision has no rational basis or 'is so outrageous in its denial of accepted moral standards that no sensible person who has applied his mind to the question to be decided could have arrived at it' (at 410). The *Wednesbury* test is often applied strictly and used to justify not interfering with a decision. For example, in *Brind v Secretary of State for the Home Dept* [1991] 1 AC 696, the government banned live media interviews with supporters of the Irish Republican Army (IRA). The House of Lords held that, although the ban was probably misguided, it had some rational basis as a means of denying publicity to terrorists and was therefore valid (see also *R v Radio Authority, ex p Bull* [1997] 2 All ER 561 at 577).

On the other hand, although successful challenges for unreasonableness are rare, significant errors of reasoning can make a decision *Wednesbury* unreasonable (e.g. *R (AB) v Secretary of State for Justice* [2010] 2 All ER 151: refusal to transfer a transgender prisoner to a woman's prison: misunderstanding of expert advice (at [82]–[85]); contrast *R (KM) v Cambridgeshire CC* [2012] 3 All ER 1218: errors made, but not material). In *R (Litvinenko) v Secretary of State for the Home Department* [2014] EWHC 194 (Admin)), the Home Secretary refused to hold an inquiry into the death of a man who had died in suspicious circumstances where it was suspected that poisoning by a Russian agent was involved. The High Court held that the reason for the refusal, namely that a more limited inquest which did not go into the broader issues would allay public concerns, was 'plainly unsustainable'.

Some cases seem to fall short of irrationality in the extreme sense suggested above but, concern violation of fundamental constitutional principles. For example, in *Hall & Co Ltd v Shoreham-by-Sea UDC* [1964] 1 All ER 1, a local authority planning condition required the plaintiff to dedicate a road to the public. This was held to be 'unreasonable' because it amounted to the confiscation of property without compensation. However, the condition was hardly perverse or irrational, given that the plaintiff stood to make considerable profit out of the permission. Indeed, such arrangements are nowadays commonplace.

In *R v Secretary of State for the Home Dept, ex p Daly* [2001] 2 AC 532, Lord Cooke described *Wednesbury* as 'an unfortunately retrogressive decision in English administrative law, in so far as it suggested that only a very extreme degree [of unreasonableness] can bring an administrative decision within the scope of judicial invalidation' (at [32]). He emphasised that the level of interference should vary with the subject matter: 'It may well be, however, that the law can never be satisfied in any administrative field merely by a finding that the decision under review is not capricious or absurd'.

A more flexible formula is to ask whether a reasonable decision-maker, *in light of the material properly before him*, could reasonably justify his decision, or whether a decision shows 'conduct which no sensible authority acting with *due appreciation of its responsibilities* would have decided to adopt' (*Secretary of State for Education and Science v Tameside MBC* [1977] AC 1014 at 1064 (emphasis added); see Lord Cooke in *International Trader's Ferry* [1999] at 157). This formula enables the court to apply different levels of scrutiny in different contexts and to evaluate the quality of the decision-maker's reasoning: a variable standard of review. However, it comes perilously close to enabling the court to interfere merely because it disagrees with the decision.

In particular, where important interests of the individual are at stake, the level of review is sometimes called 'heightened *Wednesbury*'. It requires the decision-maker to show that it has placed particularly close attention – 'anxious scrutiny' – to the interests in question (see *Bugdaycay v Secretary of State for the Home Dept* [1987] AC 514 at 531; *R v Ministry of Defence, ex p Smith* [1996]; *R v Lord Saville of Newdigate* [1999] 4 All ER 860). Heightened *Wednesbury* may, however, give way to other concerns. In *R v Ministry of Defence, ex p Smith* (above), the Court of Appeal refused to interfere with a decision to ban practising homosexuals from serving in the army. The court recognised that the decision affected fundamental rights and therefore called for 'anxious scrutiny', but also thought that the court was not in a position to assess the specialist needs of military service and should therefore defer to the views of the military establishment. The decision of the UK courts was later held to violate the European Convention on Human Rights (ECHR) on the ground that the UK court did not apply the 'proportionality' test (Section 22.9.2) and so did not give sufficient weight to human rights (*Smith and Grady v UK* (2000) 29 EHRR 493).

At the other end of the scale, where a decision depends on broad social, economic or political factors, or matters remote from ordinary judicial experience, courts have been cautious in interfering. In cases of this kind, at least where human rights interests are not an issue, the courts may apply a standard even lower than Lord Diplock's rationality test, interfering only where a decision is entirely capricious – an approach sometimes called 'super-*Wednesbury*'. This also applies where separation of powers issues are at stake, in particular where the decision in question is one that has been approved after a debate in Parliament.

Thus in *Hammersmith and Fulham LBC v Secretary of State for the Environment* [1991] 1 AC 521 (central grants to local government), Lord Bridge said (at 597):

> Since the statute has conferred a power on the Secretary of State which involves the formulation and implementation of national economic policy and which can only take effect with the approval of the House of Commons, it is not open to challenge on the ground of irrationality short of the extremes of bad faith, improper motive or manifest absurdity. Both the constitutional propriety and the good sense of this restriction seem to me to be clear enough. The formulation and implementation of national economic policy are matters depending essentially on political judgement. The decisions which shape them are for politicians to take and it is in the political forum of the House of Commons that they are properly to be debated and approved or disapproved on their merits. If the decisions have been taken in good faith within the four corners of the Act, the merits of the policy underlying the decisions are not susceptible to judicial review by the courts and the courts would be exceeding their proper function if they presumed to condemn the policy as unreasonable.

(See also *Nottinghamshire CC v Secretary of State for the Environment* [1986] AC 240).

It must be emphasised that Lord Bridge's remarks apply only to unreasonableness. Where a decision is *ultra vires* on some other ground, then approval by Parliament (other than in the form of a statute which cannot be challenged in judicial review due to parliamentary supremacy) does not validate it or prevent the court scrutinising it in the ordinary way. Thus, the separation of powers works in both directions. It must also be emphasised that the fact that a matter may be controversial is not in itself a reason for deference.

Sometimes the statute itself may require that a decision-maker act 'reasonably' or 'have reasonable cause' to believe or do something. In this kind of case, the court may decide for itself what is reasonable in the ordinary, non-*Wednesbury* sense (see e.g. *Nakkuda Ali v Jayaratne* [1951] AC 66; *R (Evans) v Attorney General* [2014] EWCA Civ 254 (Section 24.2.1)). On the other hand, if the decision-maker is a democratic body, the court may apply the *Wednesbury* approach even here (see e.g. *Secretary of State for Education and Science v Tameside MBC* [1977]: Secretary of State could interfere with local authority democratic decisions only on reasonable grounds: *Wednesbury* applied).

Unreasonableness/irrationality may often overlap with other grounds of review. In *Wheeler v Leicester City Council* [1985] 2 All ER 1106, a local authority refused to allow a rugby club to use its playing field. This was because the club had not prevented certain of its members from touring in South Africa during the apartheid era. The House of Lords held that the council had acted unlawfully. This could be regarded as an unreasonable infringement of individual freedom, as a decision based upon an improper political purpose, a failure to take relevant considerations into account (the council's duty to promote positive race relations), or as an unfair decision (in that the matter had been prejudged). Today *Wheeler* would probably be explained on human rights grounds, a perspective that was raised in the Court of Appeal, but that the House of Lords avoided.

18.1.1   Proportionality

In cases subject to the HRA and in EU law, a more stringent standard of review than *Wednesbury* unreasonableness applies, in the form of the doctrine of 'proportionality'. Proportionality has been imported from European law and will be discussed more fully later in the context of human rights (Section 22.9.2). Broadly speaking, a decision is proportionate only if it meets an important public goal (a 'pressing social need'), and in doing so violates the right in question as little as possible. As Lord Diplock ponderously put it in *R v Goldstein* [1983] 1 WLR 151, proportionality 'prohibits the use of a steam hammer to crack a nut if a nutcracker would do' (at 155).

There is an argument that proportionality should not be confined to human rights and EU cases but should be regarded as part of ordinary domestic law since the proportionality principle fits the 'variable standard of review' applicable under *Wednesbury*. For example, in *R v Barnsley Metropolitan BC, ex p Hook* [1976] 3 All ER 452, a market trader was dismissed by the market manager for the relatively minor wrong of urinating in the street. This was held to be an unreasonably severe penalty. In *R v Secretary of State ex parte Daly* [2001], it was government policy that a prisoner's confidential correspondence with his lawyer could be examined in the prisoner's absence. Lord Bingham based his reasoning firstly on the common law, 'heightened *Wednesbury*' approach appropriate where important rights are in issue. A reasonable minister could not have concluded that the policy was necessary for the legitimate goal of keeping order in prisons. The policy was also contrary to Article 8 of the ECHR (respect for correspondence). Lord Bingham said that under the HRA 'domestic courts must go beyond the ordinary standard and themselves form a judgment whether a Convention right has been breached, conducting such an inquiry as is necessary to form that judgment' (at 546). In that case, keeping of order could have been achieved by less intrusive, albeit more inconvenient, means. Lord Steyn applied the proportionality test, emphasising that it went beyond *Wednesbury* by requiring the court itself to decide whether the right 'balance' had been struck between the conflicting interests.

Before the HRA, English judges had objected to proportionality on the ground that it takes the court too far into the political merits (*Hone v Maze Prison Board of Visitors* [1988] 1 All ER 321, at 327–29; *Brind v Secretary of State for the Home Dept* [1991]). Therefore, English law sometimes fell foul of the ECHR because it failed to reach the standard of necessity required by the proportionality doctrine. As noted above (Section 18.1), *Smith* was condemned by the European Court of Human Rights in *Smith and Grady v UK* [2000]. It was held that even heightened *Wednesbury* failed to satisfy the ECHR because it excluded any consideration of whether the interference with the applicant's rights answered a pressing social need, or was proportionate to the military aims pursued.

There are high-level dicta that proportionality should be part of domestic law. In *CCSU* [1985], Lord Diplock suggested (at 410) that proportionality might, at a future date, become a distinct ground of domestic judicial review. In *R (Association of British Civilian Internees; Far East Region) v Secretary of State for Defence* [2003] QB 1397, Dyson LJ endorsed this (at [34]–[37]). In *R (Alconbury Developments Ltd) v Secretary of State for the Environment, Transport and the Regions* [2001] 2 All ER 929, Lord Slynn emphasised that 'the difference in practice is not as great as is sometimes supposed' (at 976). He thought that proportionality and *Wednesbury* should not be kept in separate compartments and that 'even without reference to the 1998 Act the time has come to recognise that this principle is part of English administrative law, not only when judges are dealing with Community acts but also when they are dealing with acts subject to domestic law'. Similarly, in *Kennedy v Charity Commission* [2014] UKSC 20, Lord Mance, speaking for a majority of the Supreme Court, said, *obiter*, that proportionality should apply outside ECHR cases, although Lord Carnwath thought that the matter was still too uncertain for the court to take this approach.

However, the two approaches have not yet merged. A decision can be disproportionate but pass the *Wednesbury* test. For example, in *Aguilar Quila v Secretary of State for the Home Dept* [2010] EWCA Civ 1482, a human rights case, immigration restriction on young adults to combat forced marriages was not *Wednesbury* unreasonable, but was too wide to be proportionate since less intrusive measures could have achieved the policy. Conversely, a decision might be irrational due to an error of logic or lack of evidence but not disproportionate.

In *R (Association of British Civilian Internees; Far East Region) v Secretary of State* [2003], a policy to pay compensation to people interned by the Japanese in the Second World War was limited to those with close connections with the UK. It was held that this was not *Wednesbury* unreasonable, and that proportionality could not be applied since this was not a human rights case. It was suggested that *Wednesbury* be replaced by proportionality, 'but it was not for this court to perform its burial rites' (at [36] (Dyson LJ)). And in *Keyu v Secretary of State for Foreign and Commonwealth Affairs* [2015] UKSC 69, the Supreme Court rejected an opportunity – as Lady Hale put matters (at [303]) – to 'consign the *Wednesbury* principle to the dustbin of history'. Lord Neuberger (at [132]) felt that 'it would not be appropriate for a five-Justice panel of this court to accept, or indeed to reject, this argument [ie that proportionality should replace rationality], which potentially has implications which are profound in constitutional terms and very wide in applicable scope', while Lord Kerr (at [271]) considered that 'this question will have to be frankly addressed by this court sooner rather than later'. The latter prediction may not in fact come to pass, as the grounds for review fall within the scope of the work of the Independent Review of Administrative Law (see Sections 1.9 and 17.1).

18.2 Procedural impropriety: statutory procedural requirements

This topic is an aspect of the *ultra vires* doctrine discussed in the previous chapter, focusing as it does on requirements imposed by statute. It illustrates the elastic nature of contemporary judicial review. Failure to comply with a procedural requirement laid down by statute (such as time limits, engagement in consultation, or giving required information or notice) should, in principle, make a decision *ultra vires* and so void, thus supporting the rule of law. However, the courts are reluctant to set aside a decision on purely technical grounds and have found reasons not to do so.

Traditionally, they have tried to rationalise this by distinguishing between 'mandatory' (important) and 'directory' (unimportant) procedural requirements by reference to the language of the governing statute in the abstract (see e.g. *Agricultural, Horticultural and Forestry Industry Training Board v Kent* [1970] 1 All ER 304).

However, more recent cases have rejected this approach in favour of a more flexible one that looks at the particular context. The starting point is, of course, still the language of the governing Act itself. But if this does not give a clear answer, the court takes a pragmatic approach, based on balancing the injustice to the citizen against the harm to the public interest. For example, in *R (Reilly) v Secretary of State for Work and Pensions* [2014] AC 453, the Supreme Court held that a failure to inform a claimant for jobseekers allowance about the details of a statutory jobseekers scheme was invalid only if it 'materially affected' the claimant (at [65], [69], [74]–[76]). Speaking for a unanimous court, Lord Neuberger said that, although it is a fundamental duty of the courts to ensure that the executive carries out its functions, it is also incumbent on the courts to be realistic in the standards they set for such compliance (at [49]).

Other examples include *Wang v IRC* [1995] 1 All ER 637: duty of Revenue to decide within a 'reasonable time'; late decision not invalid because Revenue has a duty to collect taxes; *Coney v Choice* [1975] 1 All ER 979: notice advertising school closure misplaced, but proposals well known and invalidity would cause disruption; *Agricultural Training Board v Aylesbury Mushrooms Ltd* [1972] 1 WLR 190: before a regulation took effect, industry representatives must be consulted; failure to consult mushroom growers made the regulation invalid only against mushroom growers as such.

If there has been 'substantial compliance', the court may overlook a defect (e.g. *R (Herron) v Parking Adjudicator* [2012] 1 All ER 709: parking signs not correctly displayed, but drivers adequately informed of restrictions).

Indeed, the court might allow a defect to be waived in the interests of justice (*R v Immigration Appeal Tribunal, ex p Jeyeanthan* [1999] 3 All ER 231: official letter sent out seriously incomplete could be corrected by generous interpretation of the governing rules).

The cases on procedural requirements show different approaches. For example, *Seal v Chief Constable of South Wales Police* [2007] 4 All ER 177 concerned a claim for false imprisonment under the Mental Health Act 1983 made without leave of the High Court, as required by the statute. A majority held that this made the claim a nullity. They took a relatively narrow approach which concentrated on the language and history of the Act. Lord Bingham started from the language of the Act, concluding that the Act struck a fair balance between a claimant's rights and its purpose of protecting those who care for the mentally ill. Lord Woolf and Baroness Hale, dissenting, took a broader approach. Baroness Hale's starting point was the 'principle of legality' that fundamental rights, in this case access to the courts, can be restricted only by express language or necessary implication. Lord Woolf agreed with this but also invoked Lord Hailsham's speech in the case of *London and Clydesdale Estates v Aberdeen District Council* (Section 17.7), emphasising that the court should decide what is fair and just in the particular circumstances.

Some procedural requirements are considered to be especially important. For example, the courts will not allow administrative convenience to override a statutory right of the public to be consulted on government proposals (see *Berkeley v Secretary of State for the Environment* [2000] 3 All ER 897 (Section 2.8.3); *R (Boyejo) v Barnet LBC* [2009] EWHC 3261 (Admin): consultation must be genuinely interactive; providing an opportunity for questions not sufficient). *R (Moseley) v Haringey LBC* [2014] UKSC 56 concerned a consultation about a proposal to increase council tax. The Supreme Court held that consultation must be at a time when proposals are still formative, must include sufficient reasons, must give adequate time for response and the outcome must conscientiously be taken into account. Options apart from the council's preference must be presented where appropriate, including realistic alternatives.

Another important requirement is the rule against delegation. An official who is entrusted with power to make a decision affecting the rights of individuals should not transfer that power to someone else (*delegatus non potest delegare*; *Barnard v National Dock Labour Board* [1953] 2 QB 18). However, applying this principle strictly would cause administrative breakdown and exceptions have been made. These are as follows:

▶ Under the *Carltona* doctrine, a minister can act through a civil servant in her or his department (Section 15.8.5). This can be rationalised as not being a true exception, in that constitutionally the minister and civil servant are one, the minister being responsible to Parliament for the act of the civil servant (see *R (Alconbury Developments Ltd) v Secretary of State for the Environment, Transport and the Regions* [2001]). On the other hand, why should political responsibility affect the legal position, particularly as we have seen that ministerial responsibility is weak and uncertain? Nevertheless (unless possibly the method of delegation is *Wednesbury* unreasonable), it seems that the courts cannot interfere. In *R v Secretary of State for the Home Dept, ex p Oladehinde* [1991] 1 AC 254, the House of Lords held that a deportation decision could be made by an immigration officer on behalf of the Secretary of State. However, Lord Templeman remarked (at 300) that the person exercising the power must be 'of suitable seniority in the Home Office for whom the minister accepts responsibility'. In *R v Minister of Agriculture, ex parte Hamble (Offshore) Fisheries* [1995] 2 All ER 714 at 732, Sedley J suggested that the *Carltona* principle does not apply to the making of policy. However, in *Re Golden Chemical Products Ltd* [1976] Ch 300, the court rejected any distinction between powers that a minister must exercise personally and those that can be delegated.

▶ *Carltona* does not apply to government agencies outside the central civil service, such as the police, local government, or statutory bodies (but see *R (Chief Constable of the West Midlands Police) v Birmingham City Justices* [2002] EWHC 1087 (Admin): basing the rule on a wider rationale of implied statutory authority and distinguishing between normal decision-making within the organisational hierarchy and cases where the statute requires a named official to act personally).

▶ Many local authority functions can be delegated by statute to committees, subcommittees, officers and other authorities, but not to individual councillors or outside bodies unless authorised by statute (see Local Government Act 1972, s 101; *R v Port Talbot BC, ex p Jones* [1988] 2 All ER 207). A committee cannot comprise one person.

▶ Many governmental functions can be transferred to private bodies (Deregulation and Contracting Out Act 1994, ss 61, 69).

▶ Functions involving little independent discretion can be delegated. Indeed, the courts seem ready to imply statutory authority to delegate in cases where it would be inconvenient for the decision-maker to do everything her or himself (*Provident Mutual Life Assurance Association v Derby City Council* [1981] 1 WLR 173). Fact-finding, making recommendations and giving advice can be delegated, but the decision-maker must not merely 'rubberstamp' the advice she or he is given. The decision-maker must have enough information before him or her, for example a summary of evidence, to make a genuine decision (*Jeffs v New Zealand Dairy Production and Marketing Board* [1967] 1 AC 551).

18.3 Procedural impropriety: the right to a fair hearing

This ground of review is of ancient common law origin and is central to the idea of the rule of law. It is called in aid by those who claim that judicial review is based on freestanding common law (Section 17.1). Until the early twentieth century, the courts applied a broad principle with biblical origins and usually labelled 'natural justice', namely that anyone whose rights were affected by an official decision was entitled to advance notice and a fair hearing before an unbiased judge (e.g. *Dr Bonham's Case* (1610) 8 Co Rep 114a; *Bagg's Case* (1615) 11 Co Rep 936; *Cooper v Wandsworth Board of Works* (1863) 14 CB (NS) 180).

The advance of the democratically supported administrative state produced a more cautious judicial approach. *Local Government Board v Arlidge* [1915] AC 120 marks a turning point, where Dicey felt that the rule of law itself was at risk. In *Arlidge,* the House of Lords held that in the case of administrative decisions (in that case, a house closure order), provided that the government can decide for itself what procedures to follow, the citizen's protection lies not in the courts but in ministerial responsibility to Parliament (see also *Board of Education v Rice* [1911] AC 179).

The courts then refused to apply natural justice to decisions other than those which they deemed 'judicial'. For this purpose, 'judicial' means the impartial application of rules to settle a dispute about the parties' existing rights, narrowly defined – essentially, what a court does. Thus, the courts removed natural justice from political, discretionary and policy-oriented decisions, which the court labelled 'administrative'. This excluded much of the welfare state from natural justice since the conferring of benefits such as education and housing does not strictly affect *existing* rights. It also excluded government powers such as planning, compulsory purchase and other forms of licensing which, although they affect rights, are usually discretionary. The main area left for natural justice was where a formal tribunal or inquiry determined a specific dispute, but even this caused problems in the case of public inquiries held as part of a larger discretionary process leading to a political decision, for example to build a new road. These were labelled 'quasi-judicial' with a right to be heard only at the judicial stage of the inquiry itself, thereby raising suspicions that the real decision was taken behind closed doors in characteristically English fashion (see e.g. *Franklin v Minister of Town and Country Planning* [1948] AC 87).

However, in *Ridge v Baldwin* [1964] AC 40, a landmark case that marks the beginning of the contemporary renaissance of judicial review, the House of Lords returned the law to its older rationale. The Chief Constable of Brighton had been dismissed by the local police authority without a hearing. The authority had statutory power to deprive him of his position for incapacity or misconduct, but not otherwise. The House of Lords held that he was entitled to a hearing for two reasons: (i) he had been deprived of an important right; (ii) the power to dismiss was limited by statute, so the authority did not have complete discretion. Lord Reid emphasised that, irrespective of whether it is 'judicial' in the above sense, a government decision that causes serious harm to an individual ought in principle to attract the right to be heard. Moreover, it was emphasised that the right to be heard applies irrespective of how clear-cut the outcome appears to be. Indeed, the protection of a hearing may be most necessary in what appears to be an open-and-shut case.

Since *Ridge v Baldwin,* the right to a hearing is no longer limited to judicial functions. The courts have extended the right to a hearing into most areas of government, including, for example, immigration and prison management (*R v Hull Prison Visitors, ex p St Germain* [1979] QB 425; *Leech v Parkhurst Prison Deputy Governor* [1988] 1 All ER 485). Although the expression 'natural justice' is still occasionally used, it has become interchangeable with 'fairness' (*Re HK* [1967] 2 QB 617). However, the concept of 'judicial' is still relevant, since a judicial decision will certainly attract a right to a hearing and this may be of a higher procedural standard than in the case of an administrative decision.

The courts have introduced limits to the right to be heard. They include the following:

▶ 'Fairness' concerns the protection of persons who are adversely affected by government action, rather than democratic participation in government. Thus, in the absence of a statutory requirement (which would attract a duty to be fair (Section 18.2)), there is no right to be consulted in respect of general policy decisions or lawmaking, unless the rule is targeted at a specific group of individuals or perhaps if the claimant can establish a legitimate expectation (Section 18.3.1) (see *Bank Mellat v HM Treasury (No. 2)* [2013] UKSC 39 (Section 25.5.6)).

▶ There is no general duty to publish government policy. However, a person against whom a decision is made must be informed of any relevant government policy which is necessary to enable the claimant to state his or her case (see *R (Lumba) v Secretary of State for the Home Department* [2012] 1 AC 245; *R (Reilly) v Secretary of State for Work and Pensions* [2014] at [65]). Advisory or preliminary governmental decisions do not attract a right to be heard unless the decision has direct adverse consequences for the individual's rights (*Norwest Holst v Trade Secretary* [1978] Ch 201: decision to start an investigation, no right to be heard; cf. *Furnell v Whangerei High Schools Board* [1973] AC 660: suspension of teacher pending investigation, hearing required).

▶ A judicial decision to remove existing legal rights usually attracts a hearing, but the refusal of a discretionary benefit in the public interest and where the claimant has no specific entitlement may not do so (see *McInnes v Onslow-Fane* [1978] 3 All ER 211: refusing a boxing referee's licence; *Findlay v Secretary of State for the Home Dept* [1985] AC 318: parole, change in policy). However, a decision to refuse a benefit that can only be made on limited grounds, that involves accusations of misconduct or bad character, or that affects a legitimate expectation (Section 18.3.1) will attract a hearing (see *R v Gaming Board, ex p Benaim and Khaida* [1970] 2 QB 417; *R v Secretary of State for the Home Dept, ex p Fayed* [1997] 1 All ER 228).

▶ Other factors might override or limit the right to a hearing, in particular national security considerations (*CCSU v Minister for the Civil Service* [1985]). The need to act quickly in an emergency will also exclude at least a prior hearing (*R v Secretary of State for Transport, ex p Pegasus Holidays Ltd* [1989] 2 All ER 481: air safety; *Calvin v Carr* [1980] AC 574 (below)). A hearing might be excluded where large numbers compete for scarce resources, for example applications for university places, or in respect of general decisions such as school closures. On the other hand, where a policy decision, for example to close an old people's home, directly affects the existing rights of the persons concerned there may be a collective right to be consulted, although not necessarily a hearing in individual cases (*R v Devon CC, ex p Baker* [1995] 1 All ER 73).

▶ Although the courts have warned against this (e.g. *Ridge v Baldwin* [1964]; *John v Rees* [1969] 2 All ER 274), a hearing may be excluded when the court thinks that the outcome of the decision was not affected, so that a hearing would be futile (*Cheall v APEX* [1983] 1 All ER 1130). In *Cinnamond v British Airports Authority* [1980] 2 All ER 368, the Court of Appeal upheld a decision to withdraw licences without a hearing from a group of Heathrow Airport taxi drivers who had been repeatedly warned about allegations of misconduct but had not responded.

▶ The same flexible concept of 'fairness' also determines the ingredients of a hearing. There are no fixed requirements. Subject to any statutory requirements, a decision-maker can decide its own procedure provided that they are 'fair' in the circumstances of the particular case (see *Lloyd v McMahon* [1987] 1 All ER 1118). Fairness means knowledge of the case against the person and a chance to answer any allegations (*Board of Education v Rice* [1911]). Thus, where a decision involves the application of a government policy, the policy must be published and transparent so that informed and meaningful representations can be made (*R (Lumba) v Secretary of State for the Home Dept* [2012]: unpublished policy of detaining offenders released from prison with a view to deportation). Moreover, if the government publishes a policy it must stick to it until it announces a change (*R (Kambadzi) v Secretary of State for the Home Department* [2011] 4 All ER 975: regular reviews of detention).

▶ The more serious the consequences for the individual, the higher the standard of hearing that is required. At one end of the scale, in the case of an investigation which does not directly affect a person's rights but which may affect his or her reputation or lead to further proceedings, a person who is criticised must, before publication, be given an outline of any accusations and a chance to answer them (*Maxwell v Dept of Trade and Industry and ors* [1974] 2 All ER 122). Known as 'Maxwellisation', this has sometimes been claimed as a reason for delay in the publication of government reports, for example the Chilcot Report into the Iraq War (see Section 4.9).

▶ At the other end of the scale, a person whose rights are in issue is normally entitled to see all the evidence and cross-examine witnesses (*R v Army Board, ex p Anderson* [1992] QB 169). Administrative convenience cannot justify refusing to permit a person to call witnesses, although the tribunal does have a residual discretion in the matter (*R v Hull Prison Visitors, ex p St Germain (No 2)* [1979] 1 WLR 1401).

▶ Fairness is a minimum standard to be balanced against the government's right to decide its own procedure. An oral hearing is not necessarily required, although an absolute rule excluding an oral hearing is not permitted (*Lloyd v McMahon* [1987]). The importance of the matter and the nature of the particular issues should be taken into account to decide whether the matter can be fairly determined without an oral hearing (see *R (Smith) v Parole Board* [2005] 1 All ER 755; *R (Dudson) v Secretary of State for the Home Dept* [2006] 1 All ER 421). Formal rules of evidence are not required.

▶ Fairness demands only that the evidence be relevant and that the parties have a chance to comment on it (*Mahon v Air New Zealand* [1984] 3 All ER 201). There is no automatic right to legal representation, but the decision-maker must not adopt an absolute rule on the matter and must allow representation where a person cannot effectively present his or her own case (*Hone v Maze Prison Board of Visitors* [1988]). However, under ECHR Article 6, a person subject to a severe penalty is entitled to legal representation (Section 21.4.1.3).

▶ Problems arise where an individual is confronted with those who claim inside knowledge but are reluctant to have this challenged. An expert decision-maker can rely on his own accumulated experience without having to disclose this to the parties. Expert assessors are sometimes used to help judges and other decision-makers; they need not disclose their advice in advance. However, where the judge disagrees with an assessor on an important matter, he should give the parties a chance to comment (*Ahmed v Governing Body of Oxford University* [2003] 1 All ER 915). If an inquiry is held, the decision-maker cannot subsequently take new evidence or advice received from an outside source into account without giving the parties an opportunity to comment (*Elmbridge BC v Secretary of State for the Environment, Transport and the Regions* [2002] Env LR 1; *AMEC Ltd v Whitefriars City Estates* [2005] 1 All ER 723). However, advice given to a minister by a civil servant in his or her department does not count as outside advice and, by virtue of the doctrine of ministerial responsibility, need not be disclosed (*Bushell v Secretary of State for the Environment* [1981] AC 75).

18.3.1 Legitimate expectations

Among the most important democratic principles are that government (i) ought to be able to change its mind on policy issues; and (ii) should be prevented from acting outside its powers. On the other hand, it may be unjust to the individual if a decision-maker misled a citizen by disregarding a previous promise or announced policy, particularly where the individual has rearranged his or her affairs in reliance on the undertaking. Suppose, for example, that a student gives up a job or pays fees for a course on the strength of a government announcement that a student of her category will be given a grant. The government later withdraws the announcement because of financial constraints. Thus, the law creates a dilemma in which fairness to the individual and legal certainty are in conflict with the public interest.

The concept of 'legitimate expectation' confronts this dilemma. There is much uncertainty about its rationale and limits. Originally expressed by Lord Denning in *Schmidt v Secretary of State for Home Affairs* [1969] 2 Ch 149, a legitimate expectation arises where the citizen has been led to believe by a statement or other conduct of the government that s/he is singled out for some benefit or advantage of which it would be unfair to deprive him. This does not create a binding right, but does require special weight to be given to the expectation. As Lord Hoffmann pointed out in *R (Reprotech (Pebsham) Ltd) v East Sussex CC* [2003] 1 WLR 348 at [33]–[35]: the more flexible concept of a 'legitimate expectation' attempts to compromise between these competing considerations by giving special weight to cases where a citizen has relied upon an official statement.

The expectation might be generated by a promise or assurance either announced generally, or given specifically to an individual (e.g. *R v Secretary of State for the Home Dept, ex p Khan* [1985] 1 All ER 40: Home Office circular stated that adoptions of children from abroad would be allowed in certain circumstances; *Preston v IRC* [1985] 2 All ER 327: letter concerning tax affairs). A legitimate expectation might also be generated by a consistent practice whereby people in the same position as the applicant have been given a benefit in the past (*CCSU v Minister for the Civil Service* [1985]: consultation with trade unions prior to changes in terms and conditions of employment).

A legitimate expectation must single out the claimant, or a group including the claimant. The statement must be an official one made by a person with power to make the decision. Unofficial statements such as an election address or media interviews cannot create a legitimate expectation (*R v Secretary of State for Education, ex p Begbie* [2000] 1 WLR 1115). There may be a legitimate expectation that the government will honour an international treaty obligation which it has ratified (*R (Abassi) v Secretary of State* [2002] EWCA Civ 1598; but cf. *R v DPP, ex p Kebilene* [2000] 2 AC 326).

Although Article 9 of the Bill of Rights prevents the courts from holding a minister liable for anything said in Parliament, a statement in Parliament might be used as evidence in judicial review proceedings and might create a legitimate expectation (see *Wilson v First County Trust* [2003] 4 All ER 97 at [140]). Article 9 does not seem to be violated since the minister is not being *penalised* for anything said in Parliament (Section 11.6.2).

Where an assurance is given to an individual, the individual must have disclosed all relevant information (*R v IRC, ex p MFK Underwriting Agents Ltd* [1990] 1 WLR 1545). The statement that gives rise to the expectation must be clear and unambiguous, and it must be reasonable for the claimant to rely upon it (see *Preston v IRC* [1985]: letter not sufficiently clear; see also *R (Bancoult) v Secretary of State for the Foreign and Commonwealth Office* [2008] 4 All ER 1055). *Abassi* (above) shows the need to define exactly what the legitimate expectation is. Lord Phillips explained that a legitimate expectation can be of 'a regular practice that the claimant can reasonably expect to continue': at [82], [92]. However, the expectation in that case was only that the Foreign Office would *consider* making diplomatic representations about the treatment of prisoners in Guantanamo Bay, not that it would actually do so.

A legitimate expectation cannot arise if the decision in question would be *ultra vires* or contrary to statute. In other words, the legitimate expectation doctrine is about a *legally valid* government statement or practice that the government subsequently withdraws. For example, in *R (Bloggs 61) v Secretary of State for the Home Dept* [2003] 1 WLR 2724 a prisoner was given an assurance by the police that he would be put into a witness protection scheme. However, since the scheme was the responsibility of the Home Office, the police had no power to give such an assurance which could not therefore give rise to a legitimate expectation.

In *Rowland v Environment Agency* [2004] 3 WLR 249, an assurance was given to a purchaser of land that a stretch of river was private, but public rights existed over it under statute. It was held that there was no legitimate expectation, since statute cannot be overcome. However, this might violate the wider principles of the ECHR, since it is clearly unfair that that public body should be able to rely on its own illegality so as to override the interests of the individual (see *Stretch v UK* (2004) 38 EHRR 12). In *Rowland* the Court of Appeal reached its conclusion reluctantly, being constrained by the *ultra vires* doctrine. It required the authority to do what it could within the law to mitigate the injustice to the claimant.

18.3.1.1 Reliance

It is sometimes suggested that the individual must rely on the statement that creates the legitimate expectation by incurring expense or other detriment in a way very similar to the doctrine of estoppel (Section 17.6.3). Thus, in *R v MoD ex p Walker* [2000] 1 WLR 806, a compensation scheme for soldiers injured by crimes of violence when serving overseas was subsequently changed. The House of Lords held that there was no legitimate expectation other than that the ministry would apply whatever its policy was, because there had been no reliance on the original scheme (at [813]–[816]). Moreover, even where the individual is relying on a government policy, the statutory context might exclude a legitimate expectation if it is directed to concerns other than the interests of the claimant (e.g. *Findlay v Secretary of State for the Home Dept* [1985]: change in parole policy intended to protect the public interest).

It must certainly be *reasonable* to rely on the statement. For example, in *Odelola v Secretary of State* [2009] 1 WLR 1230, the claimants were Nigerian doctors who had applied to work in the UK. While their applications were in progress the government changed immigration policy. The change meant that only doctors with UK qualifications would now be admitted. The House of Lords rejected the claimants' argument that the application should be assessed under the rules as they were when the application was made. There was no legitimate expectation that the policy would not change because the claimants should have realised that immigration policy frequently does so. It would, however, be irrational and 'conspicuously unfair' not to return the claimants' application fees.

However, the need for actual reliance has been denied (see *R v Minister of Agriculture, Fisheries and Food, ex p Hamble (Offshore) Fisheries* [1995]). Indeed, in the Australian case of *Minister of State for Immigration, ex p Teoh* (1995) 183 CLR 273, it was suggested that the individual need not even know of the statement. This was the case in *R (Rashid) v Secretary of State* [2005] EWCA Civ 744, where the Court of Appeal condemned as 'conspicuous unfairness' (at [52]) a refusal to give asylum to a group of Kurds fleeing Iraq. Neither the officials concerned nor the asylum-seekers knew about a government policy that relocation to an apparently safe part of Iraq should not defeat an asylum claim. In *R (Bancoult) v Secretary of State* [2008], Lord Bingham suggested (at [73]) that *detriment* was required but not reliance. This would explain *Walker* (above). However, more recently, in *In the matter of an application by Geraldine Finucane for Judicial Review (Northern Ireland)* [2019] UKSC 7, Lord Kerr rejected the notion that even detriment need be shown (at [72]).

This raises the question of what the purpose of the legitimate expectation doctrine is. In support of reliance not being needed, it might be suggested that it is to ensure good administration and consistency (the latter connecting to the rule of law; see Chapter 6). It is wrong for government to disregard serious assurances that it has given: as Lord Kerr stated in the *Finucane* case (at [72]), 'it cannot conduce to good standards of administration to permit public authorities to resile at whim from undertakings which they give simply because the person or group to whom such promises were made are unable to demonstrate a tangible disadvantage' (see also *Mandalia v Secretary of State for the Home Department* [2015] UKSC 59, at [29]). On the other hand, as suggested in *Walker,* the purpose of the doctrine could be to redress injustice suffered by the individual as an aspect of a broad principle of 'fairness'. On this basis, the principle of equality indicates that the individual should not get special treatment unless he or she has suffered in some exceptional way.

18.3.1.2 Consequences: procedural or substantive

The legitimate expectation doctrine cannot create legal rights in the strict sense, nor does it prevent a policy from being changed for the future (*O'Reilly v Mackman* [1982] 3 All ER 1124: prisoners' expectation of early release). It concerns only the possible injustice to those who have already been affected by it. In *R v North and East Devon HA, ex p Coughlan* [2000] 2 WLR 622, 644–46, three kinds of outcome were identified:

1. In all cases, a legitimate expectation is a relevant consideration which must be taken into account in making a decision (*R (Theophilus) v Lewisham BC* [2002] 3 All ER 851: student grant to study abroad). In *R (A) v Secretary of State for the Home Dept* [2006] EWHC 526 (Admin), Collins J said (at [29]): 'Legitimate expectation is grounded in fairness. The courts expect government departments and indeed all officials who make decisions affecting members of the public to honour statements of policy. To fail to do so will… mean that the decision-maker has failed to have regard to a material consideration'. On this basis, as long as the expectation is taken into account, the court will interfere only if the decision is completely unreasonable (see *R v North and East Devon HA, ex p Coughlan* [2000] at [57]).

2. At least where the claimant has relied on it, a legitimate expectation may also entitle the claimant to a fair hearing and perhaps require reasons to be given before the benefit is refused or withdrawn (*R v Secretary of State for the Home Dept, ex p Khan* [1985]). Indeed, the expectation itself may be only of a hearing (e.g. *A-G for Hong Kong v Shiu* [1983] 2 AC 629: to consider applications for citizenship on their individual merits; *R v Liverpool City Council, ex p Liverpool Taxi Fleet Operators Association* [1975] 1 All ER 379: undertaking to consult). This is called a 'procedural' expectation.

3. Where the expectation is that of an actual benefit (a 'substantive' expectation), the court may go further and in certain cases require the authority to give the citizen the benefit itself (substantive protection). In *Khan* (above), where the government stated by letter that certain policies concerning overseas adoptions would be followed, Lord Parker CJ suggested that 'vis-à-vis the recipient of such a letter, a new policy can only be implemented after such recipient has been given a full and serious consideration whether there is some overriding public interest which justifies a departure from the procedures stated in the letter' (at 48). However, the circumstances where this will be so are unclear since this would restrict the government's democratic freedom to change its policy and amount to a breach of the separation of powers by the court. In other cases, the only outcome would be a hearing (procedural protection).

Initially, the notion of substantive protection was strongly resisted. In *R v Secretary of State for Health, ex p US Tobacco International Inc* [1992] 1 All ER 212, the government had encouraged the company to manufacture snuff in the UK. After the company had incurred expense on its investment, the government withdrew its permission on medical advice. It was held that a legitimate expectation could not override a statutory discretion so that the government could withdraw its invitation. The company was entitled only to a hearing on the health issue giving it an opportunity to persuade the government to change its mind. However, in *R v Minister of Agriculture, Fisheries and Food, ex p Hamble (Offshore) Fisheries* [1995], Sedley J suggested that a legitimate expectation created a binding obligation that could be overridden only if in the court's view it was necessary to do so to achieve the objectives of the statute. But in *R v Secretary of State, ex p Hargreaves* [1997] 1 All ER 397, 412, this approach was described as 'heresy' as it went beyond the normal limits of judicial review. In that case, a prisoner's only legitimate expectation was that policies should be fairly applied to his case.

However, in *R v North and East Devon HA, ex p Coughlan* [2000], the Court of Appeal held that a severely disabled resident of a local authority nursing home could hold the local authority to a previous assurance that it would be her home for life. The authority proposed to close the home in order to transfer nursing care to the local authority. It was held that the assurance created an enforceable legitimate expectation that only an overriding public interest could displace.

The scope of this is not clear. Lord Woolf formulated a vague test, namely where 'to frustrate the expectation is so unfair that to take a new and different course will amount to an abuse of power'. In particular, the human right to respect for home and family life (ECHR, Art 8) was in issue, thereby raising the threshold of review to one of proportionality (Section 18.1.1). Lord Woolf suggested that the court should weigh the expectation against any overriding interest required by the change of policy. Although the decision to close the home had financial consequences, it did not raise general policy issues. This balancing exercise invites the court to scrutinise the merits of the decision beyond the usual limits of judicial review. Lord Woolf also distinguished between statements made to a few individuals or to a group with a common interest and statements made to large numbers of people or to diverse groups. Substantive protection may be less appropriate in the second kind of case.

The approach taken in *Coughlan* is, in effect, a proportionality test (Section 18.1.1). Thus, in *Nadarajah v Secretary of State for the Home Department* [2005] EWCA Civ 1363, Laws LJ doubted, *obiter*, that there was any difference of principle between a substantive and procedural expectation (while noting that statutory duty might more frequently dictate the frustration of a substantive expectation), stating that 'the question in either case will be whether denial of the expectation is in the circumstances proportionate to a legitimate aim pursued' (at [69]) (see also *R (Bhatt Murphy) v Independent Assessor* [2008] EWCA Civ 755 at [51] and *United Policyholders Group v AG of Trinidad and Tobago* [2016] UKPC 17 at [120]–[121]).

However, this area of law remains complex and uncertain. In *Finucane* [2019], the Supreme Court held that failure to comply with an undertaking to hold a public inquiry into the murder of a Belfast solicitor by Protestant paramilitary forces did not amount to frustration of a legitimate expectation, the Court holding that the decision whether or not to hold an inquiry was a matter for political judgement (at [76]). Here, rather than basing the lawfulness of denial of the expectation on the test of proportionality, and notwithstanding the concern expressed by Lord Carnwath in *R (Gallaher Group) v Competition and Markets Authority* [2018] UKSC 25 (at [41]) as to the creation of a principle of 'substantive unfairness' independently of existing grounds of review, Lord Kerr stated (at [62]) that 'where a clear and unambiguous undertaking has been made, the authority giving the undertaking will not be allowed to depart from it unless it is shown that it is fair to do so'. It would seem that the search for clarity on the applicable legal test in this context remains ongoing.

18.4   Procedural impropriety: bias

An impartial and independent judge is a fundamental component of the rule of law. However, complete impartiality is impossible to realise. Not only is bias inherent in human nature, but many kinds of decision-making process inevitably involve conflicts of interest. The problem is especially acute in the UK, with its culture of personal connections within the governing elite. The law therefore has to compromise and has done so by distinguishing between different kinds of decision and different kinds of bias. The general approach is the same as that applying to Article 6 of the ECHR: the right to a fair trial (see *Hanif and Khan v UK* (2012) 55 EHRR 16, [44]).

The decision-maker need not actually be biased – this would fall under the head of improper purpose or an irrelevant consideration (Section 17.6). The bias rule is importantly concerned with the risk or appearance of bias, hence the dictum of Lord Hewart in *R v Sussex Justices, ex p McCarthy* [1924] 1 KB 256, 259 that 'justice must not only be done but must manifestly and undoubtedly be seen to be done'. The rationale is not only that of fairness to the parties but also that of public confidence in the integrity of the decision-making process. A decision-maker who becomes aware that s/he is subject to a biasing factor must disqualify him or herself, irrespective of the cost, delay or inconvenience that may result (*AWG Group Ltd v Morrison* [2006] 1 All ER 967). However, the parties can consent to the bias in question (waiver) (see *Smith v Kvaerner Cementation Foundations Ltd* [2006] 3 All ER 593). The main principles are as follows:

▶ *financial interests*. A direct personal financial interest, however small, will automatically disqualify the decision-maker, the law conclusively presuming bias (*Dimes v Grand Junction Canal Co* (1852) 3 HLC 759: Lord Chancellor held shares in company appearing before him; *R v Hendon RDC, ex p Chorley* [1933] 2 KB 696: local councillor had financial interest in development for which planning permission was sought; see also *R v Camborne Justices, ex p Pearce* [1955] 1 QB 41, 47);

▶ *parties to the case*. In *R v Bow Street Stipendiary Magistrate, ex p Pinochet (No 2)* [1999] 1 All ER 577, the House of Lords extended automatic disqualification to a case where a judge was a member of an organisation that was party to the case, even though there was no financial interest. Lord Hoffmann, a Law Lord, was an unpaid director of a charitable subsidiary of Amnesty International, a human rights pressure group, which was party to an appeal concerning whether to extradite the former President of Chile to Spain to face charges of torture and genocide. *Pinochet* has been criticised on the ground that there is an important distinction between 'interest', where the judge stands to gain personally, so he is a judge in his own case and should automatically be disqualified, and 'favour', where the judge might prefer a particular outcome, so a more flexible approach is appropriate (Olowofoyeku (2000)). Other common law jurisdictions have confined automatic disqualification to strictly financial interests and, bearing in mind that *Pinochet* was a case of special political significance, it is unlikely that its rationale will be extended beyond the case where a party directly controls an organisation of which the judge is an active member (*R (Kaur) v Institute of Legal Executives (ILEX) Appeal Tribunal*

[2012] 1 All ER 1435 (see below); *Meerabux v A-G of Belize* [2005] 2 AC 513 at [21]–[22], [30]: mere membership does not disqualify, active involvement needed);

▶ *other personal connections* such as social, family or professional relationships with the parties, previous involvement with the same decision-making process, the holding of opinions or the membership of groups related to the issues. These do not automatically disqualify, and a more flexible approach is taken. The courts have tried to find a formula which, on the one hand, reflects the interest of public confidence in the impartiality of the decision-maker and, on the other, blocks challenges for flimsy or ill-informed suspicions. The current formula asks whether in the view of a 'fair-minded and informed observer', taken as knowing all the circumstances, there is a 'real possibility' or 'real danger' of bias (*Porter v Magill* [2002] 1 All ER 465).

This formula emerged from *R v Gough* [1993] AC 646, which replaced two earlier tests (albeit often producing the same outcome). These were, first a strict 'reasonable suspicion' test, according to which any suspicious factor as it appeared to a reasonable hypothetical observer might disqualify the judge even though if all the circumstances were known the observer might be reassured; secondly the more liberal 'real likelihood' test, which allowed the reviewing court to decide for itself whether in all the circumstances bias was likely. The problem with this test was that the court itself might be too trusting of other decision-makers, sharing the 'insider' view of public life which is endemic among the professional and official elite. The hypothetical observer device is an attempt to focus the mind of the reviewing judge on what the outside world might suspect. *Gough* tried to compromise between the two approaches. It did not include the device of the hypothetical outsider but neither did it require an overall balance, only a 'real danger' of bias. However, *Gough* seemed to be out of line with the ECHR and the practice in other English-speaking countries (see Olowofoyeku (2000)). The *Gough* test was modified by *Re Medicaments (No 2)* [2001] 1 WLR 700, which reintroduced the imagined standpoint of a hypothetical reasonable outsider which was confirmed in *Porter v Magill*. It is questionable whether this makes any difference since the outsider who knows all and is fair-minded seems to be no more than an idealised avatar for the judge (see *Virdi v Law Society* [2010] 3 All ER 653).

Each case depends on its particular circumstances. There seems to be a large element of subjective guesswork and some indulgence towards fellow professionals. Generally speaking, a conflict of interest disqualifies only if it is focused on the specific type of case. The following are examples:

▶ In *R v Gough* [1993], the accused's brother was a neighbour of a jury member, who did not, however, recognise him. The jury was not disqualified.
▶ In *R v Abdroicov* [2007] 1 WLR 2679, the House of Lords held that the presence of a policeman and a prosecuting solicitor on a jury was, in itself, acceptable in the light of the normal understandings of what citizenship and an impartial jury required. (The UK is unusual in Europe, since most states have excluded police officers from juries.) However, a majority held that, in the circumstances, there was a disqualifying bias where, in one of two related trials, disputed evidence was given by a policeman known to the policeman on the jury. However, there was no disqualification in the other trial since contested evidence was not involved. Two dissenting judges held that there was no disqualification at all because the collective good sense of the jury could be trusted. The case went to the Strasbourg court in *Hanif and Khan v UK* [2012]. That court took a stricter view. It left open the question whether a policeman on a jury would always violate Article 6 but held that, because the two cases were interrelated, there was a violation of the right to a fair trial in both cases. *Abdroicov* exemplifies the subjective nature of the reasonable outsider test and, as Olowofoyeku (2009) suggests, there is much to be said for a return to *Gough*.
▶ In *Re Medicaments (No 2)* [2001], a lay member of the Restrictive Practices Court was applying for a job with a firm one of whose members often appeared as an expert witness before the court. The Court of Appeal held that she was disqualified even though she had taken steps to minimise the conflict of interest.
▶ In *Locobail (UK) v Bayfield Properties* [2000] QB 451, the Court of Appeal stressed that *general* objections based on religious, racial, ethnic or national characteristics, gender, age, class, political views, membership

of organisations, income and sexual orientation would not normally disqualify. *Specific* connections might include personal friendships or animosity, but making adverse remarks on a previous occasion would not in itself be sufficient. The court disqualified a judge who had written polemical articles in legal journals attacking the practices of insurance companies in circumstances similar to those in the case before him. However, it did not disqualify a judge who had been a member of a solicitors' firm acting for one of the parties since he had not been personally involved, or a decision to give a licence to a betting shop where the judge was a director of a company of which the shop was a tenant. Nor did the court disqualify the chair of a tribunal that had decided both a preliminary application to proceed in a sexual harassment case and the full case later.

▶ In *AMEC Ltd v Whitefriars City Estates* [2005], the reappointment of the same adjudicator to redetermine a previous flawed arbitration constituted bias.
▶ In *Gillies v Secretary of State for Work and Pensions* [2006] 1 All ER 731, prior experience and specialist knowledge were not a disqualification.
▶ In *R v L* [2011] EWCA Crim 65, it was held that a juror who was an employee of the Crown Prosecution Service carrying out general administrative duties was disqualified.

Allegations of bias have been successfully met by the claim that professional practices ensure integrity; in other words, we should trust those in power. For example, in *Porter v Magill* [2002], a local government auditor investigating allegations of bribery had made a provisional press announcement endorsing the allegations. His later formal report confirmed his findings. The House of Lords held that he was not disqualified since the reasonable observer could assume that an experienced professional was impartial. Similarly, in *Helow v Secretary of State for the Home Dept* [2009] 2 All ER 1031, a judge who was a member of the International Association of Jewish Lawyers was presiding over an asylum application by a supporter of the Palestine Liberation Front. The House of Lords held that the fair-minded and informed person would not conclude that there would be a real possibility of bias. It would require extreme words or conduct identifying with a partisan cause to justify such a conclusion. Even though this was a campaigning organisation, it could be assumed that when putting a judicial hat on, the judge would set any private views aside.

Similarly, in *Taylor v Lawrence* [2002] 2 All ER 353, it was held that a judge was not disqualified where a solicitor appearing before him had recently transacted family business on his behalf. Lord Woolf remarked that an informed observer can be expected to be aware of 'the legal traditions and culture of this jurisdiction' (at [61]–[64]), with the implication that this would be reassuring. In *Virdi v Law Society* [2010], in a disciplinary hearing by the Law Society, the clerk, who was a Law Society employee, retired with the tribunal and drafted its report. The Court of Appeal held that there was no danger of bias because the 'well-informed reasonable person' would know that there was no impropriety.

Lawal v Northern Spirit [2004] 1 All ER 187 suggests a less complacent approach. The claimant appealed to the Employment Appeal Tribunal in respect of an allegation of racial discrimination by his employer. The senior counsel for the employer had previously sat as a part-time judge with one of the lay members of the Tribunal. The House of Lords held that the reasonable outsider might well suspect that the relationship could bias the lay member. Lord Steyn warned against complacent assumptions of professional integrity, pointing out (at [22]) that

> the indispensable requirement of public confidence in the administration of justice requires higher standards today than was the case even a decade or two ago. The informed observer of today could perhaps be expected to be aware of the legal traditions and culture of this jurisdiction ... But he might not be wholly uncritical of that culture.

Moreover, in *R (Kaur) v Institute of Legal Executives (ILEX) Appeal Tribunal* [2012], the Court of Appeal held that the Vice President of the Institute of Legal Executives was disqualified from sitting on its Appeal Tribunal in a case where a student was accused of cheating. The hypothetical fair-minded, all-knowing observer could well believe that the Vice President's concern with the reputation of the organisation would make him less than impartial. The court also discussed whether this was an example of automatic disqualification as in *Pinochet* (above). It was suggested that the automatic disqualification test which applies to financial interests and some cases where a judge is linked with a party (above) was not a separate doctrine but merely a clear example of the reasonable observer test. This means that a financial interest could sometimes be disregarded.

The bias rule is overridden where there is an unavoidable conflict of interest, in which case Parliament must be taken to have impliedly authorised the bias (see also Senior Courts Act 1981, s 11: judges as taxpayers). In the case of administrative decisions taken by politicians, conflicts of interest arising out of political policies or competing responsibilities may be built into the system by statute (*e.g. Franklin v Minister of Town and Country Planning* [1948], a case which is discredited on wider grounds but remains relevant in this context, and *R v Secretary of State for the Environment, ex p Kirkstall Valley Campaign Ltd* [1996] 3 All ER 304: local authority had interest in developing land for which it also had to decide whether to grant planning permission).

The same applies in organisations such as prisons and universities where officials have a mixture of administrative and disciplinary functions (*e.g. R v Frankland Prison Board of Visitors, ex p Lewis* [1986] 1 All ER 272: prison visitors having both judicial and investigatory roles). Of course, an avoidable bias disqualifies (*R (Al-Hasan) v Secretary of State for the Home Dept* [2005] 1 All ER 927: a deputy prison governor who had been present while the governor gave an allegedly unlawful order to carry out an intimate body search on a prisoner). Similarly, a decision may be upheld if there is no possible unbiased decision-maker (*R v Barnsley Licensing Justices* [1960] 2 QB 167: all justices members of the local Co-op).

18.5   Procedural impropriety: reasons for decisions

There is no general duty to give reasons for decisions, although many statutes impose such a duty (see *R v Criminal Injuries Compensation Board, ex p Moore* [1999] 2 All ER 90; *Stefan v GMC* [1999] 1 WLR 1293). The absence of a duty to give reasons has been justified on the grounds of cost, excessive formality, the difficulties of expressing subjective reasons and because in the case of collective decisions it may be difficult to identify specific reasons (see *McInnes v Onslow-Fane* [1978]; *R v Higher Education Funding Council, ex p Institute of Dental Surgery* [1994] 1 All ER 651; *Stefan v GMC* [1999]).

The main justification for the giving of reasons is respect for human dignity and equality. Even an admission that a decision is based on subjective judgment fulfils this requirement. The giving of reasons also strengthens public confidence in the decision-making process, concentrates the mind of the decision-maker, ensures accountability and helps identify problems.

The courts have required reasons to be given in certain cases, based on the principle of fairness which allows the court to take all the circumstances into account. In *R v Secretary of State for the Home Dept, ex p Doody* [1993] 3 All ER 92, Lord Mustill referred to 'a perceptible trend towards an insistence upon greater openness in the making of administrative decisions' (at 107). In *Oakley v South Cambridgeshire DC* [2017] EWCA Civ 71, at [30], it was stated that 'it may be more accurate to say that the common law is moving to the position whilst there is no universal obligation to give reasons in all circumstances, in general they should be given unless there is a proper justification for not doing so' (see also *Dover DC v Campaign to Protect Rural England (Kent)* [2017] UKSC 79, [54]).

Examples of cases where there is a duty to give reasons include the following:

- judicial decisions analogous to those of a court;
- cases that involve very important interests where, if reasons were not given, the individual would be at a disadvantage (e.g. *Doody* [1993]: fixing of minimum sentence for life prisoner; *Stefan v GMC* [1999]: risk of loss of livelihood, unrepresented defendant);
- cases where the particular decision is unusual or a severe penalty is involved (e.g. *R v Civil Service Appeals Board, ex p Cunningham* [1991] 4 All ER 310: compensation award out of line with that given in analogous cases by industrial tribunal; *R v DPP, ex p Manning* [2000] 3 WLR 463: decision not to prosecute after coroner's finding of unlawful killing);
- a legitimate expectation (Section 18.3.1) might also generate a duty to give reasons for overriding the expectation (*R v Secretary of State for Transport, ex p Richmond upon Thames BC (No 4)* [1996] 4 All ER 903);
- if an appeal is provided this may point to a duty to give reasons where the appeal would otherwise be pointless (*Stefan v GMC* [1999]). On the other hand, a comprehensive appeal that reopens the whole case may point against a duty to give reasons at first instance;
- in *Padfield v Minister of Agriculture, Fisheries and Food* [1968] AC 997, the House of Lords suggested that, if a minister refuses to give reasons, the court can infer that he has no proper reasons for his decision. However, in *Lonrho v Secretary of State for Trade and Industry* [1989] 2 All ER 609, the House held that a failure to give reasons does not in itself justify the drawing of an adverse inference but is at most supportive of other evidence that the decision is improper.

In answer to the complaint that a duty to give reasons would overburden officials, reasons need not be detailed or comprehensive, provided that they enable the parties to understand the basis of the decision (see *South Bucks DC v Porter* [2004] UKHL 33).

A duty to give reasons, which arises after the decision is made, should be distinguished from failing, before the decision is made, to disclose *grounds* in the sense of allegations against the applicant. Failure to disclose such grounds would normally be unfair as a breach of the right to a hearing. Moreover, once an applicant has obtained permission to apply for judicial review (see Section 19.3), there is a duty of full and frank disclosure. The authority 'owes a duty to the court to cooperate and make candid disclosure of the relevant facts and the reasoning behind the decision challenged' (Lord Walker in *Belize Alliance of Conservation NGOs v Dept of the Environment* [2003] UKPC 63 at [86]; *R v Lancashire CC, ex p Huddleston* [1986] 2 All ER 941). However, this is of no help in finding grounds for challenge in the first place.

18.6 The European Convention on Human Rights

The HRA requires all public authorities to comply with the 'Convention rights' incorporated into UK law by the Act unless primary legislation makes this impossible (Section 22.5.1). The Act provides a freestanding basis for challenge in addition to the domestic ground of judicial review, thus providing an additional and more direct remedy. The human rights perspective differs from that of domestic judicial review in that its primary focus is on the *outcome*, in the sense of the impact of the decision on the individual. Although the distinction is not an absolute one, domestic judicial review is mainly concerned with the *process* of decision-making. Thus, in a human rights case, the court itself will investigate the facts and merits and is not confined to ensuring that the decision-maker has properly considered the human rights aspects (*R (Begum) v Head Teacher of Denbigh High School* [2007] 1 AC 100; *Manchester City Council v Pinnock* [2010] 3 WLR 1441; *Thomas v Bridgend CBC* [2012] JPL 25). However, in cases where a margin of discretion is given to the decision-maker (Section 22.9.3), the court's role is closer to that of review, even in a human rights case.

The HRA also affects particular domestic grounds of review in several ways:

- The flexibility of notions such as unreasonableness and legitimate expectation means that the courts will review more intensively where a human right is engaged (e.g. *R v North and East Devon HA, ex p Coughlan* [2000]; *Rowland v Environment Agency* [2004]; *R (Reprotech (Pebsham) Ltd) v East Sussex CC* [2003]). Thus, 'proportionality', rather than *Wednesbury* unreasonableness, applies to human rights cases (Section 18.1.1).
- Article 6 of the ECHR confers a right to a fair trial where 'civil rights and obligations' are in issue (Section 21.4.1.3). This includes a right to challenge an administrative decision before a body with 'full jurisdiction'. The meaning of 'civil rights' for Article 6 purposes is narrower than the range of interests protected by the common law doctrine of fairness. For example, an alien has no civil right in relation to expulsion from the UK but is entitled only to a basic hearing, which must, however, be before an independent tribunal, to enable the answering of accusations (*IR (Sri Lanka) v Secretary of State for the Home Dept* [2011] 4 All ER 908). In deciding whether there has been a fair trial, the court will look at the process as a whole, including any right of judicial review (*Albert v Belgium* (1983) 5 EHRR 533). A particular question which especially arises here is whether the limited review on questions of fact in English law satisfies Article 6 (Section 21.4.1.3).
- The common law has been said to accord with the 'spirit' of Article 6 (*Secretary of State for the Home Dept v MB* [2008] 1 AC 440, at [24]). However, although Article 6 does require a balance between the rights of the individual and the public interest, there is an irreducible minimum standard of fairness whereas the common law duty is less strict, involving a broader balance between fairness and the public interest (*Re Officer L* [2007] 4 All ER 965; *Secretary of State for the Home Dept v MB* [2008]). Thus, except in connection with the right to a hearing in public, which can be excluded in certain circumstances (Art 6(1)), the right to a fair trial cannot be overridden by other factors, although particular aspects might be modified to deal, for example, with security matters (Section 24.6).
- As regards both the bias rule and the giving of reasons, English law seems to be compliant with the ECHR. The European Court of Human Rights has confined itself to holding that the courts, as the citizen's last protection, must give reasons for their decisions, but has not required administrative bodies to do so (*Van de Hurk v The Netherlands* (1984) 18 EHRR 481; see also *Helle v Finland* (1998) 26 EHRR 159: detailed reasons not necessary).

Summary

- The doctrine of *Wednesbury* unreasonableness comes close to interfering with the merits of a decision. The threshold of unreasonableness varies with the context on a sliding scale, determined by the impact of the decision on the individual and whether the decision involves political factors with which a court should not interfere. At one extreme, a bare 'rationality' test is applied. At the other extreme, where the HRA applies, the court itself may weigh the competing considerations, exercising what is effectively an appeal function. Between these extremes, the test appears to be whether the outcome is within the range of reasonable responses to the particular context. In effect, the court is drawing upon widely shared social and moral values.

- The principle of proportionality is applied in the human rights context and may extend to other contexts, such as legitimate expectations. This requires the court to weigh the competing factors on the basis that the interference with the right must be no greater than is necessary to achieve a legitimate objective (in the case of some rights protected by the ECHR, 'a pressing social need').

- Natural justice or fairness requires that a person adversely affected by a decision be entitled to a hearing. The requirements of a hearing are flexible and depend on the circumstances.

- In order to respect the interests of government efficiency, fairness is regarded as the minimum standard necessary to do justice. The courts are increasingly requiring reasons to be given for decisions.

- A decision-maker must also be free from the appearance of improper bias. This too depends on the circumstances. A direct financial interest automatically disqualifies the decision-maker, as perhaps does membership of an organisation which is a party to the case. In other cases, the test is whether a hypothetical, reasonable and fully informed observer would consider there to be real danger of bias.

- The rules of natural justice or procedural fairness are underpinned by the HRA, although what amounts to a fair trial depends on the context and in particular the extent to which the decision is a policy-oriented political decision.

Exercises

18.1 'I think the day will come when it will be more widely recognised that the *Wednesbury* case was an unfortunately retrogressive decision in English administrative law' (Lord Cooke). What does he mean, and do you agree?

18.2 'The difference in practice [between *Wednesbury* unreasonableness and proportionality] is not as great as is sometimes supposed ... [E]ven without reference to the 1998 [Human Rights] Act the time has come to recognise that this principle is part of English administrative law, not only when judges are dealing with Community acts but also when they are dealing with acts subject to domestic law' (Lord Slynn). Do you agree?

18.3 'Judicial review is mainly concerned with the way in which a decision is reached rather than with its outcome'. Do you agree?

18.4 There is a statutory scheme to decide whether elderly persons should be entitled to free bus passes. An applicant must satisfy a local tribunal that he or she has a special need for a bus pass due to infirmity, low income or other special circumstances. The tribunal consists of a local magistrate, a manager of a bus company and an assessor who is medically qualified. The tribunal does not hold an oral hearing but determines applications on the basis of emails from applicants and via emails between the tribunal members. Jones, who has a heart complaint and breathing difficulties, applies for a bus pass. He has no access to a computer and makes his application by letter. His application is rejected without giving reasons. Jones sends a further letter requesting to see any medical evidence in his case and to appear in person before the tribunal assisted by his lawyer. This letter is ignored. Advise Jones.

18.5 The local council is given statutory power to 'regulate the operation of cinemas'. The council introduces a system of licences for cinemas. It imposes the following conditions:

(i) Children are prohibited from attending any performance on a Sunday.

(ii) No refreshments are to be sold at the cinema. The chairman of the council owns a fast food shop next to the cinema and is a well-known Evangelical preacher.

  (a) A local cinema wishes to challenge conditions (i) and (ii). Advise it.

  (b) Another local cinema is accused of breaching condition (i), and, without giving it a hearing, the council orders it to close. Advise the council. What would be the position if a councillor had said to the cinema manager, 'Between ourselves, we are not likely to enforce the condition where a child is accompanied by a parent', and the manager had followed that advice?

18.6 Does the bias rule strike a reasonable balance between efficiency and justice?

18.7 Dan is accused of plagiarism in his dissertation at the University of Business Enterprise. His head of department holds a hearing into the matter and recommends to the University Best Practice Committee that Dan be expelled from the university. Dan appeals to the committee and is invited to a hearing. Before the hearing, Dan discovers that the chair of the committee is a business studies professor who has recently sold downloadable apps on 'how to detect plagiarism'. A member of Dan's department is also a member of the committee. Dan writes to the committee stating that he does not believe that he would get a fair hearing from 'this gang of cronies'. The chair replies that the professional integrity of colleagues is absolute. Dan appears before the committee, which confirms his expulsion from the university.

Advise Dan whether he has any grounds on which he can challenge this decision in the courts. Would your answer differ if the committee had refused to permit Dan to appear in person before it but invited him to make a written statement?

18.8 The Higher Education Act 2021 (imaginary) provides that local councils 'shall award grants to university students such as are necessary to meet their reasonable needs'. In March 2021, the Secretary of State issues guidance in a circular, sent to all schools, stating that grants will be awarded to anyone whose family income is less than £15,000, or if there is evidence of hardship. Peter, who has read the guidance, and Wendy, who has not, decided to leave their current employment to take up university places in September 2021. Their family incomes are £10,000 and £12,000, respectively. Fi wishes to take a university course in surfing studies from September 2021. Her family income is in excess of £15,000, but her family refuses to support her as they want her to study law. An official from the council writes to Fi informing her that this constitutes hardship and that she is eligible for a grant. In June 2021, the Secretary of State issues new guidance. This states: 'Due to a funding shortfall, grants will be awarded only where family income is less than £8000'. The same official now writes to Fi telling her that she will not receive a grant. Peter and Wendy are also refused grants. In Wendy's case, the local authority tells her that they will only give a grant in cases of extreme hardship.

Advise Peter, Wendy and Fi as to the likelihood of a successful challenge to these decisions in the courts and whether they are entitled to grants. Would your advice to Fi differ if the council had power to authorise its officials to make the decision concerning grants in cases such as Fi's, but had not in fact done so?

Further reading

Bell, 'The Doctrine of Legitimate Expectations: Power-Constraining or Right-Conferring Legal Standard?' [2016] PL 437

Bell, 'Reason-Giving in Administrative Law: Where Are We and Why Have the Courts Not Embraced the "General Common Law Duty to Give Reasons"?' (2019) 82 MLR 983

Craig, 'Substance and Procedure in Judicial Review' in Andenas and Fairgrieve (eds), *Tom Bingham and the Transformation of the Law* (Oxford University Press 2009)

Craig, 'Judicial Review and Anxious Scrutiny: Foundations, Evolution and Application' [2015] PL 60

Daly, *'Wednesbury's* Reason and Structure' [2011] PL 238

Elliott, 'Has the Common Law Duty to Give Reasons Come of Age Yet?' [2011] PL 56

Goodwin, 'The Last Defence of *Wednesbury*' [2012] PL 445

Gregson, 'When Should There Be an Implied Power to Delegate?' [2018] PL 408

Hannett and Busch, '*Ultra Vires* Representations and Legitimate Expectations' [2005] PL 729

Hickman, 'The Reasonableness Principle: Reassessing Its Place in the Public Sphere' (2004) 63 CLJ 166

Irvine, 'Judges and Decision Makers: The Theory and Practice of *Wednesbury* Review' [1996] PL 59

Knight, 'Expectations in Transition: Recent Developments in Legitimate Expectations' [2009] PL 15

Lee, 'Substantiating Substantive Review' [2018] PL 632

Olowofoyeku, 'The *Nemo Judex* Rule: The Case Against Automatic Disqualification' [2000] PL 456

Olowofoyeku, 'Bias and the Informed Observer: A Call for a Return to *Gough'* (2009) 68 CLJ 388

Reynolds, 'Legitimate Expectations and the Protection of Trust in Public Officials' [2011] PL 330

Rivers, 'Proportionality and the Variable Standard of Review' (2006) 65 CLJ 174

Steele, 'Substantive Legitimate Expectations: Striking the Right Balance' (2005) 121 LQR 300

Taggart, 'Proportionality, Deference, *Wednesbury'* [2008] New Zealand LJ 423

Tomlinson, 'Do We Need a Theory of Legitimate Expectations?' (2020) 40 LS 286

Tucker, 'Legitimate Expectations and the Separation of Powers' (2009) 125 LQR 233

Chapter 19

Judicial review remedies and procedure

19.1 Introduction

It could be argued that the courts (perhaps alongside tribunals: Section 20.1) provide the only open and universal means by which the individual can challenge government action. Ministerial responsibility to Parliament is of little use to the citizen directly, in that it can be called upon only by MPs, who are unlikely to be independent and cannot force ministers to disclose information. The Committee on Standards in Public Life plays a valuable monitoring role but has no enforcement powers and cannot consider individual complaints. The various 'ombudsmen' who investigate citizens' complaints against government are free to complainants and have powers of investigation into facts. However, their jurisdiction is limited to maladministration and many public bodies are excluded, they have no enforcement powers and they do not hold public hearings (Section 20.2). The courts have the advantage of sitting in public and have comprehensive power to require the disclosure of information.

Until 1977, there was no distinctive legal process for judicial review. The powers of the courts to review government action developed historically in different courts through a variety of remedies, some of which were general remedies applying also to private disputes. As we saw (Section 6.4), one aspect of the 'rule of law' emphasised by Dicey was that the common law does not distinguish between public law and private law, but applies the same principles to government and citizen alike, so that an official is in no better or worse position than a private individual. However, since Dicey's day, the powers of government have expanded enormously and this approach has become inadequate to protect the citizen, to accord public bodies which (at least in principle) act in the public interest sufficient protection from the law, and to reflect the democratic interest in governmental accountability.

Since 1977, the various remedies have been concentrated in a single jurisdiction, part of the Queen's Bench Division of the High Court and now called the Administrative Court. Originally, the Administrative Court sat only in London. However, to enhance access to justice, it now also sits in regional centres (Cardiff (with hearings taking place in Bristol, where the claimant has the closest connection to the south-west of England), Birmingham, Manchester, Leeds), the venue normally depending on the claimant's connection (see Practice Direction 54D – Administrative Court (Venue)). Collectively, these regional centres account for approximately 20 per cent of the work of the Administrative Court. It is sometimes suggested that a shortage of specialist lawyers outside London might weaken the court and dilute the idea of a distinctive jurisdiction.

The workload of the Administrative Court is substantial. However, flexibility was added by the Tribunals, Courts and Enforcement Act 2007. Under this Act, the Upper Tribunal, which also hears appeals from the main tribunals, has a judicial review jurisdiction in types of case (other than those concerning the Crown Court) designated by the Lord Chief Justice or another judge designated by him or her (ss 15, 18). The Upper Tribunal has the same status as the High Court but has a flexible membership including other senior judicial officers and lay specialists (Section 20.1). The Upper Tribunal therefore has the advantages of expertise but lacks the experience and status of the High Court in relation to the general principles of judicial review.

Up until 2012, immigration cases made up about three-quarters of the judicial review caseload. Under the Crime and Courts Act 2013 the Lord Chancellor can transfer all immigration cases to the Upper Tribunal. Most immigration and asylum cases have been so transferred, but not those raising general constitutional issues, including challenges to legislation and unlawful detention cases. Other specialist areas such as planning law may also be transferred to the Upper Tribunal, perhaps creating a general distinction between constitutional cases and cases raising issues primarily concerned with the application of particular legislation.

The law is governed by section 31 of the Senior Courts Act 1981 and Part 54 of the Civil Procedure Rules 1998 (CPR). There is a unified procedure for all the remedies. This replaces numerous technical rules that had developed over the years in relation to individual remedies. These had made challenge to government action complex and sometimes unjust, with litigants having to traverse a minefield of procedural niceties and sometimes being frustrated by choosing an inappropriate remedy in the wrong court. A Law Commission Report in 1976 (No 6407) led to the main reforms. A further Law Commission Report (No 226, 1994) led to further, relatively minor changes.

A claim for judicial review means a claim to review the lawfulness of (i) an enactment or (ii) a decision, action or failure to act in relation to the exercise of a public function (CPR 54.1). The procedure as a whole is characterised by wide discretionary powers which allow the court to choose the most appropriate remedy from the whole range. It also embodies principles concerned with the special nature of disputes between government and citizen.

These principles are of three kinds:

1. The remedies are designed to set aside unlawful government action and to send the matter back to the decision-maker or to restrain an unlawful act but not, normally, to allow the court to make a new decision itself, thus complying with the separation of powers. However, where there is only one possible decision that could lawfully be made, the court can make it itself (CPR 54.19). Moreover, the court might exceptionally correct a mistake made, for example, in a statutory instrument where it is plain that the mistake was inadvertent and when the purpose of the instrument is clear (*R (Confederation of Passenger Transport (UK)) v Humber Bridge Board* [2004] 4 All ER 533).
2. The procedure reflects the limited role of the courts. In particular, the procedure is normally based on written statements, since the court is not primarily concerned with factual disputes. However, there is power to hear witnesses if justice so requires.
3. Judicial review concerns the public interest in accountable and effective government, as well as the interests of individual claimants. The procedure gives the court a wide discretion in relation to hearing claims and giving remedies. In particular, there are barriers designed to safeguard the public interest against improper challenges (Section 19.3). To a degree, judicial review could be regarded as part of the political process, as it provides a public platform for grievances against the government so that, to a well-funded partisan, even hopeless litigation might be attractive as a means of publicising a cause. On the other hand, any restriction on the right to go to court might be seen as an affront to the rule of law. However, in cases where a person's ordinary private rights are at stake, for example if a public authority interferes with private property, an action or defence can be brought in any court, thus reflecting the traditional idea of the rule of law.

19.2 The range of remedies

Historically, there are two groups of remedies suitable for judicial review. First, from the seventeenth century, the courts developed the 'prerogative orders' (so-called because in theory they issue on the application of the Crown). These were *certiorari*, *prohibition*, and *mandamus*, and they enabled the High Court to police the powers and duties of 'inferior bodies', that is, lower courts and government officials. *Certiorari* summoned up the record of an inferior body to be examined by the court and the decision was set aside and sent back if it was invalid. *Prohibition* was issued in advance to prevent a body from exceeding its jurisdiction. *Mandamus* ordered a body to perform its duty. These orders remain the basis of the modern law of judicial review but are now called quashing orders, prohibiting orders and mandatory orders respectively (CPR 54.1). They are available only in the Administrative Court (CPR 54.2). A quashing order sets aside the offending decision and is the most common remedy.

The second group of remedies comprises declarations, injunctions and damages (Senior Courts Act 1981, s 31(2)). These are also available in other courts and are primarily private law remedies. A claimant may apply for these in the Administrative Court and must do so if he or she is seeking these remedies in addition to a prerogative order (CPR 54.3).

A declaration is a statement of the legal position which declares the rights of parties (e.g. 'X is entitled to a tax repayment'). Declarations are not enforceable, but a public authority is unlikely to disobey one. Indeed, a declaration is useful where an enforceable order would be undesirable, for example in the case of a draft government order before it is considered by Parliament or an advisory government opinion. It might, for example, be used to avoid offending Parliament (see *R v Boundary Commission, ex p Foot* [1983] 1 All ER 1099). The former prerogative orders do not lie against the Crown as such, but the declaration does. However, this is relatively unimportant because most statutory powers are conferred on ministers, and the prerogative orders lie against individual ministers.

An injunction restrains a person from breaking the law or orders a person to undo something done unlawfully (a mandatory injunction). An interim injunction can restrain government action pending a full trial. In *M v Home Office* [1993] 3 All ER 537, the House of Lords held that an injunction can be enforced against a minister of the Crown (see also *R v Minister of Agriculture, Fisheries and Food, ex p Monsanto plc* [1998] 4 All ER 321). This overturns a long tradition that the Crown and its servants cannot be the subject of enforceable orders, which still applies to ordinary civil law actions involving contract, tort or property issues (Crown Proceedings Act 1947, s 21). However, it was stressed that injunctions should be granted against ministers only as a last resort. Injunctions cannot be granted against the Crown itself.

Claimants often apply for more than one of the remedies, which may well overlap. For example, a quashing order has the same effect as a declaration that the offending decision is void. The court can issue any of the remedies in any combination and is not limited to those for which the claimant has applied (Senior Courts Act 1981, s 31(5)).

A claimant cannot seek a financial remedy, damages, restitution, or the recovery of a debt alone in judicial review proceedings but must attach it to a claim for at least one of the other remedies (CPR 54.3(2)). Moreover, *damages are not available in respect of unlawful government action as such* but can be awarded only in respect of conduct and losses which are not authorised by statute and which would be actionable in an ordinary civil action (Senior Courts Act 1981, s 31(4); Tribunals, Courts and Enforcement Act 2007, s 16(6)). In other cases, damages must be sought in an ordinary civil action.

The law relating to the liability for damages of public authorities is complex and cannot usefully be discussed without prior knowledge of the law of tort. We will not attempt to discuss the matter here, other than to remark that the courts are reluctant to impose liability in damages upon public bodies exercising statutory powers on the basis of negligence or a failure of a public duty (see e.g. *X (Minors) v Bedfordshire CC* [1995] 2 AC 633; *Marcic v Thames Water Utilities Ltd* [2004] 1 All ER 135; *Cullen v Chief Constable of the RUC* [2004] 2 All ER 237; *Anufrijeva v Southwark LBC* [2004] QB 1124). This is because the risk of paying damages might inhibit the decision-maker from exercising its powers independently (but see *Connor v Surrey CC* [2010] 3 All ER 905: existing duty in private law, public law duties should conform to this).

In four kinds of case, however, damages may be awarded on the basis of unlawful government action:

1. under the *Francovich* principle in EU law (Section 10.3.1);
2. under the tort of 'misfeasance in public office', where an authority has a specific intention to injure or knowingly acts outside its powers, being reckless as to the consequences, and causes material damage (see *Dunlop v Woollahra Municipal Council* [1982] AC 158; *Calveley v Chief Constable of Merseyside Police* [1989] AC 1228; *Racz v Home Office* [1994] 1 All ER 97; *Three Rivers DC v Bank of England (No 3)* [2003] 2 AC 1; *Watkins v Secretary of State for the Home Dept* [2006] 2 All ER 353);
3. where a right protected by the HRA is infringed (see *D v East Berkshire Community Health NHS Trust* [2005] 2 AC 373);
4. where there has been a breach of a duty specifically intended to be enforced by an individual. However, the courts, reluctant to interfere with public spending priorities, require the statute to show a clear

intention to impose such a duty on a public authority (e.g. *Marcic v Thames Water Utilities Ltd* [2004]: repairing water mains; *Ali v Bradford City Council* [2011] 3 All ER 348: clearing roads).

When it quashes a decision, the court will frequently remit the matter to the original decision-maker to decide again in accordance with the court's findings. It is fundamental to judicial review that the court's role is secondary. It cannot normally substitute its own decision for that of the designated decision-maker. However, by virtue of the Senior Courts Act 1981, s35(5)(b) as modified by section 141 of the Tribunals, Courts and Enforcement Act 2007, the court can substitute its own decision if the original decision was made by a court or tribunal, that is, not the executive, and was quashed on the ground of error of law, and without the error, there could only be one decision which the tribunal could have reached.

19.2.1 *Habeas corpus*

There is also the ancient prerogative writ of *habeas corpus* ('produce the body'). It is not part of the judicial review procedure. *Habeas corpus* is applied for in the High Court and has priority over other business. It is directed to the person who has actual control over a detained person, or at least a reasonable prospect of being able to exercise such control, and requires that person to bring the detainee (other than a convicted prisoner) immediately before a judge to justify the detention (see *Rahmatullah v Secretary of State for Defence* [2013] 1 AC 614). It provides a swift emergency remedy. Unlike judicial review, the court has no discretion whether to hear the case, and there is no time limit. *Habeas corpus* probably issues on the same grounds as those for judicial review (*Khawaja v Secretary of State for the Home Dept* [1983] 1 All ER 765). However, there is authority that *habeas corpus* applies only where a decision is *ultra vires* in the narrow sense (*R v Secretary of State for the Home Dept, ex parte Cheblak* [1991] 1 WLR 890, 894).

Habeas corpus was described as 'perhaps the most important writ known to the constitutional law of England, affording as it does a swift and imperative remedy in all cases of illegal constraint or confinement' (*Ex Parte O'Brian* [1923] 2 KB 361). According to Dicey ((1915) 118) *habeas corpus* is 'worth a hundred constitutional articles guaranteeing civil liberty' (even though it can be excluded by statute, e.g. *Re Hilali* [2008] 2 All ER 207, and has several times been suspended).

Habeas corpus may be of limited importance today, when judicial review can provide a speedy way of challenging unlawful detention. Indeed, because it cannot be used to investigate facts other than the question of who is in control of the prisoner, *habeas corpus* has been held not to provide an effective remedy under Article 5 of the ECHR: right to liberty (*X v UK* (1982) 4 EHRR 188) (see Le Sueur, 'Should We Abolish the Writ of Habeas Corpus?' [1992] PL 13; Shrimpton, 'In Defence of Habeas Corpus' [1993] PL 24; Law Com No 226, 1994, Part XI). For example, in *Rahmatullah v Secretary of State for Defence* [2013], the army had handed a prisoner in Afghanistan over to the US forces under an agreement between the two governments that such prisoner would be returned on request. The Supreme Court would not intervene, on the ground that, since the US authorities had refused to acknowledge that the UK government was arguably in control of the prisoner, it would be futile to issue the writ. However, the court pointed out that the UK government was obliged under the Geneva Convention relating to the protection of civilians in wartime to seek the prisoner's return.

19.3 The judicial review procedure: public interest safeguards

The judicial review process contains mechanisms designed to protect the public interest against improper challenges. In attempting to do this, it is vulnerable to objections relating to the right of access to the courts and the right to a fair trial under Article 6 of the ECHR, as well as contravening Dicey's version of the rule of law (Section 6.4).

The judicial review process must also be set in the wider context of the 'Woolf reforms' in civil procedure introduced in 1999 (Woolf, *Access to Justice: A Final Report to the Lord Chancellor* (Department for Constitutional Affairs 1996)). These reforms include the following general aspirations in respect of which the parties are under an obligation to assist the court (CPR 1.1):

(a) ensuring that the parties are on an equal footing;
(b) saving expense;
(c) dealing with the case in ways which are proportionate
    (i) to the amount of money involved;
    (ii) to the importance of the case;
    (iii) to the complexity of the issues;
    (iv) to the financial position of each party;
(d) ensuring that the case is dealt with expeditiously and fairly;
(e) allocating to the case an appropriate share of the court's resources while taking into account the need to allot resources to other cases.

The main distinctive features of the judicial review procedure are as follows:

▶ Permission to apply is required from a judge before proceedings can be commenced in, or transferred to, the Administrative Court (Senior Courts Act 1981, s 31(3); CPR 54.4). The procedure is *ex parte*; that is, the government side need not appear, although it must be given the opportunity to do so. At this stage, the claimant has to show that the case is 'arguable', or that she or he has a realistic prospect of success, so as to discourage spurious challenges and help the court to manage an ever-increasing case-load by filtering out hopeless cases (but see also the discussion of the Criminal Justice and Courts Act 2015, s 84 (below)). The application for permission can be renewed before another judge in open court, but not if the judge certifies the case as being 'totally without merit' (CPR 54.12(7)) (for a discussion of the meaning of this phrase, see *Wasif v Secretary of State for the Home Dept* [2016] EWCA Civ 82). In the case of a refusal of permission, there is an appeal to the Court of Appeal with its permission. If the Court of Appeal gives permission, it often then proceeds to deal with the whole matter. There is no appeal to the Supreme Court against a refusal of the Court of Appeal to give permission to appeal to itself (Access to Justice Act 1999, s 54(4)). In other cases, there is an appeal to the Supreme Court with permission.

▶ After permission for a judicial review has been granted, interim relief preventing the implementation of the government action in question can be granted pending the full hearing either by injunction (Section 19.2) or under section 31 of the Senior Courts Act 1981.

▶ The court has a discretion in relation to procedural matters. The case is normally decided on the basis of affidavits (sworn written statements), and orders for disclosure of documents are rarely made, but the court may exceptionally order disclosure, witnesses and cross-examination. The government is obliged to make full and frank disclosure of all relevant material (see *R v Secretary of State for Foreign and Commonwealth Affairs, ex p Quark Fishing Ltd* [2006] 1 AC 529; Lord Walker in *Belize Alliance of Conservation NGOs v Dept of the Environment* [2003] UKPC 63). With the agreement of the parties, the court can decide the whole matter without a hearing (CPR 54.18). It is arguable that, in view of the broad policy issues that may arise in judicial review cases, particularly under the HRA, it would be desirable that a more expansive process be used, at least in cases of major importance. One suggestion has been to appoint an Advocate General or Director of Civil Proceedings with the duty of representing the public interest before the court.

▶ Procedural flexibility is enhanced in that the Administrative Court can transfer cases to the ordinary trial process and vice versa (CPR 54.20). There is a shorter time limit than the periods of three or six years applicable to ordinary civil litigation. The law is contained in a somewhat confusing combination of section 31(6) and 31(7) of the Senior Courts Act 1981 and CPR 54.5. Under section 31(6), the court may refuse permission to make the application or refuse to give a remedy if 'undue delay' results in 'substantial hardship to any person, substantial prejudice to the rights of any person, or would be detrimental to good administration'. However, by virtue of CPR 54.5(1), the claim must be filed (i) promptly and (ii) not later than three months after the ground to make the claim first arose. In the case of a quashing order, this means the date of the decision. The time limit cannot be extended by agreement and is subject to any shorter time limit in a particular statute (CPR 54.5(3)). The time limit can, however, be extended by the court (CPR 3.1(2)). The combined effect of these provisions is that: (i) a failure to apply for permission promptly, even within three months, is undue delay. The court might then extend the time limit; (ii) if it does so, the court can still refuse relief but only on the grounds specified in section 31(6). These considerations are usually examined at the full hearing stage (see *Caswell v Dairy Produce Quota Tribunal for England and Wales* [1990] 2 All ER 434). Different time limits now apply to challenges to planning decisions (six weeks: CPR 54.5(5)) and decisions relating to public procurement under the Public Contracts Regulations 2015 (30 days: CPR 54.5(6)).

▶ The court can refuse to grant a remedy in its discretion even when a decision is *ultra vires* and, strictly speaking, void. By contrast, in ordinary litigation, an *ultra vires* decision is treated as a nullity (*Credit Suisse v Allerdale BC* [1996] 4 All ER 129; Section 17.2). The court will not set aside a decision where, for example, no injustice has been done, where the interests of third parties would be prejudiced, or where intervention would cause serious public disruption (e.g. *R v Secretary of State for the Home Dept, ex p Swati* [1986] 1 All ER 717; *R v Secretary of State for Social Services, ex p Association of Metropolitan Authorities* [1986] 1 WLR 1; and see also the discussion of the Criminal Justice and Courts Act 2015, s 84 (below)). The court might also prefer a declaration to an enforceable order where enforcement might be impracticable or hinder the governmental process (see e.g. *R v Panel on Takeovers and Mergers, ex p Datafin plc* [1987] QB 815; *Chief Constable of North Wales Police v Evans* [1982] 3 All ER 141; *R v Boundary Commission, ex p Foot* [1983] at 1116). The court will also take into account whether the claimant has made full disclosure of all relevant circumstances (*R v Lancashire CC, ex p Huddleston* [1986] 2 All ER 941). A particularly important aspect of the court's discretionary power is that judicial review is intended as a remedy of last resort. The court will not normally permit judicial review if there is another remedy, such as a right of appeal. Thus, in *R (RK (Nepal)) v Secretary of State for the Home Dept* [2009] EWCA Civ 359, it was held that, where a system of appeals was provided, judicial review would be permitted only in limited and exceptional cases. Here, an appeal could be made only from outside the country, but judicial review was not allowed. The same was held in respect of a decision of the Financial Services Authority from which there was a statutory right to a rehearing by the Upper Tribunal. The claimant unsuccessfully argued that the statutory remedy placed him at extra risk and did not address his grievance, which concerned a failure by the Authority to give adequate reasons for taking action against him in the first place (*R (Wilford) v FSA* [2013] EWCA Civ 677).

▶ However, the court will take account of whether the matters to be decided raise issues of general importance, in which case judicial review would be more appropriate. These include serious unfairness and abuses of power and where the alternative remedy is of uncertain scope (see *R (Cart) v Upper Tribunal* [2012] 1 AC 663, at [33]; *R v Chief Constable of the Merseyside Police, ex p Calveley* [1986] QB 424; *R (Sivasubramaniam) v Wandsworth BC* [2003] 1 WLR 475; *R (G) v Immigration Appeal Tribunal* [2004] 3 All ER 286; *R (Zhang) v Secretary of State* [2014] 2 All ER 560).

▶ Judicial review is a limited remedy. On the one hand, it can expose government wrongdoing by providing a public forum for a grievance and requiring officials to disclose information. On the other, it cannot guarantee a just outcome for the citizen. The court cannot usually order that a particular decision be made, but can only send the matter back to be decided again. Moreover, following an adverse court ruling, the executive, with its control of Parliament, can ensure that the law is changed. For example, in *R (Walker) v Secretary of State for Justice* [2010] 1 AC 553, under the Criminal Justice Act 2003, persons serving indeterminate sentences could be considered for release by the Parole Board if they could demonstrate that they were no longer a danger to the public. Due to lack of resources, the Secretary of State had failed to provide the necessary training and support facilities to enable prisoners to do this. This failure was held to be unlawful. Nevertheless, the claimant had no remedy. First, damages are not available in respect of invalid government action as such, and his detention was still lawful since he had no right to be released. Moreover, the detention was not arbitrary since the Parole Board hearings were not wholly an empty exercise. Thirdly, the Parole Board hearings themselves were not unfair since the Board was doing the best it could in the circumstances. Moreover, there was no violation of Article 5.4 of the ECHR (right to a speedy decision), since the delay was not so extreme as to be arbitrary (see *James v UK* (2013) 56 EHRR 12).

Section 84 of the Criminal Justice and Courts Act 2015, which amends section 31(2) of the Senior Courts Act 1981, now requires the court, in the absence of an exceptional public interest, to refuse an application for permission or the granting of a remedy if it appears 'highly likely' to the court 'that the outcome for the applicant would not have been substantially different if the conduct complained of had not occurred'. The explanatory notes to the Act provide the following illustration:

> A public authority might fail to notify a person of the existence of a consultation where they should have, and that person does not provide a response where they otherwise might have. If that person's likely arguments had been raised by others, and the public authority had taken a decision properly in the light of those arguments, then the court might conclude that the failure was highly unlikely to have affected the outcome.

This provision is therefore designed to reduce the number of legal challenges brought against government and the disruption which might be caused to the performance of public functions by litigation. It is therefore another barrier against challenge and, as such, raises rule of law concerns. If a decision or action is unlawful, should not the court be empowered to judge it as such, irrespective of whether the deficiency makes a difference to the outcome? The ability to disregard this requirement in cases of 'exceptional public interest' affords some recognition of rule of law considerations, but its meaning and scope are not yet clear.

19.4 Standing (*locus standi*)

The applicant must show that she or he has 'sufficient interest' in the matter to which the application relates (Senior Courts Act 1981, s 31(3)). Before the 1977 reforms, the law was complex and diffuse, depending primarily upon which remedy was being sought. In some cases, standing was limited to a person whose legal rights were affected by the decision in question. However, in light of the public interest aspects of judicial review, it is important, particularly in cases involving disadvantaged people, that non-governmental organisations (NGOs) such as pressure groups or representative interest groups also have access to the courts.

In *IRC v National Federation of Self-Employed and Small Businesses Ltd* [1982] AC 617, sometimes called the 'Fleet Street Casuals' or the 'Mickey Mouse Case', the House of Lords, although holding that the applications had no standing on the facts, significantly liberalised the law. The applicants were members of a pressure group representing certain business interests. They challenged a decision of the Inland Revenue not to collect arrears of tax from casual print workers who were alleged to have made false claims (in some cases under the name of 'Mickey Mouse') on the ground that the decision was politically motivated. The following propositions were laid down:

▶ The question of standing must be decided both at the preliminary permission stage, with a view to filtering out obvious busybodies and troublemakers, and at the full hearing where the entitlement to a particular remedy is in issue.
▶ Standing is not limited to a person whose legal rights are affected by the decision in question.
▶ A majority held that 'sufficient interest' depends on the nature of the interests relevant to the statute under which the decision was made. Here the applicants failed since, under the tax legislation, a taxpayer's affairs are confidential and not the concern of other taxpayers, whether individuals or groups.

Lord Diplock, with some support from the others, took a broader approach based on the importance of the matter from a public interest perspective, suggesting that the more important the matter, the more generous should be the standing requirement. In some cases affecting the whole community, any citizen should have standing. Standing should not be separate from the substance of the case. It is not clear what this means, since the two matters are conceptually distinct. It probably means that the stronger the merits, the more generous the standing test. Indeed, Lord Diplock would have given the applicants standing had they produced evidence in support of their allegations.

Upholding the rule of law is also important, so a low threshold might be appropriate if there is no other way of calling the decision-maker to account (see Rose J in *R (Bulger) v Secretary of State for the Home Dept* [2001] 3 All ER 449).

As a result of the Fleet Street Casuals case, standing has become substantially a matter of judicial discretion and is generous, especially in environmental cases. It may be that standing will be given to anyone with a serious issue to argue and where a useful purpose would be served (e.g. *R (Feakins) v Secretary of State for the Environment, Food and Rural Affairs* [2004] 1 WLR 1761; *R v North Somerset DC, ex p Dixon* [1998] Env LR 111). (The narrower approaches taken in *R v Somerset CC, ex p Garnett* [1998] Env LR 91 and *R v Secretary of State for the Environment, ex p Rose Theatre Trust* [1990] 1 QB 504 are probably now unreliable.)

Cane (1995) draws a useful distinction (albeit not one explicitly made by the courts) between different types of 'representative standing', that is, where the case is brought by an individual or group purporting to represent an interest affected by the challenged act or decision. 'Surrogate' standing, where the claimant purports to represent an *individual* with a personal interest in the claim, is not usually permitted unless there is good reason – such as age or mental capacity – why the affected person cannot bring the case themselves (see *R v Legal Aid Board, ex p Bateman* [1992] 1 WLR 711). By contrast, the courts have generally permitted 'associational' standing, that is, situations in which the claimant purports to represent a *group of persons* with a personal interest in the claim (see *R v Inspectorate of Pollution, ex p Greenpeace (No. 2)* [1994] 4 All ER 329; *R (Edwards) v Environment Agency* [2004] 3 All ER 21). A third category, according to Cane, comprises groups or individuals representing the *general public interest as opposed to the interests of particular individual(s)*. These have standing, at least where there is no other way of challenging the decision (e.g. *R v HM Treasury, ex p Smedley* [1985] QB 657: taxpayer; *R v Secretary of State for Foreign and Commonwealth Affairs, ex p Rees-Mogg* [1994] 1 All ER 457: concerned citizen (and former editor of *The Times*); *R v Secretary of State for Foreign and Commonwealth Affairs, ex p World Development Movement* [1995] 1 All ER 611: campaigning organisation; *R (Quintavalle) v Secretary of State for Health* [2003] 2 All ER 113: anti-abortion group). The contribution of pressure groups has been welcomed as adding a valuable dimension to judicial review (*R v Secretary of State for Trade and Industry, ex p Greenpeace* [1998] Env LR 415), but in 2013, the Ministry of Justice sought views on whether 'persons who had only a political or theoretical interest, such as campaigning groups' should be excluded from judicial review on the basis that such litigation could 'undermine' the principle 'that Parliament and the elected government are best placed to determine what is in the public interest' (Cm 8703, 2013, [80]). Vociferous opposition to this suggestion meant that it was not subsequently acted upon, but possible reforms to the law on standing now also form part of the work of the Independent Review of Administrative Law established in 2020.

The particular remedy is also a factor in the grant of standing. For example, in *R v Felixstowe Justices, ex p Leigh* [1987] QB 582, a newspaper editor had standing for a declaration that magistrates should not hide behind anonymity, but could not obtain a mandatory order to reveal the identity of magistrates in a particular case.

Even where the claimant lacks standing, the court may consider the substantive issues, albeit without granting a remedy (e.g. *Bulger*; *Rose Theatre*). And where a person has no standing in their own right, the court has a discretion in an action brought by someone with standing to hear any person as an 'intervener', thereby broadening the scope of the process and allowing interest groups and groups representing the public interest to have a say (CPR 54.17).

19.4.1 The costs of judicial review

As the preceding discussion suggests, judicial review has a strong public interest element. Moreover, cases are often brought by individuals or interest groups of limited means who may also intervene in cases brought by another. In respect of environmental cases, the Aarhus Convention (1998) (*Public Participation in Decision Making and Access to Justice in Environmental Matters*) requires among other matters that costs must not be prohibitive.

However, to protect an allegedly overburdened court system against politically motivated challenges, the Criminal Justice and Courts Act 2015 ss 85–90 impose severe financial restrictions on parties in judicial review proceedings, thereby arguably undermining the rule of law by limiting access to justice.

First, other than in exceptional cases, interveners must pay their own costs and can be ordered to pay the costs of another party. Second, when making a costs order, the court can look into the resources of individual members or supporters of organisations before the court, whether claimants or interveners. Third, the court can make a 'capping order' (which limits the amount a party must pay towards another party's costs if they lose the case) only after the initial permission stage, and then only if stringent conditions are fulfilled. These specify that the proceedings must be public interest proceedings (that is, an issue which is of general public importance) and that the claimant would, in the absence of a capping order, otherwise reasonably discontinue the case (ss 88(6)–(8)). The requirements of 'public interest' can be altered by the Lord Chancellor (s 88(9)). However, as a gesture to Aarhus, the Lord Chancellor may make rules departing from these principles in 'environmental' cases (s 90) (on the previous law relating to 'Protected Costs Orders' see *R (Boggis) v Natural England* [2010] 1 All ER 159).

In addition, the Civil Legal Aid (Remuneration) (Amendment) (No. 3) Regulations 2014 preclude legal aid from being paid to a claimant's lawyers if permission is refused. Moreover, under the regulations, where permission is neither granted nor refused, the Lord Chancellor has a discretion to pay legal aid. The latter provision means that she or he might refuse to pay where the government settles or the case is withdrawn before permission is determined but after costs have mounted up. These changes could therefore have a 'chilling effect', making it more difficult for poorer claimants to find competent representation.

19.5 Choice of procedure: public and private law

The judicial review procedure applies only to 'the exercise of a public function' (CPR 54.1). This implies that not all activities of government bodies are necessarily public functions and opens the possibility that some functions carried on by bodies outside government might nevertheless be public functions. Indeed, contemporary political fashion favours using private bodies to deliver public services, so that it seems anomalous that such a body should not be subject to judicial review (see the dissenting speeches of Lord Bingham and Lady Hale in *YL v Birmingham City Council* [2007] 3 All ER 957). Moreover, it is often suggested that judicial review should be about controlling any concentration of power rather than government as such. The debate about the legal basis of judicial review reflects this (Section 17.1).

The remedies provided by the HRA are also triggered by a 'public function' (Section 22.7). The meaning of public function in the two contexts is not necessarily the same. However, cases in either context can be used as guidance and the same outcome has invariably been chosen (e.g. *Weaver v London and Quadrant Housing Trust* [2009] EWCA Civ 587; *YL v Birmingham City Council* [2007]; *Hampshire CC v Beer* [2003] EWCA Civ 1056).

The courts have refused to apply a single test but have indicated a number of factors that make a function 'public'. For judicial review purposes, the focus is on the particular function that is being challenged so that a body which has a mixture of public and private functions, such as a housing association, is reviewable only in its public capacity. For example, the eviction of a tenant housed as part of its public function can be challenged but not the eviction of a tenant it houses privately (*Weaver* (above)). Conversely, a local authority might be exercising entirely private functions, as when it is dealing with a customer within an entirely commercial context based on contract (see *R (Trafford) v Blackpool Borough Council* [2014] 2 All ER 947).

It is relevant, but not enough, that the function in question is exercised in the public interest, that the body is important, or that the decision has serious consequences for those affected by it.

The main factors are as follows:

▶ Where a power exercisable for public purposes is conferred directly by statute or royal prerogative, it will normally be regarded as a public function (*R v Panel on Takeovers and Mergers, ex p Datafin plc* [1987]; *Scott v National Trust* [1998] 2 All ER 705: despite some statutory protection the Trust's *functions* are not statutory). However, a body such as an insurance company, which exercises the same commercial functions as a private body, but happens to have been created by statute, does not exercise public functions (*R (West) v Lloyds of London* [2004] 3 All ER 251). The primary consideration is not the *source* of a body's power, but the nature of the *function(s)* it performs.

▶ Secondly, a function which is intermeshed with, or 'underpinned' by, government may be public, in the sense that government bodies have control over its exercise or participate in its activities. In *R v Panel on Takeovers and Mergers, ex p Datafin plc* [1987], which is the seminal case, it was held that the Takeover Panel, a self-regulating voluntary body which acted as a City 'watchdog', was exercising public law functions. This was because it was set up in the public interest, it reported to the government and, although it did not have statutory powers itself, it was supported by the statutory powers of the Department of Trade.

▶ How much government involvement is required is a matter of degree in the particular circumstances. Relevant factors are the degree of involvement of government through finance, policy, control or regulation, and the extent to which the body in question has special powers.

▶ See, for example:

YL v Birmingham City Council [2007]: funding of a care home resident by local authority not enough without government control over the running of the home itself (Section 22.7); *Poplar Housing and Regeneration Community Association Ltd v Donoghue* [2001] 4 All ER 604: housing association formed by local authority was public; *Weaver v London and Quadrant Housing Trust* [2009]: housing association which received government funding in return for delivering government housing policy and was intensively regulated by the government was exercising public functions in respect of decisions to evict tenants since these could not be separated from its public function of allocating social housing according to government policy. It was also relevant that the association had certain special powers and was under a statutory duty to cooperate with local authorities. However, some of its functions, such as contractual arrangements with repair firms, could be private. The position of tenants who receive unsubsidised housing and pay a market rent is unclear. The dissent took a radically different and formalistic approach, regarding a function as private if it used private law powers, such as a landlord's power to evict a tenant. Housing associations have no special powers of eviction.

Hampshire CC v Beer [2003]: farmers' market run by a farmers' cooperative is exercising public functions. First, it had control over a public space in the street; second, it had previously been run by the local authority, which had now handed it over to the cooperative. This decision is questionable in the light of *Weaver*.

In *R (Trafford) v Blackpool Borough Council* [2014], it was held that a local authority was exercising a public function when it evicted a tenant (a solicitor) from office premises of which it was landlord. Here, although the matter concerned the private law of landlord and tenant, the building was publicly financed, and the decision was made under a wide statutory power to dispose of local authority land and in the context of the council's general policy. Moreover, the court took into account the particular grounds of complaint. These were characteristic public law grounds of unfairness, improper purposes and unreasonableness. This suggests an approach based on rule of law considerations.

▶ It has been held, sometimes reluctantly, that a power which is based exclusively on contract, for example the disciplinary power exercised by sports or professional associations, is a private law power (see *R v Disciplinary Committee of the Jockey Club, ex p the Aga Khan* [1993] 2 All ER 853; *R v Football Association, ex p Football League* [1993] 2 All ER 833; *R (Heather) v Leonard Cheshire Foundation* [2002] 2 All ER 936: retirement home owned by a charity). This seems artificial since many such bodies exercise their (extensive) powers for the purpose of protecting the public in much the same way as a government agency. The reality is that the individual has no choice but to submit to the jurisdiction, since the alternative is to be excluded from an area of public life in which they wish to operate. However, even in the context of government proper, it has been held that judicial review does not apply to a purely contractual relationship (compare *R v East Berkshire HA, ex p Walsh* [1985] QB 152: nurse employed under contract, with *R v Secretary of State for the Home Dept, ex p Benwell* [1985] QB 554: prison officer employed directly under statute). However, later cases such as *Blackpool* (above) suggest that, where there is an additional element of statute or governmental policy, the court may treat the matter as one of public law (*McLaren v Home Office* [1990] IRLR 338; see also Hoffmann LJ in *Aga Khan* (above), favouring the government control approach).

▶ Another possible test is whether, if the body in question did not exist, the government would have to intervene (see *R v Chief Rabbi, ex p Wachmann* [1993] 2 All ER 249). However, this is not reliable or conclusive since there is no agreement on what functions are necessary in this sense, especially in the absence of any consensus on what is meant by 'the state' in the UK. Indeed, it could apply to anything of importance. For example, if all food shops closed, no doubt the government would intervene.

19.6 Exclusivity

Although originally important and controversial, this issue has now faded into the background and will be considered only briefly. Assuming that a decision concerns a public function, must the judicial review procedure always be used or can judicial review grounds be raised in another court, such as a local county court, for example in respect of the eviction of council tenants?

The Senior Courts Act does not say that challenges in other courts are forbidden, and the remedies of declaration, injunction and damages are available in any court. When the new procedure was introduced in the late 1970s, the courts were concerned that it should not be circumvented because it is geared to the special concerns of challenging government action. The procedure was unfamiliar to lawyers, some of whom may have been reluctant or too slow to use it. The judicial review procedure is in some ways more restrictive than an ordinary action, particularly in respect of the need for permission to apply and its three-month time limit. Several cases reached the House of Lords solely on this matter, so the new procedure looked as unfriendly as the old methods.

The seminal case was *O'Reilly v Mackman* [1982] 3 All ER 1124, where prisoners sought to challenge a decision not to give them remission for good behaviour. They were outside time for judicial review and attempted to bring an ordinary civil action. Lord Diplock emphasised that a prisoner has no legal right to remission, which was an 'indulgence' from the government, but at most has a legitimate expectation that his or her case would be considered fairly. This was a matter solely of 'public law'. The House of Lords struck out their claim as an abuse of the court's process. Lord Diplock said that the judicial review procedure should normally be used in public law cases because of its safeguards which protected the government against 'groundless, unmeritorious or tardy harassment'.

Lord Diplock seemed to be staking out a position in which 'public law' was to be regarded as of special constitutional status, contrary to the notion of the rule of law eulogised by Dicey (Section 6.4). Indeed, *O'Reilly* ran counter to the recommendations of the Law Commission (Law Com No 73 (1976)) and was widely criticised as over-rigid (see Wade (1985) 101 LQR 182). The suspicion was raised that judicial review was being limited to discourage challenges to government (thus limiting access to justice, another violation of the rule of law), and to save money. In *Cocks v Thanet DC* [1983] 2 AC 286, decided soon after *O'Reilly*, the House of Lords applied *O'Reilly* harshly to hold that a claimant who had been refused housing under homelessness legislation must use judicial review rather than a more convenient action in a local county court. This was because the claimant had no right to a home, the decision being one of discretion. (The county court now has what amounts to a judicial review function in homelessness cases (Housing Act 1996; see *Runa Begum v Tower Hamlets LBC* [2003] 1 All ER 731, [7]).)

However, the cases soon drew back, and there is little left of the *O'Reilly* rule today. Indeed, in *O'Reilly* itself, Lord Diplock suggested that there should be exceptions to the exclusivity principle, but did not fully identify them. He did indicate that the judicial review procedure would not be exclusive in cases of 'collateral' challenge, where the validity of government action arises incidentally in litigation.

In *Davy v Spelthorne BC* [1984] AC 262, at 276, Lord Wilberforce expressed his distaste for the *O'Reilly* rule which he regarded as alien to English legal tradition (Section 5.1):

> The expressions "private law" and "public law" have recently been imported into the law of England from countries which unlike our own have separate systems concerning public law and private law. No doubt they are convenient expressions for descriptive purposes. In this country they must be used with caution for, typically, English law fastens, not upon principles, but upon remedies.

The courts soon began to exploit Lord Diplock's exceptions. Thus, a citizen can raise a defence in any relevant proceedings against an unlawful government claim (*Wandsworth LBC v Winder* [1985] AC 461: rent arrears; *Boddington v British Transport Police* [1998] 2 WLR 639: prosecution for smoking). An ordinary civil action might also be more appropriate if the issues are mainly factual, or where the public law aspects are peripheral (*Mercury Communications v Director General of Telecommunications* [1996] 1 All ER 575; *D v Home Office* [2006] 1 All ER 183; *Sher v Chief Constable of Greater Manchester Police* [2011] 2 All ER 364). *Roy v Kensington, Chelsea and Westminster Family Practitioner Committee* [1992] 1 AC 624 further weakened *O'Reilly*. A doctor was seeking a discretionary 'practice allowance' from the NHS. He had established entitlement to some kind of allowance, but not how much. The House of Lords suggested that whenever a litigant was protecting a 'private law right', he need not use the judicial review procedure. Alternatively, it was held that the circumstances were so closely analogous to a private claim that as a matter of discretion the action should go ahead.

Thus, it is only where the citizen has no legal rights but is making a claim based entirely on the exercise of government discretion, as was the case in *O'Reilly* itself and in *Cocks* (above), that the strict exclusivity principle applied (see also *Trustees of the Dennis Rye Pension Fund v Sheffield City Council* [1997] 4 All ER 747; *British Steel v Customs and Excise Comrs* [1997] 2 All ER 366; *Cullen v Chief Constable of the RUC* [2004], illustrating how this may turn on complex questions of statutory interpretation as to whether the citizen has a 'right' (analogous perhaps to the issue of civil rights and obligations under the ECHR (Section 21.4)).

However, the exclusivity issue has become less important. The Woolf reforms (Section 19.3) give all courts wider powers to control proceedings and require the parties to cooperate with the court in expediting proceedings. Although permission to apply is not required in an ordinary civil action, Part 24 of the CPR empowers the court to strike out a civil action at an early stage if the defendant can show that it has no reasonable chance of success. (In judicial review proceedings, however, the onus is on the *claimant* to establish a reasonable chance of success.) Moreover, cases can be transferred at any time between the Administrative Court and another court. Furthermore, the spread of the Administrative Court to regional centres and the judicial review jurisdiction of the Upper Tribunal suggest that public law is capable of being diffused among different courts.

The courts have emphasised that unless the procedure chosen is clearly inappropriate, they will not disturb it. For example, in *Clark v University of Lincolnshire and Humberside* [2000] 3 All ER 752, a student brought an action in the county court against a decision by the university to fail her. The Court of Appeal held that she was entitled to bring a civil action. Even if judicial review was appropriate, the court would not strike out a claim in another court unless the court's processes were misused, or the chosen procedure was unsuitable.

19.7 The exclusion and limitation of judicial review

19.7.1 Justiciability and 'deference'

Decisions of the High Court are not subject to judicial review at all, since the High Court has unlimited jurisdiction. In principle, all other public decision-making bodies, even those with a similar status to the High Court such as the Election Court (*R (Woolas) v Speaker of the House of Commons* [2012] QB 1) and the Upper Tribunal (*R (Cart) v Upper Tribunal* [2012]), are subject to judicial review in accordance with the rule of law, so as to ensure that special jurisdiction is coordinated with the general law. In accordance with the 'principle of legality', only clear words in a statute can exclude judicial review (*Anisminic v Foreign Compensation Commission* [1969] 2 AC 147).

However, the courts limit judicial review in many cases where interference is regarded as inappropriate because it falls outside the proper constitutional functions or expertise of the courts. The separation of powers is a primary concern. The same issue arises in human rights cases, where it is sometimes called 'margin of discretion' or, in the ECHR context, 'margin of appreciation' (Section 22.9.3).

As a common law matter, the scope of judicial review is for the courts to decide. At one extreme, there is complete refusal to decide a matter, in which case it is labelled non-justiciable. A clear example is the validity of an international treaty (Section 9.5.3). Alternatively, where it considers that the decision-maker has a high level of expertise or competence, the court may interfere only in exceptional cases. Judicial review is therefore of varying levels or thresholds (*Huang v Secretary of State* [2007] UKHL 11). The court will also respect the decisions of democratically elected bodies. It must be emphasised, however, that the fact that an issue is politically controversial or important is not in itself sufficient reason to exclude judicial review (see *R (Miller) v The Prime Minister* [2019] UKSC 41 (below)).

Some judges and writers refer to 'deference' as a description of these limits on judicial review, as signifying that the courts are accepting that the decision-maker deserves especial respect. In *R (ProLife Alliance) v BBC* [2003] 2 All ER 977 at [74]–[77], Lord Hoffmann criticised the term 'deference'. He pointed out that the matter concerns the separation of powers, namely the distinction between the role of the courts and those of the other branches of government. According to Lord Hoffmann, the courts are deferring to no one, but are upholding their constitutional function (see also Lord Bingham in *A v Secretary of State for the Home Dept* [2005] 2 AC 68 at [29]: 'relative institutional competence').

Indeed, it is arguable that deference/justiciability is not a separate doctrine but an example of the court's normal judicial review function, namely to determine the extent of the power that is under review and the weight to be attached to the justification given by the decision-maker.

Limits are of three main kinds, although in many cases they will overlap. One kind relates to the status of the decision-maker. The clearest example is that proceedings in Parliament are wholly excluded from judicial review under both the common law and Article 9 of the Bill of Rights 1688 (Section 11.6.2). This is an affirmation of the separation of powers between equal branches of government.

Other cases depend on the particular context. In *R (Cart) v Upper Tribunal* [2012], the Supreme Court held that, in view of the high status of the Upper Tribunal (Section 20.1), the court would intervene only where there is 'an important point of principle or practice, or some other compelling reason'. In *R (G) v Immigration Appeal Tribunal* [2004] it was said that, given the intention of Parliament to deal with the serious problem of delays arising from the processing of asylum cases, the court would permit judicial review only in exceptional cases. In *AXA General Insurance Ltd v HM Advocate* [2011] 3 WLR 871, it was held that the court will interfere with legislation made by the devolved democratic lawmakers within the limits of their devolved powers only if they violated fundamental principles of the rule of law (Section 16.3.1). The courts are reluctant to interfere with the decisions of independent prosecutors but will do so exceptionally where the grounds for doing so are strong and clear (*R (Corner House Research) v Director of the Serious Fraud Office (No 2)* [2008] 4 All ER 927 at [30]–[32], [58]).

The second kind of limit relates to particular grounds of review. In *Page v Hull University Visitor* [1993] 1 All ER 97, the House of Lords held that there is no review for error of law where the matter concerns specialist rules, in that case, university regulations, where the ordinary courts have less expertise than the specialist decision-maker. Where a matter concerns wide economic social or political discretion exercised by a democratically accountable body, review for reasonableness is limited (Section 18.1). Thus, in *R v Ministry of Defence, ex p Smith* [1996] QB 517, Lord Bingham said (at 556) that 'the greater the policy content of a decision and the more remote the subject is from ordinary judicial experience the more hesitant the court must necessarily be in holding a decision to be irrational'. For example, in *R (Farrakhan) v Secretary of State* [2002] QB 1391, a decision not to allow a political speaker into the UK on public interest grounds was deferred to on the basis that the Secretary of State has greater expertise and information than is available to the court and is democratically accountable for the decision (see also *R v Lichniak* [2003] 1 AC 903 at [14]). Review on the grounds of fairness and reasonableness is limited in national security cases (Section 25.1.1). In *R (Sandiford) v Secretary of State for Foreign and Commonwealth Affairs* [2014] 4 All ER 843, it was held that the rule against 'fettering discretion' does not apply to non-statutory powers (Section 17.6.3). However, the courts are unlikely to restrict review for *ultra vires* in the basic sense of outside the statutory limits.

The third and most difficult kind of limit relates to the particular subject matter of the case. This is particularly important in human rights cases. It might apply to the whole case or particular grounds of review. Some matters may make the case wholly non-justiciable. In other cases, there is a reduced intensity of review. This arises mainly in the human rights context and will be considered later (Section 22.9.3). However, it is arguable that every case depends on the particular circumstances and that there are no areas that the courts can never investigate. Indeed, it could be argued that the issue is no more than the court performing its normal task of identifying the limits of a discretionary power, in contexts where that power is unusually wide.

The following matters may be wholly outside judicial review:

> ▶ matters of international relations and foreign affairs, including the making and ratification of treaties (Section 9.5);
> ▶ matters of 'high policy': these include political decisions at the highest level of government, such as the deployment of the armed forces. However, the scope of this is uncertain. In *R v Jones (Margaret)* [2006] 2 WLR 772, Lord Hoffmann treated it as a 'constitutional principle' that the Crown's discretion to go to war was not justiciable. In *Smith v Secretary of State for Defence* [2011] 1 AC 1, Lady Hale said that the deployment of the armed forces was essentially non-justiciable. On the other hand, in *Jones* (above) Lord Bingham (at [30]) said that the courts would be slow to interfere with the conduct of foreign policy or the deployment of the armed forces but did not rule it out. In *R (Gentle) v Prime Minister* [2008] 1 AC 1356, the House of Lords refused to investigate whether the decision to invade Iraq was lawful in international law on the ground that the court had no power to decide questions of international law. However, their Lordships did not rule out intervention altogether. *R (Bancoult) v Secretary of State for the Foreign and Commonwealth Office* [2008] 4 All ER 1055 concerned a Prerogative Order in Council intended to give effect to an arrangement with the USA to provide it with a naval base. The Order excluded the former inhabitants of a UK dependency from living there. Although the challenge failed for other reasons (Section 9.4.2.1), two majority judges held that matters concerning security policy and international relations were not reviewable (at [109], [130]), Lord Hoffmann favoured a limited level of review (at [58]), and two dissenting judges held that the decision was reviewable because a fundamental right was in issue (at [72], [159]);
> ▶ the Attorney General's power to commence legal actions (*Gouriet v Union of Post Office Workers* [1978] AC 435 (Section 15.6.2));
> ▶ national security matters were once thought to be outside judicial review but are now subject to limited review (Section 25.1.1).

Many of the limits on judicial review apply to royal prerogative powers, although the royal prerogative as such is not excluded from judicial review (Section 14.6.4). This was made startlingly clear in *R (Miller) v The Prime Minister* [2019], in which the Prime Minister's advice to the Queen to prorogue Parliament, which would have had the effect of limiting debate on Brexit, was held to be justiciable. The Supreme Court acknowledged that the courts could not determine 'political questions', but observed (at [31]) that

> The fact that a legal dispute concerns the conduct of politicians, or arises from a matter of political controversy, has never been sufficient reason for the courts to refuse to consider it… almost all important decisions made by the executive have a political hue to them. Nevertheless, the courts have exercised a supervisory jurisdiction over the decisions of the executive for centuries. Many if not most of the constitutional cases in our legal history have been concerned with politics in that sense.

The Court did not consider that prime ministerial accountability to Parliament for the power of prorogation rendered it non-justiciable since such accountability was not primarily concerned with the *lawfulness* of the power, and because there would, in any event, be no possibility for Parliament to hold the Prime Minister to account if it were to be prorogued. Accordingly, determination of the question by a court was not a violation of the separation of powers but was rather upholding the principle (at [34]). The issue at hand was whether there had been an exceeding of the limits of the prerogative power in this instance, in that it had had 'the effect of frustrating or preventing, without reasonable justification, the ability of Parliament to carry out its constitutional functions as a legislature and as the body responsible for the supervision of the executive' (at [50]).

The Supreme Court's ruling that the advice given by the Prime Minister to the Queen was unlawful was highly controversial, it certainly being arguable that it represented judicial intrusion into a 'high policy' question. It was a key factor in the decision to set up an Independent Review of Administrative Law in 2020 (Sections 1.9 and 17.1), one of the tasks of which is to consider whether the principle of non-justiciability requires clarification.

What general principles identify non-justiciable issues or matters calling for deference? Jowell (2009) distinguishes between two types of deference, these being, first, constitutional principles relating to the separation of powers and respect for democracy, and second, pragmatic matters based on the practical limitations of the judicial process, bearing in mind that UK judges, unlike judges in some other countries, have limited experience of political or administrative matters. Endicott ((2018), 7.1.1) expands these into four categories: expertise, political responsibility, effective processes and respect for the allocated decision-making body (although the latter applies to all aspects of judicial review). Thus, the court is most at home with disputes with clearly defined parties and within a framework of rules; least at home with 'polycentric' matters affecting indeterminate persons and lacking agreed guidelines. Some cases, of course, fall into more than one category such as the 'high policy' cases concerning international relations and the armed forces (above).

Under Jowell's first head, matters affecting the public at large and involving a wide and nebulous range of economic, social and political factors have traditionally been regarded as unsuited to judicial resolution (see e.g. *Independent Schools Council v Charity Commission for England and Wales* [2012] 1 All ER 127 at [109]: 'public benefit'; Lord Hoffmann in *R (Alconbury) v Secretary of State* [2001] 2 All ER 929 at [76]). Under Jowell's second head are specialist decisions. These include professional judgments, aesthetic judgments such as architectural merit, moral evaluations and academic standards; here, judges lack training, resources and experience to choose between the competing arguments (*Page v Hull University Visitor* [1993]; *R (Cart) v Upper Tribunal* [2012]; *R (Sinclair Gardens Investments) v Lands Tribunal* [2005] EWCA Civ 1305; *Cooke v Secretary of State for Social Services* [2002] 3 All ER 279 at [15]–[19]; *Preston v SBAT* [1975] 1 WLR 624; *R (ProLife Alliance) v BBC* [2003]: controversial matters of morality, taste and decency).

Discretionary decisions involving the allocation of scarce resources require deference under both of Jowell's heads (see *R v Cambridge HA, ex p B* [1995] 2 All ER 129 and *R (Condliff) v North Staffs Primary Health Care Trust* [2011] EWCA Civ 910: medical treatment; *R (Douglas) v North Tyneside DC* [2004] 1 All ER 709 at [62]: student loan; *R (Bloggs61) v Secretary of State for the Home Dept* [2003] 1 WLR 2724: protection of prisoners against attack; *R (S) v Secretary of State for the Home Dept* [2013] 1 All ER 66: taxation of prisoners' wages; *Poplar Housing and Regeneration Community Association Ltd v Donoghue* [2001]: allocation of social housing; *R (Hooper) v Secretary of State for Work and Pensions* [2006] 1 All ER 487 at [32]: policy towards widows).

Both Jowell and Endicott take account of the limitations of the court's adversarial procedures in terms of the parties before the courts, procedural problems and the availability of information to the court (e.g. *R (G) v Immigration Appeal Tribunal* [2004]: delay). In *Copsey v WBB Devon Clays Ltd* [2005] EWCA Civ 932 at [39], it was said that the court should not decide general matters such as whether an employer can keep a workforce secular since it lacks the necessary consultative procedures.

The more serious the impact on individual rights, the less deference will be shown. At a very general level, it may be the uncertainty of the absence of rules or objective standards that most deters the courts from interfering.

19.7.2 Statutory exclusion of judicial review

Sometimes a statute attempts to exclude judicial review, thereby confronting a fundamental tenet of the rule of law, or 'principle of legality', that the exercise of power should be controlled by independent courts. The courts are reluctant to accept this and they construe such statutes narrowly. Clear words are required to exclude judicial review, and there are even dicta that Parliament cannot do this at all (see *R (Cart) v Upper Tribunal* [2012] at [38]). For example, a provision stating that a decision shall be 'final' does not exclude review, but merely prevents the decision-maker from reopening the matter and excludes any right of appeal that might otherwise apply (*R v Medical Appeal Tribunal, ex p Gilmore* [1957] 1 QB 574).

Even a provision stating that a 'determination of the tribunal shall not be questioned in any court of law' is ineffective to prevent review where the tribunal exceeds its 'jurisdiction' (powers). This is because the tribunal's act is a nullity and so does not amount to a 'determination'. Given that a government body exceeds its jurisdiction whenever it makes an error of law (Section 17.5), this neatly sidesteps the 'ouster clause' (*Anisminic v Foreign Compensation Commission* [1969]; see also *R (Privacy International v Investigatory Powers Tribunal* [2019] UKSC 22 (Section 25.3)).

However, given Parliament's ultimate supremacy, a sufficiently tightly drafted 'ouster clause' could surmount *Anisminic*. The court will take the policy of the Act into account. Here are some examples (for more indirect illustrations, see Elliott (2018)):

- A clause often found in statutes relating to land use planning and compulsory purchase allows challenge within six weeks and then provides that the decision 'shall not be questioned in any court of law'. The courts have interpreted this provision literally, on the ground that review is not completely excluded and that the policy of the statute is to enable development of land to be started quickly (see *R v Cornwall CC, ex p Huntingdon* [1994] 1 All ER 694).
- A provision stating that a particular action such as entry on a register or a certificate shall be 'conclusive evidence' of compliance with the Act and the matters stated in the certificate may also be effective since it does not exclude review as such but makes it impossible to prove invalidity. However, this may leave open the possibility of review for unfairness or unreasonableness (see *R v Registrar of Companies, ex p Central Bank of India* [1985] 2 All ER 79).
- Sometimes, Parliament creates a new right and, at the same time, designates exclusive machinery for deciding disputes in relation to it. This has been held effective (see *A v B (Investigatory Powers Tribunal)* [2010] 1 All ER 1149: complaints against intelligence services by a former employee against a refusal to permit him to publish his memoirs). However, the court will scrutinise the machinery to establish whether it is as good as judicial review and, if this is not the case, judicial review will be available.
- Statutes dealing with surveillance and the security services feature a clause stating that a decision cannot be challenged even on jurisdictional grounds (see Security Service Act 1989, s 5(4); Regulation of Investigatory Powers Act 2000, s 67(8)). These may exclude judicial review completely, although they do provide a right to complain to special commissioners.

Where judicial review is excluded by statute, Article 6 of the ECHR may be invoked on the ground that the ouster clause prevents a fair trial in relation to a person's 'civil rights and obligations'. The fairness of the proceedings as a whole must be considered, including the judicial review stage. On the whole, the courts have protected the right to a fair trial against attempts to restrict access to the courts (see e.g. *R (Unison) v Lord Chancellor* [2017] UKSC 51 (Section 6.1)).

Summary

▶ Judicial review is concerned with the public interest in the rule of law as well as the interests of the particular claimant. There is a special procedure for challenging decisions of public bodies in the Administrative Court. It is highly discretionary. The procedure provides the citizen with a range of remedies to quash an invalid decision, prevent unlawful action and require a duty to be complied with. Damages are only available in restricted circumstances. It provides machinery for protecting government against improper or trivial challenges. Permission to apply is required and judicial review will be refused where there is an equally convenient alternative remedy.

▶ Standing is flexible and increasingly liberal, although a third party may not be given standing where others are in a better position to challenge the decision. Apart from standing, anyone can appear with the court's permission as an intervener. However, funding constraints have been introduced with a view to preventing judicial review being used for political purposes.

▶ Judicial review applies only to public law functions, which usually include powers exercised by a wide range of bodies connected to the government or exercising statutory powers, but do not usually include powers derived exclusively from contract or consent. In some cases, the citizen may challenge public law powers outside the judicial review procedure on the basis of the rule of law principle that, where private rights are at stake, unlawful government action can be ignored.

▶ The remedies and procedure for judicial review are discretionary, so that even though an unlawful government decision is strictly speaking a nullity, the court may refuse to intervene. Delay, misbehaviour, the impact on third parties and the absence of injustice may be reasons for not interfering. Public inconvenience or administrative disruption are probably not enough in themselves but they might be relevant to the court's discretion when coupled with another factor such as delay. However, the court is now required to refuse relief where the outcome of the government decision is likely to be unaffected by the illegality.

▶ Some kinds of government power are inherently non-justiciable, but more commonly the courts are deferential to certain issues for reasons relating to the separation of powers or the limitations of judicial procedures or expertise. In these cases, judicial review may be restricted to instances of clear abuse of power.

▶ Sometimes statutes attempt to exclude judicial review. The courts are reluctant to see their powers taken away and interpret such provisions strictly. The HRA reinforces this.

Exercises

19.1 To what extent is judicial review designed to embody the public interest in accountable government and the rule of law?

19.2 To what extent have recent changes in the judicial review procedure weakened the right of the citizen to challenge government action?

19.3 What is a 'public function' for the purpose of the law of judicial review?

19.4 Claire, a civil servant working in the Cabinet Office, has evidence that the prime minister has been selling peerages to rich businesswomen in return for promises to make donations to charities specified by the prime minister's wife. Claire informs the head of her department, who replies that 'it's not possible that this has happened'. Claire now seeks judicial review. Advise her.

19.5 James, as the father of a soldier, wants to challenge the prime minister's decision to reduce the number of troops fighting overseas, on the ground that the troops are not sufficiently supported and lack resources. Advise him.

19.6 Forever Open Housing Association provides sheltered accommodation for vulnerable people. It is a charity owned by a religious sect and is part-funded and regulated by a government agency. Mary lives in a residential home owned by Forever Open, her accommodation being paid for by the local authority under its statutory obligation to arrange for care provision for the elderly. When Mary took up residence, Forever Open told her that she now had 'a home for life'. Forever Open now proposes to close the home.

  (a) Advise Mary whether she can challenge this proposal in the Administrative Court.

  (b) Suppose Mary is claiming that the fees charged by the home are unlawful. Can she sue for compensation in her local county court?

19.7 By statute (fictitious) the NHS is required to provide 'an effective health care service for all residents of England and Wales'. The statute also provides that 'the actions of any NHS hospital in relation to the provision of any service to the public shall not be questioned in any court on any ground whatsoever'. St Dave's Hospital, in the English town of Holby, is short of money and trained staff because of government financial cuts. The Secretary of State has issued a circular to all hospitals stating, among other things, that no further patients whatsoever are to be admitted for gender reassignment operations, and that hip replacement operations should normally be performed only on patients who play an active part in the economic life of the community.

(a) The Holby Transsexual Rights Society, a local pressure group, objects to the circular. It discovers the contents six months after it came into effect. Advise the society as to its chances of success in the courts.

(b) Frank, who is an unemployed resident in a hostel owned by a charity for the homeless, is refused a hip replacement operation. The charity wishes to bring an action in the Administrative Court on his behalf. Advise the charity. What would be the position if the hospital stated that, in view of Frank's general state of health and its limited resources, it would not be prepared to perform the hip replacement operation whatever the outcome of the case?

(c) The Welsh Nationalist Party wishes to challenge the circular. Advise the Party.

Further reading

Allan, 'Deference, Defiance and Doctrine: Defining the Limits of Judicial Review' (2010) 60 U Toronto LR 41

Allan, 'Judicial Deference and Judicial Review: Legal Doctrine and Legal Theory' (2011) 127 LQR 96

Cane, 'Accountability and the Public/Private Distinction' in Bamforth and Leyland (eds), *Public Law in a Multi-Layered Constitution* (Hart Publishing 2003)

Cane, 'Standing Up for the Public' [1995] PL 276

Craig, 'The Supreme Court, Prorogation and Constitutional Principle' [2020] PL 248

Elliott, 'Proportionality and Deference: The Importance of a Structured Approach' in Forsyth et al. (eds), *Effective Judicial Review: A Cornerstone of Good Governance* (Oxford University Press 2010)

Elliott, 'Through the Looking-Glass? Ouster Clauses, Statutory Interpretation and the British Constitution' in Hunt, Neudorf and Rankin (eds), *Legislating Statutory Interpretation: Perspectives from the Common Law World* (Carswell 2018)

Endicott, *Administrative Law* (4th edn, Oxford University Press 2018) ch 7

Hunt, 'Sovereignty's Blight: Why Contemporary Public Law Needs the Concept of "Due Deference"' in Bamforth and Leyland (eds), *Public Law in a Multi-layered Constitution* (Hart Publishing 2003)

Jowell, 'Judicial Deference: Servility, Civility or Institutional Incapacity?' [2003] PL 592

Jowell, 'What Decisions Should Judges Not Take?' in Andenas and Fairgrieve (eds), *Tom Bingham and the Transformation of the Law* (Oxford University Press 2009)

King, 'Institutional Approaches to Judicial Restraint' (2008) 28 OJLS 409

Mance, 'Justiciability' (2018) 67 ICLQ 739

Taggart, 'Proportionality, Deference, *Wednesbury*' [2008] New Zealand LJ 423

The term 'administrative justice' refers to a miscellaneous range of specialised bodies that make decisions affecting individuals, or that resolve disputes between the individual and the government. These range from tribunals, which have essentially become part of the judicial system, to the regulators of many business and professional activities which combine executive, legislative and judicial power.

The constitutional issues which they raise concern the separation of powers and the rule of law, the former because there are sometimes close links with the executive, the latter because the bodies may create specialised self-contained laws with their own penalties and sanctions. There are also problems of accountability since regulators are outside the central structure of ministers and Parliament. However, the ordinary courts provide supervision through their powers of judicial review, thus imposing the rule of law.

20.1 Tribunals

Numerous tribunals decide matters allocated to them by particular statutes. They are essentially simplified versions of courts of law and are created to provide a simpler, cheaper and more expert way of deciding relatively small or specialised disputes than the ordinary courts. Most tribunals hear appeals by individuals against decisions of government bodies. They therefore deal with a range of specialised and technical matters, many of which affect vulnerable people. These include education, employment, taxation, health, state benefits, transport, trading matters and land valuation, title and use. In some cases, such as employment tribunals, they decide disputes between private persons. Immigration and security services decisions have increasingly been entrusted to tribunals, thus taking important matters of individual liberty outside the ordinary courts.

Tribunals were originally called administrative tribunals, thus blurring the distinction between the judicial and executive branches and raising fears that they were not independent (see *Report of the Committee on Administrative Tribunals and Enquiries* (Cmnd 218, 1957) (the Franks Report)). Indeed, most tribunals were originally administered and funded by the very government departments that they adjudicated upon. This raises questions concerning the right to a fair trial under the ECHR.

Tribunals are usually claimed to have advantages of economy, speed and expertise compared with the ordinary courts – the price to be paid for this being rougher justice (Franks Report). Tribunal procedures are less formal than those of ordinary courts and do not necessarily involve lawyers. They are meant to be accessible to more disadvantaged people, with whom a substantial part of their work is concerned. However, they may deal with complex legal matters, and those before them are often without legal representation, so their accessibility is questionable (see Genn, 'Tribunals and Informal Justice' (1993) 56 MLR 393). Until the recent reforms (discussed below), the tribunal system had developed haphazardly, numerous tribunals having been established over the years under separate legislation. (There is a good general outline of the development of tribunals in Lady Hale's judgment in *R (Cart) v Upper Tribunal* [2012] 1 AC 663.)

Tribunals are often presided over by a lawyer chairperson sitting with one or two lay members. They are not bound by strict rules of evidence. Most tribunals must give reasons in writing for their decisions. Although legal representation is permitted, the availability of legal aid is limited. In accordance with the rule of law, tribunals are linked into the general law by virtue of the senior courts' powers of judicial review, and in many cases by rights of appeal to ordinary courts.

There is no conceptual distinction between a tribunal and a court proper. It might be important to decide whether a body is a court for the purposes of the law of contempt of court, which affects freedom of the press (Section 23.3) (see *A-G v BBC* [1981] AC 303; *General Medical Council v BBC* [1998] 1 WLR

1573), while it is necessary to rely on the definition of a court in particular statutes for particular purposes. Confusingly, some bodies have the status of a court (or 'court of record', meaning a relatively high-status court) conferred by statute, but are still called tribunals, for example the Employment Appeals Tribunal (Employment Tribunals Act 1996). Broadly speaking, a body is a court if it exercises 'judicial' functions in the sense of being required to decide questions of law relating to individual rights.

The tribunal system has been overhauled since the turn of the century. As a result of the Leggatt Report (*Tribunals for Users*, 2001), tribunals are now administered by the independent Courts and Tribunals Service, which is an Executive Agency of the Ministry of Justice. The uncoordinated range of tribunals has been systemised (see Cm 6243, 2004; Carnwath (2009)). The basic concerns were to rationalise the tribunal system, strengthen the independence of tribunals and make the tribunal system simpler, more open and user-friendly. The thrust of the reforms is to assimilate the tribunal system into the judicial branch of government.

The Tribunals, Courts and Enforcement Act 2007 gives effect to the main Leggatt reforms. In *R (Cart) v Upper Tribunal* [2011] QB 120, Sedley LJ described the reforms as a landmark in the development of the UK's 'organic constitution' (at [1]).

20.1.1   First Tier Tribunals and the Upper Tribunal

The Act creates two umbrella tribunals, which are grouped into specialist 'chambers' under powers exercised by the Lord Chancellor. These are the First Tier Tribunal and the Upper Tribunal. The First Tier Tribunal has the following Chambers: Social Entitlement; Health, Education and Social Care; General Regulatory; Tax; Immigration and Asylum; Property; War Pensions and Armed Forces Compensation. Employment tribunals do not fall within a Chamber. The Investigatory Powers Tribunal (Section 25.3) and the Proscribed Organisation Appeals Commission (see Section 25.5.2) are outside the system.

The Upper Tribunal has the status of a superior court of record which means that, like the High Court, its decisions bind lower courts (Tribunals, Courts and Enforcement Act 2007, s 3). It is primarily an appeal body from decisions of the First Tier Tribunal. The Upper Tribunal can also exercise judicial review functions similar to those of the High Court in designated cases (s 15). This is an important jurisdiction and applies to most immigration cases (Section 19.1).

The Upper Tribunal Chambers comprise the Administrative Appeals Chamber, the Tax and Chancery Chamber, the Immigration and Asylum Chamber, and the Land Chamber. The Senior President of Tribunals, who is an appellate judge, oversees and leads the tribunal judiciary (s 2). The Tribunals Procedure Committee makes procedural rules for tribunals. The Lord Chancellor has various powers of consultation and consent.

The right of appeal from First Tier decisions is only on a point of law, as opposed to fact, and permission is required from either tribunal (s 11). The right of appeal does not apply to 'excluded decisions' designated as such by the Lord Chancellor (s 11(5)).

There is a further right of appeal, again only on a matter of law, from the Upper Tribunal, to the Court of Appeal (Court of Session in Scotland). This is also subject to a requirement for permission from tribunal or court. Importantly, permission has been restricted by rules made by the Lord Chancellor to an important point of principle or practice, or some other compelling reason. This right of appeal does not apply to 'excluded' decisions. In this context, an excluded decision includes a decision by the Upper Tribunal concerning permission to appeal to itself. However, a decision of the Upper Tribunal is subject to judicial review in the High Court, albeit only in exceptional cases (see Box). In addition, both levels of tribunal can review their own decisions (ss 9, 10).

20.1.2   The independence of tribunals

Tribunal members are appointed and have security of tenure on the same basis as junior judges (Sections 7.7.3.1 and 7.7.3.2). Thus, an appointment must be selected by the Judicial Appointments

Commission. The Senior President of Tribunals makes most appointments either directly, or as advice to the Queen, but the Lord Chancellor must be consulted and, in some cases, must concur (Crime and Courts Act 2013, Sched. 13, paras 42–53). There is flexibility in deploying judges between tribunals and ordinary courts, in that certain other officials and judges of ordinary courts are *ex officio* members of both tiers (ss 4, 5, 6). Lawyer members of these tribunals are known as 'Tribunal Judges'.

Section 1 of the 2007 Act extends to tribunals the general duty to protect the independence of the judiciary imposed on the Lord Chancellor and other ministers by virtue of section 3 of the Constitutional Reform Act 2005, thus placing the tribunal system within the judicial arm of government (Section 7.4).

> The relationship between the tribunal system and the ordinary courts raises the constitutional issue of the tension between specialised areas of legal control and the rule of law in the sense of the aspiration that the same general law should apply to everyone (Section 6.4). Related to this is the wider question raised in *O'Reilly v Mackman* [1982] 3 All ER 1124 (Section 19.6) of whether public law should be a distinct legal regime concentrated in a specialised judiciary or should be diffused throughout the judicial system. The decision of the Supreme Court in *R (Cart) v Upper Tribunal* [2012] concerned whether a decision by the Upper Tribunal to refuse permission to appeal to itself was subject to judicial review. The argument against this was that the Upper Tribunal was of equivalent status to the High Court, and its members included High Court judges. Since the latter was not subject to judicial review, neither should the Upper Tribunal be. The Supreme Court held that, in principle, the Upper Tribunal was subject to judicial review. It was not completely equivalent to the High Court. Most importantly, the constitutional principle was applied that clear statutory language is required to exclude judicial review (see Section 19.7). However, the Supreme Court held that judicial review should be available only in limited circumstances. It favoured the approach taken by the Lord Chancellor's rules (above) and which relate to appeals to the Court of Appeal from the Upper Tribunal, namely that there must be an important point of principle or practice, or some other compelling reason. This test provides a filter which recognises, on the one hand, the limited resources available to the courts and the high status and level of expertise of the Upper Tribunal and, on the other, the need to comply with the rule of law by ensuring that there is independent scrutiny, and that the tribunal system is integrated into the general law. Moreover, as Lord Phillips pointed out (at [74]–[75]), the claimant has had only one hearing on the substantive issues. The court did not discuss other contexts within the tribunal system where judicial review may be available. In any case, judicial review is discretionary and the grounds of review are sufficiently flexible to accommodate the specialised context of particular tribunals (see Sections 19.1–19.3 and 19.7).

The Council of Tribunals, which previously oversaw the tribunal system and made recommendations as to procedural matters, was replaced by the Administrative Justice and Tribunals Council, which was abolished in 2013 under the Public Bodies Act 2011. An Administrative Justice Council was established in 2018 to keep the operation of the administrative justice system under review; to consider how to make the system more accessible, fair and efficient; and to provide advice to government and the judiciary on the development of the system. The Council is not part of government.

20.2 Ombudsmen

Outside the formal tribunal system, there are various mechanisms for resolving disputes between citizen and government. These include ombudsmen and internal grievance processes. The most prominent of these, and serving as a model, is the Parliamentary and Health Service Ombudsman (PHSO).

The PHSO is firmly set in the constitutional principle that the executive is primarily responsible to Parliament. It investigates, on behalf of Parliament, complaints by citizens against the central government and certain other bodies closely related to the central government (Parliamentary Commissioner Act 1967; Parliamentary and Health Services Commissioners Act 1987; Health Service Commissioners Act 1993; Parliamentary Commissioner Act 1994). The PHSO is appointed by the Crown (on the advice of the prime minister) and has security of tenure similar to that of a senior judge (Section 7.7.3.2).

Complaints about government departments and other public organisations must be made to an MP, who can decide whether to take the matter to the PHSO (complaints against Health Service bodies can be taken directly to the PHSO). This decision is not subject to judicial review by virtue of parliamentary privilege and is intended to preserve the constitutional principle that the executive is responsible to Parliament. There has been considerable criticism of this rule (the so-called 'MP filter') on the ground that MPs may be reluctant to refer to the PHSO in order to claim credit for themselves. Conversely, MPs may be unclear about the PHSO's power and refer inappropriate cases or even pass the buck by referring cases indiscriminately. The PHSO also has discretion whether or not to investigate any particular case.

The PHSO has no power to enforce its findings. It must report to the MP who referred the case. If it has found injustice caused by maladministration and considers that it has not been remedied, it may also lay a report before Parliament. The absence of direct enforcement powers may, however, be advantageous in encouraging greater frankness by those being investigated. The PHSO can see documents and interview civil servants and other witnesses, and the normal plea of government confidentiality cannot be used (Parliamentary Commissioner Act 1967, s 8(3)). However, Cabinet documents can be excluded (s 8(4)) and the PHSO must not name individual civil servants. Investigations are private (s 7(2)).

The decisions of the PHSO are subject to judicial review and are not protected by parliamentary privilege (Section 11.6; *R v Parliamentary Comr, ex p Dyer* [1994] 1 All ER 375; *R v Parliamentary Comr for Administration, ex p Balchin* [1997] JPL 917).

There are considerable limitations on the powers of the PHSO:

- Important areas of central government activity are excluded from its jurisdiction. These include foreign affairs, state security (including passports), legal proceedings, criminal investigations, government contracts, commercial activities other than compulsory purchase of land (but statutory powers exercised by contractors under privatisation arrangements are within the Ombudsman's jurisdiction), civil service employment matters, and the granting by the Crown of honours, awards and privileges.
- The PHSO can investigate only allegations of 'injustice in consequence of maladministration' (Parliamentary Commissioner Act 1967, s 5(1)). Maladministration is not defined but means broadly some defect in the *process* of decision-making as opposed to its outcome: 'bias, neglect, inattention, delay, incompetence, ineptitude, perversity, turpitude, arbitrariness and so on' (the 'Crossman Catalogue', HC Deb 18 October 1966, vol 734, col 51). The PHSO cannot directly question government policy or the merits of the exercise of a discretion (s 12; see *R v Local Comr for Administration, ex p Bradford City Council* [1979] QB 287).
- Complaints must be made in writing within 12 months of the decision that is being complained about.
- The PHSO should not investigate a matter that is appropriate to a court unless in all circumstances it would be unreasonable to expect the complainant to apply to the court. The Ombudsman can take into account the complainant's personal circumstances, but not the likelihood of success (*R v Local Comr for Administration, ex p Liverpool City Council* [2001] 1 All ER 462).

The House of Commons Public Administration and Constitutional Affairs Select Committee monitors the PHSO. Reflecting the convention of ministerial responsibility, it is for the minister concerned to decide whether to give effect to the recommendations, for example by compensating the victim of the injustice or improving departmental procedures. The executive sometimes refuses to accept the PHSO's findings (see e.g. Kirkham, 'Challenging the Authority of the Ombudsman: The Parliamentary Commissioner's Special Report on Wartime Detainees' (2006) 69 MLR 792). In this situation, the Ombudsman can lay a special report before Parliament (s 10(3)). However, in *R (Bradley) v Secretary of State for Work and Pensions* [2008] EWCA Civ 36, the Court of Appeal held that government must have 'cogent reasons' for any rejection of the PHSO's recommendations and could not lawfully simply ignore them as a matter of discretion.

Other ombudsmen include commissioners for local administration, appointed by the Crown on the recommendation of the Secretary of State, who perform a similar function in respect of local government. However, where a councillor has failed to do so, individuals can complain directly to the commissioners (Local Government Act 1974). The Local Government Ombudsman also has powers to give publicity to its recommendations. Other ombudsmen operate in a similar manner in respect of particular government bodies, for example in respect of the devolved governments of Scotland, Wales and Northern Ireland (see e.g. Public Services Ombudsman (Wales) Act 2005), European institutions, prisons and probation, social housing, the legal profession and judicial appointments (Constitutional Reform Act 2005).

In addition to ombudsmen, there are miscellaneous other bodies exercising similar functions (e.g. the Adjudicator's Office on tax matters, the Independent Complaints Reviewer for the Land Registry and the Charity Commission). These bodies often lack clear mechanisms of accountability and controls over their appointment and dismissal. However, they are likely to count as public bodies subject to judicial review (Section 19.5).

There are also internal complaints procedures offering informal hearings or alternative dispute resolution (ADR), such as mediation or arbitration within government departments and agencies. A particular example is 'administrative review' under Immigration Act 2014, s 15, in respect of decisions to remove illegal immigrants where there is no right of appeal to a tribunal (Section 9.7). These procedures are subject to the tendency of officials to prefer the informal and secretive, and a limited awareness of what independence requires. Thus, the general issue arising here is whether such internal processes are sufficiently independent to provide a fair trial in relation to a citizen's rights and obligations under the ECHR (Section 21.4.1.3), although they have the benefits of informality, speed, cheapness and responsiveness. These procedures are also subject to judicial review on normal grounds of fairness and rationality.

20.3 Inquiries

Some government decisions, particularly in relation to planning and other land use matters, are taken in the name of ministers following an inquiry held by an independent inspector. In some cases, notably routine cases under town and country planning legislation, power to make the decision is delegated to the inspector. Unlike tribunal decisions that primarily concern factual or legal issues, the subject matter of such decisions may also concern controversial political issues, relating, for example, to airport building or rural development. The inquiry system is therefore intended to provide an independent element as part of a wider process and is not a self-contained judicial process along the lines of a court.

Inquiries are sometimes described as 'quasi-judicial'. They follow a procedure broadly similar to that of a court but are more flexible and less formal. Formal rules of evidence do not apply. People whose interests are affected by the decision in question have a right to appear and give evidence. Others can speak at the discretion of the inspector, who can also allow cross-examination. This discretion is usually exercised liberally.

The independence and openness of inquiry procedures are partly safeguarded by the Tribunals and Inquiries Act 1992. This requires, in particular, that evidence must be disclosed in advance, reasons must be given for decisions, and where the minister overrules the inspector the parties must be given a chance to comment and, in the case of disagreement about facts, to reopen the inquiry.

Unlike tribunals, inquiries are primarily part of a larger administrative process and therefore not independent of political influence. Nevertheless, provided that judicial review is available, this distinctively British process has been upheld as compliant with the right to a fair trial under the ECHR. This is because there is a substantial policy or political element involved which is appropriate for the injection of a democratic element, as opposed to the impartiality expected from a court of law (see R (Alconbury Developments) v Secretary of State for the Environment, Transport and the Regions [2001] 2 All ER 929). Furthermore, the involvement of ministers and civil servants, with their close, secretive relationship, means that policy advice may not be subject to independent scrutiny at the inquiry (see *Bushell v Secretary of State for the Environment* [1981] AC 75).

Special inquiries can be held to investigate matters of public concern, for example the Leveson Inquiry (Section 23.3.3). Under the Inquiries Act 2005, a minister may establish such an inquiry, decide its terms of reference and appoint the person to hold it. There is provision for such inquiries to be open and accessible but, characteristically, the chairman and the minister have wide power to limit this. Evidence can be taken under oath, making this type of inquiry legalistic and perhaps slow. The inquiry reports to the minister. A person with a direct interest in the subject of the inquiry or a close associate cannot be appointed unless the minister considers that impartiality would not reasonably be affected (s 9). The minister must make a statement to Parliament setting out the membership of the inquiry and its terms of reference (s 6).

The inquiry chairman must 'take such steps as he considers reasonable' to ensure public access to the inquiry and its evidence. However, the minister can restrict public access to the inquiry (ss 18, 19). In particular, information must not be revealed where there is a risk of damage to the economy unless the panel is satisfied that public interest in the information outweighs the risk (s 23).

The inquiry report must be published in full subject to the minister's powers to restrict publication on grounds of 'public interest' (s 25). No time limit for publication is laid down so that a minister could delay publication for political reasons. However, judicial review would be available in such circumstances. The published parts of the inquiry report must be laid before Parliament (s 26).

A constitutional difficulty with this type of inquiry arises because senior judges are often asked to hold them. Unless the inquiry is purely a fact-finding one, this may appear to compromise the independence of the judiciary (see Beatson (2005)). Under section 10 of the Inquiries Act 2005, the Lord Chief Justice must first be consulted when it is proposed to appoint a judge to hold an inquiry.

Another form of inquiry is a Royal Commission. Again, this is established by ministers, in this case under the royal prerogative. The members of a Royal Commission are usually persons with previous links with government. The report of the Commission is usually laid before Parliament. Royal Commissions have no power to compel attendance or disclosure of information. They are sometimes employed to consider general constitutional issues, for example the Royal Commission on the House of Lords (Section 12.3).

A possible weakness of an inquiry or Royal Commission is that it does not provide any means of enforcement and may subvert more stringent methods of accountability. An inquiry may take many months or even years, during which possible legal actions or intervention by Parliament may be suspended (e.g. the Saville Inquiry into the 'Bloody Sunday' killings lasted ten years). The outcome of an inquiry is not binding, and while it may attract temporary publicity, it may thereafter be ignored. Furthermore, the terms of reference of an inquiry may be limited.

There are also parliamentary inquiries established by Parliament under its own internal powers. These comprise a mixture of MPs and outsiders. They may be more appropriate to political issues than a judicial inquiry. However, although Parliament has the power to require it, evidence is not usually on oath and the politician members of the inquiry may be ill-informed, biased and unskilled at asking probing questions. This kind of inquiry was set up in July 2012 to investigate the alleged malpractices of the banking industry.

Ministers often prefer to set up non-statutory inquiries presided over by persons of their own choosing and with procedures and terms of reference set by themselves (e.g. the Hutton (2003), Butler (2004) and Chilcot (2011) inquiries concerned with the invasion of Iraq). These sometimes sit in public but have no legal powers to compel witnesses to attend, to examine documents or to take evidence on oath, under which lying would be a criminal offence. For example, in January 2011 the Cabinet Secretary refused to permit the Chilcot Inquiry to make public letters sent by the then prime minister, Tony Blair, to George Bush, the US President.

The courts have developed the following principle in dealing with statutory government decision-making procedures: whether in the view of a 'fair-minded and informed observer' taken as knowing all the circumstances there is a 'real possibility' or 'real danger' of bias (Section 18.4). Does the appointment of inquiry chairs meet these standards, and should it? For example, in 2010 a retired judge, Sir Peter Gibson, was appointed to hold an inquiry into allegations that members of the security services had been involved in torture. Sir Peter had been the statutory overseer of the security services. He had issued reports describing the security services as 'trustworthy, conscientious and dependable'. The government maintained that, for non-statutory inquiries, there is no duty to pass legally relevant tests of impartiality and independence (see *Guardian* 30 July 2010). The Gibson Inquiry was suspended in favour of an investigation by the less independent Intelligence and Security Committee of Parliament (Section 25.3).

Illustrating that public pressures can be effective, an inquiry was established to investigate the Hillsborough stadium disaster of 1989 when 96 people were killed following the overcrowding of the stadium. Judicial inquiries and an inquest, all with limited terms of reference, had failed to satisfy the relatives of the victims. An independent panel appointed by the Home Secretary and reporting to the House of Commons was given access to all documents. Its report (HC 2012, 581) revealed wrongdoing by the police and other agencies attempting to cover up mistakes by blaming members of the public. The success of this inquiry seemed to have been due to the independence of its membership, chaired by the Bishop of Liverpool, and full public access to its proceedings. In contrast, in February 2015, a New Zealand High Court judge, Dame Lowell Goddard, was appointed to chair the independent inquiry into historic allegations of child sex abuse. This followed unsuccessful attempts to find a sufficiently independent local candidate. However, she subsequently resigned, amid disclosures as to time spent away from the inquiry and allegations that she had lost the confidence of senior staff and members of the inquiry panel (see *Guardian* 5 August 2016).

20.4   Regulators

A regulator is a public official with the power to control and channel conduct in a given area. Of course, all government could be described in these terms, but regulation has the distinctive feature that specialist officials, usually outside the main governmental bodies, directly supervise the persons or bodies under their control and intervene not only to prevent or punish misconduct, but also to impose desired policies. Regulation mainly concerns business activities but also includes charities, education bodies, health and other social welfare bodies, both public and private. Regulators make binding rules, sometimes provide finance, carry out other executive functions, such as investigations and consents or licences, and impose penalties, thus raising questions about the separation of powers and impartiality.

Most regulatory bodies are quangos or non-ministerial government departments, and so are to some extent independent from ministers (Sections 15.9 and 15.10). There is an increasing cohort of regulators, albeit with only limited powers, concerned with intrusive activities by the police and other public authorities raising the age-old question '*quis custodiet ipsos custodies?*' ('who shall guard the guards?'). These include the Information Commissioner (Section 24.2), the Investigatory Powers Commissioner's Office, the Office of Surveillance Commissioners and the Biometrics Commissioner.

There is no systematic method of accountability; this depends upon the particular statute. Analogous in this respect to tribunals, regulation creates specialised self-contained sub-systems of law which, unless there is strong connection with the ordinary courts, place the rule of law at risk. Regulation also illustrates the organic nature of the constitution, which can be changed by the accumulation of innovations introduced over time for short-term reasons. Regulation is an example of the increasing juridification of the constitution, in that the proliferation of regulatory bodies and legal mechanisms has to some extent displaced traditional modes of resolving disputes based on negotiation within personal networks.

Regulation has existed for many centuries, from the days of medieval guilds and markets, when it was a useful source of government income. During the nineteenth century, factory legislation began to impose health and safety standards which protected vulnerable workers. Environmental regulation concerning pollution originated in the nineteenth century and has developed into a leading regulatory regime. The problems of complexity and overlapping of regulators were recognised in the 1970s by the Robens Report into health and safety at work (Cmnd 5034, 1972). This did not deter the subsequent proliferation of regulators.

A new form of regulation was introduced in the 1980s as part of a policy of privatisation of public utilities including energy generation and supply, water, telecommunications, broadcasting, and public transport. These were transferred from government ownership to private companies. It was assumed, first, that market forces produced greater efficiency than state control, and second, that, provided that there was regulation, ownership was not important in relation to public benefit. The companies concerned were given special powers and privileges in order to lessen risks and so encourage investors. They are therefore hybrids between the public and private sectors rather than genuine market participants. For some purposes, they have the status of public bodies making them subject to EU directives (Section 10.3), and possibly the HRA (Section 22.7).

There is limited room for competition in these privatised industries, so the standard justification for private enterprise is missing. Regulators are therefore a substitute for competition, and their roles are complex and sometimes conflicting. Regulators provide a means of accountability to ensure that the businesses are run efficiently, they protect what competition there is, they impose public interest values (e.g. by protecting vulnerable groups in relation to electricity and gas supplies) and they act as a tool of government policy. It has been argued in the context of media regulation that the regulatory system attempts to reconcile the incommensurables of market liberalism (Section 2.3.4) and welfare liberalism (Section 2.3.5) (Vick, 'Regulatory Convergence?' (2006) 26 LS 26).

Regulation is not confined to privatised industries. Since the 1980s, regulation has proliferated, and some form of regulatory body affects most business and financial activity dealing, for example with consumer protection, environmental risks, social housing, data security, financial dealings and the governance of organisations such as professions. Bodies have been created to regulate standards in public life, including MPs (Section 11.7). The number of regulators fluctuates over time, and their functions overlap.

There is a network of diverse connections made by uncoordinated legislation between regulators, local authorities, EU bodies and the central executive. There is no single model regulatory structure, the constitution of each body depending on its particular terms of reference. Patronage is a unifying feature since the members of regulatory bodies are normally appointed by ministers, albeit sometimes with representative elements. Ministers can also often prescribe general policies.

The diversity and lack of coordination of regulators make accountability unclear and incomplete, as was the case originally with tribunals (Section 20.1). Sometimes the same body both funds and regulates its subjects, thereby raising suspicions of conflict of interest which are not necessarily removed by internal 'firewalls' within the body concerned. The right to a fair trial under the ECHR may be an issue in this context. Some regulators operate within the main government departments and are therefore fully accountable to Parliament through ministers. Many regulators are non-ministerial departments, the heads of which are directly accountable to Parliament; albeit without the day-to-day accountability provided by ministers (Section 15.9), for example the Competition and Markets Authority, the Food Standards Agency and the various utility regulators. Some are quangos outside the central government structure, the accountability of which depends on the particular statute (Section 15.10), for example the Environment Agency and the Pensions Regulator.

The BBC, which exists under the royal prerogative and is funded by government grant financed by a licence fee charged to all television users, has a curious system of semi-independent regulation in the form of the BBC Trust. This has mainly advisory powers, to ensure that the BBC acts in the public interest. Its chair is appointed by the government. It is of course important that the BBC and other broadcasters are independent of political interference. Other broadcasters are financed by advertising and regulated by Ofcom, a quango the members of which are appointed by the Secretary of State (Office of Communications Act 2002; Communications Act 2003). Ofcom now also holds the BBC's performance and editorial standards to account and regulates the competitive effects of its services.

There are also non-statutory regulators set up by an industry itself on a voluntary basis, thus creating weak accountability and conflicts of interest, for example the Press Complaints Commission, the Advertising Standards Authority and various sporting regulators. Judicial control over these bodies is problematic since they may not be regarded as 'public bodies' subject to judicial review and the HRA (Sections 19.5 and 22.7).

The Regulatory Reform Act 2001 gave ministers wide powers to intervene in the organisation and powers of regulators. The Hampton Report, *Reducing Administrative Burdens: Effective Inspection and Enforcement* (2005), concluded that there were too many regulators and that their powers overlapped unnecessarily and were insufficiently flexible and too burdensome. It recommended that there should be a reduced number of regulators operating on a more systematic basis with tougher penalties at their disposal. Key principles should include accountability; 'proportionate and meaningful sanctions for persistent defaulters'; intervention only in clear cases based on risk; easy and cheap access to advice; and avoiding duplication.

This led to the Regulatory Reform Act 2006, which gave ministers even wider powers including powers to issue codes of practice, and to alter or repeal statutes for the purposes of reorganising or abolishing individual regulators, to create criminal offences subject to limits. These abnormally wide powers are subject to the special form of parliamentary scrutiny known as the 'super affirmative procedure' (Section 13.5.5).

The McRory Report, *Regulatory Justice, Making Sanctions Effective* (2006), further widened the scope of regulation by endorsing long-standing proposals for a standardised system of flexible administrative sanctions which regulators could apply on a sliding scale of increasing stringency. The possibility of challenge in the ordinary courts should be limited. The sanctions include persuasion, warnings, the suspension or revocation of a licence, enforcement notices requiring action to be taken, stop notices preventing actions, fixed or variable civil financial penalties such as fines, and criminal sanctions in the ordinary courts. The criminal courts should have powers to impose penalties by way of restorative justice. The notion of administrative penalties is contrary to traditional ideas of the rule of law, according to which no one should be punished except for a breach of the law established in the ordinary courts (Section 6.4).

The McRory Report, other than the proposals concerning criminal prosecutions, was implemented by the Regulatory Enforcement and Sanctions Act 2008. This applies to the main national regulators, but there are exceptions including the regulators of the privatised utility companies. Ministers can make orders empowering regulators to impose civil sanctions as suggested by McRory. Safeguards include compliance with 'regulatory principles'. These require any person exercising a regulatory function to be 'transparent, accountable, proportionate, consistent' and to 'target cases only in which action is needed'. Regulators must publish reports of what enforcement action has been taken.

The term of office of a regulator depends upon the particular statute. A regulator is typically appointed by a minister for a fixed period, which can be renewed, and the regulator can be dismissed by the Secretary of State within that period on specified grounds, including misconduct (see e.g. Office of Communications Act 2002, Sched.). The appointment processes of many regulators are to some extent supervised by the Commissioner for Public Appointments in an attempt to ensure that powers of patronage are not abused (Section 15.10). However, characteristic of external safeguards over executive bodies, the Commissioner's role is only advisory. The constitutional problems raised by regulation thus exemplify the general problems of accountability in the UK Constitution, namely lack of coherence which allows blame to be transferred to others, influence, patronage and secrecy (House of Lords Constitution Committee, HL 2003–04, 68).

Methods of regulation vary with changing fashions in government. The traditional method, 'command and control', consists of imposing penalties for conduct disapproved of by the regulator. This requires inspections and audits and ultimately depends on the criminal law. Unlike the case with tribunals, the discretion of the regulator means that negotiation and compromise is a regulatory tool. This can lead to allegations of 'regulatory capture' according to which there is a risk that regulators, anxious to be approved of, either identify with the interests of those they regulate or try to please the government, in both cases compromising their independence. From the late 1990s, 'self-regulation' or 'light touch' regulation became fashionable, appearing to fit the prevailing ideology of market liberalism as well as the informal networks characteristic of UK government. This involved the regulator intervening only on the basis of 'risk', and required the regulatee to monitor itself, including assessment of risk. As banking scandals from 2008 onward illustrate, this method of regulation increases the risk of abuse, but without reducing that of regulatory capture. For example, the Financial Services Authority, which until 2013 regulated banks and other financial institutions, assisted the bodies that it regulated in various lobbying campaigns (*Guardian* 13 July 2012). Moreover, internal methods of regulation raise the problem of bias, where a regulator is a member of the governing body of the organisation itself, and so has a vested interest in its well-being (see *R (Kaur) v ILEX Appeal Tribunal* [2012] 1 All ER 1435, [18]–[24]: vice president of organisation disqualified from sitting on appeal tribunal (Section 18.4)).

One response to concerns about the discretion exercised by regulators is to favour objective methods of regulation, using quantitative data such as statistics devised in the light of prescribed targets or indexes. However, these may lead to unfairness and a failure to take relevant factors into account, which are grounds for judicial review. An extreme version of objective regulation not used in the UK relies on what Brownsword (2005) calls a 'technical fix' whereby computer technology embeds required patterns of behaviour in the operations of the business being regulated so that undesirable behaviour is difficult (e.g. speed and distance monitoring on a vehicle which cuts off power when prescribed limits are exceeded). This may be cheap and reliable as a method of control but it is open to fraud, and, as Brownsword points out, it puts openness and accountability at risk and arguably affronts human dignity.

As discussed previously (Section 15.7), accountability has two aspects. First, it requires a method by which decisions can be corrected and the official punished for failure. The former is provided primarily by the courts in the same way as over other public officials. However, judicial review is limited to serious failures of procedure or abuse of power, and the wide discretion given to a regulator may limit the scope of judicial review (see e.g. *Interbrew SA v Competition Commission* [2001] EWHC 367 (Admin)). Otherwise, accountability is haphazard. There is no automatic right of appeal, but a minister can provide for an appeal to a tribunal. Depending on the particular regime there are sometimes rights of appeal to the court or a special tribunal, sometimes an ombudsman. Moreover, the McRory Report (above) favoured an appeal to a tribunal rather than to the ordinary courts. There is a General Regulatory Chamber of the First Tier Tribunal.

Regulators are accountable to ministers and (at least in the case of those that are non-ministerial departments) to Parliament (Section 15.9). However, because regulators exist outside the normal chain of responsibility that applies between a minister, his or her department and Parliament, there is limited opportunity for scrutiny. Their annual reports and accounts must be presented to Parliament and their leaders often appear before select committees (Section 13.5.3). The minister's accountability may be confused because he or she is not directly responsible for the regulator's decisions, except where the regulator is part of the minister's own department (Section 15.7).

Accountability also means providing the public with information and explanation. Methods of accountability, such as duties to consult, to hold meetings in public and to publish information about policies and decisions, depend on particular statutes (see e.g. Utilities Act 2000; Communications Act 2003; Postal Services Act 2000; Railways Act 2005). These devices are increasingly being used, at least by the utilities regulators. As public bodies, most regulators are subject to the Freedom of Information Act 2000, which requires some information to be disclosed on request (Section 24.2). However, exemptions in the Act, notably 'commercial confidentiality' may provide a justification for refusal.

Summary

▶ Tribunals adjudicate relatively minor and specialised disputes between government and individual. They are relatively informal but subject to special safeguards to secure their independence and fairness. Reforms have rationalised the tribunal system and bedded tribunals more firmly into the judicial branch of government.

▶ A range of ombudsmen investigate complaints of maladministration against government and other bodies on behalf of the citizen. To preserve the constitutional principle of ministerial responsibility the Parliamentary and Health Service Ombudsman reports to Parliament and has jurisdiction, in respect of government department and public organisations, only through an MP. Ombudsmen do not normally have enforcement powers.

▶ Internal complaints procedures raise the problem of whether they are sufficiently independent to provide a fair trial in relation to a citizen's civil rights and obligations under the ECHR, but they offer responsive, speedy and informal means of resolving small-scale disputes.

▶ Public inquiries form part of the process for making some governmental decisions. They are presided over by independent inspectors, have an element of public participation and are subject to special safeguards. Ministers may set up special inquiries into particular events or issues. These have limited independence.

▶ The use of regulators to control a wide range of private bodies has increased in recent years. They have substantial powers, combining lawmaking, executive and judicial functions including the imposition of penalties. Regulators take several forms and their accountability is complex and uncertain.

Exercises

20.1 Are tribunals properly termed 'administrative tribunals'?

20.2 Outline the constitutional problems raised by the following:

(i) inquiries;

(ii) regulation.

20.3 Imagine that you are a minister with responsibility for regulating the admission of students to university. What structure would you set up for dealing with complaints and how would it be accountable, if at all?

20.4 Compare the merits of the ombudsmen and judicial review as methods of resolving disputes between the individual and the government.

20.5 There have been widespread allegations in the press that politicians and civil servants have been receiving payments and other benefits, such as retirement jobs and holiday homes, in return for giving favours to the leaders of banks and other influential financial organisations, both domestic and overseas. The government sets up an inquiry under the Inquiries Act 2005. The inquiry's terms of reference exclude any investigation into overseas organisations. The minister appoints Lord Bray, a former banker who was recently given a peerage, to hold the inquiry. Lord Bray announces that members of the public may attend the inquiry in person but will have no access to any written or electronic material unless they pay a charge. He appoints two bankers with whom he has worked in the past to advise the inquiry. The eventual inquiry report largely exonerates any high-level public official. However, at the same time as the report is delivered to the minister, Lord Bray is photographed by a journalist receiving a large bundle of banknotes from a special adviser to the prime minister in a London hotel. The minister responsible for the inquiry report postpones its publication indefinitely.

Advise the Campaign for Cleaner Government, a pressure group, as to any legal remedies available to them in respect of these events (chapters on judicial review might also be consulted).

Further reading

Ambler and Boyfield, *Reforming the Regulators* (Adam Smith Institute 2010)

Black, 'Regulatory Accountability: Capacities, Challenges and Prospects' in Bamforth and Leyland (eds), *Accountability in the Contemporary Constitution* (Oxford University Press 2013)

Brownsword, 'Code, Control and Choice: Why East is East and West is West' (2005) 25 LS 1

Beatson, 'Should Judges Conduct Public Inquiries?' (2005) 121 LQR 221

Carnwath, 'Tribunal Justice: A New Start' [2009] PL 48

Elliott, 'Ombudsmen, Tribunals, Inquiries: Re-fashioning Accountability beyond the Courts' in Bamforth and Leyland (eds), *Accountability in the Contemporary Constitution* (Oxford University Press 2013)

Kirkham, 'Judicial Review and Ombuds; a Systematic Analysis' [2020] PL 680

Kirkham and Gill (eds), *A Manifesto for Ombudsman Reform* (Palgrave Macmillan 2020)

Laurie, 'Assessing the Upper Tribunal's Potential to Deliver Administrative Justice' [2012] PL 288

Loughlin, *Foundations of Public Law* (Oxford University Press 2010) ch 15

Oliver, Prosser and Rawlings (eds), *The Regulatory State: Constitutional Implications* (Hart Publishing 2010)

Skelcher, 'Reforming the Oversight of Administrative Justice 2010–14: Does the UK Need a New Leggatt Report?' [2015] PL 215

Thomas, 'The Future of Public Inquiries' [2015] PL 225

Thomas, 'Administrative Justice, Better Decisions, and Organisational Learning' [2015] PL 111

Part VI

Fundamental rights

Chapter 21

Human rights and civil liberties

21.1 Introduction: the nature of human rights

The concept of human rights attempts to identify fundamental interests common to all human beings which have a special status, in the sense that they should not be violated, either at all or only in extreme circumstances. In *Surrey County Council v P* [2014] AC 896, [36], Lady Hale remarked that 'the whole point about human rights is their universal character'. Human rights did not become a prominent legal issue in the UK until the aftermath of the Second World War, which produced a worldwide reaction against the atrocities of the Nazis. Human rights concern basic needs such as physical integrity, personal freedom, property, privacy and religious choice; political interests such as freedom of expression and association; social interests such as education and family life; and the protection of the rule of law, in the form of the right to a fair trial.

Three interrelated issues underlie human rights law. First, what is a human right? Is it anything other than a political claim? Attitudes to this question influence the importance we attach to human rights law. The classic Enlightenment writers, notably Locke (Section 2.3.2), thought that there were certain natural rights given by God which it is the state's duty to protect. In his case, these were life, health, liberty and property. For Hobbes, by contrast, there are no rights other than those created and enforced by law. To Hobbes, 'natural rights' are essentially rational reasons for action rather than rights as such. They include primarily self-defence, 'do-as-you-would-be-done-by' and the honouring of promises.

There is no agreement as to how we identify a human right. Some claim that they are revealed by God; others, without explaining why, claim that humans have a special 'dignity'. For example, the UN Universal Declaration of Human Rights (Cmd 7226, 1948) is founded on the 'inherent dignity … of all members of the human family', equality, rationality and 'brotherhood' (Preamble, Article 1). Others, following Kant, derive human rights from apparently self-evident rational truths such as 'equality' or 'autonomy'. For example, Dworkin (*Freedom's Law* (Oxford University Press 1996)) argues that certain interests, such as freedom of expression and the right to a fair trial, are non-negotiable conditions of a democratic society because they underpin equality, this being the nearest we can get to a bedrock principle. A more modest claim derives from Hume (Section 2.3.3), namely that human rights are driven by our natural sympathy for others and that we create customs underpinning particular ways of life which we desire to preserve.

Grandiose theoretical and universal claims for human rights face the difficulty that they may be too vague to be directly applied and different cultures may understand particular rights and their limits in different ways. From a utilitarian perspective, Jeremy Bentham, albeit in the different context of the French political manifesto of *The Rights of Man*, regarded the notion of rights as 'nonsense on stilts', except in the sense of interests protected by particular laws. His argument was that abstract rights are too vague to apply in practice so as to decide when they should give way to other concerns. This is a central issue today. Politicians and officials drafting laws or international treaties might take refuge in vagueness as a way of producing agreement while leaving the hard questions to be decided later by the courts. Indeed, this was the case with the ECHR (see Marston, 'The UK's Part in the Preparation of the ECHR' (1993) 42 ICLQ 796).

This leads to the second issue. What is the legal basis for a statement of fundamental rights? The UK relies primarily on the ECHR and the European Court of Human Rights in Strasbourg which, under the HRA, are partly incorporated into domestic law. The ECHR came into force in 1953 as an international treaty under the auspices of the Council of Europe, which was established in 1949 and has 47 members. It is partly based on the Universal Declaration of Human Rights, a resolution of the UN General Assembly (1948) as a response to Nazi atrocities. The ECHR concentrates on the protection of individual freedom against state interference, rather than on what are known as 'second-and third-generation rights', these being respectively social claims such as housing or health care and collective interests such as environmental quality.

Other treaties deal with these matters but are not binding in UK law (see e.g. UN International Covenant on Social, Economic and Cultural Rights (1976)). The EU Charter of Rights overlaps with the ECHR and also includes economic and social rights. It is partly binding through EU law but only in respect of rights similar to the ECHR (Section 10.3.2) but no longer applies to the UK after Brexit. There are also important treaties dealing with specific human rights, such as the UN Refugee Conventions (1951 and 1957) and the UN Convention against Torture (1987). These have been incorporated into UK law (Section 9.7.4; Criminal Justice Act 1988, s 134). The UN Convention on the Rights of the Child (1989), Council of Europe Conventions on Action Against Trafficking in Human Beings (2008) and the Protection of Children against Sexual Exploitation and Sexual Abuse (2010) have not been incorporated into UK law, but have effect indirectly under the HRA since the Strasbourg cases require that relevant treaties be taken into account.

A particular problem with a written charter of rights, such as the ECHR, is that it is vulnerable to different views as to how flexibly it should be interpreted. The contest is akin to that in relation to domestic statutes, that is, whether the literal language should be strictly followed, or a broader approach taken, based on the purpose of the legislation. In respect of the ECHR, the Strasbourg court has adopted the 'living instrument' principle, which enables it to adjust the application of the Convention to meet new circumstances over time. This has led to claims that court is overreaching itself, comparable to the debate in the USA between those who claim that the Constitution should be interpreted according to the 'original intention' of its eighteenth-century founders and those who take a broader view (Section 21.3). The common law, which undoubtedly responds to changing times, also provides a basis for human rights arguments (Section 21.2).

The third issue is: who should have the last word in human rights disputes? In particular, should there be a bill of rights protected against being overridden by the democratic lawmaker? Even if we accept that the concept of human rights is meaningful and should be embedded in the law, nothing follows automatically from this as to what is the best mechanism for protecting it. The ultimate decision-maker might, for example, be a court as in the US, an elected lawmaker as in the UK or a special body as in France.

There is a continuing debate as to whether the courts or the democratic Parliament should have the last word. Human rights disputes differ significantly from those with which the courts traditionally deal. There is fundamental and apparently never-ending disagreement about the meaning and application of human rights concepts, and a court often has a wide discretion to make a subjective value judgment. Dissenting judgments are common. Human rights cases often require a judge to decide the extent to which a right should be sacrificed to another right or to some important public goal using the subjective notion of 'proportionality' meaning, broadly, that an interference with a right must not be excessive (Section 22.9.2).

Lawyers often use the metaphors of 'balance' and 'weighing' in the human rights context. However, human rights may be incommensurable, meaning that, when they conflict, there is no objective standard or common measure which can be applied to choose between them or to weigh them against other values (e.g. freedom of expression v privacy, family life v security). Sometimes, legislation sets out a pecking order representing a democratic choice (e.g. Immigration Act 2014, s 19 (Section 9.7.4)). Often, especially in privacy cases, a utilitarian approach is taken: the greatest good of the greatest number. However, this contradicts the purpose of a human right, which is that certain individual rights cannot be outweighed by the majority good, for example when torture is contemplated that might save the lives of hostages.

While judges are good at interpreting and logically applying definite rules, human rights occupy territory where judges have no special expertise, requiring them to be either political philosophers or politicians, or to resort to semantic evasion. For instance, issues about how far personal freedom should be curtailed for security reasons may turn upon the question of the line between a 'deprivation of liberty' and a 'restriction on liberty' (Section 21.4). The judge must inevitably be influenced by his or her subjective values.

21.2 The common law

English lawyers have traditionally used the terminology of negative freedom (Section 2.4) and civil liberties, rather than the positive language of rights. The traditional common law standpoint has been residual, namely that everyone is free to do whatever the law does not specifically prohibit. In Hobbes's words, 'freedom lies in the silence of the laws'. Judges and other commentators from Dicey onwards have regularly praised the common law as a buttress of freedom and individual rights (see Gearty, *On Fantasy Island: Britain, Europe and Human Rights* (Oxford University Press 2016)).

In the UK Constitution, based as it is on unlimited parliamentary power that can readily be harnessed by political parties in thrall to vested interests and volatile public opinion, it may be difficult to ensure that the laws are indeed silent. Moreover, the notion of negative freedom assumes that all freedoms are of equal value. Thus, Dicey may appear complacent: 'English law no more favours and provides for the holding of public meetings than for the giving of public concerts... A man has a right to hear an orator as he has a right to hear a band or eat a bun' ((1915) 353).

The common law's residual approach therefore depends on trusting the lawmaker not to enact intrusive laws, and trusting the courts to interpret laws in a way sympathetic to individual liberty. This violates republican principles by treating us as 'happy slaves' content with a kind master. The common law can develop in two directions. First, it can draw on Strasbourg jurisprudence by analogy to the ECHR, and second, it can develop its own jurisprudence. This could include rights both within and outside those protected by the HRA. Should this result in more limited protection than that afforded by the HRA, the Act would prevail.

The courts have developed common law principles analogous to human rights in the form of the 'principle of legality', according to which fundamental rights can be overridden only by clear statutory language (Sections 6.6, 8.5.6 and 17.4). In *R (Osborn) v Parole Board* [2013] UKSC 61, [56]–[57] which involved the common law right to a fair hearing, the Supreme Court emphasised that the protection of human rights is not a separate area of law under the HRA but permeates the domestic legal system, and that compliance with domestic law underpins the ECHR (see also *Kennedy v Charity Commission* [2014] UKSC 20; *DSD v Commissioner of Police of the Metropolis* [2015] 3 WLR 966, [64]–[68]). In this context, the label of 'constitutional rights' has been applied, albeit this is of uncertain meaning (see *R v Lord Chancellor ex parte Lightfoot* [2000] QB 597, 609).

The principle of legality is part of the common law of judicial review, independently of the concept of human rights. However, the principle apparently applies only to domestic legislation and cannot therefore be called in aid to help interpret a treaty (Section 9.5.5; *R (Al-Saadoon) v Secretary of State for Defence* [2015] EWHC 715 (Admin), [269]). Although customary international law is a source of the common law and could be invoked to protect a fundamental right, customary law cannot apparently be used directly to develop the law in an area covered by statute, in this case, the ECHR and the HRA (at [273]).

The judicial review concept of 'unreasonableness' (Section 18.1) can also be used to protect a fundamental right. This overlaps with the human rights standard of proportionality. However, the interrelation between the concepts, and indeed the whole question of unreasonableness, has become a morass of confusion. It has been constantly reiterated that the depth in which the court can review government action depends on the particular context. Notions of 'sliding scale', 'variable standard', 'intensity of review', 'anxious scrutiny', and 'deference' have been used to express this, but without an overall structure. Nor has it been established whether proportionality should apply to domestic law challenges outside ECHR and EU cases (see Section 18.1.1; and *Keyu v Secretary of State for Foreign and Commonwealth Affairs* [2015] UKSC 69; *Kennedy v Charity Commission* [2014], [51] [272]–[273]; *Pham v Secretary of State for the Home Department* [2015] 1 WLR 1591, [96], [113], [115]; *R (Youssef) v Secretary of State for Foreign and Commonwealth Affairs* [2016] 2 WLR 509).

But the common law cannot surmount the creeping erosion of liberty by the accumulation of statutes, which, taken individually, are relatively innocuous, but together add up to a formidable armoury of state powers. For example, numerous provisions were enacted on behalf of the governments of 1997–2010, restricting individual liberty and increasing surveillance to combat anti-social behaviour and terrorism. Moreover, legislation enacted to deal with a particular problem may be used for other purposes. The Terrorism Act 2000, for example, was used to remove an elderly heckler from the 2005 Labour Party Conference. Reminiscent of the eighteenth century, the Serious Organised Crime and Police Act 2005 was used to arrest a demonstrator for possession of a magazine article criticising the government (see HL Deb 1 February 2006, vol 678, cols 231, 239). Anti-terrorism powers in the Regulation of Investigatory Powers Act 2000 have been used by local government employees to spy on citizens in order to enforce minor transgressions. A notorious gap in the common law was that it did not recognise a right of privacy (*Malone v MPC* [1979] Ch 344) (Section 25.3).

It is claimed that the common law, being open to any argument and treating all parties as equals, is especially suitable for a liberal society (Allan, *Constitutional Justice* (Oxford University Press 2001)). Indeed, until the HRA, the UK had resisted incorporation of the ECHR on the basis that the common law provided equivalent protection (see *Brind v Secretary of State for the Home Dept* [1991] 1 AC 696; Lord Goff in *A-G v Guardian Newspapers (No 2)* [1990] 1 AC 109, 283). However, the two approaches are different, in that ECHR requires special justification to override a right, whereas in the common law any sufficiently clearly worded statute will do.

21.3 The European Convention on Human Rights

The legal role of the ECHR centres on its court in Strasbourg, France. The Council of Europe also has a wider political role in assessing and monitoring human rights matters. The Strasbourg court comprises 47 judges, one from each Member State. A judge must either have held high judicial office or be a 'jurisconsult of recognised competence', a term which includes academic lawyers. The judges are elected by the Parliamentary Assembly of the Council of Europe for a non-renewable term of nine years, with an age limit of 70 (Art 22). The Assembly comprises representatives from the parliaments of the Member States. Each member nominates three candidates.

The court sits in Chambers comprising seven judges, including a judge from the state involved. The Grand Chamber, comprising the senior members of the court and other judges chosen by lot, is reserved for the most important cases referred to it from a Chamber. The court system and the implementation of the court's judgments are monitored by the Committee of Ministers of the Council of Europe and, in the UK, by the Parliamentary Joint Committee on Human Rights.

The ECHR has three roles under the UK Constitution:

1. Individuals can petition the European Court of Human Rights in Strasbourg alleging that the state has violated their rights under the Convention. A petition to Strasbourg can be made only if the claimant has first exhausted all remedies in domestic courts. The court may award compensation or require the state to change its law. However, its decisions are binding only in international law. Indeed, the Strasbourg court has sought to emphasise that the protection of human rights is primarily the responsibility of national courts, with the court offering a dialogue between domestic and international jurisdictions (see *Belgian-Linguistic Case* (1979–80) 1 EHRR 252, [10]). The Court applies the Convention in the context of international law and other treaties (see *Demir v Turkey* (2009) 48 EHRR 54 [65], [67], [85]). Thus, an unincorporated treaty can enter UK law through Strasbourg, although there may be disagreement as to whether this is the case in relation to a particular right (e.g. *R (SG) v Secretary of State for Work and Pensions* [2015] UKSC 16: International Convention on the Rights of the Child).

2. The HRA incorporates into UK law the main rights listed in the Convention, but not the Convention itself, and provides a special mechanism for enforcing them which is designed to preserve parliamentary supremacy. As Lord Bingham pointed out in *R (Al-Skeini) v Secretary of State* [2008] 1 AC 153, [10], rights *under* the Convention differ from rights created by the 1998 Act *by reference to* the Convention

(see also Lord Nicholls in *Re McKerr* [2004] 1 WLR 807, [25]). However, the Act requires the court to take into account Strasbourg jurisprudence, a provision which has inspired extensive debate (Section 22.2). Thus, the HRA exists side by side with the Convention itself.

3. Independently of the HRA, as a treaty, the Convention should be taken into account by domestic courts when interpreting statutes, at least where they are ambiguous (Section 9.5.5). In *R (SG) v Secretary of State for Work and Pensions* [2015], at [254]–[255], Lord Kerr suggested that all human rights treaties should automatically be legally binding. The rationale behind this appears to be that the international rule of law embodied in human rights values should be all-pervading. The common law should probably also be developed in the light of the Convention. Thus, the Convention serves as a baseline against which the law can be assessed and reformed. For example, the Convention notion of proportionality has been much employed in the drafting of security and anti-terrorism legislation (Chapter 25).

The application of the ECHR by Strasbourg brings considerable flexibility and uncertainty. This has been promoted by the Strasbourg court's claim that the ECHR is a 'living instrument' to be interpreted in the light of changing times (e.g. *Scalk and Kopf v Austria* [2010] ECHR 1996: same-sex couples). For example, in *Hirst v UK (No 2)* (2006) 42 EHRR 849, the decision that the UK's blanket ban on convicted prisoners voting was contrary to the right to 'free and fair elections' was justified on the basis that, in the light of modern-day penal policy and current human rights standards, valid and convincing reasons must be put forward for the continued justification of maintaining such a general restriction.

Flexibility and uncertainty are also promoted by the Strasbourg court's doctrine that the rule of law in the sense of non-arbitrariness runs through the whole Convention (*James v UK* (2013) 56 EHRR 12: discretionary power to release prisoners). The meaning of 'arbitrariness' varies with the context. In relation to imprisonment after a conviction, for example, it has the narrow meaning that the detention conforms to the objects of the governing legislation. In other contexts, it might require a decision to be made in good faith and to be proportionate (not excessive) to the legitimate aims of the state (*Saadi v UK* (2008) 47 EHRR 17, [69]; *R (Haney) v Secretary of State for Justice* [2014] UKSC 66, [25]).

A principle of 'fair balance' between individual rights and the wider interests of society also runs through the whole Convention (e.g. *MT (Algeria) v Secretary of State for the Home Office* [2010] 2 AC 110 [207]). These doctrines have become the focus of virulent political attacks on the Strasbourg court, which is said to be extending its reach at the expense of national sovereignty. The concept of the 'margin of appreciation' (below) attempts to meet this concern, meaning that the state is sometimes allowed discretion as to the application of the Convention.

Another device that has enraged opponents of Strasbourg is the doctrine that the Convention concepts are 'autonomous' in the sense that the court gives them its own meaning irrespective of their meaning in national law (e.g. *Kostovski v Netherlands* (1989) 12 EHRR 434: 'witness').

The court requires practical and effective remedies to enforce the rights under the Convention (*Siliadin v France* (2006) 43 EHRR 16: forced labour).

There have been many Strasbourg decisions adverse to the UK, notably in connection with restrictions on publications (Section 23.3), treatment of prisoners (e.g. *James v UK* [2013], security and anti-terrorism powers (Section 25.5), detention of mental patients (*X v UK* (1981) 4 EHRR 188) and military justice (*Findlay v UK* (1997) 24 EHRR 221). In response to adverse Strasbourg decisions, Parliament usually changes the law, albeit not necessarily in a generous direction (e.g. changing the Immigration Rules to prevent both wives and husbands of persons settled here entering the country in response to the Strasbourg ruling in *Abulaziz v UK* (1985) 7 EHRR 471, which held that the previous rule was discriminatory in allowing wives but not husbands to enter). The government may also respond to adverse Strasbourg decisions by delaying change (e.g. *Goodwin v UK* (2002) 35 EHRR 18: transsexuals' ability to marry; *Hirst v UK* [2006]: prisoners' voting rights: see Section 12.5.5) or by derogating from (opting out) of parts of the Convention (Section 21.4).

21.3.1 The margin of appreciation

The concept of the 'margin of appreciation' is a central feature of the relationship between the Strasbourg court and the national governments. It means that the Strasbourg court gives national authorities a substantial measure of freedom in applying the Convention to their own circumstances. It plays two roles. First, it is a safety valve where there are national differences in political, cultural, religious or moral values or practices, since if an international tribunal intervened it might forfeit respect. Second, it applies in areas that are considered unsuitable for a court to decide, namely controversial social, economic and political areas, or areas involving special expertise.

Under the ECHR, the margin of appreciation derives from the duty of all states under Art 1 of the Convention 'to secure to everyone within their jurisdiction the rights and freedoms defined (in the Convention)', coupled with Art 19, which requires the court to ensure that this is done. Under the margin of appreciation, the court lays down general standards, leaving it to individual states to decide, within limits, how to apply them. Where the margin of appreciation applies, the Strasbourg court will not substitute its views for those of the state but will intervene only where the decision is clearly flawed or out of line with widely shared values (see *Handyside v UK* (1976) 1 EHRR 737 (the foundational case): pornography).

There is a similar doctrine in domestic law, usually called a 'margin of discretion', but its application differs from the Strasbourg model (Section 22.9.3).

21.3.2 Positive duties

The ECHR has traditionally been concerned mainly with 'negative' rights protected against state interference, as opposed to imposing a positive duty on the state to provide a benefit. There are two kinds of positive duty. The first is where the state is required to provide some positive benefit or facility, such as welfare services. In a democracy, courts are reluctant to impose this kind of duty on the state since it may involve choices about public spending that are regarded as more appropriate to an elected body. However, positive duties are sometimes imposed on the basis that as a 'living instrument' the Convention must respond to contemporary problems. One such case is that of extreme hardship (Section 21.4.1). The courts have constantly asserted that there is normally no duty under human rights law to provide public services such as welfare benefits, housing and education, although, if they are provided, they must comply with human rights principles such as non-discrimination (e.g. *R (Tigere) v Secretary of State for Business, Innovation and Skills* [2015] 1 WLR 3820: higher education; *R (SG) v Secretary of State for Work and Pensions* [2015]: welfare benefits). Moreover, some kinds of liberal may object to the impact of positive rights on the free market and the possible conflict with individual liberty and initiative (Section 2.3; see Sunstein, 'Against Positive Rights' (1993) 2 *East European Constitutional Review* 35).

The second kind of positive duty is more common. By virtue of Art 13 (duty to provide an effective remedy), the state must take positive steps to prevent a right being violated. First, this requires the state to enact the laws necessary to protect the right against interference both by officials and private persons; and, second, it imposes a procedural duty to enforce them properly and to investigate violations, such as deaths of persons in custody. For example, the courts must ensure not only that the media is free to inform the public, but also that the privately owned press acts responsibly and respects the privacy of individuals (*Douglas v Hello!* [2001] 2 All ER 289, [91] (Section 23.5)). Similarly, the courts must ensure that private employers do not discriminate on grounds of religion or sexual preferences (*Eweida v UK* [2013] ECHR 37).

In *Keegan v Ireland* (1994) 18 EHRR 342 [49], it was said that the boundaries between the state's positive and negative obligations do not lend themselves to precise definition, and that regard must be had to the fair balance throughout the Convention between the competing interests of the individual and of the community as a whole. The state's positive obligation is therefore not absolute, and what is required varies according to the importance of the right in question. For example, torture requires especially stringent protection (*Cestaro v Italy* [2015] ECHR 352), but violations of Art 8 (privacy) less so (*X and Y v Netherlands* (1985) 8 EHRR 235). To make the obligation absolute would place an unacceptable burden on the state, and the court will give the government a substantial margin of appreciation in relation to the measures it takes (see Fredman, 'Human Rights Transformed: Positive Duties and Positive Rights' [2006] PL 562).

21.4 The main Convention rights

The structure of the Convention rights is as follows. There are three kinds of right:

1. Some rights, which are either especially important or very narrow, namely Articles 3 (torture or inhuman or degrading treatment), 4(1) (slavery), 6 (fair trial), 12 (marriage) and Protocol 1, Article 2 (education) are absolute rights. These cannot in any circumstances be overridden.
2. Some important rights are absolute, but subject to exceptions. This means that the prescribed exceptions fall outside the Convention altogether, but otherwise, the right cannot be overridden. Articles 2 (life), 4(2) (forced labour), 5 (physical liberty) and 7 (retrospective crimes) fall into this category of 'conditional' (or 'limited') rights.
3. The other rights, broader in nature, are 'qualified rights' meaning that they can be overridden if the court thinks appropriate on defined grounds relating to the public interest and the rights of others (Arts 7–11; Art 14 (indirectly); Protocol 1, Art 1). The court is required to balance the right against the competing concerns. The question of overriding qualified rights will be discussed in the next chapter (Section 22.9).

The difference between the qualified rights and the other kinds of right may sometimes be blurred, since the definition of a Convention right is often vague, enabling the courts to use public interest arguments to limit its meaning or application even where there is no override available (e.g. the meaning of 'deprivation' of liberty as opposed to 'restriction' of liberty (e.g. *Austin v UK* (2012) 55 EHRR 14, Section 21.4.2.3)). Usually, this works against the claimant who has to bring him or herself within the scope of the right in question, whereas in applying the separate public interest overrides, the onus is on the state to justify interfering with the right. The court may also narrowly define the right even where an override is available (e.g. respect for family life: (*R (Countryside Alliance) v A-G* [2008] 1 AC 719; freedom of religion: *R (Williamson) v Secretary of State for Education and Employment* [2005] 2 All ER 1, [66]; *R (Begum) v Head Teacher and Governors of Denbigh High School* [2007] 1 AC 100).

This manipulation has been explained by the assertion of the general principle of 'fair balance' (e.g. *MT (Algeria) v Secretary of State for the Home Office*, [207]; *Kay v Lambeth LBC* [2006] 2 AC 465, [32]). For example, in *D v Secretary of State for the Home Department* [2015] 1 WLR 2217, it was held that whether a restriction under anti-terrorism law of a person with mental health problems was 'inhuman or degrading treatment or punishment' depended on balancing the risk to the public against the cost of the care measures available. There is also room for public interest balancing arguments in cases where there is an ostensibly absolute duty to do something positive, such as to hold an investigation into a death or to provide medical care. This may involve the use of limited resources and includes matters varying in gravity and urgency.

Under Article 15 of the Convention, states can 'derogate' (completely opt out) from some rights under the Convention 'in time of war or other public emergency threatening the life of the nation' but 'only to the extent strictly required by the exigencies of the situation' (Section 25.1.2). Under Article 57, a state can make a reservation from the Convention in respect of a particular law. A reservation cannot be of a 'general character'.

It must be borne in mind that rights under particular articles may overlap. For example, as well as Article 6 (right to a fair trial), Article 5 (personal liberty) and Article 8 (privacy and family life) also attract requirements of fair procedures in court decisions.

21.4.1 Absolute rights with no exceptions

21.4.1.1 Article 3: torture or inhuman or degrading treatment or punishment

Torture is defined by the UN Torture Convention, Art 1, as the intentional causing of severe physical or mental pain or suffering by, or at the instigation of, or with the consent or acquiescence of, a public official or other person acting in an official capacity. Thus, torture is prohibited by international law as *ius cogens*, and, as such, the Torture Convention is incorporated into the ECHR (Section 9.6.1). It is also incorporated into UK law by the Criminal Justice Act 1988, s 134. There is also a 'prohibited purpose' ingredient in the Convention, although this is not conclusive (*Cestaro v Italy* [2015]: police beating up demonstrators). The prohibited purposes are 'obtaining information or a confession, punishment, intimidation or coercion, or for any reason based on discrimination of any kind'.

The prohibition of torture is the most absolute right. However, even this is diluted, since there is an exception in the Torture Convention for 'pain arising out of lawful sanctions', and a defence of 'lawful justification' to a prosecution for torture in s 134 (4) of the Criminal Justice Act 1988. This might raise the doctrine of 'necessity', under which it is lawful to use 'reasonable' force in self-defence or to save the lives of others. There is a large body of literature on this (see Cohan, 'Torture and the Necessity Doctrine' (2007) 141 Val ULR 1587).

The state must not use torture itself or rely on torture-tainted evidence from another state. Under the UN Refugee Conventions as applied through the EHCR, the state has an absolute obligation not to remove a person from the country if s/he would face the risk of torture or inhuman or degrading treatment or punishment (*Chahal v UK* (1996) 23 EHRR 413, Section 9.6.3.2). However, provided that the Secretary of State does not knowingly use torture-tainted evidence, there is apparently no duty to inquire whether another state has used torture (*R (Youssef) v Secretary of State for Foreign and Commonwealth Affairs* [2016]). Furthermore, although the meaning of 'torture or inhuman and degrading treatment' might be redefined according to changing sensibilities and political pressures (*Z v UK* (2002) 34 EHRR 3); as often is the case with the ECHR, the language is vague and so invites discretion.

Discretion is also possible with the notions of inhuman or degrading treatment since these include an unspecified lesser degree of pain or suffering than in the case of torture and also include lack of medical attention or extreme forms of social deprivation, all of which notions are vague (see *Ireland v UK* [1978] ECHR 1, [167]): hooding, sleep and food deprivation; *Costello-Roberts v UK* (1993) 19 EHRR 112: severe corporal punishment; *Florea v Judicial Authority Carei Courthouse Romania* [2015] 1 WLR 1953: overcrowded prison). In *Vintner v UK* [2013] ECHR 645, one of several cases involving the UK's draconian punitive arrangements, the Grand Chamber held that a whole life prison sentence was inhuman punishment unless there was a regular review with a genuine possibility of release.

Inhuman or degrading treatment can in an extreme case include social deprivation (*R (Limbuela) v Secretary of State for Social Security* [2007] 1 All ER 951: withdrawal of welfare support from asylum-seekers where to withdraw it would result in destitution). It was emphasised in *Limbuela* that the ECHR does not confer a right to be provided with welfare services as such. In that case, the inhuman treatment resulted from a specific exclusion of failed asylum-seekers from the normal provision. Article 3 was engaged only when, taking account of all the claimant's circumstances, the claimant was reduced to a sense of despair and humiliation, for example by having no access to toilet or washing facilities. In *GS (India) v Secretary of State for the Home Department* [2015] 1 WLR 3312, the Court of Appeal held that Art 3 does not apply to deporting a seriously ill person even though treatment is not available in their home state and it is likely that they will die. There can be exceptions in urgent cases where immediate death would otherwise occur or in death bed cases where inadequate care to die with dignity is not available.

Art 3 often overlaps with Art 8 (respect for privacy and family life). However, a public interest override applies to Art 8.

21.4.1.2 Arts 4(1) (slavery or servitude) and 4(2) (forced or compulsory labour)

Slavery and servitude are absolutely prohibited, whereas the prohibition of forced labour is conditional. The exceptions are work required in the 'ordinary course of' prison or parole, military service, emergency or calamity, and 'normal civic obligations'.

Slavery is where a human being is effectively treated as property at the whim of another. It need not involve physical coercion. It differs from forced labour in that the victim may be bought and sold. Cultural factors such as marriage payments to families are a relevant factor. *Servitude* is treated as slavery. It is aggravated forced labour where the victim is required to live in another's property and feels that his or her condition is permanent. *Forced labour* is where a person who has not volunteered is compelled to work by means of a threat or a penalty (*Siliadin v France* [2006]: 15-year-old child required to work long hours as a domestic servant without pay was forced labour but not slavery). The court looks at all the circumstances, including whether the workload is disproportionate (see e.g. *Van der Mussele v Belgium* (1983) 6 EHRR 163: trainee lawyer required to defend clients free of charge not forced labour; *M v Italy and Bulgaria*, App.40020/03 (2012)). In *R (Reilly) v Secretary of State for Work and Pensions* [2014] AC 453, [81], [83], [90], the Supreme Court held that a government scheme that withdrew benefits from claimants who did not accept low-paid work was not forced labour, because the purpose of the Convention is to prevent the exploitation of labour, not to regulate state benefits.

Both overlap with Art 3 (inhuman or degrading treatment or punishment), and the state has a positive duty to prevent violations and also to investigate those that have occurred. The Strasbourg court has made it clear that the contemporary problems of human trafficking of migrants fall within Art 4, however classified, involving sometimes as they do debt bonding, confinement and sexual abuse as well as compulsory labour for little or no pay (*CN v UK* (2013) 56 EHRR 24: UK law failed to provide adequate protection; see now Modern Slavery Act 2015).

21.4.1.3 Article 6: right to a fair trial

In relation to civil rights and obligations and the determination of any criminal charges against them, individuals have a right to a fair trial in public before an independent and impartial tribunal established by law. The press and public may be excluded from all or any part of the proceedings in the interests of morals, public order or national security in a democratic society, where the interests of juveniles or the protection of the private lives of the parties so require, or to the extent strictly necessary in the opinion of the court in special circumstances where publicity would prejudice the interests of justice. Judgment must be pronounced in public except where it would subvert the special reasons for holding the hearing in private.

Article 6 is therefore central to the rule of law. It normally requires an adversarial procedure and 'equality of arms' (*Tariq v Home Office* [2012] 1 AC 452, [139]). There must be a hearing on all questions of fact by a body with 'full jurisdiction' (*R (Alconbury Developments) v Secretary of State* [2001] 2 All ER 929). The requirements of Art 6 are normally satisfied by the common law rules governing the right to a fair hearing. However, unlike domestic law (Section 18.3), Article 6 usually includes a right to legal representation (*R (G) v Governors of X School* [2012] 1 AC 167). The tribunal must be independent. In this context, the domestic law test of whether, in the view of a 'fair-minded and informed observer' taken as knowing all the circumstances, there is a 'real possibility' or 'real danger' of bias (Section 18.4), seems to satisfy Art 6 (see *R v Spear* [2003] 1 AC 734: courts martial: president and advocates part of military staff but independence protected).

Article 6 applies to the procedure of the court, not to the substantive content of the right that is being enforced. Thus, in *Wilson v First County Trust* [2003] 4 All ER 97, a statutory provision that made a pawnbroking agreement 'unenforceable' if it was not correctly signed was held not to violate Article 6 since the matter was not merely one of procedure (see also *Matthews v Ministry of Defence* [2003] 1 AC 1163: immunity of MoD from being sued by soldier does not violate the right to a fair trial because it is a matter of substantive law).

Although Article 6 is absolute and cannot be overridden on public interest grounds, the courts have introduced a public interest element into the ingredients of 'fairness'. The particular circumstances must be considered. Thus, in *Secretary of State for the Home Dept v MB* [2008] 1 All ER 657, the House of Lords held that Article 6 allows a 'fair balance' to be struck between the interests of the community and those of the individual. For example, in security cases, a controversial 'closed material procedure' can sometimes be used where an accused person is denied the right to see all the evidence against him (Section 24.6).

In *Brown v Stott* [2001] 2 All ER 97, the House of Lords held that a requirement to disclose the name of the driver involved in an accident was not in breach of the right against self-incrimination due to the public importance of the matter (see also *O'Halloran and Francis v UK* (2008) 46 EHRR 397: speed cameras, duty to give information as to identity of driver; *Sheldrake v DPP* [2005] 1 AC 264: defendant must prove no risk of drink-driving; not unfair since driver in best position to know).

The international ban on torture applies to Art 6. In *A v Secretary of State for the Home Dept (No 2)* [2006] 2 AC 221, the House of Lords held that evidence obtained by torture whether here or overseas was not admissible, regarding this as a 'constitutional principle' reflecting the fact that the international ban on torture is absolute. Their Lordships disagreed as to the standard of proof. A majority held that it must be shown on a balance of probabilities that the evidence was tainted, whereas the minority thought that it was enough to show that there was a 'real risk' (see also *Secretary of State for the Home Dept v Rehman* [2003] 1 AC 153). In *Othman (Abu Qatada) v UK* [2012] ECHR 56, the Strasbourg court agreed that the test is that of a real risk.

An important limit on Article 6 is that it applies only to 'civil rights and obligations'. A civil *obligation* arises where there is a legal duty towards the state, for example to pay taxes. The meaning of 'civil rights' is more difficult. The right in question must be recognised as such in domestic law. It includes, but is not restricted to, private law rights such as property (e.g. *Winterwerp v Netherlands* (1979) 2 EHRR 387). However, it does not apply to purely public law rights such as a legitimate expectation (*R (Alconbury Developments) v Secretary of State* [2001]).

The underlying principle seems to be that, for a civil right, the decision in question must involve some kind of *entitlement*. Therefore, there is no civil right where entitlement to a benefit depends on a discretionary decision. For example, in *Ali v Birmingham Corp* [2010] 2 All ER 175, a claim to be housed under homelessness legislation did not create a civil right because there was a substantial element of discretion (but see *Ali v UK* (2016) 63 EHRR 20, in which the Strasbourg Court took a somewhat different view on the relevance of the extent of discretion). Conversely, in *Feldbrugge v The Netherlands* (1986) 8 EHRR 425 and *Salesi v Italy* (1993) 26 EHRR 187, entitlement to health insurance from the state on proof of certain facts was held to concern civil rights.

The matter depends on the nature of the particular action. For example, in *RB (Algeria) v Secretary of State* [2010] 2 AC 110, the claimant was facing deportation. It was held that, although there may be some protection under Art 8 (respect for family life), the entry, stay and deportation of an alien do not engage a civil right since an alien has no right to remain in the UK, but depend on the discretionary powers of the Home Secretary (Section 9.6.4) (see also *R (BB) v SIAC* [2012] 1 All ER 229). Although an alien may have rights concerning his or her detention, the claimant was not challenging his detention as such, but only the fairness of the procedures used to deport him (at [90], [176], [178], [228]). In *R (G) v Governors of X School* [2012], the Supreme Court held that a process must be examined broadly as a whole. Thus, a hearing may fall within Art 6 even if it does not itself decide the civil right in question provided that it is linked with other proceedings that do so (school governors' meeting led to disqualification of teacher by the Independent Safeguarding Authority).

The removal of an existing benefit will normally engage a civil right. In *Tre Tractorer Aktebolag v Sweden* (1989) 13 EHRR 309, it was held that the revocation of a liquor licence engaged a civil right (see also *Benthem v Netherlands* (1986) 8 EHRR 1: petrol storage licence affecting operation of business). Dismissal from a particular job does not engage Article 6. However, a decision which imposes general harm on important personal or social interests including entitlement to work does so (see *R (G) v Governors of X School* [2012]: statutory barring of a teacher from professional practice; *R (Wright) v Secretary of State* [2009] 2 All ER 129: placing of a care worker on a blacklist).

Compromise in Art 6 standards?

The casual attitude of UK political culture to the qualities of independent decision-making has raised issues involving Article 6. In *R (Alconbury Developments) v Secretary of State* [2001], there was a challenge to the standard procedure used by government in making planning, compulsory purchase and other land use decisions. This procedure involves an inquiry held by a semi-independent inspector who reports to the Secretary of State who may be the promoter of the decision or policy. The Court of Appeal held that the procedure violates the right to a fair trial before an independent tribunal. However, the House of Lords drew back from holding that a widespread practice which fits the culture of UK government should be sacrificed.

Their Lordships applied the 'curative principle' according to which the process should be looked at as a whole including any appeal or judicial review element (see also *R (G) v Governors of X School* [2012], [84]; *Ali v UK* [2016]). They held that, although the procedure itself was not independent, any failure was put right because judicial review was available. A problem with this is that judicial review is not comprehensive in relation to questions of fact (Section 17.5.2) and so does not seem to satisfy the requirement of Article 6 that an independent tribunal must have 'full jurisdiction'. However, this has been dealt with by defining full jurisdiction as 'full jurisdiction to deal with the case as the nature of the decision requires' (see *Runa Begum v Tower Hamlets London BC* [2003] 1 All ER 731, 736). In this way, the limited scope of judicial review in relation to findings of fact has sometimes been held to satisfy Article 6. The courts have made a distinction between, on the one hand, a decision where a citizen has a definite entitlement on proof of certain facts (e.g. to a pension based on prescribed contributions) and, on the other, a decision where the facts are part of a larger policy or politically oriented process where the decision-maker has to balance facts against competing considerations and has a discretion as to the outcome, for example a decision to build a motorway (*Alconbury*, above).

In the first, 'factual' kind of case, the reach of judicial review into the facts is not far enough, so that an independent procedure such as a tribunal is required which can examine all questions of fact (*Runa Begum*, above, *Tsfayo v UK* (2009) 48 EHRR 18). This type of case arises where there is 'self-regulation' within an organisation (Section 20.4). In the second 'policy' kind of case, it has been held that since respect for democratic decision-making is involved, judicial review may suffice as a safety net. It can be decided which category a case falls within only by looking closely at the particular decision-making process and its goals. It is clear that the wider the view taken on the question of the meaning of 'civil right' (above), the more likely it is that the case will fall within the 'policy' category (*Runa Begum* (above), [5]).

In a criminal case, Article 6 requires further safeguards. These include a right 'to be informed promptly and in a language he understands and in detail, of the nature and cause of the accusation', adequate time and facilities to prepare a defence, a right to choose a lawyer and free legal assistance 'when the interests of justice so require', a right to call witnesses and to examine opposing witnesses on equal terms, and a right to an interpreter. However, 'charged with a criminal offence' has been defined narrowly to exclude matters relating to sentencing and bail (*Phillips v UK* [2001] ECHR 437; *R (DPP) v Havering Magistrates Court* [2001] 3 All ER 997).

Overlapping with Art 6, Art 5 (personal liberty) and Art 8 (respect for privacy and family life) also require procedural safeguards, albeit in the case of Art 8, which is only a qualified right, these may be more basic than Art 6 requires.

21.4.1.4 *Article 7: no retrospective criminal laws*

Except in respect of acts which were criminal when committed according to the general principles of law recognised by civilised nations.

21.4.1.5 *Article 12: right to marry and found a family according to national laws governing the exercise of the right*

In *R (Baiai) v Secretary of State for the Home Dept* [2007] 4 All ER 199, it was held that the courts must be vigilant to protect the right to marry, but that it carries less weight than the fundamental rights of personal liberty, freedom of expression and access to the courts. In that case, a requirement of Home

Office consent for non-Anglican marriages by immigrants was held invalid on the basis that the immigration authority could only interfere with the right to marry in the case of a sham marriage, and it must be shown that the marriages targeted made substantial inroads into the scheme of immigration control. 'Marriage' was traditionally narrowly interpreted as referring only to traditional marriages between biological men and women, leaving it to individual states to determine policy on this sensitive issue (e.g. *Chapin & Charpentier v France* [2016] ECHR 504), although this now also needs to be read against a growing consensus towards some form of legal recognition of same-sex relationships, which may raise issues under Articles 8 and 14 (below).

21.4.1.6 Protocol 1, Article 2: education

No person shall be denied the right to education. In the exercise of any functions which it assumes in relation to education and teaching, the state shall respect the right of parents to ensure such education and teaching is in conformity with their own religious and philosophical convictions.

This is a limited right. It does not confer a right to be educated. Its purpose is to combat state discrimination and indoctrination (*R (Williamson) v Secretary of State for Education and Employment* [2005] 2 All ER 1, [22]). It does not require the state to provide or to fund education. It means only a right not to be arbitrarily excluded from whatever education or funding the state provides (*A v Head Teacher and Governors of Lord Grey School* [2004] 4 All ER 628; *R (Douglas) v North Tyneside DC* [2004] 1 All ER 709; *R (Begum) v Head Teacher and Governors of Denbigh High School* [2007]; *R (Tigere) v Secretary of State for Business, Innovation and Skills* [2015] (Section 21.4.4).

The UK has made a reservation, to go only so far as compatible with 'the provision of efficient instruction and training and the avoidance of unreasonable public expenditure'.

21.4.1.7 Protocol 1, Article 3: free elections to the legislature at reasonable intervals by secret ballot (see Section 12.5.5)

In *Moohan v Lord Advocate* [2015] AC 901, the Supreme Court held that the right does not apply to referendums.

21.4.2　Conditional rights

21.4.2.1 Article 2: right to life

With exceptions for capital punishment following criminal conviction, defence against unlawful violence, lawful arrest or prevention of unlawful escape, lawful action for quelling riot or insurrection.

In addition, Protocol 6 requires the abolition of the death penalty in peacetime. Although this Protocol was not incorporated into the HRA, the Act abolished the last remaining death penalty provisions in the UK (s 21(5)). Moreover, in *Al Saadoon v UK* [2010] ECHR 282, which concerned the handing over by the army of a prisoner to the Iraq government which had reintroduced capital punishment, the Strasbourg court held that capital punishment in itself violated Art 3, which has no exceptions, thus effectively outlawing all capital punishment. However, the court's reasoning raises questions since this was based on the anguish which such a sentence brings, an argument that could be applied to lesser sentences, particularly in the context of bad prison conditions.

Article 2 has been described as the most fundamental right, requiring the highest level of scrutiny (*R (Bloggs 61) v Secretary of State for the Home Dept* [2003] 1 WLR 2724). It has three distinct aspects:

First, Article 2 requires the state not to take life in any circumstances outside the designated exceptions – the 'primary substantive' duty. It has been interpreted narrowly so as not to authorise voluntary euthanasia (*R (Pretty) v DPP* [2002] 1 All ER 1: the right to life is the right not to be killed, not to have control over one's own lifespan). In *Pretty*, the court emphasised that the Convention is not meant to intervene in controversial moral issues around which there is no consensus. This is one way in which the court deals with the problem that it lacks democratic legitimacy.

Second, the state has a duty of care to persons under its control both in the UK and overseas, for example prisoners or patients detained under the Mental Health Acts or members of the armed forces on active service (see *Osman v UK* (1998) 29 EHRR 245, [115]–[116], 'real and immediate risk to life'; *Smith v Ministry of Defence* [2014] AC 52). The state must provide 'a framework of laws, precautions, procedures and means of enforcement' which will to the greatest extent reasonably practicable protect life. This includes, for example, trying to prevent prisoners or mental patients committing suicide (see *R (Middleton) v West Somerset Coroner* [2004] 2 AC 182 (the leading case): prisoner hanged himself; *Rabone v Pennine Care NHS Foundation Trust* [2012] 2 AC 72: suicide of voluntary mental patient on home visit; killing or injuring civilians in Iraq both in custody and in the street (*R (Al-Saadoon) v Secretary of State for Defence* [2015]).

The nature of the care required depends on the circumstances and the victim's vulnerability since this kind of duty involving limited resources cannot be absolute. In this kind of case, the court invariably emphasises the need for a margin of appreciation, which broadly means that the court will interfere only if the state acts 'manifestly unreasonably' (Section 22.9.3). For example, in *R (Bloggs 61) v Secretary of State for the Home Department* [2003], prison authorities refused to transfer the claimant to a witness protection scheme, but the court accepted the risk assessment of the prison authorities. In *R (Long) v Secretary of State for Defence* [2015] EWCA Civ 770, a soldier was killed by an Iraqi mob. Due to administrative confusion, there were no satellite phones to use in emergencies. The Court of Appeal held that the state had a wide discretion in military operational cases. Art 2 could be engaged if there was a negligent systems error or a failure of control, but not merely individual human error. The Court had to avoid imposing unrealistic or disproportionate burdens. Moreover, Art 2 may not apply to high-level political or policy judgments, nor in actual combat conditions (Section 22.3).

The positive duty extends beyond persons directly under state control to other cases where the state creates a risk. (See e.g. *Van Colle v Chief Constable of Hertfordshire Police* [2006] 3 All ER 963: protection of witness; *Re Officer L* [2007] 4 All ER 965: police spy: no duty to protect against financial loss; *Sarjantson v Chief Constable of Humberside Police* [2014] 1 All ER 960: delay in police response to street attack: police need not be aware of identity of victims; *Budayeva v Russia* (2014) 59 EHRR 2: landslide with large loss of life, obligation to take preventive measures and to warn the public.)

Third, under the 'procedural duty', the state has a duty to hold a prompt, open, effective and thorough investigation into a death or serious injury for which the state may be responsible (Section 21.4.3).

21.4.2.2 Article 4(2): forced or compulsory labour

See Sections 21.4.1 and 21.4.1.2.

21.4.2.3 Article 5: liberty and security of person

Except in prescribed cases in accordance with a procedure prescribed by law, this is a right that cannot be overridden. Its purpose is to prevent arbitrary detention. It provides an exhaustive definition of when a person can be detained and must be given a narrow construction (*Zenati v Commissioner of Police of the Metropolis* [2015] EWCA Civ 80, [17]). The right to personal liberty has especially high importance in the common law and in *R (Lumba) v Secretary of State for the Home Dept* [2012] 1 AC 245, the Supreme Court emphasised that the liberty of the subject is a fundamental constitutional principle (at [219]). Art 5 reflects the centuries of struggle in England against arbitrary government.

The main exceptions are criminal convictions, disobedience to a court order, control of children, infection (this exception meaning that restrictions imposed during the COVID-19 pandemic do not necessarily amount to a breach of the Convention), mental health, alcoholism, drug addiction, vagrancy and in order to prevent illegal immigration or with a view to deportation or extradition (Art 5.1).

In *James v UK* [2012], the Strasbourg court condemned the UK's indeterminate sentence legislation under Art 5.1 as contrary to the rule of law in the sense of being arbitrary. This legislation prevented a prisoner being released until he satisfied the Parole Board that he was no longer a danger to society. The UK had argued unsuccessfully that, to comply with the rule of law, it was enough that the conviction was lawful and the continued detention was related to it. The Strasbourg court held that the state must make arrangements to guide such a prisoner's progress towards release.

There are safeguards to ensure a speedy trial and adequate remedies against unlawful detention. A person arrested must be informed promptly of the reasons for the arrest (Art 5.2). In criminal cases, a person arrested shall be brought promptly before a judicial officer and entitled to trial within a reasonable time or to bail (Art 5.3) and 'shall be entitled to take proceedings by which the lawfulness of his detention shall be decided speedily by a court and his release ordered if the detention is not lawful' (Art 5.4). In *James v UK* (above), it was held that this required a regular review of an indeterminate sentence. There is a right to compensation for wrongful detention.

The requirement for judicial review of a detention apparently does not apply where the detention is ordered by a court or other judicial tribunal (*De Wilde v Belgium* (1979–80) 1 EHRR 373; *Hutchinson-Reid v UK* [2003] ECHR 94). To this extent, domestic law with its general requirement of judicial review goes further. However, in *Clooth v Belgium* (1992) 14 EHRR 717, [36], the Strasbourg court emphasised that a court must exercise 'special diligence' when dealing with a person in custody awaiting trial.

In *Zenati v Commissioner of Police of the Metropolis* [2015], a person suspected of passport fraud was held in detention for nearly three weeks awaiting trial, even though the police had become aware that there was no substance to the charge. The reason for the delay was unclear but apparently lay with the prosecuting authority. However, the Court of Appeal in a preliminary hearing held that the prosecuting authority should not be distinguished from the Court itself for the purpose of Art 5. But the Court recognised that an impossible burden must not be put on authorities with limited resources so that the duty is to do the best they can. Similarly, Art 5 is modified in cases of military combat, in this case by the International Humanitarian Convention (*R (Al-Saadoon) v Secretary of State for Defence* [2015], [110–11]), since it would be impractical to require, for example, an independent judicial review.

The requirement to be informed promptly of the reasons for an arrest is satisfied by the common law requirement which permits very general reasons to be given at the time of the arrest. A failure to give further information at a later stage does not invalidate the detention (*Lee-Hirons v Secretary of State for Justice* [2016] UKSC 46).

Article 5 has been weakened by drawing a distinction between 'deprivation of liberty' and 'restrictions upon liberty'. The latter does not fall within Article 5 but falls within Protocol 4, Article 2, which the UK has not ratified, and so does not apply. The main problem is that interferences with personal freedom are of many different kinds and degrees of intensity, ranging from the paradigm case of a prisoner in a cell, to protective measures over a vulnerable person subject to controls that permit considerable free movement. In *Guzzardi v Italy* (1981) 3 EHRR 333, the exile of a suspected Mafioso to live under supervision on a small island was held to be a deprivation of liberty. The Strasbourg court emphasised that the matter was one of degree and not substance.

There is, therefore, a temptation to manipulate the definition of 'deprivation' to protect actions of which the court approves. *Austin v Metropolitan Police Comr* [2009] 3 All ER 455 seems to be a case in point. The House of Lords held that 'kettling' – police confinement of a crowd for two hours within a cordon on the road in uncomfortable conditions in order to prevent disorder – was only a 'restriction' on liberty and so was not unlawful (Section 23.7.2). (The exceptions to Article 5 do not seem to include police powers to keep order, although counsel in *Austin* argued that they did.) Their Lordships held that the test was not merely the length of time of the detention but was also a matter of 'degree and intensity' requiring a subjective judgment. This included a range of factors relating to the specific situation of the individual and the context in which the restriction occurred. They crucially held that the purpose of the confinement could be taken into account and that, because this was a matter of public safety and was proportionate, there was no deprivation of liberty. Since Art 5 has no public interest override, the question of proportionality was not strictly relevant.

Austin was upheld by the Strasbourg court (2012) 55 EHRR 14, with three dissenting judges. The Court's rationale is obscure. Even though it held that the purpose of a restriction is not relevant (at [58]; see also *Creanga v Romania* (2013) 56 EHRR 11, [93]), 'the court does not consider that such commonly occurring restrictions on movement, so long as they are rendered unavoidable as a result of circumstances beyond the control of the authorities and are necessary to avoid a real risk of serious injury or damage, and are kept to the minimum required for that purpose can properly be described as deprivations of liberty'. The court stressed the 'specific and exceptional' circumstances so that *Austin* might be regarded as limited to emergency situations (at [68]). Otherwise, it makes little sense since the people in question were confined almost as much as if they were imprisoned in a cell.

The law seems unclear. The principle may be that detention for a specific limited purpose for a short time to combat an immediate risk does not fall within Art 5 (see also *R (McClure) v Commissioner of Police of the Metropolis* [2012] EWCA 12). In *Gillan and Quinton v UK* [2010] ECHR 28, the UK courts had held that a police 'stop and search' involving complete coercion for 30 minutes was not a deprivation of liberty. The European Court condemned the police action under Article 8: privacy and did not decide this particular point. However, it was suggested (at [57]) that coercion of this kind did indeed fall within Article 5, in which case any justification would be irrelevant since searching is not a permissible purpose, under Art 5. Perhaps, unlike *Austin*, there was no emergency. In *Beghal v DPP* [2015] UKSC 49, the Supreme Court suggested that a detention for a period no longer than is needed for questioning and search does not fall within Art 5.

In a different context, that of the supervision of mental patients, the courts have been troubled by the variety of conditions involved, ranging from supervised freedom to complete confinement. The Strasbourg cases are difficult to reconcile (see Stone (2012)). However, the Supreme Court has now taken a straightforward approach. In *P v Cheshire West & Chester Council* [2014] UKSC 19, the claimants were mental patients who had been placed in ordinary housing with different degrees of supervision and support, rather than a care home. They did not object and were happy with their placements. The majority of the Supreme Court held that they were nonetheless deprived of liberty. The test should be the same for everyone, namely the existence of constraint, that is, that the person concerned was under continuous supervision and control for a not-negligible time and was not free to leave. There is also a subjective element in that positive consent prevents deprivation of liberty. However, the person's passive compliance or lack of objection is irrelevant, as is the purpose of the detention whether good or bad, and whether or not it is intended to benefit the person. Whether conditions are 'normal' or comfortable is also irrelevant. Thus, there was a deprivation of liberty in all the cases. Lady Hale remarked (at [36]) that the whole point about human rights is their universal character and that 'in the end it is the constraints that matter' (at [56]).

However, the dissenting judges, Lords Carnwath, Hodge and Clarke, held that the Strasbourg jurisprudence required a broader approach based on the 'ordinary' meaning of deprivation as a question of fact in all the circumstances. They took the view that living under benign supervision for one's own good in a domestic setting was not a deprivation of liberty. This invokes the notion of 'positive freedom', according to which freedom means freedom to do good things (Section 2.4). As the majority pointed out, this leads to uncertainty and blurs the question of whether liberty is removed with whether this is justified.

21.4.3 The duty to investigate violations

There are separate duties arising out of the most fundamental of the absolute and conditional rights, namely Art 2 (right to life), Art 3 (inhuman and degrading treatment) and Art 4(1) (torture), to investigate alleged violations. In *Re McCaughey* [2011] UKSC 20, which concerned shooting of suspects by the army in Northern Ireland under an alleged 'shoot to kill policy', this extension of Art 2 was explained as an aspect of the 'living instrument' nature of the ECHR. A similar duty applies to Art 5 (deprivation of liberty), but only in cases of 'enforced disappearance' (*R (Al-Saadoon) v Secretary of State for Defence* [2015], [294]). In cases where it is alleged that the government has handed a person over to another state to be abused ('refoulment') it seems that an inquiry must be held only where the government is knowingly complicit, or possibly turns a blind eye (ibid).

The purposes of the inquiry are to ensure that the full facts are brought to light, that those responsible are accountable, that unjustified suspicions are allayed, that dangerous practices are remedied and that the victims and their relatives are consoled (*R (Amin) v Secretary of State for the Home Department* [2004] 1 AC 653, [31]). The procedural duty cannot arise independently and is triggered only where there has been a breach of a substantive Art 2 duty (see *Edwards v UK* (2002) 35 EHRR 487; *R (Middleton) v West Somerset Coroner* [2004], [3], [4]; *Smith v Ministry of Defence* [2011] 1 AC 1).

However, once established, the procedural duty is 'detachable' from the primary duty so that it exists in its own right. For example, the primary duty may be unenforceable as being out of time, whereas the procedural duty might still be enforceable, albeit vulnerable to its own time limits (*Silih v Slovenia* (2009) 49 EHRR 37: death taking place before the Convention came into force). In the interests of certainty, the Strasbourg court has adopted a time limit normally of ten years in such cases (see *Keyu v Secretary of State for Foreign and Commonwealth Affairs* [2015], Section 22.4).

In *Smith* (above), the Supreme Court held that such an inquiry must be subject to public scrutiny, must be independent of an agent who may be responsible for the death, must involve the relatives of the deceased and must be prompt and effective. No particular model of inquiry is required. An 'enhanced' inquest procedure is usually sufficient, in which there is an investigation to bring the full facts to light not only in terms of the cause of death but also the surrounding circumstances, and the jury gives a narrative account (*Middleton* (above); *R (Antoniou) v Central and North London NHS Trust* [2013] EWHC 3055 (Admin): suicide of voluntary mental patient). A Coroner must hold an inquest into all deaths in state custody. A Coroner is an independent judicial officer, the hearing is in public and relatives of the deceased have a right to be heard (see Coroners Act 2009, ss 1, 7).

However, a separate public inquiry may sometimes be required, although, except where no inquest is held, it is not clear when this would be the case (see *R (Amin) v Secretary of State for the Home Department* [2004]: murder by cellmate; *R (L) v Secretary of State for Justice* [2009] 1 AC 588: attempted suicide in prison). One example may be where there is a direct killing by a state agent, calling for a high degree of public confidence in the procedure. Suicides and killings by prisoners (*Middleton* (above)) and mental patients (*Antoniou* (above)) have been held not normally to require a separate inquiry. In *Long* [2015] it was held, rather curiously, that there was no need for a separate inquiry since all relevant facts had been established by the military authorities.

There must also be an investigation into violations by private persons (*Commissioner of Police of the Metropolis v DSD* [2018] UKSC 11: multiple serious assaults on women by taxi drivers). As with other positive obligations, there is a margin of appreciation, and the extent of the duty to investigate varies with the circumstances since the gravity of the matter varies from torture by state agents at the top to carelessness in private organisations at the bottom (such as ill-treatment of the elderly in a care home). In *DSD*, there was a division between the judges as to whether serious operational failings attract liability under Art 3 or whether failures of control or systems must be shown, the majority preferring the former view.

21.4.4   Rights subject to being overridden (qualified rights)

The overriding decision that is being challenged must first be 'in accordance with' or 'prescribed by' law. This has a wide meaning to include values associated with the rule of law, such as certainty and accountability. Secondly, the decision must be 'necessary in a democratic society'. The Strasbourg court has applied this broadly to mean that the decision must meet a 'pressing social need' and must pass the test of 'proportionality' (*Connors v UK* (2004) 40 EHRR 189, [81]–[83] is regarded as a classic statement). Thirdly, the decision must fall into one of the categories listed, which vary slightly under each Article. The judicial process is especially problematic in this area. Here we shall consider the rights themselves. The balancing exercise based on proportionality is discussed in the next chapter (Section 22.9).

21.4.4.1 Article 8: respect for privacy, family life, home and correspondence

Overrides: There shall be no interference by a public authority with an Article 8 right except such as is in accordance with the law and is necessary in a democratic society in the interests of national security, public safety or the economic wellbeing of the country, for the prevention of disorder or crime, for the protection of health or morals, or for the protection of the rights and freedoms of others.

Article 8 is the vaguest and most wide-ranging Article of the ECHR. Indeed, uniquely, Article 8 gives only an entitlement to 'respect', meaning that decision-makers must give it particular weight but not that it necessarily creates definite rights (*Secretary of State for Work and Pensions v M* [2006] UKHL 11, [62]). Thus, in *Wainwright v Home Office* [2003] 4 All ER 969, 979 (strip searches), Lord Hoffmann said that values such as privacy cannot easily be embodied in clear rules, so that they are best undefined as providing only a general sense of direction or an attitude.

In *Connors v UK* [2004], [82], the scope of Art 8 was summarised as being to protect 'rights of central importance to the individual's identity, self-determination, physical and moral integrity, maintenance of relationships with others and a settled and secure place in the community'. In *Secretary of State for Work and Pensions v M* [2006], Lord Bingham (at [5]) referred to 'love, trust, confidence, mutual dependence and unconstrained social intercourse which are the essence of family life' and to 'the sphere of personal and sexual autonomy which are of the essence of private life'.

Art 8 has four aspects linked by the notion of personal autonomy:

1. It protects against intrusion and surveillance (Section 25.3).
2. It protects against disclosure and retention of information about oneself. This applies in particular to the retention by the police of any personal information, ranging from a name and address to genetic information, although the seriousness of the intrusion affects any countervailing justification (see *S and Marper v UK* (2008) 48 EHRR 50; Section 22.9.3.2).
3. It protects the home and intimate family relationships. We have already seen this in immigration cases which separate close relatives (Section 9.7.4). However, in *Secretary of State for Work and Pensions v M* [2006], Lord Nicholls and Lord Mance (at [24]–[29]) took the view that 'family life' did not include same-sex couples on the ground that there was no Europe-wide consensus at the time the issue arose and that Article 8 does not confer a general right to self-determination. A consensus in favour of same-sex couples has now emerged (see *Vallianatos v Greece* [2013] ECHR 1110).
4. It embraces respect for personal identity, dignity and development as a member of society. This includes lifestyle, reputation (*Pfeifer v Austria* (2007) 48 EHRR 175, [33]) and social relationships. It includes employment, but only insofar as it affects wider relationships, gender, sexual preferences, culture and lifestyle: 'those features which are integral to a person's identity or ability to function socially as a person' (Lord Bingham in *R (Razgar) v Secretary of State for the Home Dept* [2004] 3 All ER 821, [9]; *Von Hannover v Germany* (2005) 40 EHRR 1, [50]: 'a person's physical and psychological integrity ... the development, without outside interference, of the personality of each individual in his relations with other human beings'). There is therefore a social zone in a public context, which may fall within the scope of 'private life'.

Art 8 concerns dignity, but not life itself. In *R (Purdy) v DPP* [2009] 4 All ER 1147 and *Pretty v UK* (2002) 35 EHRR 1, it was held that there is no right to assisted suicide because Art 8 is concerned with the quality of life, not its continuance. However, a patient may be entitled to pain relief even if this shortens life. In *McDonald v UK* [2014] ECHR 492, the withdrawal of night care from a disabled person by a local authority in principle fell within Art 8 as a matter of respect for human dignity.

Art 8 is therefore very broad, and its application varies across individual states with their different lifestyle practices, thus requiring a flexible approach. In *Pretty v UK* [2002], [61], the Strasbourg court recognised that its scope could not be comprehensively defined. Article 8 reflects Mill's version of liberalism, namely that in the context of the good of society as a whole, people are happier when they choose for themselves what form of life and lifestyle to adopt (Section 2.3.3). Art 8 cases also raise the question of whether the state must take positive action to secure a right as opposed to not interfering with one, for example by providing medical care. Courts are reluctant to allocate public resources and will impose a positive obligation only exceptionally. Art 8 often attracts a wide margin of appreciation.

As well as giving substantive protection, Art 8 requires a fair procedure before an independent body (*IR (Sri Lanka) v Secretary of State for the Home Dept* [2011] 4 All ER 908). Article 6 (right to a fair trial) is not applicable to the expulsion of aliens, but this provides some procedural protection.

Article 8 examples

R (Steinfeld & Keidan) v Secretary of State for International Development [2018] UKSC 32: Civil Partnership Act 2004 incompatible with Arts. 8 and 14 in precluding different-sex couple from entering into civil partnerships (see now Civil Partnerships, Marriages and Deaths (Registration etc) Act 2019).

Beghal v DPP [2015] UKSC 49; *R (Roberts) v Metropolitan Police Commissioner* [2015] UKSC 79: police 'stop and search' powers.

Catt v UK [2019] ECHR 76: police surveillance and retention of information (Section 22.9.1).

GS (India) v Secretary of State for the Home Department [2015]: Art 8 can be engaged where deportation limits access to medical care (Section 9.7.4), but no general obligation to provide medical care.

Winspear v City Hospitals Sunderland NHS Foundation Trust [2016] 2 WLR 1089: placing 'do not resuscitate' notice on record of patient lacking mental capacity without consulting carer.

But *R (Condliff) v North Staffs Primary Health Care Trust* [2011] EWCA Civ 910: hospital policy to refuse gastric bypass surgery to combat obesity except in special cases to be decided solely on clinical grounds was valid. The Court should be cautious in imposing a positive obligation where state benefits are concerned an1d that respect for family life was satisfied by the hospital's policy which was fair (at [34],[40]).

R (AB) v Secretary of State for Justice [2010] 2 All ER 151: refusal to transfer transsexual prisoner to woman's prison goes to heart of identity.

R (Wright) v Secretary of State for Health [2009]: restriction of employment, where there is a stigma or social exclusion: child abuse register.

Connors v UK [2004]: provision of gypsy encampment.

Marcic v Thames Water Utilities [2004] 1 All ER 135: flooding of home; but responsible public authority entitled to determine priorities.

Hatton v UK (2003) 37 EHRR 28: airport noise disturbing residents; state has wide margin of appreciation (Section 22.9.3).

Guerra v Italy (1998) 26 EHRR 357: procedural duty to assess environmental impact of waste plant.

Autronic AG v Switzerland (1990) 12 EHRR 485: immigrant lifestyle; access to satellite TV from overseas.

The UK courts have sometimes given Article 8 limited weight. Senior lawyers and civil servants who may have been accustomed since childhood to a gregarious life in highly conformist institutions may underestimate the importance to others of privacy. In *MM v UK* [2012] ECHR 1906, the Strasbourg court criticised the generosity of the UK's approach to the official keeping of personal data.

In *S and Marper v UK* (2008) 48 EHRR 50, the European Court condemned the UK practice of retaining indefinitely DNA samples from both adults and children arrested or charged with offences irrespective of whether they were subsequently convicted. The Court disagreed with the House of Lords (Baroness Hale dissenting) who, in *R (S) v Chief Constable of the South Yorkshire Police* [2004] 4 All ER 193, held that the retention of DNA samples was not a significant enough intrusion to fall within Art 8. Similarly, in *Gaughran v UK* [2020] ECHR 144, the Strasbourg Court held that the indiscriminate nature of the powers of retention of the DNA profile, fingerprints and photograph of a person convicted of an offence, even if spent, without reference to the seriousness of the offence or the need for indefinite retention and in the absence of any real possibility of review, failed to strike a fair balance between the competing public and private interests.

In *R (Gillan) v MPC* [2006] 4 All ER 1041, the House of Lords upheld a police power to stop and search suspected terrorists without the need to show grounds for suspicion. Lord Bingham suggested (at [28]) that routine security checks at airports do not reach a sufficient 'level of seriousness' to qualify for Article 8 protection (see also Lord Scott (at [63])). In *Gillan and Quinton v UK* [2010], the Strasbourg court disagreed. One reason for doing so was that the House of Lords may have under-valued the importance of privacy under Art 8.

21.4.4.2 Limits to Art 8

A limit to Article 8 seems to be that it must involve a personal, in the sense of intimate, element. In *R (Countryside Alliance) v A-G* [2008] 1 AC 719, it was argued unsuccessfully that the Hunting Act 2004, which outlaws hunting wild mammals with dogs, violated Article 8, in that there was a right to par-ticipate in hunting as an aspect of countryside life and as a social activity integral to the personality. The House of Lords held that the Act does not attract Article 8 because at the heart of Article 8 is the idea of the personal and intimate, whereas hunting is carried out in public. Moreover, hunters were not a distinctive group so as to claim an identity analogous to an ethnic group. Some of the claimants were workers who serviced the hunt. It was held that Article 8 can apply to loss of livelihood, but only where the loss of a job seriously impinges on the person's social relationships or status in society or involves loss of a home. Article 8 protects the inviolability of the home. As is the case with other welfare services, Art 8 does not normally confer a positive right to be provided with a home, but only a right to be protected as to the use of an existing home, for example against eviction. Thus, where a public authority evicts a tenant, the court must look at all the circumstances in the light of Article 8 to decide whether the eviction is proportionate (*Manchester City Council v Pinnock* [2010] 3 WLR 1441: anti-social behaviour of tenant's children).

As we have seen, courts are reluctant to impose a positive obligation on the state (Section 21.3.1). However, in cases involving especially vulnerable people experiencing serious difficulties, Article 8, referring as it does to 'respect', may impose a positive duty on the state to provide a benefit (e.g. *R (Bernard) v Enfield LBC* [2002] EWHC 2282 (Admin): disabled with children; *Anufrijeva v Southwark LBC* [2004] QB 1124: asylum-seekers). There must be culpability in the sense of a deliberate or negli-gent failure to act which has foreseeably serious consequences (*Anufrijeva*).

21.4.4.3 Article 9: freedom of thought, conscience and religion

Overrides: Freedom to manifest one's religion or beliefs shall be subject only to such limitations as are prescribed by law and are necessary in a democratic society in the interests of public safety, for the protection of public order, health or morals or for the protection of the rights and freedoms of others.

The desire for religious toleration to bring about peace was one of the original driving forces of liberalism (Section 2.2). In today's diverse society, religious quarrels are still active, and religious freedom is equally important. On the other hand, problems arise when particular groups claim to be exempted from the general law for religious reasons since this threatens the rule of law.

Article 9 therefore distinguishes between the right to hold a belief, which is absolute so that no one can be penalised for what they believe, and the right to 'manifest' a belief, meaning the interaction with others, which can be restricted.

Manifesting religion or belief includes worship, teaching, practice and observance (Art 9(1)). Teaching can include evangelising, in the sense of trying to convert others. However, there is a dis-tinction between this and proselytising, meaning the use of intrusive or improper methods of persua-sion. This may be outside Article 9 altogether, although it may be difficult to draw a line between proselytising and vigorous evangelising. Alternatively, the state can regulate religious propaganda under the override of protecting the rights of others (see *Kokkinakis v Greece* (1994) 17 EHRR 397: Jehovah's Witnesses).

In the case of practices, the particular practice must be 'intimately connected' with the belief and not merely be consistent with it (see *Pretty v UK* [2002]: voluntary euthanasia not within Art 9; *R (Williamson) v Secretary of State for Education and Employment* [2005], [32], [63]: corporal punishment in a Christian school was within Article 9 because it was important to the parents' beliefs). It need not, however, be *required* by the religion (*Eweida v UK* [2013]).

In order to avoid appearing biased, the courts have denied that they are making an evaluation of any belief. However, they also accept the need for a filter to prevent spurious claims. They have done this by insisting that restrictions apply only to the question of *manifestation* and not to the belief itself, then applying various criteria to this (below).

The courts do not try to identify the meaning of religion itself, beyond requiring some form of ideological belief (e.g. pacifism, vegetarianism, teetotalism, atheism or communism) (see *Arrowsmith v UK* (1978) 3 EHRR 218: distributing leaflets encouraging soldiers not to fight; *Campbell and Cosans v UK* (1982) 4 EHRR 293; *Angelini v Sweden* (1986) 51 DR 41; *Hazar and Acik v Turkey* (1991) 72 DR 200). In *R (Williamson) v Secretary of State for Education and Employment* [2005], [55], Lord Walker emphasised that Article 9 is concerned with ethical and philosophical beliefs, as much as with religion. Lord Nichols said that a non-religious belief must relate to an aspect of human life or behaviour of similar importance to a religious belief (at [24]).

Williamson was an action against a group of schools run by a Christian sect that practised 'light' corporal punishment in accordance with parents' wishes and their understanding of the Bible, and in the belief that the child would benefit as Christians. The House of Lords refused to pronounce on the validity of these beliefs, and its investigation was limited to deciding whether the belief was genuinely held (at [22]). However, it indicated that the 'manifestation' of religion was subject to modest objective minimum requirements based on 'seriousness, coherence, importance and compatibility with human dignity' (at [23], [76]). Lord Walker expressed serious doubt as to whether these tests were suitable for a court to apply (at [60]) but accepted them in the context of manifestation of the belief, not the belief itself (at [64]). It was held that the practice did qualify for protection under these tests. Crucially, the court did not consider that all forms of corporal punishment violated human dignity (at [29], [76]–[77]). The upshot of *Williamson*, however, was that the religious practice was outweighed by the public interest in child protection, as evidenced by parliamentary opinion.

In *R (Begum) v Head Teacher and Governors of Denbigh High School* [2007], an extreme version of Muslim dress at school was held not to be protected by Article 9, partly because it did not represent the mainstream, and also because freedom was not thought to be seriously affected because the child could go to another school. An alternative and perhaps better analysis, favoured by Baroness Hale, was that the Article 9 right was overridden by the public interest in social cohesion. Thus, orthodox and familiar practices are more likely to be protected than unusual practices. Moreover, although Lord Bingham (at [111]) emphasised the pluralistic, multicultural nature of our society, religion is sometimes regarded – as in the Protestant tradition, but not universally – as primarily a private matter (*Williamson*, [15]–[19]). However, in *Ahmad v UK* (1981) 4 EHRR 126, collective worship fell within Article 9, albeit overridden (below).

Public concerns seem ready to override minority religious practices as in *Williamson* and *Begum* (above) (see also *Chappell v UK* (1987) 53 DR 241: the freedom of Druids to hold a Solstice ceremony at Stonehenge gave way to the interests of historic conservation; *Pendragon v UK* (App 31416/96, 19 Oct 1998): crowd control at Stonehenge; *ISKCON v UK* (1994) 76A DR 90: local amenity restrictions on religious commune). Similarly, in the employment sphere, the right to manifest religion in public easily gives way to the interests of the employer. It is violated only where the employer fails to take reasonable steps to accommodate the religious requirements of the employee with its own interests. Here also the distinction between the right being engaged and it being overridden by other concerns is blurred.

In *Copsey v WBB Devon Clays Ltd* [2005] EWCA Civ 932, an employee was dismissed for refusing to work on a Sunday. The employer had compelling economic reasons for Sunday working, had engaged in a long consultation process on the matter and had offered the employee an alternative position which was refused. The Court of Appeal held that, in these circumstances, Article 9 had not been violated (see also *Ahmad v UK* (above): teacher attending a mosque gave way to the requirements of the school system; *Eweida v UK* [2013]: entitled to discipline an employee who refused to obey instructions on religious grounds, but only if justified on health and safety grounds in respect of wearing religious insignia or to prevent other forms of discrimination, in that case, discrimination against homosexuals).

In one respect, however, religion seems to be generously protected since, contrary to the usual principles governing freedom of expression, religious believers can apparently be protected against being offended (Section 23.6.2).

21.4.4.4 Article 10: freedom of expression

This right shall include freedom to hold opinions and to receive and impart information and ideas without interference by public authority and regardless of frontiers. This article shall not prevent states from requiring the licensing of broadcasting, television or cinema enterprise.

Overrides: The exercise of these freedoms, since it carries with it duties and responsibilities, may be subject to such formalities, conditions, restrictions or penalties as are prescribed by law and are necessary in a democratic society in the interests of national security, territorial integrity or public safety, for the prevention of disorder or crime, for the protection of health or morals, for the protection of the reputation or rights of others, for preventing the disclosure of information received in confidence or for maintaining the authority and impartiality of the judiciary.

Freedom of expression is discussed in Chapter 23.

21.4.4.5 Article 11: freedom of peaceful assembly and association

Everyone has the right to freedom of peaceful assembly and to freedom of association with others, including the right to form and to join trade unions for the protection of his interests.

Overrides: No restrictions shall be placed on these rights other than such as are prescribed by law and are necessary in a democratic society in the interests of national security or public safety, for the prevention of disorder or crime, for the protection of health or morals or for the protection of the rights and freedoms of others. This article shall not prevent the imposition of lawful restrictions on the exercise of those rights by members of the armed forces, of the police or of the administration of the state.

Freedom of assembly is also discussed in Chapter 23.

21.4.4.6 Protocol 1, Article 1 (P1A1): private property

Every natural or legal person is entitled to the peaceful enjoyment of his possessions. No one shall be deprived of his possessions except in the public interest and subject to the conditions provided for by law and by the general principles of international law. The preceding provisions shall not, however, in any way impair the right of a state to enforce such laws as it deems necessary to control the use of property in accordance with the general interest or to secure the payment of taxes and or other contributions or penalties.

P1A1 protects property rights against confiscation without compensation but does not confer a positive right to acquire property (*Marckx v Belgium* (1979) 2 EHRR 330). Property includes financial assets, such as bank accounts and welfare benefits (see *R (SG) v Secretary of State for Work and Pensions* [2015], [60]–[61]), as well as physical property such as land goods. It includes intangible rights such as the goodwill of a business, but not future profits.

The use of property can be restricted in the public interest, provided that there is a 'fair balance' between the interests concerned (*Fredin v Sweden* (1991) 13 EHRR 784: protection of the environment). This can include paying compensation for the confiscation of property, but not necessarily for restricting its use.

Property rights may have a lower level of protection than the other human rights, and the rights of the state to override them are wider and less specific. For example, in *Wilson v First County Trust* [2003], a statutory provision that made a pawnbroking agreement 'unenforceable' if it was not correctly signed was held to override the right to property, since extortionate loans were a serious social problem, and the provision struck a fair balance. Restrictions on the use of property imposed in the public interest, for example environmental and rent controls, are valid without compensation, although the line between use and confiscation is notoriously difficult to draw (*Mellacher v Austria* (1989) 12 EHRR 391). What, for example, if a restriction on use, which is imposed to conserve wildlife, makes a piece of land unsaleable?

Excessive government charges are deprivations of property. For example, in *Breyer Group v Department of Energy and Climate Change* [2015] 1 WLR 4559, the Court of Appeal held that a government proposal to advance the termination date for a scheme to subsidise energy companies – a 'feed-in tariff system' – was unlawful. The scheme required energy supply companies to pay installers of small-scale energy systems. The aim of the proposal was legitimate, to deal with the problem of excessive burden on consumers caused by an unexpectedly large take-up of the scheme. But there was no fair balance since large investments had been positively encouraged by the government, and the proposal would save the government £1.6 billion against having to pay only £200 million compensation.

In *In re Recovery of Medical Costs for Asbestos Diseases* [2015] 2 WLR 481, a Welsh Assembly bill seeking to recover the NHS costs of treating asbestos disease from insurers was held to violate P1A1, again because there was no fair balance. The Supreme Court held that, although considerable deference must be given to a democratic lawmaker, the retrospective alteration of property rights requires special justification in order to strike a fair balance, and the proceedings of the Assembly did not indicate that this approach had been taken.

The state has a positive obligation to protect property against a natural disaster but only to do what is reasonable in the circumstances as opposed to all in the state's power. When it comes to the public spending priorities, the state has a wide 'margin of appreciation' so that 'reasonable' may mean little more than that serious consideration has been given to the matter (*Budayeva v Russia* [2014]; *Marcic v Thames Water Utilities* ([2004]).

The courts are not willing to use the Convention in cases where a property right is restricted by the exercise of other property rights (see *Aston Cantlow and Wilmcote with Billesley Parochial Church Council v Wallbank* [2003] 3 All ER 1213: charge to repair church roof taking effect as a common law right). This is because the Convention primarily concerns the liability of the state, not that of private persons (see also *McDonald v McDonald* [2016] UKSC 28 (Section 22.8)).

21.4.5   Article 14: discrimination

The enjoyment of the rights and freedoms set forth in this Convention shall be secured without discrimination on any ground such as sex, race, colour, language, religion, political or other opinion, national or social origin, association with a national minority, property, birth or other status. (However, by virtue of Article 16: 'Articles 10, 11 and 14 shall not prevent a state from imposing restrictions on the political activities of aliens'.)

As Baroness Hale pointed out in *Re G (Adoption) (Unmarried Couple)* [2009] 1 AC 173, [122], the protection of unpopular minorities is a particular duty of the courts. Article 14 was described by Lord Nicholls in *Ghaidan v Mendoza* [2004] 3 All ER 411 as fundamental to the rule of law and calling for close scrutiny (at [9], [19]), and by Baroness Hale as 'essential to democracy which is founded on the principle that each individual has equal value' (at [132]).

Art 14 does not outlaw all discrimination. Article 14 applies only where discrimination takes place in relation to one or more of the other Convention rights. However, no such right need actually have been violated. For example, although there is no right under Art 8 to be housed, aspects of housing fall within Art 8, so that refusing housing for discriminatory reasons is unlawful (*R (Morris) v Westminster City Council* [2005] 1 All ER 351: refusal of housing because a dependent child had no immigration rights). Thus, Art 14 substantially extends the protection of the Convention.

However, the discrimination must be 'within the ambit' of the other right (*Botta v Italy* [1998], [39]). In *Secretary of State for Work and Pensions v M* [2006], the House of Lords held that a rule which denied recognition to a same-sex partner in connection with a child support allowance claim did not violate Art 14. Any connection with Art 8 was tenuous, since the parent's relationship with the child, and her home and private life were not affected (compare *Ghaidan v Mendoza* [2004], which directly involved enjoyment of the home). Lord Nicholls (at [13]–[14]) was critical of the notion of 'within the ambit' as virtually meaningless, a not uncommon criticism of the language of the Strasbourg court.

Since it refers to 'such as' (another elusive term), Article 14 extends to forms of discrimination other than those listed (e.g. *A v Secretary of State* [2005] 2 AC 68: nationality; *Ghaidan v Mendoza* (above): sexual orientation; *R (Douglas) v North Tyneside DC* [2004]: age; *Wandsworth LBC v Michalak* [2002] 4 All ER 1136: family membership). It is not easy to identify its limits. In *R (S) v Chief Constable of South Yorkshire Police* [2004], the House of Lords took the view that the discrimination must relate to a 'personal characteristic or status' shared by the disadvantaged group, as opposed to a matter of behaviour only. Article 14 was therefore not engaged by a policy of retaining DNA samples taken lawfully from suspects who were later found to be innocent since the general category of 'innocent persons' was not capable of being a protected category. In another instance, 'the hunting community' was not held to be a protected category (*R (Countryside Alliance) v A-G* [2008]).

On the other hand, 'overseas resident', immigrant and 'person responsible for a child under a residence order' have been held to be protected as having different legal rights and duties from UK citizens or residents and natural parents respectively (*R (Carson) v Secretary of State for Work and Pensions* [2006] 1 AC 173: claim to pension; *Francis v Secretary of State for Work and Pensions* [2006] 1 All ER 748: maternity grant). Being married or unmarried are both statuses because marriage attracts special legal rights and duties (*Re G (Adoption) (Unmarried Couple)* [2009]). A protected category can therefore be something voluntarily assumed as opposed to an aspect of ourselves which we cannot help. Personal characteristics can therefore include, for example, place of residence (*R (A) v Secretary of State for Health* [2017] UKSC 41, [47]).

Certain 'suspect categories', race and sex being preeminent, which are central to identity and over which the victim has no choice, enjoy a high standard of protection, in that especially strong reasons are required to justify discrimination on those grounds. On the other hand, 'age' is not a suspect category in that it is a characteristic of all of us and, provided that the purpose of the discrimination is defensible, clear lines are desirable (see Lord Walker in *Carson* (above); see also Lord Carswell at [15]–[17], [32]).

To discriminate is to treat a person worse than others who are in all relevant respects the same; in other words, like cases must be treated alike. It is also discrimination to fail to treat differently persons whose situations are significantly different (*Thlimmenos v Greece* (2000) 31 EHRR 411, [44]: refusal to accept special circumstances of Jehovah's Witness in qualifying as accountant). Since many government decisions treat different groups of people differently the problem is to decide what is a relevant respect. This relates to the purpose of the decision in question. Is it a legitimate government purpose (below)?

Both direct and indirect discrimination fall within Article 14. Direct discrimination occurs where a measure or decision is specifically targeted at a person in a protected category. Indirect discrimination occurs where a particular group is not directly targeted but is adversely affected more than others by a restriction. For example, in *R (SG) v Secretary of State for Work and Pensions* [2015], a welfare benefit cap based on average income levels disadvantaged single mothers (but was held to be justified (see Box)).

Although Article 14 has no express overrides, discrimination is nevertheless lawful if it can be 'objectively justified'. This means that the discrimination must not be arbitrary. It must pursue a legitimate aim and there must be proportionality (*Belgian Linguistics Case* [1979–80]).

Discrimination examples

R (Hooper) v Secretary of State for Work and Pensions [2006] 1 All ER 487 (property rights): widows' pensions justified as redressing past unfairness to widows.

Wandsworth LBC v Michalak [2002] (attracted by Art 8): distant relative claiming to succeed to tenancy; restriction to close relatives justified as means of rationing public resources.

A v Secretary of State for the Home Department [2005] (attracted by Art 5): discrimination against foreign terrorist suspects lacked rational connection since UK citizens could also be terrorists.

In re G (Adoption) Unmarried Couple [2009] (attracted by Art 8): restriction of adoptions to married couples unreasonably inflexible.

R (Tigere) v Secretary of State for Business, Innovation and Skills [2015] (attracted by right to education): a Nigerian student living with a single mother was denied a student loan because of her immigration status, along with others in the same predicament, even though she had been settled in the UK since childhood. The Supreme Court held that this was arbitrary discrimination in respect of her right to education since the benefits to herself and society from her university course were no different from those of non-immigrant students.

R v Blackman [2015] 1 WLR 1900 (attracted by Art 6): a soldier was convicted by a court martial of murdering an insurgent in Afghanistan. Voting was by a simple majority, although the way members had voted is not revealed. He claimed discrimination since he could have been tried in the Crown Court requiring a ten:two majority. Being a soldier was held to be a personal characteristic, but discrimination was justified by the special circumstances of military life, in particular, a need to avoid a hung jury (at [22]; not elaborated but tied up with military culture of certainty and decisiveness as tools of discipline).

R (Steinfeld & Keidan) v Secretary of State for International Development [2018] (attracted by Art 8) (Section 21.4.4.1).

In domestic law, there is a freestanding ban on discrimination in respect of certain protected characteristics: Equality Act 2010, ss 13, 19, part 2. The protected characteristics are age, disability, gender reassignment, marriage and civil partnership, pregnancy and maternity, race, religion or belief (including lack of belief), sex or sexual orientation. However, some cases fall outside both the ECHR and domestic law. In *Onu v Akwiwu* [2016] 1 WLR 2653, the unauthorised deduction of wages of an immigrant Nigerian domestic worker on the ground of her non-permanent immigrant status was held not to be unlawful discrimination. It was not discrimination in domestic law because it was not on the grounds of race, colour or nationality. The ECHR was not engaged because no Convention right was involved.

Protocol 12 of the ECHR removes the requirement from Art 14 that there must be a link with the other substantive rights and outlaws all discrimination by any public authority. However, some states, including the UK, Germany and France, have not ratified this.

21.5 Criticisms of the Strasbourg court

Criticism of the Strasbourg court has focused on the court's notion that the Convention is a 'living instrument' responsive to changes in public attitudes. It has been suggested that 'mission creep' has extended the Convention into areas where it was not originally intended to apply, such as prisoners' voting rights (Section 12.5.5) and airport noise (*Hatton v UK* [2003]) (see *R (Osborn) v Parole Board* [2014]; *Kennedy v Charity Commission* [2014]: common law protections).

Another criticism has been the alleged poor performance of some Strasbourg judges including inconsistency, lack of language skills and a background in non-democratic states. The transparency of the appointment process has also been questioned (see Miller, *The European Court of Human Rights: The Election of Judges*, HC Library SN/1A/5949 (2011)). A problem of delay is widely recognised, with many cases taking several years to be concluded. Implementation and enforcement is also slow and erratic since it depends on the cooperation of the national governments.

In the 2010 Interlaken Declaration of the Council of Europe, ministers set out a reform agenda for 'subsidiarity' in the form of closer cooperation with Member States in particular in dealing with repetitive applications. Article 35(3)(b) now enables the court to rule an application inadmissible if the applicant has suffered 'no significant disadvantage'.

In 2012, the Brighton Declaration supported a looser relationship with Strasbourg in the form of a general 'margin of appreciation' for Member States. This would reduce the Strasbourg court's role effectively to that of review where a case has been considered by domestic courts following clear Strasbourg jurisprudence. It also supported the introduction of advisory opinions and improving the process for nominating Strasbourg judges including an age limit of 65 on nomination for appointment. It was suggested that there be machinery for 'dialogue' between the Strasbourg court and the courts and government agencies. Perhaps these proposals go too far in weakening the court and its independence (see Elliott [2012] PL 619).

Protocols 15 and 16 have implemented these proposals but have not yet been ratified by all Member States.

Summary

- The human rights debate involves attempts to accommodate competing and incommensurable values without any coherent overarching principle to enable a choice to be made. It is therefore arguable that an elected body rather than a court should have the last word.

- Freedom in the common law is residual in the sense that one can do anything unless there is a specific law to the contrary. This is arguably an inadequate method of safeguarding important liberties. There is a debate as to the extent to which the common law embodies the principles of the ECHR, and it is suggested that there are important differences in the approaches of the two systems.

- The ECHR as such is not strictly binding upon English courts but can be taken into account where the law is unclear or where a judge has discretionary powers. The individual can petition the European Court of Human Rights, the decisions of which are binding in international law but, unlike those of the CJEU (in relation to European Union law), are not legally binding in domestic law.

- The HRA, while not incorporating the Convention as such, has given the main rights created by the ECHR effect in domestic law. UK legislation must be interpreted to be compatible with Convention rights, and the decisions of the Strasbourg court must be taken into account, although parliamentary supremacy is preserved.

- The Strasbourg court applies principles of international law and its jurisprudence includes broad and flexible principles and doctrines such as the 'living instrument', 'fair balance', 'margin of appreciation' and 'autonomous' doctrines. These help to mediate between international and national concerns, but the court has been accused of expansionist tendencies.

- Most Convention rights are negative rights that restrain the state from interfering with them. Some have a positive aspect by imposing a duty on the state to ensure that the right in question is complied with, or to hold an inquiry into a failure to do so. In exceptional cases only, the state has a positive duty to provide a service or benefit such as a welfare payment.

- Some rights, notably deprivation of liberty, are narrowly defined; others, notably 'respect for privacy and family life', are broad and vague.

- Some of the rights are absolute and cannot be overridden by public interest considerations, although they might be defined narrowly in the light of the public interest. Other rights are subject to exceptions, and an important group of rights can be overridden in individual cases on prescribed grounds of the public interest or of other rights.

- Some rights, notably the right to life, protection against torture, slavery, forced labour and deprivation of liberty, freedom of political expression and non-discrimination, have an especially high status as being the foundations of a democratic society. The status of freedom of religion is ambivalent, religious claims outside the mainstream often being overridden. The right to property may have a lower level of protection than other rights.

- Most forms of discrimination based on personal status are prohibited, but only where there is a solid link to one of the other rights.

- In many cases, particularly where the right in issue is broad, the Strasbourg court allows a state a 'margin of appreciation' in the sense of a discretion as to the application of the Convention to its own circumstances. This is discussed in Section 22.9.3.

- The Strasbourg court has been criticised for allegedly interfering excessively and beyond its capacity with national governments.

Exercises

21.1 'Human rights are permeated with irresolvable disagreement as to what they mean, how they apply, and as to the nature of disputes about them. The courts are therefore a hopelessly inadequate mechanism for resolving human rights problems'. Discuss.

21.2 **(i)** Assess the meaning of and justification for the margin of appreciation. What are its limits?

     (ii) The Welsh Senedd enacts a law that requires all rail season ticket holders to pay a levy towards the backlog of repairs to rural railway lines in South-West Wales. On the assumption that the matter falls within the devolved powers of the Senedd, assess whether a challenge can be made under the ECHR by an urban North-Wales commuter who never uses rural railways. What would be the position if, when the matter of rail modernisation was debated in the Senedd, this particular clause was not raised?

21.3 Jones is holding a group of people as hostages in a secret location. The police arrest him. He says that his prisoners will be blown up by a bomb in one hour. The police wish to use techniques of simulated drowning ('waterboarding'), which they believe to have been recommended by military intelligence services worldwide, to discover the whereabouts of the hostages. The Home Secretary decides to authorise waterboarding, as a result of which Jones dies. The hostages are blown up. Advise the Home Secretary and the police as to any legal liability they might incur.

21.4 Angus, an army recruit, dies while on a training exercise in a remote mountainous area. The cause of death appears to be extreme cold. His parents inform their local newspaper that they believe Angus was provided with inadequate protective clothing by the military authorities. The newspaper hears from an anonymous source that senior Ministry of Defence officials have been taking bribes to procure cheap military clothing from an overseas supplier. Advise Angus's parents whether they can invoke Article 2 of the ECHR against the army authorities and, if so, what their rights are.

21.5 The common law doctrine of fairness has been said to accord with the 'spirit' of Article 6 (*Secretary of State for the Home Dept v MB* [2008] at [24]). Do you agree? What differences, if any, are there between the two? (See also Chapter 18.)

21.6 Consider whether the ECHR has been violated in the following cases:

     (i) Sexeter School of Law requires all students, as a condition of graduating, to work unpaid for ten hours per week in local law firms.

     (ii) Jane's father refuses to pay for her university course unless she agrees to work unpaid in his chocolate factory throughout every vacation.

     (iii) Jack, who would otherwise be homeless, occupies a caravan on his uncle Fred's farm. He is required to work for 15 hours a day on the farm except for Sundays and can leave the farm only with Fred's permission.

     (iv) In assessing Mary's housing needs, Exbury Council refuses to take into account her same-sex partner.

21.7 **(i)** 'In matters of human rights the courts should not show liberal tolerance only to tolerant liberals' (Lord Walker in *R (Williamson) v Secretary of State for Education and Employment* (2005), [60]). Discuss in relation to freedom of religion.

     (ii) Charles is a member of an 'anti-religion' group. Each evening he visits homes in his town distributing leaflets and attempting to persuade householders to join his group. As a result of complaints from residents, Charles is prosecuted for breaching a local by-law forbidding advertising campaigns at night. Advise Charles as to whether he is protected by Article 9 of the ECHR.

21.8 **(i)** What is meant by a 'deprivation of liberty' under the ECHR?

     (ii) Jack, who suffers from memory loss, is an outpatient at an NHS hospital. After his latest visit, the hospital authorities lock Jack in a small office for three hours to prevent him from leaving the hospital until his wife arrives to take him home. Advise Jack, who strongly objects to this, as to any rights he might have under the ECHR. What additional facts might influence your answer?

21.9 Explain the significance of Protocol 12 of the ECHR.

Further reading

Arden, 'On Liberty and the European Convention on Human Rights' in Andenas and Fairgrieve (eds), *Tom Bingham and the Transformation of the Law* (Oxford University Press 2009)

Bratza, 'Living Instrument or Dead Letter – The Future of the European Convention on Human Rights' [2014] EHRLR 116

Clapham, *Human Rights: A Very Short Introduction* (2nd edn, Oxford University Press 2007)

Clayton, 'The Empire Strikes Back: Common Law Rights and the Human Rights Act' [2015] PL 3

Gearty, *Can Human Rights Survive?* (Cambridge University Press 2006)

Gearty, *On Fantasy Island: Britain, Europe and Human Rights* (Oxford University Press 2016)

Heydon, 'Are Bills of Rights Necessary in Common Law Systems?' (2014) 130 LQR 392

Hill and Sandberg, 'Is Nothing Sacred? Clashing Symbols in a Secular World' [2007] PL 488

Juss, 'Back to the Future: Justiciability, Religion and the Figment of "Judicial No-Man's Land"' [2016] PL 198

Laws, 'Is the High Court the Guardian of Fundamental Constitutional Rights?' [1993] PL 59

Leader, 'Freedom and Futures: Personal Priorities, Institutional Demands and Freedom of Religion' (2007) 70 MLR 713

Masterman and Wheatle, 'A Common Law Resurgence in Rights Protection' [2015] EHRLR 57

McCormick, *Institutions of Law* (Oxford University Press 2007) ch 11

Spano, 'The Future of the European Court of Human Rights – Subsidiarity, Process-Based Review and the Rule of Law' (2018) 18 HRLR 473

Stone, 'Deprivation of Liberty: The Scope of Article 5 of the European Convention on Human Rights' [2012] EHRLR 46

22.1 The scope of the Act

The extent to which the HRA is radical is controversial. It was not introduced as a British Bill of Rights, but more as a tidying-up and cost-saving operation to ensure that UK law was in line with the ECHR and to reduce petitions to Strasbourg (*Rights Brought Home: The Human Rights Bill* (1997) Cm 3782; *R (Pretty) v DPP* [2002] 1 All ER 1). Unlike a classic bill of rights, the Act does not formally override parliamentary supremacy. Under its provisions, a sufficiently clearly worded statute overrides any human right, although the court must try to avoid this outcome. The HRA does not enact the ECHR as such. It incorporates the main 'Convention rights' (listed in Sched. 1), giving them defined consequences in UK law. All legislation must be interpreted in accordance with Convention rights, and the Act provides remedies enforceable in the courts against public authorities which violate Convention rights. It also provides a mechanism for Parliament to reconsider legislation that violates a Convention right.

The Act has not incorporated Article 1 (duty to secure to everyone within the jurisdiction the rights and freedoms under the Convention), or Article 13 (effective domestic remedies for breach of the Convention). In *DSD v Commissioner of Police of the Metropolis* [2015] 3 WLR 966, at [16]–[17], Laws LJ said that the HRA gives effect 'lock stock and barrel' to the substantive rights guaranteed by the Convention, but does not include the mechanisms for giving effect to them, since the Act creates its own mechanisms. Presumably, the drafters of the Act were confident that it would comply with Arts 1 and 13. However, Arts 1 and 13 might apply indirectly where UK remedies fall short since the court must take account of the decisions of the Strasbourg court which does include them in its jurisprudence (e.g. *Smith v Ministry of Defence* [2014] AC 52; *Quark Fishing Ltd v UK* (2007) 44 EHRR SE4).

It is undeniable that the HRA adds a further dimension to the law by entitling the judges to assess an Act of Parliament in the light of supposedly higher principles, even though they cannot overturn an Act. Indeed, it has been suggested that in view of the respect attracted by a court, the HRA differs little in its effect from an 'entrenched' bill of rights that empowers courts to overturn legislation (see Klug (2007); Hiebert, 'Parliamentary Bills of Rights: An Alternative Model' (2006) 69 MLR 7). In political terms, therefore, like the devolution legislation and the EU, the HRA is a brake on parliamentary sovereignty.

The Act applies both to statutes and common law. However, the common law can, to a limited extent, respond to human rights without the support of a statute (Section 21.2). In *Kennedy v Charity Commission* [2014] UKSC 20, a case concerning the disclosure of government information, Lord Mance said that one of the most fruitful features of UK jurisprudence has been the development of common law discretions to meet Convention requirements.

The UK courts' approach to human rights issues does not display a clear philosophy. Disagreement within the highest courts is not unusual. One reason for this is disagreement about the proper limits of the court's intervention, in particular the extent to which controversial matters should be left to the democratic process (Section 21.5). Another reason, particularly for tension between the UK courts and Strasbourg, is that the approaches of the two courts to balancing competing interests may differ. The UK approach seems to be broadly pragmatic and utilitarian, in the sense that the court weighs the consequences on either side and tries to choose the least harmful overall solution. The European Court of Human Rights, by contrast, is more likely to be broad brush and to stress the value of the right in principle.

Moreover, the UK courts seem to have a greater tendency to trust the integrity of the government, the police and other officials, and to accept informal safeguards, than the European Court, which requires stronger and more legalistic safeguards (see e.g. *Gillan and Quinton v UK* (2010) 50 EHRR 45; *S and Marper v UK* (2008) 48 EHRR 50; *Hanif and Khan v UK* (2012) 55 EHRR 16). However, recent proposals which would require the Strasbourg court to give a general margin of appreciation to domestic courts as to the application of established principles could lessen the tension between the two systems (Section 21.5).

Judicial views of the HRA

These reflect disagreement as to the role of the Act, which continues to infect the cases.

In *A v Secretary of State for the Home Department* [2005] 2 AC 68, [42], Lord Bingham argued that the function of independent judges to apply the law is a cardinal feature of the modern democratic state, and that 'the courts are charged by Parliament with delineating the boundaries of a rights based democracy'.

Lord Neuberger, a previous President of the Supreme Court, commented that the Act has 'pitchforked' the judges into ruling on the controversial issues of the day and has 'changed the constitutional settlement' giving judges more power as against the legislature and the executive (*The Role of Judges in Human Rights Jurisprudence: A Comparison of the Australian and UK Experience* (8 August 2014, Supreme Court, Melbourne)). However, according to Lord Hoffmann (*R v Secretary of State for the Home, Department, ex p Simms* [2000] 2 AC 115, 131–32, the Act does little more than reinforce the existing law. Much of it, in his view, reflects common law principles; it enacts the existing 'principle of legality' according to which fundamental rights can be overridden only by clear statutory language (Section 6.6), and it forces Parliament to face squarely what it is doing. In *R (Alconbury Developments Ltd) v Secretary of State for the Environment, Transport and the Regions* [2001] 2 All ER 929, [129], Lord Hoffmann remarked that the Act 'was no doubt intended to strengthen the rule of law but not to inaugurate the rule of lawyers'.

Similarly, in *R v Lambert* [2001] 3 All ER 577, Lord Hope emphasised the need to respect the will of the legislature and to preserve the integrity of our statute law. But in *Wilson v First County Trust* [2003] 4 All ER 97, [179]–[185], Lord Rodger said that 'although the Act is not entrenched, the Convention rights that it confers have a peculiar potency. Rights that can produce such results are clearly of a higher order than the rights which people enjoy at common law or under most statutes'. And in *R v Lambert* [2001], [6], Lord Slynn remarked: '[I]t is clear that the 1998 Act must be given its full import and that long or well entrenched ideas may have to be put aside, sacred cows culled'.

22.2   Relations with the Strasbourg court

Apart from parliamentary sovereignty, the domestic courts' relationship with the Strasbourg court is the most important general issue underlying the HRA. The matter is relevant as to whether the Act is the basis of a distinctively British bill of rights. By virtue of Section 2(1), all UK courts must 'take into account' relevant decisions and opinions of the European Court of Human Rights. Thus, the Act does not expressly make Strasbourg decisions binding. A claimant can petition Strasbourg in respect of a domestic court's decision as before, but the decision of the Strasbourg court is binding only in international law.

There is a continuing debate as to how far the Act enables the UK courts to develop their own free-standing interpretation of the rights included in the Convention (see e.g. Hale, 'Argentoratum Locutum: Is Strasbourg or the Supreme Court Supreme?' [2012] EHRLR 65). On the one hand, the language of the Act does not expressly prevent them from so doing, and the margin of appreciation in Strasbourg jurisprudence allows domestic courts some freedom within the envelope of the general Convention principles (Section 22.9). Furthermore, it has been claimed that the Act requires a 'constructive dialogue' between the domestic courts and Strasbourg so that each can respond to the other in changing circumstances (*Manchester City Council v Pinnock* [2010] 3 WLR 1441, [48]). It could also be argued that, as part of international law, the Convention is a gateway to other international treaties which a court may use to help it decide cases, not all of which the UK has necessarily agreed to, so that a safety valve may be desirable.

On the other hand, an Act such as the HRA that incorporates provisions in an international treaty must be interpreted in accordance with that treaty in order to comply with the UK's international obligations, the 'mirror principle' (see *In Re McCaughey* [2011] UKSC 20, Section 22.4). Obedience to Strasbourg supports the rule of law's concern with certainty, ensures that the Convention as an international agreement will be consistently applied, and discourages a court from making controversial moral or political judgments of its own. Moreover, sticking to the Strasbourg jurisprudence could be said to reflect Parliament's intention in enacting the HRA and helps to counter claims that the courts are undemocratic. Obedience to Strasbourg also reduces the number of petitions made to the Strasbourg court. Since the HRA came into force there has been a decline in Strasbourg judgments adverse to the UK from 30 in 2002 to 5 in 2019.

On the whole, the courts have followed the Strasbourg cases. In *R (Ullah) v Special Adjudicator* [2004] 3 All ER 785, regarded as the leading case, Lord Bingham said (at [20]) that 'the duty of national courts is to keep pace with the Strasbourg jurisprudence as it evolves over time: no more but certainly no less and to follow a clear and consistent line of Strasbourg cases'. In *R (Al-Skeini) v Secretary of State for Defence* [2008] 1 AC 153, Lord Brown (at [106]) converted this into 'no less but certainly no more'. In *Secretary of State for the Home Department v AF (No 3)* [2010] 2 AC 269, Lord Rogers (at [98]) famously said, in the accessible language of the law, '*Argentoratum locutum: judicium finitum*: Strasbourg has spoken, the case is closed'.

In *Smith v Ministry of Defence* [2014], at [43], Lord Hope said that 'Parliament never intended by enacting the Human Rights Act 1998 to give the courts of this country the power to give a more generous scope to the Convention rights than that which was to be found in the jurisprudence of the Strasbourg court. To do so would have the effect of changing them from Convention rights, based on the treaty obligation into free-standing rights of the court's [that is to say, the Supreme Court's] own creation' (see also Lord Mance (at [143]); Lord Carnwath (at [156])).

The Supreme Court has performed U-turns in response to Strasbourg rulings. In *Smith* (above), it reversed its previous rulings that the HRA did not apply outside territory controlled by the UK government (Section 22.3). In *Manchester City Council v Pinnock* (above), a series of House of Lords cases were overruled in order to give effect to Strasbourg cases that required the court to investigate the individual circumstances of an eviction of a council tenant.

However, in some instances, the Supreme Court has relaxed the *Ullah* principle. Indeed, in *Moohan v Lord Advocate* [2015] AC 901, at [105], it was suggested that there was a 'retreat from Strasbourg' (see Mahoney (2014)). In *Kennedy v Charity Commission* [2014], [100] it was suggested that Lord Bingham's famous *Ullah* dictum: 'no more but certainly no less' was an invitation to strike out alone in some circumstances (at [154]) (see also Lord Kerr and Lady Hale in *Keyu v Secretary of State for Foreign and Commonwealth Affairs* [2015] UKSC 69).

Lord Neuberger's statement in *Manchester City Council v Pinnock* [2010] is much relied upon. His Lordship said (at [48]) that 'where … there is a clear and consistent line of decisions whose effect is not inconsistent with some fundamental substantive or procedural aspect of domestic law, and whose reasoning does not appear to misunderstand or overlook some argument or point of principle', it would be wrong for the Supreme Court not to follow that line. This was endorsed in *R (Chester) v Secretary of State for Justice* [2014] 1 All ER 683, [27]–[29], where the Supreme Court (Lord Sumption reluctantly) followed the Strasbourg court in holding that the UK's blanket ban on prisoners having the right to vote violated the Convention. Lord Mance stated (at [27]) that, in the case of a decision of the Grand Chamber of the European Court, only some 'truly fundamental principle of domestic law or an egregious mistake or oversight' would justify an outright refusal to follow it. However, the UK courts can refuse to follow single Chamber decisions of the Strasbourg court, 'in the confidence that a reasoned expression of a divergent national viewpoint will lead to a serious review of the position in Strasbourg'. On this basis, it was held that refusing prisoners the right to vote was not a fundamental principle (at [35]).

Departing from Strasbourg

There seem to be four kinds of case that would justify a departure from Strasbourg jurisprudence, at least by the Supreme Court:

1. Where the Strasbourg cases are unclear or leave the matter open, at least where the direction of travel is within a general principle developed by Strasbourg. In *Surrey County Council v P* [2014] AC 896, the Supreme Court extended Art 5 into the detention of mental patients in foster homes. In *Moohan v Lord Advocate* [2014], a case concerning prisoners' voting rights, a topic on which the UK has clashed with Strasbourg, Lord Wilson said (at [105]) that 'where there is no directly relevant decision with which it would be possible (even if appropriate) to keep pace, we can and must do more. We must determine for ourselves the existence or otherwise of an alleged Convention right'. However, in that case, the court agreed with Strasbourg in holding that the right to vote did not apply to referendums. Similarly in *Keyu v Secretary of State for Foreign and Commonwealth Affairs* [2015] (Section 22.4), the Supreme Court chose to follow Strasbourg guidelines relating to long passed events in the interests of certainty. A majority agreed, however, that Strasbourg did not have to be slavishly followed (Lords Neuberger and Hughes (at [90]), Lord Kerr (at [228]). Lady Hale (at [291]) did not follow Strasbourg, apparently on the ground that the Strasbourg cases were not sufficiently clear (see also *Kennedy v Charity Commission* [2014] (Section 24.2)). Similarly, in *Commissioner of Police of the Metropolis v DSD* [2018] UKSC 11, Lord Mance said (at [153]) that 'If the existence or otherwise of a Convention right is unclear, then it may be appropriate for domestic courts to make up their minds whether the Convention rights should or should not be understood to embrace it'.

2. Where it is claimed that Strasbourg has misunderstood a principle of UK law (e.g. *R v Horncastle* [2010] 2 AC 373: hearsay evidence), or that the Strasbourg reasoning is inconsistent (e.g. *R (Haney) v Secretary of State for Justice* [2014] UKSC 66: nature of duty to facilitate release of prisoner serving a discretionary sentence). In this kind of case, there might be a 'dialogue' when the Strasbourg court responds to the domestic court (e.g. *R v Spear* [2003] 1 AC 734: independence of courts martial: misunderstandings of UK law later corrected by ECtHR; *Z v UK* (2002) 34 EHRR 3; *Cooper v UK* (2004) 39 EHRR 8).

3. Where the Strasbourg ruling is contrary to a fundamental principle of UK law. In *R (Alconbury Developments Ltd) v Secretary of State for the Environment, Transport and the Regions* [2001], the UK procedures for deciding land use planning and compulsory acquisition disputes lacked the independence required by Strasbourg cases under Art 6 (right to a fair trial) as regards investigation of facts, but reflected the looser version of the separation of powers practised in the UK, namely the principle that ministers responsible to Parliament should take such decisions. However, the Strasbourg cases may not have been 'clear and consistent'. The House of Lords applied the Convention less generously than Strasbourg. Thus, this exception suits a case where the claimant might petition Strasbourg which would decide whether to allow the UK a margin of appreciation or possibly change its own mind (see *R (Animal Defenders International) v Culture Secretary* [2008] 1 AC 1312; *Animal Defenders International v UK* (2013) 57 EHRR 21: where the Court accepted the UK's view on the importance of restraints on political advertising (Section 23.3.2)).

4. The court may go beyond Strasbourg, but not contradict it, where the Strasbourg court allows a margin of appreciation (e.g. *R (Nicklinson v Ministry of Justice* [2014] UKSC 38; *Commissioner of Police of the Metropolis v DSD* [2018] (at [153]: Lord Mance). *In Re G (Adoption) (Unmarried Couple)* [2009] 1 AC 173 (at [50]); Lord Hope said that Section 2 was not a 'straightjacket' [sic] and that the court could depart from Strasbourg where a matter was within the margin of appreciation.

22.3   Extraterritorial application

The law has struggled with almost 2000 allegations of mistreatment both of prisoners and of civilians by British troops in Iraq and Afghanistan. The government established an Iraq Historic Allegations Team (IHAT), to review and carry out investigations in respect of allegations by Iraqi civilians. These cases concerned claims for compensation under the HRA and also judicial review claims for an inquiry into allegations of violations of Convention rights, predominantly Article 3: inhuman or degrading treatment or punishment.

Article 1 of the ECHR imposes a duty on states to secure the rights in respect of everyone 'within their jurisdiction'. The Convention was originally territorial and respects international law, which might be destabilised if the courts interfered with matters occurring abroad. For example, in *R v Secretary of State for Foreign and Commonwealth Affairs, ex p Quark Fishing Ltd* [2006] 1 AC 529, (Section 9.4.2.1), it was held that the Act does not apply to a dependent territory, unless perhaps the Convention itself has been specifically extended to it. See also *Chagos Islanders v UK* (2013) 56 EHRR SE15 (Section 9.4). The fact that the decisions were made in London was irrelevant. The Act does not apply in the Channel Islands which, however, have a similar law of their own and are subject to the ECHR (see *R (Barclay) v Secretary of State for Justice* [2014] 3 WLR 1142).

However, case-law has made substantial inroads on the territorial principle. A personal element has been introduced based on the concept of 'control'. In *Al-Skeini v UK* (2011) 53 EHRR 18, the Strasbourg court, disagreeing with the UK case of *R (Al-Skeini) v Secretary of State for Defence* [2008] 1 AC 153, held that the Convention protected a person who was under the authority or control of the state outside UK territory. The case concerned the death of Iraqi prisoners, and the UK court had held that the Act applied only to those in custody on a British base in Iraq, but not to the treatment of prisoners outside the base. The Court's reasoning was based on Art 13 of the ECHR, which requires the state to provide an effective remedy for violations of the Convention (Art 13 is not incorporated by the HRA as such). The notion of the Convention as a 'living instrument' responsive to changes in society is also relevant.

Therefore, in *Smith v Ministry of Defence* [2014], departing from its previous decision, [2011] 1 AC 1), the Supreme Court held that the government was in principle liable under the HRA to the relatives of soldiers fighting in Iraq in respect of failure to take reasonable care in relation to the right to life (Art 2). In *Smith*, soldiers were killed by 'friendly fire' and by roadside bombs, in both cases while on patrol. It was recognised that the ambit of the Convention was not exclusively territorial but could be 'divided and tailored' (at [38]). The same reasoning applies to other parts of the Convention, in particular to Art 3 (torture and inhuman or degrading treatment or punishment) and Art 5 (deprivation of liberty). This applies both to the substantive duty and to the procedural duty to hold an inquiry into violations.

The governing principle was that the soldiers were at the time in fact under the exclusive control of the state through the military command structure. The government was alleged to have failed to equip tanks properly, and to give adequate 'recognition training'. The court was not required to decide whether on the facts the government was in breach of Art 2. In particular, high-level policy matters and specialised judgments would have a margin of appreciation (Section 22.9.3).

The same principle applies to wrongs done to civilians. In *R (Al-Saadoon) v Secretary of State for Defence* [2016] EWCA Civ 811, the Court of Appeal, agreeing with most of the comprehensive judgment of Leggatt J at first instance, confirmed that the principle is one of actual physical control, irrespective of territory and formal occupation. Thus, the Convention applies both to persons in custody and to those killing or injuring civilians in the street or their homes. There are three main situations: first, where diplomats and consular agents exercise authority and control; second, where the UK exercises governmental powers such as policing with the consent or acquiescence of the government of the territory in question, for example the Convention applied when UK soldiers were policing a queue of Iraqi civilians at a petrol station; third, and most controversial, the Convention applies to the use of force by UK agents operating independently.

In one respect, the Court of Appeal differed from Leggatt J. It was held that the element of control must exist before the violence complained of, whereas Leggatt J held that the violence itself constituted control. The Court of Appeal thought this was possibly a step too far and that only Strasbourg could authorise a further extension of the Convention. In what could be a warning to Strasbourg, the Court of Appeal remarked, that there is potentially a massive expansion of the Convention and that the genie has been let out of the bottle (at [62]).

It is not clear how far the Convention would apply in actual combat conditions where the army is under fire. A very wide margin of discretion is likely to apply. Art 2 (right to life) does not apply to a lawful act of war. Art 5 (deprivation of liberty) is modified by international humanitarian law, so that judicial supervision is not required (*Hassan v UK* [2014] ECHR 936).

In 2016, the government proposed that there would be a presumption to derogate from the ECHR under Art 15 in respect of future overseas operations of armed forces. Art 15 permits derogation, strictly to the extent needed to deal with the exigencies of the situation, in times of war or public emergency threatening the life of the nation. Certain provisions cannot be derogated from. They include Art 2 (right to life) except in the case of a lawful act of war, Art 3 (torture and inhuman or degrading treatment) and Art 4(1) (slavery) (Section 21.4). A decision to derogate can be challenged in the courts. It is not wholly clear whether extraterritorial derogation is, in fact, possible especially given the requirement that there be a threat to the life of the nation. The proposal was the subject of an inquiry by the Joint Committee on Human Rights, which was cut short by the 2017 election. A subsequent private member's bill on the matter failed to complete its parliamentary passage, but an Overseas Operations (Service Personnel and Veterans) Bill 2019–21, introduced to Parliament in March 2020, will, if enacted, oblige government to consider derogation in relation to any overseas operations considered to be significant.

The meaning of 'control'

This extension of the HRA to acts done overseas depends on whether in fact the UK is in independent control. In *Keyu v Secretary of State for Foreign and Commonwealth Affairs* [2015] (Section 22.4), it was alleged that, in 1948, British soldiers had massacred civilians in Malaya (as Malaysia was then called) and that the government should hold an independent inquiry into this. The UK government was acting under a treaty under which it exercised wide security powers in Malaya. The Crown argued that responsibility was inherited by the government of Malaysia. However, the Supreme Court held that, at the time, the Crown was in control of the military campaign for its own purposes, namely to implement the treaty, and therefore in principle the HRA could apply (at [87]–[88]). However, there was no duty to hold an inquiry because of the lapse of time (Section 22.4).

Similarly, in *Mohammed v Secretary of State for Defence* [2016] 2 WLR 247, the Court of Appeal held that the detention of Afghan prisoners by the British Army fighting insurgents in Afghanistan was carried out under UK control even though the UK was part of a UN force. By contrast, the Act did not apply to the handing over of a prisoner to the Iraqi government where the UK was acting as an agent of that government and not exercising sovereign powers (*R (Al Saadoon) v Secretary of State for Defence* (above)) (see now *Al-Waheed v Ministry of Defence* [2017] 2 WLR 327).

22.4   Time limits

The Act applies to all legislation whether made before or after it came into force in October 2000, s 3(2)(a). However, the Act has been held not to be retrospective (*Re McKerr* [2004] 1 WLR 807: inquiry into a death). If this is so, violations occurring before 2 October 2000 cannot be investigated. There is an exception in the case of a defence to proceedings brought by a public authority. This applies whenever the action complained of took place. Proceedings must be commenced within one year of the act complained of, or such longer period as the court thinks equitable in all the circumstances (s 7(5)), but the time limit is subject to any rule imposing a stricter limit upon the procedure in question (thus, if a claim is brought by way of judicial review, the three-month period will apply (Section 19.3)).

The duty to hold an inquiry into a death under Art 2, or inhuman or degrading treatment under Art 3, raises special considerations. In *Silih v Slovenia* (2009) 49 EHRR 37, this duty was held to be a separate, 'detachable duty' from the event that triggers it (Section 21.4.3). The Strasbourg court has held that an inquiry can be held into events that took place many years ago. In *In Re McCaughey* [2011], which concerned an alleged 'shoot to kill policy' by the British army in Northern Ireland, the Supreme Court, Lord Rodgers dissenting, held that an inquiry must be held into a shooting in 1990 where the DPP had refused to prosecute. The principle that the HRA was not retrospective must give way to the more important principle that the Act must 'mirror' Strasbourg so as to comply with the UK's international obligations.

Thus, Strasbourg has opened the possibility of investigating historical wrongs. This is an important issue in the light of current public concerns for such inquiries, including child abuse, and alleged wrongs connected with British aggression overseas (see, in this context, the Overseas Operations (Service Personnel and Veterans Bill (above), which, if enacted, will preclude any claim being brought under the HRA for any alleged violation arising during an overseas military operation if more than six years have elapsed).

As time passes, the desire for accountability faces increasing problems of discovering the truth and finding anyone to be accountable. Thus, in the interests of certainty, the Strasbourg court later introduced limitations on looking into past events (*Janowiec v Russia* (2013) 58 EHRR 792: massacre of more than 21,000 Poles in 1940: inquiry not required). The Supreme Court seems to have accepted the Strasbourg approach. This would probably put the outer limit on such an inquiry as the date on which the Convention was ratified by the state in question (see Box). In the UK, this was 3 September 1953.

Case study: inquiries into historical abuses: coordination with Strasbourg

In any given case, several dates may be involved, and the Strasbourg cases are not entirely clear. The possible dates are:

(i)   the date of the 'triggering event', the wrong which creates the duty to hold an inquiry, e.g. a death or torture;

(ii) the date the Convention first applied to the state in question;

(iii) the date on which the right to petition Strasbourg first applied: the 'critical date' (in the UK this was 14 January 1966). Some time after this date there must be an act or omission that relates back to the original wrong;

(iv) the date the HRA came into force, 2 October 2000, since, in domestic law, there must be a fact arising after this date also. The same fact may also satisfy Strasbourg under (iii);

(v)   the date on which the claim is made, which must normally be within one year of the action complained of, for example a refusal to hold an inquiry or abandoning a previous inquiry.

In *Keyu v Secretary of State for Foreign and Commonwealth Affairs* [2015], the Supreme Court, with considerable disagreement, attempted to coordinate with Strasbourg. The government had refused to hold an inquiry into the deaths of civilians alleged to have been massacred in 1948 by British soldiers in Malaya (as it was then). There was no solid evidence until 1969 that the killings were unlawful, but compelling evidence had emerged in late 1969 and early 1970 to this effect. Despite media pressure, the government resisted demands to hold an independent inquiry on the ground that the chances of uncovering the truth were outweighed by the cost of doing so. The claimants, relatives of the dead, suspected a cover-up. On 29 November 2010, the government formally refused an inquiry.

As regards the time limits, three questions arose. First, what is the 'critical date' from which the time calculations must be made? This is the date on which the Convention becomes binding from the viewpoint of Strasbourg. Presumably, an inquiry can always look back as far as the critical date. Second, what enables the court to look back beyond the critical date? Third, in domestic law, what is the link to the HRA? The claimants argued, first, that the duty under the Convention to hold an inquiry arose in 1953 when the Convention came into force and the deaths, 'the triggering event', were sufficiently close to that date to justify the court interfering. They argued, secondly, that new information had come to light since the Act came into force in 2000.

A majority of the Supreme Court, following the Strasbourg court, reluctantly held that it could not intervene. The principles in *Janowiec* (above) endorsed by the majority were as follows:

The 'critical date' is when the right to petition Strasbourg first applied to the UK (at [89], [90]). Events occurring even before the critical date could be investigated, provided that there is a 'genuine connection' with the 'triggering event', in this case the deaths. The genuine connection must, first, comprise 'a relevant act or omission' *after* the critical date and second, there must be a reasonably short period between the deaths and the critical date. This period must normally be within ten years of the critical date (as was the case in *McCaughey* (above)).

In *Keyu*, there was a 'relevant act', namely the emergence of new evidence in 1969/70 revealing the likelihood of wrongdoing, after a previous investigation had been abandoned. However, the deaths had occurred more than ten years before the critical date, so the second test had been failed. The genuine connection can be relaxed where 'underlying values of the Convention are involved'. However, this was not the case here since the killings took place in 1948 when the Convention did not exist.

The claim therefore failed under Strasbourg rules. As regards the additional domestic requirement, namely the link to the HRA, there must be a breach of the duty after the Act came into force in 2000. According to the majority, the most recent significant event was the emergence of compelling new evidence in late 1969, relevant to Strasbourg but not to domestic law. Moreover, there is a one-year time limit for bringing proceedings under the HRA itself. Lord Neuberger and Lord Hughes, obiter (at [104]–[108]), held, also in line with Strasbourg, that the clock ran from the first time the alleged failure arose, this being late 1969, when the evidence of wrongdoing became compelling. (The claimant had argued that time should run from the government's most recent refusal to hold an inquiry in November 2010).

Lord Kerr and Lady Hale took different routes to the same conclusion. Both thought that the Strasbourg cases were unclear. Lord Kerr left matters vague. He held that the Strasbourg rules should be regarded more as arbitrary guidelines than principles, and that Strasbourg cases should not be rigidly followed (at [208]–[209]). Furthermore, the time limit for the HRA is not necessarily the same as that of the Strasbourg court, since the procedures of the two are not the same. Without being specific, he held that a cut-off point was necessary, ten years was as good as any, and that events taking place 52 years before the HRA took effect could not in any circumstances trigger the Act (at [251]–[255]). Lady Hale declined to follow Strasbourg (at [290]–[291]). She held that logically the 'critical date' should be the date the Convention came into force, namely 3 September 1953. However, she rejected what she regarded as an arid issue and held more broadly that there was no genuine connection between the massacre and a breach of the Convention simply because there was no Convention at the time. She also suggested that the duty to hold an inquiry applied only to formal inquiries leading to legal sanctions, and not to proceedings intended to uncover historical truth. This was left open by the majority. Unlike the majority, Lord Kerr and Lady Hale thought that significant new material had come to light as late as 2009, so that the claim would not have been out of time in domestic law.

It was suggested, apparently unanimously, that the general principle in *McKerr* [2004] against the HRA being retroactive should be reconsidered (see Sections 9.5.1, 21.4.3 and 22.3 for other aspects of this important case).

The common law of judicial review has one advantage over the HRA in respect of time since, in a case such as *Keyu*, historical events can be examined indefinitely. However, in *Keyu* the majority held that the government had acted both reasonably and proportionately when it decided that the remote possibility of uncovering the truth was not worth the cost of holding an inquiry. Lady Hale's strong dissent on this point is notable. While agreeing with the majority that the HRA did not apply, she held that the government had failed to take account of the wider issues of transparency and justice, public confidence, the feelings of the victims' relatives and the enormity of the allegations. The refusal to hold an inquiry was therefore one which no reasonable minister would make and so was invalid at common law.

22.5   The HRA and Parliament

The HRA makes clear that the court cannot set aside an Act of Parliament or other 'primary' legislation (ss 3(2)(b), 6(2)), thereby preserving parliamentary supremacy. For this purpose primary legislation, apart from Acts of Parliament, includes measures of the Church Assembly and the General Synod of the Church of England, and delegated legislation that brings into force or amends primary legislation. A Prerogative Order in Council is also primary legislation for this purpose, even though the courts can set it aside in judicial review proceedings on domestic grounds (s 21) (see Billings and Ponting, 'Prerogative Powers and the Human Rights Act: Elevating the Status of Orders in Council' [2001] PL 21). Acts of the devolved legislatures are not primary legislation (s 21) and can be set aside if they violate a Convention right. (In any case, outside the HRA itself, laws made by the devolved regimes are unlawful if they violate Convention rights (Section 16.3.1).)

The court can set aside subordinate legislation and other government decisions unless primary legislation makes it impossible to do so (s 3(2)).

If an Act of Parliament or a Prerogative Order in Council violates a Convention right, the court must therefore enforce it. However, the court can make a 'declaration of incompatibility' (s 4) which invites Parliament or the executive to change the law (Section 22.5.2).

22.5.1   The interpretative obligation

At the heart of the Act is the requirement that:

> So far as it is possible to do so, primary legislation and subordinate legislation must be read and given effect in a way which is compatible with Convention rights. (s 3(1))

Before section 3 is applied, the court must decide whether the right in question has been violated. If it has, then under section 3 the governing statute must be interpreted, if possible, so as to protect the right. The court must, however, keep to the right side of the border between interpretation and law-making. The government did not introduce a strong formula of the kind used in Canada, under which a statute must expressly state that it overrides the Bill of Rights (Home Office, *Rights Brought Home: The Human Rights Bill* (Cm 3782, 1997), [2.10]). Nevertheless, section 3(1) was apparently intended to be a stronger provision than the traditional one of resolving statutory ambiguities.

Thus, it is clear that the ordinary principles of statutory interpretation are modified. The court is not confined to cases where the provision is ambiguous (*R v A* [2001] 3 All ER 1; *Ghaidan v Mendoza* [2004] 3 All ER 411). In *Wilson v First County Trust* [2003], the House of Lords held that the normal assumption that the court is seeking the intention of Parliament does not apply and that it is for the court to make an independent judgment. Thus, the court cannot assess 'the quality or sufficiency of the reasons given by the promoter of the legislation' and must decide for itself whether the measure complies with the relevant human rights standards. However, in this exercise, the court can use parliamentary material to see how the reasons for enacting the measure relate to human rights issues, for example whether the aims of the measure are among the aims permitted by the Convention (at [61]–[67], [117]–[119]).

The speeches of the House of Lords in *Ghaidan v Mendoza* are widely respected (see *Janah v Libya* (2013) UKEAT/0401/12/GE). A statutory provision entitled a person who had lived with a tenant 'as husband and wife' to succeed to the tenancy on the tenant's death. A majority held that a homosexual relationship fell within the phrase 'living as husband and wife', which they made Convention-compatible by inserting the words 'if they were' after 'as'. The majority held that, even if the ordinary meaning of the statute is clear, the court could still distort its language or read in additional wording to achieve a meaning that complied with the Convention. Lord Millett dissented on the grounds that the majority's meaning unacceptably distorted the purpose of the statute.

The boundary of the court's power depends on two factors. First, the interpretation must not go against the grain of the legislation, in the sense of contradicting its underlying purpose. The court must look beyond the language itself and consider the policy context and legislative history of the statute to identify the essential features of the statutory scheme which they must not violate. In *Ghaidan*, the purpose of the statute was to protect the security of the family home. In *Benkharbouche v Embassy of the Republic of Sudan* [2015] EWCA Civ 33, at [67], it was said that a statute cannot be read in a way inconsistent with the 'fundamental features of the legislative scheme', since there is a danger of affecting the overall balance struck by the legislature while lacking Parliament's 'panoramic vision across the whole of the landscape'. Secondly, the courts must not make decisions for which they are not equipped, in the sense of producing an interpretation that raises social or economic issues that are best left to Parliament. In *Ghaidan*, the majority considered that social attitudes to gay couples were no longer controversial.

Although the court can stretch or add to the language of the statute, it cannot delete or contradict the statutory language. Lord Millett in *Ghaidan* gave the example of the word 'cat' in a statute (at [72]). In some circumstances, 'cat' might be read to include 'dog', for example where the care of pets was the underlying concern. However, if the legislation had originally stated 'Siamese cats' and later been amended to 'cats', this route would not be possible. Thus, the courts have been warned to refrain from 'judicial vandalism' (*R (Anderson) v Secretary of State for the Home Department* [2002] 4 All ER 1089).

Examples of the 'interpretative obligation'

(See also the table provided by Lord Steyn in *Ghaidan v Mendoza* [2004].)

R (Hurst) v North London District Coroner [2007] 2 All ER 1025. The governing statute required a coroner to investigate 'how' a deceased came by his death. In the case of deaths prior to the HRA 'how?' is construed narrowly to mean 'by what means?'. In the case of post-HRA deaths, 'how?' means 'in what circumstances?', thereby allowing a wider-ranging inquiry into deaths in custody.

R v Waya [2013] 1 AC 294 concerned the Proceeds of Crime Act 2002, s 6(5), which empowers the court to confiscate assets acquired by criminal means. The defendant had obtained a mortgage loan by means of a false statement. The court had made a confiscation order in respect of the whole amount of the loan. The Supreme Court read into s 6(5) a requirement that an order which interferes with property rights protected as Convention rights must be 'proportionate'. It was emphasised that interpretation under s 3 of the HRA must 'recognise and respect the essential purpose' or 'grain of the statute'. The purpose of the Act was to prevent criminals profiting from their crimes. From this perspective, the confiscation order was disproportionate, since its purpose was more akin to a deterrent. Having entered into somewhat abstruse calculations, the Supreme Court held that the proper measure of profit enjoyed by the defendant was the increase in the value of the flat attributable to the loan and that this was the proportionate application of the confiscation power.

R v Lambert [2001] 3 All ER 577. Under s 28 of the Misuse of Drugs Act 1971, it is a defence to a charge of possessing drugs for the accused to 'prove' that he neither knew of, nor suspected, nor had reason to suspect, some fact alleged by the prosecution. This conflicts with the presumption of innocence (ECHR Art 6(2)). The House of Lords gave the phrase 'to prove' the unusual meaning of 'to give sufficient evidence'. Thus, the prosecution still has the general burden of disproving the accused's claim. Lord Hope emphasised that great care must be taken to make the revised meaning blend in with the language and structure of the statute. 'Amendment' seems to be possible as long as it does not make the statute unintelligible or unworkable (see [80]–[81]).

R v A [2001] 3 All ER 1. The Youth Justice and Criminal Evidence Act 1999 prohibited evidence in rape cases of the alleged victim's previous sexual experience without the court's consent, which could be given only in specified circumstances (s 41(1)). It was held that the court could construe the Act so as to permit evidence necessary to make the trial fair, since that was the general object of the Act. Thus, additional provisions, 'subject to the right to a fair trial', could be implied into unambiguous language beyond the normal limits of statutory interpretation even if this strained the normal meaning (see Lord Steyn's speech).

S (Children) (Care Plan) [2002] 2 All ER 192. The power of the court to intervene in local authority care proceedings could not be added to the Children Act 1989; the court cannot depart substantially from a fundamental feature of a statutory scheme, particularly if it has practical consequences which the court cannot evaluate (s 38).

Bellinger v Bellinger [2003] 2 All ER 593. A statute could not be interpreted so as to treat a transsexual as female for marriage purposes since this would raise wide social issues that a court is not equipped to confront (cf. Gender Recognition Act 2004).

Janah v Libya [2013] illustrates the difference between the interpretative power under the HRA and the stronger power to 'disapply' a statute under the European Communities Act 1972 (Section 8.5.4). The claimants were domestic workers in foreign embassies in London who brought civil proceedings in respect of their working conditions against the governments in question. Under the State Immunity Act 1978, the governments were immune from liability (Section 9.6.1). The claimants relied on Article 6 of the ECHR and the European Charter of Fundamental Rights, both of which conferred a right of access to the courts in similar terms. The Employment Appeal Tribunal held that the language and purpose of the 1978 Act was so clear that Article 6 could not be applied without contradicting the Act ([41]–[42]). However, insofar as the claims raised issues of EU law, the European Charter of Rights applied. This overrode the 1978 Act, which must therefore be disapplied ([43]–[70]). Any part of the claims that were not subject to EU law would be referred to the Court of Appeal with the possibility of making a declaration of incompatibility (Section 22.5.2).

22.5.2   Declaration of incompatibility

Where it is not 'possible' to interpret 'primary legislation' in line with a Convention right, the Supreme Court, the Court of Appeal, the High Court and certain other courts of equivalent status may – but are not required to – make a 'declaration of incompatibility' (s 4). This is at the heart of the accommodation between law and democracy made by the Act. A declaration of incompatibility invites Parliament to consider whether to change the law. It has no effect on the validity of the law in question, and is not binding on the parties (s 4(6)).

Subordinate legislation that conflicts with a Convention right can be quashed by the court and reinstated by the executive in amended form under this procedure. The fast-track procedure can also be used where an incompatibility arises because of a ruling by the European Court of Human Rights and a minister considers that there are 'compelling reasons' for proceeding (s 10).

The Act does not set out criteria for making a declaration of incompatibility and there is no requirement to do so. It has been held that a declaration of incompatibility is a last resort (*R v A* [2001], [108]) and should not be used in order to avoid the task of interpreting the statute to comply with the Convention (Lord Steyn in *Ghaidan v Mendoza* [2004], [39]).

If a matter is already being considered by Parliament, the court may refrain from making a declaration (*R (Nicklinson) v Ministry of Justice* [2014] (Lady Hale dissented on the ground that the breach was clear)). Although a declaration of incompatibility does not affect the outcome of the case itself, it will be made only where there is, on the facts, a breach of a Convention right. For example, in *R (Chester) v Justice Secretary* [2014], the Supreme Court refused to make a declaration relating to a violation of the rights of prisoners to vote because the particular claimants would not necessarily have that right (see also *R (Miranda) v Secretary of State for the Home Department* [2016] 1 WLR 1505, Section 22.9.1).

Between the coming into force of the Act and July 2019, there have been 42 declarations of incompatibility. Ten of these were overturned on appeal, and a further five related to legislation which had already been amended at the time the declaration was issued (see Ministry of Justice, *Responding to Rights Judgments* (2019)).

22.5.3   Statement of compatibility

Under section 19, a minister in charge of a bill in either House of Parliament must, before the second reading of the bill (i) make a statement to the effect that in his or her view the provisions of the bill are compatible with Convention rights (a 'statement of compatibility'); or (ii) make a statement to the effect that although he or she is unable to make a statement of compatibility the government nevertheless wishes the House to proceed with the bill. The statement must be in writing and published in such manner as the minister considers appropriate. Reasons do not have to be given.

Apart from putting political pressure on the government, the effect of a statement of compatibility is not clear. As a statement of the opinion of the executive, the courts should not defer to it when interpreting the legislation in question (*Wilson v First County Trust* [2003]). However, in *R v A* [2001], at [45] Lord Steyn suggested that a section 19 statement may invite the court to modify a statute. Moreover, a statement that the government intends to proceed despite a possible incompatibility could influence the court in giving the government a margin of discretion (Section 22.9.3) since this shows the government's serious intent (*R (Animal Defenders International) v Culture Secretary* [2008] 1 AC 1312, [33]).

Parliamentary scrutiny of human rights matters is fragmented and unsystematic. A statement of compatibility means little where the statute in question confers a wide discretion on the executive, or the police. Moreover, because the statement applies only to the second reading, it does not cover amendments that might be included at later stages. Other parliamentary mechanisms include equality and regulatory impact assessments, pre-legislative scrutiny by committees and reports of the Joint Committee on Human Rights. No specific time is set aside for declarations of incompatibility or s 19 statements and there is no machinery for notifying the Joint Committee on Human Rights of relevant statutory instruments.

22.6 Remedies

The HRA must be applied by all courts. A 'public authority', including the executive and the courts, is liable for failing to comply with a Convention right. By virtue of section 6(1), 'it is unlawful for a public authority to act in a way which is incompatible with a Convention right'. For this purpose, an 'act' includes a failure to act but does not include a failure to introduce or lay before Parliament a proposal for legislation or to make any primary legislation or remedial order (s 6(6)).

However, liability is excluded by s 6(2) if (a) 'as a result of one or more provisions of primary legislation, the authority could not have acted differently' or (b) 'in the case of one or more provisions of, or made under, primary legislation which cannot be read or given effect in a way which is compatible with the Convention rights, the authority was acting so as to give effect to or enforce those provisions'. The difference between (a) and (b) is that under (b) an authority might be able to act differently, for example by not exercising a power but nevertheless has a defence if it is enforcing a statute, for example evicting a tenant or collecting taxes.

There is a wide and a narrow way of reading s 6(2)(b). In earlier cases, the House of Lords had held that if a statutory provision was being enforced, unless the statute itself was challenged, the court should assume the decision complied with the Convention. However, in *Manchester City Council v Pinnock* [2010]: eviction from council house, the Supreme Court, following Strasbourg and overruling previous House of Lords cases, held that the particular circumstances must be scrutinised in all cases to see whether a Convention right had been violated.

Section 6 effectively adds another ground to judicial review. However, because Prerogative Orders in Council are primary legislation for the purposes of the Act, only domestic grounds of review are available to overturn them. Irrespective of the HRA, the actions of the devolved regimes in Scotland, Wales and Northern Ireland are automatically invalid if they violate Convention rights since they are outside the devolved powers (Section 16.3.1).

Section 7 entitles a 'victim' to bring proceedings in respect of an act which is unlawful under section 6 and also to rely on Convention rights in any legal proceedings. 'Victim' has the same meaning as in cases brought in Strasbourg (s 7(7)). Thus, the claimant or a close relative must be directly affected, or at least very likely to be affected, by the action complained of (see *Klass v Federal Republic of Germany* (1979) 2 EHRR 214; *Open Door and Dublin Well Woman v Ireland* (1992) 15 EHRR 244). There is no standing for non-governmental organisations (NGOs) representing collective or public interests. Thus, in a judicial review case, an NGO, unless it comprises victims, can challenge a decision only on domestic grounds (s 7(3)). It appears that a public authority cannot be a victim against another public authority since both are part of the 'state' (see *Aston Cantlow and Wilmcote with Billesley Parochial Church Council v Wallbank* [2003] 3 All ER 1213). In ordinary judicial review law, the courts can review decisions of one public body against another. In principle, this restriction seems unjustifiable.

A minister can make rules designating an 'appropriate court or tribunal' for the purposes of an action under the Act (ss 7(2), (9), (10), (11)). This power has been exercised principally in relation to special tribunals concerning immigration, asylum and other cases involving national security matters. However, by means of judicial review, the ordinary courts can ensure that the designated tribunal provides an adequate process for protecting the right in issue (see *A v B (Investigatory Powers Tribunal)* [2010] 1 All ER 1149). Decisions made by courts and tribunals can be challenged only by appeal or judicial review (s 9).

The time limits are restrictive. Subject to any shorter time limit for the particular proceedings (e.g. three months for judicial review), proceedings must be commenced within one year of the date of the act complained of unless the court or tribunal extends the period (s 7 (5) (Section 22.4).

22.6.1 Damages

Under section 8, the court can award any of the remedies normally available to it 'as it considers just and appropriate'. Damages can be awarded only by a court which has power to award damages or order compensation in civil proceedings (e.g. not criminal courts and other specialist courts) and then only if the court is satisfied that 'the award is necessary to afford just satisfaction to the person in whose favour it is made' (s 8(4)). The phrase 'just satisfaction' is part of the jurisprudence of the Strasbourg court, and the court must take into account the principles applied by Strasbourg in awarding compensation (s 8(4)). However, apart from insisting that there must be substantial loss or injury, these do not give clear guidance, and the court has considerable discretion (*Z v UK* (2002) 34 EHRR 3; *Damages under the Human Rights Act 1998* (Law Com No 266, 2006); *Cullen v Chief Constable of the RUC* [2004] 2 All ER 237; *Commissioner of Police of the Metropolis v DSD* [2018] UKSC 11).

To safeguard judicial independence, where an action for damages is brought in respect of a judicial act, meaning in this context an act of a court, there is no liability in respect of an act in good faith except for an unlawful arrest or detention or for unnecessary or excessive detention as a result of failure to comply with Art 6. The action must be brought against the Crown with the judge concerned being made a party (HRA, ss 9(3)–(4)).

Under Art 5 (personal liberty) there is a right to compensation for an unlawful detention. In *Lee-Hirons v Secretary of State for Justice* [2016] UKSC 46, a relaxed approach was taken. The Secretary of State had failed to give proper reasons following the detention of a mental patient. Damages were not awarded under the general power; nor was compensation given under Art 5, because the failure did not make the detention unlawful, and the consequences were not 'grave' enough. Cursory reasons given when the arrest was made conforming to the common law requirement were held to be sufficient to validate the detention.

The court can also make a freestanding declaration, which carries no legal sanction, that a claimant's rights under the Act have been violated (*In Re G (A Child) (Same-Sex Relationship: Family Life Declaration)* [2015] 1 WLR 826).

22.7 Public authorities

The ECHR applies to states. Indeed, some of its articles, notably Articles 8 and 10, are directed explicitly to public authorities. The HRA can therefore be directly enforced only against a public authority (s 6(1)). The law as to what is a public authority is unclear and controversial, reflecting the absence of a coherent concept of the state in UK law.

The Act singles out some particular cases but does not provide a general definition. Thus, 'public authority' includes a court or tribunal (s 6(3)). However, Parliament or a person exercising functions in connection with proceedings in Parliament is not a public authority (s 6(3)). 'Public authority' also includes anybody 'certain of whose functions are functions of a public nature' (s 6(3)(b)). An individual can be a public authority (*A v Head Teacher and Governors of Lord Grey School* [2004] 4 All ER 628).

There are two kinds of public authority. First, there are bodies such as central and local government, and the police, which are inherently public. These are known as 'core' public authorities. All the activities of these bodies fall within the HRA. In *Aston Cantlow and Wilmcote with Billesley Parochial Church Council v Wallbank* [2003], the House of Lords held, overruling the Court of Appeal, that a parochial church council of the Church of England is not a core public authority, even though the Church of England has a close connection with the state and has many special legal powers and privileges. A core public authority must be 'governmental' in the sense that its activities are carried out on behalf of the general public interest, whereas the Church of England primarily benefits its own members.

Second, there are 'functional' or 'hybrid' public authorities. These include private or voluntary bodies which perform some functions on behalf of the government but also perform private functions. The 'private acts' of hybrid public bodies do not fall within the HRA (s 6(5)).

Thus, in the case of hybrid public authorities, the court must look not only at the particular *function* but also at the particular *act* within that function which is claimed to invade a Convention right. In domestic judicial review contexts, the particular function must be looked at in the case both of core and of hybrid bodies (Section 19.5). In human rights cases, this applies only to hybrid bodies. In relation to hybrid bodies, although the courts have emphasised that the purpose of the two regimes is not the same (the HRA having the more limited purpose of following the ECHR), they have usually applied the same authorities in both contexts.

The test seems to be whether the particular act is carried out either under the control of the government or on behalf of the government (*Sigurjónnson v Iceland* (1993) 16 EHRR 462). The UK courts have broadly followed this approach. They have also been influenced by the questionable belief that a body which is itself a public authority cannot claim human rights against another public authority. This is significant in relation for example to the BBC and universities, which claim freedom of expression. There is no single criterion. The matter depends on a combination of factors relating the body in question to the government. These include, in particular, the extent of government control over the body and whether it has any special powers (see also Section 19.5).

Hybrid public authorities

In *Aston Cantlow and Wilmcote with Billesley Parochial Church Council v Wallbank* (above), the House of Lords held that some aspects of the Church of England might fall into the category of *functional* public authority, for example functions in connection with marriages and funerals, since these involve public rights. *Wallbank* concerned the statutory right of a parochial church council to force a house owner to pay for the repair of a church roof under an obligation acquired with the property. A majority held that this was a private function, as enforcing a property right for the benefit of churchgoers. Lord Scott, dissenting, thought that this was a 'public' function in that it involved historical conservation for the benefit of the community enforced by special powers.

YL v Birmingham City Council [2007] 3 All ER 957 is the other main authority. The House of Lords held that a privately owned care home was not exercising a public function in relation to a resident who was placed there and financed by a local authority acting under its statutory duty to care for the vulnerable. The majority took the view that there was not a sufficiently close connection between the home and the government to attract the HRA. The home had no special powers, was not acting as the agent of the government and the relationship between the home and its resident was the same whether or not the resident was supported by the local authority. The local authority funded the individual resident and not the home as such. Lord Bingham and Baroness Hale, dissenting, took a fundamentally different approach. This was based on the principle that the state had taken on itself the function of caring for the elderly and that it should make no difference so far as human rights were concerned whether this was done through a private agency or directly by the state itself. Baroness Hale emphasised the positive duty of the state to ensure that Article 8 rights were protected, arguing that this can best be achieved by imposing liability directly on the private agency. However, the weight of authority does not seem to be concerned with social purpose as such.

In *Poplar Housing and Regeneration Community Association Ltd v Donoghue* [2001] 4 All ER 604, the Court of Appeal held that a housing association set up by a local council to take over its rented property was a public authority at least in relation to the eviction of former council tenants. The court stressed that there was no single test, but that the matter depended on accumulating factors showing 'publicness'. The court gave weight to the historical connection between the authority and the association. Moreover, the local authority remained involved with the running of the association.

In *Weaver v London and Quadrant Housing Trust* [2009] EWCA Civ 587, the Court of Appeal rejected the historical connection approach. It held that a housing association that received government funding in return for delivering government housing policy was exercising public functions both for judicial review and HRA purposes in respect of decisions to evict tenants. It was intensively regulated by the government and under a statutory duty to cooperate with local authorities. Eviction decisions, although governed by ordinary private law, could not be separated from its public function of allocating social housing according to government policy. It was also relevant that the association had certain special powers and was under a statutory duty to cooperate with local authorities.

This contrasts with *R (Macleod) v Governors of the Peabody Trust* [2016] EWHC 737 (Admin), where a scheme for sub-market letting to meet housing need in London which was not subject to government regulation was held to be private for judicial review purposes. It is unclear to what extent a body which contracts with government to provide services under privatisation policies is subject to the HRA.

22.8 Horizontal effect

On the face of it, the HRA gives a remedy only against a public authority. However, the Act sometimes has 'horizontal effect' in the sense that private persons, as well as public bodies, may be required to respect human rights. Even private legal relationships are created and defined by the state, which could therefore be regarded as responsible for ensuring that the law meets the minimum standards appropriate to a democratic society.

These are arguments both for and against horizontality. On the one hand, according to section 7, a claim under the Act can be made only by a person who would be a 'victim' for the purposes of Article 34 of the Convention if proceedings were brought in Strasbourg (ss 7(1)(b), (7)). Under Article 34, a claim in Strasbourg can be made only against a party to the Convention, usually a state. It can therefore be argued that, since the purpose of the HRA is to give effect to the ECHR, a person can be a victim only against the state.

On the other hand, all legislation must be interpreted according to the Convention, even that applying to private relationships. In *Ghaidan v Mendoza* [2004], the House of Lords applied Article 14 (discrimination) to legislation which discriminated against homosexual couples occupying property owned by private landlords (see also *Wilson v First County Trust* [2003]). Furthermore, by virtue of section 6, the courts are public authorities. Thus, a court would act 'unlawfully' if it did not apply Convention rights in every case before it, even between private persons (see Sedley LJ in *Douglas v Hello!* [2001] 2 All ER 289 (Section 23.3.4)). A less extreme version is that, while section 6 cannot create a *new cause of action* against a private body, it can require the court to apply Convention rights to the case, at least in respect of the court's own powers to make orders and grant remedies (see *Wilson v First County Trust* [2003], at [174]; Baroness Hale in *Campbell v MGN Ltd* [2004] 2 All ER 995 (at [133])).

For example, a court might invoke Art 8 (respect for family life) against a private landlord who attempted to evict a tenant from her home (*R (McLellan) v Bracknell Forest BC* [2002] 1 All ER 899, [42]). However, in *McDonald v McDonald* [2016] UKSC 28, the Supreme Court held that, in the case of a private landlord, the HRA does not apply to a contractual issue. The case concerned the eviction, under the terms of a mortgage agreement, of a private residential tenant who suffered from a personality disorder. It was held that, while Art 8 is not excluded altogether, it cannot be used to justify a different outcome than that required by the contractual relationship, at least where there is a legislative scheme which Parliament has created to balance the competing interests in general. Thus, Art 8 in the private sector may be confined to cases where the court exercises a power in its own right, as opposed to enforcing property or contract law. In *McDonald* the court suggested that the subjection of the privately owned press to privacy rights is derived from the power of the court to impose duties in the law of tort (Section 23.5).

By contrast, in *Manchester City Council v Pinnock* [2010]: eviction of a local authority tenant due to the antisocial behaviour of his children, the Supreme Court held that the court should examine all the circumstances of an eviction of a *public sector* tenant to ensure compliance with Art 8. *Pinnock* concerned a wholly public local authority landlord and the HRA s 6 requires *all* the functions of such a body to be treated as public functions. Thus, *Pinnock* might apply to the public functions of a housing association, but *McDonald* to its private functions.

Particular Convention rights may include a positive obligation on the state not only to protect the right, but also to require private persons to respect it. In *Redfearn v UK* [2012] ECHR 1878, a private company, Serco, which worked with ethnic minorities, sacked one of its drivers, an election candidate for the BNP, a racist political party. The UK courts had held that, because Serco was a private body, the claimant was not protected by the HRA. However, the Strasbourg court held that, in the light of the importance of political parties to democracy, the state had failed to take reasonable steps to protect workers from dismissal on the ground of their political associations (Art 11).

Finally, the courts might develop the common law on the basis that the ECHR contains values of general import. In *Campbell v MGN Ltd* [2004], the House of Lords used Articles 8 and 10 of the ECHR to reconfigure the common law in respect of privacy (Section 23.5). The majority did not seem to think that the matter strictly fell within the HRA (at [17]–[19], [26], [49]).

22.9   Overriding protected rights

Any workable code of fundamental rights must be expressed in general language and with sufficient filters or exceptions to permit governments to act in the public interest or to resolve conflicts between rights. It is tempting to seek an overarching principle that would 'balance' or combine the human right with a competing interest under some overall concept of the common good. However, it is doubtful whether any such overriding principle is possible. The metaphor of balancing is empty without an objective 'scale' or 'measure' against which to compare the competing interests. Nobody has yet found one that is generally accepted. Thus, some human rights may be 'incommensurable' (Section 2.4). A favourite way of trying to solve this dilemma is to take a utilitarian approach which seeks the least harmful overall solution in the light of all the particular circumstances. However, unless we know what *weight* to give to each element, this does not solve the most difficult problems.

There are three ways of accommodating competing public interest considerations. First, the right itself could be defined so that public interest concerns may affect the meaning of the right itself. Second, many of the rights are made subject to specific justifications for overriding them (overrides). Third, in an emergency, a right can be derogated from, or a reservation made (Section 21.4). In this section, we shall concentrate on the overrides.

Under Articles 8–11 (privacy, religion, freedom of expression and association) and Protocol 1, Article 1 (peaceful enjoyment of possessions) the court is required to balance the right against a specified override. The overrides vary with the particular article, but in all cases include public safety, public order, the prevention and detection of serious crime, the protection of health and morals, and the protection of the rights of others. This is broadly understood to include the rights of the public generally to have fair, reasonable and effective laws (*Kokkinakis v Greece* (1994) 17 EHRR 397). Sometimes one human right may conflict with another, for example freedom of expression and privacy (Section 23.5), but the Convention itself contains no guidance as to any ranking order.

Where there are specific overrides, the court must apply three steps:

1. Is a Convention right 'engaged'?
2. Has there been an interference with the right?
3. Is the interference 'justified' under one or more of the overrides? Strictly speaking, at steps 1 and 2, any public interest balancing is irrelevant. However, as we have seen, sometimes the court defines the right in the light of the public interest under the principle that a 'fair balance' pervades the whole Convention (Section 21.4). In doing so, the need to look at justification may be avoided.

(If the interference is not justified the court may then have to go on to decide whether a statute unavoidably overrides the right (Section 22.5.1) and, if so, whether to make a declaration of incompatibility (Section 22.5.2).)

In this section, we are concerned with justification. This has two aspects. First, the interference must be 'prescribed by law' or 'in accordance with the law'. Second, the interference must be 'necessary in a democratic society'. Although these are separate requirements, some of the same facts may be relevant to both stages.

22.9.1   'Prescribed by law' or 'in accordance with the law'

The restrictions on the right must be 'prescribed by law' or 'in accordance with the law', terms which apparently mean the same. First, the power must be exercised validly under a rule of domestic law (e.g. *Shahid v Scottish Ministers* [2015] UKSC 58: segregation in prison beyond the permitted period). Second, the law in question, irrespective of its application to the particular facts, must meet the standards of the rule of law in its wide sense. It must be sufficiently certain and clear to enable the citizen to foresee the consequences of his or her actions and with independent safeguards to hold an official to account who abuses the power (*Beghal v DPP* [2015] UKSC 49, [3], [29]–[33]; *R (Catt) v Association of Chief Police Officers* [2015] UKSC 9: police powers of search and retention of data; see also *Catt v UK* [2019] ECHR 76). While related (see *Catt v UK* (at [106]), this matter can, in principle, be separated from whether the power can be justified as proportionate in the public interest. Thus, a power may be proportionate to widely accepted social goals but involve unacceptably wide discretion.

There must be independent safeguards against the risk that a power will be misused, and an effective means of challenging a decision. For example, in *The Christian Institute v the Lord Advocate (Scotland)* [2016] UKSC 51, the Scottish Parliament had introduced a 'named person' scheme under which a person was appointed without parental consent to protect the interests of a child or young person. There was power to share confidential information with public authorities. The Supreme Court held that, although the scheme was proportionate, it was not 'in accordance with the law'. This was because there was insufficient guidance as to how the scheme was applied. In particular, information might be disclosed without the child or parent knowing about it. By contrast, in *In the matter of an application by Lorraine Gallagher for Judicial Review (Northern Ireland)* [2019] UKSC 3, a majority of the Supreme Court (Lord Kerr dissenting) considered that statutory schemes which required the disclosure of criminal convictions, even if 'spent', to an employer, were in accordance with the law because they were highly prescriptive. The categories of disclosable convictions and cautions were precisely defined, and disclosure in those categories was mandatory, even if there might be arguments for more, fewer, wider or narrower categories.

Police 'stop and search' powers have also raised this issue. The general principle under PACE s 1 requires that a person cannot be stopped and searched unless the police have reasonable grounds for suspicion of criminal activity. However, under particular statutes, reasonable grounds for suspicion need not be shown. Random stop and search powers may be justifiable in particular high-risk situations because of their deterrent effect, but they raise issues of discrimination and the possibility of being used for improper purposes such as targeting political protestors.

Case study: police powers: stop and search and data retention

With these kinds of power, and with police powers to retain information, there are miscellaneous controls and safeguards, many of them internal, and some very general such as parliamentary mechanisms and the ordinary courts themselves. The courts are required to make what appears to be a relative and impressionistic overall assessment based on the particular context. There are sometimes widely divergent outcomes from different judges.

In *Gillan and Quinton v UK* [2010] ECHR 28, a random stop and search power under s 44 of the Terrorism Act 2000 was challenged under Art 8 (privacy). The Strasbourg court held that it was not 'in accordance with the law'. This was because the power was open-ended and vague, and lacked formal legal safeguards. It applied for 28 days, renewable indefinitely, over an extended area designated by the Home Secretary, which in this case applied to the whole of Greater London. Sufficient information was not published in advance. Independent methods of challenge consisted of the general law of judicial review or a civil action, and these depended on the police or the Home Secretary keeping accurate records and disclosing information. This was enough to satisfy the House of Lords (*R (Gillan) v Metropolitan Police Comr* [2006] 4 All ER 1041), but not the Strasbourg court. The Strasbourg court also took into account that the safeguards had failed in practice and that the power could be used to interfere with the right to free expression of demonstrators and protestors. It was also suggested that the House of Lords had not treated Art 8's concern with privacy as sufficiently important. Section 44 was revised in response to *Gillan* (see Section 25.5.4).

In *Beghal v DPP* [2015] and *R (Roberts) v Metropolitan Police Commissioner* [2015] UKSC 79, the Supreme Court upheld random powers under Art 8 once more. The powers in question were more limited than that in *Gillan*. In *Beghal*, there was power under Sched. 7 of the Terrorism Act 2000 to detain and question passengers at an airport for up to nine hours (since reduced to six) in connection with terrorism. The court stressed that, unlike the street search in *Gillan*, the power was not an unusual power and was limited in time and place. Lord Kerr dissented, with the implication that a random search is in itself not in accordance with the law. He also thought that the power was disproportionate in that the aim of protecting public safety could be achieved by lesser means. In

Beghal v UK (2019) 69 EHRR 28, the European Court ruled that the powers were not in accordance with the law because they could be exercised for up to nine hours, during which time the person would be compelled to answer questions without any right to have a lawyer present, and there was no requirement for 'reasonable suspicion', which also rendered the role of judicial review limited.

The Supreme Court in *Beghal* also suggested that where Art 10 (freedom of expression) arises, stronger grounds must be shown to seize data. Thus, in *R (Miranda) v Secretary of State for the Home Department* [2016] where electronic data were seized under Sched. 7 from a journalist's spouse during a search lasting nine hours (the maximum permitted time before the reduction to six hours), the Court of Appeal held that, even though the search itself had been proportionate, judicial review was not a sufficient safeguard in itself to protect freedom of the press, and that Parliament should provide more specific safeguards. However, no declaration of incompatibility was made.

In *Roberts*, a woman was taken to a police station and searched, having given a false address when unable to pay a bus fare. It was accepted that the police action was proportionate, so the focus was solely on whether it was in accordance with the law. Under section 60 of the Criminal Justice and Public Order Act 1994, a senior police officer must have reasonable grounds to believe that the area is a hotspot for violence and designation is limited to 24 hours. The designation must be documented, and records kept. Within a designated area, a constable can stop and search without having to show grounds. The Supreme Court upheld the power on the basis that it was more restricted than the power in *Gillan*, although the safeguards consisted primarily of administrative requirements to disclose information mainly after the event. Whether these differences are enough to satisfy the *Gillan* principle in the eyes of Strasbourg is questionable. It may be that the core issues of whether a random power is permissible at all and whether stronger independent legal safeguards are required have not been adequately addressed. Nevertheless, in *Roberts*, the Supreme Court took into account empirical evidence of the public benefits and risks of a police power of random search in deciding that the power was in accordance with the law.

In *R (Catt) v Association of Chief Police Officers* [2015], the claimant, aged 91, was a supporter of a group campaigning against the operations of a weapons manufacturer, some of whose members had committed offences of violence. The claimant had never been involved in violence. Information concerning the claimant was placed on a database compiled by the police. This included his name, age, physical appearance and history of attendance at demonstrations. Records were kept indefinitely. The Supreme Court held that, although this was a wide discretionary power, the various safeguards ensured that it was in accordance with the law. The safeguards included regular reviews, a statutory *Code of Conduct*, detailed internal guidance and the requirements of the Data Protection Act 1998 which limits the purposes for which the data could be used to police purposes. These restricted sharing the information outside the police and required that the information not be excessive and be used proportionately. There were controls provided by the Information Commissioner and judicial review (for the proportionality aspect of *Catt* see Section 22.9.2). By contrast, in *Catt v UK* [2019], the Strasbourg Court considered that the question of whether the power was in accordance with the law was 'closely related' to that of whether the interference was 'necessary in a democratic society' (at [106]). It concluded that indefinite retention of the records was not, especially given the claimant's age and the 'chilling effect' that retention would have on the expression of political opinion.

'In accordance with the law' requires the citizen to know in advance how a power may be exercised. However, in a complex area where problems may not be foreseeable, it is not possible to achieve this comprehensively. In *R (Catt) v Association of Chief Police Officers* (above), the Supreme Court accepted that it may be impossible sometimes to specify in advance all the circumstances in which a power may be used. In such cases, the existence of an independent safeguard in the form of judicial review may save the power. In *R (Bright) v Secretary of State for Justice* [2015] 1 WLR 723, the prison management had power to allocate prisoners within the prison. The claimants, sexual offenders, one of whom was in a civil partnership, were separated from their partners, and contact restricted on the ground that they were engaging in sexual activity. The decision was challenged under Art 8 (respect for privacy and family life). The Court of Appeal held, first, that there was no need to publish a detailed policy stating precisely what conduct was permitted. The policy statements given to the prisoners referred in general terms to anti-social and irresponsible behaviour and indecency. These were ordinary terms sufficiently clear to be understood. Moreover, the absence of a policy statement specifically about homosexual behaviour was overcome because the constraints of judicial review prevent the discriminatory use of powers.

Sometimes the problem is the opposite, in the sense that a rigid rule is in force which permits no discretion, so that there is no rational analysis of any risk or safeguard against arbitrary treatment. This has also been held not to be in accordance with the law (*R (T) v Chief Constable of Greater Manchester Police* [2015] AC 49: police passing information to employers). However, this kind of case might better fall under the head of proportionality (below) where it can be balanced against other concerns, since sometimes the importance of the matter may justify a rigid rule (e.g. *R (Animal Defenders International) v Culture Secretary* [2008]: ban on political advertising (Section 23.3)).

Finally, the relevant law must be made in accordance with a regular, democratic and accessible lawmaking process and preferably not by judicial extension (thus going further than Dicey's version) (see *R (Purdy) v DPP* [2009]: guidance as to prosecution policy for assisted suicide made by the executive; *R (Laporte) v Chief Constable of Gloucestershire* [2007] 2 AC 105, [52]: policing demonstrations: common law, Section 23.7.2).

22.9.2 Necessary in a democratic society: proportionality

The requirement of 'necessary in a democratic society' is given effect through the concept of proportionality. This is an ancient idea that has long pervaded European legal culture and has entered the UK primarily through EU law and the HRA. Proportionality has been resisted by the common law on the ground that it requires the courts to investigate too deeply into other branches of government, although some judges now suggest that the principle should become one of general application (Section 18.1.1; *Keyu v Secretary of State for Foreign and Commonwealth Affairs* [2015]).

Proportionality mainly arises where a right has to be weighed against one of the overrides. However, the doctrine may creep into other contexts, in accordance with the notion that 'fair balance' runs through the whole Convention (Section 21.4). It applies in particular where the state has a positive duty, for example to hold an inquiry or to protect a right against interference by others, in order to avoid placing undue burdens on the government (e.g. *D v Secretary of State for the Home Department* [2015] 1 WLR 2217: whether a restriction over a person with mental health problems was 'inhuman or degrading treatment or punishment' depended on proportionality by balancing the risk to the public against the cost of the care measures available).

The basic meaning of proportionality is that an interference with a right must not be excessive. This contains an element of subjective evaluation, which opens the way to the criticism that the court is engaging in politics. Perhaps, in order to meet this criticism, the courts take a structured approach. The judgment of Lord Reed in *Bank Mellat v HM Treasury (No 2)* [2013] UKSC 39, [68]–[76], albeit dissenting on the facts, contains a good account of the development of the doctrine and sets out a widely accepted structure (see e.g. *Gaughran v Chief Constable of the Police Service of Northern Ireland* [2015] 2 WLR 1303, [20]; *In re Recovery of Medical Costs for Asbestos Diseases* [2015] 2 WLR 481, [45]; *R (Lord Carlile of Berriew) v Secretary of State for the Home Department* [2014] 3 WLR 1404).

Lord Reed set out the following four stages in an inquiry into proportionality. It is easy to see how most of them are highly subjective:

1. whether the objective of the relevant measure is sufficiently important to justify the limitation of a protected right. This means an interest, sometimes called a 'pressing social need', which is more than merely 'useful', 'reasonable' or 'desirable' (*Handyside v UK* (1976) 1 EHRR 737; *R (Laporte) v Chief Constable of Gloucestershire* [2007], [52]: public order; *Brown v Stott* [2001] 2 All ER 97: combating drink driving; *R (Williamson) v Secretary of State* [2005] 2 All ER 1, [79]: child welfare; *R (Begum) v Head Teacher and Governors of Denbigh High School* [2007] 1 AC 100: social cohesion).
2. whether the measure is rationally connected to the objective. A more stringent standard applies than in domestic law. For example, in *A v Secretary of State for the Home Department* [2005] 2 AC 68, the government attempted to derogate from the Convention in order to detain indefinitely foreign terrorist suspects against whom there was insufficient evidence to prosecute, unless they voluntarily left the country (Section 25.5). Although the power had a proper objective and had sufficient rational basis to

validate it in domestic law, the House of Lords held that it was insufficiently focused, going too far in some respects and not far enough in others. It went too far in singling out foreign nationals since the threat was no less from British terrorists, and not far enough, since by permitting them to leave the country, they remained a danger.

3. whether a less intrusive measure could have been used without unacceptably compromising the achievement of the objective. For example, in *A* (above) the terrorist threat could have been dealt with by less intrusive means such as intensive surveillance (see also *Bank Mellat v HM Treasury No 2* [2013] (Section 25.5.6); *Shahid v Scottish Ministers* [2015] UKSC 58: protection in prison of young offenders for their own safety could have been achieved by a less drastic method than segregation and no plan was in place).

4. whether balancing the severity of the measure's effects on the rights of the person to whom it applies against the importance of the objective to the extent that the measure will contribute towards its achievement, the former outweighs the latter. Do the costs outweigh the benefits? In *R (Aguilar Quila) v Secretary of State for the Home Department* [2012] 1 AC 621, [45] Lord Wilson expressed this as 'do [the measures] strike a fair balance between the rights of the individual and the interests of the community?'

For example, in *R (BBC) v Secretary of State for Justice* [2012] 2 All ER 1089, the BBC had not been permitted to film an interview with a terrorist suspect who had been detained without charge for seven years awaiting deportation. The Divisional Court held that this was not proportionate. Stages 1 and 2 and were satisfied, but the fourth test of fair balance was not since a face-to-face interview was important in the circumstances to freedom of expression, and the government could not provide evidence of concrete harm.

This stage of the exercise is highly subjective and sometimes results in extreme judicial disagreement. For example, in *R (Catt) v Association of Chief Police Officers* [2015], the issue was whether a police database holding information about a peaceful demonstrator was proportionate. The Supreme Court held that the intrusion into the claimant's Art 8 right of autonomy was not serious and, even if stored indefinitely, the information was useful for policing purposes. Moreover, it would be burdensome to filter out innocent persons such as Mr Catt. The court overruled the Court of Appeal which had taken a much stricter approach, emphasising the significance of the claimant's autonomy and the limited importance of the information to police purposes. Lord Toulson dissented on the basis that such information was excessive, made only a minor contribution to policing and there was little justification in keeping it for many years. The European Court, for its part, considered that there had been a violation (*Catt v UK* [2019]).

A right can be overridden on the ground of the public cost only in clear and weighty cases. For example, in *R (AB) v Secretary of State for Justice* [2010] 2 All ER 151, it was held that a refusal to move a transsexual prisoner to a women's prison could not be justified on the basis of cost, and in *Aguilar Quila* (above) the Supreme Court rejected the government's argument that it would be too expensive to screen individual applicants.

The Strasbourg court makes an important distinction between general measures contained in legislation and decisions made in particular cases. In the case of general measures, the measure is considered as a whole and impact on the particular case is given less weight on the grounds of fairness and certainty (rule of law) (*Animal Defenders International v UK* (2013) 57 EHRR 21, [108]–[109]: ban on political advertising which may disadvantage particular campaigning groups; *Pretty v UK* [2002]: assisted suicide). In other words, sometimes a line has to be drawn, even if there is injustice in the specific case. However, as Sedley LJ pointed out in *R (S) v Chief Constable of South Yorkshire Police* [2004] 4 All ER 193, strictly speaking, the notion of 'balancing' individual rights against the public interest means that the latter would always prevail since more people are affected. Thus, the judge cannot avoid using his or her personal preferences.

Where the competition is between two individual protected rights, a utilitarian approach that seeks the lesser evil is taken. The starting point is to treat each right as equal, then to look at each in turn in the particular circumstances, comparing the consequences in each case (e.g. *HM Advocate v Murtagh* [2010] 3 WLR 814: police records concerning a witness: right to a fair trial outweighed privacy; *R (L) v Metropolitan Police Comr* [2010] 1 All ER 113: 'enhanced criminal records certificate affecting job as school assistant: risk to children outweighed privacy'; *Campbell v MGN* [2004]: privacy out-weighed press freedom where matter was not of serious concern to public). A problem here is the assumption that each right starts as 'equal'. Why is freedom of expression (Art 10) equal to privacy (Art 8)?

Many illustrations of proportionality can be found elsewhere in the book (e.g. Sections 9.7.4, 23.5 and 23.7.2).

In the end, proportionality requires the court to make a subjective choice as to whether an interference is justified. This raises the difficult question of incommensurability since the court has to choose between different kinds of interest where there is no common measure to compare them so that the notion of 'balance' is an evasion (Section 2.4). It also creates concerns in respect of the separation of powers.

22.9.3   The margin of appreciation/discretion

The Strasbourg concept of the margin of appreciation means that the court gives latitude to the state in areas that are not suitable for a court to decide, but are more appropriate to a democratically accountable body, namely controversial moral, social, economic and political areas, especially where large public spending is involved, or areas involving special expertise. The margin of appreciation is an important ingredient since, where it applies, the court will accept the judgment of the primary decision-maker, particularly if it is a democratic body, unless the decision is 'manifestly unreasonable'.

The Supreme Court has said that the margin of appreciation is purely a Strasbourg concept and does not apply at the domestic level (*In re Recovery of Medical Costs for Asbestos Diseases* [2015], [44], [54]; *R (Nicklinson) v Ministry of Justice* [2014], [71], [163], [230]). However, a similar if not identical principle applies at a domestic level, and the courts freely draw on Strasbourg cases. Indeed, in *R (Nicklinson) v Ministry of Justice*, Lord Neuberger said (at [75]) that 'where a provision enacted by Parliament was both rational and within the margin of appreciation accorded by the Strasbourg court, a court in the United Kingdom would normally be very cautious before deciding that it infringes a Convention right'.

The labels 'deference', or 'margin of discretion', or 'margin of judgment', or 'respect' may be used instead with resulting confusion as to what these mean. The notion of 'deference' has especially been criticised as misleading since these cases are about the proper constitutional role of the court in accordance with the separation of powers (see Lord Sumption in *Mellat* (above) [21]–[31] for a useful general account; see also Lord Bingham in *A v Secretary of State for the Home Department* [2005]: 'institutional competence').

The domestic principle is grounded in the distinctive role of the courts under the separation of powers doctrine and the limitations of the courts' competence to assess specialised evidence, for example in diplomatic and security matters. *R (Lord Carlile of Berriew) v Secretary of State for the Home Department* [2014] concerned a Home Office decision to ban a radical Iranian politician from entering the country. Lord Sumption said (at [30]–[31]):

> When it comes to reviewing the compatibility of executive decisions with the Convention (ECHR), there can be no constitutional bar to any inquiry which is both relevant and necessary to enable the court to adjudicate…The traditional reticence of the courts about examining the basis for executive decisions in certain areas of policy can no longer be justified.

On the other hand, where the matter has a significant political content and where the court does not have the evidence, experience, or institutional legitimacy to form its own view with confidence, 'it must give special weight to the judgments and assessments of the primary decision-maker with special institutional competence and cannot interfere with the decision-maker's judgment or assessment if it was one reasonably open to her' (at [34]). The likely adverse reaction of a foreign state is a matter constitutionally entrusted to the executive which has specialised experience and accountability.

> In *R (Countryside Alliance) v A-G* [2008] 1 AC 719, at [45] Lord Bingham remarked that it would be undesirable if people could achieve in the courts what they had failed to achieve in the democratic Parliament; and in *R (S) v Chief Constable of South Yorkshire Police* [2004] Lord Woolf said (at [16]): 'I regard it as being fundamental that the court keeps at the forefront of its consideration its lack of any democratic credentials'.

Thus, the margin of appreciation is part of the larger debate as to the proper role of courts. There are four main kinds of case (which may overlap):

1. cases involving controversial moral, cultural or social questions;
2. where a political judgment is required in areas of high-level policy, especially at an international level, such as diplomatic relations or military operations;
3. where the case raises controversial issues of social or economic policy, especially where public spending priorities are involved, where the decision is better left to an accountable democratic body;
4. where special expertise is required which the court is not competent to evaluate, such as security or military matters.

Article 8 (respect for privacy and family life) attracts a particularly wide margin since these matters relate to personal needs, lifestyles and beliefs which are susceptible to widely different cultures and to changing public opinion (see Lord Walker and Lord Mance in *Secretary of State for Work and Pensions v M* [2006] UKHL 11: same-sex family relationships).

Art 8 also arises in cases where there is a positive duty involving the allocation of limited resources such as housing, education, and health services. In *Poplar Housing and Regeneration Community Association Ltd v Donoghue* [2001] (allocation of social housing), Lord Woolf LCJ (at [69]) said that 'the economic and other implications of any policy in this area are extremely complex and far reaching. This is an area where ... the courts must treat the decisions of Parliament as to what is in the public interest with particular deference'. In *R (Condliff) v North Staffs Primary Health Care Trust* [2011] EWCA Civ 910 (hospital treatment policy), it was said that cases involving the allocation of scarce resources are better decided by a democratically accountable body. In *R (SG) v Secretary of State for Work and Pensions* [2015] UKSC 16 (an attempt to overturn a government cap on welfare payments which disadvantaged lone mothers), a three: two majority of the Supreme Court refused to intervene because the matter was one of controversial social policy involving public spending priorities. The court referred to 'expertise, accountability and legitimacy' as the governing factors (at [92]).

Apart from Art 8, the margin often arises in connection with P1A1 (enjoyment of possessions, e.g. *In re Recovery of Medical Costs for Asbestos Diseases* [2015]; P1A2: education (*Ponomaryov v Bulgaria* (2014) 59 EHRR 20). It also arises under Art 10 (freedom of expression). However, political expression, particularly press freedom, has a high level of protection (Section 23.3). The margin also arises in cases involving positive duties where the state has to prioritise with limited resources, such as the provision of police protection or welfare services.

On the other hand, some matters are so important as to fall outside any margin of discretion. These include the right to life, at least where the state directly takes life (Section 21.4.1), personal liberties under Arts 3, 4, and 5 (*A v Secretary of State for the Home Department* [2005], [39]–[42]; *Hillingdon BC v Neary* [2011] 4 All ER 584) and the right to a fair trial (*R v A* [2001]). There is little or no margin where the case involves 'the most intimate aspects of private life' (*Dudgeon v UK* (1982) 4 EHRR 149; *Dickson v UK* (2008) 24 BHRC 19, [78]) or in respect of political rights of expression (*Lingens v Austria* (1986) 8 EHRR 407). The state's margin of appreciation is narrow in the case of personal characteristics that cannot be changed, such as racial discrimination. There is no margin in areas which are especially within the province of the court, such as the right to a fair trial (*Kennedy v Charity Commission* [2014]).

22.9.3.1 *Application of the margin*

In *Bank Mellat v HM Treasury (No 2)* [2013], Lord Reed (at [71]) pointed out that the concept of margin of appreciation does not apply in the same way in domestic courts as it does in Strasbourg, being more dependent on the particular context within the structured proportionality inquiry. In *R (Lord Carlile of Berriew) v Secretary of State for the Home Department* [2014], Lord Neuberger (at [68]) referred to a spectrum of types of decision based on the extent of the courts' expertise. It has been stressed, however, that the overall decision on proportionality at the final stage is for the court and that any margin is likely to have been used up at the earlier stages of the inquiry (*In Re Recovery of Medical Costs for Asbestos Diseases* [2015], [52]; see also *R (Tigere) v Secretary of State for Business, Innovation and Skills* [2015] 1 WLR 3820, [33]–42]).

The margin concerns the application of a right to the particular circumstances. It does not apply to the meaning of a Convention concept itself since it is important that the same principles apply to all Member States in accordance with the doctrine that Convention concepts are autonomous (e.g. 'family': *Secretary of State for Work and Pensions v M* [2006], [24]).

The main application of the margin is at stage 1 of the proportionality inquiry (Section 22.9.2), namely the importance of the government's policy objective or the extent of any risk involved since the assessment of the importance of a policy is typically a matter for a democratic body. For example, in *R (Miranda) v Secretary of State for the Home Department* [2016], the spouse of a journalist carrying data stolen from the US government was searched at an airport. It was held that the security services' assessment must be accepted in weighing the risk to public safety against journalistic freedom.

The court will also interfere at stages 2 (rational relationship between object and power (*A* (above)) and 3 (measures excessive) where there is irrationality or arbitrariness (e.g. *Bank Mellat v HM Treasury No 2* (above), [21]–[27]: order freezing the assets of an Iranian bank in order to cut off funds that might be used to develop nuclear weapons: although the measure was rational as a whole, there was no reason to single out this particular bank).

At the fourth and final stage, the court draws an overall conclusion as to whether the primary decision is proportionate as a whole. Even at this stage, the court recognises that it is not the primary decision-maker, and so will intervene only where it considers that the weight given to the competing factors is wrong or there is an element of unfairness. For example, in *R (Bright) v Secretary of State for Justice* [2015], a decision to separate prisoners from their sexual partners was held to be proportionate. The prisoners had been involved in the decision-making process, and the circumstances of their relationships had been taken into account.

In difficult cases, the margin might be a 'tie-breaker' at the final stage. In *R (Animal Defenders International) v Culture Secretary* [2008], the House of Lords upheld a statutory ban on political advertising as proportionate. Although this was an interference with the high value of political freedom of expression, there was also a vital public interest in preventing election campaigns being distorted by money. Parliament, as a democratic body, should be given a margin of discretion since it had consistently followed the same policy, had thoroughly considered the matter and had treated it as of high importance by making a statement under s 19 (Section 22.5.3), resolving to proceed despite violating Art 10.

Examples of the margin of appreciation/discretion

Cultural and moral values

Hristozov v Bulgaria [2012] ECHR 608: use of experimental drugs for terminal cancer patients.
Gough v UK [2014] ECHR 1156: public taste: the 'naked rambler' prosecution.
Eweida v UK [2013]: prevention of discrimination against homosexuals trumped religious beliefs.
Animal Defenders International v UK [2013]: political advertising.
Countryside Alliance v UK (2010) 50 EHRR SE6: ban on foxhunting.
Re G (Adoption) (Unmarried Couple) [2009]: adoption restrictions on unmarried couples.
Secretary of State for Work and Pensions v M [2006]: treatment of same-sex couples as families': a consensus did not exist at the relevant time (2001–02), although one developed later (see *Vallianatos v Greece* [2013] ECHR 1110).

R (Williamson) v Secretary of State for Education and Employment [2005]: corporal punishment in schools.
R (ProLife Alliance) v BBC [2003] 2 All ER 977: taste and decency in broadcasting.
Petrovic v Austria (1998) 33 EHRR 307, [40]–[41]: paternity leave.
Open Door and Dublin Well Woman v Ireland [1992]: abortion.

High-level policy

Smith v Ministry of Defence [2014]: military operations overseas (Section 22.3).
R (Bancoult) v Secretary of State for the Foreign and Commonwealth Office [2008] 4 All ER 1055: governance of a dependent territory (Section 9.4.2.1).
A v Secretary of State for the Home Department [2005]: existence of emergency.
See also Section 9.6.3 (international affairs).

Social and economic matters

In re Recovery of Medical Costs for Asbestos Diseases [2015]: NHS finances: held to be outside the margin due to inadequate consideration.
R (Condliff) v North Staffs Primary Health Care Trust [2011]; *McDonald v Kensington and Chelsea Royal London BC* [2011] 4 All ER 881: NHS treatments. (But see *McDonald v UK* [2014] ECHR 492: breach of Art 8 until a full review of a disabled patient's support needs had been carried out.)
Budayeva v Russia (2014) 59 EHRR 2: duty to protect against a natural disaster.
Bah v UK (2012) 54 EHRR 21, [47]: immigration.
Manchester City Council v Pinnock [2010]: housing policy.
Marcic v Thames Water Utilities [2004] 1 All ER 135: drainage repairs.
Hatton v UK (2003) 37 EHRR 28: airport noise disturbing residents.
Guerra v Italy (1998) 26 EHRR 357: environmental risks.
X and Y v Netherlands (1985) 8 EHRR 235: caring for mentally ill children.

Specialist expertise

Da Silva v UK (2016) 63 EHRR 12: investigation into police shooting of an innocent man. But the court could examine whether institution deficiencies hampered proper investigation.
R (Miranda) v Secretary of State for the Home Department [2016], [79]: anti-terrorism police stop and search power.
Bank Melatt v HM Treasury (No 2) [2013]: security.
R (Lord Carlile of Berriew) v Secretary of State for the Home Department [2014]: diplomatic relations.
R (Mohamed) v Secretary of State for Foreign Affairs [2010] 3 WLR 554: security.
R (ProLife Alliance) v BBC [2003]: broadcasting standards.
R (Bloggs 61) v Secretary of State for the Home Department [2003] 1 WLR 2724: protecting prisoner.
Secretary of State for the Home Department v Rehman [2003] 1 AC 153, [50]–[54], [57]–[58]: security.
R (Farrakhan) v Secretary of State for the Home Department [2002] QB 1391: security.

22.9.3.2 *The limits of the margin*

The width of the margin varies according to the importance of the right in question, and the extent and purpose of the interference with it. For example, education is an important right which has been held to be 'constitutive of a democratic society' (*Ponomaryov v Bulgaria* [2014]). As such, it has a narrow margin. On the other hand, education involves spending public money which points to a wider margin. In *Ponomarov*, the Strasbourg court held that the margin gets wider towards the higher end of education as this is increasingly optional and so less central to society. Nevertheless, the margin has limits even here in respect, for example, of discrimination (*R (Tigere) v Secretary of State for Business, Innovation and Skills* [2015], [27]–[32]: refusal of student loan to immigrant).

This example shows a fundamental problem with the margin concept, namely that it depends on vague language and varying combinations of facts. The expressions 'narrow,' 'wide', 'respect' and so on do not in themselves reveal the grounds on which the court might interfere. For example, within the notion of 'appropriate weight' to be given to the primary decision-maker, such as Parliament, there may be disagreement as to whether this means 'great weight' or just 'weight' and what is the difference? (See *In re Recovery of Medical Costs for Asbestos Diseases* [2015], [67], [108].) These labels give little guidance as to how intensive the level of review should be, although it is usually acknowledged that the court is not the primary decision-maker and so cannot simply remake the decision. Unlike ordinary judicial review, there are no clear markers as to the grounds for intervening.

The application of the margin seems to depend mainly on the following factors:

▶ The existence or otherwise, at the time of the infringement, of a consensus among the Member States of the Council of Europe, revealed by their changing laws and public opinion. The gradual evolution of public opinion about sexual behaviour provides a good illustration of this (see the thorough discussion by the House of Lords in *Secretary of State for Work and Pensions v M* [2006], (Section 21.4.4): single-sex partnerships; see also *Petrovic v Austria* [1998]: no consensus about paternity leave, so a margin was available). In *S and Marper v UK* [2008], [102] (retention of DNA samples), UK practice was exceptionally intrusive, so that there was no margin available. In *Goodwin v UK* (2002) 35 EHRR 18, the UK lost any margin of appreciation because, despite warnings, it dragged its heels in catching up with European opinion in respect of transsexual identity.

▶ The state must provide some supporting evidence for its claim, although this may be accepted at face value (*Hatton v UK* [2003]: need for night flights at Heathrow airport; *R (Lord Carlile of Berriew) v Secretary of State for the Home Department* [2014]: diplomatic relations; *R (Farrakhan) v Secretary of State for the Home Department* [2002]: visiting radical speaker: security).

▶ There must have been proper consideration of the matter by the responsible authority in the form, for example of a parliamentary debate. Decisions by Parliament, the highest democratic lawmaker, attract the greatest respect. Unlike a domestic court (below), the Strasbourg court can assess the quality of the debate. In *Hirst v UK (No. 2)* (2006) 42 EHRR 849, the Strasbourg court held that the UK's blanket ban on prisoners voting in parliamentary elections was outside any acceptable margin of appreciation, partly because it believed that the matter had not adequately been debated in Parliament (Section 12.5.5). By contrast, in *Animal Defenders International v UK* [2013], the Strasbourg court upheld UK legislation banning political advertising as within the margin because there was no European consensus on the matter, and there had been thorough debate in Parliament (at [114]–[116]) (see also *Countryside Alliance v UK* [2010], [58]).

▶ There is an important constraint. In view of Art 9 of the Bill of Rights 1688 (Section 11.6.3), a domestic court cannot assess the quality of debate in Parliament (*In re Recovery of Medical Costs for Asbestos Diseases* [2015], [55]–[56]; *R (SG) v Secretary of State for Work and Pensions* [2015], [16]). It may be that the court can take into account whether or not there was in fact a detailed discussion in Parliament although this comes close to forbidden territory (see *R (SG) v Secretary of State for Work and Pensions* (above), [95]–[96] where there had been substantial parliamentary discussion; *R (Williamson) v Secretary of State for Education and Employment* [2005], [50], [51]; *Matthews v Ministry of Defence* [2003] 1 AC 1163).

▶ In the case of legislative and executive bodies other than Parliament, the court can assess the adequacy of the discussion. Thus, in *In re Recovery of Medical Costs for Asbestos Diseases* [2015], it was held that the (then) Welsh Assembly had not given enough consideration to the retrospective nature of the law that it was enacting, and so the relevant legislation would be invalid. Lord Thomas, however, while agreeing with the outcome, suggested that, given the democratic nature of the devolved legislatures, their proceedings should be given the same level of respect as those of Parliament (at [122]–[123]). Does this mean, for example, that a principle, analogous to the Bill of Rights, should protect their proceedings? (See also *Miss Behavin' v Belfast City Council* [2007] 3 All ER 1007: local council.)

If the decision is inside the margin, the court can still interfere where the primary decision is 'manifestly without reasonable foundation' (*Blecic v Croatia* (2004) 41 EHRR 185: eviction of tenant). A similar approach, albeit with some disagreement, has been taken in domestic cases (*In re Recovery of Medical Costs for Asbestos Diseases* [2015], [46], [69], [114]; *R (SG) v Secretary of State for Work and Pensions* [2015], [69]). In *Carlile* [2014], the majority deferred to the government's assessment of the risk to relationships with the Iranian government. Lord Neuberger said (at [80]): 'Unless it can be shown to be based on wrong facts or law, not genuinely held or irrational, the nature of the decision in this case is such that the court would require strong reasons before it could properly substitute its own decision for that of the Secretary of State'. Lady Hale and Lord Clarke reluctantly held that the executive's assessment must be accepted in the absence of contrary evidence. Lord Kerr dissented on the basis that the government gave too much weight to the Iranian attitude which was undemocratic and unreasonable.

In *Bank Mellat v HM Treasury (No 2)* [2013], the Crown had made an Order freezing the assets of the claimant, an Iranian bank, on the ground that the Treasury believed that there was a connection with nuclear proliferation. A majority of the Supreme Court held that foreign policy and national security have a very wide margin of appreciation requiring experienced executive judgments sometimes based on secret evidence (at [21]). However, the court could intervene as the Crown's decision was irrational, in that the Order was targeted at individuals and there was no relevant reason given for distinguishing between the claimant's bank and other Iranian banks. It was also unfair because the claimant had not been given a hearing. Lords Reed and Hope dissented on the basis that greater weight should be given to the Treasury evidence about the distinctive features of this bank.

These examples may reveal underlying disagreement about the proper constitutional role of the court. For example, in *R (Nicklinson) v Ministry of Justice* [2014], the Supreme Court was divided in relation to a statute which made assisted suicide a crime. Four justices held that, in view of the wide issues involved, Parliament was the only appropriate forum. Two justices took the view that the matter was within the competence of the court, but in the circumstances refrained from intervening in order to give Parliament the opportunity to consider the matter first. Two justices were prepared to make an immediate order, holding that there was a clear breach of Article 8 of the ECHR.

Confusingly, the Strasbourg court has sometimes blurred the matter, using the expression whether the reasons given by the national authorities are 'relevant and sufficient' (*Vogt v Germany* (1996) 21 EHRR 205, [52]). Because the application of the margin varies with the context, it is frustratingly difficult to find out what this means. The Strasbourg court has not provided clear guidelines. Its reasoning is inconsistent and often perfunctory and vague to the point where it might be suspected that it uses the concept of margin of appreciation as a smokescreen to legitimate itself in the eyes of states keen to uphold their autonomy.

Note: The margin of appreciation doctrine links to the issue of how far the UK courts can depart from Strasbourg cases in defining and applying Convention rights (Section 22.2).

22.10 Reforms

The Parliamentary Joint Committee on Human Rights monitors the operation of the HRA and of the UK's involvement with the Strasbourg court. In particular, it is concerned with the responses of the government to cases where it has been held to be in breach of the ECHR. Its reports and the government's responses are a useful source of information for students.

During the past few years, there has been substantial parliamentary and media discussion on the theme of dissatisfaction with the HRA and the judges who apply it. It is claimed that the judges take too liberal a view of human rights compared with the UK's more authoritarian traditions. This has arisen particularly in the context of immigration, terrorist suspects, prisoners' rights and sex offenders, where UK culture is punitive. Unfortunately, human rights issues have sometimes been confused with the different issues created by EU law relating to immigration. There has also been criticism of the Strasbourg court concerning alleged empire building, inefficiency and low standards of decision-making (Section 21.5).

There has, however, been no agreement about what to do in response. It has often been proposed that the UK should adopt its own 'bill of rights' tailored to its history and culture (this also relates to the disagreement as to whether the UK courts should normally follow Strasbourg jurisprudence (Section 22.2)). The proposal raises several issues, all of them controversial.

First, what would be the content of a home-grown bill of rights and how, if at all, would it differ from the ECHR? Perhaps the rights which fall within the rule of law or the 'principle of legality' (Section 6.6) would qualify. More fundamentally, should a bill of rights include socio-economic and environmental rights?

Second, how would a bill of rights affect our relationship with other states? The UK is bound in international law by the ECHR and has undertaken to submit to the jurisdiction of the court. Abandoning this could make the UK a pariah state (see also Section 10.5.6).

Third, would a bill of rights make special arrangements for the devolved regimes, particularly Northern Ireland where there are serious political and religious differences?

Fourth, what role would the bill of rights play in relation to Parliament? At one extreme, it might merely be for the courts to take into account when interpreting legislation or applying case law. Or the court may be required to give the bill of rights special weight. This would range from requiring clear words to displace it, to requiring an express statement for a statute to overcome it, with the existing HRA's 'strong interpretive obligation' (Section 22.5.1) midway between the two. At the other extreme, a bill of rights might attempt to overcome parliamentary supremacy, opening up a range of possible devices such as an entrenched clause (Section 8.5.3). Conversely, a limited bill of rights would favour a political or democratic rather than a legal, approach to fundamental rights (Section 8.5.6).

There are also questions as to how a bill of rights should be enacted, similar to those arising with constitutional reform generally. If it were to be left to the ordinary parliamentary process, the bill of rights would be tainted by the prejudices of whichever party was dominant at the time.

The government appointed a Commission on a Bill of Rights which reported in 2012 (Ministry of Justice, *Commission on a Bill of Rights: A UK Bill of Rights? The Choice Before Us*). The Commission of nine did not include representatives of those affected by human rights issues, or of the opposition parties or the devolved countries. Chaired by a business-oriented former civil servant, seven of its members were male, all were White, seven were QCs, three were peers and the average age was 62. Its members comprised three Conservative lawyers not specialising in human rights law but predisposed against the HRA, three Liberal Democrat lawyers all being human rights experts, an EU judge and a Conservative campaigner against the HRA who later resigned. The Commission's terms of reference limited debate on fundamental issues by focusing on 'a Bill of Rights that incorporates and builds on all our obligations under the ECHR, ensures that these rights continue to be enshrined in our law and protects and extends our liberties'.

The Commission was divided and did not seriously address the issues outlined above. Its report tells us little apart from the personal views of its members. A majority favoured the introduction of a bill of rights based on the existing HRA. It claimed lack of expertise in recommending what rights should be included and did not suggest how the rights should be protected. Indeed, the Commission suggested that the problem was primarily cosmetic, lying in public perception generated by an ill-informed media hostile to European influences. This could be lessened by a change of name to one associated with the UK.

Individual contributions favoured limiting human rights by introducing a weaker interpretation requirement, confining full protection to citizens, imposing reciprocal obligations and withdrawing from the ECHR. A minority of two favoured retention of the HRA (see Elliott, 'A Damp Squib in the Long Grass: The Report of the Commission on a Bill of Rights' [2013] EHRLR 139; Scott-Moncrieff, 'Language and Law: Reclaiming the Human Rights Debate' [2013] EHRLR 115); Munce (2014) 67 Parl Aff 80).

The Conservative Party manifesto of 2019 contained a vague commitment to 'update the Human Rights Act… to ensure that there is a proper balance between the rights of individuals, our vital national security and effective government'. Accordingly, an independent review panel was set up in December 2020. The panel, which is expected to report by summer 2021, has been tasked with considering the relationship between domestic courts and the Strasbourg Court, including the operation of s 2; the impact of the HRA on the relationship between the judiciary, executive and Parliament, and whether domestic courts are being unduly drawn into areas of policy; and the extra-territorial application of the Act. The government has indicated that it has no intention of making any alteration to the rights themselves, or of withdrawing from the ECHR machinery altogether. This appears to meet one of the concerns which arose in the Brexit negotiations between the UK and EU, especially in relation to future cooperation on security matters (see Section 10.5.6).

Summary

- The HRA, while not incorporating the ECHR as such, has given the main rights created by it effect in domestic law. UK legislation must be interpreted to be compatible with Convention rights, and public bodies other than Parliament must comply with Convention rights. The courts must take the decisions of the ECHR into account but are not bound by them. However, the UK courts take a cautious approach and follow Strasbourg unless there are special circumstances.

- The Act is probably not retrospective generally and proceedings must normally be commenced within one year of the alleged breach. However, in the case of an inquiry into a death or other serious violation, where there is a breach of the duty to hold an inquiry after the Act came into force, the court can investigate back for a period of ten years before the date on which the right to petition Strasbourg took effect, provided that there is a 'genuine connection' between the violation and the events in question consisting of a relevant event after that date such as the emergence of important new evidence. A longer period is possible where underlying Convention values are in issue.

- The Act was originally primarily territorial. However, it can now be 'divided and tailored' so as to apply outside the UK where the victim is subject to the control of the UK government: this has proved controversial in relation to military action overseas.

- Parliamentary supremacy is preserved in that Convention rights must give way where they are incompatible with a statute. The courts have taken a moderate approach in relation to the obligation to interpret statutes, 'so far as it is possible to do so', to be compatible with Convention rights. However, there are differences of emphasis between judges as to the assumptions on which interpretation should be approached, in particular the extent to which established English law should be respected.

- Where primary legislation is incompatible, the court can draw attention to violations by making a declaration of incompatibility. There is a 'fast-track' procedure available in special circumstances to enable amendments to legislation to be made. The government must be explicit as to any intention to override Convention rights.

- The HRA can be directly enforced only against public authorities and by a 'victim', defined in accordance with the case law of the European Court.

- 'Public authority' includes all the activities of government bodies proper, and courts and tribunals, but in relation to bodies that have a mixture of public and private functions (e.g. social landlords) only to their public 'acts'. The courts seem to be taking a similar approach to the question of what constitutes a public function as in judicial review cases.

- 'Horizontal effect' may be direct, where the court is required to enforce a right against a private person, or indirect, where the state is required to protect against violations by private persons.

- Some Convention rights can be overridden by prescribed public interest concerns, or other rights. In balancing such a right against a government decision taken in the public interest, the courts are guided by the concept of proportionality which requires that the decision interferes with the right no further than is necessary to achieve an important public objective and that the benefits outweigh the costs. This helps to structure and rationalise decision-making but requires the court to make a subjective political judgment. Where one right falls to balance against another right, proportionality requires that the least harmful outcome be sought.

- The courts have applied the notion of 'margin of appreciation' or 'margin of discretion', to particular issues. The width of the margin depends on the particular combination of elements in the case. These include the importance of the right in question, the level and democratic content of the decision and the extent to which the matter involves controversial political, social or economic choices or requires specialist knowledge which a court lacks the capacity to assess. Where a matter falls within a margin the court will normally interfere only where the decision is 'manifestly unreasonable'.

- It remains controversial whether the courts provide the best method of protecting fundamental rights, and there have been proposals for some form of reform of the HRA for a number of years.

Exercises

(You should also refer to material in Chapter 21.)

22.1 What is meant by describing the HRA as creating a 'constitutional dialogue'? Do you agree with this description?

22.2 'Parliament never intended by enacting the Human Rights Act 1998 to give the courts of this country the power to give a more generous scope to the Convention rights than that which was to be found in the jurisprudence of the Strasbourg Court. To do so would have the effect of changing them from Convention rights, based on the treaty obligations, into freestanding rights of the court's [ie, the Supreme Court's] own creation' (Lord Hope).

Explain and critically discuss.

22.3 According to Lord Bingham, the court's role under the HRA is democratic because Parliament has given the courts 'a very specific wholly democratic mandate' *(A v Secretary of State for the Home Department* [2005] at [42]). Do you agree?

22.4 Explain and compare the constitutional significance of the declaration of incompatibility and the statement of compatibility.

22.5 'My impression is that two factors are contributing to a misunderstanding of the remedial scheme of the 1998 Act. First, there is the constant refrain that a judicial reading down or reading in would flout the will of Parliament. The second factor may be an excessive concentration on linguistic factors of the particular statute' (Lord Steyn in *Ghaidan v Mendoza* [2004]).

Explain and critically evaluate this statement.

22.6 **(i)** New evidence emerged last year that Richard III murdered the 'Princes in the Tower' in 1483 but the government refuses to investigate the matter. Who, if anyone, can challenge the decision under the HRA?

(ii) Last month, the government decided to abandon an inquiry into allegations of torture in certain prisons between 1990 and 2000. Advise the alleged victims whether they have a remedy under the HRA and, if so, how they might establish such a right.

(b) Advise on the chances of success of challenges to each of the following under the HRA:

(i) The alleged beating up of refugees in a refugee camp in Utopia by British soldiers working in Utopia as part of a force led by an international relief agency.

(ii) British soldiers stationed in Utopia at the request of the Utopian government are alleged to have shot and killed Utopian civilians in the mistaken belief that they were looting a Utopian government food relief distribution centre. Would the position be different if the Utopian government had asked the British army to police the centre?

(iii) An alleged failure of the British army to provide protective combat equipment for overseas engagements comparable with that provided to the soldiers of other countries.

22.7 The Railway Premises (Public Safety) Act 2021 (fictitious) empowers a police officer to detain and search any person for the purpose of preventing 'inappropriate behaviour' within any designated railway station. Any railway station can be designated by its station manager. A designation can last for up to 28 days. A notice must be placed near the entrance to a designated station drawing attention to the power. Eggesford Station has been designated under the Act. A notice to that effect was placed in the ticket office window. Keith, a pensioner, is a railway enthusiast and often spends time on the platform at Eggesford station photographing the trains. One day last week, hearing that the Royal Train was scheduled to call at Eggesford in connection with a royal visit to a nearby military base, Keith set up his camera on the platform. Constable Spoiler stopped Keith and detained him for one hour in the station manager's office until the Royal Train had left. He searched Keith's rucksack and anorak and destroyed the pictures in his camera.

Advise Keith of any rights he may have under the HRA.

22.8 Advise Trebangor Council whether the following decisions are vulnerable to a successful challenge under the HRA:

(i) Trebangor Council evicts Mary, who has occupied a home owned by the Council for many years. The reason the council gives for the eviction is that there is a housing shortage in the area and that Mary is a troublemaker with a record of anti-social behaviour.

What would be the position if Mary's landlord were a private company and Mary was evicted for non-payment of rent?

(ii) Trebangor Council provides health services to married couples only if they are of different sexes.

(iii) The Trebangor area is prone to flooding. The Council is short of funds and decides to build flood defences to protect the Council offices, rather than divert a stream away from three cottages owned by farmworkers. There is an unusually severe flood which engulfs the cottages. One of the occupants is killed. The cottages had to be destroyed. The farmworkers demand an inquiry into the Council's decision.

(iv) Donald purchases a piece of farmland in the countryside outside Trebangor upon which he intends to develop as a golf course and hotel. The Council subsequently designates the land as part of a protected wildlife area which means that it cannot be developed without government consent. Donald finds that he cannot sell the site.

22.9 Discuss the following scenarios:

(i) Matthew, who is serving a long prison sentence for a banking fraud, requests to be moved to a prison nearer his home so that his young children will not lose touch with him. He also claims that he is at risk of death in his present prison because some of his fellow prisoners were victims of his crime. The prison authorities refuse this request on the ground that moving him is too expensive and the risk to him can be minimised by keeping him in solitary confinement.

(ii) The government orders the slaughter of a flock of birds which are owned by a religious community to whom they are sacred. The government's reason is that the presence of the birds creates a risk to human health. The community leaders believe that any risk can be minimised by suitable protective measures.

Further reading

Brady, *Proportionality and Deference Under the UK Human Rights Act* (Cambridge University Press 2010)

Buxton, 'The Future of Declarations of Incompatibility' [2010] PL 261

Chandrachud, 'Reconfiguring the Discourse on Political Responses to Declarations of Incompatibility' [2014] PL 624

Ewing and Than, 'The Continuing Futility of the Human Rights Act' [2008] PL 668

Grieve, 'Can a Bill of Rights Do Better than the Human Rights Act?' [2016] PL 223

Hickman, 'Constitutional Dialogue, Constitutional Theories and the Human Rights Act 1998' [2005] PL 306

Hickman, 'The Courts and Politics After the Human Rights Act' [2008] PL 84

Hickman, 'The Substance and Structure of Proportionality' [2008] PL 694

Hiebert, 'Governing Under the Human Rights Act: The Limitations of Wishful Thinking' [2012] PL 27

Horne and Conway, 'Parliament and Human Rights' in Horne and Drewry (eds), *Parliament and the Law* (2nd edn, Hart Publishing 2019)

Hunt, Hooper and Yowell (eds), *Parliament and Human Rights: Addressing the Democratic Deficit* (Hart Publishing 2015)

Irvine, 'A British Interpretation of Convention Rights' [2012] PL 236

Kavanagh, 'Judging the Judges Under the Human Rights Act' [2009] PL 287

Klug, 'A Bill of Rights: Do We Need One or Do We Already Have One?' [2007] PL 701

Lakin, 'How to Make Sense of the Human Rights Act 1998: The Ises and Oughts of the British Constitution' (2010) 30 OJLS 399

Lester, 'The Utility of the Human Rights Act: A Reply to Keith Ewing' [2005] PL 249

Mahoney, 'The Relationship Between the Strasbourg Court and the National Courts' (2014) 130 LQR 568

O'Cinneide, 'Human Rights Law in the UK – Is There a Need for Fundamental Reform?' [2012] EHRLR 595

O'Cinneide, 'Human Rights and the UK Constitution' in Jowell and O'Cinneide (eds), *The Changing Constitution* (9th edn, Oxford University Press 2019)

Sales, 'Strasbourg Jurisprudence and the Human Rights Act: A Response to Lord Irvine' [2012] PL 253

Sales and Ekins, 'Rights-Consistent Interpretation and the Human Rights Act 1998' (2011) 127 LQR 217

Further reading cont'd

Skinner, 'Deference, Proportionality and the Margin of Appreciation in Lethal Force Case Law Under Article 2 of the ECHR' [2014] EHRLR 32

Williams, 'A Fresh Perspective on Hybrid Public Authorities Under the Human Rights Act: Private Contractors, Rights-Stripping and Chameleonic Horizontal Effect' [2011] PL 139

Wright, 'Interpreting Section 2 of the Human Rights Act: Towards an Indigenous Jurisprudence of Human Rights' [2009] PL 595

Wright, 'The Impact of Section 6 HRA on the Common Law' [2014] PL 289

Young, 'In Defence of Due Deference' (2009) 72 MLR 554

Young, 'Is Dialogue Working Under the Human Rights Act?' [2011] PL 773

Chapter 23

Freedoms of expression and assembly

23.1 Introduction: justifications for freedom of expression

The arguments for freedom of expression were identified by Mill (Section 2.3.3) as democracy, self-fulfillment and the testing of truth. They were taken up by Lord Steyn in *R v Secretary of State for the Home Dept, ex parte Simms* [2000] 2 AC 115, [34]–[41]; see also *R (BBC) v Secretary of State for Justice* [2012] 2 All ER 1089, [35]–[43]. As regards democracy, Lord Steyn emphasised freedom of expression in informing debate, as a safety valve to encourage consent and as a brake on the abuse of power. Democracy can flourish only in circumstances where there is a free press with access to government. Thus, in *Hector v A-G of Antigua and Bermuda* [1990] 2 All ER 103. Lord Bridge said that 'in a free democratic society… those who hold office in government must always be open to criticism. Any attempt to stifle or fetter such criticism amounts to political censorship of the most insidious and objectionable kind.' However, in *R v Shayler* [2002] 2 All ER 477, Lord Hutton suggested, redolent of the 'dignified constitution' (Section 1.6), that freedom of expression might undesirably weaken confidence in those who govern us (although the opposite might be said).

Free expression requires not only the right to criticise government and challenge orthodoxy, but also fair opportunities at elections and other public debates (*Handyside v UK* (1976) 1 EHRR 737; *Bowman v UK* (1998) 26 EHRR 1; *Castells v Spain* (1992) 14 EHRR 445). This may include protecting even false statements so as not to inhibit debate, thus conflicting with the goal of truth. Under the ECHR, freedom of political speech is especially important and has only a limited margin of appreciation, meaning that the state must strongly justify its interference (*Animal Defenders International v UK* (2013) 57 EHRR 21 [102]; R (*Animal Defenders International*) v Culture Secretary [2008] 1 AC 1312, [26]). An issue here is whether freedom of expression should apply to those who reject democracy itself. In *Kuznetov v Russia* [2008] ECHR 1170, [45] the Strasbourg court appeared to suggest that freedom of assembly could be restricted if rejection of democratic principles are involved. However, it is arguably wrong to exclude discussion of other possible forms of government.

The argument that freedom of expression supports self-fulfilment is well established in the jurisprudence of the Strasbourg court (*Mouvement Raelien Suisse v Switzerland* (2013) 56 EHRR 14, [48]). It starts with the proposition that the proper end of humanity is the realisation of individual potential, which cannot flourish without freedom of expression. However, self-fulfilment also requires protection for privacy, so there is a conflict between these fundamental human rights (*Von Hannover v Germany* (2005) 40 EHRR 1). Thus, a balance must be struck between the right to respect for privacy and family life under Article 8 and freedom of expression under Article 10 (*Lingens v Austria* (1986) 8 EHRR 407, [42]; *Lindon v France* [2007] ECHR 836).

Freedom of expression also includes the right, essential to human dignity, not to be forced to express a view. As Lord Dyson said in *RT (Zimbabwe) v Secretary of State for the Home Department* [2013] 1 AC 152, at [44]: 'The idea that "if you are not with us you are against us" pervades the thinking of dictators'. In that case, an asylum-seeker was protected who feared retribution for failing to promote loyalty to the governing regime.

The argument that freedom of expression facilitates the pursuit of truth and the acquisition of knowledge suppressed by official orthodoxy was expressed in the seventeenth century by John Milton in his *Areopagitica*. Mill argued that 'truth', which he equated with the general good, can best be discovered and preserved by constant questioning in the expectation that the good will drives out the bad. (Supported by Lord Bingham in R (*Animal Defenders International*) v Culture Secretary [2008], [28]. Karl Popper states that free critical discussion at least provides a means by which to eliminate errors in our thinking (*The Open Society and Its Enemies* (Routledge 1996).)

However, this provides relatively weak support since truth is not always necessarily conducive to the general welfare and the good will not necessarily drive out the bad. It could be argued, most obviously in relation to elections, that freedom of expression allows the loudest (best-funded) voice to prevail (see *R (Animal Defenders International) v UK* [2013]; *R (Animal Defenders International) v Culture Secretary* [2008], [28]).

From a liberal perspective, one point of freedom of expression is arguably to keep diversity and disagreement alive. Thus, Bollinger suggests that freedom of expression facilitates 'the development of [a] capacity for tolerance' ('The Tolerance Society' [1990] CLR 979). A capacity for tolerance weakens 'a general bias against receiving or acknowledging new ideas' (ibid.). As Locke recognised (*On Tolerance* (1698)), it is particularly valuable as a means of keeping the peace in large and complex societies containing people with varied beliefs and interests.

Freedom of expression is not absolute. Not all aspects of it are equally important, and it may be overridden by other factors (Section 23.2). This leads to the danger, identified by Berlin (Section 2.4), of freedom of expression being regarded as a 'positive freedom' conditional upon those in power assessing its worthiness. Thus, in *City of London Corp v Samede* [2012] 2 All ER 1039, [41], Lord Neuberger MR warned against giving particular weight to matters which the judge considers to be especially important, or with which s/he agrees. In an attempt to resolve such conflicts, Mill distinguished between causing *harm* which should be prohibited, and causing *offence* or outrage which should not. This has been endorsed by the Strasbourg court (see *Handyside v UK* [1976]; *Baskaya and Okcuola v Turkey* (2001) 31 EHRR 292). However, being offended or shocked might be considered good, as stimulating thought (see Lord Scott (dissenting) in *R (ProLife Alliance) v BBC* [2003] (Section 23.3.1)). Moreover, it is not clear what counts as harm. Mill took harm to mean interfering with someone's rights or interests, but this begs the questions what counts as an 'interest'. Am I harmed if I am seriously upset by someone attacking my religion? This raises the difficult issue of 'hate speech' (Section 23.6). The domestic courts have held that protection against public offence is a valid ground for restricting freedom of expression (see *R (ProLife Alliance) v BBC* [2003] 2 All ER 977: anti-abortion television broadcast; *R (Core Issues Trust) v Transport for London* [2014] EWCA Civ 34: bus advert for gay rights. However, in these cases there was no complete ban (below)).

23.1.1 Prior restraint

In the eighteenth century, Blackstone introduced the distinction between 'prior restraint – censorship', requiring government approval in advance, and punishing the speaker after the event (*Commentaries* (1765) III, 17). Prior restraint is regarded as an especially serious violation of freedom of expression because it removes from the public sphere the possibility of assessing the matter, whereas punishment may be regarded as a legitimate compromise between competing goods. Prior restraint should therefore be only a last resort, particularly in the case of news, 'which is a perishable commodity' (see *Observer and Guardian Newspapers v UK* (1992) 14 EHRR 153). In *Open Door and Dublin Well Woman v Ireland* (1992) 15 EHRR 244, five judges thought that prior restraint should never be tolerated. On the other hand, if there are serious penalties such as fines for publication after the event, these are likely to have a 'chilling' effect by discouraging publication, so that Blackstone's distinction may be somewhat illusory.

Prior restraint includes both the *content* of what is said and the form and place where it is expressed. In *R (ProLife Alliance) v BBC* [2003], which concerned a ban on a televised party-political broadcast regarded as offensive, Lord Hoffmann drew a distinction between a complete ban and refusing to give someone a platform to disseminate offensive material. Just as no one has a right to have his or her work published by a particular publisher, no one has a right to appear on television. He emphasised the pervasive influence of television, with the implication that protective measures are especially justified. Lord Scott, dissenting, thought that, given the importance of television as a medium of political communication and the state's positive duty to ensure the dissemination of opinion, this distinction was unreal (Section 23.3.1).

Lord Scott's approach was followed in *R (BBC) v Secretary of State for Justice* [2012]. The government had refused to allow a live interview by the BBC with a person who had been detained for seven years without charge, pending extradition. In overruling the government's refusal as disproportionate, the Divisional Court emphasised the watchdog role of the press and the importance of the immediacy and personal nature of television. No countervailing security consideration was raised by the government relating to the particular circumstances. General objections to giving publicity to suspected terrorists were not enough. However, in *R (Lord Carlile of Berriew) v Secretary of State for the Home Department* [2014] UKSC 60 the Supreme Court, not without disagreement, upheld the refusal of the government to allow a prominent Iranian dissident to enter the UK in order to meet a group of MPs. The government's reason was to avoid upsetting the government of Iran. The majority were influenced primarily by the need to give a large margin of discretion to the government in diplomatic matters (Section 22.9.3), but also stressed the fact that the ban did not prevent discussion in other forms of the matters which the MPs wished to raise. Attempts to limit communications to the media by prisoners also raise the question of a restriction as opposed to a complete ban. There is a public interest in some degree of restriction where material might create a risk to security or (perhaps) celebrate crimes, but a complete ban on communications with the media is disproportionate (see *R v Secretary of State for the Home Dept, ex parte Simms* [2000]; *R (Hirst) v Secretary of State for the Home Department* [2002] EWHC 602 (Admin); *Bamber v UK* ECHR App.33724/96 (1997): 'ordinary and reasonable requirements of imprisonment'; *R (Nilsen) v Governor of Full Sutton Prison* [2004] EWCA Civ 1540: ban on autobiography of serial killer upheld).

23.2 The legal basis of freedom of expression

Article 10 of the ECHR provides:

[T]his right shall include freedom to hold opinions and to receive and impart information and ideas without interference by a public authority and regardless of frontiers. This article shall not prevent states from requiring the licensing of broadcasting, television or cinema enterprise.

Overrides: The exercise of these freedoms, since it carries with it duties and responsibilities, may be subject to such formalities, conditions, restrictions or penalties as are prescribed by law and are necessary in a democratic society in the interests of national security, territorial integrity or public safety, for the prevention of disorder or crime, for the protection of health or morals, for the protection of the reputation or rights of others, for preventing the disclosure of information received in confidence or for maintaining the authority and impartiality of the judiciary.

Article 11 on freedom of peaceful assembly and association provides:

Everyone has the right to freedom of peaceful assembly and to freedom of association with others, including the right to form and to join trade unions for the protection of his interests.

Overrides: No restrictions shall be placed on these rights other than such as are prescribed by law and are necessary in a democratic society in the interests of national security or public safety, for the prevention of disorder or crime, for the protection of health or morals or for the protection of the rights and freedoms of others. This article shall not prevent the imposition of lawful restrictions on the exercise of those rights by members of the armed forces, of the police or of the administration of the state.

The European Court has stressed that freedom of political debate and of the press is at the very core of the concept of a democratic society which prevails throughout the Convention (see *Castells v Spain* [1992]; *Jersild v Denmark* (1994) 19 EHRR 1; *Baskaya and Okcuola v Turkey* [2001]). Great weight is also given to open justice in the form of the publication of fully reasoned court judgments since this is a means of holding the judiciary to account *(R (Mohamed) v Secretary of State for Foreign Affairs* [2010] 3 WLR 554; Section 23.3.4).

Less weight is given to commercial expression, such as advertising, and possibly the least weight is given to lifestyle matters such as pornography (*City of London Corp v Samede* [2012], [41]: 'political and economic views are at the top end of the scale, pornography and vapid tittle-tattle towards the bottom'). In *R v Secretary of State for the Home Dept, ex p Simms* [2000], a prisoner was entitled to have access to a journalist in order to publicise his claim that he was wrongly convicted, but Lord Steyn thought that he would not have had such access to indulge in pornography or even in a general political or economic debate (see also *R (British American Tobacco UK Ltd) v Secretary of State for Health* [2004] EWHC 2493 (Admin): advertising; *Miss Behavin' v Belfast City Council* [2007] 3 All ER 1007: sexual services).

It is not clear how much weight is given to cultural matters such as theatre and works of art. Where these conflict with religious susceptibilities, at least those of influential sections of the community, it seems that the latter carry greater weight (*Otto Preminger Institut v Austria* (1994) 19 EHRR 34). This seems to violate Mill's distinction between 'harm' and 'offence', although religion might be a special case in view of its discriminatory and public order dimensions.

Some statutes give specific protection to political freedom of expression. The main examples are the Bill of Rights 1688, the Parliamentary Papers Act 1840 (Section 11.6.5) and the Defamation Acts 1952 and 1996 (Section 23.4). The Education (No. 2) Act 1986 imposes a duty on universities to protect freedom of speech on their premises. Sometimes statutes protect freedom of expression against some general restriction (e.g. Environmental Protection Act 1990, s 79(6A): noise controls, political demonstrations exempted).

23.3   Limits on freedom of expression

Article 10 confers the right of freedom of expression subject to 'duties and responsibilities'. These entitle the state to limit freedom of expression for the following purposes. The court must balance these against freedom of expression in the particular circumstances of each case, according to the principle of proportionality (Section 22.9):

- national security;
- territorial integrity or public safety;
- prevention of disorder or crime;
- protection of health or morals;
- protection of the reputation or rights of others. Thus, freedom of expression may be compromised by the right to a fair trial (Art 6), privacy (Art 8) and freedom of religion (Art 9);
- preventing the disclosure of information received in confidence;
- maintaining the authority and impartiality of the judiciary.

Statutes restricting freedom of expression

Numerous statutes have restricted freedom of expression for the following main purposes. These conform to Article 10 in principle. However, any restriction must be proportionate in the specific circumstances:

- security, public order and safety;
- reputation;
- privacy and confidentiality: protection of personal data, for example medical records and student records held by universities (Data Protection Act 2018); professional and business confidentiality;
- sexual morality (Obscene Publications Act 1959: 'deprave and corrupt' subject to defence of artistic merit; Cinemas Act 1985: local authorities licensing of cinema performances; Video Recordings Act 2010);
- child protection, particularly in relation to reporting court proceedings (Children Act 1989, s 97(2); Magistrates Courts Act 1980, s 69(2)(c); combating racial, religious and sexual hatred;
- protection against misleading advertising and professional claims;
- intellectual property such as copyright; in this context an exception for parody is a recognition of freedom of expression.

23.3.1 Press freedom and censorship

Political expression is especially important as a means of both holding government to account and participating in democracy. Article 10 specifically includes the right to *receive* information and ideas. By virtue of its 'duties and responsibilities' under Article 10, the press is the public's watchdog for this purpose. Thus, Lord Bingham in *McCartan Turkington Breen v Times Newspapers Ltd* [2001] 2 AC 277 stressed the importance of a free, active, professional and inquiring media to a modern participatory democracy, pointing out that ordinary citizens cannot usually participate directly but can do so indirectly through the media (at 290–91).

The European Court has held that the state has a duty to safeguard the free flow of information and opinion through the media, even in respect of objectionable opinions. (See *Jersild v Denmark* [1994]: a television interview was entitled to include racist views provided that the interviewer did not associate himself with them.) In *Animal Defenders International v UK* [2013], [102] it was said that the margin of appreciation is narrowed by the strong interest of a democratic society in the press exercising its vital role as a public watchdog: 'It is incumbent on the press to impart information and ideas on subjects of public interest and the public also has a right to receive them'.

The permissible limits of freedom of expression are wider against the government than against an individual. Thus, press freedom includes the need to give some journalistic latitude in order to prevent the chilling effect of vague restrictions which may discourage the media from bold investigations of wrongdoing among the powerful (see *Thomas v Luxembourg* (2003) 36 EHRR 359, 373; *Fressoz v France* (1999) 5 BHRC 654, 656; *Selisto v Finland* (2006) 42 EHRR 8).

The media has no special privileges under the common law. Its position therefore depends on statute and on its rights under the Human Rights Act. There are statutory provisions in several contexts which safeguard press freedom. The main ones are discussed in the following sections. Another example is provided by Schedule 2, Part 5 of the Data Protection Act 2018, which exempt journalistic, literary or artistic material processed with a view to publication from listed data protection principles. The exemption applies where the data controller reasonably believes that publication would be in the public interest, taking into account the special importance of the public interest in freedom of expression and information. Journalistic material is also protected under particular statutes from police search and seizure powers, where a court order is required.

23.3.2 Broadcasting

The media is not uniformly regulated. There is significant regulation of radio and television, mainly in the Communications Act 2003. There are specific requirements which interfere with freedom of expression, including impartiality and taste, policed by the Office of Communications (Ofcom), which replaced a variety of other bodies (Communications Act 2003). The BBC is created and governed by royal charter, which imposes similar requirements enforceable as an agreement between the BBC and the Crown, but with Ofcom being given some regulatory functions (Communications Act 2003, s 198); since 2017, Ofcom has held the BBC's performance and editorial standards to account, and regulates the competitive effects of its services. In an emergency, the Secretary of State may require the BBC to make announcements or to censor broadcasts. There is a non-legally-binding Broadcasting Code applicable to all broadcasters, which concerns moral standards, privacy and fairness.

The BBC is a designated public authority under the Freedom of Information Act 2000 (FoIA) and so is liable to disclose information if requested (Section 24.2). However, it is a public authority only in respect of information held for purposes other than those of journalism, art or literature. In *Sugar (Deceased) v BBC* [2012] UKSC 4, the claimant was a member of a pro-Israeli pressure group who believed that the BBC's coverage of the Israeli–Palestinian conflict was biased. The BBC commissioned a report on the matter intended as an internal briefing document which made recommendations concerning internal management matters. The claimant sought disclosure of this under the

FoIA. He argued that, where a document contained both journalistic and non-journalistic material, the non-journalistic material should be disclosed. A majority of the Supreme Court held that the whole of a mixed document should be protected in the interests of journalistic freedom. Lord Wilson, however, would give protection only where the predominant purpose of the document was journalistic.

Broadcasting regulation was originally justified in that, unlike the print media, access to the airwaves has been limited, being effectively a government-controlled monopoly offering the public limited choice. However, technical developments including the Internet and social media have opened up so many different outlets that detailed regulation may now be less appropriate.

Where there is a regulatory mechanism, the courts are reluctant to impose their own judgments, short of reviewing unreasonable decisions. In *R (ProLife Alliance) v BBC* [2003], a majority of the House of Lords left it to the BBC to decide whether a requirement to ensure that programmes do not offend 'good taste and decency' overrode the right to freedom of expression of the Alliance, which wished to include in an election broadcast images of the process of abortion. Lord Scott dissented on classical liberal grounds. Far from wishing to protect the public against offence, he claimed that 'the public in a mature democracy are not entitled to be offended by the broadcasting of such a programme', that a ban would be 'positively inimical to the values of a democratic society to which values it must be assumed that the public adheres' (at [98]), and that 'a broadcaster's mind-set that rejects a party election television programme on the ground that large numbers of the voting public would find the programme "offensive" denigrates the voting public, treats them like children who need to be protected from the unpleasant realities of life, seriously undervalues their political maturity and can only promote [voter apathy]' (at [99]).

A specific limitation on the broadcast media (as distinct from social media) is that there is a blanket ban on political advertising (Communications Act 2003, ss 319–21). Advertising consists of material that, independently of the advertiser's motives, is directed towards persuasion in favour of a political objective. 'Political' is defined widely to include social campaigning as well as party political matters and law reform. Thus, pressure groups and charities are subject to restrictions even if they are outside party politics.

The ban sets two aspects of freedom of expression in conflict. On the one hand, the purpose of the ban is to prevent politics from becoming an auction dominated by wealthy vested interests, for instance multinational companies objecting to climate change legislation. English law can in this respect be contrasted with the USA, where strident television advertising is a prominent feature of election campaigns, protected by the primacy of freedom of expression in the US Constitution. On the other hand, the ban restricts the freedom of expression of campaigning groups promoting valuable ideas such as animal protection by denying them influential media outlets (see *Jersild v Denmark* [1994]), although since the rise of social media, this is perhaps less problematic than was once the case.

In *R (Animal Defenders International) v Culture Secretary* [2008] the House of Lords upheld the ban on political advertising as proportionate under the Human Rights Act. Although this was an interference with the high value of political freedom of expression, it did not completely prevent the pressure group from campaigning, and there was a vital public interest in preventing election campaigns being distorted by money. Parliament, as a democratic body more competent than judges in this context, should be given a margin of discretion since it had consistently followed the same policy, had thoroughly considered the matter, and had treated it as of high importance by resolving to proceed even though there was a possible violation of Art 10. A general rule was necessary even if this produced hard cases since no workable compromise had been found (at [33]). It was also important that other outlets were available for the claimant's campaign such as the internet.

The Strasbourg court upheld the House of Lords, holding that there is no European consensus on the matter, therefore requiring a margin of appreciation (*Animal Defenders International v UK* [2013]). It was important that there had been thorough parliamentary debate. The court revised its previous position, indicating that it may have given too little weight to the problems of political advertising (see also *Murphy v Ireland* (2004) 38 EHRR 212: general ban on religious advertising upheld for similar reasons). However, a dissenting minority held that the ban was too indiscriminate to outweigh freedom of expression.

The meaning of 'political advertising' is wide, including as it does *any* advertisement by a body whose objects are of a political nature (s 321(2)(a)) and any advertisement influencing public opinion on a matter of public controversy (s 321(3)(f)). In *R (Animal Defenders International) v Culture Secretary* [2008], Lord Scott warned that the extent of the ban might be too wide in that it included advertisements which in themselves had no political content, such as for a car boot sale or to encourage voting at elections. Furthermore, given the broadcasters' duty of impartiality, the ban would chill debate by preventing a pressure group from countering TV adverts by businesses, for example in favour of eating meat (at [41]); see also Lord Bingham (at [34]).

In *R (London Christian Radio Ltd) v Radio Advertising Clearance Centre* [2014] 1 WLR 307, the Court of Appeal held that an advertisement calling for information about discrimination against Christians at work, 'to help make a fairer society', could be prohibited, even though the advert itself did not directly persuade in favour of law reform but could be read merely as inviting research. Elias LJ's dissent is attractive, invoking the 'principle of legality' according to which fundamental rights should not be restricted without clear statutory language (Section 6.6).

23.3.3 Press self-regulation

By contrast with the broadcast media, since the abolition in 1695 of state licensing of printing presses, the government has no censorship powers over the printed word. This is regarded as an essential safeguard for the press against state interference. For many years, voluntary regulation was carried out by the Press Complaints Commission, controlled by the industry itself, which had no investigatory or enforcement powers and was widely regarded as ineffectual and lacking independence.

The Leveson Report (HC 2012, 780) recommended a form of state regulation. The report was a response to substantial abuses by journalists of the privacy of individuals, primarily by 'hacking' emails and mobile phones. These resulted in criminal convictions. There were also unproven allegations of corrupt payments made by journalists to public officials.

Leveson stressed that there should be no power to prevent publication and no direct government regulation of the press. He recommended that a new 'independent self-regulatory' body should be created by statute with powers to arbitrate disputes, investigate complaints from the public and investigate on its own initiative. Its process and membership should be independent of press and government interests. There would be another independent body to appoint members of the regulator.

The scheme would be voluntary, but those who joined it would have the incentive of reduced liability to damages and costs in the courts. It has been suggested that penalising those who did not join the regulator would violate Article 10 of the ECHR. Indeed, a substantial proportion of the press objected to the scheme as a form of state licensing. In October 2016, the government announced that it was not, for the time being, implementing section 40 of the Crime and Courts Act 2013, which gives effect to this, and a similar provision was withdrawn from the Investigatory Powers Act 2016.

The government responded to Leveson in March 2013 by proposing that the regulator be validated by a charter under the royal prerogative rather than statute. Since a royal charter is a form of law under the control of ministers, this arrangement does nothing to protect the press. However, under the Enterprise and Regulatory Reform Act 2013, a royal charter cannot be amended except under its own terms, in this case, a requirement of a two-thirds vote in Parliament (of course, this lock could be removed by an ordinary statute). The charter was granted on 30 October 2013 after private negotiations between the political parties. The Home Office has appointed a chair (David Wolfe QC), of the 'Press Recognition Panel', which, under the charter, appoints and monitors the regulator. A regulator (IMPRESS) promoted by privacy campaigners was approved in October 2016 but only a few, mainly local, publications have accepted it.

Most of the industry has rejected the charter arrangements and has created its own regulatory machinery on a similar basis. This is the Independent Press Standards Organisation (IPSO) presided over by Lord Faulks, a barrister and former Justice Minister. Representatives from the industry are members of IPSO's regulator but do not form a majority. IPSO has been accepted by 90 per cent of the industry, but it is claimed that IPSO is merely a version of the discredited Press Complaints Commission.

23.3.4 The courts' censorship powers

The courts have general prior restraint powers in the form of an injunction, carrying imprisonment for contempt of court. The Attorney General can seek an injunction in the name of the public interest, most notably in the case of publications that risk prejudicing legal proceedings, such as newspaper comments on matters related to pending litigation (contempt of court) and in the interests of government confidentiality or national security (Section 24.4). A temporary injunction pending a full trial can be granted on the basis that there is an arguable case, since, once material is published, the harm is done.

A temporary injunction prevents anyone, whether a party or not, publishing the material with the intention to impede the court's purpose in granting the injunction (*A-G v Observer Ltd* [1988] 1 All ER 385; *A-G v Times Newspapers Ltd* [1991] 2 All ER 398). This can include a 'super-injunction' which prevents reports even of the fact that the injunction has been granted. However, an injunction will be granted only if it serves a useful purpose. Once material becomes public, even if unlawfully, the press has a duty to disseminate it and further restraint cannot normally be justified (see *Observer and Guardian Newspapers v UK* [1992]).

The importance of press freedom is reinforced by section 12 of the HRA. This provides, first, that a court order limiting the 'Convention right of freedom of expression' cannot normally be granted in the absence of the respondent. This affects interim injunctions which might be sought as an emergency measure. Secondly, section 12 prevents an interim order being made unless the applicant is likely to establish that publication should not be allowed. Thirdly, section 12 requires the court to have particular regard to freedom of expression and,

> where the proceedings relate to material which the respondent claims or which appears to the court to be journalistic, literary or artistic material (or to conduct connected with such material), to [have regard to] (a) the extent to which (i) the material has, or is about to, become available to the public; or (ii) it is, or would be, in the public interest for the material to be published; and (b) any relevant privacy code.

However, in *Douglas and Zeta-Jones v Hello! Ltd* [2001] 2 All ER 289, the Court of Appeal held that section 12 merely ensures that the competing rights in question are taken into account at the interim stage and does not give special weight to press freedom. In *Cream Holdings v Banerjee* [2004] 4 All ER 617 the House of Lords held that the normal threshold is that the applicant would 'more likely than not' succeed at the trial. However, the approach must be flexible; for example, if publication would cause serious harm, a lower threshold would be justified (e.g. *Thompson and Venables v News Group Newspapers Ltd* [2001] 1 All ER 908: disclosure of new identities of released prisoners at risk of threats to life).

23.3.5 Press sources

The protection of journalists' sources from exposure is a vital aspect of press freedom in order to prevent important information from drying up. In *R v Central Criminal Court, ex p Bright, Alton and Rusbridger* [2001] 2 All ER 244 the Court of Appeal quashed a production order sought by the Crown against the editors of the *Guardian* and the *Observer* to disclose information received from David Shayler, a former MI5 agent. It was held that disclosure would inhibit press freedom without there being a compelling reason for the disclosure.

Under the HRA, press freedom must be weighed against other public interests. In *R (Miranda) v Secretary of State for The Home Department* [2016] 1 WLR 1505, data on memory sticks were seized from a journalist's spouse during a search at the request of the security services at Heathrow Airport under anti-terrorist powers. The data consisted of material stolen from the US and UK governments which might create a security risk. The Court of Appeal held that the seizure was lawful, even though there was no evidence that sensitive material would in fact be published. This was because the opinion of the security service that there was a serious risk to public safety should have a wide margin of discretion, the material was stolen and no existing source would be exposed. However, it was not made clear whether the position would be different if the material had not been stolen. It was also held that the statutory power in question was flawed because it lacked independent safeguards for journalists, although the court did not make any order on this ground (Section 22.9.1). Under the general law, journalist material can be searched for and taken only with the consent of a circuit judge (Police and Criminal Evidence Act 1984, s 9).

Press sources have specific statutory protection. Section 10 of the Contempt of Court Act 1981 protects the anonymity of a publisher's sources of information, except where the court thinks that disclosure is necessary on the grounds of the interests of justice, national security, or the prevention of crime and disorder. Section 10 enables the court to exercise a discretion between the competing concerns. Before the HRA the courts interpreted the exceptions broadly against the press, influenced by the common law idea that the press should have no special privileges (e.g. *X Ltd v Morgan Grampian Publishers Ltd* [1991] 1 AC 1: commercial interest outweighed press freedom). This was strongly criticised by the European Court in *Goodwin v UK* (1996) 22 EHRR 123 on the ground that the protection of journalistic confidentiality is crucial to press freedom.

It had also been held that where national security or wrongdoing is involved the court will usually order disclosure (*X v Morgan Grampian* [1991]; *Ashworth Hospital v MGN Ltd* [2001] 1 All ER 991). However, in *John v Express Newspapers Ltd* [2000] 3 All ER 257, which concerned the leaking of legal advice, it was held following *Goodwin* that a confidential source should be publicly disclosed only as a last resort (see also *Financial Times v UK* [2009] ECHR 2065: sources should be protected unless clear evidence of damage or harmful intent).

23.3.6   Open justice and the media

In *R (C) v Secretary of State for Justice* [2016] UKSC 2, [1], Lady Hale described open justice as one of the most precious principles in our law. It has been said to be fundamental to the rule of law (*R (Mohamed) v Secretary of State for Foreign Affairs* [2010], [39]–[42]). The principle is embodied in the common law, in statutory rules of procedure (Civil Procedure Rules 39.2) and in the right to a fair trial under Art 6 of the ECHR. An important aspect of press freedom concerns open justice in court proceedings. This requires not only that court proceedings be open to the press, but also that the press can choose for itself what to report.

Open justice is, first, a means of holding the court itself to account so that interested parties, the wider public and the media can know what is going on (*C* (above), at [1]–[2]). In *Scott v Scott* [1913] AC 417, 457 it was described, following Bentham, as 'the security of securities: where there is no publicity there is no justice'. Secondly, open justice has the wider functions of upholding freedom of expression and diversity in the media. Thirdly, in cases involving the government, open justice helps to ensure that the executive is democratically accountable. The requirement that the identities of the parties must normally be published has been explained on the basis that this human interest encourages public attention to what might otherwise be dull (*Re Guardian News and Media Ltd* [2010] 2 All ER 799, at [63]).

Under the common law principle of open justice, the public are normally entitled to attend court proceedings. This includes the right of the press (but not the broadcast media) to attend and report. The reasoning of the court must also be published. In *Kennedy v Charity Commission* [2014] UKSC 20 (Section 24.2.1) the Supreme Court suggested that the common law could also give the press a right to government information which had been used in connection with judicial proceedings (see also *R (Guardian Newspapers) v City of Westminster Magistrates Court* [2013] QB 618).

However, as usual, there are exceptions where open justice must be balanced against competing concerns. Article 6 of the ECHR, the right to a fair trial, requires proceedings to be held in public although the public can be excluded in certain cases. The right of the press to give and that of the public to receive information is also protected under Art 10. Any restriction must be justified as proportionate either on public interest grounds such as security or the authority of the court or to protect the rights of others. The European Court has given states a margin of appreciation in this area (see e.g. *B v UK* (2001) 11 BHRC 667, (39); *V v UK* (2000) 30 EHRR 121, [87]). Art 6 does not expressly allow the right to a fair trial to be balanced against other concerns. However, the notion of 'fair' in itself requires the balancing of competing concerns (Section 21.4.1).

In *C* (above), the Supreme Court upheld the anonymity of a mental patient serving a sentence for murder because publicity would place his rehabilitation into the community at risk and also have a 'chilling effect' on his future treatment and that of others. In *A v BBC* [2014] 2 All ER 1037, as a last resort, the Supreme Court protected the identity of a sex offender subject to deportation. This was to prevent attack by vigilantes in his home country and also to uphold the authority of the court in connection with the deportation proceedings which would otherwise have been undermined. It was held that the common law principle of open justice was a constitutional principle existing side by side with the Convention right of freedom of expression (at [27]).

The common law principle is that secrecy is justified only in exceptional circumstances where the trial itself is at risk (*Scott v Scott* [1913], 437; *Official Solicitor v K* [1965] AC 201, 238, 239; *A-G v Leveller Magazine Ltd* [1979] AC 440). In *Bank Mellat v HM Treasury No. 1* [2013] 3 WLR 179, at [1], Lord Neuberger described the common law principle as fundamental to the dispensation of justice in a modern democratic society and able to be limited only if a private hearing was necessary to do justice between the parties and then only to an absolute minimum.

Under both common law and statute, the court has power to hold a trial in secret (*in camera*) and to impose lesser restrictions such as relaxing reporting restrictions or withholding particular information or allowing parties or witnesses to remain anonymous. Under the Civil Procedure Rules 39.2 the court can restrict publicity 'if necessary in the interests of justice' as well as on various specific grounds. These include cases such as intellectual property where publicity would defeat the purpose of the trial, national security, damage to confidential information, protecting children or mental patients, and injustice in the case of applications without notice.

Most drastically there is statutory power used in security cases to hold 'closed proceedings' in which evidence is denied even to the parties themselves (Section 24.6). Where restrictions apply, the press cannot publish details of the proceedings and perhaps even that proceedings have taken place (Contempt of Court Act 1981, s 11). Thus, accountability becomes difficult.

Press comment is also restricted on pending trials that create a 'substantial risk' that the course of justice will be seriously impeded or prejudiced (Contempt of Court Act 1981, s 2). The risk here is that the jury might be influenced by what they have read in the press. There is an important defence that the publication contains a discussion in good faith of public affairs where the risk of prejudice is merely incidental to the discussion (see *Sunday Times v UK* (1979) 2 EHRR 245; *A-G v English* [1983] 1 AC 116). In view of the importance of open justice it has been said that where a judgment has been given, 'any disapplication of the open justice principle must be rigidly contained, and, even within the small number of permissible exceptions, it should be rare indeed for the court to order that any part of the reasoning … should be redacted' (*R (Mohamed) v Secretary of State for Foreign Affairs* [2010], at [41]).

A limit on open justice in criminal cases is that it is an offence for anyone to publish information as to what was said in a jury room (Contempt of Court Act 1981, s 8(1)). This protects the independence of the jury, but seriously limits debate and research as to the merits of the jury system. However, the archaic common law offence of 'scandalising the judiciary' by making personal criticisms of a judge was abolished by the Crime and Courts Act 2013, s 33.

Open justice and national security

Most problematic are cases in which the government relies on national security to prevent publicity since it is easy to suspect that this is an excuse to hide failings.

In *R (Mohamed) v Secretary of State for Foreign Affairs* [2010] the government unsuccessfully called upon the so-called control principle, according to which information given by another government might dry up if it were made public. The case concerned allegations that the UK government was complicit in the torture of Muslim prisoners by the United States authorities in Guantanamo Bay. Certain passages concerning information received from the USA about the claimant's treatment had been excluded from a judgment in earlier proceedings in which the claimant had asked for the information to be used for his defence on terrorism charges. The question was now whether this judgment could be published. The Court of Appeal held that the government's statement that national security was threatened was not conclusive but must be given considerable weight. It would be overruled only if it was irrational or without evidence. In this case, the control principle made the matter finely balanced, but the material would be disclosed. The important factors were that the material in question was not in itself sensitive and, crucially, had been revealed in public in a United States case, so that there was no reason to believe that the control principle was at stake.

In *Guardian News and Media Ltd v Incedal* [2014] EWCA Crim 1861, the Court of Appeal reached a compromise. The government sought to have the whole of a prosecution for terrorist offences conducted in secret including the names of the defendants and even the fact of the ban. The government argued that it might otherwise drop the case. The Court of Appeal drew back from this but still imposed severe restrictions. It held that most of the case should be in secret, subject to approved reporters being present and the court deciding what they can report. The court stated that it could not envisage a situation where both the evidence and the identities of the parties should be concealed.

The right to privacy under Art 8 of the ECHR may also arise, but this is usually outweighed by the interests of open justice. For example, in *Re S (A Child)* [2004] 4 All ER 683, the competition was between press freedom in reporting the identity of the parties in court proceedings, and the privacy of a child in care whose mother had been convicted of murdering his brother. The Court of Appeal preferred the press interest. It held that the importance of open justice and drawing public attention to child abuse outweighed the child's interest since the additional publicity would cause relatively limited upset over and above that which had already occurred. *W(B) v M (Official Solicitor)* [2011] 4 All ER 1295 concerned a child in a minimally conscious state where the child's mother applied to the court to withhold life support. The Court of Protection permitted the press to report the evidence and arguments, but not the identities of the parties. The public interest in medical cases was in the general issues, not in the individuals concerned. In *Re Guardian News and Media Ltd* [2010], the Supreme Court overturned an anonymity order which had prevented publication of the names of terrorist suspects whose assets had been frozen by the court pending further proceedings. In view of public concerns about terrorism, the information was of public interest and any damage to reputation was not specific. It was assumed that the public are capable of understanding the difference between accusation and guilt.

(*See also AH v West London Mental Health Tribunal* [2011] UKUT 74; *Independent News and Media Ltd v A* [2010] EWCA Civ 343; *A-G's Reference (No 3 of 1999)* [2009] UKHL 34; Davies, 'The Rights Approach to the Right to a Public Hearing' [2012] PL 11.)

23.4 Press freedom and reputation: defamation

In general, the press is subject to the law of defamation in the same way as anyone else. Defamation concerns personal reputation, which is protected by the ECHR (Art 8). In *Reynolds v Times Newspapers Ltd* [2001] 2 AC 127, Lord Nicholls described reputation as 'an integral and important part of the dignity of the individual' (at 201). However, freedom of expression is also part of individual dignity. Moreover, both interests secure autonomy by providing protection against arbitrary interference. Hence agonising and politically controversial choices must be made between conflicting rights of apparently equal status with no agreed method of choosing between them.

The English law of defamation is widely regarded as relatively unsympathetic to the press, and English courts are often chosen as a forum for defamation actions as opposed, for example, to the US, where freedom of expression is enshrined in the Constitution. A major difference is that in English law the defendant media have to prove the truth of any allegations they make, thus chilling free expression. The law was revised by the Defamation Act 2013, the provisions of which significantly strengthen freedom of expression, albeit largely by building on existing law without introducing fundamental new principles (see Mullis and Scott, 'Tilting at Windmills: The Defamation Act 2013' (2014) 77 MLR 87).

A claimant must prove that the relevant material (i) is defamatory; (ii) has been published; and (iii) refers to him or her.

Material is defamatory if it reflects on the claimant's reputation so as to lower him or her in the estimation of right-thinking members of society generally (*Sim v Stretch* [1936] 2 All ER 1237) or tends to cause the claimant to be shunned or avoided (*Youssoupoff v Metro-Goldwyn-Mayer Pictures Ltd* [1934] 50 TLR 581) or would bring the claimant into ridicule or contempt (*Dunlop Rubber Co Ltd v Dunlop* [1921] 1 AC 367). Under the Defamation Act 2013, s 1, to be defamatory the statement must also have caused or be likely to cause 'serious harm' to the claimant's reputation. In the case of a business trading for profit, the statement must have caused or be likely to cause serious financial loss. In *Lachaux v Independent Print Ltd* [2019] UKSC 27, the Supreme Court indicated that the Act had altered the common law, by introducing the new threshold of serious harm, this being a proposition of fact that could be established only by reference to its actual impact, not just the inherent meaning of the words themselves.

Defamation takes one of two forms: libel and slander. Material is libellous if it is published in a permanent form, for example writing or another recorded medium, or on the internet. It is slanderous if it takes a less than permanent form, for example word of mouth. At common law, except in special cases including a statement that a person is inadequate professionally, slander is actionable only where 'special', that is to say, specific, damage has occurred, whereas libel is actionable even without proof of special damage.

Publication means merely communication to another person, so each time an item is repeated or passed on (e.g. from journalist to newsroom to newsagent) there is a separate publication. This might be regarded as unfair to news vendors and similar who innocently pass on the material. The Defamation Act 2013 goes some way to lessen the injustice involved. Firstly, section 10 partly protects such secondary publishers by allowing actions against them only where it would not be reasonably practicable to sue the author, editor or a commercial publisher. Secondly, a website operator has a defence if it did not post the offending material unless the claimant could not have identified the author and had posted a notice of complaint which was not responded to (s 5).

Thirdly, in the case of a publication to the public or to a section of the public, a 'single publication' rule has been introduced. Thus, in calculating the time limit for an action (three years), the clock starts running after the first publication unless the later publication by the same person is 'materially different' (s 8). This particularly affects internet searches and raises the question of what is meant by materially different. This can include prominence and extent as well as content (s 8(5)).

Defamation law recognises the importance of freedom of expression. For example, a public authority cannot sue for defamation. In *Derbyshire CC v Times Newspapers Ltd* [1993] 1 All ER 1011, the *Sunday Times* published an allegation of mismanagement of pension funds by the council. Lord Keith explained that 'it is of the highest public importance that a democratically elected body...should be open to uninhibited public criticism' (at 1017). The House of Lords did not base its decision on the ECHR but also found support in 'the common law of England'. The same principle applies to political parties (see *Goldsmith v Bhoyrul* [1998] QB 459, 493).

However, Lord Keith indicated that individual public officials can sue in defamation on the same basis as private individuals. This reflects Dicey's notion of the rule of law, namely that officials and private persons should be subject to the same general law (Section 6.4.2). Unfortunately, however, Dicey assumed that this would invariably protect the citizen. The House of Lords could thus be criticised for failing to follow the US Supreme Court's lead in *New York Times Co v Sullivan* 376 US 254 (1964) by introducing the 'actual malice' rule into UK law in relation to individuals. This rule protects statements against both public institutions and individual public officials made in the absence of malice and without knowledge that they are false. This would have helped to protect political expression and would have brought the law of defamation into closer alignment with the Strasbourg court. This treats Article 10 as requiring two distinctions; namely, political figures should receive less protection from defamation law than private individuals, and governmental bodies (and political parties) should receive even less protection from the law than political figures (see *Lingens v Austria* [1986]; *Castells v Spain* [1992]; *Oberschlick v Austria* (1995) 19 EHRR 389).

23.4.1 Defences

The following particular defences protect freedom of expression:

1. Truth (previously called 'justification'). The defendant must show that the imputation complained of is substantially true (Defamation Act 2013, s 2). Subject to an exception under section 8 of the Rehabilitation of Offenders Act 1974, this can be pleaded even where a defendant has been actuated by malice (i.e. spite or ill will). The placing of the burden on the defendant is sometimes regarded as 'chilling' freedom of expression since it might encourage journalists and other writers to be excessively cautious, particularly those with limited money.
2. Absolute privilege. Liability cannot be imposed in respect of:
   (i) parliamentary proceedings (Section 11.6.3);
   (ii) judicial proceedings and contemporaneous reports of judicial proceedings (Defamation Act 1996, s 14);
   (iii) high-level government communications (*Chatterton v Secretary of State for India* (1895) 2 QB 189).
3. Qualified privilege. This is a common law defence supplemented by statute. It applies only where the defendant honestly believes what s/he says to be true. Traditionally, qualified privilege has applied where the defendant meets the following two requirements:
   (i) the defendant has an interest or a duty (legal, social or moral) to communicate the relevant material to another or others;
   (ii) the recipient of the material must have a corresponding interest or duty to receive it (e.g. *Clift v Slough BC* [2009] 4 All ER 756: circular about anti-social staff member circulated more widely than necessary). Thus, qualified privilege may protect officials who inadvertently circulate false information about members of the public and also members of the public who complain about the conduct of officials.
   Qualified privilege also applies to a range of 'fair and accurate' reports of official proceedings, including those of legislatures, courts, inquiries, conferences and international organisations. Some, including copies of government information notices, reports of public meetings and company meetings, are subject to explanation or correction (Defamation Act 1996, s 15). The Defamation Act 2013, s 7, extends the list to an increased number of overseas and international bodies thus reflecting the progress of globalisation.
   Qualified privilege also applies to material in academic and scientific journals provided that it is independently 'peer' reviewed and reviewed by the editor (Defamation Act 2013, s 6).
   The following two defences introduced by the Defamation Act 2013 are of considerable general importance:
4. Section 3: 'Honest opinion'. Replacing the common law defence of 'fair comment', this is intended to protect free speech even if intemperate. The defence requires:
   (i) that the statement is one of opinion;
   (ii) that it indicates the factual basis of the opinion. In *Joseph v Spiller* [2011] 1 All ER 947, in the context of the previous common law defence, the Supreme Court held that the comment need not identify the facts on which it was based in detail but must identify in general terms what led the

commentator to make the comment so that the reader could understand what it was about and call for further explanation. This seems equally applicable to the new statutory version;

(iii) that the opinion is one that an honest person could have held on the basis either of facts that existed at the time it was published, or of a privileged statement published *before* the opinion was published, for example a report of a public meeting (s 3(4)(b)). Thus, under section 3, the facts must have a basis in truth. However, if the opinion is based on facts that were themselves previously published, the previous publication, if untrue, must be protected by a privilege (for example a newspaper report of a public meeting having qualified privilege or one that falls within s 4 ('public interest' (below)). But if the opinion and the factual statement are published at the same time, for example a comment about a report in the same edition of a newspaper, the facts must always be true. What is the rationale for this?

The defence of honest opinion applies even if the defendant was unaware of the facts and even if they did not form the basis of the actual statement, as long as an honest person could have made that comment on the basis of them. However, the defence is defeated by showing that the defendant did not hold the opinion in question or, where he repeats the opinion of another person, that he knew the other person did not hold it (s 3(5), (6)).

It may be difficult to distinguish between fact and opinion. An opinion is essentially a value, but can also include a fact inferred from other facts, for example a scientific hypothesis. In this context, support to freedom of expression was provided in *British Chiropractic Association v Singh* [2010] EWCA Civ 350. The Court of Appeal held that a statement in a scientific journal concerning contested scientific conclusions was to be treated as an expression of *opinion*, not a statement of fact. Thus, the defendant would not be faced with the virtually impossible task of proving that the statement was true. The Court remarked that to treat matters of scientific controversy as matters of fact would be a disproportionate interference with freedom of expression: an Orwellian Ministry of Truth (see [18]–[23]). Many scientific papers will also be protected by the special privilege for peer-reviewed journals (above).

5. Section 4: Matters of public interest. As we saw above, the defence of qualified privilege has traditionally required a special relationship between the publisher of the statement and the recipient. This has caused difficulty vis-à-vis factual material communicated to the public at large, but judges have been reluctant to create an open-ended 'public interest' defence. However, in *Reynolds v Times Newspapers Ltd* [2001], the House of Lords held that qualified privilege can in some circumstances be pleaded where political material is disseminated to the general public. This became known as the *Reynolds* defence and caused considerable controversy.

A similar idea has been enshrined in Section 4 which abolishes the common law *Reynolds* defence (s 4(6)). In *Serafin v Malkiewicz* [2020] UKSC 23, the Supreme Court observed that the principles underpinning *Reynolds* remained relevant to the interpretation of s 4, but that the latter was a statutory defence in its own right; thus, the factors outlined in *Reynolds* should not be considered a mandatory checklist for journalists. The requirements of s 4 are as follows:

(i) the statement must be or form part of a statement on a matter of public interest; and

(ii) the publisher must show a reasonable belief that it is in the public interest to publish the statement.

(iii) The statement can be one of fact or one of opinion. This creates a confusing overlap with the defence of honest opinion in s 3 (above) (see Box).

The defence of public interest is open to anyone, including 'citizen journalists' or bloggers, who may not be required to meet the same standard as professional journalists (*Economou v de Freitas* [2018] EWCA Civ 2591). However, it is likely mainly to be used by the public media. Previously, controversy centred upon the extent to which there was a requirement of 'responsible journalism', meaning that the journalist must carefully check his or her sources of information, ensuring that the statement makes a real contribution to the public interest and that the steps taken to obtain the information are reasonable and fair (see *Jameel v Wall Street Journal Europe* [2006] 4 All ER 1279, [48] [51] [53] [147]; *Flood v Times Newspapers* [2012] UKSC 11, [113]).

The problems here are threefold. First, should judges define standards of good journalistic practice and decide what the public should know? It is far from obvious that this is a task that they are well equipped to undertake. Secondly, there is uncertainty and so the chilling effect. Thirdly, there is no agreement as to what 'public interest' means. Is it, for example, limited to matters which directly affect the public? If not, what else is included? Are lurid stories about the sexual conduct of media personalities or politicians matters of public interest?

The Act does not contain a specific requirement of responsible journalism. However, its requirement of 'reasonable belief' that the matter is one of public interest could be read as importing the same idea (rather than the more basic legal meaning of reasonable as having a rational basis). Thus, section 4 requires the court to have regard to 'all the circumstances'. However, as a gesture to freedom of expression section 4(4) requires the court to make such allowance for editorial judgment as it considers appropriate. Under section 4(3), in the case of an 'accurate and impartial' account of a dispute to which the claimant is a party, the court 'must disregard any omission by the defendant to verify the truth of the imputation'. In this context, *reportage* offered a common law defence and might now be an aspect of the statutory reasonableness test. This applies to a person, including a journalist or social media user, who merely repeats an allegation made by another, for example a statement that accusations have been made against X. It must be shown clearly that, when read as a whole, the author did not in any way support the statement in question. Thus, very careful journalistic expression is required (*Chapman v Orion Publishing Group* [2008] 1 All ER 750; *Galloway v Telegraph Group* [2006] EWCA Civ 17). For example, there are distinctions between three levels of allegation: 'guilty of wrongdoing', 'reasonable grounds to suspect guilty of wrongdoing', and 'reasonable grounds to investigate whether he or she has engaged in wrongdoing' (*Chase v News Group Newspapers* [2003] EMLR 218).

Mullis and Scott (above, 96) suggest that the honest belief and public interest defences offer only limited protection to people who comment on social media on the basis of facts they learn second-hand and so cannot check. Such comment is a legitimate part of democratic activity and deserves legal protection. Under section 4, the main question is whether a person who recycles information from the television or press has the necessary reasonable belief that the matter is one of public interest. Thus, the ability of the defendant to check the facts would be one factor in a balancing exercise to be weighed against the importance of the public interest issue involved. It is not clear whether an honest but unreasonable belief that the facts are true would ever suffice for this.

The overlap between 'honest opinion' and 'public interest' privileges

Suppose D, a student, learns from a newspaper report that X, her tutor, has been accused of involvement in a tax evasion venture along with sundry well-known MPs. She immediately tweets that she knew X was a dodgy character who should not be around students. The newspaper report is false because the reporter Z had confused X with Y, an MP. D will not have the defence of honest opinion since the facts are false unless she can establish that the newspaper had the public interest privilege provided by s 4.

Suppose, alternatively, that D is the editor of the college student newspaper and publishes a blistering attack on X based on a report in the same newspaper of the AGM of a research company of which X is a director. D will not have a defence under s 3 based on the privileged occasion (the company meeting) or s 4 since the privileged publication was not made before the comment. However, D might have a defence of public interest in her own right under s 4 if the requirements of public interest, reasonableness and editorial judgment are established since s 4 applies to untrue facts.

Two other features of the law have in the past protected freedom of expression: (i) the institution of the jury; and (ii) the limited availability of an injunction. Defamation actions (which are heard in the High Court) were usually tried with a jury, which is regarded as providing a safeguard against official bias (see *Seven Bishops Case* (1688) 12 St Tr 133; Fox's Libel Act 1792). On the other hand, the jury's power to decide the amount of damages has sometimes resulted in large awards that have a chilling effect on freedom of expression suggesting that the jury is not an effective guarantor of freedom of speech. This is another reason why litigation in England has been popular.

Under the Defamation Act 2013, s 11, there is no longer a jury in a defamation case unless the court orders otherwise. This was raised in *Yeo v Times Newspapers Ltd* [2015] 1 WLR 971. A prominent MP and former minister sued the owners of the *Sunday Times* over a series of articles which concerned claims that MPs were selling their services to private organisations. The defendants, who were worried that a single judge might be biased in favour of an important person, sought jury trial claiming that it was a 'constitutional right'. It was held that, under the Act, jury trial is no longer a constitutional right and the previous approach is not relevant. The fact that the claimant held power or authority in the state and that the case involved great questions of national interest were no longer important considerations. However, jury trial might be ordered if there was a risk that the particular judge might be influenced by the status of a party.

Moreover, under s 8 of the Courts and Legal Services Act 1990 the Court of Appeal has the power, where a jury has awarded 'excessive' compensation, to substitute a lower sum. In *Rantzen v Mirror Group Newspapers Ltd* [1994] QB 670, the award was reduced from £250,000 to £110,000. While the Court based its decision on the Act, it also justified it by reference to Article 10 of the ECHR (see *Tolstoy Miloslavsky v UK* (1995) 20 EHRR 442). In *John v Mirror Group Newspapers Ltd* [1996] 3 WLR 593 the Court of Appeal held that awards of exemplary or punitive damages going beyond compensation could be recovered only where the defendant knowingly or recklessly published untruths having cynically calculated that the profit accruing from the publication would be likely to exceed any damages. Lord Bingham stated that 'freedom of expression should not be restricted by awards of exemplary damages save to the extent shown to be strictly necessary for the protection of reputations' (at [58]).

In support of freedom of speech, the judiciary has long been reluctant to grant injunctions in defamation cases. Hence, this remedy will not be granted unless the plaintiff can satisfy a number of exacting conditions, in particular that there is no ground for supposing that the defendant may avoid liability by pleading truth, privilege or fair comment (*Bonnard v Perryman* [1891] 2 Ch 269). It is uncertain whether the introduction of the 2013 Act with its greater safeguards for freedom of expression will change this attitude. In any case, judges are reluctant to grant interim (or interlocutory) injunctions which restrain the offending expression pending a full trial. Such injunctions are only granted where (i) a court is satisfied that publication will result in immediate and irreparable injury and (ii) damages would not provide an adequate remedy (*Monson v Tussauds Ltd* [1894] 1 QB 671; see also HRA 1998, s 12 (Section 23.3)).

Finally, the Defamation Act 2013, s 9, combats libel tourism by requiring that the court must be satisfied that, of all the places where the statement has been published, England and Wales is clearly the most appropriate jurisdiction to bring the action. However, this only applies where the action is brought against a person not domiciled in the UK or the EU, or a state which is party to the Lugano Convention 2007 on Jurisdiction and Enforcement (in addition to EU members this includes Iceland, Norway and Switzerland).

23.5 Press freedom and privacy

The issue of public interest strongly arises in connection with the right to privacy. Article 8 of the ECHR states that 'everyone has a right to respect for his family and private life'. Privacy relates among other things to dignity, independence, self-respect and the desire to control personal information (Section 21.4). There is therefore a clash with Article 10. Newspapers are privately owned, so the protection of privacy against the press is an example of the possible horizontal impact of the Human

Rights Act (Section 22.8). In *McDonald v McDonald* [2016] UKSC 28, the Supreme Court suggested that the Human Rights Act applied to privacy cases because the duties in question were directly imposed by the court as opposed to the court's responsibility in typically private cases to enforce private contracts or property rights.

Before the Human Rights Act, English law had no separate right to privacy and was accordingly in violation of the ECHR (*Malone v UK* (1984) 7 EHRR 14). At best, privacy was regarded as a value that influenced specific causes of action, most importantly breach of confidence, which originally concerned wrongful disclosure of information arising out of a confidential relationship (e.g. *Wainwright v Home Office* [2003] 4 All ER 969; *Kaye v Robertson* [1991] FSR 62).

However, under the influence of the Human Rights Act, the law of confidence has become a more general right of privacy detached from the need to show a specific confidential relationship or some special quality in the information. The test of proportionality applies. In *Campbell v MGN Ltd* [2004] 2 All ER 995, the *Daily Mirror* had published information and photographs about the treatment for drug addiction undergone by a famous fashion model. The House of Lords regarded freedom of expression and privacy as of equal importance and looked closely at all the circumstances with the aim of producing the least harmful outcome. Lord Hoffmann remarked (at [51]) that the law had shifted in emphasis from the notion of good faith to that of protecting autonomy and dignity and the control of information about one's private life.

The main requirements are as follows:

1. The context is one where there is a 'legitimate' or 'reasonable' expectation of privacy. In *Campbell*, this test was preferred to the stronger one used in some jurisdictions that the disclosure be highly offensive to a person of ordinary susceptibilities (at [21]–[22], [83], [134]–[135]). This relates primarily to the situation or relationship in which the information is revealed, for example in the home or a diary.

   A matter might still be protected even in a public place. In *Von Hannover v Germany (No. 2)* (2012) 55 EHRR 388, a magazine published photos of the applicants, related to Prince Rainier of Monaco, on holiday in Switzerland. The Strasbourg court held that Article 8 included a right to protect one's image, including in some circumstances the right to prevent photos being taken in a public place. The criteria to be applied included the contribution made to a debate of general interest; the role or function of the person concerned and the nature of the activities portrayed; the prior conduct of the person concerned; the content, form and consequence of publication; and the circumstances in which the photos were taken. The court emphasised that both rights deserve equal respect.

   It was held that photos coupled with a report about the conduct of the royal family during the illness of Prince Rainier did raise matters of public interest and the photos and the circumstances in which they were taken were not offensive. Thus, there was no breach of Article 8.

2. There must be an unauthorised use of the relevant information with knowledge of the confidence and for a purpose other than that for which it was imparted.

   There is a defence that disclosure of the relevant material is in the public interest and that this outweighs the interest in preserving confidentiality.

   Privacy must therefore be balanced against the right to freedom of expression and other ECHR rights. The main technique used by the courts when a conflict arises is to start by treating the competing rights as having equal weight, then to look at the impact on each right in turn in all the circumstances, asking whether the harm done to the privacy interest is *in its own terms* more serious than the harm done to freedom of expression.

   This rough utilitarianism founders upon the problem that there is no common denominator against which to compare the harms, and no agreement as to the proper relationship between a person's private and public lives. It is sometimes believed that privacy has been strengthened at the cost of restricting press freedom since press freedom is important *in itself* irrespective of the content of the particular press report. As usual, the judges must make a subjective choice. The uncertainty generated by this risks inhibiting freedom of expression.

Examples of balancing press freedom and privacy

In *Campbell v MGN Ltd* (above), it was held first that the fact that the claimant had been a drug addict was not protected since she had repeatedly told the media that she was not on drugs, and to that extent had given up her privacy. However, it was also held that the details of her treatment should not have been published since these were inherently private and personal in nature. Importantly, there were no political or democratic values in issue of a kind that supported press freedom. Lords Nicholls and Hoffmann dissented, taking a wider view of press freedom, that a newspaper should be able to add colour and detail to its reporting and that journalists should be entitled to some latitude in the wider interests of a healthy press. A restrictive approach might inhibit the press and so hamper democracy.

In *Weller v Associated Newspapers* [2016] 1 WLR 1541, photos of the children of a famous musician were taken in a café while they were on a day out with their father and published with an article in a newspaper. The Court of Appeal held that they had a reasonable expectation of privacy. Although there is no separate right of privacy for a child, some factors are especially relevant to children. In particular, an older child has greater expectation of privacy than a younger child, together with the question of parental consent and security considerations. The best interests of a child are always relevant, and so evidence of harm is not always needed. There was a reasonable expectation of privacy because this was a family occasion, a child was upset, there was no parental consent to the photos and the article identified the children by name. The matter was not of public interest since the claimants had little public profile and there had been no previous publication.

In *Richard v BBC* [2018] EWHC 1837 (Ch), the BBC had reported upon a police investigation of the veteran entertainer Cliff Richard in respect of an allegation of historical sex abuse (no arrest or charge followed). The High Court held that Richard's Art 8 rights were not outweighed by the right to freedom of expression, given the serious consequences of the disclosure to him, and the sensationalist nature of the reporting. Although there was a genuine public interest in investigations of historical sex abuse, knowledge of the identity of the person being investigated did not contribute materially to that public interest, even if it 'might be of interest to the gossip-mongers' (at [282]).

In Re JR38 [2015] 3 WLR 155 the police published photos of a 14-year-old child at a riot as part of a 'name and shame' policy. A majority of the Supreme Court held that an objective test of reasonable expectation of privacy needed to be applied. Here, Art 8 was not engaged at all because its purpose is far removed from that of protecting criminal activity. However, two dissenting judges held that in, the context of privacy, the main focus should be on the victim, not on the activity in which he was engaged. In *JIH v News Group Newspapers Ltd* [2011] EWCA Civ 42, the Court of Appeal said that no special treatment should be given to public figures or celebrities. However, where publication of the information was permitted, an anonymity order could be made, but only where there was a clear case for doing so.

In *HRH Prince of Wales v Associated Newspapers* [2007] 2 All ER 139, the Court of Appeal prohibited the press from publishing extracts from the personal journals of the Prince of Wales containing his impressions of the appearance and character of the Chinese leaders during an official visit to China. The most important factor was that the information was leaked by an employee in breach of contract. It is a matter of public interest in itself that confidential employment relationships be protected. It was also relevant that the information made only a 'minimal' contribution to the public interest.

Privacy issues also arise in connection with considerations of open justice and Article 6: the right to a fair trial. Although Art 6 is an absolute right, interest balancing is possible because of the flexible notion of 'fairness' and the principle that 'fair balance' runs through the whole Convention (Section 21.4). In this context, the interests of open justice as a basic constitutional principle add further weight to press freedom (Section 23.3.4).

In *Phillips v News Group Newspapers* [2013] 1 AC 1, which concerned telephone tapping of famous personalities, the Supreme Court held that information protected by the law of privacy was not 'intellectual property'. It is therefore protected in criminal proceedings only by the general privilege against self-incrimination, unless it also falls into one of the specific commercially based exceptions prescribed by statute.

23.6 'Hate speech'

Hate speech involves attacks on racial, ethnic, religious or cultural groups, including lifestyle matters such as sexuality. Hate speech may be directed at other vulnerable groups such as the elderly, immigrants, and the disabled. Hate speech involves matter that shocks or offends, thereby raising the overrides of public morality and the rights of others and providing a hard test of the rationales for freedom of expression.

It could be argued, with Mill, that being offended or shocked is not harmful since it challenges orthodoxy and does not limit freedom. On the other hand, there is an argument for suppressing the expression of opinions that offend others where there is a risk to public safety or the welfare of vulnerable groups. However, this leads to oppressive or lazy enforcement since it is often cheaper and easier to suppress a speaker than to police those who cause a disturbance because they are offended.

The notion of ideas and information as underlying freedom of expression has enabled it to be claimed that some forms of hate speech should not be protected since they contain no worthy ideas. This avoids the difficulty that causing offence in itself should not be banned (Section 23.6.2).

Pornography is also susceptible to this argument. For example, the publication of material that is likely to deprave and corrupt a significant proportion of those exposed to it is prohibited (the 'harm' principle), but subject to a defence of literary or artistic merit (Obscene Publications Act 1959). However, this elevates the truth rationale for freedom of expression at the expense of that of self-fulfilment and raises Berlin's fear that freedom can be perverted to include only those freedoms that the rulers enjoy (Section 2.4).

As usual, the law must find an accommodation. One way of doing so is by attempting to distinguish between expressing opinions, however distasteful, and inciting unlawful behaviour, especially violence. However, in the case of especially vulnerable groups, this line is breached and some forms of expression that are offensive to such groups are prohibited irrespective of violence. The law is sensitive to particular historical circumstances. For example, there is protection in respect of racial and religious hate expression but not age, gender, or class hate expression as such. These fall within more general offences (Section 23.7.3). However, a Law Commission consultation begun in 2020 may eventually lead to an expansion in the protected categories, with 'women, sex or gender' the most likely to be added (Law Commission, *Hate Crime Laws*, Consultation Paper 250 (2020)).

In respect of some forms of communication that are especially open to abuse, offence is prohibited generally. Thus, the Communications Act 2003, while having social inclusion as one of its aims, makes it an offence to send online or by telephone any 'grossly offensive message' (s 127(1)). The same Act imposes restrictions on the broadcast media as does the Charter of the BBC (Section 23.3.1).

23.6.1 Racism

Racism has been so widely condemned throughout Europe as to amount to a special case. The International Convention on the Elimination of All Forms of Racial Discrimination (1965) (CERD) has been ratified by most members of the Council of Europe. Article 4 of this Convention requires signatories to create offences in relation to 'all dissemination of ideas based on racial supremacy or hatred, incitement to racial discrimination, as well as acts of violence or incitement to such acts against any race or group of persons of another colour or ethnic origin'. Article 4 also requires states to have 'due regard' to (among other things) the right to freedom of opinion and expression.

The main offences are contained in sections 17–23 of the Public Order Act 1986. A person is guilty if he or she uses 'threatening, abusive or insulting words or behaviour or displays written material which is threatening, abusive or insulting if (a) he intends to stir up racial hatred or (b) having regard to all the circumstances, such hatred is likely to be stirred up thereby' (s 18). Race includes colour, race, nationality and ethnic or national origins (s 17). An ethnic group can be defined by cultural as well as physical characteristics (see *Mandla v Dowell-Lee* [1983] 1 All ER 1062: Sikhs; *Commission for Racial Equality v Dutton* [1989] QB 783: gypsies, but not other travellers).

The offences can be committed in public or private places except exclusively within a dwelling (s 18(2)(4)). Public disorder is not required, nor is the presence at the time of any member of the targeted racial group. For example, the offence could apply to an academic paper read to an audience in a university or club. However, there is a defence if the accused did not intend to stir up racial hatred and did not intend his or her words or behaviour to be, and was not aware that it might be, threatening, abusive or insulting (s 18(2)(5)).

It is also an offence to publish or distribute written material in the same circumstances (s 17), and to possess racially inflammatory material (s 23). Similar provisions apply to a public performance of a play (s 20), to distributing, showing or playing recordings, and to broadcasting or cable services except from the BBC and ITV (ss 22(7), 23(4)). These broadcasting bodies are governed by special systems of regulation. Contemporaneous reports of parliamentary, court or tribunal proceedings are exempted (s 26).

The offences are arrestable, and the police have wide powers of entry and search (s 24). The consent of the Attorney General is required for a prosecution, which might be regarded as a safeguard for freedom of expression (s 27).

There are increased sentences for offences of assault, criminal damage, public order and harassment committed wholly or partly with religious or racial motivations (Crime and Disorder Act 1998, ss 28, 32). At the time of committing the offence or immediately before or after, the offender must demonstrate hostility towards the victim based on the victim's membership (or presumed membership) of a racial or religious group.

23.6.2   Religion and sexuality

In principle, all religions have equal status in human rights law. Although the Church of England is closely associated with the state, Christianity as such is not part of English law (*Bowman v Secular Society* [1917] AC 406). The main restrictions on freedom of speech concerning religion, namely the common law offences of blasphemy and blasphemous libel, which favoured Christianity, were abolished by the Criminal Justice and Immigration Act 2008, s 79. In the context of charity law, which is based on the public interest, religion is not limited to a belief in a supernatural deity but may apply to any set of spiritual values (see Charities Act 2006, s 3 (a)(ii)).

Article 9 of the ECHR concerns freedom of thought, conscience and religion, thus including beliefs such as atheism (Section 21.4). Article 9 may overlap with Article 10 since many, if not all, manifestations of a belief could also be regarded as an expression of an opinion. Where both point in the same direction, the Strasbourg court does not appear to give Article 9 considerations any special weight (see *Incal v Turkey* (2000) 29 EHRR 449, [60]).

However, the two rights may conflict where freedom of expression is used to attack or pressurise a religion or its supporters. Here religion seems to be especially favoured in that freedom of expression can be restricted to protect believers from being offended or shocked. In *Otto Preminger Institut v Austria* [1994] the state seized a film depicting Christ and his mother as in league with the Devil which offended the Roman Catholic majority in the Tyrol. The Court held that the seizure was lawful for the purpose of protecting the rights of others. This seems to come close to censorship based on majority sentiment. The Court said that

> in the context of religious opinion and beliefs...may legitimately be included an obligation to avoid as far as possible expressions that are gratuitously offensive to others and thus an infringement of their rights, and which therefore do not contribute to any form of public debate capable of furthering progress in human affairs.

(See also *Wingrove v UK* (1997) 24 EHRR 1: homoerotic imagery discomforting to some Christians; ban upheld with strong dissent.)

The HRA requires courts to have particular regard in matters involving religious organisations to the importance of freedom of thought, conscience and religion (s 13). However, this seems to apply only to religion in a narrower sense than the full Article 9 protection would cover, and it is difficult to know what this means. Section 13 could be read as permitting religious organisations to override other rights such as privacy or to discriminate on religious grounds.

The Racial and Religious Hatred Act 2006, adding Part 3A to the Public Order Act 1986, creates various offences of intention to stir up religious hatred broadly similar to, but narrower than, those applying to racial hatred. Religious hatred means hatred towards a group of persons defined by reference to religious belief or lack of religious belief. Thus, atheists are protected by the Act. Religion is not defined. Threatening words or behaviour are required and there must be a direct intention to stir up hatred, not merely that hatred is likely. As with other public order offences, conduct taking effect entirely within a private dwelling is excluded. Prosecution requires the consent of the Attorney General.

The Act attempts to protect freedom of expression by stating (s 29J Public Order Act 1986):

> Nothing in this Part shall be read or given effect in a way which prohibits discussion, criticism or expressions of antipathy, dislike, ridicule, insult, or abuse of particular religions or the beliefs or practices of their adherents, or of any other belief system or the beliefs of its adherents, or proselytising or urging the adherents of a different religion or belief system to cease practising their religion or belief system.

Since the offence requires threatening words or behaviour, it may be that this provision limits the offence to personal abuse. Can threats of hellfire be used as part of an evangelising recruitment drive?

Under section 74 of the Criminal Justice and Immigration Act 2008, this offence has been extended to stirring up hatred on the ground of sexual orientation. Again, there is some protection for freedom of expression. By virtue of Schedule 16, the discussion or criticism of sexual conduct or practices or the urging of persons to refrain or modify such conduct or practices shall not be taken of itself to be threatening or intended to stir up hatred.

Sections 145 and 146 of the Criminal Justice Act 2003 provide for increased penalties for certain offences where the offence is racially or religiously aggravated or is motivated by hostility towards sexual orientation, disability or transgender status.

23.6.3 Political protest

Under the ECHR, the limits of permissible criticism are wider with regard to the government than in relation to a private citizen or an individual politician (*Castells v Spain* [1992], [46]).

The old common law harshly penalised dissent. The offence of seditious libel consisted of publishing material with the intention to incite hostility towards the government or its institutions or possibly to promote hostility between different classes of 'Her Majesty's subjects' (*R v Burns* (1886) 16 Cox CC 395). Seditious libel has now been abolished but echoes remain in the broad discretionary powers that modern law gives to the police, under which disagreement with government policy might be regarded by a police officer as evidence of unlawful intent.

There are other offences related to sedition that are little used, but because of their vague language remain potential threats against political dissenters. The Incitement to Disaffection Act 1934 makes it an offence maliciously and advisedly to endeavour to seduce any member of the armed forces from his or her duty. The Police Act 1996 creates a similar offence in relation to the police (s 91), and the Aliens Restrictions (Amendment) Act 1917 prohibits an alien from attempting to cause sedition or disaffection, and also from promoting or interfering in an industrial dispute in an industry in which he or she has not been employed for at least two years immediately before the offence. It is questionable whether these provisions, particularly the latter, are compliant with the HRA.

The Terrorism Act 2006 outlaws the publication or dissemination of a statement which directly or indirectly encourages terrorism (ss 1, 2). Encouragement includes 'glorifying' (which includes praising or celebrating), the commission or preparation (whether in the past, future, or generally) of acts of terrorism in such a way that members of the public could be expected to infer that they should emulate the conduct in question in existing circumstances. However, the accused must intend or be reckless as to the consequences of publication and there is a defence that the statement did not express his or her views and did not have his or her endorsement.

The definition of terrorism is wide (TA 2000, s 1; TA 2006, s 34; Counter-Terrorism Act 2008; Section 25.5.1). It includes any act or the threat of an act that involves serious violence against a person or property, or that endangers life or creates a serious risk to the health or safety of the public or a section of the public, or seriously disrupts or interferes with an electronic system. The action must be intended to advance a political, religious, racial or ideological cause. The act must be designed to influence the government or an international governmental organisation or to coerce the public or a section of it.

23.7   Freedom of assembly: demonstrations and meetings

Article 11 of the ECHR confers a right to freedom of assembly and association. This is subject to the following overrides: national security or public safety, the prevention of disorder or crime, the protection of health or morals, or the protection of the rights and freedoms of others. Also: 'this article shall not prevent the imposition of lawful restrictions on the exercise of those rights by members of the armed forces, of the police or of the administration of the state'. In *Ezelin v France* (1992) 14 EHRR 362, it was held that Arts 10 and 11 are complementary and that Art 11 is in effect a particular application of the general principle of freedom of expression in Art 10. There are few Strasbourg cases from the UK and the cases suggest that, in this area, UK law on the whole complies with the ECHR.

The right of freedom of assembly applies to assembly for political purposes, but not to assemblies for sports or other recreational purposes (*R (Countryside Alliance) v A-G* [2008] 1 AC 719 at [58], [119]; see also *Anderson v UK* [1997] ECHR 150). The right to meet in public is particularly important because, unlike many other forms of expression which depend on access to the media and therefore on money or influence, this right is open to all.

The main limits on freedom of assembly concern the protection of property rights and the protection of the public against violence. However, in *Kuznetov v Russia* [2008], at [45] the Strasbourg court appeared to suggest that freedom of assembly could be restricted if rejection of democratic principles is involved.

The law has developed as a series of pragmatic responses to particular problems and political agendas, and has become more restrictive in recent years. For example, the Public Order Act 1936 was a response to fears of fascism and communism. It was superseded by the Public Order Act 1986, which was provoked by race riots. Further legislation has been aimed at miscellaneous targets of the government of the day. These have included anti-nuclear demonstrations, hunt saboteurs, travellers, 'stalkers', football hooligans, anti-war demonstrators, terrorists and animal rights groups (see Criminal Justice and Public Order Act 1994, ss 60, 60AA; Protection from Harassment Act 1997; Crime and Disorder Act 1998; Football (Offences and Disorder) Act 1999; Football (Disorder) Act 2000; Serious Organised Crime and Police Act 2005; Terrorism Acts 2000, 2006). The legislation may be drafted loosely enough to include wider political activities, thereby attracting human rights arguments based on uncertainty, proportionality and discrimination.

This illustrates the weakness of the traditional residual approach to liberty under which, according to Dicey, the right to hold a public procession is in principle no different from the right to eat a bun. The notion that everything is permitted unless forbidden is particularly ironic in the case of public meetings. All meetings and processions take place on land. All land, even a public highway, is owned by someone, whether a private body, a local authority, the Crown or a government department. Holding a meeting without the consent of a private owner is a trespass, so that the owner can bring a civil action to evict the trespasser (see *Harrison v Duke of Rutland* [1893] 1 QB 142).

In the case of the public highway, the traditional view was that the public has a right only to 'pass or repass' on a highway (i.e. to travel) and also to stop on the highway for purposes that are reasonably incidental such as 'reasonable rest and refreshment' (*Hickman v Maisey* [1900] 1 QB 752). In *Hubbard v Pitt* [1976] QB 142, for example, the Court of Appeal held that peaceful picketing by a protest group which distributed leaflets and questionnaires was not a lawful use of the highway.

Lord Denning dissented in support of a right to demonstrate on matters of public concern. Dicey thought that a procession, but not a static meeting, would usually be lawful because processions comprise a large number of individuals exercising their right to travel at the same time.

In *DPP v Jones* [1999] 2 All ER 257, the House of Lords marginally upheld a right of peaceful demonstration by environmentalists on the highway at Stonehenge. Lord Irvine LC asserted that the law should now recognise a public right to use the highway for any reasonable purpose. Lord Hutton considered that the common law should now recognise that the right of assembly, which is one of the fundamental rights of citizens in this country, is unduly restricted unless it can be exercised 'in some circumstances' on the public highway. Lords Hope and Slynn dissented, Lord Hope because of the effect of such a right on property owners who were not before the Court to defend their interests, and Lord Slynn because of a reluctance to unsettle established law (see also *Tabernacle v Secretary of State for Defence* [2009] EWCA Civ 23: protest camp held regularly over 20 years without disruption: eviction unlawful).

As regards public land, the matter now depends on proportionality, balancing the right of assembly against the interests of the property owner and other aspects of the public interest. It seems that the right to assembly is outweighed if substantial interference with others is involved. In *City of London Corp v Samede* [2012], the *Occupy Movement*, demonstrating against corporate greed, set up a camp for several weeks in an open space outside St Paul's Cathedral in London. The land was owned by a public body which sought to remove the tents. It was held that it was proportionate to do so. The occupation was a trespass, raised health risks and caused disruption to local businesses. Moreover, the particular location was not vital to the political causes being espoused (see also *Mayor of London v Hall* [2011] 1 WLR 504: protest camp lawfully evicted from Parliament Square other than long-term protester whose occupation did not cause disruption).

In the case of privately owned land, such as many retail parks and shopping centres, the Human Rights Act may not apply because the issue is one of private property rights (see *McDonald v McDonald* [2016], Section 22.7). A private owner can exclude anyone from the premises. Whether the Human Rights Act could impose a positive duty on the state to protect freedom of assembly in such places on the basis that they are in effect public spaces is questionable. In *Appleby v UK* [2003] ECHR 222 the European Court held that the owner of a shopping mall could prevent environmental campaigners from setting up a stall and distributing leaflets. However, the Court stressed that they had other means of communicating their concerns, and that any restrictions must have a rational justification (see Mead [2013] PL 100).

23.7.1 Statutory police powers

The police have wide powers to regulate public meetings and processions. These are supplemented by powers relating to particular places (Seditious Meetings Act 1817, s 3: meetings of 50 or more people in the vicinity of Westminster when Parliament is sitting; Serious Organised Crime and Police Act 2005). The main general police powers are as follows:

▶ The organiser of a public procession intended (i) to demonstrate support for or opposition to the views or actions of any person or body of persons, (ii) to publicise a campaign or cause, or (iii) to mark or commemorate an event must give advance notice to the police (Public Order Act 1986, s 11). There are certain exceptions. These include:
  (i) processions commonly or customarily held in the area. This only applies if the route remains the same. This can apply even if the route is not fixed in advance (*Kay v Metropolitan Police Comr* [2008] UKHL 69: mass cycle ride through London);
  (ii) funeral processions organised by a funeral director in the normal course of business;
  (iii) cases where it is not reasonably practicable to give advance notice (e.g. a spontaneous march (see *Kay*, above)).

- There is no power to ban a procession for failing to give notice. However, if a 'senior police officer' reasonably believes (i) that any public procession may result in serious public disorder, serious damage to property, or serious disruption to the life of the community; or (ii) that the purpose of the organisers is to intimidate people into doing something they have a right not to do, or not doing something they have a right to do, the senior officer can impose such conditions as appear to him or her to be necessary to prevent such disorder, damage, disruption or intimidation, including conditions as to the route of the procession or to prohibit it from entering any public place specified in the directions (Public Order Act 1986, s 12). A 'senior police officer' is either the Chief Constable or the Metropolitan Police Commissioner, or the senior officer present on the scene (s 12(2)). Intimidation requires more than merely causing discomfort and must contain an element of compulsion.
- All public processions, or any class of public procession, can be banned if the Chief Constable or Metropolitan Police Commissioner reasonably believes that the power to impose conditions is not adequate in the circumstances (Public Order Act 1986, s 13). The decision is for the local authority with the consent of a Secretary of State (in practice the Home Secretary), thus injecting a nominal element of democracy.
- There are police powers to impose conditions upon public meetings for the same purposes as in the case of processions (Public Order Act 1986, s 14). For this purpose, a public assembly is an assembly of 20 or more people in a public place that is wholly or partly open to the air (s 16). Unlike processions, the police have no general power to ban a lawful assembly but can control its location and timing and the numbers attending.
- Section 70 of the Criminal Justice and Public Order Act 1994 (inserting ss 14A–C into the Public Order Act 1986) confers power on a local authority with the consent of the Secretary of State to ban certain kinds of assembly. This includes private land and buildings where the public is invited, for example ancient monuments such as Stonehenge, meeting rooms, shops, sports and entertainment centres and libraries. The Chief Constable must reasonably believe that an assembly (i) is a 'trespassory' assembly likely to be held without the permission of the occupier or outside the public's rights of access; and (ii) may result in serious disruption to the life of the community or may result in significant damage to land, buildings or monuments of historical, architectural or scientific importance. A ban can last for up to four days within an area of up to five miles. The ban covers all trespassory assemblies and cannot be confined to particular assemblies.
- Under the Serious Organised Crime and Police Act 2005, it is an offence to organise or take part in a demonstration within a designated area without police permission, for which written notice must be given if reasonably practicable at least six clear days in advance, and in any case not less than 24 hours in advance. In relation to 'taking part', a demonstration can be by one person. If proper notice is given, the police must give authorisation, but this can be subject to conditions, including limits on the number of people who may take part, noise levels and the number and size of banners and placards. These provisions do not apply to public processions that fall within the Public Order Act 1896 or to lawful trade union activity.
- A previous ban on demonstrations near the Houses of Parliament was abolished by the Police Reform and Social Responsibility Act 2011, ss 142–49. This restricts activities such as using loudspeakers and camping gear in Parliament Square Gardens and its vicinity.
- In *Primov v Russia* [2014] ECHR 605, which concerned a refusal of permission for a public meeting criticising the local administration of a village, the Strasbourg court held that requirements of notification and consent are valid provided that the powers are used only to guarantee the smooth conduct of the meeting. Moreover, enforcement must be proportionate, meaning that the police must consider alternative solutions before banning a meeting. For example, it is not sufficient merely to claim that the site is too small.

23.7.2 Common law police powers

Where a breach of the peace is taking place or is imminent, the police have a wide common law power to arrest anyone who refuses to obey their reasonable requirements (*Albert v Lavin* [1982] AC 546). The power to prevent a breach of the peace includes a power to remove a speaker (*Duncan v Jones* [1936] 1 KB 218) and a right of entry to private premises (*Thomas v Sawkins* [1935] 2 KB 249). A charge of obstructing the police is also possible (Police Act 1996, ss 8, 9(1)) and magistrates can 'bind over' a person to keep the peace.

Before the HRA, the courts were reluctant to interfere with police discretion. The main consideration was efficiency in giving the police the power to control the disturbance as they saw fit within the resources available to them. Therefore, even where a peaceful and lawful meeting is disrupted by hooligans or political opponents, the police could prevent a likely breach of the peace by ordering the speaker to stop in preference to controlling the troublemakers (*Duncan v Jones* (above)).

Although the police must act even-handedly (*Harris v Sheffield United Football Club* [1988] QB 77, 95), there is a risk that they will exercise their discretion in favour of interests supported by the government. For example, during the miners' strike of 1984–5 the police restricted the activities of demonstrators in order to protect the 'right to work' of non-strikers, going as far as to escort non-strikers to work. A result of these events is that confidence in the police has been damaged (see also *R v Coventry City Council, ex p Phoenix Aviation* [1995] 3 All ER 37: duty to protect business interests). On the other hand, in *R v Chief Constable of Sussex, ex p International Trader's Ferry Ltd* [1999] 1 All ER 129 and *R v Chief Constable of Devon and Cornwall Constabulary, ex p Central Electricity Generating Board* [1981] 3 All ER 826, police restrictions on lawful business activities favoured animal rights and anti-nuclear protesters, respectively. In both cases, it was held that the matter was one of discretion.

A breach of the peace means violence or threatened violence (see *R v Howell* [1982] QB 416; *R (Laporte) v Chief Constable of Gloucestershire* [2007] 2 AC 105, [27]). Under the ECHR, the police are required to give priority to freedom of expression. as long as the person concerned does not himself commit a wrongful act, unless there is a serious risk of disruption. In *Plattform 'Arzte fur das Leben' v Austria* (1988) 13 EHRR 204 the ECtHR held, in the context of an anti-abortion demonstration, that there was a positive duty to protect a peaceful demonstration even though it might annoy or give offence to persons opposed to the ideas and claims which it was seeking to promote. Thus, in *McLeod v UK* (1999) 27 EHRR 493 it was held that breach of the peace powers can satisfy the test of legality only where the individual causes or is likely to cause harm or acts in a manner the natural consequences of which would be to provoke violence in others (see also *Ezelin v France* [1992]; *Primov v Russia* [2014]).

Mixed protection of the right to demonstrate

▶ In *R (Laporte) v Chief Constable of Gloucestershire* [2006], the police had stopped, searched, and then turned back with a police escort a coachload of anti-Iraq War protesters who were travelling to a demonstration at a military site. Although this took place several miles from the site, the police claimed that their powers extended to taking action whenever they reasonably anticipated that a breach of the peace was likely, whether committed by the persons in question or by others. The House of Lords, invoking the importance of freedom of expression, held that the common law power to prevent a breach of the peace was confined to a situation where the breach of peace was actually taking place or was imminent. It was also held that freedom of expression should be limited only as a last resort and that the police should attempt initially to target the actual troublemakers.

▶ But in *Austin v Metropolitan Police Comr* [2009] 3 All ER 455, during a political demonstration, the police detained a crowd, including bystanders, behind a cordon on the highway for two hours in conditions of discomfort in order to prevent a violent demonstration ('kettling'). Previous attempts to disperse the crowd had been met with violence. It was held that the actions of the police did not constitute a 'deprivation of liberty' under the ECHR, but only a 'restriction' of liberty which is not protected as such (Section 21.4.2). The police action was also lawful at common law as necessary to keep order. *Austin* was upheld by the Strasbourg court in *Austin v UK* (2012) 55 EHRR 14. The court held that there was no deprivation of liberty within Article 5, since the kettling was for a limited purpose and justified as a last resort to prevent serious disorder. (However, Art 5 has no override covering justification.) The court stressed the importance of freedom of assembly and said that kettling should be used only in extreme circumstances where necessary to prevent serious injury or damage.

▶ In *Pentikinen v Finland* [2014] ECHR 106, the Strasbourg court held that the police have a margin of discretion, in assessing the necessity of action and as to the measures to be taken. In that case, a special area at a demonstration was penned off for the press. The claimant, a journalist and photographer, refused to stay in the pen and was arrested when the demonstration turned violent. The court upheld the arrest but stressed that the claimant would not have been prevented while in the pen from taking photos. This decision opens up the possibility of officials 'editing' journalism.

Short of causing distress by harassment, police surveillance, including taking photos, is lawful in itself since in a public place there is normally no reasonable expectation of privacy (Section 23.5). Police surveillance of public meetings, and the association in the official mind of political protest with crime, has a chilling effect on freedom of association and also may interfere with the right to respect for privacy under Article 8 of the Convention.

Originally, there was a clear line between information about convicted persons and information about the innocent. Thus, in *Kinloch v HM Advocate* [2013] 2 AC 93, the Supreme Court held that the retention of police observation notes concerning the behaviour of a suspect in public who was subsequently convicted did not violate Article 8. The crucial factor was that the behaviour recorded was criminal. However, the retention by the police of photographs of demonstrators not suspected of any offence was an unlawful infringement of privacy.

In *R (Wood) v Metropolitan Police Commissioner* [2009] 4 All ER 951, the police photographed the claimant as he was leaving a meeting of a group which campaigned against the arms trade. The Court of Appeal held that, although the taking of a person's photograph in a public place did not in itself engage Article 8, the conduct of the police in subsequently retaining and storing the pictures was an infringement of privacy and not proportionate. There was no evidence to link the claimant to any crime, and the surveillance concerned relatively low-level crime as opposed to such matters as terrorism. Similarly, in *R (RMC) v Metropolitan Police Commissioner* [2012] 4 All ER 510, the High Court held that Article 8 was violated when the police refused to destroy photographs taken at a police station of suspects who were subsequently not prosecuted. It was disproportionate not to distinguish between innocent people and those convicted. However, it was justifiable to retain a record on the Police National Database of an individual's encounter with the police since the interference with privacy was relatively minor and the information would be relevant to any future encounter.

In *R (Catt) v Association of Chief Police Officers* [2015] UKSC 9, a majority of the Supreme Court took a step further. It was held that basic information including attendance at demonstrations taken from a 91-year-old peaceful protester with no convictions could be held indefinitely. Given the existence of internal safeguards against sharing the information, the interests of policing outweighed what the majority considered to be a relatively minor infringement of Art 8. However, in *Catt v UK* [2019] ECHR 76, the Strasbourg Court considered that indefinite retention violated the Convention (Section 22.9.1).

23.7.3 Public order offences

Specific public order offences strike primarily at people who intentionally cause violence, but sometimes go beyond that. They overlap, allowing police discretion in relation to the penalties. Moreover, the police can arrest on the basis of reasonable suspicion for any offence (Police and Criminal Evidence Act 1984 (PACE), s 24, as modified by the Serious Organised Crime and Police Act 2005). However,

even minor punishments or disciplinary measures might be condemned under the ECHR as disproportionate or uncertain and so chilling the right of assembly (*Ezelin v France* [1992]).

The main offences are as follows:

1. Under the Highways Act 1980, it is an offence to obstruct the highway, and the police can remove the
   offender (s 137). It is not necessary that the highway be completely blocked or even that people are
   inconvenienced. Here the accused's intentions are irrelevant (*Arrowsmith v Jenkins* [1963] 2 QB 561;
   Homer v Cadman (1886) 16 Cox CC 51; *Hirst and Agu v West Yorkshire Chief Constable* (1987) 85 Crim App
   Rep 143). However, in the light of the HRA, a non-obstructive peaceful demonstration would probably
   not be unlawful (Section 23.7). There are also numerous local statutes and by-laws regulating public
   meetings in particular places.
2. The Public Order Act 1986 creates several offences, replacing a clutch of ancient and ill-defined common law offences (rout, riot, affray and unlawful assembly). However, the old case of *Beatty v Gillbanks*
   (1882) 9 QBD 308, often cited as an endorsement of freedom of assembly, may still apply to them. A
   temperance march by the Salvation Army was disrupted by a gang known as the Skeleton Army, sponsored by brewery interests. The organisers of the march were held not to be guilty of the offence of
   unlawful assembly (replaced by the Public Order Act 1986) on the ground that their behaviour was in
   itself lawful, and the disruption was caused by their opponents. Thus, even though in one sense the
   Salvationists were provoking their opponents, the court was in effect ascribing moral blame.

The offences under the Public Order Act 1986 are as follows (in descending order of seriousness):

▶ Section 1: *riot*. Where 12 or more people act in concert and use or threaten unlawful violence for a common purpose, each person using violence is guilty of the offence.
▶ Section 2: *violent disorder.* At least three people acting in concert and using or threatening unlawful
  violence.
▶ Section 3: *affray*. One person suffices. Using or threatening unlawful violence is sufficient, but threats
  by words alone do not count.

The above offences may be committed in public or in private, and the conduct must be such 'as
would cause a person of reasonable firmness present at the scene to fear for his personal safety'. No
such person need actually be on the scene. The defendant must either intend to threaten or use violence, or be aware that his or her conduct may be violent or threaten violence (s 6). 'Violence' is
broadly defined to include violent conduct to property and persons and is not restricted to conduct
intended to cause injury or damage (s 8).

▶ Section 4: *fear or provocation of violence*. Here the law begins to impinge on freedom of expression, but
  by focusing on violence does not cross Mill's line between 'harm' and 'offence' (Section 23.1). A person
  is guilty who uses 'threatening, abusive or insulting words or behaviour or distributes or displays any
  writing, sign or visible representation that is threatening, abusive or insulting'. The meaning of 'threatening, abusive or insulting' is left to the jury (see *Brutus v Cozens* [1973] AC 854) but the accused must
  be aware that his words are threatening, abusive or insulting (s 6(3)). The act must be aimed at another
  person with the intention either to cause that person to believe that immediate unlawful violence will
  be used or to provoke that person into immediate unlawful violence. Alternatively, the accused's conduct must be likely to have that effect even though he or she does not so intend. The violence must be
  likely within a short time of the behaviour in question. The offence can be committed in a public or a
  private place except exclusively within a dwelling or between dwellings (s 8).
▶ Section 4A: *threatening, abusive or insulting words or behaviour or disorderly behaviour or distributing or
  displaying any writing, sign or visible representation that is threatening, abusive or insulting' with intent to
  cause harassment, alarm and distress where harassment, alarm or distress is actually caused*. This and the following offence cross the line between harm and offence since no violence is involved. However, in
  both cases, as with section 4, a susceptible person must actually be present.

- Section 5: *harassment, alarm, or distress*. This is the widest offence. It applies to threatening, abusive words or behaviour or disorderly behaviour or 'distributing or displaying any writing, sign or visible representation that is threatening, or abusive'. However, a previous inclusion of 'insulting' behaviour was removed by the Crime and Courts Act 2013, s 57 in favour of freedom of speech.

This offence requires only that a person who actually sees or hears the conduct must be 'likely' to be caused harassment, alarm or distress. However, there are the defences that (i) the accused had no reason to believe that any such person was present; (ii) he did not intend or know that his words or actions were threatening, abusive or disorderly (see *DPP v Clarke* [1992] Crim LR 60); and (iii) his conduct was 'reasonable'. The police have a summary power of arrest in relation to all the above offences, but under section 5 must first warn the accused to stop.

It is unlikely that the offences under sections 1–4 in themselves are contrary to the ECHR in that they aim at preventing violence. However, individual cases are subject to proportionality, albeit the police are likely to have a margin of discretion. Before the HRA, it was held in relation to section 4 that whether the other person's reaction is reasonable is irrelevant and that a speaker 'takes his audience as he finds it'. Thus, provoking a hostile or extremist audience would be an offence (*Jordan v Burgoyne* [1963] 2 QB 744; *R v Horseferry Road Metropolitan Stipendiary Magistrate Court, ex p Siadatan* [1991] 1 QB 260). However, the Strasbourg principle that troublemakers must be controlled first could apply here (Section 23.7.2).

Sections 4A and 5 are more vulnerable. They threaten freedom of expression in that they move away from the important safeguards that the conduct in question must involve violence. Thus, these provisions are arguably disproportionate. They apply also to 'disorderly behaviour', an expression which is vague and not defined. They arguably run counter to the view of the European Court that conduct which shocks and offends is a price to be paid for democracy (Section 23.1).

There are other offences. Section 1 of the Public Order Act 1936, enacted at a time of civil unrest, prohibits the wearing of a uniform associated with a political organisation or the promotion of a political object, in any public place or public meeting without police consent, which can be obtained for ceremonial or special occasions. 'Uniform' includes any garment that has political significance, for example a black beret (*O'Moran v DPP* [1975] 1 All ER 473). Political association can be identified from any of the circumstances, or from historical evidence. The consent of the Attorney General, a politician, is required for a prosecution. Section 1 may be vulnerable to challenge as violating both Art 8 and Art 10.

Aggravated trespass gives the police a weapon against political demonstrators. Aimed originally at anti-hunting protesters, it occurs where a person who trespasses on land does anything which, in relation to any lawful activity that persons are engaging or about to engage in on that land or on adjoining land, is intended to have the effect (i) of intimidating those persons or any one of them so as to deter them or any one of them from engaging in that lawful activity; (ii) of obstructing that activity; or (iii) of disrupting that activity (Criminal Justice and Public Order Act 1994, s 68). For this purpose, a lawful activity is any activity that is not a criminal offence or a trespass (s 68(2)). An unlawful act that is not being committed as part of the activity carried out by the occupier on the land is apparently irrelevant. (See *Richardson v DPP* [2014] 2 All ER 20: protesters demonstrating outside a shop against Israeli occupation of claimed Palestinian territory, allegation that goods sold in the shop were acquired unlawfully from the occupied territories not relevant.) There is no defence of reasonableness, and violence is not required. The police can order a person who is committing or has committed or intends to commit an offence to leave the land (s 69). It is an offence to return within three months. It is not clear whether passive conduct such as lying down would be an offence. However, in view of the limitation of the offence to a trespasser, it is unlikely that a Human Rights Act challenge would succeed.

Moreover, under the Serious Organised Crime and Police Act 2005, any trespass on a site in England and Wales or Northern Ireland designated by the Secretary of State (s 128) is an offence. Except in the case of land owned by the Crown, which covers most central government land, and by the Queen or the immediate heir to the throne in their private capacity, this power can be used only in the interests of national security. However, the courts are reluctant to interfere with the government's view as to what national security requires.

Under the Protection from Harassment Act 1997, as amended by the Serious Organised Crime and Police Act 2005, a course of conduct (meaning conduct on at least two occasions relating to one person or on one occasion in the case of two or more persons) which the perpetrator knows or ought to know amounts to or involves the harassment of another is an offence. The test is whether a reasonable person in possession of the same information as the accused would think the conduct likely to cause harassment (s 1(2)). Aimed originally at animal rights activists, this provision can be used against political demonstrations in general.

Harassment is a wide term and may be vulnerable to challenge under the HRA. It includes trying to persuade someone not to do something lawful or to do something unlawful and can include 'collective' harassment by a group (Criminal Justice and Police Act 2001, s 44). Thus, the anti-abortion protesters in *DPP v Fidler* [1992] 1 WLR 91, who were acquitted because they intended to persuade rather than to prevent women entering an abortion clinic, would now probably be convicted. There are defences of preventing or detecting crime and acting under lawful authority and a broad defence of 'reasonableness' (s 1(3)(c)). This may allow the press to claim that its duty to inform the public overrides the victim's right of privacy. It may also allow religious enthusiasts to evangelise (cf. Section 23.6.2).

Summary

- The justifications for freedom of expression concern the advancement of truth, the protection of democracy and the rule of law, and self-fulfilment. Press freedom is particularly important in a democracy. Freedom of expression involves the state not only abstaining from interference but, in some cases, particularly in relation to the press, taking positive steps to protect freedom of expression.

- Freedom of expression may conflict with other rights, notably religion and privacy. It may also be overridden by public interest concerns such as the integrity of the judicial process.

- We distinguished between prior restraint (censorship) and punishments after the event. UK law has some direct censorship by the executive in relation to the broadcast and film media. More general powers of censorship are available by applying to the courts for injunctions. These may be too broad in the light of the HRA.

- Open justice, including press access to the courts and their decisions, is essential to the rule of law and to the accountability of the judges. Open justice is protected by both the ECHR and the common law. However, the court has an ill-defined power to override open justice if the interests of a fair trial so require. This may give rise to government arguments in favour of national security.

- Defamation protects a person's interest in reputation. Public bodies are not protected by the law of defamation, although, perhaps unjustifiably, individual public officials are. The Defamation Act 2013 contains specific measures which enhance freedom of expression especially in relation to the press, but does not introduce new general principles.

- English domestic law had not developed a distinct right of privacy, which protects interests in self-esteem, dignity and autonomy. However, under the HRA, which has stimulated common law development of a right of privacy, freedom of expression must be balanced against privacy as an independent right. Both have equal weight in the abstract and the court will compare the seriousness of the consequences in the individual circumstances. Protection for press freedom is based on establishing a public interest in disclosure.

- The interests of open justice also compete with the right to privacy and may add further weight to press freedom.

- Police powers of surveillance of demonstrators and the retention of information, including photographs and biometric data, conflict with privacy and indirectly with freedom of expression. There are specific protections against hate speech in relation to race, religion and sexual orientation. These have savings to protect freedom of expression, but the line is difficult to draw.

- The law relating to public meetings and processions sets freedom of expression and assembly against public order. This is characterised by broad police discretion. A range of statutes responding to perceived threats has created various offences that restrict freedom of expression and give the police extensive powers to regulate public meetings and processions and demonstrations by individuals and groups. The police also have wide common law powers to prevent imminent breaches of the peace. Under the HRA, these powers must be exercised in accordance with the principle of proportionality in order to safeguard freedom of expression and association.

Exercises

23.1 Chablis and Merlot, aged 15, the twin daughters of Ben, a famous sports personality, are photographed by a newspaper reporter serving as baristas at a coffee shop in the local high street during school hours. In a recent newspaper interview, their father had said that his daughters are 'always studying hard at school'. The *Daily Troll* contacts Ben and explains that it intends to publish the photos the next day. Advise Ben.

23.2 'The independence of lawyers and other professionals is not compromised by government regulation: why should this not apply also in relation to the press?'

23.3 **(i)** 'Youth Onto Bigots' (YOB) is an organisation that campaigns against all religious beliefs. YOB publishes a magazine, which it gives away on the street, detailing atrocities committed in the past by religious groups and containing the message on its cover: 'You are stupid, dangerous and are wasting your life if you believe in a god.' Advise the local religious leaders whether they have any lawful means of preventing the campaign.

(ii) Members of YOB, including Jez, a student activist, hold a demonstration and distribute leaflets outside an army recruitment office in a shopping centre in Pittsville every Saturday morning. The centre is owned by an insurance company. The leaflets include appeals not to join the army and praise the nineteenth-century Chartists who demonstrated violently against the government for equality and democracy. Last week, the police visited the centre and took photographs of the leaflet distributors. Jez was identified from one of these photographs and his name and address were recorded and stored in a secret police database of 'potential subversives'. The police share information from the database with the Home Office if requested. Discuss the legality of these events. Have any offences been committed?

23.4 To what extent does the Defamation Act 2013 enhance freedom of expression?

23.5 D, a student, hears from another student, A, via Twitter that X, her tutor, is being investigated by the college authorities for harassment of female students. D immediately tweets to her 20 followers that she knew X was a dodgy character who should not be around students. The story is false, A having confused X with Y, a tutor in another college. Advise D and A whether they may be legally liable. What would be the position if D was the editor of the college student newspaper and had published a blistering attack on X based on the information from A?

23.6 Tim, a newspaper reporter, is returning from a trip to Utopia, a country with which the UK is currently negotiating a large arms contract. He is carrying a sound recording which apparently depicts a Utopian politician receiving a bribe from a UK official. The recording was given to Tim by the official in question subject to a promise of anonymity. On Tim's arrival in the UK, an airport official searches his baggage and confiscates the recording. Discuss the legality of this.

23.7 'A function of free expression is to invite dispute. It may indeed best serve its purpose when it induces a condition of unrest, creates dissatisfaction with conditions as they are and even stirs people to anger' (Mr Justice Douglas in *Terminiello v Chicago* 337 US 1 (1949)). To what extent does English law recognise this?

23.8 Jacques, a prominent member of the English Independence Party, has been invited to address a rally in a local park. A press release announces that Jacques will argue that transgender people should not be allowed to marry. He will also claim that non-Christians should be 'run out of the country'. Police permission was sought for the rally. It was granted on condition that the press would be limited to a pen at the back of the site and photography is not allowed. A pressure group, 'Transgender Christians (TC)', proposes to attend the rally travelling by coach. Fearing that there may be violence at the rally and, having insufficient resources to provide adequate policing at the rally itself, the police stop the TC coach at a motorway service area some five miles from the park. They refuse to allow any passengers to disembark and detain the coach for about three hours until the rally has finished.

The rally is held as planned. Several hundred people are present, including six policemen who patrol the press 'pen'. Jacques makes his address at the rally wearing a jacket embroidered with the party slogan. Debbie, a journalist, leaves the pen and takes photographs of the speaker. A policeman arrests her.

Discuss the legality of these events and consider what, if any, offences have been committed.

Further reading

Ahdar and Leigh, *Religious Freedom in the Liberal State* (Oxford University Press 2005)

Barendt, 'Incitement to and Glorification of Terrorism' in Hare and Weinstein (eds), *Extreme Speech and Democracy* (Oxford University Press 2009)

Blom-Cooper, 'Press Freedom: Constitutional Right or Cultural Assumption?' [2008] PL 260

Cram, 'The Danish Cartoons, Offensive Expression and Democratic Legitimacy' in Hare and Weinstein (eds), *Extreme Speech and Democracy* (Oxford University Press 2009)

Fenwick, 'Marginalising Human Rights: Breach of the Peace, "Kettling", the Human Rights Act and Public Protest' [2009] PL 737

Foster, 'Media Responsibility, Public Interest Broadcasting and the Judgment in *Richard v BBC*' [2018] EHRLR 490

Finnis, 'Endorsing Discrimination Between Faiths: A Case of Extreme Speech?' in Hare and Weinstein (eds), *Extreme Speech and Democracy* (Oxford University Press 2009)

Gligorijevic, 'Privacy at the Intersection of Public Law and Private Law' [2019] PL 563

Greenawalt, 'Free Speech Justifications' (1989) 89 Columbia L R 119

Leigh, 'Homophobic Speech, Equality Denial and Religious Expression' in Hare and Weinstein (eds), *Extreme Speech and Democracy* (Oxford University Press 2009)

Malik, 'Extreme Speech and Liberalism' in Hare and Weinstein (eds), *Extreme Speech and Democracy* (Oxford University Press 2009)

Mead, *The New Law of Peaceful Protest: Rights and Regulation in the Human Rights Act Era* (Hart Publishing 2010)

Moreham, 'Privacy in the Common Law: A Doctrinal and Theoretical Analysis' (2005) 121 LQR 628

Rowbottom, 'In the Shadow of the Big Media: Freedom of Expression, Participation and the Production of Knowledge Online' [2014] PL 491

Schweppe and Haynes, 'You Can't Have One Without the Other One: "Gender" in Hate Crime Legislation' [2020] Crim LR 148

Williams, 'Hate Speech in the United Kingdom: An Historical Overview' in Hare and Weinstein (eds), *Extreme Speech and Democracy* (Oxford University Press 2009)

Chapter 24

Government secrecy

24.1 Access to government information: open government

In *Kennedy v Charity Commission* [2014] UKSC 20 Lord Mance said (at [1]):

> Information is the key to sound decision-making, to accountability and development, it underpins democracy and assists in combating poverty, oppression, corruption, prejudice and in efficiency. Unwillingness to disclose information may arise through habits of secrecy or reasons of self-protection. But information can be genuinely private, confidential or sensitive and these interests merit respect in their own right and, in the case of those who depend on information to fulfil their functions, because this may not otherwise be forthcoming.

Knight suggests that the traditional rationales which support freedom of expression, namely truth, democracy and self-realisation, also support a right of access to government information ([2013] PL 468). If this is so, then Article 10 of the ECHR can provide a basis for a right of access to information, at least for the press. The legal rationale is that, under Article 10, freedom of expression in relation to the press carries with it a duty to inform the public (Section 23.3). However, in *Burmah Oil Co Ltd v Bank of England* [1980] AC 1090, 1112, Lord Wilberforce did not believe that the courts should support open government.

The conventional view is that Article 10 does not found a right of access to information. Thus, Art 10 refers only to 'the right to receive and impart information and ideas without interference by a public authority'. The main Strasbourg decisions support this (see *Sugar (Deceased) v BBC* [2012] UKSC 4, [94]; *Leander v Sweden* (1987) 9 EHRR 433). However, more recent Strasbourg cases suggest that Article 10 can be extended to include a right to acquire information in the interests of government accountability and the free flow of ideas (*Tarsasag v Hungary* (2011) 53 EHRR 3: access by NGO described as 'social watchdog'; *Kenedi v Hungary* (2009) 27 BHRC 335; *Gillberg v Sweden* (2013) 31 BHRC 247, [93]–[94]: access by researchers).

A five to two Supreme Court has upheld the conventional view of Art 10, but also expressed support for the principle of freedom of information. *Kennedy v Charity Commission* [2014] concerned an attempt by a journalist to gain information held by the Charity Commission concerning an inquiry under the Charities Act 2011 into the affairs of a charity relating to Iraq. The Commission successfully claimed an exemption from disclosure under the Freedom of Information Act (below), and it was held that there was no right under the HRA to overcome this. The majority also held, obiter, that Art 10 does not directly give a right to receive information from public authorities. The Court refused to follow recent ECHR cases on the basis that they were not sufficiently clear. Lords Wilson and Carnwath (dissenting) thought that Article 10 should include a right to government information.

However, the Supreme Court in *Kennedy* went on to suggest that, under the law of judicial review, there is a home-grown common law presumption in favour of disclosure of information based on the principle of open justice, at least in the context of courts of law and other bodies exercising judicial powers. This is comparable with Art 10 of the ECHR.

Thus, in *R (Privacy International) v Revenue and Customs Commissioners* [2015] 1 WLR 397, the claimant believed that internet surveillance software was being exported to oppressive governments and used for human rights abuses. It requested the Revenue, which is responsible for regulating export control, to give information as to what investigations had taken place and what action it intended to take. The Revenue refused to disclose any information, initially denying that it had power to do so, but later admitting that it did have such power under the Commissioners of Revenue and Customs Act 2005 s 18(2). It still refused to disclose information on the grounds that it might forewarn a suspect, cause harm to reputations and breach confidentiality. Green J held that the Revenue's decision was unlawful and irrational because it did not consider the matter in sufficient depth, merely giving blanket reasons and not balancing competing considerations. Public confidence is also a relevant factor, as is the 'constitutional right' to challenge a decision in the courts.

There may be a right to information for particular purposes under Article 2 (deaths in official custody) (Section 21.4.2), Article 6 (right to a fair trial) and Article 8 (respect for family life) (e.g. *Guerra v Italy* (1998) 26 EHRR 357: environmental risks; *Gaskin v UK* (1990) 12 EHRR 36: adoption records).

24.2 The Freedom of Information Act 2000

There are certain statutory rights to information, of which the Freedom of Information Act 2000 is the most general. The scope of the Freedom of Information Act 2000 is potentially wide. Subject to many exemptions, the Act requires public authorities in England, Wales and Northern Ireland to disclose information on request and also to confirm or deny whether the information exists (s 1) (see also Freedom of Information (Scotland) Act 2002).

The operation of the Act is supervised and enforced by an Information Commissioner, who also has advisory and promotional functions. As so often in the UK Constitution, the Act depends heavily on the ability of the Information Commissioner, a government appointee, to stand up to the government and to be adequately resourced by government.

The Act does not prevent a public authority disclosing information voluntarily (s 78). Its only function is to require disclosure in certain circumstances. As we have seen, the EHCR probably does not give a right to information and in any case, in *Kennedy v Charity Commission* [2014], Lord Sumption (at [154]–[157]) thought that the Act was compatible with the EHCR, since it balances the right to information against the public interest in secrecy.

Public authorities are exhaustively listed in Schedule 1, thereby avoiding the difficulties arising in other areas of law in defining a public authority. Most central government departments, Parliament (subject to exceptions for residential and travelling arrangements of members), the Welsh Senedd (but not the Scottish Parliament (s 80)), local authorities, the police, the armed forces, state educational bodies and NHS bodies are automatically public authorities, as are a long list of other specified bodies, including companies which are wholly owned by other public authorities (s 6), such as Network Rail and universities, including UCAS. The Cabinet, the royal household and the security services are not public authorities under the Act.

The Secretary of State may designate other bodies, officeholders or persons as public authorities who appear to him to be exercising 'functions of a public nature' or who provide services under a contract with a public authority whose functions include the provision of those services (s 3(1)). This might include a charity or a company acting on behalf of a government agency. The Secretary of State can also limit the kind of information that the listed bodies can disclose (s 7), for example, information held by the BBC for purposes of journalism, art or literature material. Where a body holds information for mixed purposes only some of which are exempt, there need be no disclosure (*Sugar (Deceased) v BBC* [2012], Section 23.3.2).

Section 8 gives a right to any person to request in writing information held by the authority on its own behalf or held by another on behalf of the authority (s 3(2)). Information is construed liberally to include pictures, logos, etc. and includes entitlement to copies (*IPSA v Information Commissioner* [2015] EWCA Civ 388). The person making the request is entitled to be told whether or not the authority possesses the information ('the duty to confirm or deny') and to have the information communicated to him or her (s 1(1)).

Reasons do not normally have to be given for the request. Nor does the information have to be useful, and the applicant's purpose or motive is irrelevant. However, disclosure can be refused if the applicant has not provided such further information as the authority reasonably requires to enable the requested information to be found (s 1), although the authority must provide reasonable advice and assistance (s 16). A request can also be refused if the cost of compliance exceeds a limit set by the Secretary of State or where the request is vexatious or repetitive (s 14). A fee regulated by the Secretary of State can be charged (s 9). The authority must respond 'promptly' and within 20 working days, although there is no penalty for failure to do so (s 10). However, if the matter might involve an exemption (below) there is no time limit other than a 'reasonable' time to make a decision. Thus, there is considerable scope for bureaucratic obfuscation and delay, and for lying as to the existence of a document. There have sometimes been delays of over a year in responding to requests.

There are 23 exemptions (Part II). These apply both to the information itself, and usually to the duty to confirm or deny (but in looking at each exemption the distinction should be borne in mind). Nine are absolute exemptions for whole classes of information. Others are 'qualified exemptions' which apply to the individual document. This enables a request to be refused on public interest grounds. In some cases, release of the information must 'prejudice' the interest in question. The government originally wanted a 'substantial prejudice' test (*Your Right to Know: Freedom of Information* (Cm 3818, 1997)).

Freedom of Information Act: the main exemptions

(a) The absolute exemptions are as follows:

- information which is already reasonably accessible to the public even if payment is required (s 21);
- information certified by a minister as supplied by or relating to the intelligence and security services (s 23);
- information contained in court records (widely defined) given for the purpose of the proceedings (s 32): see *Kennedy v Charity Commission* [2014];
- information protected by parliamentary privilege (s 34). In *Corporate Officer of the House of Commons v Information Comr* [2009] 3 All ER 403, an attempt to prevent disclosure of MPs' expenses claims on the grounds of parliamentary privilege was unsuccessful (Section 11.6.2). However, information held by Parliament is exempt if the Speaker or, in the case of the House of Lords, the Clerk of the Parliaments, so certifies (s 34(1));
- information that would prejudice the conduct of public affairs in the House of Commons or the House of Lords (s 36);
- communications with the sovereign, the heir to the throne and the second in line to the throne (s.37; Constitutional Reform and Governance Act 2010, Sched. 7). This protects correspondence from the Prince of Wales who, as heir to the throne, is required to be politically neutral but has allegedly lobbied ministers in order to influence government policy. However, this immunity may not apply to environmental material (Section 24.3);
- personal information, protected under the Data Protection Act 2018 (s 40);
- information the disclosure of which would be an actionable breach of confidence (s 41);
- information protected by other legal obligations such as contempt of court or European law (s 44).

(b) In the following cases, the exemption applies only where it 'appears to the authority' that 'the public interest in maintaining the secrecy of the information outweighs the public interest in disclosure' (s 2(1)(b)):

- information which is held at the time of the request with a view to being published in the future, including pre-publication research information (ss 22, 22A). No particular time for publication need be set although it must be reasonable that the information be withheld; information required for the purpose of safeguarding national security (s 24). There is provision for a minister's certificate as under section 23 (above);
- defence (s 26);
- international relations (s 27);
- relations with the devolved governments (s 28);
- the economy (s 29), meaning the public finances;
- criminal proceedings or investigations and inquiries conducted by public authorities which may lead to criminal proceedings or relate to information provided by confidential sources (s 30). This would include many inquiries into matters of public concern;
- law enforcement (s 31);
- audit functions (s 33);
- information concerning the 'formulation or development' of government policy (s 35). This wide exemption includes communications between ministers, advice from civil servants, law officers and special advisers. A political party is not a public authority, so that party-orientated advice is not subject to the Act in any event. Once a decision has been taken, statistical background information can be released. It is not clear whether this exemption includes reviews of government policy already made;

- other information which 'in the reasonable opinion of a qualified person' would or would be likely to prejudice collective ministerial responsibility, or which would or would be likely to inhibit 'free and frank' provision of advice or exchange of views, or 'would otherwise prejudice or be likely to prejudice the effective conduct of public affairs' (s 36). This overlaps with s 35 (above) and again ensures that civil service and ministerial discussions remain secret. A 'qualified person' is the minister or other official in charge of the department. 'Frankness' therefore shields politicians, officials and their associates from criticism and indeed is conducive to dishonesty by lowering the risk of being caught out;
- communications with other members of the royal family (s 37); health and safety (s 38);
- environmental information (s 39): (this is subject to special provisions; Section 24.3);
- information where disclosure would be an actionable breach of confidence (s 41);
- legal professional privilege (s 42);
- trade secrets and commercial confidentiality (s 43), potentially a wide exemption given the government's prolific use of private contractors.

24.2.1 Challenging a refusal to disclose

The Information Commissioner can require the authority to disclose information either on her or his own initiative (enforcement notice, s 52) or on the application of a complainant whose request has been refused (decision notice, s 50). Reasons must be given for a refusal, and the Commissioner can, where appropriate, inspect the information in question and also require further information. Both sides may appeal to the Information Tribunal on the merits (s 57), with a further appeal to the Upper Tribunal. In security cases, the tribunal can only apply judicial review principles (s 60). The right to information can be enforced by the courts through the law of contempt, but no civil action is possible (s 56).

However, the executive has a general veto. An 'accountable person' (a Cabinet minister or the Attorney General, or their equivalents in Wales, Scotland and Northern Ireland) can serve a certificate on the Commissioner, 'stating that he has on reasonable grounds formed the opinion' that there was no failure to comply with the duty to disclose the information (s 53). Reasons must be given and the certificate must be laid before Parliament.

The veto was only used seven times in the first ten years of the lifetime of the Act (although enacted in 2000, it did not come into force until 2005). For example, in 2012 the Health Secretary Andrew Lansley vetoed publication of the government's assessment of the risks of health service reforms, and ministers have vetoed publication of the minutes of Cabinet meetings prior to the invasion of Iraq.

In *R (Evans) v Attorney General* [2015] UKSC 21, the Supreme Court (a panel of seven), overturned an attempt by the Attorney General to veto the publication of letters from the Prince of Wales to ministers advocating policy changes. The Attorney argued, in line with Plato's 'noble lie' (Section 1.6), that publication would weaken public confidence in the monarchy. The Information Commissioner and, on appeal, the Upper Tribunal, had decided that the letters should be disclosed in the interests of public knowledge of the processes of government.

The Supreme Court held that the Attorney could not override the Upper Tribunal's decision unless he objectively had reasonable grounds to do so. The majority held that it was an affront to the rule of law if the executive could overturn the decision of a court merely because it disagreed with it, and that only a 'crystal clear' statutory provision can authorise such a power (at [52]–[58], [90]). Thus, the case provides an illustration of the fundamental 'principle of legality' (Section 6.6). The majority held that s 53 allows the Attorney to intervene only if he could show 'properly explained and solid reasons', which he had not done in this case (at [129]–[130]). A minority went further and held that the Attorney could intervene only where there are new factors, or an error has been made. However, Lord Wilson dissented on the ground that only a democratically elected body should make this kind of decision (at [172]). Thus, the case illustrates once more a fundamental split in judicial attitudes to their constitutional role. Letters from the heir to the throne now have absolute immunity (above), but *Evans* is of wider significance.

Despite these safeguards, the Freedom of Information Act may reinforce the informal networking characteristic of UK government, because officials might make decisions in private without keeping records. The Butler Report (HC 2003–04, 898, Section 15.7.1) on the government's decision-making process concerning the invasion of Iraq in 2002 referred critically to 'sofa government' which side-stepped formal meetings. The long-awaited Chilcot Report (HC 2016–17, 265, Section 4.9) on the Iraq War and its aftermath made similar criticisms of the then Prime Minister's disregard of constitutional convention.

Proposals to protect ministers and senior officials from challenge

The Independent Commission on Freedom of Information comprised five government insiders: two former senior politicians (both of whom had been Home Secretaries and, as such, particularly vulnerable to FoI requests), the chair of Ofcom, the former independent reviewer of terrorism legislation and a former senior civil servant. It was established in 2015 to review the Act. The Commission's report concluded that, as a whole, the Act was working well. Apart from minor administrative changes intended to reduce delay and to facilitate disclosure by low-level bodies, its recommendations concentrated on revising sections 35 and 36 so to undo *Evans* (above). The Commission wished to protect a 'safe space' for ministers and civil servants for the 'free and frank exchange of views and advice for the purposes of deliberation'. This would apply to Cabinet and ministerial discussions and discussions by ministers and civil servants of government policy both being made and after it was made, thus preventing internal government reviews of unsuccessful polices being publicised.

The Commission's proposals on this matter were as follows:

The executive veto should be exercised only against the decision of the Information Commissioner. This removes the constitutional objection made in Evans to the executive overturning a court decision.

Where the veto is exercised there should be no right of appeal, leaving only judicial review. In other cases, an appeal against the Commissioner would be to the Upper Tribunal only and limited to a point of law.

It should be made 'clear beyond doubt' that the ministerial veto can be exercised when the minister 'takes a different view' from the Information Commissioner.

Where the Information Commissioner decides that the information should not be disclosed, the executive should have a 'confirmatory veto' which blocks any appeal.

The Commission provisionally suggested that large government contractors should be subject to the Act as regards their government work, but rejected the argument that universities should no longer be subject to the Act.

The government agreed to comply with the first proposal but otherwise only to 'carefully consider' the Commission's recommendations (written statement to House of Commons, 1 March 2016).

24.3 Other statutory rights to information

Other statutory rights to information are characterised by broad exceptions and weak or non-existent enforcement mechanisms. None of them gives access to the contemporary inner workings of the central government. The most important of them are as follows:

▶ historical records. Part VI of the Freedom of Information Act 2000 has replaced a series of Public Records Acts. A government document becomes a historical record after 20 years (reduced from 30 years by the Constitutional Reform and Governance Act 2010, Sched. 7), at which point the document is placed in the National Archives available to the public; this is enforced by the Information Commissioner. However, the Act exempts much government data, including national security matters, law and tax enforcement matters, personal data, legal proceedings and other investigations which directly affect individuals and data 'relating to the exercise of statutory functions';

▶ local government information. The Local Government (Access to Information) Act 1985 gives a public right to attend local authority meetings, including those of committees and subcommittees, and to see background papers, agendas, reports and minutes. There are wide exemptions, which include decisions taken by officers, confidential information, information from central government, personal matters excluded by the relevant committee and 'the financial or business affairs of any person'. The Act appears to be easy to evade by using officers or informal groups to make decisions. It is not clear what counts as a background paper;

- the Public Bodies (Admission to Meetings) Act 1960 gives a right to attend meetings of parish councils and certain other public bodies. The public can be excluded on the grounds of public interest (see *R v Brent HA, ex p Francis* [1985] 1 All ER 74);

- the Access to Personal Files Act 1987 authorises access to local authority housing and social work records by the subject of the records and in accordance with regulations made by the Secretary of State (see also Housing Act 1985, s 106(5));

- the EU Environmental Information Regulations, 2003/4/EC require public authorities to disclose certain information about environmental standards and measures. This is enforced by the Information Commissioner under the Freedom of Information Act 2000. Requests can be refused on grounds including manifest unreasonableness or a too general request, confidentiality, increasing the likelihood of environmental damage, information voluntarily supplied unless the supplier consents, international relations and national security. There must be a review by an independent body of a refusal to disclose information and this in turn must be reviewable by a court (Art 6). Since this is an EU requirement, the executive's power of veto (Section 24.2.1) cannot override Article 6 (*R (Evans) v Attorney General* [2014]). In EU law, the Commission can refuse access to environmental information on the familiar ground of ensuring 'thinking space' and trust between insiders: (Case T-424/14 and T-424/15 *Client Earth v Commission* (2015)). The Regulations continue to apply after Brexit.

The Data Protection Act 2018 restricts access to personal data and certain other kinds of information held by public bodies and private entities and requires such information to be protected by certain 'Data Principles' intended to ensure that the data can be used only for authorised purposes.

24.4 State secrecy: suppression of information

The state often claims to suppress information held by itself and by others, such as the media. Here the state is interfering with common law rights, and also the right of freedom of expression under Article 10 of the ECHR. The onus is therefore on the state to justify its intervention. In relation to government information, secrecy is reinforced by statutes, notably the Official Secrets Act 1989, forbidding disclosure of certain information, by the civil law of breach of confidence and by employment contracts.

24.4.1 The Official Secrets Act 1989: criminal law

The Official Secrets Act 1989 protects certain kinds of government information from unauthorised disclosure. It was enacted in response to long-standing and widespread criticism of section 2 of the Official Secrets Act 1911, which covered all information, however innocuous, concerning the central government and allowed no defence on public interest grounds (see *Departmental Committee on Section 2 of the Official Secrets Act 1911,* Cmnd 5104, 1972, the Franks Report). A series of controversial prosecutions culminated in the trial of a civil servant, Clive Ponting, in 1985, who gave information to an MP concerning alleged governmental malpractice during the Falklands War. Ponting was acquitted by a jury against the judge's summing up. Ponting's acquittal meant that the government could no longer resist reform.

Section 1 of the 1911 Act, which concerns spying activities, remains in force, but section 2 has been repealed. The Official Secrets Act 1989 is narrower but more sharply focused.

It identifies four protected areas of government activity and provides defences which vary with each area. The aim is to make enforcement more effective in respect of the more sensitive areas of government. In each case, it is an offence to disclose information without 'lawful authority'. In the case of a Crown servant or 'notified person' (below), this means 'in accordance with his official duty' (s 7). In the case of a government contractor, lawful authority means either with official authorisation or disclosure for the purpose of his or her functions as such, for example giving information to a subcontractor.

In the case of others, such as a former civil servant, lawful authority means disclosure to a Crown servant for the purpose of his or her functions as such (ss 7(3)(a), 12(1)), for example to a minister or the Director of Public Prosecutions, but not to a Member of Parliament or the police since these are not Crown servants. Alternatively, lawful authority means in accordance with an official authorisation, presumably by the head of the relevant department (ss 7(3)(b), 7(5)).

The protected areas are as follows:

Security and intelligence (s 1). This applies (i) to a member or former member of the security and intelligence services; (ii) to anyone else who is 'notified' by a minister that he or she is within this provision; (iii) to any other existing or former Crown servant or government contractor. In the cases of (i) and (ii), any disclosure is an offence unless the accused did not know and had no reasonable cause to believe that the information related to security or intelligence. The nature of the information is irrelevant. In the case of (iii), the disclosure must be 'damaging' or where the information or document is of a kind where disclosure is likely to be damaging (s 1(4)). 'Damaging' does not concern the public interest generally, but means only damaging to 'the work of the security and intelligence services'. This might include, for example, informing MPs that security agents are breaking the law. It is a defence that the accused did not know and had no reasonable cause to believe that the disclosure would be damaging.

Defence (s 2). This applies to any present or former Crown servant or government contractor. In all cases, the disclosure must be damaging. Here, damaging means hampering the armed forces, leading to death or injury of military personnel or serious damage to military equipment or installations. A similar defence of ignorance applies as under section 1.

International relations (s 3). Again, this applies to any present or former Crown servant or government contractor. Two kinds of information are covered: (i) any information concerning international relations; (ii) any confidential information obtained from a foreign state or an international organisation. The disclosure must again be damaging. 'Damaging' here refers to endangering the interests of the UK abroad or endangering the safety of British citizens abroad. The fact that information in this class is confidential in its 'nature or contents' may be sufficient in itself to establish that the disclosure is damaging (s 3(3)). There is a defence of ignorance on the same basis as under section 1 (s 3(4));

Crime and special investigation powers (s 4). This applies to present or former Crown servants or contractors and covers information relating to the commission of offences, escapes from custody, crime prevention, detection or prosecution work. 'Special investigations' include telephone tapping and electronic surveillance by the police or security services and entering on private property by the security services. Section 4 does not require that the information be damaging as such, because damage is implicit in its nature. There is, however, a defence of 'ignorance of the nature' of the information (ss 4(4)–(5)).

Section 5 makes it an offence to pass on protected information, for example by the press. Protected information is information falling within the above provisions which has come into a person's possession as a result of having been (i) 'disclosed' (whether to him or another) by a Crown servant or government contractor without lawful authority; or (ii) entrusted to him in confidence; or (iii) disclosed to him by a person to whom it was entrusted in confidence (see *Lord Advocate v The Scotsman Publications Ltd* [1990] 1 AC 812). Section 5 may not apply to a person who accidentally finds protected information, for example where a civil servant leaves her briefcase in a restaurant. Is this a 'disclosure'? It is an offence for a Crown servant or government contractor not to look after the protected information and for anyone to fail to hand it back if officially required to do so (s 8). The Crown must prove that the accused knew or had reasonable cause to believe that the information was protected under the Act and that it came into his or her possession contrary to the Act. As in the case of information falling under sections 1–3, the Crown must also show that disclosure is 'damaging' and that the accused knew or had reasonable cause to believe that this was so.

Case study: Official Secrets and the ECHR

In *R v Shayler* [2002] 2 All ER 477, the House of Lords held that section 1 did not violate the right to freedom of expression. The accused, a former member of the security services, had handed over documents to journalists which, according to him, revealed criminal behaviour by members of the services. His motive was to remove a public danger. The House of Lords held that the interference with the right to freedom of expression was proportionate. The main reason for this was that the restriction was not absolute. It allowed information to be released with 'lawful authority', thereby inviting the claimant to approach a range of 'senior and responsible Crown servants' such as the Metropolitan Police Commissioner and the Security and Intelligence Commission (at [103]). The consent of the Attorney General is required for a prosecution, although it is questionable whether this provides independence.

Lord Hutton (at [99]–[101]) went further than the others in stressing that the need to protect the secrecy of intelligence and military operations was justified as a 'pressing social need' even where the disclosure was not itself harmful to the public interest (cf. Lord Scott at [120]). This was to protect confidence in the security services. Moreover, an individual whistleblower may not be sufficiently informed of the consequences of his actions. Lord Hutton (at [105]–[106]) also rejected the argument that senior officials or politicians might be reluctant to investigate complaints of wrongdoing, holding that the court must assume that the relevant legislation is being applied properly. By contrast, Lord Hope asserted that 'institutions tend to protect their own and to resist criticism from wherever it may come' (at [70]).

The Court of Appeal had left open the possibility that a defence of necessity might apply to the Official Secrets Act 1989. This would apply only in extreme circumstances where disclosure was needed to avert an immediate threat to life, or perhaps property. The House of Lords did not comment on this issue.

24.4.2 Civil liability: breach of confidence

As we saw in Chapter 23, the publication of information given in confidence can be prevented by means of an injunction. The Crown can take advantage of this. However, a public authority must show positively that secrecy is in the public interest, which the court will balance against any countervailing public interest in disclosure. A public authority can rely on a public interest in disclosure in order to override private confidentiality even where the information has been given only for a specific purpose (see *Hellewell v Chief Constable of Derbyshire* [1995] 4 All ER 473; *Woolgar v Chief Constable of the Sussex Police* [1999] 3 All ER 604).

A civil action for breach of confidence may be attractive to governments since it avoids a jury trial; it can be speedy and requires a lower standard of proof than in a criminal case. Indeed, under common law, a temporary injunction, which against the press may destroy a topical story, could be obtained from a judge at any time on the basis merely of an arguable case (*A-G v Guardian Newspapers* [1987] 3 All ER 316).

In *A-G v Guardian Newspapers Ltd (No 2)* [1990] 1 AC 109 ('*Spycatcher*'), the House of Lords in principle supported the interests of government secrecy. Peter Wright, a retired member of the security service, had published his memoirs widely abroad, revealing possible criminality within the service, including a plot to destabilise the then Labour government. Their Lordships refused to grant a permanent injunction, but only because the memoirs were no longer secret. It was held that the relationship between the member of the security service and the Crown was one of confidence for life, and that the Crown could probably obtain compensation from Wright and from newspapers (see also *A-G v Blake* [1998] 1 All ER 833).

The position is probably the same under the HRA, subject to the limited protection provided by section 12 of the Act (Section 23.3). In *Observer and Guardian Newspapers v UK* (1992) 14 EHRR 153, the ECHR, with a strong dissent from Morenilla J, held that in the area of national security, an injunction is justifiable to protect confidential information even where the content of the particular information is not in itself harmful (see also *Sunday Times (No 2) v UK* (1992) 14 EHRR 229; *A-G v Jonathan Cape Ltd* [1976] QB 752).

The exposure of 'iniquity' (serious wrongdoing or crime) by government officers can justify disclosure (e.g. *Lion Laboratories v Evans* [1985] QB 526). In *Spycatcher,* serious iniquity was not established and it remains to be seen whether 'iniquity' overrides national security. The method of disclosure must be reasonable and the discloser must probably complain internally before going public (*Francome v Mirror Group Newspapers* [1984] 2 All ER 408).

24.5 Public interest immunity

An important aspect of government secrecy concerns the doctrine once called 'Crown privilege' and now 'public interest immunity' (PII). A party to a legal action is normally required to disclose relevant documents and other evidence in his or her possession. Where PII applies, such information must not be disclosed and cannot be used in the case (*Al Rawi v Secretary of State for the Home Department* [2012] 1 All ER 1).

In deciding whether to accept a claim of PII, the court is required to 'balance' the public interest in the administration of justice against the public interest in confidentiality. At one time, the courts would always accept the government's word that disclosure should be prohibited. However, as a result of *Conway v Rimmer* [1968] AC 910, the court itself does the balancing exercise.

Public interest immunity applies both to civil and to criminal proceedings (see Criminal Procedure and Investigations Act 1996, ss 3(6), 7(5)). Any person can raise a claim of PII. Claims are often made by ministers following advice from the Attorney General, ostensibly acting independently of the government. It appears that a minister is not under a duty to make a claim even if s/he believes that there is a public interest at stake, but must personally do an initial balancing exercise. In *R v Brown* [1993] 2 All ER 75, the court emphasised that it was objectionable for a minister automatically to accept the Attorney General's advice.

Where a PII certificate is issued, the person seeking disclosure must first satisfy the court that the document is likely to be necessary for fairly disposing of the case, or in a criminal case of assisting the defence – a less difficult burden (see *Air Canada v Secretary of State for Trade (No 2)* [1983] 2 AC 394; *Goodridge v Chief Constable of Hampshire Constabulary* [1999] 1 All ER 896; Criminal Procedure and Investigations Act 1996, s 3). The court can inspect the documents at this stage but is reluctant to do so in order to discourage 'fishing expeditions' (*Burmah Oil Co Ltd v Bank of England* [1980] AC 1090). The court will then 'balance' the competing public interests involved, at this stage inspecting the documents. The court will give great weight to statements by ministers, particularly in relation to security issues. The decision is, however, for the court, taking into account all the circumstances.

Grounds for refusing disclosure include, for example, national security, the protection of anonymous informers, or covert surveillance operations (*Rogers v Secretary of State for the Home Dept* [1973] AC 388; *D v NSPCC* [1978] AC 171), financially or commercially sensitive material such as communications between the government and the Bank of England and between the Bank and private businesses (*Burmah Oil v Bank of England* [1980]), and relationships with foreign governments.

It has also been said that preventing 'ill-informed or premature criticism of the government' is in the public interest (*Conway v Rimmer* [1968]). There is no automatic immunity for high-level documents such as Cabinet minutes, but a strong case must be made for their disclosure (see *Burmah Oil Co Ltd v Bank of England* [1980]; *Air Canada v Secretary of State for Trade (No 2)* [1983]).

The desire to protect candour and frankness within the public service may also be a justification (*Burmah Oil Co Ltd v Bank of England* [1980], at 1132) (but see *Conway v Rimmer* [1968] at 957, 976, 993–95; *R v West Midlands Chief Constable, ex p Wiley* [1994] 3 All ER 420; *Williams v Home Office (No 1)* [1981] 1 All ER 1151, 1155; *Science Research Council v Nasse* [1980] AC 1028, which contain contrary dicta).

A distinction has been made between 'class claims' and 'contents claims'. In a class claim, even if the contents of a document are innocuous, the document should still be protected because it is a member of a class of documents whose disclosure would prevent the efficient working of government, such as policy advice given by civil servants or diplomatic communications. *In R v West*

Midlands Chief Constable, ex p Wiley [1994], it was claimed that evidence given to the Police Complaints Authority was protected by class immunity. The House of Lords rejected this blanket claim, holding that immunity depended on whether the *contents* of the particular document raised a public interest, which on the facts they did not. It is not clear whether the notion of a class claim as such survives this case since their Lordships rejected the claim only in relation to that particular class of document. However, Lord Templeman remarked (at 424) that the distinction between a class and a contents claim loses 'much of its significance'.

In *R v H and C* [2004] UKHL 3, the House of Lords specified principles that must be applied, at least in a criminal case, to minimise unfairness. The government must show a pressing social need that cannot be met by less intrusive means. The parties must be given an opportunity to argue the reasons for the claim in open court and also for the procedure to be adopted. As much as possible of the material must be disclosed. Where a conviction is likely to be unsafe as a result of PII, the trial must probably be discontinued. Lord Bingham remarked that it is axiomatic that, if a person charged with a criminal offence cannot receive a fair trial, he should not be tried at all. The court should consider possible safeguards which would allow the material to be disclosed such as anonymity or inspection in a special place, or producing a summary.

If the PII claim fails, the material must be disclosed unless the person holding it concedes the issue to which it relates. The government can also abandon the case when faced with an unsuccessful PII claim. Thus, whatever the outcome, there may be unfairness. A claimant may not get the evidence he needs but, in order to protect its secrecy, the state may be unable to defend itself.

PII as such has been held not to violate the ECHR provided that the trial overall is 'fair' (*Edwards and Lewis v UK* (2003) 15 BHRC 189; *Rowe and Davies v UK* (2000) 30 EHRR 1; *Jasper v UK* (2000) 30 EHRR 441; *Fitt v UK* (2000) 30 EHRR 480).

24.6 Closed material procedure and special advocates

In certain cases involving secret evidence, such as security services cases, immigration cases heard by the Special Immigration Appeals Commission (SIAC), terrorism cases and hearings by the Parole Board, material not disclosed to the accused can be used: closed material procedure (CMP).

CMP creates unfairness to the individual by confronting him or her with evidence s/he never hears and cannot answer and violates the principle that justice must be seen to be done. This confronts the rule of law in the form of open justice, the right to a fair trial and 'equality of arms' under Article 6 of the ECHR, the right to personal freedom under Article 5(4), and freedom of expression under Article 10 of the ECHR in the form of the public right through the press to know what is being done in its name (Section 23.3.4). Closed material procedure was described by Lord Dyson as the very antithesis of public interest immunity (*Al Rawi v Secretary of State for the Home Department* [2012], [41]) since with PII, all the evidence relied on is normally heard in public and material protected by PII cannot be used at all. There is a stark choice whether to use or not use the material in issue or to abandon the case. In the case of CMP, the protected material is heard in secret. The main justification for CMP is therefore that the alternative may be no trial at all, creating unfairness to the state when it seeks to protect its security interests. Again there is a stark choice since, if PII is granted, the same material cannot later be introduced under CMP, even in the interests of the claimant (*CF v Security Service* [2014] 2 All ER 378, [56]–[58]).

An imperfect method of accommodating the conflicting concerns of fairness and security is the device of a 'special advocate'. This is a lawyer appointed by the court subject to security vetting, who acts on the accused's behalf and might see the material, but without disclosing it to the parties. A special advocate has no duty to the claimant or to take instructions from the claimant, after seeing the closed material. The special advocate's duty is only to the court. Thus, the claimant may not be able to give adequate instructions to his lawyer. This device therefore creates serious problems of fairness and raises ethical issues relating to the confidence inherent in the lawyer–client relationship.

CMP has been strongly opposed by many lawyers, and the courts have only reluctantly accepted it. In *R (Roberts) v Parole Board* [2006] 1 All ER 39, [18], Lord Bingham described the closed material procedure as 'taking blind shots at a hidden target' and thought that it could be used only where no serious unfairness was involved, for example where the relevant information could be edited or was not relied upon (at [19]) (see also Lord Dyson in *W (Algeria) v Secretary of State* [2012] 2 All ER 699, [35]; *R (BB) v SIAC* [2011] 4 All ER 210, [19]; *Tariq v Home Office* [2012] 1 AC 452, [139]). Closed material procedure has gradually been extended, providing an example of creeping erosion of individual rights in the unwritten constitution. It was originally accepted by the European Court of Human Rights in cases designated by statute before special security tribunals, provided that the person affected is given an opportunity to answer the case against him and any disadvantage is counterbalanced (*A v UK* (2009) 49 EHRR 29 [216]–[220]; *Kennedy v UK* (2011) 52 EHRR 4).

In *Home Office v Tariq* [2012], CMP was extended beyond cases where it is specifically authorised by statute. A majority of the Supreme Court upheld CMP under subordinate regulations in a case where the claimant who had been suspended from work as an immigration officer on alleged security grounds was alleging racial and religious discrimination before an employment tribunal. This was because the nature of his employment involved security vetting, and the tribunal's procedure was sufficiently flexible to provide safeguards to ensure fairness.

In *Bank Mellat v HM Treasury (No 1)* [2013] 3 WLR 179, the Supreme Court, as a panel of nine judges, reluctantly adopted CMP without clear statutory authority, even though the government could not establish that the material would affect the outcome of the appeal, or give any specific reasons why CMP should be adopted. The case concerned a Treasury Order to shut down the UK operations of an Iranian bank under counter-terrorism powers. The Supreme Court (in a five-to-four decision) held that it had an implied power under its governing statute (Constitutional Reform Act 2005) to adopt CMP. The majority's reasoning was that unless it were able to reconsider a closed judgment made at first instance to identify a possible mistake, there was a risk that injustice would be done. It transpired, however, that the material would not have affected the outcome, so CMP was not necessary. The minority, Lords Dyson, Hope, Kerr and Reed, held that CMP should not be used because the Treasury could not establish the relevance of the material. Lords Hope, Kerr and Reed went further and held that, under the 'principle of legality', the court should not have the power even in principle to use CMP without express statutory authority.

In *Al Rawi v Secretary of State for the Home Department* [2012], the Supreme Court drew the line by refusing to recognise CMP as part of the common law. It did not allow the use of closed material procedure in an ordinary civil action, in that case an action against the government for alleged complicity in torture. The court relied on the common law principle of the rule of law, as well as on the ECHR. It was held that the court has no inherent power to order the use of closed material. Any such power must come from Parliament.

Parliament duly responded at the behest of the executive. The Justice and Security Act 2013, Part 2 gives the High Court and courts above it power in all civil proceedings to use CMP. It is therefore more difficult for a claimant to challenge government evidence especially in cases where torture or mistreatment of prisoners by the government is alleged. 'Civil proceedings' do not extend to judicial review of a decision made in a criminal cause, such as a decision not to prosecute: *Belhaj v DPP* [2018] UKSC 33.

There is a two-stage process. At stage one, on an application by the Secretary of State or any party or of its own motion, the court 'may' make a declaration that 'the proceedings are proceedings in which a closed material procedure application may be made to the court' (s 6). This applies if:

1. a party would otherwise be required to disclose 'sensitive material' or would have been were it not for PII or other protection. 'Sensitive material' is material the disclosure of which would be damaging to the interests of national security (s 6(11));
2. it is in the 'interests of the fair and effective administration of justice to make a declaration' (s 6(5)).

There is no requirement that PII proceedings must first have taken place.

At stage two, on an application, the court is 'required' to limit disclosure of the sensitive information other than to the court, a special advocate or the Secretary of State (s 8). The application must always be heard in the absence of all other parties.

Rules of Court may restrict the giving of reasons for decisions, provide for a decision without a hearing, limit evidence and legal representation, and provide for hearings in the absence of parties and lawyers (s 11).

There are provisions which aim slightly to mitigate the unfairness inherent in this procedure:

1. Before making an application, the Secretary of State must consider the possibility of using PII (s 6(7)).
2. All parties must be informed of any application and its outcome (s 6(9) (10)).
3. The Act provides for the appointment of a special advocate but makes clear that the special advocate is not responsible to the person whose interests he or she represents (s 9).
4. The court must keep the declaration under review and must revoke it if it considers it to be no longer in the interests of justice (s 7).
5. The court must consider requiring the parties to be provided with a summary of material that is withheld (s 8(1)(d)).
6. Where a party chooses to withhold material without the court ordering it not to do so or chooses not to provide a summary as required by the court, the court may order that party not to rely on the relevant points.
7. The Secretary of State must report annually to Parliament on the use made of CMP in that year (s 12) and must commission a review (not necessarily by an independent person) of the working of the procedure after five years from the coming into force of the Act (s 13).

There are limits to the use of CMP under the requirement of the 'fair and effective administration of justice'. The trial must not be seriously unfair. In particular, a defendant must always have access to enough material to be able to answer the allegations against him. The overall test is whether the person concerned is given sufficient information about the allegations against him to enable him to give effective instructions (*A v UK* [2009]; *Secretary of State for the Home Dept v AF* [2010] 2 AC 269, [59]).

Relevant factors include the importance of the material to the case, what steps had been taken to safeguard the claimant's interests, alternative methods of protecting the information such as PII or a 'confidentiality ring' which limits those with access to the information, how effectively the special advocate was able to act on behalf of the claimant, caution in drawing inferences, and what difference disclosure would make. In the first case under the Act, *CF v Security Service* [2014], important factors in favour of making the declaration were that the material was essential to the case which could not be tried without it (at [43]), that alternative mechanisms would be unreliable (at [51]), and that the particular issues were raised by the claimants themselves (at [53]). However, while CMP might minimise the unfairness to the claimant, it cannot overcome the problem that justice cannot be seen to have been done (at [52]).

It seems that interference with a basic right cannot be made on the ground of closed evidence alone. In *BM v Secretary of State for the Home Dept* [2010] 1 All ER 847, the minister ordered the claimant to move to another city under a Control Order, alleging that there was a risk that he might abscond. The court set aside the minister's decision on the ground that the 'open material' showed no support for the allegation. Similarly, the majority in *Tariq* [2012] distinguished cases where detention was involved where Article 5 ECHR (personal freedom) was also in issue. In such cases, the victim should always have enough information to answer any specific allegations against him.

CMP is usually claimed by the government. However, it can also protect the individual. In *W (Algeria) v Secretary of State* [2012], the government objected to the use of closed material procedure where witnesses in a deportation case before SIAC would give evidence only in secret because they feared for the safety of their families. The Supreme Court held that CMP could be used by a claimant. Lord Dyson (at [38]) held that this applied only where Articles 2 (life) and 3 (torture) of the ECHR were at issue and not to protect Article 8 (privacy and family life).

Summary

▶ There is no general right to the disclosure of governmental information. The Freedom of Information Act 2000 confers a right to 'request' the disclosure of documents held by public authorities. However, this can often be overridden by the government and is subject to many exceptions, particularly in relation to central government policy. The Supreme Court has limited the scope of the executive veto, and the government has accepted that it will be used infrequently.

▶ There are certain statutory rights to the disclosure of specified information, but these are outnumbered by many statutes prohibiting the disclosure of particular information.

▶ Under the Official Secrets Act 1989, defined categories of information are protected by criminal penalties. Disclosure of the information must usually be damaging. There is also a defence of ignorance.

▶ The law of confidence requires the court to balance the public interest in openness against the public interest in effective government. The balance is struck differently according to context.

▶ The courts have endorsed the importance of freedom of expression, and a public body is required to show a public interest in secrecy. The main remedy is an injunction. Third parties such as the press are not directly bound by an injunction but might be liable for contempt of court if they knowingly frustrate its purpose.

▶ Public interest immunity allows the government to withhold evidence. The court makes the decision on the basis of 'balancing' the public interest in the administration of justice against the public interest in effective government. The courts' approach to public interest immunity is affected by the HRA, which requires that any claim preserve the essentials of the right to a fair trial.

▶ Proceedings might be 'closed' proceedings, where the defendant is denied direct access to the evidence against him and the public and press are excluded. Again, the essentials of the right to a fair trial must be preserved. There is also a conflict with the rule of law and Article 10 of the ECHR (freedom of the press). The device of a special advocate might be used.

Exercises

24.1 Compare public interest immunity and closed material procedure in the context of open justice and the right to a fair trial.

24.2 While on holiday in Devon, the prime minister accidentally leaves her personal diary on a train. Another passenger finds it and is delighted to see that it contains disparaging remarks about the prime minister's Cabinet colleagues. He hands it in at the office of the *Sunday Stir*. The editor informs the Prime Minister's Office that extracts from the diary will be published in next Sunday's edition. Advise the prime minister as to any legal remedy she might have.

24.3 Derek, a civil servant in the Department of Health, believes that the Cabinet minister in charge of his department has been ordering government statisticians to alter the latest NHS performance figures to show that government policies are working. Derek gives this information to the editor of the *Daily Whinge*, who contacts the relevant minister for his comments. The Attorney General immediately applies for a temporary injunction and commences an action for breach of confidence against Derek. The minister commences an action for defamation against Derek and the *Whinge*. Derek requests the production of letters between civil servants and the minister (the existence of which he learned from an anonymous email), which he claims would support his version of events. The government issues a PII certificate on the ground that the information is in a category the disclosure of which would inhibit free and frank discussion within the Cabinet. The minister who signed the certificate did not examine the information personally, but relied on advice from the Attorney General that the 'certificate will cover us for all Cabinet-level documents'. Advise Derek and the *Whinge*.

24.4 Tom has recently retired from a senior post in the intelligence services. He possesses recordings of conversations by service officials which suggest that senior ministers have requested them to fabricate evidence supporting a proposed invasion of an African country. He wishes to pass the recordings to Jerry, a journalist. Advise Tom whether he and Jerry are at risk of conviction under the Official Secrets Act 1989.

24.5 To what extent does the law adequately safeguard individual privacy against (i) police surveillance and (ii) surveillance by the security services?

24.6 Critically discuss the application of the Freedom of Information Act to discussions between ministers and between ministers and officials. To what extent does the Independent Commission on the FOIA make a useful contribution?

Further reading

Birkinshaw, 'Information; Public Access, Protecting Privacy and Surveillance' in Jowell and O'Cinneide (eds), *The Changing Constitution* (9th edn, Oxford University Press 2019)

Elliott, 'A Tangled Constitutional Web: The Black Spider Memos and the British Constitution's Relational Architecture' [2015] PL 539

Hazell and Busfield-Birch, 'Opening the Cabinet Door: Freedom of Information and Government Policy Making' [2011] PL 260

Jackson, 'Justice, Security and the Right to a Fair Trial: Is the Use of Secret Evidence Ever Fair?' [2013] PL 720

Stratford and Johnston, 'The Snowden "Revelations": Is GCHQ Breaking the Law?' [2014] EHRLR 129

Tomkins, 'National Security and Due Process of Law' (2011) 64 CLP 215

Worthy, 'More Open But Not More Trusted? The Effect of the Freedom of Information Act 2000 on UK Central Government' (2010) 23 *Governance* 561

Worthy, *The Politics of Freedom of Information* (Manchester University Press 2017)

Chapter 25

Exceptional powers: security, emergencies and terrorism

25.1 Introduction: the nature of security and emergency measures

The rule of law requires that government powers be defined by clear laws and that there should be safeguards for individual freedom. Accountability requires that citizens should be fully informed as to what government is doing. As against this, the Hobbesian minimum duty of the state is to safeguard human life by keeping order (Section 2.3.1). Hobbes believed that the people must entrust open-ended and absolute powers to government. He thought that the risk of government abusing its power was a price worth paying for security. Today, international terrorism is the outstanding risk calling for special powers.

Wide powers to deal with exceptional perils are particularly prone to fears that they may be misused. They sometimes have to be conferred and used swiftly without the normal safeguards, and they sometimes require secrecy including evidence of whether an exceptional peril exists. Thus, considerable trust must be placed in officials without the normal means of accountability. Trust is problematic because of fears that politicians and officials may be overzealous in the pursuit of their goals or may have limited competence in distinguishing between proper and improper use of their powers. Parliamentary scrutiny of legislation may be rushed or truncated, so that the laws are effectively made by a small group within the executive without consultation or checks and balances. This was the case in July 2014 when the Data Retention and Investigatory Powers Act was passed by Parliament in two days with little discussion.

Thus, Marshal J, dissenting in *Skinner v Railway Labor Executives' Association* 489 US 602 (1989), remarked (at 635–636): 'When we allow fundamental freedoms to be sacrificed in the name of real or perceived exigency, we invariably come to regret it'.

A pervasive issue is that of secrecy (Chapter 24). Openness is important for democratic accountability, trust in government and fairness in the courts. On the other hand, secrecy is justifiable to prevent hostile elements from countering measures and to protect the safety of government agents and confidential sources. Secrecy may also be needed in the interests of cooperation with foreign governments.

Secrecy can also be justified for purposes unrelated specifically to special powers, such as the protection of personal privacy, protection of trade secrets and professional confidentiality between lawyer and client. More dubiously, secrecy is claimed to enhance government efficiency by encouraging frank discussion within official circles and by enabling decisions to be taken by experts without the danger of public panic if disclosures are misunderstood, or policymaking inhibited by premature criticism, or the quality of discussion diluted by the temptation to play to the gallery. It has even been suggested that secrecy, by hiding weaknesses, enhances public confidence in government (Section 1.6).

25.1.1 Security and the courts

Emergency action may violate the rule of law in several respects.

There may be a temptation to use torture or detention without trial. Torture is absolutely prohibited by the ECHR (Section 21.4.1).

Vaguely defined powers, such as random stop and search, or intrusive surveillance, may be misapplied because the needs of an emergency favour flexibility. For example, in 2009, on the pretext of community protection against local anti-social behaviour, the West Midlands police established large-scale CCTV surveillance in a predominantly Muslim area of Birmingham without local oversight and concealing its true purpose, which was national counterterrorism (*Guardian* 1 October

2010). Minorities might also be targeted in the belief that those who do not support majority lifestyles are a security risk.

Safeguards such as judicial review might be restricted, or the judicial review doctrine that powers must be used reasonably and for proper purposes frustrated by the wide terms in which the powers are conferred.

Evidence in legal proceedings may be restricted and open justice impeded by secret court hearings (Section 24.6).

Measures introduced to meet an emergency may become permanent and be increased over time. A 'sunset clause' can be included under which a measure lapses unless renewed by a vote in Parliament. However, obtaining such a vote is not difficult.

Jury trial may be removed (e.g. Northern Ireland (Emergency Provisions) Act 1978).

Measures intended to deal with serious threats might be used against trivial offences, or for political purposes. Laws cast in wide terms are not necessarily ambiguous, so ministerial reassurances about the scope of the legislation cannot be used as an aid to interpretation under the *Pepper v Hart* [1993] AC 593 doctrine (Section 7.7.2). For example, anti-terrorist powers have been used against peace protesters (*Gillan v UK* [2010] ECHR 28) and against an elderly person who objected to the invasion of Iraq at a Labour Party conference (*Guardian* 8 October 2005).

25.1.2 Derogation

A state can derogate from some Articles of the ECHR in times of war or other public emergency threatening 'the life of the nation' (Art 15; HRA, ss 1(2), 14, 15). Article 2 (the right to life) cannot be derogated from except in respect of deaths resulting from lawful acts of war; nor can Article 3 (torture and inhuman and degrading treatment), Article 4(1) (slavery), Article 7 (retrospective punishment) or Protocol 6 (capital punishment).

The state must show that the threat is current or imminent, that the measures are a necessary response to the emergency and that other international obligations are not violated. There must also be judicial review by an independent court (*Chahal v UK* (1996) 23 EHRR 413). The European Court has given states a wide margin of appreciation and is reluctant to attribute improper motives to a government (see *Lawless v Ireland (No 3)* (1961) 1 EHRR 15; *Brannigan and McBride v UK* (1993) 17 EHRR 539; *Klass v Federal Republic of Germany* (1979) 2 EHRR 214; *Brogan v UK* (1989) 11 EHRR 117).

The definition of 'emergency' is not clear. The criteria are that the threat be actual or imminent, that its effects involve the whole nation, that the organised life of the community be at risk, and that the crisis be exceptional so that normal measures are plainly inadequate (see *Lawless v Ireland (No 3)* [1961]). *A v Secretary of State for the Home Dept* [2005] 2 AC 68 concerned a derogation order to give effect to Section 23 of the Anti-Terrorism, Crime and Security Act 2001 authorising the indefinite detention of foreign terrorist suspects. A majority of the House of Lords deferred to the government's view that an emergency existed in the shape of the terrorist threat following the 9/11 attacks. Lord Hoffmann took a different view. He suggested that an emergency existed only when the basic principles of democracy and the rule of law were threatened, and that a high risk of terrorist attack was not in itself evidence of this. Indeed, he suggested that government measures of the type in issue were a greater threat to democracy.

However, on the separate question of the necessity of the response, the House set aside the derogation order on the ground that it was disproportionate and made a declaration of incompatibility in respect of the statute (Section 22.5.2).

In deciding whether an exceptional interference with a Convention right is justified, the courts are particularly concerned with safeguards to prevent an abuse of power. These try to strike a balance by requiring basic standards of the rule of law. They include:

▶ powers being defined in detail by clear publicly announced laws (see *R (Gillan) v Metropolitan Police Commissioner* [2006] 4 All ER 1041, [31]);

- the safeguards of access to a lawyer and judicial supervision;
- the right to a fair trial, including the right to challenge evidence (*Secretary of State for the Home Department v MB* [2008] 1 All ER 657).

Traditionally, the UK courts regarded matters of national security as non-justiciable, relying on ministerial accountability to Parliament as a safeguard. *Liversidge v Anderson* [1942] AC 206 was a notorious case where the governing legislation stated that the minister must have 'reasonable cause' to believe that a person was an enemy alien, but still the House of Lords refused to intervene (but note Lord Atkin's classic dissent accusing the majority of trashing the statute). However, in *R v IRC ex p Rossminster* [1980] 1 All ER 80, at 93, Lord Diplock said that the time has come to acknowledge that the *Liversidge* majority were wrong (see also Lord Scarman, at 104).

Lord Diplock also said in *Council of Civil Service Unions (CCSU) v Minister for the Civil Service* [1985] AC 374: '[N]ational security is par excellence a non-justiciable question. The judicial process is totally inept to deal with the type of problems which it involves'. However, even in the *CCSU* case, the government had to show that it was acting in good faith and that the matter (the effectiveness of GCHQ, the government's centre for electronic interception) was genuinely one of national security.

In recent years, the UK courts have been more willing to interfere with national security powers. The jurisprudence of the ECHR has invited the courts to apply the proportionality principle, thus increasing the intensity of review (e.g. *A v Secretary of State for the Home Dept*, above).

On the other hand, the 'margin of discretion' enables the courts to defer particularly to the government's use of information, its assessment of risk and its use of secrecy since these are matters with which judicial experience is not comfortable (Section 22.9.3; see Poole (2008)). For example, in *R (Mohamed) v Secretary of State for Foreign Affairs* [2010] 3 WLR 554, the Court of Appeal held that a statement of the government that national security was threatened was not conclusive but would be overruled only if it was irrational or without evidence (see also *Secretary of State for Foreign and Commonwealth Affairs v Assistant Deputy Coroner for North London* [2013] EWHC 3724 (Admin), [57]).

25.2 The security and intelligence services

The 'secret services' comprise the security services, the intelligence services and the government communications centre, GCHQ. Traditionally, they have operated under the general law without special powers other than the possibility of royal prerogative power. They were, in principle, accountable to ministers, ultimately the prime minister, but there was no formal mechanism for parliamentary accountability. Their role has been primarily that of information gathering. Where powers of arrest or interference with property were required, the assistance of the police was requested. However, the *Spycatcher* litigation (see Section 24.4.2) brought to a head recurrent concerns that security agents were out of control and unaccountable, and they have now been placed within a statutory framework. This relies heavily on the discretionary powers of ministers, but contains certain safeguards, albeit judicial review is restricted.

The security services (formerly MI5) deal with internal security (Security Service Act 1989, as amended by Intelligence Services Act 1994). They report to the prime minister. Their responsibilities include:

> the protection of national security and, in particular, its protection against threats from espionage, terrorism and sabotage, from the activities of agents of foreign powers, and from actions intended to overthrow or undermine parliamentary democracy by political or violent means. (s 1)

Section 1(3) includes the safeguarding of 'the economic well-being of the UK against threats posed by the actions or intentions of persons outside the British Islands'. This is extremely wide and could extend, for example, to the lawful activities of environmental non-governmental organisations (NGOs). The Security Service Act 1996 extends the functions of the security services to include assisting the police in the prevention and detection of serious crime. This includes the use of violence, crimes resulting in substantial financial gain, conduct by a large number of persons in pursuit of a common purpose, or crimes carrying a sentence of three years or more. This is wide enough to include political public order offences and industrial disputes and may violate ECHR notions of clarity and proportionality.

The intelligence services (formerly MI6, now SIS, and GCHQ) deal with threats from outside the UK. They are governed by the Intelligence Services Act 1994. They are under the control of the Foreign Office but also report to the prime minister. Their functions are 'to obtain and provide information relating to the actions and intentions of persons outside the British Islands' and 'to perform other tasks relating to the actions and intentions of such persons'. GCHQ monitors electronic communications and 'other emissions' and can provide advice and information to the armed forces and other organisations specified by the prime minister. Reflecting the ECHR, their powers are limited to national security, with particular reference to defence and foreign policies, the economic wellbeing of the UK in relation to the actions and intentions of persons outside the British Islands, and the prevention and detection of serious crime (ss 1(2), 3(2)).

Neither service must take action to further the interests of any political party (Security Service Act 1989, s 52(2); Intelligence Services Act 1994, s 2(3)).

Under sections 5 and 6 of the Intelligence Services Act 1994, all the intelligence agencies can enter property or interfere with wireless telegraphy under a warrant issued by the Secretary of State or Scottish ministers. Contravention is 'unlawful', but not a criminal offence. In the case of SIS and GCHQ, a warrant cannot relate to property in the UK, but the Secretary of State can authorise SIS and GCHQ to carry out actions overseas that would be a crime or civil wrong in the UK (s 7). (This does not of course affect any liability in the overseas country concerned.) In relation to the police support role of the security service, a warrant can be issued only in the case of more serious crimes (see Intelligence Services Act 1994, s 5, as amended by Security Service Act 1996).

25.3   Surveillance, interception and acquisition of information

The problem of the state amassing information about individuals is of concern because of increasingly sophisticated surveillance and data storage and transfer technology. This is not only because of the risk to democratic freedoms of the abuse of power, but also because of the accidental escape or misuse of information. On the other hand, public opinion generally does not appear to object to mass surveillance. Many, if not most, people are prepared to place information about themselves on the internet, even though this potentially becomes available to anyone.

The common law originally provided little protection to the individual. It did not recognise a right of privacy and assumed that royal prerogative power to intercept the mail could extend to telephone tapping (see *Malone v MPC* [1979] Ch 344). However, this has been changed by the ECHR. Under Article 8 (privacy), there must be safeguards in respect of surveillance. These must include clearly defined limits on the power and supervision by an independent court (*Malone v UK* (1984) 7 EHRR 14; *Khan v UK* (2001) 31 EHRR 1016). Moreover, retaining data falling within Article 8 after it has been used for the authorised purposes is a violation, unless there is a particular reason for suspicion against that person (*Amann v Switzerland* [2000] ECHR 88) (see also Section 23.7.2).

An elaborate network of provisions authorising various forms of surveillance and interception has emerged over the years. These provisions include both human and electronic surveillance, the interception of phone and internet communications, and the acquisition of data, as well as the retention of data harvested from electronic systems including the internet both targeted at individuals and in bulk including data from people not suspected of any wrongdoing ('bulk personal datasets', see Investigatory Powers Act 2016, Parts 6 and 7). These powers are subject to Art 8 of the ECHR (respect for privacy) and, in the case of journalistic matters, to Art 10 (freedom of expression). Thus, they must be shown to be necessary and proportionate and used only for specified purposes, such as national security, the economic wellbeing of the country, then public interest in preventing or detecting serious crime (see e.g. Investigatory Powers Act 2016, s.2).

The present law is based upon the Regulation of Investigatory Powers Act 2000 (RIPA), as substantially modified by the Investigatory Powers Act 2016 (IPA), which rationalises the present array of powers. The powers available to the intelligence services, the police and certain other public bodies include warrants for the interception and examination of data, authorisations for obtaining 'communications data' (which are data concerning the source or destination of a message, but not its content), requiring service providers such as internet companies to retain communications data, and giving access to the government, warrants for equipment interference, and 'bulk' warrants which enable the security services to intercept data from unspecified persons. The 2016 Act broadly continues the same powers as contained in earlier legislation but adds controversial new powers, especially in respect of the retention of data (below). The provisions of IPA came into force in stages, with the final provisions taking effect in 2020.

In most cases, a warrant from or authorisation of the Secretary of State or a member of the Scottish government, acting personally, is required (IPA, s 30). There are more stringent thresholds and safeguards for issuing warrants or authorisations in respect of particular kinds of data, such as personal information. For example, 'bulk personal datasets' (IPA, Part 7) consist of personal information about several persons, most of which are of no interest to the security services. There is protection in this case for health records and sensitive personal information. There is additional protection for MPs and the devolved legislatures (permission of the prime minister is required), legal professional privilege, and journalistic material and sources, albeit these seem to require only that special consideration be given to these matters (e.g. IPA, ss 26, 27, 28 and 29). The Secretary of State must make 'arrangements' to prevent data being used for purposes other than those for which it was acquired or falling into the hands of other persons, although there is no systematic policing of this (e.g. IPA, ss 150–153).

In addition to a warrant from the Secretary of State, or authorisation by a senior public official, authorisation from a judge is required in many cases: 'the double lock'. However, the last usually requires only the judicial review level of scrutiny, so that the judge does not investigate factual issues unless there is a clear error. The judicial review powers of the courts are further limited by the wide powers involved, the court's traditional reluctance to investigate security matters deeply and the use of public interest immunity (Section 24.5) and closed material procedure (Section 24.6).

Under various statutes, there was a profusion of special regulators to supervise the exercise of surveillance, interception and data retention powers by the security and intelligence services and by the police and other bodies, albeit the same persons sometimes combined several offices. The protection a regulator offers is limited, since the victim may be unaware of the conduct in question. Much depends upon trusting officials to behave lawfully and internal auditing and monitoring to be carried out conscientiously. Thus, apart from the specific regulators, the Secretary of State or Scottish Ministers are responsible for ensuring that warrants are issued for proper purposes and are proportionate (see e.g. IPA, ss 19–21).

Part 8 of the 2016 Act replaces the different regulators by a single body comprising Judicial Commissioners, who must be judges of High Court level or above, led by an Investigatory Powers Commissioner (IPC) who is also a senior judge. Judicial Commissioners authorise the issue of warrants and other authorisations under the Act. The IPC keeps the operation of the Act under review but has no investigatory or enforcement powers in individual cases. It reports to the prime minister, who must lay its Annual Report before Parliament. The IPC and the Judicial Commissioner are formally appointed by the prime minister, who must act on the recommendation of the Lord Chancellor, the heads of the judiciary in England and Wales, Scotland and Northern Ireland and, in the case of the other Judicial Commissioners, the IPC. However, the prime minister decides the number of Judicial Commissioners.

There is also an Investigatory Powers Tribunal which hears allegations of misuse of power by the security services and other public officials. Its procedure includes special powers to hear evidence in secret (Section 24.6). In human rights cases, it has been designated as the only forum for human rights challenges against any of the intelligence services (HRA, s 7). The tribunal may award compensation, quash warrants or authorisations, and order records to be destroyed. The tribunal is required to apply judicial review principles (RIPA, s 67, as amended by IPA, s 243). In view of the wide powers involved, this affords only a low level of review.

Previously, decisions of the tribunal could not be questioned in the courts, even on jurisdictional grounds (RIPA, s 67(8)). However, in *R (Privacy International v Investigatory Powers Tribunal* [2019] UKSC 22, a majority of the Supreme Court, applying the *Anisminic* principle (Section 19.7.2) determined that only a legally valid decision as to jurisdiction was immune from judicial review. Lord Sumption, dissenting, considered that the rule of law was sufficiently protected by the judicial character of the tribunal. IPA, s 242 now provides for appeal on a point of law from the tribunal to the Court of Appeal or the Court of Session.

There is an Intelligence and Security Committee composed of backbench members of both Houses, which examines the spending, administration and policy of the intelligence services (Justice and Security Act 2013, Part 1). The committee can review the expenditure, administration, policy and operations of the security services and GCHQ and, subject to a 'memorandum of understanding' with the government, can consider intelligence and security relating to other government departments. The Act also requires the Intelligence Services Commissioner, if directed by the prime minister, to keep under review designated activities of the intelligence services or their heads, the armed forces, and the Ministry of Defence (s 5).

However, the committee is under substantial executive control, lacking the full independence of a normal parliamentary committee. In particular, its members must be nominated by the prime minister in consultation with the leader of the Opposition. Its powers to review operational matters are limited by the need for the consent of the prime minister. It can require the disclosure of information, but subject to a veto by the Secretary of State on the grounds that the information is 'sensitive' or in the interests of national security or on the various grounds that restrict requests for information by other parliamentary committees (see Sched. 1).

The committee's annual report is laid before Parliament but can be censored beforehand by the prime minister after consultation with the committee. The committee is therefore not a normal parliamentary committee responsible only to the House.

Types of investigatory power covered by RIPA and IPA

In *AJA and Others v Metropolitan Police Commissioner* [2013] EWCA Civ 1342, [8], [9], Lord Dyson MR summarised the regulatory requirements of RIPA as applying to the following six covert investigatory powers in descending order of intrusiveness:

  (i) interception of communications including telephone tapping and internet surveillance (Section 25.3.2);
  (ii) intrusive surveillance (above);
  (iii) demands for decryption;
  (iv) CHIS (covert human intelligence sources);
  (v) directed surveillance (above);
  (vi) acquisition of communications data such as origins and destinations of phone messages and websites visited, but not content (Section 25.3.3).

In the following sections, certain particular powers will be discussed.

25.3.1 Surveillance

Surveillance means intelligence-gathering activity without the awareness or participation of the person subject to it (*Re a Complaint of Surveillance* [2014] 2 All ER 576). Under Section 48(2) of RIPA it includes: (a) monitoring, observing or listening to persons, their movements, their conversations or their other activities or communications; (b) recording anything monitored, observed or listened to in the course of surveillance. However, recording a voluntary interview with an official is apparently not surveillance, even if the subject is unaware of the recording (*Re a Complaint of Surveillance* (above)).

'Directed surveillance' is covert surveillance undertaken as part of a specific operation to obtain private information about a person (RIPA, s 26), and 'intrusive surveillance'. Intrusive surveillance is covert surveillance carried out in relation to anything taking place on residential premises, or in a private vehicle where an individual is planted or a covert surveillance device is used.

RIPA also regulates the use of covert human intelligence (ss 26, 29). This includes undercover officers, spies and informers, for example police officers joining political activist groups.

Low-level public bodies such as local councils have been using their surveillance powers casually. Local authorities have allegedly authorised directed surveillance powers routinely to combat relatively minor matters such as litter dropping and school attendance. However, the Protection of Freedoms Act 2012, ss 37 and 38, introduces a requirement for approval by a magistrate of local authority authorisations for surveillance and covert human intelligence.

The use of covert surveillance devices by the police is also regulated by the Police Act 1997, and the two regimes overlap. Part III of the 1997 Act authorises the police to interfere with property for the purpose of preventing or detecting 'serious crime'. For this purpose, serious crime means crime involving violence, substantial financial gain, or conduct by a large number of persons in pursuit of a common purpose (s 93(4)). Thus, political groups may be vulnerable. The action must be 'necessary' and 'proportionate'. The exercise of the power must be authorised by a designated senior police officer, a military officer, a customs and revenue officer, or an officer of certain other law enforcement agencies. In certain cases, the authorisation must be by a Judicial Commissioner (Section 25.3.3). This includes dwellings, hotel bedrooms and offices, and matters likely to involve legal professional privilege, confidential personal information or confidential journalistic material. The 1997 Act also imposes duties on private communication providers such as internet service providers (ISPs) to cooperate with the authorities.

25.3.2 Interception of postal, telephone and internet communications

By virtue of IPA s 3, it is an offence intentionally and without lawful authority to intercept a communication while it is being transmitted by means of a public postal service or a public telecommunications system (which includes any electronic means of transmission such as emails and social media on the internet). It is also an offence intentionally and without lawful authority to intercept a communication transmitted through a private telecommunications system (e.g. a company network, except by the controller of the system or with his or her consent (*R v Sargent* [2003] 1 AC 347)).

'Lawful authority' is conferred on a range of public officers. Under s 18, the leaders of law enforcement and intelligence agencies, including tax authorities, can seek interception warrants from the Secretary of State via a Crown officer. Interception powers must normally identify the persons or premises concerned. However, the Secretary of State can issue a 'bulk warrant', which is in effect a general warrant authorising the blanket interception of material of any number of unidentified persons in respect of 'overseas-related communications', that is, communications which are either sent or received outside the British Islands (IPA, Parts 6 and 7). Since most commercial internet companies operate outside the UK, this covers perhaps millions of ordinary citizens who use social networks. However, such powers were held not to be incompatible with Arts 8 and 10 ECHR in *R (Liberty) v Secretary of State for the Home Department* [2019] EWHC 2057 (Admin), as the 2016 Act had put in place sufficient safeguards against the risk of abuse of such powers. Warrants to interfere with electronic equipment can also be issued by the Secretary of State and Scottish Ministers on the application of the intelligence services, and senior law enforcement officers (IPA, Part 5). In all cases, there is a 'double lock' in that the approval of a Judicial Commissioner is also required.

Anyone in lawful possession of intercepted information can require the disclosure of the key to protected (encrypted) data on the grounds of national security, prevention or detection of crime, in the interests of the economic wellbeing of the UK, or, more dubiously, that it is necessary for the purpose of securing the effective exercise or proper performance by any public authority of any statutory power or statutory duty (RIPA, s 49). A disclosure notice must be authorised by a circuit judge. A disclosure notice requested by the police, the security services or the customs and excise commissioners can also impose a lifelong secrecy requirement as to the existence of the notice (RIPA, s 54).

There are wide restrictions on disclosing interception matters in legal proceedings. Evidence cannot normally be given disclosing any content of an intercepted communication or secondary data obtained from such a communication, or 'tending to suggest' that there has been or is about to be 'interception-related conduct' (IPA, s 56). Information obtained by interception is not therefore admissible. There are exceptions, mainly for proceedings concerning the surveillance legislation itself. However, information obtained from interception can be used in police interviews and presumably by the executive for other purposes (*R v Sargent* [2003]). Information obtained by other bugging devices, and undercover agents, is admissible in court (*R v Khan (Sultan)* [1996] 3 All ER 289).

25.3.3 Communications data

A senior public official including the police and a local authority can obtain electronic 'communications data' from postal or telephone companies (IPA, Part 3). Communications data do not include the content of a message. They include 'source data' identifying the person using the service, 'traffic data' identifying the source and destination of a message, 'use data' (e.g. billing data) and any other information which the service provider holds about the user and the source and destination of a message (see IPA, ss 261(5), 262(3)).

Although this power might be regarded as less intrusive, in light of the decision of the CJEU in C-203/15 and C-698/15 *Tele2 Sverige AB v Post-och telestyrelsen and Secretary of State for the Home Department v Watson and Others* [2017] QB 771 that access to communications data must normally be subject to prior review by a court or an independent administrative body, the government conceded that most communications data requests should be subject to independent authorisation. This is carried out by the IPC (IPA, s 60A), who delegates the function to an Office for Communications Data Authorisations. Authorisation can only be obtained for a limited range of purposes specified in s 60A(7), and the conduct authorised must be proportionate to what is sought to be achieved.

The *retention* of communications data is also controversial. On the one hand, there is increasing use of the internet by terrorists and other criminals. On the other hand, there are fears that the government may abuse the power, for example by using it for trivial purposes, or by making data available to foreign governments or to commercial companies. The government used to rely on an EU directive authorising the general retention of data (Directive 2006/25/EC). However, this was set aside by the CJEU on the ground that it violated the European Charter of Rights (similar to the ECHR in this context). Its purpose, to combat terrorism and serious crime, was valid, but it was disproportionate in that it lacked clear rules about safeguards, the time limit was too long, it did not require the irreversible destruction of retained data, and it did not require the data to be retained within the EU (Cases C-293/12 and C-594/12 *Digital Rights Ireland v Minister for Communications, Marine and Natural Resources* [2014] ECR I-238).

The Data Retention and Investigatory Powers Act 2014, which conferred new powers to retain communications data, was rushed through Parliament without detailed discussion in two days in order to overcome the loss of the Directive. This Act automatically expired at the end of December 2016 by virtue of a 'sunset clause'. Section 1 of this Act was determined to have been inconsistent with EU law in *Secretary of State for the Home Department v Watson* [2018] EWCA Civ 70, following the *Tele 2 Sverige* case (above). Meantime, new powers in respect of the obtaining and retention of communications data were enacted by IPA, Part 4.

The Act empowers the Secretary of State to issue a 'Data Retention Notice' requiring service providers to retain and disclose communications data and specifying the method and time of retention for a maximum of 12 months and to make further regulations. Again, communication data can only be retained for a limited range of purposes, that which relates to 'the economic well-being of the UK' only where national security is also involved, thus lessening the risk that the government will sell data to business interests (s 87). Following the *Watson* case and *R (Liberty) v Secretary of State for the Home Department* [2018] EWHC 975 (Admin), only the prevention or detection of *serious* crime is now a permissible purpose. A Data Retention Notice must be authorised by a Judicial Commissioner (s 89). The 2016 Act also consolidates other powers of surveillance and interception and repeals various such powers under other legislation.

The 2016 Act also gives the Secretary of State powers, subject to judicial approval, to interfere with the systems and arrangements made by service providers. These include 'technical capability notices' (s 253), which require service providers to provide assistance in relation to warrants or authorisations and 'national security notices' which require service providers to assist the security services in other respects (s 252). It is not clear whether service providers must decrypt data under these powers. Service providers can also be required to put in place filtering arrangements in order to select material for retention (s 67).

25.3.4   CCTV cameras

Apart from the general law of privacy (Section 23.5), there are no restrictions on the use of CCTV cameras in public places. The Protection of Freedoms Act 2012, Part 2 introduces a familiar weak version of regulation. The Act requires the Secretary of State to prepare and publish a code of practice containing guidance about the use of surveillance cameras and information obtained from them. Various local government bodies must 'have regard to' the code when exercising their functions. The code is admissible as evidence but is not directly enforceable (s 33). A Surveillance Camera Commissioner has advisory powers and publishes an annual report to be laid before Parliament.

It seems that the risk of being photographed in public must be regarded as one of the 'ordinary incidents of living in a free community' (*Campbell v MGN* [2004] 2 All ER 995, at [122]). However, the matter depends on the particular context. It is important to consider the purposes of the intrusion and what are the normal conditions to be expected in public encounters. For example, in *R (Gillan) v MPC* [2006], at [28] Lord Bingham suggested that routine security checks at airports do not reach a sufficient 'level of seriousness' to qualify for Article 8 protection. The same probably applies to ordinary CCTV coverage in commercial premises and on public transport, at least if a public warning of the presence of the cameras is given. By contrast, in *Peck v UK* (2003) 13 BHRC 669, CCTV footage taken for security purposes was subsequently published to show the applicant attempting to commit suicide. This was held to go far beyond any security observation that he could have foreseen when in that street. It is arguable that training a camera on a specific individual without good reason for suspicion is an infringement of Article 8 ECHR.

25.4   Emergency powers

It was established in the eighteenth century that, under the common law, the executive has no special powers in an emergency, but only the power available to anyone of self-defence, the defence of others, and of preventing a breach of the peace; thus illustrating Dicey's version of the rule of law. The police have a general common law power to prevent a breach of the peace (Section 23.7.2). There is no legal obstacle to the armed forces, or indeed anyone else, being used in support of this. Indeed, perhaps everyone has a duty to aid the civil power in quelling a disturbance (*Charge to the Bristol Grand Jury* (1832) 5 C & P 535). An individual, whether policeman, soldier or private person acting in self-defence is, however, liable for the excessive use of force. The force used must be no more than is reasonable in the circumstances for self-defence or the defence of others (see Criminal Law Act 1967, s 3). In deciding what is reasonable the court will take into account the pressure of the circumstances (see *A-G for Northern Ireland's Reference (No. 1)* [1977] AC 105; *McCann v UK* (1995) 21 EHRR 97). Obedience to orders as such is probably not a defence (*Keighley v Bell* (1866) 4 F and F 763) but should be taken into account as an aspect of reasonableness.

Under the royal prerogative, subject to the common law principles above, the armed forces can be deployed at the discretion of the Crown, and the Crown can also arm the police (Section 14.6.1). The Crown may also enter private property in an emergency but must pay compensation for any damage caused other than in wartime (War Damage Act 1965; *Saltpetre Case* (1607) 12 Co Rep 12; *A-G v De Keyser's Royal Hotel* [1920] AC 508).

Beyond this is the possibility that where there is such a serious disruption to public order that the courts cannot function, the military may assume control under a state of martial law. Dicey denied that martial law is part of English law ((1915) ch 8). However, martial law has been applied in colonial territories (and was declared in Ireland in 1920). The House of Lords accepted that the courts could, in principle, control the activities of the military under martial law (*Re Clifford and O'Sullivan* [1921] 2 AC 570). However, even with the ritual of 'reading the Riot Act', martial law can probably confer no greater powers than those available under the common law (above) (see *Marais v General Officer Commanding* [1902] AC 109).

Statute, of course, has no such limits and exceptional executive powers can be conferred by emergency regulations (Civil Contingencies Act 2004 (CCA)). They can be made by Order in Council, or, if this would cause serious delay, by a senior minister, if the relevant authority is satisfied that an emergency exists or is imminent, that there is an urgent need to deal with it, and that existing legislation is inadequate for the purpose. Thus, there need be no declaration of a formal state of emergency or approval by Parliament to trigger the powers. However, the powers lapse unless approved by Parliament within seven days (s 27) and must be renewed at 30-day intervals (s 27(4)).

An emergency is more widely defined than for the purpose of derogating from the ECHR (Section 25.1). An emergency means:

> an event or situation which threatens serious damage to human welfare or the environment in the United Kingdom or in a part or region, or war or terrorism which threatens serious damage to the security of the United Kingdom. (s 19(1))

These threats are widely drawn. Human welfare includes loss of life, illness or injury, homelessness, property damage, disruption of supplies of money, food, water, energy and fuel, or disruption of a communication system, facilities for transport or health services. Environmental damage is limited to biological, chemical or radioactive contamination or disruption to or destruction of plant or animal life (ss 19(2)–(3)). An emergency might include, for example, a general strike, a natural disaster or epidemic, or a terrorist threat.

It is clear that the COVID-19 pandemic falls within the Act and it is interesting to speculate why government instead asked Parliament to enact specific primary legislation in this context (Coronavirus Act 2020) and has additionally created numerous pieces of delegated legislation, much of it under other statutory powers such as the Public Health (Control of Disease) Act 1984 (as amended). One possibility is that the government wished to circumvent protections associated with duration. Under the CCA, Parliament must meet within five days and the regulations lapse unless approved by Parliament within seven days and in any event after 30 days. In both cases, they can be renewed (ss 26, 27). However, s 98 of the 2020 Act permits a Commons debate on the continuation of the Act only after six months.

The CCA allows individual ministers to alter statutes. It confers powers on ministers to deploy the armed forces, to require people to perform unpaid functions and provide information, to restrict freedom of movement and assembly, to take or destroy property without compensation (s 22), and to extend the power to detain without trial. There are similar powers conferred by the Coronavirus Act 2020 for ministers and the devolved governments to alter primary legislation through secondary legislation (s 92).

The CCA contains safeguards based on the ECHR. These include proportionality and compliance with Convention rights. The powers can be used only for the specific purpose of dealing with the threats created by the emergency. There can be no military conscription or outlawing of industrial action. No offence can be created except one triable summarily by magistrates or the Sheriff's Court in Scotland and not punishable with more than three months' imprisonment. Criminal procedure cannot be altered, nor HRA (CCA, s 23). Judicial review is not specifically preserved, but 'regard' must be had to its importance (CCA, s 22(5)).

25.5 Anti-terrorism measures

The UK's anti-terrorism laws illustrate the phenomenon of 'creep', as increasingly wide powers introduced in response to particular events are becoming absorbed into the general law. They also illustrate the importance of safeguards comprising access to independent courts, monitoring bodies and parliamentary mechanisms. The problem of terrorism tests the limits of human rights law. Terrorist activities present challenges going beyond ordinary crimes, and so require special legislation. In particular, in view of the large, random and horrific nature of the consequences intended to frighten and demoralise the public, and the ruthlessness of the perpetrators, often working within secretive well-organised networks, there is a need for precautionary action at an early stage and for secrecy and specialist expertise with resulting limitations on judicial review. On the other hand, treating terrorism as different from ordinary crime may help to give the perpetrators the publicity that they seek.

To legitimise special measures, the rhetoric of 'war on terror' is sometimes substituted for that of law enforcement. This rhetoric and the publicity generated may encourage the very terrorism that it seeks to combat. Moreover, the width of the powers which are sometimes not limited to terrorism means that they may be used against non-violent people whose activities the government dislikes or whom the police or local officials find it convenient to target. For example, anti-terrorist legislation was used to remove a member who objected to the invasion of Iraq from a Labour Party conference (*Guardian* 8 October 2005).

Special anti-terrorism laws were originally enacted as emergency provisions in response to the conflict in Northern Ireland (see Northern Ireland (Emergency Provisions) Act 1978 (EPA); Prevention of Terrorism (Temporary Provisions) Act 1974 (PTA)). These Acts created two distinct anti-terrorism regimes in the UK since there were additional measures in Northern Ireland (e.g. trial without a jury and detention without trial). The EPA and PTA were intended to be temporary and only apply to terrorism cases but were repeatedly re-enacted, extended and modified. Some of the powers in the PTAs and EPAs were mirrored in new laws to deal with ordinary crime in the UK as a whole. Thus, the extraordinary powers had become ordinary.

The law is now based on the Terrorism Act 2000 (TA) which, following the Lloyd Report (Cm 3420, 1996), created a permanent comprehensive code. In response to a series of terrorist atrocities and also to adverse court rulings (e.g. *A v Secretary of State for the Home Dept* [2005]; *Secretary of State for the Home Department v JJ* [2008] 1 All ER 613), this was amended and supplemented by the Anti-Terrorism, Crime and Security Act 2001 (ATCSA), the Prevention of Terrorism Act 2005, the Terrorism Act 2006, the Counter-Terrorism Act 2008, the Terrorism Prevention and Investigation Measures Act 2011, the Counter-Terrorism and Security Act 2015 and the Counter-Terrorism and Border Security Act 2019.

These measures have fluctuated between liberalising and strengthening the law in response to short-term political considerations. A terrorist suspect may invoke most of the main human rights including Article 3 (torture and inhuman or degrading treatment or punishment), Article 5 (personal liberty), Article 6 (fair trial), Article 8 (privacy), Article 9 (freedom of religion), Article 10 (freedom of expression), Article 11 (freedom of association), and Article 14 (discrimination) (see *Review of Counter-Terrorism and Security Powers* Cm 8004, 2011).

There is an independent reviewer of terrorism legislation, currently Jonathan Hall QC, appointed by the Home Secretary (Terrorism Act 2006, s 36 as amended; Terrorism Prevention and Investigation Measures Act 2011, ss 20, 21). Unusually, the reviewer is not subject to procedural restrictions and can investigate both publicly and in private. He reports to Parliament (see Anderson, 'The Independent Review of Terrorism Laws' [2014] PL 403). The Counter-Terrorism and Security Act 2015 empowers the Secretary of State to form a 'Privacy and Civil Liberties Board' to support the activities of the reviewer. The government chose not to establish such a Board, but the reviewer has appointed a special adviser to work with him in the exercise of his functions.

25.5.1 Narrowing the definition of terrorism

The definition of terrorism (TA, s 1) is complex, 'sweepingly broad and extraordinarily vague' (Richards J in *R (Kurdistan Workers' Party) v Secretary of State for the Home Dept* [2002] EWHC 644 (Admin)). It has three elements which can be summarised as the use for political ends of fear induced by violence (*Al Sirri v Secretary of State for the Home Department* [2013] 1 AC 745, [39]):

1. There must be use or threat of action that falls into one or more of five categories: serious violence against a person; serious damage to property; endangering life; creating a risk to the health or safety of the public or a section of the public; designed seriously to interfere with or seriously to disrupt an electronic system.
2. The action must be intended to advance a political, religious, racial or ideological cause.
3. Except where firearms or explosives are involved, the action must be designed to influence the government or intimidate the public or a section of it, or an international governmental organisation. It is not necessary for the action to be carried out on UK soil, or against a UK citizen or property owned by a UK citizen. The breadth of the definition means that it could include a wide variety of actions and persons, some of which might not be a significant threat to national security. For example, the definition could apply to political journalism, social media, publications and political campaigns, such as environmental protesters who chain themselves to trees to protect a wildlife habitat or anti-abortion demonstrators. Given the breadth of the definition and the wide range of offences involved, many of them intended to cover indirect or preparatory activities, ministers and the police have considerable discretion in deciding who is or is not a terrorist.

In *R (Gul) v Secretary of State for the Home Department* [2014] AC 1260, the Supreme Court held that, in view of the deliberately wide definition of terrorism, members of armed groups fighting wicked regimes were nevertheless terrorists and, as such, guilty of an offence for posting videos on the internet encouraging military action by armed resistance groups in a civil war. Concern was expressed over the width of the definition. It was recognised, however, that the unpredictable nature of terrorism and changing political circumstances required this. Thus, there appears to be no distinction between terrorism and armed resistance by a people struggling for self-determination.

However, in *R (Miranda) v Secretary of State for the Home Department* [2016] 1 WLR 1505, the Court of Appeal, not without difficulty, held that the literal meaning of the definition should be cut down so as to avoid people who take part in legitimate political activities being considered as terrorists. The court assumed that Parliament must have intended the 'ordinary' understanding of terrorism. It therefore read into the definition of a terrorist a requirement that the person concerned must intend to create the risk in question or be reckless as to the risk (at [45]–[56]). The case concerned the spouse of a journalist who was stopped and questioned at an airport on suspicion of being a terrorist. However, the court also held that the possibility of such an intention was enough to justify the use of the power in question in the particular case (see Section 25.5.4).

25.5.2 Proscription

One of the key elements of the anti-terrorism regime is the banning of terrorist organisations. The laws on proscription are serious restrictions on freedom of expression and association. They were controversial when first enacted but are now among the least problematic of the anti-terrorism laws.

It is an offence to belong to or to support a proscribed organisation (TA, ss 11, 12, as amended by Counter-Terrorism and Border Security Act 2019, s 1). The proscribed organisations are listed in TA, Schedule 2, or have the same name as one listed, or are proscribed by statutory instrument. The organisation remains proscribed irrespective of any change in name (Terrorism Act 2006, s 21). This raises the Convention rights of freedom of expression and freedom of association, which overlap in this context.

The Home Secretary can add other organisations to the list if she or he believes the organisation is 'concerned in terrorism' (TA, s 3; Terrorism Act 2006, s 21). This means committing or participating in acts of terrorism, preparing for terrorism, promoting, encouraging or unlawfully 'glorifying' terrorism, or otherwise being concerned with terrorism. Glorifying terrorism, which includes praise or celebration, is unlawful if it can reasonably be inferred to refer to conduct that should be emulated in present circumstances. The Home Secretary does not have to show reasonable grounds for her belief.

It is an offence to be, or to profess to be, a member of a proscribed organisation (TA, s 11), to express support for or invite support for a proscribed organisation (TA, s 12), or to express an opinion or belief that is supportive of a proscribed organisation, being reckless as to whether a person to whom the expression is directed will be encouraged to support a proscribed organisation (Counter-Terrorism and Border Security Act 2019, s 1). In *Sheldrake v DPP* [2005] 1 AC 264, the House of Lords did not decide whether this very wide provision violated the right of freedom of expression. (However, Lord Bingham thought that it would be justified as proportionate (at [54]).) TA, s 11(2) imposes a burden of proof on the accused to show that she or he has not taken part in the activities of the organisation at a time when it was proscribed. This was held to be unfair as a violation of Article 6 of the ECHR (right to a fair trial), and the legislation fell to be interpreted subject to Article 6 via s 3 HRA.

It is also an offence to address a meeting (of three or more persons) with the purpose of encouraging support for a proscribed organisation or furthering its activities, or to arrange or help to arrange a meeting which the person knows supports or furthers the activities of a proscribed organisation or which is addressed by a person who belongs to or professes to belong to a proscribed organisation, irrespective of the subject of the meeting (TA, s 12(2)). In the case of a private meeting, there is a defence that the person has no reasonable cause to believe that the address would support a proscribed organisation or further its activities (TA, s 12(4)). It is also an offence to wear clothing or an item in public that would arouse reasonable suspicion that the person is a member of a proscribed organisation (s 13) or to publish an image of such clothing or item (Counter-Terrorism and Border Security Act 2019, s 2).

25.5.3 Arrest and detention

A constable may arrest without warrant and search a person whom he reasonably suspects to be a terrorist (TA, ss 41, 43(2)). Unlike ordinary powers of arrest, this power does not tie the arrest to a specific offence (*R v Officer in Charge of Police Office Castlereagh Belfast, ex p Lynch* [1980] NI 126). Significant in the context of liberal values of human dignity, the officer does not need to disclose to the arrestee the grounds for his suspicions (*Oscar v Chief Constable RUC* [1992] NI 290).

Article 5 ECHR requires that a suspect must be brought promptly before a court (PACE, s 46: as soon as 'practicable'). *In Brogan v UK* [1989], UK anti-terrorist legislation fell foul of this, and it has since been refined several times. Currently, a terrorist suspect can be detained for up to 48 hours by the police alone. To detain a person from 48 hours up to a maximum of 14 days, the police must apply to a court (TA, Sched. 8, modified by Protection of Freedoms Act 2012, s 57). (The equivalent periods for other offences are 24 hours, which can be extended to 36 hours in some cases, and 96 hours with a warrant from a court (PACE, ss 41–43).)

The 14-day period can be temporarily extended to 28 days by the Secretary of State 'if he considers it urgent'. The approval of a senior judge is required. This power applies only when Parliament is dissolved or until the first Queen's speech after a dissolution. The Order lasts for up to three months but must be approved by Parliament after 20 days (Protection of Freedoms Act 2012, s 58).

An extension can be granted if the detention is necessary to obtain or preserve evidence or to carry out an examination or analysis and the investigation is being conducted diligently and expeditiously (ibid), but again, the police investigation does not need to be tied to a specific crime. The detention must be reviewed regularly. The accused is entitled to legal representation but can be excluded from any part of the hearing and sensitive material can be withheld from the accused and his or her advisers (ibid).

25.5.4 Stop and search powers and power of entry

Under TA, s 43, as modified by the Protection of Freedoms Act 2012, ss 60(2), (3), a constable may stop and search anyone whom he reasonably suspects to be a terrorist. He may also search any vehicle stopped under this power, but not passengers unless they too are suspected of being terrorists. However, if he reasonably suspects that a vehicle is being used for terrorism, anything on or in the vehicle or carried by the driver or passengers can be searched and seized.

There are also more drastic powers. Originally, under TA, ss 44–45, a policeman in uniform, even without reasonable grounds, could stop and search any person for articles of a kind that could be used in connection with terrorism. This applied within an area authorised for up to 28 days by a senior officer again without needing reasonable grounds. In *R (Gillan) v MPC* [2006], a policeman used section 44 against a student demonstrator and a journalist at an arms sale fair supported by the government. The decision of the House of Lords upholding this was condemned by the ECHR (*Gillan and Quinton v UK* [2010] ECHR 28). It was held that section 44 engaged at least Article 8 of the ECHR as a clear interference with privacy and that the power was too vague and lacked essential safeguards, including judicial supervision. It was not therefore 'in accordance with the law' (Section 22.9.1).

The Protection of Freedoms Act 2012, s 61, replaces section 44 with more restricted powers aiming to satisfy the requirement of proportionality. A senior officer must 'reasonably suspect' that an act of terrorism will take place and 'reasonably consider' that the authorisation is necessary to prevent this, and that the area or place is no greater than necessary, and that the duration of the order is no longer than necessary. A constable in uniform can then stop and search vehicles and pedestrians without himself having reasonable grounds for doing so. However, there must be reasonable grounds to seize and take away evidence. The power can be exercised only to discover evidence of terrorism.

The Secretary of State must prepare and publish a code of practice to which a police officer must have regard when exercising these powers (Protection of Freedoms Act 2012, s 62).

Under TA, s 89, a member of the armed forces on duty, or a police officer, may stop any person so long as it is necessary in order to question him or her for the purpose of ascertaining that person's identity or movements and what she or he knows about a recent explosion or incident.

Under Sched. 7 of the TA 2000, a passenger at an airport can be stopped by a police officer without having reasonable grounds to do so, questioned for up to six hours and required to hand over any documents in his or her possession. In *Beghal v DPP* [2015] UKSC 49, the Supreme Court held that this power satisfied Art 8 ECHR (privacy) as far as ordinary travellers are concerned since it was limited in scope and there was provision for accountability; however, the Strasbourg court disagreed in *Beghal v UK* (2019) 69 EHRR 28, (Section 22.9.1). In *R (Miranda) v Secretary of State for the Home Department* [2016], the Security Services had requested that Miranda be stopped because he was the spouse of a journalist and suspected of carrying data famously stolen from the US government by Edward Snowden which they believed might include material which created a risk to state agents (although Snowden had apparently filtered the material). The Court of Appeal held that, since there was no requirement of reasonable suspicion, the possibility of a person being a terrorist was enough to justify the use of Sched. 7. However, the court also held that Sched. 7 was not 'prescribed by law' because it lacked sufficient safeguards for journalists to comply with Art 10 (freedom of expression), in that there was no check by an independent authority (Section 22.9.1).

There are also search powers over private premises. Normally, unless following an arrest (PACE, s 18), a police officer can enter and search private premises only with a warrant from a magistrate on the ground that it is reasonable to suspect that there is material on the premises that is likely to be of substantial value to the investigation of an indictable offence (i.e. a more serious one triable in the

Crown Court), and is likely to be relevant evidence (PACE, s 8). Section 42 of the TA 2000 confers wider powers. A magistrate may issue a search warrant for the search of any premises if a constable has reasonable grounds to suspect that a person concerned with the commission, preparation or instigation of acts of terrorism is to be found there. The Counter-Terrorism Act 2008 adds a power to remove documents, including electronic data, for examination and retain them for up to 96 hours (s 1): however, this provision has not yet been brought into force.

25.5.5 Terrorism prevention and investigation measures

There is a problem in dealing with terrorist suspects against whom there is insufficient admissible evidence to take to a court, sometimes due to the rule that electronic interception evidence cannot be used (Section 25.3.2). Deportation may also be ruled out because the suspect faces human rights violations overseas. The government's initial attempts to deal with the problem were famously frustrated by the courts.

In *A v Secretary of State for the Home Department* [2005], the government attempted to derogate from Art 5 ECHR in order to detain indefinitely foreign terrorist suspects unless they voluntarily left the country (Section 22.9.2). The House of Lords held that the power in question was insufficiently focused on its object, going too far in some respects and not far enough in others. It went too far in singling out foreign nationals since the threat was no less from British terrorists who could not be deported and not far enough by permitting them to leave the country since they were also a danger when abroad. The government then introduced 'Control Orders' which restricted freedom movement short of detention. They could include provision for house arrest in certain circumstances and require the subject to reside in a prescribed area. However, these also fell foul of the courts as being detention in all but name (*Secretary of State for the Home Dept v JJ* [2008]).

The Terrorism Prevention and Investigation Measures Act 2011 (TPIM), as modified by the Counter-Terrorism and Security Act 2015, is the most recent attempt to deal with the problem. The Secretary of State can impose a TPIM notice restricting a person's freedom of movement and communications if s/he has a reasonable belief that that person is or has been involved in terrorism. This is subject to a two-year time limit which can be extended for a further year. 'Involvement' includes the commission, preparation and instigation of acts of terrorism, or facilitating, encouraging supporting or assisting acts of terrorism which need not be specific acts. The standard of proof of 'reasonable belief' is the civil standard of 'balance of probability'.

The Secretary of State must reasonably consider that the measures are necessary to protect the public from a risk of terrorism and are necessary for purposes connected with preventing or restricting the individual's involvement in terrorism. The prior permission of the court is required, except in urgent cases when the matter must be referred to the court immediately after imposing the restriction. However, the court can refuse permission only if the measure is 'obviously flawed' on the basis of judicial review principles.

A TPIM can impose limited residence conditions including an overnight curfew, travel restrictions which prevent the subject leaving or entering a specified area and can require compliance with police directions. The Counter-Terrorism and Security Act 2015 increases these powers by enabling suspects to be relocated to a different part of the country and with increased monitoring powers. There are also restrictions on access to bank accounts and the transfer of assets abroad, restrictions on the use of electronic communication devices, and restrictions on communication or association with others. A subject can be required to report to a police station and allow photographs to be taken, wear a tracking device, and allow official access to his or her home. The Secretary of State must report to Parliament every three months as to the use made of these powers. The powers expire after five years but can be extended for another five years subject to an affirmative vote of both Houses of Parliament (TPIM, s 21).

25.5.6   Terrorist assets

There is a range of powers enabling the government to combat the financing of terrorist activities.

Under section 1 of the Anti-Terrorism, Crime and Security Act 2001 (ATCSA), a magistrate in civil proceedings can order the forfeiture of cash which is intended to be used for terrorist purposes, or which belongs to a proscribed organisation, or which is or represents property obtained through terrorism.

Under ATCSA, ss 4 and 5, the Treasury can freeze the assets of any person resident in the UK or any UK citizen or company if it reasonably believes (i) that action to the detriment of the UK economy (or part of it) has been or is likely to be taken; or (ii) that action constituting a threat to the life or property of one or more UK nationals has been or is likely to be taken, in both cases either by an overseas government or by an overseas resident. These powers are therefore not limited to terrorists but could, for example, be used to protect trade interests against overseas competition. They include power to require public bodies to disclose confidential information, again not limited to terrorist offences (ATCSA, s 17). The freezing order can prevent benefits being paid to the person in question or to any person the Treasury reasonably believes has assisted or is likely to assist them.

By virtue of Orders in Council made under the United Nations Act 1947 section 1, the Treasury can give directions for the freezing of terrorist assets to give effect to United Nations Security Council Resolutions. This drastic power can involve placing serious restrictions as to all spending upon the persons concerned other than for essential needs.

In *HM Treasury v Ahmed* [2010] 2 AC 534, the Supreme Court held that an order made under the 1947 Act which triggered asset freezing on 'reasonable suspicion' was invalid as violating the principle of legality, under which only clear statutory language can deprive a person of property (Section 6.6). The Terrorist Asset Freezing (Temporary Provisions) Act 2010 retrospectively validated the use of these powers. The Terrorist Asset-Freezing Etc Act 2011 puts the reasonable suspicion test into full statutory form.

In *Bank Mellat v HM Treasury (No 2)* [2013] UKSC 39, the Supreme Court held that a Treasury Direction with the aim of shutting off selected Iranian banks from the UK financial sector was invalid. Under the HRA, the Direction was an irrational, disproportionate and discriminatory interference with property rights because it did not apply to other banks in a similar position and the possibility of less intrusive measures had not been considered. There was also procedural unfairness, in that the measures were targeted at particular banks which had not been given an opportunity to object. *Bank Mellat* therefore illustrates that anti-terrorist measures cannot be targeted crudely, although in a borderline case, the government might be given a margin of discretion. Where a person has been convicted of certain funding and money laundering offences the court concerned may order assets connected with the offence to be seized (TA 2000, s 23). The Counter-Terrorism Act 2008 has extended this power and introduces provisions for compensating the injured out of the convicted person's assets.

The Counter-Terrorism and Security Act 2015 clarifies the law by making it an offence for a UK-based insurance company to cover a terrorist ransom payment.

25.5.7   Supporting terrorism: the 'Prevent' strategy

The TA 2006, ss 1–4, as amended by the Counter-Terrorism and Border Security Act 2019, s 5 introduces measures aimed at those who support and encourage terrorism and the dissemination of terrorist publications, including internet communications. It is an offence to make a statement 'that is likely to be understood by a reasonable person as a direct or indirect encouragement or other inducement to some or all of the members of the public to whom it is published to the commission, preparation or instigation of acts of terrorism'. This includes the notorious notion of 'glorifying' terrorism, thus potentially exposing historical analysis, for example of the English Civil War, to the criminal law.

The Counter-Terrorism and Security Act 2015 requires local authorities, educational and health institutions and the police to have regard to 'the need to prevent people being drawn into terrorism'. This is intended to counter extremist speakers. The government can issue 'guidance' to the bodies concerned, which can be enforced by court order. Judicial functions and the functions of Parliament and the devolved lawmakers are excluded. The Secretary of State can extend the duty to other bodies, but not to the military, the security services, or the Church of England. This Act was originally intended to empower ministers to ban 'extremist' speakers, but this proposal was withdrawn in the light of extreme controversy as to what this means.

Recent atrocities committed in Syria and Iraq involved UK subjects travelling to those countries to join extremist Jihadi fighters. Under the Counter-Terrorism and Security Act 2015, the Secretary of State can impose a 'temporary exclusion order' for up to two years on a citizen or other person with a 'right of abode' in the UK for the purpose of preventing the return to the UK of someone 'reasonably' suspected of involvement in terrorism-related activities. A terrorism-related activity consists of committing, preparing or instigating acts of terrorism, which need not be specific acts, or facilitating, assisting or supporting such acts. These are also offences in their own right.

This provision does not affect nationality as such, so may not violate international law which forbids a state from making a citizen stateless (UNHCR Convention Relating to the Status of Stateless Persons 1954; Convention on Reduction of Statelessness 1961). Moreover, the Act does not completely exclude the right to reside in the UK since a person is entitled to a 'permit to return' subject to his or her movements being monitored (see further Section 9.3.1). The main problem is that no court order is required for an exclusion order, so the only protection is the possibility of judicial review, activated from outside the UK.

The police are empowered to confiscate the passport of an outgoing traveller similarly suspected, for up to 14 days, but in this case, it is renewable thereafter by application to a court. During this time, the Secretary of State may consider revoking the passport. Since there is no legal right to a passport this provision is less controversial.

The 2015 Act reinforces the government's 'Prevent' strategy (see *Prevent Strategy Review* (Cm 8092, 2011)). This is intended to combat terrorism of all kinds by persuasion, education, training and guidance, backed up by the various powers under terrorism and public order legislation (Sections 23.6.2 and 23.7.3). The objects of the policy are to challenge extremist ideologies, to protect vulnerable people and to support sectors and institutions where there are risks of radicalisation. It is implemented by the Home Office through public bodies such as the police, local authorities and educational bodies, and also through voluntary bodies the funding of which may depend on commitment to mainstream democratic values. The 2015 Act provides for local panels to be set up to safeguard vulnerable persons (as defined by the panel) against being drawn into terrorism (see also Counter-Terrorism and Border Security Act 2019, s 20).

Some 'Prevent' devices, such as the 'safe space', which insulates its participants from unpleasant opinions, may raise issues of freedom of expression. For example, the Education (No 2) Act 1986 imposes a duty on universities to protect freedom of speech on their premises which 'safe spaces' may hamper.

Miscellaneous powers and offences are:

1. preparation of terrorist acts (TA 2006, s 5). This is not confined to a specific act of terrorism but could include, for example, buying materials capable of being made into bombs;
2. giving or receiving instruction or training for terrorism (TA 2006, s 6). This is also wide, including the use of any method or technique for doing anything that is capable of being done for the purpose of terrorism (s 6(3)(b)). For example, it could include IT skills. However, the instructor must know that the pupil intends to use the skills for terrorist purposes;
3. attendance at a place used for terrorist training (TA 2006, s 8);
4. offences relating to radioactive devices or materials for terrorist purposes (TA 2006, ss 9–11);

5. the Secretary of State can authorise the taking of land or a road closure or restriction if s/he considers it necessary for the preservation of peace or the maintenance of order (TA 2000, ss 91, 94). A member of the armed forces on duty or a constable may order a road closure or restriction if he considers it immediately necessary for the preservation of peace or the maintenance of order (TA 2000, s 92);

6. the Counter-Terrorism Act 2008 introduces increased penalties for any offence with a terrorist connection;

7. the Counter-Terrorism Act 2008 confers wide powers on any person to disclose information to any of the intelligence services for the purpose of its functions (s 19), with a corresponding power given to the intelligence services also to disclose information. This does not appear to be limited to terrorist offences.

Summary

▶ The courts give the executive a wide margin of discretion in relation to security matters. Under the ECHR, there is also a wide margin, and states can derogate from some of its provisions in the event of an emergency. However, the courts protect fundamental rights by requiring safeguards, in particular independent judicial supervision.

▶ The security and intelligence services are subject to a certain degree of control, largely outside the ordinary courts.

▶ There is regulation of electronic and other forms of surveillance by the police and other law enforcement agencies, also outside the ordinary courts. The overlapping regimes of the Police Act 1997 and the Regulation of Investigatory Powers Act 2000 give the government wide powers of interception and surveillance subject to procedural safeguards and limits derived from the ECHR as to permissible purposes and proportionality. The Investigatory Powers Act 2016 seeks to rationalise the law and extends the power of government to examine internet data.

▶ In an emergency, the police, supported by the armed forces, may take action to keep the peace and can use reasonable force in self-defence and the defence of others. It is questionable whether martial law as such is part of English law. The Civil Contingencies Act 2004 gives the executive wide powers to deal with an emergency but was not used for the COVID-19 pandemic. These powers are subject to limited control by Parliament and safeguards based on the ECHR.

▶ Increasingly restrictive anti-terrorist measures have been introduced in response to a series of threats and incidents. These have sometimes required derogation from the ECHR's protection for personal liberty. They also involve restrictions on the right to a fair trial. The courts have condemned a significant number of these powers and criticised others. However, there is no consensus on how to accommodate security and respect for freedom.

Exercises

25.1 Are there adequate safeguards against (a) unlawful interception of phone conversations; (b) electronic communications data; (c) CCTV surveillance?

25.2 To what extent are civil liberties protected in the event of a state of emergency?

25.3 Julie, a university lecturer, is a keen campaigner in favour of any cause that invites media attention. Last week she chained herself to a tree in support of an anti-development campaign. The previous week, she took part in a demonstration against a hospital closure which involved blocking access to the staff toilets. This week she is joining a campaign against the privatisation of higher education, which involves disabling the computers in the university's 'Enterprise and Profit Centre'. Her blog recommends resistance by force if necessary to oppressive and capitalist regimes everywhere. Her university vice chancellor consults you to find out whether Julie can be treated as a terrorist. Advise him.

25.4 **(i)** The Students' Union of Westchester University invites James, a writer of historical novels, to give an address open to the public promoting his view that the present monarchy is illegitimate and should be replaced by a descendant of the Stuart dynasty, by force if necessary. Advise the university whether it can ban the event.

(ii) Suppose the University Literary Society advertised a 'safe space' meeting on Victorian literature. The advertisement stipulated that there must be no expression of 'offensive opinions'. Advise the university whether it should provide a room for the meeting.

Further reading

Arden, 'Human Rights in the Age of Terrorism' (2005) 121 LQR 609

Barak, 'Human Rights in Times of Terror: A Judicial Point of View' (2008) 28 LS 492

Birkinshaw, 'Information; Public Access, Protecting Privacy and Surveillance' in Jowell and O'Cinneide (eds), *The Changing Constitution* (9th edn, Oxford University Press 2019)

Clayton and Tomlinson, 'Lord Bingham and the Human Rights Act: The Search for Democratic Legitimacy During the "War on Terror"' in Andenas and Fairgrieve (eds), *Tom Bingham and the Transformation of the Law* (Oxford University Press 2009)

Dyzenhaus, *The Constitution of Law: Legality in a Time of Emergency* (Cambridge University Press 2008)

Feldman, 'Human Rights, Terrorism and Risk: The Roles of Politicians and Judges' [2006] PL 364

Fenwick, 'Terrorism and the Control Orders/TPIMs Saga: A Vindication of the Human Rights Act or a Manifestation of "Defensive Democracy"?' [2017] PL 609

Gearty, 'Human Rights in an Age of Counter Terrorism: Injurious, Irrelevant or Indispensable?' (2005) 58 CLP 25

Poole, 'Courts and Conditions of Uncertainty in Times of Crisis' [2008] PL 234

Squires, 'Terrorism and Pre-emptive Civil Processes' (2016) 20 Int J HR 684

Stanford, 'The Multi-faceted Challenges to Free Speech in Higher Education: Frustrating the Rights of Political Participation on Campus' [2018] PL 708

Sumption, 'Government by Decree: Covid-19 and the Constitution' Cambridge Freshfields Annual Lecture 2020, https://resources.law.cam.ac.uk/privatelaw/Freshfields_Lecture_2020_Government_by_Decree.pdf

Syrett, 'The United Kingdom' in Roach (ed), *Comparative Counter-Terrorism Law* (Cambridge University Press 2015)

Walker, 'The Legal Definition of Terrorism in the United Kingdom and Beyond' [2007] PL 331

Walker, *Terrorism and the Law* (2nd edn, Oxford University Press 2011)

Walker and Broderick, *The Civil Contingencies Act 2004* (Oxford University Press 2006)